Ezekiel 1–20

CONCORDIA COMMENTARY

A Theological Exposition of Sacred Scripture

EZEKIEL 1–20

Horace D. Hummel

THE SCRIPTURES TESTIFY TO ME

Concordia Publishing House
Saint Louis

Copyright © 2005 Concordia Publishing House
3558 S. Jefferson Avenue, St. Louis, MO 63118-3968
1-800-325-3040 • www.cph.org

Unless otherwise indicated, Scripture quotations are the author's translation.

The SymbolGreek II, NewJerusalem, JacobiteLS, and TranslitLS fonts used to print this work are available from Linguist's Software, Inc., PO Box 580, Edmonds, WA 98020-0580, USA; telephone (425) 775-1130; www.linguistsoftware.com.

Manufactured in the United States of America

Library of Congress Cataloging-in-Publication Data

Hummel, Horace D.
    Ezekiel 1–20 / Horace D. Hummel.
        p.   cm. — (Concordia commentary)
    Includes bibliographical references (p.).
    ISBN 0-7586-0315-0
    1. Bible. O.T. Ezekiel I–XX—Commentaries. I. Title. II. Series.

    BX8627.H79   2005
    224'.4077—dc22

                              2005009047

1 2 3 4 5 6 7 8 9 10   14 13 12 11 10 09 08 07 06 05

To Ruth
The desire of my eyes
(See מַחְמַד עֵינֶיךָ, Ezek 24:16)

Contents

Commentary on the following sections and indexes for both volumes are in *Ezekiel 21–48*.

Commentary on 21:1 (ET 20:45)–24:27

III. Oracles against Other Nations (Ezekiel 25–32)

IV. Oracles of Israel's Eschatological Restoration (Ezekiel 33–39)

V. Vision of the New Jerusalem and the New Creation (Ezekiel 40–48)

Editors' Preface

What may a reader expect from the Concordia Commentary: A Theological Exposition of Sacred Scripture?

The purpose of this series, simply put, is to assist pastors, missionaries, and teachers of the Scriptures to convey God's Word with greater clarity, understanding, and faithfulness to the divine intent of the text.

Since every interpreter approaches the exegetical task from a certain perspective, honesty calls for an outline of the presuppositions held by those who have shaped this commentary series. This also serves, then, as a description of the characteristics of the commentaries.

First in importance is the conviction that the content of the scriptural testimony is Jesus Christ. The Lord himself enunciated this when he said, "The Scriptures ... testify to me" (Jn 5:39), words that have been incorporated into the logo of this series. The message of the Scriptures is the Good News of God's work to reconcile the world to himself through the life, death, resurrection, ascension, and everlasting session of Jesus Christ at the right hand of God the Father. Under the guidance of the same Spirit who inspired the writing of the Scriptures, these commentaries seek to find in every passage of every canonical book "that which promotes Christ" (as Luther's hermeneutic is often described). They are Christ-centered, *Christological* commentaries.

As they unfold the scriptural testimony to Jesus Christ, these commentaries expound Law and Gospel. This approach arises from a second conviction—that Law and Gospel are the overarching doctrines of the Bible itself and that to understand them in their proper distinction and relationship to one another is a key for understanding the self-revelation of God and his plan of salvation in Jesus Christ.

Now, Law and Gospel do not always appear in Scripture labeled as such. The palette of language in Scripture is multicolored, with many and rich hues. The dialectic of a pericope may be fallen creation and new creation, darkness and light, death and life, wandering and promised land, exile and return, ignorance and wisdom, demon possession and the kingdom of God, sickness and healing, lost and found, guilt and righteousness, flesh and Spirit, fear and joy, hunger and feast, or Babylon and the new Jerusalem. But the common element is God's gracious work of restoring fallen humanity through the Gospel of his Son. Since the predominant characteristic of these commentaries is the proclamation of that Gospel, they are, in the proper sense of the term, *evangelical*.

A third, related conviction is that the Scriptures are God's vehicle for communicating the Gospel. The editors and authors accept without reservation that the canonical books of the Old and New Testaments are, in their entirety, the inspired and inerrant Word of God. The triune God is the ultimate author of the Bible; every word is inspired by the Holy Spirit, who did also, at the same time, make use of the knowledge, particular interests, and styles of the human writers. Thus, while individual books surely are marked by distinctive features, the canon of Scripture has its own inner unity, and each passage must be understood in harmony with the larger context of the whole. This commentary series pays heed to the smallest of details because of its acceptance of *plenary and verbal inspiration* and interprets in accord with the analogy of faith following the principle that *Scripture interprets Scripture.* Both are necessary because the entirety of the Bible is God's Word, *sacred* Scripture, calling for *theological* exposition.

A fourth conviction is that, even as the God of the Gospel came into this world in Jesus Christ (the Word incarnate), the scriptural Gospel has been given to and through the people of God, for the benefit of all humanity. God did not intend his Scriptures to have a life separated from the church. He gave them through servants of his choosing: prophets, sages, evangelists, and apostles. He gave them to the church and through the church, to be cherished in the church for admonition and comfort and to be used by the church for proclamation and catechesis. The living context of Scripture is ever the church, where the Lord's ministry of preaching, baptizing, forgiving sins, teaching, and celebrating the Lord's Supper continues. Aware of the way in which the incarnation of the Son of God has as a consequence the close union of Scripture and church, of Word and Sacraments, this commentary series features expositions that are *incarnational* and *sacramental.*

This Gospel Word of God, moreover, creates a unity among all those in whom it works the obedience of faith and who confess the truth of God revealed in it. This is the unity of the one holy Christian and apostolic church, which extends through world history. The church is to be found wherever the marks of the church are present: the Gospel in the Word and the Sacraments. These have been proclaimed, confessed, and celebrated in many different cultures and are in no way limited nor especially attached to any single culture or people. As this commentary series seeks to articulate the universal truth of the Gospel, it acknowledges and affirms the confession of the scriptural truth in all the many times and places where the one true church has been found. Aiming to promote *concord* in the confession of the one scriptural Gospel, these commentaries seek to be, in the best sense of the terms, *confessional, ecumenical,* and *catholic.*

All of those convictions and characteristics describe the theological heritage of Martin Luther and of the confessors who subscribe to the *Book of Concord* (1580)—those who have come to be known as Lutherans. The editors and authors forthrightly confess their subscription to the doctrinal exposition of Scripture in the *Book of Concord.* As the publishing arm of The Lutheran Church—Missouri Synod, Concordia Publishing House is bound to doctrinal agreement with the Scriptures and the Lutheran Confessions and seeks to herald the true Christian doctrine to the ends of the earth. To that end, the series has enlisted confessional Lutheran authors from other church bodies around the world who share the evangelical mission of promoting theological concord.

The authors and editors acknowledge their debt to Martin Luther as an exegete, particularly the example of his hermeneutical method. Luther's method (practiced by many others as well) included (1) interpreting Scripture with Scripture according to the analogy of faith (that is, in harmony with the whole of Christian doctrine revealed in the Word); (2) following the contours of the grammar of the original languages; (3) seeking the intended meaning of the text, the "plain" or "literal" sense, aware that the language of Scripture ranges from narrative to discourse, from formal prose to creative poetry, from archaic to acrostic to apocalyptic, and it uses metaphor, type, parable, and other figures; (4) drawing on philology, linguistics, literature, philosophy, history, and other fields in the quest for a better understanding of the text; (5) considering the history of the church's interpretation; (6) applying the text as authoritative also in the present milieu of the interpreter; and (7) above all, seeing the present application and fulfillment of the text in terms of Jesus Christ and his corporate church; upholding the Word, Baptism, and the Supper as the means through which Christ imparts salvation today; and affirming the inauguration, already now, of the eternal benefits of that salvation that is yet to come.

To be sure, the authors and editors do not feel bound always to agree with every detail of Luther's exegesis. Nor do they imagine that the interpretations presented here are the final word about every crux and enigmatic passage. But the work has been done in the spirit of Luther and in harmony with the confession of the church: grace alone, faith alone, Scripture alone, Christ alone.

The editors wish to acknowledge their debt of gratitude for all who have helped make possible this series. It was conceived at CPH in 1990, and a couple of years of planning and prayer to the Lord of the church preceded its formal launch on July 2, 1992. During that time, Dr. J. A. O. Preus II volunteered his enthusiasm for the project because, in his view, it would nurture and advance the proclamation of the Christian faith as understood by confessors of the Lutheran church. The financial support that has underwritten the series was provided by a gracious donor who wished to remain anonymous. Those two faithful servants of God were called to heavenly rest a few short years later.

During the early years, former CPH presidents Dr. John W. Gerber and Dr. Stephen J. Carter had the foresight to recognize the potential benefit of such a landmark work for the church at large. CPH allowed Dr. Christopher W. Mitchell to devote his time and energy to the conception and initial development of the project. Dr. Mitchell has remained the CPH editor and is also the Old Testament editor. Dr. Dean O. Wenthe has served on the project since its official start in 1992 and is the general editor, as well as a commentary author. Mrs. Julene Gernant Dumit (M.A.R.) has been the CPH production editor for the entire series. In 1999 Dr. Jeffrey A. Gibbs, already a commentary author, joined the editorial board as the New Testament editor.

CPH thanks Concordia Theological Seminary, Fort Wayne, Indiana, for kindly allowing its president, Dr. Dean O. Wenthe, to serve as the general editor of the series and to dedicate a substantial portion of his time to it for many years. CPH also thanks Concordia Seminary, St. Louis, Missouri, for permitting Dr. Jeffrey A. Gibbs to devote a significant share of his time to his capacity as the New Testament editor. Those two seminaries have thereby extended their ministries in selfless service for the benefit of the church.

The editors pray that the beneficence of their institutions may be reflected in this series by an evangelical orientation, a steadfast Christological perspective, an eschatological view toward the ultimate good of Christ's bride, and a concern that the wedding feast of the King's Son may be filled with all manner of guests (Mt 22:1–14).

> Now to him who is able to establish you by my Gospel and the preaching of Jesus Christ, by the revelation of the mystery kept secret for ages past but now revealed also through the prophetic Scriptures, made known to all the nations by order of the eternal God unto the obedience of faith—to the only wise God, through Jesus Christ, be the glory forever. Amen! (Rom 16:25–27)

Author's Preface

There is a German saying that can be freely translated "When I am finished, I also begin." That is hyperbolic, but still true, at least in my case, at the conclusion of essaying a commentary on a book as opaque as Ezekiel sometimes seems.

Inevitably, there are afterthoughts. When there were clear choices between equally viable options, did I make the right choice? Certain sections of the book remain question marks in my mind.

Writing a somewhat technical commentary, based on the original language, inevitably reinforces in one's mind the truism that "every translation is an interpretation." Hence, a comparison of the renditions in the major English translations was often at least as enlightening as reading other commentaries. (I limited myself to the versions that are in most common use by our congregations and members.)

Perhaps the major overriding issue for me throughout was the simultaneous tension and unity of the historical and the Christological. It is axiomatic among us that a confessional commentary must do justice to both aspects. But the task is far easier said than done! The exposition in this book is structured with the text's philological and Christological perspectives divided into the textual notes and commentary, respectively. But their distinction is often artificial. For the grammatical aspects, there are relatively clear and commonly agreed upon rules to follow. But what rules shall one follow in expounding the Christological sense of an OT text? There are, of course, certain general hermeneutical principles to follow, but, except where there is a clear NT reference (rare for Ezekiel), one can only pray that the Holy Spirit, working through the entirety of the Scriptures, has informed the interpreter of Ezekiel sufficiently. The user of this commentary must be the final judge of especially that aspect of my efforts.

Or, to put the matter differently, it is a reminder of the extent to which the church must always steer between the Scylla of historicism on the one hand and the Charybdis of allegory on the other. Modern commentaries have tended, to one degree or the other, to succumb to the former, leaving especially the OT as an ancient, largely irrelevant record of Israelite "spirituality." Even in conservative churches, at least since the Enlightenment (and certainly no less so in our era), secular cultural changes always seek to infiltrate exegesis. We may have exorcized the grosser manifestations of historicism (JEPD, imagined Second and Third Isaiahs, etc.), but in subtler ways those pressures never cease to threaten. No further evidence is needed than to note the distinctly subcanonical status the OT holds in the doctrinal formulations, liturgical and homiletical practice, and actual piety of the church.

No less a perennial threat are the countless sermons and meditations one hears that, at best, can only be labeled "allegorical."[1] Even though we can hardly endorse that precise method, at least its overriding concern was with the text's message about the triune God who has revealed himself in the life, death, and resurrection of our Savior. In a good sense, concern with historical matters has entered our consciousness in a way not found in antiquity, and, if properly deployed, it lends reinforcement to basic doctrines such as the incarnation, the resurrection of the body, and the Sacraments.

When it comes to those to whom I owe special thanks, I hardly know where to start. Perhaps I must begin with the sainted Dr. Walter Roehrs at Concordia Seminary, St. Louis, who first introduced me to the hidden treasures of the Hebrew language and its ancient Near Eastern environment. I had taught electives in Ezekiel several times before embarking on this commentary, and inevitably, one learns from interaction with the students. Here I must single out Carl Hanson, now a missionary in Taiwan, who compiled an exhaustive bibliography on Ezekiel for me. (The vast majority of the titles, if accessible, I found to be either too popular for my purposes or too "far out" even to merit refutation.) Series editors Dr. Christopher Mitchell and Mrs. Julene Dumit have labored over and improved my manuscript to a greater extent than I will ever know. And last, but by no means least, I must remember my wife, Ruth, who tolerated no little neglect of other matters while I wrestled with Ezekiel.

July 21, 2005
St. Ezekiel the Prophet[2]

---

[1] A very instructive illustration of patristic exegesis, which, in its own way, was also text-based, is the study of ancient Christian commentary on Ezekiel 1 by Christman: "What Did Ezekiel See?"

[2] The *Lutheran Service Book* follows the Maronite calendar in commemorating St. Ezekiel on July 21. In the Greek Orthodox calendar, the day for Ezekiel is July 23.

Principal Abbreviations

Books of the Bible

Gen	2 Ki	Is	Nah	Rom	Titus
Ex	1 Chr	Jer	Hab	1 Cor	Philemon
Lev	2 Chr	Lam	Zeph	2 Cor	Heb
Num	Ezra	Ezek	Hag	Gal	James
Deut	Neh	Dan	Zech	Eph	1 Pet
Josh	Esth	Hos	Mal	Phil	2 Pet
Judg	Job	Joel	Mt	Col	1 Jn
Ruth	Ps (pl. Pss)	Amos	Mk	1 Thess	2 Jn
1 Sam	Prov	Obad	Lk	2 Thess	3 Jn
2 Sam	Eccl	Jonah	Jn	1 Tim	Jude
1 Ki	Song	Micah	Acts	2 Tim	Rev

Books of the Apocrypha and Other Noncanonical Books of the Septuagint

1–2 Esdras	1–2 Esdras
Tobit	Tobit
Judith	Judith
Add Esth	Additions to Esther
Wis Sol	Wisdom of Solomon
Sirach	Sirach/Ecclesiasticus
Baruch	Baruch
Ep Jer	Epistle of Jeremiah
Azariah	Prayer of Azariah
Song of the Three	Song of the Three Young Men
Susanna	Susanna
Bel	Bel and the Dragon
Manasseh	Prayer of Manasseh
1–2 Macc	1–2 Maccabees
3–4 Macc	3–4 Maccabees
Ps 151	Psalm 151
Odes	Odes
Ps(s) Sol	Psalm(s) of Solomon

Reference Works and Scripture Versions

ABD	*Anchor Bible Dictionary.* Edited by D. N. Freedman. 6 vols. New York: Doubleday, 1992
AC	Augsburg Confession
AE	American ed. of *Luther's Works.* 55 vols. St. Louis: Concordia; Philadelphia: Fortress, 1955–1986
ANEP	*The Ancient Near East in Pictures Relating to the Old Testament.* Edited by J. B. Pritchard. 2d ed. Princeton: Princeton University Press, 1969
ANET	*Ancient Near Eastern Texts Relating to the Old Testament.* Edited by J. B. Pritchard. 3d ed. Princeton: Princeton University Press, 1969
ANF	*The Ante-Nicene Fathers.* Edited by A. Roberts and J. Donaldson. 10 vols. Repr. Peabody, Mass.: Hendrickson, 1994
Ap	Apology of the Augsburg Confession
BAR	*Biblical Archaeology Review*
BDB	Brown, F., S. R. Driver, and C. A. Briggs. *A Hebrew and English Lexicon of the Old Testament.* Oxford: Clarendon, 1979
BHS	*Biblia Hebraica Stuttgartensia*
BKAT	Biblischer Kommentar, Altes Testament
BWAT	Beiträge zur Wissenschaft vom Alten Testament
BZAW	Beihefte zur Zeitschrift für die alttestamentliche Wissenschaft
CCSL	Corpus Christianorum: Series latina. Turnhout: Brepols, 1953–
DCH	*The Dictionary of Classical Hebrew.* Edited by D. J. A. Clines. Sheffield: Sheffield Academic Press, 1993–
Ep	Epitome of the Formula of Concord
ESV	English Standard Version of the Bible
ET	English translation
FC	Formula of Concord
GKC	*Gesenius' Hebrew Grammar.* Edited by E. Kautzsch. Translated by A. E. Cowley. 2d ed. Oxford: Clarendon, 1910
HALOT	Koehler, L., W. Baumgartner, and J. J. Stamm. *The Hebrew and Aramaic Lexicon of the Old Testament.* Translated and edited under the supervision of M. E. J. Richardson. 5 vols. Leiden: Brill, 1994–2000
IDB	*The Interpreter's Dictionary of the Bible.* Edited by G. A. Buttrick. 5 vols. Nashville: Abingdon, 1962, 1976

JANESCU	*Journal of the Ancient Near Eastern Society of Columbia University*
JAOS	*Journal of the American Oriental Society*
Jastrow	Jastrow, M., comp. *A Dictionary of the Targumim, the Talmud Babli and Yerushalmi, and the Midrashic Literature.* 2 vols. Brooklyn: P. Shalom, 1967
JBL	*Journal of Biblical Literature*
Joüon	Joüon, P. *A Grammar of Biblical Hebrew.* Translated and revised by T. Muraoka. 2 vols. Subsidia biblica 14/1–2. Rome: Editrice Pontificio Istituto Biblico, 1991
JSOTSup	Journal for the Study of the Old Testament: Supplement Series
KJV	King James Version of the Bible
LEH	Lust, J., E. Eynikel, and K. Hauspie. *A Greek-English Lexicon of the Septuagint.* 2 vols. Stuttgart: Deutsche Bibelgesellschaft, 1992–1996
LW	*Lutheran Worship.* St. Louis: Concordia, 1982
LXX	Septuagint
MT	Masoretic Text of the Hebrew Old Testament
NA^{27}	Nestle, E. and E., K. and B. Aland, et al. *Novum Testamentum Graece.* 27th ed. Stuttgart: Deutsche Bibelgesellschaft, 1993
NASB	New American Standard Bible
NIV	New International Version of the Bible
NKJV	New King James Version of the Bible
NPNF[1]	*The Nicene and Post-Nicene Fathers.* Series 1. Edited by P. Schaff. 14 vols. Repr. Peabody, Mass.: Hendrickson, 1994
NRSV	New Revised Standard Version of the Bible
NT	New Testament
OT	Old Testament
PEQ	*Palestine Exploration Quarterly*
PG	Patrologia graeca. Edited by J.-P. Migne. 162 vols. Paris, 1857–1886
PL	Patrologia latina. Edited by J.-P. Migne. 217 vols. Paris, 1844–1864
RSV	Revised Standard Version of the Bible
SC	Small Catechism by M. Luther
SD	Solid Declaration of the Formula of Concord
Soncino ed.	Hebrew-English Edition of the Babylonian Talmud. Edited by I. Epstein. 30 vols. London: Soncino, 1984–1990

TDNT	*Theological Dictionary of the New Testament.* Edited by G. Kittel and G. Friedrich. Translated by G. W. Bromiley. 10 vols. Grand Rapids: Eerdmans, 1964–1976
TLH	*The Lutheran Hymnal.* St. Louis: Concordia, 1941
UBS[4]	*The Greek New Testament.* 4th rev. ed. Stuttgart: Deutsche Bibelgesellschaft, 1994
VT	*Vetus Testamentum*
VTSup	Supplements to Vetus Testamentum
Waltke-O'Connor	Waltke, B. K., and M. O'Connor. *An Introduction to Biblical Hebrew Syntax.* Winona Lake, Ind.: Eisenbrauns, 1990
ZTK	*Zeitschrift für Theologie und Kirche*

Icons

These icons are used in the margins of this commentary to highlight the following themes:

Trinity

Temple, Tabernacle

Incarnation

Passion, Atonement

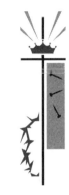

Death and Resurrection,
Theology of the Cross,
the Great Reversal

Christus Victor,
Christology

Baptism

Catechesis,
Instruction, Revelation

Lord's Supper

Ministry of Word and Sacrament,
Office of the Keys

The Church

Worship

Sin, Law, Death

Hope of Heaven,
Eschatology

Justification

Bibliography

Alexander, Ralph. *Ezekiel*. Chicago: Moody, 1976.

Allen, Leslie C. *Ezekiel*. 2 vols. Word Biblical Commentary 28–29. Dallas: Word, 1990 (vol. 2), 1994 (vol. 1).

Block, Daniel I. *The Book of Ezekiel*. 2 vols. New International Commentary on the Old Testament. Grand Rapids: Eerdmans, 1997–1998.

Boadt, Lawrence E. "Mythological Themes and the Unity of Ezekiel." Pages 211–31 in *Literary Structure and Rhetorical Strategies in the Hebrew Bible*. Edited by L. J. de Regt, J. de Waard, and J. P. Fokkelman. Assen, The Netherlands: Van Gorcum, 1996.

Bøe, Sverre. *Gog and Magog: Ezekiel 38–39 as Pre-Text for Revelation 19,17–21 and 20,7–10*, Wissenschaftliche Untersuchungen zum Neuen Testament 2/135. Tübingen: Mohr Siebeck, 2001.

Bright, John. *A History of Israel*. 3d ed. Philadelphia: Westminster, 1981.

Brighton, Louis A. *Revelation*. Concordia Commentary. St. Louis: Concordia, 1999.

Brownlee, William H. *Ezekiel 1–19*. Word Biblical Commentary 28. Waco: Word, 1986.

Calvin, John. *Commentaries on the First Twenty Chapters of the Book of the Prophet Ezekiel*. Translated by Thomas Myers. 2 vols. 1849. Repr., Grand Rapids: Eerdmans, 1948.

Chemnitz, Martin. *Examination of the Council of Trent*. Part 2. Translated by Fred Kramer. St. Louis: Concordia, 1978.

———. *The Two Natures in Christ*. Translated by J. A. O. Preus. St. Louis: Concordia, 1971.

Christman, Angela Russell. "What Did Ezekiel See? Patristic Exegesis of Ezekiel 1 and Debates about God's Incomprehensibility." *Pro Ecclesia* 8/3 (Summer 1999): 338–63.

Coogan, Michael David, ed. and trans. *Stories from Ancient Canaan*. Philadelphia: Westminster, 1978.

Cook, Stephen L., and Corrine L. Patton, ed. *Ezekiel's Hierarchical World: Wrestling with a Tiered Reality*. Leiden: Brill, 2004.

Cooke, G. A. *A Critical and Exegetical Commentary on the Book of Ezekiel*. International Critical Commentary 21. Edinburgh: T&T Clark, 1936.

Dijk, H. J. van. *Ezekiel's Prophecy on Tyre (Ez. 26,1–28,19): A New Approach*. Biblica et orientalia 20. Rome: Pontifical Biblical Institute, 1968.

Driver, G. R. "Difficult Words in the Hebrew Prophets." Pages 52–72 in *Studies in Old Testament Prophecy*. Edited by H. H. Rowley. New York: Scribner, 1950.

Eichrodt, Walther. *Ezekiel: A Commentary*. Translated by Cosslett Quin. Old Testament Library. Philadelphia: Westminster, 1970.

Eisenman, Robert, and Michael Wise. *The Dead Sea Scrolls Uncovered: The First Complete Translation and Interpretation of 50 Key Documents Withheld for over 35 Years* Rockport, Mass.: Element, 1992.

Fohrer, Georg. *Ezechiel.* Handbuch zum Alten Testament (First Series) 13. Tübingen: Mohr (Siebeck), 1955.

———. *Die symbolischen Handlungen der Propheten.* 2d ed. Zurich: Zwingli Verlag, 1968.

Fretheim, Terence E. *The Suffering of God: An Old Testament Perspective.* Philadelphia: Fortress, 1984.

Friebel, Kelvin. *Jeremiah's and Ezekiel's Sign-Acts: Rhetorical Nonverbal Communication.* Journal for the Study of the Old Testament: Supplement Series 283. Sheffield: Sheffield Academic Press, 1999.

Garfinkel, S. P. *Studies in Akkadian Influences in the Book of Ezekiel.* Ann Arbor: University Microfilms, 1983.

Gibson, John C. L. *Canaanite Myths and Legends.* Edinburgh: T&T Clark, 1977.

———. *Textbook of Syrian Semitic Inscriptions.* 3 vols. Oxford: Clarendon, 1971–1982.

Gieschen, Charles A. *Angelomorphic Christology: Antecedents and Early Evidence.* Leiden: Brill, 1998.

Greenberg, Moshe. *Ezekiel.* 2 vols. Anchor Bible 22–22A. Garden City, N.Y.: Doubleday, 1983–1997.

Grillmeier, Aloys. *Christ in Christian Tradition.* Vol. 1: *From the Apostolic Age to Chalcedon (451).* Translated by John Bowden. 2nd rev. ed. Atlanta: John Knox, 1975.

Hals, Ronald M. *Ezekiel.* The Forms of the Old Testament Literature 19. Grand Rapids: Eerdmans, 1989.

Harstad, Adolph L. *Joshua.* Concordia Commentary. St. Louis: Concordia, 2004.

Haussleiter, Johannes, ed. *Victorini Episcopi Petavionensis Opera.* Corpus Scriptorum Ecclesiasticorum Latinorum 49. Repr., New York: Johnson Reprint Co., 1965.

Hengstenberg, E. W. *Christology of the Old Testament and a Commentary on the Messianic Predictions.* Translated by James Martin. 2d ed. Vol. 3. Edinburgh: T&T Clark, 1864.

Herrmann, Johannes. *Ezechiel.* Kommentar zum alten Testament 11. Leipzig: Deichert, 1924.

Hugenberger, Gordon P. *Marriage as a Covenant: Biblical Law and Ethics as Developed from Malachi.* Grand Rapids: Baker, 1998.

Jensen, R. B. "Of Cherubim and Gospel Symbols." *Biblical Archaeology Review* 21/4 (1995): 42–43, 65.

Just, Arthur A., Jr. *Luke 1:1–9:50.* Concordia Commentary. St. Louis: Concordia, 1996.

———. *Luke 9:51–24:53*. Concordia Commentary. St. Louis: Concordia, 1997.

Kaufmann, Yehezkel. *The Religion of Israel*. Translated and abridged by Moshe Greenberg. London: George Allen and Unwin, 1961.

Keel, Othmar. *Jahwe—Visionen und Siegelkunst*. Stuttgart: Katholisches Bibelwerk, 1977.

Keil, Carl Friedrich. *Biblical Commentary on the Prophecies of Ezekiel*. Translated by James Martin. 2 vols. Edinburgh: T&T Clark, 1876. Repr., Grand Rapids: Eerdmans, 1978. Translation of *Biblischer Commentar über den Propheten Ezechiel*. Biblischer Commentar über das Alte Testament, vol. 3 of part 3, by C. F. Keil and Franz Delitzsch. Leipzig: Dörffling & Franke, 1868.

Kelly, J. N. D. *Early Christian Creeds*. 3d ed. New York: Longman, 1972.

Kleinig, John W. *Leviticus*. Concordia Commentary. St. Louis: Concordia, 2003.

Kutsko, John F. *Between Heaven and Earth: Divine Presence and Absence in the Book of Ezekiel*. Winona Lake, Ind.: Eisenbrauns, 2000.

Levy, Abraham J. *Rashi's Commentary on Ezekiel 40–48*. Philadelphia: Dropsie College, 1931.

Lieberman, Saul. *Greek in Jewish Palestine: Studies in the Life and Manners of Jewish Palestine in the II–IV Centuries C.E.* New York: Jewish Theological Seminary of America, 1942.

———. *Hellenism in Jewish Palestine: Studies in the Literary Transmission, Beliefs and Manners of Palestine in the I Century B.C.E.–IV Century C.E.* New York: Jewish Theological Seminary of America, 1950.

Lockwood, Gregory J. *1 Corinthians*. Concordia Commentary. St. Louis: Concordia, 2000.

Malul, Meir. "Adoption of Foundlings in the Bible and Mesopotamian Documents: A Study of Some Legal Metaphors in Ezekiel 16.1–7." *Journal for the Study of the Old Testament* 46 (1990): 97–126.

Manning, Gary T. *Echoes of a Prophet: The Use of Ezekiel in the Gospel of John and in Literature of the Second Temple Period*. London: T&T Clark, 2004.

Mitchell, Christopher W. *The Song of Songs*. Concordia Commentary. St. Louis: Concordia, 2003.

Mounce, Robert H. *The Book of Revelation*. The New International Commentary on the New Testament. Grand Rapids: Eerdmans, 1977.

Pieper, Francis. *Christian Dogmatics*. 3 vols. St. Louis: Concordia, 1950–1953.

Rad, Gerhard von. *Old Testament Theology*. Translated by D. M. G. Stalker. 2 vols. New York: Harper/Harper & Row, 1962–1965.

Schürer, Emil. *The History of the Jewish People in the Age of Jesus Christ*. New English ed. 3 vols. in 4. Edinburgh: T&T Clark, 1973–1987.

Steinmann, Andrew. *The Oracles of God: The Old Testament Canon*. St. Louis: Concordia, 1999.

Swete, Henry Barclay. *The Apocalypse of St. John.* Repr., Grand Rapids: Eerdmans, 1968.

———. *The Gospel according to St. Mark.* 3d ed. Repr., Grand Rapids: Eerdmans, 1956.

Taylor, John B. *Ezekiel: An Introduction and Commentary.* Tyndale Old Testament Commentaries. Downers Grove, Ill.: Inter-Varsity, 1969.

Tov, Emanuel. *Textual Criticism of the Hebrew Bible.* 2d rev. ed. Minneapolis: Fortress, 1992, 2001.

Tuell, Steven Shawn. *The Law of the Temple in Ezekiel 40–48.* Harvard Semitic Monographs 49. Atlanta: Scholars Press, 1992.

Ulrich, Dean. "Dissonant Prophecy in Ezekiel 26 and 29." *Bulletin for Biblical Research* 10/1 (2000): 121–41.

Woollcombe, K. J. "The Biblical Origins and Patristic Development of Typology." Pages 39–75 in *Essays on Typology.* London: SCM Press, 1957.

Yeivin, Israel. *Introduction to the Tiberian Masorah.* Translated and edited by E. J. Revell. Masoretic Studies 5. Missoula, Mont.: Scholars Press, 1980.

York, A. D. "Ezekiel 1: Inaugural and Restoration Visions." *Vetus Testamentum* 27 (1977): 82–98.

Zimmerli, Walther. *Ezekiel.* Translated by Ronald E. Clements. 2 vols. Hermeneia. Philadelphia: Fortress, 1979–1983.

Introduction

Our Christian Method of Interpretation

Hermeneutics, after languishing in benign neglect for years, has recently become a popular avocation among exegetes, or at least among academics. This is not the venue even to begin to summarize or evaluate all those discussions—or even consider more traditional hermeneutics.[1]

Obviously, to a large extent, exactly the same principles of interpretation apply to Ezekiel as to the rest of the Bible, and specifically to the OT. Every passage of Scripture is interpreted by the Scriptures as a whole. There are the rules of general hermeneutics, which apply to all human discourse, as well as those of special hermeneutics, which are unique to the Scriptures, since they are the inspired, inerrant, and authoritative Word of God. All of the rules of general and special hermeneutics must be adapted to the specific type of literature one is confronting.

A specifically Lutheran approach like ours will accent such themes as Christology, the dynamics of Law and Gospel, and God's means of grace for bringing people to faith and preserving them unto salvation—his Word and Sacraments. How these themes may be applied to Ezekiel will be discussed in "Outline and Theological Emphases" below as well as throughout the commentary wherever relevant. Given the Christological interpretation of the "Glory" (כָּבוֹד) in the opening vision (Ezekiel 1, especially 1:26–28) and elsewhere in the book (especially chapters 10 and 43), it is legitimate, now using NT language and thought, to interpret *Christ as the divine speaker throughout the book* and the one in whose name and by whose authority the prophet gives his messages.

The dialectic of Law and Gospel will then be integrated with the axis of the cross and resurrection, which extends throughout the entire Scriptures. OT passages about judgment and salvation must be interpreted in light of Christ: God's judgment ultimately falls upon the sinless Christ on the cross, who thereby atones for the sins of all humanity. Christ's resurrection manifests God's verdict of justification *propter Christum* and the promise of resurrection to eternal life for all baptized believers in Christ. One day Christ will return in glory to bring this world to its end. On that day all the dead shall be raised. All

---

[1] The classic Lutheran treatment of hermeneutics is *Philologia sacra* by the seventeenth-century theologian Salomon Glassius (Jenae: Steinmann, 1623–1636). It was the standard textbook for over a century, until the advent of *Institutiones theologiae exegeticae in usum academicarum praelectionum adornatae* by Carl Gottlob Hofmann (Wittenberg: Io. Ioach. Ahlfeldivm, 1754; reprinted under the auspices of The Lutheran Church—Missouri Synod in St. Louis in 1876). Hofmann's textbook was the one from which the founders of the LCMS learned their hermeneutics.

those in Christ shall inherit the new heavens and new earth (compare Ezekiel 40–48 to Revelation 21–22), whereas all unbelievers will go "into everlasting fire" (Athanasian Creed).[2]

Traditionally, it has not been difficult to interpret the messianic and eschatological sections of Ezekiel in light of the first and second advents of Christ and the salvation entailed in each advent.

To do the obverse with the judgment oracles has generally proven much more difficult, at least in practice. Commentators on Ezekiel may not in principle deny the association between the judgment oracles and the meting out of God's judgment at Christ's first and second advents, but they tend not to implement that association in their interpretations. That naturally creates a severe problem in the interpretation of Ezekiel, since the first half of the book consists mainly of oracles of judgment or doom for Israel (chapters 1–24), and the next eight chapters are judgment oracles against other nations (chapters 25–32). That the judgment oracles are often bizarre in form and extreme in expression does not help to facilitate their interpretation. I consider this difficulty in explaining the judgment oracles to be an indictment of Lutheran practice in general: in our proclamation, the Law part of the paradox of Law and Gospel—judgment and salvation—often tends to come through weakly or nominally, if at all. This indictment against weak Law interpretation and proclamation is not intended to counter the dictum that the Gospel element should predominate. But if the Law part of the paradox is not proclaimed clearly and forcefully, neither can the Gospel be, and the question must soon arise whether some other "gospel" is being preached.

Regarding Word and Sacrament, the verbal prophecies in the OT obviously stand in continuity with the preaching of the Word in the church era. Like the NT, the OT too has its "sacramental" rites and institutions in which the forgiveness of sins is connected to physical means appointed by God. However, dogmatically speaking, the NT Sacraments—Christian Baptism and the Lord's Supper—are not present in the OT, that is, before Christ had come and instituted them. But just as there is a fundamental unity to the Word in both Testaments, so too a unity of the same sort exists in regard to the Sacraments. The difficulty is partly semantic. While "Word" is used in both Testaments, "Sacrament" is not a biblical vocable at all. But since the dogmatic term "Sacrament" applies to the physical, external means of grace to which God's Word and salvation are attached, we may regard such physical means of grace in the OT as the land, the temple, and the sacrifices to be "sacramental." I know of no better umbrella term to suggest the underlying unity of the peculiar means of salvation chosen by God in both Testaments than "sacramental." When I use the word in reference to the OT, I always enclose it in quotation marks to indicate

---

[2] This summary of biblical eschatology and the Christian faith is succinctly expressed in the Apostles', Nicene, and Athanasian Creeds.

that there is also an aspect of discontinuity and escalation between the OT prophecy and the greater NT fulfillment.

In Ezekiel, as anywhere in the OT, when topics such as these appear, we have to deal with the "ceremonial laws," which have been fulfilled in Christ and are no longer binding for the NT church. Inevitably, that means that certain details in those pericopes can only be interpreted within purely OT horizons. To one degree or the other, however, they usually have some kind of more general applicability to the time of the church.[3]

To establish that applicability we must invoke the dual hermeneutical principles uniting the two Testaments: prophecy-fulfillment and type-antitype. The extent to which these two pairs of terms are virtually two ways of saying the same thing becomes especially clear in a book like Ezekiel. Ezekiel utters prophecies about many ceremonial topics, but one unpacks their applicability to the Christian via typology. In short, Christ is the "new temple," and his sacrifice both fulfills and terminates the OT sacrificial and ceremonial rites (the topic of the book of Hebrews).

The hermeneutic for interpreting the land of Israel is harder, but, typically, Ezekiel's messianic oracles are inseparable from a restored "land" over which the Messiah and his people will rule. The NT antitype, when viewed eschatologically, includes the parousia and the eternal state, so we rightly understand the OT land to find its fulfillment in the new heavens and new earth to be inaugurated after Christ returns in glory (Ezekiel 40–48; Revelation 21–22). Even "glory" too rightly describes our eternal homeland. But how the land of Israel, as an OT type, applies to the first coming of Christ and the present era of the church is harder to understand. The NT itself generally avoids relating Israel's land to the present kingdom of God in Christ. That silence is understandable because of the territorial implications of the land in the ongoing Jewish revolt against Rome. Christ did not come to give Christians any particular piece of land on this present earth, but a portion in the life of the world to come.[4]

This same issue, in slightly different guise, still bedevils us whenever church-state relations appear. No earthly kingdom, nation, or people can be equated with OT Israel; it is Christians, scattered throughout the world, who comprise the true "Israel of God" (Gal 6:16). This issue appears whenever the theme of God's kingdom is articulated, as in the Lord's Prayer ("Thy kingdom come …"). Historically, Lutheranism has always nuanced the term "kingdom" differently from both Reformed and Catholic-Orthodox interpretations (themselves, of course, different from each other). Partly in reaction to Catholic claims of authority over and in the state, and to the reconstructionist efforts of

---

[3] See the kinds of Christian interpretations and ecclesiastical applications of OT ceremonial laws in Kleinig, *Leviticus*.

[4] One may see the Christian exposition of the significance of the land of Israel in "The Central Theme" in Harstad, *Joshua*, 25–31.

some Reformed churches to establish a "Christian" civil realm, Lutheranism has tended to limit the term "kingdom" to Christ's spiritual reign in the hearts of believers. The importance of that application is certainly not to be minimized, but it surely falls short of the great Pauline accent on the church as the "*body* of Christ" and related material accents such as the Sacraments, the resurrection of the body, and so on. The kingdom of God is comprised of flesh-and-blood people gathered around Word and Sacrament, awaiting the visible return of Christ and the resurrection to life everlasting in the physical paradise. The Holy Spirit is no "spiritualist"; the Christian faith involves far more than ethereal "spirituality."

That point provides an easy transition to a final topic in this section. The entire hermeneutical posture we have been summarizing has tended to be called "spiritual" or "pneumatic" exegesis. That label has its basis in the NT itself (e.g., 1 Cor 2:13–15), and such exegesis was practiced in the early church and for many centuries later. After the Enlightenment, when the historical-critical method "freed" its practitioners from all traditional and churchly commitments to the teachings of Scripture, "spiritual" exegesis was viewed as the antithesis of the critical agenda. A brief respite during the twentieth-century era of "biblical theology" was ultimately unable to turn the tide. The currently popular relativistic "postmodern" methods of interpretation have proved to be the least sympathetic of all to the scriptural witness. But the obvious abundance of Christological, spiritual, and Trinitarian exegesis of the OT throughout the NT itself (not to mention the consistent ecclesiastical use of that sort of OT exegesis in the faithful church throughout the ages) constrains us to follow that exegetical method and excludes critical and postmodern orientations.

Part of the modern objection to Christological, pneumatic exegesis is based on a misunderstanding of the terminology. Critics tend to pillory "spiritual" and "typological" interpretation as "allegorical," which they allege is the antipode of "historical" interpretation. To be sure, allegory, especially in the early church, was sometimes deployed in a way that disregarded the historical aspect of the biblical text. However, the term "allegory" itself does not intrinsically imply such an extreme; see St. Paul's use of ἀλληγορούμενα, "interpreted allegorically" (ESV), in Gal 4:24 and his Christological method of interpretation in Gal 4:21–5:6. Catholic interpreters, with their greater emphases on the Sacraments and the church, have tended to use the word "allegory" and methods that critics might label as such more frequently and positively than Protestant or Lutheran expositors. Nevertheless, since the word "allegory" has such overwhelmingly negative connotations today, it is probably best avoided.

The crucial issue is the way interpretation relates the biblical text to history. At one extreme, we have the histor*icism* of the critics, who think that they have exhaustively determined the meaning of the text if they believe they have discerned the intention of the original author in his own context (about which they rarely reach any agreement). At the other extreme, which might be called pure allegory, the interpretation floats clear of history, abandoning itself to the subjective whims and opinions of the modern interpreter. Some "postmodern" interpreters explicitly disregard the "intentionality" of the original author(s).

There is a responsible via media that takes seriously the historicity of the unique, original word or event recorded in Scripture as well as its theological continuity with succeeding words and events in history under God, all the way to the consummation of all history at the parousia of Christ. "Prophecy-fulfill-ment" and "typology" are the usual shorthand terms for what I like to call that "sacramental" view of history, in which the saving Christ truly is present "in, with, and under" the original word and historical event recorded in Scripture—in the OT as well as the NT. This Christological and eschatological interpre-tive perspective avoids the common truncation that thinks that OT passages "dead-end" in the first advent of Christ. To be sure, it is essential for the procla-mation of the Gospel to affirm that *the fulfillment* came in the incarnation, life, ministry, death, resurrection, and ascension of Christ, who is the pivot of all interpretation and of all Scripture. But at the same time, OT and NT passages continue to be "fulfilled" as the Holy Spirit (the Spirit of Christ) works in the life of the individual believer (beginning with Baptism) and of the corporate church, until the ultimate τέλος ("goal, end," as in Mt 10:22; 24:13–14) arrives at the return of Christ, whereupon follow the resurrection of the dead and eter-nal life in the new creation for all whose names are written in the Lamb's book of life.[a]

(a) Ex 32:32–33; Ps 69:29 (ET 69:28); Phil 4:3; Rev 3:5; 13:8; 20:12, 15; 21:27

With such a hermeneutic, even the famous *quadriga* (a team of four horses, applied to four senses) of classical allegorism can be affirmed. However, we do not think of four discrete senses, but of one, unified *fourfold* sense of Scrip-ture:

1. The historical meaning of the biblical passage remains factual and foundational.
2. Creedal and doctrinal conclusions follow, based on the text.
3. "Tropological" or moral implications are part of the message.
4. And, finally, the "anagogical" or eschatological scope of the passage must be con-sidered: all of history and life should be viewed *sub specie aeternitatis*, as part of God's eternal plan.

Specific applications of what I have summarized must be applied to each pericope in its particularity. No absolute rules can be posited to ensure a "cor-rect" exegesis of each unit. Often equally faithful exegetes will reach different conclusions about the same text. But if it is a genuinely Christian and Spiritual exegesis, it will inevitably fall within certain parameters. The broad outlines of those parameters have already been sketched. We often stress in the use of typology that as long as we remain close to the central course of redemptive history—from the original creation to the new creation, with Christ at the cen-ter—the danger of straying into the pseudospiritualism of allegory is all but eliminated.

Last, but not least, the role of the homiletician must be kept in mind. Is what the faithful preacher proclaims from the text part of its "meaning"? Tra-ditionally, the "meaning" of the text has been reserved specifically for the fruit

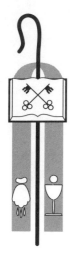

of the exegetical study of it, while the "application" of the text has been applied to the preacher's work. Such a distinction may or may not be valid.

If there is a complete discontinuity between the text's meaning and the sermon, obviously the pastor has abandoned textual, expository preaching. On the other hand, a lecture or Bible class that sets forth the expository meaning of the text is not a sermon. Undoubtedly, the preacher has a certain necessary freedom in applying the text to the particularities of his congregation's setting and his own circumstances. Ultimately, however, the faithful preacher too must yield to the same Spirit who inspired the text and who, through the Scriptures, disciplines the exegete. And the hallmark of a sermon is the proclamation (rather than "teaching") of Law and Gospel to the hearts of the sinner-saints who comprise the congregation gathered around Word and Sacrament.

Text and Style in Ezekiel

The state of the Hebrew text of the book of Ezekiel and the prophet's writing style are two distinct and disparate topics. Yet the two interact, and issues of biblical text and style may overlap nowhere more closely than in Ezekiel. A difficult style is likely to multiply textual variations among translators and copyists. Conversely, a difficult text may make it difficult to determine what the intended sense and literary style of the original words written by the prophet were.

A glance at the plethora of textual notes in *BHS* will suffice to indicate just how difficult many passages in Ezekiel actually are. Textual critics generally assert that the Masoretic Text of Ezekiel is the worst of the major prophets, with only Hosea, Samuel, and some psalms in even worse shape. Some of the textual notes in *BHS* (and other critical editions) are simply modern conjectures, passed off as "corrections." Others are based on actual evidence from Hebrew manuscripts and/or the ancient versions, especially the LXX. In many cases, the LXX has a shorter text than the MT (although not nearly to the degree that we meet almost throughout Jeremiah and Job, with even more radical divergences in Daniel). Was the original Hebrew text amplified on the way to becoming the MT or condensed in the Greek tradition? The divergence simply means that one of the two is further removed from the autograph. However, we hasten to add that rarely is the basic gist of the text in dispute, and virtually never anything of doctrinal concern.

The traditional view has been to assume the originality and correctness of the Hebrew, which is, after all, the language in which Ezekiel himself wrote. That tradition is followed in this commentary, but we note exceptional instances of textual variants. In each case, the exegete finally must make a judgment call, and each instance must be considered on its own merits.

Many of the older historical critics tended to prefer the LXX text. However, the pendulum is starting to swing back toward a more balanced view, with many more today preferring the Hebrew. Part of the reason for the change is that recent studies have shown that different Greek translators and copyists (recognizable by their choices of vocabulary) worked on the LXX version of Ezekiel. Also, some papyrus discoveries offer a different Greek text from the traditional LXX. Hence, it seems apparent that the Greek variations reflect their own various translational traditions and were not simply reproducing faithfully a Hebrew *Vorlage* different than the MT.

The other ancient versions do not significantly change the picture. The legible fragments of Ezekiel found at Qumran (a complete scroll of which could not be opened) follow the MT quite closely. The Targum is, of course, a paraphrase, but basically follows the Hebrew equally closely. About the same picture emerges in the Syriac Peshitta.

All of this leaves us with the question of Ezekiel's style itself. Adjectives such as "convoluted," "prolix," "repetitious," or the like are commonly used to describe it. Critics once blamed much of it on the clumsiness or insensitivity of later redactors or editors (and to a certain extent they still tend to do so), but there never was much consensus among the critics on the details. Except where the LXX seemed to support their conjectures, the entire approach was about as speculative as could be.

We must assume that the Hebrew is basically the way Ezekiel wanted it to be, and that the MT is as close as we are likely ever to get to the original autograph by the prophet himself. But how are we to parse or explain his style? Some of what strikes us as odd may be cultural: ancient Semitic compositions had different canons and conventions than modern types of literature do. Among those is the prominence of recapitulation or repetition. Yet even here Ezekiel does not follow the patterns typical of earlier classical Hebrew. The collapse of ancient Semitic cultures, specifically the Israelite monarchy, attendant on the invasions, migrations, and deportations climaxing around Ezekiel's time may have something to do with it. Even when he writes poetry, Ezekiel is far from the literary elegance of Isaiah, who wrote a century to a century and a half earlier (ca. 740–681 B.C.). It would help if we knew whether our text of Ezekiel is, in effect, a transcription of sermons he originally delivered orally, or whether he wrote them before preaching them. Oral discourses (especially sermons!) tend to be more expansive than written compositions. But, of course, writers, then as now, differ widely in style.

The issue could be related to the question of the nature of Ezekiel's speechlessness. A majority of the book's oracles come from the period when Ezekiel is so described. In 3:26 God states, "You will be speechless," and that condition endures from Ezekiel's initial commissioning to be a prophet until 33:22 (fulfilling 24:25–27), when word came that Jerusalem had actually fallen. If the prophet was in fact totally silent throughout that period, that would imply that he originally wrote at least that part of the book (chapters 1–33) before he preached it. However, 3:27 seems to indicate that he was mute except when God gave him an oracle, and then he could speak, though he could only utter God's words ("you must speak my words to them," 2:7; similar is 3:4). Even so, that does not answer the question of which came first, his preaching or his writing. Neither does it answer the question of whether the book's style reflects his oral manner of speaking or whether he wrote in his particular style with his readers (rather than his listeners) in mind.

Some of his unusual vocabulary may stem from Ezekiel's formation as a priest (1:3); as a priest, he would have a natural propensity to use liturgical language. Parts of the book approach what we know as "apocalyptic" style, with its own distinctive conventions. Ezekiel certainly does have his own characteristic Hebrew vocabulary, some of which will even be apparent to readers of the book in English, but most of it is not. The earlier prophets seem to have avoided ascribing their words to Yahweh's "Spirit," perhaps because that idiom had been hijacked by false prophets (e.g., 1 Ki 22:24), even as Montanists early in the Christian era and modern heretics too may appeal to new revelations by the "Spirit" (or some spirit!) to legitimate their false doctrines.[b]

(b) Cf. 1 Cor 12:10; 14:32; 2 Pet 1:21; Rev 19:10; 22:6

(c) E.g., Ezek 2:2; 3:12–14, 24; 8:3; 11:1, 5, 24

Ezekiel, however, regularly refers to his animation and inspiration by the "Spirit,"[c] even though false prophets, preaching Jerusalem's imminent deliverance, were still active (11:1–4 and especially chapter 13). Aramaisms are quite common (though some are disputed), probably due to the Babylonian context, where Aramaic was the lingua franca. In addition, one scholar has counted twenty-four definite, fourteen probable, and twelve possible Akkadianisms.[5] Ezekiel contains some one hundred thirty hapax legomena—words found only once in the OT—and they probably indicate his further distance from the language and culture of Jerusalem. The book lacks some key terms in OT theological vocabulary, for example, חֶסֶד ("grace, mercy"); אֱמוּנָה ("faithfulness"); and דַּעַת ("knowledge").

On the other hand, certain words and phrases are very common in Ezekiel, and some of these are unique to him. Most striking, and unique in the OT as a vocative, is God's consistent address to him as "son of man" (ninety-three times in the book), emphasizing that he is a mere human in contrast to God's transcendent and glorious divinity (see the textual notes and commentary on 2:1).

At the same time, various formulae are employed to emphasize that the prophet's words are really God's. What is commonly labeled the "word-event formula" occurs fifty times in Ezekiel (more often than in the other prophets): "the Word of Yahweh came (to me)." That formula tends to hypostasize the divine Word (דָּבָר) as *someone* who comes to the prophet and who also is the content of his preaching and writing. If so, this points to the incarnation of Jesus Christ, the Word who became flesh (Jn 1:1, 14; Rev 19:13) and who is the content of all Christian proclamation, as he is of the entire Scriptures. Also not unique to Ezekiel, but common in it (122 times), is the "citation formula," כֹּה אָמַר אֲדֹנָי יְהוִה, "thus says the Lord Yahweh." It usually occurs at the beginning of an oracle, but may also appear in the middle. The "signatory formula," נְאֻם אֲדֹנָי יְהוִה, "the oracle/speech of the Lord Yahweh" (the precise

---

[5] Garfinkel, *Studies in Akkadian Influences in the Book of Ezekiel.*

meaning of נְאֻם is unknown), is common in the prophets, but about one-fourth of its usages appear in Ezekiel (eighty-five times). It usually concludes an oracle, or at least a topic within the oracle.

Both the citation formula and the signatory formula are overwhelmingly used in Ezekiel with the long form of the divine name, "the Lord Yahweh." The use of both the title ("the Lord") and the proper name ("Yahweh") emphasizes the authority of the one who established his covenant and authorized his prophet to speak his Word. It also highlights the covenantal status of the people, even though they have apostatized from their Lord and his covenant.

Correspondingly, Ezekiel thirteen times terms his audience בֵּית הַמֶּרִי/ בֵּית מְרִי, literally, "(the) house of rebellion" or "(the) rebellious house." That may be a sardonic play on his much more common term (eighty-three times) for the people as בֵּית יִשְׂרָאֵל,[6] "the house of Israel." "House of Israel" was the old covenant name for the people, only temporarily preempted politically by the apostate and now defunct northern kingdom of "Israel." For the exiles in Babylon, the covenant name would have been particularly poignant, recalling their lineage and family status. We might compare it to the designation of the church as the "household of God" (Eph 2:19; 1 Tim 3:15; 1 Pet 4:17), "body of Christ" (1 Cor 12:27; Eph 4:12), and "the Israel of God" (Gal 6:16).

Yahweh's "oath formula" חַי־אָנִי, "as I live," is common in Ezekiel (sixteen times). Somewhat similarly, we meet fourteen times, especially at the end of oracles, אֲנִי יְהוָה דִּבַּרְתִּי, "I, Yahweh, have spoken," which underscores the performative power of his Word. Often we meet God's "self-introduction formula" alone, אֲנִי יְהוָה, "I am Yahweh." In the so-called "Holiness Code" of Leviticus (chapters 17–26), with its many affinities to Ezekiel, that declaration is often the only reason given why something is commanded or forbidden by God. In Ezekiel, it often appears at the end of a result clause, "then you/they will know that I am Yahweh." Alternatively, we meet "(then) they will know that a [true] prophet has been among them" (2:5; 33:33). These are usually known as variants of the "recognition formula," but we may also follow Zimmerli in labeling such expressions proof-sayings because the divine action or event announced by the prophet will prove to the people that Yahweh "is who he claims to be in his name."[7] Those idioms affirm what the Torah of Moses had said long ago—that God acts, both in judgment and in salvation, so that people will know that he is Yahweh.[d]

Among other common refrains is the "hostile orientation formula," where God says, "Behold, I am against …" (הִנְנִי אֶל/עַל).[e] To express such hostility, God directs his prophet, "Set your face against/toward" (שִׂים פָּנֶיךָ אֶל/עַל/דֶּרֶךְ).[f]

Besides specific words or phrases, Ezekiel uses a great variety of forms or genres of literature. Most striking are his uses of extended allegories to drive

(d) E.g., Ex 6:7; 7:5, 17; 10:2; 14:4; 16:6; Deut 4:35, 39; 7:9; 29:4–5 (ET 29:5–6)

(e) Ezek 5:8; 13:8, 20; 21:8 (ET 21:3); 26:3; 28:22; 29:3, 10; 30:22; 34:10; 35:3; 36:9; 38:3; 39:1

(f) Ezek 6:2; 13:17; 21:2 (ET 20:46); 21:7 (ET 21:2); 25:2; 28:21; 29:2; 35:2; 38:2

---

[6] See the textual notes and commentary on 2:3, 5; 3:1.

[7] Zimmerli, *Ezekiel*, 1:38.

(g) Ezek
15:1–8;
16:1–43;
17:1–24;
23:1–49;
27:1–36;
28:12–19;
31:1–18

(h) Ezek
19:1–14;
26:15–18;
28:11–19;
32:1–16

home his points.ᵍ Hermeneutically, "allegory" is the appropriate term here because it is not *we* who allegorize his literal text, but Ezekiel who, at God's command, writes allegories, then interprets them. Besides allegories, we find mocking laments over the dead,ʰ an extended historical recital of Israel's innumerable sins (20:3–26), legal disputations (18:1–32; 23:36–48), wisdom proverbs as starts for diatribes (12:22; 16:44; 18:2), and many other forms. As starting points for sermons, Ezekiel delights in using citations or quotations of the people against themselves.

We must mention Ezekiel's use of striking "action prophecies" to parallel his words. This provides a sort of Word-Sacrament synonymity. These are often called "symbolic actions" or considered a sort of street-theater as a teaching aid. Such labels are perhaps not entirely inappropriate, but they are all too weak; "sacramental" and "performative" are much better. Other prophets use such acted-out prophecies too, but none as often as Ezekiel, nor as bizarre as Ezekiel's often are (especially chapters 4–5).

As scholars have increasingly stopped trying to solve their difficulties by hypothesizing scenarios of editorial amplifications of a putative shorter original text, and have seriously analyzed the Hebrew text as it stands, they have increasingly discovered just how many and how intricate are the various artistic devices employed in Ezekiel. Here Greenberg in his Anchor Bible commentaries has made signal contributions in calling attention to patterns such as spiraling techniques, by which an oracle moves to a higher or more intense level; "halving," in which a shorter oracle follows a longer one, almost as an echo; panels, in which parts are constructed parallel to each other; and many others. We hope that future scholarly efforts will be directed in that same generally constructive direction so as to shed greater light on the sophisticated literary techniques with which the prophet conveys his message.

Outline and Theological Emphases

As in the preceding introductory section, again we are treating two discrete topics in one breath, as it were. That procedure seems appropriate for a book like Ezekiel, since the two are so closely intertwined.

There is not much point in trying to offer more than a four or five point outline of the book, for delving into more detail would necessitate making each chapter a point in the outline (see the detailed outline that forms the table of contents). There can be little debate about the following:

1. Chapters 1–3 are the prophet's inaugural vision and commissioning.
2. Chapters 4–24 are prophecies of judgment against the Israelites, mostly condemning those still living in Judah, but also the exiles to a certain extent.
3. Chapters 25–32 are Gentile oracles—oracles against foreign nations.
4. Chapters 33–39 are mostly oracles of Israel's eschatological restoration.
5. Chapters 40–48 are a vision of the "new Jerusalem" and the "new creation" surrounding it. (This fifth section could be treated as the concluding part of the eschatological restoration, with chapters 33–39 as the initial part.)

Before we analyze the above outline theologically, we may also note what I have called an "internal outline" centering on three appearances of the "Glory" (כָּבוֹד). First, this Glory in the form of a man (1:26–28), a preincarnate Christophany, is the substance of the inaugural vision. Second, in chapters 8–11 Ezekiel again witnesses the "Glory" (כָּבוֹד), which forsakes the hopelessly corrupt temple in Jerusalem and goes into "exile" on the Mount of Olives across the Kidron.[i] Yahweh is abandoning the city and temple to its now inevitable destruction. Finally, in 43:1–5 the prophet sees the same "Glory" (כָּבוֹד) return to the restored and holy eschatological temple, which is the center of the new Israel, a type of the church triumphant—the eternal dwelling place of all believers.

(i) Ezek 8:4; 9:3; 10:4, 18–19; 11:22–23

Something similar to that "internal outline" in Ezekiel is in the book of Revelation. First, the glorified Christ appears to the apostle John (Rev 1:12–20). Second, in chapters 4–5 the apostle John witnesses the heavenly throne scene, which includes four living creatures that seem to be the same ones described by Ezekiel in Ezekiel 1 and 10. Prophecies of judgment and destruction, intermixed with scenes of salvation for those in Christ, follow in Revelation 6–20. Finally, the book concludes with a glorious vision of the eschatological state, where the Jerusalem temple has been replaced with God and the Lamb, dwelling forever among the redeemed in Christ (compare Revelation 21–22 to Ezekiel 40–48).

Let us return to the main outline of Ezekiel. I have often referred to the sequence exhibited in Ezekiel as the "classical prophetic outline." That may be a bit of an overstatement, but the same outline is clearly used in Isaiah 1–27; in the LXX arrangement of Jeremiah; and in Zephaniah.[8] What gives it special cogency in Ezekiel is that its theological import coincides perfectly with the historical events that occurred during the time when each of the main sections of the prophecy were being proclaimed. That theological import, in Ezekiel and in other OT and NT books, may be summarized under the phrase "Law and Gospel." In general terms, the outline can be summarized in this way:

1. God's judgment falls upon Judah and Jerusalem. Judgment begins with the household of God (1 Pet 4:17).

2. God's judgment falls upon pagan nations (Gentile unbelievers). "If it [judgment] begins with us, what will be the end of those who disbelieve the Gospel of God?" (1 Pet 4:17).

3. God brings salvation for all who repent and believe.

The theology implicit in this classical prophetic outline is summarized by St. Paul in Rom 3:22–24:

---

8 Some commentators are of the opinion that the classical prophetic outline originated with Ezekiel, but that is based on the hypothesis of a long gap between Isaiah's activity and the final edition of his book. That opinion is too close to the usual critical dating of the beginnings of canonical formation of most of the OT not to arouse suspicion.

The righteousness of God [is] through faith in Jesus Christ for all who believe. For there is no distinction [between Jew and Gentile], for all have sinned and fall short of the glory of God, being justified freely by his grace through the redemption that is in Christ Jesus.

When we read the outline of Ezekiel in that way, the most profound theology is enshrined in what otherwise would simply be an inert arrangement of material.

No particular theological meaning attaches to the precise datings that occur throughout the book. There are many of these in Jeremiah too, but not at all in chronological order. All of those in Ezekiel are chronological, save one, and all are pegged to the year of the exile of King Jehoiachin, save one. These dates appear at fourteen points in the book: 1:1–2; 3:16; 8:1; 20:1; 24:1; 26:1; 29:1; 29:17; 30:20; 31:1; 32:1; 32:17; 33:21; and 40:1. The only date that is not in reference to the exile of Jehoiachin is the "thirtieth year" in 1:1, which probably is from the prophet's birth, and hence gives his age at the time of his call. The only one that is not in chronological order is 29:17, which is the latest date in the entire book. Apparently because of the interposition in the overall outline, which groups the Gentile oracles together, the prophecy on Egypt in 29:17–21 was placed after a much earlier oracle on Egypt in 29:1–16, even though it seems to be the last prophecy of Ezekiel (of which we have record).

Another editorial device apparent in Ezekiel, although by no means unique to him, is what I like to style as "the alternation of weal and woe." (The archaic English word "weal" means "welfare" and is retained by many commentators for the sake of assonance with "woe.") In essence, this is the alternation of Law and Gospel. One of the most striking examples in the book occurs toward the end of chapter 16, beginning at 16:53 and climaxing in 16:60–63. After a long chapter detailing the utter depravity of Jerusalem, we suddenly hear of the restoration of fortunes and God remembering his covenant. Since there is no indication that his audience had repented, it is doubtful that Ezekiel would have so suddenly changed emphases based on any change in them. But by the composition of his book, he reminds all generations that, as always, the antecedent purpose of God's judgment or "Law" (God's "alien work"; see Is 28:21) is to elicit repentance and so prepare for the Gospel of pure grace, by which God accomplishes his "proper work" (indirectly derived from Is 29:14) of justifying the sinner for Christ's sake. This rhetorical feature thus reinforces the theological thrust of the classical prophetic outline. The "woe" passages are generally more precisely dated than the "weal" ones, possibly as a way of saying that God's "anger is but for a moment; in his favor is [everlasting] life" (Ps 30:6 [ET 30:5]).

Beyond these "Law-Gospel" themes that are built into the very structure of the book, there are many others that must be stressed. It is more important to do this with Ezekiel because, in my estimation, it is the least known—that is, the most neglected—of the major prophets. We have already noted some of the reasons for this neglect: Ezekiel's accent on judgment or "Law"—a theme that, functionally at least, the church finds uncomfortable and tends to treat quite perfunctorily. The problem is surely intensified by the often weird and verbose ways in which Ezekiel makes the point.

The obverse reason for the neglect of the book by the church is its relatively brief overtly messianic material. If we define "messianic" too narrowly and then unconsciously try to reduce the entire OT to the narrow theme of prophecy explicitly predictive of the person and work of Christ (which I think we have often been guilty of doing), then we will have special difficulties with Ezekiel. If one understands "Messiah" primarily in royal terms—the new Son of David and King of Israel—the explicit references to the new "David" who will be the "shepherd" and "king" are Ezek 34:23–24 and 37:24–25. Those passages are often read in conjunction with Jeremiah 23; John 10; and other "shepherd" passages in the Bible. But if one defines "messianic" broadly of all prophecies of Israel's restoration, the book is full of them, even in the earlier sections. And it should be noted that, as the prophets commonly do, Ezekiel immediately broadens the application to apply not only to what we NT believers know to be Christ's first advent but also to Christ's second coming. The distinction between the two is hard enough to discern in the OT, and even in the NT it must be handled carefully, so that the necessary distinction does not degenerate into a divorce.

The enigmatic "Prince" (נָשִׂיא, 44:3; 45:7; etc.) in chapters 40–48 is not depicted with all of the same kind of "messianic" vocabulary and imagery familiar from the other prophets. We shall discuss his role in the commentary on those chapters, also in relation to the new "David" who is the "shepherd" and "king" in Ezek 34:23–24 and 37:24–25, since that Davidide is identified as "Prince" (נָשִׂיא) in 34:24 and 37:25. The main role of "David" in chapters 34 and 37, and the "Prince" in chapters 40–48, seems to be to rule in Jerusalem after *Yahweh* has delivered his people. Inevitably, some critics have seen a contradiction here with other depictions of the Messiah as the active agent of peace, righteousness, and so on who is the one to deliver the people. But there is no contradiction because from a NT perspective, the OT descriptions of "Yahweh" and "Messiah" refer to one and the same triune God.

All commentators agree that Ezekiel places a tremendous accent on the might, majesty, and transcendence of Yahweh. This is apparent from the opening vision (chapter 1), as well as from Yahweh's consistent address to the prophet as "son of man"—a mere mortal—throughout the book. Ezekiel does not explicitly speak of Yahweh's holiness, which is so prominent in especially Isaiah, but does highlight the obverse of Yahweh's holiness, namely, his glory. An often-quoted formula asserts that God's holiness is his glory concealed, and his glory is his holiness revealed. Sometimes, Yahweh's "Glory" (כָּבוֹד) has hypostatic or "incarnational" significance, as we shall stress in chapter 1.[9] But at other times it is used in a more general sense. For example, by defeating the horde of Gog, Yahweh says, "I will establish my glory" (נָתַתִּי אֶת־כְּבוֹדִי) among

---

[9] See the textual notes and commentary on 1:26–28.

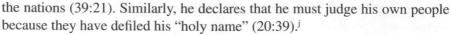

(j) See also
Ezek
36:20–22;
39:7, 25;
43:7–8

the nations (39:21). Similarly, he declares that he must judge his own people because they have defiled his "holy name" (20:39).[j]

Ezekiel witnesses to his awareness of the vast gulf between himself and Yahweh by addressing and referring to him 217 times as אֲדֹנָי יְהוִה, "the Lord Yahweh," using a plural of majesty for "Lord" (אֲדֹנָי), the vowels of which were usually added to the Tetragrammaton itself after the sacred name began to be considered unpronounceable (see the textual note on this phrase in 2:4).

Corresponding to Yahweh's exaltedness is a heightened awareness of mediatorial creatures who help bridge the gulf between Yahweh and man. Some mediating features, such as the "hand" of Yahweh (e.g., 1:3; 8:1; 33:22) seem to be hypostatic for God himself, but other mediators may be what will come to be known as "angels." Such are the "living creatures" in chapter 1, who reappear in chapters 10–11, where Ezekiel will call them "cherubim."[10]

As for the "man" who serves as Ezekiel's spiritual guide above the Jerusalem temple in chapters 8–11, and the "man" who guides him through the new Jerusalem in chapters 40–48, it is debatable whether he is angelic or a hypostasis of God, perhaps the preincarnate Christ.[11] The existence of angels had already been revealed in the oldest parts of the Scriptures (e.g., Gen 3:24; Job 38:7), but beginning especially with Ezekiel, and continuing in Daniel and Zechariah, more attention is paid to them, and their descriptions and roles in these OT books are much greater than in any preceding biblical book.

It may not be quite accurate to call Ezekiel the "father of apocalyptic," especially in light of the role played by his contemporary Daniel, but apocalyptic themes will grow in frequency in the later Scriptures (e.g., Zechariah) and the intertestamental literature. In this respect, Ezekiel plays a prominent role in the *praeparatio evangelica*, the "preparation for the Gospel" of Jesus Christ, preparation for when the Word would become flesh and angels would play prominent roles in the accompanying events (the annunciation, the angelic choir, etc.).

Attention must also be called to the relatively large amount of consideration Ezekiel gives to the cultic, liturgical, and "sacramental" aspect of revelation. Being a priest by training, it is scarcely surprising to see him steeped in the vocabulary and concerns that predominate in Leviticus. In certain other prophetic respects, Ezekiel has much in common with his older contemporary Jeremiah, but in respect to priestly concerns and liturgy, Ezekiel and Jeremiah, on the surface at least, occupy opposite poles.

However, we should not make more out of that difference than the biblical facts will bear. Virtually all the prophets address liturgical matters when

---

[10] See the textual note on חַיּוֹת in 1:5.

[11] The same debate pertains to the glorious "man" in Daniel 10 and the "mighty angel" in Revelation 10: are they truly angels, or are they Christophanies? See "The Identity and Function of the Mighty Angel of Revelation 10" in Brighton, *Revelation*, 274–78, and Gieschen, *Angelomorphic Christology*.

condemning abuses of the liturgy, especially the practice of rituals divorced from theology, faith, and ethics. Ezekiel certainly condemns those abuses too.[12] However, his whole book is cast in a liturgical milieu. That is especially obvious at both the beginning and end of the book: the call vision features the winged living creatures, clearly reflecting the cherubim above the ark of the covenant in the temple,[13] and the last nine chapters (Ezekiel 40–48) center on the eschatological temple. Furthermore, Ezekiel tends to use plenty of Levitical vocabulary, such as describing sin as "uncleanness."[14]

Although in one sense, then, Ezekiel is still very much in the *Old* Testament, his eschatological prophecies make plain that the advent and parousia of Jesus Christ will not simply effect a restoration of the old covenant, which Israel had broken. Perhaps the clearest evidence of that is Ezekiel's use of the "mountain" motif. The theme appears in chapters 6; 17 (see 17:22–23); 18 (see 18:6, 11, 15); 20 (see 20:40); 28 (see 28:14, 16); 34–36; 38–39; and 40–43 (see 40:2; 43:12).[k] The defilement of Israel's mountains by the people's pagan practices will be replaced by the true God's rule from those same mountains. In such a context, one would expect to see the motif of Mount Zion—the temple mount and dwelling place of Yahweh—featured prominently, as in Isaiah and Jeremiah,[l] but in Ezekiel it is not. "Zion" is even absent from the vision of the eschatological temple on the mountain in Ezekiel 40–48.[15] The model in Ezekiel 40–48 appears to be a new theophany and theocracy unlike anything before, a reality beyond the OT itself. Its eschatological temple far transcends the Solomonic temple on Zion, and its arrangement of the twelve tribes of Israel in the restored land differs radically from that prescribed in Joshua (the preliminary fulfillment of the Torah). The picture in Ezekiel 40–48 most closely resembles that of the eschaton in Revelation 21–22 (although there the temple has been replaced by God and the Lamb, Rev 21:22).

Ezekiel's priestly stamp characterizes the entire book to one degree or the other. It is hard to prove or even measure, but I suspect that this poses special problems for many Lutherans, at least to the extent that they identify with

(k) See also Ezek 19:9; 22:9; 28:14–16; 31:12; 32:5–6; 33:28; 37:22

(l) E.g., Is 2:1–5; 4:2–6; 28:16; 51:3; 52:7–8; 61:3; Jer 31:6, 12; 50:5; 51:10

---

[12] The Lutheran confessors cited Ezekiel in that vein to combat sacerdotalism: "Nor dare we assume that the church immediately approves or accepts whatever the pontiffs decide, especially when Scripture prophesies about bishops and pastors in the words of Ezekiel (7:26), 'The law perishes from the priest' " (Ap XXII 17). See also the citation of Ezek 20:18–19 in Ap XV 14.

[13] The creatures he first sees in 1:5–12 he will call "cherubim" (Ezek 10:1–20; 11:22) when he sees them again. He refers to cherub(im) also in 9:3; 28:14, 16; 41:18, 20, 25. See further the textual notes and commentary on 1:5–12.

[14] For example, 22:15; 24:11, 13. See also 4:13–14, which deals with unclean food. For the Levitical background, see, for example, Lev 5:3; 7:19–21; chapter 11.

[15] The vision in Ezekiel 40–48 seems more reminiscent of Mount Sinai than of Mount Zion. Ezekiel 40–48 emphasizes scrupulous obedience to priestly laws (recalling the Sinai legislation), although those laws in Ezekiel differ in some key respects from the laws in the Torah, for reasons that are debated (see later discussion). While the name "Zion" is frequent in Isaiah and Jeremiah, it is completely absent from the book of Ezekiel.

Protestantism more than with their catholic heritage. Ezekiel was a prophet as well as a priest (1:3). He exhibits many continuities with the whole "goodly fellowship of the prophets" (Te Deum Laudamus) even as he expresses his prophecy in liturgical and "sacramental" terms. Thus, he is one of our best exemplars of a minister who combines the Abrahamic and Mosaic strands of OT theology, which are comparable to the Pauline and Petrine strands, respectively, in NT theology.[16] Ezekiel, like other prophets, calls the people away from cultic abuses and back to the justifying faith of Abraham (Gen 15:6), as does St. Paul in Galatians 3–4. At the same time, he, like a faithful priest, calls the people to a renewal of right worship after the manner of the OT divine service in liturgical purity (cf. the priestly language of the apostle Peter in 1 Peter 2). As a book combining prophetic (faith) and priestly (liturgical, sacramental) concerns, the closest NT parallel may be the book of Hebrews.

We might recall Tillich's famous phrases (although we use them with different understandings than his), "Protestant principle" and "Catholic substance."[17] The biblical accent on the necessity of personal faith and accountability before God (which, without a proper understanding of the means of grace, could degenerate into subjectivism) must be accompanied by the biblical accent on the objective grace of God proffered in Scripture and the Sacraments (which, without a right understanding of faith, could degenerate into *ex opere operato* [by the mere performance of the act] ritualism or objectivism). In the United States, our Protestant, "evangelical" (Arminian) church context and the individualistic "choice" culture of our secular age combine in a way that makes the biblical stress on the Sacraments in liturgical worship the most difficult of these themes for many Christians to appreciate. American Christianity has been oriented far more toward the Word than to the Sacraments.

The book of Ezekiel provides a needed corrective to that imbalance. Virtually everything else that can be asserted of Ezekiel must be heard in that perspective: through him, God's objective "Word and Sacrament" confronts the hearers "whether they listen or do not" (2:5, 7; 3:11; cf. 3:27).

Perhaps more than any other prophet, Ezekiel is the "prophet of the paradox." Maybe his position on the "continental divide" of OT history—on the cusp of the exile, the watershed event—helps explain it. It may be hyperbolic to equate that divide with the far greater divide between B.C. and A.D., but there are similarities nonetheless. All the same paradoxes that virtually constitute Lutheranism are proclaimed with extraordinary force in Ezekiel as an old era

---

[16] One may see the discussion of the Abrahamic and Mosaic covenants in relation to the new covenant in Christ in the excursus "Covenant" in Harstad, *Joshua*, 744–49. As for Pauline and Petrine theology, we reject the critical construal of them as opposed to one another. Rather, both apostles proclaimed justification by grace alone and through faith alone. Nevertheless, each retained distinctive emphases: Paul was apostle to the Gentiles, who had no prior connection to the Mosaic Torah, while Peter was apostle to the Jews, for whom the Torah had been foundational (Gal 2:8–9).

[17] Paul Tillich, *Systematic Theology* (Chicago: University of Chicago Press, 1963), 3:6, 245.

disappears forever under God's judgment and a new era of God's grace dawns. The Israelites who would return to Judea from Babylon after Cyrus' edict would make pitiful attempts to return to the status quo ante, but the times could never again be the same. And, although the transition came too gradually for us to pinpoint it exactly, by about 200 B.C., the religion of many Israelites had changed from "Yahwism" (the OT religion) to "Judaism," which by NT times was essentially established in the Pharisaic party, although codification did not come until A.D. 200 with the writing down of the Mishnah (the core of the Talmud).

We, of course, do not read the OT through the lens of the Talmud, but through that of Christ and the NT. Through that lens, we can see so much in Ezekiel that anticipates Christ. Like all the prophets, he predicts the (as yet unknown) future by analogy with the (known) past and present. I like to compare that aspect of the prophets to the way the NT describes heaven in terms that are familiar to us from our present existence, yet also in terms that transcend it. Hence we, just like the OT prophets, have a picture of the future that is true and accurate (as revealed in Scripture) but also beyond our ken (cf. 1 Cor 13:12).

Paradoxes proclaimed with special vigor in Ezekiel are those that we Lutherans call Law and Gospel; simultaneously sinner and saint; the two kingdoms (church and state, the kingdom of God and the kingdoms of this world); and the eschatological tension between "already now" and "not yet." Perhaps no prophet brings out so clearly the motif, so dominant in Luther, of *sub contrario*: God works through apparent opposites. He kills in order to make alive (1 Sam 2:6); he punishes and disciplines in order to bless; he chooses things that are not to reduce to nothing things that are (1 Cor 1:28). That motif, of course, centers on the death and resurrection of Jesus Christ, our baptismal incorporation into his death that we may be raised with him (Romans 6), and the weakness and folly of the cross, which is the power and wisdom of God for the salvation of everyone who believes (1 Cor 1:18–31).

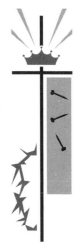

For Israel in Ezekiel's day, the nation's "death" is the exile, and while the return will be a small "resurrection," not until the advent of Christ (the new "David" promised in Ezek 34:23–24; 37:24–25) will God reconstitute his Israel (the church, consisting of Jews and Gentiles alike in Christ) with the full power of the Messiah's resurrection and the Spirit poured out in his name (Ezekiel 37; 40–48).

In Ezekiel, the pivot of the two eons comes in chapter 33, and more particularly 33:21–22. When a messenger arrives with the news that Jerusalem has indeed fallen, the prophet is no longer mute. Moreover, he can cease accenting God's *opus alienum* (judgment under the Law) and accent rather his *opus proprium* (justification according to the Gospel). Chapter 33 is the beginning of the fourth part of the "classical prophetic outline" (oracles of Israel's eschatological restoration; see above). Hence the theology Ezekiel begins to preach in chapter 33 is at the same time illustrated by the current event. The fall of Jerusalem can be likened to the death of Christ: it appears to be utter defeat, yet paradoxically it is the event that signals the start of the new era of salvation. We recall that Jeremiah's Lamentations, a dirge about fallen Jerusalem, has been a traditional lectionary reading for Good Friday or Holy Saturday.

If one knows Bach, "the fifth evangelist," the "theology of the cross" expounded in Ezekiel 33 is expressed unforgettably in his *St. John Passion*, where the doleful aria "It is finished" is momentarily interrupted with the joyful paean "The hero from Judah has triumphed in strength." A similar thought is expressed in liturgical art in the so-called *Christus rex*, "Christ the King." Christ is depicted on the cross clad in Eucharistic vestments. The message, then, is not only Christ's resurrection triumph after his crucifixion, but also that he delivers that same triumph to us "as often as you eat this bread and drink the cup" (1 Cor 11:26).

Other paradoxes come into focus in Ezekiel as well: God's otherness as well as his nearness (cf. Ezek 11:16—God as a "sanctuary" to the Israelites, even in exile in Babylon); eschatology and ethics; faith and works; promise and fulfillment; the individual believer and the community (the believer in church and society); particularism and universalism (the prophet's messages for Israel in particular and universally for all nations).

Von Rad has well written:

> No other prophet feels so great a need to think out problems so thoroughly and to explain them with such complete consistency. In other words, Ezekiel is not only a prophet, but a theologian as well. And this double office was essential for him, because he confronted a presumptuous and indeed rebellious generation for which a prophet's preaching was not enough: he had to debate and argue with it.[18]

In that light, Ezekiel's language and perhaps sometimes tiresome reading can be seen in a much more positive light.

Let us add one final note. Ezekiel is also called to be a pastor, a "watchman" of the flock, as he styles it (3:17–21; 33:1–7). God charges him to proclaim the divine Word, which is a matter of death and life, both for himself and his hearers, and both now and for eternity (see the commentary on 3:17–21). His responsibility depends not at all upon whether the sinners to whom he preaches do or do not repent. His "success" is measured only by his fidelity in preaching judgment and eschatological salvation. If he fails to warn the sinner, God will hold him responsible for the sinner's blood. If he carries out his duty to preach the Word, he will have saved his own life—and that of the sinner too, if he repents, just as St. Paul says to young Pastor Timothy in 1 Tim 4:6. Hence Ezekiel's ministry is a model for all pastors in these latter days when the pressure is so great to scratch itching ears (2 Tim 4:3), and the imminent event is not the destruction of Jerusalem, but the dissolution of the entire world, to be followed by the new and eternal creation.

---

[18]   Von Rad, *Old Testament Theology*, 2:223.

Preach you the Word and plant it home
    To men who like or like it not,
The Word that shall endure and stand
    When flow'rs and men shall be forgot.[19]

Historical Context of the Book of Ezekiel

Fortunately, we are about as well-informed about the history of the ancient Near East in Ezekiel's time as of any period in the OT. Much of our knowledge comes from the Bible itself, especially 2 Kings 22–25 and 2 Chronicles 34–36, and much of the last half of the book of Jeremiah. In addition, we have fairly detailed records from Babylon, which was a world power for only a relatively short time, but that time coincided fairly closely with Ezekiel's own lifetime. If the "thirtieth year" in Ezek 1:1 refers to Ezekiel's age at the time of his call, that would place his birth at about 627 B.C. or shortly afterward. At the moment, Assyria still ruled in all its glory and ostensibly at the height of its power. Yet by the time Ezekiel came of age, Assyria had disappeared as a nation.

Externally, and ultimately fatally, the major challenge to Assyria came from a Chaldean (Aramean) people, the Babylonians, led by Nabopolassar, Nebuchadnezzar's father, and their allies from the northeast, the Medes. See the map in the back of this book. The ancient capital Asshur[20] fell in 614, and Nineveh fell two years later. Assyria made its last stand at Haran, but this city too fell in 610, when Ezekiel was about seventeen. The Egyptians, under Pharaoh Neco, marched to Assyria's aid. At the Megiddo pass in 609, the Judean king Josiah lost his life in a futile attempt to stop Neco's march north. The Assyrians, with the help of their Egyptian allies, attempted to retake Haran in 609 and failed. The Assyrian defeat left Egypt and Babylon to contend for the succession to Assyria's world hegemony. That contest was decided at the battles of Carchemish and Hamath in 605, with Nebuchadnezzar himself leading the victorious Babylonian army. The battle of Carchemish is mentioned by name in Jer 46:2.

Shortly after Nebuchadnezzar's great victories, his father died, and he had to return home to secure his throne before he could consolidate his power in the Levant. But in short order the Babylonians returned, and Jehoiakim (Josiah's son) became Nebuchadnezzar's vassal. He remained a vassal for three years (probably from 604 to 602), but then rebelled, partly relying on Egypt's hollow promises of aid. In December 598 Jehoiakim died (he was probably assassinated) before retribution for his rebellion arrived, and his son Jehoiachin succeeded him—and was left to pay the price for his father's folly. In that same month, the Babylonian army marched against Judah, and on March 16, 597, Jerusalem surrendered. Not only King Jehoiachin, but much of the nobility, including Ezekiel, as a member of a priestly family, was exiled. Not surprisingly,

---

[19] From "Preach You the Word," by Martin Franzmann (*LW* 259.1). Copyright 1971 Mrs. Martin Franzmann. Used by permission of the Martin H. Franzmann family.

[20] "Asshur" can denote the whole of Assyria as well as its capital city.

the deportees were settled in old Chaldean territory in southeastern Mesopotamia (modern Iraq).

Five years into the exile, in 593, Ezekiel's call came. This was the "fifth year" (1:2), counting inclusively (the usual way of counting time in the OT). Almost two-thirds of the book records the prophet's words and actions from then until the final catastrophe in 587. In 33:21 come the words of a messenger with the dreaded news that "the city [Jerusalem] has fallen." The rest of the book is eschatological: in God's own good time the recent sad history will be reversed.

We know that still another insurrection and probably still another deportation occurred around 582, apparently upon the assassination of Gedaliah, whom the Babylonians had installed as regent in Judah (Jeremiah 40–41), but we hear nothing of this in Ezekiel. The last dated prophecy in the book (Ezek 29:17) is in the "twenty-seventh year" after Jehoiachin's (and Ezekiel's) exile, that is, in 571, which gives the prophet a total recorded ministry of somewhat over twenty years.

History of Interpretation of the Book of Ezekiel

Most modern commentaries consider only how the book has fared at the hands of higher critics. That is hardly fair, because there had been over two millennia of interpretation of the book as canonical before the critical era began. The history of the OT canon is beyond our purview here,[21] but one can make as good a case as for any biblical book that Ezekiel commended itself almost immediately as inspired by God, as conservatives have tended to argue throughout the ages. The reason is that "history" had vindicated Ezekiel in as direct and immediate a way as possible: Jerusalem and its temple had indeed been destroyed!

We should begin with what the rest of the canon itself has to say about Ezekiel. Modern criticism often makes a lot out of what it calls "inner-biblical interpretation." At critical hands, that phrase is usually bound up with tradition-historical theories about how a book allegedly was edited and reedited to suit later circumstances, until at some point the process was more or less halted. But we can use the phrase rightly of books later than Ezekiel that in some way attest the prophet's message and his own writing of his book.

We can begin with Ezekiel's younger contemporary, Daniel. Some surface connection is visible in the prominence of "son of man" in both books, even if we cannot trace a dependency. The referents of the phrase are almost completely different: in Ezekiel it refers to the prophet (see 2:1), whereas in Daniel it refers to the preincarnate Christ, who receives from the Ancient of Days the kingdom of God, over which he reigns forever, and the worship of men (Dan 7:13–14). Nevertheless, the "Son of Man" in Daniel comes on the clouds of heaven to receive "glory" (Dan 7:13), and in Ezekiel 1 the enthroned "Glory" (1:28) in the form of "a man" (1:26) arrives in a wind-storm (1:4). More gen-

---

[21] One may see Steinmann, *The Oracles of God.*

erally, to the extent that Ezekiel is the "father of apocalyptic," as to some extent he may rightly be called, that genre of literature is even more apparent in Daniel (especially chapters 7–12).

Zechariah also exhibits apocalyptic qualities, and perhaps the precise dating in both Zechariah and Haggai may be part of Ezekiel's legacy, although that honor would have to be shared with Jeremiah, who also supplies precise dates at various points in his prophecy.

Apocryphal and pseudepigraphical texts mention Ezekiel: Sirach 49:8 refers to his call, and 4 Macc 18:17 alludes to the resurrection scene in Ezekiel 37 by quoting 37:3.

Josephus in *Antiquities* makes two comments that are not fully understood—and hence have stimulated much discussion and speculation. First, after referring to Jeremiah and Ezekiel, he reports that Ezekiel "was the first person that wrote."[22] Often, it has been assumed that poetry was originally disseminated in oral form, so this remark of Josephus may refer to the overwhelmingly prose idiom of Ezekiel. Josephus may be saying that Ezekiel was the first prophet to write in prose. However, Josephus provides no further explanation of what he meant by his remark, and scholars offer various other explanations of it.

Second, and even more enigmatically, Josephus reports that Ezekiel "left behind him in writing *two* books, concerning these events [the fall of Jerusalem and the exile]."[23] What could be his second book? Some think of chapters 40–48, about the eschatological temple, which many critics have declared to be a secondary addition, but Josephus would not have subscribed to modern critical theory. More likely, Josephus refers to the *Apocryphon of Ezekiel*, written in the first century B.C. or the first century A.D. Only four fragments of it in secondary literature and one fragment of the apocryphon itself have survived, but its main theme seems to have been the doctrine of the resurrection, perhaps a sort of midrash on Ezekiel 37.

At Qumran, Ezekiel's influence was apparently considerable. A large scroll of the prophet, found in cave 11, could not be opened, but several fragments of Ezekiel have been recovered from other caves.[24] The sectarian writings from Qumran contain many similarities to Ezekiel. The description of the eschatological temple in the *Temple Scroll* is not identical with Ezekiel's description in chapters 40–48, but it has many commonalties. The emphasis on the Zadokite priesthood in the *Damascus Document* may be compared to Ezekiel's priestly orientation. Finally, the heavy use of the heavenly throne-chariot (מֶרְכָּבָה, *merkavah*) in the *Songs of the Sabbath Sacrifice* recalls Ezekiel 1 and 10.

---

[22] Josephus, *Antiquities*, 10.79 (10.5.1); William Whiston, trans., *The Works of Josephus* (complete and unabridged; new updated ed.; Peabody, Mass.: Hendrickson, 1987), 271.

[23] Josephus, *Antiquities*, 10.79 (10.5.1), Whiston, *The Works of Josephus*, 271; emphasis added.

[24] See Zimmerli, *Ezekiel*, 1:75.

The throne-chariot (*merkavah*) became a topic of extensive speculation in the writings of the mystical Kabbalah branch of Judaism. That motif had an ambivalent influence on more orthodox (rabbinic) Judaism. On the one hand, the tendency of such speculation to degenerate into quasi-Gnostic beliefs, as well as orthodox Judaism's misgivings about possible contradictions between the priestly laws in Ezekiel 40–48 and the laws of the Pentateuch, made Ezekiel problematic for orthodox Judaism. On the other hand, especially after the Roman destruction of Jerusalem in A.D. 70, the throne-chariot motif must have served as a vivid way to conceptualize God's transcendent power and presence. Apparently that ambivalence led to the rabbinic rule, noted by Jerome, that a Jew was not to read the beginning or ending of Ezekiel (presumably chapters 1 and 40–48) until he was thirty years old, since that was the age at which one would enter the ministry.[25] That was also Ezekiel's own age at his call (1:1).

Ezekiel is never named in the NT, but there are a few quotations, and allusions to Ezekiel abound, especially in Revelation.[26]

Patristic and medieval interest in Ezekiel continued to concentrate on the call vision (chapter 1) and on the symbolism of the numbers in the eschatological temple vision (chapters 40–48).

Calvin wrote a commentary on the first twenty chapters of Ezekiel; that was as far as he got before he died. It is available in English translation.[27] Like most of Calvin's commentaries, it is useable by Lutherans with relatively little need for theological adaptation.

As far as I know, Luther devoted no particular attention to Ezekiel. It comes as a slight surprise, then, to note that there are over a dozen references to Ezekiel in the *Book of Concord*. The Lutheran confessors cite the prophet to support a variety of doctrines, including justification through faith alone;[28] election and God's desire for all people to be saved, contrary to double predestination;[29] the authority of Scripture alone versus ecclesiastical decrees and human traditions;[30] and divine monergism in conversion and regeneration.[31]

Modern "evangelical" interest in the book has been especially prominent among those who espouse dispensational premillennialism. There is consider-

---

[25] Jerome, *Commentariorum in Hiezechielem*, prologue to book 1 (CCSL 75:3–4).

[26] Parts of Ezek 37:5, 10 are quoted in Rev 11:11, and Ezek 37:27b is quoted in 2 Cor 6:16. See the list of numerous allusions to Ezekiel in the back of NA[27] or UBS[4]. This commentary often cites NT parallels; see especially those in Revelation cited in the commentary on Ezekiel 1 and 40–48.

[27] Calvin, *Commentaries on the First Twenty Chapters of the Book of the Prophet Ezekiel*.

[28] Ezek 18:21–22 is cited in Ap IV ("Justification") 263.

[29] In this regard, Ezek 18:23 is cited in FC Ep XI 10; SD XI 81, and Ezek 33:11 is cited in FC Ep XI 10; SD II 49; XI 81, 84. Ezek 33:11 is also cited in Ap XII 94 regarding faith in God's promise to forgive the penitent.

[30] Ap XXII 17 cites Ezek 7:26, and Ezek 20:18–19 is cited in Ap XV 14. See also the quote of Ezek 20:5 in Ap XXVII 30.

[31] On this topic, FC SD II 19 makes reference to Ezek 36:26, and FC SD II 26 cites Ezek 11:19; 36:26.

able literature on the role of Gog and Magog (chapters 38–39) in the end-time battles, as well as in the role of the temple and its worship in the millennium. Lutherans and other amillennialists have no interest in such misuses of biblical prophecy, although something may be salvaged from some details of commentaries written from that viewpoint.[32]

I wish I could report a comparable interest in Ezekiel among modern Lutherans. But whether confessional or liberal, there is virtually nothing to report, except for a handful of popular treatments. This near vacuum probably is a result of the de facto problems Lutherans tend to have with the OT in general, and with the priestly and liturgical character of Ezekiel in particular. I venture to assert that, with the exception of the call vision (chapter 1) and that of the dry bones (chapter 37), the book is virtually unknown to most Lutherans.

Pericopal preaching might help rectify that biblical illiteracy. Yet how often are the OT texts fully utilized by Lutheran preachers, even when one of the OT pericopes is chosen? The one-year lectionary in *Lutheran Worship* includes four selections from Ezekiel for Sunday services.[33] In the three-year lectionary in *Lutheran Worship*, Series A offers three and a half selections (a half when Ezekiel is one of two options),[34] Series B three,[35] and Series C none. Readings from Ezekiel are appointed for several feast days.[36] The one-year series in *Lutheran Service Book* has three selections for Sunday services.[37] In the three-year lectionary in *Lutheran Service Book*, Series A has four readings,[38] Series B three,[39] and Series C two.[40] There are two selections from Ezekiel for feast days.[41]

The history of "higher critical" study of Ezekiel is probably of less interest (and importance) to the users of this commentary. One could hardly find a better example of that approach's virtually unprincipled subjectivism and re-

---

[32] For a history of millennialism and the Lutheran perspective on it, see the excursus "The Millennium" in Brighton, *Revelation*, 533–41.

[33] Second Sunday of Easter: Ezek 37:1–14; Fourth Sunday of Easter: Ezek 34:11–16; Seventh Sunday of Easter: Ezek 36:24–27; Twenty-fifth Sunday after Pentecost: Ezek 33:10–16.

[34] Fifth Sunday in Lent: Ezek 37:1–3 (4–10) 11–14; Sixteenth Sunday after Pentecost: Ezek 33:7–9; Nineteenth Sunday after Pentecost: Ezek 18:1–4, 25–32; Last Sunday in the Church Year: Ezek 34:11–16, 23–24 (optional reading).

[35] Day of Pentecost: Ezek 37:1–14; Fourth Sunday after Pentecost: Ezek 17:22–24; Seventh Sunday after Pentecost: Ezek 2:1–5.

[36] Ezek 34:7–16 is appointed for Saints Peter and Paul (June 29) in the one-year lectionary. In the three-year lectionary, Ezek 3:16–21 is appointed for St. Andrew (November 30); Ezek 34:11–16 for St. Timothy (January 24), St. Titus (January 26), and Saints Peter and Paul (June 29); Ezek 20:40–42 for St. Laurence (August 10); and Ezek 2:8–3:11 for St. Matthew (September 21).

[37] First Sunday after Easter: Ezek 37:1–14; Second Sunday after Easter: Ezek 34:11–16; Sixth Sunday after Easter: Ezek 36:22–28.

[38] Fifth Sunday in Lent: Ezek 37:1–14; Proper 18: Ezek 33:7–9; Proper 21: Ezek 18:1–4, 25–32; Proper 29: Ezek 34:11–16, 20–24.

[39] Day of Pentecost: Ezek 37:1–14; Proper 6: Ezek 17:22–24; Proper 9: Ezek 2:1–5.

[40] Third Sunday in Lent: Ezek 33:7–20; Proper 19: Ezek 34:11–24.

[41] St. Andrew (November 30): Ezek 3:16–21; St. Matthew (September 21): Ezek 2:8–3:11.

sultant vast spectrum of results than in critical commentaries on Ezekiel. Nevertheless, as I observed about millennialist expositions of Ezekiel, so too some insights in critical commentaries, especially those of a more philological sort, may be useful.

Strange as it may seem, until well into the twentieth century, Ezekiel almost completely escaped the radical treatment to which much of the rest of the Bible was subjected. It is not entirely clear why; perhaps the tendency of critics to concentrate their efforts on the eighth-century prophets left the later prophets as also-rans. That Ezekiel was a priest probably contributed to critical aversion of it: the common viewpoint was that the priestly was totally antithetical to the prophetic. Also, the clear signs of the book's overall plan and its clear structure may have made scholars reluctant to challenge its unity.

After 1900 a few minor questions were raised, but no major assault came until the work of Gustav Hölscher in 1924, who, following a common assumption that early prophecy was cast in poetry, left only 144 verses (in whole or in part) of Ezekiel (out of a total of 1,273) as genuine.[42] The rest of the book was supposedly comprised of later adaptations, applications, and so on. Even more radical was C. C. Torrey of Yale, who in 1930 argued, on the one hand, that the prophecies in Ezekiel originated in the seventh century as a polemic against Manasseh's idolatries and, on the other hand, that the book itself wasn't written until the Seleucid period (in about 230 B.C., and further edited around 200).[43] And so it went.[44]

The pendulum began to swing back after World War II. Most noteworthy, perhaps, were studies published by C. G. Howie (a student of W. F. Albright) in 1950[45] and by G. Fohrer in 1952,[46] who stressed various aspects of the book that fit the period in which the book claims to have been written. Major critical doubts remained, however, about the apocalyptic style of chapters 38–39, the eschatological vision of the new temple and land in chapters 40–48, as well as the generally longer text of the MT, compared with the LXX, throughout the book.

A high point of resurgence of respect for the Hebrew text (at least from within criticism's own horizons) came with Walther Zimmerli's massive two-volume commentary in 1969 (translated into English in 1979 and 1983).[47] In

---

[42] Gustav Hölscher, *Hesekiel, der Dichter und das Buch: Eine literarkritische Untersuchung* (BZAW 39; Giessen: Töpelmann, 1924).

[43] C. C. Torrey, *Pseudo-Ezekiel and the Original Prophecy* (New Haven: Yale University Press, 1930).

[44] For a detailed treatment of this era, see Zimmerli, *Ezekiel*, 1:3–9.

[45] Carl Gordon Howie, *The Date and Composition of Ezekiel* (Philadelphia : Society of Biblical Literature, 1950).

[46] Georg Fohrer, *Die Hauptprobleme des Buches Ezechiel* (BZAW 72; Berlin: Töpelmann, 1952).

[47] Walther Zimmerli, *Ezechiel* (2 vols.; BKAT 13/1 and 2; Neukirchen-Vluyn: NeuKirchener Verlag des Erziehungsvereins, 1969); ET: *Ezekiel* (trans. Ronald E. Clements; 2 vols.; Hermeneia; Philadelphia: Fortress, 1979–1983).

many respects Zimmerli was a classical form- and tradition-critical scholar. Although he posited a substantial amount of the text to be genuine, he still hypothesized a complicated process of editorial additions by later disciples. Those negatives were somewhat balanced by the theological sensitivity of many of his comments, which are typical of many of the earlier commentaries in the series, which were still under the influence of the "biblical theology" movement.

With Zimmerli we enter what may be labeled the contemporary era, where the perspective is still too recent to attempt much of an evaluation, let alone a forecast of what can be expected in the future. One may perhaps generalize by saying that the conservatizing trend has continued, although to various degrees and in various ways. Typical of most current biblical scholarship, "every man does what is right in his own eyes" (cf. Judg 21:25). As far as I am aware, the radical hermeneutics of postmodernism have not affected the exegesis of Ezekiel, at least not in any overt way.

Perhaps I can best adopt a more personal tone here and indicate which current commentaries I have found most useful and which I can recommend as helpful parallels to my own. Ironically, two of the best, in my judgment, are anything but contemporary. Nearly a century and half old is the commentary of C. F. Keil in the Keil-Delitzsch series.[48] He had the advantage of writing before the full onslaught of the historical-critical method. Although he interacts with his own (now mostly forgotten) contemporaries, his work remains unfailingly helpful—and, to the conservative mind, always essentially on target. While he was a Lutheran, his perspective is not specifically or pointedly Lutheran. The high quality of his commentary (and the entire Keil-Delitzsch series) reminds us that the much touted "advances" in modern biblical studies are pitifully few and far between.

From an entirely different perspective—yet with some convergences with Keil—is the commentary of Walther Eichrodt.[49] Best known for his two-volume *Theology of the Old Testament*,[50] he writes from a "biblical theology" perspective that generally includes acceptance of higher criticism. But, on the whole, the work is not nearly as helpful as one might anticipate.

Two more recent works compete in the "ratings" for the works most helpful to me. First in chronological order is the two-volume commentary of the late Israeli scholar Moshe Greenberg.[51] Before his death, Greenberg was able

---

[48] Carl Friedrich Keil, *Biblischer Commentar über den Propheten Ezechiel* (Biblischer Commentar über das Alte Testament, vol. 3 of part 3, by C. F. Keil and Franz Delitzsch; Leipzig: Dörffling & Franke, 1868); ET: *Biblical Commentary on the Prophecies of Ezekiel* (trans. James Martin; 2 vols.; Edinburgh: T&T Clark, 1876; repr., Grand Rapids: Eerdmans, 1978).

[49] Walther Eichrodt, *Der Prophet Hesekiel: Übersetzt und erklärt* (2 vols.; Das Alte Testament Deutsch 22/1 and 2; Göttingen: Vandenhoeck & Ruprecht, 1959–1966); ET: *Ezekiel: A Commentary* (trans. Cosslett Quin; Old Testament Library; Philadelphia: Westminster, 1970).

[50] Walther Eichrodt, *Theology of the Old Testament* (trans. J. A. Baker; 2 vols.; Philadelphia: Westminster, 1961–1967).

[51] Moshe Greenberg, *Ezekiel* (2 vols.; Anchor Bible 22–22A; Garden City, N.Y.: Doubleday, 1983–1997).

to finish writing on only thirty-seven chapters. Had he lived, he might have been most helpful on chapters 40–48. From a purely philological perspective, Greenberg is about as "conservative" as can be. While not ruling out any copyist's errors in the *hebraica veritas* ("the true Hebrew text," as St. Jerome called it) and even discerning a handful of such "errors," Greenberg works valiantly and persuasively to make sense of the text as it stands. Naturally, one will not expect to find here any Christian insights, but he often shows respectful awareness of them. At least for what is always the foundational task of exegesis, that is, simply struggling to "hear" what the text says in its own historical context, I regard Greenberg as helpful without a peer.

A new entry in my "honor roll" is Daniel Block's two-volume commentary in the New International Commentary on the Old Testament.[52] In many ways one has the best of both worlds here: a quite conservative attitude toward the Hebrew text (explained in footnotes, though not so detailed as Greenberg's notes on the text) and a clear consciousness of Christian connections.

Some may regard my inclusion of John Taylor's little commentary in the Tyndale series[53] strange. In the best sense of the term, Taylor's work (like the entire series) is "popular," that is, it is intended at least as much for the layperson as it is for any professional. Yet it is a veritable *multum in parvo*, and not the least of its virtues is its explicitly Christian perspective, paralleled perhaps only by Keil.

I turn now to less helpful studies. No less than three full-fledged volumes of commentary on Ezekiel have been published in the Word Biblical Commentary series. All are quite detailed (especially in textual notes), and all are sometimes helpful. But, in balance, I found all three ultimately disappointing. First came William Brownlee's commentary on chapters 1–19, published posthumously (1986).[54] Leslie Allen was assigned chapters 20–48 (1990). After Brownlee's death, he was given the task of writing another commentary on chapters 1–19 (1994),[55] both to give an overall unity in approach to the entire book of Ezekiel in the WBC series and also because of certain idiosyncrasies in Brownlee's approach, especially his argument that most of Ezekiel's ministry took place near Gilgal on the lower Jordan. (He argued that "Gilgal" was the original behind the supposedly corrupted Hebrew גּוֹלָה, "exile," in 1:1.) How Brownlee might have proceeded with chapters 20–48 had he lived may be discerned from his commentary in *The Interpreter's One Volume Commentary on the Bible*.[56] In certain respects, both Allen and Brownlee might fit un-

---

[52] Daniel I. Block, *The Book of Ezekiel* (2 vols.; New International Commentary on the Old Testament; Grand Rapids: Eerdmans, 1997–1998).

[53] John B. Taylor, *Ezekiel: An Introduction and Commentary* (Tyndale Old Testament Commentaries; Downers Grove, Ill.: Inter-Varsity, 1969).

[54] William H. Brownlee, *Ezekiel 1–19* (Word Biblical Commentary 28; Waco: Word, 1986).

[55] Leslie C. Allen, *Ezekiel* (2 vols.; Word Biblical Commentary 28–29; Dallas: Word, 1990 [vol. 2], 1994 [vol. 1]).

[56] William Hugh Brownlee, "The Book of Ezekiel," in *The Interpreter's One Volume Commentary on the Bible* (ed. Charles M. Laymon; Nashville: Abingdon, 1971), 411–35.

der some "big tent" definition of "conservative," but both, in my judgment, often miss the mark. Especially in textual matters, Allen often tends toward the radical, particularly in the alacrity with which he opts for the LXX text over the Hebrew; such is true also of his three-stage hypothesis about the composition of the book and the Rube Goldberg-esque speculations on the history of the text when he perceives problems.

For various reasons, a number of others may be classified as also-rans. Completely popular studies or those focused on only a portion of the book are not considered here. Fully as conservative as Keil's but more general (not concentrating so closely on the text) is Hengstenberg's commentary.[57] Much more recent chronologically, but light-years further removed theologically, is G. A. Cooke's volume in the International Critical Commentary series (finished completely only through chapter 24).[58] Although the viewpoint is more or less in line with the critical thought of the time, a wealth of erudition is displayed, especially in the "critical notes." Ronald Hals (a Lutheran of the old Capitol Seminary), in volume 19 of the series The Forms of the Old Testament Literature, is somewhat restricted by the scope of that series, but otherwise he is only mildly critical.[59]

Joseph Blenkinsopp of Notre Dame wrote the commentary on Ezekiel in the Interpretation series.[60] The series styles itself "A Bible Commentary for Teaching and Preaching." It fails on both counts, at least for the conservative reader. In addition, it rarely addresses the original text directly. An equally popular commentary in the International Theological Commentary series was coauthored by Bruce Vawter and Leslie Hoppe, both Roman Catholics. The commentary is entitled *A New Heart*,[61] underscoring one valid element of the last part of the book (especially chapter 36), but easily oversimplifying the impact of the book as a whole. Another relatively popular work in The New American Commentary series, which relates to the NIV English text, is by Lamar Cooper Sr.[62] The commentary is aware of NT parallels and implications but is also millennialistic, which limits its usefulness.

---

[57] Ernst W. Hengstenberg, *Die Weissagungen des Propheten Ezechiel für solche die in der Schrift forschen erläutert* (2 vols.; Berlin: Schlawitz, 1867–1868).

[58] G. A. Cooke, *A Critical and Exegetical Commentary on the Book of Ezekiel* (International Critical Commentary 21; Edinburgh: T&T Clark, 1936).

[59] Ronald M. Hals, *Ezekiel* (The Forms of the Old Testament Literature 19; Grand Rapids: Eerdmans, 1989).

[60] Joseph Blenkinsopp, *Ezekiel* (Interpretation; Louisville, Ky.: John Knox, 1990).

[61] Bruce Vawter and Leslie J. Hoppe, *A New Heart: A Commentary on the Book of Ezekiel* (International Theological Commentary; Grand Rapids: Eerdmans, 1991).

[62] Lamar Eugene Cooper Sr., *Ezekiel* (The New American Commentary 17; Nashville: Broadman & Holman, 1994).

Ezekiel 1–3

Ezekiel's Inaugural Vision and Commissioning

A. Ezekiel's Inaugural Vision (1:1–28)
B. The Prophetic Commissioning of Ezekiel: Part 1 (2:1–10)
C. The Prophetic Commissioning of Ezekiel: Part 2 (3:1–27)

Ezekiel's Inaugural Vision

Translation

1 ¹In the thirtieth year, in the fourth [month], on the fifth [day] of the month, when I was among the exiles by the Kebar Canal, the heavens were opened, and I saw a divine vision. ²On the fifth of the month, that is, in the fifth year of the captivity of the king Jehoiachin, ³the Word of Yahweh came forcefully to Ezekiel, the son of Buzi, the priest, in the land of the Chaldeans, by the Kebar Canal, and the hand of Yahweh was upon him there. ⁴As I looked, behold, a wind-storm was coming from the north—a large cloud and fire flashing and a radiance to it round about, and in the middle of it was something like the appearance of electrum—in the middle of the fire. ⁵In the middle of it was the likeness of four living creatures. This was their appearance: they had the likeness of a man. ⁶But there were four faces belonging to each one, and four wings belonging to each one of them. ⁷Their legs—[each was] a straight leg, and the soles of their feet were like the soles of a calf's hoof, and gleaming like polished bronze. ⁸The hands of a man were under their wings on all four of their sides; the four of them had faces and wings. ⁹Their wings were touching one another. They did not turn when they moved, but each one went straight ahead. ¹⁰The likeness of their face(s) was the face of a man [on the front], and the face of a lion was on the right for the four of them, and the face of an ox on the left for the four of them, and the face of an eagle [on the back] for the four of them. ¹¹Their faces and their wings were spread out upward. Each had a pair [of wings] touching [the wings of] each [neighbor], and a pair [of wings] covering their bodies. ¹²Each one went straight ahead. Wherever the S/spirit wanted to go, they went. They did not turn as they went. ¹³As for the form of the living creatures, their appearance was like coals of fire, burning like the appearance of torches. It [fire] was moving back and forth among the living creatures. The fire had brightness, and from the fire lightning was going out. ¹⁴The creatures darted forth and back like the appearance of a flash of lightning.

¹⁵As I looked at the living creatures, behold, one wheel was on the ground beside the living creatures, each with its four faces. ¹⁶The appearance of the wheels and their design was like the appearance of tarshish, and the four of them had one appearance. Their appearance and their design were as a wheel would be in the midst of a wheel. ¹⁷Toward any of their four sides they went when they moved; they did not turn aside when they moved. ¹⁸As for their rims, they had height and fear, and their rims were full of eyes all around—all four of them. ¹⁹Whenever the living creatures moved, the wheels moved beside them, and whenever the living creatures would rise from the ground, the wheels rose too. ²⁰To wherever the S/spirit wanted to go, they would go—to where the S/spirit wanted to go—and the wheels would rise together with them, because the spirit

of the living creature was in the wheels. ²¹Whenever they [the living creatures] moved, they [the wheels] would move; when they [the living creatures] stood still, they [the wheels] would stand still; and when they [the living creatures] rose from on the ground, the wheels would rise together with them, because the spirit of the living creature was in the wheels.

²²There was something over the heads of the living creatures like a dome, looking like awesome ice, stretched out over their heads above. ²³Under the dome, their wings [were stretched out] straight, one to the other, and each had two [wings] covering themselves, each had two [wings] covering themselves—[covering] their bodies. ²⁴I heard the sound of their wings, like the sound of many waters, like the voice of the Almighty when they moved—a sound of commotion like the sound of an army camp. When they stood still, they relaxed their wings.

²⁵There was a sound from above the dome that was over their heads. When they stood still, they relaxed their wings. ²⁶Above the dome that was over their heads was something like the appearance of stone of sapphire—the likeness of a throne. Above the likeness of the throne was the likeness of the appearance of a man, upon it above. ²⁷I saw something like electrum with the appearance of fire within and surrounding it, from what appeared to be his waist and upward. From what appeared to be his waist and downward I saw what appeared to be fire, and a radiance surrounding him. ²⁸Like the appearance of the bow that is in the clouds on a day of rain, so was the appearance of the radiance surrounding [him]. That was the appearance of the Glory of Yahweh, and when I saw, I fell on my face, and I heard a voice speaking.

Textual Notes

Introductory comment: Any user of a text-critical edition of the Hebrew Bible will see a plethora of notes on chapter 1. In fact, only chapter 41 has more noteworthy textual variants than chapter 1. Some of the kinds of problems in chapter 1 are found throughout Ezekiel. The LXX often offers a shorter text, and it is debated whether or not it was translated from the same Hebrew text represented by the Masoretic tradition. (See "Text and Style in Ezekiel" in the introduction.) A reasonable explanation for the abundance of problems in chapter 1 lies in the subject matter itself and the psychological effect the vision had on the prophet. "A divine vision" (1:1) is going to defy accurate and lucid verbal description. That is part of the reason for the repeated use of similes or analogies ("likeness," "appearance"), climaxing in 1:28. The prophet is so stunned and overwhelmed by the God and angels he sees that his descriptions are characterized by "asyndetic constructions, redundancies, choppy staccato sentences, abrupt insertions."[1] That appears to be confirmed by the fact that when Ezekiel sees a second extended vision of the divine Glory in chapter 10, its description is much smoother, even when material from chapter 1 is repeated. The prophet is calmer in chapter 10 because he had seen the divine Glory before.

---

[1] Block, *Ezekiel*, 1:89.

Theologically, regarding the dogma of the verbal inspiration of Scripture, Ezekiel 1 prompts two observations. First, better evidence could hardly be found that the process of inspiration was not "mechanical" (a matter of dictation). This chapter conveys the very human author's response to God's self-revelation. Second, the difficult text attests authorship by Ezekiel alone. If, as critical interpreters assume, later disciples of Ezekiel made multiple editorial passes through the book, that would surely have resulted in a much smoother and more grammatically conventional description of the vision.

1:1 וַיְהִי—The first circumstantial clause in the verse gives the date (year, month, and day) when the inaugural vision took place . It begins with the common וַיְהִי, "now it came to pass" (KJV), "and it happened," or, literally, "and it was." Often a *waw* consecutive implies that the clause is a continuation of a previous clause or sentence. However, the usage had long since become fossilized, and so the *waw* consecutive frequently is used at the beginning of an entirely different narrative or even a new book, as here. Six other OT books begin with וַיְהִי: Joshua, Judges, 1 Samuel, 2 Samuel, Ruth, and Esther. This *waw* consecutive is commonly omitted in translation (as in mine) because it results in redundant English.

וַאֲנִי בְתוֹךְ־הַגּוֹלָה—This second circumstantial clause gives the location where Ezekiel received his inaugural vision. "Exiles" translates the singular noun גּוֹלָה. Technically, the word is an abstract noun, "exile" or "captivity." In Hebrew, abstract concepts are usually expressed by grammatically feminine forms. Here the word may be either abstract or concrete, which yields more idiomatic English here: the "exiles," the individuals constituting the exiled community.

נִפְתְּחוּ הַשָּׁמַיִם—This is the first of the two main clauses of the verse. When וַיְהִי begins a verse (as it does 1:1), the following main clause usually begins with another *waw*. However, נִפְתְּחוּ (Niphal of פָּתַח, "to be opened") lacks a *waw,* and its lack of conjunction is attested by the versions except for two LXX uncials. Hence its syntax is asyndetic.

I render הַשָּׁמַיִם as "the heavens" because the noun is dual (in form at least) and is regularly used with a plural verb, as here (נִפְתְּחוּ). "Sky" sounds too naturalistic, especially in this context of divine revelation.

וָאֶרְאֶה מַרְאוֹת אֱלֹהִים:— This second main clause follows the first one so as to indicate divine purpose: the heavens were opened (purposefully by God) so that Ezekiel could see "a divine vision." One might translate מַרְאוֹת אֱלֹהִים literalistically as "visions of God," as the LXX and Vulgate did already, and as do many English translations. But, as both Greenberg and Block argue,[2] that is probably incorrect. If Ezekiel had meant "visions of God," his usual usage suggests that he would not have used אֱלֹהִים, but אֲדֹנָי יְהוִה. Second, in Ezekiel אֱלֹהִים is not usually a proper, but a common noun ("divinity"), although there are exceptions, especially in his quotations of the common covenant formula "I will be your God." Also מַרְאוֹת is probably not an ordinary plural but an intensive plural (cf. GKC, § 124 e) or plural of generalization (Joüon, § 136 j), as plurals are often used in Hebrew.

---

[2] Greenberg, *Ezekiel*, 1:41; Block, *Ezekiel*, 1:84–85.

Above all, although what follows in chapter 1 could conceivably be construed as a vision of *God*, that construal would not work at all the other two times Ezekiel uses the phrase (8:3; 40:2). Even in chapter 1, the heavenly figure Ezekiel eventually sees on the throne is described in such qualified circumlocutions, climaxing in כָּבוֹד, "Glory" (see below), that the translation "visions of God" belies Ezekiel's own words.

In the OT, there is only one other possible parallel to actually "seeing God" (Ex 24:9–11), but that episode must be interpreted in the light of Ex 33:18–23, where Moses is permitted to see only the "back" of God's "glory," not his face, because "man shall not see me and live" (Ex 33:20).

Hence, one is not surprised that also at the climax of this vision, the text labors, especially through the hypostatic כָּבוֹד to make unmistakable the gulf between God's aseity (God as he is in himself) and a human being, a בֶּן־אָדָם, "son of man," as God consistently addresses the prophet throughout the book (starting in 2:1).

1:2 הִיא הַשָּׁנָה הַחֲמִישִׁית לְגָלוּת הַמֶּלֶךְ יוֹיָכִין—The third person references to Ezekiel in 1:2–3 interrupt the first person narration that began in 1:1 and resumes in 1:4. See the commentary below for a discussion of the relationship between 1:1 and 1:2–3. Whatever the actual relationship, both grammatically and in content, we have in 1:2–3 a close approximation of the "normal" superscription of a prophetic book. There are always some variations; no two superscriptions are identical.

The dating scheme in 1:2 is explicitly pegged to the exile of Jehoiachin (which coincides with the exile of Ezekiel too) in 597 B.C., as is the case with other dates throughout the book. The pronoun הִיא ("that is") presumably distinguishes that departure point commencing here (dating from the year of exile) from the dating point of reference of the "thirtieth year" (probably from Ezekiel's birth) in 1:1. The fifth year of Jehoiachin's captivity is then (counting inclusively) 593 B.C., the year when the inaugural vision came and Ezekiel's public ministry began.

The noun גָּלוּת ("captivity, exile") is from the same Hebrew root (גלה) as the synonym גּוֹלָה in 1:1. The feminine ending ־וּת is common on abstract nouns (cf. English "-ness" or "-hood"), though this noun too can have either an abstract or concrete denotation. Here the abstract translation seems required.

1:3 The verse division is artificial because 1:2–3 is one sentence. Ezek 1:2 consists of a temporal phrase introducing 1:3, which consists of two main clauses. Each of those clauses is introduced by הָיָה, which sometimes is not translated at all in idiomatic English (I did not translate it in 1:1). הָיָה may also be translated by "was/became/came/happened."

הָיֹה הָיָה דְבַר־יְהוָה—In this first clause, the Hebrew underscores the verb by use of the infinitive absolute (הָיֹה) with the perfect form (הָיָה). Ordinarily the infinitive absolute is rendered in English by some intensifying adverb like "certainly." The infinitive absolute of הָיָה is never found elsewhere with the common formula "the Word of Yahweh," which occurs fifty-eight times in Ezekiel. Critics often allege dittography of הָיָה at some point in the textual transmission and cite the absence of any confirmation of the presence of a Hebrew infinitive absolute in the originals from which the ancient versions were translated. However, equivalents of an infinitive absolute are rare in languages other than Hebrew, so that is scarcely definitive proof. Our rule of thumb is *not* to emend the Masoretic Text if possible.

Since what follows in Ezekiel 1 is a vision, not a spoken "word" in any ordinary sense, we are reminded how closely divine visions and words are linked in prophetic books—so closely, in fact, that they are virtually interchangeable. A prophetic "vision" does not necessarily imply a visual experience, nor does "the Word of Yahweh" require an aural one. The verbal part of "the Word of Yahweh" would be the speech that begins in 2:1.

יְחֶזְקֵאל—The prophet's name, Ezekiel, occurs only one more time in the book and in the whole Bible: in 24:24 among words Yahweh commanded him to speak to the exiled Israelites. One other person in the OT bears the same Hebrew name: another priest, mentioned in 1 Chr 24:16, though his is traditionally transliterated (much closer to the Hebrew pronunciation) as Jehezkel. יְחֶזְקֵאל is a typical Israelite name. Like many OT names it is theophoric, ending with the generic name for God, אֵל, "El." A century earlier, King Hezekiah had almost the same name but with a shortened form of God's personal name, "Yahweh," in place of "El."[3] Ezekiel's name is confessional and perhaps a prayer. It expresses a typical prayer or confession of a pious couple at the birth of a child: "may God make (the child) strong" or "God will strengthen." Ezek 3:8–9 appears to play on Ezekiel's name: no matter how hostile his audience, God will give the prophet grace to live up to his name by making him "strong" (the adjective חָזָק, thrice in 3:8–9).

One may observe in passing that it once was commonly understood in Christendom that the giving of the "Christian" name at Baptism was a real confession of faith and an affirmation of the "christening," that is, that Holy Baptism made the recipient a Christian. The annual anniversary, often called the "name day," would be observed religiously. That this is no longer the usual case testifies not only to our secularization in general, but specifically to the functional weakness of our theology of Baptism.

בֶּן־בּוּזִי—Little can be said about the name of Ezekiel's father, Buzi. The ending (ִי-) may be gentilic, in which case the name would mean "Buzite," either a descendant from a man named Buz or an inhabitant of a region called Buz. Job 32:2 and 32:6 so use "Buzite" in the ancestry of Elihu, and the personal name Buz occurs in Gen 22:21; Jer 25:23; and 1 Chr 5:14, but none of these have any obvious connection with Ezekiel's father.

הַכֹּהֵן—The attributive "the priest" could syntactically refer to either Buzi or to Ezekiel. Presumably it applies to both, since a priest's son normally would be a priest too. However, it is possible that Ezekiel was exiled before he could actually serve as a priest. There is nothing else in the book that indicates whether or not Ezekiel had served as a priest. However, his outlook and vocabulary are more sacerdotal than those of any other prophet.

כַּשְׂדִּים—In both Akkadian and Greek the name is spelled with an "l," as we have inherited it: "Chaldean(s)." It is a matter of no moment, but the שׂ may well be origi-

---

[3] Sometimes Hezekiah is spelled יְחִזְקִיָּה (Micah 1:1) or יְחִזְקִיָּהוּ (2 Chr 28:12), but most often it is חִזְקִיָּהוּ.

nal, because we know the people to have been of Aramean stock. Apparently somewhere around 1,000 B.C. they migrated from the Aramean homeland in the northland ("Aram" became "Syria" in Western translation) to the marshland of southern Mesopotamia (modern Iraq). There they had long been a thorn in the side of the Neo-Assyrian Empire (cf. Merodach-Baladan in 2 Ki 20:12–19) and finally were able to gain dominance after Assyria's precipitous collapse at the end of the seventh century. Historians often refer to their empire, of which Nebuchadnezzar is the best-known representative, as "neo-Babylonian" to distinguish it from a much earlier "Babylonian" empire in the second millennium. Often the Bible uses "Chaldea(ns)" almost interchangeably with "Babylonia(ns)," as in Ezek 12:13; 23:15, 23. The Chaldeans' presumed Aramaic background probably explains why several chapters in Daniel are written in Aramaic, and why, under their successors in imperial rule, Aramaic became the lingua franca of the empire. Some Aramaisms also seem to appear in Ezekiel, but their number is disputed. Older Hebrew lexicons refer to Aramaic as "Chaldee," but that term is now obsolete.

וַתְּהִי עָלָיו שָׁם יַד־יְהוָה:—Ezekiel uses similar expressions about "the hand of Yahweh" coming upon him (with the preposition עַל or אֶל) in 3:14, 22; 33:22; 37:1; 40:1 to indicate divine influence upon him and revelation to him. Similar expressions with עַל that denote "the hand of Yahweh" aiding or strengthening people are in 2 Ki 3:15; Ezra 7:6, 28; 1 Chr 28:19. In contrast, most passages that speak of the "hand of Yahweh" with the preposition בְּ ("on" meaning "against" someone) refer to Yahweh striking or destroying enemies (e.g., Ex 9:3; Deut 2:15; Judg 2:15; 1 Sam 7:13).

This is the second main clause in 1:3. A form of הָיָה is repeated at the beginning of this second clause too. Some of the subsequent date formulas also have two main clauses following (e.g., 8:1; 20:1). The third person suffix on the preposition (עָלָיו) is required by the third person references to Ezekiel in the rest of 1:2–3. A few Hebrew manuscripts, as well as the LXX and Peshitta have "upon me," instead of "upon him." No change in meaning would ensue, but the first person would mean that the last clause of 1:3 should be joined to 1:4.

1:4 וָאֵרֶא—Hebrew, as usual, has another coordinate clause with *waw*. Our translation subordinates it ("as I looked …").

וְהִנֵּה רוּחַ סְעָרָה בָּאָה—Literally, וְהִנֵּה means "and behold." Another *waw* introduces this exceedingly common interjection. A contemporary substitute might be "look!" It highlights what follows, but often only slightly. Modern translations often omit it.

The noun רוּחַ can refer to "wind" (5:2; 12:14; 37:9b). It can refer to God's "Spirit" (11:5; 37:1); the human "spirit" of a person; or the "S/spirit" of the (angelic) living creatures (1:20b–21). Sometimes Ezekiel plays on those different possible meanings (37:1–10, 14). Here one minor version inserts "the Lord's," which would make this refer to the Holy Spirit. Biblically speaking, God sends all winds, and this one too, in particular. However, the following noun (סְעָרָה) requires רוּחַ to mean "wind" here. The noun סְעָרָה means "tempest, storm-wind" (BDB) or "whirlwind" (KJV). Hence the construct chain is literally "wind-storm." סְעָרָה connotes a fierce and overpowering storm, as in 13:11, 13, where it is accompanied by hail and destruction (see also Is 29:6; Jer 23:19). Yahweh speaks from out of a storm-wind (סְעָרָה) in Job 38:1; 40:6.

וְאֵשׁ מִתְלַקַּחַת—The Hithpael feminine singular participle of לָקַח apparently means something like "taking/chasing itself," that is, "flashing here and there." The Hithpael occurs only once elsewhere: this identical phrase is in Ex 9:24, describing the lightning that accompanied a hailstorm in one of the plagues preceding the exodus.

וְנֹגַהּ לוֹ סָבִיב וּמִתּוֹכָהּ—The noun נֹגַהּ means "radiance, brightness, shining," a natural description of fire, as also in Ezek 1:13, 27 and other biblical theophanies. The preposition לְ is used here (and often later in this chapter) to denote possession: "a radiance to it" means "it had radiance." The antecedent of the third masculine singular pronoun ("it") on the preposition (לוֹ) is evidently the "fire" (if not the "large cloud"), but אֵשׁ is usually feminine in Hebrew, as indicated by the feminine suffix on מִתּוֹכָהּ ("in the middle of it"). There are, however, other instances where the same sequence of changing genders for "fire" is found, for example, Jer 20:9; Job 20:26.

כְּעֵין הַחַשְׁמַל—In addition to "eye," the noun עַיִן can mean "appearance, look" (HALOT, 3 a), and with the preposition כְּ, the combination כְּעֵין means "something like," "like the appearance/color of," or simply "like." The combination appears again in 1:7, 16, 22, 27; 8:2; 10:9. Like other circumlocutions in the following text, it tries to express the indescribability of what Ezekiel sees. There simply are no adequate words. Already here the infinite gulf between Creator and creature is indicated.

The meaning of חַשְׁמַל is uncertain (cf. BDB; HALOT). Ironically, we are not sure of the meaning of the simile, which is intended to help us know the unknowable. The noun occurs in the OT only here and in 1:27 and 8:2, all describing a theophany. The LXX (ἤλεκτρον) and Vulgate (electrum) both have "electrum," which is an alloy of gold and silver. A possible Akkadian cognate suggests "amber." The nearby references to "fire" suggest something yellowish or reddish and brilliant.

מִתּוֹךְ הָאֵשׁ:—This final phrase, "in the middle of the fire," clarifies that "it" in the preceding וּמִתּוֹכָהּ, "in the middle of it," referred to the "fire." This somewhat redundant explanation suggests Ezekiel's surprise and excitement at the otherworldly scene unfolding before his eyes.

1:5 וּמִתּוֹכָהּ—This is the third instance of תָּוֶךְ, "middle," in 1:4–5. It is unclear whether this is simply consecutive narration by Ezekiel (not all aspects of the vision could be reported at once) or whether things gradually come into clearer focus as the storm cloud draws closer. Assuming the latter, many translations insert *came* from its midst" or the like.

חַיּוֹת—The noun חַיָּה is from the root חָיָה, "to live, be alive." The noun, which I translate as "living creature," often means "animal," but that would be misleading in this context. The description of the features of these living creatures that follows includes some animal features, but Ezekiel stresses first their anthropoid appearance. The description of what may be these same angelic beings in Rev 4:6–9 uses ζῷα (plural of ζῷον), which likewise means "living creature" (from ζάω, "to live").

Later Ezekiel will call these living creatures cherubim (Ezek 10:1–20; 11:22), and he refers to cherubim also in 9:3; 28:14, 16; 41:18, 20, 25. Some commentators propose that Ezekiel is reluctant to call the creatures in chapter 1 "cherubim" because they have four wings, whereas Ex 25:18–20 and 1 Ki 6:23–29 imply that the cherubim on the ark and in the temple had two wings (although those passages do not say that the cherubim had no more than two wings). The biblical passages with cherubim are summarized by Brighton:

> In Ex 25:17–22 Moses was commanded to fashion two cherubim out of hammered gold. One was placed at each end of the lid of the ark [of the covenant]; they faced each other with their wings outstretched over the lid. God promised to meet with Moses between the cherubim over the ark and speak with him (Ex 25:22; Num 7:89). Cherubim were also woven into curtains for the tabernacle and later the temple (Ex 26:1, 31; 2 Chr 3:14). For the temple, Solomon had two cherubim made of olive wood and overlaid with gold, ten cubits in height. They were placed in the temple's Holy of Holies, and their wings overshadowed the ark, which was moved there when the temple was finished (1 Ki 6:23–28; 8:6–7; 2 Chr 3:10–13; 5:7–8). Solomon's temple also had cherubim carved on the walls of both the Holy Place and the Holy of Holies, and also on the doors (1 Ki 6:29–35). Cherubim adorned the stands for the moveable bronze basins used in the courtyard of the temple (1 Ki 7:27–29, 36). And cherubim were carved all around the eschatological temple Ezekiel saw in a vision (Ezek 41:17–20, 25).
>
> The cherubim in the Holy of Holies over the ark served as God's throne, the place of his majestic presence.[4] In addition, the cherubim David planned for Solomon to build for the temple, whose wings were "for spreading and covering the ark of the covenant of Yahweh," are said to be God's chariot (1 Chr 28:18). Therefore Yahweh is said to ride upon the cherubim (Ps 18:10 [MT 18:11]; cf. Ezek 9:3). …
>
> The picture, then, that the OT presents is that wherever God's heavenly throne and majesty are revealed or described in detail, the cherubim always attend him. They either are the throne of his majestic presence, as in the Holy of Holies, or they attend his presence to serve and enhance that glorious presence and to sing his praises.[5]

Apparently these "living creatures" are a type of those created heavenly beings that will commonly come to be called "angels," as Christian tradition classifies them. While the grammatical gender of חַיָּה is feminine, the description of the living creatures does not emphasize any features that relate to human gender (masculine or feminine). See the next textual note, and compare Mt 22:30 ‖ Mk 12:25 ‖ Lk 20:35–36, where Jesus states that after the resurrection, Christians will not engage in marriage but will be like angels (who, presumably, do not marry or procreate, which would require gender). See further the commentary on Ezek 1:5–11.

דְּמוּת אָדָם לָהֵנָּה—This is literally "the likeness of human [belonged] to them." "Likeness" (דְּמוּת) is another favorite circumlocution of Ezekiel. Its most famous usage is in Gen 1:26, where it both parallels and qualifies God's creation of man in his

---

[4]   See 1 Sam 4:4; 2 Sam 6:2; Pss 80:2 (ET 80:1); 99:1; Is 37:16.

[5]   Brighton, *Revelation*, 125.

"image" (צֶלֶם). Ezekiel is too aware that he is witnessing a vision to use a word more indicative of materiality like צֶלֶם.

The context here requires אָדָם to be understood in its common generic sense in traditional English, not "man" in the sense of "male." Most languages have different words for the two senses and Hebrew has אִישׁ, "a man, male." Grammatically, חַיּוֹת ("living creatures") is feminine, but the inconsistency of the gender of the verbal and pronominal references to them in the following verses underscores that gender is beside the point here. Of the forty-five such references to them in this and the following verses, only twelve are the technically correct feminine. Sometimes the grammatical inconsistency in gender spills over into the description of the wheels too.

1:6 וְאַרְבָּעָה פָנִים—As nearly always, another *waw* connects the clauses, but the context requires that it be translated adversatively ("But …"): no ordinary אָדָם has *four* faces or wings!

וְאַרְבַּע כְּנָפַיִם—The "four wings" of these creatures (later called cherubim in 10:1–20, 11:22) contrasts with the seraphim in Isaiah's inaugural prophetic vision (Isaiah 6), which had six wings apiece. The difference in number is noteworthy because the number four (which occurs over fifty times in the book) seems to have special significance for Ezekiel, as we shall see at various points, climaxing in the vision of the "foursquare" eschatological temple in chapters 40–43. We will shortly meet four wheels (1:15); chapter 8 describes four especially sinful acts; four plagues are highlighted in chapter 14; and the winds come from the four points of the compass in chapter 37. If the number is to be pressed symbolically, the latter illustration would seem to be the most indicative: totality, completeness, and perhaps the ability to travel all over the earth, just as the four faces enabled the living creatures to see in every direction. Compare similar uses of four in Ezekiel's near contemporaries: the four world eras of Daniel 2 and Daniel 7; the four horns demolished by four smiths in Zech 2:1–4 (ET 1:18–21); the four chariots of the "Lord of the whole earth" in Zech 6:1–8.[6]

The cherubim statues on the lid of the ark of the covenant had wings, but Ex 25:17–22 does not specify how many. The description of the cherubim in the temple (but not on the ark) in 1 Ki 6:27 implies that they have (at least) two wings.

Zimmerli attempts to find significance in the fact that the wings of the creatures (cherubim) in Ezekiel, like those of the cherubim in the tabernacle and temple (but unlike those of the seraphim in Isaiah 6), are not explicitly described as used for flight. Zimmerli gives a negative interpretation to the alleged attitude of priestly writers, including Ezekiel, which "takes on an aspect of hieratic rigidity and ornamental fixity which distinguished it from the lively mobility of the figures of Is 6."[7] But that comparison is insidious. Zimmerli's view may simply contradict 1:24 later, where moving wings make a loud noise, and the wings are let down when movement stops. In Ezekiel the wheels may do most of the moving, but it is hard to see any "hieratic rigid-

---

6   Regarding the biblical symbolism of the number four, see Brighton, *Revelation*, 181–82.

7   Zimmerli, *Ezekiel*, 1:121.

ity" in either the entire vision or in the function of any of the components. Zimmerli simply betrays his continuing dependence on attitudes (basically Protestant and especially German) that have characterized higher criticism throughout its history: an anti-priestly, anti-liturgical prejudice in favor of an idealized notion of the prophets as Reformed iconoclasts.

1:7 וְרַגְלֵיהֶם רֶגֶל יְשָׁרָה—The first clause in Hebrew is literally "their legs—a straight leg," with the plural רַגְלֵיהֶם followed by the singular רֶגֶל. The singular could imply that each creature had only one leg, or it could imply that each leg was straight, however many each had. Although aspects of both man and beast are present, we do not seem to be dealing with quadrupeds here; most likely each creature had two legs. "Straight" (יָשָׁר) could mean "unjointed," without a knee; no joint was needed because they flew instead of walking, but in 1:23 יָשָׁר is used again to denote *extended* wings when the creatures were in flight. So here it probably is better taken to mean that the creatures were standing upright, not reclining with their legs bent beneath their bodies.

וְכַף רַגְלֵיהֶם כְּכַף רֶגֶל עֵגֶל—In this context we must translate רֶגֶל as "foot" instead of "leg." כַּף is used in Hebrew of either the "palm" of one's hand or the "sole" of one's foot. Obviously, the latter applies here. But what, then, is the "sole" of the calf's foot? I have rendered it "hoof." The Targum paraphrases "calf's foot" as "round," that is, while a man's foot points in one particular direction, the feet of these creatures do not, so they are able to move in any direction (just as their four faces look in every direction). That may be the point here.

וְנֹצְצִים כְּעֵין נְחֹשֶׁת קָלָל:—The Qal of נָצַץ occurs only here (though cognates with the same meaning occur in Mishnaic Hebrew and Aramaic), and it means "to sparkle" (*HALOT*) or "gleam." The form is the masculine plural participle, but we would expect it to be feminine, since its antecedent is feminine (either רֶגֶל or רַגְלֵיהֶם), but see the last textual note on 1:5 on this common feature of Ezekiel's diction. Ezekiel uses כְּעֵין again (as in 1:4) to introduce the simile, instead of the simple כְּ used earlier in 1:7. This longer alternative seems to be used by Ezekiel for a simile of entire entity, not just part of it, so the subject may be the four living creatures, not merely their legs or feet. Ezekiel's younger contemporary Daniel uses the identical phrase כְּעֵין נְחֹשֶׁת קָלָל (Dan 10:6) to describe the "man" (Dan 10:5) who appears to Daniel along the Tigris River, who may be an angel or even the preincarnate Christ (compare Daniel 10 to Rev 1:12–20).

1:8 וְיָדֵו אָדָם מִתַּחַת כַּנְפֵיהֶם עַל אַרְבַּעַת רִבְעֵיהֶם—I follow the Qere וִידֵי: "hands" of a man were under their wings. The last part of this clause literally says, "on the four of their fourths," which evidently means "on all four sides" of each four-sided creature, as I have translated. Each creature had four faces, four wings, and perhaps four hands under the wings, or perhaps four pairs of hands, corresponding to the way a human has one *pair* of hands and one face. However, although acknowledging those possibilities, which have been advocated by earlier exegetes, Greenberg argues that just as each creature had only one wheel (1:15; 10:9), so each had only one pair of hands.[8]

---

[8] Greenberg, *Ezekiel*, 1:44.

וּפְנֵיהֶם וְכַנְפֵיהֶם לְאַרְבַּעְתָּם:—These last three Hebrew words may fit better if read as the beginning of the sentence that continues in 1:9a than as the ending of the sentence in 1:8a.

1:9 The wings are treated first (in 1:9a), then the faces (in 1:9b–10), which is the reverse of the order in the last three words of 1:8. The idiom אֶל־עֵבֶר פָּנָיו at the end of 1:9, which is translated "straight ahead," literally contains the word "face" (פָּנִים). The LXX has a condensed version of 1:8b–9 that does not discuss their wings at all. (It is common for the LXX of Ezekiel to be shorter than the MT, although to a lesser degree than the LXX of Jeremiah.) Ezek 1:11–12 to some extent duplicates 1:8b–9, although there is also mutual complementarity. Both the textual variation and the seeming verbosity lead some scholars to attempt to reconstruct an "original" text, but the degree of sheer speculation involved is high. I shall continue to follow the *hebraica veritas* (Jerome), unless there seem to be compelling reasons not to.

חֹבְרֹת אִשָּׁה אֶל־אֲחוֹתָהּ כַּנְפֵיהֶם—"Touching" may be too weak a rendering of the Hebrew participle of חָבַר. It is feminine plural to match כַּנְפֵיהֶם, since כָּנָף ("wing") is a feminine noun. (The derived noun חָבֵר means "comrade, companion.") As for the two large cherubim Solomon constructed for the temple, apparently they each faced forward, toward the ark, since their inner wings touched and the outer wing of each touched a side wall of the Holy of Holies (1 Ki 6:27). That verse uses נָגַע, "touch." This verb, חָבַר, is used for the overlapping of the various curtains that made up the tabernacle (Ex 26:3–11). Hence, "joined" may be a better translation, meaning that the wing tips were actually joined, and so the wings of each creature moved in perfect concert with those of the others. Such a picture of the harmonious relation of the wings would fit perfectly with description in 1:9b of their faces moving straight ahead without turning.

1:10 וּדְמוּת פְּנֵיהֶם—The opening word is דְּמוּת ("likeness"), used also in 1:5. The plural פָּנִים can refer to either one face or to many. Hence פְּנֵיהֶם may refer only to "their [first] face," which presumably is the face on the front of each creature—the face Ezekiel sees first. In that case the verse would begin, "The likeness of their [first] face was the face of a man," and we could assume that each of the other three faces too was a "likeness" (rather than an exact equivalent) of the kind of creature's face, even though דְּמוּת is not repeated in the verse again. Or פְּנֵיהֶם may refer to all four of the faces, in which case we could translate, "The likeness of their faces was this: the face of a man and the face of a lion …" The Hebrew does not specify which faces were on the front and back, but because of the references to the faces on the "right" and "left," we may assume that the first face is on the front and the last one is on the back.

Throughout Ezekiel 1 the descriptions appear to reflect the order in which the various features come into sight, and that is true in 1:10. That is, Ezekiel initially noticed the humanoid face looking straight ahead (1:9); then the leonine and bovine faces to the right and left, respectively; and finally he was able to discern that an eagle-like face was on the back. נֶשֶׁר could refer to a "vulture" as well as an "eagle," but the latter has always been preferred in passages such as this and Ex 19:4; Is 40:31.

1:11 וּפְנֵיהֶם וְכַנְפֵיהֶם פְּרֻדוֹת מִלְמָעְלָה—It is easy to understand how "their wings" (כַנְפֵיהֶם) would be "spread out" (פְּרֻדוֹת, Qal passive participle of פָּרַד) "upwards"

(מִלְמָעְלָה) or "above." But what sense does that make for "their faces" (פְּנֵיהֶם)? Traditional exegetes have attempted various desperate expedients. We could fault the versification and take וּפְנֵיהֶם as the conclusion of 1:10, "thus were their faces." The LXX lacks any translation of "their faces," and it would be easiest to omit it here.

The rest of 1:11 is compact but clear. First, there is a statement similar to 1:9a about their wings "touching" or "being joined," with the additional information that this was true about only "two" of each creature's four wings. Next, the lower pair of wings is described as "covering" (מְכַסּוֹת, Piel participle of כָּסָה) "their bodies" (גְּוִיֹתֵיהֶנָה, with an unusual form of the third feminine plural suffix), undoubtedly out of modesty. Similarly, for the six-winged seraphim in Is 6:2, one pair of wings covers their faces and another pair covers their legs.

1:12 אֶל אֲשֶׁר יִהְיֶה־שָּׁמָּה הָרוּחַ לָלֶכֶת יֵלֵכוּ—This verse in effect repeats 1:9b, but with a significant addition: the creatures go (יֵלֵכוּ) wherever the "S/spirit" (רוּחַ) desires them to go (לָלֶכֶת, Qal infinitive construct of הָלַךְ with לְ). In 1:4 רוּחַ meant "wind," though the storm-wind will reveal the triune God. In 1:20–21 and 10:17 we meet assertions that the רוּחַ ("spirit") of the living creatures was in the wheels. Does רוּחַ here likewise refer to the "spirit" of the four living creatures?

Or does it refer to the divine "Spirit" as the one who determines where God's throne is to go? The OT (as well as the NT) testifies to "the Spirit of God" (e.g., Gen 1:2; Ezek 11:24) as a distinct person of the one true God; that "Spirit" is the Holy Spirit, the third person of the Trinity. Ezekiel refers to "the Spirit of Yahweh" falling upon him in 11:5. In 37:1 Ezekiel says that Yahweh brought him out by "the Spirit of Yahweh" and set him down in a valley. This would be the same "Spirit" who enters him in 2:2 and 3:24 and who lifts him up and sometimes carries him various places (e.g., 3:12, 14; 8:3).

The OT also speak of humans and animals possessing a God-given "spirit of life" (רוּחַ חַיִּים, Gen 6:17; 7:15, 22). Hence, in Ezek 1:12 רוּחַ could refer to the "spirit" of these living creatures—the spirit that vivifies them. Other possibilities include their "mind," "disposition," "will," or "volitional impulse," understood as ultimately directed by Yahweh, who is enthroned above (Ezek 1:25–28). As bearers of God's throne, they would not convey God wherever they themselves please. They must be subject to the will of Yahweh and carry the divine throne wherever the Spirit of God desires them to go (as when the Glory of Yahweh departs from Jerusalem in chapter 10 and returns to it in chapter 43).

Since 1:12 in its context leaves the identity of רוּחַ here an open question, I have translated it "S/spirit."

1:13 וּדְמוּת הַחַיּוֹת—The syntax of this verse is difficult. The ancient versions vary considerably in their treatments of it. I translate this first phrase as a *casus pendens*. The first word is דְּמוּת, which in its previous uses (1:5, 10) I translated as "likeness." It represents Ezekiel's attempt to verbalize a sight beyond human language and description.

מַרְאֵיהֶם כְּגַחֲלֵי־אֵשׁ בֹּעֲרוֹת כְּמַרְאֵה הַלַּפִּדִים—The noun מַרְאֶה (twice in this clause) is a synonym of דְּמוּת (see the preceding textual note). "Their appearance" (מַרְאֵיהֶם) is the subject, and the predicate nominative has two phrases, the second in apposition to the first, and each uses כְּ: "like coals of fire, burning like the appearance of torches." In the last phrase the use of both כְּ and מַרְאֵה underscores Ezekiel's sense of the vision's transcendence and the impossibility of giving a precise description of it. The statement in 10:2 that these coals were amidst the creatures expands on the description given here but does not conflict with it.

הִיא מִתְהַלֶּכֶת בֵּין הַחַיּוֹת וְנֹגַהּ לָאֵשׁ וּמִן־הָאֵשׁ יוֹצֵא בָרָק:—The remainder of 1:13 might well be separated into two sentences. The first begins with הִיא, the feminine demonstrative pronoun, which must refer to the feminine noun אֵשׁ ("fire") earlier in the verse. אֵשׁ itself occurs twice in the second sentence.

1:14 וְהַחַיּוֹת רָצוֹא וָשׁוֹב כְּמַרְאֵה הַבָּזָק:—This short verse is missing entirely in the LXX. For reasons unknown, the LXX very often presents a shorter text than the MT. I proceed based on the assumption of the priority of the Hebrew text.

This verse's references to lightning and darting movement are similar to 1:13. It conveys Ezekiel's excitement at what he sees. Two Qal infinitive absolutes, רָצוֹא וָשׁוֹב, are used instead of finite verbal forms. Besides the most common use of an infinitive absolute as an intensifier before a finite verb (as in 1:3), the infinitive absolute can be used as a surrogate for any inflected verb form. The first verb, רָצוֹא, a hapax legomenon, probably is what lexicographers call a "byform" of the common verb רוּץ, "to run" (*HALOT*, s.v. רצא I, though *HALOT* prefers to follow the Vulgate's *ibant* and read יָצוֹא). Byforms may be dialectical variants or alternate forms of weak Hebrew verbs. שׁוֹב often means to "return." The two infinitives together have an iterative meaning: the creatures "were *running* and *returning*" (Waltke-O'Connor, § 35.5.3a, example 1), that is, they kept darting forth and back, to and fro.

Like the verse's first word, its last word, בָּזָק, is a hapax legomenon in the OT. At the end of 1:13, the usual word for "lightning," בָּרָק was used. For בָּזָק, an Aramaic cognate supports the meaning "flash of lighting" (*HALOT*).

1:15 וָאֵרֶא הַחַיּוֹת—As Ezekiel is watching the living creatures, the wheels will come into view. Most modern English versions begin a new paragraph about the wheels (1:15–21). These first two Hebrew words function as a dependent clause introducing the following main clause. Both this clause and the following one begin with *waw*.

וְהִנֵּה אוֹפַן אֶחָד בָּאָרֶץ—Often אֶרֶץ is rendered "earth" or "land," but "ground" seems more appropriate here. Its mention appears proleptic here, anticipating 1:24b, where the throne-vehicle finally "lands."[9]

לְאַרְבַּעַת פָּנָיו:—This is, literally, "for/with respect to [לְ] its four faces." One could paraphrase "one [wheel] for each of the four of them [the living creatures]" (NRSV), but since the "living creatures" were mentioned last, I render this as "each [creature] with its four faces." The antecedent of the Hebrew pronominal suffix must both logically and syntactically be taken to be the creatures, as previously described.

---

9 Kaufmann (*Religion of Israel*, 437), a noted Israeli scholar, connects the "earth/ground" here with the "firmament" (רָקִיעַ) in 1:22–23, 25–26, which is the same term used in Gen 1:6–20, giving a cosmic symbolism to the entire spectacle. That cosmic symbolism is thoroughly consonant with the vision as a whole, but a connection between the "earth/ground" here and the "firmament" in 1:22–23, 25–26 is beyond what is exegetically sustainable.

The LXX (also the Syriac, Vulgate, and many Targum manuscripts) begins the next verse (1:16) with a translation of a conjunctive *waw*, which is absent in the MT (מַרְאֵה). That has led to the conjecture that a *waw* originally began 1:16 (וּמַרְאֵה) but was mistakenly attached to the end of 1:15 as the suffix on פָּנָיו. We recall that the versification is a medieval development and not intrinsic to the autograph, but if one follows the LXX, so many other changes follow in both verses that one hesitates to do that. Another conjecture is that לְאַרְבַּעַת originally was לְאַרבעתם, "according to the four of them." Supposedly, after a loss of the final mem on לארבעתם in 1:15, פָּנָיו was added to fill out the sense. פָּנָיו repeats the final two consonants of אוֹפָן earlier in 1:15.

1:16 מַרְאֵה הָאוֹפַנִּים וּמַעֲשֵׂיהֶם כְּעֵין תַּרְשִׁישׁ—The two nouns "appearance" (מַרְאֵה) and "design" (מַעֲשֶׂה) both occur twice in 1:16. The verse makes good sense as it is, but "design" is missing in the LXX of 1:16a and "appearance" in 1:16b. To avoid a third instance of "appearance" in English I translate כְּעֵין simply as "like" (rather than "like the appearance of"); see the textual note on it in 1:4.

The meaning of תַּרְשִׁישׁ is uncertain, so I have simply transliterated it. The LXX too transliterates it here and in some other passages, though in others the LXX renders it as "chrysolite," a bright yellow precious stone, or as "anthrax," a dark red stone.[10] Targum Onkelos indicates a "sea color," that is, bluish-green. In 28:13 *tarshish* is in the Edenic garden of God, and it was also one of the precious stones in the breast-piece of the high priest (Ex 28:20; 39:13). It also seems "likely that the OT passages with תַּרְשִׁישׁ and סַפִּיר are part of the OT background for the eschatological depiction of *God's redeemed in Christ as the new Jerusalem, constructed with gems and precious materials*" in Revelation 21, particularly "chrysolite" in Rev 21:20.[11]

וּדְמוּת אֶחָד לְאַרְבַּעְתָּן—Literally, "one likeness [was] to the four of them," this means that all four looked alike. דְּמוּת is feminine, while the adjectival אֶחָד is masculine, but similar gender inconsistencies abound in Ezekiel 1.

כַּאֲשֶׁר יִהְיֶה הָאוֹפַן בְּתוֹךְ הָאוֹפָן:—Literally, "as a wheel would be in the midst of a wheel," this has traditionally been taken to imply a second wheel inserted at a right angle (NIV: "intersecting"). That interpretation has in its favor the possibility of movement in any of the four directions without being turned. Mechanically simpler would be two concentric circles, a construction which can be illustrated by a depiction of the throne-chariot of Sargon of Assyria (roughly a century before Ezekiel).

1:17 עַל־אַרְבַּעַת רִבְעֵיהֶן בְּלֶכְתָּם יֵלֵכוּ—This means that "when they moved" (בְּלֶכְתָּם) "they went" (יֵלֵכוּ) "toward [any of] the four of their sides." עַל, which usually means "on, upon," frequently is used interchangeably with אֶל, "to, towards." "Their four sides" are the four directions the creatures faced—one face in each of the four directions. (We again note the inconsistency in grammatical gender: the suffix on רִבְעֵיהֶן is feminine plural, while the verb יֵלֵכוּ is masculine plural even though the implied subject is feminine plural, הַחַיּוֹת [1:15].)

---

[10] For a discussion of how the LXX translates it, see Mitchell, *The Song of Songs*, 930, n. 57.

[11] Mitchell, *The Song of Songs*, 931. See the discussion on pages 929–32 and "Solomon in Song 5:9–16 as a Type of Christ" on pages 944–62.

לֹא יִסַּבּוּ בְּלֶכְתָּן:—The negated Niphal (third masculine plural imperfect) of סָבַב apparently means "without turning aside, changing direction, veering off."

1:18 וְגַבֵּיהֶן וְגֹבַהּ לָהֶם וְיִרְאָה לָהֶם—The syntax is awkward, but the sense is clear. גַּב can refer to a variety of curved objects, and here it means "rim … of a wheel" (*HALOT*, s.v. גַּב I, 3), as also in 1 Ki 7:33. Here the plural גַּבֵּיהֶן is masculine (with third feminine plural suffix), but later in the verse is a feminine plural form (וְגַבֹּתָם, with third masculine plural suffix). Literally, this is "and [as for] their rims, height to them and fear to them." Most English translations render the nouns גֹּבַהּ ("height") and יִרְאָה ("fear") as if they were adjectives, for example, ESV: "their rims were tall and awesome."

Many emendations have been suggested and even appear in popular translations (e.g., the "spokes" of RSV). The LXX apparently misread the Hebrew יִרְאָה, "fear," as a form of רָאָה, "to see," and so translated καὶ εἶδον, "and I saw." But no suggestion is as compelling as leaving the Hebrew text as it is.

1:20 עַל אֲשֶׁר יִהְיֶה־שָּׁם הָרוּחַ לָלֶכֶת יֵלֵכוּ שָׁמָּה הָרוּחַ לָלֶכֶת—This elaborates on the second clause in 1:12; see the textual note and commentary there.

Most critical scholars are certain that this Hebrew line contains a dittograph. The last three words (שָׁמָּה הָרוּחַ לָלֶכֶת, which I set off by dashes: "—to where the S/spirit wanted to go—") are said to be a corrected repetition of the earlier three words שָּׁם הָרוּחַ לָלֶכֶת. In the earlier phrase, one would expect שָׁם ("there") to have the directive ending (הָ-), as it does in the last phrase (שָׁמָּה, "to there"). Hence critics assert that the last three words are a scribal correction, originally written above the line or in the margin, and apparently later inserted in the text itself. Allegedly, the problem arose because of scribal haplography: the first phrase originally had שמההרוח but one ה (on the end of שָׁמָּה) was inadvertently omitted because the following word also began with a ה, the definite article (הָרוּחַ).

All aspects of that reconstruction are based on well-known principles of textual criticism. That it is not sheer speculation is confirmed by the fact that the repetitious three words do not appear in the LXX. But on the other hand, so convoluted an explanation may be unnecessary, because Ezekiel is not consistent in his use of the two forms שָׁם and שָׁמָּה. For example, 4:13 too has שָׁם where one would expect שָׁמָּה, and the final word of the book is שָׁמָּה, where one would expect שָׁם (48:35).

כִּי רוּחַ הַחַיָּה בָּאוֹפַנִּים:—The singular הַחַיָּה here and in the parallel phrase at the end of 1:21 may be collective ("the living creature*s*"), as in 1:22, or it may be distributive ("[each] living creature"). Here רוּחַ refers to the "spirit" of the living creatures themselves, and not to the Holy Spirit. This was one of the two possibilities for רוּחַ discussed in the textual notes on 1:12.

1:21 No subjects of the verbs are explicitly stated until the "wheels" and "living creature" (see the preceding textual note) toward the end of the verse, but the sense is perfectly clear. The verse reiterates 1:20 and underscores the absolute unity of the entire angelic ensemble.

וּדְמוּת עַל־רָאשֵׁי הַחַיָּה רָקִיעַ—See the textual note on דְּמוּת ("something like") in 1:5. The singular הַחַיָּה must be collective ("living creature*s*") as shown by the plural pronoun on רָאשֵׁיהֶם ("their heads") later in the verse. Possibly the singular is intended to indicate the fundamental unity of the four, who move in unison.

I use "dome" to translate רָקִיעַ. Traditionally, it has been rendered "firmament" (*HALOT*; KJV of Gen 1:6–8, 14–15, 17, 20), meaning "the vault of heaven."[12] The word denotes an inverted bowl, as the sky stretching out to the horizon appears to the naked eye. In Genesis 1 it serves to separate the waters above from the waters below, and as the setting for the sun, moon, and stars. The etymology of רָקִיעַ suggests something hammered smooth, as a bowl might be (see *HALOT*, s.v. רקע). Meanings of words are not usually determined by their etymological history, and, hence, not as much should be made of it as many commentators do. Here, as one sees from the following context, the רָקִיעַ functions as a platform for God's throne. That might imply a more level surface, but, especially in a vision, that kind of detail should be qualified at least as much as Ezekiel keeps qualifying his descriptions ("something like," etc.).

כְּעֵין הַקֶּרַח הַנּוֹרָא—Usually קֶרַח means "ice" or "frost." For here *HALOT* (3) gives "crystal," based on the LXX's κρύσταλλος, which is also in the "recycling" of Ezekiel's vision in Rev 4:6: "a sea of glass, like crystal." A description of the celestial foundation of God's presence as crystalline appears already at the sealing of the old covenant in Ex 24:10: "They saw the God of Israel, and under his feet was something made like a pavement of lapis lazuli, as the essence of heaven in clarity."

The Niphal participle of יָרֵא can mean "to be feared, terrible," but here it probably means "awesome" (*HALOT*, Niphal, 2 d). It has the definite article (הַנּוֹרָא), as though the reference were to something well-known, perhaps the crystal pavement already seen by Israel's elders in Ex 24:10. The best analogy I can think of is the face of a newly calved glacier, with its indescribably deep, rich blue color.

1:23 Many emendations are proposed, partly based on the LXX, but none are compelling to me. "[Stretched out] straight" is a rather clipped construction, but the verbal idea can easily be supplied.

לְאִישׁ שְׁתַּיִם מְכַסּוֹת לָהֵנָה—It is common Hebrew style to repeat a phrase that refers distributively to a number of like objects. My translation repeats this phrase ("each had two [wings] covering themselves") to reflect the Hebrew. The LXX does not repeat the phrase, so one must choose between explaining the shorter Greek text as a "translator's simplification"[13] or deeming the MT to have a dittograph. I choose the former; the repetition has distributive force. The repeated phrase says that each of the creatures (grammatically feminine) had two wings covering themselves. לָהֵנָה probably is the longer form (הֵנָה) of the third feminine plural pronominal suffix "them" (usually הֵן) with the preposition לְ, rather than the adverb הֵנָה, "hither, thither."

אֶת גְּוִיֹּתֵיהֶם:—This clarifies that the previous, repeated phrase means that each had two wings covering "their bodies." Thus, in this vision one pair of the cherubic

---

12 *The Random House Dictionary of the English Language*, second ed., unabridged (New York: Random House, 1987), 723.

13 Greenberg, *Ezekiel*, 1:48.

46

wing tips touch each other (1:9–11), as above the ark in the temple, and a second pair of wings cover their bodies, somewhat as in Isaiah's vision (Is 6:2).

1:24 וָאֶשְׁמַע אֶת־קוֹל כַּנְפֵיהֶם—The noun קוֹל occurs five times in this verse. It may be translated either "sound" or "voice," depending on context. Since English has no one word covering both, the translation necessarily loses the Hebrew unity as we shift to "voice" when the reference is to God's. Ezekiel piles up three graphic similes of the "sound of their wings" to indicate an otherworldliness evident to the ear (like the previous similes of otherworldly appearance to the eye). The LXX omits the second and third similes, triggering the usual rash of changes suggested by scholars (e.g., the incredible number suggested by Allen[14]).

כְּקוֹל מַיִם רַבִּים—The first simile is to "the sound of many waters." The same simile reappears in 43:2 of the sound of the return of God's "Glory" (כָּבוֹד) to the eschatological temple. This simile recalls the awesome roar of ocean breakers (Ps 93:4).

כְּקוֹל־שַׁדַּי—The second simile is to the "voice of Shaddai/the Almighty." We hear no words of the Almighty yet, but we will shortly—in chapter 2, which is the call proper of Ezekiel. Ezek 10:5, a parallel verse, expands this to כְּקוֹל אֵל־שַׁדַּי, "like the voice of God Almighty."

Shaddai/Almighty is an undisputed epithet of Yahweh. It is ancient and most common in the patriarchal period (as God explains in Ex 6:3) as well as Job and Ruth. It would take another essay to discuss the term fully. What its etymology and original meaning may have been are matters of speculation, and there has been much. One etymology frequently ventured relates Shaddai to the Akkadian *shadu*, "mountain," and understands it as describing Yahweh as a "mountain God," not in the pagan sense, but in reference to Mount Sinai. A recent inscription found at Deir Allah (probably the biblical Succoth on the Jabbok River, just east of its debouchment into the Jordan), famous for its reference to Balaam, also seems to depict Shaddai as the head of the divine assembly.

If any specific overtones can be induced from its appearances in the Bible, passages with Shaddai/Almighty seem to emphasize God's power, often potentially destructive in judgment. Thus, I cannot improve upon its traditional rendering as "Almighty," following a fanciful rabbinic etymology and the usual LXX rendition as παντοκράτωρ (also used to translate צְבָאוֹת [e.g., 2 Sam 5:10]), which also appears in the NT (e.g., Rev 1:8). The theme of the glorified Christ as παντοκράτωρ continues to play a prominent role in the piety, iconography, and church architecture of Eastern Orthodoxy.

קוֹל הֲמֻלָּה כְּקוֹל מַחֲנֶה—This third simile is of the din and clamor of a military camp (מַחֲנֶה). הֲמֻלָּה appears elsewhere in the OT only in Jer 11:16. Based on Ugaritic it may refer to a "(tumultuous) **crowd**" (*HALOT*).

1:25 While 1:24 was about the sound of the creatures' wings, this verse refers to a sound (or voice?) from above the dome, hence from God. Parts of the verse are virtually identical to parts of the preceding and following verses. Since parts of 1:25 are missing in

---

[14] Allen, *Ezekiel*, 1:8–9.

some versions and Hebrew manuscripts, we encounter the usual morass of critical speculations. Without going into detail, I shall only observe that it is easier to explain the MT as the basis of the variants than vice versa, and this is a cardinal rule of textual criticism that points to the authenticity of the MT. As the verse stands, it emphasizes that the noise does not come from the creatures, but from the direction of the dome above them. When the creatures are silent, the prophet is able to recognize God's voice, or perhaps when God is going to speak, the creatures then stand still (in deference) and relax their wings so no other sound will obscure or detract from God's words.

1:26 Ezekiel's cautious descriptions climax as he approaches the climax of the vision, God himself. Three times in this verse we meet דְּמוּת ("likeness") and twice מַרְאֶה ("appearance"). Although the Hebrew סַפִּיר is etymologically related to the English "sapphire," most scholars agree that it refers to lapis lazuli. Archaeology also indicates how highly prized lapis was in antiquity, while what we know as sapphire was scarcely known. In Ex 24:10 the pavement under God's presence was made of סַפִּיר (see the textual notes on 1:22), but Ezekiel clearly attributes it to the throne, both here and in 10:1.

דְּמוּת כְּמַרְאֵה אָדָם—Ezekiel's eyes finally focus on God himself. The prophet's description is especially cautious: he uses both "likeness" and "appearance," the latter further circumscribed by the preposition כְּ, "like." Yet he clearly states that God's form is that of אָדָם, "a man."

1:27 The Hebrew seems to indicate that the upper part of the divine man was like electrum and fire together, while his lower part was like fire alone. If חַשְׁמַל really is electrum (see the textual note on it in 1:4), then it is amber in color, as fire is too, so the upper and lower portions are similar but not quite identical. The LXX speaks simply of electrum (no fire) above the figure's waist and of fire below the waist. Ezek 8:2, which is parallel to 1:27, also makes that simple distinction. Probably 8:2 merely abbreviates 1:27 by omitting fire from the description of the electrum-like upper part.

כְּמַרְאֵה־אֵשׁ בֵּית־לָהּ סָבִיב—Here בֵּית is used as a preposition, "within" (*HALOT*, A 3). But what is the antecedent of the pronoun on לָהּ ("within *it*")? Most likely, the antecedent is the preceding construct phrase כְּעֵין חַשְׁמַל. The noun עַיִן is feminine, while the gender of חַשְׁמַל is uncertain. Apparently it looked as though fire were encased in the electrum-like upper torso, and fire also surrounded it (the adverb סָבִיב).

מִמַּרְאֵה מָתְנָיו—Here the noun מַרְאֶה in construct (and with מִן) is best translated *"from what appeared to be* his waist" rather than "appearance" as in earlier verses. I have translated מָתְנַיִם as "waist" rather than the traditional "loins." "Hips" might be another alternative, but anatomically the difference is slight, and in a vision such as this, precise measurement is not to be expected.

וְנֹגַהּ לוֹ סָבִיב—This phrase ("and a radiance surrounding him") uses the same preposition לְ that is in the phrase two textual notes above, but here its suffix is masculine (לוֹ) instead of feminine (לָהּ). Again we must inquire what the antecedent is. The most likely referent is אָדָם ("a man") in 1:26. A certain radiance surrounds the entire figure (not just his lower half). That fits the description of his upper part being as of electrum and fire (see the first textual note on 1:27), and it is still compatible with 8:2, which mentions only electrum for his upper body.

1:28 The first half of the verse elaborates the appearance of the "radiance" that was mentioned briefly at the end of 1:27.

הוּא מַרְאֵה דְמוּת כְּבוֹד־יְהוָה—Here, הוּא could be either a demonstrative adjective ("that") or the personal pronoun "he," consistent with the reference to "him" at the end of 1:27. The use of a demonstrative adjective before the noun it modifies appears elsewhere in Ezekiel and is usually taken as an Aramaism. A literal translation is "That was the appearance/manifestation of the Glory of Yahweh."

כְּבוֹד־יְהוָה—The divine "Glory" (כָּבוֹד) reappears often in the book.[a] I have capitalized "Glory" because the reference is obviously to a divine figure; here God is in the form of "a man" (1:26). That כָּבוֹד may even refer to such a human figure is paralleled elsewhere in the OT only in Ex 33:18–22. Moses asks Yahweh, "Show me, now, your Glory" (Ex 33:18). Yahweh covers Moses with his hand until his Glory has passed by, and then Yahweh allows Moses to see his back, but not his face, lest Moses die.

(a) Ezek 3:12, 23; 8:4; 9:3; 10:4, 18–19; 11:22–23; 43:2–5; 44:4; cf. 39:21

When כָּבוֹד is used of a visible manifestation of God, "Glory" is really a woefully inadequate translation because the word in ordinary English usage conveys none of that meaning. But I am at a loss to suggest any viable alternative. As I detail in the theological commentary, it is a major OT means of expressing the λόγος ἄσαρκος, the "not-yet enfleshed Word," the preincarnate Christ. From our NT vantage point, we can see how the contours of the divine Glory revealed in the OT are wholly congruent with the full revelation of divine Glory in the God-man, Jesus Christ.

וָאֶשְׁמַע קוֹל מְדַבֵּר׃—Ezekiel hears the same קוֹל that began as "a sound from above the dome" in 1:25, only now Ezekiel can make out words—God's call to the prophet (Ezekiel 2). He hears "the voice of the Almighty" to which he had likened the sound of the creatures' wings in 1:24.

The final phrase could be understood as a construct phrase with the participle מְדַבֵּר as a substantive: "I heard a voice of one [masculine singular] speaking." Or the participle could serve as a (present-tense) verb with קוֹל as its subject: "I heard a voice speaking." The decision here determines what will be understood to be the subject of the verb that begins 2:1.

A similar issue pertains to the start of Is 40:3 and 40:6. Mt 3:3 translates Is 40:3 as "The voice of one calling" rather than "A voice calling." However, Is 40:6 must be "A voice saying …"

Commentary

The opening chapter affords Ezekiel, the prophet-priest, a vision into the opened heavens of the enthroned Glory of God. Thus the book of Ezekiel grants a proleptic view in heaven of what the apostles would see on earth: "The Word became flesh and tabernacled among us, and we beheld his glory, the glory of the only-begotten from the Father, full of grace and truth" (Jn 1:14). The incarnate Glory of God would atone for the sins of the world by his death on the cross and rise again from the dead. He then would ascend and, as our High Priest, be "seated at the right hand of the throne of the Majesty in the heavens" (Heb 8:1). In Revelation the apostle John sees through the opened heavens the enthroned Christ and the divine liturgy of the heavenly host. In particular, Revelation 4 recalls Ezekiel 1, down to the details of the mysterious creatures who support the divine throne in heaven.

As we ponder this most mysterious prophetic book, then, we bear in mind that the realities we strive to understand through Ezekiel's eyes find their fulfillment in Jesus Christ. The vision of divine Glory in chapter 1, though it transcends human comprehension, reveals the divine Glory to be manifested in the God-man, Christ our Lord. Likewise, when Yahweh speaks throughout the rest of the book (beginning in chapter 2), the words can rightly be regarded as those of Christ, the Word made flesh.

The Superscription (1:1)

1:1 The first verse of Ezekiel is not the usual type of superscription common in other prophetic books. Those superscriptions vary considerably, but they usually have one or more of the following elements: the prophet's name, his hometown, his paternity, and the date, and what follows is often called a חָזוֹן, "vision," דָּבָר, "word," or מַשָּׂא, "oracle." In Ezekiel, such elements appear in 1:2–3, which are in the third person, as is usually the case in prophetic superscriptions. However, 1:1 and 1:4–28 are in the first person as Ezekiel speaks. Hence, a major question arises at the outset: how is 1:1 connected with what follows?

The easiest solution is to assume that Ezekiel was the editor or "redactor" of the entire book that bears his name, and that he himself added 1:1 when his entire book was ready for "publication." In fact, I would argue similarly for the other prophetic books, and for most of the rest of the Bible as well. It should be obvious, if one stops to think, that virtually everything written has an editor—who most often is the writer himself. We almost automatically "proofread" virtually anything intended for any eyes but our own, and we often edit, add, and subtract as we go along. The Bible is literature written by humans under the inspiration of the Holy Spirit (2 Tim 3:16 and 2 Pet 1:19–21), and there is no reason why the human authors should not have applied the finishing touches, under inspiration, to the writings God moved them to produce.[15]

A major issue is the referent of the "thirtieth year" in Ezek 1:1. Here there is no unanimity whatsoever.[16] Throughout the rest of the book, beginning in 1:2, dates are in reference to the year of King Jehoiachin's exile, which was

---

[15] The biblical doctrine of inspiration does not automatically rule out other editors, such as disciples or other close associates of the primary or earlier author(s), especially for books that span generations of history, such as Samuel, Kings, and Chronicles. However, any such assumption would have to be clearly distinguished from higher-critical theories of redaction, which normally posit pseudonymous authors and anonymous editors who continued to alter the substance of the message over long periods of time, until canonization artificially ended the process of "reinterpretation," "contemporization," and the like. Nothing in the book of Ezekiel indicates authorship by anyone other than the prophet himself.

[16] For a summary of all the ancient and modern guesses, see York, "Ezekiel 1: Inaugural and Restoration Visions."

597 B.C. If the "thirtieth year" in 1:1 had the same referent, the prophet would inexplicably have put the latest date in the book first. (Ezek 29:17 refers to "the twenty-seventh year," which is the latest date in the book, unless 1:1 is later.) Since 1:2 refers to the fifth year of Jehoiachin's exile, if 1:1 refers to the thirtieth year of that exile, then 1:1 would predate by twenty-five years the succession of dates (which is chronological with one exception) in the rest of the book beginning in the following verse (1:2).

One could assume that the "thirtieth year" in 1:1 is the *same* as the "fifth year" in 1:2, only counting from a different starting point. If so, one might consider the Targum's guess that "the thirtieth year" pivots on the year when Hilkiah the high priest found the book of the Torah in the temple (2 Ki 22:8). That hypothesis has a certain plausibility, because no other prophet is so characterized by both the language and the content of the Pentateuch as Ezekiel. On the other hand, neither in Ezekiel nor elsewhere in the OT is there ever any hint that Hilkiah's discovery was ever used as the beginning year for chronological calculations.

Possibly the most common—and, in my judgment, the best—presumption is that "the thirtieth year" refers to the prophet's *age* at the time he received his inaugural vision, Ezekiel 1. (This suggestion goes as far back as Origen.[17]) Hebrew would not ordinarily express age in quite this way, but it is possible. Ezekiel plainly is a priest (1:3). Evidently that is the reason why he himself, as part of the leading group of Jerusalem's citizenry, had been deported together with Jehoiachin in 597 B.C., when Ezekiel (if "the thirtieth year" refers to his age) was twenty-five years old and eligible to begin some priestly activity. When he turned thirty, he would have been painfully aware of the fact that, were he still in Jerusalem, he would now have become eligible to begin his full priestly service in the temple, after a five-year preliminary period. These stipulations for priestly service are given in Num 8:24 and Num 4:29–30.

We may note that Christ himself began his public ministry in his thirtieth year of his earthly life (Lk 3:23), and probably John the Baptizer did too, given that he was six months older than Christ (humanly speaking) and the commencement of his ministry preceded that of Christ.

"In the fourth [month]" (Ezek 1:1) would be the summer month called Tammuz (roughly overlapping parts of June and July) if we begin the year in the spring according to the liturgical calendar of Israel, which began with the month of redemption: the exodus and Passover (Ex 12:2). See the commentary on Ezek 45:21, which refers to the Passover.

Ezekiel was "among the exiles" (1:1). Ezekiel uses the prepositional phrase בְּתוֹךְ ("among") over one hundred times. Here it may simply indicate his general location in the exiled community. Although Ezekiel was living in that community, he may have temporarily gone to the banks of the river on the edge of the settlement, as 3:15 seems to imply. "Among the exiles" (1:1) may imply a

---

[17] Origen, *Selecta in Ezechielem* (PG 13:768–69).

consciousness on the part of the prophet that what he witnesses and speaks at God's command is of central significance, not only for him and the little exilic community, but for all Israel. Because he was at the center of God's work of judgment and salvation, his life and work has significance for the whole world and for all times.

"The Kebar Canal" (1:1) probably was a large feeder canal, which, then as now, can often be as big as many rivers. נָהָר usually means "river" and often refers to the Euphrates, but here "canal" is the accurate translation. This canal was large enough to receive a proper name, "Kebar." Its precise location eludes us. It has often been identified with the modern, dry Sha en-Nil. We hear of it again somewhat over a century later in the archives of the Jewish Murashu family, whose members were bankers in the Babylonian city of Nippur. (See the map in the back of this book.) However, there it is described as merely "near" Nippur, not running through the middle of it, as the Sha en-Nil did in antiquity.

Ezekiel was standing by a stream of flowing (living) water on the occasion of his inaugural vision. Some of Daniel's visions also came by streams: the Ulai (Daniel 8) was in Susa (in modern Iran), and the vision recorded in Daniel 10 occurred by "the great river, the Tigris" (Dan 10:4), roughly halfway between the Ulai and the Kebar. Since foreign lands were considered unclean (see Amos 7:17), exiled Israelites might naturally seek communion with God near flowing water, which was often used in purification rites (see "living water" in Lev 14:5–6, 50–52; 15:13; Num 19:17). The triune God is the source of "living water" for his people (Jer 2:13; 17:13; Zech 14:8; Song 4:15).[18] Israelites would also recall God's miracles of redemption through water such as the dry crossing of the Red Sea (Exodus 14–15); the dry crossing of the Jordan River (Joshua 3–4); and the salvation of Noah and his family through the flood waters (Genesis 6–9), which is a type of Christian Baptism (1 Pet 3:18–22). Flowing water would recall the river of Eden (Gen 2:10–14). It would also anticipate the eschatological, life-giving river in the new creation that flows from the temple (Ezek 47:1–12), which seems to be (in OT imagery) the same "river of the water of life" that flows from the throne of God and the Lamb (Rev 22:1–2).

At the Baptism of our Lord, Jesus, like Ezekiel, sees the heavens opened and hears the spoken words of God by a river (Mt 3:16–17 ‖ Lk 3:21–22). Compare also Acts 16:13 and the long history of Christian preference for using living water for Baptism, if possible, as in the *Didache*:

> Concerning Baptism, baptize thus: having first instructed all these things, baptize "in the name of the Father and of the Son and of the Holy Spirit" in living water. But if you do not have living water, baptize in other water: if you are not able [to baptize] in cold water, then [baptize] in warm. If you do not have both, then pour out water on the head three times "in the name of the Father and of the Son and of the Holy Spirit." (*Didache* 7:1–3)

---

[18] For the connection between such OT passages with "living water," Jesus' promise in Jn 4:14 and 7:38–39 to give "living water," and the Sacrament of Holy Baptism, see Mitchell, *The Song of Songs*, 29–31, 263–74, 837–47, 868–73.

In "the heavens were opened" (Ezek 1:1), the passive (Niphal) form of the verb should be emphasized: the unspoken agent is God himself. The expression is unique in the OT (most similar is Gen 7:11). In some other theophanies, the heavens are "torn" open (קָרַע in Is 63:19 [ET 64:1]) or "stretched" open (נָטָה) like the curtains of a tent (2 Sam 22:10 ‖ Ps 18:10 [ET 18:9]). In Ezek 1:1 the verb "open" (פָּתַח) may be evocative of the opening of the "windows" (אֲרֻבּוֹת) of heaven for either judgment (the deluge in Gen 7:11) or for blessing (2 Ki 7:2; Mal 3:10). The immediate import in Ezekiel 1–24 will be judgment upon unfaithful Israel, but God's ultimate purpose is to reveal the Gospel (Ezekiel 25–48; see "Outline and Theological Emphases" in the introduction). In the NT, the heavens are opened by God to reveal his salvation in Jesus Christ: at Jesus' Baptism (Mt 3:16–17; Lk 3:21–22); for angels to do his bidding (Jn 1:51); to reveal to Peter that the Gospel is for the Gentiles too (Acts 10:11); and to show the apostle John the revelation (Rev 4:1; 19:11; cf. 11:19; 15:5).

The opened heavens revealed to Ezekiel "a divine vision" (1:1). There are more divine visions in Ezekiel than in any other OT book except for Daniel, and than in any NT book save Revelation. In Ezek 8:3 and 40:2 also, Ezekiel will receive what he calls "a divine vision," and in those verses that phrase introduces the extended visions in chapters 8–11 and chapters 40–48, respectively. If 1:1 is Ezekiel's editorial superscription to the entire book (see the commentary above), the phrase "divine vision" in 1:1 may encompass those and the other visions throughout the book. Those visions came from God, and some psychological or other purely naturalistic explanation is not to be sought. Eichrodt comments about the heavens opened to reveal the divine vision:

> [This] was also inseparably associated with a painful paralysis of every human endeavour at self-determination or self-assurance. ... Ezekiel therefore possesses an unshakable certitude, that the indescribable vision which he has been found worthy to see does not proceed from his own spiritual power, but that God in person is introducing him into a new dimension of reality, the strangeness and terrifying sublimity of which far transcend all that is imaginable to man.[19]

The Date Formula (1:2)

1:2   It is of no little significance that the date formula in this verse and in all other dates throughout the rest of the book (besides "the thirtieth year" in 1:1) is anchored to the date of King Jehoiachin's exile. Jehoiachin was a son of David, and as long as he lived, he was the only legitimate claimant to the throne in Jerusalem. Both the Israelites and the Babylonians knew that. Thus, by no accident, 2 Kings 25 (and its doublet in Jeremiah 52) ends on the positive note that special favors, befitting royalty, had been shown to the exiled Jehoiachin by Nebuchadnezzar's son and successor, Evil-Merodach. That favor (as well as some previous favor by Nebuchadnezzar himself) is also attested

---

[19]   Eichrodt, *Ezekiel*, 54.

extrabiblically in Babylonian sources. Zedekiah (Jehoiachin's uncle) had been placed on the throne after Jehoiachin's deportation in 597 B.C. Zedekiah is often considered the last king of Judah, but he was really no more than a puppet of the Babylonians, and he obviously enjoyed the respect of neither his masters nor his subjects.

Thus, not only do the Israelites' political hopes rest on Jehoiachin, but their religious ones as well. The messianic promise of the Savior, first given right after the fall into sin (Gen 3:15), explained further to Abraham (Gen 12:1–3) and his descendants, and elaborated especially by Nathan to King David (2 Samuel 7), rested on Jehoiachin and his heirs: his "house" would never fail until the advent of Christ, who would reign on David's throne forever (e.g., Is 9:5–6 [ET 9:6–7]). By no means were all the implications of that promise understood until after the ascension of Christ (see Acts 1:6–9), and even we Christians today may not fully "understand" them. Nevertheless, this chronological framework of the book of Ezekiel remains a major part of the implicit theology of the book. The exile of Jehoiachin attests that God had executed judgment on unfaithful Israel, but his continued life, albeit in exile, signifies that God will still fulfill his promise of salvation for the entire world through the greater Son of David and King of Israel.

Up to a point, Ezekiel and his audience doubtless agreed on Jehoiachin's importance. On a key point, however, they totally disagree. The populace, encouraged by false prophets, cherished the false expectation that their exile would be of short duration; if they had sinned, their transgression was mild, and the punishment they had already received was enough, or was even more than was fair (Ezekiel 18). They expected that they would be released soon, the Davidic monarchy would be restored in Jerusalem, and life could continue at least as well as before; perhaps even a truly "messianic" era would be instituted shortly. Virtually the first two-thirds of the book of Ezekiel is devoted to demolishing such false hopes. On this point, Ezekiel and Jeremiah are in total agreement, as Jeremiah now preaches to those still in Jerusalem, who were not included in the deportation in 597. Superficially, Ezekiel's initial message is sometimes compared to Cato's diatribes to the Roman senate: *Carthago delenda est*, "Carthage [here substitute Jerusalem] must be destroyed."

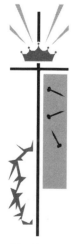

Only after all such false hopes have been dashed and the people were driven to repent and learned to depend solely on God's promise of salvation by grace alone—whenever and however he sees fit to implement that promise in history (cf. Gal 4:4)—could salvation come to them. In Christological terms, this is Law and Gospel, a theology of the cross, a cruciform way of believing and living. The Christian recognizes in Ezekiel's message the foreshadowing of Good Friday, when God's judgment climaxed in the death of his own Son, and Easter Sunday, when God's verdict of justification by grace alone was published to the whole world. The Christian pastor who preaches and teaches Ezekiel proclaims its message of Law and Gospel as part and parcel of God's constant action *sub contrario* (working through apparent opposites). Ezekiel's message is not rendered irrelevant by its climactic expression in Christ; rather, through Christ and his Spirit, it has been made part of the history of *our* salvation.

The Means of Divine Revelation (1:3)

1:3   Here two more expressions (in addition to "a divine vision" in 1:1) describe the divine origin and content of not only what immediately follows, but also of the entire book: "the Word [דְּבָר] of Yahweh came forcefully to Ezekiel" and "the hand [יַד] of Yahweh was upon him." Expressions with all three of these key terms, divine "vision(s)" (מַרְאָה) and Yahweh's "Word" (דְּבָר) and "hand" (יַד), recur throughout the book. Of these three, God's "Word" is easily the most important, both from the Ezekielian context and that of the entire Scriptures. Typically, we are told nothing of the precise process by which what we know as "verbal inspiration" took place. The emphasis is simply on the fact that what the prophet spoke and wrote is God's Word, which came to be (usually some form of הָיָה as here) present and audible to the prophet from outside himself, and was by no means merely a verbalization of some inner spiritual experience of his own. Ezekiel's own personality remains slightly evident throughout his book, and to a far lesser degree than Jeremiah's, but to a greater degree than in many biblical writings where the author's persona recedes drastically, sometimes to the extent that we do not even know the author's name.

The formula of the coming (הָיָה לְ) of Yahweh's Word, here and repeatedly throughout the book, surely implies the personal agency of God. Words emanate from people, who use words to communicate. If the speaker is God, an anthropomorphism is implied, and probably a personal, "incarnational" element as well. The sort of element that is merely implied here is made explicit in 3:17, for example, where the Lord refers to Ezekiel hearing "a word *from my mouth.*" In chapter 1, the incarnational element is even more up front because the vision described in the following verses obviously depicts the invisible God in anthropomorphic terms (albeit highly circumscribed, so no literalistic and idolatrous misunderstandings might ensue). Especially since the divine "Glory" (כָּבוֹד, 1:28) reappears often in the book,[b] that personal form of the God who utters the divine Word is reinforced throughout the book. Sometimes in the OT too, the divine Word is a hypostasis of God, just as in the NT Christ is the incarnate Word of God—the Word who *is* God (e.g., Jn 1:1–3, 14; Rev 19:13).[20]

The third, related expression, which appears for the first time in Ezek 1:3, is "the hand of Yahweh." This expression too is anything but unique to Ezekiel, since it and similar expressions occur throughout the OT. God's almighty

(b) Ezek 3:12, 23; 8:4; 9:3; 10:4, 18–19; 11:22–23; 43:2–5; 44:4

---

[20]   For the Christological nature of the divine "Glory," see the commentary on Ezek 1:28. Throughout this commentary, I intend the reader to understand my use of the terms "person(al)" and "hypostasis" to reflect the church's traditional language and theology as expressed in the creeds of the early church and in the Lutheran Confessions. See further the commentary on 1:25–28.

"hand" may bring either judgment and destruction or salvation and eternal life.[21] Its role is such that it could almost be counted as another of the OT hypostases, pointing to the Trinity and the incarnation of Christ. However, since the divine "hand" is qualified by "of Yahweh" rather than standing independently, it is usually classified rather as one of the major anthropomorphisms. Its classical expression probably comes in connection with the exodus: God redeemed his people "with a mighty hand and an outstretched arm" (e.g., Deut 4:34; 5:15). In many other contexts, it refers to God's (active) power or omnipotence. This biblical significance continues in the familiar assertion in the Apostles' Creed of our risen Lord's session "at the right *hand* of God the Father Almighty" (similar phrases occur in the Nicene and Athanasian Creeds).

Ezekiel refers to "the hand of Yahweh" six times,[c] usually with הָיָה and עָלַי ("was … upon me"), as here, although sometimes stronger language is used (e.g., the adjective חָזָק, "strong," in 3:14 and the verb נָפַל, "fall," in 8:1). Thus "the hand of Yahweh" embodies divine urgency, pressure, or compulsion upon the prophet to do something. One may compare the effect of Yahweh's hand on this OT prophet to the way Jesus, the supreme Prophet, used δεῖ, "it is necessary,"[d] to describe his obligation to make his way to Calvary. The most striking applications of "the hand of Yahweh" in Ezekiel are his transportations from Babylon to Jerusalem in 8:1–3 and 40:1, where we shall have to discuss the expression further. Most often in Ezekiel, Yahweh's "hand" is associated with the prophet's personal receipt of a vision.

(c) Ezek 1:3; 3:14, 22; 33:22; 37:1; 40:1 (see also 8:1)

(d) Lk 9:22; 13:33; 17:25; 22:37; 24:7, 26, 44 (cf. 4:43)

The Theophany and the Living Creatures (1:4–14)

1:4 Ezekiel's description of the theophany begins in a way similar to many biblical theophanies: a storm, lightning, and other awe-inspiring phenomena. Sometimes volcanic and/or seismic phenomena appear too, as at Sinai (Ex 19:16–19). It is probably noteworthy that in "As I looked …" (1:4), Ezekiel uses the everyday Hebrew verb for "see, look" (רָאָה, from the same root as the noun translated "vision" in 1:1). 1 Sam 9:9 tells us that the participial form of that verb, רֹאֶה, "seer," had been a common term for a prophet in Israel prior to the era of Samuel, but was largely replaced by נָבִיא, the usual Hebrew noun for "prophet." However, as Ezek 1:4 and many other verses indicate, the verb רָאָה by no means ceased to be used altogether for prophetic experience. The verb חָזָה, "to see," and the noun חָזוֹן, "vision," appear to be used more frequently in the writing prophets for the prophetic "second sight" or inspiration by the Holy Spirit (cf. 2 Pet 1:21), but that verb too is sometimes used of seeing with ordinary, everyday vision (e.g., Is 33:17, 20; Prov 24:32). Hence this general vocabulary, along with the phrases about the "Word" and "hand of Yahweh" already mentioned, are just about all that Ezekiel (and the rest of the Bible)

---

[21] See the textual note on it in 1:3. Some scholars have tried to associate Yahweh's hand being upon the prophet with some sort of trance or ecstatic experience on the prophet's part, but this is, at best, speculative, a secularizing shift from theological to anthropological categories.

gives in lieu of a precise, empirical description of how exactly God communicated to and inspired the biblical writers.

What is to be made of the storm cloud coming "from the north" (Ezek 1:4)? It may simply be another case where something ostensibly quite ordinary is transmuted into a divine appearance (cf. the burning bush of Exodus 3). In this case, it would be God's use of a natural meteorological circumstance. The head of the Persian Gulf is dominated by a zone of very low pressure during the summer months, often producing severe sand or dust storms. Various details of the vision might be read as "transfigurations" of a storm. However, "north" (צָפוֹן) is often the direction from which evil—especially military invasions—comes upon Israel and Judah in the judgment oracles of the prophets. This direction is determined by geography: Canaan sat at the western leg of the Fertile Crescent, while the Persian Gulf forms the end of the eastern leg (with mostly desert in between).

It may be relevant that in Canaanite mythology Mount North (צָפוֹן, the classical Mount Cassius, on the Mediterranean coast at what today is the Turkish-Syrian border) was the equivalent of the Greek Mount Olympus, the abode of the gods. Isaiah 14, a polemic against the king of Babylon, who thought himself to be a god, includes a polemic against that Canaanite myth (Is 14:13). It is hard to imagine Ezekiel (of all the prophets) adapting so central a pagan idea. Yet, the fact that a psalmist can exmythologically apply the picture to Mount Zion (Ps 48:2–3 [ET 48:1–2]) does open up the possibility.[22]

At any rate, whether the whole theophany was, humanly speaking, simply a vision with no external starting point visible to anyone besides Ezekiel, or whether it was a sort of "transfiguration" of a natural phenomenon others could see, by the end of 1:4 it begins to be clear that we are hearing a description of far more than a desert storm. חַשְׁמַל (translated "electrum") is of uncertain meaning, but its other uses by Ezekiel (in 1:27 and 8:2), as well as an apparent Akkadian cognate (*elmeshu*, a quasi-mythical precious stone), indicate something of a dazzling brilliance. The word prepares us for the supernatural description that follows.

1:5–11 Either the vision only gradually comes into focus, or Ezekiel, perhaps initially dazed, only gradually makes out its various components. The prophet first notices the strange "living creatures" (1:5). They are humanoid and stand upright, but they each have four faces, looking to the four points of the compass; four wings, with human hands under them; and the soles of their feet are like a calf's hoof.

One should be cautious about assigning specific significances to all the individual features of the vision, though the implications of some features are

---

[22] By exmythologically we mean that the OT sometimes alludes to pagan myths in its polemic against them. The Scriptures may appropriate mythological language or imagery in order to declare that the God of Israel is Lord over all the deities and forces worshiped in pagan myths. What was taken literally in mythology now becomes in the OT merely metaphorical of the power of Yahweh.

clear. While the living beings are creatures, some of their features point to attributes of the God whose throne rests upon them. Their four faces looking simultaneously in all directions certainly suggest God's omniscience and omnipresence. The specific forms of the faces seem to represent the crown of four aspects of God's creation: man is the crown of all creation, and thus this face is first and forward; the lion and the ox are supreme among the wild and the domestic animals, respectively; and the eagle is preeminent among birds. The calves' hooves are of uncertain significance, but if they are round (see the second textual note on 1:7), they may suggest God's omnipresence by their ability to move in any direction.

Apparently the creatures form a square by being joined at their wing-tips. This should imply that no matter from what angle the four were viewed, a person could see at least one of each of the four kinds of faces at the same time.

The seraphim in Isaiah's vision (Isaiah 6) had six wings apiece and used two to fly. Ezekiel's creatures do not fly, but merely support the superstructure—the throne of God. The two visions do have in common a concern for modesty and humility in the presence of the divinity above. Here Ezekiel does not specifically label the creatures he sees, but later he will call them cherubim (Ezek 10:1–20; 11:22; cf. 9:3). The cherubim on the ark (Ex 25:17–22) and in the temple (1 Ki 6:27) likewise were winged. In later angelology, the cherubim and seraphim were ranked as the two highest orders of angels, but that kind of systematization does not appear in the Bible. The cherubim were ranked at the top, presumably because representations of them appeared above the ark of the covenant; God's throne rests on them in Ezekiel 10; and God is described as riding on a cherub (Ps 18:11 [ET 18:10] ‖ 2 Sam 22:11; this psalm has many other affinities with Ezekiel 1).[23]

The book of Revelation draws on Ezekiel in many ways (e.g., compare Ezekiel 40–48 to Revelation 21–22). The theophany revealed to the apostle John includes four angelic beings in Rev 4:6–9, and John calls them "living creatures," using the Greek equivalent (ζῷα, plural of ζῷον) of Ezekiel's Hebrew term for them (חַיּוֹת, plural of חַיָּה). The four "living creatures" in Rev 4:6–9 surround God's throne, rather than support it (as in Ezekiel), and in some ways they also resemble the seraphim in Isaiah 6: they have six wings and lead the celestial worship of God with the Trisagion, "Holy, holy, holy is the Lord …" (Rev 4:8, quoting Is 6:3). Brighton comments on the similarities and differences between the creatures in Isaiah 6; Ezekiel 1 and 10; and Revelation 4:

> In comparing the three visions of Isaiah, Ezekiel, and John, one notes similarities and dissimilarities in the appearances of the winged creatures. John mentions that each winged creature had one particular appearance or *face*,

---

[23] For a summary of Jewish views of the cherubim among the ranks of angels, see Brighton, *Revelation*, 125–26. For Christian views, one may see Pseudo-Dionysius the Areopagite, *On the Celestial Hierarchy*, and John of Damascus, *De sacris imaginibus*.

that of a lion, an ox, a man, or an eagle.[24] Isaiah does not mention facial appearances. Ezekiel says that *each creature* had four faces, the face of a man, on the right side the face of a lion, on the left side the face of an ox, and then also each had the face of an eagle (נֶשֶׁר; LXX ἀετός [Ezek 1:10]).[25] In the second appearance of the winged creatures to Ezekiel, in Ezek 10:14, each creature again had the four faces, but with one difference. The face of a cherub (כְּרוּב; LXX Vaticanus: χερούβ) has taken the place of that of the ox.[26] Perhaps John saw only one face for each winged creature because they were stationary, while Ezekiel saw each with four faces because they were moving—hence also the wheels that each creature had (Ezek 1:19–24; 10:15–17), which John does not mention.[27] …

In John's vision the winged creatures are *full of eyes*, both "in front and in back" (Rev 4:6b) and "around and within" their wings (4:8a). Isaiah does not mention eyes. … [In Ezekiel] the bodies and the wings of the creatures were full of eyes [10:12].

Both Isaiah and John hear the winged creatures *singing a hymn of praise*, a Te Deum. Ezekiel hears no hymn, but he does hear a loud rumbling-like sound or voice (קוֹל רַעַשׁ גָּדוֹל; LXX: φωνὴν σεισμοῦ μεγάλου), which says, "Blessed is the glory of Yahweh from his place" (בָּרוּךְ כְּבוֹד־יְהוָה מִמְּקוֹמוֹ; LXX: εὐλογημένη ἡ δόξα κυρίου ἐκ τοῦ τόπου αὐτοῦ [Ezek 3:12–13]). Ezekiel hears this blessing in connection with the sound of the winged creatures. …

The four winged creatures that John saw are, then, *a particular order of angels*.[28] In his vision of God's heavenly glory and throne, they are closer to God than any other creature, angelic or saintly. As such they form an "exalt-

---

[24] ἀετός means a bird of swiftness and one which feeds on carrion. It was used to refer to an eagle or to a vulture (see Mt 24:28; Lk 17:37), depending on the context. Here in Rev 4:7 because of the modifier πετομένος ("flying"), an eagle is most likely meant (cf. [Rev] 8:13; 12:14). Josephus, *Antiquities*, 8.81–84 (8.3.6), calls the cherubim that were on the bases of the ten moveable basins in Solomon's temple (1 Ki 7:27–29) "eagles." [This and the following notes within the block quote are also from Brighton.]

[25] In Ezekiel's eschatological vision of a new temple in 41:17–26, the cherubim which were carved on the entrance to the inner sanctuary of the temple and on the walls had two faces each, those of a man and of a lion (41:17–19).

[26] In Mesopotamian lore the cherub was sometimes pictured as a winged bull or ox. For references see E. Lohse, "Χερουβίν," *TDNT* 9:438–39, and T. H. Gaster, "Angel," *IDB* 1:131–32; for a description see E. Borowski, "Cherubim: God's Throne?" *BAR* 21 (July/August 1995): 36–41.

[27] Ezekiel's description (1:4–18) of the winged creatures is more detailed than that of either Isaiah or John. For example, in Ezekiel the creatures first appear in flashes of lightning and fire, and their appearances were like that of a man with four faces each. They each had legs and their feet were like those of calves. Under their wings each had hands of a man, and they each had a wheel. Isaiah refers to the fact that the winged creatures he saw had faces (6:2), but it is not clear from the text of what sort or how many they were.

[28] They are angels not in the sense of ἄγγελος as "messenger," for their duty is not to carry messages from God to people as heavenly mediators. Rather, their role is one of service and praise. Perhaps a better designation would be "heavenly figures or attending spirits." But the word "angel" in common usage today conveys also this meaning.

ed order of angelic beings,"[29] whose glorious task is to lead the heavenly host in the praise and adoration of God. They could be thought of as the choir masters of the heavenly choir, whose joy and thanksgiving it is to sing the praises of their Lord and Creator. They initiate the worship (Rev 4:9), and the saints and angels in heaven follow their lead (4:10–11; 5:11–12).[30]

In fact, Rev 4:8 asserts that the four living creatures "never cease" singing the Trisagion. Since that scene occurs in a vision, one cannot press the point, but the suggestion certainly is that they had continuously been doing so at least since Isaiah overheard them, and, furthermore, that they continue to do so today and into eternity. Hence, it is almost an understatement when our Communion liturgy introduces the Sanctus with the words "with angels and archangels …"[31] Our song uses words on loan from the heavenly choirs and makes us apprentices of what will occupy us throughout eternity. (See also the Te Deum: "To you cherubim and seraphim continually do cry: Holy, holy, holy …"[32])

Brighton comments on the symbolism of the faces:

Since these four winged creatures have different faces, which are likenesses from the animate part of God's creation, commentators throughout the Christian centuries have ascribed various symbolical meanings to the faces. Victorinus, the earliest Latin commentator (third century), says that the four creatures are *the four gospels*. The lion is Mark; the man is Matthew; the ox is Luke; and the eagle is John.[33] Irenaeus associated the four winged creatures with *four aspects of Christ's work*. The lion represents Christ's royal office, the ox his priestly office or character, the face of a man Christ's human nature, and the flying eagle the gift of the Spirit, which he gives to his church. According to Irenaeus the four evangelists reflect these four characteristics of Christ's ministry. The eagle thus symbolizes Mark, the man Matthew, the ox Luke, and the lion John.[34] Irenaeus also states that because there are four zones or directions of the earth and four winds, it is fitting that the church with the Gospel should have "four pillars," that is, a Gospel with or under four aspects.[35] Pseudo-Athanasius suggested that the man was Matthew, the ox Mark, the lion Luke, and the eagle John.[36] Augustine has the lion as Matthew, the man as Mark, the ox as Luke, and the eagle as John.[37] …

[29] R. Mounce, *Revelation*, 138.

[30] Brighton, *Revelation*, 123–26.

[31] For example, *LW*, p. 146.

[32] For example, *LW*, p. 214.

[33] J. Haussleiter, ed., *Victorini Episcopi Petavionensis Opera*, 48. Victorinus also states reasons why he thinks each creature is (or represents) one of the four gospels. For example, he says that the ox is Luke because Luke relates how Zechariah was a priest who officiated before the altar in the temple, where sacrifices (including oxen) were offered (pp. 50, 52). [Again, this and the following notes within the block quote are also from Brighton.]

[34] *Against Heresies*, 3.11.8.

[35] *Against Heresies*, 3.11.8.

[36] *Synopsis Scripturæ Sacræ* (PG 28:432).

[37] *De Consensu Evangelistarum*, 1.9 (PL 34:1046), cited in H. B. Swete, *Mark*, xxxviii.

The winged creatures are, properly, representatives of God's total creation in worship before his heavenly throne (see [Rev] 5:13–14). The fact that they are full of eyes suggests that God in his "ceaseless vigilance"[38] oversees his creation as it is represented by the four winged creatures. The four would represent the entire creation of God as it was before the fall and/or as it will be when restored (see Rom 8:18–25; Rev 21:1). The four could then also symbolize the four gospels because through the gospels the message of the Lord Christ is sent out into "the four corners of the earth" ([Rev] 7:1), and as a result of Christ's victory all creation will be restored at the End.[39]

Using the acronym "mloe," a common interpretation is that the four evangelists, in spite of their variations, all proclaim one and the same Gospel.

1:12–14 Remarkably, despite the multiple components of the creatures, they all move in absolute unison. The animating force in their motion is the "S/spirit." It would take another volume to explore all the nuances of the Hebrew רוּחַ. If the word here meant "wind," it would connect the vision with the storm (1:4), though this is no ordinary storm-wind, but a theophany. Jesus himself explained the operation of the Holy Spirit by analogy to the wind; as in Hebrew, so too in Greek the same word can denote either or both:

The wind [πνεῦμα] blows [πνεῖ] where it wills, and you hear its sound, but you do not know whence it comes and where it goes; thus is everyone who is born of the Spirit [πνεῦμα]. (Jn 3:8)

Much like our own human spirit and our spirituality as baptized believers in Christ who are indwelt by the Holy Spirit, the term here may refer to God-given energy and life internal to the creatures or to the divine impulse of the Lord acting upon them by means of the Holy Spirit—the third person of the Trinity. These are not mutually exclusive ideas, but the frequency with which Ezekiel later refers to Yahweh's Spirit suggests that priority be given to the latter (see the textual notes on 1:12).

Interpretation inevitably raises the question of whether this "Spirit," then, should be identified with the third person of the Trinity. The biblical confession that one and the same God is the subject of both Testaments demands that we do justice to their theological continuity. The OT supports the later dogmatic systematization of the one triune God in three distinct but inseparable divine persons, which the early church formulated in the ecumenical Creeds after considerable struggle. Yet the full revelation of the personhood of the Holy Spirit, who "proceeds from the Father and the Son" (Nicene Creed), does not come until Pentecost, after the Son has been clearly revealed. The OT knows of no sense of רוּחַ, not even when it means simply "wind," where God is not the ultimate subject. Hence, God must somehow be the source of the S/spirit here too, even if his Spirit's activity is not so unmistakably revealed as Christologically and salvifically as it will be later in NT contexts, which affirm that

---

[38] H. B. Swete, *Apocalypse*, 71.

[39] Brighton, *Revelation*, 126–27.

the Spirit in the Christian is "the Spirit of Christ" (Rom 8:9) and that the OT prophets too had "the Spirit of Christ in them" (1 Pet 1:11). All of this can and should be developed more in homiletical contexts than is possible here.

The Spirit (רוּחַ) plays a prominent role throughout Ezekiel, most famously in the vision of the dry bones in chapter 37. The Spirit works in conjunction with God's Word, as affirmed in Lutheran theology; when God speaks (e.g., 2:1–2) or the prophet speaks for God (chapter 37), the Spirit is at work and accomplishes God's purpose. The prominence of the Spirit throughout Ezekiel is especially striking when one compares it to the relatively few overt references to the Spirit in the prophets who preceded Ezekiel, and in the priestly oriented portions of the OT, such as Leviticus. At times in earlier periods and OT writings, the "Spirit" does appear quite prominently, as in the time of the judges, but he is conspicuous by his infrequency in the earlier writing prophets. One explanation is that the frequent claims of pneumatic activity by the false prophets (see, e.g., 1 Ki 22:21–24) caused the true prophets to be more reserved. That explanation is plausible, and, if so, it explains why the earlier prophets prefer to accent the agency of God's "Word." False prophecy had not ceased in Ezekiel's time, nor has it ceased today (together with false claims about the activity of the "Spirit" apart from God's Word), but the false gospel of "cheap grace" with which the preexilic false prophets were identified received a body blow in the fall of Jerusalem. Already in Ezekiel, then, we detect the eschatological overtones of the Spirit, who accompanies "the Word of Yahweh" (Ezek 1:3). Hence we should hear Ezekiel's rehabilitation of the word as part of the *praeparatio evangelica*,[40] the "preparation for the Gospel" of Jesus Christ, apprehended in faith wrought by the Spirit.

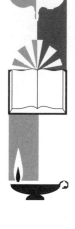

When the creatures do move, Ezekiel compares them to flashes of lightning (1:14), which again suggests an actual storm as the background. "Coals of fire, burning like the appearance of torches" appear in an additional simile (1:13). Another term for "burning coal" appeared in Isaiah's vision (רִצְפָּה, Is 6:6), and "torch(es)" (לַפִּיד, as in Ezek 1:13) indicated God's presence with Abraham in Gen 15:17 and with Moses in Ex 20:18. Fire can be an agent of purification, but also of judgment and wrath (see לַפִּיד, "torch," in Nah 2:5 [ET 2:4]; Zech 12:6; cf. Is 66:16, 24; Ps 18:9 [ET 18:8]). John the Baptist both warns and promises that Jesus Christ "will baptize you with the Holy Spirit and with fire," but "the chaff he will burn with unquenchable fire" (Mt 3:11–12). The message of Ezekiel following the vision is initially one of judgment, but ultimately of salvation: the Law prepares for the Gospel.

The Wheels and the Dome (1:15–24)

1:15–21 The prophet's eyes turn to the wheels. Whether the picture implied by "as a wheel would be in the midst of a wheel" (1:16) is that of two wheels intersecting at right angles, or (less likely) that of concentric rims, the

---

[40] *Praeparatio evangelica* is the name of a pamphlet by Eusebius.

point is the universal mobility of the vehicle. The wheels can move in any of the four directions without being turned. Since the Lord's throne is above, his throne can move freely in any direction. As a modern equivalent, we might think of a chair with a spherical castor on each leg, allowing the chair to roll in any direction—wherever the occupant desired—without turning the orientation of the chair.

That suggests that the One who is enthroned can see in all directions at once; he is omniscient. He has no need to turn his throne in a particular direction first to see whether he desires to go there. That the wheels themselves were full of eyes seems to imply that they too were alive, perceptive, and under the guidance of the Spirit (see the commentary on 1:12 and 2:1–2). In 10:12 Ezekiel will notice that the living creatures too are full of eyes.

1:22–24 Finally, the prophet dares to look up at the "dome" or "firmament" supported by the chariot. Some of the descriptions again appear to be spin-offs of storm phenomena. If the "dome" here is not the sky itself, it is something that looked very much like it. The Hebrew noun is the same as that in Gen 1:6–8, 14–20, where it refers to the "firmament" that is the "heavens," into which God places the sun, moon, and stars. The implication of the term here in Ezekiel 1, where it is beneath God's throne, may be that the entirety of creation (the universe as we humans know it) is under the lordship of Yahweh, who reigns as King and who administers his kingdom for the sake of the people he has chosen in his grace. King Jehoiachin has been dethroned (1:2), but the real King of Israel continues to reign unhindered.

This points toward the advent of God's kingdom in Jesus Christ. After his death and resurrection will come his session on the divine throne in glory, with all things under his feet (Psalm 110; Phil 2:5–11), in subjection to him who governs the universe for the sake of his church and the ministry of Word and Sacrament (Eph 4:4–16).

As the palanquin moves, the living creatures emit awesome, powerful sounds, the likes of which one might also hear in a thunderstorm or battle (Ezek 1:24). "Many waters" (1:24; also 43:2) in some biblical contexts (e.g., Pss 18:17 [ET 18:16]; 144:7; Song 8:7) alludes not only to the destructive flood waters of the universal deluge, but also to God's salvation of his redeemed people through water: the flood, the Red Sea, the Jordan River, and especially Holy Baptism.[41] In some passages (e.g., Pss 32:6; 93:4), the phrase "many waters" probably has exmythological connotations. The pagan Canaanites venerated Yam, the god who was the personification of the ocean, but in the OT that Canaanite myth is subverted by declaring that Yahweh is the triumphant God over the chaotic waters (Pss 65:8 [ET 65:7]; 93:3–5), which represent the forces

---

[41] See the study of "many waters" in the OT and NT in Mitchell, *The Song of Songs*, 1194–97, 1227–29. The "many waters" in Ezek 26:19; 27:26; and 31:15 have connotations of the destructive flood waters and God's judgment. However, the "many waters" in Ezek 17:5, 8; 19:10; 31:5, 7; (cf. 32:13) are abundant waters for life and growth of plants (which are metaphors for people).

of disorder and evil, even "the old evil foe" (*LW* 298:1), that is, Satan (cf. Is 27:1; Job 41:25 [ET 41:33]).

The military imagery evoked by the wings of the living creatures, which emit "the sound of an army camp" (Ezek 1:24), connects these angelic beings with the whole host of heaven. The God of Israel is "Yahweh of hosts" (e.g., 1 Sam 1:3; 1 Ki 18:15), who commands the angelic hosts and also the hosts of his people on earth—the church militant. Even though Israel's military hosts have been rendered impotent by the Babylonian invasion and are in disarray, God's might, as reflected by the bearers of his throne, remains unabated.

The repeated assertion that when the living creatures "stood still, they relaxed their wings" (1:24–25) means that the loud sounds of their wings would cease, probably in preparation for hearing the actual "voice of the Almighty," which their wings merely sounded like (1:24). "Yahweh is in his holy temple; let all the earth be silent before him" (Hab 2:20). He will begin to speak in Ezekiel 2, when he issues Ezekiel's call into the prophetic ministry.

The Glory of God to Be Incarnate in Jesus Christ (1:25–28)

1:25–28   Here we approach the climax of the vision. Precisely when the prophet became aware that the vision was of God speaking to him is not specified. Ezek 1:24 hints at it, and all doubt disappears in 1:28. When in 1:25, Ezekiel ventures to peer above the dome and realizes that it is the Almighty himself, he is even more reticent than before about describing what he sees. The throne is made of a precious gemstone, and the figure on it is "the likeness of the appearance of a man" (1:26). Like other OT theophanies in which the Lord or his Angel (the preincarnate Christ) appears as a man (e.g., Genesis 18; 32:24–30; Josh 5:13–15),[42] this points toward the incarnation of Jesus Christ as true man, fully human (without sin) and yet fully God.[43]

The term here is אָדָם, "a man, a human; Adam," rather than אִישׁ ("a man, a male," as in Gen 18:2; 32:25; Josh 5:13), but that does not detract from the Christological implication. The most frequent use of אָדָם in Ezekiel is in Yahweh's addresses to the prophet as "son of man" (2:1, etc.; see the commentary there; cf. the "Son of Man" coming on the clouds of heaven in Dan 7:13). The use of *'adam* here, if it is to be pressed, may recall that God created *'adam* (Adam; the man; the first man and woman; humanity) in his own image (e.g., Gen 1:26–27; 2:7–8, 20), even as the "dome" or "firmament" in Ezek 1:22–26 may recall that which God created in Genesis 1.

This divine man is composed of various brilliances of what looked like fire and electrum from his waist and above, and of fire below, with a rainbow-like nimbus entirely surrounding him (1:27–28). Despite Ezekiel's caution and awe,

---

[42] As noted by Harstad, *Joshua*, 254, regarding Josh 5:13–15, Luther and many Lutheran exegetes down to the present day have interpreted OT appearances of "the angel of the Lord" as the preincarnate Christ.

[43] See the classic exposition by the sixteenth-century reformer Martin Chemnitz, *The Two Natures in Christ*, which includes abundant OT passages that speak of this mystery of Christ's incarnation (e.g., Is 7:14; 53:11; Jer 23:5–6; 1 Chr 17:17) as well as NT passages and references from early church fathers.

he gives a fuller eyewitness "description" of Yahweh than one can find anywhere else in the OT, except in Dan 7:9–14. Even Isaiah had seen only Yahweh's "train" (Is 6:1). The portrait here finds its closest parallels in those of the
glorified Christ at his transfiguration (Mt 17:2; Mk 9:2–3; Lk 9:29) and in his
revelation to the apostle John (Rev 1:12–20), especially John's vision of the
throne scene in Revelation 4, which has many specific affinities to Ezekiel 1.[44]

Ezekiel realizes that what he is gazing upon is "the appearance of the Glory
of Yahweh" (1:28). The textual note explained that "Glory," even when capitalized, does not begin to do justice to the divine כָּבוֹד, which reappears often
in the book.[e] This "Glory of Yahweh" is the climax of all the similitudes
throughout the chapter. In OT usage Yahweh's "Glory" (כָּבוֹד) often describes
God as he "incarnationally" appears on earth (e.g., Ex 33:18–22; Ps 26:8). The
first revelations of the divine Glory in Scripture are as Yahweh redeems his
people from Egypt (Ex 16:7, 10), appears to them on Sinai (Ex 24:16–17), and
comes to dwell among them semi-permanently at the tabernacle (Ex 29:43;
40:34–35), which is the OT site of atoning sacrifice for the forgiveness of sins,
life, and salvation.

I have never been able to find a better word for this "form" (Phil 2:6) of
the divinity than "hypostasis" (a transliteration of the Greek ὑπόστασις, as in
Heb 1:3), which has been used as a dogmatic term from the time of the early
church and in the Chalcedonian creed to refer to Christ as the second person
of the Trinity.[45] The treatise *The Two Natures in Christ*, written by Martin
Chemnitz in the sixteenth century, defines it thus:

(e) Ezek
3:12, 23;
8:4; 9:3;
10:4, 18–19;
11:22–23;
43:2–5; 44:4

> In the language of the church of our day ... the terms subsistence (ὑφισ-
> τάμενον), hypostasis or substance (ὑπόστασις), person (πρόσωπον), and
> individual (ἄτομον) are all synonyms, designating a singular thing which
> possesses the total and perfect substance of the same species. ... We speak of
> the divine nature and the human nature [of Christ], the divine essence and the
> human substance. The names of the person are God, man, Logos, the Second
> Person of the Trinity, the Son of God, the Son of Man, Christ, and so forth.[46]

Chemnitz further states:

> These two natures [divine and human] have been joined together and united
> to constitute *in the incarnate Christ one hypostasis*. ... Although there are
> and remain two natures in Christ without conversion or commingling, ... yet
> there are not two but only one Christ (Rom. 5:18–19 and Gal. 3:16), one Lord
> (1 Cor. 8:6 and Eph. 4:5), and one Mediator (1 Tim. 2:5). Likewise, the rec-
> onciliation, justification, obedience, grace, and life belong to the one Christ
> (Rom. 5:18).[47]

---

[44] See especially the textual notes and commentary on 1:5–11.

[45] For hypostasis in the Chalcedonian creed, see Grillmeier, *Christ in Christian Tradition*,
1:544, 549. For a discussion of its meaning as used by early church fathers, see Kelly, *Early
Christian Creeds*, 240–42.

[46] Chemnitz, *The Two Natures in Christ*, 29.

[47] Chemnitz, *The Two Natures in Christ*, 77; emphasis added.

Two of the similes based on biblical themes used by the church fathers to attempt to explain the mystery of the hypostatic union of the divine and human natures in the one Christ are especially relevant for the "man" composed of "electrum" and "fire" surrounded by "radiance" (Ezek 1:26–28):

> One is that of light and the sun. … For in Heb. 1:3 the Son is called *the splendor or brightness of God's glory*, as a light from the light. He is also called the Sun of righteousness in Mal. 4:2 [MT 3:20]; and light shone from His body in Matt. 17:2 and Acts 9:3. …

> Another simile of the ancient church is that of the lighted mass. …

> This simile seems to be taken from the burning bush, which burned totally and yet was not consumed. In this bush the Son of God prefigured His future incarnation and appeared to Moses (Ex. 3:2). In Rev. 1:7 the likeness of the Son of Man is shown to John in His appearance in the air in a furnace of fire and heat [cf. Dan 3:25].[48]

The relationship between "the Glory of Yahweh" (Ezek 1:28) and God himself is the same as that (to be fully revealed in the NT) between Jesus Christ and God the Father, as described in, for example, John 17 and Heb 1:3. Our Lord will pray, "Now glorify me, Father, in your presence with the glory I had with you before the world came to be. … I desire that where I myself am, they too may be with me, in order that *they may see my glory*" (Jn 17:5, 24). In the OT, manifestations of Yahweh's glory often are associated with the angel of Yahweh (e.g., Ex 14:17–20), God's name (Is 59:17; Pss 79:9; 102:16 [ET 102:15]), and his speaking or his Word (e.g., Ex 16:10–11; Deut 5:24; Is 40:5). Even after the incarnation of our Lord, the NT often uses δόξα ("glory") in essentially the same sense as the OT uses כָּבוֹד ("Glory").[f] The NT even explains whose glory it was that the OT prophets saw: "Isaiah … saw his [Christ's] glory, and spoke about him" (Jn 12:41).

In traditional language, we have here the λόγος ἄσαρκος, the "Word not-yet made flesh," the preincarnate Christ. Dogmatically, we cannot divide the works of the "economic Trinity," since *opera ad extra indivisa sunt.*[49] Therefore, we should not say that Yahweh's "Glory" (כָּבוֹד) consists exclusively of the second person of the Trinity, which would communicate a kind of unitarian "Yahweh." (What Ezek 1:12 and 2:2 say about the Spirit also militates against that view; see the commentary on those verses.) But the more common error is to interpret Yahweh's "Glory" (כָּבוֹד) without realizing the full extent to which it is an OT revelation of God the Son. To see the connection, one may compare the Glory enthroned on angels in the storm cloud in Ezekiel 1 to corresponding NT passages that picture *Christ* as the one who comes in glory on the clouds of heaven with his angels in attendance (e.g., Mt 24:30; cf. Mt 16:27)

(f) See, e.g., Jn 1:14; Acts 7:55; 1 Cor 2:8; 2 Cor 4:4, 6; Titus 2:13

---

48 Chemnitz, *The Two Natures in Christ*, 88, 90; emphasis added. The reference to Rev 1:7 may point toward the fiery features of Christ in Rev 1:14–16.

49 This Latin clause means that the three persons of the Trinity are united and inseparable in the works of the triune God toward the created world.

and *Christ* as the one who is seated on the divine throne in glory (Mt 19:28; 25:31).

When Ezekiel finally realizes what and whom he is beholding, he adopts the only proper posture by prostrating himself in abject worship: "When I saw, I fell on my face, and I heard a voice speaking" (Ezek 1:28). "So the 'vision of God' attains its objective only when, from amid the flames ablaze around him, the Lord of this world and of all worlds speaks to the man whom he has reduced to such a state of dissolution."[50]

What was the point of it all? Why such an elaborate, even bizarre display? Beyond a point, of course, human answers to such questions are impossible. No other prophet, not even Isaiah, experiences so baroque a vision. Many other eccentric things are related in the book of Ezekiel, so it is possible that God is merely accommodating himself to Ezekiel's own propensities (although such an approach may come close to an attempt to "psychoanalyze" the prophet). Block seriously entertains the possibility that Ezekiel was a reluctant or even rebellious prophet.[51] However, only in 4:14 does Ezekiel protest a directive from God (a directive he found to be especially vile), so I find that speculation wide of the mark. I would argue just the opposite. Under God's control, Ezekiel will go to virtually any length, verbal or otherwise, to get his unpalatable message across. (Ezekiel does "remonstrate" with God in an intercessory way in 9:8 and 11:13.)

There is no way of knowing whether Ezekiel communicated the vision of chapter 1 to the people or kept it to himself—at least until his "publication" of his scroll. In essence, the vision is repeated at two other pivotal points in his ministry: in chapters 10–11, which foresee God's abandonment of the "holy city" to its destruction, and briefly in chapter 43, when the "Glory" (כָּבוֹד) returns to the eschatological temple and city, anticipating Revelation 21.

A first purpose of the vision is to impress upon the prophet—and, indirectly, upon his readers and hearers—the immeasurable gulf between the God of Israel and man. Thus, it is the counterpart of the way God addresses the prophet throughout the book: "son of man" (2:1, etc.), that is, a mortal, finite, and sinful descendant of Adam.

A second, related purpose is to show that Israel's God reigns over Babylon too, with his power not at all diminished by the great distance (some one thousand miles) that separates the Kebar Canal (1:1) from his temple in Jerusalem. Initially, the exiles, who do not appear to have had a particularly orthodox theology, may have at least partially shared the notion common in ancient pagan religions that a god and his nation, land, and city were inseparable, and thus every god was quite localized in his authority. Gods were often little but personifications of their adherents in their particular localities, and when

---

[50] Eichrodt, *Ezekiel*, 59.

[51] Block, *Ezekiel*, 1:11–12 and passim.

they (the gods and their people) were conquered and absorbed by some other people with their own national deity, a certain syncretism and unionism followed easily. Such syncretism may be compared to modern "ecumenism," in which the false prophets of our day urge the acceptance of other religions as legitimate (at least for their adherents) modes of worship, probably of the same Deity to whom Jesus claimed to be the exclusive way (e.g., Jn 14:6).

Ezekiel was no syncretist, but he would have been attached to Jerusalem and the temple, especially because of his lineage as a priest (1:3). The vision would have forcibly assured him that God, who had chosen to dwell between the cherubim in Jerusalem, was by no means bound to that locality and could manifest his glory wherever, whenever, and however he saw fit.

Initially, Yahweh's unrestricted power would enable him to do the unthinkable and abandon his own temple (chapter 10) to destruction (finally reported to Ezekiel as accomplished in 33:21). But the execution of judgment according to his Law was not God's ultimate purpose. His wrath served the greater purpose of the Gospel. He has the power to kill and the power to resurrect to new life (1 Sam 2:6).

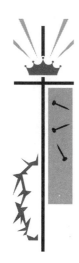

When the city finally did fall and the exiles lamented that they were only "dry bones" (Ezekiel 37), that is, hopeless, without a future, and dead, God could and would keep his ancient promises (Gen 3:15, etc.) and raise the dead bones (cf. 2 Ki 13:21) to become his living people. A new temple would be built, to which God's Glory would return (Ezekiel 43). God would restore his Israel ("the Israel of God," consisting of all baptized believers in Christ [Gal 6:16]) and dwell in the midst of his people forever through the ministry of "the Prince" (Ezekiel 40–48; Revelation 21–22). All these strands shall be knit together by the Glory's incarnation as a man, his earthly human life, atoning sacrifice, resurrection, and enthronement (Heb 10:5–18).

Seen thus, the vision becomes a preview and summary of the prophet's entire message.

Parallels to Ezekiel's Vision

When God communicates, he may do so at least in part using language and imagery already familiar to the recipients, perhaps because they are common parlance in their culture. Many "parallels" to elements in Ezekiel 1 can be found in Mesopotamian culture. The art, iconography, and religious thought of the ancient Near East was full of hybrid creatures of all sorts: cherubs, seraphs, sphinxes, griffins, and other multi-faced and winged creatures. Many commentaries and studies discuss aspects that possibly may be compared to this chapter.[52] We can find examples of gods with four identical human faces, but none with four different faces. Throne-chariots borne by various creatures are

---

[52] One of the most thorough and pertinent to Ezekiel 1 is Keel, *Jahwe—Visionen und Siegelkunst.*

common. Some of these features may have been somewhat familiar to the Israelites long before the exile because, politically and culturally, Canaan had been within the Assyro-Babylonian orbit to one degree or the other for several centuries. But, even if so, the impact would have been much greater when, uprooted from their native soil, the Israelites now in Babylon would have encountered that culture in their daily lives.

Thus, one can hardly rule out such influences in the composition of Ezekiel's vision. But I am inclined to place much more emphasis on biblical parallels. Ezekiel's entire background, priestly training and orientation, and concern for orthodox faith in Yahweh make it likely that the major parallels are to be sought in the OT itself. Preeminent among these must surely be the cherubim on the lid of the ark of the covenant and on the walls of the Jerusalem temple (see the textual notes on 1:5). The ark of the covenant was Yahweh's earthly throne, the focal point of his "house" (בַּיִת, as it is usually called in the OT), where he heard his people's prayers (1 Kings 8) and provided his forgiving grace for all his people's sins (Leviticus 16). Hence, its כַּפֹּרֶת (literally, "place/means of atonement") or cover is traditionally called the "mercy seat" (Ex 25:17–22 KJV). The LXX translates כַּפֹּרֶת with ἱλαστήριον, which St. Paul uses to define Christ in Rom 3:25. This "incarnational" presence of Yahweh, enthroned between the wings of the cherubim over the ark, was as much of a localization of the omnipresent God as was possible until the incarnation of Jesus Christ himself who, Gabriel announced, would reign on the throne of David forever (Lk 1:32–33).

But God was not imprisoned on his throne above the ark. As part of his election of his people Israel and his covenant with them,[53] he had freely chosen to make the ark and the temple central to his salvific work. But when Israel was unfaithful to that covenant, then God also could freely abandon that abode, and that such was the case is the burden of the first half of Ezekiel (chapters 1–24). And, paradoxically, all the time that God was indwelling his earthly temple, his ultimate temple and throne were in heaven:

> Yahweh is in his holy temple;
>> Yahweh—in the heavens is his throne. (Ps 11:4)

The tabernacle, where Yahweh's Glory came to dwell (Ex 40:34–35), was an earthly (vertical) type constructed to model the sanctuary in heaven (Ex 25:9, 40; cf. Heb 8:5). From that perspective, the ark was not his throne, but his footstool. Parts of the description of Yahweh in a Davidic psalm can apply in part to him taking up residence above the ark, but the couplet as a whole transcends any limitation to the earthly temple:

---

[53] For a description of God's OT covenants, their stipulations, and their fulfillment in the new covenant of Christ, see the excursus "Covenant" in Harstad, *Joshua*, 744–56.

He pulled aside the heavens and descended,
> deep darkness under his feet;
he rode upon a cherub and flew,
> he appeared on the wings of wind/Spirit. (2 Sam 22:10–11)[54]

Putting together those OT texts from the eras of Moses and David provides an already-ancient precedent for what happened in the sixth century when "the heavens were opened" and Ezekiel saw "a divine vision" (1:1) in the form of Yahweh's "Glory" (כָּבוֹד, 1:28).

In addition to the cherubim, we have already mentioned the scene at the end of Exodus 24 after the sealing of the covenant. Moses and others saw a pavement of sapphire or lapis lazuli under God's feet (Ex 24:10). In Ezekiel's vision, God's throne itself is made of that same gemstone (1:26; 10:1).

We also should not forget the description of Elijah's translation in "a chariot of fire [אֵשׁ, as in Ezek 1:4, 13, 27] and horses of fire. … And Elijah went up by a storm-wind [סְעָרָה, as in Ezek 1:4] into heaven" (2 Ki 2:11). No further details are given, but there are some similarities to the stormy, fiery conveyance, with animal-like creatures propelling it, in Ezekiel's vision.

Finally, we must mention again God's frequent association with fire in theophany. God appeared as "a smoking furnace and a burning lamp" when he ratified his covenant with Abraham (Gen 15:17). He appeared and spoke to Moses in the form of the burning bush (Exodus 3). He was manifest "incarnationally" in the pillar of fire that led the Israelites by night in the wilderness (Ex 13:21–22; 14:24; Num 14:14; recalled in Neh 9:12, 19).[55]

Later Writings Influenced by Ezekiel's Vision

With the possible exception of the valley of dry bones in chapter 37, it is safe to assert that no other part of the book has had nearly the impact upon later generations than Ezekiel's call vision has. This holds true of both Christianity and Judaism. It is hard to say in which of the two religions the influence has been the greater, but, naturally, our main interest is in Christianity, since it is in Christ that the vision finds its fulfillment.

In the OT itself, there surely is some connection with Daniel's crucial vision of the "Son of Man" in Daniel 7, which must have occurred not too long after Ezekiel's call. Ezekiel may refer to Daniel, his (younger?) contemporary, in Ezek 14:14, 20; 28:3 (although Daniel, more typically of prophets, does not refer to other prophets). "Son of Man" appears as a simile in Dan 7:13 (Aramaic: כְּבַר אֱנָשׁ), and the reference is to a divine figure, so the import of that phrase is essentially the same as "the likeness of the appearance of a man"

---

54 The parallel verse to 2 Sam 22:11, Ps 18:11 (ET 18:10), has "glided" (see *HALOT*, s.v. דאה) instead of "appeared." For the ambiguity of רוּחַ as "wind" or "Spirit," see the textual notes and commentary on Ezek 1:4, 12.

55 See the Christological interpretation of the exodus by St. Paul in 1 Cor 10:1–4. One may also see the Christological exposition of the pillar of fire and cloud in relation to God's glory in Mitchell, *The Song of Songs*, 763–64, 777–83, and 414–15, 419, 422, 425–27.

(דְּמוּת כְּמַרְאֵה אָדָם) Ezekiel describes in 1:26.[56] And when Ezekiel in 1:28 more closely describes what he sees on the throne as "the appearance of the Glory of Yahweh" (דְּמוּת כְּבוֹד־יְהוָה), with "Glory" being used hypostatically, it turns out to be a case of the same Person being portrayed in different words. The "Son of Man" from Daniel 7 became important to Christianity when Jesus made it his own favored self-designation, as recorded in the Gospels. Besides Dan 7:13–14, one finds a verbal correspondence to Ezekiel 1 that in some respects is even closer in Dan 10:5, in Daniel's description of the heavenly "man" who has been relieved by the archangel Michael from his celestial warfare to come and explain for Daniel the meaning of the seventy week-years (Dan 9:2, 24).

In the intertestamental period, Ezekiel's vision is mentioned in the apocryphal Sir 49:8. The influence is even greater in the pseudepigraphic *1 Enoch* (second century B.C.–first century A.D.), where "Enoch" describes a journey to heaven, where he sees "a lofty throne—its appearance was like crystal and its wheels like the shining sun" (*1 Enoch* 14:18).[57] Elsewhere, *1 Enoch* makes prominent use of the "son of man" title.

In *1 Enoch* 14:18, however, we pick up beginnings of motifs that flourished in Judaism. The verse refers to "the voice of the cherubim," reflecting a line of interpretation that saw the cherubim in the light of Isaiah's description of the seraphim, that is, as continuously praising Yahweh (Is 6:3; cf. the discussion of Rev 4:8 above). We see that interpretation in practice in the "angelic liturgy" of Qumran, especially in the *Songs of the Sabbath Sacrifice*. The central object of praise is the "chariot" (מֶרְכָּבָה, *merkavah*), which becomes a hypostasis of God and plays a prominent role in Jewish speculative mysticism, especially the Kabbalah (which in recent years has seen a resurgence in the West, also attracting many celebrities).

Popular as that line of interpretation was and became, orthodox (rabbinic) Judaism reacted negatively to it, in part because of the Gnostic and theosophical notions attached to it. Eventually within mainstream Jewish circles, the rule was established that one must be at least thirty years old to read the beginning and ending of Ezekiel, that is, as mature as Ezekiel himself was when the vision came "in the thirtieth year" (1:1).[58]

The impact of Ezekiel's vision is also obvious in the NT. St. Paul's doctrine of Jesus' "glory" (δόξα) is surely indebted to it (see the commentary on 1:25–28). But Ezekiel's influence is most obvious in St. John's description of the heavenly throne in Revelation 4. About a dozen of the apostle John's ex-

---

[56] See Hengstenberg, *Christology of the Old Testament*, 3:85–86.

[57] James H. Charlesworth, ed., *The Old Testament Pseudepigrapha*, vol. 1: *Apocalyptic Literature and Testaments* (Garden City, NY: Doubleday, 1983), 21.

[58] This Jewish prohibition about Ezekiel was noted by Jerome, *Commentariorum in Hiezechielem*, prologue to book 1 (CCSL 75:3–4). According to Jerome, the same Jewish prohibition forbade reading the Song of Songs prior to age thirty. For a discussion of both prohibitions, see Mitchell, *The Song of Songs*, 277–78, 286–88, especially footnote 167.

pressions there are borrowed directly from Ezekiel 1, intermingled with elements of Isaiah's vision: the six wings of the creatures, who initiate the celestial worship of the Lord (see the commentary on Ezek 1:5–11).

Finally, we should not forget the early association in Christian art of the four faces of the cherubim with the four evangelists, who have written four distinct Gospels, yet they together are ultimately one portrait of the "Glory" (כָּבוֹד) incarnate, Jesus Christ. Just which face was to be associated with which evangelist fluctuated initially, especially between the Eastern and Western branches of the church. But, at least in the West, what came to be summarized under the acronym "mloe" became standard: *m*an, *l*ion, *o*x, and *e*agle stand for the four evangelists in their canonical order: Matthew, Mark, Luke, and John.[59]

If a personal reminiscence may be permitted, the reredos of the Nebraska church where I spent my childhood was adorned with a statue of Christ, flanked by two apostles, Saints Peter and Paul, accompanied by a lion and an ox, respectively, reflecting the early association between St. Peter and Mark the Evangelist, and between St. Paul and Luke the Evangelist. Those two animals fueled many childish fantasies, but not a single soul ever explained to me what "a lion and a cow" were doing above the altar. It was not until much later, in the course of my own studies, that it all became clear to me. Much later, long after I had left home, the church underwent what I can only label a Protestantizing, iconoclastic "renovation," and today nothing but a bare cross stands above the altar. The worship life of the church is poorer for the loss.

---

[59] For an easy and accessible summary, see Jensen, "Of Cherubim and Gospel Symbols."

Ezekiel 2:1–10

The Prophetic Commissioning
of Ezekiel: Part 1

Translation

2 ¹He said to me, "Son of man, stand on your feet, and I will speak with you."
²The Spirit entered into me as he spoke to me and made me stand on my feet.
Then I heard him speaking to me.

³He said to me, "Son of man, I am sending you to the sons of Israel, to nations rebelling, who have rebelled against me. They and their fathers have revolted against me to this very day. ⁴The sons—brazen-faced and hard-hearted—I am sending you to them, and you must say to them, 'Thus says the Lord Yahweh.' ⁵Then they, whether they listen or do not—for they are a rebellious house—they will know that a prophet has been among them.

⁶"And you, son of man, do not be afraid of them, and of their words do not be afraid. Even though briars and thorns are with you and on scorpions you are sitting, do not be afraid of their words, and by their looks do not be intimidated, for they are a rebellious house. ⁷You must speak my words to them whether they listen or do not, for they are rebellious.

⁸"You, son of man, listen to whatever I am telling you. Do not be rebellious like the rebellious house. Open your mouth and eat whatever I am giving you."
⁹Then I looked, and behold, a hand was stretched out toward me, and behold, in it was a rolled-up scroll. ¹⁰He unrolled it before me, and it was written on front and back. Written on it was "Laments, Moaning, and Woe."

Textual Notes

2:1 The later division of Ezekiel's call narrative into two separate chapters is infelicitous. The last three words in the Hebrew of 1:28 really go with 2:1 because it is there that the transition from sight to speech occurs. A similar situation occurs at the end of chapter 2, since there is only a minor shift in accent at 3:1. A greater transition comes between 2:7 and 2:8.

Our present chapter divisions are largely medieval. Sometimes they coincide with the older Masoretic divisions, which, along with the vocalization (vowels and accents), were written down in the sixth–ninth centuries A.D. How much earlier than that the Masoretic traditions ("Masorah" means "tradition") may extend is beyond tracing. Some of the same kinds of space divisors indicated by the Masoretes appear, in effect, already in the Qumran scrolls, and thus are of relatively high antiquity.

The division between 1:28 and 2:1 coincides with a Masoretic ס in the Hebrew text. The ס indicates a "closed" (סְתוּמָה) space: the space after 1:28 was in the middle of the line, with the first words of 2:1 following the space on the same line. The ס indicates a lesser division than a פ, which occurs after 2:2 and after 2:7. The פ in-

73

dicates an "open" (פְּתוּחָה) space: the space extends to the end of the line, and the next verse starts on the next line.

בֶּן־אָדָם—For the first time, we meet God's consistent way of addressing Ezekiel throughout the book. God calls him "son of man" instead of using his name, יְחֶזְקֵאל (1:3). God calls him by this phrase ninety-three times. I have opted to retain the traditional and literal "son of man" in no little part because of its prominence in the NT in reference to Christ. Older translations and commentaries are virtually unanimous in rendering it as "son of man."

However, in recent decades in Western academic circles has arisen the alien ideological agenda of neutralizing the biblical language and theology of sexuality. That agenda mandates altering Scripture's distinctive vocabulary for male headship, both in reference to God (e.g., God the Father; God the Son as true man) and in reference to humanity (e.g., the husband as the head of the wife). However, biblical soteriology depends on the proper understanding of such vocabulary and theology: Adam is the head of sinful humanity, doomed to die, while Christ is the head of redeemed and justified humanity, whose members receive eternal life through faith in him (Rom 5:12–21). Scripture's gendered terminology cannot be altered without perverting the Gospel itself.

Any quick check of modern commentaries and translations will show that there is no unanimity about the translation. The alternatives offered reflect slight variations in understanding the nuances of the term. For example, "mortal" (NRSV) is not entirely incorrect, but fails to bring out the major thrust of the phrase. Mortality is part of the fallen human condition ever since Adam and Eve fell into sin (Genesis 3), hence Ezek 31:14 refers to "sons of man" after death. Every son of Adam and daughter of Eve now is mortal. But the accent of "son of man" as a term for Ezekiel is much more on the vast distance between the weakness of humanity (cf. Ps 8:4–5 [ET 8:3–4]) and the power of the Almighty, who gives his prophet the capacity to speak, who uses that prophet as an instrument of his Word, and who has the power to discipline Israel (through the ministry of his prophets and through other historical events, particularly the exile), but who ultimately will use his power to redeem his people.

Besides meaning "son" in the literal sense ("the son of Buzi," Ezek 1:3), בֵּן can be idiomatic for being a (male) member of a class, "a single individual in a group." Hence in construct with אָדָם, it can mean "a human being" (*HALOT*, s.v. בֵּן I, 4) or "individual man" (*HALOT*, s.v. אָדָם I, 1 c). Translations such as "human (being)," "man," and "person" are possibly more to the point than "mortal," but come across as rather abrupt, even brusque, and are inferior to the literal "son of man." While אָדָם can have the general meaning "man, mankind" (BDB, 2), one should not forget that it is also the proper name of the progenitor of the human race, "Adam" (e.g., Gen 2:20; 3:17, 21; 4:25; 5:1–5).

וַאֲדַבֵּר אֹתָךְ:—The *waw* may form a purpose clause: "so/in order that I may speak with you." אֹתָךְ is the pausal form of אֹתְךָ, using the second masculine singular suffix.

Ezekiel often uses אֵת־ or אוֹת־ in contexts where (as here) it must mean "with." We notice a similar phenomenon in 1 and 2 Kings and Jeremiah. BDB (s.v. אֵת II, 1 d β) parses it here and often in Ezekiel as a variant spelling of the preposition "with," which with a suffix normally is אֵת־. *HALOT* (s.v. אֵת I, 4 d) speculates that Ezekiel frequently used the sign of the direct object with the meaning "with" because the preposition אֵת, "with," was lacking in the biblical Hebrew of this era, but *HALOT* offers no evidence for that assertion.

2:2 וַתָּבֹא בִי רוּחַ כַּאֲשֶׁר דִּבֶּר אֵלַי וַתַּעֲמִדֵנִי—As Lutheran theology classically emphasizes, the Spirit (רוּחַ) works through God's Word and so enters Ezekiel when God speaks. The Spirit, who is "the Lord and giver of life" (Nicene Creed), is the subject of the third feminine singular Hiphil verb וַתַּעֲמִדֵנִי (since רוּחַ is grammatically feminine). While Ezekiel had fallen down (1:28) at the theophany as though dead (as did the apostle John in Rev 1:17), the same "Spirit of him who raised Jesus from the dead" (Rom 8:11; cf. Rom 1:4) raises Ezekiel and stands him on his feet.

וָאֶשְׁמַע אֵת מִדַּבֵּר אֵלַי:—The form מִדַּבֵּר is the Hithpael masculine singular participle with the ת (originally מִתְדַּבֵּר) assimilated and marked by the *daghesh forte* in the *dalet* (-דּ-). The identical form occurs also in Num 7:89; 2 Sam 14:13; Ezek 43:6. The speaker is always God, except for 2 Sam 14:13, where it is God's king. Here I have added "him" as object ("I heard *him* speaking to me") for the sake of a fluent translation, as already the LXX found expedient to do. Even though the participle is indefinite, it is preceded by אֵת to mark it as the direct object (see Waltke-O'Connor, § 37.5a, including example 5).

Instead of the Masoretic pointing of the consonants מדבר as a Hithpael, they could be pointed as a Piel (מְדַבֵּר), which seems almost required by the preposition אֶל in its ordinary sense of "(un)to." Greenberg is probably correct that the Hithpael pointing is "artificial—an exploitation of a textual opening for introducing a later reverential linguistic conceit." That is, the Hithpael means that Ezekiel would only *over-hear* the divine speech, thus allegedly preserving the vast gulf between Creator and creature.[1] This would not totally contradict a genuine Ezekielian theme, but the point here is that God *does* come down and speak to Ezekiel, as he did climactically in the incarnation of the Word made flesh.

2:3 שׁוֹלֵחַ אֲנִי אוֹתְךָ—The Qal participle of שׁלח is intrinsically tenseless. Here the context requires a present sense extending into the indefinite future. The English language is fortunate to have a periphrastic idiom that connotes both present and future: "I am sending you."

בְּנֵי יִשְׂרָאֵל—"Sons of Israel" is often rendered generically as "children of Israel," but see the textual note on "son of man" in 2:1. As with that phrase, so too "sons of Israel" has in view the individual man (Israel/Jacob) who is the progenitor of his people. The gentilic form יִשְׂרְאֵלִי, "Israelite," is rarely used in the OT (only Lev 24:10–11; 2 Sam 17:25) and today has been preempted by its use in reference to the modern state of Israel. The literal "sons of Israel" corresponds nicely to the "fathers," that is, ancestors, later in 2:3. The theme of hereditary guilt or original sin can be deduced from

---

[1] Greenberg, *Ezekiel*, 1:62, who quotes Rashi (a major medieval Jewish exegete): "The Shekinah [the immanent divine presence] speaks in its majesty to itself; its messengers only over-hear it."

this phrase. Ezekiel uses the phrase בְּנֵי יִשְׂרָאֵל ("sons of Israel") only 11 times, compared to a total of 636 occurrences in the OT. By contrast, he uses "house [בֵּית] of Israel" 83 times, out of a total of 147 in the OT. Thus the ratio in Ezekiel is just the opposite of that in the OT as a whole. The "house" idiom expresses Israel's family solidarity more. See the textual notes on "rebellious house" in 2:5 and "house of Israel" in 3:1.

As throughout the OT, "Israel" is the covenant or "baptismal" name of God's chosen people, derived from Jacob's encounter with the preincarnate Christ (God in the form of a "man") in Gen 32:25–31 (ET 32:24–30; see the textual notes and commentary on "man" in Ezek 1:26). The ten apostate northern tribes tarnished the name's meaning when they co-opted it for themselves (1 Ki 12:16), and the name often came to refer to northern "Israel" in contrast to southern "Judah," which retained the Davidic monarchy. But human apostasy does not invalidate the divine promise associated with the name, "for the gracious gifts and the call of God are irrevocable" (Rom 11:29). Ezekiel thus can use "Israel" for (1) the northern kingdom, even though it had long ceased to exist; (2) for the exiles with him in Babylon; and (3) for those Israelites still left in "the land of Israel" (33:24) even after the destruction of Jerusalem in 587 B.C.

אֶל־גּוֹיִם הַמּוֹרְדִים אֲשֶׁר מָרְדוּ־בִי—The noun גּוֹיִם is anarthrous but the following adjectival participle, הַמּוֹרְדִים, has the article; such exceptions to normal Hebrew syntax are found in later style (Waltke-O'Connor § 37.5b, including examples 13 and 14). Many English versions, starting with the KJV, follow the Peshitta in reading the singular גּוֹי, apparently taking the singular as a collective, which can be followed by a plural (הַמּוֹרְדִים). (The LXX lacks any translation of גּוֹיִם.) But the MT plural should stand.

The varied usage of "Israel" (see the preceding textual note) may help explain this phrase. Often, but not always, גּוֹי refers to a non-Israelite "nation." גּוֹי is basically a political entity, while עַם is an ethnic, cultural, and religious one. OT Israel was both a religious and political people. God had originally promised to make Abraham into a great "nation" (the singular גּוֹי in Gen 12:2). God reiterated and expanded that promise to Jacob/Israel, promising also that a multitude of "nations" (plural גּוֹיִם) would issue from him (Gen 35:11).

The "nations rebelling" (Ezek 2:3), then, might refer (1) to all twelve tribes, who are descended from Jacob/Israel; (2) to the three tribes theoretically constituting the southern kingdom (Judah, Benjamin, and Simeon), or (3) the two kingdoms of (northern) Israel and Judah, who are called "two nations" in Ezek 35:10; 37:22 (cf. 36:13–36). In any case, some of the sense of "pagan" (or "Gentile" as it is often translated) may cling to the word in its context here. Without fidelity to the covenant, the people were just another heathen nation.

The repetition of the verb that was in the form of the participle (הַמּוֹרְדִים), this time as a finite form (מָרְדוּ), reinforces the rebellion of the nations of Israel. (See the next textual note.) Ezekiel uses מָרַד again in 17:15 and 20:38 (together with פָּשַׁע in 20:38 as here in 2:3).

הֵמָּה וַאֲבוֹתָם פָּשְׁעוּ בִי—The verb in this indictment, פָּשַׁע, is nearly synonymous with מָרַד, the verb twice in the preceding part of the verse. Both can be translated "to rebel," though to indicate the different Hebrew we render this as "revolt." Ezekiel uses פָּשַׁע also in 18:31 and 20:38 and the related noun פֶּשַׁע ten times. Later Ezekiel will use a third synonym for "to rebel," מָרָה (5:6; 20:8, 13, 21), and the noun derived from that verb, מְרִי, "rebellion" (e.g., 2:5–8). Perhaps מָרָה is the most general of the three verbs, although in Deut 21:18–21 it refers especially to a child's insubordination toward parents. As an antonym of עָבַד, "to serve," מָרַד means "to refuse to serve; to be disloyal to one's master." פָּשַׁע has that connotation too, but very often takes on moral or religious coloration, "to transgress" against God's commands. The noun פֶּשַׁע is one of the three most frequent OT terms for "sin, transgression," alongside עָוֹן and חַטָּאת, and the three co-occur in Ezek 21:29 (cf. 18:30; 33:10).

2:4 אֲנִי שׁוֹלֵחַ אוֹתְךָ ... וְהַבָּנִים—Ezek 2:3 and 2:4a stand in a sort of chiastic relation to each other: literally, "sending [am] I you to sons" (2:3) and "sons … I [am] sending you" (2:4a). "Sons," as descendants of the patriarchs and heirs of God's promises, may continue to picture the Israelites as Yahweh's adopted children as in 2:3, but the accent here is even more strongly on the present generation.

קְשֵׁי פָּנִים—"Brazen-faced" is literally "hard of face." This precise expression is unique, but the similar expression קְשֵׁה־עֹרֶף (traditionally "stiff-necked") is common describing recalcitrant Israel (e.g., Ex 32:9; 33:3, 5). The singling out of "face" here is a more pointed parallel to the exhortation to Ezekiel, "and by their looks [וּמִפְּנֵיהֶם] do not be intimidated" in 2:6 and (in reverse word order) 3:9. The picture is not just of impassive, expressionless faces listening to the prophet's messages, but of hostile, threatening ones.

וְחִזְקֵי־לֵב—"Hard-hearted" is another expression that is unique in the OT, though similar ones are in 3:7. The adjective חָזָק usually means "strong," but "strong of heart" would be misleading; more appropriate would be "obdurate of heart." Most of the combinations of the root חזק and noun לֵב are with the verb חָזַק in references to Pharaoh's heart being hard (e.g., Ex 7:13, 22), or to God hardening Pharaoh's heart (e.g., Ex 4:21; 9:12; cf. Josh 11:20, where God hardens the heart of the Canaanites). In this context the phrase is plainly negative, of an obdurate people, adamant in their refusal to listen. לֵב ("heart") requires various translations into English. Rarely is there accent on the physical organ as such. Usually it refers to spiritual disposition involving the mind and will (volition), though the emotions are usually involved. Hebrew idiom was nothing if not psychosomatic. Some of this usage has carried over into English metaphors involving "heart." In 11:19 and 36:26 Ezekiel describes this kind of unrepentant, unbelieving heart as "a heart of stone," which Yahweh will replace with a "heart of flesh."

כֹּה אָמַר אֲדֹנָי יְהוִה:—This whole clause will occur 122 times in Ezekiel, usually introducing an oracle. It has Ezekiel's characteristic double appellation of God as אֲדֹנָי יְהוִה, "the Lord Yahweh." That double appellation is not unique to Ezekiel, but much more frequent in his prophecy (217 times) than in the rest of the OT (84 times in other books), so that it almost becomes Ezekiel's signature—or better, God's signature, a sort of counterpart to God's consistent address to the prophet as בֶּן־אָדָם (e.g., 2:1).

The form אֲדֹנָי ("Adonai, Lord") is from אָדוֹן, which can be used as a title of respect for ordinary human lords as well as of God. When used of God, it always, as here, has the unusual vocalization of the suffix (ָי). The usual form of the first common singular suffix on the plural "lords" (אֲדֹנָי, "my lords," as in Gen 19:2) would be this (יַ‑) if it were in pause, but frequently אֲדֹנָי is not in pause, and is not here, so that cannot be the explanation for the form. The precise reason for the Masoretic vocalization is thus somewhat of a mystery. The most likely explanation is that it is intended as a sort of "plural of majesty," perhaps by extension from the usual plural form of the Hebrew word for the one true God (אֱלֹהִים).

The Tetragrammaton, יהוה, is the personal name of the true God. Its original pronunciation probably was "Yahweh." However, Jews came to consider the name too sacred to utter. Throughout the Hebrew Bible, Jewish scribes artificially placed the vowels of אֲדֹנָי under the consonants of יהוה. Later Jewish readers and cantors knew to read this "perpetual Qere" as "Adonai." Medieval Christians, however, were not so instructed, and thus arose its pronunciation as "Jehovah."

How far back into history the Jewish avoidance of "Yahweh" goes is uncertain, but it is obviously reflected in the LXX's usual translation of יהוה as κύριος, which is also the usual NT practice, leading to the liturgical Kyrie. English translations, virtually without exception, render the Tetragrammaton pointed with the vowels of Adonai as "Lᴏʀᴅ" (all four letters capitalized, in contrast to "Lord," which is the usual translation of אֲדֹנָי). This should be pointed out and explained to laypeople. My experience is that they rarely understand it—or perhaps even notice the difference.

What happens, then, when אֲדֹנָי ("Adonai, Lord") is followed by the actual Tetragrammaton, יהוה, as here, throughout Ezekiel, and many other times in the OT? In such cases יהוה is outfitted with the vowels of אֱלֹהִים ("Elohim, God"). So Hebrew scribes read יְהֹוִה as if it were אֱלֹהִים, and English versions usually translate it as "Gᴏᴅ" (all capitals) to signal the underlying Tetragrammaton. As long as the reluctance to reproduce the sacred name "Yahweh" itself continues, any deep reading of the biblical text requires understanding these conventions.

In instances such as we have here, the LXX translators, if they had followed their usual conventions, would have rendered the double appellation as the repetitious κύριος κύριος, but apparently they often simply omitted one of them. Hence, usually throughout Ezekiel, as here, the LXX has only one κύριος. Until recently, critical commentators tended to favor the shorter LXX text (with only one "Lord"). Throughout his two-volume commentary, Zimmerli seems to favor the LXX reading, but recants in his appendix.[2] I see no reason to abandon the MT and believe it adds to the message (see the commentary).

An additional wrinkle can be added. Hebrew manuscript evidence indicates that Jewish scribes often wrote the Tetragrammaton in the archaic, paleo-Hebrew (today often called "Phoenician") script. Later Christian copyists rendered this to-them meaningless writing with κύριος (or θεός). When a double κύριος resulted, again the tendency was to retain only one.

2:5 וְהֵמָּה אִם־יִשְׁמְעוּ וְאִם־יֶחְדָּלוּ—Alliteration joins 2:4b with 2:5: אָמַר ("say") occurs twice near the end of 2:4, and אִם ("if") occurs twice here at the start of 2:5. But the connection between these verses is more one of theology that links together Yah-

---

[2]   Zimmerli, *Ezekiel*, 2:556–62.

weh, his prophet, and the recalcitrant audience. Yahweh sends the prophet, who is to speak Yahweh's words, despite the fact that the hearers most likely will not listen.

The text is elliptical, almost a shorthand caption for what will follow. The initial וְהֵמָּה ("they") does not find its predicate ("they will know …") until after two intervening clauses. Like the English "hear," the Hebrew שָׁמַע may imply mere audition but is regularly used in the sense of "listen, obey." Its antonym in this clause, חָדַל, implies refusing or at least desisting from doing what preceded. The traditional "forbear" sounds archaic to me, and "refuse," while it fits this context, implies a bit more than the Hebrew. "Listen or do not" is the most natural way of reproducing in idiomatic English the text's intent. The implicit assumption is that it will be the second option the Israelites will follow: they will not listen, and the reason why is explained by the following כִּי clause.

כִּי בֵּית מְרִי הֵמָּה—This is another "signature" phrase of Ezekiel since it occurs seven times in the book and nowhere else in the OT.[3] Ezekiel's label for the people as "a rebellious house" may be in deliberate opposition to the common phrase "house of Israel," which Ezekiel will begin using in 3:1 (see the textual note and commentary there).

Hebrew often uses a construct chain (here, literally, "house of rebellion") to express what English does with an adjective ("rebellious house"). The phrase is the third in the triad of characterizations of the people. The earlier two, "brazen-faced" and "hard-hearted," were in 2:4. This adds a third characterization of Israel's contumacy: בֵּית מְרִי. The noun מְרִי, "rebellion," is derived from the verb מָרָה, which is a synonym of מָרַד and פָּשַׁע (see the textual notes on those two verbs in 2:3). מְרִי recurs in 2:6–8 and a total of sixteen times in Ezekiel.

2:6 Stylistically, we encounter in this verse a type of writing (reflecting the divine speech) that has poetic features and is quite characteristic of Ezekiel. The first clause has chiasm, which I have reproduced in translation: "*do not be afraid* **of them**, and **of their words** *do not be afraid*." The following four clauses each consist of two parallel clauses, with key words in the same order. The first is "*briars and thorns* are with **you** and on *scorpions* **you** are sitting." The second is, literally, "*from their words* **do not be afraid**, and *from their looks* **do not be intimidated**." English translations may convey some of the repetition, chiasm, and parallelism that is present in the Hebrew, but not the alliteration (e.g., סָרָבִים וְסַלּוֹנִים). These literary features are found in other parts of chapter 2 as well. All of that gives a poetic cast to the composition, although it can hardly be labeled poetry. Possibly this kind of writing (in contrast to the ancient tradition of classical Hebrew poetry) reflects all the political and cultural scramblings of Ezekiel's time and earlier. Probably the intent of the poetic features was to emphasize or prolong the development of the themes to make sure they "sank in."

סָרָב (in plural, "briars") is a hapax legomenon, and its presumed meaning is derived from context. Its mate, סַלּוֹן, is rare, but Semitic cognates mean "thorn"

---

[3] Ezek 2:5, 6; 3:9, 26, 27; 12:2 (with הֵם instead of הֵמָּה); 12:3. Even just the combination בֵּית מְרִי occurs nowhere else in the OT. The phrase בֵּית הַמֶּרִי (with the article) occurs six times in Ezekiel: 2:8; 12:2, 9, 25; 17:12; 24:3.

(*HALOT*). It recurs in 28:24, where it is pointed סַלּוֹן and is parallel to קוֹץ, a common word for "thorn" or "thornbush." These two words plus "scorpions" (עַקְרַבִּים) are obviously metaphors for nettlesome or hostile people. "Scorpion" troubles some commentators because the reference is not to a plant as with the first two, and hence we technically have a mixed metaphor. Some would take it as a popular or otherwise unknown name of still a third type of thorn in order to resolve the perceived problem. Anyone who has spent time in the Near East knows that there is no lack of thistles and thorns of various sorts, especially obnoxious in the summer after the winter rains have stopped. But we should not force עַקְרַבִּים to have anything other than its well-attested meaning, "scorpions." The metaphors used here are vaguely reminiscent of those describing enemies in the Psalter, although there the pictures are usually derived from the animal kingdom (e.g., Pss 7:2–6 [ET 7:1–5]; 22:13–14, 17 [ET 22:12–13, 16]).

After three instances of the common verb "to fear, be afraid" (יָרֵא), Ezekiel uses (the Qal second masculine singular jussive of) the verb חָתַת. It is partly synonymous, although generally somewhat stronger. I have ventured "be intimidated," while others translate it as "be dismayed," "be daunted," or so on. "By their looks" translates a literal "from their faces."

God will again speak parallel exhortations not to be afraid (יָרֵא) and not to be intimidated or dismayed (חָתַת) to Ezekiel in 3:9. That same pair of exhortations was spoken by God to Israel through Moses (Deut 1:21; 31:8), by God to Joshua (Josh 8:1), by Joshua to Israel (Josh 10:25), and by God through other prophets (e.g., Is 51:7; Jer 30:10; 46:27).

2:7 וְדִבַּרְתָּ אֶת־דְּבָרַי אֲלֵיהֶם—Like many imperfects, the perfect with *waw* consecutive is often used as a strong, standing imperative. Hence, "You *must* speak my words," like "you must say to them" in 2:4. Note that the verb דִּבֶּר takes its cognate accusative, דָּבָר.

This is a thoroughly repetitious (and thus emphasizing) verse at the end of a unit, 2:3–7. Here we have מְרִי ("rebellion") without a preceding בֵּית ("house"), in contrast to the usual combination "rebellious house" as in 2:5. The versions and even many Hebrew manuscripts do include "house" here. The shorter MT is certainly the more difficult reading and hence receives a certain automatic preference according to one of the most basic canons of textual criticism. No emendation is necessary. If anything, the stark "rebellion" is stronger, almost as though this stance was of their very essence. Hebrew frequently uses abstract nouns (here, "rebellion") adjectivally, and so we have translated the noun as a predicate adjective, "they are rebellious." Stylistically, the bare "rebellion" here ties in with the admonition to the prophet in the next verse not to be "rebellion" himself.

2:8 "You, son of man," repeating "son of man" from 2:3 and 2:6, signals that a new paragraph is beginning. As we read on, it soon becomes apparent that 2:8–10 is transitional, both on the verbal and thought levels. We see both the continuation of the divine commissioning of Ezekiel as God's prophet and the introduction of a new element: the scroll.

"Whatever" in "listen to whatever I am telling you" translates אֵת אֲשֶׁר (the direct object indicator followed by the relative pronoun: "that which"). That combination occurs in three consecutive commands, twice in this verse and once in 3:1. It underscores the unconditional obedience God is requiring from Ezekiel.

אַל־תְּהִי־מֶרִי כְּבֵית הַמֶּרִי—The prophet is not to be "rebellion" (מֶרִי, pausal of מְרִי), the stark noun applied to Israel as the "rebellious house" (2:5, 8) and at the end of 2:7. Here again I have translated it with the adjective "rebellious." Here again (like 2:5, but in contrast to 2:7) "house" is used of Israel. Already KJV somewhat freely used the demonstrative pronoun, "*that* rebellious house," but the Hebrew simply has the definite article. The line between the article and the demonstrative is often porous. The article is probably used here to say that Israel's rebelliousness is an established fact so ingrained that "the rebellious house" can almost be their proper name, just as it, in intent, is a substitute for "house of Israel" (see the textual note on "rebellious house" in 2:5).

2:9 יָד שְׁלוּחָה אֵלָי וְהִנֵּה־בוֹ מְגִלַּת־סֵפֶר—The Qal passive participle שְׁלוּחָה ("stretched out") is feminine, agreeing with יָד, "hand," since parts of the body that occur in pairs are feminine (except for שָׁדַיִם). However, the suffix (referring to the "hand") on the preposition, בוֹ, is masculine. As noted already in chapter 1, such perplexing gender variation is not rare in Ezekiel.

The construct phrase מְגִלַּת־סֵפֶר is not easy to translate. סֵפֶר usually refers to a "scroll." "Book" is out of the question because books (codices), as we know them, hardly antedate NT times. Because Christian literature tended to be written on books, they virtually became symbols of the true biblical faith. This is in contrast to Judaism; down to this day, the scroll plays a prominent role in synagogue worship. מְגִלָּה too usually refers to a "scroll." In later Jewish terminology, the five liturgical readings (propers, in Christian terminology) for major Jewish festivals, grouped together in the Hebrew canon, are called the *Megilloth*. In this context, however, the etymological force of the word (from גָּלַל, "to roll") must come to the fore. The entire phrase then means "rolled-up scroll." The common rendering, "written scroll," while compatible in the context, is a bit of a paraphrase.

Some debate whether the scroll would have been made of papyrus or skin. Except for the command to eat it (2:8), the question might be purely academic. Papyrus is almost certainly the correct choice, since it was the more common writing material in biblical times. The technique of preparing skins so that they could be written on on both sides was not developed until Christian times. Papyrus is much less edible than skin might be.

2:10 וַיִּפְרֹשׂ אוֹתָהּ לְפָנַי—Since it was a "rolled-up scroll," the most natural way to understand the verb פָּרַשׂ, usually "to spread out," is "to unroll." "Open" might too easily make a modern reader think of a book.

וְהִיא כְתוּבָה פָנִים וְאָחוֹר—The feminine pronoun הִיא corresponds to the gender of מְגִלָּה. The Hebrew idiom is, literally, "written face and back," meaning that it is written on both its front and its back—on both sides.

וְכָתוּב אֵלֶיהָ קִנִים וָהֶגֶה וָהִי:—The Qal passive participle in וְכָתוּב is singular, which suggests that the last three words in the verse are a heading or title, which

Ezekiel could read at a glance. Writing titles on the outside of scrolls is a practice well-attested throughout antiquity. I have capitalized the title: "Laments, Moaning, and Woe." This interpretation helps solve the problem (according to some commentators) that the words do not correspond precisely to the contents of the book of Ezekiel. (Only the second of the three words is really subject to that criticism anyway; see below.) Even if the words in the title are not exact, technical labels for the contents of the book, they easily describe what Ezekiel's audience will perceive the content of his message to be when the judgments he predicts come true.

The first word, קִנִים, "laments," appears masculine (plural) in form. However, its singular form is feminine, קִינָה. The plural occurs in only one other verse, where it is feminine in form: קִינוֹת (2 Chr 35:25). The masculine form here could be another example of Ezekiel's grammatical gender anomalies. Or this word, like others, may have both forms for its plurals. Or the masculine plural form could be meant to signal some specialized meaning. For example, for the feminine noun תְּהִלָּה, "song (of praise)," the plural normally is feminine in form, but as the Hebrew title of the canonical book of Psalms, it is the masculine תְּהִלִּים. The LXX here has a singular form, as are the other two words in the title. Text critically the preference is for the MT, which is the harder form.

In any case, laments or dirges (wailed at funerals) are common in the OT as a whole, and also in the judgment oracles in the book of Ezekiel. See קִינָה in 19:1, 14; 26:17; 27:2, 32; 28:12; 32:2, 16, and see further "Introduction to Eekiel 19" in the commentary on chapter 19.

The second noun, הֶגֶה, is basically clear, but also elusive enough to make finding the best English equivalent rather difficult. It occurs only two other times in the OT: Ps 90:9; Job 37:2. However, the verb הָגָה is fairly frequent. The verb can describe various noises made by animals: "to coo" (e.g., Is 38:14) and "to growl" (Is 31:4). The verb can also refer to reading to oneself out loud, as when meditating on Scripture (Ps 1:2; see *HALOT*, 2 c, d). Most relevant for Ezek 2:10 are passages where it refers to humans who "moan" (*HALOT*, 2 b, citing Is 16:7; Jer 48:31). Here the context requires the noun to mean "sighing," "moaning," or the like—the groans and sighs associated with grief.

The third noun, הִי, is a hapax legomenon. The LXX (οὐαί) and Vulgate (*vae*; 2:9b) take it as an interjection expressing grief. Here it is used as a noun, "woe" (*HALOT*). Some think those translations reflect confusion with הוֹי or אוֹי (both meaning "woe" and used later by Ezekiel). Others think הִי is a by-form of the verb נָהָה (Ezek 32:18) or the noun נְהִי (five times in Jeremiah). But such expedients are not necessary. Mishnaic Hebrew also knows it as an interjection, a usage that may have begun here.

Commentary

2:1 Chapters 2 and 3 are sometimes labeled the verbal "call" or "commissioning" of the prophet to distinguish them from the "inaugural vision" of chapter 1. But that kind of division may mislead; ultimately, chapters 1–3 are one unit. The division between chapters 2 and 3 is even less felicitous than that between chapters 1 and 2, since 2:8–3:3 is a subunit about the scroll.

This entire unit (chapters 1–3) remains visionary, but the change between chapters 1 and 2 is that now God reveals himself more to the prophet's ears than to his eyes. However, neither here nor generally in prophetic literature is that distinction absolute. Hearing had played a role already in 1:24, and sight plays a role again in 2:9. Fretheim has well observed: "There is a kind of sacramentalism evident in the combination of the word and the visible vehicles in and through which the word is … 'enfleshed' and conveyed."[4] The unity of "Word and Sacrament" in this context consists of the God who has revealed himself in a theophany of judgment (the usual context of most of the elements in chapter 1) now calling Ezekiel to be, initially, a prophet of judgment.

For that purpose, here as throughout Scripture, the God who appears as "a man" (1:26), anticipating the incarnation of Christ, uses an ordinary human being to carry out his ministry. However, lest Ezekiel be tempted to forget God's condescension in calling him, God continually addresses him as "son of man" (see the textual note on that title in 2:1), never by his name.

The scene evoked by the call of the enthroned God in human form (1:26) is based on common practice in royal chambers. Anyone who was favored enough to be ushered into royal chambers would prostrate himself. Ezekiel employs the reverent gesture of prostration and submission (וָאֶפֹּל עַל־פָּנַי, "I fell on my face") in 1:28; 3:23; 43:3; and 44:4. (In 11:13 grief-stricken Ezekiel employs that same gesture in supplication to God.) The prostrated subject would rise only when bidden to do so by the monarch.

That bidding begins this chapter: "He said to me, 'Son of man, stand on your feet, and I will speak with you' " (2:1). One might debate the subject of the verb "said" (וַיֹּאמֶר), although it is, no doubt, ultimately God. At the end of 1:28 Ezekiel said he heard either "the voice of one speaking" or "a voice speaking" (see the textual note there). It would be entirely consonant with Ezekiel's extreme guardedness about describing God in anthropomorphic terms (1:26) that he would merely say that "a voice" spoke to him (1:28), and hence that voice would be the subject of 2:1. Compare Is 40:3 and 40:6, where that prophet hears a "voice" (קוֹל).

The command to Ezekiel is "stand on your feet" (2:1), that is, be poised and ready to do whatever further God may command, to go wherever God may send him. Greenberg well summarizes: "The biblical visionary must be in possession of himself in order to receive the divine word. The ecstasy of biblical prophecy consists in a Godward concentration of consciousness that obliterates circumstances, in contrast to the ecstasy of pagan prophets, in which consciousness itself was obliterated."[5]

2:2 "Spirit" is anarthrous here, as also seven other times in the book.[a] As a result, a few commentators want to limit its meaning to the psychological

(a) Ezek 3:12, 14, 24; 8:3; 11:1, 24; 43:5

---

[4] Fretheim, *The Suffering of God*, 84.

[5] Greenberg, *Ezekiel*, 1:62.

("life, consciousness, vigor, courage," or the like), but that is certainly wrong. That this is God's Spirit (with the word capitalized!) is signaled by the Hiphil or causative form of the verb following: the Spirit *made me stand* on my feet." That clearly implies some objective force outside the prophet. God's Spirit is likewise involved in creation (Gen 1:2) and many other divine acts. The preceding ("as he spoke") and following ("him speaking") references to the utterance of God's Word connect the operation of the Holy Spirit with the divine Word.

2:3 God declares both here and in the following verse that he is "sending" (שׁוֹלֵחַ) Ezekiel as his minister. That verb figures prominently also in other prophetic calls (Is 6:8; Jer 1:7). Yahweh denounces false prophets by asserting that he has *not* sent them (Jer 14:14–15). Of more immediate significance for Ezekiel, in Jeremiah's letter to the exiles in Babylon (Jeremiah 29), he uses the same language to denounce false prophets among the people who claim that the exile will be of short duration: Yahweh declares that he did not send (שָׁלַח) those false prophets (Jer 29:9, 31). He had sent (שָׁלַח) his Word by his servants, the (true) prophets (Jer 29:19; and he had sent the exiles to Babylon [Jer 29:20]). Ezekiel does not use precisely the same language in denouncing the false prophets in his own midst, but especially in chapter 13 he uses words that amount to the same thing to condemn prophets and prophetesses who proclaim "peace" when "there is no peace" (13:10, 16).

In contexts where God calls and "sends" his prophets, the Hebrew verb שָׁלַח in many ways parallels the NT vocabulary of God "sending" (ἀποστέλλω) his "apostles" (ἀπόστολος; e.g., Matthew 10), although the Hebrew verb never developed the semi-technical connotations of the NT counterpart.

We shall hear echoes or expressions of Ezek 2:3 throughout virtually all the rest of the book. Ezekiel is not called to preach to any ordinary community or to be a missionary to some new pagan culture, but to a covenant community that has rebellion in its genes, as it were. The fathers and their sons had rebelled and been unfaithful time and again, and continued to behave that way down "to this very day." That emphasizes both original sin, inherited from Adam and all subsequent fathers, and the actual sin committed by the fathers and sons alike. Like us, Israel is a people that cannot not sin, that has rebelled against the Lord, personally rejecting the personal God and Father who had created and redeemed them. As most pastors today know only too well, people who have left the church are usually far harder to gain than those who have never confessed the Gospel.

It is to the "sons," the present generation, to whom Ezekiel must preach.

2:4 The two adjectival phrases "brazen-faced" and "hard-hearted" cover the entirety of the people. Both in exterior mien ("brazen-faced") and in interior determination ("hard-hearted"), they are thoroughly refractory.

God directs Ezekiel, "You must say to them, 'Thus says the Lord Yahweh.'" The common prophetic citation formula "thus says the Lord Yahweh" occurs 122 times in Ezekiel. Its double designation of God ("the Lord Yahweh") is the functional obverse of Ezekiel's own constant reminder that he is not to speak his own mind, since he is merely a "son of man" (2:1). Ezekiel does not speak out of merely personal, private conviction, but as a mouthpiece of the Almighty. The double appellation of the Deity ("the Lord Yahweh") underscores precisely who the sender of the message is. First, he is "the Lord" clearly in the sense of Deity, not merely some faceless numen. Second, he is none other than Yahweh, the personal, covenant Deity who is a "jealous God, visiting the iniquity of the fathers upon the children to the third and fourth generation of those who hate me" (Ex 20:5).

2:5   God holds out the possibility that the Israelites may listen to Ezekiel and repent when they hear his prophetic warnings of judgment. After all, even the pagan Ninevites had repented and believed in God because of the ministry of an Israelite prophet (Jonah 3:5). But the prophet is not to tailor his message to his audience; he is to preach what he has been given to say "whether they listen or do not" (Ezek 2:5). If they do listen, believe, and are saved, it will be only due to the efficacy of the divine Word, just as the divine Word had the power to raise up Ezekiel himself and enable him to carry out his prophetic office (2:1–3).

If they do not listen, then the fault will not be God's nor that of the faithful prophet (as God elaborates in 3:17–21). The following clause assigns the blame: "for they are a rebellious house" (2:5). "Rebellious house" is the third in the triad of terms in 2:4–5 describing Israel's determined apostasy. "Rebellious house" may indicate a sort of dynasty of original and actual sin as a sarcastic play on "house of Israel" (3:1), the covenant people. Or it may take off from the idea of family, "like father, like son," since "they and their fathers have revolted against me to this very day" (2:3).

Later God will describe the "rebellious house" as unable to see or hear (12:2). Nevertheless, the people shall be without excuse. When the judgment the prophet has to proclaim comes to pass, there will be no denying that his oracles of doom were not his own invention, but that Yahweh had indeed sent him: "they will know that a prophet has been among them" (2:5). "Know" is here used in its full biblical sense: the God-given realization of the truthfulness of the Word faithfully spoken by his messenger. The clause also implies "true" modifying "prophet." Of false prophets there was no lack (then as now), but they will be exposed as no prophets of the true God at all.

That final clause of 2:5 is usually classified as a variant of the recognition formula so characteristic of Ezekiel: "then you/they will know that I am Yahweh" (e.g., 6:7, 13–14).[6] In 33:33 the formulation found in 2:5 is repeated in somewhat more detail, including an implied attack on false prophets. The use of the wording "they will know that *a prophet* ..." (2:5; 33:33) shows that

---

6   Variations of expression occur around seventy-two times in Ezekiel, occasionally with subjects other than "you" or "they."

knowledge of God comes through his prophetic Word. Already Deut 18:18–22 had specified fulfillment of his predictions as a major validation of a true prophet.

Much of the phraseology in this verse is repeated (sometimes verbatim) and/or expanded later. The "whether they listen or do not" clause defines the call of every prophet, and every pastor. He is not called to be successful (as measured externally), but to be faithful. The clause, at first glance, might leave the impression that Israel would repent before it was too late. Most prophets and preachers surely hope that their ministries will change many lives. But if Ezekiel harbors any expectations that his ministry might avert the fall of Jerusalem, Yahweh in the same breath disabuses him of them.

2:6 Three times in this verse Ezekiel receives a reassuring "do not be afraid" from God (and one "do not be intimidated"). That common phrase is found also in the theophany to Abraham (Gen 15:1), to Israel through Isaiah (e.g., Is 10:24; 35:4), in Jeremiah's call (Jer 1:8), and elsewhere. Sometimes it is accompanied by God's further assurance that he is "with" his people (Deut 20:1; Jer 1:8; 1 Chr 28:20; cf. Mt 28:19–20). Properly construed, "do not be afraid" is one facet of the Gospel. It may be compared to "Peace be with you" as spoken by Christ (see Jn 14:27; also Jn 20:19, 21, 26). It applies to believers, especially those called into the ministry, in the face of pressures exerted by this world (ministry is "countercultural") and otherworldly, satanic threats.

"Briars," "thorns," "scorpions," and intimidating "looks" (Ezek 2:6) are all heaped up to underscore the intensity of the opposition Ezekiel must expect. Pastors today may think of various kinds of opponents to their faithful ministry, such as "alligators"—a metaphor for church members whose goal seems to be to usurp the pastor's rightful authority and hinder his ministry. The preaching of the Law is never popular, and the pure Gospel has always had its opponents, even within the church. See, for example, Gal 1:6–3:1; 1 Jn 2:15–23; 4:1–6.

The repetition of "for they are a rebellious house" (Ezek 2:5–6) should not be misunderstood as an extenuating circumstance: "That's just the way they are. They can't help it." That is not the line of thought. Hardened, habitual, obdurate sinfulness is anything but an excuse before God. Neither should this be construed as saying that the Israelites were worse than other people. Rather, this is a commentary on the total depravity of the human nature of all people ever since the fall of Adam and Eve into sin. Natural man rebels against God (Gen 6:5; 8:21; Rom 1:18–32; 1 Cor 2:14). See FC Ep I, "Original Sin."

2:7 This brief verse, although completely repetitious, serves as a succinct, powerful summary of God's commissioning of Ezekiel this far. The repetition suggests the conclusion of a subsection: in 2:3–7 Yahweh has spoken to Ezekiel about his ministry to Israel. New elements are introduced in the next verses, where the focus is on Ezekiel's relationship to Yahweh himself and the prophetic words Yahweh gives to him.

2:8 A new phase in the commissioning of the prophet begins in the final three verses of chapter 2. After being commanded to "stand" (2:1) following the inaugural vision (chapter 1), he is now commanded to "listen/obey" (שְׁמַע), although that has also been implied all along. Some interpret this new command to imply that Ezekiel was reluctant or initially even unwilling to accept his call. At best, that view *over*-interprets. The injunction "not to let himself be infected by the Israelite disease,"[7] that is, not to be "rebellious," underscores the previous encouragements not to fear or be intimidated (2:6). Twice in this verse and again in 3:1, "whatever" is the object of God's command: he requires Ezekiel's unconditional surrender to the divine will and Word.

Likewise, the Christian pastor is called to proclaim the full counsel of God in his Word, "whatever" that Word contains. The avoidance of doctrines or teachings because they are distasteful to the pastor or to his hearers is not an option. Neither should the pastor adjust his message depending on "whether they listen or do not, for they are rebellious" (2:7). Catering to what people want to hear is a sure route to apostasy (2 Tim 4:3), as "user-friendly" worship services easily may be also.

The eating of a scroll is then introduced (Ezek 2:8–9), which will occupy the text through 3:3. It is a test of the prophet's willingness to ingest the divine Word, which is necessary before he can preach it to others. After God commands, "Open your mouth and eat whatever I am giving you" (2:8), the prophet would naturally think of food, but that is not the case.

The subject of testing is a major one in the Bible and in the Christian life. Sometimes it involves food. God fed the Israelites manna in the wilderness to test them (Deut 8:16). Daniel and his companions were tested regarding unclean foods (Daniel 1). The Lord Jesus tested his apostles before feeding the five thousand (Jn 6:5–6). In a vision St. Peter was commanded to dine on food that included animals unclean according to the OT—and hence was reprehensible to the apostle—but eating it represented the new phase of preaching the Gospel and baptizing Gentiles (Acts 10–11).

One of the major tests in the OT is that of Abraham, whom God called to sacrifice his son Isaac (Genesis 22). Even our Lord was tested "forty days and nights" in the wilderness, and the devil tempted him to turn stones into bread (Mt 4:1–11). In the Sixth Petition we regularly pray, "Lead us not into temptation," which Luther's Small Catechism explains with these words:

> God tempts no one. We pray in this petition that God would guard and keep us so that the devil, the world, and our sinful nature may not deceive us or mislead us into false belief, despair, and other great shame and vice. Although we are attacked by these things, we pray that we may finally overcome them and win the victory.[8]

---

[7] Block, *Ezekiel*, 1:123.

[8] *Luther's Small Catechism with Explanation* (St. Louis: Concordia, 1986, 1991), 19.

As Ezek 2:8–10 and other passages cited above show, those whom God calls into the ministry are not immune from testing, and they may actually be tempted more severely than others. It seems that the devil puts a higher priority on the attempted corruption of clergy because of the greater damage to the church that ensues should a minister succumb.

2:9–10 Ezekiel's sight of a "hand" returns us, at least momentarily, to the more visionary mode of revelation used throughout chapter 1, with its anthropomorphic theophany of the preincarnate Christ (1:26). One notes how closely divine speech and theophanic sight are connected here, which can be compared to the interrelatedness of Word and Sacrament.

The text does not specify whose hand it is, nor whose voice when speech resumes in 3:1. But Ezekiel obviously had no doubt, nor do we, that Yahweh is the subject throughout this section about the scroll (2:8–3:3).

Yahweh's "hand" plays a fairly prominent role throughout Ezekiel. Another vision of the outstretched divine hand occurs in 8:3 (and a cherub stretches out his hand in 10:7). In other references, such as "the hand of Yahweh" in, for example, 1:3 and 3:14, 22, and the warning that God would stretch out his hand in judgment (e.g., 6:14; 14:9, 13; 16:27), it is doubtful that any actual vision of a hand was involved. Instead, "the hand of Yahweh" in, for example, 1:3; 3:14, 22 (see also 8:1) appears to function as a metaphor for Yahweh's overpowering strength, which prompts various actions—not unlike the metaphorical use of the word "hand" many other times in Scripture, and still in the language of the Apostles' and Nicene Creeds, which refer to Christ's session "at the right hand" of God the Father.

The use of שָׁלַח (the passive here in 2:9 idiomatically meaning that the hand was "stretched out, extended") verbally connects this verse with 2:4 and 3:5–6, where the verb is used technically of Yahweh "apostolically" sending Ezekiel into prophetic ministry.

The fact that the message given Ezekiel to eat is written on a scroll indicates that, at least in Ezekiel's time, prophetic oracles were commonly written, either by the prophet himself or perhaps by a scribe. In light of Ezekiel's dumbness (3:26), he may have written down his prophecies initially, before delivering them. A comparable situation obviously obtained with Jeremiah and his scribe, Baruch (see especially Jeremiah 36). Evidence for writing is less direct, if present at all, for other prophets, but there is no reason at all why the practice could not have been customary long before Jeremiah and Ezekiel.

One must be cautious about equating the scroll seen in the vision here with the entire, canonical book of Ezekiel. However, one certainly gets the impression that the connection is close. A scroll written on both sides could probably accommodate all forty-eight chapters of the book without difficulty.

Two false conclusions have at times been based on these verses. One is that these verses point to a doctrine of inspiration that amounts to mechanical dictation. That charge comes, of course, from opponents of the doctrine of special divine revelation and the consequent inerrancy of the Scriptures. "Dictation" is, indeed, one metaphor used of the mystery of inspiration, but in the totality of Scripture, it certainly is not the whole picture. Nor is it what conservatives have understood by what Scripture teaches about the supernatural process, which is beyond rational explanation (see, e.g., 2 Tim 3:16; 2 Pet 1:21).

A second faulty conclusion, allegedly based on the triad in Ezek 2:10 ("Laments, Moaning, and Woe") and the triad of "sword," "famine," and "pestilence" found in both Jeremiah (e.g., Jer 14:12; 24:10; 34:17) and Ezekiel (e.g., Ezek 5:12; 6:11–12), once was virtually a higher-critical dogma: true pre-exilic prophecy consisted only of judgment. Everything else (especially the clear messianic, Gospel portions) in those books had to be later, presumably added to soften the harshness of the earlier oracles for later generations, who were probably exilic or later, after the judgment had already occurred. No doubt, judgment was a predominant accent of the earlier prophets, because the Law's condemnation was what the unfaithful, covenant-violating people needed to hear. That was also true of the first seven years of Ezekiel's ministry (preceding the fall of Jerusalem). But it is absurd to assert that those prophets could not and did not proclaim Gospel as well as the Law in all its severity. To be blunt, that assertion was based on a developmental, evolutionary premise. It went in search of "proof texts" and could only be sustained by excising large portions of the actual texts as not original or "genuine."

The Prophetic Commissioning
of Ezekiel: Part 2

Translation

3 **¹**Then he said to me, "Son of man, what you receive, eat. Eat this scroll, and then go, speak to the house of Israel." **²**I opened my mouth, and he caused me to eat this scroll. **³**Then he said to me, "Son of man, feed your stomach and fill your innards with this scroll that I am giving you." I ate, and it was in my mouth like honey in sweetness.

⁴He then said to me, "Son of man, go now to the house of Israel and speak with my words to them. **⁵**For not to a people of incomprehensible speech or of difficult language are you being sent, but to the house of Israel, **⁶**nor to many peoples of incomprehensible speech or of difficult language, whose words you would not understand. Surely, if I sent you to them, they would listen to you. **⁷**But the house of Israel will not be willing to listen to you because they are not willing to listen to me, for the whole house of Israel is hard-headed and hard-hearted. **⁸**Look, I have made your face just as strong as their faces and your forehead just as strong as their forehead. **⁹**Like the hardest stone, harder than flint have I made your forehead. Do not fear them, and do not be intimidated by their looks, for they are a rebellious house." **¹⁰**Then he said to me, "Son of man, all my words that I will speak to you, receive in your heart, and with your ears listen. **¹¹**Go now to the exiles, to the sons of your people. You shall speak to them and you shall say to them, 'Thus says the Lord Yahweh,' whether they listen or do not."

¹²Then the Spirit lifted me up, and I heard behind me a loud rumbling sound—blessed be the Glory of Yahweh from his place— **¹³**the sound of the wings of the living creatures touching each to the other and the sound of the wheels beside them, a loud rumbling sound. **¹⁴**The Spirit lifted me up and took me away, and I went bitter, in the fury of my spirit, and the hand of Yahweh was strongly upon me. **¹⁵**I came to the exiles at Tel Abib who were living by the Kebar Canal, where they were living. I sat there among them for seven days—devastated.

¹⁶At the end of seven days the Word of Yahweh came to me as follows: **¹⁷**"Son of man, I have appointed you a watchman for the house of Israel. When you hear a word from my mouth, you must give them warning against me. **¹⁸**When I announce to a wicked man, 'You shall surely die,' and you do not warn him and you do not speak to warn the wicked man against his wicked way to make him live, he, a wicked man, shall die because of his iniquity, and I will seek his blood from your hand. **¹⁹**But you, if you warn the wicked man, and he does not repent of his wickedness or of his wicked way, he shall die because of his iniquity, but you yourself will have saved your life.

[20]"Or when a righteous man apostatizes from his righteousness, does unrighteousness, and I place a stumbling block in front of him, he shall die. If you have not warned him, he shall die because of his sin, and his righteous deeds which he had done will not be remembered, and I will seek his blood from your hand. [21]But you, if you do warn him, a righteous man, not to sin, being a righteous man, and he does not sin, he shall surely live because he heeded the warning, and you yourself will have saved your life."

[22]Then the hand of Yahweh was upon me there, and he said to me, "Get up, go out to the valley plain, and there I will speak with you." [23]So I got up and went out to the valley plain, and behold, there the Glory of Yahweh was standing, just like the Glory that I had seen by the Kebar Canal, and I fell on my face. [24]But the Spirit entered into me and made me stand on my feet. Then he spoke to me and he said to me, "Go, shut yourself up inside your house. [25]And as for you, son of man, behold, they have placed upon you ropes, and they have tied you up with them so that you will not be able to go out among them. [26]I will make your tongue stick to the roof of your mouth so that you will be speechless and you will not be to them a man who reproves, for they are a rebellious house. [27]But whenever I speak to you, I will open your mouth, and you shall say to them, 'Thus says the Lord Yahweh.' Whoever listens, let him listen, and whoever refuses [to listen], let him refuse, for they are a rebellious house."

Textual Notes

3:1 בֶּן־אָדָם אֵת אֲשֶׁר־תִּמְצָא אֱכוֹל—This first full clause of God's command is not found in the LXX, which provides a convenient alibi for critics who argue that it was not part of the original text. Good reasons can be adduced for retaining it, however. God's next instruction repeats the command to "eat" (אֱכוֹל), and repetition is so integral a part of Ezekiel's style that objections to that feature carry little weight. Second, eliminating the clause also eliminates the chiasm in the form of AB‖B'A': "what you receive" (object) "eat" (imperative) ‖ "eat" (imperative) "this scroll" (object). Such chiasm is thoroughly compatible with Ezekiel's various artistic touches (see the chiasm and parallel clauses in 2:6, for example).

The Qal of מָצָא commonly means "to find," but here it does not imply a search or accidental discovery. The context refers to the scroll God had just extended to Ezekiel in a hand and then had unrolled in Ezekiel's sight (2:9–10). The verb can mean "obtain, gain" (*DCH*, s.v. מצא I, 8), and here most appropriate is "receive" because the scroll is presented to him. Various paraphrases include "what is offered to you" (RSV) and "what is before you" (NIV).

וְלֵךְ דַּבֵּר—For the sake of fluency, I have added "then" to this pair of imperatives: "and then go, speak …" The text plainly coordinates the eating and the speaking. The added "then" accents that just as Ezekiel is not at liberty to choose his message (it must be the message given him by God), so too he is not at liberty to refuse to preach.

אֶל־בֵּית יִשְׂרָאֵל:—Many manuscripts and versions have "sons of Israel" instead of the MT's "house of Israel." We will meet this variation again, but there is no good reason to abandon the MT. The two phrases are essentially synonymous. "House of Israel" combines elements of other phrases in Ezekiel, "sons of Israel" and "rebellious house" (see the textual notes on those phrases in 2:3 and 2:5, respectively). By Ezekiel's time "house of Israel" was already an ancient formulation for the people, found as early as the exodus under Moses (Ex 16:31; 40:38). A common Near Eastern way of describing countries was in dynastic terms, with "house" followed by the name of the current king. Ezekiel may use "house of Israel" to stress the unity of "Israel" under God even without a reigning king, since King Jehoiachin is now in exile (1:2).

The earlier prophets Isaiah and Jeremiah often referred to "the house of Israel" and occasionally also to "the house of David" (Is 7:2, 13; 22:22; Jer 21:12; but absent in Ezekiel) while the Davidic monarchy was still intact in the southern kingdom of Judah. Isaiah appealed to Israel as "the house of David" when he issued his famous prophecy of the virgin birth of Christ (Is 7:13–14), who would reign forever on the throne of David (Is 9:5–6 [ET 9:6–7]). "House of David" is now attested extrabiblically from archaeological excavations at Dan.

3:2   וַיַּאֲכִלֵנִי אֵת הַמְּגִלָּה הַזֹּאת׃—Most render the Hiphil of אָכַל, which is, literally, "he caused me to eat," with a weaker "he gave me to eat." (God will use the participle of נָתַן in the clause "I am giving" in the next verse.) Here the accent is on the divine causation, but it does not imply compulsion by force or some involuntary reflex by the prophet. It follows the Qal imperative אֱכֹל (twice in 3:1), so God enables Ezekiel to do what he himself had commanded him. "God is the one who works in you both to will and to do according to his good pleasure" (Phil 2:13).

Many commentators and translators omit the demonstrative "this" with "scroll." The LXX does not have it, and it is often argued that, while it was appropriate on God's lips in the previous verse, it is not on Ezekiel's here. It may be countered that Ezekiel's repetition of God's very word was deliberate. He had no choice of *which* scroll to eat, no option to eat a different scroll with more palatable contents.

3:3   בִּטְנְךָ תַאֲכֵל וּמֵעֶיךָ תְמַלֵּא—The verbs in God's two commands are jussive. The jussive may appear the same as the imperfect (as does תְמַלֵּא), but is shortened when possible (hence תַאֲכֵל instead of תַּאֲכִיל). The jussive is common in the third person. In the second person it is normally used with the adverb of negation אַל instead of the imperative, but other uses in the second person, such as the usage here, are rare (Joüon, § 114 g). The meaning is equivalent to an imperative, as I have translated. תַאֲכֵל is the Hiphil of אָכַל again (as in 3:2). תְמַלֵּא is Piel, which is the causative ("to fill") of the verb's stative Qal meaning, "to be full."

Both verbs take two direct objects. The first object of each precedes it, and the "scroll" does double duty as the second object of each. Literally, the commands can be translated, "cause your stomach to eat [this scroll] and fill your innards [with] this scroll." The two objects that each precede its verb for emphasis are essentially synonyms and almost standard parallels. "Belly" I judged too inelegant for בֶּטֶן, although it is not quite as anatomically precise as "stomach." For מֵעִים, "bowels" was fine when KJV was translated but is no longer. "Innards" is literal and appropriate. ("Innards" recurs in 7:19.)

וָאֹכְלָה—This is the lengthened (with "paragogic" *he*: הָ-) form of the Qal first common singular imperfect of אָכַל with *waw* consecutive (cf. GKC, § 49 e). Most of the versions translate it as if there were a *mappiq* in the *he*, הּ-, which would make that the third feminine singular suffix, referring back to the scroll ("I ate *it*").

כִּדְבַשׁ לְמָתוֹק:—The honey of wild bees was always known to the Israelites (e.g., 1 Sam 14:25–27), but the product was apparently not produced in artificial hives until much later. Often the word seems to refer to thickened date or grape syrup.[1]

3:4 לֶךְ־בֹּא אֶל־בֵּית יִשְׂרָאֵל—This is, literally, "go, come to the house of Israel." When used with another imperative, the imperative of הָלַךְ becomes a nearly inert proclitic, as indicated by the lack of accent and the *maqqeph*. I have tried to preserve a bit of its force by using "now"—although there is no particular accent on the present tense. The combination of the same two imperatives recurs in 3:11: לֵךְ בֹּא.

וְדִבַּרְתָּ בִדְבָרַי—The Piel דִּבֶּר with the preposition בְּ attached to what is to be spoken can mean "to recite (verbatim)" as in Deut 6:7, or it can refer to speaking the prophetic "Word of Yahweh" (1 Ki 13:18). In this context the nuance seems to be a verbatim repetition of what Ezekiel had ingested in the scroll—no more, less, or other words—in absolute obedience to the divine imperative. Compare also "speak my words" in 2:7, where that nuance is not so clear with the use of אֶת (the direct object marker) instead of בְּ. But the point is not lost, and possibly this paves the way for the prophet's dumbness (3:26).

3:5 כִּי לֹא אֶל־עַם עִמְקֵי שָׂפָה וְכִבְדֵי לָשׁוֹן—"Incomprehensible speech" and "difficult language" in this and the next verse render expressions that literally are "deep of lips" and "heavy of tongue." "Lip" and "tongue" can virtually mean "language." The adjectives in construct, עָמֵק and כָּבֵד, are plural, probably referring to the many members of the "people" (עַם). עָמֵק occurs only here and in Is 33:19. Its etymological meaning would be "deep," but here it does not imply profundity, but refers to language that is "unfathomable" or "incomprehensible." Isaiah uses "too deep of lip to understand" to describe the speech of the Assyrians, from whom Israel will be delivered (Is 33:19). כָּבֵד often means "heavy" and implies that the tongues are clumsy and inarticulate. "Heavy of mouth" and "heavy of tongue" was Moses' alibi for not answering God's call in Ex 4:10, but there the phrases denote lack of eloquence or the like. Is 28:11–12 uses similar language to describe the painful way Yahweh will "teach" his people Israel who would not accept his own Word: by forcing them to learn a foreign language that sounds to them like gibberish.

אֶל־בֵּית יִשְׂרָאֵל:—Our translation supplies "but," which is absent in Hebrew. Apparently the preceding אַתָּה שָׁלוּחַ does double duty: not to the kind of people described in the first half of the verse "you are being sent, [but you *are* being sent] to the house of Israel."

3:6 אִם־לֹא—This combination is an emphatic affirmative when in the context of oaths (BDB, s.v. אִם, 1 b (2)). It will later be used in that sense several times in Ezekiel (e.g., 5:11; 20:33; 34:8). Here it is not in an oath, and its meaning "is very difficult" to determine (see the discussion in BDB, s.v. אִם, 1 c (ε)). Probably it means "surely."

---

[1] See Kleinig, *Leviticus*, 73, who translates it as "fruit syrup."

3:7 חִזְקֵי־מֵצַח וּקְשֵׁי־לֵב —These two construct phrases serve as compound predicate adjectives describing Israel. They are clear enough in meaning, but not easy to reproduce in idiomatic English. Literally, the Hebrew says, "strong of forehead" and "hard/difficult of heart." The figurative use of "forehead" also appears in Jer 3:3, "the forehead of a harlot," and Is 48:4, "bronzed forehead" (cf. English "effrontery"). The two expressions here in Ezek 3:7 are similar to those in 2:4. Here, variety is provided by substituting "forehead" for "face," and the two adjectives are reversed, so "strong" goes with the external noun "forehead" and "hard/difficult" with the internal "heart." "Heart" in Hebrew usage has a lot to do with the will, strengthening the double use of the negated verb אָבָה (not to "be willing") in this verse. I am venturing "hardheaded" and "hard-hearted" in an attempt to reproduce the Hebrew lilt.

3:8 נָתַתִּי ... וְאֶת־מִצְחֲךָ חָזָק לְעֻמַּת מִצְחָם: —The downside of my translation of 3:7 comes in this verse, where I saw no real way to avoid the literal "forehead," but the linguistic connection with 3:7 (which uses the same Hebrew term, מֵצַח) is inevitably lost. "Made" is also somewhat weaker than the idiomatic Hebrew use of נָתַן, "set, establish, institute." "Just as" renders לְעֻמַּת, "matching, corresponding to."

3:9 כְּשָׁמִיר —There is debate about the meaning of שָׁמִיר. *HALOT* (s.v. שָׁמִיר II) argues for the traditional understanding of it as "diamond," which is the meaning of cognates in rabbinic Hebrew and Aramaic. "Adamant" is also possible, but is not well-known as a noun today. With the NIV I have avoided the debate and merely reproduced the force of the metaphor by "hardest stone."

For the pair of verbs יָרֵא and חָתַת, see the textual notes on 2:6. While 3:9 is parallel to 2:6, the Hebrew here uses the direct object אוֹתָם after "fear" rather than the idiomatic מִן plus suffix (מֵהֶם), "be afraid *of* them," as after the first אַל־תִּירָא in 2:6. Since the direct object works just as well in English too, I have translated the Hebrew literally. Here, as in 2:6, מִפְּנֵיהֶם goes with negated חָתַת.

3:10 In Hebrew the object "all my words" is placed first for emphasis. "Receive in your heart, and with your ears listen" is more metaphorical, but corresponds to the physical eating of the scroll with God's words at the beginning of the chapter. We might logically have expected the imperatives to be in reverse order: "with your ears listen" and then "receive in your heart," since the audible words would first be heard, then taken to heart. Maybe the reason is to bring "heart" back into consideration. Ezek 3:8–9 had focused on "face" and "forehead," while "heart" had not been mentioned since 3:7. In any case, we have an example of the figure of speech known as hysteron proteron ("last first"), where the second in an order is placed first because of its immediate impact (cf. English, "thunder and lightning," even though the light arrives before the sound).

3:11 As in 1:1, the abstract הַגּוֹלָה ("the exile") is used idiomatically for the concrete "exiles." "The sons of my/your/their people" can refer to close blood relatives or more broadly to "countrymen" or fellow Israelites (e.g., Gen 23:11; Lev 20:17). Here the emphasis is on family bonds between Ezekiel and the other Israelites that are primarily covenantal or "baptismal" rather than merely genetic or ethnic. In Ezekiel all but one (37:18) of the other uses of the phrase appear in chapter 33 (33:2, 12, 17, 30), which has the same "watchman" theme as 3:17–21. The repetition of that theme in both chapters 3 and 33 is not a result of redactional doubling. Rather, the original author has mortised together the very structure of the book far more tightly than most readers realize.

3:12 This is surely the same Spirit (רוּחַ) who stood Ezekiel on his feet in 2:2. Here Ezekiel does not just stand, but the Spirit lifts him up. Some commentators offer a "Spirit-wind" dual translation (cf. my commentary on 1:4, 12, 20–21). Ezekiel's sensation may have been that of a blowing wind, and that would fit in with the meteorological cast of the entire call vision, starting at 1:4. However, the Hebrew word here neither requires nor excludes that exegesis. In the subsequent verses, Ezekiel describes himself as going (3:14) and coming (3:15) and sitting (3:15), all of which seems to signal his emergence from a visionary state to the ordinary world of sensory experience. At the same time, the distinction cannot be pressed, because God's Spirit is certainly just as active in this physical world through his Word and Sacraments as he is active in the "spiritual" realm of prophetic visions (including also NT ones such as in Revelation).

Locomotion by the Spirit (called "the Spirit of Yahweh" in 11:5) occurs again in 8:3; 11:1, 24; 37:1; and 43:5, when again it is unclear whether or not these are purely visionary experiences. Usually, as here, רוּחַ is anarthrous, perhaps due to Ezekiel's reserve in describing supernatural matters (cf. his abundant use of "likeness" and "appearance" in chapter 1).

קוֹל רַעַשׁ גָּדוֹל—The noun רַעַשׁ is used more often in Ezekiel than in any other book. Most often it refers to an earthquake (e.g., Amos 1:1), but it can refer more generally to a roar or rumbling.

בָּרוּךְ כְּבוֹד־יְהוָה מִמְּקוֹמוֹ:—This clause is a major textual crux. I have translated it literally, as, in effect, do the ancient versions, without exception. Some modern translations do so as well (e.g., ESV, NIV, NASB). One commentator who follows the MT is Greenberg.[2] But other translations (e.g., RSV, NRSV) and many commentators emend בָּרוּךְ ("*blessed be …*") to בְּרוּם (Qal infinitive construct of רוּם with בְּ), "*when* the Glory of Yahweh *arose* from its place." The basis for the emendation, proposed already in the middle of the nineteenth century, is the similarity of a *mem* and a *kaph* in the archaic (paleo-Hebrew or "Phoenician") script. However, if so, the misreading by some copyist must have occurred at an extremely early date, since "blessed" is attested by the unanimity of the MT and ancient versions, and the adoption of the square Aramaic script must have been beginning already in Ezekiel's day. (Aramaic was the native language of the Neo-Babylonian or "Chaldean" Empire.) The result of the emendation would be that the divine Glory (כָּבוֹד) had stood still on the ground since 1:24, because that is when Ezekiel mentioned the great noise created when the living creatures (who supported the Glory) moved. Then, instead of a sudden doxology in 3:12, we would have a simple temporal clause, explaining when Ezekiel heard the noise.

If we follow the maxim that the more difficult reading is to be preferred, the traditional text ("blessed") wins hands down. The traditional text is harder—but by no

---

[2] Greenberg, *Ezekiel*, 1:70–71.

means impossible—to explain. It must be a spontaneous doxological salute to the departing כָּבוֹד. Elsewhere in the OT, many similar benedictions celebrate Yahweh's deeds or praise his name (e.g., Pss 41:14 [ET 41:13]; 72:18–19; 89:53 [89:52]; 106:48), even though no other doxology praises the divine Glory (כָּבוֹד).

The sense of the final word of the doxology (מִמְּקוֹמוֹ, "from its/his place") is unclear. מָקוֹם is the common generic Hebrew noun for a "place, location," although in some contexts it can refer to a "sacred site" (*HALOT*, 6), "holy place, sanctuary." (The Arabic cognate *maqam* usually has similar force.) That is apparently the logic of NIV's rendering, "his dwelling place." The idea then might be that just as the כָּבוֹד normally dwelt in Zion and was praised there ("blessed be Yahweh from Zion," Ps 135:21), so now he can be praised wherever he has localized himself "incarnationally" (cf. Ezek 1:26; 11:16).

It would stretch the Hebrew syntax to link the final word with the main clause: "I heard behind me a loud rumbling sound *from his place*, 'Blessed be the Glory of Yahweh' " (so Keil, who argues that it makes no difference whether the suffix ["his"] refers to Yahweh or to the Glory).[3] Less forced is the interpretation that the whole doxology, including "from his place," is a verbalization of the rumbling Ezekiel heard (so KJV, which inserts in italics "saying" before the doxology). The Syriac and Targum have similar connectives.

In sum, in spite of its manifold challenges, I follow the Hebrew text (supported by the ancient versions), which is thoroughly compatible with the tenor and theology of the rest of the book.

3:13 The Hiphil feminine plural participle מַשִּׁיקוֹת is not the participle of the common verb נָשַׁק, "to kiss," but of a rare homonym, whose Hiphil (occurring only here) means "to touch one another" (*HALOT*, s.v. נשק II) or perhaps "keep in line." The immense sound created by the moving wings was described by powerful similes in 1:24. The sound contributed by the wheels is apparently their rumbling at "takeoff." The wheels were described at great length in 1:15–21, but nothing was said there about their sound. The final phrase of 3:13 repeats the one in 3:12 that introduces what Ezekiel hears, thus forming an inclusion. The prophet apparently does not see the action (he hears it "behind" him, 3:12), but the sounds were familiar enough to him from the landing of the vehicle in the inaugural vision (chapter 1) that he could identify them.

3:14 וְרוּחַ נְשָׂאַתְנִי וַתִּקָּחֵנִי—The first two words essentially repeat the first two of 3:12, but in reverse order and with the perfect verb here. Here, the subject, רוּחַ, precedes both of the verbs of which it is the subject. The unusual order emphasizes the subject, *God's* "Spirit." Possibly this order helps distinguish this divine רוּחַ from רוּחַ later in the verse.

מַר בַּחֲמַת רוּחִי—In "bitter, in the fury of my spirit," רוּחַ here refers to Ezekiel's *human* spirit. When רוּחַ refers to the human psyche, it corresponds broadly to the anthropological usage of the English "spirit" (minus the secularistic, purely humanistic overtones often present in modern culture). Hebrew usage of anthropological רוּחַ

---

[3] Keil, *Ezekiel*, 1:56–57.

overlaps to some extent with לֵב ("heart") and נֶפֶשׁ ("self, soul"). "Mood/disposition" might also be a possible translation in this context.

The noun חֵמָה is common in Ezekiel, which has thirty-three out of one hundred twenty-five OT occurrences. Usually it refers to God's wrath at human sin, and often it is parallel to אַף.

וְיַד־יְהוָה עָלַי חָזָקָה:—The verb חָזָקָה is the pausal form of the Qal third feminine singular perfect of חָזַק. Literally, the clause is "the hand of Yahweh upon me was strong," but that seems almost platitudinous, and so it is probably better rendered as "the hand of Yahweh was strongly upon me" or "was heavy upon me." (Compare the adjective חָזָק, "strong," which was frequent in 3:7–9 and describes "hand" in 20:33–34.)

The connotations of this language seem harsh and forceful, which may explain Ezekiel's embittered spirit. This clause is unique in the OT, but there are many other passages that describe Yahweh (or people) acting with (usually בְּ) a "strong hand." The adjectival phrase in 20:33–34 describes how Yahweh will gather his scattered people with his "strong hand" and outstretched arm for the purpose of pouring out his wrath and judgment on them. Similar connotations of force and even violence attend the adjectival phrase in Ex 3:19; 6:1; 13:9; Num 20:20; and many others. Hence we may conclude that this clause emphasizes Ezekiel's prophetic compulsion to carry out his call with complete obedience.

The operation of Yahweh's "Spirit" upon Ezekiel earlier in the verse seems to have some close association with "the hand of Yahweh" that is upon him here. Both God's hand and his Spirit play prominent roles in Ezekiel in ways that are not easy to distinguish. While 3:13 states that the "Spirit" lifted him up, in 8:3 the Lord's "hand," as well as his "Spirit," plays a role in transporting Ezekiel too.

3:15 The verbosity and repetition of my translation literally reflects that of the MT. I follow the Kethib, אשר, to be vocalized אֲשֶׁר ("where"), rather than the marginal Qere אשב, to be vocalized with the vowels the Masoretes placed on the Kethib, yielding אֵשֵׁב, "I sat" (the same word indisputably appearing four words later). Even KJV, following the Qere, was forced to be a little free: "I sat where they sat, and remained there … seven days." The Qere reading can be defended only by another appeal (as in 3:12) to the ancient "Phoenician" script, where the forms *resh* and *bet* are fairly similar.

Most scholars assume the MT to have conflated two readings: (1) "who were living by the Kebar Canal" and (2) "where they were living." But (naturally!) there is no agreement on which of the two was original. Most commentators, partially appealing to the Syriac version (the only significant departure from MT in antiquity), retain the second (Zimmerli, Greenberg, Allen[4]), while some translations (RSV, NRSV) prefer the first. The more conservative translations (e.g., NIV) basically retain the MT, as also does Block in his commentary.[5] There I also have cast my lot.

---

4 Zimmerli, *Ezekiel*, 1:95; Greenberg, *Ezekiel*, 1:71; Allen, *Ezekiel*, 1:4, 13.

5 Block, *Ezekiel*, 1:132.

As the text stands, "Tel Abib" is an adverbial accusative (without either directive ה‎- or preposition). A more phonetic transcription would yield Tel Aviv ("v" for aspirated *bet*, without *daghesh*), but "Tel Abib" is traditionally retained in this context to distinguish it from the modern Israeli metropolis. The original Akkadian was *til abūbi*, "mound of the flood," that is, a long abandoned tell believed to be the site of a city destroyed by the primeval flood. (The best known Mesopotamian "parallel" to the biblical account of the flood is tablet 11 of the Gilgamesh epic.) Various ancient Akkadian texts indicate that the name almost became generic, even of cities destroyed in contemporary wars. Whatever its real antiquity, on one of those vacant mounds the Judahite exiles had been settled (a pattern of occupation still common today—usually to the dismay of archaeologists). Since both elements of the Akkadian name have Hebrew cognates, it is not unlikely that already the exiles gave it the ordinary Hebrew meaning of "mound of spring grain/fruit."

This verse raises questions about the relation between the mound and the Kebar Canal, especially in light of 1:3, which states that Ezekiel's vision and call came to him while he was at the canal. If 1:3 is understood as a general statement of the area where the exiles lived, the difficulties vanish. The text requires neither that the exiles lived precisely on the banks of the canal, nor that the prophet's vision and commission occurred precisely there. All that can be asserted with any certainty is that he was somewhere alone outside the settlement at the time of his call and now returns to the settlement to exercise his ministry. (Compare also the question of the location of the "valley plain" in 3:22–23.)

מַשְׁמִים בְּתוֹכָם‎:—Describing Ezekiel's state of mind upon his return is the Hiphil masculine singular participle of שָׁמֵם‎, which in Qal means "to be devastated" or "appalled." (Qal and Poel participles of the verb denote the "abomination of desolation [causing the destruction of the temple]" in Dan 9:27; 11:31; 12:11.) Hiphils are usually transitive, and that is theoretically possible here too: Ezekiel may have been "causing onlookers to be awe-struck, dumbfounded, disconcerted" (cf. *HALOT*, Hiphil, 2, citing also 1 Sam 5:6). But much more likely in this context is that the Hiphil is intransitive, as also in Job 21:5. For these two verses BDB (Hiphil, 2 b) gives "shewing horror," that is, "horrified," but "devastated" preserves a connection to the more common meaning of the verb. Other possible translations are "disconcerted, disoriented, distressed, stunned, disturbed, overwhelmed, in shock." A similar scene (with somewhat different vocabulary) is described by Jeremiah (15:17).

3:16 At this point an isagogical excursus is necessary. The long space in the middle of 3:16, indicated by פ‎ (see the textual notes on 2:1), indicates the beginning of a new paragraph (or pericope) at 3:16b. Normally a new paragraph begins at the start of a verse, rather than in its middle. However, scores of times in the OT a division marker appears in the middle of a verse. There is no consensus about why division markers sometimes appear in mid-verse, but many seem persuaded (as are Greenberg and I) by Talmon's suggestion that "the break often occurs where supplementary information—from elsewhere in the Bible (e.g., parallel texts) or from extrabiblical writings … is available on the event in question."[6] The parallel to 3:16–21 would be 33:1–9.

---

[6] Greenberg, *Ezekiel*, 1:83, citing S. Talmon, "Pisqa Beʿemṣa Pasuq and 11 Q Psᵃ," *Textus* 5 (1966): 11–21.

Ezek 3:17–19 is an almost verbatim counterpart to 33:7–9. Inevitably, the parallelism triggers all sorts of critical speculation about the use of "doublets" in the editorial history of the book. Most commonly 3:16b–21 is taken as a secondary insertion, perhaps to enhance the prophet's authority, or perhaps to form a sort of "inclusion" bracketing his judgment oracles (chapters 4–32). From a purely literary standpoint, a certain intrusiveness of 3:16b–21 is undeniable. Without it, the narrative would flow smoothly from 3:16a to 3:22. We have two introductory phrases in 3:16: first a time notice (continuing 3:15) and second is a word-event formula, which is very common in Ezekiel ("the Word of Yahweh came (to me)"; see further below).

However, there is no compelling reason on literary or historical grounds why we need be so critical of the received text. Repetition is a hallmark of Ezekiel's style. And for all the verbal contacts between 3:16b–21 and 33:1–9, the differences should not be minimized. The text before us is clearly a private message for the prophet alone, while 33:1–9 is to be proclaimed to the people. The contexts are different too. Here the concern is that the message of judgment is conveyed unambiguously, whereas in chapter 33, after the dreaded message had come that Jerusalem had fallen (33:21), emphasis is placed on the possibility of repentance. If the present passage is seen as an integral part of Ezekiel's commissioning (initially to be a prophet primarily of judgment), chapter 33 emerges as his virtual recommissioning as a prophet of salvation. Finally, one may note that it is characteristic of Ezekiel's style to rework earlier oracles in later, different situations, usually in expanded form. In that light it is thoroughly plausible to view 33:1–9 as a reworking of 3:16–21.

"The Word of Yahweh came (to me)" (3:16b) may be called the word-event formula because "there lies in the mention of the coming of Yahweh's word a reference to its eminently historical character and its relation to events."[7] The advent of the divine Word causes events to take place, as is supremely true in the advent of Jesus Christ, the Word made flesh. The word-event formula comes close to being Ezekiel's trademark since it occurs fifty times in Ezekiel, in contrast to twenty-four occurrences in Jeremiah and some in the postexilic prophets Haggai (five times) and Zechariah (nine). It does occur fairly frequently in the much earlier prophetic narratives in monarchical times (Samuel, Kings, Chronicles), and so its frequency in Ezekiel and later may represent a sort of archaizing trend.

Here the verse begins with וַיְהִי and then after the division marker (פ) there is another וַיְהִי that resumes the narrative. The same sequence as here (וַיְהִי ... וַיְהִי, with the second having a resumptive meaning) occurs also in Ex 19:16; Judg 19:1; 2 Sam 7:4 (‖ 1 Chr 17:3); 1 Ki 13:20; Jer 42:7; and Ruth 1:1 (in 1 Ki 13:20 the verbs are separated by a division marker as here). Especially similar to Ezek 3:16 are 2 Sam 7:4 (‖ 1 Chr 17:3); 1 Ki 13:20; and Jer 42:7 in that they all use the word-event formula, with "the Word of Yahweh" coming to a prophet.

"Came to" translates the idiomatic הָיָה אֶל. See BDB, s.v. הָיָה, Qal, II 1 b.

---

[7]   Zimmerli, *Ezekiel*, 1:145. See the discussion on 1:24–26, 144–45.

3:17 Attention must be given to literary structure throughout the following section (3:17–21). Typical legal constructions commence in 3:18, where further analysis will be necessary.

In this initial verse, God declares that he has "appointed" the prophet to be a watchman. The verb נָתַן in its sense of formal, and especially divine action, is often interchangeable with the more general שִׂים or הֵקִים.

The literary pivot of the section is צֹפֶה, the Qal participle of צָפָה, "to keep watch, look out," hence meaning a "watchman, sentry, lookout," such as would be stationed on the city wall to alert the city in the face of danger or attack. The entire pericope is an extended metaphor of the prophet viewed through that lens. It is a sort of a formal induction into the prophet's ministry, underscoring his accountability—both to the God who appointed him and to the people he is called to warn. One could almost style his role as "liturgical" (always implying a certain formality), considering the unity of the whole "Torah" (OT revelation), and avoiding later, retrospective divisions of duties into "religious," "ceremonial," and "political" categories. Just how much judicial authority OT priests actually had is not totally clear, though the Torah assigned them responsibility to adjudicate certain legal/moral/religious cases such as uncleanness (e.g., Leviticus 13–14), adultery (Num 5:11–31), and bloodshed (Deut 17:8–9). In any event, Ezekiel, a priest-prophet (Ezek 1:3) in exile, was in a class by himself.

The following two perfect *waw* consecutives (וְהִזְהַרְתָּ ... וְשָׁמַעְתָּ, "hear ... warn") are part of hypothetical statements. The added "when" and "must" in my translation are technically interpretive but clearly required by the context: "*When* you hear a word from my mouth, you *must* give them warning against me." "Word" translates דָּבָר, but as is clear from the next verse, it implies a verdict or decree of doom. The nuance evident here is often present in the phrase "the Word of Yahweh," especially in the earlier half of Ezekiel. God is the ultimate Judge, and when his messenger, the prophet, hears his verdict, he is obligated to relay it to those who stand under judgment.

וְהִזְהַרְתָּ—The Hiphil of זָהַר, meaning "to warn about" (*HALOT*, s.v. זהר II), is found with מִן only here in 3:17–18 and in the parallel 33:7–8. The preposition could be translated "from." However, the use of the same verb in the next verse, where the meaning is clearly to warn the "wicked man" against the consequences of his behavior, suggests that here too the meaning is to warn sinners "against" Yahweh, who is the righteous Judge, and hence is the "enemy" who threatens disaster for the sinner. The concept of God as the enemy of sinners is not novel, but is implicit in many of the complaint psalms too.[8]

3:18–21 This series of four verses is couched in the typical legal language of the Torah. Especially with his priestly training, Ezekiel would be thoroughly familiar with its idioms, which appear frequently in the book. Four hypothetical cases of various responses to prophetic warnings are given, each with its consequences. The form is that of casuistic or case law: "If/in the case that ... then ..." Typically in the Torah

---

8   Cf. Ingvar Fløysvik, *When God Becomes My Enemy: The Theology of the Complaint Psalms* (St. Louis: Concordia, 1997).

and also in extrabiblical examples,[9] the cases are framed in the singular ("if a man …"), not in plural or the collective (as NRSV wrongly translates for the sake of "inclusive" language!). The cases are applicable to each individual member of the whole people. The corporate nature of the people is presupposed too, because individual transgressions do damage to the whole congregation, the collective "the house of Israel" (3:17).

The conceptuality is judicial throughout: culpability, accountability, and the verdict of life or death. We know little of actual judicial practice in ancient Israel (and it undoubtedly changed over time, especially under the monarchy), but, as far as we know, the actual verdicts of ultimate matters such as life and death, being ultimately God's, were communicated through the prophets (e.g., Nathan to David [2 Samuel 12], Isaiah to Hezekiah [2 Kings 19–20], Jeremiah to Zedekiah [Jeremiah 21]), using the priestly idiom. Here clearly Ezekiel is a priest-prophet (Ezek 1:3).

Exactly how the judicial verdict "You shall surely die" (3:18) was normally carried out is not clear. Did it refer to capital punishment or to some untimely death in circumstances caused by God alone? Similar uncertainty attaches to comparable expressions in the Torah, such as the offender being "cut off" from Israel (e.g., Ex 12:15; Lev 7:20–21), perhaps referring to something like excommunication.[10] See further the commentary below.

Critical scholars have misinterpreted the accent on the individual in Jeremiah and Ezekiel. They allege that Jeremiah (Ezekiel's older contemporary) pioneered the real breakthrough in "liberating" religion from its earlier corporate, cultic, and group expressions and developing it into a matter of "inwardness," of a "personal relationship with God" instead of intellectual assent to doctrinal propositions. Jeremiah supposedly had inculcated a "religion of the heart" and advocated the dispensability of external worship forms, such as temple, liturgy, and "sacraments," with an almost solipsistic accountability to God alone.

Ezekiel is an invaluable corrective to such a misguided reading of Jeremiah. If anything, the accent on the individual is more prominent in Ezekiel than in Jeremiah. Not only is it prominent here in 3:16–21 and its parallel in 33:1–9, but chapter 18 is devoted almost exclusively to the topic of individual accountability to God. But the reverse is true as well: Jeremiah also prevents the typical Protestant/liberal denigration of Ezekiel (unless one erects his own "canon within the canon," preventing Scripture from interpreting Scripture). As reconstructed by critics, Ezekiel is the beginning of a fatal compromise, a relapse into priestly institutionalism and legalism, from which Jesus would once again rescue us. But that critical view misunderstands the proper, biblical balance between collective and individual accountability. Above all, it denigrates the worth of corporate, liturgical, and sacramental worship forms, as well as

---

9 Cf. *ANET*, 159–98; 523–28.

10 Kleinig, *Leviticus*, 163, explains that the passive construction implies that God carries out this penalty of cutting off, or excommunicating, the offender from his people and that the penalty also has an "eschatological dimension, suggesting that even if the offender escapes obvious punishment in this life, he would be separated from God's people in the afterlife."

the divinely instituted OT offices of priest and prophet and the NT office of pastor, through which God lavishes his grace upon his people.

As noted above, the simultaneously individual and collective concern of case-law formulations harks back to ancient Near Eastern tradition, long before the main biblical period. In the upheavals of the exile—when religious, political, and societal institutions crumbled and it was largely "every man for himself"—Ezekiel almost inevitably places somewhat greater accent on individual responsibility and accountability. But the idea popularized by critical scholars that the institutional church, its clergy, and its rites (to use modern terminology) were dispensable and even harmful to true piety was as unthinkable to Ezekiel as it is to the biblical and churchly tradition as a whole. The critical perspective has been fostered by pietism and Protestantism (both "evangelical" and liberal) and is abetted today by the radical individualism of secular culture (deconstructionism, postmodernism). In the face of that, the church catholic must struggle mightily to regain and retain the simultaneously priestly and prophetic perspective of Ezekiel.

3:18 לָרָשָׁע—This initial "wicked man" has a definite article; the second does not. English idiom requires just the reverse. The initial article indicates a type, class, or category of person.

וְלֹא הִזְהַרְתּוֹ וְלֹא …—The repeated וְ ("and") here is essentially synonymous with כִּי ("if") in 3:19 and 3:21. The following verbs function as the protasis of a conditional sentence. Typical again of priestly legislation is the use of the perfect verb (הִזְהַרְתּוֹ, Hiphil second masculine singular with third masculine singular suffix) to set up a hypothetical case in which an event has already occurred (Ezekiel has failed to warn the wicked man), and the following imperfect verbs (יָמוּת and אֲבַקֵּשׁ) describe what the consequences would then be.

לְחַיֹּתוֹ—The Piel of חָיָה has a causative meaning compared to the Qal, "to live," and can mean "to cause to live, to make someone live," or even "bring back to life, resurrect." The translation is fraught with theological interpretation. The result of this Piel, "to make him live," is the same as described in 3:21 with the Qal (חָיֹה יִחְיֶה), "he shall surely live." Compare the different phraseology translated "saved your life" in 3:19, 21. The prophet's preaching aims to bring the person to repentance and life with God through faith; in that way the preached Word would "make him live," not just temporally and spiritually, but also everlastingly after the resurrection (e.g., Dan 12:2–3).

הוּא רָשָׁע בַּעֲוֺנוֹ יָמוּת—The syntax is puzzling (so also in 33:8). הוּא רָשָׁע could be an Aramaism meaning "that wicked man." More likely it means, literally, "he, [being] a wicked man."

Ezekiel often uses the preposition בְּ with the noun עָוֹן, "iniquity." The preposition has a causal meaning, "on account of … because of" his iniquity (BDB, s.v. בְּ, III 5; cf. *HALOT*, 19). The combination occurs in 3:18–19; 4:17; 7:13, 16; 18:17–20; 24:23; 33:6, 8, 9; 39:23. Similar is בְּ with חַטָּאת, "because of his/your sin(s)," in 3:20; 16:52; 18:24. "The wages of sin is death" (Rom 6:23). See the causal clause describing the opposite situation in Ezek 3:21, where a man repents and lives "because [כִּי] he heeded the warning."

Alternatively, עָוֹן could have the nuance of "*judgment* for iniquity," in which case בְּ would have a locative meaning: to perish "in" the divine judgment.

וְדָמוֹ מִיָּדְךָ אֲבַקֵּשׁ:—"I will seek his blood from your hand" means "I will hold you responsible for his death." The nuance of the Piʿel בִּקֵּשׁ is "to demand, to require" (*HALOT*, 3). By a common synecdoche, the "blood" (דָּם) of the wicked man who dies represents his death. Compare Lev 17:11 on atonement by sacrifice: "The life of the flesh is in the blood."

3:19 וְאַתָּה֙ כִּי־הִזְהַרְתָּ רָשָׁע—The pronoun אַתָּה, "you," is emphatic, both by its position at the beginning of the sentence and by its redundancy, since the conjugated verb by itself means "you warn." This is no mere abstract enumeration of case law, but a forceful, personal address and admonition to the prophet ("you"). The same structure recurs at the beginning of 3:21.

וְלֹא־שָׁב֙ מֵרִשְׁעוֹ֙ וּמִדַּרְכּוֹ הָרְשָׁעָה—The verb שׁוּב with the preposition מִן (repeated here) is a common, idiomatic way of saying "repent from" (though the combination has the opposite meaning in 3:20). The usual English idiom is "repent *of* (sin, etc.)." *HALOT* explains the verb "in a theological sense: to turn back to God (Yahweh) be devoted to God … be converted" (s.v. שׁוּב, Qal, 2 and 2 a). BDB gives "of spiritual relations … *turn back* to God (= seek penitently) … *repent*" (Qal, 6, 6 c, and 6 d). Repentance is a return to God and the life of faith, thereby turning away from the alternative into which one has fallen. God's verdict of death for the wicked man (3:18) drives the person to realize that he is on the way to temporal death and eternal perdition in Sheol/hell if he does not repent.

Sometimes a contrast is attempted between this Hebrew idiom and the Greek μετανοέω, "repent" (literalistically, "change one's mind"), as though the NT concept were more intellectual than the allegedly more holistic OT view. But that distinction is fallacious; it builds too much on etymology in contrast to usage, which fails to sustain such a distinction.

Some interpreters see a subtle distinction between "of his wickedness" (מֵרִשְׁעוֹ) as his being or orientation and "of his wicked way" (מִדַּרְכּוֹ הָרְשָׁעָה) as his resultant discrete acts, but Hebrew does not typically make such distinctions. Many critics excise the second phrase because of its absence in the parallel 33:8, but that is scarcely determinative. Possibly the two expressions represent a structural parallel with the first two clauses of the next verse. In both verses, the two virtually synonymous phrases reinforce one another. "Wickedness" here translates a masculine noun רֶשַׁע (there is also a synonymous feminine noun). In the next verse, we meet the masculine צֶדֶק ("righteousness"), probably in symmetry. See the textual note on it there.

Like ὁδός in the NT, דֶּרֶךְ may be used concretely of a "way," that is, a street or road, or more figuratively of a "way of life," that is, a mode or pattern of behavior. The figurative meaning is common in both Testaments, and "those belonging to the Way [ὁδός]" (Acts 9:2) was the first name of those later dubbed "Christians" at Antioch (Acts 11:26).

וְאַתָּה אֶת־נַפְשְׁךָ הִצַּלְתָּ:—The redundant pronoun אַתָּה again emphasizes "you yourself," as also when the entire clause is repeated at the end of 3:21.

English idiom requires a future perfect translation here: "you yourself *will have saved* your life." The Hebrew verbal system has no such "tense" and so must use the simple perfect. The Hiphil of נָצַל is a virtual synonym of the Hiphil of יָשַׁע, which is part of the name "Jesus."[11] Both verbs are commonly translated "to save," although "to rescue" or "to deliver" is also possible.

The object, נֶפֶשׁ, defies accurate translation. The KJV rendered it "thou hast delivered thy *soul.*" While "saving souls" (a modern idiom) may be part of the implication here, such a translation does not reproduce the force of the Hebrew, which does not dichotomize "body" and "soul," as became common in the West. To summarize, נֶפֶשׁ is what distinguishes a corpse from a living person. Hence it pertains to the mystery of life itself—not mere biological life, but God-given life in all its fullness, including what is unique to each individual life. Hence, "life" is the usual modern translation here. In this context it is functionally parallel to the Piel of חָיָה in 3:18, "to make him [a wicked man] live" by calling him to repentance and everlasting life through faith.

3:20 The sentence structure in 3:20, which is the third of the four cases in 3:18–21, is easily the most complicated. Yet it is not untypical of the casuistic tradition and of Ezekiel's style in general. Perhaps the more complicated syntax of 3:20 is intended to correspond to the most disturbing of the four situations in 3:18–21, namely, when a righteous person apostatizes (see the commentary). In the first sentence of 3:20, three conditional protases ("when a righteous man apostatizes … does unrighteousness … I place a stumbling block") precede the apodosis ("he shall die"). Then in the second sentence of 3:20, the prophet's dereliction is considered, as well as three consequences of it.

וּבְשׁוּב צַדִּיק מִצִּדְקוֹ—In contrast to 3:19, where it meant "repent of," here the combination of the verb שׁוּב and preposition מִן (on מִצִּדְקוֹ) means "to turn away from, abandon" (*HALOT*, Qal, 3) "his righteousness," that is, to "apostatize" (BDB, 6 a). In both cases I have translated with precise theological language instead of "turn/return." There is a "returning" in both cases, but two different starting points. (In other conjugations of the verb and in cognate nouns, the two contrasting meanings also appear.)

"Righteousness" (see the commentary) here translates the masculine noun צֶדֶק, which Ezekiel uses only here and in 45:10. This verse also uses the feminine synonym צְדָקָה, which is most common in chapters 18 and 33. The immediate reason for the masculine here may be to obtain symmetry with the corresponding masculine noun רֶשַׁע ("wickedness") in 3:19 (see the textual note there). As often in Hebrew, both masculine and feminine forms of a noun exist without discernible difference in meaning.

וְעָשָׂה עָוֶל ... בְּחַטָּאתוֹ יָמוּת—Two words for "sin" are new in Ezekiel. Instead of עָוֹן as in 3:18–19, here we first meet עָוֶל, "unrighteousness" (BDB, under the root עול III). (*HALOT* [1 a], which often avoids theological meanings, gives "perversity, injustice.") Hence it is a direct antonym to צֶדֶק, "righteousness." Ezekiel will use עָוֶל again in the similar passages 18:8, 24, 26; 33:13, 15, 18 (as well as 28:18). Because

---

[11] One may see the explanation of the name "Joshua/Jesus" in "The Man Joshua" in the introduction of Harstad, *Joshua*, 12–13.

it is less frequent, it is not usually reckoned among the major Hebrew words for sin, but it might as well be.

The much more common noun חַטָּאת is almost universally translated as "sin" (or, especially in Leviticus, "sin offering"). The clause בְּחַטָּאתוֹ יָמוּת ("he shall die because of his sin," with causal בְּ) is parallel to בַּעֲוֹנוֹ יָמוּת ("he shall die because of his iniquity") twice in 3:18–19. Given the parallel clauses, one should not strain to distinguish a significant difference in the meaning Ezekiel intends here for the nouns rendered "iniquity" and "sin," nor between either of them and "unrighteousness."

וְנָתַתִּי מִכְשׁוֹל לְפָנָיו—This third protasis causes the most problems because it describes something not done overtly by the backslider, but by God himself: "and I place a stumbling block in front of him."

The verb כָּשַׁל means to "*stumble* at, over, something" (BDB, Qal, 1), or, more metaphorically, "*bring injury* or *ruin ... cause overthrow*" (BDB, Hiphil, 1 a, b). The noun מִכְשׁוֹל is usually translated "stumbling-block" (BDB), meaning "something on which someone stumbles, **hindrance, offence** ... on which someone trips" (*HALOT*). In Lev 19:14 the Israelite is forbidden to "put a stumbling block in front of a blind man," and that is the only other verse where we have the same phrase as here (מִכְשׁוֹל and לְפָנֵי). This noun is especially characteristic of Ezekiel's vocabulary: eight of the fourteen OT occurrences are in Ezekiel. Six are in the phrase מִכְשׁוֹל עָוֹן ("stumbling block of iniquity," 7:19; 14:3, 4, 7; 18:30; 44:12). The noun is in the absolute state in 3:20 and 21:20. In all these cases, it describes something placed in the sinner's way, forcing him to make a decision—either to heed the final warning and repent before he dies or to allow the evil that has been germinating within him to come to open expression and lead him into the abyss.

Here in 3:20, it is clear that *God's intent is to save the apostate through the prophet's ministry, but the apostate spurns God's prophetic Word.* He plunges headlong toward his doom, heedless of the warning. Hence the "stumbling block" is tantamount to a death sentence. It is the same as in 3:18, where God says, "When I announce to a wicked man, 'You shall surely die' ..." But there is no determinism: God neither wanted nor caused the apostate man's impenitence and damnation. It did not have to be so.

In 33:12 we have an instance of a positive outcome. (That verse uses the verb כָּשַׁל instead of the noun as here.)

Here, Ezekiel is enjoined to warn the apostate, but the prophet defaults. In the first sentence of 3:20, why is the prophet's failure to warn not mentioned before the wicked man's death? (It was in 3:18.) Apparently, part of the reason is the parallelism between 3:18–19 and 3:20–21. In both pairs of verses, the first instance (3:18 and 3:20) is an example of the prophet's malfeasance, and the second (3:19 and 3:21) is one of his faithfulness. However, the circumstances in 3:20 are materially different than in 3:18. In 3:18 the prophetic warning is announced by God right at the start, because the man is already wicked. In contrast, 3:20 begins with a man who is righteous, but then apostatizes; the process is parceled out in stages, in any one of which the prophet's warning might have arrested the ultimately fatal defection (see the commentary below).

וְלֹא תִזָּכַרְןָ צִדְקֹתָו—The Kethib is צִדְקָתוֹ, "his righteousness," while the Qere is צִדְקֹתָיו, "his righteous deeds," which agrees with the plural verb (third feminine plural Niphal imperfect of זָכַר). The same Kethib-Qere variation is in 33:13. The variation reflects the history of Hebrew orthography. The Kethib reflects an older, "defective" spelling, while the Qere attests the later *plene* form. As often in Hebrew, a word may have both abstract and concrete meanings. In this context, the singular would be abstract ("righteousness"), although theoretically it could refer to a concrete righteous deed. Similarly, the plural here probably is concrete, but the abstract is not impossible. (When Yahweh is the one doing צְדָקוֹת, it is often translated as his *saving* deeds," that is, the deeds he has performed according to his own promises of imputing righteousness and accomplishing salvation for his people.)

3:21 My literal translation reflects the verbosity of the text, which is characteristic of Ezekiel's style. After the third masculine singular suffix ("him") on הִזְהַרְתּוֹ, the noun צַדִּיק ("a righteous man") is not necessary. Or the suffix could have been omitted from the verb, as in the parallel clause beginning 3:19, which has just רָשָׁע.

לְבִלְתִּי חֲטֹא צַדִּיק—This second צַדִּיק in the verse is equally redundant. The sense is that the prophet warns him "not to sin, [since the man is] a righteous man." The warning is for the righteous man not to fall into sin. The LXX associates this second צַדִּיק with "shall certainly live," which suggests a different textual history, but the sense is ultimately unaffected.

חָיוֹ יִחְיֶה—"He shall surely live" uses the Qal of חָיָה, which has a stative meaning, compared to the causative Piel in 3:18. The form of the Qal infinitive absolute here is חָיוֹ instead of the "normal" חָיֹה.

כִּי נִזְהָר—The Niphal (third masculine singular perfect in pause) of זָהַר here means "to heed a warning" (*HALOT*, s.v. זהר II, Niphal, 1) rather than the simple passive, "to be warned" (*HALOT*, 2). This same form with the same meaning recurs in 33:4–6. Sometimes the Niphal has a "tolerative" meaning, which here would be "he tolerated/let himself be warned." Compare the textual note on the Hiphil in 3:17.

3:22 Here we rejoin the main narrative after the digressive "watchman" admonitions of 3:16b–21. The phraseology of Yahweh's "hand" being upon Ezekiel "there" resembles that in 1:3. More recently, Yahweh's "hand" rested heavily upon Ezekiel in 3:14. It will appear again in 8:1; 37:1; and 40:1. In the other instances, some action ensues, but here divine speech follows. The "hand" comes close to being a hypostasis of God, a precursor of his incarnation in Jesus Christ, and an anthropomorphism of God's power that gives urgency to the situation. In 8:3 the Spirit (who will appear in 3:24) transports Ezekiel to Jerusalem, and in 37:1 apparently to the same place as here. But in 3:22, Ezekiel is apparently to make his own way, as he also does shortly in 3:24b after he is told to go home.

Here in 3:22, he is commanded to leave his home in Tel Abib (3:15) and go outside the settlement to the בִּקְעָה, one of various Hebrew words for "valley," often used of a broad alluvial plain between the hills or bluffs lining a river, as, for example, of the Ghor of the Jordan. It might be translated "plain," but if it were on a highland plateau, Hebrew would ordinarily use מִישׁוֹר (e.g., Is 40:4). Hence, I have used the compound expression, "valley plain." A transliteration of בִּקְעָה survives in modern geography as the *Bekáa* Valley between the Lebanon and Anti-Lebanon Mountains, between Beirut and Damascus (geologically, a northward extension of the Jordan Valley to the south). Here it refers to the wide plain of the lower Euphrates, which, away from the canals and irrigation, was wasteland. As an isolated, uninhabited spot, it was especially suitable for a private divine vision. Apparently, it is the same place where Ezekiel returns for the famous vision of the dry bones in chapter 37 (see 37:1–2). We do not know enough of the geography even to speculate on its distance from Tel Abib, which was located near the Kebar Canal (3:15).

3:23 וְהִנֵּה־שָׁם כְּבוֹד־יְהוָה—Here הִנֵּה signals an element of surprise or astonishment. It is unclear whether "the Glory of Yahweh" refers to the divine figure alone ("the Glory of Yahweh" in 1:28; see the textual notes there) or whether it refers to the entire scene of chapter 1—the creatures bearing the throne-chariot with the enthroned human figure above. In 8:4 Ezekiel explains that "the Glory of the God of Israel" is the same as "the vision that I had seen on the valley plain," and that, as well as other language used in 43:2, indicates that here in 3:23 Ezekiel is referring to the entire scene he had described in chapter 1. Since those two reappearances of the Glory in chapters 8 and 43 are comprehensive in their reference, it would seem likely that the same is true here too.

The concluding clause of 3:23 is repeated verbatim from 1:28.

3:24a וַתָּבֹא־בִי רוּחַ וַתַּעֲמִדֵנִי עַל־רַגְלָי—This is verbatim the same as in 2:2 except for an additional phrase there (see the textual notes there). In 3:23 Ezekiel saw the Glory "standing" (עֹמֵד, Qal participle), and here the Hiphil of the same verb (וַתַּעֲמִדֵנִי) refers to the vertical position the Spirit is able to effect on the prophet. He is to "stand at attention" as his first real "marching orders" are to commence.

וַיְדַבֵּר אֹתִי וַיֹּאמֶר—Since רוּחַ ("Spirit") is feminine, and these verbs of speaking are masculine, we must understand Yahweh or his Glory to be the subject of the verbs.

3:24b–27 Since no time notice is given, apparently the commands in 3:24b–27 were given more or less immediately after the previous instructions in 3:16b–21. Some have hypothesized a long interval of time in between, perhaps including an abortive ministry and a self-imposed confinement after that, but there is no hint of anything of that sort in the text.

Yahweh addresses Ezekiel abruptly in 3:24b, not even prefacing his speech with the usual "son of man" (it does not appear until 3:25). The speech has three parts: (1) the order to go home and confine himself to his house (3:24b); (2) that cords or ropes will tie him up (3:25); and (3) that he will be made dumb or at least speechless (3:26). The words themselves are clear enough, but they cry out for interpretation.

Zimmerli labels 3:24b–27 "one of the most difficult passages in the whole book."[12] Exegetically, that is only a slight overstatement. The major questions have to do with (1) whether some or all these commands are to be taken literally or figuratively and (2) whether these verses are to be taken as a conclusion of the entire call and commissioning episode (chapters 1–3) or as the beginning of the series of sign

---

[12] Zimmerli, *Ezekiel*, 1:158.

actions (partially involving Ezekiel's very person; cf. אוֹת in 4:3 and מוֹפֵת in 24:24) that will dominate chapters 4–5.

הִסָּגֵר בְּתוֹךְ בֵּיתֶךָ:—"Shut yourself up" translates the Niphal masculine singular imperative of the common verb סָגַר. A Niphal can be either passive or reflexive (middle) in meaning; the context here calls for the latter.

3:25 וְאַתָּה בֶן־אָדָם—The reason for the delay of the "son of man" address (expected in 3:24b, but delayed until the start of 3:25) emerges in this verse: to signal the shift in focus from the prophet as subject to object. Perhaps it also interjects a note of sympathy for him as well.[13]

נָתְנוּ עָלֶיךָ עֲבוֹתִים וַאֲסָרוּךָ בָּהֶם—The combination of the first verb (נָתַן) and noun (plural of עֲבֹת) will recur in 4:8 with the same meaning.

Two questions arise about the two verbs in "they have placed [נָתְנוּ] upon you ropes, and they have tied you up [וַאֲסָרוּךָ] with them." First, why are they perfects when all the surrounding verbs are imperfects? I am of the persuasion that they are a species of what we often call "prophetic perfects": the future is foreseen so vividly that it is described as already past and completed, as, for example, in Is 60:1. Here we do not exactly have predictive prophecy, but something close—something already as good as done, but with an eye primarily toward future application. Some translators simply render them with a future tense translation, as I was tempted to do. (Even KJV is not consistent in what English tense it uses to translate prophetic perfects.)

Second, who are the subjects of these plural verbs? Translating them as passive would eliminate the need to identify the actors, but that would clash with the following active verbs. Already the LXX and Vulgate translated the first verb as passive; NIV translates the second as passive; and RSV and ESV render both in the passive (ESV: "cords will be placed upon you, and you shall be bound with them"). The passives clash with the plural suffix at the end of the verse ("among *them*"), and so NIV, RSV, and ESV paraphrase that last phrase as "among the people." That may ultimately be correct, but an inordinate amount of de facto emendation has taken place.

So who are the subjects of the action? At first blush, the most natural assumption would seem to be the Israelites in exile, who show their hostility toward Ezekiel by tying him up. Such behavior would accord with that given Jeremiah, who is beaten and put in the stocks by the priest Pashhur (chapter 20), nearly lynched by a mob enraged by his prophecies of the fall of Jerusalem (chapter 26), and so on. But the book of Ezekiel simply does not evidence any similar violent abuse of Ezekiel. As Block points out:

> On the contrary, they seek him out; and in less serious moments they treat him as a curiosity, an entertainer (33:30–33). Indeed, public apathy toward his message seems to have been a more serious problem than malevolence toward his person.[14]

If not his audience, then who? The textual apparatus of *BHS* proposes emending the verbs to the first person, making God ("I") the subject. While theologically there

---

[13] Allen, *Ezekiel*, 1:61.

[14] Block, *Ezekiel*, 1:155.

surely is some truth there, not an iota of textual support exists for that change. Keil follows the Hebrew text but explains the plurals by appealing to "heavenly powers" who bind Ezekiel, not with material cords, but by a spiritual power, so that the expression is not to be taken literally.[15] No conservative would argue that Keil's explanation is impossible, but it certainly goes far beyond what can be demonstrated by this passage or the larger context.

In my judgment, Keil is half right—right in arguing for a non-literal reading of the verse. Evidence has been adduced above for a relationship between Ezekiel and the people that does not involve physical violence, but does involve spiritual and emotional hostility. Hence the people are the subjects, but their action is metaphorical. I judge Greenberg's solution to be perhaps the best: "The public repulsion toward you is so great, it has as good as driven you off the streets and confined you to your quarters."[16] I would add only that, while God announces this as fact, God's Word is tantamount to a prediction, which may account for the prophetic perfects. The people will do God's will without being aware of whom they serve. See the similar situation with Caiaphas' unwitting prophecy about Christ in Jn 11:49–51.

In 4:8 God will again refer to this binding of Ezekiel with ropes, but there God will declare himself to be the subject: "I have placed upon you ropes." God is the author of the people's actions in 3:25.

3:26 וּלְשֹׁונְךָ֙ אַדְבִּ֣יק אֶל־חִכֶּ֔ךָ—Here God describes himself as acting directly, rather than working through human instruments (as in 3:25). "*I will make* your tongue *stick* … " translates the Hiphil of דָּבַק. Older translations used "cleave," as does KJV for the Qal in Gen 2:24. More recent translations use "cling" (ESV) or "stick" (NIV), which I prefer. חֵךְ could be translated "palate," but "roof of mouth" is more common in everyday speech.

וְנֶאֱלַ֖מְתָּ—The major debates in this verse (and later in the book) turn on this verb, which refers to Ezekiel again (in different forms) in 24:27 and 33:22. In the OT אָלַם is almost always in the Niphal and with a meaning that is deponent (intransitive), not passive. Traditionally, it was taken to mean "*be dumb*, i.e. silent … unable to speak" (BDB, 1). To prevent the misunderstanding that it implies stupidity, modern parlance is to use "be mute." Likewise, for the adjective and noun אִלֵּם (e.g., Ex 4:11; Is 35:6; 56:10), the preferred English is now "mute" instead of the traditional "dumb" (BDB).

Speculative interpreters supposed that the prophet was afflicted with an irreversible physiological condition. With that understanding secular psychoanalysts have had a "field day" with Ezekiel. They have "posthumously diagnosed [him] as suffering from a wide range of pathological and psychological maladies."[17]

Physiological speechlessness may, indeed, be the right meaning of the verb. It cannot merely be another metaphor (as 3:25 had). The fact that later (24:27) Ezekiel's condition is called a "sign" (מֹופֵת) requires that we take it literally. However, I, with

---

[15] Keil, *Ezekiel*, 1:65.

[16] Greenberg, *Ezekiel*, 1:102.

[17] Block, *Ezekiel*, 1:154.

many others, think that it does not refer to a *permanent* speechlessness. The Niphal of אָלַם can have the literal meaning of "speechlessness *under certain circumstances*."

Probably the closest parallel verse with the Niphal of אָלַם is Is 53:7, since it also includes vocabulary found in the clause "I will open your mouth" in Ezek 3:27. The Suffering Servant (Jesus Christ) was afflicted, yet by his own choice "he did not open his mouth" (וְלֹא יִפְתַּח־פִּיו, twice), and he is likened to a sheep that "is silent" (נֶאֱלָמָה) when it is being sheared (Is 53:7). Yet Jesus did speak occasionally during his trials and from the cross, so his silence was not continual or absolute. Another close parallel is Ps 39:10 (ET 39:9), where David states that because of God's chastisements, "I am mute; I do not open my mouth" (נֶאֱלַמְתִּי לֹא אֶפְתַּח־פִּי). Yet David is uttering his psalm, so his muteness is not permanent or continual, but temporary (and also self-imposed, though that does not seem to be the case with Ezekiel, since God imposes it on the prophet). See the Niphal also in Pss 31:19 (ET 31:18); 39:3 (ET 39:2); Dan 10:15.

The wider context of the book indicates that Ezekiel was physically able to speak at various times. Elders or others of his audience frequently come to the prophet to hear his message (8:1; 14:1–4; 20:1) or to request an explanation of his action prophecies (12:9; 21:12 [ET 21:7]; 24:19), and obviously they assume that he is able to speak. And, as a matter of fact, he frequently does address audiences orally, delivering messages he has received from Yahweh. It can be argued that in all these cases Yahweh temporarily reverses the prophet's physical muteness. Yet I believe we need not press things that far. Both the immediate exegetical requirements of this verse and the context (especially the following verse) are met by understanding Ezekiel's behavior as an *intermittent, divinely imposed* silence, or, at the very least, a command for a voluntary self-imposed silence. The perfect here, "You will be speechless," can be taken as an imperative if not as a prophetic perfect.

My view that the muteness is temporary is supported by 3:27 (see below) and by the later passages in Ezekiel where the same verb (Niphal of אָלַם) refers to the prophet. In 24:27 Ezekiel is told that he will again be able to speak freely when the news of Jerusalem's fall comes, and in 33:22 Ezekiel reports that happening. But of that future terminus we are told nothing here. The following clause too helps define the way in which Ezekiel will be mute, though it does not directly answer the question of whether his speechlessness was physiological or spiritual, permanent or intermittent (see the next textual note).

וְלֹא־תִהְיֶה לָהֶם לְאִישׁ מוֹכִיחַ—Ezekiel is told he will not be able to exercise this role as a result of his speechlessness. There is much controversy over the precise meaning of אִישׁ מוֹכִיחַ. Literally the phrase means "a man, a reprover." Some think that אִישׁ before the participle signifies an official office in Israelite society, but evidence of such a position is scanty at best. Is 29:21 and Amos 5:10 refer to a "reprover" (מוֹכִיחַ) acting "in the gate" of the city, but it is doubtful if such a "reprover" or public censor had an official office to act as such. Any faithful man could carry out that role, and whoever undertook the role merely fulfilled general biblical injunctions to be his "brother's keeper" (cf. Gen 4:9; Lev 19:17; Prov 9:7).

The meaning "reprover" is contextually derived. מוֹכִיחַ is the Hiphil masculine singular participle of יָכַח, whose Hiphil can have condemnatory meanings such as "to rebuke, reprove, judge, convict, chasten, punish" or more neutral meanings, "to mediate, arbitrate." BDB includes Ezek 3:26 under "reprove" (Hiphil, 5 b), while *HALOT* defines the participle here as "someone who administers a reprimand" (Hiphil, 2). Often the context in which יָכַח is used is in the courtroom, but exactly what role it describes must be inferred. It may be the prosecutor, the defense attorney, or a mediator between two disputing parties. It has the latter sense in Job 9:33, one of the precursor passages to the famous "Redeemer" (גֹּאֵל) declaration of Job 19:25–27. Some commentators build on the mediator idea and translate it here as "intercessor" or the like. Prophets often did intercede on behalf of their people, but it is doubtful if the participle מוֹכִיחַ ever has that connotation.

3:27 וּבְדַבְּרִי אוֹתְךָ—See the textual notes on the similar clause in 2:1.

אֶפְתַּח אֶת־פִּיךָ—God promises Ezekiel, "I will open your mouth," which will relieve the (temporary) muteness God imposed on him in 3:26 so that he can speak the prophetic Word given him. Ezek 24:27 and 33:22 state that after the fall of Jerusalem, God will open the prophet's mouth and his divinely imposed speechlessness will end. In Num 22:28 God opens the mouth of a donkey so she can speak his prophetic word to Balaam. Compare Dan 10:16 and Ps 51:17 (ET 51:15): "O Lord, open my lips, and my mouth shall declare your praise." (The nominal phrase "opening of mouth" [BDB, s.v. פִּתְחוֹן] occurs in Ezek 16:63 and 29:21 but in totally different contexts.)

Oddly, Block, in an otherwise excellent commentary, connects the expression with the Akkadian *pīt pî*, "opening of the mouth," a ceremony by which a statue was thought to be transformed into an idol indwelt by the spirit of the god it represented. (A similar ritual is known from other cultures.) Thus, he argues that Yahweh intends to make a "living idol" out of Ezekiel, and he connects it with Ezekiel's value as a מוֹפֵת ("sign") to the people in chapters 12 and 24.[18] He even finds superficial parallels with the well-known Babylonian lament *Ludlul bēl nēmeqi*[19] ("I will praise the lord of wisdom," that is, Marduk). However, in all this I fear Block is badly misguided. All of Yahweh's prophets were to combat paganism (as called ministers still are), and Ezekiel, exiled in the midst of a pagan milieu, would be most unlikely to let himself be influenced by it.

Greenberg suggests that Ezekiel's dumbness and confinement to his home both were the result of the people's rejection of him. His despondency deprived him of "the capacity for normal human contact," and so he only spoke to the people when he was given a divine oracle to proclaim to them. The fall of Jerusalem seven years later finally vindicated Ezekiel, and the opening of his mouth at that time reflected the Israelites' receptivity to his message.[20] But Greenberg's view attributes too much influence to Ezekiel's audience and downplays God's work in Ezekiel himself, both now and after Jerusalem's fall.

---

[18] Block, *Ezekiel*, 1:158–59, citing J. M. Kennedy, "Hebrew *pithôn peh* in the Book of Ezekiel," *VT* 41 (1991): 233–35.

[19] Block, *Ezekiel*, 1:159–60.

[20] Greenberg, *Ezekiel*, 1:120–21.

Commentary

3:1 The command for Ezekiel to "eat" the scroll in 2:8 is repeated two more times in 3:1, and it will be expanded in 3:3. All that repetition, plus the fact that in this verse the object ("whatever you receive") is placed first in the chiastic structure of the double command to "eat," has been taken to imply that Ezekiel was reluctant to eat something so unappetizing; perhaps he was resisting. The supposition is not implausible. Moses, Isaiah, and Jeremiah voiced reservations when they were called into the ministry (Ex 3:11; 4:10; Is 6:5; Jer 1:6–7). But Ezekiel does not raise any explicit objection to God's call and command to eat. A comparable double command, with double obedience by Ezekiel, occurs in Ezekiel 37, when the prophet prophesies to the dry bones (37:4, 7, 9–10).

Some commentators are too eager to deny that the eaten scroll represents a preexistent heavenly text that Ezekiel is to ingest and then recite. The title of the scroll (2:10) suggests that its contents do correspond to most of Ezekiel's preaching through chapter 32, since his main emphasis is on judgment, although the totality of Ezekiel's preaching also includes Gospel (which will predominate in chapters 33–48). But the main point of the scene is not to describe the exact process of all prophetic inspiration. Rather, it is that Yahweh gives to Ezekiel the divine message he is to proclaim, and Yahweh will protect his prophet from the fierce opposition to God's Word that he will have to face. The scroll is God's Word in an external, physical ("sacramental") form that the prophet must ingest if he is to carry out the formidable task ahead of him. This is similar to the traditional phrasing of the Collect for the Word in the Lutheran liturgy:

> Blessed Lord, who hast caused all Holy Scriptures to be written for our learning, grant that we may in such wise hear them, read, mark, learn, and *inwardly digest* them, that by patience and comfort of Thy holy Word we may embrace, and ever hold fast, the blessed hope of everlasting life, which Thou hast given us in our Savior Jesus Christ, who liveth and reigneth with Thee and the Holy Ghost, ever one God, world without end.[21]

The part of the collect about inwardly digesting the Scriptures is based on this episode in Ezekiel. We might compare Ezekiel's ingestion and digestion of the Word in scroll form to the way in which in the Lord's Supper the Word made flesh is received by mouth and ingested to permeate the body of the communicant, who is a member of Christ's one body (1 Cor 10:16–17).

In *Lutheran Worship*, "inwardly digest them" was altered to "take them to heart."[22] The change removes us one step from the language of Scripture. The increasing biblical illiteracy of modern worshipers may render the origin of the phrase less obvious. But, if so, it provides a standing opportunity for the pas-

---

[21] *TLH*, p. 14; emphasis added.

[22] *LW*, p. 156.

tor to instruct the congregation about the origin of the liturgy in the Bible itself.

For all the other prophets of whose calls we have a biblical record, God performs some comparable sign involving their mouth in order to consecrate them for the preaching ministry. Moses complains about his deficient oratory skills (Ex 4:10, 14–16), but he is given the divine name, "Yahweh," to utter, as well as miraculous signs to perform and Aaron as his own prophet (Exodus 3–4). God promises Moses, "I will be with your mouth and his mouth, and I will teach you what to do" (Ex 4:15). The seraph touches Isaiah's lips with a burning coal (Is 6:6–7). Yahweh's hand touches Jeremiah's mouth (Jer 1:9). In all these cases, the signs came in response to expressions of inadequacy by the man called to preach. If Ezekiel is reluctant to eat the scroll, his hesitancy would be due to his knowledge that, as a sinful human being ("son of man," as God first calls him in 2:1), he is wholly unworthy for the task of proclaiming the divine Word ("my words," 3:4).

The double command to "eat" in 3:1 is followed in virtually the same breath by a reiteration of the command to preach to an apostate people ("then go, speak to the house of Israel"). The extraordinary experience was not an end in itself, but a prerequisite for ministry.

3:2–3 The causative forms of "eat" in these verses perhaps imply a supernaturally aided act. The picturesque reiteration of the command in 3:3 involving "stomach" and "innards" implies that Ezekiel's entire body is to be permeated with the ingested divine Word. Faith is never a matter of either "head" (intellect) or "heart" (spiritual disposition) alone, but of both. That principle applies to a called messenger of the Word in a special way, and in Ezekiel that point is made most dramatically: the scroll of God's Word enters through his mouth (head) and is to be digested in his innards (in the vicinity of his heart). The objective Word, coming to him entirely from outside himself, must be "internalized." Even his physical life is to be grasped, owned by the Word. One immediately thinks of the many subsequent action prophecies of Ezekiel (especially in chapters 4–5) that involve his body. Since hostility and rejection were also his lot, one might also invoke a certain "theology of the cross" here.[23]

The sweet taste of the strange food has been allegorized broadly into the sweetness of the Gospel, or even the promise of salvation after the announcement of judgment. But Eichrodt is basically on target in his explanation "that it points to our experience that even strange and apparently unintelligible demands on the part of God, when they are once fulfilled by us, bestow an inward satisfaction which takes away all their bitterness."[24] The Word will give Ezekiel spiritual joy in his ministry despite the divine mandate to preach sear-

---

[23] I regard Greenberg's interpretation (*Ezekiel*, 1:67–68), following Kimchi's medieval gloss, that the point of the commands in 3:3 is to keep Ezekiel from vomiting the indigestible papyrus, as gratuitous, at best.

[24] Eichrodt, *Ezekiel*, 65.

ing Law (especially in chapters 4–24) as well as comforting Gospel (especially chapters 33–48).

A question surrounding the entire scene involving eating the scroll is this: shall we take it literally as referring to a physical scroll, or is it simply a vivid metaphor in a vision? The boundaries between vision and reality are often indistinct—not only in Ezekiel, but in other prophets as well (for example, Isaiah's call and the visions of Daniel and Zechariah).

Elsewhere Scripture uses honey's sweetness as a metaphor, although usually in a somewhat more general application than in Ezekiel, and often without any mention of eating. In both Pss 19:11 (ET 19:10) and 119:103 the metaphor is applied to God's word(s) in general. In Prov 16:24 and 24:13 the application is to true wisdom (God's revelation) or its results. Undoubtedly, the closest parallel (although without mention of honey) is in Jer 15:16: "Thy words were found, and I did eat them; and thy word was unto me the joy and rejoicing of mine heart" (KJV). It is one of many close parallels between the two virtually contemporary prophets, and, as usual, Ezekiel's version tends to be more expansive. We also should include the echo of Ezekiel's vision in Revelation 10, where the seer of Patmos is given a "little book" to eat, and it makes his stomach bitter, but in his mouth it is as sweet as honey (Rev 10:8–10).[25] Thus Jeremiah, Ezekiel, and the apostle John are the three prophets in Scripture who eat God's words.[26]

The parallel in Jeremiah seems to be purely metaphorical, standing, as the passage does, at the beginning of one of his laments and with no divine command to eat a scroll. This situation is not so clear cut in Revelation. Both eating the scroll from God and its taste like honey are mentioned, but the whole context is so visionary that the episode probably has to be classified as a vision.

What is really surprising, especially in the light of all these near parallels (and even more so in light of the congenital skepticism of higher criticism), is the virtual unanimity of commentators of every stripe that the eating of the scroll by Ezekiel should be taken literally.[27] Allen[28] is the only significant exception of which I am aware. And the construal of the act's meaning varies little either: God's message must permeate even the prophet's bones and marrow, as it were, so that he preaches the message with every fiber of his being. His consumption of the divine Word causes a sort of inner reformation that enables

---

[25] See Brighton, *Revelation*, 270–73.

[26] John can be called a prophet because Revelation is called a prophecy (Rev 1:3; 22:7–19).

[27] At this writing, the latest treatment of the topic is by Margaret S. Odell, "You Are What You Eat: Ezekiel and the Scroll," *JBL* 117/2 (Summer 1998): 229–48. The treatment is somewhat idiosyncratic. Building on Milgrom's interpretation that "the priestly absolution of guilt is accomplished through the priests' eating the purification offerings," she argues that Ezekiel's eating of the scroll is a key element in his transformation from priestly to prophetic status—a process she would see continuing through Ezekiel 5. (The quote is from page 239, where Odell cites Jacob Milgrom, *Leviticus 1–16* [New York: Doubleday, 1991], 637.)

[28] Allen, *Ezekiel*, 1:40–41.

him to accept and internalize even the strangest and harshest prophecies given to him, and then also to proclaim them as part of God's overarching design of love. In the life of every Christian, one might compare some of our classical hymns: "What God Ordains Is Always Good," "God's Time Is the Best Time," and so on.

Commentators often point out that, externally, Ezekiel's act has parallels in other religions, especially in certain types of trances in mysticism. "Parallels" are to be found already in ancient Egyptian records, as well as from later Jewish and Arab mystics. But these pagan "parallels" are theologically without significance. Nothing depends on whether or not Ezekiel's strange behavior can be duplicated superficially elsewhere.

3:4 Ezek 3:4–11 is a unit that basically repeats 2:3–7, although heightening virtually every detail. Ingesting the scroll (3:1–3) has prepared Ezekiel interiorly for his task, and the accent in these verses is on his exterior preparation. He will be supplied with God's very words (3:4). In comparison with 2:3, the stress shifts from Yahweh's appointment to Ezekiel's responsibility to be absolutely obedient in delivering the divine Word to Israel.

3:5 Ezekiel is not to be a "foreign missionary" to peoples who speak languages unintelligible to the prophet, nor is he even to have a cross-cultural ministry. He is to minister to his own people, who have the same language and culture as he does. They will have no difficulty understanding his tongue. If they refuse to listen, it will be due to their rebellious sinful nature.

All preachers face a perennial temptation to be "user-friendly" by softening or avoiding altogether those aspects of the divine Word that their listeners find offensive. But Ezekiel is commanded not to adapt his message to his audience's preferences. To do so would be for him to rebel against God (2:8). May we preachers today take this to heart!

Previously, the primary accent on the Israelite audience had been vertical: their rebellion against God (2:3–8). Now there is also a horizontal contrast between the chosen people and other nations.

3:6 The new thought in this verse uses a contrary-to-fact assertion: if Ezekiel had been sent to some other people besides Israel, they would have listened. In 3:5, the foreign "people" mentioned would most likely be the Babylonians, among whom the Israelites had been forced to live. In 3:6 one would probably think of any of the various other ethnic groups who had also been exiled to the vicinity of Nippur. The best OT example of the situation God describes is the people of Nineveh, who had repented at Jonah's preaching (despite that prophet's own initial refusal to preach). This point is probably also implicit in the oracles to the other nations, found in virtually all the prophetic books (including Ezekiel 25–32), although the situation is more complicated there. At the very least, other nations are subject to God's judgment because they have not obeyed "natural law," the law written in their hearts (especially evident in Amos 1–2; cf. Rom 2:12–15). Jesus makes a similar point, asserting that Tyre and Sidon, even Sodom, would have responded better to his mighty works than did the Jewish communities at Bethsaida, Capernaum, and Chorazin (Mt 11:20–24).

Instead of "whose words you would not understand" (Ezek 3:6), we would expect "who would not understand your words." The point is apparently to state the situation from Ezekiel's own viewpoint. But the result is the same: there would be no communication between the prophet and his audience.

3:7 This dismal forecast of Ezekiel's failure is obviously intended as comfort to Ezekiel. The present, continuing refusal of Israel to listen to God ("they are not willing to listen to me," with the negated participle אֹבִים) guarantees their future refusal to listen to God's prophet ("Israel will not be willing to listen to you," with the negated imperfect יֹאבוּ). "Convince a man against his will, he's of the same opinion still" applies with double force to repentance and conversion, which can only be accomplished by the Holy Spirit, who works through the Word. No merely human devices or persuasive techniques will work. "No one is so deaf as someone who does not want to hear."

"The whole house of Israel" appears to include both past generations and the present one, as we saw already in 2:3–4 and as Israel is presented throughout the book. There had never been a time in Israel's existence when it had not been refractory and confrontational. The people's behavior is both an old family tradition (they are a "house") and also one that they almost spontaneously reaffirm themselves.

Their rejection is not of Ezekiel personally, but of the one who sent him, just as Yahweh said to Samuel in 1 Sam 8:7. It is a refrain heard throughout Scripture. So Jesus expressed "*the Christological principle of representation* according to which the emissaries bear in themselves the person of Christ":[29]

> The one who listens to you listens to me, and the one who rejects you rejects me. But the one who rejects me rejects the one who sent me. (Lk 10:16 and parallels)

The most striking application of that Christological principle today is in the office of the keys (confession and absolution), wherein the pastor forgives or retains sins in the stead and by the command of his Lord Jesus Christ.[30] The principle also has countless other applications, also among laymen and women.

3:8 Such adamancy on the part of the people requires a counter-adamancy. Compare Jeremiah's call: "I make you this day a fortified city and an iron pillar and bronze walls against all the land" (Jer 1:18). In Jeremiah some words of comfort accompany the promise of the requisite fortitude for the task. Ezek 3:8 should not be construed to imply some grim insensitivity on Ezekiel's part, although the personalities of the two prophets are a study in contrasts. Jeremiah is given to expressing his emotions and pathos, while Ezekiel is re-

---

[29] Just, *Luke 9:51–24:53*, 442. See Just's exposition of this in terms of the theology of the cross on pages 438–39, 441–43.

[30] See Luther's explanation in SC, Confession.

served and resolute, even when his wife dies (Ezekiel 24). God still uses "all sorts and conditions of men" in the ministry.

The diamond-hard countenance given Ezekiel (3:7–9) is apparently a deliberate play on Ezekiel's name. Three times in 3:8–9 the Hebrew adjective חָזָק, "strong," applies to Ezekiel, and his name is compounded of that same root ("God will strengthen"; see the textual note on it in 1:3). Ezekiel's whole life, as well as his name, is to be an action prophecy, a type (in the theological sense) of the hard words of judgment he has to speak.

3:9 The first part of the verse is a metaphorical restatement of 3:8, and the rest is a nearly verbatim restatement of elements of 2:6–7. The verse does not necessarily indicate that Ezekiel was particularly fearful; it simply illustrates again the repetitiousness that is characteristic of his book.

3:10–11 A new direct address to the prophet introduces this final short speech at the end of Ezekiel's commissioning. Much of it is a reiteration of what has been said earlier. In a straightforward explanation of the implication of the eating of the scroll, Yahweh insists that his prophet listen to his words (unlike Israel, which heard but did not listen) and transmit his words verbatim to Israel, regardless of their reaction. As Zimmerli points out, the Hebrew imperfect ("I will speak") refers not just to past revelations, but indicates that Ezekiel must continue to be a listener and pass on God's future messages.[31] Ezekiel conveys only what he has received, and he is answerable to God only for delivering the Word faithfully. As such he is a model for the ministry of all God's servants.

The new element in 3:11 is that the "sons of Israel" (2:3) to whom the prophet shall preach are specified for the first time as "the exiles"—not those still left in Canaan who had escaped this deportation. Ezekiel is to have no part in "decrying absentees from church to the congregation at hand." God is not only more specific, but also more intimate. The prophet must preach to "the sons of your people," bound to the same Father by the covenant and its promises, as in the full sense of the NT κοινωνία, "the communion of saints," initiation into which comes in the Sacrament of Baptism.[32]

3:12 A new paragraph (3:12–15) begins here, which is a resumption of the narrative begun in 1:1. There are many echoes of earlier parts of the story at the same time that the prophet's initiatory encounter with Yahweh is concluded.

The Spirit who had earlier empowered him to stand (2:1–2; and later, 3:24) now transports him. The last part of 3:12 is a spontaneous doxological salute to the departing Glory (כָּבוֹד), presumably uttered by heavenly, angelic creatures, and conceivably joined by the prophet himself (although it would be Ezekiel's only utterance in chapters 1–3). The closest parallels to Ezek 3:12

---

[31] Zimmerli, *Ezekiel*, 1:138.

[32] See "Baptism in Luke-Acts" in Just, *Luke 1:1–9:50*, 135–43.

117

are Rev 5:8–14 and Rev 7:9–12, where the four living creatures (who seem to be the same ones as in Ezekiel's vision) around God's throne in heaven, along with other angels and the elders (saints in glory), sing doxological praises to God and the Lamb. Based on those NT parallels, the four living creatures (and/or other unnamed angelic beings) most likely are the ones who utter the doxology in Ezek 3:12.

In 1:28 and 10:4, 18, the "Glory of Yahweh" refers specifically to the man-like form of God on the throne (1:26; cf. 8:2), but here it is apparently used by synecdoche for the whole ensemble: the divine figure, his throne, the dome, and the living creatures supporting the structure. "His place" could refer to the heavenly throne or to the "place" on earth where God was "incarnationally" present, normally between the cherubim of the tabernacle and (later) the Jerusalem temple, but now for a time even in the Babylonian exile, thousands of miles away from any sacred earthly structure (a thought picked up again in 11:16). These two places are linked by the vertical typology that pervades all biblical thinking—the correspondence between heaven and earth under God, as acclaimed in worship ("thy will be done on earth as it is in heaven"; "therefore with angels and archangels and with all the company of heaven we laud and magnify your glorious name …"[33]). This vertical typology is brought out in the doxology sung by the angels at the birth of Jesus Christ:

> Glory to God in the highest,
> and on earth, peace to men of his good will. (Lk 2:14)

God's glory was revealed on earth through the incarnate Word (Jn 1:14), and his incarnation is cause for celebration both on earth and in the highest heavens. The celestial and terrestrial choirs join in unison to laud the "King of glory" at his advent (Ps 24:7–10).

3:14 The precise connection between the movement of the Glory and the transportation of Ezekiel by God's Spirit is not specified, but it recalls the way other prophets, such as Elijah, were whisked away by the Spirit to do God's bidding (cf. 1 Ki 18:12; 2 Ki 2:16), and even Philip in the NT had a similar experience (Acts 8:39–40).

Many commentators are disposed to make a great deal out of the clustering of vocabulary in this verse which may have special associations with pre-classical prophecy. Yahweh's Spirit could have lifted up (נָשָׂא) or "spirited away" Elijah (1 Ki 18:12; 2 Ki 2:16), which is the action that takes place here, as Ezekiel states: "The Spirit lifted me up and took me away." The second verb, לָקַח, "to take," with Yahweh as subject, was used of Elijah's assumption in 2 Kings 2, just as it had been already of Enoch's assumption in Gen 5:24. (Similarly and more generally, see its use in Pss 49:16 [ET 49:15] and 73:24.) The reference to Yahweh's "hand" (יַד) certainly harks back to Ezek 1:3, but may also allude to Elijah's movement from Carmel to Jezreel (1 Ki 18:46). Thus,

---

[33] For example, *LW*, p. 146.

we certainly have a significant collection of ancient, traditional prophetic vocabulary in this verse. However, I am inclined to doubt that its use is intended to authenticate Ezekiel's credentials as equal to those of the earlier prophets. In my view, Yahweh's theophany and call in Ezekiel 1–3 provides all the authentication needed.

For a prophet who rarely shares his emotions with us, the raw anger in "bitter, in the fury of my spirit" (3:14) is striking. "Bitter, embittered" (מַר) in a psychological sense is often combined idiomatically with נֶפֶשׁ in the sense of "mood." Perhaps נֶפֶשׁ is absent here because the "spirit" (רוּחַ) often has that sense too and is to be thought of as doing double duty (his spirit was both bitter and furious).

The bigger problem is *why* Ezekiel was bitter and angry. I would exclude any extrapolation that it resulted from Ezekiel's unwillingness to accept his call. It might, however, reflect his awareness of the thankless and dangerous task God has given him. Such a mood would reflect the "Laments, Moaning, and Woe" that had been written on the scroll he had eaten (2:10), even though his bitterness contrasts with the "sweetness" of the eaten scroll (3:3; מַר, "bitter," and מָתוֹק, "sweet," are contrasted in Is 5:20 and Prov 27:7). He may share God's wrath at the impenitence of the people. Some wordplay between מַר, "bitter," and מְרִי, the people's "rebellion" (in "rebellious house," e.g., 3:9), may also reinforce the sense. Similarly, I would prefer not to understand the חֵמָה ("fury, rage") as the prophet's anger at his divine call (which would represent disobedience to God's command in 2:8), but as a reflection of God's own wrath (to which the word often refers elsewhere) against his disobedient people. In that sense, חֵמָה is very common in Ezekiel[34] and is often paralleled with אַף, "anger."

Some of Ezekiel's bitter anger may have been kindled already by his own forced exile, the devastation of Judah by the invading Babylonians, and his anguish at the impending doom of his recalcitrant people. The apostle Paul could express divine wrath (Rom 1:18) but also deep anguish for the unbelieving Jews of his day (Rom 9:1–5; 10:1).

That God's "hand" upon Ezekiel was "strong" (or perhaps "heavy") is not easy to interpret. That "hand" had first come upon him at the beginning of the inaugural vision (1:3). The adjective, "strong," in 3:7–9 entailed a play on the meaning of his name, "God will strengthen," and the phrase here may possibly be another play on the prophet's name. His opposition will be strong, but Yahweh's hand upon him is far stronger (cf. 1 Jn 4:4). Greenberg suggests the phrase means that the divine hand overpowered or overwhelmed him.[35] Some interpretation consonant with his bitter anger earlier in the verse and his devastated condition at the end of 3:15 is required.

---

[34] חֵמָה occurs thirty-three times in Ezekiel out of one hundred twenty-five OT occurrences.

[35] Greenberg, *Ezekiel*, 1:71.

All in all, Ezekiel's sense is not one of "liberation," but of overmastering compulsion to carry out God's call. Once he has received the divine Word, he is compelled to preach it, as was his older contemporary Jeremiah (Jer 20:9) and the apostles (Acts 4:20; 10:42), including Paul (1 Cor 9:16).

3:15–16   When Ezekiel returns from somewhere outside the settlement of Tel Abib, at the conclusion of the call-commissioning vision, he sits or lives among the other exiles, but is completely overwhelmed and probably disoriented or stunned. This may be a prelude to his speechlessness, which begins at the end of the chapter (3:26).

Why *seven* days? There is no reason to dismiss the number as purely symbolic, but one should not miss the important biblical symbolism often attached to the number. One naturally thinks first of the seven days of creation, from Sabbath to Sabbath. Job's "friends" sat with him for seven days and nights as if in mourning before they began to speak to him (Job 2:13). Much more pertinent is the role the number seven played in the consecration of priests (Ex 29:29–37; Lev 8:33–35; cf. 2 Chr 7:9). It is quite plausible that God meant for Ezekiel to understand these seven days as a sort of ordination to his prophetic priesthood. Comparable periods of less than seven days might be Ezra's shocked silence at the extent of the returnees' apostasy until the evening sacrifice (Ezra 9:4, which uses מְשׁוֹמֵם, the same verb used here in Ezek 3:15) and Saul's three-day fast after the Damascus-road Christophany (Acts 9:9).

Psychologically, it is understandable that the excitement of the previous day would end in nervous exhaustion, but that is surely the least of it. It was a period of adjustment, to be sure, but far more than merely emotionally. He must live among his own people, but begin to "dance to the beat of a different drummer." Allen asks:

> Did priestly rank in ancient Israel tend to inculcate an attitude toward God such as professional military training does toward superior officers (cf. 1 Sam 2:35)? Be that as it may, there is evidence that the absolute "yes" of Ezekiel's response to God took a psychological toll, in the disorientation of 3:15. Theologically, however, Ezekiel's passive subjection conveys an assurance that his oracles are the true, unalloyed word of God.[36]

Eichrodt presses the significance of what begins here a bit further, and, in principle, I think rightly so:

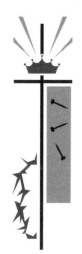

> It means that he, as a weak human being, must always share all the human sufferings of his time, and that he is under an obligation to be one with his fellows and to share in the troubles destined for them. At the same time, he imparts an exemplary significance and a representative character to this suffering of his, through his call to prophesy to a people who have frittered away their birthright as the elect. ... This son of man is stripped by God of all the pretensions of his birth and position. He has to descend into the depths of humiliation in order that, by his work of mediation, a new work of salvation may begin and a new people of God come into being. He thus comes remark-

---

[36]   Allen, *Ezekiel*, 1:45.

ably near to the servant of God in Isa. 53, and can only be understood fully within his own historical context and significance, when the line on which he stands is extended towards the Son of Man in the New Testament. ... Jeremiah's relationship to Jesus is much more generally recognized. ... But we must recognize, in Ezekiel no less than in Jeremiah, a living inward connection with the greatest of all prophets, or, with the words of Calvin, a *praeludium eius mysterii.*[37]

3:17   The metaphor of the prophet as a "watchman" has a long history of association with prophecy. Almost in the nature of the case, the watchman's duty (in virtually any setting) is to warn against impending danger or even doom. In a broader context, the idea usually is that a timely warning will make it possible for those forewarned to avoid or be delivered from danger, but that is not the immediate application of the word in Ezekiel's context.

The metaphor appears already among Isaiah's Gentile oracles, twice in chapter 21. In Is 21:6–10, a watchman stationed on a watchtower hears and passes along the message "Fallen, fallen is Babylon" (echoed in Rev 18:2). In the immediately following Is 21:11–12, someone from Dumah/Seir cries out, "Watchman, what of the night?" and receives an enigmatic reply, apparently connoting the hopelessness of Seir's situation. (See also Is 56:10 on "blind watchmen," meaning false prophets.) Also in the eighth century Hos 9:8 is explicit: "The prophet is the watchman of Ephraim." Hosea alludes to the theme also in 5:8 and 8:1. Close to Ezekiel's own day, Habakkuk writes: "I will take my stand to watch—on the tower—and look forth to see what he [God] will say to me" (Hab 2:1). And, as one might expect, the closest situational parallel is found in Jer 6:1 and elsewhere in that contemporary of Ezekiel.

Ezekiel's conscription to be a watchman involves the ultimate issues, as the repeated alternatives of life and death in connection with the theme make plain. Hence this passage needs to be read in an eschatological perspective. Although we might be reluctant to "read into" Ezekiel's charge all the fullness that NT revelation will bring to it, I am convinced that that same fuller revelation obligates the Christian expositor to read eschatology out from this text— that is, to think of more than merely the immediate concerns of physical survival. God—and Ezekiel—is not just concerned with natural, temporal life, but also with spiritual and eternal life. The divine sentence of death ultimately results in perdition in hell, while the divine verdict of life portends "the resurrection of the body, and the life everlasting" (Apostles' Creed).

By no accident, the themes of watching and prophetic vigilance figure prominently in the NT, usually in clearly eschatological contexts. Jesus' parable of the

---

[37] Eichrodt, *Ezekiel*, 73–74, citing Calvin's commentary on 1:26: "the likeness of the appearance of a man" (*Corpus Reformatorum*, 68:53). See Calvin, *Ezekiel*, 1.97. "I willingly embrace the opinion of those fathers who say that this is *the prelude to that mystery* which was afterwards displayed to the world, and which Paul magnificently extols when he exclaims—'Great is this mystery—God is manifest in the flesh' [1 Tim 3:16]" (emphasis added).

ten virgins (Mt 25:1–13) is the best known application. Our Lord's summary admonition in Mk 13:37 is, "What I say to you, I say to all: 'Watch!' "

This theme is clearly expressed in the church's liturgical worship. In the brief order for Compline, each day is a sort of miniature of one's short life, "life's little day." On a broader canvas, the church year, reviewing the life of our Lord and, indeed, of history itself, is very eschatologically conscious in Advent and even more so at the end of the church year. The theme of each Christian as a watchman found classical expression in what is often known as the "king of Lutheran chorales," Philipp Nicolai's "Wachet auf," "Wake, Awake." Nor can one overlook J. S. Bach's powerful musical setting of the hymn in his cantata 140. The temptation is strong to let the existential eclipse the eschatological, but the result would only be a caricature of the biblical message.

The prophet's role as "watchman" readily applies to the pastoral office today (see further below) and, in a broader sense, to all Christians. The pastor faces so much pressure to make his people feel comfortable rather than to exercise the role of eschatological prophet of woe (Law) and weal (Gospel). However, Ezekiel's warning that God himself becomes the enemy if the people abandon the true faith is a powerful call to repentance that excludes the simplistic "smile, God loves you" theology of popular, comfortable pseudo-Christianity. To be sure, the ultimate purpose in that warning is to elicit repentance in preparation for the Gospel, but the immediate emphasis of Ezekiel in the ensuing chapters will be judgment. Nevertheless, the book as a whole represents a sturdy Law-Gospel stance.

3:18 The first example is where the watchman fails to warn the "wicked man" that God has declared "You shall surely die." The man dies because of his iniquity, but the prophet is held responsible for his death because of his dereliction. The principle applies directly to modern ministry. The burden of the office of the ministry is not to be taken lightly, nor is the responsibility of each Christian to admonish his erring brother. In the world's eyes—and sadly, in the estimation of much of visible Christendom—it is not a "capital crime" for a pastor to be remiss in warning about God's verdict of death, that is, in preaching the Law, but the pastor is sure to be held accountable by a higher Judge. The pastor is no mere "spiritual advisor," "counselor," or "enabler," but the public holder of the office of the keys—Christ's keys, "the keys of death and Hades" (Rev 1:18; cf. Mt 16:19; Rev 3:7).

Key terms throughout Ezek 3:18–21 are רָשָׁע and צַדִּיק, traditionally rendered "wicked man" and "righteous man," respectively. Besides these adjectival forms, both have important verb and noun counterparts. רָשָׁע ("wicked man") is widely used in the OT with various negative applications (but is rarely used in cognate languages). It is especially frequent in the Psalms and Wisdom literature. Its twenty-nine occurrences in Ezekiel are proportionately higher than in any other prophetic book, and of those twenty-nine, twenty-three are found in this pericope and its congeners in chapters 18 and 33. Over eighty times in the OT the terms צַדִּיק ("righteous man") and רָשָׁע ("wicked man") are paired antithetically. Each one is what the other is not. The problem with the usual translations of the two is that the modern audience is likely to hear them as primarily—if not exclusively—moralistic terms. The misapprehensions very easily slip into Hollywoodish stereotypes of "good guys" and "bad guys."

No doubt, behavior figures prominently in the usage of these words. Or, to use NT language, "sanctification" is prominent. However, the sanctified life of the righteous person that shows forth fruits of righteousness is itself the result of the person's justification. See AC IV, "Justification," and VI, "The New Obedience" and especially Ap IV, "Justification," which expounds the relationship between justification, sanctification, and good works.

The Hiphil of both cognate verbs, צָדַק and רָשַׁע, often refers, respectively, to the judicial verdicts of "justify, declare righteous, acquit"[a] and "declare guilty, condemn," or even "damn."[b] On one hand, the OT does not yet reveal all the fullness of the doctrines of justification, eternal salvation, and damnation that St. Paul will express using similar language in the light of Christ's death and resurrection. But on the other hand, I judge that the greatest danger for OT exegesis is to fail to "read out" of the OT context what by the Bible's own testimony necessarily leads to Christ. Exegetically, it remains necessary to try to hear the OT on its own terms first, but hermeneutically and homiletically it is indispensable that the fullness of the cross be expounded, because the OT Scriptures testify to Christ.[38]

A strictly OT formulation would begin with the gift of the covenant and its ensuing obligations. Although not intrinsically legalistic, a legal or judicial analogy or metaphor underlies the word. A covenant could be either unilateral, given to someone as a donor, as in adoption, that is, "election," or it could be bilateral, a contract with obligations, rewards, or penalties for both parties. However, God's covenants with Israel express divine monergism in salvation, and Israel's obedience to the covenant is a fruit of God-given faith and a response to the salvation God himself accomplishes for his people.[39] The forensic or courtroom picture is implicit in the doctrine of justification that is central in the establishment of the Abrahamic and Mosaic covenants. The general assumption of God's courtroom (or throne room, divine council) decisions determining history (and certainly ultimate outcomes) is constitutive of the OT view of history, as it continues to be for unsecularized Christianity.

A רָשָׁע ("wicked man"), then, is someone who has been found guilty and has been convicted before God and his heavenly court (cf. the decision about Ahab in 1 Ki 22:19–22). Ostensibly, the "wicked man" is part of Israel, since Ezekiel's warnings are addressed to "the house of Israel" in exile (3:1–7, 17). Thus the "wicked man" belongs to Israel in the sense of it being "the visible

(a) E.g., Ex 23:7; Deut 25:1; 1 Ki 8:32; Is 50:8; 53:11; Ps 82:3; Prov 17:15

(b) E.g., Ex 22:8 (ET 22:9); Deut 25:1; 1 Ki 8:32; Ps 37:33; Job 10:2; 40:8; Prov 17:15

---

[38] Jn 5:39; also Lk 24:27, 45; Acts 17:2, 11; cf. "The OT Witness to Christ" in Just, *Luke 9:51–24:53*, 1021–36.

[39] See the excursus "Covenant" in Harstad, *Joshua*, 744–56.

church." Outwardly, he is part of the covenant community, but his heart is elsewhere; he is not a member of the "true, invisible church," the Israel of faith, which is comprised of all believers of both Testaments (Romans 9–11; Gal 6:16). He may be grossly and obviously wicked, or, before men at least, guilty only of peccadilloes. He may keep the ceremonial laws scrupulously, but violate the weightier theological aspects of being among the elect, who are justified through faith alone. (There certainly are passages, in both Testaments, that score such superficial, hypocritical behavior, but Protestantism with its aversion to liturgy or virtual equation of ritual with ritual*ism*, has tended to exaggerate that particular failing.) Ultimately, of course, only God can judge.

Almost precisely the opposite must be asserted of the "righteous man" (צַדִּיק). He will not be flagrantly lawless, of course, but neither will he be absolutely perfect; he is justified by grace alone and through faith alone, not through good works, which, however, are not lacking in his life. In Wisdom terminology, he is תָּם, "blameless" (Job 1:1, 8; 2:3), as was Job, whom God commended in his heavenly court, even as Satan sought to condemn him (Job 1–2). Such a person will be aware of his sins, which he freely confesses and for which he seeks God's forgiveness, as in the "penitential psalms" (see especially David in Psalms 32 and 51). He will make diligent use of the OT "sacraments," the sacrifices and eucharistic/thanksgiving gifts that God employs as "means of grace" (e.g., as prescribed in Leviticus).

The "righteous man" (צַדִּיק) is characterized by God's gift of "rightness," objective norms of truth established by Yahweh, the "righteous judge" (שׁוֹפֵט צַדִּיק, Ps 7:12). The righteous man's "righteousness" (צְדָקָה) is imputed to him through faith alone, as is stated about Abraham (Gen 15:6). His righteousness, while itself invisible, does produce evidence of itself by the man's willing, joyful obedience (as much as God gives him power) to God's Word and revealed norms (Psalm 119). This evidence is the result, not the cause or means of earning or meriting God's favor.

These words in OT usage ("righteous, righteousness; justification") are virtually twins of מִשְׁפָּט and its cognates. מִשְׁפָּט is usually misleadingly translated "judgment" (heard negatively in the sense of condemnation rather than simply the neutral "verdict") or as "justice" (today easily confused with secular, humanistic norms). But it mainly refers to God's undeserved acquittal of the sinner, who is righteous through faith, as in "*justi*fication," and who leads a life concordant with that status. See, for example, how Isaiah declares that the Suffering Servant (Jesus Christ) brings מִשְׁפָּט, "justification," to the nations (Is 42:1–4) as their light (Is 51:4). As with the "wicked man," so too only God can see into the heart of the "righteous man"; he alone knows those who are his. There is no reason to believe that, in principle, men could usurp that role any more easily in the OT than in the NT.

This whole effort to define "wicked" and "righteous" as theological terms, and not as confined to legalistic, moralistic behavior, comes to a head in the recurrent reference to life and death as the two outcomes throughout Ezekiel 3 and the similar pericopes in chapters 18 and 33. Again, we deal with concepts that dare not be looked at atomistically (only with reference to the immediate context), but which resound throughout the Scriptures—the NT as well as the OT (see especially Romans 1–8).

The immediate concern in Ezekiel has to do, no doubt, with the aftermath of the impending fall of Jerusalem, especially for those already in exile. After their vain hopes of shortly resuming "life" in Jerusalem will collapse, what then? Ordinarily, to die would imply a sudden, premature, and possibly violent death. To live would imply somehow surviving the catastrophe. But is physical life or death all that is in view? Hardly!

In the light of the rest of the book (and the Scriptures as a whole) it surely must involve at the very least sharing in the covenant promises given to Abraham and through Moses, escaping the loss of identity through syncretism and intermarriage with pagan neighbors, possibly even in sharing in the promised return to Jerusalem and Judah—if not personally, at least through their progeny. Yet we must extend these concepts much further, given how already the OT attests the promise of the resurrection of the body, eternal life for the righteous, and eternal punishment for the wicked (e.g., Isaiah 65–66; Job 19:25–27; Dan 12:2–3).

Among liberals the dogma is simply de rigueur that such doctrines do not surface until shortly before the NT era. Even some "evangelicals" espouse such teachings. I beg to dissent. There is no point in arguing that such beliefs were as clearly and fully revealed in the OT as in the NT. But to deny their presence in the OT is to sever the unity of the Testaments and make OT faith into a purely this-worldly one—one that then leads almost inevitably into Judaism rather than into Christianity. As so often, one must "distinguish, but not divorce" the two Testaments. One should not "read into" OT texts a fullness not yet revealed, but the far greater danger here is that we fail to "read out" of them the fulfillment of which we are the beneficiaries in Christ. We are not expounding texts in synagogues, but in Christian churches. Only in Christ is the veil removed so that the reader of the OT Scriptures can see their true meaning (2 Corinthians 3).

There is yet another angle to be pursued on this matter. To assume that Ezekiel believed and preached that there was some immediate, almost mechanical and empirically predictable connection between one's response to his warnings and that person's physical fate is to view him as an incredibly naive person. By ignoring the eschatological dimensions of life and death as preached by the prophets, liberal critics imply that the prophets had such a naive view—and not just Ezekiel. In some circles it is virtual dogma that "orthodox" (Deuteronomistic) OT faith held just such a mechanical view of retribution or reward limited to this earthly life.

We must not discount the OT emphasis that justification (or unbelief) directly impacts a person's present life. Even St. Paul can write that "whatever man sows, that he will also reap" (Gal 6:7), and he can also talk of the believer's "reward" (e.g., 1 Cor 3:14). But all of these words and concepts communicate in a different tongue if read in the light of the messianic promise throughout the OT, which is the bud of the same Gospel of Jesus Christ that flowers in the NT. To mechanize retribution and to limit it to this present existence and world (excluding eternity, the new heavens and new earth, and hell for the damned) is to change OT religion into a matter of merit and works. The liberal view cannot pass the test of interpreting Psalm 1 or Psalm 23, for example, both of which end with a clear intimation of eternity. Nor can it explain what Ezekiel will envision in chapters 40–48 (compare Revelation 21–22).

3:19 This verse presents case 2, which is identical to case 1 (3:18), except that here the watchman has done his duty, and when the warning is rejected and the wicked man dies as a result of his iniquity, the watchman has saved his own life. Just how the fact that the prophet saves his life was conceptualized and what all that concept entails must parallel what has already been discussed in the previous verse. It underscores that faith is always personal (even though not isolated from the community, OT Israel and the NT church); no one can believe for someone else. It also emphasizes that faith manifests itself in love for one's neighbor (Gal 5:6).

Love for the lost mandates warning that eternal death awaits the wicked man, even as eternal life is God's gift to the righteous man, such as the prophet who "saves his life." To take the easy route and to fail to warn the sinner—or worse yet, to preach a "gospel" that does not require repentance from sin and trust in Christ as the only Savior—is to hate one's neighbor and to face God's judgment for failure to be a watchman. Christ may echo this Ezekiel passage when he warns and promises:

> For whoever wishes to save his life will lose it, but whoever loses his life for the sake of me and the Gospel will save it. (Mk 8:35)

The definition of the Gospel and an example of how even a called apostle (Peter) can take offense at it are provided in the preceding context (Mk 8:31–34).

Something else about Ezek 3:19–22 should not escape our notice. In earlier verses it had often sounded as though the "rebellious house" (3:1–7, 17) was so hardened and incorrigible in their rebellion that any hope for repentance was futile (see also 2:3–7). Here we see that there was a certain hyperbole in such earlier statements. The people are not predestined by God to certain and collective doom, but stand at the crossroads between life and death. There is still time between their present general impenitence and the final death knell. Humanly speaking, each must still "choose" to accept or reject the Lord's proffered grace.[40] Even to those who finally spurn the offer, God makes plain that the intent of the warning was to save his life.

As becomes plain in chapter 33, after all human hopes have been dashed, having heeded the warning will open the gates to a promised land, to a "new

---

[40] Cf. the interpretation of the famous "choose … whom you will serve" passage, Josh 24:14–15, in Harstad, *Joshua*, 778–87.

Jerusalem" far beyond present imaginings (cf. Revelation 21). As the closely related chapter 18 will make plain, the people cannot charge that God is unfair by trying to shift blame on the "fathers" and thus trying to exculpate themselves. "It is not how one begins the race that counts, but how one ends."[41] Allen's lovely literary reference applies to the Israelites at this juncture in their earthly life: "Like Christian in Bunyan's *Pilgrim's Progress*, Ezekiel was made to see that 'there was a way to hell even from the gates of heaven, as well as from the City of Destruction.' "[42]

3:20 Case 3 contemplates the sad case, all too familiar in Israel and the church, a "righteous man" (צַדִּיק), by all human measures a faithful member of the community, who apostatizes—who abandons or even renounces the faith and life he once professed. To compound the tragedy, the "watchman" also, for whatever reason, fails to give timely warnings and so is held accountable by God for the apostate's death. This is a reminder that, to use Lutheran language, the *iustus* ("saint" or "justified person") needs to hear God's Law just as much as the *peccator* ("sinner") precisely because we are always (throughout this life) simultaneously both (*simul iustus et peccator*). The pastor needs to contemplate case 3 even more than every Christian does. His holy office does not shield him from God's wrath if he fails to exercise it. On the contrary, "to whomsoever is given much, much shall be required from him" (Lk 12:48).

The tripartite protasis in the first sentence almost gives us a "biography" of the process of falling away. First, the righteous man "apostatizes from his righteousness." He returns to his preconversion, precircumcision or prebaptism state and mentality. This initial change may be known only to God, perhaps barely acknowledged by the man himself. Second, he "does unrighteousness" as he begins to act out the new priorities and values in his heart. At this point no one should be unaware of the change. Finally, God says, "I place a stumbling block in front of him." God gives him the "acid test" of putting a "stumbling block" in his path, which might, even at the last minute, alert him to the mortal danger on the path ahead—but which he fails to heed.

It is *God* who places the "stumbling block" in front of him. Modern sentimental notions of God as "love" in some simplistic or even universalistic sense make this a very unpalatable statement. If it were misunderstood to say that God *caused* the righteous man to sin, we would have problems, perhaps double predestination. But if we diagram the sentence carefully, we note that this is still one of the protases ("when ..."). The apodosis, the final death sentence ("he shall die"), is imminent, but here in the last protasis, we have, as it were, God's "last ditch" attempt to arrest the man's decline down the slippery slope before he finally crosses the point of no return. God seeks to rescue the man by issuing the call through the prophet (or the modern pastor) for the man

---

[41] Block, *Ezekiel*, 1:149.
[42] Allen, *Ezekiel*, 1:59.

to repent. However, the man may reject and so trip and fall over God's warning, and if he does, then his fall is God's judgment on his refusal to heed the prophetic Word that God intended to save him.

The formulation of this theological point antedates Ezekiel. A more familiar articulation of the thought occurs in Isaiah. Wicked King Ahaz (representing apostate Israel) refused to ask for a sign of God's proffered salvation. Yet the people's unbelief was no obstacle to God accomplishing redemption for all: God himself would provide the sign, namely, Immanuel, born of a virgin (Isaiah 7). But for those people who reject his Immanuel promise (Is 8:6–8), Yahweh himself will become a "stone of stumbling and a rock of offense" (Is 8:14).

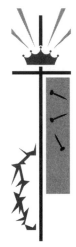

The corresponding terms πρόσκομμα ("stumbling block") and σκάνδαλον ("offense") play a prominent role in the NT. St. Paul cites Is 8:14 and alludes to Ezek 3:20 in Rom 9:32–33 as he describes the failure of the Jews as a whole to believe in the promised Christ, although Gentiles did. And St. Peter applies this language to all who reject Christ (1 Pet 2:8). In Gal 5:11 St. Paul speaks of the "offense of the cross," and just before his crucifixion our Lord warns his protesting disciples that all of them "will be offended" because of him that night (Mt 26:31).

In more recent theological parlance, these passages have often been summarized in the phrase "the scandal of particularity." (Although "scandal" transliterates the Greek σκάνδαλον, probably "offense" or the like would be a better English rendering.) The point is that salvation is through one particular person: Jesus Christ, and him alone; in one particular way: by grace alone and through faith alone; as revealed authoritatively by the inerrant and normative Scriptures (Scripture alone). These elements of the Gospel are intrinsically offensive to all universalism and synergism.

Ezek 3:20 finally warns that the righteous man who apostatizes "shall die because of his sin, and his righteous deeds which he had done will not be remembered." No one, no matter how righteous, can earn (or acquire from some other, "more righteous" saint) a "treasury of merit," some accumulation of previous good deeds that might now outweigh his evil. God will not finally judge using some "scales of justice," in which the good must be heavier than the bad—a common figure in ancient Egyptian depictions of a man's final judgment, and still prominent in modern, populist religion or spirituality. This line of thought will be especially prominent in chapter 18: God judges according to people's status *coram Deo* at the time of death, neither crediting them for past faith from which they have lapsed, nor holding repented and forgiven sin against them. Instead of balancing scales, it is all or nothing: with righteousness through faith (ultimately in Christ), all sin is forgotten (Jer 31:34), whereas without such justifying faith, any prior good is forgotten (Heb 6:4–8).

3:21 Here, in case 4, in a way, is the positive motivation for the prophet to undertake his calling despite its bleak prospects. Not all of Israel is incorrigibly wicked and doomed to die. To return to the language of 3:20, there is an interval between a person's first stirrings of apostatizing (perhaps even sub-consciously) and his actual implementation of a return to his natural, fallen state. During this interval, it is always possible, by God's grace, that the prophet's warning may take effect. And, if the man (and the prophet) is "faith-ful unto death," God's promise is sure: "I will give you the crown of life" (Rev 2:10). No person merits or chooses life of his own free will, but he is free to spurn or forfeit it.[43]

This is a familiar theme in the prophets, and throughout Scripture. We see it already in Isaiah's call (Isaiah 6): after Isaiah's response to the divine call, God depicts how obdurate Israel will be toward his prophet; nevertheless, in the final verse, he promises that a "holy seed" will sprout from the burnt and apparently lifeless stump of Israel (Is 6:13). It is a theme that Isaiah and other prophets will formulate as the promise of a remnant (e.g., Is 10:21–22). Before God, the mark of success in ministry does not lie in numbers. As Christ said, "Woe to you when all men speak well of you, for so their fathers did to the false prophets" (Lk 6:26).

3:22–23 Zimmerli makes an appropriate comparison of Ezekiel's com-mand to go out somewhere in the wide valley with the angel's summons to St. Philip in Acts 8:26 to go somewhere "without first knowing what is to happen there."[44] Yahweh's Glory, which appeared in Ezekiel 1, reappears here (and will later in chapters 10 and 43). Perhaps the reappearance here is intended to re-mind Ezekiel again that he is a mere creature, time- and space-bound, mortal. At any rate, Ezekiel responds with the same overwhelming awe as he had the first time (1:28b). His relationship with the holy God never becomes casual or chummy, and one may seriously ask whether Christians who espouse such a "relationship" are worshiping the God of Israel or a figment of their imagina-tion. *Lex orandi, lex credendi*: how one worships reflects (and also creates) how one believes. Worship and doctrine affect and reflect each other.

3:24 The command to Ezekiel to seclude himself in his house is the first of the injunctions in 3:24–27, all of which on their face appear to inhibit the normal exercise of his calling. But a closer reading makes clear that they all prepare him for the successful performance of his task. He is to say and do nothing in public except when he is clearly "moved by the Holy Spirit" (2 Pet 1:21). The main point of the confinement in his house is Ezekiel's seclusion from the public, a point to be reinforced by the following commands. It seems that all the locations of his preaching that are indicated in the book are at his house (8:1), since the elders or people come to him (14:1; 20:1; 33:30–31).

3:25–27 The remaining verses of the chapter amplify the impression cre-ated by 3:24. Each verse contains exegetical questions already discussed (see the textual notes). The basic issue has always been whether we are to take the

---

[43] Again, see the commentary on Josh 24:14–15 in Harstad, *Joshua*, 778–87.

[44] Zimmerli, *Ezekiel*, 1:157.

verses metaphorically or literally. My answer has always been to take them literally, but not literalistically, since literalistic interpretations of them would simply conflict with other data in the book. The major issue is Ezekiel's muteness. It is certainly possible that God imposed a physical inability to speak, but the Hebrew does not have to be so understood. I have preferred "speechlessness," either divinely imposed or voluntarily undertaken at God's command. Whatever its precise nature, 3:27 makes absolutely clear that the condition could be suspended whenever God willed, and the rest of the book, until the news of Jerusalem's fall terminates the speechlessness (33:22, fulfilling the promise in 24:27), bears that out.

These verses may be the first of Ezekiel's action prophecies, which will occupy virtually all of chapters 4–5 (which calls into question the aptness of the chapter divisions). Sometimes these are referred to as "symbolical actions," but that is much too weak. Slightly better is "sign acts," which builds on the Hebrew מוֹפֵת, "portent, sign," a term that will be applied to Ezekiel (12:6, 11; 24:24, 27), as it had been to Isaiah and his sons (Is 8:18; cf. Ex 4:21; 11:10). But מוֹפֵת (like אוֹת, "sign," with which it is often paired) is a multivalent word. Among other meanings, it may virtually mean "type" in the theological sense, an event which initially is an unverbalized prophecy. Words usually follow the event, however, making the meaning of the event unequivocal. The clear analogy to the pairing of "Word" and "Sacrament" to serve as joint means of grace should not escape us.

If that hermeneutic is applied to Ezek 3:24–27, we have action prophecies of the siege and fall of Jerusalem. Its inhabitants too will be confined—if not to their individual houses, certainly within the walls of the city. Its inhabitants too will be "tied up" in the sense of being sharply restricted in their movements. Above all, when Jerusalem does fall, all who survive will be stunned into speechlessness—at the very time when Ezekiel's muteness will cease, since his prophecies of the fall will have been fulfilled (33:22).

Chapter 3 and the whole inaugural vision and prophetic call (chapters 1–3) end with a prophecy that Ezekiel's preaching will continue in absolute faithfulness to Yahweh, whenever Yahweh wills: "Whenever I speak to you, I will open your mouth, and you shall say to them, 'Thus says the Lord Yahweh.'" Ezekiel will not be able to serve as "a man who reproves" or "a prosecuting attorney" of the people in the ordinary sense (3:26), but perhaps with greater impact than if he had enjoyed the relative liberty of other prophets. Although the last words of the chapter reiterate that Israel is a "rebellious house," the preceding words again leave open the possibility of repentance for individuals. No inexorable Greek μοῖρα, "fate," or other determinism characterizes God's judgment. The two alternatives (and there are only two!) are summarized in an almost formulaic restatement of the simple, but stark, alternatives: "Whoever listens, let him listen, and whoever refuses [to listen], let him refuse" (3:27). The negative alternative reminds one of the end of Isaiah's call (Is 6:9), appropriated by our Lord himself to explain his ministry of preaching in parables

(Mt 13:14–15 and parallels). And the positive, "Whoever listens, let him listen" (Ezek 3:27), is the prototype of one of Jesus' favorite formulae: "The one who has ears to hear, let him hear!" (e.g., Lk 8:8).[45]

And on a similar note the entire Scriptures end: "Outside are the dogs [homosexuals] and sorcerers and fornicators and murderers and idolaters and everyone who loves and makes a lie. ... The Spirit and the bride say, 'Come.' And let him who hears say, 'Come.' And let him who is thirsty come; let him who desires take the water of life without price. ... He who testifies to these things says, 'Surely, I am coming soon.' Amen. Come, Lord Jesus" (Rev 22:15, 17, 20).

---

[45] For an exposition of this verse and the questions it raises, see Just, *Luke 1:1–9:50*, 342–45. See also Just's exposition of the related theme of opened and closed eyes on pages 120–22.

Ezekiel 4–24

Prophecies of Judgment against Israel

A. The First Action Prophecies of Jerusalem's Siege and Exile (4:1–17)

B. More Action Prophecies and the First Judgment Oracle (5:1–17)

C. Judgment for Idolatry on the Mountains (6:1–14)

D. "The End Has Come" (7:1–27)

E. The Glory of God versus Four Abominations in the Temple (8:1–18)

F. Those without the Mark Are Slain (9:1–11)

G. The Glory Mounts the Throne over the Cherubim and Wheels (10:1–22)

H. After Promising "One Heart" and "a New Spirit," the Glory Departs the Temple (11:1–25)

I. An Action Prophecy of the Prince's Exile and Two False Proverbs about True Prophecy (12:1–28)

J. False Prophets and Prophetesses (13:1–23)

K. Cases of Casuistry (14:1–23)

L. Jerusalem Is a Useless Vine (15:1–8)

M. Jerusalem the Whore (16:1–63)

N. The Allegory of the Cedar Sprig and the Messiah Planted by Yahweh (17:1–24)

O. The Wicked Will Die and the Righteous Will Live (18:1–32)

P. A Lament for Israel's Princes (19:1–14)

Q. Review of the Old Covenant and Promise of the New (20:1–44)

Commentary on 21:1 (ET 20:45)–24:27 is in *Ezekiel 21–48*.

The First Action Prophecies
of Jerusalem's Siege and Exile

Translation

4 ¹"Now, you, son of man, take for yourself a brick, put it in front of you, and sketch on it a city, namely, Jerusalem. ²Lay siege against it, build a siege wall against it, throw up a ramp against it, set up camps against it, and station battering rams against it all around. ³And you, take for yourself an iron griddle and set it as an iron wall between you and the city. Direct your face toward it, so that it will be under siege as you besiege it. This is a sign for the house of Israel.

⁴"And you, lie down on your left side, and lay the iniquity of the house of Israel on it. For as many days as you lie on it, you shall bear their iniquity. ⁵But I myself have converted for you the years of their iniquity into the number of days: three hundred ninety days. And you shall bear the iniquity of the house of Israel. ⁶When you have finished these, you shall lie down a second time on your right side, and you shall bear the iniquity of the house of Judah for forty days; a day for each year have I converted it for you. ⁷You shall direct your face toward the siege of Jerusalem, with your arm bared, and you shall prophesy against it. ⁸See, I have placed upon you ropes so that you will not turn from your one side to your other side until you finish the days of your siege.

⁹"And you, take for yourself some wheat, barley, beans, lentils, millet, and emmer. You shall put them in a single dish, and make them into bread for yourself. During the number of days that you are lying on your side—three hundred ninety days—you shall eat it. ¹⁰Your food which you shall eat shall be by weight twenty shekels a day. At the same time each day you shall eat it. ¹¹Also you shall drink water by measure: one sixth of a hin. At the same time each day you shall drink. ¹²And a flat barley loaf—you shall eat it, and it you shall bake upon pellets of human dung in their sight."

¹³Then Yahweh said, "Thus shall the sons of Israel eat their food, unclean, among the Gentiles where I will banish them."

¹⁴Then I said, "Ah, Lord Yahweh, behold, my throat has never been defiled. A carcass or something torn by wild animals I have not eaten, from my youth until now, neither has rotten meat entered my mouth."

¹⁵Then he answered me, "Look, I designate for you droppings of cattle instead of human dung-pellets, and you shall make your bread upon them."

¹⁶Furthermore, he said to me: "Son of man, behold, I am about to break the staff of bread in Jerusalem, and they shall eat bread by weight and in fear, and they shall drink water by measure and in horror, ¹⁷so that they shall lack food and water, and they will be horrified, each man and his brother, and they shall waste away because of their iniquity."

Textual Notes

4:1 Formally, the speech of Yahweh's כָּבוֹד ("Glory") that began in 2:1 simply continues here. We may question the aptness of the insertion of a chapter division between the call vision (chapters 1–3) and chapter 4.

If, however, we adhere to the traditional chapter divisions, it should not be overlooked that with chapter 4 we begin the second major division of the book. We considered chapters 1–3 as a unit: the call of the prophet. This new unit runs from chapter 4 through chapter 24 and contains assorted messages of judgment and doom upon Judah and Jerusalem. A thematic arrangement may be discerned: chapters 8–11, concentrating on the temple, bisect two unequal sections, chapters 4–7 (judgment on the city and the land) and chapters 12–24 (a miscellany of judgment oracles). This gives us a sort of ABA' pattern of arrangement.

וְאַתָּה בֶן־אָדָם קַח־לְךָ לְבֵנָה—The pronoun with *waw*, וְאַתָּה, "and you," begins 4:1, 3, 4, 9. In these contexts Yahweh is addressing Ezekiel personally. Each of these verses begins a new subdivision in the text. The translation indicates this by beginning a new paragraph at 4:1; 4:4; and 4:9. (While 4:3 introduces a new action, it does not begin a new paragraph because it is part of the action prophecy in 4:1–3.)

In 4:1, 3, 4, 9 the second masculine singular pronoun (וְאַתָּה) is followed by a second masculine singular imperative. Immediately following the imperatives in 4:1, 3, 9 (קַח) is לְךָ, "for yourself." Grammarians call this use of the preposition לְ a dative of interest/advantage or an ethical dative (see *HALOT*, s.v. לְ, 9).

Ezekiel, whom Yahweh again calls a "son of man" (4:1; see 2:1), is commanded to take a brick and sketch a city on it. לְבֵנָה, a "brick" or "tile," does not refer to a kiln-fired brick, common in our culture, but to a sun-dried brick, still widely used for buildings in much of the Near East. Israelites in Jerusalem, in the Palestinian highlands, preferred to use the plentiful stone, but the exiles are in lower Mesopotamia. The brick Ezekiel used will not have hardened yet so that sketches could easily be made upon it. (We might compare it to newly poured concrete.)

וְחַקּוֹתָ עָלֶיהָ עִיר אֶת־יְרוּשָׁלָם:—The verb חָקַק can mean "to engrave" and is sometimes so translated here. But that seems to imply a more careful, perhaps official, inscription than is probably to be envisioned here; hence, I have translated it as "sketch." From excavations, we know of such sketches of ancient cities on mud bricks, including, interestingly, one of the city of Nippur, located not far from Tel Abib.[1] (The common noun חֹק, "statute," is derived from this same verb by metonymy, referring to a law that could be inscribed in stone.) The final phrase, אֶת־יְרוּשָׁלָם, in apposition to עִיר, could simply mean that the city he is to sketch is Jerusalem, but it may also indicate that he is to write "Jerusalem" on the brick so that the spectators have no doubt about its significance.

4:2 The verse describes the well-known course of action in laying siege to an ancient walled city.[2] The text does not specify whether the items in this verse were

---

[1] *ANEP*, § 260.

[2] The classical discussion of the subject is by Yigael Yadin, *The Art of Warfare in Biblical Lands* (2 vols.; New York: McGraw-Hill, 1963).

sketched on the brick or whether models or miniatures of them were built around the brick. The use of different verbs (rather than חָקַק, "to sketch," in 4:1) suggests the latter alternative. That conclusion is supported by considerations of space: it is not easy to see how all of this detail could have been drawn on a single brick.

Structurally, continuing the syntax of the previous verse, 4:2 begins with four co-ordinate clauses in parataxis, each consisting of three words, and each beginning with a perfect with *waw* consecutive (imperative in meaning). Each verb is followed by עָלֶיהָ ("against her/it," that is, the city) and a direct object. Only in the fifth and last clause is there minor variation, since it uses an imperative (וְשִׂים).

The first object, מָצוֹר, may be abstract ("siege") or concrete ("siege works"). I have opted for the first alternative, but, if the second were followed, the clause might more literally be translated, "set siege works/appliances against her." In either case, the clause is a general introduction, with the individual components to follow.

The דָּיֵק or "siege wall" was a continuous mound or rampart, or a series of them around the city. The purpose of the circumvallation was generally to keep watch on the city, both to prevent escapes and to intercept fresh supplies, keeping them from reaching the city. The specific fulfillment of this prediction, Nebuchadnezzar's con-struction of the siege wall against Jerusalem, is described in 2 Ki 25:1 (‖ Jer 52:4).

The סֹלְלָה was a "ramp" constructed from the ground at the foot of the city (an-cient cities were usually built at the tops of hills) and built up to the face of the city wall so that battering rams could be brought up the ramp and into position to attempt to breach the wall. The verb here, שָׁפַךְ, literally means to "pour out," undoubtedly a reference to the thousands of baskets of dirt, gravel, rock, and so on that would have to be poured out by human porters in the construction of such a ramp. Both literary and excavational evidence indicates that a rather precise recipe or method for build-ing such ramps was in use. Visitors to the site of biblical Lachish, southwest of Jerusalem, can plainly see the ramp used by the Assyrians to capture and destroy that city in 701 B.C., during the same campaign when Sennacherib also challenged Jerusalem (2 Ki 18:14; Is 36:2; 37:8; 2 Chr 32:9). Ussishkin, the latest excavator at Lachish, sectioned the siege ramp there.[3]

The "camps" (מַחֲנוֹת) are separate military camps for parts of the besieging army, strategically positioned around the city walls. All of the military appurtenances men-tioned so far in this verse are clearly visible to the visitor to the famous site of Masada on the western shore of the Dead Sea, where the dry desert air has preserved them phenomenally well for two millennia.

Last come the כָּרִים, "battering rams," frequently pictured in Assyrian reliefs[4] and perhaps invented by the Assyrians. The word כַּר may mean "ram/he-goat" as well as a military implement, and the latter, metaphorical meaning was probably derived from the former, famous for its butting activity (although a derivation from כָּרָה, "to dig,"

---

[3] The results may be read in David Ussishkin, "Excavations at Tel Lachish 1978–1983," *Tel Aviv* 10/2 (1983): 137–41; and Israel Eph'al, "The Assyrian Siege Ramp at Lachish," *Tel Aviv* 11/1 (1984): 60–70. See the drawing of Lachish and the photo of the site, including the siege ramp, in D. Ussishkin, "Lachish," *ABD* 4:122–23.

[4] E.g., *ANEP*, §§ 367 and 369.

is also possible). At the tip of the "ram" was a metal rod, usually shaped like a spear head or ax blade, which rammed between the stones of a wall. Once it penetrated the wall, it could be moved from side to side, dislodging bricks and perhaps causing whole sections of the wall to collapse.

4:3 The Hebrew מַחֲבַת is not quite so specific as "griddle." It could denote any kind of metal plate, but "griddle" is generally agreed to be most likely. It was a common household utensil, usually convex in shape and placed directly over an open fire with its edges resting on stones or bricks surrounding the fire. Flat cakes or bread could be baked on it. Since Lev 2:4–8 specifies that grain sacrifices could be prepared in griddles, pans, or ovens with only the griddled offerings being broken, many agree with Zimmerli that the griddle probably was fairly large.[5]

וַהֲכִינֹתָה אֶת־פָּנֶיךָ אֵלֶיהָ—This idiom, the Hiphil of כּוּן with פָּנִים, means "to direct one's face" (*HALOT*, s.v. כּוּן, Hiphil, 5), or perhaps "glare at," "fix your gaze," or the like. The idiom occurs in the OT only here and shortly again in Ezek 4:7. It is an intensification of the common "set [שִׂים] your face," used in 6:2 and repeatedly afterward (also in the rest of the OT). The prepositions אֶל (usually "toward") and עַל ("over," "against") are so often interchanged in Ezekiel especially that very possibly we should translate "direct your face *against*" the city, since עַל repeatedly had that hostile meaning in 4:2.

וְהָיְתָה בַמָּצוֹר וְצַרְתָּ עָלֶיהָ—The noun מָצוֹר, "siege" in the first of these two clauses is from the same root as the following verb, וְצַרְתָּ, namely, צוּר, **"lay siege to … a city"** (*HALOT*, s.v. צוּר I, 3 a). I have taken the first clause as a purpose clause and the second as a temporal, circumstantial clause: "so that it will be under siege as you besiege it."

אוֹת הִיא לְבֵית יִשְׂרָאֵל:—The verse "closes with a terse colophonic declaration on the significance of the dramatization."[6] "Sign" is a correct, but probably minimalistic translation of אוֹת. The word is often theologically loaded, meaning "type" or the like. In the series of Ezekiel's symbolical actions or word acts in chapter 4, the word occurs only here, but it may refer to the whole drama in 4:1–3. We meet the word three other times in Ezekiel (14:8; 20:12, 20). In about half of its occurrences in the OT, it is paired with מוֹפֵת, "portent," though in Ezekiel אוֹת is absent from the passages with מוֹפֵת (12:6, 11; 24:24, 27). The LXX usually renders אוֹת and מוֹפֵת by σημεῖον and τέρας, respectively. Many NT verses likewise pair σημεῖον and τέρας to speak of eschatological "signs" and "portents/wonders" in language reminiscent of the OT.[a] Both אוֹת and מוֹפֵת overlap somewhat in meaning with פֶּלֶא, "wonder, miracle," and forms of the cognate verb פָּלָא.

Jesus' signs (denoted by σημεῖον) figure prominently in the Gospel of John, of course (e.g., Jn 2:11, 23). The signs and portents in Ezekiel (denoted by אוֹת and מוֹפֵת) are comparable in that they convey divine "sacramental" significance through earthly elements. However, those in Ezekiel convey judgment (Law) rather than salvation (Gospel).

(a) Acts 2:19; 7:36; see also Jn 4:48; Acts 2:22, 43; 4:30; Rom 15:19; Heb 2:4

---

5 Zimmerli, *Ezekiel*, 1:162.

6 Block, *Ezekiel*, 1:174.

4:4   The phrases "put/lay iniquity [עָוֹן] on" and the resultant "bear [נָשָׂא] iniquity" recur throughout this section (4:4–8) and are analyzed more carefully in the commentary below. The idea is clearly that of assuming or bearing a burden. The antecedent of עָלָיו ("on it") twice in 4:4 must be Ezekiel's left side (צִדְּךָ הַשְּׂמָאלִי). Yahweh does not give Ezekiel any sermon or other explanation by which the prophet would communicate to the people that his actions represent the transfer or imputation of iniquity and punishment, but one assumes that somehow the audience was apprised of that meaning.

The emendation of וְשַׂמְתָּ ... עָלָיו to "I will lay ... on you"[7] (making God the subject of the action) was once quite popular (so RSV) but has more recently tended to be abandoned (so NRSV and ESV) in recognition of the fact that the change anticipates the explicit divine action in 4:5.

מִסְפַּר הַיָּמִים אֲשֶׁר—This might more literalistically be translated "the number of the days which ..." but it is idiomatic Hebrew for "however many days" or "as many days as," technically a compound relative consisting of a nominal phrase ("the number of the days") and the common Hebrew relative אֲשֶׁר. A similar idiom with מָקוֹם meaning "wherever" or "each place where" will be used in 6:13.

4:5   וַאֲנִי נָתַתִּי לְךָ אֶת־שְׁנֵי עֲוֹנָם לְמִסְפַּר יָמִים—The redundant pronoun "I" referring to God is emphatic: literally, "but *I myself* have given to you the years of their iniquity for the number of days." God has exchanged or converted the number of years into the same number of days, so that the mortal "son of man" (4:1) could represent the entire period of 390 years. English idiom requires a free translation of נָתַתִּי. "Assigned" is sometimes used, but "converted" seems clearer to me.

A similar but opposite conversion occurs in Num 14:33–34: days of iniquity are converted into years of punishment. The Israelite spies scouted out the land of Canaan for 40 days, and their lack of faith in God's promise that Israel could conquer the land is converted into 40 years of punishment, during which Israel will wander in the desert.

In Daniel 9 the 70 years of exile are converted typologically into 70 year-weeks. Somewhat comparable is the computation of a Babylonian exile lasting 70 years, based on the number of sabbatical years the land had been deprived of its rest (2 Chr 36:20–21).

וְנָשָׂאתָ עֲוֹן בֵּית־יִשְׂרָאֵל:—The noun עָוֹן can refer either to "iniquity" or to "punishment" for it. Here and in the similar clause in 4:6, this probably means "you shall bear the *punishment* ..." but since it is punishment for iniquity, I have retained the same translation for עָוֹן as earlier in 4:5, "iniquity."

4:6   וְשָׁכַבְתָּ עַל־צִדְּךָ הַיְמָונִי שֵׁנִית—A "second time" (שֵׁנִית) Ezekiel is to lie down, this time on his right side. "Second" is to be taken adverbially in reference to וְשָׁכַבְתָּ עַל־צִדְּךָ (he is to lie on his side a second time, but this time on the right side), not in reference to the whole preceding clause, including הַיְמָונִי (as though he were to lie on his right side a second time). The Qere, הַיְמָנִי, is the adjective "right" with article, while the Kethib, הַיְמָונִי, is otherwise unknown. Perhaps the Kethib is a

---

7   Zimmerli, *Ezekiel*, 1:148, and Allen, *Ezekiel*, 1:50, attribute this suggested emendation to Wellhausen.

variation of יְמִינִי but with the second *yod* incorrectly read or copied as the longer *waw*. Ordinarily יְמִינִי means "Benjaminite," but it could mean "right," since the two are etymologically related.

יוֹם לַשָּׁנָה יוֹם לַשָּׁנָה—The conversion here, "a day for each year," corresponds to the conversion of the years into the days in 4:5. The Hebrew formulation is slightly different than in 4:5, but the upshot is the same. Literally, the Hebrew here has "a day for a year, a day for a year," which is a verbatim repetition from Num 14:34 (see the first textual note on Ezek 4:5). We shall meet a similar distributive reduplication again in 10:9; 14:4, 7; 24:6; 46:1.

4:7 וְאֶל־מְצוֹר יְרוּשָׁלִַם תָּכִין פָּנֶיךָ—This has the same idiom for "direct your face" or "glare, stare at" as in 4:3 (Hiphil of כּוּן plus פָּנִים). As in 4:3, the object of the preposition אֶל is the model of the siege of Jerusalem.

וּזְרֹעֲךָ חֲשׂוּפָה—The "arm bared" indicates readiness for battle. "Unrolled sleeve" in idiomatic English would have the same import.

וְנִבֵּאתָ עָלֶיהָ:—The combination of the Piel verb נָבָא and preposition עַל usually implies a negative message, "prophesy *against*." The preposition אֶל is sometimes used in the same sense ("against"), or it may emphasize the direction of the message (prophesy "toward") rather than its content. In Amos 7:15–16 both combinations are used, and the distinction between the two is clear.

4:8 נָתַתִּי עָלֶיךָ עֲבוֹתִים—The binding with ropes echoes 3:25, with the same verb (נָתַן) and noun (plural of עֲבֹת). In both cases, whether the expression is to be taken literally or figuratively is a matter of interpretation. See the textual notes and commentary on 3:25–27.

4:9–17 This whole section is about food. Some translations and interpreters consider the entire section to describe a single symbolic diet for Ezekiel, which is prophetic of what the Israelites will endure. It is possible that when a "barley loaf" is mentioned in 4:12, Ezekiel is simply using the common term used by the lower classes, regardless of the ingredients. If so, there is no contradiction with the list of ingredients in 4:9.

However, it seems better to understand this section as God's description of two distinct diets, representing distinct circumstances and events. The diets are to be eaten by Ezekiel as distinct action prophecies, each representing a different set of conditions for the Israelites. A diet indicating the starvation rations of the Israelites in Jerusalem while the city is under siege is prescribed for Ezekiel in 4:9–11 and is interpreted in 4:16–17. Another diet, representing the subsistence level of the Israelites during their exile in Babylon, is prescribed for Ezekiel in 4:12, explained in 4:13, and modified in 4:14–15. This forms a chiastic structure:[8]

A   Siege diet (4:9–11)
  B   Exilic diet (4:12)
  B'   Exilic diet explained (4:13) and modified (4:14–15)
A'   Siege diet explained (4:16–17)

4:9 חִטִּין וּשְׂעֹרִים וּפוֹל וַעֲדָשִׁים וְדֹחַן וְכֻסְּמִים—Most of these foods are common in the Hebrew OT and in other Semitic languages. The only one not mentioned else-

---

[8]   So Block, *Ezekiel*, 1:169.

where in the OT is דֹחַן, but its meaning, "millet," is clear from its Akkadian cognate *duḫnu*. Conversely, עֲדָשִׁים ("lentils") appears to be unique to Hebrew, but since it is used three other times in the OT, there is no doubt as to its meaning. Many of these names are plural in form, referring to the fact that many kernels are normally ground together before being eaten. חִטִּין ("wheat") has the Aramaic plural ending (ין-) instead of the Hebrew (ים-). Ezekiel's choice of the Aramaic form is a portent of the imminent replacement of Hebrew by Aramaic in much everyday speech during the exilic era. "Wheat" and "barley" (שְׂעֹרִים) are often paired in the Bible, representing the two main grains from which bread was made, although barley bread was generally limited to those too poor to afford wheat.

"Beans" (פּוֹל) and "lentils" (עֲדָשִׁים), both legumes, could be used in bread, but ordinarily were eaten in a sort of soup or stew. As is still true in much of the world today, beans were often the major food of the poor. "Millet" (דֹחַן) could be eaten by humans, but was probably more often grown for livestock. כֻּסְּמִים (the plural of כֻּסֶּמֶת in Ex 9:32; Is 28:25) means "emmer," a species of wheat other than the common durum variety mentioned first (חִטִּין). Emmer was considered inferior because it could not easily be threshed, but it did provide people with a fall-sown wheat. The view that כֻּסְּמִים is "spelt" (so BDB; *DCH*; and *HALOT*) is almost certainly erroneous, because that is an entirely different (hexaploid) variety of wheat, which is not grown in that part of the world. (Of the modern versions consulted [e.g., NRSV, NIV], ESV appears to be the first to translate the word correctly as "emmer.") KJV's archaic "fitches," that is, modern "vetch," is a legume and even further afield.

The triplet of "wheat," "barley," and "emmer" occurs in Is 28:25 as well as in Ugaritic. As mentioned earlier, "wheat" and "barley" are often paired. Thus the list in this verse has an ABA' order, two cereals at beginning and end, with two legumes in the middle.

Lev 19:19 (cf. Deut 22:9) prohibits the sowing of two kinds of seed in the same field, but there is no prohibition of mixing different grains to make flour or bread. Even so, the mixture of cereal flour with legume meal is unusual. The Babylonian Talmud (*Erubin*, 81a) records a third century A.D. experiment using this mixture to make bread, but reports that it was not eaten but given to a dog! As this commentary is being published (A.D. 2005), an "Ezekiel bread" is being marketed on the West Coast of the United States. Ezek 4:9 is quoted, and the bread claims to use the ingredients mentioned (although spelt instead of emmer). It is a heavy, slightly coarse bread, but easily edible.

בִּכְלִי אֶחָד—Since Hebrew really has no indefinite article, the use of אֶחָד here seems to mandate "a *single* dish" rather than merely "a/one dish." The point is that all the items are to be thoroughly mixed together into the dough for the bread.

וְעָשִׂיתָ אוֹתָם לְךָ לְלָחֶם—The idiom of עָשָׂה with an accusative (אוֹתָם) and לְ (לְלָחֶם) can mean "to make something [accusative] into [לְ] something else" (see BDB, s.v. עָשָׂה I, Qal, II 1 g; cf. *HALOT*, s.v. עשׂה I, Qal, 7 a).

4:10–11 These two verses, which describe siege rations of food and drink, are arranged symmetrically; compare 4:16. A shekel weighed about four-tenths of an ounce, so twenty shekels of food was about eight ounces. A hin was roughly a gallon, so the daily ration of water was about two-thirds of a quart. By almost any criterion, this is clearly a starvation diet. Especially in hotter times of the year, the small amount of water would not go far. At the end of the chapter, 4:16–17 returns to the same picture verbally, and in 5:10 even direr circumstances are prophesied. From here on, there are many parallels with the curses for Israel's disobedience in Leviticus 26. Lev 26:26 is similar to Ezek 4:10 with its phrase "by weight" but also includes "and you shall not be satisfied."

Ezekiel's rations are prophetic of the famine that will grip Jerusalem during its siege. We can compare these figures with the actual situation in the last days of Jerusalem as reported by Jeremiah. While under house arrest, Jeremiah was allowed one loaf a day "until all the bread from the city was gone" (Jer 37:21). When he subsequently was lowered into a cistern, "there was no water in the cistern, only mud, and Jeremiah sank in the mud" (Jer 38:6).

מֵעֵת עַד־עֵת—This phrase, in both 4:10 and 4:11, literally says that Ezekiel is to eat and drink his rations "from time to time" (*HALOT*, s.v. עֵת, 5 d), which might mean whenever he is hungry or thirsty (which would be most of the time). However, in Mishnaic Hebrew the similar phrase מֵעֵת לְעֵת can refer to a period of twenty-four hours (see Jastrow, s.v. עֵת; cf. מֵעֵת אֶל־עֵת in 1 Chr 9:25). Hence God apparently commands Ezekiel to eat and drink the rations prescribed in 4:9–11 just once each day, and at the same time each day. The implication may be that Ezekiel is to partake of these rations only—and only at the set time—while he is engaged in public ministry. Such a restriction would only increase the agony of the audience as it waits for the appointed time. Yet it might be possible that Ezekiel would be permitted to partake of other sustenance in private while not on duty as a prophet (see the commentary below).

4:12 וְעֻגַת שְׂעֹרִים תֹּאכֲלֶנָּה—The phrase with עֻגָה in construct is literally "a loaf of barley," but I have translated it as "a flat barley loaf." "Barley" was generally regarded as inferior to wheat, and so barley bread was eaten mostly by the poor. Many translations have "cake," but that sounds like dessert to us. The "loaf" is not our raised bread, but is similar to Near Eastern pita or similar flat bread. The noun עֻגָה occurs in other OT passages, such as in reference to the unleavened *matsoth* eaten at the exodus after the Passover in Ex 12:39, and the small loaf Elijah requested from the widow of Zarephath in 1 Ki 17:13. It is related to the verb עוּג, "to bake," which occurs later in Ezek 4:12 and only there in the OT. The verb may refer to the baking of bread directly on hot stones or ashes without the use of a pan, and so the noun may refer to bread baked in that way. The LXX translates עֻגָה quite appropriately as ἐγκρυφίας, a "cake baked hidden in the ashes" (LEH). Ezek 4:12 does not use the usual Hebrew verb אָפָה, "to bake," nor לֶחֶם, the common noun for "bread" baked in the ordinary way. (לֶחֶם was in 4:9.)

Many translations (e.g., KJV, RSV, NIV) and commentators consider 4:12 to refer to how Ezekiel is to prepare the same bread to which 4:9–10 refers. If so, וְעֻגַת שְׂעֹרִים would be an adverbial accusative: "And you shall eat it as a barley cake" (RSV). However, here the third singular pronominal suffix on the verb תֹּאכֲלֶנָּה (Qal second masculine singular imperfect of אָכַל) is feminine (as also is the following pronoun וְהִיא

and the suffix on תְּעֻגֶנָה), while the three occurrences of the same verb in 4:9–10 had a masculine (third singular) suffix (תֹּאכֲלֶנּוּ), referring to the masculine nouns לֶחֶם in 4:9 and מַאֲכָל in 4:10. In 4:12, the feminine suffix on תֹּאכֲלֶנָה refers to the feminine noun עֻגָה. Therefore it is best to take this phrase as a *casus pendens*[9] that introduces a new loaf (different from that in 4:9–10), literally, "and a loaf of barley—you shall eat it …" Instructions for baking this loaf then follow in 4:12.

Thus 4:12 describes a food that is different from the siege diet in 4:9–11 (see the textual note on 4:9–17 above). Hence this "flat loaf" (עֻגָה) is not to be taken as synonymous with the "bread" (לֶחֶם) made out of the various grains in 4:9. So also, there is no contradiction between the stipulation that this "loaf" is to be of "barley" (שְׂעֹרִים, 4:12), while the "bread" made in 4:9 included many additional ingredients.

וְהִיא בְּגֶלְלֵי צֵאַת הָאָדָם—The feminine pronoun הִיא refers to the "loaf" introduced at the start of 4:12. Baking bread upon *animal* dung (what God will grant Ezekiel in 4:15) was common and is still not unknown in poorer rural villages and among the nomadic Bedouin of the Near East. This method is the result not only of poverty, but of the scarcity of wood and other fuels in much of that part of the world. Edward Robinson recorded his experience in the nineteenth century:

> The men were baking a large round flat cake of bread in the embers of a fire of camel's and cow-dung. Taking it out when done, they brushed off the ashes and divided it among the party. … I tasted it, and found it quite as good as the common bread of the country. … This is the common fare of persons travelling in this manner.[10]

"Upon" is the proper translation of בְּ here (on בְּגֶלְלֵי), as confirmed by the parallel use of עַל in 4:15. The dough is placed directly on the hot embers of burning dung, and when the loaf is done baking, the ashes are cleaned off (as best as can be) and the bread is ready for eating. A few of the ashes may possibly cling to the bread, but, if so, the heat will have sanitized them.

גֶלְלֵי is the masculine plural construct of גֵּל, "dung." In its two other OT occurrences, it refers to human feces also in Job 20:7, but to animal feces in Ezek 4:15. The root גָּלַל means to "roll" and hence usually implies something round. The noun bespeaks the natural shape of feces after defecation, as does our euphemistic "cow pie" or vulgar "turd." I have used the (plural) word "pellets" here in 4:12 (and "dung-pellets" in 4:15, where the word is not further qualified by צֵאָה, "dung," as here). גֵּל is a dialectical variant of גָּלָל, "dung, feces" (1 Ki 14:10; Zeph 1:17). Both are related etymologically to גִּלּוּלִים, "fecal deities," one of Ezekiel's favorite contemptuous terms for idols (thirty-nine times; e.g., 6:4–6). Yahweh styles idols as pellets of dung (see the textual note on גִּלּוּלֵיכֶם in 6:4), intentionally eliciting disgust.

Likewise, God's command in Ezek 4:12 is intended to evoke abhorrence at the vulgarity. More vulgarities of a different sort will be present in chapters 16 and 23.

---

[9] So Block, *Ezekiel*, 1:181, n. 83, who cites *casus pendens* constructions also in 30:18b and 32:7b.

[10] Edward Robinson, *Biblical Researches* (London: J. Murray, 1841), 2:76, quoted in Greenberg, *Ezekiel*, 1:107.

Were Ezekiel preaching today, his God-given vocabulary would no doubt cause outrage among listeners who knew the true meaning of the Hebrew terms.

The noun צֵאָה, "dung, excrement," (*HALOT*), occurs elsewhere in the OT only in Deut 23:14 (ET 23:13), where its contextual meaning is clear. Probably it derives from the verb יָצָא and hence denotes "what goes out" of a person, as does the Latin etymology of "excrement." The slightly more common noun צֹאָה[b] shares the same etymology and meaning. In 2 Ki 18:27 and Is 36:12 Sennacherib's field commander threatens that conditions during an Assyrian siege of Jerusalem would even cause the eating and drinking of one's own waste. OT passages with these words are considered so offensive that English translations commonly paraphrase them. However, such bowdlerization removes some of the scandal of the Hebrew terms. It weakens the force when, for example, God uses צֹאָה to characterize the vulgarity of attempts at justification by works (Prov 30:12; cf. Is 4:4). OT passages with such vocabulary may be the background of the saying of Jesus in Mk 7:18–23.

(b) 2 Ki 18:27; Is 4:4; 28:8; 36:12; Prov 30:12

Ezek 4:12 would not be particularly surprising if it merely referred to animal dung, but the use of *human* excrement for cooking was revolting. God had commanded the Israelites in Deut 23:13–15 (ET 23:12–14):

> You shall have a marked place outside the camp, and you shall go there, outside, and you shall have a trowel among your implements, and when you sit outside, you shall dig with it, then turn and cover your excrement [צֵאָה, as in Ezek 4:12], because Yahweh your God walks about in the midst of your camp to save you … so your camp shall be holy, so that he shall not see something indecent and depart from you.

But this is not clearly relevant. Before being used as fuel, dung (of whatever source) is dried and virtually odorless.

תְּעֻגֶנָה לְעֵינֵיהֶם:—This is the verb "to bake" (Qal second masculine singular imperfect of עוג with third feminine singular pronominal suffix) that is related to the noun עֻגָה, "loaf" (used earlier in the verse).

Ezekiel is to perform his bizarre cooking "to their eyes" (לְעֵינֵיהֶם), in public view of the exiled Israelites. This is the first command in the book for the prophet to perform an act in public, but similar commands will recur later (e.g., 12:2–7). It was necessary that the people see this action so they would understand (if not immediately, then at least later, after the fall of Jerusalem) that it was a prediction of their fate. Undoubtedly his earlier actions prescribed in chapter 4 were also to be done in public, but the command to act publicly becomes even more important now as Ezekiel ratchets up the portrayal of the judgments to come.

4:13 The LXX varies significantly from the MT, mostly by abbreviation. Allen[11] and others are disposed to follow the LXX, but I see no good reason to do so. The verse has unique features. This is the only place in the book where we find "Yahweh said" (וַיֹּאמֶר יְהוָה) without the addition of "to him" or the like. That gives the verse more the character of a solemn pronouncement than of another communication to the prophet which he, in turn, should pass on to the people.

---

[11] Allen, *Ezekiel*, 1:51.

אֶת־לַחְמָם טָמֵא—This (לֶחֶם) is the ordinary noun for "bread" (as in 4:9), but here (as often) it has the wider significance of "food." "Unclean" (טָמֵא) is part of the priestly vocabulary from Leviticus that is common in this prophetic book by a priest (1:3). See the commentary below.

בַּגּוֹיִם אֲשֶׁר אַדִּיחֵם שָׁם:—The Hiphil of נדח, meaning "to banish, expel, drive out," is a relatively strong expression. That the form is first person imperfect indicates (1) that the exile of those remaining in Jerusalem is still in the future and (2) that Yahweh will personally execute this punishment. It will not be merely another meaningless turn in the wheel of history or fate. Since the clause has the plural "nations" (גּוֹיִם), it points beyond the pending Babylonian exile to the Diaspora, when Israelites will be scattered throughout virtually all the rest of the known world (cf. Jeremiah 40–44).

4:14 Ezekiel's priestly formation (1:3) comes to the fore in this verse, not only in his remonstrance itself, but by the vocabulary used, which does not easily lend itself to translation.

אֲהָהּ אֲדֹנָי יהוה—The combination of these three words has a semi-formulaic quality about it, seeing that Ezekiel uses it three more times (9:8; 11:13; 21:5 [ET 20:49]). The interjection אֲהָהּ, "ah, alas!" is commonly associated with alarm. The sense of urgency is heightened by its connection with a fuller form of the divine name, "the Lord Yahweh" (see the textual notes and commentary on 2:4).[12]

I regard it of considerable importance that English readers note the use of God's *personal* name, not merely another generic name or title for the Deity. (English translations conventionally indicate the personal name in אֲדֹנָי יהוה by translating it "Lord GOD/GOD" [KJV, RSV, ESV], using capital letters for "God.") The whole biblical "theology" (in the narrow sense) follows from this proper name. Only this personal Deity, the one true God (Deut 6:4), has become incarnate, taking on a true human body at the conception of Jesus Christ. Because he did so and lived as a true man, suffered, died, and rose again, he is able to promise that all baptized believers in him shall be raised bodily on the Last Day and enter as whole people (body and soul) into the salvation he has prepared. Mere "God" (instead of "GOD") or mere "Lord" (versus "LORD") for the Tetragrammaton[13] may fail to convey this. Early Christians readily thought of Yahweh, the personal God of Israel, when "Lord" (κύριος) was used, but modern audiences do not. The incarnate Deity was named "Jesus" (Mt 1:21), meaning "Yahweh saves." "Jesus is Lord" (1 Cor 12:3) is usually considered the earliest Christian creed, the progenitor of the later Apostles', Nicene, and Athanasian Creeds.

נַפְשִׁי לֹא מְטֻמָּאָה—Often נֶפֶשׁ can mean "throat" (*HALOT*, 1) or, more technically, the gullet or esophagus. Thus, like much Hebrew anatomical language ("heart," etc.), it has a physical meaning before its expansion into emotional and spiritual meanings. Hebrew usage is thus "psychosomatic." The transferred meanings of נֶפֶשׁ are con-

---

[12] Zimmerli has a comprehensive analysis of the use of the divine name in Ezekiel in his first appendix, in *Ezekiel*, 2:556–62.

[13] In English translations "LORD" is traditionally used for the Tetragrammaton when it appears alone without אֲדֹנָי, "Lord."

nected to "throat" by the obvious fact that life is dependent on the intake of food, drink, and air (cf. Gen 2:7). Thus, it is regularly translated as "life, self, person, personality," and so on. Traditionally, it was rendered "soul" in KJV (including here), but "soul" has taken on so many other connotations that in modern English that translation can no longer be regarded as acceptable.

The Pual participle מְטֻמָּאָה ("defiled") is feminine, matching the gender of נֶפֶשׁ.

Ezekiel goes on to list three egregious examples of meat that would have rendered him unclean had he ever eaten them. In the first two examples, the concern is that the blood has not been drained properly (Lev 17:10–13), a cardinal concern of "kosher" laws (to use the postbiblical, Jewish term). נְבֵלָה refers to the "carcass" of an animal that had died a natural death. טְרֵפָה applies to an animal that had been torn in pieces by predators, and in later Judaism, it virtually became a generic term for food that is not kosher. Meat from these two sources was forbidden to both laity (Ex 22:30 [ET 22:31]; Deut 14:21; cf. Lev 17:15) and to priests (Lev 22:8; Ezek 44:31), who would be disqualified from divine service. The third term, פִּגּוּל ("rotten meat"), was prohibited for priests and is a little harder to translate accurately. Certain sacrificial meat went to priests as part of their emolument, but it had to be eaten before the third day, before it would have begun to decompose in the warm climate (Lev 7:18; 19:7). Hence *HALOT* defines פִּגּוּל as sacrificial meat "**which has become unclean** because it has been kept too long (until the third day …)." In Is 65:4 פִּגּוּל is parallel with "pig's meat," that is, pork.

4:15 נָתַתִּי לָךְ—Here נָתַן has the nuance of "to allow, grant." We have met it repeatedly in a statutory sense, and so I have translated it "designate" here. But the word's basic meaning is "give," and from Ezekiel's standpoint, the "gift" element in God's concession is also apparent. All of God's commandments were ultimately intended as gifts to his people, whom he had saved (Ex 20:2; Deut 5:6).

אֶת־צְפוּעֵי הַבָּקָר תַּחַת גֶּלְלֵי הָאָדָם—Here the Kethib of the word (plural in construct) for animal dung is צְפוּעֵי, but the Qere is צְפִיעֵי. By either spelling, the noun occurs only here in the OT and means "animal droppings, dung" (*HALOT*, s.v. צָפִיעַ). For the cooking method and for גֶּלְלֵי הָאָדָם, see the textual notes above on 4:12. Greenberg opines that if the "the prophet's act was to carry its original meaning, it must be supposed that—for ritual reasons?—priests were known not to use animal dung as fuel."[14] That seems to be a reasonable inference. In any case, preparing food in an unclean land would result in unclean food.

4:16–17 The introductory formula "he said to me" and the address to the prophet as "son of man" indicate that a new subsection is beginning—a verbal interpretation of the action prophecy of 4:9–11.

These last two verses are really one extended sentence. They have a certain stereotypical quality. "I am about to break the staff of bread" in 4:16 echoes Lev 26:26, and "they shall waste away because of their iniquity" in Ezek 4:17 echoes Lev 26:39. Clauses nearly identical to the first are found also in Ezek 5:16 and 14:13, and clauses similar to the second recur in 24:23 and 33:10. All of 4:16b is similar to 12:18–19.

---

[14] Greenberg, *Ezekiel*, 1:108.

Echoes of Leviticus 26, the peroration of the so-called "Holiness Code"[15] in Leviticus 17–26, continue throughout Ezekiel 5–6 as well.

The sermonic quality of 4:16–17 anticipates the general tone of most of the rest of Ezekiel's oracles after one more action prophecy at the beginning of chapter 5. They function as a sort of commentary on the preceding action prophecies, in case their import was not obvious to the observers. We are not told whether or not Ezekiel relayed these verses orally to Israel at this time or whether the explanation was spoken only to the prophet, who subsequently wrote it down.

4:16 הִנְנִי שֹׁבֵר מַטֵּה־לֶחֶם בִּירוּשָׁלַם—Common in prophetic oracles is הִנֵּה followed by a participle, indicating imminent divine action—the so-called *futurum instans* ("imminent future"; see Waltke-O'Connor, § 37.6 f, and GKC, § 116 p). The perspective is God's. As people count time, the chronological imminence of the event God announces may or may not be evident to them, although in this case the Israelites will learn of Jerusalem's fall in a few short years. Sometimes, however, the imminence may be eschatological and apparent only to the eyes of faith. We should understand the judgment upon Jerusalem as a type of the eschatological judgment for all humanity's sin that was executed upon the crucified Christ, and then, via the cross, as a type of the final judgment at the end of the world (Revelation 20). At all times Christians are to consider the return of Christ and the final judgment to be imminent, whether or not they are so according to the world's way of reckoning time.

The idiom "to break [שָׁבַר] the staff [מַטֵּה] of bread [לֶחֶם]" can be translated literally because "staff of bread" has found its way into English. Bread is the "staff" (walking stick, crutch) upon which man leans for life. If the staff is broken, then human life will fail. This idiom will be repeated in similar warnings of divine judgment in 5:16 and 14:13.

וְאָכְלוּ־לֶחֶם בְּמִשְׁקָל וּבִדְאָגָה—They will eat their "bread," or, more generally, "food" (לֶחֶם) "by weight" (בְּמִשְׁקָל) means that their rations will be precisely weighed out because they are so small. מִשְׁקָל denotes a unit of measure by weight.

וּמַיִם בִּמְשׂוּרָה וּבְשִׁמָּמוֹן יִשְׁתּוּ:—Likewise, the scant available water would be carefully apportioned "by measure" (בִּמְשׂוּרָה) to each person. מְשׂוּרָה is a "measure of volume of liquids" (*HALOT*).

Shared vocabulary ties 4:16 to 4:9–11: "eat," "bread," "drink," "water," and the two phrases for "by weight/measure."[16] This supports the view that 4:9–11 and 4:16 are about a siege diet, whereas 4:12 and 4:13 are about an exilic diet (see the textual note above on 4:9–17).

The last two clauses in the Hebrew of 4:16 are structured in a chiastic style: "eat" is first and "drink" is last, and between those two verbs are corresponding terms: "and

---

[15] That critical caption for Leviticus 17–26 is unobjectionable if we simply hear it as a convenient title for a discrete section of the Pentateuch. Critical proponents of the old "documentary hypothesis" often hypothesized that Ezekiel came from the same circle of priests that composed that "document." In conservative eyes, the echoes of Leviticus in Ezekiel simply reflect vividly Ezekiel's priestly formation (1:3).

[16] בִּמְשׂוּרָה is in both 4:11 and 4:16. בְּמִשְׁקוֹל in 4:10 is only slightly different from בְּמִשְׁקָל in 4:16.

they shall eat bread by weight and in fear, and water by measure and in horror they shall drink."

In the OT the noun שִׁמָּמוֹן, "horror," occurs only here (4:16) and in 12:19, but the root שׁמם is very common, especially in the book of Ezekiel, occurring nearly fifty times (almost a third of the root's occurrences in the OT). The Niphal (וְנָשַׁמּוּ) of the verb שָׁמֵם occurs in 4:17, where I have used the same English stem in translation ("horrified"). These words are strong and could be translated many ways; for example, the noun could be translated "shock," "dread," and so on. The same root (שׁמם) appears in Daniel's well-known "abomination of desolation [causing destruction, horror]" (Dan 9:27; 11:31; 12:11). Ezekiel will expatiate on this theme later, describing the people's horror in terms of self-loathing (6:9; 20:43; 36:31).

4:17 לְמַעַן יַחְסְרוּ לֶחֶם וָמָיִם—Either a purpose or result clause can be introduced by לְמַעַן. With a following imperfect verb (as here) it commonly means "so that" (*HALOT*, s.v. מַעַן, 2 b). Here it may logically follow the first declaration of Yahweh in 4:16: "I am about to break the staff of bread in Jerusalem … so that they shall lack food and water." However, its precise force here can be—and is—debated. Ezekiel seems to use it frequently in conclusions (6:6; 12:19; 14:5; 16:63). The rest of 4:17 exhibits usual Hebrew parataxis (a series of coordinate clauses).

וְנָשַׁמּוּ אִישׁ וְאָחִיו וְנָמַקּוּ בַּעֲוֹנָם:—The subject of נָשַׁמּוּ is literally "a man and his brother." Some translators offer "every single person" or the like.

The combination of בְּ with עָוֹן occurred in 3:18–19. See the textual notes on בַּעֲוֹנוֹ in 3:18.

Commentary

Ezekiel's Action Prophecies

With this new section of the book (see the textual note on 4:1), we are thrown abruptly into something for which Ezekiel is probably better known than for his sermons and which is probably the major factor in this common assessment of him: "No stranger figure can be found in all the goodly fellowship of the prophets."[17]

The immediate question is how to label the topic of this section. And what label we use tends to reveal how we understand and interpret it. Possibly the most common label has been "symbolical actions."[18] In a rather similar vein, they are sometimes considered a form of "street theater" or "sermon illustrations." While there is probably a germ of truth in all those labels, they all fall far short of getting at the actions' true significance.

Block's favored term is "sign-act,"[19] building on God's characterization of at least one of them in 4:3 (see below). My own preferred term is "action

---

[17] Bright, *A History of Israel*, 336.

[18] So a major and influential German study: Fohrer, *Die symbolischen Handlungen der Propheten*.

[19] Block, *Ezekiel*, 1:173 and passim.

prophecy," that is, a prophecy that is not verbalized (at least not initially), but rather is acted out, yet with the same predictive force as the prophet's verbalized sermons. Virtually always an interpretation of the actions does ensue, partly so that the audience is not left guessing what their predictive force is. "If actions speak louder than words, here they were a megaphone for the prophetic words."[20]

A Lutheran naturally considers this unity of act and verbalization as analogous to our understanding of Word and Sacrament as simply two forms of the divine "Word" in its broader sense, whose content is Jesus Christ, the Word made flesh (Jn 1:14). This is a classical instance where the interpreter's hermeneutical presuppositions will play a determinative role. If a real sacramentology is lacking, such an interpretation will hardly be acceptable. Also, one must add that a conviction of the reality of predictive prophecy is a necessary prerequisite, whether we are speaking of the "spoken sacrament" or of the "visible word."

We must therefore avoid the under-interpretation that the prophetic actions (or the Sacraments) are merely symbolic, without real power and devoid of the efficacious real presence of God in them. Likewise, a certain over-interpretation must also be avoided. Sometimes the recognition that these acts were not mere symbols, but the *verbum visibile* ("the Word made visible") is accompanied by a conviction that such behavior is *ex opere operato*, akin to magic. The two extremes may meet: one is reminded how Protestants on the one hand and Roman Catholics and the Orthodox on the other may have difficulty distinguishing real biblical sacramentology from magic—though for opposite reasons!

At least for the sake of argument, it might be conceded that such kinds of prophetic behavior may have been used also by pagans and that Yahweh "baptized" the method of acting out prophecy, placing it into an entirely different context when done by true prophets. For example, in Jeremiah 27–28 we have the spectacle of a "contest" of action prophecies between Jeremiah and the false prophet Hananiah, and in 1 Ki 22:11, the false prophet Zedekiah made iron horns to accompany his vain prophecy of victory. Pagans and apostate Israelites may not have seen the difference between such false prophetic actions and those of Ezekiel. However, the Bible is clear in its denunciation of magic. For orthodox Yahwism—the OT faith, which finds its necessary fulfillment in Jesus Christ—the prophetic action had no intrinsic power to effect anything apart from the will and activity of the triune God according to his Word, as neither did verbalized predictions. It was Yahweh himself who validated and fulfilled both the action and verbal prophecies that he had inspired.

Ezekiel is by no means the only prophet who uses action prophecies, but both in frequency and in strangeness, his stand out. As usually counted, Ezekiel's total of twelve action prophecies exceeds the ten of Jeremiah by only

---

[20] Allen, *Ezekiel*, 1:66.

two. Isaiah performs only one (Is 20:2–4). But whatever the numbers, such actions accompanied much true prophecy, beginning at least with Ahijah (1 Ki 11:30) through Agabus in the NT (Acts 21:10–11).

The Model Siege of Jerusalem (4:1–3)

4:1–3 In 4:1–2, Ezekiel mimes in miniature and in detail the regular course of the siege of an ancient walled city. It may be debated whether the action of 4:3 is to be linked with those of 4:1–2, but it seems more likely that it is to be taken as part of the same prophecy. However, there is no clear connection in 4:3 with the ordinary procedures of ancient warfare, unless we are to think of the metal plating or shields used to protect the wooden battering rams from the defenders' attempts to set them afire. Probably the iron griddle was intended to represent the impenetrable barrier Yahweh had erected between himself and the city. He had hidden his face from the once-chosen city (cf. 7:22). Several commentators cite the similar lament of Lam 3:44: "You have covered yourself with a cloud so that no prayer can pass through."

Presumably still part of the one action prophecy are the final commands to Ezekiel in 4:3 to glare at his miniature city and to besiege it himself. God's wrath toward the unfaithful city expresses itself not only in a passive silence, but also in an active hostility to be expressed by his spokesman, the prophet.

The final clause on the *sign*ificance of the prophecy, "This is a sign for the house of Israel," probably applies to all of 4:1–3 (and spills over to the rest of chapters 4–5 too). "Sign" (אוֹת) is not used again in the remaining action prophecies in chapters 4–5, but there is no reason why it could not have been. Its accurate translation is difficult, especially in a culture as deficient in sacramental and supernatural consciousness as ours. "Sacrament/miracle" is usually part of its meaning. As such, the word is the perfect Hebrew term for action prophecy. It is nearly synonymous with מוֹפֵת (usually translated "portent"), with which it is often paired, making a virtual hendiadys. If one can distinguish the two, מוֹפֵת seems to be applied more to the person of the prophet almost as a surrogate for Yahweh himself (so in 12:6, 11 and 24:24, 27). The two words are used together for Isaiah and his two sons (who had prophetic names): "Behold, here am I and the children whom Yahweh has given me as signs and portents in Israel from Yahweh of hosts, who dwells on Mount Zion" (Is 8:18).

The similarity of this whole complex of words and ideas to the hermeneutical concept of "typology" should not be overlooked. In fact, "type" would often pass as a translation of these two key Hebrew words and their equivalents in the Greek NT, σημεῖον and τέρας (see the textual notes on 4:3). "Typology" implies a person, event, institution, or place with futuristic significance whose full import would not be evident if it were not elucidated by some verbalization of the divine Word (which, for many OT types, does not come until the NT). So it is with the action prophecies. The same bilateral relationship continues in the Word-Sacrament structure of the church's worship. The physical elements (water, bread, wine) would not be Sacraments without the accompanying divine Word (the triune name for Baptism; the Verba for the Supper),

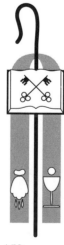

and the preaching of the Word of the Gospel must be accompanied by the proper administration of the Sacraments if the church is to increase in faith and size (e.g., Acts 2:38–47; 10:44–48).

Ezekiel Bears Iniquity for 390 and 40 Days (4:4–8)

4:4–6   Here we encounter one of the more difficult sections of the book. Scripture passages where numbers are used in some symbolical way often are particularly hard to interpret (cf. Daniel 9; Rev 7:4; 14:1–3; 20:1–7). Since Ezekiel does not specify what his *termini a quo* (starting point of the count) and *ad quem* (end) are for the periods of 390 and 40 days (representing years), and since some of his idioms are capable of more than one meaning, interpretations have inevitably differed in the course of history and still do today. We shall consider matters in the order in which they occur in the text.

The abrupt "and you" (4:4) signals a new series of action prophecies. Instead of representing Yahweh to Israel, the prophet now acts as a priest representing Israel, bearing the burden of his people's sins. More precisely, he can be taken as typifying Jesus Christ, who is "Israel reduced to one," and who bore the entire sin of the people (Is 53:5–6, 11–12).

As Ezekiel lies on his left side, assuming that his feet pointed toward the east (the normal direction of orientation in antiquity), the prophet would be facing north. This, plus the fact that the left was considered the less auspicious side (cf. Gen 48:13–19; Eccl 10:2), would suggest that the following scene is directed against the northern kingdom, which was "Israel" (versus "Judah") in the political sense. However, matters are not so simple. His left side is to bear "the iniquity of the house of Israel" (4:4–5), but "Israel" in what sense? "The house of Israel" had also appeared at the end of 4:3, as it will again in 5:4, and in both of those instances, the context makes plain that the reference is to the exiled Judeans.

A concordance study of "Israel" and "Judah," which appear 186 and only 15 times in Ezekiel, respectively, shows that when the two appear together in the book, often they are used interchangeably. In passages where the northern kingdom is contrasted with Judah, Ezekiel often avoids the name "Israel" or uses substitutes. For example, "Oholah" and "Oholibah" represent Samaria (the capital of northern Israel) and Jerusalem (the capital of Judah), respectively (23:4), or Joseph/Ephraim (northern Israel) versus Judah in 37:16 and 37:19. Since northern "Israel" in the political sense had disappeared over a century earlier in 722 B.C., Ezekiel may be thinking of the southern kingdom as the surviving remnant of the once united people of God. In many other passages throughout Ezekiel, "Israel" is used in its theological sense, comprising all the heirs of the covenant, regardless of political allegiances. Below we will return to the question of the identity of "the house of Israel" in 4:4–5 as we survey various interpretations of the numbers in the passage.

Thrice in 4:4–6, Ezekiel is commanded to "bear the iniquity" (נְשָׂא עָוֹן), first of the "house of Israel" (4:4–5) and then of the "house of Judah" (4:6). Initially, in 4:4 he is commanded to "lay/put/place" (שִׂים) that "iniquity" (עָוֹן)

on his left side. I have translated עָוֹן as "iniquity" consistently, but the word has various connotations (all related to "iniquity") in different contexts. In fact, almost the whole of the biblical doctrine of sin (hamartiology) can be expressed by this single vocable. It can mean (1) a single iniquitous action; (2) the sinful human condition, original sin, the total depravity of human nature since the fall of Adam and Eve (e.g., Ps 51:7 [ET 51:5]); (3) the guilt resulting from iniquitous behavior (e.g., Jer 2:22; 3:13); or (4) the divine punishment that is the result of iniquity (e.g., Num 14:33–34). A fifth meaning is when God is the one who bears iniquity, as in Ex 34:7 (part of "the close of the commandments"), where God "bears" or "forgives" (as it is usually translated) iniquity. In the fullness of time, this activity of God will be brought to completion with Christ on the cross, as constantly reiterated in the *Agnus Dei* of the liturgy.

That Ezekiel is first commanded to "lay the iniquity" on his left side in 4:4 seems to be simply a matter of logic: before the side (or a person) can bear a burden, it must first be placed on it (or on him), either by the person himself (as here) or by someone else.

Very similar language is used in the scapegoat ritual of the Day of Atonement (Lev 16:21–22). The sins of the people are first placed (נָתַן is the verb used there) on the head of the goat before the goat bears (נָשָׂא) them and carries them off into the desert.

Comparable language is used of the high priests. It appears in Ex 28:36–38, part of the investiture ceremony of Aaron (the prototypical high priest), specifically in his obligation to wear a turban or miter on his forehead with a golden plate so that he could "bear the iniquity of the holy things" offered by the faithful (to make up for any lapse or deficiency) so that the offerings "may be accepted before Yahweh." (There רָצוֹן, "favor, acceptance" is used, but the meaning is ultimately the same as that of the idiom "to bear sin"; offerings given in the wrong spirit are unacceptable.) Even more explicit is Lev 10:16–17, where Moses expresses concerns about the improper behavior of Aaron's two surviving sons with respect to the sin offering, which, he reminds them, "has been given to you to bear the iniquity of the congregation, to make atonement [לְכַפֵּר] for them before Yahweh."

From passages such as these, it might be a small step to conclude that Ezekiel's actions here were expiatory also. Beginning with Rashi in the Middle Ages, many Jewish exegetes have so interpreted this text.[21] However, it should be noted that while Ezekiel had a priestly lineage (1:3), he had *not* assumed the office of priest, which happened at age 30; he was in exile in his thirtieth year, according to 1:1. Hence he could not officiate in any temple ceremony, even though he probably had been schooled in how to do so. That alone renders any simple equation of Ezekiel's singular action prophecies with priestly rituals impossible, despite the fact that his frequent use of priestly language, as here, clearly reflects that background.

---

[21] Reflected still in Greenberg, *Ezekiel*, 1:104; cf. also Brownlee, *Ezekiel 1–19*, 67.

Ezekiel's "bearing sin" must be taken as *representative*, not expiatory. And it must be added that even the genuine priestly sacrifices did not function *ex opere operato* (mechanically or magically). The view that they did is the result of a theology of righteousness by works:

> This wicked idea about works has always clung to the world. The Gentiles had sacrifices which they took over from the patriarchs. They imitated their works but did not keep their faith, believing that these works were a propitiation and price that reconciled God to them. The people of the Old Testament [unbelieving Israelites] imitated these sacrifices with the notion that on account of them they had a gracious God, so to say, *ex opere operato*. Here we see how vehemently the prophets rebuke the people. … Such passages [as Ps 50:8; Jer 7:22] do not condemn the sacrifices that God surely commanded … but they do condemn the wicked belief of those who did away with faith. (Ap IV 206–7)

Neither were OT sacrifices efficacious by virtue of the priest's "indelible character" (to borrow Roman language rejected by Lutheran reformers).[22] Rather, the priests were types of Jesus Christ, the great High Priest (Hebrews 4–8). God graciously appointed them as his ministers in the OT era to provide forgiveness and expiation of sin through the sacrifices he also ordained—and all of that only by virtue of their ultimate connection with the perfect sacrifice to be offered by the Messiah on Calvary (see Ap XXIV 53–65). Likewise, God has graciously established the NT office of the ministry to provide forgiveness and salvation as he works through his appointed means of grace, his Word and Sacraments (AC V). Like the OT sacrifices, the Christian Sacraments have efficacy only in connection with what occurred on Calvary. The forgiveness of sins conferred through Holy Baptism (e.g., Acts 2:38–39; 22:16) and the Lord's Supper (Mt 26:28) is that procured by Christ's atonement through the offering up of his body and the shedding of his blood. The forgiveness God proffers through the Sacraments is received through faith, not through the mere performance of ritual *ex opere operato* (AC IX, X, XIII, and XXIV 28–29).

This theological context and import of the passage is clear enough, but the issue of the significance of the numbers in the passage is complex. There are questions about where the computation begins; of the relation, if any, between the numbers 390 and 40 (whether they are concurrent, successive, or overlapping); and, not least, of how literally we should press the numbers: to what extent, if at all, are they symbolic? We shall concentrate initially on 390, but it is ultimately impossible to treat the two numbers separately. On all these questions, predictably, there is a wide range of commentator opinion, both ancient and modern. Few, if any, of the answers are without any difficulty.

In general, one may say that ancient and medieval interpretations tried to fit both of the numbers into a single frame of reference, while modern commentators tend not to. One major question is whether עָוֹן in 4:4–6 means prior

---

22 See Chemnitz, *Examination of the Council of Trent*, 2:90–95.

"iniquity" or subsequent "punishment." Another major issue is whether the numbers of years are to be considered literal or symbolic.

A first possibility is to take עָוֹן in 4:4–6 to refer to "iniquity" committed in the past. Since the northern kingdom of Israel only lasted for about two centuries (ca. 922–722 B.C.), the 390 years of "iniquity" by "Israel" cannot refer just to the northern kingdom. Instead, "Israel" must refer to the elect nation as a whole. Assuming that it does, the number of 390 years works fairly well if taken literally. If we count back 390 years from the beginning of Ezekiel's ministry in 593 B.C. (see the textual notes on 1:1), we arrive at 983 B.C., which falls in David's 40-year reign (which began ca. 1010–1000 B.C. and ended ca. 970–960 B.C.). After David's adultery with Bathsheba, the latter part of his reign was marked by conflict (2 Samuel 10–20). He was succeeded by his son Solomon, who began well and built the temple. But in the latter part of Solomon's 40-year reign (which began ca. 970–960 B.C. and ended ca. 930–920) he lapsed into idolatry and saw the beginning of the schism that would rend the ten northern tribes away from Judah (1 Kings 11). Subsequently northern Israel apostatized, and Judah's faithfulness was at best sporadic. Therefore, the history of Israel as a whole since the latter part of David's reign may be taken as an era of overriding sinfulness.

However, a similar interpretation of the 40 years is difficult. Ezek 4:6 says the 40 years pertain to "Judah," which (in contrast to "Israel") presumably refers to the southern kingdom after the division of the monarchy in ca. 922 B.C. If עָוֹן refers to past "iniquity" and we count back 40 years from 593 B.C., we arrive at 633 B.C., during the reign of Josiah (640–609 B.C.). Josiah's reign, especially his reformation in ca. 622 B.C., was one of the last periods of repentance and faithfulness in Judah (2 Ki 22:1–23:30). Josiah is commended as one of the best kings because he adhered to the rediscovered Torah of Moses, restored the Passover, and abolished idolatry (2 Ki 23:21–25). Yet even at the end of his reign, "Yahweh still did not turn from the great burning of his anger. His anger was hot against Judah because of all the provocations by which Manasseh had provoked him. So Yahweh said, 'Judah too I will remove from before me, just as I removed Israel' " (2 Ki 23:26–27). Therefore it is plausible that Yahweh was angry at Judah during the 40 years preceding Ezekiel's call (633–593 B.C.). However, it is hard to understand why the starting point of this period of anger would be during the reign of faithful King Josiah. It is equally difficult to explain why the period of anger would be only those preceding 40 years in the history of Judah and not extend back farther, for example, to the reign of Manasseh (ca. 687–642 B.C.).

A second possibility for both numbers is to understand עָוֹן as consequent "punishment," rather than prior "iniquity," and to take the numbers figuratively. It works well to consider the 40 years for Judah as symbolic and representing the years of exile in Babylon. Most of those years are after Ezekiel's call. Even though Jeremiah gave the actual historical length of the exile as a literal 70 years (Jer 25:11–12; 29:10), the 40 years of punishment in Ezek 4:4–6 may be a typological number, calculated using the 40 years of Israel wandering in the desert under Moses as the prototype. This is supported by Ezek 29:11–13, where Ezekiel will use "forty years" in a typological way as the duration of future punishment for Egypt.

However, if עָוֹן means "punishment," there is no easy way to interpret the 390 years for the northern kingdom of "Israel" (or for "Israel" as the whole nation) in the same typological way as the 40 years can apply to Judah's "punishment." No other Scripture passage uses the number 390 in a symbolic or typological manner. (It is the product of 13 x 3 x 10, and while the numbers 3 and 10 can have symbolic meaning elsewhere in Scripture, the number 13 has no clear symbolic import elsewhere.) The difficulty remains even if we assume that 390 years is the total of 40 for Judah plus 350 for northern Israel; the resulting number of 350 has no clear typological meaning.

As often happens with numbers, the LXX has a different set from the MT. According to the LXX, the prophet is to lie on his left side 150 days (the number is inserted in the text in the middle of 4:4) and 40 on his right (4:6, as also in the MT). The LXX of 4:5 and 4:9 states that the total of those is 190 days.[23] If we take עָוֹן as "punishment," the LXX numbers are capable of being incorporated into a single interpretation: they could mean that northern Israel's exile will last 150 years and Judah's exile will last 40 years, and the numbers are consecutive (not overlapping), so the total adds up to 190. The actual fall of Samaria was in 722 B.C., and Jerusalem's fall was in 587 B.C., so that time interval could be rounded up to 150 years and considered the time of northern Israel's punishment. For Judah, if we count down from 593 B.C. (Ezekiel's call) or from 587 B.C. (Jerusalem's fall), we are within two decades of the edict of Cyrus in 538 B.C., which allowed the Israelites to return to Judah. The total elapsed time from 722 B.C. to 538 B.C. is 184 years, which is close to the total of 190 years, which the LXX has in both 4:5 and 4:9.

The LXX's figures are very neat, but both their neatness and "their two iniquities" in LXX 4:5 raise the suspicion that they are a harmonizing artifice of the LXX translator, and not an accurate translation of a different Hebrew tradition than the MT. Most commentators have viewed the LXX numbers with appropriate suspicion. (We shall meet another numerical disparity in 5:2, where the LXX speaks of four parts of hair instead of the three in the MT.) Presumably, the LXX worked back from 4:8 with its mention of the siege of Jerusalem and so understood 4:4–5 in terms of bearing punishment and managed a consistent exegesis of 4:4–8. Greenberg cites an observation by Freedman that the LXX's figures here have a "curious relationship" to the number of days in the deluge: it rains for 40 days (Gen 7:12, 17) and the waters "prevail over" the land for 150 days (Gen 7:24).[24]

---

[23] When arriving at that total, the LXX refers to "their two iniquities" (4:5), but the Hebrew clearly has the singular of "iniquity" ("the years of their iniquity").

[24] Greenberg, *Ezekiel*, 1:106, citing a private observation by David Noel Freedman.

If we then disregard the LXX numbers, we must return to the MT and try to find a coherent interpretation of them.

One way out of the difficulties we have noted so far is to take the numbers of the MT (390 for Israel and 40 for Judah) as basically typological. Probably not as popular today as it once was, nevertheless, this view has an ancient pedigree, apparently beginning already in intertestamental times (see the reference to the *Damascus Document* below). It may even find its justification in the Scriptures themselves when they interpret earlier events in Israel's history typologically.

To begin, we may add the two periods of 390 and 40 together, since Ezekiel is to lie first on one side and then later the other (without overlapping the two actions), and the total of the times spent on his two sides represents the siege of Jerusalem. The resultant total of 430 years immediately recalls the 430 years of Israelite bondage in Egypt (Ex 12:40), as had already been prophesied to Abraham in his covenant initiation ceremony (as the round number of 400 years in Gen 15:13). The use of this period as a type first surfaces in Deut 28:68, where Moses prophesies that if the Israelites are disobedient, God will again bring them back to Egypt (a prophecy that must be taken typologically, since historically they did not return there). The theme of a (typological, judgmental) return to "Egypt" resurfaces in Hos 8:13; 9:3; 9:6 (in Hos 9:3 "Egypt" is paralleled with "Assyria"). On the positive side, a typological "new exodus," when God will call forth Israel, his son, from Egypt, appears in the well-known Hos 11:1, which is ultimately fulfilled in Christ. After the holy family's flight to Egypt, God calls forth from there his Son, who is "Israel reduced to (embodied in) one" (see Mt 2:13–15). The same idea must underlie the prophetic allusions to the return from Babylonian exile as a "second exodus" in Hos 2:16–25 (ET 2:14–23); Is 11:15–16; 52:12; and many other passages. This typological use of Gentile nations as being like Egypt (God's people are in bondage among the nations, as ancient Israel was in Egypt, until God brings them forth) is essentially parallel to the hermeneutics underlying the Gentile oracles in Ezekiel 25–32 and in virtually all the prophets.

The typological use of the number 40 is even easier because it had appeared repeatedly in earlier history: most obviously the 40 years of Israel wandering in the wilderness, but also in the 40 days of rain at the deluge (Gen 7:12, 17), possibly even in the 40 years Moses was obligated to remain in Midian before God called him back to deliver his people (Acts 7:30 on Ex 2:11–3:10).

In terms of Israel's past history, it is thus relatively easy to find reference points. It is not so easy, however, to determine what beginning and ending points Yahweh had in mind for the application of these numbers. But is searching for such points even a valid quest? In a prophet who uses various symbolisms as often as Ezekiel does, perhaps we should not even ask, or at least avoid any attempt at precision. In general terms, the longer period (390 years) assigned to the northern kingdom would correspond to their longer period of exile, and the much earlier fall of Samaria (in 722 B.C.) compared to the later fall of Jerusalem (587 B.C.). Regardless of whether the two periods are concurrent or consecutive, the ending point probably relates to Ezekiel's prophecy that the two kingdoms would be reunited after the return from exile (37:15–28).

Backhandedly, Ezekiel's prophecy of 40 years' exile for Judah speaks for its authenticity, because Jeremiah spoke of a literal (and historically accurate) 70-year period (Jer 25:11–12; 29:10; cf. Dan 9:2). Yet the seventy years itself may be a partially symbolic number, as evidenced by the two different biblical calculations of the *termini* of the period. One is from 605 B.C. (the battle of Carchemish and the first deportation to Babylon)[25] to 538 B.C. (the edict of Cyrus allowing the exiles to return to Judah); this encompasses 67 years. The other is from 587/586 B.C. (the fall of Jerusalem) to 516 B.C., when the rebuilding of the temple was finished; thus the temple had been in ruins for 70 years (but the exile itself ended earlier when the Israelites returned after the edict of Cyrus). Elsewhere in Ezekiel, "forty years" appears as a typological number for the length of Egypt's eschatological punishment (Ezek 29:11–13).

Many exegetes through the centuries (e.g., Calvin, Alexander[26]) have not been content to leave the historical application of the numbers as vague as I have suggested, but the widely varying calculations would seem to suggest that the attempt to arrive at precise historical dates is fundamentally misguided.

One ancient interpretation must be given some attention, however. St. Jerome attests it.[27] And the *Damascus Document* (fragments of which were found among the Qumran scrolls) clearly reflects it, indicating that it antedates the Christian era. This ancient tradition takes the 390 years (if the 40 years are concurrent with them) or the 430 years (if the two periods are consecutive) as a type of the final judgment. The calculation usually begins with the fall of Jerusalem in 587 and ends sometime in or near the Maccabean period. In general, the hermeneutic here is reminiscent of the 70 hebdomads or "year-weeks" (that total 490) in Daniel 9 (whose exegesis is beyond our scope here).

I frankly find a cautious typological hermeneutic for these enigmatic numbers very attractive, although I am not willing to commit myself to specific chronological applications. I am tempted to make a virtue out of that uncertainty: although some historical anchorage must be assumed (if we are not allegorizing), much of the value of typological approaches in general is that they are applicable to history itself *sub specie aeternitatis*, as part of God's eternal plan, including our present time of the church until the end of all earthly time. In the light of the unity of Scripture, it is essential to place Calvary as the fulcrum of the entire understanding. *Die Weltgeschichte ist das Weltgericht* ("the history of the world is [the history of] the world's judgment").

---

[25] In 605 B.C. Nebuchadnezzar besieged Jerusalem and carried off to Babylon some of the articles from the temple as well as some of Jerusalem's citizens (2 Ki 24:1; Dan 1:1–4). Daniel was included in that first deportation.

[26] Calvin, *Ezekiel*, 1:173–77; Alexander, *Ezekiel*, 24.

[27] Jerome, *Commentariorum in Ezechielem* (PL 25:44).

Nevertheless, the tides of current scholarly opinion are not moving in that direction. As mentioned earlier, most are convinced that the two numbers cannot be fitted into a single frame of reference. A common opinion is that the first figure of 390 years should be taken as retrospective rather than predictive, and hence that עָוֹן here should not be translated as "punishment," but as "iniquity" committed by Israel in the past. Some of the initial reluctance to accept this opinion stemmed from Fohrer's dogmatic assertion in his influential study that prophetic acts, like magical acts, must describe future events, not past ones.[28] Usually they do, but such rigidity is not sustainable.

If one does compute 390 years back from 587 B.C., one derives a date of 987 B.C., not far from the time when the כָּבוֹד moved from the tabernacle to the temple newly built by Solomon (1 Ki 8:10–11; ca. 960–950 B.C.). But the biblical record goes on to relate that only a relatively short time later, Solomon's apostasy began—an apostasy that only worsened in Israel's subsequent history. In spite of ephemeral efforts at reformation, especially by Kings Hezekiah and Josiah, Israel's apostasy never really abated as long as the temple stood. Thus by lying prostrate on his left side for the corresponding number of days, Ezekiel, in a priestly way, bore the iniquity of the people. This nonverbal action corresponds to the verbal accusations he will deliver later, as recorded in 5:6–7, where Yahweh recounts the past iniquities of Israel.

In contrast with the debates about 390, there is little disagreement in understanding the 40 years of 4:6 as predictive and in translating נָשָׂא עָוֹן as "bear punishment." The verbatim links with Num 14:34 are a nearly indisputable indication that Ezekiel intends this prediction of exile to be a repetition, in essence, of the earlier punishment when Israel wandered for 40 years in the desert. Forty was the conventional figure for a generation, and, in both cases (in Moses' day and in Ezekiel's), the idea is that the old, rebellious generation must die off before a "rebirth" of Israel in a new generation could take place. As the 390 years (referring to Israel's past "iniquity") relate to 5:6–7, so also the 40 years (assuming they refer to the coming "punishment" in exile) relate to the judgments to be prophesied in 5:8–17.

We probably should not take these verses literalistically and assume that the prophet will lie *continuously* (round-the-clock) on his side—first for 390 days on his left, then turning once for the 40 days on his right. The issue is comparable to the understanding of Ezekiel's dumbness in 3:25–27; compare the mention of "ropes" or "cords" in connection with both (3:25 and 4:8). A more likely and realistic scenario is that Ezekiel would lie on the appointed side for several hours each day while engaged in prophetic ministry—probably during the busiest part of the day, when the most people would see him and probably report the strange sight throughout the community of exiles. During the rest of the day, and especially at night, he would perform his normal activities in the

---

[28] Fohrer, *Die symbolischen Handlungen der Propheten*, 110.

privacy of his house. Additional commands in subsequent verses support such a view (see the discussion of his diet in the commentary on 4:9–17 below).

We should be aware that the internal chronology of the book of Ezekiel leaves adequate space for the days of such behavior. Fourteen months elapse between the last date, in 1:2, and the next date, in 8:1. A proper lunar (synodic) month is 29 1/2 days (so in a lunar calendar months alternate between 29 and 30 days), and 14 lunar months total 413 days. This easily accommodates the 390 days, but if it is also to include the 40 days, we must assume that the 390 and the 40 days were at least partly concurrent, as some commentators do. If we assume that the fourteen months included a lunar leap year, when an intercalary month of 29 days was added, the total extends to 442 days. That would leave room for consecutive periods of 390 and then 40 days, as well as the seven days in 3:15–16 and the time required for the action prophecies of 5:1–4. Then we probably would have to assume that the oracles in chapters 6–7 are placed there for literary reasons (and are not chronological), and that there is no overlap with the visions (?) of chapters 8–11.

Ezekiel obviously did not deem it important enough to provide such detailed information about how exactly we are to account for the 390 and 40 days. We must be thankful that he has given us as much chronological data as he has—more than any other prophet, with the possible exception of his contemporary, Jeremiah.

Finally, it must be noted that many commentators are exercised over what appears to them to be an intertwining of two different metaphors: (1) the siege of Jerusalem and (2) exile among the nations. They commonly posit a dichotomy between verses that accent the iniquitous guilt that warranted the siege of Jerusalem (4:7–11, 16–17, and probably 4:4–5) with those that assume or describe the exile (4:12–13, and probably 4:6). They commonly label 4:13 as a redactional insertion that attempts to harmonize the two pictures (siege and exile). Critics usually advance theories of later editing to update the original message for different circumstances to explain the alleged mixture.

It is undeniable that chapter 4 does contain both metaphors (see especially the textual note above on 4:9–17). One could think of Ezekiel himself editing and contemporizing his earlier prophecies before releasing the final edition of his book. But I seriously doubt that there is any real "problem" to be "solved." The Israelites and other ancient peoples were only too aware that sieges were commonly followed by exile—if those under siege survived the fall of their city! I do not believe that Ezekiel's original audience would have been surprised in the least by his oscillation between guilt and punishment, and between siege pictures and those of exile. Theologically, the two are hardly separable. Sin and its consequences are treated in one breath, as it were, throughout Scripture. Also in Christian theology and preaching, they may be distinguished theoretically, but one follows the other: "the wages of sin is death" (Rom 6:23).

4:7 This verse adds the detail that while lying on his side, Ezekiel is to stare at the model of the city, as already commanded in 4:3b. No mention is made of which side the prophet should be lying on. Since the verse closely follows 4:6, it might apply only to the 40-day period. But if Ezekiel lay on opposite sides of the model (to its left while on his left side, then to its right while on his right side), the command could apply to the preceding 390 days too.

The prophet's "arm bared" vividly acts out that God is the enemy of Jerusalem. Yet because Ezekiel is also bearing the iniquity of the people, he embodies both the Accuser and the accused. We may compare this to the "sacrificial" and "sacramental" postures assumed by the pastor at the altar: facing the congregation when representing God and facing the altar when representing the congregation.

The same Hebrew noun and verb in "arm bared" (4:7) appear in Is 52:10[29] in the positive sense of Yahweh fighting *for* Jerusalem: "Yahweh has bared his holy arm in the sight of all the nations, and all the ends of the earth shall see the salvation of our God." The phrase recalls similar ones that are strongly associated with the exodus, such as God's promise, "I will redeem you with an outstretched arm" (Ex 6:6).[c] So it is conceivable, as some commentators assert, that Ezekiel's audience originally might have misunderstood him to be predicting the deliverance of Jerusalem, just as the false prophets were predicting. But Jeremiah (21:5) too uses exodus language ("with an outstretched hand and a strong arm") to portray Yahweh as warring *against* unfaithful Jerusalem.

(c) See also, e.g., Ex 15:16; Deut 4:34; 5:15; 7:19

Any doubt is removed by the concluding clause of Ezek 4:7: Ezekiel is to "prophesy against" the model of Jerusalem. "Prophesy" might be used in a broad sense to include the action prophecies being described, but the word usually implies verbalization. Conceivably, then, Ezekiel may have preached at the same time he acted. It seems more likely, however, that this refers to the verbal prophecies that will come a little later (perhaps including 4:13, 16–17, but especially those that commence in chapter 5).

4:8 As in 3:25, it is debatable whether the "ropes" placed on Ezekiel are metaphorical. I am inclined to see metaphor in both instances (see the textual notes and commentary on 3:25–27). But I think that it is more conceivable here than in the first instance that, either by Ezekiel's own actions or by those of aides, his body was trussed with ropes while he lay on his sides. (In 3:25 it was hard to see how the *people* would literally tie him up.)

The import here is the same whether or not physical ropes were used. In 3:25 the binding with ropes pertained to his ministry as a whole; here it pertains only to the action prophecy of lying on his sides. But, in a broader sense, the application is the same in both cases: Yahweh is in total control of his prophet's activity—both his oral messages (the only breaks in his speechlessness, which began in 3:25–27) and his action prophecies. Ezekiel is not free to do anything of his own volition or fabrication.

---

[29] Is 52:7–10 is the Old Testament Lesson for Christmas Dawn in all three series of the three-year lectionary in *Lutheran Worship*.

In principle, the application to the modern pastor is obvious. In the exercise of the ministry of Word and Sacrament, he is to obey the "thus says Yahweh" of his divine call. He is to preach God's Word as revealed in the Scriptures—nothing more and nothing less. His actions are circumscribed by that same divine Word: while conducting his ministry, he is to act with the proper reverence and decorum that befits the holy Lord in whose presence, and on whose behalf, he serves. Even while "off duty" (though he never vacates the office), he is to adorn his pastoral office with a righteous "private" life of Christian faith. If he teaches false doctrine (contravening the Word) or if he engages in conduct unbecoming the office (whether in the church or at home), he may be removed.

Ezekiel's Siege and Exilic Diets (4:9–17)

4:9–12   The point of Ezekiel's mixture of flour and vegetable meal is an action prophecy of the siege diet the people will be forced to eat (4:9–11). There will not be enough of any one grain to make a loaf of bread. One can survive only by mixing together whatever remainders one can find, and even that product will be unpalatable.

Several interpretative problems confront us in these verses. First, 4:9b specifies that the siege diet was to last 390 days, that is, during the time the prophet lay on his left side. Nothing is said about what he would eat during the subsequent 40 days on his right side. Keil offers the explanation that mention of the 390 days was quite sufficient to make the point and that "the 40 days of Judah were omitted for the sake of brevity."[30] Perhaps that is as good a hypothesis as any.

Second, a single loaf of bread is not enough to sustain a man for 390 days (much less for 430 days, if the same diet was also for the subsequent 40 days). Nothing is said about any divine miracle of the sort in 1 Ki 17:10–16 or Mt 14:13–21. Neither could the meager ration of water in 4:11 prevent dehydration (especially for a man who daily lay in the hot sun). Evidently, we must think of Ezekiel taking one small bite of the loaf daily while lying on his side. "At the same time each day" in 4:10–11 may indicate that Ezekiel performed his public ministry for a few hours each day and ate and drank once daily in public at a set time, but then when the regular hours of his daily ministry were over, he could sustain himself normally during his "off duty" hours in private.

Third, the "barley loaf" in 4:12 seems to be different than the bread in 4:9, which included other ingredients. The "barley loaf" was to be baked in a vulgar way, whereas no special cooking instructions are given for the bread in 4:9. God says nothing about rationing the "barley loaf" in 4:12 (contrast the ration in 4:10 for the bread in 4:9). The two verses use some different Hebrew ter-

---

[30]   Keil, *Ezekiel*, 1:80.

minology (see the textual notes). On the part of critics, this apparent discrepancy triggered radical textual surgery; they assumed that the text mixed and confused pictures of the siege of Jerusalem and the later exile.

The best explanation appears to be that 4:9–11 and 4:12 speak of two separate action prophecies. They are both concerned with scarcity of food, but the diet in 4:9–11 represents that of the residents of Jerusalem during its siege, whereas 4:12 represents the diet of the Israelites in exile, as God explains in 4:13. God's explanation for 4:9–11 will come in 4:16–17. (See the textual note on 4:9–17.)

4:13 The series of action prophecies on the horrors of the coming siege, the fall of Jerusalem, and the exile among the nations essentially comes to a climax with this personal statement from Yahweh. It is almost statutory in impact because there is no explicit command for Ezekiel to proclaim it, but, no doubt, that is what God intended.

Two words in the verse require special comment. The first is טָמֵא, "unclean." The biblical distinction between clean and unclean is not an easy concept to explain to modern Westerners or for us to grasp.[31] In many respects, "clean" overlaps with "holy." "Holiness" has a more obviously ethical content, but biblical usage itself by no means limits that concept to some moral or "spiritual" sphere. "Clean" has a more clearly ritual or ceremonial application, but it also pertains to the whole life of the believer. Some of the problems Christians have in understanding both categories basically stem from the NT invalidation of OT "ceremonial" laws (cf. St. Peter's reaction to eating unclean foods in Acts 10), although one must be aware that the OT itself does not make a clear-cut distinction between "moral" and "ceremonial" laws.

As secularism has enveloped the Christian world, especially since the "Enlightenment," both terms have been attenuated even further. "Holiness" tends to be invested *only* with ethical meaning, and "clean" is heard *only* in a hygienic sense. In OT usage, if "clean" had anything at all to do with hygiene, the connection was purely coincidental. "Holiness" is often attributed to God as well as his people, while "clean" and "unclean" are categories that only apply to people, not to God. Yet the OT passages about both holiness and cleanness have a primary concern to preserve the people's relationship with and faith in the one true, triune God.

Lands outside of Israel were intrinsically unclean, not because Yahweh's reign was limited to the "Holy Land," but because those lands and their peoples were cut off from the divine covenant and temple, and because of the idolatrous practices that held sway in other lands (cf. Josh 22:19; Amos 7:17; and Ezek 36:18b). Most ancient nations were "theocracies," as was Israel, but with false gods at their head. Hence, people living in those lands were necessarily

---

[31] For a broad, Christian explanation of the categories of clean and unclean, holy and profane, see Kleinig, *Leviticus*, 5–13. For clean and unclean foods, which is the specific background of Ezek 4:13–14, see pages 256–62.

"unclean," and the food they ate was necessarily "unclean," because they were under the dominion of demons (cf. 1 Cor 10:20–21). One might compare their foods with the "unclean food" and "mourners' bread" that exiled Israelites would eat in Assyria according to the prophetic judgment in Hos 9:3–4 (cf. Deut 26:14).

The second word is גּוֹיִם (Ezek 4:13). In this context I have chosen to retain the ancient, traditional translation of it as "Gentiles" rather than "nations." In other contexts "nations" may be preferable, but not here. Our secular culture tends to hear "nation" purely in the sense of "country," basically a geographical idea. "Gentiles," however, if heard correctly, accents the fact that we are dealing with people outside Yahweh's covenant, who by definition then worshiped other gods and were unclean. To sojourn among such people and their gods is the fate of the Israelites whom God will banish in exile.

4:14 There may have been an oral tradition, but no written law forbids the use of human dung for cooking. One can well imagine that it was not normally done, or, at least, that priests avoided the practice. In any case, Ezekiel responds to the command in a way comparable to St. Peter's dissent when the Lord told him to feast on unclean animals (Acts 10:13–16). Modern readers of Ezek 4:12 may be disgusted by the hygienic impurity, but for ancient Israelites, the revulsion would be more akin to St. Paul's attitude toward eating meat sacrificed to idols (e.g., 1 Corinthians 8–10). Ezekiel's remonstration (4:14) takes the positive form of a declaration of his scrupulosity in observing matters of ceremonial purity. Ezekiel's observance undoubtedly was heightened by his priestly background (1:3).

This verse is the only example of Ezekiel's resistance to God's commands, no matter how bizarre they seemed. (Ezekiel does "remonstrate" with God in an intercessory way in 9:8 and 11:13.) Throughout the rest of the book, his simple acquiescence to God provides a vivid contrast with his contemporary, Jeremiah, who ultimately obeys Yahweh but often bitterly laments his calling as a prophet. Some commentators think they detect other examples of Ezekiel's reluctance to obey, but one must "read between the lines" quite substantially to support that position (see, e.g., the commentary on 2:8). God uses "all sorts and conditions" of people to accomplish his purposes.

The Christian reader will sympathetically understand Ezekiel's dilemma. We recall again that what we simply categorize as OT "ceremonial" law, now abrogated in Christ, was in OT times inseparable from theological and moral imperatives. A natural application of Ezekiel's concern is to the call for Christian sanctification or the third use of the law. Compare 1 Cor 6:13–20 on the sanctification of the Christian's body and the command to refrain from sins of the flesh.

4:15 God's concession to Ezekiel's protest reveals God as compassionate even when executing his *opus alienum* (his prophet is to condemn Israel's sin according to the Law). It is comparable to the way God allowed Abraham to bargain with him about sparing Sodom (Gen 18:22–33), even though the destruction of the city would be fully justified (Genesis 19). We might compare it to Jesus' parables about persistence in prayer (e.g., Lk 18:1–8) and the way Jesus conceded to the Canaanite woman (Mt 15:22–28). Even with the concession to Ezekiel, the point of the action prophecy would still come through clearly: the shame of those in exile with Ezekiel, who would be forced to eat unclean food among the Gentiles (Ezek 4:13).

4:16–17 In case anyone had doubts about the meaning of Ezekiel's action prophecy in 4:9–11, which portrayed the plight of people in a city under siege, God here verbalizes the message in stark language. And, if not right then, at some point in his ministry, Ezekiel would proclaim this to his fellow exiles. In fact, he proclaims it repeatedly in principle, because these verses are virtually a miniature of the rest of his judgment oracles, especially through chapter 24.

Nor shall it be overlooked that in these verses, as throughout chapters 5–6, we have quotations or paraphrases of the covenant curses in Leviticus 26 (see the textual notes on Ezek 4:16–17). Many of the Israelites in Ezekiel's audience would have known those words of Moses very well. But then as now, knowing the Bible and heeding it in faith are two different matters! Both the old covenant and the new one in Christ contain blessing promises—climaxing in Christ and his beatitudes—for those who believe and heed God's Word, but curses that warn of judgment and woe for those who disbelieve and transgress the divine covenant.[32] Since the Israelites had broken faith with Yahweh (not the other way around, as they later complain, especially in chapter 18), here Yahweh, through his prophet, "affirms his determination to keep the covenant, and to hold his people to the fine print, the letter, of the Torah."[33] As Yahweh will say in 5:6–8, since the Israelites had failed to perform his judgments, Yahweh himself will perform his judgments on them, thus fulfilling the terms of his covenant with them.

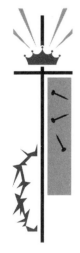

Both the old and the new covenants must be read Christologically.[34] Both aspects of each covenant (the blessings and the curses) must be related organically to the cross (Gal 3:8–14). That is where all of God's covenant curses were executed in full upon his sinless Son. On the accursed tree, Christ was cursed vicariously for the sins of all mankind. Therefore, the cross is also the heart and climax of the covenant blessings in both Testaments. Through faith alone we, like Abraham (Gen 15:6), receive justification, the forgiveness of sins, and all the blessings of God's grace summarized in his unilateral covenant promise to Abraham long ago.

---

[32] For an exposition of the covenant blessings and curses in Leviticus 26, see Kleinig, *Leviticus*, 568–82. For the covenant blessings and curses in Deuteronomy, which are pronounced in Josh 8:34, one may see Harstad, *Joshua*, 366–71. For a Christological exposition of the Lukan beatitudes and woes, which include Lk 6:20–26, see Just, *Luke 1:1–9:50*, 267–91.

[33] Block, *Ezekiel*, 1:188.

[34] See the excursus "Covenant" in Harstad, *Joshua*, 744–56.

The covenant blessings and curses are also eschatological.[35] Christ has already suffered the end-time judgment from which all believers in him shall be spared, and they shall inherit the kingdom prepared for them from the foundation of the world (Mt 25:34). But by the same token, the covenant curses that were fulfilled in the destruction of the kingdom of Israel and subsequent exile from the land were portents of the eternal fate of all unbelievers, who shall be damned. "Do you not know that the unrighteous shall not inherit the kingdom of God?" asks St. Paul (1 Cor 6:9). The NT declarations of the wicked who shall be excluded from the eternal kingdom[d] echo the OT covenant curses and Ezekiel's accusations against the Israelites who "shall waste away because of their iniquity" (4:17).

(d) E.g., 1 Cor 6:9–10; Gal 5:19–21; Rev 22:15

---

[35] The eschatological import is especially obvious in the beatitudes in Rev 14:13; 19:9; 20:6; 22:7, 14.

More Action Prophecies and the First Judgment Oracle

Translation

5 ¹"And you, son of man, take for yourself a sharp sword. Like the barbers' razor, you shall take it for yourself and cause [it] to pass over upon your head and upon your beard. Then you shall take for yourself scales for weighing and divide them [the hairs]. ²A third you shall burn in fire inside the city when the days of siege are completed. And you shall take the [second] third and strike it with the sword all around the city. The [final] third you shall scatter to the wind, and I will unsheathe the sword after them. ³But you shall take from there a few in number and wrap them in the folds of your robe, ⁴and from them again you shall take some and throw them into the midst of the fire and burn them in the fire. From it a fire will spread to the whole house of Israel.

⁵"Thus says the Lord Yahweh: This is Jerusalem. I have set her in the middle of the nations, and all around her are countries. ⁶But she rebelled against my ordinances, becoming more wicked than the nations, and [she rebelled] against my statutes more than the countries around her, because they [the Israelites] rejected my ordinances, and my statutes—they did not walk in them.

⁷"Therefore, thus says the Lord Yahweh: Because you have been more flagrant than the nations around you, and you have not walked in my statutes, and you have not performed my ordinances, and you have not even acted according to the ordinances of the nations around you, ⁸therefore, thus says the Lord Yahweh: Behold, I am against you, even I, and I will perform judgments in your midst in the sight of the nations. ⁹I will do among you something that I have never done before and the likes of which I shall never do again, because of all your abominations. ¹⁰Surely, fathers will eat sons in your midst, and sons will eat their fathers. I will execute judgments upon you, and I will scatter any of your remnant to every wind.

¹¹"Therefore, as surely as I live, says the Lord Yahweh, surely because you have defiled my sanctuary by all your detestable practices and all your abominations, even I—I will do the shaving. My eye will not pity, and I myself will have no compassion. ¹²A third of you will die in the plague or perish in the famine in your midst; a third will fall by the sword all around you; and a third I will scatter to every wind, and I will unsheathe the sword after them. ¹³Then my anger will be fulfilled, I will let my wrath at them rest, and I will be satisfied. Then they will know that I, Yahweh, have spoken in my jealousy when I exhaust my wrath at them. ¹⁴I will make you into a ruin and a reproach among the nations around you, in the sight of everyone who passes by. ¹⁵She will be a reproach and a taunt,

a warning and an object of horror to the nations around you when I execute judgments upon you in anger, in wrath, and in furious chastisements—I, Yahweh, have spoken— [16]when I send deadly arrows of famine against them, [arrows] that shall become a destroyer, [arrows] that I will send to destroy you. I will increase famine upon you and break your staff of bread. [17]I will send against you famine and wild animals, and they will bereave you. Plague and bloodshed will pass through you, and I will bring the sword upon you. I, Yahweh, have spoken."

Textual Notes

5:1 חֶרֶב—We translate this here as "sword" (its usual meaning) instead of "razor" to facilitate the action prophecy's application of the "sword" in 5:2, 12, 17 as a major instrument of God's punishment. Unwieldy though it would be for shaving, an actual sword may be the intended sense, partly also to dramatize the action. On the other hand, חֶרֶב is sometimes used more generally (cf. Ex 20:25; Josh 5:2–3; Ezek 26:9), so Greenberg's translation, "blade,"[1] is attractive.

תַּעַר הַגַּלָּבִים—The construct phrase is an adverbial accusative: Ezekiel is to use the sword "*like/as* the barbers' razor." The noun גַּלָּבִים ("barbers") occurs only here in the OT, but cognates are attested in Akkadian, Phoenician, and Punic. It has the *qattāl* formation, standard for a *nomen opificum* (name of a profession or occupation). In such contexts Hebrew commonly uses the definite article, which idiomatic English does not require.

תִּקָּחֶנָּה לָּךְ—The imperfect (from לָקַח) is parallel to the preceding imperative קַח. Hebrew can use second person imperfect or perfect verbs with the force of an imperative (especially after an imperative), and that is true of all the second person verbs in 5:1–4. The antecedent of the verb's feminine suffix (נָּ-ה) probably is "sword" rather than "razor" since חֶרֶב is regularly construed as feminine, whereas elsewhere תַּעַר is always masculine except in Is 7:20, which may be a sort of antecedent to the present context.

וְהַעֲבַרְתָּ—The Hiphil of עָבַר has no object, but plainly what he is to "cause to pass over" his head and beard is the sword, using it as a razor for shaving. Hebrew idiom omits an obvious object more readily than English.

וְחִלַּקְתָּם:—The plural object suffix ("them") lacks an antecedent. We must supply "the hairs," although the plural of "hair" never appears in the Hebrew.

5:2 שְׁלִשִׁית—Ezek 5:1 had concluded with the command to divide the hair up by weight. This verse specifies what Ezekiel is to do with each "third" he had weighed out. Curiously, the LXX refers to each portion as a "fourth" (τέταρτον), even though there are only three of them in 5:2. The Hebrew of 5:12 likewise refers to three parts, each called a "third" (שְׁלִשִׁית), but the LXX translates 5:12 so that there are four parts. In 14:21 both the Hebrew and the LXX refer to four parts. Apparently the fourths in LXX 5:2 arose from the attempt to harmonize LXX 5:2 with LXX 5:12 and with (MT

---

[1] Greenberg, *Ezekiel*, 1:108.

and LXX) 14:21. In LXX 5:12 and in (MT and LXX) 14:21, "plague" and "famine" are counted as separate judgments. However, in MT 5:12, "plague" and "famine" are judgments that befall the same "third" of the people.

בָּאוּר תַּבְעִיר בְּתוֹךְ הָעִיר—The uncommon noun אוּר can mean "firelight" or, as here, "fire" (*HALOT*, s.v. אוּר I, 1). Obviously it is related to the common noun אוֹר, "light." The usual noun for "fire" (אֵשׁ) will be used several times in 5:4, presumably in correspondence with the other sibilants in that verse. Probably the uncommon word was chosen here to achieve a certain alliterative effect: it, the following Hiphil verb (תַּבְעִיר), and the noun עִיר all sound somewhat alike.

כִּמְלֹאת יְמֵי הַמָּצוֹר—The Qal infinitive construct of מָלֵא used gerundively with כְּ might more literalistically be translated "at the being full of the days of the siege." The idea that time is a vessel that is filled often underlies Hebrew temporal idioms. God is the one who determines the vessel's volume of time, then acts when it is full (cf. Gen 15:16). In the NT the Greek equivalent πληρόω is often translated "to fulfill" (meaning "to fill to the full") and usually is laden with theological content: God's plan of salvation is fulfilled in Christ. Similar is the sense of πλήρωμα in Gal 4:4 (Christ came in the "fullness" of time) and elsewhere.

תַּכֶּה—"Strike" in the context of the action prophecy might more appropriately be rendered "chop up" or the like. The verb (Hiphil second masculine singular imperfect of נָכָה) is both asyndetic and suffixless. The latter is not unusual (the context easily supplies the object: the second third of the hair), and the expected conjunction had appeared at the beginning of the previous clause (וְלָקַחְתָּ, "*And* you shall take …"). The syntax is choppy, and various text-critical proposals purport to "correct" it, but in a book like Ezekiel, it is best to leave well enough alone and follow the Hebrew.

וְחֶרֶב אָרִיק אַחֲרֵיהֶם:—"I will unsheathe" translates אָרִיק, the Hiphil (first common singular imperfect) of רִיק, "to empty out" the sheathe by drawing the sword out of it. The idiom is also known in Akkadian. What is startling is the sudden switch to first person speech, that is, Yahweh himself ("I") declares that he will perform this action. Naturally, some critics would attempt an easy way out by excising it as a gloss or later addition. But Yahweh has been speaking (commanding) all along. Furthermore, personal interpositions by Yahweh himself appear elsewhere in the book. These remind the hearer/reader that the prophet's strange actions have historico-theological import, which will be elaborated shortly.

As did 4:16–17, so also 5:2 describes a fulfillment of the covenant curses upon disobedient Israel in Leviticus 26, which reverberate throughout the rest of the chapter. Ezekiel's action with the last third is especially close to Lev 26:33, which likewise connects "unsheathe the sword" with "scatter."

5:3 וְלָקַחְתָּ מִשָּׁם—I have rendered the copula as "But …" because, logically, one would expect that the disposal of the three thirds in 5:2 would have been the end of all the hair. However, the punishments signified by that threefold division in 5:2 are not the whole story of God's future punishments of his people. The fact that a few hairs remain (but to be punished further) may also suggest that some will be preserved for the purpose of salvation, but the prophet's emphasis in chapters 4–24 is on judgment. The prophet will preach salvation for the faithful remnant in chapters 33–48.

"From there" (מִשָּׁם) leaves unanswered the question of where the few remaining hairs are to be found. Perhaps not all of the final third were blown away by the wind, or perhaps a few remained on the ground after the prophet's shaving and weighing of them.

וְצַרְתָּ אֹתָם בִּכְנָפֶיךָ:—Here the Qal of צוּר means "to tie up" or "to bind (hair) in the skirt of the garment" (*HALOT*, s.v. צור I, 1 a and c, respectively). It is the same verb that in 4:3 meant "to besiege" the model of Jerusalem. Greenberg sees it here as redolent of 4:3: "there a hostile act, here a friendly act."[2] בִּכְנָפֶיךָ is literally "in your wings," but here, in Hebrew idiom, it refers to the folds in the loose fitting outer garment commonly worn (still today) in much of the Near East. In the many folds and wrinkles of the loose garment, it was easy to hide, fasten, or wrap small objects, especially something as light as hair. I prefer "robe" to "skirt" because we usually associate that word with female dress.

5:4 וְשָׂרַפְתָּ אֹתָם בָּאֵשׁ—Hebrew commonly adds בָּאֵשׁ ("in the fire") after verbs of burning, such as שָׂרַף, but English translations often omit it.

מִמֶּנּוּ תֵצֵא־אֵשׁ—The antecedent of "from *it*" is uncertain. The suffix is masculine. If the reference is to the fire Ezekiel just kindled, we would expect a feminine suffix because אֵשׁ is usually feminine. If the reference is to that last act of judgment, we still would expect a feminine suffix because abstractions (such as an action or idea) usually are expressed by the feminine in Hebrew. However, both those conventions are not without exception.

5:5 פ כֹּה אָמַר אֲדֹנָי יְהֹוִה—The space in the MT (indicated by the פ between 5:4 and 5:5) signals that we have a major transition here (see the first textual note on 2:1). The transition is reinforced by the use of the citation formula, "thus says the Lord Yahweh."[3] In 2:4 and 3:11 that formula had been a sort of shorthand for messages of judgment, and that is what we have in the rest of this chapter.

The following material (5:5–17) is very complicated. Block describes it as a "remarkable collage of sayings" and surmises that they represent a "literary synthesis" of "fragments or summaries of the oral explanations offered in association with the various acts as they were performed."[4] There is no way to test such a hypothesis, but it is a plausible one, and there is no reason why Ezekiel himself should not have been responsible for composing it.

זֹאת יְרוּשָׁלַם—The demonstratives זֶה and זֹאת often point forward, but here זֹאת points back to the city sketched in the brick (4:1) and, in application, to the city itself and perhaps to the entire land of which she was the capital and to all the inhabitants.

הַגּוֹיִם—The term can mean "Gentiles, pagans," but, although that implication remains here, the emphasis is simply upon "(foreign) nations/political entities." Parallel to it at the end of the verse is אֲרָצוֹת, "countries/lands." Sometimes Ezekiel uses עַמִּים ("peoples, ethnic or cultural units," although easily interchangeable with גּוֹיִם)

---

[2] Greenberg, *Ezekiel*, 1:110.

[3] Cf. "Text and Style in Ezekiel" in the introduction.

[4] Block, *Ezekiel*, 1:196.

instead of אֲרָצוֹת. The parallel placement of any two of these three terms is typical of Ezekiel.

5:6 וַתֶּמֶר אֶת־מִשְׁפָּטַי ... וְאֶת־חֻקּוֹתַי—This Hiphil (third feminine singular imperfect) of מָרָה "to rebel" may have the same meaning as the Qal, or it may be an "elative" Hiphil, perhaps implying a long-term, studied intransigence toward God's Word.

"Ordinances" and "statutes" translate מִשְׁפָּטִים and חֻקּוֹת, respectively. The two words are a nearly constant pair throughout the Bible, together virtually forming a hendiadys. One might be tempted to translate מִשְׁפָּט (from שָׁפַט, "to judge") as "judgments," except that in modern English usage that word is usually heard negatively. Here it denotes the decisions or verdicts of God as the judge and the giver of the Torah, which doctrinally encompasses both his Law and his Gospel. מִשְׁפָּט has a wide semantic range and is one of the most difficult of all Hebrew words to reproduce accurately. Ezekiel may be deliberately introducing a play on the word here: in 5:7 it will mean something like "custom" and in 5:8 "punishment." חֻקָּה (as well as חֹק, its masculine equivalent) is derived from חָקַק, "to engrave, inscribe" (or "sketch" in 4:1). Undoubtedly, edicts or statutes were sometimes promulgated by inscribing them in stone, but the noun derivatives do not require that nuance.

לְרִשְׁעָה מִן־הַגּוֹיִם—This result clause states the consequence of Israel's rebellion. רִשְׁעָה might be a so-called feminine form of the Qal infinitive construct (see GKC, § 45 d; Joüon, § 49 d) from רָשַׁע, "to be wicked, guilty." However, most lexicons consider it to be a feminine noun, so literally the clause states that Israel became "wickedness" (personified or embodied). The following preposition מִן forms a comparative construction: "becoming *more* wicked than the nations."

בְמִשְׁפָּטַי מָאָסוּ—The change from the earlier third person feminine singular forms to this third person plural verb makes this a verbatim citation from Lev 26:43, where it is stated as grounds for exile if/when Israel violates the divine covenant. Other parts of Ezekiel (e.g., 22:3–12, 25–30) contain a virtual catalogue of the specific sins implied by the generalizations at the end of 5:6.

5:7 לָכֵן—"Therefore" introduces the citation formula ("thus says the Lord Yahweh") twenty-five times in the book of Ezekiel. לָכֵן is used thirty-eight other times as well, for a total of sixty-three times (more than Isaiah's twenty-seven and Jeremiah's fifty-five). Usually, as here, it connects the preceding indictment or description of wrongdoing with the following punishment, legal sentence, or remedy. This connection will be even more evident in the next verse. (One may divide the announcement of judgment in 5:7–17 into two parts [5:7–10 and 5:11–17] based on לָכֵן again in 5:11.) The shift from the preceding third person forms to the second person of direct address ("you") signals the same transition to the sentencing. The use of לָכֵן four times in 5:7–11 implies the direness of the situation and emphasizes the climactic warning of the impending judgment, which Israel so well deserves.

יַעַן הֲמָנְכֶם מִן־הַגּוֹיִם—After the preceding לָכֵן, the indictment is introduced further here by יַעַן, "because." Sometimes יַעַן comes first. Here it can be construed as leading into the following verse (5:8). At other times יַעַן is not used, and לָכֵן introduces the judgment directly. Sometimes then לָכֵן can be translated "surely" or the like, as in 5:10.

הֲמָנְכֶם is somewhat of a crux. The MT is presupposed by the early versions, but they vary widely in their interpretations. Possibly it is an irregular form of the noun הָמוֹן, "tumult, crowd," with second masculine plural suffix ("your tumult"). However, it would be unusual for a noun to follow יַעַן (though a noun phrase follows it in 5:9). The form can be a Qal infinitive construct of a verb הָמַן with suffix, which would be a normal syntactical construction after יַעַן.[5] However, there is no other instance of such a verb in the OT. Some (including *HALOT*, s.v. הָמוֹן) wish to emend. Most prefer to construe it as the infinitive of an otherwise unknown verb that is denominative from הָמוֹן, and hence would mean "be tumultuous, turbulent." Since the accent is not on noisiness, I have chosen "be flagrant."

וּכְמִשְׁפְּטֵי הַגּוֹיִם ... לֹא עֲשִׂיתֶם:—English idiom requires different translations ("have ... performed" and "have ... acted") for the two matching uses of עָשָׂה in the latter part of the verse. This clause appears to be a direct contradiction of 11:12, where God makes the accusation that the Israelites *did* act according to the ordinances (conform to the pagan practices) of the other nations. Therefore many manuscripts and editions, followed by RSV and NRSV, omit the negative here. But the received text is not hard to understand (see the commentary below). The negative clause beginning with וְלֹא in 16:47 probably should be understood in the same way.

5:8 In a way, this verse functions as the apodosis to 5:7: "because" Israel acted as described in 5:7, "therefore" the judgment described in 5:8–10 is the just punishment. But לָכֵן and the citation formula, which begin 5:7, are repeated here to emphasize judgment. Nearly every element in the rest of the verse also has the function of emphasis.

הִנְנִי עָלַיִךְ גַּם־אָנִי—"Behold, I ..." is intended to grab the people's attention even more. Usually a participle follows הִנֵּה, often indicating imminence of action ("about to do"). But here a suffixed form of the preposition עַל ensues. The suffix (like other forms in the following verses) is feminine singular ("you"), referring to Jerusalem as the personification of the people.

In Ezekiel God's emphatic גַּם־אָנִי ("even I") is characteristically found in his announcements of punishment (never in promises of salvation). It will also occur in 5:11 (twice); 8:18; 9:10; 16:43; 20:15, 23, 25; 21:22 (ET 21:17); 24:9.

5:10 לָכֵן—Here לָכֵן may be asseverative ("surely") rather than introducing the legal sentence (as in 5:7 and 5:11) after the indictment (5:5–6). Some even think it indicates God is swearing an oath. What follows in 5:10 is a paraphrase of Lev 26:29, which speaks of a siege-induced famine in the same dire terms: parents cannibalizing their own sons and daughters.

וְעָשִׂיתִי בָךְ שְׁפָטִים—This time the "judgments" God executes (עָשָׂה) are denoted by שְׁפָטִים, which commonly has that meaning, whereas מִשְׁפָּטִים was used in that same sense in 5:8, where literary concerns prevailed: the "judgments" (מִשְׁפָּטִים, 5:8) resulted from Israel's violation of God's "ordinances" (also מִשְׁפָּטִים, 5:7).

שְׁאֵרִיתֵךְ—This is one of the key vocables used by the prophets to refer to the "remnant," which usually is a remainder of the people who will be kept by God's

---

[5] So, for example, Keil, *Ezekiel*, 1:89, and, influentially, BDB, s.v. הָמַן.

grace in faith and faithfulness, and who will be saved. The context here (and in 6:12, which uses the Niphal participle of שָׁאַר) points in the opposite direction: only a remnant of Israel will be left, and they too will be subject to judgment. Ezekiel uses the word again similarly in 9:8 and 11:13, where he fears that God will annihilate all Israel, including the last "remnant" of the people. In later passages Ezekiel uses it of other peoples who will fall under God's judgment: in 25:16 it refers to the "remnant" of the Philistine coastland, which Yahweh will destroy, and in 36:3–5 he speaks against "the remnant of the nations" who invaded Israel.

5:11 Ezek 5:11–17 is sometimes outlined as a second announcement of judgment upon Jerusalem. It begins with לָכֵן, which again (as in 5:7, but unlike in 5:10) functions in its usual way, enunciating the sentence of punishment after the guilty verdict given in 5:5–6.

חַי־אָנִי—When Yahweh is the speaker, there is no higher authority than himself to swear by. Probably חַי is the noun "life" rather than the homographic adjective "living, alive." The pronoun אָנִי must function solecistically as a noun in the genitive: literally, "by the life of I." The phrase is commonly translated with an English verb, "as I live." Yahweh swears by himself using חַי־אָנִי six times in other OT books[a] but sixteen times in Ezekiel.[b] Most of the time it is in passages where the Lord swears to execute judgment, but occasionally it is in a positive affirmation (33:11). This first person formula may be compared to the common third person formula חַי־יְהוה, "by the life of Yahweh" (translated "as Yahweh lives") used in oaths (e.g., 1 Sam 14:39, 45).

(a) Num 14:21, 28; Is 49:18; Jer 22:24; 46:18; Zeph 2:9

(b) Ezek 5:11; 14:16, 18, 20; 16:48; 17:16, 19; 18:3; 20:3, 31, 33; 33:11, 27; 34:8; 35:6, 11

נְאֻם אֲדֹנָי יְהוה—This phrase is sometimes called the "signatory formula" because it serves as a kind of signature by Yahweh attesting an oracle as his. It occurs 81 times in Ezekiel and 11 times elsewhere in the OT. The shorter phrase נְאֻם־יְהוה occurs 4 times in Ezekiel (13:6, 7; 16:58; 37:14) and 264 times elsewhere in the OT. Despite the frequency of these phrases, נְאֻם is technically a bit of a crux. It occurs only in oracle formulas. The form appears to be the construct of נְאֻם, though that presumed absolute form never occurs. Neither has any convincing etymology or cognate of the word been found. Some suggest that it means God's "whispering" or "announcement" (*HALOT*) in the prophet's ear, but there is no certain basis for that.

The elusiveness of this term's exact meaning is a classic illustration that the Bible clearly affirms the *fact* of verbal inspiration, but does not explain much about exactly *how* it occurred. That lack of explanation is, in a way, an affirmation that inspiration was miraculous.

Functionally, the two phrases with נְאֻם that are common in Ezekiel are interchangeable with כֹּה אָמַר יְהוה, "thus says Yahweh" (11:5; 21:8; 30:6). נְאֻם־יְהוה tends to occur at the end of a speech or section. It is especially common in Ezekiel and Jeremiah, partly due, no doubt, to the prominence of battles with false prophets in the careers of both of them. In Ezekiel, it frequently appears after the oath "as I live," as here.

אִם־לֹא—This begins the second asseveration ("surely because …") that follows the initial "therefore" (the first asseveration was "as surely as I live"). We have already met אִם־לֹא in Ezek 3:6, and here too it is not part of an oath, but emphasizes what follows.

יַעַן אֶת־מִקְדָּשִׁי טִמֵּאת—This ("because …") introduces further detail about the accusation that was presented in general terms in 5:5–6. The accusation is the reason for the punishment whose description begins later in 5:11 and extends through 5:17. The reason given for the coming doom is that Jerusalem (she is implied by the feminine singular verb) "defiled, polluted, made unclean" God's "sanctuary." The verb is the factitive Piel (second feminine singular perfect) of טָמֵא, "unclean." "Sanctuary" (from the Latin *sanctus*) is etymologically an exact equivalent of מִקְדָּשׁ, whose root is "holy" (קדשׁ). Usually in the Bible, it refers to the tabernacle or (as here) the temple, the place God had sanctified by his election and presence.

This phrase adumbrates chapters 8 and 11, which will reveal in considerable detail how Israel had "defiled" God's "sanctuary."

בְּכָל־שִׁקּוּצַיִךְ וּבְכָל־תּוֹעֲבֹתָיִךְ—The noun שִׁקּוּץ ("detestable practice") is close to synonymous with תּוֹעֵבָה ("abomination"), with which it is paired here. To the extent they are distinguishable, שִׁקּוּץ refers more specifically to idols or idolatrous practices. The word's most famous use is in Daniel's שִׁקּוּץ שֹׁמֵם, "desolating abomination" or "abomination of desolation" (Dan 12:11; Dan 9:27 and 11:31 have variations of the phrase), that is, an abomination so bad that it causes the holy city and temple to be destroyed.

וְגַם־אֲנִי אֶגְרַע—As in 5:8, the redundant גַּם־אֲנִי ("even I") is emphatic. The verb is somewhat problematic. Clearly it is the first common singular Qal imperfect of גָּרַע, which can mean "to shave" (*HALOT*, 1, citing Jer 48:37 and Ezek 5:11). It can also mean "to **cut down**," "withdraw," or "diminish" (*HALOT*, 2, 3, and 4). English translations vary from "will I also diminish thee" (KJV) to "I will cut you down" (RSV) to "I myself will withdraw my favor" (NIV) to "I will withdraw" (ESV). In my judgment (and according to *HALOT*, 1), "shave" is best. This harks back to Ezekiel shaving off his hair in 5:1. Now God says, "even I—I will do the shaving." The next verse (5:12) too will hark back to Ezekiel's action prophecy (specifically 5:2) and apply it further.

The same picture of God shaving people in judgment (though with some different vocabulary) appears in Is 7:20. The "baldness" in Is 15:2 and Jer 48:37 likewise is the result of shaving imposed as divine punishment.

וְלֹא־תָחוֹס עֵינִי וְגַם־אֲנִי לֹא אֶחְמוֹל:—Two clauses emphasize Yahweh's mercilessness in carrying out his judgment. These clauses or slight variations of them are paired together four more times in Ezekiel (7:4, 9; 8:18; 9:10). The two verbs here are also paired in the divine command in 9:5 and in the impersonal construction in 16:5 (while just חוּס occurs in 20:17; 24:14 and just חָמַל in 36:21). I have rendered the first idiom literally as "My eye will not pity." In 7:4 (and 16:5) it is followed by the prepositional phrase "on you." The second verb, חָמַל, most often means "to have compassion." When it takes a prepositional phrase with an object, it can mean "to spare (someone)," so the negated absolute verb here could mean "I will spare no one." However, in Ezekiel חָמַל is used absolutely, without a prepositional phrase, except in the impersonal construction in 16:5 and in 36:21.

All the Ezekiel passages with either of these two verbs express merciless divine judgment, except for 20:17 ("My eye spared them/had pity on them") and 36:21 ("I had compassion on my holy name").

5:12 This verse is obviously intended as an explanation of Ezekiel's action prophecy in 5:1–2. The connection is evidenced by the nearly verbatim repetitions of phrases we encountered in 5:2.

שְׁלִשָׁתֵ֫יךְ—The meaning is clear ("your third"), but we would expect the form of the suffix to be ךָ- instead of יךְ- (as if the noun were plural: "your thirds"). Some conjecture that a copyist transposed the *yod* and *taw* in the presumed original שְׁלִשִׁיתֵךְ.

בַּדֶּ֫בֶר ... וּבָרָעָב֮—These two aspects of the judgment, death "in the plague" and "in the famine," apply to the first third of the people. Apparently both are explanations of the burning of the first third of Ezekiel's hair "in fire" in 5:2. "In your midst" (5:12) implies that the people who die of plague and famine will be "inside the city" (5:2).

The "pestilence" or "plague" (דֶּבֶר) is commonly assumed to be the bubonic plague. All together, "famine" (רָעָב) and the related adjective "hungry" (רָעֵב) occur sixteen times in Ezekiel. The triple threat of "plague," "famine," and "sword" also appears in Jeremiah (e.g., Jer 14:12; 21:7, 9), and we will meet it again in Ezekiel.[c] The pairing of plague and famine appears to be another echo of the covenant curses in Lev 26:25–26. In a besieged city, the starving residents are especially susceptible to disease because of their malnutrition, and the crowded, dirty conditions within the city facilitate the spread of disease.

(c) Ezek 6:11, 12; 7:15; 12:16; cf. 5:17; 14:21

The LXX of Ezek 5:12 applies "plague" and "famine" to different groups of people and so ends up with four divisions ("fourths") instead of thirds. See the first textual note on 5:2.

בַּחֶ֫רֶב ... סְבִיבוֹתָ֫יִךְ—The third who perish "by the sword" will fall "all around you," meaning outside but near the city. That is well illustrated by Zechariah's fate after he escaped from the city (2 Ki 25:4–7).

5:13 In the first half of the verse, three virtually synonymous clauses are piled up to emphasize that God's righteous wrath must—and will—accomplish its purpose: the satisfaction of God's justice.

וְכָלָה—The verb כָּלָה will be repeated toward the end of the verse (the Piel infinitive בְּכַלּוֹתִי). The Qal here may simply mean "be finished, completed, ended," but it often implies that some purpose or objective is accomplished or "fulfilled," as I have chosen to translate it. The Piel of כָּלָה is causative, and I have translated the final clause of 5:13 as "when I exhaust my wrath at them." Yahweh makes similar statements using the Piel in 6:12; 7:8; 13:15; 20:8, 21.

וַהֲנִחֹ֫תִי—The Hiphil of נוּחַ may mean "give rest" in some neutral sense, but often it too indicates when some objective has been achieved.

וְהִנֶּחָ֫מְתִּי—The Hithpael of נָחַם often means "be comforted, satisfied" in any ordinary sense, but the overtones are considerably different when God is "satisfied" after executing his wrath. The *taw* in the Hithpael preformative (הִתְ-) has been assimilated into the *nun* as marked by the *daghesh* (הִנֶּ-). The unusual vowels (נֶחָ-) are because it is in pause, as indicated by the *athnach*. The LXX has no translation for this verb, leading some to speculate that it is a later addition. The Qumran fragment of 5:11–17 does not have room for the whole Masoretic version of the text, which might suggest that the Hebrew Qumran text was of the same text type as the LXX, but that does not necessarily mean it is the original or better text. There appears to me to be no overriding reason to abandon the MT.

בְּקִנְאָתִי—The noun קִנְאָה is traditionally translated "jealousy," and related adjectives as "jealous." Applied to God, these must not be understood in a petty human sense, but in the sense that God demands his people to be faithful to him alone. See the commentary below.

5:14 וְאֶתְּנֵךְ לְחָרְבָּה וּלְחֶרְפָּה—The idiom נָתַן לְ means "make (something or someone) into" or even "give/surrender someone up to." The second feminine singular pronominal suffix on the verb (וְאֶתְּנֵךְ), "you," must refer to Jerusalem (since cities are grammatically feminine in Hebrew), but the city represents all the Israelites.

The Hebrew assonance of חָרְבָּה and חֶרְפָּה can be matched by the English "ruin" and "reproach," respectively. Often חֶרְפָּה refers to the act of reviling someone or to "disgrace, shame," but in 5:14–15 it denotes one who is ashamed and the object of taunting. The terms are yet another echo of the covenant curses in Leviticus 26 (specifically Lev 26:31). They are common in Jeremiah too and are paired in Jer 49:13.

The LXX omits the second member of the pair (חֶרְפָּה). Some scholars then treat it as a gloss, but with even less justification than for וְהִנַּחְמָתִי in 5:13.

כָּל־עוֹבֵר:—Like Jeremiah (e.g., Jer 18:16; 19:8), Ezekiel refers to "every passerby" here and in Ezek 36:34 to magnify the extent of the shame to be heaped upon Jerusalem. Compare the same phrase also in 16:15, 25.

5:15 וְהָיְתָה—The feminine singular verb refers to Jerusalem in the third person: "She will be …" That is a switch from the surrounding phrases, which have second person (feminine singular) forms. The ancient versions, and apparently also fragments from Qumran, read this verb as second feminine singular: "You will be …" However, the first clause of 5:16 too refers to the audience in the third person ("against them"; see the textual note below) then shifts to second person in the rest of 5:16. Such shifts are common in Hebrew.

חֶרְפָּה וּגְדוּפָה מוּסָר וּמְשַׁמָּה—The noun חֶרְפָּה is repeated from 5:14. Here it is paired with גְדוּפָה, which is a hapax legomenon, but similar words from the same root leave no doubt as to its meaning: "a taunt, reviling." It could mean that Jerusalem is the object of taunting or that people will use the name of Jerusalem as a taunt-word because she is a well-known example of one who has suffered destruction and shame. (The verb גָּדַף in 20:27, where God is the object, means "to blaspheme.") מוּסָר is one of Jeremiah's favorite words for God's "discipline" or "chastisement" to be applied to Israel, but in this context it probably means "a warning, reminder (of God's punishment)." מְשַׁמָּה (from the root שׁמם) means "something that causes people to be horrified, appalled."

בַּעֲשׂוֹתִי—God states that all of these emotive words will apply to Jerusalem "when I execute judgments upon you in anger, in wrath, and in furious chastisements" (5:15). One commentator compares the expression here with a well-known verse that uses the verb (יָכַח) cognate to the noun תּוֹכָחוֹת ("chastisements") here: "Yahweh chastises him whom he loves" (Prov 3:12). That aspect of God's judgment is not expressed in this Ezekiel passage, but in the total context of the book as a whole, one would have to agree that it is relevant.

אֲנִי יְהוָה דִּבַּרְתִּי:—This final clause in the verse is an independent sentence. It is repeated at the end of 5:17 to conclude the chapter. However, the syntax earlier in 5:15 (God speaking to Jerusalem) will continue in the following verse, so that this short sentence stands as an interjection between 5:15 and 5:16.

5:16 The long first half of the verse is a wordy (for emphasis!) circumstantial clause that is parallel to the second half of 5:15. Both half-verses begin with an infinitive construct with the preposition בְּ in a temporal sense: "when I execute [בַּעֲשׂוֹתִי] … when I send [בְּשַׁלְּחִי] …" Echoes of Leviticus 26 and Deuteronomy 28 and 32 reverberate throughout Ezek 5:16–17. Most of the passage is couched in the second person plural. However, like the beginning of 5:15, which referred to Jerusalem in the third person ("she"), the first part of 5:16 refers to the Israelites in the third person (בָּהֶם, "against them"). The rest of the verse refers to the Israelites in the corresponding second person masculine plural, which differs from the feminine singular references to Jerusalem in earlier verses, though the two kinds of forms are indistinguishable in English translation; both are "you." The LXX omits sizable portions of 5:16.

בְּשַׁלְּחִי אֶת־חִצֵּי הָרָעָב הָרָעִים—The Piel of שָׁלַח is used twice in this verse. The intensive stem implies not only "send" (as does the Qal, which too is frequent in Ezekiel), but often adds the nuance of "unleash, let loose."

"Arrows of famine" is a striking turn of a phrase that recalls Deut 32:23–24. Deut 32:23 speaks of God sending arrows against his people, and Deut 32:24 continues by speaking of רֶשֶׁף ("plague"), which appears also in the archaizing poem of Habakkuk 3 as one of Yahweh's attendants (Hab 3:5). It appears likely that "exmythological" usage underlies רֶשֶׁף in Deut 32:24. A god by the name of Reshef is quite well-known in the Ugaritic texts (from northern Canaan of about the fourteenth century B.C.) and is the personification of disease and other evils. Among other things, Reshef is known in Ugaritic as "lord of the arrow," that is, the arrow was his symbol. The OT often takes pagan, mythological language and, using it with theologically proper meaning, poetically applies it to the one true God and his whole monotheistic revelation. Whether the mythology found in Ugaritic was still known in Ezekiel's time or whether the language had simply entered into the fabric of Hebrew poetic expression is impossible to say.

"Deadly" is a common translation of רַע here. The major Hebrew word describing moral evil or wickedness is רָשָׁע, "wicked, evil" (as in Ezek 3:18–19). Often רַע is translated the same way, but doing so here might wrongly make Yahweh the author of evil. While רַע may encompass the moral dimension of evil, it is much more versatile in meaning and can refer to all kinds of things or circumstances (including divine punishments) that are (perceived by sinful humans) as harmful, tragic, undesirable, and so forth.

אֲשֶׁר הָיוּ לְמַשְׁחִית אֲשֶׁר־אֲשַׁלַּח אוֹתָם לְשַׁחֶתְכֶם—These two relative clauses each begin with אֲשֶׁר and feature a form of the verb שָׁחַת, "to destroy." In the translation I have repeated the antecedent of אֲשֶׁר in brackets, "[arrows] which … ," to clarify the sense.

The Hiphil participle מַשְׁחִית, "destroyer," is the same term for the "destroyer" who struck down the firstborn in Egypt (Ex 12:23), and it also describes Yahweh destroying Sodom (Gen 19:14; cf. Ezek 16:49–50). The implication may be that Israel has become like those reprobate peoples whom Yahweh punished. The same participle with מַלְאָךְ also appears in 2 Sam 24:16, referring to "the angel who was destroying" Israel in punishment for David's sin of counting the fighting men. In all three of these other passages the punishment is executed personally by Yahweh and/or an angel he sends. These comparisons accord with the general tenor of the whole context of Ezekiel 5 with its reversal: once Israel's enemies were the target of divine punishment, but now it is Israel itself.

וְרָעָב אֹסֵף עֲלֵיכֶם—Things will go from bad to worse. אֹסֵף is the Hiphil first common singular jussive of יָסַף, though its meaning is the same as the imperfect (אוֹסִיף). The Hiphil can mean "to add, increase, do again or more." Lev 26:21 and Deut 32:23 are both in the background.

וְשָׁבַרְתִּי לָכֶם מַטֵּה־לָחֶם:—The last clause cites Lev 26:26. The metaphorical idiom of God breaking the staff of bread was in Ezek 4:16 (see the textual note on the phrase there) and will be repeated in 14:13.

5:17 וְשִׁלַּחְתִּי עֲלֵיכֶם ... וְחַיָּה רָעָה וְשִׁכְּלָךְ—The new punishment introduced in this verse is חַיָּה, a singular collective that can mean "wild animals, beasts of prey" (*HALOT*, s.v. חַיָּה 1, 2), especially when modified by the adjective רַע (feminine רָעָה). (That adjective had also modified the "arrows of famine" in 5:16.)

The verb וְשִׁכְּלָךְ is the Piel of שָׁכַל and is third masculine plural, even though its subject is the feminine singular חַיָּה because that means "animals." The suffix is second feminine singular, referring to Jerusalem as "you," as in 5:11–12, 14–15. The literal "bereave you" means that the animals will kill your children. *HALOT* (s.v. שָׁכַל, Piel, 1 a) suggests "wild animals will rob you of your children."

Yahweh promises to send wild animals as agents of judgment two more times (14:21; 33:27), but he also promises their elimination in the eschatological reversal of salvation in 34:25–31. They appear elsewhere in the Bible as well as in extrabiblical treaty curses. The mention of both wild animals and the curse that "they will bereave you" is another reverberation of Deut 32:24–25 and Lev 26:22.

וְדֶבֶר וָדָם יַעֲבָר־בָּךְ—The first three Hebrew words are alliterative. The first two ("plague and bloodshed") probably function as a hendiadys, "a fatal plague." In nations and religions outside Israel, דֶּבֶר ("plague, disease") was personified as a demon, and here too it may be a personification. דָּם may mean simply "blood," but in both singular and plural forms the word is used metonymically for "murder, bloodshed." Perhaps here, and more clearly elsewhere in the book, it is virtually personified as an agent of death.

וְחֶרֶב—The final mention of the "sword" (previously in 5:1–2, 12) is almost shorthand for "war" itself.

אֲנִי יְהוָה דִּבַּרְתִּי:—This is repeated from 5:13 and 5:15. One final time Yahweh avers that he is the actual speaker and actualizer of all the horrors mentioned.

Commentary

Chapter 5 divides into two uneven parts. First is the last of the inaugural action prophecies (5:1–4). Second comes a rather generic judgment oracle comprising the rest of the chapter (5:5–17). In the second part, only 5:12 is a specific reference to and commentary on the action prophecy in the first part (especially 5:2). The second part (5:5–17) is a virtual synopsis of much of the rest of the book, especially through chapter 24. It follows that most of the basic hermeneutical and theological problems of the rest of the book must be confronted here too, and, as pertinent, they will be addressed below.

The second part of the chapter (5:5–17) can be outlined further as follows:

A. Indictment or accusation (5:5–6)
B. Judgment or punishment (5:7–17)
  1. First pronouncement of judgment (5:7–10): "Therefore …"
  2. Second pronouncement of judgment (5:11–17): "Therefore …"

5:1 One is surprised that Ezekiel does not react as negatively to the command to shave his head and face as he had to the earlier command to eat bread baked over human excrement (4:12–14). There are clear prohibitions against priests shaving their heads or beards (Lev 21:5; Ezek 44:20), but despite them, Ezekiel maintains his usual posture of unquestioning obedience. In addition to the religious stigma, under ordinary circumstances it was also dishonorable culturally for a man to appear beardless (2 Sam 10:4 ‖ 1 Chr 19:4). Shaving of the head is frequently associated with mourning rites (cf. Deut 14:10), and Ezekiel's audience may have inferred that Ezekiel was mourning proleptically at the fall of Jerusalem (if they got the message at all). By being the one shaved, Ezekiel assumes the role of the people in the city. That the city is the ultimate object of the shaving becomes clear shortly, and in that application it also emerges that Yahweh is the real wielder of the judgment sword (5:2, 12, 17).

5:2 Most theological comment on this verse can wait until the texts' own explication of it in 5:12. The mention of "the city" in connection with the first third of the hair connects this action of the prophet with the sketch of Jerusalem on a brick in 4:1–3. The audience should not be tempted to think for a moment that Ezekiel is prophesying about anything but Jerusalem—and so, ultimately, themselves. "Fire" is a common symbol of destruction and sometimes of God himself as punisher, partly because of the common practice, ancient and modern, of torching conquered cities (e.g., Josh 6:24 and 11:11, which use the same vocabulary as Ezek 5:4). The initial completion of the "days of the siege" would have been the 390 days Ezekiel lay on his left side (4:4–5).

The "sword" is the agent of destruction for the second third of hair, and Yahweh will pursue the last third, scattered to the wind, with his own "sword." The term appears ninety-one times in Ezekiel and is especially prominent in chapter 21, with its Song of the Sword (21:13–22 [ET 21:8–17]).

5:3 Since Yahweh does not provide his own exegesis of this verse later (as he does of 5:2 in 5:12), we must attempt one here. If the previous verse represents God's various judgments on the inhabitants of Jerusalem, this action prophecy predicts that a tiny remnant, "few in number," will somehow survive the catastrophe (see also, e.g., 6:8, 12; 9:1–6; 12:16; 14:22). That will not be a matter of "luck," however, but of God's own gracious intervention. (Contrast the biblical view with the tremendous popularity of Tyche, the Greek goddess of luck—and the careless way in which Christians often speak today, even of "Lady Luck.") Elsewhere, the OT prophets develop the theme of the "remnant" considerably, and it ultimately undergirds what we know as "church versus state" in Israel's theocratic community. Only some of those in the nation of Israel truly belonged to theological Israel, the OT church, as St. Paul explains in Romans 9–11. The same distinction applies to the NT church, "the Israel of God" (Gal 6:16), in terms of the "visible" church (all who belong to a church) versus the "invisible" church comprised of all baptized believers in Christ. "The church in the proper sense is the assembly of saints who truly believe the Gospel of Christ and who have the Holy Spirit. Nevertheless, we grant that the many hypocrites and evil men who are mingled with them in this life share an association in the outward marks" (Ap VII/VIII 28).

5:4 Even that small act of divine mercy (5:3) is immediately qualified. Not all who escape the immediate conflagration will ultimately survive. The long arm of Yahweh's wrath will reach even those in exile. Echoes of the curses in Lev 26:36–39 for covenant violation are again apparent here. The ancient message of Moses (some eight centuries before Ezekiel) was not new to those acquainted with the Scriptures, but Ezekiel's audience needed to be reminded of its applicability to them.

This interpretation assumes that fire is an agent of destruction throughout this section. Keil and a few other commentators, however, sense a contradiction here to the act of saving a remnant in 5:3. Hence, the argument is that this fire "has not merely a destructive, but also a cleansing, purifying, and quickening power."[6] The idea is present in some OT passages. Isaiah 6 and Mal 3:1–4, for example, develop it at some length. Appeal is also made to Ezek 6:8–10, where those who escape do repent (although "fire" is not mentioned). I, however, view it unlikely that "fire" would be given two disparate significations in the same context here.

5:5 The citation formula, already associated with divine judgment in the book (2:4; 3:11), here introduces a major block of such material.

One might picture Ezekiel pointing at the sketched brick (4:1) as he reminds the audience of what his action prophecies have all been about. Block also thinks of a courtroom scene, where "this is Jerusalem" introduces the accused to the court.[7]

The statement that Jerusalem was "in the middle of the nations" includes the idea that God had placed her in the thick and thin of human politics and commerce. It was taken in later Jewish and Christian thought in a literalistic, geographical sense. We have medieval maps so depicting Jerusalem at the cen-

---

6   Keil, *Ezekiel*, 1:85.

7   Block, *Ezekiel*, 1:197.

ter of the known world. The precise age and origin of this idea is unknown. It can be documented in the pseudepigraphical *Jubilees* (8:12, 19) from the intertestamental period. A plaque in the floor under the high dome of the Church of the Holy Sepulcher in present-day Jerusalem still identifies it as the center of the world. Closely related is the metaphor of Jerusalem as the "navel of the earth" (Ezek 38:12), that is, the place from which the earth was formed.[8]

However, these passages are not so much about the geographic centrality of Jerusalem (and it is doubtful if the ancients would have understood them that way). Rather, their point is that Jerusalem is the *theological* center of God's activity, the locus of his salvation, both in the OT era and in its fulfillment in Christ, who died and rose there. If one reads them theologically, they are powerful metaphors. That Jerusalem had been chosen as the center of God's salvific activity is often accented with its epithet "Zion."

In that sense, Jerusalem/Zion is all but inseparable from the election of David and his house—and thus of the promised Son of David, Jesus Christ, who shall reign on David's throne forever. Zion and the promised Davidic King are linked explicitly in, for example, Pss 2:6; 132:10–14. In that vein one can, indeed, speak of Calvary as the center of God's whole soteriological activity, as the "navel" from which the new creation has been born and is being formed. The new birth into God's kingdom comes through Holy Baptism ("water and the Spirit," Jn 3:5) into Christ's death and resurrection (Rom 6:1–4), and this "living water" offered by Jesus is not confined to any particular geographical locale (John 4). To be sure, the church's mission begins in Jerusalem, but then it fans out to the ends of the earth (Acts 1:8).

The theological centrality of Jerusalem is obviously in the background of Ezekiel's thought here and elsewhere. However, right now the perversion of the "theology of Zion," that is, making the theological centrality of Jerusalem into a magical guarantee of the city's and the people's impregnability, was precisely the notion that Ezekiel had to demolish. In the present context, the point is that all the grace and kindness that God has showered on Jerusalem has not taken place in a private corner, nor has her behavior gone unnoticed. Neither will the forthcoming judgment upon Israel for its ingratitude and infidelity be private and concealed from public view.

5:6 *This verse is Ezekiel's whole indictment of Jerusalem in a nutshell.* It is the same basic indictment voiced by many other prophets as well. "To whom is given much, much shall be required from him" (Lk 12:48). Jerusalem is targeted for theological reasons. As the focal custodian of God's promises (land, temple, king, Messiah), Jerusalem also had special responsibilities. But now she had become a model for paganism. As Isaiah (1:21) had trenchantly summarized, "How the faithful city has become a whore!"

---

[8] Greenberg says that "the later Jewish cosmogonic doctrine ... that Jerusalem was 'the navel of the earth' " was "derived probably from Greek thought" (*Ezekiel*, 1:110–11, citing I. Seeligmann, "Jerusalem in Hellenistic-Jewish Thought," in *Judah and Jerusalem* [Hebrew; Jerusalem: Israel Exploration Society, 1957], 204, n. 37, and S. Talmon, "Tabûr Ha'aretz and the Comparative Method" [Hebrew], *Tarbiz* 45 [1976], 163–77).

Deut 4:7–8 describes Israel's covenant relationship as the envy of the nations: none of them had the one true God living in their midst, and none had received such beneficial and "righteous" (צַדִּיק) laws as Israel. As Deuteronomy makes clear (perhaps more than any other part of the OT), Israel's covenant relationship with God was established and continued solely by his grace and love, through and through. When we (like Ezekiel) refer to the OT laws, statutes, and so on, we must be careful to expound them within their setting: they were given after Yahweh had already redeemed his undeserving people from Egypt and claimed them as his own. The laws can function according to the first, second, and third uses of the (doctrinal) Law (to use classic Lutheran terminology); they never were (and are not now) a means to obtain God's favor. Otherwise, the OT would have expounded an entirely different type of religion than the NT, and the one in the NT would have been the abrogation, not the fulfillment of the OT faith. (In principle, Marcion would have been right!)

Instead of treasuring God's gifts of grace and showing its gratitude by obedience, Israel had followed the behavior patterns of its Gentile neighbors. In fact, says Yahweh, Israel had become even more wicked and rebellious than the surrounding heathen (Ezek 5:6)! It was not merely a case of Israel's assimilation or acculturation, but of its calculated rebellion and rejection of the Abrahamic and Mosaic covenants.[9]

The accusation against Jerusalem is not intended to praise the pagan nations round about her, of course. They cannot have rebelled against God's Torah (special revelation), because God had not given it to any of them (cf. Ps 147:20). But a doctrine of "natural law" (as in Rom 1:18–32) underlies the thought here, as in many other places in Scripture, such as the covenant with Noah in Genesis 9; Amos 1:3–2:3; and, ultimately, most of the Gentile oracles in the prophetic corpus, including Ezekiel 25–32. Yahweh prophesies against the Gentile nations too, because of their hubris and inhumanity toward others. Despite how evil they are, the law written on their hearts had kept them on a higher level than the depravity to which Israel had sunk in her rebellion, says Yahweh here (Ezek 5:6). This thought had been adumbrated already in 3:6b. St. Paul makes a similar point in Rom 2:12–14. The Gentiles, unlike Israel, had sinned ἀνόμως ("without the Law"), and so they shall perish ἀνόμως. Israel had sinned while having the Law and so shall be judged according to the Law, as Ezekiel is doing here.

5:7 Both the beginning and the end of this verse make the same point articulated in 5:6: Israel's behavior has been even worse than that of the pagan nations. The precise force of the first clause is uncertain (see the textual notes), but it appears to charge that Israel has been even more "flagrant" (as I have translated it), brazen, and/or riotous in its misbehavior than the nations. There probably is an element of hyperbole in such a statement, upping the common

---

[9] Compare the excursus "Covenant" in Harstad, *Joshua*, 744–56.

charge that Israel was as bad as the nations. But we must also hear it in the light of the extra culpability Israel bears because it is the beneficiary of God's gracious, special revelation.

As the textual notes point out, many translations omit the negative in the last clause of the verse in order to eliminate the apparent contradiction with not only the first part of the verse, but also with 11:12. (That omission would give "you *have* acted according to the ordinances of the nations" instead of "you have *not even* acted …") But such an expedient is hasty and superficial. Much of the solution lies in grasping the multivalence in meaning of מִשְׁפָּט ("ordinance"). Here in 5:7b it does not mean God's will revealed in Scripture, as it did in 5:6–7a, but the standards of justice or societal norms (remnants of conscience, left even after the fall into sin) by which the nations governed themselves. (I have retained the translation "ordinance" to convey the connection to the uses of the same word in 5:6–7a.)

It is still true that unbelievers may externally lead a more lawful life than some members of the visible church (especially weak or nominal Christians, but sometimes even clergy!), who may display behavior of which even secular society disapproves, both in sins of omission and of commission.

5:8 By repetition of the formulaic signal of punishment that also began 5:7 ("Therefore, thus says the Lord Yahweh"; see the textual notes) and by an accumulation of other devices, this verse underscores the gravity of the divine verdict against Israel. The following formula, "Behold, I am against you," occurs here for the first time in the book of Ezekiel. This Hebrew formula (sometimes called the hostile orientation formula) is thought to have originally been a challenge to a duel in face-to-face combat (e.g., Samson and the Philistines in Judg 16:9), but more characteristically it announces imminent retribution upon the enemies of God's people (e.g., Nah 2:14 [ET 2:13]). But now Israel has proved to be God's enemy, and so the phrase is applied to Israel itself. In Ezekiel God uses the formula "Behold, I am [הִנְנִי] against [עַל or אֶל] …" fourteen times,[d] more than any other prophet.

(d) Ezek 5:8; 13:8, 20; 21:8 (ET 21:3); 26:3; 28:22; 29:3, 10; 30:22; 34:10; 35:3; 36:9; 38:3; 39:1

Lest there be any misunderstanding about who the agent of judgment is, Yahweh adds, "even I." This is no mechanical working out of some impersonal principle of retribution or cycle of karma, but is God's personal execution of the curses for disobedience inherent in the covenant. This climaxes on the cross, where Christ is cursed on our behalf (Gal 3:13). Since we have been baptized into his death, we would die in our sins if we did not also daily rise with him to newness of life (Romans 6; 8:13).

The punishment will fit the crime precisely. The Hebrew conveys the correspondence clearly, but it is impossible to reproduce in English. In Ezek 5:7 Yahweh used the negated verb עָשָׂה twice to refer to Israel's evil behavior and sins of omission ("you have *not performed* my ordinances, and you have *not even acted* …"). Now in 5:8–9 he uses the same verb twice to express what he himself will do: "I will *perform* judgments in your midst. … I will *do* …" The term for the punishments is מִשְׁפָּטִים, which is the same noun translated "ordinances" in 5:6 and 5:7, but here it must mean "judgments." God will perform what his unfaithful people failed to perform, but to their condemnation. Often the related noun שְׁפָטִים is used for "judgments," and God uses that noun with עָשָׂה ("perform") to describe his punishment of Israel in 5:10, 15; 11:9. God had performed (עָשָׂה) judgments (שְׁפָטִים) against Egypt in the exodus narrative (Ex 12:12; Num 33:4; cf. "judgments" in Ex 6:6 and 7:4). Ezekiel may intend that the Israelites now see themselves before God in the same role as the Egyptians appeared then. Later, Ezekiel will speak of God performing (עָשָׂה) judgments (שְׁפָטִים or מִשְׁפָּטִים) against Israel's enemies.[e]

(e) Ezek 25:11; 28:22, 26; 30:14, 19; 39:21

The appropriate divine judgment will take place where the rebellion occurred, "in your midst" (5:8) and "among you" (5:9), that is, in Jerusalem. God's acts of judgment there will also be "in the sight of the nations" (5:8). Since Jerusalem is located among the nations and she had acted even more flagrantly than the surrounding nations (5:7), her insolence had been evident to all. So it will also be with her comeuppance.

5:9 Her unprecedented sin will bring unprecedented punishment. A concrete example will be given in the next verse. The reason is all her "abominations," that all-purpose word for everything that is incompatible with God's Word and provokes his wrath. The word's forty-three occurrences in Ezekiel far outnumber its appearances in all the other prophets combined.

5:10 The horrors of cannibalism, even within one's own family, are not unparalleled in desperate siege conditions elsewhere in world history, but that God himself would instigate it now among his chosen people was unprecedented. While the language is masculine ("fathers" and "sons"), the practice undoubtedly would not discriminate between genders. The threat of cannibalism often occurs in ancient secular Near Eastern treaty curses. The possibility is referred to in other biblical passages, most fully in Deut 28:53–57, as part of the curses should Israel break the Mosaic covenant.

"To every wind" here (Ezek 5:10) is stronger than would be "the four winds" (e.g., 37:9). God will disperse the remnant in every direction imaginable. Here we may pick up an echo of the action prophecy in 5:2, but the explicit connection to 5:2 will come in 5:12.

5:11 By an accumulation of oaths, emphatics, and stress on God himself as the speaker and the one who threatens, this verse leads into the climax in the next verse (5:12), where the specifics of the action prophecy at the head of the chapter (5:1–4) are interpreted. The transition is prepared by Yahweh's use of the metaphor "I will do the shaving" (5:11, recalling 5:1) to describe his coming judgment.

Yahweh adduces Israel's climactic offense as reason for the fury of his judgment: "because you have defiled my sanctuary." The clause adumbrates what will be described in considerable detail in chapters 8 and 11. God's laws in Leviticus had the purpose of keeping his holiness, which was incarnate at the tabernacle and temple, separate from and undefiled by the unclean things

183

of the people.[10] Israel violated the entire divine purpose as well as the letter of those laws.

The verse ends with two parallel assertions of Yahweh's pitilessness and mercilessness in carrying out the judgment: "My eye will not pity, and I myself will have no compassion." There may be a slight element of hyperbole (since "a few" still remain in 5:3), but it brings out forcefully Yahweh's "grim resolve"[11] to carry out his threats. No sentimentality will be allowed to interfere. "My eye" is used anthropomorphically parallel to Yahweh ("I myself") because grief or horror are readily perceived by and expressed in the eyes, perhaps to the point of shedding tears.

Still, the fact that God here declares that he will have no mercy shows, in a backhanded way, "that the normal, basic attitude of God toward Israel is not determined merely by law, but by love. It is his proper manner to spare and pity, but there is a level of human guilt at which this mode is set aside, and the standard of his judicial righteousness comes into force."[12]

That point bears constant emphasis in order to correct the canard that the God of the OT (sometimes caricatured as a lesser or different god, as by Marcion) was characterized by wrath and judgment, with his love and forgiveness first becoming apparent only in the NT triumph of the cross and resurrection of Christ. That misunderstanding is especially easy to fall into when reading a book like Ezekiel, which, on the surface, abounds in wrath and judgment. But the *cantus firmus* of the OT—the "constant song"[13] of God's overriding love for his people, even when he must punish—finds its maximal expression in the Gospel proclamation of him "who did not spare his own Son, but gave him up for us all" (Rom 8:32).

5:12   Here we are given God's own exegesis of the action prophecy of 5:1–4. It is striking, however, that there is not even a hint of the few hairs tucked in the folds of the prophet's robe (5:3)—that is, of a tiny surviving remnant of Israelites. The account of the fulfillment—the fall and exile of Jerusalem—appears three times in the Bible: 2 Ki 25:1–21; 2 Chr 36:17–21; Jer 39:1–18.

5:13   In 5:13–17, words commonly used of Yahweh's wrath against his enemies are used against his own unfaithful people (see the textual notes). In the first sentence of 5:13 ("Then my anger will be fulfilled, I will let my wrath at them rest, and I will be satisfied"), three clauses are accumulated to describe Yahweh's determination to honor his threats to the fullest, so that his ultimate objective—restoration of a remnant to faith and faithfulness—may be achieved.

---

[10] See Kleinig, *Leviticus*, 6–13.

[11] Block, *Ezekiel*, 1:210.

[12] Herrmann, *Ezechiel*, 65–66, commenting on 9:10, quoted by Greenberg, *Ezekiel*, 1:115.

[13] For a Lutheran description of the Gospel as the *cantus firmus* or "constant song" that pervades the OT as well as the NT, see Mitchell, *The Song of Songs*, 16–17.

To a modern reader who has only a one-sided conception of God's love and lacks comprehension of the biblical dynamic of Law and Gospel, these sorts of statements will cause problems. As noted in the commentary on 5:11, they easily lead to the misunderstanding that the God (god?) of the OT was vengeful, or arbitrary and excessive in his exercise of judgment. But from a proper Christian standpoint, they remind us that the depravity of humanity's sin—including our own—fully deserves such terrible retribution, and that from God's judgment we have absolutely no escape except through the vicarious satisfaction of Jesus Christ. Revealed in these verses is the ferocity of God's wrath at the sin of his own people (again, including us) that could only be sated through the bloody sacrifice of his own perfect Son. The atonement of Jesus Christ expiated our sin (and that of the whole world) and also propitiated God: his fierce wrath is satisfied by the sacrifice he himself provided, so that his disposition toward us in Christ is love. But for all those who perish without Christ, God's wrath will only be satisfied by their damnation to eternal perdition.

The OT depiction of God meting out his seemingly unquenchable wrath on his unfaithful people points to the inability of sinful humans to do anything themselves to atone for their sins. Yet this recognition is not intended by God to dead-end in total despair; his goal is repentance and renewal in faith. In the text, the purposefulness of Yahweh's action is emphasized by an expansion of the recognition formula: "Then they will know that I, Yahweh, have spoken in my jealousy when I exhaust my wrath at them" (5:13). The shorter formula "I, Yahweh, have spoken" (5:13) will be repeated two more times before the chapter ends (it concludes 5:15 and 5:17).

Whatever false notions the Israelites may have developed about God, his drastic acts of judgment, no less than his signal acts of deliverance, were in fulfillment of predictions uttered long ago and were intended to remind the people of the covenant he had made with them. The curses for covenant disobedience in Leviticus 26 echo throughout the chapter. Yahweh's efficacious Word, spoken by Moses over eight hundred years earlier, soon will be fulfilled in concrete action. Since the curses of God's Law upon their sin are fulfilled so dramatically, how much more confident can God's people be that his Gospel promises of salvation in Christ shall be brought to completion in their entirety (cf. Rom 5:6–10)!

That Yahweh declares, "I ... have spoken *in my jealousy*" (Ezek 5:13), reveals much. This (קִנְאָה) and related Hebrew terms apply to God frequently in Ezekiel, and, indeed, throughout the OT. In the Torah God had commanded his people to avoid provoking him because he is "a jealous God" (אֵל קַנָּא).[f] Since Yahweh's relationship with his people is so frequently described as a marriage, this language indicates that God is a husband who will not share his "wife" with any other god and who will take appropriate action when the

(f) Ex 20:5; 34:14; Deut 4:24; 5:9; 6:15

(g) Num 5:11–31; Prov 6:34; cf. Mt 19:9; Jn 8:3–4

marriage covenant is broken.[14] The same dynamic pertains to human marriage.[g]

God is "monogamous" also in religion. "Because he loves so deeply, he must respond vigorously."[15] He tolerates no spiritual adultery or harlotry with other gods, no syncretism or unionism of any sort. Ezekiel in chapters 16 and 23 will expound at length Israel's spiritual harlotry in terms of sexual infidelity, and the two usually go together, both in the OT and in the NT.[h] Perverted practices in the ancient world such as homosexuality and cultic prostitution were commonly part of the worship of other gods. Today too, the church must affirm that extramarital intercourse and homosexuality incur God's wrath.

All this relates to the First Commandment: "You shall have no other gods!" (Ex 20:3; Deut 5:7). Other "gods" really are not divinities at all, but demons (1 Cor 10:20–21). They have diabolical power and attraction, but cannot be tolerated among God's people, lest God pour out his wrath in his jealousy. In NT application, Jesus insists that "no man comes to the Father except by me" (Jn 14:6). Any compromise of the Gospel of salvation through Christ alone constitutes accommodation or acceptance of false gods. An orthodox church is always on its guard against any kind of universalism or false ecumenism.

(h) E.g., Numbers 25; Jn 4:16–20; 1 Cor 5:1–13; 6:12–20

5:14   In 5:14–15 the focus shifts from Yahweh's anger to the emotional and psychological effects of Jerusalem's devastation, especially among the surrounding nations. One might entitle these two verses "a great reversal"—not the common biblical one of justification by grace alone,[16] but its very opposite. Jerusalem, who was called to be a "light to the nations" (Is 42:6; 49:6), is reduced to rubble. Whatever pride and glory she had achieved, as judged by human standards, will now be changed into reproach and shame. Under God's blessing, Jerusalem was the holy city, the city set on a hill (Mount Zion; cf. Mt 5:14), but since she has defiled her sacred status with abominations, she will be brought to ruin—as every person without God is but dust and ashes.

5:15   We have four overlapping Hebrew nouns of invective reflecting "the richness of the Hebrew vocabulary of contempt."[17] Jerusalem will be "a reproach and a taunt, a warning and an object of horror." With its heaping up of words describing onlookers' reactions, the final clause ("I, Yahweh, have spoken") emphasizes (as had 5:13 and as 5:17 will again) that it is all the result of God's exercise of his almighty Word.

5:16–17   Ezekiel's first major judgment sermon comes to a climax in these verses, both summarizing and heightening themes that appeared earlier.

---

[14]   One may see the survey of OT and NT texts that depict God's relationship with his people as a marriage in Mitchell, *The Song of Songs*, 40–66.

[15]   Block, *Ezekiel*, 1:211.

[16]   As expressed in, for example, the Magnificat (Lk 1:46–55) and the Beatitudes (Mt 5:3–12), God in his grace eschatologically reverses the sinful condition and the world's estimate of his people: he exalts the humble but humbles the exalted; the first shall be last, and the last shall be first; and so on.

[17]   Block, *Ezekiel*, 1:212.

The background of Leviticus 26 and Deuteronomy 28 and 32 reminds the audience that God is as good as his ancient Word—in judgment as well as grace.[18] Yahweh's zeal ("jealousy," 5:13) in fulfilling his covenant promises and curses is manifested by his summoning all kinds of agents to carry out his will.

---

[18] This is expressed in, for example, Josh 23:14–16, after God had fulfilled his Torah promise to bring the Israelites into the land:

> You know with all your heart and with all your soul that not one promise has fallen from all the good promises that the LORD your God promised to you. ... But just as has come true for you all the good promise that the LORD your God promised to you, likewise the LORD will bring upon you all the evil warning until he has destroyed you from upon this good ground that the LORD your God gave you when you transgress the covenant of the LORD your God which he commanded you and [when] you go and you serve other gods and you bow down to them.

> For this translation and the view that 23:16 is not just hypothetical but foresees the time "*when* [not 'if'] you transgress the covenant," see Harstad, *Joshua*, 737–43.

Judgment for Idolatry on the Mountains

Translation

6 ¹The Word of Yahweh came to me: ²"Son of man, set your face toward the mountains of Israel and prophesy against them. ³You shall say, 'O mountains of Israel, hear the Word of the Lord Yahweh. Thus says the Lord Yahweh to the mountains and to the hills, to the ravines and to the valleys: Behold, I am about to bring against you a sword, and I will destroy your high places. ⁴Your altars will be demolished, and your chapels will be smashed, and I will throw down your slain in front of your fecal deities. ⁵I will lay the corpses of the sons of Israel in front of their fecal deities, and I will scatter your bones around your altars. ⁶In all the places you live, the towns will be laid waste, and the high places will be demolished, so that your altars will be laid waste and demolished, your fecal deities smashed and cease to be, your chapels broken in pieces, and your works wiped out. ⁷The slain will fall in your midst, and then you will know that I am Yahweh. ⁸Yet I will leave a remnant when you have some who escape the sword among the nations, when you are scattered in various countries. ⁹Then, those of you who escape will remember me in the nations where they have been carried captive, how I was heartbroken by their whoring heart which turned away from me and by their eyes which whored after their fecal deities. They will loathe themselves for all the evils they have done, for all their abominations. ¹⁰And they will know that I, Yahweh, did not speak in vain about doing to them this disaster.'

¹¹"Thus says the Lord Yahweh: Clap your hands, stomp with your foot, and say, 'Ah,' on account of all the vile abominations of the house of Israel, for they will fall by the sword, famine, and the plague. ¹²He who is far away will die of the plague, and he who is near will fall by the sword, and he who remains under siege will die of famine. Thus I will exhaust my wrath upon them. ¹³Then you will know that I am Yahweh when their slain lie among their fecal deities around their altars, on every high hill and on all the mountaintops, under every green tree and under every leafy oak, each place where they offered fragrant sacrifice to all their fecal deities. ¹⁴I will stretch out my hand against them, and I will make the land a desolate waste from the desert to Riblah, in all the places they live. Then they will know that I am Yahweh."

Textual Notes

6:1 The chapter division here is very apt. Both 6:1 and 7:1 open with "the Word of Yahweh came to me," which has been called the "message-reception formula" or "word-event formula." Chapter 6 divides itself into two oracles, 6:2–10 and 6:11–14. Each oracle begins with a physical gesture and ends with a variation of the recognition formula, "And they will know that I, Yahweh, did not speak in vain ..." (6:10), or the recognition formula itself, "Then they will know that I am Yahweh" (6:14). Internally, the chapter is dominated by Ezekiel's characteristic practice of "halving." That is, each oracle constitutes about half of the chapter, and each has a main section (6:3–7 and 6:11–13a) followed by a sort of echo, which many commentators refer to as an "afterwave" (6:8–10 and 6:13b–14).

This unity in variation is characteristic of the entire chapter, which is tightly bound together by "lexical and syntactical repetitions and resumptions" and uses "rhyme, alliteration, parallelism, synonymy."[1] As in chapter 5 (also 4:10–11, 16–17; 12:19–20; 14:12–23), the covenant curses for Israel's disobedience in Leviticus 26 exert a pervasive influence on this chapter too, although not often in the form of verbatim quotes.

As we also noted in the previous chapter, the LXX has a considerably shorter text than the MT. Greenberg summarizes the relationship: "MT exhibits a maximizing occasionally conflate text, consistent in texture and rich in literary devices; G, a sparser text, occasionally contracted, otherwise plainer and literarily poorer."[2]

6:2 בֶּן־אָדָם—See the textual note on "son of man" in 2:1.

שִׂים פָּנֶיךָ אֶל־הָרֵי יִשְׂרָאֵל—The idiom "set/direct your face toward" was in 4:3 (there with the Hiphil of כּוּן). Here and at the end of the verse, the preposition אֶל is used. Its primary force is direction "toward," but it is so often used interchangeably with עַל ("on, against") that it is often a toss-up which meaning was intended. At the end of the verse, the sense demands "against." That would also be possible here at the beginning of the verse, although I have chosen "toward." The decision turns somewhat upon whether one regards the clause as purely literary, or whether an action prophecy is intended. Since the second section of the chapter (6:11) clearly opens with action, the symmetry that characterizes the chapter as a whole suggests that we have one here too. If the exiles were already beginning to face Jerusalem when praying (cf. Dan 6:11 [ET 6:10]), it would be especially poignant for Ezekiel to face the city when prophesying against it.

By addressing the "mountains of Israel," Ezekiel expands his scope from besieged Jerusalem (the focus in chapters 3–5) to the whole land of Israel, of which Jerusalem was the historic capital. Ezekiel uses "mountains of Israel" sixteen times in the book, and he is the only biblical author to use it.[a] (The singular "mountain/hill country of Israel" is in Josh 11:16, 21.) The phrase will be amplified in the next verse, and the ultimate reason for addressing the mountains (idolatry upon them) will become obvious at the end of 6:3 and in the following verses.

(a) Ezek 6:2, 3; 19:9; 33:28; 34:13, 14; 35:12; 36:1, 4, 8, 37:22; 38:8; 39:2, 4, 17

There is probably another reason why Ezekiel addresses the mountains: nostalgia for the landscape of the homeland in contrast to the relatively flat, featureless terrain of southern Babylonia. Allen says: "It expresses such nostalgia as a native of Switzerland feels who has to reside in Holland, or a Welshman who must live in East

---

[1] Block, *Ezekiel*, 1:218.

[2] Greenberg, *Ezekiel*, 1:139.

Anglia."[3] Ezekiel's point is to make vivid to the Israelites the enormity of their loss, which their behavior had brought upon them.

Yahweh's intended audience surely is the people of Israel, beginning with Ezekiel's fellow exiles, but in chapter 6 he mainly refers to them as third-party bystanders who would overhear Ezekiel's speech to Israel's mountains.[4] To explain why Ezekiel does not primarily address the people, Greenberg quotes Calvin: "Thus God obliquely signifies, first, that the Israelites were deaf, and then unworthy of the trouble which Ezekiel would spend in teaching them."[5]

The sequel to chapter 6 comes in chapter 36, where "the mountains of Israel" are again addressed. Much of the other language of chapter 6 is repeated there too. But chapter 36 is a great reversal. In contrast to the judgment forecast here, chapter 36 promises Israel's eschatological return to the mountains.

6:3 לֶהָרִים וְלַגְּבָעוֹת לָאֲפִי^{dd}קִים וְלַגֵּאָיֹת—The inanimate objects of the prophet's denunciation are expanded: "to the mountains and to the hills, to the ravines and to the valleys." The distinctions between the two members of each pair are somewhat arbitrary. The main Israelite occupation of Canaan had centered on the central mountain spine with its heights of various altitudes running virtually the entire north-south length of the country. These could be called either "mountains" or "hills." Running generally at right angles (east-west) to the line of mountains were the many "ravines" and "valleys." A "ravine" (אָפִיק, *aphik*) generally was fed by a spring at its head, with water coursing down it. Hence "Aphek" is part of many place names. A "valley" (גַּיְא) may denote either a wide or narrow depression. Most often it is used with the name of a specific valley. Hebrew has still other words for specific types of valleys.

The Qere marginal note attests to textual confusion about (or perhaps dialectical variants of) the plural of גַּיְא. The Qere form (גֵּאָיֹות) appears five other times in Ezekiel, while the Kethib (גֵּאָיֹת) occurs only here. In Ezek 35:8 we also find the plural גֵּאָיֹות.

בָּמוֹתֵיכֶם:—With this last word in the verse we reach the gravamen of Ezekiel's concern in this chapter. בָּמָה is conventionally translated as "high place," but "high" should probably be heard more in the sense of "religiously important" than of altitude. (If altitude were the salient point, רָמָה would probably be used.) Heights were apparently preferred for these shrines or places of worship (see 6:13), but "high places" could also be constructed in valleys and inside cities.

---

[3]   Allen, *Ezekiel*, 1:86.

[4]   Most of the time in chapter 6 God refers to the Israelites in the third person masculine, usually plural ("they," "their," "them"), but singular ("he") in 6:12. In the context of 6:2–3, the second masculine plural forms ("you," "your") in 6:3 clearly are spoken to the mountains. Then there is a transition and ambiguity in 6:4 (also 6:6) since the second person masculine plural forms ("your altars … your chapels … your slain … your fecal deities") pertain to the Israelites, even if "your" could be understood to refer to the mountains in the sense that the altars and corpses are on the mountains. The second person masculine plural forms in 6:5 (especially "your bones") and 6:6, 8–9, 13 seem to address the Israelites, but interspersed with them are third person masculine plural references to the Israelites in 6:5, 9, 10, 11, 12, 13, 14. The second person masculine plural forms in 6:7 seem perhaps addressed again to the mountains.

[5]   Calvin, *Ezekiel*, 1:219, quoted in Greenberg, *Ezekiel*, 1:139.

Considering that "high places" are mentioned in the Bible about eighty times in the sense discussed here, it is surprising how little we know about them. Apparently, they usually were an open-air sanctuary (in contrast to a temple, which often is called a "house"), but 1 Sam 9:22 speaks of a structure (perhaps a "hall") at one. Perhaps there was no complete standardization of a "high place." One might expect archaeological excavations to elucidate the matter, but widely varying features have been so identified. The unknown can hardly explain the unknown. One of the best candidates is the (varying phases of) the massive rectangular platform unearthed at Dan. It probably harks back to the time when Jeroboam I selected Dan and Bethel to replace Jerusalem. A huge circular structure from Late Bronze (pre-Israelite) Megiddo is often identified as a "high place." Of an entirely different character is the row of ten monoliths at Gezer, traditionally also called a "high place."

The biblical texts regularly speak of sacrifice and burning of incense in connection with high places. Thus, 6:4 speaks of altars and one other feature ("chapels"?) of at least some high places. Albright associated high places with pagan funerary cults,[6] but his view has not been widely followed (even though the latter part of 6:4 and also 43:7 refer to corpses there). Ezek 6:13 will refer to "every green tree," and burials sometimes were under oak trees (Gen 35:8; 1 Chr 10:12), which might suggest ancestor worship there, but even if so, such a tree by itself (without an altar and perhaps other features) probably was not enough to constitute a "high place."

Ezekiel never refers to אֲשֵׁרִים (singular אֲשֵׁרָה) and mentions מַצֵּבוֹת (singular מַצֵּבָה) only in 26:11. However, in other OT books they are regularly associated with high places. Neither word is easy to translate, partly because of questions about their appearance and function. The latter (מַצֵּבָה) was apparently, in essence, a generic word for a stela, pillar, or standing stone of almost any sort. Hence, the word is sometimes, especially in early Israelite periods, used in a perfectly neutral or positive sense. But in connection with a high place, it had entirely different (pagan) connotations. אֲשֵׁרָה, with which מַצֵּבָה is often paired, is even more difficult. We now know that "Asherah" was also the name of a major Canaanite goddess, who was the wife of El and "mother of the gods." The figure at the high places was somehow related to her, but precisely how is not clear. It apparently was not a statue representing her (carved figures are sometimes mentioned separately). It was of wood, probably a pole, although possibly a living tree (hence KJV's "grove"). The Asherah, then, represented the female principle of the universe (in pagan thought). The standing pillar (מַצֵּבָה) correspondingly represented the male principle (probably phallic). That explains the frequent association of cultic prostitution with the high places, and, undoubtedly, was a major reason for their popularity.

In early Israelite history, some "high places" apparently were used for acceptable worship of Yahweh. Both Samuel (1 Sam 9:11–25; 10:5) and Solomon (1 Kings 3) engaged in worship at them, although 1 Ki 3:3 concedes that as a peccadillo by

---

[6] W. F. Albright, "The High Place in Ancient Palestine," in *Volume du Congrès: Strasbourg, 1956* (VTSup 4; Leiden: Brill, 1957), 242–58.

Solomon. The Jerusalem temple was supposed to have become the sole location for the liturgical worship of Yahweh (1 Kings 8), and so by the end of Solomon's reign and thereafter, the "high place" became so inextricably associated with paganism that it became a major focus of orthodox denunciation. After the division of the kingdoms, Judahite kings periodically made efforts at reformation, although they often stopped short of the drastic step of outlawing the high places. Only Hezekiah and Josiah succeeded in doing that, but the efforts of both were promptly reversed by their successors. In Ezekiel's time, the high places were obviously still flourishing in Canaan.

6:4 וְנָשַׁמּוּ מִזְבְּחוֹתֵיכֶם—Usually the Niphal of שָׁמֵם carries the meaning "be desolated, deserted." Here, however, since the subject is "your altars," the translation "be demolished" is more appropriate. Qal forms of by-forms of this verb probably occur in 6:6, where I have translated them the same way.

וְנִשְׁבְּרוּ חַמָּנֵיכֶם—The noun חַמָּן has been rendered in quite a variety of ways in the history of translation. Its meaning still cannot be said to have been settled definitively. Older translators and commentators often rendered it "sun pillars" or "images" and associated it with the patron deity of Carthage, Baal-*Hammon*. They derived the word from חָמַם, "to be hot." But Ugaritic evidence falsifies that derivation, and it has generally been abandoned.

Most current translations have "incense altar" (so *HALOT*) or "incense stand." That is certainly plausible, and archaeological evidence for it is abundant. Little four-horned, limestone incense altars have been found in many places, and ceramic stands of great variety (usually, but arguably, associated with incense) are also frequent. The evidence from Nabatean and Palmyrene inscriptions is ambiguous. It may support the translation "incense stand/burner," but also "chapel/sanctuary" of some sort. I have chosen the latter translation since it accords well with 2 Chr 34:4, which speaks of חַמָּנִים "above" altars.[7]

וְהִפַּלְתִּי חַלְלֵיכֶם—The shift from the preceding passive verbs to this first person verb (Hiphil of נָפַל) stresses Yahweh's personal activity. חָלָל can serve as either an adjective or noun meaning "pierced with the sword; … **slain**" (*HALOT*, 1 a). It occurs thirty-six times in Ezekiel. It may mean simply "wounded," but usually implies the "mortally wounded," especially when in construct with חֶרֶב ("by the sword"), as in, for example, 31:17–18; 32:20–21.

לִפְנֵי גִּלּוּלֵיכֶם:—This is the first passage in Ezekiel with גִּלּוּל (always in plural) one of his most contemptuous terms for an idol. Ezekiel includes thirty-nine of its forty-eight occurrences in the OT. It is etymologically related to גֵּל, "feces" (Ezek 4:12, 15; Job 20:7; see the textual note on it in 4:12), and גָּלָל, "dung, feces" (1 Ki 14:10; Zeph 1:17). Thus Yahweh styles "idols" as "feces, turds," intentionally eliciting disgust. Most agree that the vocalization of גִּלּוּל is patterned after שִׁקּוּץ ("abomination"). I agree with Block:

> Modern sensitivities prevent translators from rendering this expression as Ezekiel intended it to be heard, but had he been preaching today, he would probably have identified these idols with a four-letter word for excrement.[8]

---

[7] Cf. Block, *Ezekiel*, 1:225, nn. 38–39.

[8] Block, *Ezekiel*, 1:226.

Most English translations avoid conveying the actual sense of the term so as not to offend modern readers, but the scatological term was chosen deliberately to be offensive. This commentary usually translates it as "fecal deities" to convey the sense, but occasionally has another translation if the context so indicates (e.g., 22:3–4). If anything, our translation is still a bit "sanitized."

6:5 פִּגְרֵי בְּנֵי יִשְׂרָאֵל—Hebrew פֶּגֶר is from the common Semitic root for "corpse." The first half of 6:5 refers to "the sons of Israel" in the third person, whereas 6:4b and 6:5b seem to refer to the Israelites (if not to the mountains) in the second person. The third person reference here clarifies that the "corpses" are those of the Israelites, not of the mountains. Ezekiel is alluding to the covenant curse in Lev 26:30, which refers to "your corpses"; that verse and its context are addressed to the Israelites. Since the first clause of Ezek 6:5 is missing entirely in the LXX, some scholars assume that it is an editorial gloss, but even Zimmerli defends its originality,[9] and most recent commentators have agreed.

6:6 בְּכֹל מוֹשְׁבוֹתֵיכֶם—This phrase is literally "in all your settlements" (see also the similar one in 6:14). It is a common phrase in Pentateuchal laws.[b]

הֶעָרִים תֶּחֱרַבְנָה—Conventionally עִיר (plural עָרִים) is translated "city." The line between a "city" and a "town" is admittedly subjective, but the usage of עִיר indicates that it can refer to either a walled or an unwalled population center. The large walled cities had historically been bastions of the Canaanites. Archaeological evidence indicates that the vast majority of the Israelites lived in small agricultural villages, nearly always unwalled. The major exception, especially after the defection of the northern kingdom (which had more walled cities), was fortified Jerusalem.

תִּישַׁמְנָה ... וְיֶאְשְׁמוּ—These two anomalous verb forms appear to be Qal imperfects from the roots יָשַׁם and אָשַׁם, respectively, but most commentators and lexica agree that they are Qal by-forms of שָׁמַם, "be desolated, deserted" (whose Niphal was in 4:17; 6:4). Partly for the sake of consistency, I have translated both as "be demolished" as also for the Niphal in 6:4. By-forms of one sort or another are especially frequent with geminate verbs. Another verb form in 12:19 and 19:7 (also Gen 47:19) also appears to be from יָשַׁם. A dismantled altar would be just another pile of stones.

וְנִשְׁבְּרוּ וְנִשְׁבְּתוּ גִּלּוּלֵיכֶם—The alliteration with the two verbs is striking. "Cease to be" is my rendition of the Niphal of שָׁבַת (probably related to "Sabbath"). Literalistically, it might be translated "be brought to an end; disappear."

וְנִגְדְּעוּ חַמָּנֵיכֶם—"Broken in pieces" translates the Niphal of גָּדַע, from whose root is the name Gideon. His name matches his action of destroying an altar of Baal and its accompanying Asherah, although this verb is not used in that passage and for that feat he was called Jerubaal (Judg 6:25–32). Later verses (Judg 8:29, 35) suggest that Jerubaal may have been his original given name.

וְנִמְחוּ מַעֲשֵׂיכֶם:—"Be wiped out" is a literal translation of the Niphal of מָחָה. God repeatedly used the Qal of the verb in the flood narrative to declare that he would "wipe out" reprobate humanity (Gen 6:7; 7:4, 23). In 2 Ki 21:13 Yahweh threatens to wipe out Jerusalem as one wipes a dish.

(b) E.g., Ex 35:3; Lev 3:17; 7:26; 23:3, 14

---

9   Zimmerli, *Ezekiel*, 1:183.

6:7 חָלָל—Here the singular "slain" is a way of expressing the indefinite general or collective. Compare the individualizing plural in 6:4, 13.

6:8 וְהוֹתַרְתִּי בִּהְיוֹת לָכֶם פְּלִיטֵי חֶרֶב—My free translation of this clause is necessitated both by syntactical issues and radically different idioms in Hebrew compared to English. Literalistically, it is "I will leave in the being to you escapees of the sword." The Hiphil of יָתַר is usually transitive, but here it lacks an object. It is followed immediately by an infinitive clause that is the usual way of expressing a circumstantial (temporal) clause. In Ezekiel that construction often follows the recognition formula ("then you/they will know that I am Yahweh"), which makes וְהוֹתַרְתִּי look even more intrusive. Critics commonly allege that 6:8 is a conflated text, artificially combining two different continuations of 6:7, but that is too easy a way out. The *lectio difficilior* principle is that the harder text is more likely to be original. Of the ancient versions, only the LXX omits the verb. Ezek 6:8 does not seem to be a simple continuation of 6:7, but rather introduces a somewhat new topic.

For the OT theme of God preserving a faithful remnant of his people, the verb יָתַר and cognate nouns are less frequently used than שָׁאַר and cognate nouns (as in the name of Isaiah's son [Is 7:3]). Yet both can pertain to any remnant or remainder, whatever is left behind. שָׁאַר is used in a neutral sense in 6:12 below.

פָּלִיט is a common noun for "refugee, escapee." The related verb פָּלַט is sometimes used in a context of salvation.[c]

(c) E.g., Pss 17:13; 18:3, 44, 49 (ET 18:2, 43, 48); cf. Ezek 7:16

בְּהִזָּרוֹתִיכֶם—The second masculine plural suffix on this Niphal infinitive construct of זָרָה is peculiar in that it has a *yod* (-ִי-). That is the proper form of the suffix when attached to a feminine plural noun. Ezekiel seems to have used that form of suffix because the verb's ending (-וֹת) is the same as that of a feminine plural noun. The same thing happens again in 16:31.

6:9 נִשְׁבַּרְתִּי אֶת־לִבָּם—The major grammatical challenge in this verse is how to construe this clause. אֵת can be the preposition "with" or the inert sign of the direct object. Elsewhere the Niphal of שָׁבַר is always either passive ("be broken") or intransitive (something "breaks"), never transitive ("to break" something). Most likely it is passive here, so אֵת must be the preposition "with," and the clause literally means "I am broken with their whorish heart" (KJV). More idiomatic English is "broken by" or "broken over" (ESV).

Some hypothesize that the prefix נ on the Niphal verb was mistakenly added by a copyist influenced by the נ on the previous verb (נִשְׁבּוּ, Niphal of שָׁבָה). Hence they emend the verb to the transitive Qal, in which case אֶת־לִבָּם would be the direct object: "I have broken their wanton heart" (RSV). The only ancient version that might support a transitive reading is the Syriac, but the Syriac cognate of שָׁבַר means "to be heartbroken," which fits perfectly here.

The following phrase וְאֵת עֵינֵיהֶם ("by their eyes") is governed by the same verb, and "heartbroken" fits there too, while a transitive translation ("I will break their eyes") makes no sense. Finally, one may compare this idiom with a Hophal of שָׁבַר with the same passive meaning in Jer 8:21. Both "heart" and "eyes" still play a prominent role in our modern thought and language about love and religion.

הַזּוֹנָה ... הַזֹּנוֹת—These are Qal participles of the verb זָנָה, which is used especially of a wife who "commits adultery," but it can also refer to fornication and prostitution. The image of Israel as a harlot will be developed in great detail in chapters 16 and 23. Compare also Hosea 1–3. This common biblical metaphor of idolatry as adultery is the obverse of the metaphor of God's covenant with Israel as a marriage (see the textual notes and commentary on "jealousy" in Ezek 5:13). The native Canaanite fertility religion had a strong component of immoral sexual "worship" as a literal part of it.

וְנָקֹטוּ בִּפְנֵיהֶם—This clause ("they will loathe themselves") with the Niphal of קוּט is literalistically "they will feel disgust in their own faces." Similar idioms with this verb appear in 20:43 and 36:31.

הָרָעוֹת אֲשֶׁר עָשׂוּ—Here and in 6:11 the noun רָעָה clearly means "evil," "wickedness," or a synonym referring to sinful human conduct which the Israelites "have done" (עָשׂוּ). The same noun and verb recur in 6:10 but in a different sense.

6:10 This verse offers a slight variation on the common recognition formula, "then you/they will know that I am Yahweh" (e.g., 6:7, 14). What they will come to know is not just Yahweh himself, but that his Word does not return to him empty or in vain (Is 55:11). That is true of his Word of promise and blessing, but also of his threats of punishment, as here. As דִּבֶּר can often be translated "to promise," so here דִּבַּרְתִּי could be translated "I threaten."

לַעֲשׂוֹת לָהֶם הָרָעָה—The idiom עָשָׂה רָעָה is the same as in 6:9, but now with God as subject. Besides this verse, God is the subject of this idiom elsewhere only in Ex 32:14 (after Israel made the golden calf) and Jonah 3:10. In these instances it would be wrong to translate רָעָה as God doing "evil," since God never is the author of evil, and because the people fully deserved the just punishment. Instead, רָעָה means "calamity, disaster" (*HALOT*, 5 a).

6:11 Just as the first oracle in the chapter (6:1–10) began with God commanding Ezekiel to perform an apparent action prophecy ("set your face," 6:2), so too does the second oracle (6:11–14): "Clap your hands, stomp your feet, and say, 'Ah!' " These actions may convey emphasis or attract attention. The meaning of the gestures themselves is debated. Even today, different cultures may attach different significances to these same gestures. For example, in America the clapping of hands is the common way of expressing applause, but in many parts of Europe applause is communicated by stomping the feet (which is mentioned next here, but not necessarily with the same meaning as clapping the hands).

הַכֵּה בְכַפְּךָ—The Hiphil imperative of נָכָה with כַּף literally commands Ezekiel, "strike with your hand." Similar forms of this idiom occur in 2 Ki 11:12 and Ezek 21:19, 22 (ET 21:14, 17); 22:13. Since it would be difficult to clap with just one hand, the phrase here probably is a shortened form of the longer phrase "strike hand upon hand" in 21:19. Other OT passages use different idioms to refer to clapping the hands. Quite a number of dispositions are associated with handclapping in the OT, and to decide the significance, the interpreter must depend on context, which is not always unambiguous. Here many commentators interpret the emotion as delight: Ezekiel,

195

representing Yahweh, is to clap to show God's pleasure that the apostates are being punished. I am inclined, however, to agree with those who see this gesture as expressing God's anger—the same kind of divine fury executed at the end of 6:12.

God uses this same idiom in 21:19, 22 (ET 21:14, 17), where he again commands Ezekiel to clap his hands, then explains that it signifies his execution of his wrath at Israel. Similarly, God uses the same idiom in 22:13 when he claps his hand in anger at the enumerated sins of Israel.

When the gesture means something else, Ezekiel uses a different verb. Thus 25:6 uses the idiom מָחָא יָד for Ammon clapping its hands in gleeful malice at the demise of Israel (but the following idiom for stomping the feet is the same as in 6:11.)

וּרְקַע בְּרַגְלְךָ—Ezekiel literally is told, "Stomp with your foot," but as with the preceding idiom for clapping the hands, we may assume that he would stomp with both feet. In the OT this idiom (רָקַע and רֶגֶל) occurs only here and in 25:6, where Ammon stomped his feet in sinister delight in the destruction of Israel. (In 25:6 this idiom is parallel to an expression for clapping the hands, מָחָא יָד, different from the one on 6:11). In 2 Sam 22:43 the Qal of רָקַע refers to trampling enemies. If this is an action prophecy, Ezekiel's action on Yahweh's behalf probably indicates divine wrath as Yahweh executes judgment and thus tramples his own people who had become his enemies by their rebellion against him.

וֶאֱמָר־אָח—While Ezekiel claps and stomps, he is to utter the interjection אָח. The word is onomatopoetic. Like English "ah," it may arise in various circumstances. Commentators advocate different interpretations of it here. Some take it as expressing "malicious glee"[10] or even translate it "hurrah!"[11] In my judgment, however, a more plausible construal in this context is that by it the prophet expresses God's lamentation that Israel's sin had been so grievous as to require the punishment in 6:11b–12.

The interjection אָח occurs elsewhere in Ezekiel only in 21:20 (ET 21:15). It is often taken to be a short form of הֶאָח, which appears in 25:3; 26:2; 36:2. Block has observed, however, that there is a clear distinction: the shorter form אָח connotes lamentation or indignation, while the longer form הֶאָח expresses derision or joy. He further perceives a correlation between these two forms and the choice of verbs used to express clapping (הִכָּה with אָח and מָחָא with הֶאָח).[12] He is probably right.

כָּל־תּוֹעֲבוֹת רָעוֹת בֵּית יִשְׂרָאֵל—"Abominations" (תּוֹעֵבוֹת) is strong enough without the adjective "evil, vile" (feminine plural of רַע). The adjective almost appears superfluous after a noun that itself connotes consummate depravity. It is almost as though human language is an inadequate vehicle for articulating the quality and extent of depravity.

אֲשֶׁר בַּחֶרֶב בָּרָעָב וּבַדֶּבֶר יִפֹּלוּ:—Here אֲשֶׁר functions as a causal conjunction (BDB, 8 c) introducing the reason for the previous three action prophecies. The triad of "sword," "famine," and "plague" occurred (in varying order) in 5:12, 17 and will

---

[10] Greenberg, *Ezekiel*, 1:135.

[11] Taylor, *Ezekiel*, 91.

[12] Block, *Ezekiel*, 1:235, including n. 83.

recur in 6:12; 7:15; 12:16; 14:21. In 5:12, 17 (explaining 5:1–2) the focus was on Jerusalem, but here in 6:11 the three afflict the entire "house of Israel." This verse echoes the covenant curses in Leviticus 26. In Lev 26:25–26 God threatens to bring the sword and plague, then describes a famine. The triad is most common in Jeremiah,[d] who issues the same kind of prophecies for Israel's disobedience as does Ezekiel. The triad refers to the same three punishments between which David had to choose in 1 Chr 21:12 (cf. also 2 Chr 20:9).

(d) Jer 14:12; 21:7, 9; 24:10; 27:8, 13; 29:17–18; 32:24, 36; 34:17; 38:2; 42:17, 22; 44:13

6:12 The triadic scheme continues in 6:12, listing Yahweh's agents in a different order. Apparently "he who is far away" refers to Israelites scattered throughout the land; "he who is near" refers to Israelites just outside the walls of Jerusalem; and "he who remains under siege" refers to Israelites inside the city. In Ezekiel, "famine" is consistently placed inside the city, while "plague" and "sword" may appear anywhere.

וְהַנִּשְׁאָר֙ וְהַנָּצ֔וּר—These two participles are, literally, "he who is left and he who is guarded," but I have taken them as a hendiadys: "he who remains under siege." The first is a Niphal participle from the root שׁאר, whose noun and verb forms often refer to the righteous remnant, the true Israel that will survive the final judgment. Here, however, it does not have that theological implication because it refers to those who perish in the famine. The second is the Qal passive participle of נָצַר, "keep watch, guard." Since נָצַר can also mean "protect, preserve," many interpret and translate it in a positive sense, "he who is spared, preserved," but that appears inappropriate in the context of judgment here. The picture at this point is one of total annihilation.

וְכִלֵּיתִ֥י חֲמָתִ֖י בָּֽם׃—Only after the triad completes its fatal work will Yahweh "exhaust, spend; finish, fulfill" (Piel of כָּלָה) his "wrath, fury" (חֵמָה) against them (בָּם). The clause is similar to clauses at the beginning and end of 5:13. See the textual note on וְכָלָה in 5:13. Yahweh makes similar statements using the Piel in 7:8; 13:15; 20:8, 13, 21; 22:31.

6:13 As in 5:13, the fulfillment of Yahweh's wrath against Israel (6:12b) leads into the recognition formula ("then you will know that I am Yahweh"). Its second person form here ("you") is grammatically inconsistent with the surrounding third person references to the Israelites ("they," "them," "their"), and when the formula is repeated at the end of the chapter it is in the third person. The reason for the momentary inconsistency is because the prophet's real audience is the exiles who are listening to him, even though he is speaking about those Israelites still in Judah, upon whom God's "final judgment" has not yet fallen. Yahweh's ultimate goal is to cause both groups to recognize who he truly is, both in judgment and salvation, but the impenitent and arrogant people first need judgment. "His passionate intervention in comprehensive judgment was the only means by which his people could be taught the demands of his being and so of his covenant requirements."[13]

The rest of the chapter (6:13b–14) is the "afterwave" of 6:11–13a, and it returns to the theme of 6:4–7: the pagan hilltop worship sites where Israel's rebellion manifested itself most visibly and abominably. As in 6:4–7, Yahweh declares that the

---

[13] Allen, *Ezekiel*, 1:90.

corpses of the Israelites will be scattered around their altars and their idols, who are feces (see the textual note on 6:4). This will be the scene throughout the land.

אֶל כָּל־גִּבְעָה רָמָה ... וְתַחַת כָּל־עֵץ רַעֲנָן—Ezekiel echoes the familiar phrase "on every high hill and under every green tree" (עַל כָּל־גִּבְעָה גְבֹהָה וְתַחַת כָּל־עֵץ רַעֲנָן),[e] but substitutes the synonym רָמָה (Qal feminine singular participle of רוּם) in place of גְּבֹהַ, "high," as also in 20:28 and 34:6. (In the OT only these three Ezekiel verses have the phrase גִּבְעָה רָמָה.) Ezekiel amplifies that familiar phrase by adding parallel phrases "on all the mountaintops" (בְּכֹל ׀ רָאשֵׁי הֶהָרִים) and "under every leafy oak" (וְתַחַת כָּל־אֵלָה עֲבֻתָּה). "On all the mountaintops" perhaps is derived from Hos 4:13.

(e) 1 Ki 14:23; 2 Ki 17:10; Jer 2:20; cf. Deut 12:2; 2 Ki 16:4; Jer 3:6; 2 Chr 28:4

רֵיחַ נִיחֹחַ—This is literally "an odor of soothing" or "odor of appeasement." It is commonly associated with incense but can be used of the smell of any God-pleasing sacrifice. Hence it could be rendered as "an aroma that is pleasing [to God]," but since the aroma was produced by offering a sacrifice (perhaps accompanied by incense), I have translated it as "fragrant sacrifice." This phrase is frequent in Leviticus in God's prescriptions for the divine service. In the sacred worship of Yahweh in the OT, it refers to an offering for which Yahweh has made provision and that he promises to accept as pleasing to himself when it is offered according to his Word. These offerings were types of the vicarious atonement of Jesus Christ, whose once-for-all sacrifice is the only one that truly and fully appeases God's anger at our sin.[14]

The first word of the alliterative Hebrew phrase, רֵיחַ, is a noun related to רוּחַ ("spirit, breath") and means "aroma, odor." The second word, נִיחֹחַ, is a noun derived from the Polel infinitive of the verb נוּחַ, "to rest" (*HALOT*, s.v. נִיחֹחַ), and signifies something that gives rest or appeases. It indicates that the sacrifice is received by God favorably or pleasurably. Compare 5:13, where Yahweh uses the Hiphil of נוּחַ to state that after he executes judgment on Israel, "I will let my wrath at them rest."

Adherents of pagan religions thought that they could appease or propitiate their gods by virtue of their sacrifices. Yahweh's anger at human sin must be propitiated and appeased, but this cannot be accomplished by human action or effort as such; it is only accomplished by God's gracious gift of the means (received and offered in faith) by which his righteousness is satisfied. Finally and climactically, that is accomplished by the sacrifice offered by Jesus Christ for the sins of the whole world.

The phrase occurs three more times in Ezekiel. The first two (16:19; 20:28), like 6:13, refer to idolatrous worship by apostate Israel. However, the third (20:41) is in a brief salvation oracle promising that after the exile and restoration, God will receive the repentant Israelites themselves as a "fragrant sacrifice."

6:14 וְנָטִיתִי אֶת־יָדִי עֲלֵיהֶם—God's "hand" can bring either judgment or salvation (see the textual note on it in 1:3), but this expression clearly refers to God acting in judgment. Similar phrases recur in 14:9, 13; 16:27; 25:7, 13, 16; 35:3.

שְׁמָמָה וּמְשַׁמָּה—Literally, "desolation and desolation," this is a hendiadys ("a desolate waste"). Both words derive from the root שׁמם, hence these synonyms sound alike (assonance). The result is a superlative, expressing the completeness of the action.

---

[14] See Kleinig, *Leviticus*, 42–43, 57–58, 66–68.

מִמִּדְבַּר דִּבְלָתָה—This is an ancient text-critical crux. The MT points מִמִּדְבַּר as in the construct state and apparently understands the preposition מִן as denoting comparison: "more than the desert of Diblathah." However, if the ending on דִּבְלָתָה is the *he* directive (הָ-), and if מִמִּדְבַּר were not in construct, then the phrase would mean "from the desert to Diblah," implying that מִדְבָּר is the southern border of the land, as stated in Ex 23:31. KJV combines both possibilities: "more desolate than the wilderness toward Diblath."

דִּבְלָתָה may be the same place as דִּבְלָתָיִם (a dual form) in Jer 48:22, where it is preceded by בֵּית (Beth-Diblataim). דִּבְלָתָיִם also appears in Num 33:46–47 with the *he* directive (דִּבְלָתָיְמָה) and preceded by עַלְמֹן. In both passages the location is clearly in northern Moab, just south of Mount Nebo. A specific *desert* of Diblah is unknown; it would have to be to the east of the city. All the ancient versions attest to "Diblah" or "Diblotha," and NKJV retains "Diblah."

Nevertheless, virtually all other modern translations and commentaries assume that the name was originally *Riblah*, but was miscopied as Diblah very early (prior to the LXX translation). Orthographically, the confusion is an easy one (and occurs a number of times) because, both in the paleo-Hebrew (Phoenician) and the modern (Aramaic) script, the forms of *resh* and *daleth* are very similar.

In contrast to an obscure transjordanic "Diblah," Riblah was a very well-known location in the territory of Hamath in central Syria (north of Damascus) on the Orontes River. (Another Riblah, in Num 34:11, is a different location entirely, somewhere on the northeast boundary of Israel, apparently northeast of the Sea of Galilee.) Riblah is just a bit north of Lebo Hamath ("entrance to Hamath," probably a pass through the Anti-Lebanon Mountains), which is specified in Num 34:8 as the northern limits of "greater Israel," and similarly Hamath in Ezek 47:17 is the northern limit of eschatological Israel. Thus "from the desert to Riblah" would be an alternate (south to north) way of saying much the same thing as "from Dan to Beersheba" (e.g., Judg 20:1; 1 Sam 3:20), which goes from north to south and is somewhat smaller in scope.

If Riblah is the correct reading here (and this commentary assumes that it is), then מִמִּדְבַּר probably should be revocalized to מִמִּדְבָּר so that it is not in construct. The preposition מִן indicates the starting point ("from") or terminus a quo. רִבְלָתָה would be Riblah with the *he* directive.

If so, Riblah may have been chosen for alliteration with מִדְבָּר.[15] But more likely it would have been chosen because of its painful historical associations. Pharaoh Neco had imprisoned wicked King Jehoahaz, son and successor of King Josiah, at Riblah (2 Ki 23:33). The place name would remind the Israelites that the reformation instituted by Josiah was cut short by his untimely death (2 Ki 22:1–23:30; cf. the commentary on Ezek 4:4–6) and that the imprisonment of his son at Riblah marked the end of Israel's hopes of political independence. When Ezekiel's prophecies were fulfilled in the actual fall of Jerusalem a few years later, Riblah was Nebuchadnezzar's headquarters. After King Zedekiah's futile attempt to escape, he was brought to Ri-

---

[15] Greenberg, *Ezekiel*, 1:137.

blah, and his sons were slain just before his eyes were put out and he was taken to Babylon in chains (2 Ki 25:4–7).

Commentary

This chapter introduces Ezekiel's mountain motif. See the broad sketch of this motif in "Outline and Theological Emphases" in the introduction and the commentary on 17:22–23 and 20:40. The motif involves both Law (judgment) and Gospel (salvation), but in this chapter the emphasis obviously is on judgment because of the idolatry practiced by the Israelites upon the mountains. The chapter is replete with echoes of the covenant curses in Leviticus 26 that warned of the consequences of Israel's disobedience. Ultimately, this chapter points toward the execution of God's judgment in full on Christ upon "Mount Calvary," where he was cursed vicariously for the sin of all humanity (Gal 3:13). We might envision Christ himself expressing the full extent of divine grief at our sin as he suffered on the cross: "I was heartbroken by their whoring heart" (Ezek 6:9).

Yet this chapter also holds the promise of a remnant that will be restored by God in his grace (6:8). That faithful remnant begins with a single man: the risen Christ. His atonement makes possible the eschatological restoration of "all Israel" (Rom 11:26; the church of both Testaments) and its eternal state upon the temple mount depicted in Ezekiel 40–48 and (with no temple) in Revelation 21–22.

One may also think of NT passages where Law and Gospel are proclaimed upon a mountain but with the accent falling on the Gospel. These passages point to the great reversal in that lofty places once defiled by idolatry become sacred space by the presence and Word of Jesus Christ. Such would include the place where the Beatitudes (the blessings of the new covenant in Christ) were pronounced by Jesus in his Sermon on the Mount (Matthew 5–7); the mount of transfiguration, upon which Christ revealed his glory in fulfillment of the Torah and the Prophets, represented by Moses and Elijah, respectively (Mt 17:1–13); and the Mount of Olives, the site of his eschatological discourse (Mt 24:3–25:46), passion prayer (Gethsemane, Mt 26:30, 36–46) and ascension (Acts 1:9–12).

6:1–7 The prolixity that characterizes Ezekiel is much in evidence in the entire chapter. Time and again, often with repetition of identical vocabulary, the point is driven home that Israel's idolatries will be exterminated. The precise connotation of many words is uncertain or disputed (reminding us how little we really know about the details of Canaanite paganism), but the gist is unmistakably clear nonetheless. Much of it is summed up in the final clause of 6:6: everything the Israelites have made (none of it dedicated *ad maiorem Dei gloriam*) will be "wiped out." And the chapter ends with the now-familiar refrain "then you/they will know that I am Yahweh" (6:7, 14; and expanded in 6:10, 13)—the one true and triune God who brooks no rivals.

The initial address to the "mountains" (6:2–3) extends the scope of Yahweh's judgment (which had centered on Jerusalem in chapters 4–5) to the entire land of Israel, and that idea is seconded by "in all the places you live" in 6:6.

Various motifs converge in the warning that the Israelites' corpses will lie in front of their idols, and their bones will be scattered around their altars (6:4–5). The threat evokes the horror of ignominy that the ancient world attached to the lack of a decent burial (much more so than is the case today). Ancient texts frequently speak of invaders deliberately exhuming the bodies of their enemies in the course of warfare, especially as punishment for a broken treaty oath or covenant. An element of sarcasm is probably involved here as well: instead of standing, kneeling, and prostrating themselves as live worshipers would, the apostate Israelites' bodies will lie motionless, almost as though in mockery of their idols. The close contact with the dead would defile the pagan sanctuaries. 2 Ki 23:16–20 describes how Josiah deliberately defiled the altar and high place at Bethel by exhuming bones and burning them on the altar. Jer 8:1–3 prophesies that the dead apostate Jerusalemites will be exhumed and spread out before the heavenly bodies they had worshiped. This implies a deliberate challenge to the idols to defend their worshipers and themselves— if they really are deities. (Such was the response of Gideon's father to devotees of Baal who protested the destruction of his altar in Judg 6:31.)

The last clause in Ezek 6:6 summarizes the entire chapter (and much of the rest of the first half of Ezekiel): "your works [מַעֲשֵׂיכֶם] (will be) wiped out." "Works" is a very generic noun (as is the verb "work"), but the Hebrew word frequently has connotations of whatever people make or do in disregard for and defiance of the true God. For example, the account in 1 Ki 12:28–33 of the construction of the pagan temples in Dan and Bethel by Jeroboam I and his liturgical innovations contrary to the OT divine service repeatedly uses the verb עָשָׂה ("he made"). In Isaiah the verb and its derived nouns are used of men's apostate cultic inventions (e.g., Is 2:8, 20). In many instances in the Bible, "(all) the works of their hands" or a similar phrase (e.g., 2 Ki 22:17; 2 Chr 34:25; Acts 7:41; Rev 9:20) refers to infractions against the First Commandment (see עָשָׂה in Ex 20:4, 23). Today the phrase applies just as easily to technology or other forms of "fine idolatry." Against all such works, biblical theology proclaims salvation *sola gratia*, "by grace alone," not by human "works" presumed to be meritorious, much less by "works" of idolatry or the occult.

The result of divine judgment is that "you will know that I am Yahweh" (6:7). This so-called "recognition formula" characteristically comes at the end of Ezekiel's oracles or sections. It is repeated (in various forms) in 6:7, 10, 13, 14 and occurs close to sixty times in the book. It refers to knowing and confessing that Yahweh both speaks and fulfills his Word—a faith-based recognition of his basic character and the consequences for all who believe or disbelieve. Repeatedly after commands in the Pentateuch (e.g., Leviticus 18), we meet simply, "I am Yahweh." The very name implies, among other things, his sovereign power, holiness, and power to save.[16]

---

[16] See the excursus "The Lord (יהוה)" in Harstad, *Joshua*, 47–51.

The obedience of God's people does not require them first to authenticate his claims by their own reason or experience. Rather, obedience simply follows faith: alignment with Yahweh's own character takes place as he works through his Word and sacramental means of grace. In Ezekiel's context, the accent is on Yahweh's omnipotent power to punish and to rescue. Yahweh's nature is more fully revealed in the NT by his incarnation in Jesus Christ, but the nature of the believers' relationship to the triune God remains the same in both Testaments (*sola gratia* and *sola fide*). All circumcised Israelites were incorporated into the Abrahamic and Mosaic covenants.[17] "For as many of you as were baptized into Christ have been clothed with Christ. ... And if you are of Christ, then you are Abraham's seed and heirs according to the promise" (Gal 3:27, 29).

6:8 In a partial digression, Yahweh for the first time in Ezekiel broaches the idea of the "remnant," although he had hinted at it in 5:3 by instructing the prophet to hide a few hairs in the folds of his garment.

Critics have commonly considered such promises of a remnant to have been added to the text after the destruction of Jerusalem in 587 B.C., making them, in effect, *vaticinia ex eventu*, "prophecies from an outcome," that is, after the fact (a contradiction in terms). But such a stance is totally unwarranted and is the product of theological skepticism. The critical view denies the possibility of genuine supernatural and predictive prophecy and flies in the face of all Scripture. From Gen 3:15 to the end of Revelation the motif of Law and *Gospel* rings loud and clear. God does not "wish that any should perish" (2 Pet 3:9). As the dogmaticians say, that is God's "antecedent will." That he condemns and punishes unbelievers is his "consequent will," due solely to their own refusal to repent and believe.

The covenant curses in Leviticus 26, which reverberate so strongly in Ezekiel, themselves keep the door open for a converted remnant (Lev 26:40–45). The remnant theme (expressed with a variety of vocabulary) is also prominent in the prophets preceding Ezekiel. Once Ezekiel's earlier prophecies of the fall of Jerusalem are fulfilled, God's restoration of the remnant becomes the overriding theme (Ezekiel 33–48). Even before that, after this passage, each time when the remnant theme resurfaces, it is gradually expanded.[f] The Gospel grows louder.

6:9–10 These verses serve as a classic description of contrition after the Law has done its work of judgment. One might wish that such depictions of repentance were considered most characteristic of Ezekiel, rather than those passages that, if isolated from the total context, seem to know only of God's relentless judgment.

(f) Ezek 7:16; 11:16–21; 12:15–16; 14:22–23; 16:60–63

Three main verbs describe the mental state of those who had escaped with their lives, but live as lonely refugees in foreign lands. First, Yahweh says they

---

17 For an exposition of those covenants in relation to the new covenant in Christ, see the excursus "Covenant" in Harstad, *Joshua*, 744–56.

"will remember [יִזְכְּרוּ] me" (6:9). Like much Hebrew vocabulary, the word would be misunderstood if it were taken to refer exclusively to an intellectual exercise (as it tends to be in our usage). The cognitive element is certainly part of it: repentant believers confess the *fides quae creditur*, the objective "faith which is believed," the body of Christian doctrine drawn from the Scriptures and expressed in the Creeds and confessions of the church. The greater accent in 6:9–10, however, is on the implementation of this knowledge of God—receiving it in faith (*fides qua creditur*, the individual's subjective "faith by which it is believed"), internalizing it, and acting accordingly. In Christian worship, the idea climaxes in the remembrance of Christ in the celebration of the Lord's Supper (Lk 22:19), with the faithful reception of his true body and blood for the forgiveness of sins according to his Words of Institution.

What the repentant Israelites will remember is surprising: "how I was heartbroken by their whoring heart" (Ezek 6:9). In NT language, this is not narcissistic bemoaning of the cross they must bear, but remembrance of the cross of Christ in which they share. God was (anthropopathically) "heartbroken" at their prostitution. The same covenant God who married Israel as his wife, then became jealous at her repeated infidelity (5:13; also chapters 16 and 23), can at the same time be "heartbroken" by the way the love he has shown his people is repaid with harlotry. God's grieving is not unique to Ezekiel; compare also, for example, Ps 78:40; Is 63:10; Micah 6:3–4.

The repentant people realize that they have been unfaithful in both their "whoring heart" (that is, their will) and "their eyes which whored" (that is, their allegiance). The idioms here remind one of the similar phrases in 1 Jn 2:16: "the lust of the flesh and the lust of the eyes."

The second main verb is that when the people are brought to repentance, "they will loathe themselves," not merely for having been caught and punished, as it were, but at the realization of how depraved they had become. All the humanistic psychobabble that extols "feeling good about yourself," about "rights" to sin and live as you please, and every notion that one's heritage (such as being part of the covenant nation) somehow affords a privileged position before God—all this bursts like a soap bubble. What worth and dignity the people had resulted from their creation in the image of God, and as long as they refused to repent, they had forfeited even that. Now, like St. Paul, they consider their former lives to be dung (Phil 3:8).

Third, when they really "know" Yahweh (6:10; virtually synonymous with "remember me" in 6:9), they will confess the power of his Word, also in judgment. They realize more than that he has been justified in his actions in general. In particular, they will know that the warnings he gave long ago through Moses (especially Leviticus 26, which intellectually they "knew" perfectly well) were a matter of God's faithfulness to his covenant, even in judgment.

6:11–12 The last third of the chapter is essentially a reprise of the first third. Many of the same words or phrases are repeated or paralleled. Unlike in

6:8–10, but as in 6:1–7, there is no hint of a change of heart by the people, and certainly God appears to have nothing but judgment in mind at the moment.

6:13 Yahweh emphasizes the comprehensiveness of his judgment, particularly against the high places. The phrases with "every" and "all" may have described the pervasiveness of Israel's defiant apostasy, but now they describe the universality of God's judgment. "Where 'his' [Yahweh's] people had gathered to secure the blessing of the gods, there they will be gathered as corpses, heaped up and strewn about in the ultimate act of desecration. Rather than offering life to the devotees, the pagan sanctuaries have become symbols of death."[18]

6:14 The "hand" of Yahweh is stretched out for a great variety of purposes (see the textual notes on 1:3 and 6:14), but in the final verse of the chapter it becomes a summary formula for the comprehensive "scorched earth" judgment soon to come. "In all the places they live" implies that God's long hand will reach them everywhere; there will be no hiding. For the fourth time in chapter 6 alone, they will know that he is Yahweh, learning it the hard way. Only after God's judgment has brought them to a realization of their depravity will it be possible for his grace to work in them a new life (the dynamic of God's Law as the necessary prerequisite for his Gospel).

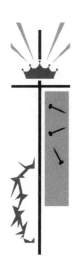

"History does not repeat itself," so the particular form of the judgment that befell Israel may not also be the form of ours. Yet the theological pattern remains the same. God works *sub contrario*: he kills in order to make alive; Good Friday was necessary before Easter Sunday; and we are baptized into Christ's death in order that we may also be raised with Christ (Rom 6:1–4; Col 2:11–13). For Ezekiel's prophecies of doom and destruction, we can access some of the pertinence for ourselves via the hermeneutic of typology. Especially in Advent the church thinks and sings of being "captive Israel" "that mourns in lonely exile here."[19] That implies that ancient Israel's experience has been recapitulated in us who are "exiles" in the "diaspora" (1 Pet 1:1; 2:11; James 1:1) as daily we live out our Baptism, dying with Christ and rising with him to newness of life (Romans 6), awaiting our "return" to the promised land—our eternal home, the heavenly Jerusalem (Gal 4:26; Heb 12:22; Rev 3:12; Revelation 21).

---

[18] Block, *Ezekiel*, 1:237.

[19] From "Oh, Come, Oh, Come, Emmanuel" (*LW* 31:1).

"The End Has Come"

Translation

7 ¹The Word of Yahweh came to me: ²"You, son of man, thus says the Lord Yahweh to the land of Israel:

"An end!
>   The end has come upon the four corners of the earth.
³Now that the end is upon you,
>   I will let loose my anger against you.
I will punish you according to your ways,
>   and I will place on you [the penalty for] all your abominations.
⁴My eye will not have pity on you,
>   and I will have no compassion,
for [the penalty for] your ways I will place on you,
>   and [the punishment for] your abominations will be in your midst.
Then you will know that I am Yahweh!"

⁵"Thus says the Lord Yahweh:
Disaster!
>   A unique disaster!
>   Look, it comes!
⁶An end has come!
>   The end has come!
It has awakened against you.
>   Look, it comes!
⁷The doom has come upon you,
>   O inhabitant of the land,
The time has come,
>   the day is near—
of panic,
>   not joy on the mountains.
⁸Now very soon I will pour out my wrath upon you,
>   and I will exhaust my anger against you.
I will punish you according to your ways,
>   and I will place upon you [the penalty for] all your abominations.
⁹My eye will not pity,
>   and I will have no compassion.
According to your ways I will place [the penalty] upon you,
>   and [the punishment for] your abominations will be in your midst.
Then you will know that I, Yahweh, am the smiter!"

¹⁰"Behold, the day—
  behold, it comes.
Doom has burst out,
  the rod has budded,
  insolence has blossomed.
¹¹Violence has grown into a rod of wickedness.
None of them [will remain]—
  none of their multitude,
none of their wealth,
  not a thing of value among them.
¹²The time has come,
  the day has arrived.
Let not the buyer rejoice,
  nor the seller grieve,
for wrath is upon all its wealth.
¹³For the seller will not return to the land he has sold,
  even if they are still alive.
For the vision concerning all its wealth will not be reversed,
  and each man, because of his iniquity in his life, will have no strength.
¹⁴They blow the horn and make everything ready,
  but no one goes to battle,
for my wrath is upon all its wealth.
¹⁵The sword is outside,
  and plague and famine are inside.
Anyone in the country will die by the sword,
  and anyone in the city—plague and famine will devour him.
¹⁶Any who escape will flee to the mountains like valley doves,
  all of them moaning, each in his iniquity.
¹⁷All hands will be limp,
  and all knees will flow with water.
¹⁸They will put on sackcloth,
  and shuddering will cover them.
On every face will be shame,
  and on all their heads baldness.
¹⁹They will throw their silver into the streets,
  and their gold will become an unclean thing.
Their silver and their gold will not be able to rescue them
  on the day of Yahweh's fury.
They will not satisfy their appetites or fill their stomachs,
  because it was the iniquitous cause of their downfall.
²⁰His beautiful ornament they made into arrogance,
  and they made from it their abominable and disgusting images.

"Therefore, I will make it an unclean thing for them.

²¹I will place it in the hand of foreigners as booty,
    to the most wicked people of the earth as plunder,
and they will desecrate it.
²²I will turn my face away from them
    so that they may desecrate my treasure,
and so that robbers may enter it and desecrate it.
²³Prepare the chain,
    for the earth is full of judicial murder,
and the city is full of violence.
²⁴I will bring the most wicked of the nations,
    and they will take possession of their houses.
I will put an end to the pride of the mighty,
    and their sanctuaries will be desecrated.
²⁵Terror comes;
    they will seek peace, but there will be none.
²⁶Disaster after disaster will come,
    and rumor after rumor will be.
They will seek a vision from the prophet;
    instruction will perish from the priest,
and counsel from the elders.
²⁷The king will mourn,
    the prince will be clothed with horror,
and the hands of the citizenry will be paralyzed.
According to their own conduct I will deal with them,
    and by their own judgments I will judge them.
Then they will know that I am Yahweh."

Textual Notes

7:1–27 Linguistically, this chapter presents at least as many problems as the inaugural vision in chapter 1. Let two major contemporary commentators summarize it: Block says: "The passage is replete with redundancies, confusion of gender, omitted articles, missing verbs, obscure allusions, incomplete and garbled statements (v 11), as well as words, forms, and constructions unheard of elsewhere."[1] Greenberg notes:

> Language and ideas characteristic of Ezekiel are combined in our chapter with an unusually rich array of poetic elements echoing passages from elsewhere in the Bible. Abrupt changes in perspective, obscurity, even incoherence (vs. 11b), bespeak a passion and excitement that could not be contained in the prophet's usual prosaic framework, and that sought release in language and figures drawn from the reservoir of Hebrew poetry evidently known to him. As in the few other instances in which he demonstrated his poetic range (e.g., chs. 21; 28:11–19), the modern interpreter encounters insuperable difficulties in following him.[2]

---

[1] Block, *Ezekiel*, 1:241.

[2] Greenberg, *Ezekiel*, 1:163.

This chapter has a relatively high number of hapax legomena and rare words. The divergence of the LXX from the MT is even more pronounced than usual, for reasons which elude us.

7:2 The citation formula ("thus says …") often is preceded by a command to speak: "say (to) …" But here and often elsewhere (e.g., 5:5, 7, 8; 6:11; 7:5) it is not.

לְאַדְמַת יִשְׂרָאֵל—The phrase "the land of Israel," using אֲדָמָה rather than אֶרֶץ, is unique to Ezekiel, in which it is common.[a] The address "to the *land* of Israel" may be intended to have a psychological effect comparable to the focus of chapter 6 on the mountains of Israel. The word אֲדָמָה overlaps with אֶרֶץ at the end of 7:2 (see the commentary below), but is not simply synonymous. אֲדָמָה might be translated "soil," and so would have special poignancy for an agriculturally oriented community such as that of the Israelite exiles. At least until the rise of modern "agribusinesses," farmers characteristically knew and cherished every contour of the "family farm."

קֵץ—The sermon begins abruptly with one word: קֵץ, "end."[3] Hebrew has no indefinite article, but English idiom requires the insertion of "an." (In Latin, which has no articles, a simple *finis* would correspond exactly to the Hebrew.) The word's very brevity and suddenness would both attract attention and summarize the coming message. Not until it is repeated in the next clause does it even have a predicate. It occurs a total of five times in 7:2–6.

בָּא הַקֵּץ—When קֵץ is repeated, its ominous predicate verb is בָּא, "has come." בָּא and בָּאָה together occur a total of nine times in the first twelve verses. בָּא could be the masculine singular participle, but the many other perfect verbs in the context suggest that it too is the perfect. It and the others are classic examples of the so-called "prophetic perfect." The prophet sees the future so vividly that he describes it as having already occurred.

Likewise, בָּאָה (7:5, 6, 7, 10) could be either the feminine singular participle or third feminine singular perfect. It is accented as the participle (בָּאָ֫ה) in 7:5, 6, 10 and so is translated "comes," but it is accented as the perfect (בָּ֫אָה, "has come") in 7:7.

עַל־אַרְבַּעַת כַּנְפוֹת הָאָרֶץ:—The marginal Qere (אַרְבַּע, "four") is the "correct" masculine form, since normally the masculine forms of the numerals 3–10 are used with feminine nouns (such as כַּנְפוֹת), and feminine forms of those numerals are used with masculine nouns (so-called "chiastic concord"). The Kethib is the feminine אַרְבַּעַת. The word for "corners" (כַּנְפוֹת) is, literally, "wings." (Compare 5:3, where it refers to the "folds" in Ezekiel's robe.) An anatomical part that occurs in pairs in nature is normally feminine and uses a dual form instead of a plural. When it has some extended or specialized meaning, however, various changes in the noun's declension may occur. The underlying metaphor here is of the earth spread out like a cloth with

(a) Ezek 7:2;
11:17; 12:19,
22; 13:9;
18:2; 20:38,
42; 21:7, 8
(ET 21:2, 3);
25:3, 6;
33:24; 36:6;
37:12;
38:18, 19

---

[3] The beginning of 7:6 largely repeats 7:2c, and there both occurrences of the noun have a predicate verb, forming a chiastic construction (קֵץ בָּא בָּא הַקֵּץ). Some interpreters argue that בָּא fell out of the original beginning of the sermon (which then would have been בָּא קֵץ) via haplography. There is a little text-critical support for that emendation, but there is no overriding reason why the MT should not be retained. Ezek 7:6–9 parallels 7:2c–4 closely but not precisely. The critical assumption has often been that they are merely different recensions of the same sermon.

its four corners. This is a popular, everyday idiom and does not represent some pre-scientific "flat earth" teaching.

7:3 The opening "now" (עַתָּה) underscores the imminence of the end. Likewise, "upon you" (עָלַיִךְ, somewhat as in 5:8, where Yahweh was the subject) implies something about to commence or overtake. God's anger is pictured as an entity in itself. The Piel of שָׁלַח is used as in 5:16–17 of God releasing the agents of his wrath, who are impatiently waiting to carry out their work.

"I will punish you" translates וּשְׁפַטְתִּיךְ, which could be rendered "I will judge you" (i.e., render a verdict), but in this context it is obvious that the verdict is "guilty on all counts." It is not an arbitrary verdict, but well substantiated by the people's conduct ("ways").

וְנָתַתִּי עָלַיִךְ—This idiom (נָתַן עַל) with the perfect *waw* consecutive is repeated in 7:8 and with the verb in the imperfect in 7:4, 9. Literally, it is "I will lay upon you," and the implied object is something like "your well-deserved penalty," so our translation supplies "penalty." The punishment will correspond to the abominable behavior. "Whatever a man sows, that he will also reap" (Gal 6:7).

7:4 This verse will be repeated with minor variations in 7:9. The first two clauses are repeated almost verbatim from the end of 5:11 (see the textual note there). The people have not repented from their heinous sin, and so they are excluded from God's pity and compassion.

וְתוֹעֲבוֹתַיִךְ בְּתוֹכֵךְ תִּהְיֶיןָ—This clause (repeated verbatim in 7:9) is, literally, "and your abominations will be in your midst." However, the abominations are already present in the midst of Jerusalem, as Ezekiel will be shown in detail in chapter 8 (see also 9:4). Hence this clause may be pregnant (as are the clauses in 7:3, 4, 8, 9 where I have supplied "penalty"), and so it means "and [the punishment for] your abominations will be in your midst" or "… will be imposed on you." "To the Hebr[ew] mind guilt carried with it the punishment of guilt."[4] Greenberg translates, "your abominations shall fester within you,"[5] which is endorsed by Allen.[6] Greenberg compares it to the curse of 24:7, where the shed blood has not been covered with dirt, but poured on bare rock. "The guilty evidence will not be obliterated, but, ever present, will call down retribution upon the culprits."[7] The same picture occurs in God's indictment of Cain in Gen 4:10.

7:5 The second announcement of doom (7:5–9) obviously has many parallels with the first one (7:2–4). Much critical thought has assumed that the two sections are doublets, that is, variants of a single original, which scholars attempt to reconstruct by selecting elements from each. Some appeal to the periphrastic Targumic rendition, which exhibits a text of that sort. The LXX has a considerably different text, and Zimmerli conjectures a reconstruction of both it and the MT.[8] Even other critics, however,

---

4   Cooke, *Ezekiel*, 77.

5   Greenberg, *Ezekiel*, 1:147.

6   Allen, *Ezekiel*, 1:107.

7   Greenberg, *Ezekiel*, 1:147.

8   Zimmerli, *Ezekiel*, 1:193–94.

have argued that the very repetitiveness of the MT argues for its genuineness. Block speaks of it as a "one-two punch."[9]

The staccato style of the Hebrew is impossible to reproduce completely. Two indications of it are the sixfold repetition of "comes/has come" in the section (7:5–9) and the two uses of הִנֵּה, "behold, look!"

This message too (like "An end!" in 7:2) begins anarthrously, this time with the noun רָעָה, translated "disaster." It is one of six different words used in this section to describe the calamity. The heightened "unique disaster" represents unique Hebrew (אַחַת רָעָה) in that the adjective (feminine of the numeral "one") precedes the noun it modifies. Presumably this was done for emphasis. The interpretation that the phrase refers to a unique disaster goes back at least as far as Rashi and is followed by Keil,[10] NIV, KJV, Block,[11] Greenberg,[12] and others. Some modern translations follow the Targum and the Hebrew manuscripts that have אַחַר instead of אַחַת, and so give "disaster after disaster" (e.g., RSV, ESV). However, militating against that reading is the use of an entirely different preposition (עַל) to express that idea in 7:26.

7:6 קֵץ בָּא—The beginning of 7:6 is very similar to 7:2b. Here, however, anarthrous קֵץ precedes its verb. This is the opposite of usual Hebrew word order. It must be another device for emphasis.

בָּא הַקֵּץ—This repeats the previous clause, but in the opposite and normal word order (verb, subject).

הֵקִיץ אֵלָיִךְ—The verb הֵקִיץ creates assonance with the preceding noun הַקֵּץ. The Hiphil of קִיץ means "awaken, wake up" and occurs fairly often in either a transitive or intransitive sense; here it must be intransitive. BDB, *HALOT*, and various commentators have understood it to be a by-form of יָקַץ, which also means "awaken." Greenberg associates the verb with קָיִץ, "ripe summer fruit," and the pun with קֵץ in Amos 8:2.[13] קִיץ in the Qal does seem to have a comparable meaning in Is 18:6. Greenberg then translates Ezek 7:6 as "it is ripe for you."[14] A harvest metaphor does appear in Ezek 7:10c–11a, but that view appears rather forced here. Zimmerli,[15] followed by Block,[16] abandons the Masoretic pointing and takes it as a *plene* spelling (הַקֵּיץ) of the preceding word, the noun (with article) הַקֵּץ. That emendation would result in "end" occurring three times in a row in the verse.

הִנֵּה בָּאָה:—Since קֵץ is a masculine noun, and it is the implied subject of the masculine verb הֵקִיץ in the preceding clause, why is the verb here בָּאָה, the feminine singular participle? Perhaps קֵץ is not implied to be the subject here, and the verb is to

---

9   Block, *Ezekiel*, 1:243.

10   Keil, *Ezekiel*, 1:100–101.

11   Block, *Ezekiel*, 1:250, including n. 37.

12   Greenberg, *Ezekiel*, 1:148.

13   Greenberg, *Ezekiel*, 1:148.

14   Greenberg, *Ezekiel*, 1:148.

15   Zimmerli, *Ezekiel*, 1:195.

16   Block, *Ezekiel*, 1:250, including n. 39.

be construed impersonally: "It comes," that is, every horrible thing that the end brings with it. Such an abstract idea (for which we use the neuter) is normally expressed in Hebrew by the feminine.

Others have suggested that the final word of 7:6 (בָּאָה) may be a dittograph of the first word of 7:7 (בָּאָה), whose feminine form is determined by its feminine subject, the following feminine noun (צְפִירָה). A related suggestion is that the last two words of 7:6 should be the first two words of 7:7, yielding "Behold, it comes! The doom has come."

7:7   The noun צְפִירָה, which occurs again in 7:10, is a major crux. There are detailed discussions of it in Zimmerli[17] and Greenberg.[18] It (or a homonym) appears in Is 28:5 in the sense of "garland, crown, wreath," but no such meaning is appropriate for Ezek 7:7, 10. Any connection with the (same?) word in Isaiah must be only etymological because the contexts are so different. Various Semitic languages have cognates with meanings like "a twist, braid, plait" or the like. "Chain, leash, net" and so on are suggested as possibly related to a victor's garland, and while such suggestions are amenable to the context in 7:7, 10, they are speculative nonetheless. The LXX does not translate the word at all, either because it was working with an entirely different text or because it simply did not understand the word. The context seems to require something similar to the nouns קֵץ ("end") or רָעָה ("disaster") in earlier verses. Most translations and many commentators offer "doom" or the like, often admitting that "doom" is as good a guess as any. For the lack of a convincing alternative, I have translated "doom" also.

Whether or not הַצְּפִירָה in 7:7 relates to Is 28:5, two later parts of the verse are in all likelihood allusions to earlier prophecies; see the last two textual notes on Ezek 7:7.

יוֹשֵׁב הָאָרֶץ—The switch from addressing the land in the second person (feminine singular) to this vocative address to "the inhabitant of the land" may appear intrusive, but we have met this feature before and will again. See, for example, the alternation between second person (singular) and third person (singular and plural) forms in 5:12–15. Although Yahweh often speaks of or to (7:2) the land, his primary concern is with the people who live in it.

קָרוֹב הַיּוֹם—"The day is near" is very close to Zeph 1:14 and may be a deliberate allusion to it.

מְהוּמָה וְלֹא־הֵד הָרִים:—The association of מְהוּמָה with the "day" in the preceding clause appears to be an echo of one of Isaiah's inimitable triple alliterations describing the Day of Yahweh (Is 22:5). מְהוּמָה means "confusion, tumult, riot, panic," often in martial contexts. It stands in explicit contrast to the final construct chain, הֵד הָרִים.

The noun הֵד is a hapax legomenon. *HALOT* proposes "thunderbolt" based on Ugaritic and Arabic cognates. Many others assume that it is an abbreviated form of הֵידָד, which can be either a "cheer, jubilant shout" or a "war cry." In Is 16:9–10 הֵידָד refers to shouts of joy or celebration at harvest time. Many other OT passages depict

---

[17]   Zimmerli, *Ezekiel*, 1:195.

[18]   Greenberg, *Ezekiel*, 1:148.

the harvest as a time of rejoicing, although with various terminology; compare Is 9:2 (ET 9:3), metaphorically of the messianic era.

7:8 "Very soon" (מִקָּרוֹב) is an idiomatic extension of "near" (קָרוֹב) in 7:7. Similar to "I will let loose my anger" (וְשִׁלַּחְתִּי אַפִּי) in 7:3 is "I will pour out my wrath" (אֶשְׁפּוֹךְ חֲמָתִי) in 7:8. This is the first occurrence of the idiom (שָׁפַךְ חֵמָה) in Ezekiel, but it is common later.[b] The metaphor is clearly derived from the practice of defenders who stand upon the city wall and pour a boiling liquid down upon the attackers below. For "and I will exhaust my anger" (וְכִלֵּיתִי אַפִּי), see the textual notes on the similar expressions in 5:13 and 6:12.

(b) Ezek 9:8;
14:19; 20:8,
13, 21, 33,
34; 22:22;
30:15; 36:18

7:9 This verse repeats 7:4 almost verbatim. The recognition formula at the end of the verse is expanded by a predicate participle (מַכֶּה, "smiter," the Hiphil of נכה). Yahweh was the "smiter" of Egypt in the exodus redemption of Israel (מַכֶּה, Ex 7:17; Ps 136:10, 17). However, Isaiah spoke of Yahweh as the "smiter" who punished Israel for her sin (מַכֶּה, Is 9:12 [ET 9:13]) as Ezekiel does here. In contrast, according to Ezek 20:12 and 37:28, it will be known that Yahweh is the "sanctifier."

7:10 This third (7:10–27) and longest of the oracles of doom in chapter 7 opens in just as agitated a vein as the previous two (7:2–4 and 7:5–9) but becomes more sedate as it proceeds.

צְפִירָה is again translated "doom" as in 7:7. It is the subject of the common verb יָצָא, which here probably has a botanical meaning such as "burst out," as in the messianic passage Is 11:1. Two more botanical verbs with overlapping meaning follow, צִיץ and פָּרַח, each of which can mean "sprout," "bud," or "blossom." If translated progressively (as a plant first sprouts, then buds, and finally blossoms), the three more or less synonymous clauses of 7:10b may gradually move toward a climax in terms of a harvest. The verbs in 7:10b and 7:12a are perfect, in contrast to the participial or adjectival forms dominant earlier. Past, present, and future should probably be thought of as all linked or in a continuum—an idea to which the technically tenseless Hebrew verbal system easily links itself.

Many critics are tempted to repoint מַטֶּה ("rod") as מֻטֶּה, which in form is the Hophal participle of נָטָה, referring to justice that is "warped, bent, perverted" (see the textual note on מֻטֶּה in 9:9). That would nicely parallel the following זָדוֹן ("insolence") but would deviate from the harvest metaphor inherent in the verse. There is no manuscript or versional support for the change, so the MT is preferred. מַטֶּה also appears in the next verse (7:11), where too it should not be emended.

7:11 הֶחָמָס ׀ קָם לְמַטֵּה־רֶשַׁע[d]—I have taken the verb קוּם as a continuation of the botanical metaphors of 7:10: "violence has grown" as does a plant. But the ambiguity about the "rod" (מַטֶּה) in 7:10 continues in 7:11. Does the "rod of wickedness" represent the wicked actions of the apostate Israelites? Or is it God's "rod" that he will now use to punish Israel's "wickedness"? I incline toward the second alternative. If so, "violence" is another epithet of the Babylonians (as "insolence" was in 7:10), who now have grown strong enough to conquer Israel (with God's consent).

The rest of 7:11 is quite obscure in Hebrew. It appears as if the prophet's emotion leads to a fourfold repetition of the negative particle לֹא ("not"), each time without any verb, resulting in what appear to be a series of alliterative exclamations. The third plural suffixes ("them, their") lack antecedents, but probably refer to the Israelites.

לֹא־מֵהֶם—The preposition מִן appears to be used in a partitive sense here and in the next two exclamations. At the end of this first exclamation, I have supplied "will remain," and that idea applies to the rest of the verse: whatever the intended specifics, the gist of the rest of the verse is that nothing of them will remain after the "day" (7:10).

וְלֹא מֵהֲמוֹנָם וְלֹא מֶהֱמֵהֶם—The two nouns in these two alliterative phrases probably are both from the verb הָמָה, which occurs in 7:16 ("moaning"). Block suggests that "the words may signify onomatopoeic expressions of alarm or grief."[19] I have followed Keil[20] in understanding the first derivative noun, הָמוֹן, to apply to the "multitude" of the Israelites and the second noun, הֶמֶה, to refer to the multitude of their possessions, that is their "wealth."

The noun הָמוֹן occurs in 7:11–14. Its meanings can range from "turmoil, din, roar" to "crowd, multitude" to "wealth, riches." BDB (3 b) prefers "crowd, multitude" (my translation in 7:11), while *HALOT* (4) prefers "procession, pomp" for 7:11–14. In 7:12–14 I have translated it "wealth" (see the textual note on it in 7:12).

The noun הֶמֶה is a hapax legomenon. (*HALOT* advocates "noise.") Since it is from the same root as הָמוֹן, its meaning probably is the same as one of the wide-ranging meanings of הָמוֹן.

וְלֹא־נֹהַּ בָּהֶם:—The noun נֹהַּ is another hapax legomenon. Based on the LXX, BDB (under the root נוה) understands it to mean "eminency, distinction." It may be related to an Arabic cognate that means "to be raised high" (*HALOT*). Most likely it refers to something of value or glamour/honor.

7:12 The first two lines resume the theme of 7:10 (and earlier verses) about the imminence of the day of judgment and end. The topic of the next three lines (with the first of three successive כִּי clauses) shifts to a major result of the end: the cessation of all commercial life. This topic continues into 7:13a.

The buyer would rejoice if he got a bargain price, but his bargain means nothing if disaster looms. That the seller would grieve leaves the impression that he is selling under duress and cannot hold out for as good a price as he would ordinarily expect. The context is the Oriental bazaar, where fixed prices are rare and bargaining is the order of the day. For a wry comment on the atmosphere, see Prov 20:14.

"Wrath" (חָרוֹן) in Hebrew idiom rarely stands by itself, as it does here and in Ezek 7:14. Usually it is in construct with אַף (literalistically: "the *glow* of your/his [God's] nose"). Its self-standing use may be semi-poetic (e.g., Ex 15:7; Ps 2:5). Its isolation makes its parallel with the assonant חָזוֹן ("oracle, vision") in Ezek 7:13 more prominent, which may be another indication of the semi-poetic character of this section.

The feminine suffix on הֲמוֹנָהּ ("*its* wealth") here and in 7:13, 14 probably refers to the land of Israel, since אֶרֶץ is a feminine noun. See the textual note on הָמוֹן in 7:11. It

---

[19] Block, *Ezekiel*, 1:256.

[20] Keil, *Ezekiel*, 1:103.

is used sixteen times in the oracle against Egypt in chapters 29–32 with implications of "pride, insolence," and Eichrodt and Block favor that interpretation also here.[21] However, I have opted for "wealth" in 7:12–14 because the immediate concern of the verses is buying and selling.

7:13 אֶל־הַמִּמְכָּר לֹא יָשׁוּב—This clause evokes the laws of the Jubilee Year (Lev 25: 13–17) according to which any property sold during the past half century would revert to its original owner (or heir) without compensation. This negated clause implies that when judgment and exile overtake buyer and seller, such a law will be irrelevant.[22]

וְעוֹד בַּחַיִּים חַיָּתָם—This is, literally, "while still in life is their life." The noun חַיָּה (repeated later in the verse) is a rare, poetic word (ordinarily we would expect נֶפֶשׁ). Its plural suffix ("they") refers to the buyer and seller.

חָזוֹן ... לֹא יָשׁוּב—The noun חָזוֹן ("vision") refers to the prophecy of doom. It differs from חָרוֹן ("wrath") in 7:12, 14 by only one consonant. It and the verb from which it is derived, חָזָה, are frequently used of prophetic oracles, even when there is no particular accent on the faculty of sight, as when paired with דָּבָר ("word"). Hence, although we translate it "vision," that English word must not be pressed literalistically. The usage of such Hebrew words is classical evidence that the Bible is not concerned with the mechanics of inspiration (how exactly the prophet sees or hears the oracle from God), but with the fact of inspiration—the divine origin and authority of the message.

This second instance of לֹא יָשׁוּב in the verse has an entirely different meaning ("will not be reversed/revoked") than the earlier one ("will not return"). This use is apparently parallel to a Hiphil use of the idiom as a refrain in Amos' Gentile oracles (Amos 1:3–2:3). The "vision" delivered to Ezekiel is a final decision of the heavenly court, beyond which there is no appeal (cf. Is 55:10–11).

וְאִישׁ בַּעֲוֹנוֹ חַיָּתוֹ לֹא יִתְחַזָּקוּ—Literally, we seem to have "each man because of his iniquity his life, they shall not be strong/strengthened." אִישׁ is used distributively ("each man"), which explains the plural of the Hithpael verb. For the combination of עָוֹן and the preposition בְּ, see the textual note on 3:18. (It recurs in 7:16 but probably with a different nuance.) The Hithpael of חָזַק can have the intransitive meanings "be courageous; be strong" or the passive "be strengthened." If the loss of the provision for the Jubilee Year is still part of the picture here (as it seems to be at the start of 7:13), then the sense may be that, in its absence, a man will have no way to strengthen or enrich himself. Or the idea could be that because each man's life is characterized by iniquity, the people shall have no strength or courage to withstand the divine judgment. The following verse may favor that understanding: no one will have sufficient strength to fight or resist the enemy.

Many (even Block[23]) follow the LXX, which translated as though the form of חָזַק were Hiphil, which often means "grasp, keep hold of." Many English translations fol-

---

[21] Eichrodt, *Ezekiel*, 102–3; Block, *Ezekiel*, 1:258–59.

[22] All the material between the two occurrences of לֹא יָשׁוּב in 7:13 is missing in the LXX. Critical opinion favors the LXX (e.g., Zimmerli, *Ezekiel*, 1:197, and Allen, *Ezekiel*, 1:101). However, homoioteleuton seems to suffice as an explanation for the LXX: the scribe's eye skipped from one יָשׁוּב to the next.

[23] Block, *Ezekiel*, 1:257, including n. 72.

low that and assume (contrary to the construction in the LXX) that the verb's object is "his life," as does ESV: "because of his iniquity, none can maintain his life." The sense is fitting, but is hard to justify linguistically.

7:14 תִּקְעוּ בַתָּ֯קוֹעַ—The noun תָּקוֹעַ is a hapax legomenon (but resembles the place name תְּקוֹעַ, "Tekoa"). Most ancient versions translate it as a musical instrument, probably a trumpet (so LXX). A reminiscence of Jer 6:1, "Blow the shophar in Tekoa," may have determined Ezekiel's choice of words. (Critics often propose deleting the בְ, leaving תָּקוֹעַ as an infinitive absolute of the preceding verb.)

וְהָכִין—Especially in later Hebrew, the infinitive absolute (this one is Hiphil) can be used as a finite verb when it follows a preceding finite verb (here: תִּקְעוּ). Its meaning is the same as if it were the same form as the preceding finite verb (GKC, § 113 z; Joüon, § 123 x). Hence after "they blow the horn," this means "and *they make ready* everything."

With the exception of the pronominal suffix on חֲרוֹנִי ("my wrath"), the כִּי clause at the end of 7:14 is identical with that at the end of 7:12. One might infer that God's wrath is really upon the people, so הֲמוֹנָהּ could be translated as "its [Israel's] crowd/multitude," but I have retained "wealth" (as in 7:12–13) for the sake of consistency.

7:16 The Hebrew begins with a cognate construction, literally "escapees will escape." My translation takes וְהָיוּ אֶל־הֶהָרִים as meaning "they will flee to the mountains." Greenberg takes אֶל ("to") as a surrogate for עַל, so that the escapees "shall haunt [literally, 'shall be on'] the mountains."[24]

The point of the simile "like valley doves" is not entirely clear. One would think that doves would prefer valleys, where vegetation and food are more plentiful, but they readily flee to the inaccessible caves and crags of the mountains when pursued. See Song 2:14.

כֻּלָּם הֹמוֹת אִישׁ בַּעֲוֹנוֹ׃—The verb הָמָה is used of various sounds, generally of low volume. With doves, one might use "coo," except that it probably does not convey the intent of the verse. English idiom knows of "mourning doves," and "mourning" is also appropriate for the escapees. It may be saying too much, however, if it implies repentance from their sins, rather than just remorse because of the punishment for them. There is lament, but no confession of sin. Even if they fled to the mountains, they would not escape their real problem: their guilt, their fundamentally misguided relationship with Yahweh.

Mountains often figure as places of refuge in the Bible (e.g., Lot in Gen 19:17; David from Saul in 1 Sam 23:24–29; 26:1–25). They also appear in Jesus' eschatological discourse (Mt 24:16 ‖ Mk 13:14). The picture of Yahweh's enemies fleeing like birds to the mountains appears also in Is 16:2 and Jer 48:28, both in Gentile oracles, but in the light of the metaphor's frequency, one need posit no dependence on those verses by Ezekiel.

The incongruity of the masculine plural suffix on כֻּלָּם and the feminine plural participle הֹמוֹת can be explained in this case by a fusion of figure and fact, of (feminine plural) doves and men. The comprehensive "all" is qualified by the distributive אִישׁ ("each man"). Usually in Ezekiel בְּ with עָוֹן has a causal meaning (see the tex-

---

[24] Greenberg, *Ezekiel*, 1:143, 151.

tual notes on 3:18), but here a locative meaning is more suitable ("in his iniquity"), especially since "because of his iniquity" here could imply repentance, which is not part of the picture yet. (The prophecies of chapters 33–48 are for the penitent people after the destruction of Jerusalem.)

7:17 This verse contains two psychosomatic expressions of sheer terror. The Hebrew uses "all" with the duals of יָד and בֶּרֶךְ. For "hands" to hang "limp" implies more than discouragement and despair; a stronger, physiological reaction is signified, such as paralysis from fear.

The second, parallel expression is harder. Most translations say the knees will be or become "weak as water" (RSV, NIV) or "turn to water" (ESV). Neither does justice to תֵּלַכְנָה, since הָלַךְ with water, streams, and so on often means "flow" (see the verses cited in BDB, Qal, 3, including Joel 4:18 [ET 3:18], which describes hills flowing with milk). The following מַיִם is apparently an adverbial accusative, "will flow *with water*," that is, water shall flow down the knees. It is not a simile ("be like water"), which normally would use כְּ. Modern translations are probably euphemistic for the sake of public reading. The LXX appears to have caught the gist with its πάντες μηροὶ μολυνθήσονται ὑγρασίᾳ, "all thighs will be defiled with moisture." That is, the "water" probably refers to involuntary micturition: loss of bladder control in moments of sudden, extreme fright. Greenberg suggests that knees are specified because of the knee-length shirts worn by Egyptian and Assyrian soldiers.[25]

In Hebrew synonymous poetic parallelism, the second member of the pair tends to be slightly stronger than the first. That is, the verse as a whole says more than simply that both hands and knees were temporarily immobilized by fear.

7:18 The expressions of grief are arranged chiastically: the first and last expressions speak of voluntary actions, the two middle cola of involuntary ones. The first and last actions, the wearing of sackcloth and the shaving of one's head (resulting in "baldness"), are frequently referred to as nonverbal expression of distress. Lev 21:5 forbids priests to shave their heads in mourning (Lev 21:1–4), but there is no clear biblical indication that all Israelites were forbidden to shave their heads in all circumstances. The donning of sackcloth is followed by the two middle cola: the donning of two figurative articles of clothing, "shuddering" and "shame." פַּלָּצוּת ("shuddering") is a rare poetic word, but with no uncertainty of meaning.

7:19 This verse is usually taken as the beginning of the second half of the oracle. The initial section, extending through 7:24, somewhat parallels 7:12–13 in the oracle's first half. The accent is now more on the religious effects of the Day of Yahweh. In contrast to the commercial concerns of 7:12–13, the focus here is on the underlying sin of materialism and its bankruptcy.

"Unclean thing" translates נִדָּה in 7:19–20. As usual in the OT, the "uncleanness" is not hygienic or even moral, as such, but ritual and theological. The primary application of the Hebrew word is to menstrual "impurity" (Lev 12:2, 5; 15:19–24, 33; 18:19; Ezek 18:6), though it can refer more broadly to immoral sexual relations (Lev 20:21; Ezek

---

[25] Greenberg, *Ezekiel*, 1:152.

22:10) or other kinds of impurity (Num 19:9, 13, 20–21). Metaphorically, it can refer to anything polluted, including idols and idolatry, as here and in Ezek 36:17.

The middle sentence is almost identical with Zeph 1:18, of which it may well be an echo. "Silver" and "gold" are treated as a hendiadys (that is, money), so the verb יוּכָל is singular. The sentence ends with the theologically loaded phrase בְּיוֹם עֶבְרַת יְהוָה, "on the day of Yahweh's fury," which occurs elsewhere only in Zeph 1:18. Yahweh will refer to "the fire of my fury" in 21:36 (ET 21:31); 22:21, 31; 38:19.

כִּי־מִכְשׁוֹל עֲוֺנָם הָיָה׃—See the textual notes and commentary on מִכְשׁוֹל in 3:20. Conventionally translated "stumbling block," here it actually means something more like "downfall," as I have translated. Both verbal and nominal forms of כשל are especially prominent in Ezekiel, and the phrase here, מִכְשׁוֹל עָוֺן (literally, "stumbling block of iniquity"), is peculiar to him (7:19; 14:3, 4, 7; 18:30; 44:12; just מִכְשׁוֹל appears in 3:20; 21:20 [ET 21:15]). In 14:3, 4, 7 the phrase is applied to idols; in 18:30 to unrepented transgression; and in 44:12 to Levites serving at apostate shrines. The second member of this construct chain must be considered epexegetical: "their iniquity" (עֲוֺנָם) is the cause of their "downfall" (see the textual note on the phrase in 18:30). The suffix ("their") on עֲוֺנָם refers to the entire phrase, hence I have translated, "their downfall." Throughout this verse, people are consistently referred to in the plural.

Just how silver and gold became "the iniquitous cause of their downfall" is specified in the following verse.

7:20 The verse teems with difficulties, not so much textual as interpretative. As a glance at translations and commentaries will show, there are various options, and it is not easy to be dogmatic about one's ultimate choices. In any case, the translation offered must attempt to convey the translator's conclusions about the verse's message.

וּצְבִי עֶדְיוֹ לְגָאוֹן שָׂמָהוּ—This is, literally, "the beauty of his ornament—into pride he made it." The phrase that functions as the direct object of the verb is placed first for emphasis: "the beauty of his ornament" is idiomatic Hebrew for "his beautiful ornament." Since עֲדִי ("ornament, decoration") is often used of women's jewelry, the first option is to interpret it as such here, as many do. The word is then a collective, and so too is the following singular suffix on עֶדְיוֹ ("his" means "their"); most ancient versions translate the suffix as a plural, but emendation is unnecessary (so Zimmerli[26] and Greenberg[27]). It is readily understandable that the Israelites might melt down their gold and silver jewelry to make idols, as they did to make the golden calf in Exodus 32. This understanding has in its favor the ease with which it allows the "unclean thing" in both 7:19 and later in 7:20 to have essentially the same referent: their idols.

The second option, which I prefer, is to understand עֲדִי as a reference to the temple, which also served as the national treasury,[c] as was generally true of temples in antiquity. We should understand that some of the contents of the temple (particularly gold and silver stored there), not the structure itself, was converted into idols. While עֲדִי does not refer to the temple elsewhere in the OT, the word in construct with it

(c) 1 Ki 15:15, 18; 2 Ki 12:19 (ET 12:18); 14:14; 16:8; 24:13

---

[26] Zimmerli, *Ezekiel*, 1:199.

[27] Greenberg, *Ezekiel*, 1:153.

here, צְבִי ("beauty, splendor"), may refer to the temple in Dan 8:9; 11:16, 41, 45. The suffix on עֶדְיוֹ is then a reference to Yahweh ("*his* ornament"). In this section of Ezekiel 7, Yahweh usually speaks in the first person, but speakers in the OT may switch to referring to themselves in the third person.

The interpretation that the phrase here refers to the temple goes back at least to the Targum and was followed by many of the great Jewish commentators (Rashi, Kimchi). Such an understanding highlights the heinousness of the people's behavior.

Greenberg prefers the first option but suggests that between 7:19, which speaks only of silver and gold, and 7:24, which explicitly mentions sanctuaries, "vss. 20–22 form a bridge whose terms are sufficiently ambiguous they can be understood as applying to either, or (and perhaps this is intended) to both."[28]

The verb שָׂמָהוּ is שִׂים (with third masculine singular suffix), which with the preposition לְ (on לְגָאוֹן) means "make/fashion into" or the like (see BDB, s.v. שִׂים, Qal, 5 a, b; similar is Is 60:15). It is similar to עָשָׂה בְ in the next line and essentially synonymous to נָתַן לְ in the verse's final clause. Because of its position at the end of the line, the object suffix on שָׂמָהוּ ("made *it*," omitted in the translation) is resumptive, referring back to the "beautiful ornament." The verb is singular with an unspecified subject, which could refer to King Manasseh or be a collective referring to Israel in general ("they").

גָּאוֹן ("pride") can refer to what one is justifiably proud of, or even what God is proud of (Is 60:15). But frequently it is used *in malem partem* of evil pride or "arrogance," as I have taken it. (In Ezek 7:24 it recurs similarly in "the *pride* of the mighty.") This could mean that the Israelites became arrogant because they took the wrong kind of pride in the temple, as if it made them immune from accountability and divine judgment (see 24:21, 25). Or concretely, it could refer to the idols they fashioned and in which they took pride.

וְצַלְמֵי תוֹעֲבֹתָם שִׁקּוּצֵיהֶם עָשׂוּ בוֹ—However one understands the previous line, this makes plain that the subject is cultic infractions and idolatry. Again the direct object comes first in Hebrew: literally, "the images of their abominations [and] their disgusting things they made from it." In my English translation, I have made the second and third nouns into adjectives ("abominable" and "disgusting") that both modify "their images."

צֶלֶם, "image," can be used positively (Gen 1:26–27), but in this context it obviously refers to idols, as also in its two other appearances in Ezekiel (the obscene 16:17, where Jerusalem makes them from Yahweh's gold and silver, and 23:14).

תּוֹעֵבָה and שִׁקּוּץ are paired as in 5:11 (see the textual note on them there). They may be essentially synonymous, or, since the second term has no copula, it could refer to other abhorrent pagan practices not immediately connected with the "images of their abominations." The second term is lacking in the LXX; the translator may have telescoped the two synonyms. The syntax is a bit strange: first a construct chain (וְצַלְמֵי תוֹעֲבֹתָם) and then שִׁקּוּצֵיהֶם, "their disgusting objects/practices," which is asyndetic (except for a few Hebrew manuscripts and later versions, which add a copula to it).

---

[28] Greenberg, *Ezekiel*, 1:153–54.

The preposition בְּ (בוֹ) could be locative: they made their idols "in it [the temple]." That idols were in the temple is clear from 8:5, 10. But more likely is an accusative of material (as in Ex 31:4): "they [the people] made [their idols] from/out of it," that is, from the gold and silver in the temple (Ezek 7:19).

עַל־כֵּן נְתַתִּיו לָהֶם לְנִדָּה:—"Therefore" (עַל־כֵּן) signals the beginning of a new paragraph. The topic changes from what the Israelites have done to what God will do. The first of Yahweh's four reactions is that he will make the temple and/or its appurtenances odious in the people's eyes. The other three follow in 7:21–24.

Here נָתַן לְ parallels שִׂים לְ in 7:20a, but God is the subject. Thus his action is the appropriate punishment for the people's actions. We have a repetitive strengthening of the menstrual metaphor (נִדָּה, "unclean thing") from 7:19. The people's changed attitude toward the temple will not merely "happen," but will be part of God's judgment. Chapters 8–11 will discuss in detail God's abandonment of the temple, because it is no longer *his* "house."

7:21 The second judgment is that Yahweh "will place" the temple "in the hand of foreigners." זָר can mean "stranger," "(non-Israelite) foreigner," or even "enemy,"[29] but the implication is the same regardless of which nuance one selects here. The verb וּנְתַתִּיו also governs the second colon. בַּז ("booty") and שָׁלָל ("plunder") are standard pairs, virtual synonyms, as in the name of Isaiah's son Maher-*shalal-hash-baz* (Is 8:1–3). The construct phrase רִשְׁעֵי הָאָרֶץ is found otherwise only in the Psalms (e.g., Ps 75:9 [ET 75:8]). It may be translated as a superlative ("the *most* wicked people of the earth"), like a similar construct chain in Ezek 7:24. Nebuchadnezzar's armies are described similarly in 30:11–12, and even without that parallel passage there would be little doubt as to whom Ezekiel has in mind. The fearful picture of the invaders here and in the following verses matches the predictions of Deut 28:49–57. Compare similarly Jer 6:23.

וְחִלְּלָהּ:—The Kethib apparently is וְחִלְּלָהּ, with a third feminine singular object suffix. The Qere וְחִלְּלוּהוּ reads the suffix as masculine, which probably is preferable because a masculine suffix was used with the first verb in the verse (וּנְתַתִּיו). However, the last part of the next verse (7:22) uses feminine pronouns (בָהּ ... וְחִלְּלוּהָ), and 7:23 uses feminine verbs and nouns ("land," "city"). Hence a feminine suffix here may refer to Jerusalem or the land of Israel (as 7:23 clearly does). Possibly Ezekiel intended this verb and its suffix as transitional from the preceding masculine forms to the subsequent feminine ones.

7:22 The third judgment is that Yahweh will allow invaders to profane the temple and/or land. In another expression of Yahweh's direct involvement, Yahweh says, "I will turn my face away from them"—either away from the Israelites (abandoning them) or away from the depredations of the invaders, which could take place only with Yahweh's permission, however unaware of his omnipotence they may have been.

צְפוּנִי is the Qal passive participle of צָפַן, "to hide; store; treasure." The reference might be specifically to the temple treasury. The feminine suffixes following indicate

---

[29] Block, *Ezekiel*, 1:266, prefers "foreigners" but refers to an Akkadian cognate that means "enemy."

that it may be an epithet of Jerusalem or the land (both are mentioned in 7:23). Thus the Targum paraphrases: "the land in which my presence dwells." The church fathers usually interpreted it as a reference to the temple and specifically the Holy of Holies. This possibility seems less likely in the context, and the feminine suffixes militate against it. Some (including BDB, 1) translate "[my] treasured, cherished place," which might suggest anthropopathic overtones, namely, that God too suffers at the destruction. That idea is biblical, but it seems foreign to this context where God is pouring out his wrath .

The noun פָּרִיצִים derives from פָּרַץ, which usually means "to break through/down, break into." Both verb and noun are used in quite a variety of applications. "Robbers" or the like is the usual rendition. Compare our legalese "break and enter."

7:23 The fourth judgment (7:23–24) is that Yahweh will also hold the Israelites accountable for social crimes.

עֲשֵׂה הָרַתּוֹק—The noun רַתּוֹק is a hapax legomenon, although a feminine equivalent in the plural may appear in Is 40:19. The verb רָתַק occurs twice (Nah 3:10; Eccl 12:6) and means "to fetter, chain." Hence the noun assumedly means "a chain." Prophetic idiom sometimes uses imperatives in the sense of future predictions, so the imperative "prepare" (עֲשֵׂה) is intelligible as a command to prepare a long chain to tie the captive Israelites together to form a long train to be led into exile.

Of the ancient versions only the Targum clearly supports the MT. Greenberg summarizes: "The versions guess desperately and we can do little better."[30] The LXX connects the clause with the previous verse and translates, "… and will cause confusion." Some critics emend רַתּוֹק to בַּתּוֹק, which does not occur in the OT but would mean "slaughter" based on the verb (itself a hapax!) in Ezek 16:40 meaning "cut down." But the context is not so much concerned with loss of life as with material destruction. RSV was apparently influenced by the LXX in its translation, "and make a desolation." ESV ("Forge a chain!") follows the MT.

The following כִּי clause gives two reasons for the judgment. Previously the accent had been on cultic abominations; now social crimes are included. Those whose relationship with the true God is skewed show it not only by their corrupt worship, but also in their inhumane treatment of others, even within the body of believers (Israel as the visible church). Highlighted here is their skewed judicial system.

מִשְׁפַּט דָּמִים is found only here in the Bible. Since מִשְׁפַּט is in construct, "judgments/verdicts of bloodshed" is the probable literal translation. The picture is not one of the "bloody crimes" (RSV, ESV) as such, but of a corrupt judicial system that is not really concerned with the proper administration of justice (as מִשְׁפָּט often means). Rather, the system uses its authority wrongly, using rights, legal fictions, or shenanigans to maintain the power structure and give legal cover to criminal behavior. Human life is cheap in "kangaroo courts." This interpretation is confirmed by two parallel statements in 9:9 and similar accusations in 11:6 and chapter 22.

חָמָס is a noun with a broad meaning, conventionally translated "violence." "Might makes right" might well summarize the underlying attitude. Those with the

---

[30] Greenberg, *Ezekiel*, 1:154.

power, wealth, or influence will stop at nothing to have their way. Almost the same clause as here is used to explain the reason for God sending the universal flood in Gen 6:11, and a similar one is in Gen 6:13.

7:24 רָעֵי גוֹיִם is probably to be taken as a superlative, parallel to רִשְׁעֵי הָאָרֶץ in 7:21. רָשָׁע is more explicitly "evil" *coram Deo*, but the less specific רַע can easily be used synonymously. We are not told what criterion is used to characterize the invaders as "the *most* wicked of the nations." The atrocities of the Babylonians are well documented in extrabiblical sources, although the Assyrians had excelled in cruelty too.

וְיָרְשׁוּ אֶת־בָּתֵּיהֶם—This clause with the verb יָרַשׁ, "inherit, take possession of," is loaded with overtones of the Israelite conquest of Canaan. Because of the depravity of the Canaanites, God caused the Israelites to inherit their land and take possession of their houses.[d] Now the tables will be turned.

גְּאוֹן עַזִּים—"The pride of the mighty" continues the "might makes right" motif of the previous verse. The exact phrase is unique, although Ezekiel refers to "the pride of your/her strength" in 24:21; 30:6, 18; 33:28. The phrase may well be sarcastic; their "strength" is ephemeral and will soon be toppled. The LXX translated 7:24 as though it read גְּאוֹן עֻזָּם, "their proud strength."

וְנִחֲלוּ מְקַדְשֵׁיהֶם:—The verb probably is the Niphal of חָלַל, "to profane," whose Piel was in 7:21–22. Ezekiel uses the Niphal for the defiling of a holy place also in 25:3 and for the profanation of God's name in 20:9, 14, 22.

The verb form in 7:24 could also be the Piel of נָחַל, "to give as a possession" (see the Piel in Josh 13:32; 14:1; 19:51), which would relate to יָרַשׁ earlier in the verse (see the textual note on it above) and continue the theme that as Israel once took possession of Canaan from its pagan inhabitants, so Babylon will now do to apostate Israel. One suspects that the not-so-subtle approximation to what Israel regarded as her inheritance was no accident; it was an effective way of (almost painfully) underscoring the magnitude of their loss.

The unique form מְקַדְשֵׁיהֶם may be the Piel participle of קָדַשׁ with third masculine plural suffix, which would mean "men/places who sanctify them [the Israelites]." If so, it might refer to apostate clergy of the sort ordained by Jeroboam (1 Ki 12:31) or to pagan shrines that the Israelites thought would provide a kind of sanctification. But more likely it is an anomalous pointing of "their sanctuaries" (whose conventional form would be מִקְדְּשֵׁיהֶם). That is how the LXX and many modern translations render it. The strange vocalization is probably a deliberate distortion to convey the idea that these are illegitimate sanctuaries, not sanctioned by Yahweh. I have translated it "sanctuaries," but it is one of those cases where commentary is necessary to convey the nuance of the text as it stands.

In any case, the clause seems to imply that the religious institutions were in league with the corrupt judges and others to maintain the iniquitous state of affairs. That "their sanctuaries" is plural indicates the presence of rival pagan shrines besides the Jerusalem temple. Elsewhere in the Bible we have copious evidence of such shrines. **7:25** The final three verses of chapter 7 are perhaps a distinguishable subsection, no longer concentrating on the religious effects of the day of Yahweh's judgment, but on the political ones.

(d) See Deut 19:1; also Deut 6:11; Josh 1:11, 15; 3:10; 12:1

קְפָדָה־בָא—The noun קְפָדָה is another hapax. The probable meaning of "terror, anguish" is based on the ancient Greek and Latin versions and a Syriac cognate. It may be related to the rare OT noun קִפֹּד, "porcupine, hedgehog; short-eared owl." If קְפָדָה were feminine, it would clash with the following masculine verb. However, the Masoretic accents place the stress on the penultima (-פָ-), hence it probably is an archaic masculine form with unaccented דָ ending. The verb בָא is either third masculine singular perfect or masculine singular participle; either way ("has come" or "comes") it may be called a prophetic perfect in contrast to the imperfects in 7:26. Compare the syntax to 7:6.

וּבִקְשׁוּ שָׁלוֹם וָאָיִן:—In this context, "peace" is an appropriate translation of שָׁלוֹם, but we should not forget that the Hebrew noun usually is much broader, including, above all, peace with God, and also welfare, health, prosperity, wholeness, and so forth. One cannot help but think of Jeremiah's refrain: false prophets preach "peace, peace, but there is no peace" (Jer 6:14; 8:11; cf. Is 48:22; 57:21; Jer 12:12; 30:5). **7:26** הֹוָה עַל־הֹוָה תָּבוֹא—The noun הֹוָה occurs elsewhere only in Is 47:11 and means "disaster" (*HALOT*). It is related to the more common noun הַוָּה, "destruction." The construction with עַל ("after") could also be rendered "disaster upon disaster."

וּשְׁמֻעָה אֶל־שְׁמוּעָה תִּהְיֶה—The structure of this phrase is precisely parallel to that of the preceding one. The talk of rumors (שְׁמוּעָה) reminds us of our Lord's eschatological prediction of "wars and rumors of wars" (Mt 24:6 ‖ Mk 13:7).

The people turn desperately to anyone who might be in a position to give them some answers or help, but, as Ezek 7:27 goes on to say, they find none. " Seek" (וּבִקְשׁוּ) ties in with the identical form in 7:25. "Vision" is the conventional translation of חָזוֹן, but its accent is on revelation itself, regardless of the means God uses to deliver it. In 1 Sam 3:1 it is parallel to "the word of Yahweh," meaning any revelatory word(s) from him. See it also in Ezek 12:22–24, 27. One thinks of Prov 29:18: "Where there is no vision, the people perish," which is often misused as though the "vision" were human foresight or imagination, not God's salvific revelation.[31]

Neither will the priest be able to offer תּוֹרָה. The noun can refer to the Torah (its transliteration) of Moses, the Pentateuch, as in Josh 1:7; 8:31–32. Since the priests were the custodians and teachers of the Torah (Deut 17:18; 31:9, 26; 33:10), that may be its sense here. The word can also have a more generic meaning of "instruction, revelation." It is traditionally translated "Law," but that is so multivalent a word that it often misleads. To the extent that "Law" might be an adequate translation, dogmatically we would insist that it is the *third* use of the Law (FC VI) that is being spoken of here if we are dealing with believers who want to know what to do. If the people have become apostate unbelievers, they will inevitably hear the *second* use of the Law, for *lex semper accusat.*

---

[31] Many scholars theorize that after "they will seek a vision from the prophet" (Ezek 7:26), we should expect a half-verse with אַיִן ("there will be none") or the like, as at the end of 7:25. But Greenberg, *Ezekiel*, 1:155, plausibly argues that precisely because "seek" is repeated from 7:25, where it is followed by "there will be none," the audience can easily finish the sentence in 7:26 themselves.

Finally, the "elders," who are the traditional repositories of wisdom in Israelite society, will have no עֵצָה to give. The word is conventionally translated "counsel" and is often associated with proverbs, maxims, or wisdom sayings from a professional class of the "wise" or wisdom teachers. In a common schematization, דָּבָר, "word," characterizes prophetic speech; תּוֹרָה, "law," that of the priests; and עֵצָה that of the wise (cf. Jer 18:18). The scheme is helpful but inevitably oversimplified and probably at its weakest in the limitation of עֵצָה to a special group of teachers or administrators. This verse illustrates a wider possible source for "counsel."

7:27 Here we have another tripartite division. The first two entities are officials who, in the OT era, had important civic and religious/theological duties. The third group is broader and includes those who didn't necessarily hold an office.

הַמֶּלֶךְ ... וְנָשִׂיא—Ezekiel generally is reluctant to use the otherwise common noun מֶלֶךְ, "king," in reference to the human head of Israel. In the prediction of 34:23–24, even when the eschatological "David" is referred to by name, he is referred to as רֹעֶה, "shepherd" (a common ancient Near Eastern royal metaphor), or נָשִׂיא, "prince" (the word used in the next clause of 7:27). In 37:24–25, the coming "David" is foretold to be "king"—but promptly "shepherd" and "prince" also. Throughout the eschatological chapters 40–48, the role of the "prince" (נָשִׂיא) in the new era is mentioned frequently, but we hear nothing of a "king" (מֶלֶךְ). Ezekiel's apparent antipathy to the title "king" is understood as resulting from his acute realization that the Davidic monarchy, far from being a force for a faithful Israel, had, more often than not, been the fountainhead of all sorts of apostasy and syncretism.

What is הַמֶּלֶךְ doing here then? Possibly, Ezekiel, for a change, is simply recognizing the preexilic state of affairs; the reference to "the king" here is certainly not complimentary! One suggestion (Greenberg, following Freedman[32]) is that "king" and "prince" are synonymous here. It may be that the king was commonly called נָשִׂיא, but, outside of Ezekiel, there would be little evidence of that. The LXX omits the first clause with "king" and the conjunction that connects it to the next clause.

All this turns to the precise meaning of (anarthrous) נָשִׂיא. If "prince" implies royalty, that translation may be misleading. In premonarchical Israel, the נָשִׂיא was apparently a leader or chief of one of the twelve tribes (Num 2.3–31). Elsewhere שַׂר is often translated "prince" also. Compare Ezekiel's contemporary, Jeremiah, in Jer 44:21, with a tripartite division of society with שָׂרִים as the middle members; compare also the well-known messianic שַׂר־שָׁלוֹם of Is 9:5 (ET 9:6). The lack of a definite article on נָשִׂיא here may indicate a class noun: all those who could be titled נָשִׂיא, whatever the precise meaning. I have retained the traditional "prince" for lack of any certain alternative.

עַם־הָאָרֶץ—The third societal division here is not pellucid either. Sometimes in the Bible the phrase "the people of the land" seems to have as its surface meaning "all the citizenry." But frequently in Jeremiah (1:18; 34:19; 37:2; 44:21; 52:25) and in Ezekiel (here and in 22:29), it seems to indicate the "landed gentry," property own-

---

[32] Greenberg, *Ezekiel*, 1:156–57, citing a private observation by David Noel Freedman.

ers with some influence. The context would suggest that they were supporters of the Davidic dynasty, which had apostatized.

The verbs used with the three groups, while not strict synonyms, all point in the same general direction. If anything they come in ascending degrees of severity.

For "the king," the Hithpael of אָבַל, "to mourn," may be a bit stronger than the simple Qal, perhaps "to exert oneself in mourning (rites?)."

The "prince" wears or is clothed in "horror," although the noun שְׁמָמָה often means "desolation, devastation" (as in, e.g., 6:14; 12:20). The "wearing" of horror may be metaphorical, or may refer to horrid clothes worn by prisoners and exiles. The common sackcloth and ashes hardly seem appropriate because they signify repentance—hardly the mentality of the Israelite leaders at this point.

For "the citizenry" it is hard to get a translation strong enough for תִּבָּהַלְנָה. The Niphal of בָּהַל is "deponent," since its meaning is active. I have used "paralyzed," but "be in a state of sheer terror" is the idea. To return to the accent at the beginning of the chapter, the people know that the "end" has come (7:6).

The rest of the verse (which might better have been numbered as a separate verse) is a final summary statement by Yahweh. It recapitulates and gives a final emphasis to a theme heard repeatedly in the first part of the chapter. The following two statements will parallel this one by St. Paul: "Whatever a man sows, that he will also reap" (Gal 6:7).

מִדַּרְכָּם אֶעֱשֶׂה אוֹתָם—As often in Ezekiel, the preposition אֵת, "with," with an object suffix is written אוֹתָם instead of the regular אִתָּם.

The noun דֶּרֶךְ, "way," is commonly used of one's conduct, way of life, and basic goal and orientation in life. Both with דֶּרֶךְ and its counterpart in the next colon (וּבְמִשְׁפְּטֵיהֶם), we would expect the preposition כְּ, "as, like, corresponding to." However, different prepositions are used in both cases. מִן is used with דֶּרֶךְ. In this context, מִן must mean "on account of"; Greenberg suggests "out of (the repertoire of)," which approximates its common meaning "from."[33]

וּבְמִשְׁפְּטֵיהֶם אֶשְׁפְּטֵם—Parallel to מִדַּרְכָּם in the preceding clause is וּבְמִשְׁפְּטֵיהֶם, "by their own judgments." The preposition בְּ has the sense of introducing a standard of measurement or computation (BDB, III 8). The noun מִשְׁפָּט is obviously cognate with the following verb, שָׁפַט.

After the long diatribe of chapter 7, the repetition (see 7:4, 9) of the recognition formula ("then they will know that I am Yahweh") comes as another stroke of the death knell.

Commentary

Neither text nor context gives us a clue as to any special circumstances surrounding the delivery of this excitatory sermon. Some of its jerky style may be rhetorical, intended to arouse the listeners too, but that should not be misunderstood as superficial affectation. Evidence for the view that the chapter is in the form the author intended, and perhaps identical to the form of it he preached,

---

[33] Greenberg, *Ezekiel*, 1:157.

may be seen in the fact that when it came to the final editing of the book (presumably by Ezekiel himself), no attempt was made to smooth out its terse and abrupt rhetoric. "The end is at hand. There is no time to worry about fine literary style."[34]

The body of the chapter may be divided into three announcements of Israel's end: (1) 7:2–4; (2) 7:5–9; and (3) 7:10–27. There are many parallels between 7:2–4 and 7:5–9, and sometimes phrases from the first section are repeated verbatim in the second. Both the first and second sections begin with the citation formula ("thus says the Lord Yahweh"), and all three sections conclude with a form of the recognition formula ("then you/they will know that I am Yahweh"). The agitated tone of the first two sections lessens considerably in the third section, where the land is no longer addressed in the second person, but in the third, as the effects of Yahweh's judgment upon it are pronounced.

"An End" (7:1–4)

7:1–4 "End!" With this short, anarthrous word (קֵץ in 7:2c), Ezekiel ushers in a chapter with a distinct eschatological, sometimes an almost apocalyptic, flavor. Beginning with chapter 34 that tone will become frequent, but until chapter 7 it has been relatively subdued and only implicit in the book. When "end" is repeated in 7:2, it is with a verb (בָּא, "*has* come") that is a prophetic perfect, typical of eschatological prophecy. The chapter contains various other words or metaphors that are commonly associated with eschatology, such as "the day" (7:7, 10, 12, 19) and harvest imagery (7:10–11). (See the commentary on those verses.)

In Dan 8:17, 19, קֵץ ("end") clearly refers to the eschatological end time. In Ezekiel its import is not quite so precise, but we are close. Perhaps we are at the same point as with the pun in the last of Amos' visions (Amos 8:1–3) on קֵץ, "end," and קָיִץ, "ripe summer fruit" (which does not appear in Ezekiel). In Amos 8, the target is primarily the imminent fall of the northern kingdom, but the situation is comparable to Ezekiel's application to Jerusalem and Judah. How much of a harvest metaphor we should hear in connection with the word "end" is debatable, but the harvest metaphor surfaces clearly in 7:10c–11 and may be implicit in the "joy" of 7:7c. Our idioms of harvest joy ("bringing in the sheaves") and judgment (the Grim Reaper; see Jer 9:20–21 [ET 9:21–22]) are both rooted in Scripture.

Eschatological and apocalyptic implications appear already at the end of 7:2 in "the four corners of the earth [אֶרֶץ]." That phrase is universal in import, in contrast to "the land [אֲדָמָה] of Israel" earlier in the verse. "Land" is earthy in a literal sense (referring to the soil or territory), and its immediate application is to Jerusalem and the rest of "the land of Israel," but since God's enemies—the objects of his judgment—are also the heathen nations, a sort of

---

[34] Block, *Ezekiel*, 1:243.

typology is built into the treatment of "the land of Israel." The doom of unbelieving Israel ("the land") is a miniature and a portent of the end and judgment of the entire world ("the earth"). The same is true in 7:23, where אֶרֶץ could refer just to the land of Israel, but the language recalls the state of the whole "earth" prior to the universal flood (Gen 6:11, 13).

Ezekiel was by no means the first prophet to make that linkage between the land of Israel and the whole earth. The oracles of judgment upon the surrounding Gentile nations in Amos 1–2 lead into judgment on Israel and Judah in Amos 3–9. The same kind of connection is implicit in the extended sections of Gentile oracles in many other prophets, including Ezekiel 25–32. The powerful second chapter of Isaiah moves from Israel's judgment to the condemnation of all human presumption. The inclusion of the world at large is as explicit as can be in Zeph 1:2–18.

At the same time that it looks forward to the end of the whole world, the "end" of Israel (Ezek 7:2) is also an antitype that looks back to "the end of all flesh" upon the whole "earth" in universal deluge in the days of Noah (Gen 6:13). (Ezekiel will refer to Noah in 14:14, 20.) The Christian can hardly contemplate such passages about the "end" without integrating them with Jesus' declaration "It is finished/ended" (τετέλεσται, Jn 19:30) on Calvary, where God's judgment was concentrated on his own Son, who is Israel embodied in one person. At the same time, when the entirety of God's wrath was "finished/ended" upon his Son, that opened the way of escape for all who confess that his was indeed the judgment they deserved. It is a judgment that is repeated daily in the Christian life of repentance and faith, as we die with Christ to sin and rise with Christ to new life in Baptism, which is the antitype of the flood in the days of Noah (when only eight were saved), and "which also now saves you" (1 Pet 3:21).

The underlying spiritual and theological problems of the Israelites that Ezekiel addresses are the same problems that have always plagued God's people and still afflict the church and the unbelieving world today. The human tendency is to embrace one-sidedly God's promises of salvation for those who believe, while disregarding God's threat of judgment upon those who do not believe—and to glibly assume, without self-examination, that the divine judgment certainly cannot apply to oneself.

The other temptation is to relegate the entire subject of the "end" to a far distant, essentially irrelevant time. Not for nothing are the Gospels full of admonitions such as "Watch, therefore, for you know neither the day nor the hour" (Mt 25:13). 2 Pet 3:3–4 is the classic passage illustrating how already the early church faced an indifference defended by the delay of the parousia. The modern church, even when relatively orthodox in theory, is notorious for collapsing the Gospel into merely the present, existential moment before God. Empirically, this is obvious when it comes to the usual way we lead our personal lives (living for the moment and as if this life will never end). But if we so easily disregard the inevitable end of our own personal lives, how much easier is it to ignore the cosmic end of all things created?

Biblical eschatology is always simultaneously existential (vertical) and horizontal (extending from creation to the cross and to the end of the world at Christ's return). Ezekiel 7 drives home that point by its proclamation of both the people's existential status *coram Deo* (under his judgment) and the arrival of the "end" already now.

"The Day" (7:5–9)

In connection with the "end," 7:7 introduces "the day" (הַיּוֹם), a term that plays a prominent role in biblical thought and that is still evident in theological discourse today. In contexts like this, "the day" (7:7, 10, 12) is shorthand for the likes of "the day of Yahweh's fury" (7:19) and especially "the Day of Yahweh" (13:5). In poetic parallelism to "the day" we also meet "the time" (הָעֵת, 7:7). In the OT "the time" never took on the theological freight that "the day" did, but in the NT καιρός is quite prominent as a term for the "time" when God acts, either in judgment or salvation or both, for example, the appointed "time" of Christ's first advent (Mk 1:15), of Christ's passion (Mt 26:18), of Christ's second advent (Mk 13:33), of the "harvest" at the end of the world (Mt 13:30), or the time of the final judgment of the demons (Mt 8:29).

Yahweh's "day" is a time of encounter with him, the details of which will be determined by him alone. The word may be used of moments of deliverance or salvation (e.g., Is 49:8, quoted in 2 Cor 6:2). And, before we proceed, here is a place to correct the common misunderstanding of "Judgment Day" to the effect that it is only the time of the damnation of the unfaithful. In fact, "judgment" in that phrase is used in the common biblical sense of a "verdict" rendered by a judge. For the believer, then, that day will be the time of God's public verdict of "not guilty" for Christ's sake—justification by grace alone and through faith alone in Christ's vicarious atonement.

However, more often in biblical usage of "the day," and certainly in Ezekiel, the accent is on judgment in the sense of condemnation. That was no more congenial an idea to people living in the OT era than it is with many popular conceptions of God today. The clearest evidence for this is in the famous passage Amos 5:18–20. Against popular fantasies, Amos insists that the Day of Yahweh "is darkness and not light, as if a man fled from a lion and a bear met him."[35]

Ezekiel had many prophetic predecessors besides Amos, so Ezekiel is able to mention "the day" briefly since it was a well-established concept. Isaiah is particularly rich in his development of it. Much of Isaiah 2 (especially 2:12–22) speaks of the exaltation of Yahweh's "day" over everything "that is proud and lofty … lifted up and high." The common treasury of language and imagery

---

[35] Amos is often credited with having originated the concept of the "Day of Yahweh," but the text itself indicates that the idea antedated him. There are many other speculations about its origins, but, typically, the Bible itself shows little, if any, interest in such diachronic speculations of the sort that have preoccupied critical scholarship.

throughout Ezekiel 7 is even closer to Is 13:1–6, a Gentile oracle against Babylon, which in Ezekiel 7 is recycled against Israel. Stylistic and conceptual links to Ezekiel 7 are also clear in Zeph 1:14–16, which is the basis of the famous medieval hymn *Dies irae*, "Day of Wrath" (*TLH* 607, unfortunately omitted in *LW*).

Ezekiel 7 speaks only of "the day" (7:7, 10, 12) and "the day of Yahweh's fury" (7:19), but throughout the prophets there are many variant expressions with the same import. Often it is simply "that day" (הַיּוֹם הַהוּא, e.g., Is 2:11, 17, 20) or "those days" (e.g., הַיָּמִים הָהֵם, Jer 31:33) or "the last days" (אַחֲרִית הַיָּמִים, e.g., Is 2:2). "Day" may be in construct with נָקָם, when it is usually translated as "day of vengeance," but better would be "day of vindication" (Is 34:8; 61:2; 63:4). Sometimes "day" is in construct with a name that refers to a specific historical divine intervention, such as "the day of Egypt" (Ezek 30:9); "the day of Jezreel" (Hos 2:2 [ET 1:11]); or "the day of Midian" (Is 9:3). Sometimes Yahweh's day is the time when he will offer a זֶבַח ("sacrifice; peace offering; sacrificial meal"), as in Zeph 1:7–8, where Israel itself will be sacrificed; compare Is 34:6; Jer 46:10; and, more positively, Ezek 39:17.

7:9   To the recognition formula ("then you will know that I, Yahweh") is added the predicate participle "am the smiter." That underscores the same point made in earlier passages: Yahweh himself has become the enemy[36]—not because he has abandoned his covenant promise, but because Israel has abandoned it. In Is 53:4 God uses the corresponding passive participle (Hophal of נָכָה) of the (Hiphil) active participle here to declare that the Suffering Servant is the one who is "smitten":

> Truly he bore our sicknesses
>> and carried our pains,
> but we had deemed him stricken,
>> *smitten* by God and afflicted.

Christ is Israel embodied in one man. He was "smitten" as he suffered the sum total of the punishment for humanity's sin meted out by "Yahweh … the smiter." The apparent paradox between Is 53:4 and Ezek 7:9 is resolved only by Christ on the cross. The *Agnus Dei* bears the iniquity of us all.

Doom, Plunder, and Horror (7:10–27)

7:10–11a   The precise thrust of these Hebrew lines is much debated. Already the LXX appears to have been thoroughly befuddled. The obscure צְפִירָה ("doom"?) appears again (as in 7:7).

There seems to be a botanical analogy to a plant that has grown ripe for harvest—the time of judgment. A possible link between קֵץ, which is the "end" in 7:2–3, 6, and קַיִץ, "ripe summer fruit," based on the wordplay of Amos 8 (see the commentary on 7:1–4), may mean that a harvest picture has lurked just beneath the surface of the chapter all along, but it first comes to the fore here

---

[36]   See, for example, the last textual note on 3:17.

(unless הֵד in 7:7 refers specifically to *harvest* shouts, as Greenberg[37] believes). Harvest is easily associated metaphorically with judgment because the activities of cutting down, sweeping clean, separating the grain from the chaff, and so on can easily be applied to the ravages of an invader—and to God's eschatological judgment, the separation of believers from unbelievers, the salvation of believers and the fiery torment of the damned.

Other prophets certainly exploit the picture. Isaiah predictably is rich in such passages, but is by no means alone. The verb אָסַף ("gather in harvest") is often used in such contexts (Jer 8:13; Zeph 1:2; cf. Micah 7:1). In the NT, harvest imagery abounds.[e]

In trying to determine how far to press the botanical imagery in Ezek 7:10–11, much depends on the interpretation of מַטֶּה, "rod" (7:10–11). Some connection with Aaron's rod which budded in Num 17:23 (ET 17:8) naturally suggests itself, because two of the verbs used here also occur there. A "rod" is often associated with rulership and discipline, even of God's chastisement upon his own people. For example, God calls Assyria "the rod of my anger" upon godless Israel in Is 10:5. Maybe that is the point here: what in the case of Aaron had been a sign of legitimate authority and supernatural life is now progressively becoming "an emblematic cudgel of oppression and wickedness."[38] But the Hebrew grammar leaves open the question of whether Israel is the subject of the misbehavior here or the object of the rod's blows.

A similar ambiguity attends "insolence" (זָדוֹן) in Ezek 7:10. Is it Israel's attitude that now "has blossomed"? Or is "insolence" the epithet of the Babylonian enemy, whom God will employ for his purpose, but whom God will then put in his place. Greenberg notes that "insolence" (זָדוֹן) is used of Babylon in such a way in Jer 50:31–32.[39]

7:11b–13   The effects of God's wrath are highlighted. First is the collapse of all commercial and business life. That topic recurs in 7:19. A buyer would not be able to rejoice in any bargain he has found, nor will the seller lament any poor transaction, because in the catastrophe both will lose all. There is not even the possibility of economic rebalancing during the Jubilee Year (see the textual notes on 7:13).

Even in the ordinary course of human affairs, the possibility of divine intervention makes all commercial and financial plans contingent upon his will (*Deo volente*, James 4:13–15). How much more is this true when projected upon an eschatological screen (cf. Mt 24:40–41 ‖ Lk 17:34–35).

7:14–15   The thought now shifts to the futility of human preparations in the face of the devastating judgment. The people may plan to fight back, but when they sound the trumpet, calling their forces to do battle, they will be so

(e) E.g., Mt 9:37–38; 13:1–43; Lk 3:17; Rom 1:13; 2 Cor 9:10; James 3:18; Rev 14:14–20

---

[37] Greenberg, *Ezekiel*, 1:148.

[38] Block, *Ezekiel*, 1:256.

[39] Greenberg, *Ezekiel*, 1:149.

petrified that they will be unable to mount any significant resistance to the agent of God's judgment. The trio of "sword, " "plague," and "famine" from chapter 5 (5:12, 17) reappear and overtake them all.

7:16–18   As in 5:3–4, again the door is left slightly ajar to accommodate the possibility of a handful of survivors who manage to escape. But those who make it to the mountains exist in almost a living death, "all of them moaning" (7:16), and the following verses will expand that thought. The last phrase of 7:16, "each in his iniquity," will not let us forget the real problem: the people's sin, which they cannot escape. They may bemoan their guilt, but are not about to repent of it. All will be involved, but the theme of individual accountability, which Ezekiel will later accent so strongly (especially chapter 18), also makes an appearance here ("each in *his* iniquity").

7:19   Materialism is by no means only a modern malady, since it is endemic to the fallen human condition. As this and the following verse make plain, it always entails idolatry: the worship of the created instead of the Creator. The culpability is even greater for recipients of divine revelation; "everyone to whom is given much, much shall be required from him" (Lk 12:48). As an "-ism" intrinsically at odds with God's plan of redemption, materialism inevitably triggers God's wrath. It is not merely a closed-circuited, this-worldly human conclusion that a person's deepest needs cannot be satisfied by the "abundance of things he possesses" (Lk 12:15), but materialism is an orientation that brings judgment, unless repented of and forgiven.

As usual in Ezekiel, the judgment ("the day of Yahweh's fury," 7:19) will find an immediate fulfillment in the fall of Jerusalem in 587 B.C. But eschatological overtones are implicit, as the church recognizes in its use of the *dies irae* theme in its hymnody and liturgy.

Also as usual in Ezekiel, English translations soften the impact of the Hebrew terminology. The "unclean thing" (7:19–20) that their gold will become has its roots in the ceremonial laws of uncleanness, especially for menstruation (see the textual notes on 7:19). The ceremonial (and civil) laws of the OT cannot be taken over mechanically by the NT church, but the moral laws do apply to the church. However, the OT itself often does not make a clear-cut distinction between the ceremonial and the moral. Already in the OT (as in 7:19–20; 36:17), the vocabulary of "unclean(ness)" is used in a broader theological sense, and in the NT uncleanness/impurity results not only from sexual immorality, but also from greed and idolatry.[f] To regard material goods as containing no intrinsic worth apart from the Giver of all good gifts (James 1:17) may at least be the first step in praise and thanksgiving before God. The final clause in Ezek 7:19 is virtually a paraphrase of the well-known dictum of St. Paul in 1 Tim 6:10: "The love of money is a root of all evils."

(f) E.g., Rom 1:23–27; Gal 5:19–20; Eph 4:19; 5:3; Col 3:5

7:20   Whatever the precise force of this difficult verse, it is a reminder of how easily God's gifts are not received with thanksgiving, but become ultimate ends or pursuits, that is, become idols. If my reading of the verse is correct (see the textual notes), it describes how the Israelites used gold and silver from God's temple as the precious metals from which they fashioned their idols. The same thing, spiritually if not literally, can be done by Christians in the church. The visible church can easily be turned into a caricature of what God intends by that highest of all gifts—his indwelling presence in the person of Christ. The Christian's very body too is a temple that is defiled by immorality (1 Cor 6:9–20). *Corruptio optimi pessima*, "the corruption of the best is the worst of all."

7:21–27   The rest of the chapter continues to paint in the blackest colors Israel's estrangement from God's redemptive intent so that the only remaining outcome is his *opus alienum*, his "alien/strange work," that is, executing judgment according to his Law. "Foreigners" (unbelievers) and "the most wicked people of the earth" (7:21; cf. 7:24) will possess and then inevitably desecrate what God had called and made holy. The people's pride in what they should have been ashamed of will turn into utter chaos and despair as they stare into the abyss. As King Saul once sought in vain for a word from God (1 Sam 28:6), so will they, but the point of no return has been passed; they have no true repentance or faith in God's promises.

The antepenultimate and penultimate clauses of the chapter are chilling ("According to their own conduct I will deal with them, and by their own judgments I will judge them," 7:27). These are clear statements of Law for all who would be saved by the Law (see Rev 20:12–13). "And Yahweh alone will be exalted in that day" (Is 2:11).

The Glory of God versus Four Abominations in the Temple

Translation

8   ¹In the sixth year, in the sixth [month], on the fifth day of the month, I was sitting in my house and the elders of Judah were sitting in front of me. The hand of the Lord Yahweh fell upon me there. ²I looked, and behold—a figure with an appearance like a man. From what appeared to be his waist and downward was fire, and from his waist and above was an appearance of brilliance, something like electrum. ³He stretched out the form of a hand and seized me by a lock from my head. Then the Spirit lifted me up between earth and heaven and brought me to Jerusalem in a divine vision, to the entrance of the gate of the inner court that faces northward; there was seated the statue of jealousy which provokes jealousy. ⁴And behold, there was the Glory of the God of Israel, like the vision that I had seen on the valley plain.

⁵He said to me, "Son of man, look northward." So I looked northward, and behold, north of the altar gate was this statue of jealousy at the entrance. ⁶He said to me, "Son of man, do you see what they are doing—great abominations which the house of Israel is practicing here, distancing themselves from my sanctuary? But you will see even greater abominations."

⁷Next, he brought me to the entrance to the court, and I looked, and behold—a hole in the wall. ⁸He said to me, "Son of man, dig through the wall." So I dug through the wall, and behold—an entranceway. ⁹He said to me, "Go in and observe the vile abominations that they are committing here." ¹⁰When I entered, I looked, and behold, every kind of figure of creeping things and of detestable beasts and of all the fecal deities of the house of Israel engraved on the wall, all around. ¹¹Seventy men of the elders of the house of Israel—with Jaazaniah the son of Shaphan standing in their center—were standing before them [the images], each with his censer in his hand, and the scent of the incense cloud was ascending. ¹²He said to me, "Do you see, son of man, what the elders of the house of Israel are doing in the darkness, each in his image-chambers? For they are saying, 'Yahweh does not see us; Yahweh has forsaken the land.' " ¹³Then he said to me, "You will see even greater abominations which they are practicing."

¹⁴Next, he brought me to the entrance of the gateway to the house of Yahweh that is on the north, and behold, there the women were sitting, bewailing Tammuz. ¹⁵He said to me, "Do you see, son of man? You will see even greater abominations than these."

¹⁶Finally, he brought me to the inner court of the house of Yahweh, and behold, at the entrance to the temple of Yahweh, between the vestibule and the al-

tar, were twenty-five men—their backsides to the temple of Yahweh, and their faces eastward—and they were prostrating themselves eastward to the sun. [17]Then he said to me, "Have you seen, son of man? Is it too trivial for the house of Judah to commit the abominations they do here that they [also] fill the land with violence, and thus they provoke me more and more? They are even sticking the branch up my nose! [18]But I also will act in wrath. My eye will not pity, and I will have no compassion. They will call in my ears with a loud cry, but I will not hear them."

Textual Notes

8:1   The LXX dates the vision in the fifth rather than in the sixth month. A most natural conclusion would be that the translators inadvertently wrote "fifth" twice (in the Hebrew the dating of the month precedes that of the day). Nevertheless, there has been considerable critical preference for the LXX alternative on the dubious grounds that the allegedly secondary MT had tried to clear the 430 days of the previous action prophecy (4:4–7) by adding a month's interval. (Zimmerli's influential arguments to the contrary[1] may reverse that tide, however.) We need not rehash the problem of those numbers. There is really no way of being sure whether the earlier action prophecy and this vision overlapped or not. Nor does it really seem to matter. There is no compelling reason why the prophet could not have experienced a vision during his long immobility.

8:2   See the textual notes on the parallel passage, 1:26–27. With the LXX and most commentators I have read the first instance of אֵשׁ ("fire") in the verse as אִשׁ, the defectively written form of אִישׁ "a man." "Man" is usually written with a full (*plene*) vowel (אִישׁ), but there are exceptions, of which this appears to be one. "Man" provides a more natural antecedent to the following possessives ("his"). In the parallel, 1:26, אָדָם is used for "man." The first אֵשׁ in MT may have arisen by assimilation to the second אֵשׁ, "fire," at the end of the next clause; both words are in pause. The same phenomenon may explain the strange form of the last word of the verse, הַחַשְׁמַלָה. The normal form of חַשְׁמַל (1:4, 27) with definite article has received the ending הָ apparently by assimilation to לְמַעְלָה, and both of these words too are in pause. (Others explain the form of הַחַשְׁמַלָה as expressing a sort of climax to a grandiose description, but such ad hoc morphology is less likely.)

זֹהַר appears elsewhere in the Bible only in Dan 12:3 ("the wise will shine with the *brightness* of the firmament"). It corresponds to נֹגַהּ in 1:4, 27. Greenberg notes that the association of זֹהַר here with a divine figure and with heaven in Daniel "made the term fitting for the title of the 'bible' of Jewish mystics, the Zohar."[2]

8:3   בְּצִיצִת רֹאשִׁי—The rare noun צִיצִת is used elsewhere only in Num 15:38–39, where it refers to the fringe or tassels on the hem of a garment. Here it refers to a lock of Ezekiel's hair. (The apocryphal story of the angel carrying Habakkuk in the same way to bring food to Daniel in the lions' den was probably influenced by this text.)

---

[1]   Zimmerli, *Ezekiel*, 1:216.

[2]   Greenberg, *Ezekiel*, 1:167.

בְּמַרְאוֹת אֱלֹהִים—See the textual note on this same phrase (but without בְּ) in 1:1.

שַׁעַר הַפְּנִימִית—Since שַׁעַר ("gate") is masculine, "the inner" (הַפְּנִימִית), which is feminine, does not modify it. Most commentators assume that הֶחָצֵר ("the court"), which may be masculine but is usually feminine, is assumed, and so my translation supplies "the inner *court*." Ezek 10:5 uses חָצֵר to refer to the outer "court."

מוֹשָׁב—The noun מוֹשָׁב (derived from יָשַׁב) can mean "seat" (as well as "residence" in other contexts), and so I have translated it verbally: "was seated." The statue or idol may well have been in a sitting position, of which many examples have been found. But also possible is a more general meaning, such as "was situated" or even the statue's "stand, pedestal."

סֵמֶל הַקִּנְאָה הַמַּקְנֶה:—This is, literally, "the statue of jealousy that causes/provokes jealousy," though many translators choose "outrage" instead of "jealousy." The first two words will be repeated in 8:5. סֵמֶל is an infrequent noun for "image, statue" that in Ezekiel occurs only in 8:3, 5. We met the noun קִנְאָה before in 5:13, where "jealousy" connoted Yahweh's wrath at the infidelity of Israel, his espoused "wife." His wrath at her harlotry is also the theme of chapters 16 and 23. The only true God cannot and does not brook rivals.

The Hiphil participle הַמַּקְנֶה is from the verb קָנָא, from which also the noun קִנְאָה is derived. The Hiphil of קָנָא occurs elsewhere only in Deut 32:16, 21 and Ps 78:58 and has a causative meaning. That the statue "causes/provokes [God's] jealousy" explains what is meant when it is called "the statue of jealousy." הַמַּקְנֶה is unusual because it is formed as if the root were קָנָה. The "normal" form of the Hiphil participle of קָנָא would be מַקְנִיא. The two phonemes (א and ה) were close enough in Hebrew that interchange often took place. See GKC, § 75 qq.

8:4 See the textual notes on 1:26–28 and 3:22–23.

8:5 בֶּן־אָדָם—See the textual note on "son of man" in 2:1.

שָׂא־נָא עֵינֶיךָ דֶּרֶךְ צָפוֹנָה וָאֶשָּׂא עֵינַי דֶּרֶךְ צָפוֹנָה—Both times I have translated the idiom "to lift up [נָשָׂא] one's eyes" simply as "look." Ezekiel frequently uses דֶּרֶךְ ("way, road") as a preposition, especially in chapters 40–48. I have translated דֶּרֶךְ צָפוֹנָה simply as "northward."

בַּבִּאָה:—The noun בִּאָה, translated "entrance," is a hapax legomenon. It presumably is derived from the common verb בּוֹא. The noun still leaves the precise location of the statue a bit uncertain, whether on the outer side of the entrance or somewhere in the entranceway. Others attempt to relate the word to the Akkadian *bi'u*, an architectural term meaning "drainage opening," "drainpipe," or "passageway," but if that is its meaning, it still does not pinpoint the statue's location.

8:6 הֲרֹאֶה—Some take the interrogative *he* with the participle רֹאֶה ("seeing") as also having an exclamatory nuance. Such a force is more likely when הֲ is used with the perfect verbs in 8:12, 15, 17, but it might also apply to the participle used here. I have not attempted to bring such a nuance out in translation, because the context alone seems to suffice to express it.

The form מֵהֶם ("what they") is unique. Apparently it is a contraction of מָה הֵם, which is the Qere. This is the only instance where the *he* of the interrogative מָה has coalesced before a guttural (another *he*; cf. Waltke-O'Connor, § 18.1e, n. 5). Before non-gutturals this happens occasionally; for example, מַזֶּה in Ex 4:2 is a contraction of מַה־זֶּה, "What is this?"

לְרָחֳקָה מֵעַל מִקְדָּשִׁי—A major issue is the implied subject of לְרָחֳקָה. The form is a feminine-type Qal infinitive construct of the stative verb רָחַק, "to be distant, far away." Modern scholars have tended to prefer "Yahweh" as the subject, as already Jerome had done: God says, *ut procul recedam a sanctuario meo*, "so that I must withdraw far from my sanctuary."[3] This alternative is very attractive and anticipates Yahweh's subsequent departure from the temple, which is the major motif of chapters 8–11.

However, the weight of evidence seems to point toward a continuation of the people as the subject; they have moved far away from God. That view was already reflected in the translations of the LXX, the Syriac, the Targum, Aquila, and Theodotion. Greenberg observes that רָחַק מֵעַל "implies more than a physical distancing; it includes sentiments of indifference or hostility. ... Alternatively, there may be an allusion here to a compulsory alienation [of the Israelites] from the sanctuary in the form of exile."[4] It could also refer to the Israelites worshiping outside (away from) the temple at other sites. One may think of Jeremiah's reference (Jer 11:13) to gods as numerous as Judean towns and altars "as numerous as the streets of Jerusalem." The people may have thought their behavior was licit and that their deviant worship implied no denial of their faith in Yahweh. Is it not always so with heresies? But, as Allen observes, such worship would have been wicked not only because it is pagan but also because it is being practiced at locations other than the one sanctioned place of sacrifice, namely, the Jerusalem temple. "The God of Ezekiel cannot be associated with so liberal a notion."[5]

וְעוֹד תָּשׁוּב תִּרְאֶה תּוֹעֵבוֹת גְּדֹלוֹת׃—This clause will be repeated in 8:13 and 8:15. It means "*thou shalt see yet* greater abominations" (BDB, s.v. שׁוּב, Qal, 8; cf. *HALOT*, s.v. שׁוּב, Qal, 5; Joüon, § 177 b). When the verb שׁוּב is coordinated with a second verb (here: תִּרְאֶה), it can mean "to do again," especially when accompanied by the adverb עוֹד, "yet, more, even." Following that phrase, the adjective גָּדוֹל has comparative force ("greater"). This comparative force is made explicit in 8:15 with the prepositional phrase מֵאֵלֶּה, "greater *than these*."

8:7 חֹר־אֶחָד—Here and in 8:8 the numeral אֶחָד functions as an indefinite article, hence "*a* hole" (8:7) and "*an* entranceway" (8:8).[6]

---

[3] Cf. Jerome, *Commentariorum in Ezechielem* (PL 25:79).

[4] Greenberg, *Ezekiel*, 1:168–69. The idiom occurs in Jer 2:5; 27:10; Ezek 8:6; 11:15; 44:10; Joel 2:20; 4:6 (ET 3:6); Prov 5:8.

[5] Allen, *Ezekiel*, 1:143.

[6] The entire last half of 8:7 (following "the court" with *athnach*) is missing in the LXX. Critics have proposed various reconstructions of the "original" text based on the LXX. Often they assume that the narrative moved originally from 8:7a (the prophet was brought to the entrance of the court) to 8:9 (God's order for him to enter). The simple sequence was supposedly complicated by an early addition of 8:8 and a later one of 8:7b (according to, for example, Zimmerli, *Ezekiel*, 1:218–19, 240). The reconstructed shorter text does have the advantage of being closer structurally to the other three scenes in this part of the vision. But

8:8　חֲתָר־נָא בַקִּ֔יר[dd]—"Dig through" translates the imperative of חָתַר (which can be distinguished from חָפַר, simply "dig"). This verb is precisely the one required in the context, that is, in the sense of "enlarge." Already St. Jerome proposed the most likely meaning of 8:7b–8: the prophet is commanded to enlarge the existing hole in the wall until it becomes large enough for him to squeeze through.[7]

8:9　הַתּוֹעֵבוֹת הָרָעוֹת—The adjective רַע can imply moral and/or religious "evil," but in this context that seems too weak a translation, so I have used "vile" (so also RSV, ESV).

8:10　כָּל־תַּבְנִית—The noun תַּבְנִית can refer to the *figure, image … of idols in form of animals* (BDB, 3, under the root בנה), as also in Deut 4:17–18 and Ps 106:20, or to idolatrous images of people (Deut 4:16; Is 44:13). The end of the verse will make clear that these figures were not statues, but were "engraved on the wall" (see the textual note on this phrase below). תַּבְנִית is in construct with three following nouns, indicating three kinds of figures: of "creeping things" (רֶמֶשׂ) and of "beasts" (וּבְהֵמָה) and of "the fecal deities" (גִּלּוּלֵי). See the textual note on "fecal deities" in Ezek 6:4.

The LXX omits a translation of כָּל־תַּבְנִית, which produces a smoother reading, but that hardly proves that Hebrew copyists amplified the original by adding the phrase.

רֶמֶשׂ וּבְהֵמָה שֶׁקֶץ—In Gen 1:24–26 the nouns רֶמֶשׂ (singular as collective: "creeping things") and בְּהֵמָה (singular as collective: "beasts") refer to animals that were part of God's good creation and were not intrinsically unclean or evil. In Gen 1:24 "beasts" (בְּהֵמָה) and "creeping things" (רֶמֶשׂ) occur in the reverse order as here. Deut 4:16–18 forbids the making of images (תַּבְנִית) of beasts (בְּהֵמָה) and creeping things (רֶמֶשׂ) using the same phraseology here in Ezek 8:10. There it is not the creatures themselves but the making of idolatrous images of them that is evil.

In the phrase וּבְהֵמָה שֶׁקֶץ, the noun שֶׁקֶץ ("detestable thing") is in apposition to בְּהֵמָה ("beasts"), and so it is translated as an adjective: "detestable beasts." Alternatively, the two could be taken separately ("beasts and detestable things"), though one would expect שֶׁקֶץ to have a conjunctive *waw*.[8] In Lev 11:10–13, 20, 23, 41–42, שֶׁקֶץ refers to those creatures that the Israelites were forbidden to eat because they were declared unclean (cf. also Lev 7:21). In the obscure verse Is 66:17, שֶׁקֶץ pertains to some idolatrous practice.

מְחֻקֶּה עַל־הַקִּ֔יר[dd]—The Pual participle of חקה leaves some uncertainty about precisely what kind of process was used in making the wall representations. The root

---

we have already noted that none of the four is exactly like another. Hence there is no reason why this scene should not be longer—and perhaps compensated for by the unusually short third scene that follows (8:14–15).

[7]　Jerome, *Commentariorum in Ezechielem* (PL 25:80).

The LXX omits the reference to the "wall" (קִיר) both here and in 8:10. In 8:10 the LXX renders "on the wall" (עַל־הַקִּיר) as "on it." So Zimmerli (*Ezekiel*, 1:219) supposes that the LXX did not understand קִיר, even though it is a quite common Hebrew word! The LXX does translate it correctly three times in chapter 12 (12:5, 7, 12). Obviously, the LXX either translated from some different prototype, or some other distortion beyond recovery occurred in the LXX.

[8]　Greenberg, *Ezekiel*, 1:165, takes the two words serially.

seems to imply something scratched, incised, carved, or engraved. Inlaid tiles are a possibility. I have used "engraved," which implies something formal and planned, not mere graffiti.

סָבִיב | סָבִיב:—Ezekiel uses the double סָבִיב also in 37:2 and frequently in chapters 40–43. The duplication is emphatic; here it implies that the engraved figures covered the walls. The only occurrence of double סָבִיב outside Ezekiel is in 2 Chr 4:3.

8:11 The parenthetical remark about Jaazaniah separates the subject ("seventy men") from its predicate participle (עֹמְדִים, "were standing"). The LXX smoothes out the syntax a bit. Critics often delete the parenthetical remark as a gloss,[9] but Block sagely observes that "if smoothness were a test of authenticity, most parenthetical clauses would be eliminated."[10]

מִקְטֶרֶת, "censer," is a late Hebrew word, used elsewhere in the OT only in 2 Chr 26:19, although the verbal root קָטַר is ancient and found throughout the OT. The more common classical Hebrew noun for "censer" was מַחְתָּה, a "fire pan" for carrying the coals upon which the incense was placed (e.g., Ex 25:38; 38:3; Lev 10:1; 16:12).

The noun עָתָר is a hapax legomenon, and hence its meaning is not entirely certain. It seems to be cognate to Arabic and Syriac words meaning "scent, perfume, vapor," especially of sacrifices, and it may have had pagan overtones. The LXX does not translate עָתָר, perhaps indicating that the translators did not know what it means.[11] Critics often assume that עֲנָן is a gloss added to explain the meaning of עָתָר, but that assumption is without justification.

8:12 אִישׁ בְּחַדְרֵי מַשְׂכִּיתוֹ—The noun חֶדֶר is quite generic for a "room," although tending to imply some inner room, such as a "bedroom" (e.g., Song 1:4; 3:4). In this context, the word might imply a space set aside as a sort of chapel, or simply some recess, niche, closet, or so on, which had been pressed into service ad hoc for religious purposes. The construction with the plural חַדְרֵי ("chambers") in construct with the singular מַשְׂכִּיתוֹ ("his image") is unusual. It apparently arises from the ambiguity of the distributive אִישׁ, "each/every," which is singular but pertains to all seventy of the elders. The ancient versions generally have a singular ("chamber"), but probably only for idiomatic reasons. I have retained the MT's ambiguity in my translation. The infrequent noun מַשְׂכִּית is one of the many Hebrew words for a type of idol and refers to a relief carved on stone. It appears in idolatrous contexts in Lev 26:1 and Num 33:52. A cognate, meaning "statue," is also known in Aramaic.

8:14 The third temple scene (8:14–15) is described most briefly of all. Structurally, it balances the extraordinarily long and detailed one preceding (8:7–13) and prepares for the climactic one in 8:16–18.

Ezekiel is brought to a gateway on the north, but it may be futile to attempt to determine precisely where this gateway was located. The whole section (8:5–18) gives the impression that we are gradually moving closer to the inner court of the temple

---

[9] Cf. Zimmerli, *Ezekiel*, 1:220.

[10] Block, *Ezekiel*, 1:288, n. 30.

[11] The LXX translates וַעֲתַר עֲנַן־הַקְּטֹרֶת by καὶ ἡ ἀτμὶς τοῦ θυμιάματος, which is also its translation of just עֲנַן הַקְּטֹרֶת (without עָתָר) in Lev 16:13.

itself. That is explicitly where the final scene (8:16–18) is located. Therefore, in this part of the vision, we are probably situated just outside it.

הַנָּשִׁים—The Hebrew has the definite article with "the women," as I have literally translated it. (The LXX omits the article.) A similar use of הַנָּשִׁים followed by a participle occurs in 2 Ki 23:7, where "the women were weaving" something ("hangings" according to KJV and RSV; the MT has "houses," and the versions make what appear to be many guesses) for the worship of Asherah that involved male cult prostitutes at the house of Yahweh. The Hebrew article can be used with nouns that are "*definite in the imagination*," marking certain people who are "understood to be present or vividly portraying someone whose identity is not otherwise indicated" (Waltke-O'Connor, § 13.5.1e). It may be that this kind of mourning was especially associated with women, or the article could imply a semiprofessional club or sorority that devoted itself to this ritual. In any event, most of the information we have about Tammuz concerns women who were mythologically involved with him.

יֹשְׁבוֹת—The first predicate participle indicates that the women were "sitting," which often was the posture of mourners (cf. Ezek 26:16; Jonah 3:6; Job 2:8).

מְבַכּוֹת אֶת־הַתַּמּוּז:—The second predicate participle (feminine plural) is the Piel of בָּכָה. The Piel occurs elsewhere only in Jer 31:15, where the feminine singular participle is followed by a prepositional phrase, מְבַכָּה עַל־בָּנֶיהָ (Rachel is bitterly "weeping over her sons" because they are no more; cf. Mt 2:18). The common Qal means "weep, mourn, bewail," and the Piel apparently has the same meaning. The Hebrew has the sign of the direct object and the definite article with "Tammuz," suggesting that the usual translation, "mourning *for* Tammuz," is not quite correct. Literally, the women were "bewailing the Tammuz." Perhaps the construction (Piel participle and direct object) has a particular nuance, such as intensive or prolonged mourning, or the performance of a special type of lament or liturgy bewailing the god. One might compare our idiom "chant the Te Deum." Alternatively, the article ("the Tammuz") may polemically reduce the proper noun to a common one, such as we often meet in "the *baals* and the *ashtoreths*" (e.g., 1 Sam 12:10), thus "reducing them to fetishes."[12] In my translation, I have retained the transitive sense of the verb, but not the article.

8:16   The final temple scene is easy to locate. We find ourselves inside the gateway in the inner court, specifically "between the vestibule [הָאוּלָם] and the altar." (Most translations render הָאוּלָם as "the porch," but that strikes me as too jejune for a temple.) The אוּלָם was akin to the "narthex" in a church. It was the outermost chamber of the three parts (Holy of Holies; Holy Place or sanctuary; vestibule) of Solomon's temple. For its construction, see 1 Ki 6:3; 7:19, 21. (The tabernacle only had the Holy of Holies and the Holy Place and lacked a vestibule.) The eschatological temple too will have an אוּלָם (Ezekiel 40 passim).

This was an area reserved for priests. Already for the tabernacle it appears that laymen could not approach the sanctuary more closely than the great altar of burnt offering,[13] and these men are closer to the vestibule than was the altar. Joel 2:17 specifies that

---

[12]   Greenberg, *Ezekiel*, 1:171.

[13]   See figure 6 in Kleinig, *Leviticus*, 48.

"between the vestibule and the altar" is the area where the priests gathered for lamentation at a public ceremony of repentance—precisely what should be going on in the space as Ezekiel watches. In Mt 23:35 Jesus refers to the murder of the priest-prophet Zechariah as especially heinous partly because it occurred in this same area.

Ezekiel estimates that "twenty-five men" have gathered in this space for their pagan rite. The preposition כְּ in כְּעֶשְׂרִים וַחֲמִשָּׁה can mean "about," but sometimes it is used to introduce an exact number.[14] The LXX reads just "twenty," and some have favored that number, both as more suitable as an approximation and on the assumption that sun worship had begun in Mesopotamia, where the number twenty was sacred to Shamash, the sun god. But that eastern provenance for sun worship has been challenged, and Greenberg points out that twenty-five is a favorite number of Ezekiel, "who uses it more frequently than any other biblical author."[15] The same number of "twenty-five men" (but different men than the ones here) appear again in this vision in 11:1, where the number does not have the preposition כְּ.

אֲחֹרֵיהֶם אֶל־הֵיכַל יְהוָה—The plural of אָחוֹר is uncommon in the OT. אָחוֹר can refer to the "hinder side, back part" (BDB) or "hindquarter, backside" of men (only here in the OT) or animals (the oxen in 1 Ki 7:25). The Talmud interpreted the biblical phrase to mean "that they [the men] uncovered themselves and committed a nuisance" toward God.[16] The rabbinic Hebrew מתריזין, rendered "committed a nuisance," can literally mean "to have diarrhea" (Jastrow, s.v. תָּרַז).

מִשְׁתַּחֲוִיתֶם—Different forms of this verb occur in 46:2, 3, 9 and often elsewhere in the OT for the true worship of Yahweh. Older grammarians explained them as forms of the Hithpael of שָׁחָה with metathesis of the *taw* and *shin*. Modern philologists accept that the root is חָוָה and that the conjugation is Hishtaphel, with an infixed *taw*. This is the only verb to occur in that conjugation in the OT, although Hishtaphel forms regularly occur in other Semitic languages.

The form here clearly means "prostrating themselves" but requires comment. The normal form of the masculine plural participle is מִשְׁתַּחֲוִים, which several non-Masoretic Hebrew manuscripts read here, and which occurs in several other OT passages (e.g., Gen 37:9; Zeph 1:5; Esther 3:2). The form here is identical but with the addition of a *taw* (-תֶ-) in its ending, which makes its ending the normal suffix of the second masculine plural perfect of a third-*he* verb (-יתֶם). Medieval grammarians call this a "mixed form," that is, a form that combines the prefix of the participle (-מִ) and the suffix of the perfect.

8:17   הֲנָקֵל לְבֵית יְהוּדָה מֵעֲשׂוֹת—The Niphal of קָלַל means "to be small, insignificant, trivial." הֲנָקֵל probably is the Niphal participle (so GKC, § 67 t; Joüon, § 82 c), rather than the perfect, and it has the interrogative -הֲ. To express the comparative idea

---

[14]   For example, כְּ introduces the exact number of thirty-six men in Josh 7:5. See the textual note on that phrase in Josh 7:5 in Harstad, *Joshua*, 303.

[15]   Greenberg, *Ezekiel*, 1:172. The number occurs in Ezek 8:16; 11:1; 40:1, 13, 21, 25, 29, 30, 33, 36; 45:12. These are eleven of the twenty-five occurrences of "twenty-five" or "twenty-fifth" in the Bible.

[16]   *Yoma*, 77a (Soncino ed.).

of "too small/little" (or "too big/much") Hebrew can use it (and other expressions) together with the preposition מִן attached to an infinitive construct (here: מֵעֲשׂוֹת). See GKC, § 133 c, and Joüon, § 141 i. The construction here asks, "Is it too trivial for the house of Judah to commit" the temple abominations? A similar sarcastic question with the interrogative *he* on the same Niphal participle (הֲנָקֵל) is in 1 Ki 16:31: "Was it too small/trivial for him [Ahab] to walk in the sins of Jeroboam the son of Nebat that he [also] took for his wife Jezebel … and he served Baal and worshiped him?" The same construction with נָקֵל (without the interrogative *he*) and מִן on an infinitive occurs in Is 49:6: "it is too small" for the Suffering Servant only to restore the tribes of Israel; God will also make him "a light for the nations" so that the Lord's salvation may extend "to the end of the earth" (cf. also 2 Ki 20:10).

כִּי־מָלְאוּ אֶת־הָאָרֶץ חָמָס—Usually the Qal of מָלֵא is intransitive, as in "the earth *was full* of violence" (Gen 6:13). Ezekiel says essentially the same thing with מָלֵא in 7:23; 9:9.[a] But the Qal of מָלֵא can also be transitive, as here: "*fill* the land with violence."

(a) Cf. also
Is 1:15; Jer
23:10; 51:5;
Ps 26:10

וַיָּשֻׁבוּ לְהַכְעִיסֵנִי—More literally this might be rendered "they keep returning to provoke me." שׁוּב is often used idiomatically with another verb to express repetition of the action denoted by the other verb (BDB, Qal 8), hence "they keep on provoking me" or "they provoke me more and more." Compare תָּשׁוּב תִּרְאֶה in 8:6, 13, 15, meaning "you shall see again/even greater …"

Many observe correctly that this use of the Hiphil infinitive construct of כָּעַס occurs in Deuteronomy of Israel provoking Yahweh to anger (Deut 4:25; 9:18; 31:29; and finite forms in Deut 32:16; cf. God provoking the people to anger in Deut 32:21). The Hiphil is also fairly common in 1–2 Kings in the same sense, sometimes with a first common singular suffix, as here ("provoke me"). While it is undeniable that Ezekiel's diction is generally quite distinguishable from that labeled "deuteronomic," we have already seen instances where Ezekiel evidences a clear knowledge of Deuteronomy and the rest of the Torah of Moses, especially Leviticus,[17] as we would expect from his lineage as a priest (Ezek 1:3).

The LXX lacks a translation of this clause, inevitably triggering critical scholars to issue a spate of emendations. Zimmerli argues that the two Hebrew words represent a later insertion to smooth out the connection between the preceding social sin ("violence") and the following cultic(?) action with the "branch,"[18] but one must have evidence to make such a charge.

Frequently in Ezekiel, cultic and social sins are condemned side by side (so in chapter 9; see also 22:4; 33:25–26). But here the previous examples of cultic misbehavior and the additional social sins ("violence") of the nation are eclipsed in gravity by the final cultic insult to Yahweh with the "branch." "The provoking of Yahweh to anger provides the final scaffolding for a literary framework borrowed from Deut 32:16 ([and 32:]21) and first represented in [Ezek 8:]3."[19]

---

[17] For example, echoes of Leviticus 26 and Deuteronomy 28 and 32 reverberate throughout Ezek 5:16–17 (see the textual notes on those verses).

[18] Zimmerli, *Ezekiel*, 1:221–22.

[19] Allen, *Ezekiel*, 1:145.

וְהִנָּם שֹׁלְחִים אֶת־הַזְּמוֹרָה אֶל־אַפָּם:—This final clause of 8:17 is a famous crux. Neither among ancient or modern commentators is there any consensus as to its exact meaning.

The first part is clear enough: the pronoun on הִנָּם (literally, "behold, they") serves as the subject of the masculine participle of שָׁלַח, which can mean "to reach out, extend" a rod or something else held with the hand.

The two major problems are (1) the reading אַפָּם and (2) the meaning of הַזְּמוֹרָה.

The MT reads אַפָּם, "their nose." However, according to a Masoretic note, this is one of eighteen (by one count) תִּיקּוּנֵי סוֹפְרִים, "corrections of the scribes" in the OT. These "scribes" were textual scholars and copyists who probably antedated the Masoretes of the sixth–tenth centuries A.D. and the Masoretic Kethib-Qere system they developed for recording textual variants. Most of the "corrections of the scribes" are in verses with language that could be deemed offensive to God. In this instance, the Jewish tradition may suggest that the original text was אַפִּי, "my [Yahweh's] nose,"[20] which could be an objectionable anthropomorphism of God or describe an obscene gesture toward God.

However, many scholars question whether the "corrections of the scribes" really refer to changes made in the Hebrew text. The "correction" may in fact be a Jewish scribal explanation of the meaning of a euphemism in the Hebrew text, which the scribes did not alter.[21] Hence the MT may indeed be the original text. In this case, the scribes may be saying that even though the Hebrew text is (and has always been) אַפָּם ("their nose"), that reading is a euphemism, and the meaning of that euphemism (literally, "lifting the branch to their nose") is that the worshipers were lifting the branch to Yahweh's nose. Hence the meaning may be that Yahweh is saying, "They are even sticking the branch up my nose!"

The details of the exegesis of the clause will depend on one's decision on this textual matter. The context clearly suggests some provocative gesture. An idolatrous rite that the Israelites did to themselves ("to their nose") would not be nearly so insulting as something they did personally to Yahweh ("to my [Yahweh's] nose"). For that reason, my translation gives the meaning that Jewish tradition claims is the original text, or is the meaning of the euphemism in the MT, which may be the original text. Whatever the gesture was, it appears to have been part of the sun worship being described in 8:16–17 as the worst of the four "abominations" in the vision of chapter 8. The rabbis regarded it as obscene and blasphemous, hence it became one of the "corrections of the scribes."

---

[20] According to *Tanhuma, Beshalah,* 16, "the verse (Ezek. 8:17) '*to My nose*' was corrected by them: '*to their nose,*'" but this and other verses listed "were corrected by the men of the Great Synagogue" (Lieberman, *Hellenism in Jewish Palestine,* 29, citing the Hebrew in n. 6). That a change was made to Ezek 8:17 is also stated in *Mekilta, Shirta,* 6 (*Mekilta de Rabbi Ishmael* [ed. Jacob Z. Lauterbach; Philadelphia: Jewish Publication Society of America, 1933], 44, line 25 of the Hebrew).

[21] One may see the discussion in Lieberman, *Hellenism in Jewish Palestine,* 28–37; Tov, *Textual Criticism of the Hebrew Bible,* 65–67; and Yeivin, *Introduction to the Tiberian Masorah,* § 89.

In the ancient versions it is not clear whether the translators were aware of the alleged scribal alteration, were translating freely, or translated from a different Hebrew textual tradition. The LXX has "and behold, they were as turning up the nose/showing contempt" (καὶ ἰδοὺ αὐτοὶ ὡς μυκτηρίζοντες). The Vulgate has *et ecce adplicant ramum ad nares suas*, "and behold, they place a branch to their noses." The Targum has "and behold, they were bringing shame/nakedness [בַּהֲתָא] to their noses."

Interpretation of the clause also depends on how we understand זְמוֹרָה. Elsewhere it means "branch of a vine," as in Ezek 15:2. Here it may be used figuratively or metaphorically.

Some medieval commentators followed the Talmud's scatological interpretation of the men's "backsides" in 8:16 (see the textual note above) and took the expression here as a figure for breaking wind.[22] If the men were passing gas, their idolatrous worship truly was a stench in God's nostrils. Many moderns have endorsed that understanding (Zimmerli,[23] Eichrodt,[24] and a number of others). Equally ancient, with its roots in Jewish tradition, is a phallic interpretation, taking זְמוֹרָה as "rod" in the sense of penis. In the light of Ezekiel's use of frank, even crude language elsewhere (e.g., 4:12–15; "fecal deities" in, e.g., 6:4; chapters 16 and 23), such interpretations are thoroughly credible. Ezekiel may well have been quoting some popular euphemism for flatulence, but there is no way to prove or disprove such understandings.

Many recent interpreters have thought that the clause simply describes another pagan cultic gesture. Job 31:26–27 refers to hand-kissing the mouth in connection with worship of the sun or the moon (Job swears, literally, that "my hand has not kissed my mouth" in idolatrous worship). Some seek a parallel in the Akkadian idiom *laban appi*, which involved both hand and nose and was intended to express humility before either gods or humans. The so-called "Bavian relief" shows Sennacherib worshiping Assyrian gods, holding an object that may be a branch to his nose.[25] From Syria comes a representation of a king holding a flower on a stalk in front of his beard and clenching his right fist in front of his mouth as he worships heavenly bodies.[26]

Greenberg argues that these cultic parallels are irrelevant because the obscure clause is not part of the idolatrous rites described earlier in 8:17, but pertains to the immediately preceding social crimes ("violence").[27] Personally, I am inclined to say "both and": the religious apostasy and social corruption together have become intolerable before the holy and righteous God of Israel.

8:18 The two idioms "my eye will not pity, and I will have no compassion" are the same as in 5:11; 7:4, 9; and 9:10 (see the textual note on them in 5:11).

---

[22] Lieberman, *Hellenism in Jewish Palestine,* 33, n. 37, cites some rabbinic sources for this and other rabbinic interpretations of the meaning as obscene.

[23] Zimmerli, *Ezekiel,* 1:244.

[24] Eichrodt, *Ezekiel,* 128.

[25] Mayer I. Gruber, "Akkadian *laban appi* in the Light of Art and Literature," *JANESCU* 7 (1975): 73–83.

[26] *ANEP,* § 281.

[27] Greenberg, *Ezekiel,* 1:172–73.

Since the last resolution by Yahweh in this verse ("They will call …") is missing in the LXX, many critics assert that it is a duplication from 9:1, but the repetition serves to bind chapter 8 to the next section of the vision, chapter 9.

Commentary

Introduction to Ezekiel 8–11

By any reckoning, the visionary narrative of chapters 8–11 is a pivotal one in the book. It probably is not as well-known to the average reader as the call vision (chapter 1) and the vision of the dry bones (chapter 37). But that, of course, does not diminish its intrinsic importance.

I have often referred to these chapters as the second part of the "internal outline" of the book that centers on the "incarnational" form of Yahweh, namely, his כָּבוֹד, "Glory."[28] Chapters 8–11 relate how Yahweh's "Glory" abandons the Jerusalem temple to destruction. The counterpart is the return of the "Glory" to the eschatological temple in Ezekiel's vision in 43:1–4.

Chapters 8–11 are also important in illustrating the "vertical typology" intrinsic to biblical thought. Greenberg summarizes it well:

> The visionary destruction is a glimpse, rare in prophecy, of the "upper story" of events (cf., e.g., I Kings 22:19–23). Human agents would eventually execute judgment on Jerusalem and Judah, but they would only be translating a prior heavenly reality into an earthly one. Basically, the enemy was God; the Babylonian army was but a later projection of his celestial executioners.[29]

Ezekiel 8–11 contains many scenes that are echoed in the book of Revelation, where the apostle John is given visions of the same heavenly realities witnessed by Ezekiel. These echoes reveal the continuity between OT and NT prophecy. They also confirm that Ezekiel's visions ultimately center in the person and work of Christ, as the visions of St. John do immediately. One may compare the divine "man" in Ezek 8:2–3 to the appearance of the risen Christ in Rev 1:13–16 and probably Rev 10:1–3 (cf. also Dan 10:4–6 and Acts 9:3–7; 26:13–18). Particularly striking is the correspondence between Ezekiel 9 and Rev 7:1–8; 9:4, where the repentant Israelites (Ezek 9:4), corresponding to baptized believers in Christ (Revelation), are sealed with the mark of Christ on their foreheads (the *taw* in Ezek 9:4 is shaped like a cross). All those without the mark are subject to God's judgments, but those with the divine seal shall be saved, even though they must endure various kinds of sufferings while God pours out his wrath upon unbelieving humanity.

Chapters 8–11 may be outlined in various ways, but there seems to be considerable agreement that a chiastic arrangement, accenting the visionary character of the whole, frames the entire section:

---

[28] For the incarnational Glory of Yahweh, see further the textual notes on 1:26; the commentary on 1:26–28; and "Outline and Theological Emphases" in the introduction, which also explains the "internal outline" of the book.

[29] Greenberg, *Ezekiel*, 1:202–3.

A 8:1a: The context of the vision (date, location, audience of exiled elders)
  B 8:1b: The beginning of the vision (God's hand falls on the prophet so that he sees the vision)
    C 8:2–3: The divine man appears, and the Spirit transports Ezekiel to Jerusalem in divine visions
      D 8:4: The appearance of the divine Glory
      D' 11:22–23: The appearance of the divine Glory
    C' 11:24a: The Spirit transports the prophet back to Jerusalem in a divine vision
  B' 11:24b: The vision goes up from the prophet (that is, it ends)
A' 11:25: The prophet tells the exiles what he has seen

Within this chiastic framework, at least three aspects of the vision may be distinguished: (1) the departure of the כָּבוֹד, "Glory" (9:3; 10:1–22; 11:22–23); (2) the various idolatrous abominations occurring in the temple (8:5–18); and (3) the judgments upon Jerusalem (9:1–11).

There is other material in the four chapters, however, that does not easily fit into an outline and sometimes even seems disruptive of the narrative flow. The narrative about the movement of the departing Glory comprises just a few verses (8:4; 9:3; 10:4, 15, 18–19; 11:22–23) and long descriptive passages intervene.

Some commentators perceive a problem in that chapter 8 is concerned with cultic offenses, while in 11:1–6 members of the nobility ("leaders of the people," 11:1) are accused of social crimes. However, liturgical and social abuses go hand in hand. The perception of a problem does not rest on a biblical distinction, but on modern ideas—that theology and worship practices are somehow less important than societal "justice," or that an individual can engage in false worship without doing damage to the church at large and to society.

Various critics find still other alleged inconsistencies. Often they devote pages to attempting to establish an "original" biblical text before later additions and modifications supposedly took place. In my judgment, such approaches generally tell us much more about the commentator than about the text. There is no a priori reason why some editorial work might not have occurred when the author issued the final form of his work, but even if something might qualify as a "gloss," there is no reason why the glossator might not have been Ezekiel himself.

One major issue is whether a remnant will be spared. Some passages might seem to imply that all Israel shall be annihilated (e.g., 5:1–4; 7:1–13; 8:18; Yahweh's answer in 9:9–10 to Ezekiel's question about this in 9:8; and Ezekiel's perception in 11:13). However, earlier passages had hinted at a remnant (e.g., 5:10; 6:8–10), as do some other passages soon after the temple vision (12:16; 14:12–23). So it is not inconsistent for chapters 8–11 to include that theme, as when the penitent are marked with a cross so they will not be executed with the infidels (9:4, 6, 11).

Allegedly even more disjunctive is the salvation oracle about a regenerated remnant in 11:14–20, which contrasts with the predominant theme of judgment throughout Ezekiel 1–24. However, this salvation oracle is an excellent example of what I like to call the "alternation of weal and woe," the dialectic of Law and Gospel that is found in virtually all of the prophets. Later chapters expand on parts of that oracle, such as Yahweh's promised gifts of a new "heart" and "S/spirit" (11:19), elaborated in 36:26–27 and 37:1–14.

Clearly, the text of chapters 8–11 presents itself as a single visionary experience. And the very fact that we are dealing with a vision should make us reluctant to press ordinary principles of logic and chronology too hard. The theme of Yahweh's abandonment of Jerusalem obviously dominates the entire section. Even most of chapter 11, which theoretically might have been experienced independently (later) by the prophet, fits the context; it shares the concern of chapters 8–10 about the inhabitants of Jerusalem before its final fall. Furthermore, the prophet's personal interactions with the Jerusalemites described in chapter 11 could only have been possible in visionary form.[30] At very least, it can confidently be argued that there is nothing about any of the material in chapters 8–11 in which Ezekiel could not have been personally involved. Hence, further speculation about possible editorial work must be regarded as unproductive.

The Context and Beginning of the Vision (8:1)

8:1 The vision is dated exactly fourteen months after Ezekiel's first vision (1:1–2). On our calendar the date would be about September 18, 592 B.C. In the interval since his first vision, the prophet clearly had become recognized and respected as a prophet: "the elders of Judah were sitting in front of" him (8:1), evidently waiting for an oracle—although there probably was no way for Ezekiel or his audience to know when—or even if—one would come. We will encounter the same scene in 14:1; 20:1; and 33:30–31. In 20:1 the elders are specifically reported to have inquired of God through Ezekiel. They never received the message of Jerusalem's deliverance they vainly kept hoping for even after news of the city's fall had reached them, as 33:30–31 makes clear.

The "elders of Judah" (8:1) are apparently members of whatever system of self-government the exiles established to substitute for that of the homeland. Jeremiah too mentions the "elders" in exile as among those who were recipients of the letter he sent ("the remnant of the elders of the exiles," Jer 29:1). The book of Ezra (5:5, 9; 6:7, 8, 14) indicates that this system of rule continued into at least the early postexilic period.

The expression "the *hand* of the Lord Yahweh *fell* upon me" (Ezek 8:1) is unique.[31] By it Ezekiel indicates the suddenness of the onset of the vision, and perhaps also its overpowering nature (cf. "the hand of Yahweh upon me was strong" in 3:14; cf. also Is 8:11). The expression is more dramatic than "the hand of Yahweh was upon me" in Ezek 3:22, and it contrasts to the usual "the

---

[30] Radical critics once commonly argued that Ezekiel actually exercised all or part of his ministry in Jerusalem, in which case he could have interacted physically with Jerusalemites as pictured in chapter 11. However, this commentary accepts Ezekiel's statements in his book (beginning in 1:1) that his ministry and life was among the exiles in Babylon.

[31] Only here in the OT is יָד, "hand," the subject of נָפַל, "to fall." In other passages Ezekiel says that Yahweh's "hand" (יָד) "was/came" (הָיָה) upon him (1:3; 3:22; 33:22; 37:1; 40:1).

Word of Yahweh came to me" (e.g., 1:3; 3:16; 6:1; 7:1). The verb (נָפַל) will be used again in 11:5 when the prophet states, "The Spirit of Yahweh fell upon me." When the vision ends and Ezekiel relates its contents to the elders in 11:24–25, it appears that he had remained in body in exile during the vision, and so we are dealing with something like a trance. Apparently the prophet was not physically transported to Jerusalem to see what was going on there. (In contrast, evidently in 3:14–15, Ezekiel was physically translated from one place by the Kebar Canal to another nearby location.)

The Divine Man Reappears and the Spirit Transports Ezekiel (8:2–3a)

8:2   Ezekiel describes the same human, yet also supernatural, form of Yahweh's Glory he had perceived at the end of the inaugural vision (1:26b–28). This is no angelic messenger or interpreter as in chapters 40–48, but clearly Yahweh himself in a form "like a man" (8:2). *This is another appearance of the preincarnate Christ.*[32] Here we have the "same groping for vocabulary, the prominence of terms for brilliance," and the same division of the figure's appearance like electrum above his waist and like fire below his waist as in 1:26–28.[33]

8:3a   What is new in this theophany (compared to chapters 1–3) is that the divine "man" stretches out "the form of a hand" to transport Ezekiel to Jerusalem. Whereas in 8:1 Yahweh's "hand" had been more metaphorical for God's overwhelming power, here it takes on more concrete form. But since it is God's, we still meet a certain reticence about naming it; Ezekiel calls it "the *form* of a hand" (rather than the straightforward "Yahweh's hand"). The Hebrew expression occurs only here and (referring to the humanlike hand of the cherubim) in 10:8. תַּבְנִית ("form") means a "structure," usually in the sense of a model, copy, miniature, and so on. It is so used of the "pattern" of the earthly tabernacle and its furnishings built as a "copy" or "type" of the heavenly prototype (Ex 25:9, 40, translated by τύπος, "type," in Acts 7:44; Heb 8:5) and also of the "plan" of Solomon's temple drawn up by David (1 Chr 28:11, 12; cf. 28:19). A similar sense occurs in Josh 22:28, where war is averted when the Transjordan tribes of Israel convince the Cisjordan Israelites that they have built an altar that is only a תַּבְנִית ("model, copy") of the one true altar of Yahweh; they promise not to offer sacrifice on the "copy," because then it would compete against the one orthodox altar.

The sense of תַּבְנִית ("form") in Ezek 8:3 is similar to its meaning ("figure, resemblance") in 8:10 and 10:8. It then parallels what Ezekiel otherwise expresses by דְּמוּת ("likeness") or מַרְאָה ("appearance"), both of which are com-

---

[32]   See further the textual notes on 1:26; the commentary on 1:26–28; and "Outline and Theological Emphases" in the introduction.

[33]   Block, *Ezekiel,* 1:279. Block notes that the order in 1:27 (above his waist discussed first) is reversed in 8:2 (below his waist described first).

mon in chapters 1 and 10 and are used to describe the divine vision in similitudes. Thus, Ezekiel saw what looked like a human hand, but one that belonged to no mere human; again, the "man" (8:2) is none other than the preincarnate Christ.

However, it is not the "hand" (יָד, 8:3) that transports Ezekiel to Jerusalem in the vision, but רוּחַ. The word may mean "wind," of course (as in 5:2, 10, 12), but in this context it surely must refer to the divine Spirit, who in the fullness of time would be revealed as the third person of the Trinity. See the textual notes on רוּחַ in 1:4, 12, and the commentary on 1:12–14. The fact that the "Spirit" (8:3) acts immediately after the appearance of the divine "man" (8:2) may be adduced to support the creedal explanations of the Trinity, particularly that the Holy Spirit "proceeds from the Father and the Son [*filioque*]" (Nicene Creed), and that *opera ad extra indivisa sunt*.[34]

Some commentators speculate whether or not the elders observed any levitation, but such a debate seems frivolous. Since it evidently was a vision internal to Ezekiel's mind (to the extent that we can even analyze such a phenomenon), the answer probably would be negative.

Nothing is said about whether the fiery "man" (8:2) accompanies Ezekiel on the journey, or, for that matter, about his location during the rest of Ezekiel's vision.

"The Statue of Jealousy" Opposes "the Glory of the God of Israel" (8:3b–4)

8:3b   This is Ezekiel's first sighting of "the statue of jealousy" (8:3), which is the first of the four abominations he will see in the temple. He will see the statue again in 8:5 in the first temple scene (8:5–6). The purpose of this initial sighting of this abomination is to place it in the starkest contrast to the divine "Glory" he sees immediately afterward in 8:4.

Ezekiel is set down at the north gate of the inner court. This "inner court" is mentioned again in 8:16 and 10:3. Ezek 10:5 refers to the "outer court." As we learn already in 2 Ki 21:5 and 23:12, by late monarchic times the Jerusalem temple had two courts. (Later Ezekiel will also envision two courts in the eschatological temple in 40:17–19 and 40:28–34.) The "gate of the inner court" (8:3) is the gateway (as שַׁעַר usually should be translated) through the inner wall by which one could enter the courtyard around the temple itself. There probably were at least two other entranceways; this one happened to be on the north. This one was probably very important: since it is usually assumed that the royal palace was on the north side of the temple, the king would have used it whenever he came to the temple to worship. It probably is the same as the "altar gate" in 8:5, because the great altar of sacrifice was visible through this gate, and sacrificial animals were slaughtered "on the north side of the al-

---

[34] This Latin clause means that the three persons of the Trinity are united and inseparable in the works of the triune God toward the created world.

tar before Yahweh" (Lev 1:11). Apparently, Ezekiel finds himself just outside this gate, that is, in the outer court just north of the entrance to the inner gate.[35]

There is considerable debate when it comes to tracing Ezekiel's route through the temple in the remainder of the vision of chapters 8–11. His route has been described as "zigzag."[36] Sometimes the problems seem to arise from simple *hyper*criticism; sometimes they may arise from our lack of full knowledge of the architecture and layout of the temple precincts; and throughout we must keep reminding ourselves that it is all a *vision.*

Furthermore, Ezekiel describes *four types of abominations* that are typical of what was happening in various sections of the Jerusalem community, and the order in which they are presented may have a logic of its own that is not intended to correspond to any particular route through the temple precincts. Since Ezekiel would have been trained to become a priest (1:3), he may well have had firsthand knowledge of these practices before being carried into captivity. There doubtless was enough communication between the exiles and those still in Jerusalem that the continuation of such behavior would be common knowledge.

The first thing that strikes Ezekiel's eye is a "statue" (סֵמֶל). The Hebrew word occurs in only two other contexts in the OT (although it is known in Phoenician in the sense of any statue of either a human or of a deity). In Deut 4:16 God had prohibited the construction of פֶּסֶל תְּמוּנַת כָּל־סָמֶל, "a graven image in the form of any statue," that is, any sculptured idol that detracted from exclusive worship of Yahweh. Moreover, that prohibition included any "representation of male or female" (תַּבְנִית זָכָר אוֹ נְקֵבָה, Deut 4:16), which would include any figure connected to the fertility cult (with its practices such as sacral prostitution).

We know that such a statue was made, in violation of that command. 2 Chr 33:7 refers to פֶּסֶל הַסֶּמֶל ("the carved image of the idol," ESV) that evil King Manasseh had erected in the Jerusalem temple. Probably Josiah removed it as part of his reformation after the rediscovery of the Torah in around 622 B.C. Although it is not explicitly mentioned again, Ezek 8:3 is reason enough to believe that its cult had returned under King Jehoiakim, and probably a majority of commentators think that it is the abomination referred to here.

Even more precise than 2 Chr 33:7 is the parallel text, 2 Ki 21:7, which describes Manasseh's idol as פֶּסֶל הָאֲשֵׁרָה, "the carved image of Asherah" (ESV). This reference indicates the gravity of the offense. Asherah is now quite well-known, both as the highest goddess in the Canaanite pantheon and as the consort of El, the highest god. She may be the "queen of heaven" (Jer 44:17–19, 25) worshiped by the Judean refugees who had fled to Egypt with Johanan (Je-

---

[35] Cf. the discussion by Zimmerli, *Ezekiel*, 1:237.

[36] Allen, *Ezekiel*, 1:139, cites a discussion by Siegfried Sprank, *Ezechielstudien* (BWAT 3.4; Stuttgart: Kohlhammer, 1926), who outlines a straight course, countering earlier proposals that he described as involving a "zigzag course."

remiah 43–44). The same word (אֲשֵׁרָה, "an Asherah," e.g., 1 Ki 16:33) is used of cult objects representing her, apparently sometimes sculpted, sometimes of trees, but apparently always made of wood.

In pagan mythology, Asherah was the mother of seventy lesser gods, including Baal. But in popular piety, she was apparently identified with Astarte as a goddess of fertility and worshiped alongside Baal (cf. 2 Ki 23:4). The OT frequently refers to and condemns the worship of her on the "high places" (בָּמוֹת), where she is the feminine principle alongside the masculine, which is represented either by the Baals (Judg 3:7; 6:26–30) or by מַצֵּבוֹת (cult pillars of stone; Deut 16:21–22; 1 Ki 14:23; and passim). Recent excavations have confirmed how widespread in popular religion a syncretism of Yahweh and Asherah had become. Both at a site called Kuntillet 'Ajrud in the Sinai and at Khirbet el-Kom, west of Hebron, inscriptions have been found speaking of Yahweh and "his Asherah."[37]

Thus, if the סֶמֶל in Ezek 8:3 is indeed an Asherah, as seems plausible, it is easy to understand why it represented the heart and core of Canaanite idolatry and the primary enemy of Yahweh as he sought the faithful and undivided love of his beloved people Israel. It is obvious why their adulterous love affair with Asherah would provoke the passionate outrage or "jealousy" (5:13; 8:3, 5) of the one true God, who was their jilted husband and who had married them in his grace despite their wretchedness (Ezekiel 16 and 23; note his "jealousy" in 16:38, 42; 23:25). Apparently a seated figure ("was seated," 8:3), she was a direct challenge to Yahweh, who was enthroned above the cherubim inside the Holy of Holies. Both Block and Greenberg observe how fitting it is that this alien goddess should be referred to by a foreign loan word (סֶמֶל).[38]

Since the statue represented the prostitution of Israel, one readily thinks of NT parallels. The church, the virgin bride of Christ, is called to exclusive fidelity to her faithful Lord and Bridegroom. His call requires the forsaking of all other lords and gods, notably those whose worship involves sexual immorality; Christians can have no union, syncretism, or compromise with them.[b]

8:4 But something else also catches the prophet's eye, which throws the apostasy just described into bold relief. It is almost as though Ezekiel deliberately takes note of the glaring contrast by placing this verse at this point. The adverb שָׁם ("there") repeated in both 8:3–4 explicitly links the two verses together. But Yahweh and the idol ultimately *cannot* coexist "there" simultaneously! It is finally the question of truth. For intrinsically "ecumenical," unionistic, or syncretistic paganism this might have been no problem, but for

(b) See, e.g.,
1 Cor
6:12–20;
10:6–22;
2 Cor
11:2–3;
Eph
5:21–33;
1 Jn 5:21;
Rev 2:14, 20

---

[37] The literature on Asherah is immense; I will call attention only to Walter A. Maier III, *ʾAšerah: Extrabiblical Evidence* (Harvard Semitic Monographs 37; Atlanta: Scholars, 1986). Unlike Maier, much contemporary critical scholarship simply assumes that such pagan syncretism or pluralism was standard Israelite practice until strict monotheism was introduced later, at which time the biblical narrative was composed or rewritten accordingly.

[38] Block, *Ezekiel*, 1:281; Greenberg, *Ezekiel*, 1:168.

Yahweh it was an utter impossibility. Yahweh's "incarnational" presence is often called just כְּבוֹד־יְהוָה, "the Glory of Yahweh," but here we have the כְּבוֹד אֱלֹהֵי יִשְׂרָאֵל, "the glory of the God of Israel," as a way of stressing that this Glory alone has the legitimate claim on "the Israel of God" (Gal 6:16), that is, the church of both Testaments. If Israel goes whoring after other gods, she ceases to be his people Israel. What is true of unbelieving ethnic Israel is all the more true of Gentiles should they forsake the God of Israel's exclusive claim on them through Jesus Christ (Romans 9–11).

This verse does not specify whether Ezekiel sees the entire throne-chariot that he had seen in the plain in chapter 1, or just the divine man who is the Glory (1:26–28). But the reference to a personage with a hand and a waist in 8:2 would indicate that the main focus from here through the end of chapter 11 is on the divine man, although aspects of the cherubim, wheels, and the rest of the vehicle from chapter 1 will reappear in chapter 10 (the cherubim are also in 9:3 and 11:22).

Four Scenes Reveal the Four Abominations in the Temple (8:5–18)

8:5–18   Block correctly observes that the rest of the chapter "forms one of the most tightly knit literary units in the entire book."[39] A tour guide points out four shocking pagan rites to the prophet. Ezekiel never explicitly identifies who the guide is, but several features indicate that he is Yahweh himself. In 8:5, the nearest antecedent to "he said to me" is the "God of Israel." In 8:6 the sanctuary has a first person pronominal suffix ("*my* sanctuary"), and in 8:17 the object suffix of "provoke" is also first person ("provoke *me*"). Finally, the conclusion in 8:18 repeats words ("my eye will not pity, and I will have no compassion") we heard from the mouth of Yahweh before, in 5:11 and 7:4, 9. That illustrates a favorite Ezekielian literary device, sometimes called "resumptive exposition." Already in 5:11 Yahweh had declared that he would punish the defilement of his sanctuary mercilessly, and in 8:18 he resumes the threat of merciless punishment against the backdrop of the brazen idolatries the prophet has observed in the temple in 8:5–17.

There are four scenes: 8:5–6; 8:7–13; 8:14–15; and 8:16–18. Each of the four scenes follows essentially the same pattern: the location; the abomination; Yahweh's question, "Do you see, son of man?"; and finally, "You will see even greater abominations" except for the fourth time, since the fourth is the greatest abomination. The first and second scenes begin with commands, followed by a report of the prophet's obedience. The second is rather complex, involving Ezekiel's own activity in digging through a wall into a dark room. The third is very simple. And the fourth serves as a conclusion to all four scenes, announcing Yahweh's resolve to pay no attention to any pleas for mercy.

The four scenes escalate in severity. This is because the locations of the abominations seem to move progressively from the probable location of the

---

[39]   Block, *Ezekiel*, 1:283.

first in the outer court closer and closer to the Holy of Holies. Also, the abominations become more hideous; the fourth and climactic one apparently involves an outrage done to Yahweh himself ("their backsides to the temple of Yahweh," 8:16; "sticking the branch up my nose!" 8:17).

As further introduction, we should note the three different expressions used for the temple. In 8:6 we have מִקְדָּשׁ, "sanctuary," referring to the entire temple compound. In 8:14 and 8:16 we meet בֵּית־יְהוָה, "the house of Yahweh," indicating the temple as Yahweh's earthly, "incarnational" dwelling, which had been usurped by idolatrous squatters, as it were. And finally twice in 8:16 we find הֵיכַל יְהוָה, "the temple of Yahweh." הֵיכַל can refer to a king's "palace" in secular usage, but when it is Yahweh's, it always refers to the temple, specifically the Holy Place or nave of the building. The three terms represent increasing degrees of sanctity as one moves from the entire compound inward toward the heart of the temple.

The First Temple Scene: "The Statue of Jealousy" Again (8:5–6)

8:5 In the first of the four scenes comprising the rest of the chapter, Ezekiel again sees "the statue of jealousy," which was the first abomination (see the commentary above on 8:3b–4). Three times 8:5 emphasizes the northerly direction. It may be coincidental, but there may also be a deliberate allusion to "Mount North," the modern Jebel Akra or the classical Mount Casius (today located on the Turkish-Syrian border, slightly inland from the Mediterranean). It was the Canaanite "Mount Olympus," the home of the gods and specifically (in this context) of Asherah, whose image appears to be the "statue." Yahweh, of course, had his own mountain, Mount Zion, which he had elected within the order of history, where a mythological nature goddess could have no legitimate role. In the fullness of time, Mount Zion would be the place where the incarnate Son of God (the divine man) would offer the all-sufficient sacrifice for the sins of the world, then rise again.

8:6 Depending on the interpretation of the "distancing" (see the textual note), this verse describes the statue either as alienating Yahweh from his own sanctuary (he cannot share his house with another object of worship) or as expressing the people's alienation of themselves from the sanctuary by their adulterous behavior. My translation favors the latter alternative, but the issue is debatable. The end result is the same in either case: the destruction of the temple after God abandons it because of the people's persistent apostasy.

The Second Temple Scene: Engraved Images on the Walls (8:7–13)

8:7 This second scene, revealing the second abomination in the temple, is the most detailed. The exact location of Ezekiel in the temple during this second part of the vision is impossible to determine precisely—all the more so because it is part of a vision. But since the previous vision had been "north of the altar gate" (8:5), here we would appear to be on the inner side of the gateway, facing the outer court of the temple. Perhaps while standing within the gateway itself, or near its exit, Ezekiel notices a curious hole in the wall.

8:8 Upon God's command to enlarge (see the textual note) the hole, the prophet discovers an "opening" or "entranceway" into another chamber. 1 Ki 6:5–6 mentions side chambers around the Solomonic temple, and Ezekiel will envision rooms along the walls of the outer court of the eschatological temple (Ezek 40:17). We are never informed of the purpose of these rooms, but they could have had any number of legitimate uses for preparation, maintenance, and storage for the divine worship liturgies (cf. the vestry, sacristy, and narthex of a church). One would suppose that the "entranceway" to which God directs the prophet was not the usual entrance into the room. From it Ezekiel would be able to observe what is happening in the room without himself being observed.

8:9–10 Ezekiel obeys Yahweh's command to enter the room and looks around. We will be informed in 8:12 that the room is dark, but he is still able to see the iconography and occupants of the room. The exact nature of what he sees is not entirely clear, nor is it clear what cult(s) the figures belong to. We are left to infer, but we have even less biblical data than we had for "the statue of jealousy" (8:3, 5). Perhaps the images are a conglomeration of all the alien cults flourishing in Jerusalem. There may be a deliberate contrast between them and the orthodox temple engravings of 1 Ki 6:29, 32, 35. Babylon's famous Ishtar gate had images of men, lions, and serpent-dragons, and scholars often adduce it as a parallel. The relevance of that parallel is supported by the reference to the Babylonian god Tammuz in Ezek 8:14, and to Judah-Oholibah lusting after Babylonians when she sees their pictures engraved in red in 23:14. Other scholars think of the thereomorphic (beast-shaped) deities of Egypt, often found in tomb niches. Canaanite influences and archaeological finds from northern Syria (Carchemish, Gozan) could also be cited. As for "the fecal deities" (8:10), see the textual note on them in 6:4.

What can be said with certainty is that the worship of "creeping things" and "beasts" turns the order of creation upside down. In Genesis 1 God had created "creeping things" and "beasts" (see the textual notes on Ezek 8:10). God then created man as the one who would rule and have dominion over these creatures (Gen 1:26–28). Here the human worshipers degrade themselves by submitting to these lesser creatures as their gods. This is the same process St. Paul describes:

> They exchanged the glory of the immortal God for the likeness of the image of mortal man and of birds and quadrupeds and reptiles. Therefore God gave them over in the lusts of their hearts to uncleanness, to the dishonoring of their bodies among themselves, who indeed exchanged the truth of God for a lie and worshiped and served the creature rather than the Creator, who is blessed forever! Amen. (Rom 1:23–25)

The apostle's reference to God's "glory" (Rom 1:23) may be compared to "the Glory of the God of Israel" in Ezek 8:4, and the "uncleanness" (Rom 1:24) to which the idolaters are consigned may recall the *detestable* beasts" in Ezek 8:10, since that Hebrew term (שֶׁקֶץ) refers to animals that are declared "unclean" in Lev 11:10–43.

8:11 Ezekiel sees that seventy men were "standing before" the images, and that phrase (עָמַד לִפְנֵי) itself often connotes worship.[40] The number seventy (seven times ten) may be partly symbolic of perfection (seven) and completeness (ten), thus representing the whole nation. The number immediately reminds one of the seventy who assisted Moses in governing the Israelites in the desert (Ex 24:1, 9; Num 11:16, 24, 25). One may also compare the seventy-one members of the postexilic Sanhedrin[41] and the seventy(-two) disciples whom Jesus sent out.[42] According to Ezek 7:26 "elders" normally would offer "counsel" and wisdom. Officials and probably all who had risen to political prominence in Judah after the deportation of Jehoiachin would be considered "elders." Compare 8:1, where there is a corresponding (but probably much smaller) group of "elders" in exile with Ezekiel.

Special mention is made of the man standing in the center of the group, who may be their leader: "Jaazaniah the son of Shaphan." He is singled out because of his prominence and the importance of his family elsewhere in the OT.[43] Three generations of the family of Shaphan are prominent in the book of Jeremiah. They agreed with Jeremiah's stance that Israel should submit to Babylon. Jeremiah's reason was that Babylon was the agent of God's wrath at apostate Israel. Most members of the Shaphan family seem to have agreed with Jeremiah's theology, although the Babylonians probably perceived that agreement as politically motivated in the face of Babylon's overwhelming military superiority. The family's "pro-Babylonian" reputation may explain why so prominent a family escaped deportation at the same time that Ezekiel and King Jehoiachin suffered it. The Babylonians probably favored them as useful political allies.

This[44] Jaazaniah's father, "Shaphan," had been state secretary or scribe (סֹפֵר) under Josiah, and to him the lost book of the Torah was turned over when it was found during the repair of the temple (2 Ki 22:3–14). Three of Shaphan's sons played prominent roles alongside Jeremiah: (1) Ahikam, who had saved Jeremiah from being lynched by a mob enraged by his prediction of the destruction of the temple (Jer 26:24); (2) Elasah, who delivered Jeremiah's letter to the exiles in Babylonia (Jer 29:3); (3) and Gemariah, who tried to prevent Jehoiakim from burning Jeremiah's scroll (Jer 36:25; cf. Jer 36:10–12). Ahikam was the father of Gedaliah, whom the Babylonians made governor of

---

[40] See, for example, Abraham standing before Yahweh in Gen 18:22, and the same idiom in Lev 9:5; Deut 4:10; 10:8; 18:7.

[41] See Schürer, *The History of the Jewish People in the Age of Jesus Christ*, 2:210–11.

[42] See Just, *Luke 9:51–24:53*, 436.

[43] Shaphan and/or his relatives are mentioned in 2 Kings 22; 25:22; Jer 26:24; 29:3; 36:10–12; 39:14; 40:5, 9, 11; 41:2; 43:6; 2 Chronicles 34. We are assuming that all these refer to the same man by that name.

[44] This "Jaazaniah" is said to be "the son of Shaphan" to distinguish him from another "Jaazaniah" in Ezek 11:1 who is "the son of Azzur."

the conquered province at Mizpah after the fall of Jerusalem (2 Ki 25:22–25). Nebuchadnezzar had ordered that Jeremiah not be harmed, and he was turned over to Gedaliah for safekeeping (Jer 39:11–14).

It is usually assumed that this is the Gedaliah mentioned on a seal, dating from this period, found in excavations at Lachish. The seal describes him as עַל־הַבַּיִת, [45] "over the house," that is, a vizier or chief minister of the king. He is not so described in the Bible, but that description could easily refer to his administrative position under Zechariah or to his later role as a representative of the Babylonians.

Thus, in all likelihood, Ezekiel knew "Jaazaniah the son of Shaphan" (Ezek 8:11) before the prophet was deported to Babylon. Perhaps already then Ezekiel knew him to be the idolatrous "stray sheep" in a family that had been faithful for generations. One supposes that he must have been at odds with most of his relatives on almost everything.

Block notes that the name "Jaazaniah" does not appear in the OT and its environs until the end of the seventh century B.C. The name (יַאֲזַנְיָהוּ) apparently means "Yahweh listens" (a form of the verb אָזַן, "to give ear; hear" with the theophoric ending יָהוּ, "Yahu", that is, "Yahweh"). Block suggests that "its emergence and remarkable popularity during Jerusalem's last critical years probably reflects a general longing in Judah for the divine ear." In the last verse of this chapter (8:18), God declares that he will not hear Israel's prayers even when they call "in my ears" (בְּאָזְנַי), and the noun "ear" (אֹזֶן) has the same consonantal root that is in "Jaazaniah." Block argues that God's declaration in Ezek 8:18 "involves an intentional play on the name, and may account for the insertion of this stylistically intrusive note" in 8:11 about Jaazaniah standing in the center of the seventy elders.[46] This may well be true, assuming that the Israelites were far more mindful of the etymological meaning of names than our culture is.

Incense was so commonly used in ancient Near Eastern worship that we would almost be surprised if it were not mentioned here. In pagan use it was thought to placate angry or capricious deities. Various Egyptian reliefs show men on the walls of cities under siege with arms stretched upward in prayer, whose worship leader is a man with a censer. The men in Ezekiel's vision may be attempting to avert the present Babylonian incursion into Judah, or the vision may portend the future siege of Jerusalem (as did most of Ezekiel's action prophecies in chapter 4).

Incense also played a prominent role in the divine services Yahweh prescribed for proper worship.[c] Yet the abuse of it incurred God's wrath.[d] Its idolatrous use in Ezek 8:11 may be a parody of its prominence in the Yom Kippur ritual, where once a year the high priest (and he alone) entered the Holy of

(c) E.g., Exodus 30; 1 Chr 6:34 (ET 6:49); 2 Chr 2:3 (ET 2:4); 13:11

(d) E.g., Lev 10:1–2; Is 1:13; Ezek 16:18; 23:41; 2 Chr 26:16–19

[45] See S. H. Hooke, "A Scarab and Sealing from Tell Duweir," *PEQ* 67 (1935): 195–96.

[46] Block, *Ezekiel*, 1:290.

Holies and by the cloud of incense shielded the sacred "mercy seat" (above which God was "incarnationally" enthroned) from human eyes, so the high priest would not die (Lev 16:1–2, 12–13). Perhaps that sacred rite was being aped by the seventy "elders," who presumably (since they are not called "priests") either were unordained or should not have been ordained because they were not of priestly lineage (cf. the idolatrous priesthood ordained by wicked King Jeroboam in 1 Ki 12:31; 13:33). One may be reminded that the Christian church traditionally has prohibited uncalled laymen (and all women) from the pastoral office and regular performance of its distinctive duties, though in modern times the biblical qualifications for the pastoral office have been compromised in many denominations—a modern abomination.

Yahweh gave directions for building the incense altar in Ex 30:7–8, and prescribed the ingredients for the holy incense in Ex 30:34–38, also prohibiting the making or use of it for any other purpose besides divine worship. In Ezek 16:18 and 23:41, Yahweh refers to it as "my incense." By Yahweh's own appointment, the incense was a potent propitiator (Num 17:11–12 [ET 16:46–47], in connection with Korah's rebellion). In the Blessing of Moses, incense is parallel to whole burnt offering as a means of atonement (Deut 33:10).

Incense continued to be used in the early church (cf. Rev 5:8; 8:3–5) and many tradition-minded churches, especially those of the Eastern rite, still employ it. Its modern significance is the same as in the Scriptures. From God's side, in the Divine Service his presence is revealed through Word and Sacrament, yet also "veiled" as he comes to the worshipers through those means, even as the smoke recalls the cloud that both revealed and veiled the divine Glory, whose presence among sinners is made possible only by atoning sacrifice—ultimately, the sacrifice of Christ, whose pleasing aroma is represented by the pungent smell of the incense (cf. Eph 5:2; also 2 Cor 2:14, 16; Phil 4:18). From man's side, incense represents prayer arising to God's throne of grace (Ps 141:2; Rev 5:8; 8:3–4; cf. Lk 1:10: "the whole multitude of the people was praying outside at the hour of incense").

8:12–13 The focus changes a bit from a wide-angle scene of all the seventy elders to an individualization of each one at his private devotions in his own image chamber—a room where perhaps he worshiped his own patron deity. Why are their rites carried on "in the darkness"? Is it to be taken as another caricature of the Holy of Holies or of Yahweh dwelling in "deep darkness" (עֲרָפֶל, 1 Ki 8:12)? Did their cult require the cover of darkness? Is it to be taken figuratively of the spiritual state of the people who can no longer find true light (cf. Is 8:19–22; 59:9–10; Jn 12:46)? Are they ashamed of what they are doing in secret? People will do sins in darkness that they would never consider doing in daylight (cf. Jn 3:19–21; Eph 5:12).

If the worshipers think that the darkness conceals the shame of their idolatry, they are wrong. Their rationalizations for their activities, "Yahweh does not see us; Yahweh has forsaken the land" (Ezek 8:12; essentially repeated, but in reverse order, in 9:9), are ironic because Yahweh himself calls the prophet's attention to the furtiveness of their behavior. The cover of secrecy for aberrant worship is a motif that surfaces in other texts (e.g., Deut 13:7–9 [ET 13:6–8]; 27:15; Is 29:15; Job 31:27), but "God will bring every deed into the judgment, even every secret thing, whether good or evil" (Eccl 12:14). God sees what is done in secret (Mt 6:4, 6, 18; cf. Lk 8:17). The arrogant presumption that God does not see or hear sinful actions or words appears in other passages as well, for example, Pss 10:1–11; 94:1–7; Job 22:13–14; Zeph 1:12. Jeremiah apparently had to combat the same two rationalizations (that Yahweh could not see and was absent): "'Can a man hide himself in hidden places so I cannot see him?' declares Yahweh. 'Do I not fill heaven and earth?' declares Yahweh" (Jer 23:24).

If the elders are not engaging in the kind of practical atheism that has probably always existed, we may suggest at least two theological misunderstandings that may be feeding the desperate behavior Ezekiel witnesses. One is the quasi-pagan notion that virtually identifies a deity with his or her land. Because that conception was so common among Israel's neighbors, it would have been strange if the synergistic "Yahwism" of Judah's last years did not harbor it also. But, if so, it would have been dealt a body blow with the various defeats, deportations, and occupations by foreign powers around 600 B.C. that devastated Yahweh's land. Those events required the conclusion (according to that way of thinking) that either Yahweh was impotent to protect his people, or he had forsaken his land and his people. If Yahweh could not protect them, they had good reason to turn to other deities for help. If Yahweh had forsaken them, there was no point in continuing to worship him. In either case, if Yahweh were impotent or absent, they would have no reason to fear his punishment for their supplications toward other gods.

A second likely reason for the elders' false worship would have to do with the absolutization of the inviolability of Zion as preached by Isaiah over a century earlier when Assyria had threatened Jerusalem.[e] Isaiah had not proclaimed the inviolability of *Jerusalem* as such—merely another city—but the inviolability of *Zion*, the "invisible church" of both Testaments, against which the gates of hell can never prevail (Mt 16:18). But the distinction between the visible church (the nation of Israel), represented by her capital city, and the true, invisible church (Israel comprised of all OT and NT believers, Jew and Gentile alike in Christ) was lost on most Israelites of that era. In fact, the more desperate Jerusalem's situation became, the more desperately they clung to their own caricature of the doctrines of election and preservation.[47] That is evident also in Jeremiah's invective against the Jerusalemites' almost magical trust in the temple (Jeremiah 7 and 26).

(e) E.g., Is 1:27; 2:3; 4:3–5; 10:24; 12:6; 14:32; 18:7; 28:16

---

[47] What Christian theology calls the doctrines of election (by grace alone) and preservation in the faith (again by grace alone) pertain to OT Israel just as much as to NT believers. See FC Ep and SD XI.

To true believers, of course, the certainty that God *does* see (e.g., Gen 16:13; Ps 10:14) and *has not* forsaken his "land"—that is, his church, gathered around his Word purely taught and his Sacraments rightly administered—is a matter of great comfort, as is often expressed in Scripture, including the NT theology of "Zion" fulfilled in Christ.[f] In Christ, all the promises of God find their yes (2 Cor 1:20). Contrariwise, it is of great concern to the faithful when they perceive or assume that their way is hidden from God (1 Sam 1:11; Is 63:15; Ps 80:15 [ET 80:14]). But the pitiable likes of the people in Ezekiel's vision have abandoned the scriptural orbit of concern altogether. Like the people of Isaiah's time who turn everywhere except to "Torah and testimony [of Yahweh]," there is no dawn (Is 8:19–22). Like many in our so-called "post-Christian" society, they embrace "spiritualities" and esoteric cults of every conceivable sort under the sad delusion that the Christian faith no longer offers "answers" that are absolutely and universally true.

(f) E.g., Mt 21:5; Rom 9:33; 11:26; Heb 12:22; 1 Pet 2:6; Rev 14:1

The supreme irony in the seventy elders' rationalization is that it becomes a self-fulfilling prophecy. What they say ("Yahweh does not see us") is false about Yahweh, but true about the images they are worshiping ("they have eyes but do not see," Pss 115:5; 135:16; cf. Dan 5:23). In fact, Yahweh's ability to see not only the hidden recesses of the temple but also the darkest corners of human hearts is precisely what distinguishes Yahweh from all would-be competitors. The "claim that Yahweh has left the country was a boast of impunity,"[48] but it would come true all too soon: his Glory begins to depart the temple in Ezek 9:3 and forsakes it in 11:22–23. Thus the elders forecast the substance of the remainder of Ezekiel's visionary visit to Jerusalem (chapters 8–11).

The Third Temple Scene: Bewailing Tammuz (8:14–15)

8:14–15   The shocking thing about this third abomination is that, as we apparently move close to the Holy of Holies, where Yahweh sits enthroned above the cherubim, the idolatry becomes even more brazen. The weeping for Tammuz (or perhaps the Hebrew means "performing the Tammuz ritual"; see the textual notes) is not being carried on secretly in darkness (as was the activity in 8:12), but publicly in broad daylight. Women in the OT could serve at the divine sanctuary in a God-pleasing role (e.g., 1 Sam 2:22), but these women, like those in 2 Ki 23:7, were aiding Israel's apostasy by practicing a ritual about a dead god instead of worshiping the living God.

Our knowledge of Tammuz is sketchy. The Sumerian King List (third millennium B.C.) lists two kings by the name Dumu-zi/Tammuz, one an antediluvian shepherd king and the other postdiluvian, Gilgamesh's predecessor at Uruk. By that time Tammuz had been deified, and a complex mythology had developed around him. It centered in his death and banishment to the underworld by his wife, the goddess Inanna. The cult apparently had something to do with the end of spring and the cessation of the rains, and the ensuing "death"

---

[48]   Allen, *Ezekiel*, 1:144.

of nature (the hot and arid season) was to be counteracted by weeping and mourning. Just how much, if any, of this myth is connected with the annual "dying and rising" of a fertility god is debated. The fourth month of the Mesopotamian calendar was named after Tammuz, and several forms of lament over him were widely practiced as women's rite for centuries. As late as the tenth century A.D., the pagan Sabaeans of Haran (today near the Turkish-Syrian border) observed a mourning ceremony for Tammuz in his month.

The rite was probably imported into Judah directly or indirectly from Mesopotamia. This verse is the only certain reference to it in the OT. Commentators usually assume that Tammuz worship coalesced to some degree with the worship of Baal-Hadad in Canaan and of Adonis in Greece (as recognized already by St. Jerome[49] and Cyril of Alexandria[50]). Based on that assumption, Is 17:10–11 is usually interpreted to refer to some form of that cult (נַעֲמָנִים is usually taken as a deliberate distortion of an epithet for Adonis/Tammuz, for whom the Israelites are planting vegetation). There may well be other allusions to Tammuz worship elsewhere in the OT, but our knowledge of ancient pagan practices is still too meager for us to discern the (usually) brief allusions.

We are left to guess whether the women have syncretistically identified Yahweh with Tammuz (an "ecumenical" and "inclusive" assumption that the different names both link to the same deity) or whether they have substituted him for Yahweh. Nor is it clear why this rite is being observed in Jerusalem in the sixth month (8:1) instead of in the fourth month, which was the month named after Tammuz (June/July on our calendar). If the cult was relatively new in Jerusalem, the women may not have been properly informed, or the prophet may be deliberately caricaturing the indiscriminate syncretism of the city. Again, since we are dealing with a vision, we probably should not press the point.

The Fourth Temple Scene: Sun Worship (8:16–18)

8:16 Three times Yahweh had promised that Ezekiel would see "greater abominations" (8:6, 13, 15), and now this one is the greatest. Probably it is worst both because of its location "between the vestibule and the altar" (8:16), which is probably closer to the Holy of Holies than any of the previous abominations, and because of its content. One may discern in it three offenses: worship of the sun, filling the land with violence, and "sticking the branch up my [Yahweh's] nose!" which, whatever its precise significance, was deemed so offensive that Jewish scribes may have felt compelled to alter the Hebrew text (see the textual notes). The first and third of those offenses may be cultic or liturgical abuses. But the social crimes summarized as "violence" (חָמָס, 8:17)

---

[49] The Vulgate translates the last clause of 8:14 as *et ecce ibi mulieres sedebant plangentes Adonidem*, "and behold, in that place women were sitting, striking themselves in lamentation on account of Adonis." See also Jerome's commentary on 8:14 (*Commentariorum in Ezechielem* [PL 25:82]) or the quotation from it in Zimmerli, *Ezekiel*, 1:242.

[50] Cyril of Alexandria, *Commentarius in Isaiam Prophetam*, on Is 18:1–2 (PG 70:441).

should not be disassociated from the cultic abominations. The implication of Yahweh's declaration is that idolatry has a pernicious effect on the entire society. The worship abuses in the temple cause a moral decline throughout the land, so that "they fill the land with violence" (8:17). Probably it is the total, cumulative effect of both (idolatry and widespread violence) that is goading God to fury.

Keil argues that the twenty-five men are the twenty-four leaders of the divisions of priests, with the high priest at the head.[51] Thus, he argues, the entire priesthood is symbolically represented as apostate, just as the seventy elders in 8:11 represented the entire apostate nation. Keil's argument is attractive. 1 Chr 24:7–19 supports an organization of the priesthood into twenty-four divisions in the time of David.[52] Among contemporary commentators, Zimmerli favors the view that they are priests.[53] Taylor assumes they are priests and observes that "when church leadership becomes corrupted there is no end to the chaos that is caused to the life of the nation."[54] There can be no quarreling with that conclusion (regardless of who the twenty-five are).

Evidence for sun worship in Israel is sparse, but it was known early on because it is condemned by Moses in Deut 4:19 and 17:3 (ca. 1400 B.C.). The personified sun was commonly at the head of pagan pantheons because of its supreme importance in the daily and annual cycles of nature. It was no great difficulty for the fallen "religious" mind to realize that, humanly speaking, all life on earth ultimately depends on the sun.

In Israel, sun worship seems to have been at its zenith in the seventh and sixth centuries B.C. (overlapping Ezekiel's era). In the "dark ages" for Yahwism in the seventh century B.C., it received official state sponsorship. Manasseh is reported to have "built altars for all the host of heaven in the two courts of the house of Yahweh" (2 Ki 21:5, included in a list of other outrages). Josiah's reformation (ca. 622 B.C.) deposed the priests who made offerings to the sun and other heavenly bodies (2 Ki 23:5), and the king also "removed the horses that the kings of Judah had dedicated to the sun at the entrance to the house of Yahweh, ... and he burned the chariots of the sun with fire" (2 Ki 23:11). But after Josiah's untimely death, the old pagan practices must have returned with a vengeance, as reflected in Ezekiel's vision.

The tabernacle was oriented with the Holy of Holies toward the west (Ex 27:13–14; Num 3:23, 38). Josephus' description of the Herodian temple indicates that it too faced west.[55] Most likely the Solomonic temple was oriented

---

[51] Keil, *Ezekiel*, 1:123, citing Lightfoot's *Chronology of O.T.*, opp. 1:124.

[52] For the history of the priestly divisions, see Schürer, *The History of the Jewish People in the Age of Jesus Christ*, 2:245–50.

[53] Zimmerli, *Ezekiel*, 1:243. He says that Ezekiel may have avoided calling them priests for polemical reasons (to imply that they were not true, faithful priests).

[54] Taylor, *Ezekiel*, 100.

[55] Josephus, *Antiquities*, 15.418–19 (15.11.5).

to the west, like its predecessor (the tabernacle) and its successor (Herod's temple). That would explain Ezekiel's statement that the idolaters have their backs toward "the temple of Yahweh" as they face east to worship the sun (8:16). This westward orientation may have been precisely to distinguish Yahwism from the widespread deification of the sun, whose worship was oriented toward its rising.

The church, in contrast, has always preferred an eastward orientation. Since churches began to be built only after Jewish Christians were expelled from the synagogues, one suspects that the Christians' desire to distinguish themselves from the temple and synagogue played a role in their choice of orientation. But the main reasons probably are to be found in the identification of Christ with Malachi's prophecy (Mal 3:20 [ET 4:2]) of "the sun of righteousness"; Christ's resurrection at dawn on Easter; and Christ's promise about his return (that might be taken as indicating it will start from the east): "As the lightning goes out from the east and shines as far as the west, thus shall be the parousia of the Son of Man" (Mt 24:27). Likewise, the traditional preference for orienting Christian graves toward the east reflects the belief in "the resurrection of the body" (Apostles' Creed) based on Christ's resurrection at dawn.

It is worth noting that in both cases—the OT tabernacle and temple, and the Christian church—the need to distinguish the true faith from competing false alternatives (sun worship; Judaism) led to "countercultural" worship practices, rather than adopting or conforming to heathen worship forms.

As the sun worshipers prostrate themselves eastward, they have their "backsides" toward "the temple of Yahweh" (Ezek 8:16), that is, toward the sanctuary/nave and the Holy of Holies. The significance of their posture is obvious. While the Hebrew phraseology here is unique, the OT has some not unrelated idioms that represent idolatry and apostasy, such as "They turned toward me the (back of the) neck and not the face" (Jer 2:27) and "They turned their faces away from the dwelling place of Yahweh and presented the (back of the) neck" (2 Chr 29:6). In this vision the men's physical posture corresponds with their spiritual disposition. They were prostrating themselves to the sun as to a sovereign deity. Even if perchance the twenty-five men had intended their sun worship as a legitimate extension of Yahwism,[56] they were in fact perverting the role of legitimate priests and were venerating the sun as a rival deity in place of Yahweh.

No one can have it both ways. Yahweh is a "jealous God" (e.g., Ex 20:5; see "jealousy" in Ezek 5:13 and the statue provoking his "jealousy" in 8:3, 5). The biblical faith, which in its OT form may be called "Yahwism," is particularistic and exclusive. Hence, very understandably, these gestures of supreme and ultimate contempt for Yahweh are considered the fourth and climactic abomination. Likewise in Christianity, the NT form of the same biblical faith

---

[56] As argued by Zimmerli, *Ezekiel*, 1:243–44.

in the same triune God, there is but "one Lord, one faith" (Eph 4:5; cf. 1 Cor 8:6), and believers must not compromise the exclusive lordship of Jesus Christ.

8:17 This long verse seems to summarize all the manifestations of rank apostasy that Yahweh has just shown Ezekiel, to which are now even added social crimes. "They fill the land with violence" evokes the flood narrative, when God sent the universal deluge because "the earth was full of violence" (Gen 6:13; cf. 6:11). The final clause about the "branch" describes some supremely insulting physical gesture that euphemistically describes how Yahweh feels about the countless ways his subjects have demonstrated their contempt for him (see the textual note).

The specific forms of idolatry that Ezekiel has witnessed in the temple throughout chapter 8 probably were practiced only during a limited period of Israel's history. Nevertheless, the matters that seem to have been involved in those abominations, including infractions against the priestly office, sexual immorality, and deviant worship practices, have analogies that have continued to plague the Christian church. Throughout church history, and no less in the modern era, abominations of various sorts have arisen in parts of the visible church that involve distortions of the pastoral office, immorality, and worship practices that contravene the Word of God.

While no complete catalogue can be offered here, the foremost worship "abomination" is the failure to proclaim God's Law and Gospel faithfully and administer his Sacraments according to his institution. The denial of the inspiration and authority of the Scriptures allows the Gospel to be supplanted with other "gospels" disguising social, political, and philosophical agendas. The perennial "health and wealth" gospel is as old as the ancient fertility religions. Clergy scandals have eroded respect for the pastoral office. Most recently in the West, some denominations have begun to ordain women and condone or even ordain homosexuals and lesbians. Such are on par with "sticking the branch up my [God's] nose" (8:17).

8:18 This final verse of the chapter, which looks forward to chapters 9–10, is expressed in emotional terms of wrath and mercilessness that relate to the expressions of divine exasperation we have heard throughout the chapter: the Lord's "jealousy" (8:3, 5), the repeated abominations, and the exclamatory questions he repeatedly addressed to the prophet. The verse contains three sentences of judgment.

The first declaration is that Yahweh's rebellious subjects have so provoked him that he "will act in wrath." That is the message of virtually the whole first part of the book (Ezekiel 1–24).

His avowal that "My eye will not pity, and I will have no compassion" articulates his wrath with idioms that are familiar from 5:11 and 7:4, 9.

Yahweh's final declaration, ",.. I will not hear them" (8:18), is new in the book. However, he had used the same Hebrew verb when he predicted that "Israel will not be willing to listen to you because they are not willing to listen to me" (3:7). Now his refusal to listen to them is the just punishment. Possibly it is a rebuttal to the name of "Jaazaniah" in 8:11, which means "Yahweh listens" (see the commentary on 8:11). The divine promise implicit in Jaazaniah's name has been voided by his outrageous behavior and that of his accomplices (the seventy elders, representing the whole "house of Israel," 8:11). Especially in the prophets, the lack of mercy is frequently expressed by this theme of God's refusal to answer prayer (e.g., Jer 11:11; Micah 3:4; Zech 7:13).

By the three statements in Ezek 8:18, Yahweh adamantly declares that "this time there will be no second chance, no renaissance of relationship with [him]. … He will not allow his heart to overrule his head."[57]

---

[57] Block, *Ezekiel*, 1:300.

Ezekiel 9:1–11

Those without the Mark Are Slain

Translation

9 ¹Then he called out in my hearing in a loud voice, "Bring here the supervisors of the city, each with his weapon of destruction in his hand." ²And behold, six men were coming from the direction of the upper gate that faces north, each with his weapon—a club—in his hand. There was one man in their midst, dressed in linen, with a scribe's kit at his waist. They entered and stood beside the bronze altar. ³Now, the Glory of the God of Israel ascended from being on the cherub, on which it had been, to the threshold of the temple. He called out to the man who was dressed in linen, who had the scribe's kit at his waist.

⁴Yahweh said to him: "Go through the city, through Jerusalem, and you shall mark a *taw* on the foreheads of those who moan and groan over the abominations being committed in her." ⁵To the others he said in my hearing, "Go through the city after him and slaughter. Do not let your eye pity, and do not have compassion. ⁶Old and young man, girl, little children, and women you shall kill to destruction. But do not go near anyone who has the *taw* on him. Begin from my sanctuary." So they began with the old men who were in front of the temple. ⁷Then he said to them, "Defile the temple and fill the courts with the slain. Go!" So they went and slaughtered in the city. ⁸While they were slaughtering and I was left alone, I fell face down and cried out, "Ah, Lord Yahweh! Are you destroying the entire remnant of Israel as you pour out your wrath upon Jerusalem?"

⁹He said to me, "The guilt of the house of Israel and Judah is extremely great, the land is filled with bloodshed, and the city is full of injustice, for they say, 'Yahweh has forsaken the land,' and 'Yahweh does not see.' ¹⁰Hence, as for me, my eye will not pity, and I will have no compassion. I will place their conduct on their own head."

¹¹And behold, the man dressed in linen who had the scribe's kit at his waist was reporting, "I have done just as you commanded me."

Textual Notes

9:1 The continuity between chapters 8 and 9 comes through by the repetition of the vocabulary קָרָא בְאָזְנַי קוֹל גָּדוֹל, "call in my ears/hearing with a loud cry," in both 8:18 and 9:1. However, the context is quite different. In 8:18 the "ears" were those of God, to whom the impenitent Israelites would cry loudly without him hearing their entreaties. Here the "ears" are those of Ezekiel, who merely overhears what God loudly commands others to do. Possibly the picture is that God's loud cry in 9:1 drowns out the sinners' loud cries for mercy in 8:18. The repetition of identical words or phrases but with different meanings is characteristic of Ezekiel. Another connecting link is the *waw* consecutive (rendered "then") that begins 9:1, indicating a continuation of the earlier narrative sequence. Other links appear as chapter 9 continues. "City" is a key word in the entire section (chapters 8–11), although the entire Judean community is ultimately in view.

קִרְבוּ פְּקֻדּוֹת הָעִיר—The verb could be the Qal third common plural perfect of קָרַב, as reflected in the LXX and Vulgate, in which case פְּקֻדּוֹת הָעִיר would be the subject: "the supervisors of the city have come." But since the following verse (9:2) will picture the men as "coming" then, this verb must be an imperative. The Targum and Syriac Peshitta translate as if it were the Qal imperative קִרְבוּ, telling the supervisors to "come near." But if קִרְבוּ is an imperative, it is the second masculine plural imperative of the Piel, which has a transitive meaning, "to bring (something/someone) near." (The identical form occurs in Is 41:21 and is the Piel imperative.) Hence פְּקֻדּוֹת הָעִיר is its object: "Bring near the supervisors of the city." Most English translations follow that understanding. Yahweh issues his command to unspecified (angelic?) attendants, who would bring near the supervisors.[1]

The divine command intimates the setting of a royal court or judicial courtroom, with Yahweh as the King and/or Judge who summons the supervisors or executioners. The prophet is a witness of Yahweh's actions vis-à-vis his people. The common pattern in prophetic judgment oracles of formal indictment and execution of sentence is evident in the relationship between 8:5–18 and 9:1–11. Some of the vocabulary has possible legal overtones. The same Piel imperative, קִרְבוּ, in Is 41:21 is in the context of God's order, "present your case." Here the פְּקֻדּוֹת (see below) may resemble court bailiffs or the like. The dispatch with which the scribe reports that the sentence has been executed (9:11) also suggests a forensic setting.

Nouns for abstract ideas are usually feminine in Hebrew. The noun פְּקֻדָּה (like the verb from which it is derived, פָּקַד) can have a variety of nuances, including "punishment" (as the LXX renders it here), "gracious visitation, care," "oversight, supervision" (see BDB and *HALOT*). It is sometimes used for (supervisory) "office, service" (Num 3:32; Is 60:17) and often in Chronicles for the "appointed service" of the presiding priests. It occurs in those senses in both singular and plural. But it is also used in the concrete sense of people who occupy those administrative or supervisory offices, and Ezek 9:1b–2 demands such a meaning in 9:1. The translations of it here are numerous. Following Cooke,[2] many, including Greenberg,[3] RSV, and ESV, have "executioners." Functionally, that is appropriate in the following context, but, as a translation in 9:1, it is probably premature. I have ventured "supervisors."

וְאִישׁ כְּלִי מַשְׁחֵתוֹ בְּיָדוֹ:—The noun כְּלִי is a generic word for almost any "implement" or "instrument" (much like English "thing" or Latin *res*), so "weapon" is a natural translation in this context. The noun מַשְׁחֵת is a hapax legomenon, but its meaning ("destruction") is unmistakable. The closely related מַשְׁחִית (in form the Hiphil par-

---

[1]   So Block, *Ezekiel*, 1:300, n. 1, and Greenberg, *Ezekiel*, 1:175, who calls it an "authoritative (royal) imperative" (citing, e.g., the imperatives spoken by Joseph to "implicit attendants" in Gen 43:31; 45:1; and by God in Is 40:1–2).

[2]   Cooke, *Ezekiel*, 103.

[3]   Greenberg, *Ezekiel*, 1:174.

ticiple of שָׁחַת), "destroyer" or "destruction," appeared in 5:16 and will reappear in 9:6, 8; 21:36 (ET 21:31); 25:15. מַשְׁחִית was also used in the exodus narrative of the "destruction" Yahweh brought upon Egypt (Ex 12:13), and with the definite article was personalized a few verses later as "the destroyer" himself (Ex 12:23). Similarly, in 1 Chr 21:15 Yahweh sends his מַלְאָךְ הַמַּשְׁחִית, "destroying messenger/angel," to punish David for taking a census of his people.

9:2 שִׁשָּׁה אֲנָשִׁים בָּאִים—The participle בָּאִים ("were coming") enables the reader to see the action in progress, even as Ezekiel did. So also does the participle מֵשִׁיב ("was reporting") in 9:11.

These "six men" plus the scribe to be mentioned shortly make a total of seven—a common symbolic number for completion of a divine work, as in the seven days of creation. There is a possible connection between this aspect of Ezekiel's vision and Babylonian mythology. Among the seven planetary Babylonian deities was the scribe god Nabu, called "Nebo" in Is 46:1 and present in names such as *Nebuchad-nezzar*. A possibly closer parallel is to be found in the seven gods who execute Erra's judgment in the so-called "Poem of Erra." But we should be reluctant to posit influence from pagan Babylonian culture on so strict and orthodox an Israelite as Ezekiel. It is more plausible that this part of Ezekiel's vision may be the precedent for the seven angels in *1 Enoch* 19:1–20:7, and especially for the apostle John's vision of the seven angels who execute divine wrath in Revelation 8–10. Among the detailed connections between Ezekiel 8–11 and Revelation is the similarity between Ezek 9:4–6 and Rev 7:2–3; 9:4.

The six "men" are not further identified, but presumably they (and the scribe) are angels (see the commentary). In many other biblical passages, angels are called "men" (e.g., the "two angels" in Gen 19:1 were two of the "three men" in Gen 18:2). If so, Allen's comment is appropriate: "God's people were no longer on the side of the angels!"[4]

שַׁעַר הָעֶלְיוֹן אֲשֶׁר ׀ מָפְנֶה צָפוֹנָה—The gate from which the six are coming is as hard to identify as the other gates mentioned in 8:3, 5, 14. Commentators disagree about its location. Perhaps it is called "upper" because the inner court stood on a higher level than the surrounding area (cf. 40:28–32). If it is a gate into the inner court, then it probably is the same gate through which Ezekiel had been led into the inner court in 8:16, since the prophet too had come from the north (8:3, 14). This gate in 9:2 is usually identified with "the upper Gate of Benjamin in the house of Yahweh" (Jer 20:2). Jotham is reported to have built "the upper gate of the house of Yahweh" (2 Ki 15:35), which may or may not be the same as the one as here in Ezek 9:2. In 2 Chr 23:20 a party going from the temple to the palace goes through an "upper gate," though it may be a gate to the palace rather than the temple.

"Faces" translates מָפְנֶה, Hophal participle of פָּנָה, which occurs in Hophal elsewhere only in Jer 49:8. To indicate a direction of orientation Ezekiel often uses the Qal participle of פָּנָה or a relative clause with אֲשֶׁר. That it "faces" the north may re-

---

4   Allen, *Ezekiel*, 1:146.

flect the same exmythological imagery appearing in the inaugural vision (see the commentary on 1:4).

כְּלִי מַפָּצוֹ—The "implement, weapon" (כְּלִי) that each of the six men has is defined more specifically here than in 9:1. The noun מַפָּץ is a hapax legomenon. It may have the abstract meaning "**smashing**, destruction" (*HALOT*), based on its derivation from the verb נָפַץ, "to smash," in which case the construct phrase means "his weapon for smashing." Or it may have the concrete meaning of a "club" or "cudgel" since the similar noun מַפֵּץ, which occurs only in Jer 51:20, denotes a battle mace. In that case the construct phrase is epexegetical, specifying that "his weapon" is "a club." In either case the pronoun on the *nomen rectum* semantically goes with the *nomen regens* ("his weapon").

לְבֻשׁ בַּדִּים—The seventh figure is described in more detail. First, he is "dressed" (לְבֻשׁ, Qal passive participle) in "linen" (בַּדִּים, plural of בַּד). Since linen was ordinarily bleached, this implies the color white. Linen (שֵׁשׁ) was used in the tabernacle curtains (e.g., Ex 26:1, 31) and in the high priest's ephod and other vestments (e.g., Ex 28:4–6, 8, 15, 39; בַּד is used in Lev 16:4). All the priests were to wear linen (בַּד) underpants while ministering or they would die (Ex 28:42–43; cf. Lev 6:3 [ET 6:10]; Ezek 44:17–18). Angels, who are also engaged in direct divine service, are depicted as wearing "linen" (בַּד, Dan 10:5; 12:6–7; see also Rev 15:6; 19:14; cf. Ezek 40:3) or some kind of white garb (e.g., Mt 28:3; Mk 16:5). The saints in glory wear white robes (Rev 7:9, 14). At the second coming of Christ, his bride, the church, is clothed in bright linen, and "the linen is the righteous deeds of the saints" (Rev 19:7–8).

A second detail is that the seventh "man" (Ezek 9:2; see the commentary) has a קֶסֶת at his waist. The word appears only in 9:2, 3, 11. It appears to be a loanword from the Egyptian *gśtj*, denoting a scribe's palette or writing kit.[5] Sometimes it is pictured in Egyptian tomb paintings; it is a board with a slot for a pen and hollowed places where ink was kept—usually two kinds of ink, one black and one red.[6] We also know of palettes containing wax into which temporary notations could be incised and presumably transferred later to some more permanent register. But we are not given details about this palette.

9:3 The first sentence is parenthetical since it interrupts the narrative about the supervisors, which began 9:1–2 and continues in 9:3b. I assume that Yahweh had been seated on his throne-chariot supported by the cherubim, as implied by 8:4, but then in 9:3a he ascends from the cherub(im) to stand in the threshold, where he will give instructions to the man dressed in linen and the six other men. The fact that he ascended from the cherub(im) will be repeated in 10:4 as part of the larger narrative of the Glory's departure from the temple in chapter 10.

Another possibility is that the Glory actually ascended in 10:4, and the statement here in 9:3a about the Glory's movement is proleptic, anticipating 10:4. If so, 9:3a does not mean that the Glory's departure occurred now, but it links his (later but imminent) departure with this context.

---

[5]   Thomas O. Lambdin, "Egyptian Loan Words in the Old Testament," *JAOS* 73 (1953): 154.

[6]   *ANEP*, §§ 232–34.

In either case, his movement represents the first stage of his abandonment of the temple, where he had dwelt "incarnationally" since the time of Solomon.[7] His drastic action of forsaking his dwelling place is a direct consequence of his people's apostasy, and it is parallel to the other judgments executed in chapters 9–10. Ironically, the people's false rationalization that Yahweh had already abandoned them (8:12; 9:9) is about to be fulfilled (see the commentary on 8:12).

הַכְּרוּב—This is the first reference in the book to "cherub(im)" by that name. In chapter 1 Ezekiel had called the angelic beings who support God's throne "living creatures" (1:5–22), and he will call those same creatures "cherubim" in 10:1–20 and 11:22. He refers to cherub(im) also in 28:14, 16; 41:18, 20, 25. The Hebrew of 9:3 and of the parallel phrase in 10:4 has the singular, literally, "the cherub." The LXX has the plural here and in 10:4. Many translators take the singular here as a collective. However, the singular "cherub" agrees with the suffix on the following preposition (עָלָיו). Ezekiel, with his background as a priest (1:3), would have known that there were two cherubim of a piece with the lid of the ark. However, someone looking into the Holy of Holies (as Ezekiel does in this vision) might speak of the whole as a unit. Thus Allen translates the singular as "cherubim-structure."[8] Some commentators wish to make more of the difference in number than that.[9]

The two cherubim on the lid of the ark faced each other in a position of reverence (Ex 25:18–22; 37:7–9). The Torah speaks of Yahweh's presence upon those two cherubim on the lid of the ark (Ex 25:22; Num 7:89). The tabernacle had additional cherubim woven into the design of the curtains (Ex 26:1, 31; 36:35). Solomon's temple housed the ark with its two cherubim on the lid. Solomon made two other large cherubim for the Holy of Holies, and they faced forward with their wings outstretched—one wing touching the outer wall and the other wing touching that of the other cherub (1 Ki 6:23–28). Solomon's temple also had other cherubim that were carved and engraved on the walls and doors (1 Ki 6:29, 32, 35; see also 1 Ki 7:29, 36).

Thus the statement that "the Glory of the God of Israel had ascended from being on the cherub" (Ezek 9:3) does not answer the question of *which* cherub had been the resting place of the Glory.

With that question in mind, we also begin to comprehend another challenge running throughout the vision, namely, that of determining the successive locations of the departing Glory and the supporting cherubim. References to the Glory repeatedly interrupt the narrative flow: here in 9:3, as previously in 8:4, and later in 10:1, 3–5. The description of the Glory in 10:8–18 interrupts the narrative completely. In 10:18 the narrative resumes with the flight of the cherubim, only to be interrupted again in

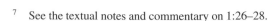

[7] See the textual notes and commentary on 1:26–28.

[8] Allen, *Ezekiel*, 1:116, 122.

[9] Zimmerli, *Ezekiel*, 1:232, 254, uses it as a redactional criterion. In his reconstruction of the history of the text, the plural refers to the mobile throne of the inaugural vision with its four "living creatures" (chapters 1 and 10), while the singular refers to the pair of cherubim on the ark in the earthly sanctuary.

10:20–22 with a detailed assertion that Ezekiel identifies the cherubim as the same "living creatures" he saw in chapter 1. The vision of chapters 8–11 ends with the account of the departure of the Glory and the cherubim from the city in 11:22–23.

This much is clear based on 9:3: at some time previous to Yahweh's command that summoned the six supervisors and the scribe, the כָּבוֹד ("Glory") had begun to exit by moving from on a "cherub" (presumably in the Holy of Holies) to the "threshold of the temple," that is, between the הֵיכָל or Holy Place (nave) and the porch or vestibule.

9:4 וַיֹּאמֶר יְהוָה—The Tetragrammaton, which is the subject of the sentence, usually does not appear within vision narratives. The LXX omits a translation of it here. One might have expected it with the main verb וַיִּקְרָא ("he called") in 9:3b after the parenthetical first half of 9:3. However, Greenberg makes a convincing case for its appropriateness, pointing to a parallel situation in Ex 40:34–Lev 1:1. The narrative at the end of Exodus is about the cloud (עָנָן) of Yahweh's Glory (כָּבוֹד, Ex 40:34–35), and Lev 1:1 continues that narrative. Thus the implicit subject of the first verb in Lev 1:1, which is וַיִּקְרָא ("he called," the same verb as in Ezek 9:3b), is the divine Glory, manifested as the cloud by day and fire by night (Ex 40:38). The second verb in Lev 1:1 has Yahweh as the subject (וַיְדַבֵּר יְהוָה). Hence Lev 1:1 implies that the Glory is a manifestation of Yahweh himself and the two are really one and the same Divinity.

That same implication is present in Ezek 9:3–4, about which Greenberg says:

> Now, had YHWH appeared as the subject of the verb immediately following mention of the *kabod* [וַיִּקְרָא, "he called," in 9:3b], it would have impressed on the reader a contrast between the two [between the Glory and Yahweh] that was, in its turn, unwanted; in the present text, the identification comes upon one gradually through means of coordinate verbs, only the second of which [וַיֹּאמֶר, "he said," in 9:4] has YHWH as its subject.[10]

Thus the sequence in Ezek 9:3–4 affirms that the Glory is of the same divine essence as Yahweh and can be equated with Yahweh himself. As Jesus will affirm, "Whoever has seen me has seen the Father" (Jn 14:9). While the doctrine of the Trinity remains a mystery, the fuller NT revelation declares that the divine Glory became incarnate in the person of Jesus Christ, the second person of the Godhead. See the textual notes and commentary on Ezek 1:26–28.

וְהִתְוִיתָ תָּו—Literally, "and you shall *taw* a *taw*," this is a cognate accusative construction, since the verb (Hiphil second masculine singular perfect of תָּוָה with *waw* consecutive) and its direct object (the noun תָּו) are from the same root. The Hiphil of תָּוָה occurs only here and means "to mark with a *taw*, make a *taw* sign." The Piel occurs in 1 Sam 21:14 (ET 21:13) and means "to make a mark, scribble." Besides Ezek 9:4, 6, the noun תָּו occurs elsewhere only in Job 31:35, where it denotes Job's written "signature." *Taw* is the last letter of the Hebrew alphabet. In the old preexilic script it had the shape of two crossing lines. The commentary below discusses its shape further.

---

[10] Greenberg, *Ezekiel*, 1:176–77.

הַנֶּאֱנָחִים֙ וְהַנֶּאֱנָקִ֔ים—"Moan and groan," a not uncommon translation, is an attempt to reproduce the rhyme and assonance of the two Niphal masculine plural participles, of אָנַח and אָנַק. The Niphal of אָנַח will reappear in 21:11–12 (ET 21:6–7) in an action prophecy where Ezekiel is commanded to groan to portend intense grief at the impending doom. In 24:17 God will use the Niphal of אָנַק to command Ezekiel to "groan"—but silently—in mourning at the death of his wife.

9:5 The tandem idioms of one's eye not showing pity and of having no compassion first appeared in 5:11; see the textual note on them there. In this chapter, they will reappear in 9:10.

Two Qere notes grace the margins of this verse. The first reads the negative particle אַל (which must be the correct reading) instead of the preposition עַל before the verb תָּחֹס. The preposition might be an aural scribal error (since the two sound alike), but the Aramaic tendency to have *ayin* where Hebrew has *alef* may be exerting its influence already. The second Qere reads the singular עֵינְכֶם, "your eye," as the subject in agreement with the singular verb תָּחֹס. (This idiom occurs a number of times in Ezekiel, and in every other instance, the singular "eye" is used.)

9:6 זָקֵן בָּחוּר וּבְתוּלָה וְטַף וְנָשִׁים—For emphasis the Hebrew places the five direct objects first, before the verb. The first four are singular in a generic sense.

תַּהַרְגוּ לְמַשְׁחִית—The verb is the Qal imperfect of הרג. מַשְׁחִית will recur in 9:8, where it clearly is the Hiphil participle of שָׁחַת. But here most lexica consider it to be a noun meaning "destruction" (BDB), as also in 5:16; 21:36 (ET 21:31); 25:15. Thus it is a synonym of the noun מַשְׁחֵת in 9:1 (see the textual note on that word above). The addition of לְמַשְׁחִית, literally, "you shall kill *to destruction*," makes the command more forceful and underscores the impossibility of any exemptions—except for those with the saving mark.

תָּחֵלּוּ וַיָּחֵלּוּ—The repeated verb (Hiphil of חָלַל) "begin" may be a punning anticipation of the "slain" (חֲלָלִים) in 9:7.

הַזְּקֵנִים אֲשֶׁר לִפְנֵי הַבָּיִת:—There is debate about the identity of these "old men/elders" who were in front of the temple." At the start of the verse the generic "old man" was the first category of people to be killed. In chapter 8 Ezekiel saw seventy idolatrous "elders" in their dark chambers in 8:11–12 and in 8:16 twenty-five sun worshipers who were in a location that was in front of the temple. Yet the expression here is too general to draw definite conclusions. Probably it refers to any and all elders who had come to the temple for whatever specific reason.

9:7 Killing "the old men" (or any people) "who were in front of the temple" (9:6) would desecrate the building (cf. 2 Ki 23:15–16, 20). The command to fill the courts with corpses overlaps with the command in 9:6 to begin at the temple. It serves as "an explicit divine license to commit an unthinkable desecration."[11]

טַמְּאוּ—The Qal of טָמֵא, "to be unclean," is primarily used of cultic uncleanness (see the textual notes and commentary on 4:13–14). The Piel has the causative mean-

---

[11] Greenberg, *Ezekiel*, 1:178.

ing "to defile, render unclean." In 5:11 and 23:38, the Piel refers to the Israelites de-filing the sanctuary by their abominations. In 18:6, 11, 15; 23:17, it refers to sexual immorality, which defiles. Here the Piel may link the present desecration of the tem-ple with that already committed by the aberrant worship practices described in chap-ter 8. (The Piel of חָלַל can mean "to profane," and in 23:38 it occurs as a synonym together with the Piel of טָמֵא, but the use of the Hiphil of חָלַל, meaning "to begin," twice in 9:6 may have influenced the choice of the Piel of טָמֵא here.)

וְיָצְאוּ וְהִכּוּ בָעִיר׃—The report of the fulfillment of a command is ordinarily ex-pressed by an imperfect with *waw* consecutive, but the two verbs here are perfects with conjunctive *waw*. Yet such unusual features do not surprise one in Ezekiel as much as they might elsewhere. (The LXX and Syriac translate as if the verbs were imperatives.)

9:8 וְנֵאשַׁאֲר אָנִי—This apparently is another "mixed form" (as was מִשְׁתַּחֲוִיתֶם in 8:16). It is a conflation of two forms of the Niphal of שָׁאַר, the masculine singular par-ticiple וְנִשְׁאָר (with which the following pronoun אָנִי is necessary to define the sub-ject) and the first common singular imperfect with *waw* consecutive, וָאֶשָּׁאֵר (with which the redundant pronoun אָנִי is emphatic). See GKC, § 64 i. In either case, the meaning is the same. Each of those readings is attested by some Hebrew manuscripts. The mixed form might be an attempt to preserve both readings.

וָאֶפְּלָה—With this ending (הָ-), the form of the verb is the first common singular cohortative (with *waw* consecutive). However, such forms often have the same mean-ing as a regular imperfect (with *waw* consecutive), so Waltke-O'Connor calls such forms "pseudo-cohortative" (§§ 33.1.1c and 34.5.3).

אֲהָהּ—This is the same interjection of alarm as in 4:14, where Ezekiel reacted to the command to eat bread cooked on human excrement. Here and in 11:13 Ezekiel uses it when he assumes that all Israel will be exterminated.

הֲמַשְׁחִית אַתָּה אֵת כָּל־שְׁאֵרִית יִשְׂרָאֵל—The word מַשְׁחִית (here, Hiphil participle with interrogative הֲ-) links the question to previous verses with the same form that announced God's judgment (5:16; 9:6). The participle describes what Ezekiel sees happening in the present before his eyes (albeit in a vision). For שְׁאֵרִית, "remnant," see the textual note on it in 5:10. See also the textual notes on related terminology in 6:8, 12 and the commentary on 6:8.

9:9 עֲוֹן בֵּית־יִשְׂרָאֵל וִיהוּדָה—The noun עָוֹן can refer to "iniquity, sin," or to the di-vine "punishment" due to the accumulated consequence of the people's transgres-sions. See the commentary on 4:4–6, which refers to the עָוֹן of Israel and Judah, as does 9:9. Here the emphasis is on their extreme "iniquity," which warrants their ex-treme punishment.

The long construct phrase is unusual because it has two governed nouns, "Israel and Judah." The single phrase here (in contrast to two phrases, e.g., "the iniquity of the house of Israel and the iniquity of the house of Judah") implies that the same "in-iquity" is shared by both houses, that of "Israel" and "Judah." Both houses are equally guilty; neither is better than the other. Hence this situation contrasts with 4:4–6, where "the house of Israel" had 390 years worth of "iniquity/punishment," whereas "the house of Judah" only had 40 years worth. Each of these two houses have been mentioned before, but always as distinct from each other, never together as they are here.[12] Here they are lumped together to indicate that the apostasy was so widespread it had permeated the entire people. The expression explains why Ezekiel perceived that Yahweh would destroy "the *entire* remnant of Israel" in 9:8.

גָּדוֹל בִּמְאֹד מְאֹד—This expression for the extreme gravity of the "iniquity" is more literally "very, very great," but "extremely great" is more idiomatic. When מְאֹד is repeated, the first one often is strengthened by the addition of the preposition בְּ (see BDB, s.v. מְאֹד, 2 e: "with muchness, muchness").

וַתִּמָּלֵא הָאָרֶץ דָּמִים וְהָעִיר מָלְאָה מֻטֶּה—These two clauses both use feminine forms of the verb מָלֵא because both subjects (הָאָרֶץ and הָעִיר) are feminine. The first clause has the (passive) Niphal, "be filled," followed by an accusative of material (דָּמִים, "bloodshed"). The second has the more common Qal, "be full," with a direct object (מֻטֶּה, "injustice"). I have reproduced the variation in my literal translation.

In form מֻטֶּה ("injustice") is a Hophal participle of נָטָה, "to stretch out." The Hophal would mean "stretched out" or perhaps "bent, perverted." BDB and *HALOT* both list the word as a noun that occurs only here in the OT and that means "bending, twisting" (*HALOT*) or "that which is perverted, perverted justice" (BDB). It could refer to a ruler's staff being extended so as to exercise authority, here apparently meaning illegitimate governmental or judicial tyranny. If it means "bent, twisted," the implication is that justice is being perverted. Its common rendition, "injustice," is not completely inaccurate, but changes the vivid word picture of the Hebrew into an abstraction. Yet I know of no way to improve upon it.

The following כִּי clause repeats the people's two rationalizations in 8:12, but in inverted order—a common feature of literary quotation.

9:10 For the two idioms "my eye will not pity" and "I will have no compassion" (also used in 9:5), see the textual note on them in 5:11.

דַּרְכָּם בְּרֹאשָׁם נָתָתִּי—This idiom, literally, "I will place on their head their way," will recur verbatim in 11:21 and 22:31 and with slight variation in 16:43. דֶּרֶךְ frequently means "way, manner of life, things done in life, conduct," and is used more often in a bad sense than in a good one (see BDB, s.v. דֶּרֶךְ, 6 c, d). This clause probably involves an ellipsis: "I will place on their head [the punishment for] their way." Similar idioms occurred earlier, including "your ways I will place on you" (7:4) and "I will place upon you all your abominations" (7:8; cf. 7:3, 9). Similar too is "his blood would be on his own head" (33:4), meaning that the impenitent sinner would be responsible for his own blood being shed when God judges him.

9:11 מֵשִׁיב דָּבָר—The idiom with the Hiphil participle of שׁוּב is, literally, "bringing back/returning word," meaning that he gave a report of what he had done (see BDB, s.v. שׁוּב, Hiphil, 3).

כַּאֲשֶׁר צִוִּיתָנִי[d]—The marginal Qere instructs us to read כְּכֹל אֲשֶׁר, "according to everything which," instead of the Kethib, כַּאֲשֶׁר, "just as." This is a rare case where

---

[12] For "house of Israel," see 3:1, 4, 5, 7, 17; 4:3–5; 5:4; 6:11; 8:6, 10, 11, 12. For "house of Judah," see 4:6; 8:17.

I believe the Kethib should be retained. The ancient versions support the Kethib. Elsewhere Ezekiel uses כְּכֹל אֲשֶׁר only in 24:24, whereas he uses כַּאֲשֶׁר often (e.g., 1:16; 2:2; 10:10; 12:7).

Commentary

For the place of this chapter in the extended vision of the Glory's departure from the temple, see "Introduction to Ezekiel 8–11," which begins the commentary on chapter 8. Chapter 9 is set off from the preceding and following chapters by a structural difference. Chapters 8 and 10 are full of visual images with only occasional verbal comment. In contrast, the "story line" of chapter 9 is carried by direct discourse, with a total of seven speeches.

9:1 The vision hastens toward the final judgment of God's apostate people. In this chapter, the judgment begins to fall upon the unfaithful people in the city and ultimately upon the city itself. This chapter is closely connected to chapter 8 (see the first textual note on 9:1).

The speaker of 9:1 evidently is the "figure with an appearance like a man" (8:2), who is Ezekiel's guide throughout the vision of chapters 8–11. He is the divine "Glory" (כָּבוֹד, 8:4), if not Yahweh himself, although the text is reluctant to be too specific. The Glory is Yahweh's incarnational presence and may be identified as the preincarnate Jesus Christ, the second person of the Trinity.[13]

In 9:1 he seems to order angelic attendants to "bring here the supervisors of the city." The supervisors themselves may be angels who had been stationed over the city to protect it during physical and spiritual warfare (cf. 2 Ki 6:15–17; Is 62:6; Dan 10:13–21). The eschatological city of Jerusalem will have twelve angels, each stationed over one of the city gates (Rev 21:12). However, since the earthly Jerusalem is now apostate, the function of these supervisors is to execute judgment. That each of the supervisors is to have his "weapon of destruction" (Ezek 9:1) recalls the angelic "destroyer" Yahweh sent to slay the firstborn of Egypt (see the textual notes on 9:1). Compare also the two angels involved in the destruction of Sodom and Gomorrah (Genesis 19) and Ps 78:49.

9:2 That the six "men" come from the north may reflect the same exmythological motif that appeared in the call vision, where the divine Glory came from the north (see the commentary on 1:4). The concept was "baptized" and applied positively to Zion, envisioned as Yahweh's abode in the far north (Ps 48:2–3 [ET 48:1–2]). However, in the OT the import of the "north" is generally negative, since that is the direction from which God's judgment comes, as prominently in the prophecies of Jeremiah (Jer 1:13 and passim). Geographically, enemy armies would attack Jerusalem from the north because that direction gave the advantage of advancing from a higher elevation. Also, in the

---

[13] See the textual notes and commentary on 1:26–28, and see the first textual note on 9:4, which also discusses the subject of "called out" in 9:3b, which seems to be the Glory.

wider geographical perspective, armies from Mesopotamia would attack Israel by traveling down from the north along the western leg of the Fertile Crescent.

The "bronze altar" (Ezek 9:2) by which the men stand must be the Solomonic altar (1 Ki 8:64), which Ahaz had removed and placed north of the new altar he installed. His innovative, but apostate, altar was modeled after one he saw in Damascus (2 Ki 16:10–14). The fate of the true altar after the demise of Ahaz is uncertain. Perhaps the reformations of Hezekiah and Josiah did (at least temporarily) restore it to its rightful place in divine worship. However, one would not be surprised if the apostate kings that followed each of those reforming kings countermanded their efforts. The remark in this verse suggests that such was indeed the case. The "men" are taking their stand with orthodoxy, embodied by the true altar, which had been moved (once again) to the north of its ordained location in the temple court.

A seventh "man" is "dressed in linen, with a scribe's kit" (Ezek 9:2). His garb resembles that of the OT priests (see the textual note on "linen" in this verse), and his role in chapter 9 is like that of a priest or mediator who preserves the faithful from God's wrath. However, in 10:2, 6–7, he will be the one charged with executing judgment by scattering coals on the city. Block notes that Jewish tradition understood the man as Gabriel, the angel who executed God's will on earth. Some Christians have regarded him as a Christ figure. A messianic interpretation may antedate Christianity. Block quotes an excerpt from the pre-Qumran *Damascus Document*, which seems to understand him as the Messiah.[14] (Compare the discussion below about the meaning of the mark on the forehead of the righteous.) However, in my judgment, that hermeneutic confuses possible analogy with identification. One may draw an analogy between this white-robed figure and NT portraits of Christ (e.g., Rev 19:11–16, where he executes judgment), but the passages are different enough that the figures are not to be equated. A comparison of the scribe's role in Ezek 8:4–6 to that of the angel in Rev 7:2–3 (cf. Rev 9:4) suggests that more likely the scribe is an angel (see further the discussion of Rev 7:2–3; 9:4 below).

9:3 The movements of Yahweh's "Glory"—that is, his "incarnational" presence in the tabernacle and then the temple until the incarnation of our Lord himself—are not easy to follow throughout chapters 8–11. One question is which cherub or cherubim the Glory had been upon ("cherub" is singular in 9:3). Does this refer to the two cherubim on the cover of the ark or to the four "living creatures" in chapter 1, which Ezekiel will call cherubim in chapter 10? To put it bluntly, is Yahweh in his temple on earth, or is he in his heavenly temple—or both at the same time? The important theological issue is how, even in a vision, we are to distinguish between—and at the same time maintain the unity of—the two different locations of God's presence upon cherubim:

---

[14] Block, *Ezekiel*, 1:305, n. 29, citing the Talmud, *Shabbath*, 55a, for the Jewish tradition, and quoting from the *Damascus Document*, 19.9b–13 (see the citation in Block re the date of that document).

(1) God as he sits on his heavenly throne supported by four living cherubim (as pictured in Ezekiel 1 and 10) and (2) God as he dwells in his temple on earth between the wings of the cherubim statues on the mercy seat.[15]

From a Christian standpoint, this paradox has, in a sense, even been heightened by its antitype or fulfillment in the incarnation of Christ: "In him dwells all the fullness of the Deity bodily" (Col 2:9). From the moment of Christ's incarnation in the womb of the Virgin Mary, and throughout his earthly life, Jesus was the physical dwelling place of the divine Glory on earth. Yet at the same time, God's glorious presence was not limited or restricted only to the physical location of Christ.[16] Moreover, Christ himself, according to his divine nature, possesses the attribute of omnipresence, and his divine attributes are communicated to his human nature due to the hypostatic union of the two natures in the one Christ. Christian theology speaks of several modes of Christ's presence: his local, corporeal mode of presence; his illocal or intangible mode of presence; his supernatural, divine mode of presence, according to which Christ's human nature too shares his divine omnipresence; and his sacramental presence in the Lord's Supper.[17]

Regardless of how we are to interpret the location of the Glory as he ascends "from being on the cherub … to the threshold of the temple" (Ezek 9:3), it seems clear that the movement described here (and again in 10:4) represents the first stage of his ultimate abandonment of the temple. It will no longer be his house, which was protected from destruction by his presence. The vacated temple will be only another human structure, as vulnerable as any other building made of stone and wood.

Many commentators plausibly assume that Ezekiel's depiction of the Glory's departure is directly aimed at the misinterpretation of Isaiah's message of the inviolability of "Zion" by the populace of Jerusalem.[18] "Zion" in the promises of Isaiah, who preached over a century before Ezekiel, should be identified as the true "church" consisting of all believers in both Testaments; this "Zion" shall endure forever and withstand all the forces of evil. However, the popular misunderstanding of the Israelites was that the prophecies promised the inviolability of the earthly city of Jerusalem, her temple, and her inhabitants (nominal members of the outward, visible "OT church"). Back in

---

[15] Greenberg, *Ezekiel*, 1:196, observes that this kind of paradox as such was not unique to Israel in the ancient world. The pagans too had their temples (and idols) that they thought were inhabited by their gods, even while they also believed that their gods inhabited more lofty abodes, such as a mountain or the realm of heaven.

[16] See also the commentary on 1:25–28 and the following "Parallels to Ezekiel's Vision," also in the commentary on chapter 1.

[17] Pieper, *Christian Dogmatics*, 2:176–88, describes these four modes. Luther and the Lutheran Confessions spoke of three modes that included the sacramental presence of Christ. See FC SD VII 98–106, quoting Luther, *Confession concerning Christ's Supper* (AE 37:222–24).

[18] See the commentary on 8:12–13, which traces this theme into the NT.

Jerusalem, Ezekiel's older contemporary Jeremiah had to fight against that mis-understanding that the temple and city were inviolate in his "temple sermons" in chapters 7 and 26 (see also his citation of Micah 3:12 in Jer 26:18).

> God left His throne, that He might issue His command for the judgment upon Israel from the threshold of the temple, and show Himself to be the judge who would forsake the throne which He had assumed in Israel. This command He issues from the temple court, because the temple was the place whence God attested Himself to His people, both by mercy and judgment.[19]

9:4   A vast interpretive literature has arisen around the mark that the scribe was to put on the foreheads of all who lamented Jerusalem's idolatrous religious pluralism and syncretism (detailed in chapter 8). Much of this litera-ture is colored by polemic, either Jewish repudiations of any connection be-tween the mark and the cross of Jesus Christ, or Christian polemic against secularizing interpreters who would completely disconnect this text from Christ's cross.

The text states that the mark was a *taw* (תָו, 9:4, 6), the last letter of the He-brew alphabet. Perhaps beginning in the exile, and certainly in the postexilic era, the so-called square or Aramaic script was adopted for the writing of He-brew since Aramaic was the lingua franca used by the Babylonians. The square Aramaic script continues to be used today for printed editions of the Hebrew OT, and in that script the shape of the letter is ת. However, in preexilic times, the language was written in the paleo-Hebrew script, which probably was still used by Ezekiel himself. No biblical manuscripts from the preexilic or exilic eras are extant, but plentiful Northwest Semitic inscriptions attest the earlier shapes of the *taw*. In the twelfth through sixth centuries B.C., *taw* usually had one of the following shapes: +, †, †, ✗, or ✕.[20]

Most English translations render it as a "mark" (e.g., KJV, RSV, ESV), al-though a "cross" or an "x" is much more accurately descriptive of the shape. The LXX translated it simply as a "sign" (σημεῖον). More precise is the Vul-gate's "sign of a tau" (*signa thau*, 9:4), which may relate to the Greek *tau*, now printed as τ or T, but its original shape was T. That is also the shape of the cor-responding letter in many later Western alphabets, including the English cap-ital "T." A T is often called a "tau cross" and is one of the many forms in which a cross can appear (in ancient times as well as modern). Often an ✗ is called a "St. Andrew's cross," following an ancient tradition that the apostle Andrew was crucified on a cross of that shape.

Two crossing lines is one of the easiest of all marks to make. Such a mark is often used still today to set things apart or designate them as in some way special or different. For example, the Qumran scribes annotated certain pas-

---

[19]   Keil, *Ezekiel*, 1:128.

[20]   See the charts for extrabiblical Hebrew and Moabite in Gibson, *Textbook of Syrian Semitic Inscriptions*, 1:117–18, and for Phoenician inscriptions in Gibson, *Textbook of Syrian Semit-ic Inscriptions*, 3:180.

sages in one of their Isaiah scrolls by a marginal ×. In Job 31:35 the Hebrew *taw* refers to Job's "signature," and an × can still be used today (and usually is recognized for legal purposes) as a signature by those who, for one reason or another, cannot write. In ancient custom, this kind of mark could denote ownership or attestation (as in Job 31:35).

Therefore in Ezek 9:4–6 the *taw* probably is best interpreted as Yahweh's signature, or a mark that designates people who truly belong to him through faith and who are faithful to his kingdom. The passage may be compared to Is 44:5, where those who belong to Yahweh write ליהוה ("belonging to Yahweh") on their hand. (Ownership was commonly expressed by the preposition לְ before the owner's name, as we know from the OT and archaeologically from thousands of seals and jar handles.)

Instead of speaking of Ezek 9:4–6 as a direct prophecy or type of the cross of Christ, I prefer to regard it as a sort of analogous anticipation, at least in the mind of God. But who shall read the mind of God? We may, however, concur with Keil, who observes (following a certain Schmieder) that "there is something remarkable in this coincidence to the thoughtful observer of the ways of God, whose counsel has carefully considered all beforehand."[21]

Since the *taw* marked the true believers, who were to be spared from the general destruction of the population of apostate Jerusalem, various interpreters have connected it with all kinds of other saving marks in the Bible: the mark (אוֹת) that God put on Cain so that he would not be killed (Gen 4:15); the blood of the Passover lamb that the Israelites put on their lintels and doorposts so that their firstborn would not be struck dead by the destroyer (Exodus 12); the rosette on the high priest's forehead to expiate for Israel's sins (Ex 28:36–38); the phylacteries (טוֹטָפוֹת, literally, "guardians") of God's Word, worn on the hand and forehead (Ex 13:16; Deut 6:8; 11:18; cf. Mt 23:5); and the scarlet cord Rahab hung in her window so that she and her family were saved in the destruction of Jericho (Josh 2:18–21; 6:22–25).

Clear Christian echoes of Ezek 9:4–6 appear in Rev 7:1–8; 9:4. Four angels are ready to unleash destructive winds, but another angel comes and tells them not to do so until he puts a seal on the foreheads (as in Ezek 9:4) of the servants of God. A total of 144,000 faithful from the twelve tribes of Israel are sealed—a symbolic number representing the entire church militant on earth, since God's Israel consists of all Jewish and Gentile believers in Christ (Romans 9–11; Gal 6:16). The sealed believers in Christ are then spared when the demonic forces arise from hell to torment humanity (Rev 9:4). The mark put on their foreheads is "the seal of the living God" (Rev 7:2), which would be a stamp having God's name or signature. In Rev 14:1 the 144,000 are about to join the church triumphant, and there they are described as having "his [the

---

21 Keil, *Ezekiel*, 1:129.

Lamb's] name and the name of his Father written on their foreheads."[22] By analogy, that may suggest that the *taw* in Ezek 9:4–6 represents Yahweh's name or signature, designating the marked people as his very own.

Early church commentators and fathers easily and naturally expounded the *taw* in Ezek 9:4–6 as being the same shape as the cross of Jesus Christ and as a sign pointing to his cross, the Gospel, and the Sacraments. For example, Tertullian (ca. A.D. 160–ca. 225) explained that since Christ suffered, all those in Christ must suffer too:

> He signed them with that very seal of which Ezekiel spake [called Θαῦ, "*Tau*," in the Greek translation of Ezek 9:4 quoted by Tertullian]. ... Now the Greek letter *Tau* and our own letter T [are] the very form of the cross, which He predicted would be the sign on our foreheads in the true Catholic Jerusalem. ... Now, inasmuch as all these things are also found amongst you, and the sign upon the forehead, and the sacraments of the church, and the offerings of the pure sacrifice, you ought now to burst forth, and declare that the Spirit of the Creator prophesied of your Christ.[23]

Cyprian (ca. A.D. 200–258) commented on Ezek 9:4: "That the sign pertains to the passion and blood of Christ, and that whoever is found in this sign is kept safe and unharmed, is also proved by God's testimony" in Ex 12:13 about the blood of the Passover lamb. "What previously preceded by a figure [type] in the slain lamb is fulfilled in Christ, the truth which followed afterwards. ... When the world shall begin to be desolated and smitten, whoever is found in the blood and the sign of Christ alone shall escape."[24]

In NT theology, the divine sealing and the imposition of the name of God are accomplished in the Sacrament of Holy Baptism. Christian Baptism takes place in the triune name (Mt 28:19). Those baptized into Christ are adopted as sons of God and so become descendants of Abraham (and hence true Israelites) and heirs of all God's promises (e.g., Gal 3:26–29). The book of Acts records the outpouring of the Holy Spirit in conjunction with Baptism (e.g., Acts 2:38–39; 9:17–18; 10:47; 11:16), and so the NT speaks of Christians as being "sealed" with the Holy Spirit (e.g., 2 Cor 1:22; Eph 1:13; 4:30). Receiving the Spirit of sonship enables the Christian to name God as his Father (Rom 8:15).

---

[22] For the symbolism of the number of the 144,000 and its application to the church, see Brighton, *Revelation*, 180, 183–93, 364–75. Brighton explains connections between Revelation 7 and Ezekiel 9, 10, and 43. He also interprets the seal and divine name as conferred through Christian Baptism and faith in the Word of the Gospel based on NT passages.

[23] Tertullian, *Against Marcion*, 3.22 (*ANF* 3:340–41; see also n. 14 on p. 340). See also *An Answer to the Jews*, 11 (*ANF* 3:167–68), where Tertullian asserts that temporal and eternal ruin shall come to all except "he who shall have been frontally sealed with the passion of the Christ," then quotes Ezek 8:12–9:6 and declares Christ himself to be the sign promised in the OT.

[24] Cyprian, *Address to Demetrianus*, 22 (*ANF* 5:464). In *Three Books of Testimonies against the Jews*, 2:22 (*ANF* 5:525), Cyprian asserts that "in this sign of the Cross is salvation for all people who are marked on their foreheads," and immediately cites Ezek 9:4–6 as his first proof text.

That Baptism marks a Christian as belonging to Christ (and him alone) is the background of 1 Cor 1:10–17, where St. Paul must argue against the schismatic view that Christians belong to separate parties apparently based on who baptized them (cf. also Eph 4:4–6).

The church's traditional practice is to make the sign of the cross upon the baptized, and Christians in the worshiping congregation likewise make the sign of the cross at the Invocation and other parts of the service in remembrance of their Baptism. For the last time, the sign of the cross is made upon the body of the baptized Christian in the funeral and interment in anticipation of the resurrection, which is the greatest act of divine preservation and deliverance from judgment and destruction.

Some Jewish scholars concurred in principle with this kind of symbolic interpretation of the *taw*. Origen (ca. A.D. 185–ca. 254) researched the different ways in which Jews had interpreted the sign. One Jewish Christian pointed out to him that in the old Hebrew script the letter resembles the cross and so it predicts the mark placed on the foreheads of Christians. An unbelieving Jew said that it represented the Torah, whose initial letter is *taw*, and that the people so marked had lived according to the Law. Yet another said that because it is the last consonant of the alphabet, it symbolizes the perfection of those who moaned and groaned over the sinners and suffered together with them.[25] Some rabbis associated the sign with the blood of the Passover lamb and so deemed it a mark of salvation.[26]

However, an anti-Christian backlash seems to have taken place among other Jewish interpreters who interpreted the mark negatively. Although they allowed that the *taw* could be a mark of life and mercy to be placed upon the righteous, they also viewed it (especially when written in blood) as a mark of divine judgment to be placed upon the wicked. Some rabbis considered it equivalent to the Greek letter Θ, which was a mark of death. The Talmud, *Shabbath*, 55a, records the view of one rabbi that the *taw* could stand for תָּמוּת, "you shall die."[27] However, a negative view of the function of the *taw* is incompatible with the statements in Ezek 9:4, 6 that the marked Israelites were moaning over the abominations and were exempted from the execution imposed on the idolaters. They are people who grieve about the surrounding evils and vocally express

---

[25] Origen, *Selecta in Ezechielem* (PG 13:800–801), translated in Lieberman, *Greek in Jewish Palestine*, 187–88, and quoted in Block, *Ezekiel*, 1:312.

[26] See Lieberman, *Greek in Jewish Palestine*, 190.

[27] See the discussion of Jewish views in Lieberman, *Greek in Jewish Palestine*, 185–91. *Shabbath*, 55a, also records the view that a *taw* of ink was placed on the foreheads of righteous "that the destroying angels may have no power over them" and a *taw* of blood on the foreheads of the wicked "that the destroying angels may have power over them" (Soncino ed.). Among the many variations is another Jewish view that the *taw* of ink was placed on the righteous so they would die immediately and escape torture by the destroying angels (p. 190, citing *Tanḥuma*, *Tazri'*, 9). See also Block, *Ezekiel*, 1:311–12; Greenberg, *Ezekiel*, 1:177.

their opposition to it.[28] They are repentant and apparently seek to dissuade their fellow Israelites from perpetuating the abominations (cf. Mt 18:15–20; 1 Corinthians 5; 1 Jn 5:16–21).

The negative view of the *taw* raises the question of whether, in effect, any Israelites were spared from judgment. Ezekiel sometimes (and perhaps hyperbolically) seems to imply total annihilation for Israel (e.g., 5:1–4; 7:1–13; 8:18), and a negative interpretation of the *taw* might be defended (mistakenly) in light of such passages. However, the theme of a repentant remnant preserved by grace was introduced in 6:8–10 (see the commentary there) and will be repeated in 12:16 and 14:12–23. Those passages depict the remnant as small, and in 9:4–6 only one angel is devoted to exemption versus six who execute the destruction. Yet no matter how few they are, "the survivors serve to enhance the sinful status of their fellow citizens and so the fairness of divine punishment."[29]

One can hardly help but think of Gen 18:20–33, where Abraham appeals to Yahweh's character as a God who would not indiscriminately destroy the righteous along with the wicked, no matter how few in number the righteous might be. Also striking is the contrast between the unnumbered (and probably few) repentant Israelites marked with *taw* in Ezekiel 9 and the 144,000 faithful sealed in Rev 7:1–8 (although that symbolic number is now quite small compared to the world's population). Throughout the Scriptures, quantity is not the salient feature of the remnant; rather, it is their faith and faithfulness, which is the result of their salvation by grace alone (Hebrews 11).

9:5–7   These verses underscore the pitiless thoroughness of the annihilation of all but the righteous remnant. Strong, able-bodied men are conspicuous by their absence from the list of those destined for slaughter. The implication apparently is that they will already have fallen in battle. Instead, the six angels target the defenseless, who in ancient times would seek shelter behind a city's walls.

This "take no prisoners" attitude reflects that of God himself (8:18 and 9:10), and the execution is here undertaken at God's express command. Partly this may be understood as simply a reflection of the horror of war, ancient as well as modern, where innocent civilians commonly suffer as much as the actual combatants. But we may also discern the doctrine of original sin behind the thoroughness. "A little leaven leavens the whole lump" (1 Cor 5:6; Gal 5:9), regardless of which or how many actual sins have been committed. The solidarity of a "house" may also be in view; compare Josh 7:22–26, where not only Achan, but his entire estate is stoned and burned because of his transgression. What we know as the Close of the Commandments may also be relevant: God

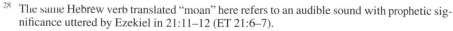

---

[28] The same Hebrew verb translated "moan" here refers to an audible sound with prophetic significance uttered by Ezekiel in 21:11–12 (ET 21:6–7).

[29] Allen, *Ezekiel*, 1:148.

visits[30] iniquity to the third and fourth generation of those who hate him (Ex 20:5).

Presuming that the six "men" (Ezek 9:2) were in fact angels, the following scene reminds us of an important aspect of angelology. With our de facto tendency one-sidedly to accent God's love, we tend to picture angels as only agents of good. They certainly are that, but they can be dispatched to carry out "the whole counsel of God" (Acts 20:27).

God's command for them to "begin from my sanctuary" (Ezek 9:6) is programmatic. As virtually an antitype to the scene here, this clause is echoed in 1 Pet 4:17, speaking of the final judgment:

> For it is the time for judgment to begin from the house[31] of God. And if it is first from us, what will be the end of those who are disbelieving the Gospel of God?

In OT times, the temple could be used for asylum (e.g., by Adonijah in 1 Ki 1:50–51; cf. 2 Ki 11:14–15). Sometimes this is imitated in modern times (usually when those under judgment by the state seek refuge in a church or mosque out of secular motives). But the main point in Ezekiel 9 is that the structure that had been God's earthly residence could no longer be that because of the persistent "abominations" (8:6, 9, 13, 15, 17; 9:4) perpetrated in and around the temple. Yahweh now pronounces the same sentence on his own former residence that he had earlier directed at pagan sanctuaries (6:4–14; see also Ex 23:24; 34:13; Deut 7:5; 12:3). Possibly this emphasis on the temple as Yahweh's now uninhabitable house is conveyed by the switch from "sanctuary" in 9:6 to בַּיִת (literally, "house") as the term for the temple in 9:6b–7, although that latter term is commonly used for the temple throughout the OT.

The idea of greater judgment upon those who have but abuse God's greater gifts certainly applies to the church and the individual Christian. As Christ said, "Everyone to whom is given much, much shall be required from him" (Lk 12:48). We easily forget that the cross is not only the maximal expression of God's love to those who believe, but also the maximal expression of his wrath to those who do not—or, as St. Paul puts it, "to one a fragrance from death to death, to the other a fragrance from life to life" (2 Cor 2:16). The crass idolatry that Ezekiel witnessed in the temple is not without its modern parallels (cf. the commentary on 8:17).

9:8 For the second time in the book, Ezekiel remonstrates with God. The first was in 4:14, where he used the same exclamation, "Ah!" There the prophet

---

[30] The verb is פָּקַד, which is the root of פְּקֻדוֹת, the "supervisors" or, as some take it, the "executioners" in Ezek 9:1.

[31] The Greek is οἶκος, "house," that is, the church as God's temple. In Ezek 9:6b–7 the term for the temple is בַּיִת, literally, "house." Since at the time Peter wrote his first epistle the actual temple either was no longer standing or had been superseded by the church, English translations of 1 Pet 4:17 commonly have "household," "family," or so on, but that changes the metaphor and loses some of the connection to Ezek 9:6.

was reluctant to carry out a vile divine command. Here Ezekiel is an observer, not an actor, and his remonstration is an intercession on behalf of the people. Intercession was a common part of prophetic ministry, paradigmatically in the intercession of Moses for the Israelites after the golden calf incident (Exodus 32–34). Ezekiel intercedes again and similarly in 11:13, but that is the only other time in the book where he clearly adopts that role. Probably the rarity of his supplications is because of the book's great accent on the imminence and inevitability of the judgment.

His petition takes the form of a question: "Are you destroying the entire remnant of Israel as you pour out your wrath upon Jerusalem?" Compare Abraham's intercessory questions to God in Gen 18:23–32. By phrasing his petition as a question, the prophet does not challenge God's authority or the justice of the well-deserved judgment, but he appeals nevertheless to the God whose heart he knows must still hold some mercy. His plea seems to be only for a faithful "remnant of Israel," since it is less likely in this context that it is a general plea for absolution for all Israel. Apparently, in his excited state of mind, Ezekiel overlooks those marked with a *taw*, whom God had commanded the executioners to spare (9:6). Perhaps Ezekiel overlooks them because they were so small in number. In any case, Taylor is on target in describing Ezekiel: "Though his forehead was made as hard as adamant (3:9), his heart was always a heart of flesh (36:26)."[32]

"Israel" (9:8) may be a religious as well as a political or demographic term. "Jerusalem" at the end of Ezekiel's question points toward the city and its inhabitants in politico-geographical terms. Yet Jerusalem plainly had representative significance for the whole people and land of Israel. With the city already decimated by the deportations of 605 B.C. (of which Daniel had been a part) and 597 B.C. (of which Ezekiel himself had been a part), Ezekiel fears that the comprehensive slaughter he is now witnessing will mean the extinction of the nation.

Nevertheless, both "Israel" and Ezekiel's reference to a "remnant" point in a transnational direction. From the time when God called Abraham, the subsequent history of the patriarchs and the later people clearly showed that "not all who are descended from Israel belong to Israel" (Rom 9:6), although it took a long time for God's chosen people to grasp the implications of that fact. The OT history of Israel is full of examples where unfaithful Israelites were cut off from the people and promises of God despite their lineage, and of still other examples where non-Israelites were fully incorporated into the covenant people by grace.

The NT makes plain that even by that time many Christians (probably both Jewish and Gentile) had not fully comprehended the distinction between ethnic Israel and the Israel of faith, nor had all fully grasped God's equal accep-

---

[32] Taylor, *Ezekiel*, 103.

tance of Jew and Gentile alike in Christ by grace alone (see, e.g., Acts 1:6; Romans 9–11; Ephesians 3–4). In modern times too, confusion about "Israel" is evident in the millennial and dispensational schemes that involve a "two covenant" theology (one covenant for Jews, another for Gentiles). A similar confusion exists in liberal ecumenism, which holds out some hope of salvation for Jews apart from faith in Christ and abhors "supersessionism," the tenet that the NT church fulfills and so supersedes OT Israel. Yet the OT theme of the preservation and salvation of the "remnant" remains one of the chief expressions by which especially the prophets articulated the same theology that now we call the distinction between the visible and the invisible church. In the OT era, the whole people of Israel were the visible church, while the faithful remnant was the true, invisible church seen and known by God (so in Ezek 9:4–6, 11, Yahweh's scribe knows exactly whom to mark).

Ezekiel's intercession is striking because it follows God's declaration that he would not heed the prayers of Israel (8:18). Perhaps Ezekiel clings to the hope that even if God is deaf to the other Israelites, possibly he will listen to his prophet. In more general terms, St. Paul urges that intercessions be made for all people (e.g., 1 Tim 2:1). The pastor in particular carries out the intercessory role, both in publicly leading intercessory prayer in the Divine Service and in his private prayers for his church members. The NT picture is that the imminence of the final judgment is all the more reason to pray (cf. Mt 24:44; 25:13; Lk 21:28).

9:9 Yahweh has ensured the salvation of the faithful remnant despite the forthcoming judgment that (in terms of its temporal consequences) will afflict the entire people and nation. However, in Yahweh's answer to the prophet's intercessory petition, his provision for the remnant is totally subordinated to the thoroughness of the punishment of the wicked. "The land is filled with bloodshed" (9:9) is a clear echo of the human condition that precipitated the flood: the earth was filled with/full of violence (Gen 6:11, 13), and so God sent the deluge to cover the face of the entire earth. As the depravity had been nearly total, so the judgment is comprehensive. In the universal flood only eight had been spared, and that salvation has typological application to the Sacrament of Christian Baptism (1 Pet 3:18–22). But Ezekiel gives no count of the marked members of the remnant here.

The objective guilt of the people is matched by their subjective stance that disclaims Yahweh's covenant claims on them and forfeits his gracious promises. The people had expressed their unbelief using the same clauses earlier ("Yahweh does not see us; Yahweh has forsaken the land" [8:12]) in the context of depraved worship. Unbelief is ultimately inseparable from the perversion of justice ("the city is full of injustice," 9:9).

9:10 Yahweh continues with a reiteration of his mercilessness in the present context. The judgment will be commensurate with the crime. "Whatever a man sows, that will he also reap" (Gal 6:7). It is too late for any possible reprieve. Reference to God's "eye" is an ironic reply to the people's arrogant assertion that he does not "see" (9:9).

9:11 This episode comes to a conclusion with the scribe's report that he has obeyed God's instructions. Since this scribe has been commissioned as an agent of protection for the penitent, this final note assures Ezekiel that a remnant will indeed be spared, even though Yahweh's immediate answer (9:9–10) to his plea (9:8) might have left the impression that none would escape.

The Glory Mounts the Throne over the Cherubim and Wheels

Translation

10 ¹Then I looked, and behold, above the dome that was over the heads of the cherubim was something like lapis lazuli stone, what appeared to be the likeness of a throne. He appeared above them. ²He said to the man dressed in linen, "Go in among the wheelwork beneath the cherubim, and fill your cupped hands with fiery coals from among the cherubim, and scatter them over the city." So he went in as I watched.

³Now the cherubim were standing on the south side of the temple when he, the man, entered, and the cloud had filled the inner court. ⁴Then the Glory of Yahweh rose from above the cherubim [and moved] to the threshold of the temple. The temple was filled with the cloud, and the court was full of the radiance of the Glory of Yahweh. ⁵The sound of the wings of the cherubim was heard as far away as the outer court, like the voice of God Almighty when he speaks.

⁶When he commanded the man dressed in linen, "Take fire from among the wheelwork, from among the cherubim," he went and stood beside the wheel. ⁷Then the cherub reached out his hand from among the cherubim to the fire that was among the cherubim. He lifted up [some coals], and he put [them] into the cupped hands of the man dressed in linen, and he [the man] took [them] and went out. ⁸There appeared to belong to the cherubim the form of a human hand under their wings.

⁹Then I looked, and behold, there were four wheels beside the cherubim, one wheel beside each cherub, and the appearance of the wheels was like a stone of beryl. ¹⁰As for their appearance, the same likeness belonged to the four of them, as though a wheel were inside each wheel. ¹¹Whenever they moved, they went in one of their four directions, and they did not turn when they went, for [to] the place where the front wheel faced, they would follow after it, and they did not turn when they went. ¹²Their entire body, their backs, their hands, their wings, and the wheels were full of eyes all around—the wheels of the four of them. ¹³As for the wheels, they were called "wheelwork" in my hearing. ¹⁴Four faces belonged to each one [of the cherubim]. The face of one was the face of the cherub; the face of the second was the face of a man; the third was the face of a lion; and the fourth was the face of an eagle. ¹⁵Then rose the cherubim; these were the living creatures that I had seen by the Kebar Canal. ¹⁶Whenever the cherubim went, the wheels went alongside them, and when the cherubim raised their wings to rise from the ground, the wheels too did not swerve from their side. ¹⁷When they [the cherubim] stood still, they [the wheels] would stand still, and when they [the

cherubim] rose, they [the wheels] would rise with them, for the spirit of the living creatures was in them [the wheels].

[18]Then the Glory of Yahweh went out from the threshold of the temple and stood above the cherubim. [19]The cherubim raised their wings and rose from the ground in my very sight as they went out, and the wheels were beside them. He stopped at the entrance of the east gate of the house of Yahweh, and the Glory of the God of Israel was upon them [the cherubim] from above. [20]These were the living creatures that I had seen beneath the God of Israel at the Kebar Canal, and I [now] knew that they were cherubim. [21]Four faces belonged to each one, and four wings belonged to each, with something like the hands of a man underneath their wings. [22]As for the appearance of their faces, they were the [same] faces that I had seen by the Kebar Canal—their appearances and themselves. Each one went straight ahead.

Textual Notes

10:1 There is a substantial amount of overlap between chapters 1 and 10. What chapter 1 had referred to rather vaguely as the חַיּוֹת ("living creatures," 1:5 and passim) are here specified as "cherubim." See the textual note on them in 1:5 and the commentary on 1:5–11 and 10:1. Much of 1:26 is repeated in 10:1 with only minor textual differences. Here כְּאֶבֶן סַפִּיר is shortened from כְּמַרְאֵה אֶבֶן סַפִּיר in 1:26. The LXX of 10:1 does not reflect the presence of either כְּמַרְאֵה or נִרְאָה ("appeared"). But if they are omitted (as many critics argue they should be), and especially if one disregards the *athnach* on כִּסֵּא, the verse would have an entirely different meaning; see the commentary below.

My translation follows the MT. The final clause, נִרְאָה עֲלֵיהֶם, is a narrative sentence ("he appeared above them") that resumes the narrative action from 9:11. The implied subject is Yahweh, who then speaks in 10:2 (and in the parallel verse 10:6). The narrative had been interrupted by the description in 10:1a. The narrative continues in 10:1b, 2, 4a, 6–7, 15a, and finally is completed in 10:18–19.

10:2 The Hebrew has וַיֹּאמֶר ("and he said") twice, once at the start of the verse and a second time immediately before the quotation of what Yahweh said. My translation combines the two. The second one is not reflected in the LXX and is omitted in some minor Hebrew manuscripts, but the twofold use occurs elsewhere (e.g., Gen 22:7; 2 Sam 24:17), so it does not warrant emendation of the Hebrew text.

אֶל־בֵּינוֹת לַגַּלְגַּל—The word בֵּינוֹת is a plural form of the preposition בֵּין. This is the first instance in Ezekiel of גַּלְגַּל, which will be repeated in 10:6, 13 (and in reference to chariot wheels in 23:24; 26:10). It is obviously a derivative of the verb גָּלַל, "to roll." Translations and commentators often render it by "wheelwork," "casters," or "rotary system." "Wheelwork" reflects that its form in 10:2, 6, 13 is singular. The term used for the same wheels in 1:15–21, and again often later in chapter 10, is אוֹפָן. The use of the less common word גַּלְגַּל has occasioned much speculation, but in 10:13 Ezekiel himself reports that he heard that the אוֹפַנִּים ("wheels") were called גַּלְגַּל ("wheelwork"). Hence, there can be no reasonable doubt that the two words are substantially synonymous.

אֶל־תַּחַת לַכְּרוּב—The combination אֶל־תַּחַת לְ occurs only here, but its meaning, "beneath," is not in dispute. The Hebrew has the singular "cherub," but it surely is collective here and most of the time later in the chapter, as it was in 9:3. Later in 10:2 the plural is used. The LXX renders it as plural here, as I have here and where appropriate later in the chapter.

חָפְנֶיךָ—In the OT the noun חֹפֶן is used only in the dual or plural number. It means "hollowed/cupped hands." Instead of cupping each hand separately, probably the two hands were cupped together to form one bowl. If so, instead of taking two handfuls, the man was to have one measure that filled both hands. This would also apply to 10:7, where a cherub places the coals into the man's cupped hands.

10:3 Mention of the cherubim triggers another digression in 10:3–5, consisting mostly of description (except for 10:4a), before the main narrative resumes in 10:6. These verses continue the description in 10:1a and fill in many details relating to the activity of the כָּבוֹד and the throne-chariot.

בְּבֹאוֹ הָאִישׁ—This is a normal Hebrew idiom for a temporal clause (בְּ on an infinitive construct functioning as the *nomen regens* of a construct chain) except for the pronominal suffix on the infinitive ("when *he* entered—the man"). Normally such an infinitive (or any word in construct) does not have a suffix.[1] However, the use of a proleptic suffix, as here, is common in later Hebrew and in Aramaic. It seems to be another instance in Ezekiel where we witness the beginning of the disappearance of Hebrew as an everyday language and its gradual replacement by Aramaic.

Ezek 10:3b and 10:4b both concern "the cloud" (הֶעָנָן) associated with the Glory and the cherubim. The definite article indicates that the reference is not to the storm cloud in 1:4 out of which Ezekiel's inaugural vision may have materialized, but rather with the cloud that is Yahweh's "real presence." See the commentary on 10:1, 3 (and textual notes and commentary on 1:26–28).

10:4 The first sentence of 10:4 repeats in only slightly different wording what was already stated in 9:3. See the textual notes and commentary on 9:3, and the first part of the commentary on chapter 10 below.

10:5 This essentially parenthetical verse basically states the same thing about the sound of the cherubim wings that 1:24 said about the sound of the wings of the living creatures. Therefore it further equates the cherubim with the living creatures. The reason why this statement is placed here probably has to do with some movement of the cherubim, since they would use their wings when they moved. Perhaps the sound of their wings was due to the movement of the cherubim to the south side of the temple (their location in 10:3).

קוֹל can mean either "sound" or "voice." English has no one word comprising both, so some of the Hebrew simile between "the sound [קוֹל] of the wings" and "the voice [קוֹל] of God Almighty" is lost in translation. "God Almighty" is the traditional rendering of אֵל־שַׁדָּי. See the textual note on the similar phrase ("the voice of the

---

[1] Zimmerli, *Ezekiel,* 1:226, supposes that metathesis of the *alef* and the *waw* has taken place, so the reading should be בְּבֹא. He notes other examples in Ezekiel of such metathesis occurring with the verb בּוֹא.

Almighty") in 1:24. The epithet's frequent association with God's power, as in Job and many patriarchal narratives, may help explain its use here.

The "outer court" (10:5) must refer to the space immediately inside the perimeter wall of the sacred enclosure. Since Ezekiel is apparently in the inner court, he must hear the reverberations of the sound throughout the temple complex.

10:6 Ezek 10:6–7 resumes the narrative of the man dressed in linen from 9:11 and 10:2 after the digression in 10:3–5. The command given in 10:2 is repeated in 10:6, followed by a more detailed account of its implementation. Because 10:6 is essentially repetitive, the verbs in the sentence might be translated as pluperfects: "when he *had* commanded [in 10:2] … he had gone and stood." In 10:1b and 10:2, the implied subject—the person who "appeared" and then spoke—is Yahweh, and so here too Yahweh is the implied person who commands the man clad in linen, who then stands beside "the wheel" (הָאוֹפָן). The definite article (literally, "the wheel") seems to imply a particular, designated wheel, but, if so, we are not told which one. Alternatively, the word may be another collective ("wheels"), essentially parallel to the preceding term לַגַּלְגַּל ("the wheelwork").

10:7 וַיִּשְׁלַח הַכְּרוּב אֶת־יָדוֹ—The definite article with the singular ("the cherub") may point to one particular cherub designated for this task (just as הָאוֹפָן in 10:6 may have referred to one particular wheel). But if "cherub" is a true singular (not a collective), to which cherub does it refer? Since the verb here and the later verbs וַיִּשָּׂא וַיִּתֵּן are singular, it seems that just one cherub performed these actions. Logically, it would only require one cherub to fill the linen-clad man's cupped hands with the coals.

10:8 This verse plays a transitional role between what precedes and what follows. With respect to the preceding, it functions almost as an afterthought, explaining the cherub's hand in 10:7. It also serves as a flashback to the living creatures' human hands mentioned in 1:8. In chapter 1 no significance was attached to their hands. Here we learn that they could be used to fetch coals from the interior of the throne-chariot. Compare Gen 3:24, which may indicate that a cherub could hold and wield a sword, and Is 6:6, where a seraph takes a coal from the heavenly altar using tongs.

Looking forward, the mention of the cherubim hands seems to trigger the description in 10:9–17, 20–22 of the cherubim in their entirety, concentrating especially on the wheels. Ezek 10:9–14 is roughly parallel to 1:8–21, but there are differences, as I shall note below.

10:9 What in English can easily be condensed to "one wheel beside each cherub" is expressed in idiomatic Hebrew by repetition of the full phrase. The LXX omits one of the phrases, perhaps by haplography.

10:11 This repetitive verse essentially repeats what was stated about the locomotion of the cherubim in 1:9, 12 and of the wheels in 1:17. However, commentators disagree about whether this verse is describing the wheels (as did 10:10) or the cherubim. It seems more likely that it describes the wheels. If so, then הָרֹאשׁ (literally, "the head") must be the "front, leading wheel," that is, the one that was in the front when the vehicle would go in a particular direction. My translation reflects that view. If, however, it describes the cherubim, הָרֹאשׁ would refer to the head of one of the cherubim, or possibly to one of the four faces of the cherubim. (In 10:1 the singular רֹאשׁ referred to the "heads" of the cherubim.)

10:12　It is even less clear than in 10:11 whether this verse is describing the wheels or the cherubim. The context might indicate that this verse is still describing the wheels, which were the topic in 10:10 (and probably 10:11) and are again in 10:13. Commentators and translators who assume "wheels" to be the subject commonly translate "backs" and "hands" as "rims" and "spokes," respectively. The plural of גַּב ("back") referred to the "rims" of the wheels in 1:18. Some interpreters see especially in 10:12 the beginning of the conversion of the "wheels" into a special class of angels (see the commentary on 10:8–17).

However, the opening phrase, וְכָל־בְּשָׂרָם (literally, "all their flesh"), seems inappropriate for wheels, but more appropriate if the subject has changed back to the cherubim, who were prominent in 10:1–8 and are the subject in 10:14–15. (The LXX omits "all their flesh," perhaps because the translators assumed the verse was about the wheels and considered that phrase inappropriate for them.) Chapter 1 only referred to the wheels as possessing "eyes" (1:18),[2] but 10:12 may be adding new information that Ezekiel did not notice earlier. Furthermore, the "living creatures" in Rev 4:6, 8, which correspond in many ways to the cherubim in Ezekiel, are "full of eyes," both "in front and in back" (Rev 4:6) and also "around and within" (4:8). One might appeal to the rule that "Scripture interprets Scripture," but not all of the features of the creatures in Revelation 4 are identical to those in Ezekiel 1 and 10, so we should not press the identification. Nevertheless, all in all, it seems best to take "cherubim" as the new subject of the description in 10:12. Ezek 10:21 supports this because it too refers to "hands" and "wings," and they clearly belong to the cherubim. (Extrabiblical parallels can be found: some figures of the Egyptian god Bes are full of eyes, but the relevance of this to Ezekiel is doubtful.)

10:13　This is a parenthetical comment about the terminology for the wheels. See the discussion of גַּלְגַּל and of אוֹפָן in the textual notes on 10:2. Some distinction seemed necessary also in translation, so I have rendered גַּלְגַּל as "wheelwork."

לָהֶם קוֹרָא—The idiom קָרָא לְ commonly means "to name." קוֹרָא is an impersonal third masculine singular Pual perfect, literally, "to them it was called." This is best translated as if the indirect object were the subject of the passive verb: "they were called."

10:14　Even though the previous verse (10:13) was about the wheels, the larger context requires us to take 10:14 as referring to the cherubim, and so my translation adds "of the cherubim" in brackets.

All of this verse is missing in the LXX. One proposed reason is that the translators found it impossible to reconcile this verse with 1:10 and so omitted it. One problem (which some modern commentators find insurmountable) is that this verse might

---

[2]　Allen, *Ezekiel,* 1:117, 125, tries to solve the problem by punctuating the verses differently (connecting 10:12a with 10:11, and making 10:12b a sentence by itself) so that the description here ascribes eyes only to the wheels. In terms of sense that is an appealing solution, but textually it is speculative because it relies on a convoluted explanation of the supposed history of the text.

appear to say that each cherub had four identical faces. If the term פְּנֵי in each of the four clauses after the first is taken as a true plural, then it could mean "the *faces* of the first were the *faces* of the cherub" and so on. Then the first would have four cherub faces, the second four human faces, the third four lion faces, and the fourth four eagle faces. In contrast, 1:10 states that each of the four cherubim had four different faces: each had one human face, one lion face, one ox face, and one eagle face.

However, 10:14 does not need to be construed so as to contradict 1:10. The plural term פָּנִים is normally used for a single face, so these clauses in 10:14 could be translated, "the *face* of the first was the *face* of the cherub" and so forth. Since Ezekiel had already mentioned in 1:10 the four different faces that each cherub possessed, perhaps here in 10:14 he only mentions the one face of each that was turned toward him. Ezek 1:10 implies that each cherub was oriented differently, with its human face in front, directed outward (away from the others). Consequently, a viewer standing in one place, such as Ezekiel, would see a different face on each cherub. Probably the seer would especially notice the one face (out of the four on each) that was directed toward him.

That same explanation may apply to Rev 4:7, where the apostle John says about the four creatures, "The first living creature was like a lion, and the second living creature was like an ox, and the third living creature had a face like that of a man, and the fourth living creature was like a flying eagle." Apparently John saw only one face per creature, but that does not necessarily mean that each creature had only one face. Perhaps John from his vantage point (like Ezekiel in 10:14) noticed and recorded only one of the four faces each creature had.

One last difficulty remains, namely, that the first face mentioned in 10:14 is פְּנֵי הַכְּרוּב, "the face of the cherub" (with the definite article, while "man," "lion," and "eagle" are anarthrous). Based on Ezek 1:10 and Rev 4:7, one would expect "ox" in place of "the cherub." Some critics simply emend the text to "ox." But it is hard to see how שׁוֹר could be corrupted into הַכְּרוּב. Even if some copyist had been extremely careless, succeeding copiers would surely have corrected it if they thought it was a mistake.

What does a cherub's head look like? Could it look like that of an ox? We are not told. Bovine-headed sphinxes are known from Mesopotamia, but it is doubtful if anything of that sort is intended here. Keil's explanation, based on the presence of the definite article, seems most satisfactory to me: "The allusion is to one particular cherub, who was either well known from what had gone before, or occupied a more prominent position than the rest."[3]

10:15 Critics allege that this verse is redundant (or premature) because 10:15a is repeated in 10:19, and 10:15b in 10:20 and 10:22. Nevertheless, it is attested in all the ancient versions, and such repetition is common throughout chapters 1 and 10.

וַיֵּרֹמּוּ הַכְּרוּבִים—This uncommon verb, repeated in 10:17, 19, is the Niphal (third masculine plural imperfect with *waw* consecutive) of רָמַם and means "to rise." It is a by-form of the common רוּם, used for the rising of the cherubim in 10:16–17.

---

[3] Keil, *Ezekiel,* 1:141.

הִיא הַחַיָּה—Here and in 10:17, 20, Hebrew feminine singular forms (here, literally, "this was the living creature") identify the masculine plural "cherubim" (10:15) with the "living creatures" of chapter 1 (e.g., 1:5, 13). The antecedent of the feminine singular pronoun הִיא is the preceding word, הַכְּרוּבִים. The singular forms must be collective and so are translated as plurals ("these were the living creatures," 10:15, 20). These verses (10:15, 17, 20) illustrate how easily the singular (collective) and plural interchange throughout the descriptions of what Ezekiel sees in chapters 1 and 10.

10:16   Before the text returns to the main theme of the departure of the כָּבוֹד from the temple (10:18–19), 10:16–17a reaffirms the harmonious movements of the wheels and the cherubim, first noted in 1:20–21.

גַּם־הֵם—Literally, "also they," this is emphatic. I have rendered it simply as "the wheels *too*."

10:17   The verse repeats what 1:20–21 stated about the relationship between the cherubim and wheels. The translation adds the referents of the Hebrew pronouns.

10:18   That the Glory "went out *from* the threshold" is somewhat free. The combination of prepositions following the verb יָצָא is actually מֵעַל, "from off of." That combination was used appropriately with the verb רוּם in 10:4, where the Glory rose from its location on/above the cherubim. Greenberg suggests that the two stages of the departure have here been telescoped into one.[4] The LXX seems to have resolved the issue by reading only "from the temple."

10:19   "The east gate of the house of Yahweh," to which the throne-chariot now moves, does not refer to the temple itself, but to the eastern gate of the outer court, the main entrance to the entire sacred enclosure. "House" (בַּיִת) can be used of the entire sacred compound surrounding the temple (as well as the building itself). Since the Glory has moved from the threshold of the temple (10:18) to this gate of the outer court, the Glory has abandoned the temple itself and is preparing to forsake the entire temple compound.

10:20–22   The remaining verses in the chapter simply repeat and underscore what has already been stated. In spite of the substitution of "the cherub" for "ox" in the list of the four faces in 10:14, these last three verses emphatically affirm the identification of the creatures Ezekiel sees in chapter 10 with those he witnessed in chapter 1: they have four faces, four wings, hands under their wings, and they move straight ahead.

10:20   This verse reiterates in slightly expanded form the brief recognition in 10:15b correlating the prophet's inaugural vision with the present one.

10:21   This verse clearly echoes 1:6 and 1:8. The repetition אַרְבָּעָה אַרְבָּעָה apparently is distributive: "four faces" are ascribed to each one of the cherubim. Compare the long phrase in 10:9 that is repeated and distributive. Here "four" need not be repeated in translation, and the LXX and Vulgate have only one "four" (leading some to regard the second "four" as a dittograph, but the versions often omit a repeated phrase; LXX 10:9 omits the second instance of the distributive phrase).

---

4   Greenberg, *Ezekiel*, 1:183.

10:22 Some freedom is imperative in translating this verse. After "Kebar Canal," the Hebrew has מַרְאֵיהֶם וְאוֹתָם, "their appearance and them(selves)." Except for the LXX, other ancient versions attest the strange wording. Apparently אוֹתָם functions as an emphatic pronoun, and the phrase stresses that the "faces" were not mere apparitions without substance. The last clause (אִישׁ אֶל־עֵבֶר פָּנָיו יֵלֵכוּ) is repeated from 1:9, 12.

Commentary

For the place of this chapter in the extended vision of the departure of the Glory from the temple, see "Introduction to Ezekiel 8–11" at the start of the commentary on chapter 8.

Chapter 10 gives exegetes a disproportionate share of grief. The basic problem is the frequent alternation between the flow of the action narrative and the descriptions of the Glory (כָּבוֹד) and cherubim. We have narrative in 10:1b–2, 4a, 6–7, 15a, and 18–19. All the rest—that is, most of the chapter—is descriptive. When certain details of the vision capture Ezekiel's attention, he tries to describe them even though they may seem incidental to the reader who is trying to follow the sequence of the action. The same alternation between narration and description will continue into chapter 11, although the two parts seem to flow together more smoothly there than here.

Especially in chapter 10 one almost gets the impression that Ezekiel is taking notes as he observes the scene before him, sometimes reporting the action, but more often attempting to verbalize what he saw. After the vision was over, Ezekiel could have converted his notes with relatively minimal change into the text we now find in his book. To be sure, this text really does not give us any more information about the external aspect of the process of its divine inspiration than other texts in the book do. But what I have submitted seems to be at least a plausible speculation.

Many modern scholars have tended to take an entirely different tack in dealing with the text. Instead of attributing its peculiarities to the particular process of inspiration that gave rise to it, they have, to varying degrees, tended to delete large portions of the present text as later glosses. Sometimes they claim to distinguish various layers in the text. They may offer reasons why the putative later layers were added, but more often they do not. Block rightly complains: "Inordinate attention tends to be devoted to isolating these layers, at the expense of interpreting each statement in the light of its current context."[5] Three examples will suffice. Eichrodt considers only 10:2 and part of 10:7 to be genuine.[6] Zimmerli finds the original core only in parts of 10:2, 4, 7, 18, and 19.[7] Each page of his commentary is arranged in two columns; a little over four columns are devoted to these allegedly original fragments,[8] while the rest of

---

[5] Block, *Ezekiel*, 1:314.

[6] Eichrodt, *Ezekiel*, 107.

[7] Zimmerli's reconstructed text is in *Ezekiel*, 1:234.

[8] Zimmerli, *Ezekiel*, 1:249–52.

the chapter seems to deserve only about three columns.[9] A little less rigidly, Allen thinks he discerns a threefold pattern in the shaping of this chapter and in much of the rest of the book.[10]

There is no theological a priori reason to deny that something approaching our modern conception of "editorial" activity may have occurred in the history of the text. But, if we speculate along those lines, the conservative's first choice of "editor" will surely be Ezekiel himself, still under the inspiration of the Spirit.

If one does not approach the text with a "hermeneutic of suspicion," one can see order and design. In terms of structure, the chapter readily divides into two parts: 10:1–8 and 10:9–22. Each part is introduced by "then I looked, and behold" (וָאֶרְאֶה וְהִנֵּה, 10:1, 9). In the chapter we see Jerusalem's imminent judgment described from two perspectives, each with a main character. These two are intertwined: (1) the earthly judgment is carried out by the man dressed in linen, who is to scatter coals on the city (10:2, 6–7); and (2) the heavenly judgment is the abandonment of the temple by the Glory (10:4, 15, 18–19).

Chapter 10 also repeatedly echoes (and, at points, virtually duplicates) previous texts. The description of the Glory enthroned upon the dome over the heads of the cherubim and their attendant wheels is largely parallel to that in chapter 1. Ezek 10:1 clearly reflects 1:26 (the heavenly throne above the dome). Ezek 10:4 echoes 9:3 since both narrate that the Glory ascended from the cherub(im) and stood at the threshold of the temple. (For the debate on the chronological relation of the two verses, see the textual notes and commentary on 9:3.) Those two verses in their contexts consider the same event with alternative accents: in 9:1–11 the accent is on Yahweh's wrath on Jerusalem with secondary consideration of his departure; in 10:1–8 the accent switches to his departure. And 10:9–22 is full of echoes of 1:16–21.

I have used the word "echo" because chapter 10 presents some refinements of earlier texts. At the inaugural vision (chapter 1), it seemed as though Ezekiel could barely describe, let alone explain, much of what he saw. In chapter 10, his second extended vision of the Glory (Ezekiel also briefly saw the Glory in 3:22–23), the details tend to be explained more fully (especially those of the wheels). While Ezekiel seemed stupefied after the first vision (see 3:14–15), he is more lucid here.

10:1 The first sentence of this verse interrupts the narrative line about Yahweh and the linen-clad man (9:11; 10:2) with description. The interruption serves a variety of purposes. Structurally, it links the throne-chariot Ezekiel describes to the following narrative: the city's judgment coincides exactly with Yahweh's abandonment of his temple. The interruption also underscores the theme of judgment. The throne-chariot had appeared at the start of the prophet's call narrative (chapters 1–3), which had stressed Yahweh's character as a judge

---

[9] Zimmerli, *Ezekiel,* 1:254–56.

[10] Allen, *Ezekiel,* especially 1:135.

and Ezekiel's call to proclaim his judgment. Now that same judgment-bearing scene reappears.

Since the first sentence mentions only the throne (not any occupant), it may be empty, but it is at hand for Yahweh to mount it, which he apparently does in 10:18. But Yahweh is not absent from the present scene. The Masoretic punctuation requires that we take Yahweh as the implied subject of the second sentence: "He appeared above them." He will continue to be the subject who speaks in the following verse. (It would be pure tautology if the implied subject were something like "*a throne* appeared above them" because the fact that the throne has become visible has already been stated.)

That the creatures who bear the throne are "cherubim" is mentioned in 10:1 for the first time in the book, almost in passing and in an anticipatory way. In 10:15 and 10:20–22 Ezekiel will make explicit the association between the "cherubim" and the "living creatures" he saw in chapter 1. Why did the prophet not realize in chapter 1 that they were "cherubim"? Perhaps there was some difference between what Ezekiel saw in his visions and the images he knew were inside the Jerusalem temple (see the textual notes on 1:5). Probably Ezekiel had never actually entered the temple itself and seen the cherubim carved on its walls and doors (1 Ki 6:29–35), since a priest did not begin his full service until he was thirty years old, which Ezekiel only attained in exile (see the commentary on Ezek 1:1, 3).[11] Nevertheless, because of Ezekiel's training as a priest, he would have been taught about the appearance of the cherubim in the temple. The OT never tells us precisely what they looked like, but the ones in the temple may have had only two wings (in contrast to the four on the creatures Ezekiel sees) and only one face (perhaps human) in contrast to the four faces (three of which were not human) in 1:10 and 10:14.

The Bible makes a lot of "vertical typology," the correspondence between the earthly sanctuary and its heavenly prototype (so Ex 25:9; 1 Kings 8 [Solomon's temple dedicatory prayer]; 1 Chr 28:19; Acts 7:44; Heb 8:5), but we are never told precisely what the heavenly prototype of the cherubim in the earthly temple looked like. Presumably Moses and Solomon were shown prototypes of the cherubim to be fashioned over the ark and in the tabernacle and temple, even if they did not see the living cherubim themselves. However, Ezekiel is the only one in the OT who attempts a description of the living cherubim based on his own observation (and that in a vision). Since they are supernatural (angelic), perhaps a precise and comprehensive description in human language is impossible. The only other description in the Bible that offers much detail is by the apostle John,[a] although the "living creatures" he sees are not al-

(a) Rev 4:6–9; cf. Rev 5:6, 8, 11, 14; 6:1–7; 7:11; 14:3; 15:7; 19:4

---

[11] The cherubim in the Holy of Holies could have been seen only by the high priest, who entered it only on the annual Day of Atonement. Lev 16:13 indicates that the smoke from the incense he was to burn when (or after) he entered the Holy of Holies covered the atonement cover, so perhaps that smoke and the darkness of the room prevented even him from seeing clearly the cherubim on the atonement cover or the wall behind the ark.

together identical to the cherubim seen by Ezekiel. Many commentators entertain possible parallels with the various hybrid figures we know from ancient Near Eastern iconography (sphinxes, griffins, etc.), but any and all such comparisons must be considered highly speculative.

(b) 1 Sam 4:4; 2 Sam 6:2; 2 Ki 19:15; 1 Chr 13:6; Ps 18:10 ‖ 2 Sam 22:11; Pss 80:2 (ET 80:1); 99:1; cf. 2 Ki 2:12; Ps 104:3

The major difference between the models of the cherubim in the tabernacle and temple and the creatures in Ezekiel 1 and 10 is that the former were static, while the cherubim here are infinitely mobile. Israelite poetry contains pictures of Yahweh enthroned or riding on a cherub,[b] with which Ezekiel was surely familiar. Somehow (we are not told precisely how) Ezekiel realizes that he has glimpsed the celestial reality of the Glory enthroned on the cherubim, who has been forced to abandon his "incarnation" in Jerusalem because of the Israelites' sin, but who nevertheless was personally present with the faithful exiles. The underlying thought approximates Yahweh's assertion shortly (11:16) that he has become to them their "sanctuary for a little while in the lands to which they have come" (see the exegesis of that verse).

The Christian will also observe that in Christ Yahweh has become permanently incarnate. Throughout eternity, Christ's divine and human natures shall ever be united inseparably (cf. the commentary on 1:25–28). But in the interim of the "not yet," after his ascension and before his return in glory to bring this world to its close, God still meets us in grace through his Word and Sacraments, which convey to us the benefits of Christ's vicarious suffering, death, and resurrection, namely, the forgiveness of sins and everlasting life with the promise of bodily resurrection. The same kind of vertical typology present in the OT underlies our entire theology of worship, as we sing in the Preface that introduces the Sanctus in the Communion liturgy: "with angels and archangels and with all the company of heaven we laud and magnify your glorious name ..."[12]

10:2 The subject of "said" is still Yahweh, even though he was last named as the speaker back in 9:4. He addresses "the man dressed in linen," who is no longer depicted with his writing kit as a scribe (9:2–3, 11), but now as an incendiary. His orders correspond to those given the other six angels in 9:5–7, who were told to kill, but his commission is to destroy the city itself. He is to enter among the cherubim and receive (cf. 10:7) in his cupped hands some coals of the heavenly fire blazing among them. His linen vestments suggest a priestly status (see the textual notes on 9:3). Without Yahweh permitting him to handle the sacred fire, we may surmise that the same judgment that befell those who abused fire in divine worship (Lev 10:1–3; Num 16:35) would have overtaken him.

Commentators argue about the precise origin of the fire. However, chapter 1 should settle the question: the appearance of the living creatures "was like coals of fire, burning like the appearance of torches. It [fire] was moving back and forth among the living creatures. The fire had brightness, and from the fire

---

[12] E.g., *LW*, p. 146.

lightning was going out" (1:13). Chapter 1 had merely mentioned the coals of fire without indicating any function for them; now chapter 10 reveals at least one purpose they could serve. In Is 6:6–7 a coal is used to purify Isaiah's mouth for ministry, but most similar to Ezek 10:2 is Rev 8:5, where coals from the heavenly altar are thrown down upon the earth to inflict judgment. Ezek 1:15 and 10:2 imply that the wheels extended beneath the cherubim, and in 10:2 Yahweh directs the man wearing linen to go in among the wheelwork (which also means he will go among the cherubim) to access the coals.

Many commentators are not satisfied with this explanation and seek others, sometimes exploiting the singular form of the Hebrew translated as the first instance of "cherubim" in 10:2, or emending the Hebrew text in one way or another. Only a couple of examples are worth mentioning here. Zimmerli eliminates all the plural references to "cherubim" as secondary and allows only a single cherub in the sanctuary. Then he speculates that perhaps גַּלְגַּל ("wheelwork") was a brazier for the incense altar, made moveable by wheels and set in front of the ark in the Holy of Holies.[13] In contrast, Eichrodt judges the reference to the wheels as an accretion and proposes the altar of incense itself to be the source of the burning coals.[14] But these and other comparable theories fail to find support in the text as it stands.

The conflagration to be wreaked on the city evokes comparisons with Sodom, the wicked city infamous for homosexuality, upon which God rained down "brimstone and fire" (Gen 19:24); Ezekiel in 16:46–56 will refer to Sodom and its destruction (16:50). Other passages that speak of similar judgments include Ps 11:6; Is 34:9; Ezek 38:22; Rev 11:5; 14:10; 19:20; 20:9; and the "lake of fire and brimstone, which is the second death," to which all who do not believe in Christ are consigned for eternity (Rev 21:8).

Yahweh directs the priestly angel here to "scatter/sprinkle/strew" the coals all over Jerusalem (Ezek 10:2). The same verb (זָרַק) was in Ex 9:8–10, where Moses threw ashes from a kiln to cause the plague of boils. The verb most commonly appears in sacrificial contexts, often for the sprinkling of blood (e.g., Ex 24:6, 8; Lev 1:5, 11; Ezek 43:18). Judgment Day can be depicted metaphorically as a sacrifice with the city and its inhabitants pictured as a sacrificial victim (e.g., Zeph 1:7–8), but that does not appear to be the case here.

The actual burning of the city by the Babylonians is described in 2 Ki 25:9 and 2 Chr 36:19 and confirmed by archaeological excavations in the city of David. Hence, via visionary experience, we meet again the "vertical typology" in which a heavenly action corresponds to very real events on earth.

10:3–4 The chariot parks (literally) "to the right of the house/temple" (מִימִין לַבַּיִת), that is, on the south side, probably more specifically south of the altar of burnt offering. No reason is given for this location, but probably it

---

[13] Zimmerli, *Ezekiel*, 1:250–51.

[14] Eichrodt, *Ezekiel*, 134.

is to be at the farthest possible remove from the "statue of jealousy" at the north gate (8:5), and possibly also because of the association of the north gate with the executioners (9:2).

"The man" who "entered" (10:3) is almost certainly still "the man dressed in linen" who was to enter the wheelwork (10:2), although some commentators entertain the possibility that it is the fiery human figure of 8:2, in which case these verses would take us back to the beginning of this vision.

"*The* cloud" (10:3–4) is to be associated with Yahweh's personal guidance of his pilgrim people in the desert (Ex 13:21), in a pre-tabernacle tent-sanctuary (Ex 33:7–10), and, more permanently, at the consecration of both the tabernacle (Ex 40:34–35) and its successor, the temple (1 Ki 8:10–11), fulfilled in the tabernacling of the Word made flesh in Jn 1:14 (see the commentary on Ezek 9:3). The reference to "the cloud" here is almost ironic because in those earlier accounts the accent was on God's gracious presence, especially as he became "incarnate" in the sanctuary where he had "caused his name to dwell [שָׁכֵן]" (e.g., Deut 12:11). (In postbiblical literature, the "Shekinah" is a term for this gracious presence, formed from the verb used of God's tabernacling presence with his people, שָׁכַן.) Here God is abandoning the structure because it has been polluted by idolatry (Ezekiel 8).

Even though the Glory had only moved to the threshold, its "radiance" (נֹגַה, 10:4) was of such magnitude that it filled the courtyard. This is a clear echo of chapter 1; the same term was in 1:4, 13, 27, 28.

10:6–7 These verses complete most of the main narrative of chapter 10. (Aside from the brief narrative insertion in 10:15a, the narrative does not resume until 10:18–19, where it is concluded.) Even so, it is sketchy enough that many questions might be raised, such as the precise position of the man in linen in relation to the various cherubim as some of the fire is withdrawn and put in his hand. Furthermore, we are never told that the man in linen actually scattered the coals over the city, as he was commanded to do in 10:2. (In contrast, in 9:11 he reported that he had completed the assignment given him in 9:4.) This is sometimes explained as an example of the literary principle of "unity of place": the narrative assumes that Ezekiel is only able to report what he would have been able to observe from his location.[15]

Parallel to 10:2, 6–7 is Rev 8:5, where the angel fills his censer with coals of fire from the incense altar in heaven, and the apostle John then does see the angel throw the coals down on the earth, causing lightning, thunder, and earthquakes.

10:8–17 A long excursus on the cherubim and especially the chariot wheels begins here. Functionally, it emphasizes the chariot's prominent role in the gradual departure of the divine Glory from the city. Some of these verses might be understood to ascribe to the wheels some of the same features pos-

---

[15] Cf. Greenberg, *Ezekiel,* 1:193.

sessed by the cherubim, for example, a "body," "backs," "hands," and "wings," though it is more likely that these belong to the cherubim (see the textual notes on 10:11–12). But it is clear that the wheels are "full of eyes all around" (10:12) and are animated because they have the same "spirit" or life force that the living creatures/cherubim have (10:17). In that sense the wheels are alive and are not simply an inert means of mobility.

Especially since the "Glory" (כָּבוֹד) can be identified with the preincarnate Christ (see the textual notes and commentary on 1:26–28), the "spirit" of the cherubim in the wheels (10:17; also 1:20–21) recalls the "S/spirit" in 1:12, 20, where the third person of the Trinity is at hand (see the textual notes on 1:12 and commentary on 1:12–14). In both the Christological and the Pneumatological exegesis of the OT, the hermeneutic is not of "reading in" NT theology alien to the OT text, but of "reading out" of the OT text its full implications in the light of the fuller NT revelation.

Critics often suspect that the description of the wheels here includes later redactions, reflecting early Jewish "exegesis" that interpreted the wheels as a class of angels. It is not clear just how and when, in the history of Jewish thought, the wheels metamorphosed into angels. Probably an impetus for it was that Jewish interpreters attributed to the wheels some of the features that probably belong to the cherubim ("body," "hands," "wings" in 10:12). The earliest attestation of an angelic triad of cherubim, seraphim, and ophanim ("wheels") appears in the pseudepigraphic *1 Enoch* 61:10 and 71:7. (That book was written apparently in stages from the second century B.C. through the first century A.D.) At Qumran, where *1 Enoch* was clearly well-known, and also at Masada, an angelic liturgy was found, usually called the *Songs of the Sabbath Sacrifice,* that involves cherubim blessing the throne-chariot. Also found at Qumran is a fragmentary text called *Foundations of Fire* that refers to אוֹפַנִּים in a description of fiery chariots of God's Glory.[16] *1 Enoch* was also highly regarded in some sectors of the early church, and some propose that it influenced the imagery of Revelation 4. However, in Revelation 4, the focus is not on the throne as such, but on him who is seated on it.

10:18–19   Here the primary narrative resumes after the long digression about the cherubic porters and wheels. We are left to assume that the angel scattered the destroying coals and reported back at the threshold before the Glory's departure.

Ezek 10:18–19 describes the second phase of Yahweh's abandonment of the temple. The first had been depicted in 10:4 (anticipated by 9:3), and the third and final phase will not come until the end of chapter 11. First, the Glory resumes his place on the throne above the cherubim, but no longer in the Holy of Holies (10:18). Next, the divine chariot moves to the main entrance to the entire temple area, poised to quit the now-defiled area completely (10:19).

---

[16] Eisenman and Wise, *The Dead Sea Scrolls Uncovered*, 226, who translate the word as "wheel-angels" (p. 228).

Interpreters can make too much out of the precise terms used of the temple or of God, but two occur in this verse that may have significant overtones. Throughout Ezekiel the usual word for the "temple" (and often so translated) has been simply בַּיִת, literally, "house." It is so commonly used that it clearly is not deprecatory per se. But only in the vision of the Glory's departure (chapters 8–11) is the Jerusalem temple called "the house of Yahweh" (8:14, 16; 10:19; 11:1). That phrase will not recur again in the book until the Glory returns—not to the Jerusalem temple, but to the eschatological one (Ezek 44:4–5). Hence we get a sense of God's increasing distance from what had been his "incarnational" dwelling ever since its dedication by Solomon (1 Kings 8), and earlier in the temple's tent predecessor, the tabernacle. Never again in Ezekiel will the present, earthly Jerusalem be the site of "the house/temple of Yahweh," but in the eschaton the city shall be called "Yahweh Is There" (48:35).

Similarly, perhaps we can mine the significance of the use of the phrase "God of Israel" instead of "Yahweh" in 10:19–20. By his departure, the God who had revealed his ineffable name to Israel was now withdrawing his gracious presence from the people who had broken his covenant. Yet this is not the permanent end of Israel, of course; God promises to reconstitute his people with a "new heart" and a "new S/spirit" (36:26) and make a new covenant with them through his shepherd and prince, the new David (34:23–25; 37:24–26). This is fulfilled in the NT church, the new Israel comprised of all baptized believers in Christ, Jews and Gentiles alike (e.g., Rom 6:1–4; chapters 9–11; Gal 3:26–29; 6:16).

10:20–22 Ezekiel's identification of the "cherubim" in chapter 10 as the same "living creatures" that he saw in chapter 1 impresses upon him that the chariot is not only the means for Yahweh to proclaim his majesty and sovereignty to his faithful exiles (chapter 1), but also the means by which Yahweh will terminate his relationship with his defiled temple and his apostate people (chapter 10). The visible church on earth (ethnic Israel in the OT; nominal members of the NT church) has no unconditional claim on God (Mt 7:21–22). If necessary, he is able to raise up children of Abraham from the stones (Mt 3:9; Lk 3:8).

Ezekiel 11:1–25

After Promising "One Heart" and "a New Spirit," the Glory Departs the Temple

Translation

11 ¹Then the Spirit lifted me up and brought me to the east gate of the temple of Yahweh, which faces eastward. There, at the entrance to the gateway, were twenty-five men, and I saw among them Jaazaniah son of Azzur and Pelatiah son of Benaiah, leaders of the people. ²He said to me, "Son of man, these are the men who are plotting evil and counseling wicked counsel in this city, ³who are saying, 'Not imminent is the building of houses. It is the pot, and we are the meat.' ⁴Therefore, prophesy against them; prophesy, son of man."

⁵Then the Spirit of Yahweh fell upon me, and he said to me, "Say, 'Thus says Yahweh: This is what you are saying, O house of Israel. I know what arises in your spirit. ⁶You have multiplied your slain in this city and filled its streets with the slain.'

⁷"Therefore, thus says the Lord Yahweh: Your slain, which you have placed within it [the city], are the meat, and it is the pot. But I will drive you out of it. ⁸The sword you have feared, and the sword I will bring upon you, says the Lord Yahweh. ⁹I will drive you out from it, give you over to the hands of foreigners, and execute judgments upon you. ¹⁰By the sword you will fall, and at the border of Israel I will judge you. Then you will know that I am Yahweh. ¹¹It [this city] will not be a pot for you, and you will not be the meat inside it. At the border of Israel I will judge you. ¹²Then you will know that I am Yahweh, whose statutes you have not walked in and whose ordinances you have not performed, but you have acted according to the ordinances of the nations around you."

¹³While I was prophesying, Pelatiah son of Benaiah died. Then I fell face-down and cried out in a loud voice; I said, "Ah, Lord Yahweh, you are making a complete destruction with the remnant of Israel!"

¹⁴Then the Word of Yahweh came to me: ¹⁵"Son of man, your brothers, brothers who are men of your redemption, and the whole house of Israel—all of it—to whom the inhabitants of Jerusalem say, 'Remove yourselves from Yahweh! To us this land has been given as a possession,' ¹⁶therefore, say, 'Thus says the Lord Yahweh: Indeed, I have removed them far away among the nations, and I have indeed scattered them among the lands. But I will be for them a sanctuary for a little while in the lands to which they have come.' ¹⁷Therefore say, 'Thus says the Lord Yahweh: Then I will gather you from the peoples and assemble you from the lands where you have been scattered, and I will give you the land of Israel.' ¹⁸When they arrive there, they will remove from it all its loathsome things and

all its abominations. [19]I will give them one heart, and a new S/spirit I will put within you; I will remove their heart of stone from their body and give them a heart of flesh [20]so that they will walk in my statutes and keep my ordinances and do them. They will be my people, and I will be their God. [21]But as for those whose heart goes after their loathsome things and abominations, I will place their conduct on their own head, says the Lord Yahweh."

[22]Then the cherubim lifted up their wings, with the wheels beside them, and the Glory of the God of Israel was upon them from above. [23]And the Glory of Yahweh went up from the middle of the city and stood on the mountain that is east of the city. [24]Then the Spirit lifted me up and brought me to Chaldea, to the exiles, in the vision by the Spirit of God. Then the vision I had seen went up from me, [25]and I told the exiles all the things of Yahweh that he had shown me.

Textual Notes

11:1 "Twenty-five men" is the same number Ezekiel saw in 8:16 (according to the MT). Here the LXX reads "about [ὡς] twenty-five." "About" (ὡς) was how the LXX translated the preposition כְּ on the number in 8:16, but there the LXX had "about twenty." There is no reason to add "about" (כְּ/ὡς) to the number here. Even without it, the "twenty-five" men both here and in 8:16 (according to the MT) create one of the clear linkages between chapter 11 and earlier parts of the temple vision (chapters 8–11). For another link, see רַע in 8:9 and 11:2.

שָׂרֵי הָעָם:—The noun שַׂר is often translated "prince," but that implies royalty, which is not in view here. These people are public officials or leaders, perhaps equivalent to זְקֵנִים ("elders"). Zimmerli thinks the generality of their label reflects the prophet's remoteness from the Jerusalem scene.[1]

11:2 The chapter continues with a private divine communication to Ezekiel (11:2–4) and then a public oracle for him to deliver (11:5–12). In 11:2–3 (the division between those verses is infelicitous) Yahweh delivers a tripartite indictment ("plotting … counseling … saying") of the twenty-five men in 11:1. The three parts of the indictment are very similar to Micah's charges a little over a century earlier and may be intended to echo them (Micah 2:1–2).

הַחֹשְׁבִים אָוֶן—The verb חָשַׁב can mean "to think, devise, plan, plot." It implies deliberate, calculated, rationalized behavior. אָוֶן may occur in Ezekiel only here (in 30:17 it is debatable). It can be a general term for "evil." "Injustice" (*HALOT*, 3) may be too narrow, since the meaning of אָוֶן is close to the other main Hebrew words for sin (cf. "wickedness," "iniquity," and "sin" in 3:19–20). It may connote deceit or fraudulence and often implies injustice or abuse of power. Almost identical to the phrase here is חֹשְׁבֵי־אָוֶן in Micah 2:1. The comparable phrase מַחְשְׁבוֹת אָוֶן ("plots of evil") in Is 59:7 and Prov 6:8 (cf. Is 55:7) uses a noun derived from חָשַׁב. Especially in the Psalms we frequently meet פֹּעֲלֵי אָוֶן (e.g., Pss 64:3 [ET 64:2]; 92:8 [ET 92:7]), traditionally translated "workers of iniquity" (KJV) or "evildoers" (NIV, ESV).

---

[1]   Zimmerli, *Ezekiel*, 1:257.

וְהַיֹּעֲצִים עֲצַת־רָע—This second part of the indictment uses a cognate accusative, literally, "counseling a counsel of wickedness." The preceding occurrence of רַע in Ezekiel was as an adjective ("vile") describing the abominations in the temple Ezekiel saw in 8:9, linking that verse to this one.

בָּעִיר הַזֹּאת:—"In this city" here sets the stage for the third part of the indictment (11:3).

11:3 This verse is in general a classical instance of the truism that translation and interpretation go hand in hand. A quick check of the versions, ancient and modern, will uncover wide variation in translation, obviously because of different understandings of what is meant.

הָאֹמְרִים לֹא בְקָרוֹב בְּנוֹת בָּתִּים—The verb אָמַר can refer to unspoken thoughts (as in 11:5b; 20:32),[2] and may do so here, but that does not significantly impact the quotation.

The combination of קָרוֹב and the preposition בְּ occurs elsewhere only in Lev 10:3, where קָרוֹב is used as a noun with a spatial and spiritual sense (people "near" to God). Here קָרוֹב might have the spatial meaning of "nearby (land)." The Babylonian army surrounding and besieging Jerusalem would make it impossible for Israelites to build "on nearby (land)" (בְּקָרוֹב), that is, land in or near the city. But more often the sense of קָרוֹב is temporal, of the "near" future (as in מִקָּרוֹב in 7:8). Here negated, "not in the near (future)" is equivalent to "not anytime soon" or "not imminent."

The infinitive construct (בְּנוֹת is from בָּנָה, "to build") can be used as the subject of a nominal clause (Joüon, § 124 b), as it is here, and have the nuance of something that should or could be done: "the building of houses is not in the near future." This might be paraphrased as "now is not the time to build houses." A favorite medieval interpretation took it as jussive in meaning ("let us build"), but grammatically that is not possible.

The "houses" (בָּתִּים) can refer to literal domiciles or to households with future descendants and lasting families. A literal interpretation here is supported by the parallel passage Micah 2:1–2. Ezek 11:2 likely reflected Micah 2:1, and Ezek 11:3 may reflect Micah 2:2, which condemns Israelites for coveting fields and (literal) houses.

The LXX takes the clause as a question referring to the recent past: "Weren't the houses built recently?" That question (with οὐχί) implies that the answer is affirmative. Ordinarily such a Hebrew question would have the interrogative *he*, although there are examples without it (GKC, § 150 a). In oral usage, the tone of voice may indicate a question, but writing normally requires some literary sign.

הִיא הַסִּיר וַאֲנַחְנוּ הַבָּשָׂר:—The understanding of the first part of the quotation from the leaders is inevitably bound up with the interpretation of this proverb or popular metaphor, "She is the pot, and we are the meat." The feminine singular pronoun undoubtedly refers to Jerusalem, since cities are feminine (and so was בָּעִיר הַזֹּאת at

---

[2] Greenberg, *Ezekiel*, 1:186–87.

the end of 11:2). As a figure, "pot" could have many applications. Ezekiel himself will use the metaphor again in 24:3–6, where the fire under a cooking pot cooks its contents: the inhabitants of Jerusalem. Here it is most improbable that the leaders would be applying that picture against themselves. In Micah 3:1–3 the oppressive rulers of Israel are pictured as cannibalizing their fellow Israelites in a cooking pot. In Jeremiah's call (Jer 1:13–16) the boiling pot to the north symbolizes impending disaster. Compare Jeremiah 19, where the prophet breaks a flask (בַּקְבֻּק, 19:1, 10) as an action prophecy that Yahweh will break Jerusalem.

The point of comparison here seems to be that as a cooking pot protects the meat inside from the flames, so the apostate Israelites assume that Jerusalem will protect them. Less likely, the pot could be a storage jar that would protect the meat from scavengers or the like.

After the first deportations, the Israelites who were left in Jerusalem apparently assumed that they had escaped the judgment and would be immune in the future. "The new rulers are the prime cuts of meat, supposedly invulnerable within the city walls, as opposed to those who have been discarded as waste (cf. v. 15) and obviously no longer enjoy the protection of God."[3]

Keil says that Ezekiel is alluding to Jer 29:5, where Jeremiah had advised the exiles to settle down and build houses because their return to Jerusalem was seventy years off. Keil understands the Jerusalemites here as scoffing at Jeremiah's words, at least as possibly applicable to themselves. The time is far off, they say, when the city would fall and they would be exiled and so need to build houses in a foreign land. This twist of meaning, Keil argues, is implied by Yahweh's subsequent reply (11:7–11).[4] His view is possible.

Greenberg notes two other possible inferences from God's rejoinder. He quotes Fohrer, who suggests, on the basis of 11:6, that the rulers feel no need to build houses because they have expropriated the property of the deportees (11:14–21) and also that of other defenseless residents of the city (the "slain" of 11:6). Alternatively, he suggests on the basis of 11:8 ("the sword you have feared") that they are arguing that all energies and resources must go into fortifying the city as the protective "pot" in preparation for their planned rebellion against Babylon.[5]

Many of those interpretations are possible and not mutually exclusive. In the lack of further specificity in the text, it is hard to be dogmatic about precisely what the Israelites meant. This much is clear, however: their attitude is motivated by a total disregard of God's warnings and by a hubris and self-confidence, undoubtedly bolstered by a misunderstanding of the nature of God's promises to Zion.[6]

11:4 הִנָּבֵא ... הִנָּבֵא—The repetition of the Niphal imperative ("prophesy") reflects the urgent need to proclaim the consequences of what had become intolerable in God's

---

[3]   Block, *Ezekiel*, 1:334.

[4]   Keil, *Ezekiel*, 1:144–45.

[5]   Greenberg, *Ezekiel*, 1:187; see Fohrer, *Ezechiel*, 60.

[6]   See the commentary on 8:12–13; 9:3.

eyes. It is unusual that an oracle is issued within a vision, but a partial parallel occurs in 37:1–14. Usually within a vision the prophet remains only an observer; that he here speaks within a vision probably underscores the urgency even more. Since in the popular mind "prophesy" tends to be heard as synonymous with "predict," I was greatly tempted to translate "preach," which gives a more accurate overall picture of prophetic activity. Of course, the element of prediction frequently is present in prophecy, as it is here and generally elsewhere.

11:5 וַתִּפֹּל עָלַי רוּחַ יְהוָה—Only here in the OT does Yahweh's "Spirit" (רוּחַ) "fall" (נָפַל) on someone. Some other passages state that God's Spirit "was/came" (הָיָה) upon someone[a] or "rushed, acted" (צָלַח) upon someone.[b] In Ezek 8:1 it was Yahweh's "hand" that "fell" (נָפַל) on the prophet, and his "hand" is on Ezekiel also in 1:3; 3:14, 22; 33:22; 37:1; 40:1.

(a) E.g., Judg 3:10; 11:29; 2 Chr 15:1; 20:14

(b) Judg 14:6, 19; 15:14; 1 Sam 10:6, 10; 11:6; 16:13

Zimmerli treats 11:5a as a later addition because it interrupts the divine speech.[7] Others allege that 11:5a is unnecessary because Ezekiel is already under the influence of the Spirit throughout chapters 8–11. However, this alleged "interruption" adds further emphasis to God's action in the process of divine revelation.

וַיֹּאמֶר אֵלַי—Since "the Spirit of Yahweh" was in the previous phrase, the subject who speaks might be either Yahweh or his Spirit. In light of the fuller revelation of the Trinity in the NT, it is almost a distinction without a difference. From the standpoint of OT usage, we probably should opt for Yahweh as the subject of the masculine verb here.

כֹּה־אָמַר יְהוָה—In Ezekiel "thus says Yahweh" occurs only in 11:5; 21:8 (ET 21:3); 30:6. It was the same formula Moses used to deliver oracles to Pharaoh (e.g., Ex 4:22; 5:1; 7:17), and it is common in other prophets, especially Jeremiah. Functionally, it is equivalent to the common phrases with נְאֻם (see the textual note on that phrase in 5:11). Throughout Ezekiel the usual citation formula is the longer כֹּה אָמַר אֲדֹנָי יְהוִה, "thus says the Lord Yahweh" (122 times: e.g., 2:4; 3:11).

כֵּן אֲמַרְתֶּם בֵּית יִשְׂרָאֵל—The oracle is directed to the "house of Israel" because the twenty-five leaders (11:1) represent and speak for virtually the entire population. But perhaps irony is intended: they certainly cannot be "Israel" in the theological sense (all believers in the one true God). As in 11:3, the verb אָמַר could refer either to what the people were "saying" or "thinking."

וּמַעֲלוֹת רוּחֲכֶם—The noun מַעֲלָה is derived from the verb עָלָה ("go/come up") and can refer to a pilgrimage of ascent (to Jerusalem) or to stairs, but only here does it have the metaphorical sense of "thoughts" (BDB; *HALOT*, 3) that arise within. Idioms with the verb עָלָה are common with "heart," referring to thoughts that "arise in the heart." Hebrew usually uses לֵב ("heart") as the seat of cognitive activity. Here, it is most interesting that the "thoughts" are of the Israelites' רוּחַ, "spirit." This is now the third time that word has appeared in 11:1–5. In the first two instances, it is Yahweh's Spirit, who transports the prophet (11:1) and gives him the words to speak (11:5a). Here, however, it is the people's "spirit," undoubtedly in the sense of "mind." Ezekiel is probably deliberately contrasting the human "spirit" with the divine

---

[7] Zimmerli, *Ezekiel*, 1:258.

"Spirit," and we should be careful to distinguish the two (e.g., by capitalizing the word when it refers to God's Spirit) whenever references to the human "spirit" and "spirituality" come up in modern discourse.

אֲנִי יְדַעְתִּיהָ—The verb comes at the end of the sentence after the redundant and emphatic אֲנִי ("I"). The verb has a feminine singular object suffix even though the antecedent (מַעֲלוֹת) is feminine plural; such a discrepancy is permissible in Hebrew, although not common. The pronoun is redundant (literally: "the thoughts of your spirit, I know it").

11:6 חַלְלֵיכֶם—In 6:4, 7, 13; 9:7, חָלָל referred to the "slain" Israelites whom Yahweh warned would be killed because of their idolatry. The word usually has a military connotation of those killed in battle, and hence in those earlier verses it may allude to the imminent Babylonian conquest of Jerusalem. However, in 11:6–7 it refers to those who had been slain in the past, and so it is best to take the word in its broadest sense as referring (literally) to victims of murder and (metaphorically) to victims of other kinds of injustice and oppression. At the end of 11:6 the singular חָלָל ("slain") is used as a collective.

11:7–12 Yahweh's counterthesis to the thoughts of the Israelites in 11:2–3 is introduced by לָכֵן ("therefore," 11:7). It is divided into two parts, 11:7–10 and 11:11–12, and each part concludes with the recognition formula ("then you will know …"; see the textual note on 11:12). The first part is further subdivided into two parts (11:7–8 and 11:9–10) by the signatory formula (נְאֻם אֲדֹנָי יְהוִה) at the end of 11:8.

11:7 וְהִיא הַסִּיר—As in 11:3, this clause refers to Jerusalem ("she/it") as the "pot."

וְאֶתְכֶם הוֹצִיא מִתּוֹכָהּ—The form of the verb is the Hiphil of יָצָא, either the infinitive construct or third masculine singular perfect. Many Hebrew manuscripts have אוֹצִיא, the first person imperfect, with Yahweh as the subject ("I will bring/drive out"). This is reflected in most of the ancient versions as well, and my translation follows that reading (as do KJV and NIV). הוֹצִיא might be understood as a prophetic perfect and an impersonal verb with an indefinite subject ("someone will bring you out"), which would be equivalent to a passive ("you will be brought out").[8] Greenberg takes the verb as the infinitive and construes it as a passive.[9] RSV and ESV translate with a passive.

Ezek 11:9 has almost the same clause but with different word order and the first common singular perfect with *waw* consecutive (וְהוֹצֵאתִי אֶתְכֶם מִתּוֹכָהּ). In both verses "drive you out" (NIV) is somewhat interpretive; a more neutral "bring out" may be preferable. The question is whether the people will come out dead or alive; see the commentary below.

11:8 חֶרֶב … וְחֶרֶב—Twice "sword" appears at the beginning of a clause for emphasis. It is anarthrous, but English usage requires the article ("the sword"). The word order is retained in my translation.

נְאֻם אֲדֹנָי יְהוִה—See the textual note on this formula in 5:11. It recurs in 11:21.

---

[8] Cf. Keil, *Ezekiel*, 1:147.

[9] Greenberg, *Ezekiel*, 1:185.

11:9 The divine discourse foretells what will happen after the city's fall. See the textual note on זָר in 7:21.

וְעָשִׂיתִי בָכֶם שְׁפָטִים:—See the textual note on the nearly identical clause in 5:10. Forms of the root שפט occur in 11:9–12: the noun שֶׁפֶט ("judgment") in 11:9, the verb שָׁפַט ("to judge") in 11:10–11, and the noun מִשְׁפָּט twice in 11:12. The root is highly multivalent. Forms of it may be difficult to translate without either losing or adding something, and they often must be translated differently in different contexts. Ezekiel repeatedly exploits the root here (as he did also in 5:6–10, 15), but the impact the Hebrew makes by repetition of the same root cannot be reproduced in English. In 11:9–11 I have used "judgment" and "judge." (For the plural of מִשְׁפָּט in 11:12 I used "ordinances," both for God's and for those of the heathen, as also in 5:7.) In English "judge/judgment" tends to connote "condemn(ation)." A more neutral rendering of "(give a) verdict" would initially be accurate, but since in this context God's verdict on apostate Israel is obviously "guilty," I have retained "judge/judgment." In some modern translations the root is often connected with "justice." Although the theologically informed can connect "justice" with "justification" or with the dialectic of Law and Gospel, "justice" today has been so preempted by liberationist secularism that it is usually of minimal usefulness.

11:10 עַל־גְּבוּל יִשְׂרָאֵל—"At the border of Israel," repeated in 11:11, is here introduced as the place of judgment. The phrase implies that the residents of Jerusalem will be expelled from the city and will be on their way into exile when they will be judged. The phrase could mean that they are still within the borders, but in this context it probably suggests somewhere beyond the border, separated from the promised land. Traditionally, 11:10–11 was taken as a prediction of the sad, bloody scene at Riblah on the upper Orontes in central Syria (2 Ki 25:18–21; Jer 52:24–27). Modern critics ironically have had the same understanding, but have been inclined to take it as a "prophecy after the event," that is, a later insertion written after the events at Riblah had occurred.[10] While indeed the believer will understand the judgment at Riblah as part of the fulfillment, the aftermath of Jerusalem's fall was far more extensive than simply that scene. And until the city actually falls (Ezek 33:21), Ezekiel consistently predicts judgment. The point here and in 11:11 highlights the failure of the "pot" to provide security or immunity from divine judgment.

11:11 הִיא לֹא־תִהְיֶה—Again the feminine singular pronoun הִיא ("she/it") refers to Jerusalem. As is frequently the case in Hebrew, the negative לֹא ("it will *not* be a pot") does double duty and negates the second clause as well ("you will *not* be the meat"). Block tries to wrest sense from the second clause without a negative by translating, without comment, "that you should become meat within it."[11] The conjunctive *waw* in Hebrew is supple enough that such a rendering is within the limits of possibility, but, it seems to me, it is much less likely. The ultimate meaning is the same in either case.

---

[10] E.g., Zimmerli, *Ezekiel*, 1:259.

[11] Block, *Ezekiel*, 1:328.

The Vaticanus manuscript of the LXX omits 11:11–12a. This is a classical instance of homoioteleuton: a copyist's eye skipped from the recognition formula ("then you will know …") at the end of 11:10 to the identical formula at the start of 11:12 and only wrote the formula once (also omitting the intervening verse, 11:11).

11:12 יְהֹוָה אֲשֶׁר בְּחֻקַּי לֹא הֲלַכְתֶּם—Israel's recognition of Yahweh will include the realization that it was his statutes and judgments that they had transgressed. There are other instances where the recognition formula ("then you/they will know that I am Yahweh") is expanded (e.g., 6:13; 12:15), but rarely to the extent found here. Three expansive clauses follow. This first one is, literally, "… Yahweh, who in my statutes you have not walked." English usage requires the construction with the relative pronoun אֲשֶׁר ("who") followed by "my statutes" and "my ordinances" to be rendered as possessive clauses: "Yahweh, *whose* statutes you have not walked in and *whose* ordinances you have not performed." In Hebrew both of those two accusations are repeated more or less verbatim from 5:7. (The same idioms, but phrased positively, will recur in 11:20.)

The third expansion, "you have acted according to the ordinances of the nations around you," on the surface is the opposite of the last statement in 5:7, but there is no contradiction; see the commentary on 5:7. Because of the repetition from 5:7 and also the apparent discrepancy, many critics predictably delete 11:12 as a secondary gloss. But why must we prohibit Ezekiel from repeating some things verbatim and from expanding others to make a unique formulation?

In 5:6–8 the appropriate translation for the plural of מִשְׁפָּט was "ordinances," which is my translation of it in 11:12 (also 11:20). Here "judgments" would have been possible and would have linked 11:12 to the verb "judge" at the end of 11:11. The plurals of מִשְׁפָּט and חֹק or חֻקָּה (conventionally translated "statute") are parallel in many passages in Ezekiel (first in 5:6–7) and throughout the OT. These words could be rendered as "laws" in a broad sense. The second instance of מִשְׁפָּט in 11:12 refers to the מִשְׁפָּטִים of the heathen, who enacted or followed their own decisions and standards of right and wrong. They probably attributed their "ordinances" to their gods, but at best, their ordinances were the product of God's natural law written on the human heart and visible in nature, but distorted by their sinful nature. At worst, some of their ordinances were demonic in origin, such as the sacrifice of children, an abomination that some of the Israelites adopted and that Yahweh never even conceived (Jer 7:31; 19:5; 32:35; see further on Ezek 16:20–21).

11:13 אֲהָהּ אֲדֹנָי יְהֹוָה—See the textual note on this phrase in 4:14. Here as in 9:8 Ezekiel uses it when he assumes that all Israel will be destroyed.

(c) Cf. Is 10:23; Jer 4:27; 5:10; 30:11; 46:28; Nahum 1:8–9

כָּלָה אַתָּה עֹשֶׂה אֵת שְׁאֵרִית יִשְׂרָאֵל:—The noun כָּלָה, "complete destruction, annihilation," is the direct object of the participle עֹשֶׂה ("you are making a complete destruction") and אֵת is the preposition ("*with* the remnant of Israel"). Similar constructions with כָּלָה, עָשָׂה, and אֵת occur in 20:17 (where אוֹתָם probably is the preposition with suffix) and Jer 5:18; Zeph 1:18.[c]

The LXX and most English translations (beginning with the KJV) translate Ezekiel's outcry as a question ("Are you completely exterminating … ?"). There is no interrogative particle (-הֲ), but Hebrew questions sometimes do without it (GKC,

§ 150 a). Some propose that a scribe omitted the -הֲ by haplography after the preceding Tetragrammaton (יְהֹוָה). If it were a question, it would be very similar to the one Ezekiel posed in 9:8. But Ezekiel had already received an answer to his earlier question: in 9:9–10 Yahweh stated that he would show no pity, but 9:4, 6, 11 also indicated that Yahweh would indeed preserve a remnant, consisting of those marked with a cross. It seems unlikely to me that Ezekiel would repeat the same question here (although that conclusion is inevitably bound up with exegesis). Rather, the horror of the event led him, at least momentarily, to conclude that God's ominous answer in 9:9–10 was beginning to be fulfilled before his very eyes. In the anguish of the moment, he forgets Yahweh's provision of the *taw* (9:4, 6, 11) and other earlier indications that a remnant would be spared. This interpretation seems to accord better with Yahweh's explicit promise shortly in 11:15–21 of a restored and regenerated remnant, especially when contrasted with 9:9–10.

11:15 This entire verse in Hebrew is an incomplete sentence. It describes the people and the situation to which the salvation oracle in 11:16–21 is addressed.

אַחֶיךָ אַחֶיךָ אַנְשֵׁי גְאֻלָּתֶךָ—The second "your brothers" (אַחֶיךָ) is in apposition to "men of your redemption," so I have added "who are." Some consider the second אַחֶיךָ a dittograph (the LXX does not have it), but repetition for the sake of emphasis or intensification is characteristic of Hebrew. Keil suggests "thy true, real brethren," in contrast to those who at the end of the verse are quoted as wishing to exclude the exiles.[12] Zimmerli understands the "whole house of Israel" in the next line as a parallel,[13] and he is probably correct.

The last two Hebrew words are literally "the men of your redemption." That should not be misunderstood to imply that the men were accomplishing redemption in terms of vicarious atonement, which only Jesus Christ accomplished. Here we have a more "secular" use, native in the realm of family law, of the noun גְאֻלָּה, "redemption, right/obligation to repurchase." It is derived from the verb גָּאַל, whose participle (גֹּאֵל, "redeemer") denotes a relative who took responsibility for needy and disadvantaged relatives, especially in preventing the loss of family property. Many laws concerning this "redemption" (גְאֻלָּה) are detailed in Lev 25:24–52. A historical example contemporary to the ministry of Ezekiel is Jeremiah's "redemption" (גְאֻלָּה, Jer 32:7–8) of his cousin's property shortly before the fall of Jerusalem (Jer 32:6–12). Another famous example is the "redemption" (גְאֻלָּה, Ruth 4:6–7) of Naomi's field by Boaz (Ruth 4:1–12).

The "men of [Ezekiel's] redemption" are relatives whom (or whose property) he could redeem, or who could redeem him and his property according to OT covenantal law. The reason for using this particular expression here becomes clear at the end of the verse, in the quotation from those who had not yet suffered exile: they consider themselves the sole heirs of the land, but Yahweh here implies that Ezekiel and his fellow exiles still retain the right of "redemption" and so remain legitimate heirs of

---

[12] Keil, *Ezekiel*, 1:149.

[13] Zimmerli, *Ezekiel*, 1:229.

the land and all the divine promises to Israel. Since the pronoun on גְּאֻלָּתֶךָ is singular ("your"), the phrase may imply that all of Ezekiel's relatives were carried into exile in 597 B.C. together with him (unless it is to be taken more figuratively or generally).

Some English translations (RSV, NRSV) follow the LXX and read "your fellow exiles." A somewhat similar Hebrew word (a form of גָּלוּת or גּוֹלָה instead of גְּאֻלָּה) would yield that translation. But such a meaning for גְּאֻלָּה is unparalleled elsewhere in the OT. Above all, it breaks up the progression of the essentially synonymous expressions, "brothers," "men of your redemption," and "house."

וְכָל־בֵּית יִשְׂרָאֵל כֻּלֹּה—The third kinship expression is commonly deleted as a gloss, but contextually it functions as an indispensable part of the thought (see the commentary below). The repetition of כֹּל ("all") is obviously emphatic and recurs in other restoration oracles (20:40 and 36:10; indirectly also in 35:15, a Gentile oracle against Edom). Here it both begins and ends the phrase. The second instance (כֻּלֹּה, with third masculine singular suffix) has the same consonants and echoes כָּלָה ("complete destruction") in 11:13, contrasting two populations: one about to be exterminated, the other with a glorious future, as Yahweh will describe (11:16–21).

רַחֲקוּ מֵעַל יְהוָה—The Qal of רָחַק with the combination of prepositions מֵעַל means to "remove oneself" (*HALOT*, s.v. רחק, 2 a) away from a person or place, as also in 8:6; 44:10. The form here is the imperative, as supported by the ancient versions. Most modern translations treat it as if it were the perfect רָחֲקוּ (e.g., "they are far away," NIV). The imperative is the *lectio difficilior*, and especially with such strong textual support, it should be retained. The imperative expresses more strongly that those still in Jerusalem consider themselves the heirs of the ancient patriarchal promises, and they wish to exclude the exiles from those promises (and thus from the God who made them).

לָנוּ הִיא נִתְּנָה הָאָרֶץ לְמוֹרָשָׁה׃—"To us" is first for emphasis in the Jerusalemites' claim. The anticipatory pronoun הִיא is feminine, agreeing with הָאָרֶץ (literally, "she … the land"). The identical phrase, but without הִיא, is repeated at the end of 33:24, where the survivors of the 587 B.C. destruction of Jerusalem make a similar claim against the exiles. That and the absence in the LXX of a translation of the pronoun lead some to delete it here, but that is unnecessary.

11:16 כִּי הִרְחַקְתִּים בַּגּוֹיִם וְכִי הֲפִיצוֹתִים—The repeated כִּי may be translated in various ways. The English tradition, beginning with the KJV, usually interprets it concessively ("although"). I have preferred to take it asseveratively ("indeed") as emphasizing more strongly Yahweh's agency in sending the Israelites into exile. The Hiphil of רָחַק ("remove"; "far away" is implied) deliberately answers the use of the same verb (but Qal) by the Jerusalemites in 11:15. It is paralleled by the Hiphil of פּוּץ, "scatter," a verb Ezekiel uses frequently (and often elsewhere paired with זָרָה, "to disperse" [e.g., 12:15; 20:23]).

וָאֱהִי לָהֶם לְמִקְדָּשׁ מְעַט—Despite his scattering of the Israelites, Yahweh promises to be a "sanctuary" for them. מִקְדָּשׁ was used of the temple in 8:6 and 9:6. Various translations are possible for מְעַט, "smallness; fewness." The LXX treats it as an adjective: ἁγίασμα μικρόν, "a *little* sanctuary." More likely it is an adverbial accusative, in which case it could refer to degree: a sanctuary "to *some extent*" (Waltke-O'Connor, § 39.3.4b, example 6; cf. BDB, 1 d; "I became a little like a holy place" [*HALOT*, 5 a]). But in the light of the next verse, which promises the return to the land, most likely it is an adverbial accusative in a temporal sense, "for a little while, temporarily" (cf. *HALOT*, 5 b).

11:17 Like 11:16, 11:17 begins with לָכֵן ("therefore"). The two verses are coordinate, together forming Yahweh's antithesis to the dismissive sentence pronounced upon the exiles by the Jerusalemites in 11:15. But 11:17 is also joined to the following verses, through 11:21. After the reminder of past judgment in 11:16a, we now have a series of promises in 11:17–20, concluding with hortatory warning in 11:21.

וְקִבַּצְתִּי אֶתְכֶם—After the citation formula ("thus says the Lord Yahweh"), the quote of what Yahweh says may begin with a *waw*, which evidently expresses continuity.[d] I have rendered the *waw* by "then." What is striking throughout this verse is the switch from third to second person object pronouns ("I will gather *you* ..."). The rest of this oracle (11:18–21) reverts to the third person.[14] The LXX, evidently for harmonistic reasons, uses the third person in 11:17. Because of the change in person in MT 11:17, some critics suspect it is a gloss, but that suspicion is groundless and arbitrary. The temporary change reflects an awareness that, although most of the entire temple vision is concerned with the situation in Jerusalem, the prophet's real addressees are his fellow exiles ("you" refers to those already now in exile). The direct address to them accords with comparable passages in 20:34–38 and 36:24–32.

(d) See also Ezek 13:13; 16:59; 17:22; 25:13; 30:10, 13; 32:3; 38:10

The verse also contains subtle vocabulary choices that are all but impossible to reproduce in English. "Gather" and "assemble" reflect קָבַץ and אָסַף, respectively, which are essentially synonymous. They are common enough in Ezekiel but are rarely paired (only in 11:17; 29:5; 39:17). One or the other (or sometimes both) are used in a constant theme in the prophets, going back even to Deut 30:3–4, that after God scatters his people in judgment, he will regather them. That theme continues in the NT, where God strikes Jesus himself, thereby scattering his sheep (Mt 26:31, quoting Zech 13:7; Jn 16:32), and God allows his church to be scattered by persecution (Acts 5:37; 8:1–4; 11:19). Yet God also makes the eschatological promise to gather the universal church (Mt 13:30; 23:37; 24:31; Jn 11:52), which consists of believing Jews and Gentiles alike in Christ, who are now scattered throughout the nations (James 1:1; 1 Pet 1:1).

While Ezek 11:16 had spoken of dispersal among the גּוֹיִם ("nations"), here God will gather his people from the עַמִּים ("peoples"). Those two words are often interchangeable throughout the OT, but the first tends to suggest a political entity, while the latter may signal a religio-cultural unit. Ezekiel generally employs גּוֹיִם when the subject is dispersal, but עַמִּים when speaking of ingathering. As here, he pairs עַמִּים with אֲרָצוֹת ("countries") when speaking of God's ingathering also in 20:34, 41; 34:13; 39:27.

11:19 וְנָתַתִּי לָהֶם לֵב אֶחָד וְרוּחַ חֲדָשָׁה—The phrase לֵב אֶחָד ("one heart") in the sense of unity in faith, will, and purpose is in the similar divine promise in Jer 32:39 (where "one heart" is paralleled by "one way") and was actually present (not just

---

[14] The only exception is בְּקִרְבְּכֶם in 11:19; see the textual note on it below.

promised) among the Israelites in 1 Chr 12:39 (ET 12:38) and 2 Chr 30:12. Similarly, God will promise a "new heart" (לֵב חָדָשׁ) in Ezek 18:31; 36:26. Ezekiel will speak of Israel having רוּחַ חֲדָשָׁה ("a new S/spirit") also in 18:31; 36:26. Compare phrases with רוּחַ and the verb חָדַשׁ in Ps 51:12 (ET 51:10) and Ps 104:30. The translation "S/spirit" conveys that רוּחַ here refers to the human spirit renewed by the power and gift of the indwelling Holy Spirit; see the commentary below. Clearly רוּחַ in Ezek 11:1, 5, 24 refers to the third person of the Trinity.

Both ancient versions and modern commentators have sought to assimilate the two adjectives ("one" and "new") in this verse in one way or another. The LXX read καρδίαν ἑτέραν ("another heart"), as if the Hebrew were אַחֵר instead of אֶחָד. The Syriac and some Hebrew manuscripts read לֵב חָדָשׁ ("new heart") here, harmonizing the phrase to that in 18:31 and 36:26.[15]

בְּקִרְבְּכֶם—The second person pronoun stands out. While all of 11:17 had been couched in the second person, all the rest of 11:18–21 is in the third person. Many Hebrew manuscripts have בְּקִרְבָּם and the ancient versions too harmonize this to the surrounding third person forms and read "within them."

לֵב הָאֶבֶן מִבְּשָׂרָם ... לֵב בָּשָׂר:—The Hebrew text uses בָּשָׂר twice, each in a different sense, and no one English word easily covers both. God will take their heart of stone "from their body/flesh" and give them "a heart of flesh." See the commentary below.

11:20 The verse continues the sentence that began in 11:19. לְמַעַן introduces it as a result clause: because of God's gifts of "one heart" and "a new S/spirit" (11:19), his people will do what this verse states. They will not only keep the letter of the Law externally, but also its spirit, and they will do so because of the gift of the Spirit, who will give them an undivided heart.

בְּחֻקֹּתַי יֵלֵכוּ וְאֶת־מִשְׁפָּטַי יִשְׁמְרוּ וְעָשׂוּ אֹתָם—These positive expressions of what Israel will do use the same vocabulary as 5:7 and 11:12, which stated what Israel failed to do. See the textual notes there.

וְהָיוּ־לִי לְעָם וַאֲנִי אֶהְיֶה לָהֶם לֵאלֹהִים:—This classic covenant formula translates literalistically as "They will be(come) to me for a people, and I will be(come) to them for a God." The idiom הָיָה לְ usually means "to become." The use of לְ in לִי and לָהֶם is that of possession, hence the formula is usually translated, "They will be my people, and I will be their God." The formula is repeated verbatim in 14:11 and 37:23 and phrased somewhat differently in 34:24, 30–31; 36:28; 37:27.

11:21 וְאֶל־לֵב שִׁקּוּצֵיהֶם וְתוֹעֲבוֹתֵיהֶם לִבָּם הֹלֵךְ—By any measure, this first half of the verse is difficult. Many emendations have been proposed, and yet, surprisingly, all end up with essentially the same translation. The LXX supports the MT, which strongly suggests that we should try to make the most of a difficult situation without emending. A literalistic translation is "To the heart of their loathsome and abominable

---

[15] Zimmerli, *Ezekiel*, 1:230, suggests that the text originally was חָדָשׁ, but its last letter was lost, becoming חַד ("one" in Aramaic), which was then Hebraized by adding *alef* in front. But this is highly speculative, and "one heart" is not discordant with the "new S/spirit" following here. There is no cogent reason to emend.

things their heart goes." There seem to be two alternatives, both of which yield a similar understanding. The first takes אֶל as "concerning, about" (equivalent in meaning to עַל, since the two often are used interchangeably in Ezekiel) in an anticipatory way and sees both instances of "heart" as referring to the heart of the apostate people: "Now concerning [their] heart—[after] their loathsome things and their abominations their heart goes." The second alternative takes אֶל in the sense of the direction "toward" which the heart of the idolatrous people is oriented. It also sees a play on "heart" in two different senses. The first לֵב ("heart") is in construct with שִׁקּוּצֵיהֶם וְתוֹעֲבוֹתֵיהֶם, meaning "the heart/essence of their loathsome things ..." (their idolatries). The second (לִבָּם, "their heart") refers to the people's heart, yielding, "toward the essence of their loathsome things and their abominations their heart goes."

In either case, the entire half verse must refer to people who fit the description: "But as for those whose heart goes after their loathsome things and abominations ..."

דַּרְכָּם בְּרֹאשָׁם נָתָתִּי—See the textual note on the identical clause in 9:10.

11:22 The words are almost identical to part of 10:19, which suggests that this verse is intended to continue the narrative that was suspended there. Regarding the cherubim, see the textual note on 1:5 and the commentary on 1:5–11.

11:23 The last previous reference to the Glory was in 10:19, where the Glory was situated at the east gate of the temple, which is tantamount to "the middle of the city" here. "The mountain that is east of the city" is, of course, better known as the Mount of Olives. In the OT it is so named only in Zech 14:4, and with "ascent" rather than "mountain" in 2 Sam 15:30.

וַיַּעֲמֹד—I have translated עָמַד literally ("stood"), as with the participle describing the Glory "standing" in 3:23. (It meant "to stand still" when referring to the living creatures in 1:21, 24, 25.) Some translations have "stopped," which might imply either a longer stay or that its stay there was only temporary. On the issue of the duration, see the commentary below.

11:24 וְרוּחַ נְשָׂאַתְנִי וַתְּבִיאֵנִי ... בְּרוּחַ אֱלֹהִים—Twice the "Spirit" (as in 11:1, 5) is mentioned: as the agent of Ezekiel's transportation and as the enabler of the vision that comprises chapters 8–11. Thus, one can assert, both exegetically and dogmatically, that the vision was inspired, even though the text may not satisfy our curiosity for more details about the mechanics or psychology of prophecy and, more broadly, the verbal inspiration of all the Scriptures. The main point is simply to affirm the fact of inspiration, as also in, for example, 2 Tim 3:16 and 2 Pet 1:21.

כַּשְׂדִּימָה—See the textual note on the "Chaldeans" in Ezek 1:3.

וַיַּעַל מֵעָלַי הַמַּרְאֶה—The statement that "the vision went up from on me" is similar to the conclusions of the theophanies in, for example, Gen 17:22 and 35:13, where "God went up from on" Abraham and Jacob, respectively. The verse division between 11:24 and 11:25 is infelicitous, since this clause can be taken to begin a sentence that continues in 11:25. The vision ends where the prophet had been bodily all along: in Chaldea, among the exiles. The language thus once more marks the entire trip in chapters 8–11 as visionary.

Commentary

For the place of this chapter in the extended vision of the departure of the Glory from the temple, see "Introduction to Ezekiel 8–11" at the start of the commentary on chapter 8. The chapter divides itself into three parts: (1) the prediction of the destruction of ungodly rulers (11:1–13); (2) the promise of a righteous, regenerated remnant (11:14–21); and (3) the definitive withdrawal of the Glory from Jerusalem and the end of the vision (11:22–25). One almost gets the impression that nearly all of 11:1–21 is intended to signal Yahweh's reluctance to leave his chosen city, even though Israel's sin had made his departure inevitable. The promise of restoration and regeneration (11:14–21) that immediately precedes the Glory's departure (11:22–25) indicates that the departure is not permanent, but is a prelude to the restoration that is the focus of chapters 33–48 and especially to the return of the Glory to the eschatological temple in chapter 43.[16]

Destruction of Ungodly Rulers (11:1–13)

11:1 For the first time since 8:3 the Spirit[17] reappears. Since then we have heard nothing about Ezekiel's own location. Now he is moved to the eastern entrance of the temple compound, the same place to which the Glory had moved in 10:19.

The twenty-five men he sees there are obviously a different group than the sun worshipers of 8:16. Here the men are labeled "leaders of the people," a term we meet otherwise only in postexilic texts (Neh 11:1; 1 Chr 21:2; 2 Chr 24:23). Here the label probably denotes those who had assumed positions of leadership or influence in the vacuum left when, together with Ezekiel, Jehoiachin and the previous leaders had been deported in 597 B.C.

Among the twenty-five men, Ezekiel recognizes at least two whom he names: Jaazaniah and Pelatiah. Perhaps he had known them before he was deported. This is not the same Jaazaniah mentioned in 8:11 (he has a different father), and Pelatiah resurfaces in 11:13. Otherwise we know nothing of them, but all four of the names mentioned in 11:1 are common ones, especially during the period at the end of the monarchy. The name "Pelatiah" is known from

---

[16] Critics have questioned the genuineness of most of this chapter, except for the final four verses, which narrate the final stage of the Glory's departure from Jerusalem. In their view the chapter, in whole or in part, either was not written at all by Ezekiel or was a separate experience that he attached to the other visions only at a later date. See, for example, Zimmerli, *Ezekiel*, 1:257–60. It is true that the first sentence (11:1a) indicates that the chapter is a new section of the temple vision that comprises chapters 8–11. The chapter has distinctive features, including some marks of a different literary genre (a typical prophetic disputation speech). But at the same time, it has many linkages and parallels with other parts of the temple vision, such as the Spirit, the east gate, the presence of twenty-five men, and the prophet's protest. These make it entirely plausible to understand it as one part of the extended vision.

[17] The capitalization is deliberate. For the "Spirit" as the third person of the Trinity, see the textual notes on 1:12 and the commentary on 1:12–14.

several seal inscriptions of the period. One may suppose that the name was especially prominent at the time because of its meaning, "Yahweh has rescued."

11:2–3 Precisely what these leaders are plotting or doing is difficult to determine (see the textual notes), but, at the very least, some malevolent self-sufficiency and possibly an unfounded arrogation of divine promises to themselves are involved.

11:5–6 The operation of Yahweh's "Spirit" (11:5), like that of his "hand" (1:3; 3:14, 22; 8:1; 33:22; 37:1; 40:1), has a certain "incarnational" quality, expressing God's real and active presence on earth while still preserving his transcendence and otherness. No rigid distinction between the two expressions can be made in Ezekiel. Later revelation (especially the NT) that pertains to the process of inspiration will develop language about God's "Spirit" much more than of his "hand." Possibly the Spirit is mentioned here because only words (that is, verbal inspiration!) ensue in 11:5–12, but no actions. However, in 11:1 the Spirit performed the action of bringing the prophet to the east gate.

In the OT the Spirit had been explicitly connected with prophecy since the days of Moses (Num 11:25–26) and, later, Samuel (1 Sam 10:6, 10). Besides Ezekiel, the other writing prophets seldom refer directly to the operation of the Spirit upon them, although Micah 3:8 is a major exception, and 1 Pet 1:11 explains that the Spirit of Christ was in them (cf. Zech 7:12; 12:10). The OT prophets usually attribute their authority to the divine "Word" (דָּבָר) instead of God's "Spirit." Some have hypothesized that false prophecy had so preempted "spirit" language that the orthodox prophets hesitated to use it.

Ezek 11:5 contrasts "the Spirit of Yahweh," who fell upon Ezekiel, with "what arises in your [the Israelites' sinful] spirit." Yahweh's Spirit knows what is in the spirit of a man,[e] and with his Spirit he answers that the way the men are behaving is incompatible with his Spirit and will, expressed in his Word. Their actions prove that their "spirit" is an evil one. Their "spirituality" is their own invention, not a gift of revelation from the true God. Any "spirit" or "spirituality" that contravenes God's Word is not of God's Spirit.

(e) Cf. Hos 4:12; 5:4; Jn 2:24–25; Rom 8:27; 1 Cor 2:10; Rev 2:23

Yahweh accuses them of filling the city with "the slain." It is hard to tell to what extent the word is to be taken literally. Similar accusations are made in 19:3 (the princes devour the people) and 22:6 (use of power to shed blood). Elsewhere in biblical literature, during this historical period, Manasseh (2 Ki 21:6) and Jehoiakim (Jer 26:20–24) are specifically accused of such bloodshed. There is no reason to assume that circumstances were any better under Zedekiah, who occupied the throne at the time of Ezekiel's vision. Religious, political, and social factors may well have converged to create an environment of literal and metaphorical murder, including assassinations. Keil cites Calvin as having given the correct explanation: "Under this form of speech he embraces all kinds of injustice. For we know that all who oppressed the poor, deprived men of their possessions, or shed innocent blood, were regarded as murderers in the sight of God."[18]

---

[18] Keil, *Ezekiel*, 1:146, n. 1 (cf. Calvin, *Ezekiel*, 1:355).

11:7 Ezekiel repeats the leaders' own words from 11:3, but gives the parts of their proverb an application precisely the opposite of their own. Far from being the secure "prime cuts" protected in the pot, they "are in fact butchers who have made stew out of the citizenry."[19] The words read almost as a condensation of Micah 3:1–3. The pot still stands for Jerusalem (as in 11:3), but directly or indirectly (depending on the text followed; see the second textual note on 11:7), Yahweh will remove the murderous Jerusalemites from the pot. The "slain" are the meat, and the others will be deported after the city has fallen.

11:8 The Hebrew text clearly has Yahweh as the subject of the second verb ("I will bring"). As so often in the Bible, God is ultimately the actor, whatever the mediate, earthly means he may use. As with "slain" in 11:6–7, the "sword" here does not necessarily imply death, although that is not excluded. It should be taken to include all the horrors of war. "The officials were living in a fools' paradise,"[20] thinking that the catastrophe that had overtaken the city in the deportation of 597 B.C. (of which Ezekiel was a part) would never happen to them. But the sword is in Yahweh's own hand, as it were, poised to bring retribution in essentially the same way they had dealt with the disadvantaged within the city (11:6).

The progression of the argument here makes use of two words that in other passages occur in the stereotyped phrase "slain by the sword."[21] In 11:6–7 the first of those words, חָלָל, "slain," had been featured thrice, and 11:8 and 11:10 feature חֶרֶב, "sword," thrice. Anyone conversant with Hebrew idiom and the NT will think of our Lord's rebuke of Peter in Mt 26:52: "All who take up the sword will perish by the sword." Later, Ezekiel will address very similar words to the survivors of Jerusalem's fall in 587 B.C. who imagined that the ancient promises of land applied to them: "You stand by your sword. ... Those who are in the ruins will fall by the sword" (33:26–27).

11:9–11 In an expansive style typical in Ezekiel, Yahweh repeats and develops the point he introduced in 11:7: their proverb about the pot and the meat (11:3) does not apply to them in the way they understood it. He hammers away at the theme of judgment ("judgments" and twice "I will judge you"). In fact, as many commentators have discerned, Yahweh implies a double punishment: not only will the leaders be expelled from the city in which they delight, but once outside the Holy Land, a still more formidable punishment will await them.

By adding the recognition formula, "then you will know that I am Yahweh," in 11:10c (repeated in 11:12a), the oracle of judgment simultaneously

---

[19] Block, *Ezekiel*, 1:336.

[20] Allen, *Ezekiel*, 1:162.

[21] That English phrase can translate either the singular חֲלַל־חֶרֶב (Num 19:16) or the plural חַלְלֵי־חֶרֶב. The plural phrase is in Ezek 31:17–18; 32:20–32; 35:8; and these other prophetic passages: Is 22:2; Jer 14:18; Lam 4:9; Zeph 2:12. Generally the phrase refers to those who have been slain under God's judgment.

becomes a divine proof saying. The punishment will publicly prove God's justice, even though the leaders' obduracy will have forced him to manifest it in a bitter penalty. They may not repent, but they will be forced, however unwillingly, to confess that he is Lord of all.

11:12   The present sermon ends with a charge we heard already in 5:6–7: Israel has become like the heathen nations. Particularly in antiquity, acculturation implied repudiation of the Israelite cultus, that is, worship of the true God. In this "Christ versus culture" clash, the pagan culture had already won. It is a battle the church must constantly fight, certainly not less in the culture wars of our present age.

11:13   The shock of Pelatiah's sudden demise leads Ezekiel to forget Yahweh's earlier promises of sparing a remnant (9:4, 6, 11), and to say, in effect, "You really *are* annihilating all Israelites." This understands Ezekiel's words as an exclamation, not a repetition of the question in 9:8 (see the textual notes on 11:13). Indirectly, however, the verse probably implies that Ezekiel is making an intercession, as he had in 9:8, and here his exclamation will be followed by the promise of salvation for the restored remnant (11:16–20). It is also further evidence of Ezekiel's humanity: he is no sadist delighting in preaching judgment, but simply obeying God's command, and grieving at the plight of his unbelieving kinsmen, just as St. Paul will grieve while expounding the remnant theme in Romans 9–11.

Possibly the death of Pelatiah had such an impact because it seemed to make a mockery of his name, which means "Yahweh has rescued." Perhaps Ezekiel took it as a token of what would happen to all sinners—as, in a sense, it surely was. God's Word of judgment and Law must kill the sinful nature of every person. But that is his alien work, preparation for his proper work through his Word of forgiveness and new life by the Gospel: the gift of his Holy Spirit, faith, and a new heart, so that the man of faith gladly walks in God's ways (Ezek 11:19–20).

Pelatiah's death inevitably raises a major question about the relationship between the divine vision and reality. There are some approximate parallels in Scripture. Ananias and Sapphira immediately fell dead at the words of judgment spoken by St. Peter because they had lied to God the Holy Spirit (Acts 5). Jeremiah prophesied the death of the false prophet Hananiah, which took place within a year (Jer 28:15–17). But even though Ezekiel states that Pelatiah died "while I was prophesying" (11:13), Ezekiel had not prophesied his death. If he had, it would scarcely have shocked him as much as it obviously did.

In the absence of more information in Ezekiel, it is hard to say more. There is certainly no reason to deny the incident's facticity or to take it as purely visionary. There clearly was a prophetic element in the mass execution in chapter 9, and so perhaps there is one here with Pelatiah's death as well. If Ezekiel perceived the event as contemporary, even though it physically occurred later in history, we may have something similar to the common Hebrew "prophetic perfect," where what Yahweh prophesies is so certain that he describes it with a perfect verb, as if it has already happened. Regardless of the timeframe, many commentators use the term "clairvoyance" or "second sight" (cf. the term "seer" as a frequent synonym of "prophet"). If such language is not construed magically but as a special gift of the Spirit, it may be suitable (cf. Elisha and Gehazi in 2 Kings 5). Since God's "Spirit" was at work (Ezek 11:1, 5, 24), it is no more difficult to believe that Ezekiel really did see what was happening in Jerusalem (or what would happen shortly) than to believe that God actually gave him the vision.

God Will Create a Righteous, Regenerated Remnant by Giving His People "One Heart" and "a New Spirit" (11:14–21)

Block beautifully entitles this entire section (11:14–21) "The Gospel according to Ezekiel."[22] Read through a Christological lens, it also summarizes *the* Gospel—period! We can distinguish, but dare not divorce, each biblical writer's way of presenting the Gospel from the Gospel itself (as summarized in the ecumenical Creeds and by dogmatic theology). This section summarizes that, as Luther loved to stress, God works *sub contrario*, that is, in a form contrary to what human reason expects. Here the issue is where the remnant—the true Israel, consisting of the legitimate heirs of God's promises—is to be found, whether among those who had experienced the exile with Ezekiel, or those still in Jerusalem who had escaped it. As powerfully proclaimed by his older contemporary Jeremiah,[23] Ezekiel insists that God's future lay with those who had "died" to their past and would miraculously be resurrected by God (see especially Ezek 11:19 and chapter 37).

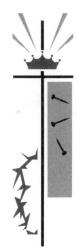

The climax of this death-resurrection pattern comes in the Good Friday–Easter Sunday nexus. We are initiated into Christ's death and resurrection in the Sacrament of Holy Baptism (e.g., Rom 6:1–4; Col 2:11–13) and are maintained in him through the application of Law and Gospel in his Word and the Sacrament of the Altar. Daily we die to sin and arise to new life in Christ. At temporal death our sinful nature dies for good, and on the Last Day, when Christ returns to bring this world to its end, our bodies shall be raised incorruptible, and we as whole persons shall inherit eternal life in the new heaven and new earth.

In the context of Ezekiel 11, these verses are Yahweh's response to Ezekiel's outcry in 11:13, where he had declared (his perception) that God had begun to exterminate Israel in its entirety. Earlier in 9:8, when Ezekiel had posed the same thought as in 11:13 but phrased (more hopefully) as a question, God's answer had accented the negative (9:9–10).[24] Now after Ezekiel's out-

---

[22] Block, *Ezekiel*, 1:341.

[23] Jeremiah's message, like that of Ezekiel, is that Israel cannot escape judgment. The future of the people lies with those who go through the "death" of exile and the subsequent "resurrection" of return after seventy years (see especially Jeremiah 29).

[24] Nevertheless, in that chapter Yahweh still made provision for sparing the repentant remnant (9:4, 6, 11).

cry in 11:13, phrased as a despairing statement, Yahweh proclaims emphatic Gospel. God's Law rightly drives the hearers to despair of their own merit and abandon hope of evading judgment. But when the penitent cast themselves upon God's mercy alone, they hear his Gospel pardon and promise of new life.

Inevitably, 11:25 raises the questions of when Ezekiel told the exiles about his vision (chapters 8–11) and, if he preached it to them immediately, whether he would have included this Gospel part, since they seem to have remained unrepentant until news of Jerusalem's fall in 587 B.C. reached them in 33:21. Predictably, critics quite unanimously assume that this section (especially 11:18–21) is a postexilic addition, but only hypercriticism would question the veridicality of God's reply to Ezekiel himself. After Jerusalem's fall, recorded in chapter 33, the Gospel message will predominate in Ezekiel, but here he still faces an audience that does not believe that such a thing will ever happen. Yet the inclusion of this section's description of what God will do *after* the judgment comes would reinforce to the exiles that the future judgment is a foregone conclusion.

This issue is not unique to Ezekiel; it is part of the "alternation of weal and woe," the pattern of Law and Gospel commonly found in all the prophets and intimated already in the Pentateuch (e.g., Leviticus 26 and Deuteronomy 30). We have met it earlier in Ezekiel (5:1–3; 6:1–9) and will meet it again later.[f] (f) Ezek 12:15–16; 14:9–11, 12–22; 16:59–63; 17:21–24; 20:30–44 Some argue plausibly that preaching both was a sign of a true prophet. False prophets proclaimed only God's "love," that is, "Gospel" in a reductionist sense of temporal peace and success, and avoided any call to repent (e.g., 1 Ki 22:5–28; Jeremiah 28), as false prophets still do today.

11:14–15 Yahweh draws three concentric circles of those who make up the present Diaspora. First of all, there are Ezekiel's "brothers," apparently his immediate family. Second, the men of his "redemption" (see the textual note), whose property he, as God's proxy, would be obligated to buy back if it were alienated from them. Finally is the "whole house of Israel," that is, the entire present Diaspora, including the deportees from the northern kingdom of Israel over a century earlier (ca. 722 B.C.), at least as many as had retained their identity as Israelites and their faithfulness to Yahweh. The destruction of Jerusalem would hardly exterminate all of Israel when all of these Israelites in the Diaspora are taken into account.

The scornful demand (the imperative "remove yourselves") of those Israelites still left in Jerusalem suggests a sort of propaganda war going on between those who (so far) had escaped exile and those now exiled in Babylon. Those in Jerusalem remained confident that they would never suffer the same fate, while the exiles, on the whole, had not abandoned all hope of returning.[25] The issue, then, was who had title to the land left behind by the exiles. At stake was not only legal inheritance of property, but also theological inheritance of

---

[25] Later in Ezekiel it will become evident that some of the exiles came to fear that they would never return. See, for example, 37:11.

God's promised grace and life. God's promises to the patriarchs had centered on the land as the place wherein he would bestow his blessings upon them, and the fulfillment of those promises was the reason why God enabled Joshua's conquest of Canaan. Essentially the same debate will erupt after Jerusalem finally does fall in 587 B.C., and again Yahweh will have to condemn the Israelites who thought they could sin with impunity and still claim the land as their own (33:23–29).

Paganism often linked worship of a national deity with residence in the land that supposedly was that deity's kingdom because the deity often was little more than a personification of that country. The argumentation of the Jerusalemites suggests that their reasoning was along those lines. In saying to the exiles, "Remove yourselves from Yahweh!" they were telling the exiles to abandon faith in Yahweh because the exiles could not worship him in a foreign land; they should adopt and worship the gods of the land in which they now resided. The Jerusalemites' mandate obviously was contested by the exiles, perhaps not so much because the exiles disputed the theological premise, but because they still thought their absence from the land of Israel was only temporary.

Yet up to a point, the link between worship and territory was a legitimate one. The erection of an altar by the tribes whose land was in Transjordan nearly precipitated a civil war shortly after the conquest (Joshua 22, especially 22:24–27). The link surfaces in the fugitive David's lament to Saul: his expulsion from the land was accompanied by the exhortation, "Go, serve other gods" (1 Sam 26:19). In Ezek 11:16, Yahweh will finesse the issue for the exiles: he will be their sanctuary even while they are in Babylon.

Before we leave the topic, we should consider briefly what "land" means theologically to Christians.[26] We have no difficulty with the eschatological application of the land of OT Israel to the new heavens and new earth, in which all the redeemed shall enjoy eternal life (Isaiah 11; 65–66; Revelation 21–22). This typology derived from the Scriptures is clear. But what of the interim, the NT era before the parousia of Christ and the creation of the new heavens and new earth?

The church learned from her incarnate Lord that she is in no way linked with any particular "land" in a geographical or political sense (as Jesus explains to the Samaritan woman in Jn 4:19–24).[27] The issue is still beclouded for many today by various nationalisms or civic religions that unfortunately affect the way Christians think about the church and their particular church. (Christians in America certainly have not escaped the temptation to equate their "land"

---

[26] See also Harstad, *Joshua*, 25–31, 489–96.

[27] Jesus was wrongly accused of (politically) trying to reclaim the land from Roman rule (e.g., "King of the Jews" in Mt 27:11, 29, 37), but emphatically declared that his kingdom was not of this world (Jn 18:33–36). After his resurrection, he continued to instruct the disciples, who at first still thought of his kingdom in nationalistic and ethnic terms (Acts 1:6–8; 10:45; 11:1–3, 18).

with that of OT Israel.) But in principle the non-territoriality of Christianity has been central to the Christian mission at least since Pentecost (Acts 2). Understandably, the early Christians in their milieu were careful not to preach that Christ brought God's kingdom in a territorial sense as the fulfillment of the OT "land" prophecies, even when, in the original OT context, prophecies of the Messiah often came in the same breath as those about the land.

If we are not to atomize the OT, we will see the "land" prophecies as fulfilled in Christ just as much as other prophetic themes. He explicitly speaks of his body as the new temple (Jn 2:19–21), and Christians are described as "living stones" in that temple (1 Pet 2:4–6). "Temple" and "land" are not synonymous, of course, but they are inextricably linked, and like all God's promises and prophecies, they merge in Christ. In that vein, the church is repeatedly described as "the body of Christ," and all Christians are incorporated as members of that body through Holy Baptism (1 Corinthians 12). Of course, spiritual language is involved, but plainly St. Paul does not consider it *merely* metaphorical, any more than he thinks of the true presence of Christ's body and blood in the Lord's Supper as merely metaphorical (1 Cor 10:16–17; 11:23–30).

Especially in light of today's individualism, and the tendency to define the church in local and sociological terms, it bears emphasizing that Christ himself is our "land." Through baptismal incorporation into him, we are heirs of all God's promises (Gal 3:6–9, 14, 26–29), including those about the land (e.g., Revelation 21–22). Indeed, through his Spirit, he must be received in faith in each individual heart, but no one is a Christian in isolation from Christ's body, the church. Christ is to be found only where he has promised to be found, that is, in his Word and Sacraments, which are dispensed in his church. Through those, his means of grace, we are already in our "promised land," although the resolution of the "now/not yet" paradox still awaits us at the return of Christ, when this world shall end, and the new heavens and new earth shall be established, "in which righteousness dwells" (2 Pet 3:13).

In terms of Ezek 11:15, unlike the Jerusalemites who said, "Remove yourselves from Yahweh!" we do not desire anyone to be "exiled" from the "land" and the "temple," that is, from Christ and his church, although some may "exile" themselves by their impenitence (cf. 1 Cor 10:16–22; 11:23–30) or neglect of public worship (cf. Heb 10:24–25). Nor do we claim this "land" as our own to the exclusion of others, as the Jerusalemites did ("*To us* this land has been given as a possession" [Ezek 11:15]). Rather, through the preaching of the Gospel we invite all those who are far off and those who are near (Eph 2:11–22) to be gathered and assembled with us to receive "the land of Israel" (Ezek 1:17), a gift of pure grace for them as for us.

11:16 Yahweh readily affirms one part of the Jerusalemites' premise, that he has sent the "house of Israel" (11:15) into exile. The plurals "nations" and "lands" (11:16) seem to envision not only the community at Tel Abib, but also the Dispersion elsewhere. The scattering of Israel would multiply almost exponentially after Jerusalem's fall in 587 B.C.

But Yahweh challenges the other part of their premise, namely, that expulsion from the land necessarily implies alienation from himself. That God was not imprisoned, as it were, in his temple and his land was, as such, not so novel a thought in the OT. After all, God had plainly been with the patriarchs and others long before he had given them the land, or before there was a temple or even a portable tabernacle. Faithful Israelites realized that Zion was not some intrinsically holy place by nature (as in pagan worship sites), but that God had elected or chosen Zion to be the place where he would "cause his name to dwell" (e.g., Deut 12:11) in a way not dissimilar from the way in which he had chosen Israel as his people (e.g., 1 Kings 8). Perhaps, however, only the remnant had that straight; the masses among the exiles probably had succumbed to pagan ways of thinking about sacred space.

In Ezek 11:16b Yahweh goes beyond merely reaffirming ancient biblical truth: "I will be for them a sanctuary for a little while in the lands to which they have come." We find a certain parallel in Jeremiah's promise to the exiles in Jer 29:11–14 and in Daniel's action (Dan 6:11 [ET 6:10]): God would be accessible to them in prayer even when they lacked the benefit of a temple. A possible anticipation of Ezekiel's statement here has been sought in Is 8:14, but just how "sanctuary" parallels "rock of offense and stone of stumbling" in that well-known passage is not clear (see commentaries).

Yahweh here unambiguously personalizes the place of worship: "*I* will be for them a sanctuary" (Ezek 11:16). The exiles had been deprived of the stone temple in Jerusalem. Even if the building still stood until 587 B.C., God's Glory or "incarnational presence" is forsaking it (11:22–25). But Yahweh promises to himself be the exiles' sanctuary, created by his abiding presence among them. Ezekiel does not yet specify how they will experience or verify God's presence in grace. Perhaps Ezekiel's own encounters with Yahweh would stand as a witness of this promise's veracity. And we may assume that at least some of the extant OT Scriptures were brought by some of the exiles (especially by clergy such as Ezekiel) and so were already available for liturgical use. In the OT in general, however, we find no parallels or sequels to the bold assertion here (for NT sequels, see especially the discussion in the commentary on 11:14–15 of John 4 and Christ's appropriation of the "temple" to himself).

The Jewish Targum found this personalizing of the sanctuary intolerable and paraphrased: "I have given them synagogues, second only to my holy temple." It is plausible that the ultimate roots of the synagogue are to be found in the exile (and Ezekiel's words here have even been adduced in support of that supposition). Yet there is no certain knowledge of the existence of synagogues until the Hellenistic period in Egypt and no archaeological evidence for special synagogue structures until the century before Christ. Synagogues do not become common until after the second destruction of Jerusalem, by Titus in A.D. 70. It may also be noted that some strains of Jewish piety associate Ezekiel's words here with religious devotions by the family in homes. We recall the Christian tradition of a "family altar," a smaller version of a church altar, which Lutherans commonly had in their homes for family devotions and prayer, and which may also be found in classrooms of Lutheran schools.

11:17 God's promise of an inheritance, including the land, still stood: "I will give you the land of Israel." The judgment of dispersal had been unavoidable, and God even makes himself available as the "sanctuary" (11:16) during that interim, but, unless his promise was to be voided, his people had to be restored to their land. What Ezekiel could not accomplish, even for his own family, Yahweh would do for his people when the full implications of the land prophecies would be revealed in Jesus Christ.

In this and the next verse there appears to be a clear echoing of the promise given to Moses in Ex 6:6–8. God will bring about a second exodus that will reverse the judgment. As Yahweh again redeems his people, he will "gather" and "assemble" them (Ezek 11:17) after having "removed" and "scattered" them (11:16). This exodus typology will, at least in essence, reappear frequently in later salvation oracles in Ezekiel.[28] The exiles' release from their wilderness and their repossession of the land will not come by an arrogant claim, such as the Jerusalemites made in 11:15, but by Yahweh freely *giving* them the land by pure grace.

The succeeding verses make plain that what Ezekiel is predicting is no mere inner-historical reversal of fortunes and reacquisition of lost real estate. As is typical of prophecy, the unknown (the future) is described in terms of the known. (The same principle will apply to NT depictions of heaven and eternal life.) This promise was indeed fulfilled in the return led by Zerubbabel—even if the response of the Israelites at that time was rather underwhelming. But as often in typology, one fulfillment becomes the springboard for another, still greater fulfillment. Hermeneutically, it is not a matter of multiple fulfillments or meanings, but of different aspects or phases of the "one literal sense." Usually, both continuity and discontinuity attend the various aspects or phases.

The greater fulfillment of this promise came with the first advent of Christ, who, through his death and resurrection, leads all who believe into his "land"— the church, the body of Christ. Yet even his first advent is not the end of the story. The final fulfillment or consummation will not be realized until his second advent, whereupon God will create the eternal "land," the new Jerusalem, where there will be no need of a temple, "for its temple is the Lord God the Almighty and the Lamb" (Rev 21:22). That is the glorious, definitive antitype of the temporary sanctuary of Yahweh's presence that he promised the exiles in Ezek 11:16.

11:18 As at the first conquest of Canaan, when the land had been given to Israel because of the flagrant behavior of its former inhabitants (see, e.g.,

---

[28] Ezek 20:33–42; 34:13; 36:24; 39:27. In many of those and other passages, Ezekiel speaks of God bringing (Hiphil of יָצָא or בּוֹא) his people into the "land" (אֶרֶץ). Ezek 11:17 does not use either of those verbs and uses אֲדָמָה, "land/soil." Nevertheless, some of those other promises (34:13; 36:24) do use "gather" (קָבַץ) and אֲדָמָה, "land/soil," as in 11:17.

Deut 18:9–13; 20:17–18), so the land had again become polluted by centuries of people doing "loathsome things" (שִׁקּוּצֶיהָ) and "abominations" (תּוֹעֲבוֹתֶיהָ; two of Ezekiel's favorite words)—this time unfaithful Israelites themselves. In biblical thought, it is not only the people who are defiled by their sin, but the land itself, just as all creation suffered under the curse because of Adam's fall (Gen 3:17–18), and in the parousia we are promised nothing less than a new creation (cf., e.g., Is 11:6; Rom 8:20–22). God will restore his people to the land, and in gratitude they will purge it of its idolatry and contaminants, and keep it pure. That God's people then and now often fail in this respect is a reminder that the parousia is not yet, and we live by the daily forgiveness of sin (cf. Romans 6–7).

11:19 This verse is of hermeneutical significance for the entire promise (11:14–21). How pivotal it is for Ezekiel's entire message is evidenced by the fact that he repeats it almost verbatim in 36:26–27. St. Paul's language in 2 Cor 3:3 also appears to be derived from it. The horizon is transhistorical, and the accent is on something that only God can do. The real problem was inside the people, a matter of the "heart," which in biblical usage accents the will and spiritual orientation. Nothing short of a supernatural "heart transplant" and gift of a new "S/spirit" will avail.

Yahweh's first promise is "I will give them one heart." A faith-filled heart that is "sincere," "undivided," "single-minded," or "unanimous" might be more idiomatic English equivalents. Its opposite would be an "insincere," "duplicitous," or "whoring heart" (6:9), or a "heart" in which idols have been set up (14:3–7). Some commentators take the "one heart" as a promise of the reunification of the northern and southern kingdoms. Although that eschatological prophecy does occur later in Ezekiel (37:15–22), as also in other prophets, that theme seems extrinsic to this context. In the natural, fallen state, each person pursues his own selfish interests; "every one of us has turned to his own way" (Is 53:6). Only God can unite all hearts by the "one thing" that "is needful" (Lk 10:42 KJV; cf. Mt 6:21; 22:37). In the infant church, after the "new" gift of the outpouring of the Holy Spirit, the disciples had "singleness of heart" (Acts 2:46) and "were of one heart and soul" (Acts 4:32). Similar expressions with "heart" that involve unity in faith are in Rom 10:8–10; Eph 6:5; Col 3:22; 1 Tim 1:5; 2 Tim 2:22; Heb 10:22; 1 Pet 1:22.

Since this transformation does not happen naturally, the "*single/one* heart" is parallel to "a *new* S/spirit" (Ezek 11:19). Theologically, all of this is a gift of the Holy Spirit, but I judge the accent here to be on the new human spirit God will grant. The same Spirit who gave the disciples one "heart" (Acts 4:32) is poured out on all who are baptized into Christ ("you will receive the gift of the Holy Spirit," Acts 2:38) and renews the human spirit of the baptized believer. The adjective "new" can modify various words in eschatological contexts, for example, "one new man" in Christ (Eph 2:15; cf. Eph 4:24; Col 3:10; the "new" Jerusalem and "new" heaven and "new" earth in Revelation 21–22).

Here in Ezek 11:19 "new" modifies "S/spirit," in parallelism with "heart" ("spirit" and "heart" are often interchangeable in biblical usage). In the close parallel in 36:26–27, God promises to give the people "a new heart" and "a heart of flesh" after removing their "heart of stone." There he also promises to bestow "a new S/spirit" that is parallel to God's Spirit: "I will give you a new heart and put a new S/spirit within you. … I will put my Spirit within you." In 37:1–14 Yahweh expands on this gift of the Spirit that effects resurrection from the grave (see especially 37:12–14). Here the "new S/spirit" is not just a renewed human will, but the gift of the Holy Spirit, who accomplishes the renewal. The same can be said about the "right S/spirit" and "willing S/spirit" God graciously places in the believer according to David's petitions in Ps 51:12, 14 (ET 51:10, 12), in light of the intervening phrase "your Holy Spirit" (Ps 51:13 [ET 51:11]).[29] Then we may speak of a new spirituality, and if we are careful to stress the capital "S" in "Spirit" (referring to the Holy Spirit, the third person of the Trinity), Ezek 11:19 can readily be expounded in concord with the affirmation that the Holy Spirit "proceeds from the Father and the Son" (Nicene Creed; cf. Jn 14:6, 26; 15:26; 16:7).

God will remove the obdurate "heart of stone" and grant in its place a "heart of flesh" (Ezek 11:19). In the NT, when "flesh" (σάρξ) is opposed to "S/spirit" (πνεῦμα), "flesh" often denotes the sinful human nature (e.g., Rom 8:1–17; 1 Cor 5:5; Gal 5:16–17; 6:8). Here, however, the "heart of flesh" is opposed to one of "stone," so "flesh" implies a heart that responds in God-given faith to the Holy Spirit's working through the Word and Sacraments (cf. Is 57:15; 61:1), versus an obdurate, unresponsive "stone" heart (cf. Gen 6:5; the hardened heart of Pharaoh, which was integral to the exodus narrative [e.g., Ex 7:3, 13, 14]; and Is 6:10). English has the native idioms "hardhearted" (cf. Ezek 2:4) and "tenderhearted" (often used as a translation of εὔσπλαγχνοι in Eph 4:32), which might be compared to "heart of stone" and "heart of flesh" (Ezek 11:19).

Except for the eschatological vista here, the basic promise that God grants his people a sincere heart and new S/spirit is not new with Ezekiel. In Moses' day God poured out his Spirit on the seventy elders (Num 11:16–30; cf. Is 63:11), and the accent on the internal appears in Deut 30:6, where circumcision of the heart is part of the promised blessing upon faithful Israel (contrast those with uncircumcised hearts in Ezek 44:7, 9). Saul's heart was "turned around" (הָפַךְ) after an encounter with Samuel (1 Sam 10:9). Through Isaiah, God had promised to place his Spirit upon his Suffering Servant (Is 42:1; 61:1) and the seed of Israel (Is 44:3). The parallel with Jer 32:39 is especially close. Ezekiel's line of thought is the same as Jeremiah's famous "new covenant/testament" prophecy of Jer 31:31–34. This will become even more obvious in the next verse.

---

[29] In the version of Ps 51:12–14 (ET 51:10–12) used as an Offertory in *LW* (pp. 143–44), "willing S/spirit" (Ps 51:14 [ET 51:12]) is rendered "your free Spirit."

11:20 This result clause speaks of true, wholehearted obedience, of God-pleasing behavior, which is only possible after the radical change (the new heart and spirit) affected by God's Spirit. The OT is well aware that mere possession of God's Torah is not sufficient for salvation, nor is mere external conformity to its stipulations (going through the motions, *ex opere operato*). Here Ezekiel does not use "Torah" (תּוֹרָה), which, in its full sense, is God's entire instruction or revelation, that is, both Law and Gospel. Instead, God refers to "my statutes" and "my ordinances," which indeed he gave in the Torah and which encompass what doctrinal theology labels both justification and sanctification. We are still in the OT, which implies historically also those laws that Christ has kept perfectly and that now those who have been baptized into the "new covenant" are no longer bound to follow. The principle of true obedience has not changed but has been "radicalized" (2 Corinthians 3). Allen[30] appropriately cites Rom 8:3–4: God has done "what the Law could not do … in order that the just requirement of the Law might be fulfilled in us, who walk not according to the flesh but according to the Spirit."

The "Gospel according to Ezekiel"[31] reaches its climax with what is commonly known as the covenant formula: "They will be my people, and I will be their God" (Ezek 11:20). Even though בְּרִית, "covenant," is not used here, it is used in similar passages, for example, in 34:25, leading up to the covenant formula in 34:30–31 and in 37:26–27. To get the full impact of the formula, one should perhaps add "truly" (as opposed to "nominally") or "fully" to both halves of the formula. In a way, it is a restatement of the First Commandment: if it were fully obeyed, no other commandments would be necessary. The good news of the new covenant is that such loyalty is the gift of grace in Christ, who was perfectly obedient to God, his Father, and whose obedience and righteousness are imputed to believers in him. But until the parousia, the "not yet" always coexists. Christians remain both saints and sinners, and as such we cannot and do not "fear, love, and trust in God above all things."[32] So, in the unique structure of Luther's Small Catechism, the Decalogue functions as condemning Law first, then, in the light of Christ's fulfillment of it, also as Gospel.

The covenant formula is usually thought to root in ancient wedding language. This may be evidenced in, for example, Ex 6:7, where it follows the verb לָקַח, "to take" (God says, "I will take you to myself …"), a verb often used for a man taking a wife. It is also supported by the covenant-like passages in the Song of Songs (2:16; 6:3; 7:11 [ET 7:10]).[33] Thus it is to be associated with the nuptial language throughout Scripture, of OT Israel as the wife of Yah-

---

[30] Allen, *Ezekiel*, 1:165.

[31] Block, *Ezekiel*, 1:341.

[32] SC, Ten Commandments, 2.

[33] One may see the exposition of this covenant theme, wherein the Shulammite's marriage to Solomon reflects Israel's marriage to Yahweh and anticipates the church's betrothal to Christ, in Mitchell, *The Song of Songs*, 395–408.

weh (e.g., Ezekiel 16 and 23) and the NT church as the bride of Christ (e.g., Rev 19:7; 21:2). Negatively, it also relates to the depiction of idolatry as adultery that provokes Yahweh's jealousy (again, Ezekiel 16 and 23; also 5:13).

Whatever its ultimate origin, the covenant formula (with variations in wording) reverberates throughout both Testaments, from Gen 17:7–8 (Abraham) to Rev 21:2–3 (the new Jerusalem as the bride of Christ). In the NT, see also 2 Cor 6:16; Heb 8:10. It will be fully realized in the eternal state, where the redeemed will be singly devoted to God like a virgin bride and God will dwell with his people personally and immediately, as in Eden, without need for mediators (no temple except God and the Lamb, Rev 21:22).

11:21 Plainly this verse contrasts the unregenerate heart with one that has been supernaturally recreated. The question is why we are suddenly again plunged into the depths of sin, as it were, after the heights of the Gospel in 11:14–20. It is probably best taken as a reminder that although the promise was sure, and it has now been accomplished in Christ, Ezekiel was still preaching in the time of the "not yet." It comes at the end of the vision and summarizes the charges laid against the Jerusalemites in chapter 8, so in context it may be understood as directed primarily to Ezekiel's immediate audience, his fellow exiles. They dare not assume that the promise was automatically theirs because they were exiles. If they did not repent, they too would surely perish. (The rest of the book indicates that few, if any, had repented before Jerusalem fell as recorded in chapter 33.)

The Glory Departs from Jerusalem and the Temple Vision Ends (11:22–25)

11:23 The last scene in the vision of chapters 8–11 represents the fulfillment of all the predictions of impending doom upon the city. Yahweh's Glory, that is, his "incarnational" presence on earth in the midst of his people,[34] now abandons his earthly "house," the Holy of Holies in the temple, and also the entire city as well. It is no longer "Zion," the elect holy city, inviolable because of the divine presence, as Isaiah had preached so forcefully a century earlier.[35] It is now only another human construction, as vulnerable to the invading Babylonians as any other.

Many authors speculate about whether "stood on the mountain that is east of the city" (11:23) means that the Glory stayed on the Mount of Olives or only halted there temporarily en route to somewhere else. The Glory reappears in 43:1–5, in a vision seen by Ezekiel twenty years after this one, but that vision is not of the earthly Jerusalem and temple; rather, it is of an eschatological temple, city, and land. There the Glory comes to fill the eschatological temple "from the east" (43:2), but that passage says nothing about the mountain. From these

---

[34] See especially the textual notes and commentary on 1:26–28.

[35] See the commentary on Ezek 8:12–13.

two visions one cannot deduce anything about the Glory's whereabouts after departing from the earthly Jerusalem temple in this vision in 592 B.C.

One conjecture is that the Glory remained on the Mount of Olives until the Jerusalem temple was rebuilt in 516 B.C., although the Bible says nothing about the Glory returning to the rebuilt earthly temple. (The Glory is notably absent from Ezra 6:13–18.) Another speculation has the Glory tarrying on the Mount of Olives only momentarily, as though in regret at having to leave the city, and then heading for Babylonia, where it would function as the "sanctuary for a little while in the lands to which they have come" (11:16), giving the exiles the same assurance Ezekiel had received in his inaugural vision. But nothing in the text explicitly supports a linkage of the Glory (כָּבוֹד) with the sanctuary (מִקְדָּשׁ), and that speculation connects the inaugural vision (chapters 1–3, which took place a little over a year earlier) too closely with the temple vision in chapters 8–11.

In the inaugural vision, the Glory had come from the north (1:4), and, it seems, from heaven. (Nothing is said in 3:12–15 about where the Glory went after the inaugural vision.) If one must speculate about its ultimate destination in 11:22–25, heaven seems to be the most defensible answer. The vertical typology underlying the temple's construction and theology would point in that direction, and the basic anthropomorphism of God's "residence" being in heaven may demand it. Daniel's vision of the Ancient of Days and the Son of Man in Dan 7:9–10, 13–14, and John's vision of the enthroned Almighty in Rev 4:1–11, also support such an assumption.

11:24–25 As in 3:14–15 at the end of the inaugural vision, here too the vision's end is signaled by the Spirit transporting Ezekiel back to the exiles, that is, out of his trance-like state and back to his natural senses. How long the elders (8:1) had been sitting before him and waiting, we are not told. At least when the vision is over, there is nothing for Ezekiel to do except to relate what he had seen and heard on his journey in the Spirit. We are told nothing about the elders' reaction or response. We shall meet them again in 14:1.

Ezekiel 12:1–28

An Action Prophecy of the Prince's Exile and Two False Proverbs about True Prophecy

Translation

12 ¹The Word of Yahweh came to me: ²"Son of man, you are living in the midst of the rebellious house, who have eyes to see, but they do not see, and ears to hear, but they do not hear, for they are a rebellious house. ³Therefore, you, son of man, make for yourself a knapsack for exile, and go into exile by day in their sight. You shall go into exile from your place to another place in their sight. Perhaps they will see that they are a rebellious house. ⁴You shall bring out your knapsack, packed as for exile, by day in their sight. Then you yourself shall go out in the evening in their sight like one of those going into exile. ⁵In their sight dig through the wall, and you shall bring out [your knapsack] through it. ⁶In their sight you shall lift it on your shoulder, and you shall carry it out at dusk. You shall cover your face so that you will not see the ground, for I have made you a portent to the house of Israel." ⁷Then I did so, just as I was commanded. I brought out my knapsack, packed as for exile, by day, and in the evening I dug through the wall by hand. At dusk I brought [it] out; I carried it on my shoulder in their sight.

⁸The Word of Yahweh came to me in the morning: ⁹"Son of man, has not the house of Israel, the rebellious house, said to you, 'What are you doing?' ¹⁰Say to them, 'Thus says the Lord Yahweh: The prince is this burden in Jerusalem, together with the whole house of Israel who are in its midst.' ¹¹Say, 'I am a portent for you': as I have done, so it will be done to them. Into exile, into captivity they will go. ¹²The prince who is in their midst will carry [his knapsack] on his shoulder at dusk and go out. They will dig through the wall to bring [him] out through it. He will cover his face, and so he will not see by eye the ground. ¹³I will spread my net for him, and he will be caught in my trap. I will bring him to Babylon, the land of the Chaldeans, but he will not see it, and there he will die. ¹⁴All those who are around him, his aides and all his troops, I will scatter to every wind, and I will unsheathe my sword after them. ¹⁵Then they will know that I am Yahweh when I scatter them among the nations and I disperse them in the countries. ¹⁶But from them I will let remain a few in number from the sword, famine, and plague, in order that they may relate all their abominations among the nations where they go. Then they will know that I am Yahweh."

¹⁷The Word of Yahweh came to me: ¹⁸"Son of man, you shall eat your food in trembling, and you shall drink your water in shuddering and in fear. ¹⁹You shall say to the people of the land, 'Thus says the Lord Yahweh about the inhabitants of Jerusalem on the soil of Israel: They will eat their food in fear and

drink their water in desolation, for its land will be desolated of its contents because of the violence of all its inhabitants. ²⁰The inhabited cities will be laid waste, and the land will be desolate. Then you will know that I am Yahweh.' "

²¹The Word of Yahweh came to me: ²²"Son of man, what is this proverb you have in the land of Israel: 'The days go by, and every vision fails'? ²³Therefore say to them, 'Thus says the Lord Yahweh: I will put an end to this proverb, and they will never use it as a proverb again in Israel.' On the contrary, say to them, 'The days are near, and the fulfillment of every vision. ²⁴For no longer will there be any vacuous vision or misleading divination within the house of Israel. ²⁵For I am Yahweh. I will speak the word I will speak, and it will be fulfilled; it will be delayed no longer. For in your own days, O rebellious house, I will speak a word and fulfill it, says the Lord Yahweh.' "

²⁶The Word of Yahweh came to me: ²⁷"Son of man, the house of Israel is saying, 'The vision that he is seeing is for many days [ahead], and for distant times he is prophesying.' ²⁸Therefore, say to them, 'Thus says the Lord Yahweh: All my words will be delayed no longer, because I will speak a word, and it will be fulfilled, says the Lord Yahweh.' "

Textual Notes

12:2 בֵּית־הַמֶּרִי—See the textual note on this Ezekielian signature phrase for Israel in 2:5 (there without the article). It occurs twice more (also without the article) in 12:2–3 as well as in 12:9, 25 (with the article).

12:3 כְּלֵי גוֹלָה—The noun כְּלִי can have a wide range of meanings, including "dish, vessel, bowl" (as in 4:9), "weapon" (as in 9:1–2), "gear," and "baggage." Here its plural is in construct with גּוֹלָה, "exile." I have translated the phrase as "a knapsack for exile" (similarly in 12:4, 7) because Ezekiel's consisted of a simple knapsack or a bag to be slung over his shoulder (12:6). Here we must think of a few items salvaged from homes on short notice. Only what could easily be carried a long distance was quickly stuffed into a bag. Ezekiel and his audience will have known that only too well from their own recent experience. Assyrian victory reliefs frequently portray a procession of captives being led away with large bags slung over their shoulders.[1] Ancient rabbinic sources mention that such bags would contain bare necessities such as a skin bottle (for flour or water and use as a pillow), a bowl, a lamp, and a mat.[2]

וּגְלֵה יוֹמָם לְעֵינֵיהֶם—The Qal imperative ("go into exile") is absent from the LXX, and hence some deem it a dittograph of the preceding noun, גּוֹלָה. But the Syriac indirectly attests to the MT because it omits the second use of the verb in the verse (וְגָלִיתָ). The Peshitta typically abridges repetitive passages.

The word יוֹמָם and the phrase לְעֵינֵיהֶם emphasize that Ezekiel is to make sure his audience sees his action prophecy. יוֹמָם ("by day," also in 12:4, 7) is one of the few true Hebrew adverbs, formed by adding the adverbial suffix ־ָם to the noun יוֹם. Greenberg suggests deleting it because it is usually balanced by לַיְלָה ("night") or עֶרֶב

---

[1] See *ANEP*, §§ 10, 366, 373.

[2] See *Midrash Rabbah Lamentations*, 1.22 (on Lam 1:2); Talmud, *Nedarim*, 40b–41a.

("evening"), as in 12:4.[3] That is true enough, but I take it to be simply a manner of emphasis. The action as a whole is introduced in 12:3, while the particulars begin to be detailed in 12:4.

Literally, "to their eyes," לְעֵינֵיהֶם is repeated seven times in 12:3–7. (The ancient versions omit some of them.)

מִמְּקוֹמְךָ אֶל־מָקוֹם אַחֵר—"From your place to another place" is imprecise, but Cooke's paraphrase is adequate: "Not necessarily far away, but far enough to show what the action meant."[4] Ezekiel's "place" at his outset is his house.

אוּלַי יִרְאוּ כִּי בֵית מְרִי הֵמָּה:—This is the only Ezekielian occurrence of אוּלַי, an adverb meaning "perhaps" and "usually expressing a hope" (BDB, 1). In prophetic usage, it is usually associated with a call to repentance so that God may repeal his decree of judgment (e.g., Jer 26:3; 36:3; Amos 5:15). That helps determine the force of כִּי at the beginning of the final clause. With verbs of seeing, believing, and the like, כִּי can introduce a subordinate clause and mean "that": "perhaps they will see that they are a rebellious house." God hopes the action prophecy will make the Israelites see that they have been rebellious, and so it would move them to repentance. However, many view the phrase more pessimistically and take כִּי as concessive ("though," NASB, ESV), introducing the reason why they probably will not repent ("they are a rebellious house").

12:4 The verbs in this verse, a perfect with *waw* consecutive and an imperfect, have the force of imperatives, as is common. כֵּלֶיךָ כִּכְלֵי גוֹלָה is, literally, "your things/belongings like the things of exile." I have translated it "your knapsack, packed as for exile" (similar is the phrase in 12:7). See the first textual note on 12:3.

כְּמוֹצָאֵי גוֹלָה:—The noun מוֹצָא (from יָצָא) can refer to a place of departure or the action of going forth, but here it refers concretely to people, *those going forth into exile* (BDB, 1 b).

12:5 חֲתָר־לְךָ בַקִּיר[dd]—This word for "wall" (קִיר) usually refers to the wall of a house, whereas חוֹמָה usually refers to the large defensive wall (often stone) of an ancient city. Since houses in Mesopotamia were (and still are) commonly built of mud brick, it was relatively easy to "dig" (imperative of חָתַר) through their walls. Ezekiel will add in 12:7 that he dug through it "by hand."

וְהוֹצֵאתָ בּוֹ:—Instead of the Hiphil of יָצָא ("bring out"), the ancient versions here and again in 12:6, 7, and 12 translate as if the verb were Qal (Ezekiel will "go out"). Many modern commentators and translations emend accordingly. Part of the perceived problem is that no object for the transitive Hiphil is given here and in 12:6, 12. But the omission of an object that can readily be supplied from the context is common in Hebrew. What Ezekiel is to "bring out" here (and in 12:6) must be his knapsack. In 12:7 the Hiphil (הוֹצֵאתִי) does have that stated direct object.

12:6 While there is no stated object, the context implies that the object of the verbs תִּשָּׂא and תוֹצִיא (what Ezekiel is to "lift" and "carry out") is his knapsack (12:3–4). The noun עֲלָטָה appears only in Gen 15:17; Ezek 12:6, 7, 12. In contrast to the "twi-

---

[3] Greenberg, *Ezekiel*, 1:209.
[4] Cooke, *Ezekiel*, 130.

light" presumably intimated by עֶרֶב in 12:4, I have translated עֲלָטָה as "dusk," which usually implies a slightly later time, but before total darkness. Some translations have "dark," but that would seem to be contradicted by "in their sight." For מוֹפֵת, see the commentary below.

12:7 בְּיָד—"By hand" is omitted in the LXX. Some consider it to be a dittograph of בַקִּיר ("through the wall"). It does not appear in 12:5, where Yahweh first gave the command for Ezekiel to dig, but it rings true, since the prophet could dig through the mud brick wall manually (see the first textual note on 12:5).

12:10 הַנָּשִׂיא הַמַּשָּׂא הַזֶּה בִּירוּשָׁלַם—A major issue is the meaning of מַשָּׂא. Some lexicons believe there are two homographs of מַשָּׂא, one meaning "load, burden" and another meaning "pronouncement, oracle," but more likely they are the same word, which can be used in either of those two senses. The word is a derivative of נָשָׂא and apparently is related to the idiom "lift up one's voice." It commonly appears at the head of prophetic sermons, especially of Gentile oracles, and is translated "oracle." However, if related to the common sense of נָשָׂא as "lift, carry" (as in 12:6, 7, 12), the translation "burden, load" is appropriate. Theoretically, the two meanings might merge if the oracle is conceived of as a load on the prophet's mind, or if it refers to the judgment that God will unload or heap upon the people who are the object of the oracle.

Ostensibly following Symmachus, the Vulgate, and the Targum, most modern translations opt for "oracle" and translate as if the clause had עַל: "This oracle/prophecy is about the prince in Jerusalem" (similar are KJV, RSV, ESV, NIV; but NASB and NKJV have "burden" instead of "oracle").

But if we follow the MT, it seems more likely that מַשָּׂא should here be translated "burden." Elsewhere Ezekiel only uses the word in 24:25, where it does not mean "oracle." Probably הַנָּשִׂיא is the subject of this verbless clause: "The prince is this burden in Jerusalem."[5] However, its meaning is that "this burden—the exile's pack—represents the chief and the Israelites of Jerusalem."[6] Hence the "burden"— the knapsack Ezekiel had carried in 12:3–7 as part of his action prophecy—now in 12:10 represents "the prince" (King Zedekiah; see the commentary below) still reigning in Jerusalem and the other Jerusalemites soon to be exiled.

This interpretation represents a shift in the significance of the knapsack. Earlier (12:3–7) it represented the belongings that a typical Jerusalemite would carry into exile after the city falls. As the prophecy proceeds, now Yahweh gives the knapsack a different significance in order to articulate a further message specifically about the reigning king. There is no reason to disallow this shift; there was also a shift in whom the prophet represents (see the commentary on 12:5). That the prophet's actions are both predictive and symbolic continues in the rest of the interpretation. To play with words or use them with more than one meaning in the same context is rather typical of Ezekiel.

---

[5] Block, *Ezekiel*, 1:363, including n. 18. Similar is Greenberg, *Ezekiel*, 1:211.

[6] Greenberg, *Ezekiel*, 1:212.

The highly alliterative phrase here הַנָּשִׂיא הַמַּשָּׂא הַזֶּה is similar to (and may even have been influenced by) the caustic reply Yahweh instructed Jeremiah to give to the people's question, "What is the burden of Yahweh?" (asking for a prophecy from Yahweh). His response was, "You are the burden, and I will cast you off!" (Jer 23:33, following a commonly accepted emendation).

The irregular pointing of "Jerusalem" (בִּירוּשָׁלַם) in Ezek 12:10 should be noted. *BHS* follows the Leningrad Codex, the oldest dated manuscript of the complete Hebrew Bible (ca. A.D. 1010). Usually a Qere perpetuum points the last consonants as ־לָם (indicating that it should be read as ־לַיִם). In Ezek 12:10, however, the usual *ḥireq* is missing in the Leningrad Codex, although a footnote in *BHS* records that many manuscripts and editions have it. Early extrabiblical evidence indicates that the city's name originally ended with ־לִים or ־לֵם (cf. the spelling in the LXX, NT, and most Western languages). The ending of the Masoretic form (־לַיִם) usually indicates a dual. To the best of my knowledge, the origin of the Masoretic form has never been adequately explained.[7]

אֲשֶׁר־הֵמָּה בְתוֹכָם:—Literalistically, these last three words say "which they in their midst." Commonly, בְתוֹכָם is emended to בְּתוֹכָהּ, "in her/its midst" (i.e., of Jerusalem). The form in the MT is explained as a vertical dittograph of the בְּתוֹכָם near the beginning of 12:12. This is possible, of course, but also the easy way out. Keil provides a possible alternative. He understands הֵמָּה ("they") to refer to the Israelites in exile and translates the entire phrase as "to whom they belong." That is, the exiles are referred to as a part of the nation, which, Keil continues, explains why in the next verse Ezekiel can tell the exiles, "I am *your* sign."[8] But if so, the Hebrew expresses the thought very obliquely by using third masculine plural forms. I have accepted the emendation as the least of various evils. (Some much more radical emendations are suggested, but in my judgment, they do not merit recounting here.)

12:12 וְהַנָּשִׂיא … יִשָּׂא —For emphasis the subject ("the prince") appears long before the verb ("will carry"). There is also a deliberate association between the two similar-sounding words. Since the noun נָשִׂיא probably is a passive formation from the verb נָשָׂא, the association emphasizes the reversal: the prince who was lifted up as a ruler over the people will have to lift up his own knapsack, just like any commoner.

וְיֵצֵא —The MT and the ancient versions attest to the Qal form of the verb: the prince will "go out." The versions generally omit the copula. Block argues that the presumed original was יוֹצֵא ("he will bring out [his knapsack]") and by metathesis it became וְיֵצֵא.[9] That would be in harmony with the Hiphil forms of יָצָא in 12:5–7, which the versions generally read as Qal, and with לְהוֹצִיא following in 12:12. But the meaning of the verse is essentially the same in either case.

בַּקִּיר[dd] יַחְתְּרוּ לְהוֹצִיא בוֹ —Since the prince would flee from Jerusalem, this clause probably refers to the wall of the city, not of a private dwelling or house. However,

---

[7]
For the orthography and meaning of the name, see the excursus "Jerusalem" in Harstad, *Joshua*, 443–48.
[8]
Keil, *Ezekiel*, 1:159.
[9]
Block, *Ezekiel*, 1:363, n. 20.

instead of switching to חוֹמָה ("city wall"), קִיר has been retained for the sake of continuity with 12:5 and 12:7. Some other passages use קִיר for a city wall (e.g., Num 35:4; Josh 2:15).

The plural verb יַחְתְּרוּ implies that the digging is done by others, perhaps Zedekiah's servants, but more likely we should think of attacking armies breaching the city wall, as apparently happened in 2 Ki 25:4. (The LXX and Syriac have a singular verb.)

No object is stated for the Hiphil infinitive לְהוֹצִיא, but it must be the נָשִׂיא, that is, Zedekiah (rather than just his knapsack), regardless of whether the diggers are the invading armies (who intend to carry the king into exile, as they did in 2 Ki 25:7) or the servants of Zedekiah, desperate to escape.

פָּנָיו יְכַסֶּה יַעַן אֲשֶׁר ...—This final sentence is difficult. In 12:6 the simple coordinate Hebrew clauses expressed purpose ("you shall cover your face *so that you will not see* the ground"). The purpose of Ezekiel's action in 12:6 was to prophesy the prince's corresponding action, described here. The combination יַעַן אֲשֶׁר usually functions as a conjunction meaning "because." However, it seems unlikely that the fleeing prince would desire not to be able to see the land. Therefore here (as in 21:9 [ET 21:4]) יַעַן אֲשֶׁר may be telic, meaning "so"[10] or introducing a result clause. The LXX understood the clause as expressing purpose (to escape recognition): "he will cover his face *so that he will not be seen by eye*, and he himself will not see the land." The Vulgate and Syriac understood it as a purpose clause, "so he will not see [Vulgate: with his eye] the land." See further the commentary below.

לֹא־יִרְאֶה לַעַיִן הוּא אֶת־הָאָרֶץ:—Literalistically, this is "he will not see by eye— he—the land." Some advocate excising one or both of the words לַעַיִן הוּא, and a large number of other emendations or reconstructions of a supposed original have been proposed. We may understand לַעַיִן as adding emphasis to the idea of seeing ("by eye"), similar to the way לְעֵינֵיהֶם ("to their eyes/in their sight") occurred seven times in 12:3–7. The use of לְ in reference to a norm or standard can mean "by" (BDB, 5 i (b), translating לַעַיִן by "*as* the eye sees it"). The redundant pronoun הוּא is emphatic, underscoring the subject of the sentence, נָשִׂיא, and is placed after the verb to effect a contrast with הָאָרֶץ.

12:13 וּפָרַשְׂתִּי אֶת־רִשְׁתִּי עָלָיו—God will spread his net "for" (עַל) the prince (not "over," which some translations have). In Prov 29:5 a net is spread for (עַל) a man's feet. רֶשֶׁת denotes a "net" either spread on the ground so the victim would be entangled in it or stretched over a pit, into which he would fall. The noun מְצוּדָה in the following clause is essentially synonymous.

בָּבֶלָה אֶרֶץ כַּשְׂדִּים—The name "Babylon" occurs here for the first time in the book. It may refer to either the city or the country; here the latter sense is needed because the exiles had not been settled in the capital city. כַּשְׂדִּים ("Chaldeans, Chaldea") here and previously in 1:3 and 11:24 is essentially a synonym, although it technically

---

[10] This is how it is translated and explained by Block in 21:9 (*Ezekiel*, 1:665, including n. 42), where the context requires it to introduce a purpose clause. GKC, § 107 q, translates it in 12:12 as "in order that."

refers to Aramaic-speaking people who had invaded the territory long ago and now ruled Babylon (cf. older lexica and grammars that refer to Aramaic as "Chaldee").

וְאוֹתָהּ לֹא־יִרְאֶה—The object pronoun "it/her" precedes the verb for emphasis. Its feminine antecedent is אֶרֶץ, the "land" of the Chaldeans. In 12:12 אֶרֶץ most likely referred to Judahite "ground," but the shift in reference is no problem.

12:14 The long compound object (similar to that in 17:21) precedes the verb (אֱזָרֶה) for emphasis. The word order was easy to retain in the translation. The Qere directs reading עֶזְרוֹ instead of the Kethib, עֶזְרֹה, which simply has an older form of the third masculine singular suffix (ה-) on עֵזֶר ("help; helper"). The older suffix form occurs eleven other places in Ezekiel (e.g., כֻּלֹּה in 11:15). The versions translate the noun as a plural, as have I ("aides"), since it can be understood in a collective sense. Note the play on עֶזְרוֹ and the following verb, אֱזָרֶה (Piel of זָרָה): "his help" God will "scatter." The same verb was used in similar prophecies of judgment in 5:2, 10, 12 (cf. 6:5, 8).

אֲגַפָּיו (plural of אֲגַף with third masculine singular suffix) may indicate that עֵזֶר had a more specific military sense, possibly "allies." אֲגַף occurs only in Ezekiel.[a] It is usually considered cognate with the Akkadian *agappu*, which means "wing," and in a military context, possibly something like "division." The more general "troops" seems to fit better in translation.

(a) Ezek 12:14; 17:21; 38:6, 9, 22; 39:4

וְחֶרֶב אָרִיק אַחֲרֵיהֶם:—This is repeated from 5:2, 12.

12:16 וְהוֹתַרְתִּי מֵהֶם אַנְשֵׁי מִסְפָּר—The Hiphil of יָתַר is sometimes used semi-technically or theologically for the theme of God's preservation of a faithful remnant by his grace, as also in 6:8. Compare the common noun for "remnant," שְׁאֵרִית, in 5:10; 9:8; 11:13. (The corresponding masculine noun שְׁאָר does not occur in Ezekiel.) אַנְשֵׁי מִסְפָּר (literally, "men of number") occurs only here in the OT. It implies that the remnant will be a group small enough to be counted easily, as did the phrase with מִסְפָּר in 5:3.

The triad of divine punishments, "sword," "famine," and "plague," occurred previously in 5:12, 17; 6:11–12; 7:15 (also 14:21).

12:17–20 These verses mandate and explain a new action prophecy by Ezekiel.

12:18 "Food" is a better rendition of לֶחֶם than "bread." The Hebrew has three prepositional phrases with בְּ. רַעַשׁ ("trembling") is often associated with earthquakes. The noun רָגְזָה ("shuddering") occurs only here, but other words from the root can denote all kinds of agitation, which may be why דְּאָגָה ("fear") is added, which would be evidenced by facial expression. The phrases with those two words can be taken together as a hendiadys: "in fearful shuddering." Some critics allege that וּבְדְאָגָה upsets the balance of the parallelism and is a secondary intrusion from the next verse, but that is hypercritical. The imperfect verbs ("you shall eat … you shall drink") function as imperatives.

Eichrodt and Zimmerli understand Ezekiel's tremors as a physiological result of the strain he allegedly felt because of his ecstatic experiences.[11] But Greenberg rightly objects that there is no textual basis for such an analysis.[12]

---

[11] Eichrodt, *Ezekiel*, 153–54; Zimmerli, *Ezekiel*, 1:278.
[12] Greenberg, *Ezekiel*, 1:225.

12:19 אֶל־אַדְמַת יִשְׂרָאֵל—As often in Ezekiel, אֶל is used with a meaning more common for עַל ("*on* the soil"). Because the verse seems to picture homeless survivors desperately seeking safety, I have translated אַדְמַת יִשְׂרָאֵל as "the soil of Israel" rather than "the land of Israel."

The description of their behavior simply reworks slightly the vocabulary used to describe Ezekiel's action prophecy in 12:18. "Trembling" (רַעַשׁ, 12:18) is not repeated, but "fear" (דְּאָנָה) is. "Shuddering" (רָגְזָה, 12:18) is replaced by an even stronger term: שִׁמָּמוֹן ("desolation"), a noun derived from the verb שָׁמֵם. A related verb occurs three words later (see the next textual note), and another noun from שָׁמֵם occurs in 12:20. The play on these words cannot readily be reproduced in English translation, but words like "desolate" or "devastate" and their cognates offer possibilities.

לְמַעַן תֵּשַׁם אַרְצָהּ מִמְּלֹאָהּ—When used as a conjunction, as here, לְמַעַן usually expresses purpose and occasionally result. When used as a preposition, it commonly implies causality. Here it apparently retains a causative meaning ("for, because") even though it serves as a conjunction.

The verb תֵּשַׁם is the Qal third feminine singular imperfect of שֵׁם (so Joüon, § 82 h) or יָשַׁם, in either case a by-form of שָׁמֵם. The identical form will recur in 19:7. (A form of יָשַׁם was used in 6:6; see the textual note there.) Hence the verb is related to the nouns שִׁמָּמוֹן earlier in 12:19 and שְׁמָמָה in 12:20.

The feminine singular suffix on אַרְצָהּ ("*its* land") probably has Jerusalem as its antecedent. The versions indicate no suffix but have a definite article; the MT is the *lectio difficilior*.

The privative מִן on מִמְּלֹאָהּ means the land will be "desolated/stripped/deprived *of* its contents." The noun מְלֹא can mean "that which fills" something. The feminine singular suffix ("*its* contents/fullness") refers to the preceding "land" (אֶרֶץ). מְלֹא recurs in 19:7; 30:12; 32:15; and 41:8 (מְלֹו).

כָּל־הַיֹּשְׁבִים בָּהּ:—This refers back to "the inhabitants of Jerusalem" earlier in the verse.

12:20 The same verb form as here, תֶּחֱרַבְנָה, was used in 6:6 to prophesy that the cities "will be laid waste." The noun שְׁמָמָה is related to the noun שִׁמָּמוֹן and the verb תֵּשַׁם in 12:19.

12:21–28 The rest of the chapter consists of two oracles, 12:21–25 and 12:26–28. Both have the same structure. They begin with the word-event formula, "the Word of Yahweh came to me" (12:21, 26). Then a popular saying follows, with God's answer contradicting it. The conclusions of both oracles make the same point: Yahweh will fulfill his prophecies quickly (12:25 and 12:28).

12:22 מָה־הַמָּשָׁל הַזֶּה לָכֶם—This oracle introduces into Ezekiel the vocabulary of the noun מָשָׁל and verb מָשַׁל (12:23). The noun and verb will occur together in 12:23; 17:2; 18:2–3; 21:5 (ET 20:49); 24:3, and the noun alone is in 14:8 and the verb in 16:44. The noun is commonly translated "proverb," but the Hebrew is much broader in meaning. It can, indeed, be used of a brief little aphorism, but it also applies to lengthier literary metaphors. Both uses appear in Ezekiel, and also in the book of Proverbs, whose Hebrew title is the plural construct (מִשְׁלֵי). Sometimes "parable" would be an appropriate translation. In 14:8 מָשָׁל, meaning "byword," will be used alongside אוֹת ("sign, object lesson"). The verb is most common in the Qal, meaning to "speak a proverb" or "use as a proverbial saying" (as in 12:23). The Piel can mean "to speak in riddles," as the Israelites accuse Ezekiel of doing in 21:5 (ET 20:49).

The idiom with מָה and the preposition לְ is, literally, "what is this proverb in relation to you?" (cf. BDB, s.v. לְ, 5 a (d)). That the suffix on the preposition is plural (לָכֶם, "you have," ESV) indicates that God includes Ezekiel himself among the people. Modern English does not distinguish singular and plural second person pronouns, but KJV could still translate "ye" here.

עַל־אַדְמַת יִשְׂרָאֵל—Some take this to mean that the proverb is *about* the land of Israel" (RSV, ESV). This is grammatically possible. But in the context עַל more likely has a locative sense (those who live "on" or "in" the land of Israel). News of the proverb's currency in Israel may have reached Ezekiel. Since the exiles had not yet really accepted their status, it may well have circulated among them too.

יַאַרְכוּ הַיָּמִים—The Qal of אָרֵךְ means "become long," but (literally) "the days become long" means "(many) days go by." Since Hebrew can use "days" synonymously with "time," a free translation of "time passes" or the like would be possible. The imperfect verb form suggests a generalization that prophecies never come true no matter how much time elapses.

כָּל־חָזוֹן:—The noun חָזוֹן can refer to a "vision" (something visual in nature), but in connection with prophecy it often (like the verb from which it is derived, חָזָה) refers to verbal divine communication, whether or not a vision accompanies Yahweh's words. See also the textual notes on it in 7:13 and 12:23. Possibly "prophecy" would be a better translation here. Such an understanding might explain why the LXX lacks a translation of כָּל־, which expresses comprehensive skepticism: no prophecy ever comes true.

12:23   הִשְׁבַּתִּי—This Hiphil perfect (of שָׁבַת) is usually taken as a prophetic perfect ("I *will* put an end"). Already the LXX translated it as a future.

כִּי־אִם—This adversative is quite emphatic ("on the contrary").

קָרְבוּ הַיָּמִים וּדְבַר כָּל־חָזוֹן:—This is God's counterproverb. The verb "be/draw near" (here קָרְבוּ is Qal perfect, not Piel imperative, as the form was in 9:1; see the textual note there) does double duty: its subject is "the days," and the verb is implied in the final noun clause, "the fulfillment of every vision [draws near]." There have been critical attempts to supply a second verb for the final clause,[13] but one is not needed. The Israelites' proverb had used both יָמִים and חָזוֹן (12:22), and so God uses both in his counterattack. Here דָּבָר (usually "word") indicates that the prophetic חָזוֹן ("vision") has verbal and predictive content. The two terms are near synonyms here. דָּבָר might have been rendered "substance" or "content," but in the context, "fulfillment" seems most appropriate.

12:24   כִּי—Both 12:24 and 12:25 are introduced with this causal conjunction ("for") and each verse gives one corollary that explains the reason for God's counterproverb in 12:23.

---

[13]   Zimmerli, *Ezekiel*, 1:279, lists them.

Two phrases are used to describe the cessation of what might generically be termed "false prophecy." The actual terms are more nuanced. First, there will no longer be any חֲזוֹן שָׁוְא, "vision of falsehood/vacuity," that is, a "vision" that lacks meaningful content or whose content is false. שָׁוְא often implies falsity and can also accent emptiness, worthlessness, or uselessness. In comparable passages, Jeremiah prefers שֶׁקֶר, which implies a simple lie (e.g., Jer 5:31; 14:14; 23:25). Ezekiel uses שָׁוְא often to characterize and condemn false prophecy,[b] but uses שֶׁקֶר only in 13:22. In 13:7 מַחֲזֵה־שָׁוְא is synonymous with the phrase here.

(b) Ezek 12:24; 13:6–9, 23; 21:28, 34 (ET 21:23, 29); 22:28

Second, there will be no more מִקְסַם חָלָק. Syntactically, putting a noun in construct with an adjective that modifies it (GKC, § 128 w) makes a stronger expression. Literally, "divination of slippery," it must be translated as "slippery/misleading divination." Synonymous is מִקְסַם כָּזָב ("divination of a lie") in 13:7.

The noun מִקְסָם occurs in Ezekiel only here and in 13:7 (the synonym קֶסֶם appears in 13:6, 23; 21:26–27 [ET 21:21–22]). It is derived from the relatively common verb קָסַם, "to divine, practice divination,"[c] which can refer to any number of manipulative, pagan techniques attempting to discern the will of the god(s). The details of such practices are quite well-known from extrabiblical literature. Ezekiel briefly refers to some methods of divination in 21:26 (ET 21:21), including hepatoscopy: examination of the livers of sacrificed animals. The entire genus of occult practices is forbidden in Israel in Deut 18:10–14. Here Ezekiel characterizes divination with חָלָק, whose literal meaning is "smooth, slippery." Hence it may imply flattery, or, like שָׁוְא, falsehood. Most English translations (already KJV) have "flattering," but that meaning is debatable in this context (see the commentary below). Allen and Greenberg think that the word has already here developed the meaning "empty," which it has in postbiblical Hebrew.[14] That is possible and would make a good parallel with שָׁוְא if earlier in the verse it referred to a vision of "emptiness," but in Ezek 12:21–14:11 Yahweh is concerned with prophecy that is false and pernicious, not just empty.

(c) Ezek 13:9, 23; 21:26, 28, 34 (ET 21:21, 23, 29); 22:28

בֵּית יִשְׂרָאֵל:—Many ancient manuscripts and versions have "sons of Israel" instead of "house of Israel," but בֵּית and בְּנֵי are frequently interchanged, and the difference is not usually significant. Compare the textual notes and commentary on "rebellious house" in 2:5 and "house of Israel" in 3:1.

12:25 אֲנִי יְהוָה אֲדַבֵּר אֵת אֲשֶׁר אֲדַבֵּר דָּבָר—My translation follows the Masoretic punctuation, although other punctuation is possible.[15] The disjunctive *rebia‘* on יְהוָה indicates that אֲנִי יְהוָה is a complete nominal sentence ("I am Yahweh"). It is the same self-introduction formula or affirmation that we meet frequently after Pentateuchal injunctions, which follow from the very nature of Yahweh himself. Many translations disregard the punctuation and take אֲנִי as an emphatic subject of the verb אֲדַבֵּר, with "Yahweh" as an appositive ("I, Yahweh, will speak …").

The rest of the verse summarizes and climaxes 12:23–25a, that is, Yahweh's counterproverb and its basis. The points will be recast only slightly differently in 12:28.

---

14 Allen, *Ezekiel*, 1:187, citing Jastrow; Greenberg, *Ezekiel*, 1:228.

15 See Zimmerli's discussion of the verse's syntax (*Ezekiel*, 1:279–81).

This verse uses the noun דָּבָר twice and its cognate verb דִּבֶּר three times. The noun could easily have been translated as "prophecy" (cf. its translation as "fulfillment" in 12:23) instead of "word" here and in 1:28.

לֹא תִמָּשֵׁךְ עוֹד—The feminine form of תִמָּשֵׁךְ (Niphal imperfect) assumes a neuter or abstract subject, which must be supplied in thought: "it [the fulfillment of whatever Yahweh speaks] will be delayed no longer."

12:26–27 The second oracle is introduced (12:26) in the same way as the first (12:21). Again the next verse quotes the people, although the quote in 12:27 had not yet become a proverbial saying like the first one (מָשָׁל, 12:22). It is only an ad hoc way of dismissing Ezekiel's prophecies of catastrophe as irrelevant. The repeated pronoun הוּא ("he") makes plain that Ezekiel is the specific target. The "days" (יָמִים, as in 12:22, 23, 25) could be rendered as "years," especially as a parallel to the following "times." The two synonymous clauses are structured chiastically: "... he is seeing is for many days" is parallel to "for distant times he is prophesying."

12:28 לֹא־תִמָּשֵׁךְ עוֹד כָּל־דְּבָרַי—This verse reaffirms 12:25, and as there, the syntax is somewhat awkward and debatable. The Masoretic accents indicate that the phrase "all my words" is the subject of the preceding feminine singular verb תִמָּשֵׁךְ, even though דְּבָרַי is masculine plural. The LXX and most English translations follow the Masoretic syntax, and Zimmerli[16] and Allen[17] argue for it. Sometimes a feminine singular verb is used when the plural subject is conceived of as a collective (Joüon, § 150 b and g), and כָּל־דְּבָרַי could be taken as "my every word." Ezekiel may have repeated the same verb used in 12:25 (where it has no expressed subject) to reinforce the point even though the verb does not agree with its subject. (The parallel in 12:25 would support ending the clause with עוֹד.) My translation of the rest of the verse attempts to reproduce the uneven Hebrew as closely as possible.

Commentary

Introduction to Ezekiel 12–24

As one subdivides the book of Ezekiel, all of the remaining chapters (12–24) until the Gentile oracles (chapters 25–32) can be lumped together as a miscellaneous collection of oracles of judgment upon Israel and Jerusalem. The section can be considered as a reprise of earlier material, especially of chapters 4–7, between the call narrative (chapters 1–3) and the visionary tour of Jerusalem (chapters 8–11). Yet beyond such generalities, this section (chapters 12–24) certainly has its various distinctives, as we shall see. No chronological data allowing us to date these oracles precisely is given until 20:1, where the date (August 14, 591 B.C.) is eleven months after the last previous date, in 8:1 (ca. September 18, 592 B.C.). All of the oracles in this section easily could have been given within that time, still well before the fall of Jerusalem itself in 587 B.C.

---

[16] Zimmerli, *Ezekiel*, 1:283.

[17] Allen, *Ezekiel*, 1:188.

The prophecies in this section vary widely in form, length, and specific subject matter. To a certain extent, their arrangement might appear random to us. Yet there are some indications of deliberate groupings of similar subject matter.

Initially, we meet a collection of two action prophecies (12:1–16 and 12:17–20). It may not be coincidental that these follow immediately after the vision of chapters 8–11, just as the first action prophecies in the book (chapters 4–5) immediately followed the call vision (chapters 1–3). The action prophecy that concludes this part of the book (24:15–27) does not follow a vision. Nevertheless, these two collections of action prophecies (12:1–20 and 24:15–27) that frame chapters 12–24 contain certain common features not found in the other action prophecies: (1) both report that the prophet was obeying a divine command; (2) both report requests by the audience that the prophet explain what the actions meant; and (3) both describe the prophet as a מוֹפֵת ("portent," 12:6, 11; 24:24, 27) for the people. The pairing of the prophet's physical props and actions with the prophetic Word from Yahweh can be compared to the pairing of God's Word and Sacraments to serve as joint means of grace for the Christian church.[18]

Two other groupings are obvious. In 12:21–14:11 five oracles are clustered about true prophecy and Ezekiel as a true prophet versus false prophecy, prophets, and prophetesses. (See further "Introduction to Ezekiel 12:21–14:11" below.) Second, in chapters 18–19, two oracles concerning the "generation gap" are put side by side, although they differ radically in form.

An Action Prophecy and an Oracle about the Prince's Exile (12:1–16)

The first unit of this chapter concerns the exile, especially of the prince. It consists of two parts: an action prophecy (12:1–7) and an oracle that explains the symbolism of the prophet's actions and props (12:8–16). The two parts extend over two days. Ezekiel is to carry out his activity during the daytime and evening of the first day, then interpret it the next morning. Similar time spans occur in 24:18 and 33:22.

An Action Prophecy with a Knapsack and Digging through the Wall (12:1–7)

12:1–2 As commonly in Ezekiel, the message opens with the word-event formula ("the Word of Yahweh came to me," 12:1) followed by the address of the prophet as "son of man" (12:2). These are repeated almost verbatim in 12:8–9, at the beginning of the second part of the unit.

Before the action prophecy itself, Yahweh gives the reason for it: the obduracy of the people, twice called a "rebellious house" (12:2). The refrain that

---

[18] See the commentary on 3:25–27.

Israel is a "rebellious house" first appeared in the prophet's commissioning (2:5–8; 3:9) and was prominent in 3:26–27, immediately before the first block of action prophecies (4:1–5:12). Its repetition here has added sharpness, because for more than a year Ezekiel has been preaching, but to no apparent avail. As Taylor comments:

> The preacher's knowledge that his words will be ignored is never to be used as an excuse for not uttering the words. ... [Ezekiel] may be regarded as the exemplar for all Christian workers in seemingly impossible situations or in singularly unfruitful spheres of service.[19]

To make his point, Ezekiel draws on an apparently well-known saying: the people "have eyes to see, but they do not see, and ears to hear, but they do not hear" (12:2). Ironically, they have become like the idols they worshiped (Pss 115:5; 135:16; cf. Rom 1:23–25). The phraseology is as old as Moses (Deut 29:3 [ET 29:4]). Yahweh's words to Ezekiel about the people are nearly identical to those he addressed to Jeremiah about them (Jer 5:21). Similar wording appears also in Yahweh's call of Isaiah (Is 6:9–10) and is echoed in Is 43:8; 44:18. It is noteworthy that our Lord cites Isaiah's similar formulation (Is 6:9–10) when explaining why he speaks to the people in parables (Mt 13:13–15 and parallels; cf. Jn 12:37–41), and his words in Mk 8:18 echo Ezek 12:2. The obduracy of ancient Israel was no greater than the stubborn unbelief Jesus Christ encountered during his ministry and that every faithful preacher of the Gospel inevitably meets. All descendants of Adam constitute a "rebellious house" congenitally, with original sin (and hence the sentence of death) inherited from the first man (cf. Rom 5:12–21).

The action prophecy itself is designed to appeal to the people's sense of sight. The vocabulary of 12:3–7 bears witness to that by its frequent use of "in their sight" (literally, "to their eyes"), "see," and various words for the time of day. The preached explanation in 12:8–16 will be directed toward their hearing.

12:3 The prophecy seems most pertinent for those still in Jerusalem, although Ezekiel's fellow exiles in Babylon were clearly still in agreement that the city would never fall. The action prophecy of going into exile begins with a general description of the mime to be carried out initially in broad daylight so all can "see." But the last part of the verse also reveals God's intent that "perhaps they will see that they are a rebellious house"—"see" in the sense of understanding and repenting. Despite being a "rebellious house," the possibility remains that the prophetic actions and words will accomplish God's salvific will among them and at least some Israelites will "see the light" (cf. Mt 4:13–16, quoting Is 8:23–9:1 [ET 9:1–2]). Deathbed conversions are possible, but relatively rare. Most people die as they lived. But as long as there is life, there is

---

[19] Taylor, *Ezekiel*, 115.

hope for repentance, faith, and salvation. God hopes, and so should we—and act accordingly.

12:4 Some details of this action prophecy need to be inferred (see the commentary on 12:5), but this verse clearly describes two initial stages. First, Ezekiel is to gather his essential belongings, pack them in a bag, and in broad daylight bring them somewhere outside his house to show that he is prepared to be forced into exile. Second, in the evening (presumably at twilight before it had become totally dark), he should actually act out the departure.

The significance of leaving at evening is debated. Medieval interpreters understood it as a cover for the ignominy of exile. Most modern commentators think of the cool of evening. Greenberg thinks of the symbolism of "calamity and termination" and compares Is 24:11 and Jer 13:16.[20] Approaching darkness can represent the coming time of judgment[d] or the (temporary) triumph of evil over good (cf. Lk 22:53; 23:44). But the question need not be decided definitely for understanding the overall import of the action prophecy.

(d) Cf.
Micah 3:6;
Jn 9:4;
12:35; Acts
2:20; 13:11;
1 Thess 5:2

12:5 This short verse raises several questions. Yahweh's command is to "dig through the wall, and you shall bring out [your knapsack] through it." Scholars commonly interpret the digging as predicting the attempt by Zedekiah and/or other Jerusalemites to escape the invading Babylonians after the city walls had been breached. However, the biblical reports in 2 Ki 25:4 and Jer 52:7 report no digging through walls, but of them leaving through "the gate between the double walls." To dig through city walls would be difficult and time consuming because they were massive and constructed of stone (versus mud bricks used for house walls). This is more than the "trifling inconsistency" Cooke makes it out to be.[21]

In addition, if that were the meaning of Ezekiel's action, he would have to dig from the inside of his house out. Yahweh had last told Ezekiel to go outside his house (12:4b). Now he commands him to dig through the wall "in their sight" (12:5). This seems to imply that he is digging from the outside in, unless the audience is inside his house (as the elders are in 8:1) or they watch from outside as he breaks through from the inside.

It seems that Ezekiel has switched roles. In 12:3–4 as he handled his knapsack he represented the Israelites who would be exiled. But as he digs in 12:5, he now represents the invading Babylonians, who will breach the city walls (2 Ki 25:4; Jer 52:7), burn down the houses—including God's house—and break down "all the walls around Jerusalem" (2 Ki 25:9–11; Jer 52:13–14). This switch should not surprise us because we met similar multiple roles in the action prophecies of Ezekiel 4–5. For example, in 4:2–3 Ezekiel represented both Yahweh and the invading Babylonians (the agents of Yahweh's wrath) as he laid siege to the model city. Then in 4:4–17 he represented the people as he

---

[20] Greenberg, *Ezekiel*, 1:210.
[21] Cooke, *Ezekiel*, 131.

bore their sin and ate meager diets. In 5:1–2, he represented both Yahweh, the punisher, by shaving, and the people in the city by being the one shaved.

As Ezekiel burrows through the wall from the outside in 12:5a, he represents the attacking enemy. Once inside his house, he switches roles in 12:5b and again (as in 12:3–4) represents the people as he brings out his knapsack through the hole he made. He continues the role of the people (and their prince) in the next verse.

12:6 At dusk, Ezekiel is to carry the knapsack out of his house, representing the beginning of the trek into captivity. But a problem emerges: in 12:4 he had brought the knapsack outside. Ezekiel has telescoped his actions somewhat, and we are not told when or how he brought the knapsack back inside his house. He may have brought it back in (through the door) promptly after displaying it outside in 12:4. Or he may have left it outside, and then after he dug through the wall into his house, Ezekiel may have returned outside and brought the knapsack inside with him (either through the door or through the wall). In any case, at dusk he came back out through the hole in the wall, carrying the knapsack outside again.

Yahweh adds another detail: Ezekiel is to cover his face as he emerges. This gesture is mentioned in many biblical passages (e.g., Gen 38:15; 2 Sam 15:30), and its significance depends on the context. Its implication here is widely debated. The only explanation Yahweh gives here is that the action prevents Ezekiel from seeing "the ground" (the most likely meaning of הָאָרֶץ in this verse). But the Hebrew word often means "land, country," and that meaning is also possible when the clause is repeated in Ezek 12:12. Many commentators have interpreted the gesture as indicating either shame or grief. Zimmerli probably is correct when he surmises that the gesture "also plaintively hides the lost homeland from the view of the exiles."[22] (See further the commentary on 12:12.)

In all of this, to the Israelites Ezekiel is to be a מוֹפֵת, "portent, sign, wonder." This term occurs in 12:6, 11; 24:24, 27, always describing the prophet as he carries out his ministry. It is a synonym of אוֹת, used in 4:3 for the "sign" Ezekiel performed (see the textual note and commentary there). "Portent(s)" had described the miracles performed by Moses and Aaron to demonstrate Yahweh's power (e.g., Ex 4:21; 7:9; 11:10; cf. Acts 7:36) and also the plagues performed by Yahweh himself, designed to move Pharaoh and the Egyptians to repentance (Ex 7:3; 11:9; Deut 4:34; 6:22; 7:19). "Sign" and "portent" may be used together, almost as a hendiadys, as when the prophet Isaiah and his sons are called "signs and portents" (Is 8:18). Thus generally we may understand the prophets in their persons, not only in their words and actions, as portending the divine message. The infant Lord is the "sign" in Lk 2:12. In Peter's Pentecost sermon he proclaimed Christ as the one who both fulfilled and performed

---

divine "portents" (τέρατα, Acts 2:19–22). He *is* the Word incarnate, and he also proclaims it. The apostles too performed "portents," in Christ's name.[e]

(e) Acts
2:43; 4:30;
5:12; 6:8;
14:3; 15:12;
Rom 15:19;
2 Cor 12:12

God had also warned that a false prophet might perform a "portent" as he attempts to seduce the people into apostasy (Deut 13:2–3), and our Lord issued a similar warning (Mt 24:24; see also 2 Thess 2:9; Rev 13:13–15). But the genuineness of Ezekiel's prophetic ministry, in contradistinction to false prophecy, will become the topic shortly (Ezek 12:21–28).

12:7 Rarely does Ezekiel report his obedience to God's commands. (He will do so again in 24:18 and 37:7). In his brief report, he both adds one detail ("by hand"; see the textual note) and omits another detail that was in the command (covering his face). The focus is on the knapsack and on his obedience in the people's sight.

Oracle Explaining the Knapsack and Digging (12:8–16)

12:8–9 These verses introduce the oracle that explains the symbolism of the preceding action prophecy (12:1–7). They show that Ezekiel has at least succeeded in attracting his audience's attention and curiosity, even if they do not (yet) "see that they are a rebellious house" (12:3). Their question, "What are you doing?" is similar to one recorded in 24:19. But in 33:30–32, Yahweh reminds the prophet that the people still basically regard him as no more than a rather comical showman; they are still uncomprehending or unrepentant or both.

12:10 Then Yahweh states that the knapsack symbolizes the king of Jerusalem and the city's inhabitants who are a "burden" (like a sack) that will be carried into exile. Symbolism and prediction merge throughout 12:10–20. The king and populace are mentioned in one breath ("The prince is this burden … together with the whole house of Israel"). In the OT and ancient Near Eastern thought, the king is considered "the head of the body." What happens to the head has implications for all.

But Yahweh does not honor the current ruler in Jerusalem with the title "king" (מֶלֶךְ). Instead, he is labeled as merely a "prince" (נָשִׂיא; see the textual note). This lesser title was applied to tribal chieftains of premonarchical times. Ezekiel may use it here even more generically and deprecatorily: the word appears to be a passive formation of the verb "lift up" (נָשָׂא) and thus could be applied to anyone who happens to be "lifted up" to a position of authority.

Here it almost certainly refers to King Zedekiah, the puppet whom the Babylonians placed over Jerusalem after the deportation in 597 B.C. and who reigned (but without any real authority) for eleven years until Jerusalem fell in 587 B.C. (counting inclusively; see 2 Ki 24:17–20). Ezekiel may even be alluding to the old objection to the monarchy that Yahweh was Israel's only real, legitimate king; see 1 Samuel 8 and Ezek 20:33, where Yahweh declares, "I will be king over you!" The legitimate earthly "king" was Jehoiachin, who had been exiled with Ezekiel in 597 B.C. (whereupon Zedekiah was installed). Ezekiel accorded Jehoiachin the title "king" in 1:2, and both the Babylonians

and those left in Jerusalem still regarded him as such, even in his exile. Yet Ezekiel's esteem for the current ruler would not have been much higher even if Jehoiachin were still on the throne, to judge from Jeremiah's oracles in chapters 21–22, with which Ezekiel would surely have agreed.

Ezekiel does use "king" (מֶלֶךְ) for the eschatological king, a true son of David, the Messiah (37:22–25), and also names him as "prince" (נָשִׂיא, 34:24). (Why Ezekiel uses "prince" in connection with the eschatological temple in chapters 45–46 is more puzzling; see the discussion in the commentary there.) For Christians, any problem in this respect disappears with the confession that Christ is both true God (and so King of kings) and Son of David, a biological descendant (Mt 1:1, 6) and the royal heir (Is 9:5–6 [ET 9:6–7]) of the anointed king whose line furnished the legitimate earthly kings who ruled over ancient Israel.

12:11 Now Ezekiel is to explain how and why he himself is a "portent" (מוֹפֵת, as in 12:6) to his present audience—his fellow exiles—but the import is ultimately about those still in Jerusalem. As in the previous verse, the symbolism still centers on the "burden" of the knapsack. "As I have done, so it will be done to them" is similar to comparisons between the prophet's behavior and the experience of the people in 24:22, 24. To underscore that the Jerusalemites await the same fate that Ezekiel and his exilic audience have already undergone, "into *exile*" (גּוֹלָה, which has been used now numerous times in Ezekiel) is backed up by a near synonym, "into *captivity*" (שְׁבִי). By using a passive verb ("it will be done to them"), the prophet momentarily refrains from identifying the executor of the judgment, whether Yahweh himself or his human agents, whom he will name in 12:13.

12:12 "The prince" (הַנָּשִׂיא) is placed first in Hebrew (unusually, before the verb) for emphasis and is emphasized further toward the end of the verse by a redundant הוּא ("he"; see the last textual note on 12:12). In 12:10 the "burden" of the knapsack represented the prince, but here he is the one who will be forced to pack his belongings himself and sling his knapsack over his shoulder, just like the rest of the exiles.

The significance of the covering of his face is debated, as it was in 12:6. The meaning may be the same in both verses. Possibly the fleeing king (represented by Ezekiel) would cover his face so that he would not be recognized and captured (LXX 12:12 points in that direction). However, the effect of the covering is to limit his vision of the land (see the textual notes on 12:12). The אֶרֶץ that he will not see still includes the "ground," but as the next verse indicates, the meaning of "land" is becoming more prominent. The next verse will focus on Babylonia, but here the primary reference may still be on Judah. That is, he (and the exiles who are still in view; see the commentary on 12:10) will never return to his native soil.

Jeremiah had uttered a similar prediction of Jehoahaz (Jer 22:10–12). The theme of never seeing one's land again was often included in extrabiblical curses. Also, in the fulfillment, Zedekiah was blinded at Riblah before being taken to Babylon (2 Ki 25:6–7). There is no reason to doubt that the covering of Ezekiel's face to limit his vision was intended by God to prophesy that event (cf. Ezek 6:14, which mentions Riblah by name).

12:13 In 12:11 Yahweh instructed Ezekiel to speak in the first person ("I am a portent …"), but now in this verse it clearly is Yahweh who is speaking in the first person through Ezekiel's mouth ("I will spread my net …"). Commonly in Scripture, quotations of direct speech by God and inspired messages by human instruments alternate or are even hard to distinguish. Theologically speaking, the difference is only formal, since the Scriptures in their entirety are the verbally inspired Word of God.

The point is that the "prince" will not ultimately be captured by Nebuchadnezzar, but by Yahweh himself, who masterminds the historical events and uses them as his means of judgment. The metaphor of Yahweh as a hunter appears frequently elsewhere in Scripture (e.g., Is 8:14; Hos 7:12; cf. Ezek 19:8). The motif is also found in extrabiblical treaty curses.

Since this prophecy corresponds so closely to what later happened in 2 Ki 25:1–7, critical commentators often assume that this is a "prophecy after the event," added later after Zedekiah's blinding at Riblah, if not still later, after Zedekiah died in prison in Babylon (Jer 52:11). But the blinding of captives (or threats to deal with disloyal vassals in that way) was such a well-known practice in antiquity that, even humanly speaking, it is no surprise to meet such a prediction. That God caused the historical fulfillment to match the prediction is no less a surprise for a believer in the one true God, who guided all history toward its culmination in the first advent of Christ, and who even now guides the course of events toward the consummation of all history at Christ's return.

12:14–16 God will remove all supports for the throne and will personally pursue the unfaithful prince with the "sword." But again at the end of a section, in 12:16 Yahweh sounds the promise of the preservation of a remnant (see 5:3 and especially 6:8–10). Yet the reason here is so that they may explain to their new neighbors that their plight was not a result of Yahweh's weakness, but their deserved punishment for their abominable past. They will simultaneously confess Yahweh's righteousness and their own sin. Instead of "*relate* all their abominations" (12:16), "confess" would have been a free but appropriate translation. Genuine confession of sin and confession of the faith go together. Both involve relating or confessing acts—the one of man's sinful behavior and the other of God's salvific deeds.

In its grammatical context in 12:16, the subjects of the recognition formula ("then they will know that I am Yahweh") could include "the nations" as well as the exiles among them, in which case the verse could envision the conversion of the heathen,[23] but that theme is hardly prominent here. Theologically, the subject of the formula here (and generally elsewhere) is "Israel" in the sense

---

[23] Cf. Zimmerli, *Ezekiel*, 1:274, and others.

of the true, invisible church of both Testaments, consisting of all believers in Christ. Only they can "relate" the full knowledge of the one true and triune God.

Action Prophecy of Eating and Drinking in Exile (12:17–20)

12:17–18 Appended to the first action prophecy in this section of the book is another brief but powerful one. There appears to be no connection with the preceding one except in form, that is, both are action prophecies about the exile. There are no chronological indicators to indicate whether or not this pantomime was performed at about the same time. However, we may surmise that it too falls within the eleven months between the dates in 8:1 and 20:1 (see "Introduction to Ezekiel 12–24" above). That would account for its placement here instead of near the action prophecies about siege and exilic diets in 4:9–17.

The action is brief, with just two parallel lines commanding it in 12:18 ("you shall eat your food in trembling" and "you shall drink your water in shuddering and in fear"). Unlike in the preceding episode (12:7), there is no account of the prophet's obedience, but this action prophecy too includes divine instructions on how to interpret the action (12:19–20a, as in 12:8–16) and concludes with the recognition formula (12:20b, as in 12:15–16).

The picture is obviously one of such extreme fright in the chaos and anarchy after Jerusalem's fall that the people will scarcely be able to manage the elementary activities of eating and drinking. The scene depicted is thus later than the one foretold in 4:9–11, 16–17, which described conditions during the siege. We should envision Ezekiel trembling so uncontrollably that he spills his drink and misses his mouth with his food.

12:19–20 The prophet is ordered to interpret his actions "to the people of the land." Ezekiel uses that phrase with various meanings, but generally it refers to property owners, people with political influence (e.g., 7:27; 22:29; 33:2; 39:13). Eichrodt detects irony here,[24] and probably correctly so. Ezekiel is addressing his fellow exiles as he prophesies "about the inhabitants of Jerusalem" (12:19). The deportation in 597 B.C., of which Ezekiel and his audience had been a part, had mostly skimmed off the "upper crust," so many in his audience probably had been (until recently) property owners and people of some influence. But now they are landless and helpless to influence events in Jerusalem. At the same time, they are given the solace that Yahweh does at least recognize their status as "the people of the land" and that the following prophecy is not directed against them.

Especially in 12:20, it seems clear that the picture is one of the devastation of the entire land (not only Jerusalem) after the coming catastrophe. The picture ultimately goes back to the covenant curses detailed in Lev 26:14–46. The words in Ezek 12:19–20 translated "desolat-" are from or are related to the root שׁמם (see the textual notes), a root also used in the covenant curses of Lev 26:22,

---

[24] Eichrodt, *Ezekiel*, 154–55.

31–35, 43. The proximate reason given for the entire land's desolation is the "violence" of its inhabitants (Ezek 12:19); see the similar accusations of "violence" (חָמָס) in 7:23 and 8:17. Surely this accusation points to lawless misbehavior throughout Israel's history (cf. 4:4–8), but the immediate focus here may be on the gangs of bandits and other criminals who were preying on Israelite victims in the social chaos between the first Babylonian incursions into Israel in 605 B.C. and the fall of Jerusalem in 587 B.C., after which time order was restored in Israel (but under Babylonian rule). The suffering of the Israelite inhabitants is attributed directly to the violence they have inflicted upon their fellow Israelites. They may once have deluded themselves into thinking that they could behave so lawlessly with impunity, but they will have to learn the hard way that violence breeds violence.

We are ill-informed on the fulfillment of this prophecy in post-587 Judah. But we probably get a good glimpse of the chaos and anarchy of the times in the events recorded in Jeremiah 40–43, for example, the assassination of Gedaliah by Ishmael and Jeremiah's own forcible removal to Egypt at the hands of Johanan's band. And yet once more, the people will be forced, however reluctantly, to acknowledge Yahweh's righteousness in bringing their own sins down on their heads ("then you will know that I am Yahweh" [Ezek 12:20]).

Introduction to Ezekiel 12:21–14:11

One might well ask whether a new chapter should begin at 12:21. If so, it might well extend through 14:11, since this entire section addresses (in one way or another) the question of true versus false prophecy, and sometimes more specifically, the people's challenges to the validity of Ezekiel's own ministry—a perennial challenge faced by all ministers of the Gospel (e.g., St. Paul in Galatians 1–2).

The word-event formula, "the Word of Yahweh came to me," occurs four times in this extended section (12:21, 26; 13:1; and in 14:2 after the elders paid Ezekiel another visit). The formula sets off four main revelatory units. The interpreter probably will make at least one more subdivision, consisting of 13:17–23, a subunit against false prophet*esses*. None of the material is dated, though it likely falls within the eleven months between 8:1 and 20:1 (see "Introduction to Ezekiel 12–24" above). All the material in 12:21–14:11 may well have been gathered together on topical grounds.

The problem of how to gauge the truth of prophecy is anything but unique to Ezekiel. Moses had addressed the question twice in Deuteronomy (13:2–6 [ET 13:1–5]; 18:15–22), his farewell sermon. His famous promise that God would raise up another Prophet like him (fulfilled in Christ, as quoted in Acts 3:22–23)[25] also warned that those who would not listen to that Prophet would be held accountable by God and that a prophet who prophesied words in God's

---

[25] Compare also "to him you shall listen" (Deut 18:15) to the Father's words at Jesus' transfiguration, "listen to him" (Mt 17:5; Mk 9:7; Lk 9:35).

name that God did not speak (or who prophesied in the name of other gods) would die (Deut 18:15–22). Hence it is a matter of eternal life and death that people know how to distinguish true prophecy (especially that of Jesus, the true Prophet) from false prophecy and believe words truly spoken from God while rejecting those that are not.

Moses gives the criterion that a prophet should be judged based on whether or not his prophecy came true (Deut 18:22). But for any given audience, that would be helpful only in the case of short-range prophecy. The apostle Peter, for example, had to deal with those who doubted the prophecy that Christ would return again, and by the time that prophecy is fulfilled, it will be too late for scoffers to repent, believe, and be saved (2 Peter 3).

Moses gave a rule of thumb that is more comprehensive, and also potentially more helpful in the short term, in Deuteronomy 13:

> If there arises among you a prophet or dreamer of dreams, and he gives you a sign or portent, and then comes true the sign or portent that he spoke to you, saying, "Let us go after other gods … ," you shall not listen to the words of that prophet or that dreamer of dreams. (Deut 13:2–4 [ET 13:1–3])

Here God allows that a false prophecy may come true and may even be accompanied by miraculous signs (see Rev 13:13–15). Therefore, the ultimate test of prophecy is its theological orthodoxy—specifically, whether it is in harmony with the First Commandment, but more broadly, whether it is supported by the whole of the Scriptures, which are the infallible source and norm for faith and life. Thus the OT test for determining orthodoxy by measuring a prophecy's fidelity to the Mosaic Torah corresponds to the church's test of "apostolicity." Following St. Peter's assertion in his Pentecost sermon that the promise to Moses had been fulfilled in Christ (Acts 3:18–23), "Mosaicity" and "apostolicity" will be linked inextricably with Christocentricity. The broader question of theological truth is at stake here, and believers must have prior agreement on the standard by which truth is determined: the Holy Scriptures, interpreted in accord with the Gospel they proclaim (Scripture interprets Scripture).

Conflict between prophets and kings and/or priests is recorded as soon as "prophecy" in a narrow sense appears during the ministry of Samuel, the pivotal prophet during the transition from the era of the judges to the monarchy (e.g., 1 Sam 13:8–15). But the first head-on confrontations between true and false prophets are recorded in 1 Kings 18 (Elijah and the prophets of Baal) and 1 Kings 22 (Micaiah versus Ahab's court prophets). Further conflicts appear in eighth-century prophecy (e.g., Is 28:7–13; Micah 2:11; 3:5–7) and seem to have become especially acute in Ezekiel's day, just before the fall of Jerusalem. His older contemporary, Jeremiah, carries on a running battle with false prophets, as recorded in, for example, Jeremiah 27–29 (especially Hananiah and Shemaiah are named).

In principle, the issue certainly did not disappear with the fall of Jerusalem. The many admonitions in the NT make plain that the problem dogged the apostolic church too. And it is almost superfluous to remind the reader that the situation is essentially unchanged in modern times. Possibly it is even more acute among those influenced by so-called "postmodernism," who deny the very possibility of absolute, objective truth. One may assert that the shape of the issue for the contemporary person who must choose between various claimants to the truth (sometimes all appealing to "Jesus" and some interpretation of "the Bible") is not fundamentally different from the choice confronting Ezekiel's audience. A major difference is that in Ezekiel's day the OT canon was incomplete, whereas we now have the benefit of the full biblical revelation, as well as the creeds and confessions of the church and the "hindsight" afforded by the many controversies and their resolution over two millennia of church history.

Two False Proverbs about True Prophecy (12:21–28)

12:21–22 Ezek 12:22 and 12:27 record two popular ways in which Israelites discounted Ezekiel's prophecies, and which scoffers (ancient and modern) could use to dismiss all true prophecy, since both evasions are perennial. The first one had been distilled into a common saying or proverbial slogan: "The days go by, and every vision fails" (12:22). It reasoned, based on the (often) long interval between a prophecy and its fulfillment, that the prophecy would never come to pass, and hence had not been valid to begin with. The saying was probably targeted at Ezekiel's earlier prophecies of judgment, although Jeremiah had made many similar prophecies and had encountered similar skepticism (see Jer 5:12; 17:15). But the formulation here in Ezekiel suggests that the intent was to cast doubt about the validity of all prophecy; "every vision" included verbal as well as visual revelation (see the last textual note on 12:22).

In the eighth century, Isaiah had countered the people's unbelief in the efficacy of God's Word (Is 55:10–11). Even if that prophecy had persuaded the Israelites in general, in time their confidence in the efficacy of the Word apparently weakened, faded, and ultimately dissipated. In any case, Ezekiel's audience could assert that he had (so far) failed one of the tests of a true prophet (Deut 18:22): his prophecies had not come true. Since the date is ca. 592–591 B.C., the fall of Jerusalem is a good four years later.

12:23 God counters by recasting the first proverb. Instead of "the days *go by*" in the popular proverb (12:22; the imperfect יַאַרְכוּ implies indefinite duration), Yahweh asserts, "The days *are near*" (12:23; the perfect form of קָרְבוּ implies imminence and reinforces the meaning of the verb itself). Again, instead of "every vision *fails/perishes*" (אָבַד, 12:22) in the proverb, God speaks of "the fulfillment of every vision" (12:23). "Every" probably intends to generalize again: God's Word *never* fails (e.g., Is 40:8; 55:11).

12:24 The popular proverb will go out of use when the judgment finally comes, because it will prove that Ezekiel's prophecies have not been false or empty (never to be fulfilled), but true and full of God's truth (as proven by their fulfillment). The prophecies that the populace had dismissed were prophecies of woe. But the phrases used in this verse ("vacuous vision," "misleading divination") characterize false prophecies of weal (welfare, peace, victory, success).

For that reason חָלָק ("slippery; misleading") is commonly translated as "flattering," as endorsed by some modern commentators. That false prophecy in general will cease may well be implied too; that theme will be taken up in chapter 13. But the major thrust here is on the cessation of false prophecies that Jerusalem will be spared from destruction and that Israel's deliverance is just around the corner.

12:25 The basis of Yahweh's counterproverb and the nullification of all false prophecy is anchored in Yahweh's own person: "For I am Yahweh." That same self-introduction formula punctuates many Mosaic regulations, especially in Leviticus 17–26, sometimes referred to as Israel's "Holiness Code" (a label that can be salutary without its original critical baggage), which has so many affinities with Ezekiel's language and theology. Anyone who knows what the name "Yahweh" signifies will understand that certain things necessarily follow from his person and name. Christians simply "recycle" that confession by use of the name "Jesus" (the Christ). Compare the early Christian creed "Jesus is Lord," that is, "Jesus is Yahweh" in 1 Cor 12:3.[26]

Yahweh's assertion "I will speak the word I will speak, and it will be fulfilled" (Ezek 12:25) does not accent God's ability to speak arbitrarily as he wishes, but in the context, it clearly accents the totality of his speech. He is not divided against himself and does not contradict himself. Everything he says—all his words—will be accomplished. This assertion of the efficacy and power of his Word is in obvious answer to the agnosticism referred to in 12:22, namely, that all prophecy is worthless or not trustworthy.

As 12:28 will accent again, the fulfillment (of judgment!) is at hand. The facts of history clearly show that this was, indeed, so—regardless of precisely when this undated oracle was uttered. The fulfillment in the face of the people's refusal to listen will be the ultimate confirmation that they really are no longer the "house of Israel" (12:24) but a "rebellious house" (12:25), as they had repeatedly been addressed earlier (e.g., 2:5–6; 3:27; 12:2). As if any further confirmation were needed, this section (12:21–25), like the next, closes with the divine imprimatur that is especially common in the prophets: "… says the Lord Yahweh."

12:26–27 Again God calls the prophet's attention to a common sentiment, this time apparently circulating among the exiles themselves and apparently in specific disregard of Ezekiel: "The vision that he is seeing is for many days [ahead], and for distant times he is prophesying." This attitude is less skeptical than the previous one, but since its import is so similar, God's response is brief and virtually identical to the refutation of the proverb in 12:21–25.

The Israelites' objection resonates in every age, in our own certainly no less than in previous ones. Scholars and theologians, as well as skeptical laypeople, may not actually deny biblical eschatology, but consign it to so dis-

---

26 See the explanation of the name "Joshua/Jesus" in "The Man Joshua" in the introduction of Harstad, *Joshua*, 12–13, and that commentary's excursus "The LORD (יהוה)" (pp. 47–51).

tant a future that, for all practical purposes, they feel they can ignore it safely. It is a truism that often in works of Christian theology, the "last things" not only come last in the book(s), but also are given very cursory treatment because time is running out (no pun intended!). Although 12:27–28 is about collective Israel, the truism certainly applies to individuals and personal eschatology, that is, each person's death and eternal welfare. The delay of Christ's parousia allowed cynics to confront the early church with a theology that seemed to be a combination of that in Ezek 12:22 and 12:27, as 2 Pet 3:3–13 makes clear. Today even Christians can lapse into thinking that the "delay" of two millennia means that the promise of Christ's return is so indefinite that it is all but irrelevant.

12:28　In Ezekiel's own circumstances, God not only reaffirms Ezekiel's credentials as a true prophet but avers once again that there will be no long delay. In that case, the verdict of "history" has long since been rendered, since Jerusalem fell about four years later, in 587 B.C.

We have no warrant to prepare any eschatological timetable (Mk 13:32), but the admonition spoken by Christ and his apostles for us always to watch (e.g., Mt 25:13) and be ready (e.g., Mt 24:44) is ever relevant. The eschatological future dare not be collapsed into the existential present. At the same time, we live every day *sub specie aeternitatis*, aware that the present moment has its place in God's eternal plan. We live in the time between the times, between what we temporally bound creatures describe as our Lord's first and second comings. But in the larger scope of biblical thought, we are just like Ezekiel in that we are part of the true "Israel of God" (Gal 6:16), living by faith, knowing that the time of judgment is imminent, but so is the consummation of the ages. And God's "time" is not ours.

False Prophets and Prophetesses

Translation

13 [1]The Word of Yahweh came to me: [2]"Son of man, prophesy against the 'prophets' of Israel who are 'prophesying.' You shall say to the 'prophets' [who 'prophesy'] out of their own heart: 'Hear the Word of Yahweh.' [3]Thus says the Lord Yahweh: Woe to the foolish 'prophets' who follow their own spirit and that which they have not seen. [4]Like jackals among ruins have your 'prophets,' O Israel, become. [5]You have not gone up into the breaks, nor have you repaired the wall for the house of Israel so that it might stand in battle on the Day of Yahweh. [6]They proclaim vacuity and lying divination—those who say, 'Yahweh says,' when Yahweh has not sent them, and they expect [him] to fulfill [their] word. [7]Have you not proclaimed a vacuous vision and spoken a lying divination when saying, 'Yahweh says,' and I have not spoken?

[8]"Therefore, thus says the Lord Yahweh: Because you have spoken vacuity and proclaimed a lie, therefore, behold, I am against you, says the Lord Yahweh. [9]My hand will come upon the 'prophets' who proclaim vacuity and divine a lie. They will not be in the council of my people, they will not be recorded in the register of the house of Israel, and they will not enter the land of Israel. Then you will know that I am the Lord Yahweh. [10]The very good reason is that they have misled my people saying, 'Peace,' when there is no peace, and when he [my people] builds a flimsy wall, behold, they [the false prophets] daub it with mud plaster. [11]Tell those who are daubing mud plaster that it [the wall] will fall. There will be driving rain; and you, O large hailstones, will fall; and a violent wind will break out, [12]and behold, the wall will fall. Will it not be said to you, 'Where is the mud plaster you daubed on?'

[13]"Therefore, thus says the Lord Yahweh: I will make a violent wind break out in my wrath, and there will be driving rain in my anger, and large hailstones in [my] wrath for destruction. [14]I will demolish the wall that you have daubed with mud plaster. I will level it to the ground so that its foundation will be exposed. It will fall and you will perish within her, and you will know that I am Yahweh. [15]Thus I will exhaust my wrath against the wall and against those who daubed it with mud plaster, and I will say to you, 'Gone is the wall, and gone are those who daubed it over— [16]the "prophets" of Israel who are "prophesying" about Jerusalem and who proclaim about her a vision of peace when there is no peace,' says the Lord Yahweh.

[17]"And you, son of man, set your face against the daughters of your people, who are 'playing the prophet' out of their own heart, and prophesy against them. [18]You shall say: 'Thus says the Lord Yahweh: Woe to those women who sew magic bands on all my wrists and who make veils for heads of every size in order to entrap people. Will you women entrap the lives of my people, but preserve your

351

own lives? [19]You women profane me among my people for handfuls of barley and scraps of bread, killing people who should not die and keeping alive people who should not live, by your lying to my people—those who listen to lies.

[20]" 'Therefore, thus says the Lord Yahweh: Behold, I am against your magic bands, where you women entrap people like birds. I will tear them from your arms, and I will set free the people whom you entrap like birds. [21]I will tear off your veils and rescue my people from your hand. They will no longer be in your hand like prey; then you will know that I am Yahweh. [22]Because you have disheartened the righteous man with delusion even though I have not aggrieved him, and you have strengthened the hands of the wicked man so that he does not repent of his evil way, and thus you do not save his life, [23]therefore, you women will no longer proclaim vacuity, and you will no longer practice divination. I will rescue my people from your hand. Then you will know that I am Yahweh.' "

Textual Notes

13:2–23 Throughout the translation of this pericope, I have added quotes in those places where "prophets" (נְבִיאִים) and "prophesy" (the Niphal of נָבָא, which regularly has an active meaning) refer to the false variety. Ezekiel concedes these terms for the male false prophets and their activity, probably because the terms were widely used thus in Israel (e.g., 1 Ki 22:6, 10–13, 22–23). However, Ezekiel makes two noteworthy distinctions in Hebrew when it comes to the women. First, Ezekiel denies them the corresponding title "prophetesses": נְבִיאָה does not occur in 13:17–23, and so "prophetesses" is not in the translation. Another distinction, which is reflected in the translation, is that instead of the Niphal of נָבָא, which Ezekiel used for the false prophesying of the men, for the women he uses the Hithpael participle הַמִּתְנַבְּאוֹת, "playing the prophet" (see the textual note on it in 13:17).

13:2 הִנָּבֵא אֶל־נְבִיאֵי יִשְׂרָאֵל הַנִּבָּאִים—The command for Ezekiel to prophesy (הִנָּבֵא, Niphal imperative) *against* those "prophets" (plural of נָבִיא) who are (falsely) "prophesying" (הַנִּבָּאִים, Niphal participle with article) is ironic and plays on the similarity of the Hebrew words. Yahweh often uses this imperative (הִנָּבֵא) with this preposition (אֶל) or with עַל to command Ezekiel to "prophesy against" various objects of his wrath.[a] The phrase נְבִיאֵי יִשְׂרָאֵל הַנִּבָּאִים will recur in 13:16 to denote "the 'prophets' of Israel who are [falsely] 'prophesying.' "

לִנְבִיאֵי מִלִּבָּם—Yahweh's polemic against the false prophets is summarized in this phrase that states the origin of their messages: their prophecies are "from [מִן] their (own) heart [לִבָּם]," not from Yahweh. Similar is the accusation that they "follow their (own) spirit" (13:3). מִן indicates source. The terse Hebrew (literally, "prophets from their heart") requires supplying "who 'prophesy' " in the translation. It is unusual (but not irregular) for the second word in a construct phrase to have a preposition (here מִלִּבָּם). For other examples, see Joüon, § 129 n.

13:3 After the citation formula ("thus says the Lord Yahweh"), the indictment of the false prophets continues in 13:3b–9. Some verses (13:3b–4, 6, 9) refer to them in the third person, but other verses (3:5, 7–8) use the second person. Critical commentators assume some fusion of different oracles or successive layers of commentary

(a) Ezek 6:2; 11:4; 13:2, 17; 21:2, 7 (ET 20:46; 21:2); 25:2; 28:21; 29:2; 34:2; 35:2; 36:1, 6; 37:4, 9; 38:2; 39:1

placed on a putative original.[1] But the obvious unity of the passage favors the explanation of "rapid changes in the mental address of the prophet"[2] or in "his vacillation between the roles of orator and writer, engaged in both confrontation and exposition."[3] Similar alternation will occur again in 26:2–21 and 28:21–23.

"Woe" is the usual translation of הוֹי. The interjection apparently originated in laments for the dead (perhaps meaning "alas"), but in prophetic literature הוֹי focuses attention on the grief that will inevitably accompany the fulfillment of oracles of doom. Ezekiel uses הוֹי thrice (13:3, 18; 34:2) and the synonym אוֹי in 16:23; 24:6, 9.

הַנְּבִיאִים הַנְּבָלִים—The alliteration might be reflected in English by something like "imprudent prophets." נָבָל ("foolish") is most common in Wisdom literature's rich vocabulary of antonyms to חָכָם ("wise"). Greenberg suggests "villainous,"[4] which would indicate ethical mendacity. "Godless" might ultimately be the best choice, because "wisdom" in biblical usage is ultimately a matter of confessing the true faith (e.g., Prov 1:7; 1 Corinthians 1–2).

הֹלְכִים אַחַר רוּחָם—The idiom with הָלַךְ and אַחַר can refer to "following after" the true God (e.g., Deut 13:5 [ET 13:4]), but often it is used of following false gods (e.g., Deut 4:3; 13:3 [ET 13:2]). Only here in the OT does someone "follow after spirit" (רוּחַ), and "their (own) spirit" is the antithesis of Yahweh's Spirit, who moves a true prophet (e.g., Ezek 11:5, 24). As the source of the false prophets' subjective "inspiration," "their own spirit" is similar to "their own heart" in 13:2.

The LXX apparently read לֵב in place of רוּחַ and also omitted הַנְּבָלִים, yielding "those prophesying from their heart." Many moderns, including Allen[5] and Zimmerli[6] prefer the LXX, but the reasons for abandoning the MT are weak. The MT's use of a synonym ("spirit") of "heart" in 13:2 (rather than repeating "heart," as the LXX does) strengthens the argument for the MT.

וּלְבִלְתִּי רָאוּ׃—This last clause is difficult. The ancient versions translate, "and they completely do not see" (LXX), "and they see nothing" (Vulgate), "who do not see a vision" (Peshitta). It is not clear whether the versions were following a slightly different text or were translating freely. Many English translations have "and have seen nothing" (KJV, ESV, NIV). Ordinarily לְבִלְתִּי introduces a negative purpose or result clause, and it is usually followed by an infinitive. Here a perfect follows, as also in some other verses, including Jer 23:14 (apparently an imperative follows in Jer 27:18). Those verses likewise are about false prophecy, and the clause with לְבִלְתִּי is a negative result (Jer 23:14) or purpose (Jer 27:18) clause. Here, if it is a negative result clause, then the sense is that because they follow "their own spirit, they do not see," that is, they are spiritually blind. Greenberg takes לְבִלְתִּי as a variant of לְבִלִי,

---

[1] See Zimmerli, *Ezekiel*, 1:291.

[2] Greenberg, *Ezekiel*, 1:243.

[3] Block, *Ezekiel*, 1:400, citing Ellen F. Davis, *Swallowing the Scroll: Textuality and the Dynamics of Discourse in Ezekiel's Prophecy* (JSOTSup 78, Sheffield: Almond, 1989).

[4] Greenberg, *Ezekiel*, 1:235.

[5] Allen, *Ezekiel*, 1:188.

[6] Zimmerli, *Ezekiel*, 1:285.

that is, "in a condition of not" (noting the equivalence of בְּלְתִּי and בְּלִי elsewhere: compare Deut 9:28 to Num 14:16 and Ps 72:7 to Job 14:12).[7] Many commentators construe the clause as a relative clause with לְ, "*according to* things which *they have not seen*,"[8] in which case the verb refers to (lack of) prophetic sight. In essence, I have followed that understanding because of its obvious parallelism with the preceding clause ("who follow their own spirit"). That they "follow … that which they have not seen" means they have not "seen" (received) any true prophetic vision from God.

13:4 הָיוּ:—The only unusual linguistic feature in this short exclamation is this verb at the end of the sentence. Without it the verse would be a normal nominal sentence, since Hebrew idiom requires no verb. However, there are parallels; the same verb also ends 22:18. One Hebrew manuscript and apparently the LXX omit it, leading to suspicions that it might be a later addition. But as used in the MT, its meaning is ingressive ("have *become*"). This may mean that earlier in Israel's history true prophets predominated, but now false prophets so outnumber true ones that the characterization ("like jackals among ruins") can be applied to the prophets as a whole.

13:5 בַּפְּרָצוֹת—The versions read a singular ("break"), but the plural is attested elsewhere, and there is no reason to abandon the MT.[9] פֶּרֶץ often refers to a "breach, break, gap" in a wall made by an attacking army that succeeds in breaking it down.

וַתִּגְדְּרוּ גָדֵר—The metaphor may shift slightly with this verb (גָּדַר) and its cognate accusative (גָּדֵר), literally, "and you walled a wall," though the לֹא that began the verse does double duty, negating this clause too ("*nor* have you repaired the wall"). גָּדֵר normally refers to a low wall, often of loose stones, around a field or vineyard. Israel is sometimes described as God's "vineyard" (e.g., Isaiah 5), but at the end of this verse the picture is plainly that of a city under siege. The Hebrew could mean to "build" a wall, but I have followed most in understanding it to refer to repairs or maintenance in the city wall that has been breached. The preposition עַל might refer to a wall "around" Israel, but "for" seems a better fit in this context.

13:6 חָזוּ שָׁוְא וְקֶסֶם כָּזָב[dd]—This echoes the vocabulary for divination and false prophecy in 12:24; see the textual notes there. Here the verb חָזָה is followed by three nouns, literally, "they have seen vacuity and divination of a lie." One might expect the third word in the sentence to be a verb (וְקָסְמוּ), "and they have divined a lie," and some emend the text to create that reading.[10] NRSV retains the MT by translating literally, "they have envisioned falsehood and lying divination." I have retained the Hebrew construction by translating חָזוּ as "they proclaim"—that is, they preach the *results* of both their visions and their divinations. The textual notes on the cognate noun חָזוֹן ("vision") in 7:13 and 12:22–23 observe that it may refer to verbal formulation (God's words), and likewise the verb (usually "see") can refer to verbal procla-

---

[7] Greenberg, *Ezekiel*, 1:236.

[8] GKC, § 152 x; Keil, *Ezekiel*, 1:165; and with questions, Cooke, *Ezekiel*, 139 and Zimmerli, *Ezekiel*, 1:286.

[9] Cooke, *Ezekiel*, 142, alleges that the plural ending וֹת- is dittographic since the same two letters begin the next word.

[10] So Cooke, *Ezekiel*, 143.

mation (here, false prophecy). So also in 13:7, 8, 9, 16, 23, the verb is translated "proclaim."

שָׁוְא usually refers to "emptiness," "vacuity," or "worthlessness" (see the textual note on it in 12:24) rather than outright falsehood, but the parallel כָּזָב is an unambiguous term for "lie, falsehood." The entire compound expression echoes 12:24. שָׁוְא is repeated in 13:6–9, 23, and is translated "vacuity" except in the construct phrase in 13:7, where it is translated with the corresponding adjective, "*vacuous* vision."

וְיִחֲלוּ לְקַיֵּם דָּבָר:—The Piel of יָחַל, "to hope, expect," is common in the OT, but this is its only occurrence in Ezekiel (the Niphal occurs in 19:5). The Piel of קוּם (the infinitive construct קַיֵּם) occurs elsewhere only in Ps 119:28, 106; Ruth 4:7; and Esther 9, so this is one of its earliest occurrences in the OT.[11] The treatment of a verb's middle ו or י radical as a consonant clearly reflects Aramaic influence on Hebrew. A comparable context in Jer 28:6, where Yahweh is the subject of the classical Hebrew Hiphil of קוּם, meaning "to fulfill" (as the Piel must mean here), leads to a common understanding, which I have followed, that Yahweh is the implied subject of the infinitive here. The Hebrew specifies no subject; others assume that the speakers (הָאֹמְרִים) are the implied subject, but even false prophets would still hope that Yahweh would fulfill their words.

13:8 לָכֵן—"Therefore" signals the transition from accusation (13:2–7) to announcement of judgment (13:8–12). (Another לָכֵן will introduce the announcement of judgment in 13:13–16 and 13:20–23.) The accusation itself begins with יַעַן and restates in two parallel cola (דַּבֶּרְכֶם שָׁוְא and וַחֲזִיתֶם כָּזָב) the charges already made twice in 13:6–7. Then לָכֵן is repeated with the accusation's result: the bare hostile orientation formula or declaration of opposition, "Behold, I am against you" (see the commentary on 5:8). The use of both the citation formula ("thus says the Lord Yahweh") and the signatory formula ("says the Lord Yahweh") underscores that Ezekiel's words are the very Word of God.

13:9 וְהָיְתָה יָדִי אֶל־הַנְּבִיאִים—Similar clauses with הָיָה, יָד, and אֶל or עַל often refer to divine inspiration or empowerment for Ezekiel himself (see the textual notes and commentary on 1:3). Here, however, the sense is clearly hostile: God's hand is against the (false) prophets. The LXX ("I will extend my hand over the prophets") seems to follow another common idiom for God stretching out (נָטָה) his hand in wrath, and some assume that to be the original here, but there is no further evidence for that. One is reminded of a recurrent refrain in Isaiah: "For all this his anger is not turned away, and still his hand is stretched out" (Is 5:25; 9:11, 16, 20 [ET 9:12, 17, 21]; 10:4).

Three parallel cola express the effects of Yahweh's hand, each beginning "they will not …" The first is "They will not be in the council of my people." Though the noun סוֹד occurs in the OT twenty-one times, it is not fully understood. It can refer to Yahweh's "counsel," which he reveals through his true prophets (Amos 3:7), or to Yahweh's heavenly "council" or "assembly," in which true prophets may stand, but

---

[11] But Block, *Ezekiel*, 1:402, may not be correct in supposing that Ezekiel has deliberately created the form.

false prophets cannot and have not (Jer 23:18, 22; see the commentary on Ezek 13:8–9). More generally it can refer to an intimate or close group or association (Ps 89:8 [ET 89:7]). It can be used as a synonym with קָהָל ("congregation," Gen 49:6) or עֵדָה ("congregation," Ps 111:1). Here it is an assembly of "my people," an endearing phrase that occurs six more times in this chapter (Ezek 13:10, 18–19, 21, 23; also 14:8–9). Generally, in the judgment oracles God sounds as though he is disowning his people, but in confrontation with self-serving "prophets," his underlying pity for Israel ("my people") is clearly aroused. No matter how unfaithful the false prophets and even his people are, he remains faithful to his Word, in judgment of them as well as in salvation of the remnant (that is, Law and Gospel).

וּבִכְתָב—The noun כְּתָב usually denotes a written document, and here (also Ezra 2:62; Neh 7:64) it specifically refers to a written "register" (*HALOT*, 2) of people's names. In form, כְּתָב is an Aramaicizing equivalent of classical Hebrew מִכְתָּב (and a synonym of סֵפֶר). Clearly it is cognate with the following Niphal verb יִכָּתֵבוּ.

13:10 יַעַן וּבְיַעַן—Literally, "because and with cause," this repetition of יַעַן occurs otherwise only in 36:3 and Lev 26:43. It is obviously emphatic. I have paraphrased, "the very good reason is that."

הִטְעוּ—This is the Hiphil of טָעָה, which occurs only here and is an Aramaic equivalent of the common classical Hebrew תָּעָה.

וְהוּא בֹּנֶה חַיִץ—It is not clear who is the antecedent of the pronoun and subject of the participle. I have taken it as עַמִּי ("my people"), a singular collective. חַיִץ is another hapax in biblical Hebrew, but חַיִץ occurs in the Mishnah and refers to "a pile of loose and uneven material" (Jastrow), a low wall or embankment built of loose stones. The Mishnah generally prohibits making sturdy and durable constructions in the field during the Sabbatical Year, but it does permit the building of a חַיִץ in the Sabbatical Year because it is flimsy.[12] Since it is made without any mortar or plaster (which is wet before hardening), it can be called a "dry wall."[13] To finish it with plaster would make it a קִיר, although in 13:12 that common word is used synonymously.

וְהִנָּם טָחִים אֹתוֹ תָּפֵל:—Again the antecedent of the pronoun and subject of the participle is unstated, but here it clearly must be "the (false) prophets" in 13:9. טָחִים is the participle of טוּחַ, "to plaster, daub," which will recur in 13:11–15 and 22:28. The precise meaning of תָּפֵל is uncertain. Most lexicons and modern translations have "whitewash," based on the rabbinic Hebrew and Aramaic טְפֵלָא or טְפֵלָה, "paste, plaster, coating" (Jastrow). (As with the verb הִטְעוּ earlier in the verse, Aramaic equivalents often have ט where Hebrew has ת.) Both the Vulgate and Targum have "mud without chaff/straw," that is, a plaster lacking an essential binder. Since such "mud plaster" would conceal the flimsiness of the wall's construction better than whitewash, I have chosen it as a more likely rendition.

13:11 Ezek 13:10 would easily lead into the announcement of judgment in 13:13. Many of a critical mind assume that 13:11[14] and perhaps also 13:12 are later scribal

---

[12] Talmud, *Shebi'ith*, 28b (Mishnah 3:8).

[13] So Greenberg, *Ezekiel*, 1:237; cf. *HALOT*.

[14] So Cooke, *Ezekiel*, 141.

additions.[15] Eichrodt, on the other hand, retains 13:11–12 and deletes 13:13–14b.[16] So much for "scholarly objectivity"! Allen, on the positive side, sees "an impressive movement" in the text in the series of uses of אָמַר: (1) the self-confident assertions of the false prophets (לֵאמֹר in 13:10); (2) Ezekiel's mocking counterspeech, which he is commanded to say (אֱמֹר in 13:11); (3) the imagined audience's shocked reaction, which will be spoken to the false prophets (יֵאָמֵר in 13:12); (4) concluding with Yahweh's twofold speech (אָמַר in 13:13 and וְאֹמַר in 13:15).[17] Still, one must admit that 13:11 has some challenging syntax.

תָפֵל—The LXX and Syriac lack a term for "plaster." In 13:10 and 13:11 both the Syriac and the LXX translate תָפֵל as a verb meaning "it will fall" (the Syriac by ܢܦܠ and the LXX by πεσεῖται), so apparently they vocalized תפל in both 13:10 and 13:11 as תִּפֹּל.[18] Since the LXX and the Syriac each have only that one verb for the two Hebrew words תָפֵל וְיִפֹּל in 13:11, apparently they ignored וְיִפֹּל or else the Hebrew text(s) they were translating lacked that verb.

וְיִפֹּל—This apparently is indirect speech: "tell … *that it will fall*" (for which we might have expected כִּי יִפֹּל). This terse clause will be expanded in the first clause of 13:12 (וְהִנֵּה נָפַל הַקִּ^{dd}יר).

הָיָה ׀ גֶּשֶׁם שׁוֹטֵף—This is the first of three clauses describing three meteorological events. It begins with a "prophetic" perfect verb, הָיָה, while the next two each have an imperfect verb. Here the LXX has καὶ ἔσται, as if its text had the *waw* consecutive, וְהָיָה. This first meteorological condition is clear enough: a "flooding/driving rain" (repeated in 13:13; 38:22). After the next two clauses in 13:11, the first clause in 13:12 will state the result of the three meteorological events: "the wall will fall."

וְאַתֵּנָה אַבְנֵי אֶלְגָּבִישׁ תִּפֹּלְנָה—This clause describes the second meteorological event. אַתֵּנָה, which will be repeated in 13:20 and 34:17, is the long form of the second person feminine plural pronoun (GKC, § 32 i). אֶבֶן is a feminine noun. The phrase is an apostrophe, an appeal to the personified elements to wreck their wrath upon the wall: literally, "and you, stones of hail, will fall" (similar are KJV, ESV, NKJV). The imperfect תִּפֹּלְנָה could also have the force of a jussive ("may you fall").

The LXX and Vulgate read וְאַתֵּנָה as if it were אֶתֵּנָה, the long form of the first person imperfect of נָתַן (as in, e.g., Gen 17:2; 34:12). The clause would then be "I will give stones of hail, which will fall" (cf. NIV). But a first person divine reference is at odds with the flow of the verse and anticipates 13:13. Zimmerli suggests that the consonants אתנה may be a dittograph of the following אַבְנֵי,[19] but the difference is too great for that to be plausible.

---

[15] As, for example, Zimmerli, *Ezekiel*, 1:290.

[16] Eichrodt, *Ezekiel*, 159–61.

[17] Allen, *Ezekiel*, 1:203.

[18] The subject of that feminine Hebrew verb, תִּפֹּל, would be קִיר, the "flimsy wall" in 13:10, which is masculine, as indicated by אֹתוֹ in 13:10, so that vocalization of the Hebrew would create a grammatical inconsistency. However, the Syriac translated קִיר by the feminine noun ܐܣܬܐ, so in Syriac the subject and verb have the same grammatical gender. Since Greek verbs are not inflected for gender, it is not an issue in the LXX.

[19] Zimmerli, *Ezekiel*, 1:287.

The "stones" are of אֶלְגָּבִישׁ. The word recurs in 13:13 and occurs elsewhere only in 38:22, together with fire and brimstone in a semi-apocalyptic context of judgment on Gog. It is traditionally translated "hail." (The common Hebrew word for hail is בָּרָד). It may be an Egyptian loanword, and cognates are known in Akkadian and Ugaritic, but are of uncertain meaning, probably referring to some type of stone. I have settled for "large hailstones" for the phrase אַבְנֵי אֶלְגָּבִישׁ.

וְרוּחַ סְעָרוֹת תְּבַקֵּעַ:—This predicts the third meteorological event. The construct phrase "a wind of storms/gales" (also in 13:13) is the same as in 1:4 except that סְעָרָה was singular there. The Piel of בָּקַע normally is transitive and can mean "break, rip up, tear to pieces" (or "to hatch eggs" [Is 59:5]). Here apparently the Piel is intransitive and means "to break out." Since it is feminine singular, its grammatical subject is רוּחַ. One might expect the Niphal, which can have the intransitive meaning "to burst open, break forth." In the similar clause in 13:13 the Piel is transitive.

13:12 נָפַל is a prophetic perfect ("*will* fall"). The impersonal Niphal יֵאָמֵר ("it will be said to you") apparently refers to what the people will say to the false prophets after their wall falls. The people are, in effect, speaking for God because their statement of the wall's demise anticipates what God himself will say in 13:15. The noun טִיחַ occurs only here but clearly means "clay-coating" (*HALOT*) or "mud plaster" and is cognate to the verb טוּחַ.

13:13 וּבִקַעְתִּי רוּחַ־סְעָרוֹת—This is similar to a clause in 13:11, but here רוּחַ סְעָרוֹת is the object (not the subject), and the Piel of בָּקַע has the transitive and factitive meaning "to make (a storm) break out" (*HALOT*, 2). The two prepositional phrases בַּחֲמָתִי and בְּאַפִּי ("in my wrath" and "in my anger") are about as interchangeable in Hebrew as they are in English. Compare the "day of wrath" theme in the commentary on 7:8.

וְאַבְנֵי אֶלְגָּבִישׁ בְּחֵמָה לְכָלָה:—This third phrase is nominal (verbless). Zimmerli proposes adding תִּפֹּלְנָה after the analogy of 13:11,[20] but there is no reason to emend. לְכָלָה, "for finishing off/destruction," has the same noun Ezekiel used in 11:13 when he feared God would leave no remnant.

(b) Ezek 13:14; 16:39; 26:4, 12; 30:4; 36:35–36; 38:20

13:14 The verb הָרַס is quite common in Ezekiel.[b] Its force is strong: "raze, demolish."

וְהִגַּעְתִּיהוּ אֶל־הָאָרֶץ—This is, literally, "I will cause it to touch the ground." The idiom is used elsewhere of leveling massive city walls or the like (Is 25:12; Lam 2:2). Any visitor to excavated archaeological sites can easily see with his own eyes the common military practice in antiquity of leveling walls down to the earth's surface.

וְנָפְלָה וּכְלִיתֶם בְּתוֹכָהּ—The metaphor changes here from the destruction of a simple terrace wall to the fall of the city of Jerusalem, as indicated by the feminine verb וְנָפְלָה and the feminine pronoun on בְּתוֹכָהּ ("within her"), which would conflict with the masculine noun קִיר and the masculine pronouns referring to it earlier in the verse. Both עִיר, "city," and cities themselves are feminine.

13:15 וְכִלֵּיתִי אֶת־חֲמָתִי—Similar clauses with the Piel of כָּלָה and חֵמָה, "wrath," or אַף, "anger," with first common singular suffix, "exhaust my wrath/anger," occurred

---

[20] Zimmerli, *Ezekiel*, 1:287.

in 5:13; 6:12; 7:8 and will recur in 20:8, 21. The verb may allude to the cognate noun כָּלָה at the end of 13:13.

וְאֹמַר—God speaks personally here, whereas in 13:12 an impersonal passive Niphal (יֵאָמֵר) introduced the speech, apparently by the people. The Syriac and Targum have passive verbs here, and some modern commentators emend וְאֹמַר to a passive, but that is arbitrary and is in poorer concord with 13:13–16 as a whole, since God speaks personally throughout.

אֵין—"Gone" is a free translation of this substantive ("nonexistence") used as a particle of negation ("there is no …").

13:16 הַנִּבְּאִים—This vocalization of the masculine plural Niphal participle is more common than the one in 13:2 (Joüon, § 78 h; 96 C b). The omission of the *daghesh* in the נ following the article is not uncommon (Joüon, § 18 m).

13:17 The beginning of the indictment against false prophetesses has obvious parallels with 13:2–3. Yet there are two major differences. The first is the use of the Hithpael of נָבָא (הַמִּתְנַבְּאוֹת, feminine plural participle) for the women instead of the Niphal used for the men (13:2, 16). Sometimes these two conjugations of נָבָא seem to be synonymous and interchangeable. For example, Ezekiel uses the Niphal in 37:7 to report, "I prophesied as I had been commanded," then in 37:10 uses the Hithpael with the identical meaning: "I prophesied as he commanded me." If the Hithpael here were synonymous with the Niphal in 13:2, 16, my translation of it as "playing the prophet" would be invidious. However, in some passages the Hithpael does carry derogatory overtones (1 Ki 22:8, 18 ‖ 2 Chr 18:7, 17; Jer 23:13; 29:26–27), and the context here clearly favors a pejorative sense. That may explain the second major difference: Ezekiel never dignifies the women with the title נְבִיאָה, "prophetess," whereas he had used נָבִיא for the men (13:2–4, 9, 16).

13:18 If we really knew what kinds of magical practices were current among the exiles, a reasonably reliable translation and exegesis of this and the following verses would be possible. As it is, however, we are almost totally in the dark, and translations, both ancient and modern, vary widely. And even if we understood the external practices, we would still be in the dark as to what precisely those practices were supposed to have accomplished. Were those practices brought along from the Israelite homeland and perhaps still practiced there too? Or do they represent the exiles' acculturation in the pagan Babylonian environment?

Somewhat corresponding to those alternatives are the major expedients in attempting to translate some of the technical vocabulary. When the words have few or no other parallels in the OT, should we look at those in postbiblical, Tannaitic Hebrew? (That would fit with the view that the practices were Israelite in origin.) Or are Akkadian cognates more helpful (as we would expect if the Israelites borrowed the practices from their Mesopotamian neighbors)? Often the argumentation relies on etymology, and the unreliability of that procedure is well-known.

לִמְתַפְּרוֹת כְּסָתוֹת—The Qal of תָּפַר means "to sew" in its three OT occurrences. So too presumably does the Piel, which occurs only here. Since the Piel participle is feminine plural, the translation is "those *women* who sew." (Other feminine plural forms in 13:18–23 will be translated similarly.) The women are sewing כְּסָתוֹת (whose assumed singular is כֶּסֶת), which occurs only here and in 13:20. The LXX and later Hebrew point in the direction of "pillows" or "cushions, pads."[21] More commonly, interpreters appeal to the Akkadian verb *kasū*, "to bind," to defend a translation like "bands" (*HALOT*), which accords better with the description that they are on the wrist or arm, and with 13:20, where Yahweh promises to "tear" (קָרַע) them off. I have adopted that translation.

עַל־כָּל־אַצִּילֵי יָדַי‎ ‏אַצִּיל—Literally, this is "on all the joints of my hands/arms." means "joint." While יָד usually means "hand," it can also refer to the arm. The ancient versions understand אַצִּילֵי יָדַי to refer to "elbows." In Jer 38:12 a similar phrase seems to refer to "armpits." Here "wrists" seems the most likely meaning. I have joined most modern translations in that rendering. יָדַי is the plural (or dual) of יָד with first common singular suffix. God is speaking, so "my hands/arms" makes sense only if God is identifying himself with his people who have been banded.[c] Greenberg cites medieval evidence for יָדַי being an anomalous plural form without a pronominal suffix, resulting in the translation "on the joints of every arm," referring to the arms of Israelites.[22] Some versions and manuscripts read the dual יָדַיִם. (According to GKC, § 87 f, some argued that יָדַי is a dual form without suffix.) The LXX has the singular of both nouns and no pronoun ("every elbow of an arm") as if the final *yod* were absent from both אַצִּילֵי and יָדַי.

(c) Cf. Is 63:9; Zech 2:12 (ET 2:8); Ps 22:17 (ET 22:16); Acts 9:4–5

הַמִּסְפָּחוֹת—The meaning of this second object the women are using is just as controverted as the first. These objects are placed on people's heads, but nothing else is clear. If it is the plural of מִסְפָּחָה (*HALOT*: "scarf, **head covering**, or veil?"), it occurs only here and in 13:21. The form could also be the plural of מִסְפַּחַת, whose singular occurs in Lev 13:6–8 and means a "scab" or "scale" on the skin, but that meaning is improbable in this context. Based on medieval Hebrew passages with the plural, Greenberg follows the view that it means "rags" and says that it is an insulting term for what the prophetesses (not their clients) had on their heads.[23] The LXX has the plural of ἐπιβόλαιον, "wrapper, mantle." Block appeals to a derivation from the verb סָפַח, "join, attach," and thinks of some sort of amulet attached by a string and worn around the neck or on the forehead "like a phylactery," reminding us that Origen in his Hexapla had used φυλακτήρια to translate both of the disputed terms in this verse, perhaps reflecting a common view of them as amulets.[24] Most commonly today, based on an Akkadian root meaning "loosen, scatter," the word is rendered "veils." I also have accepted that guess.

עַל־רֹאשׁ כָּל־קוֹמָה—Like "on all the joints of my hands" earlier, this is not quite pellucid. The noun קוֹמָה means "height" or "stature," and so כָּל־קוֹמָה probably means "people of every size" (*HALOT*, 3 a), or more broadly, people of any rank or social

---

[21] Greenberg, *Ezekiel*, 1:239. See Jastrow, s.v. כֶּסֶת, 1.

[22] Greenberg, *Ezekiel*, 1:233, 239.

[23] Greenberg, *Ezekiel*, 1:239.

[24] Block, *Ezekiel*, 1:414, including n. 29.

standing. (NIV ventures "veils of various lengths," apparently associating the idiom with הַמִּסְפָּחוֹת.)

לְצוֹדֵד נְפָשׁוֹת—The only explanation given of the women's activities is a polemical one. צוּד, "to hunt," occurs elsewhere in the Qal, but its Polel appears only in 13:18 and 13:20. The intensive Polel stem might imply an eagerness, even a fanaticism, on the part of the women who seek "to entrap people."

Twice in this verse the plural of נֶפֶשׁ is best translated "people" (the third occurrence is translated "lives"). Its traditional rendering as "soul" is misleading today. In my judgment, there is no thought here that the women were hunting for disembodied "souls." Block entertains the possibility that, although Ezekiel himself would not have accepted the idea of a disembodied soul, his language here "represents a rhetorical accommodation to the prevailing notions of his addressees without assent, a pattern observed frequently in the book."[25] Babylonian thought included various demons who controlled the fate and identity of a person, and conceivably the Israelite women were attempting to use them to entrap other Israelites. However, a dichotomy between body and soul that would allow souls alone to be caught is far removed from orthodox Israelite thought. Platonism and Gnosticism contributed to later conceptions of a "soul" as a person's true and higher self entrapped in the (evil) physical body, but that distinction is alien to the OT usage of נֶפֶשׁ and the NT usage of ψυχή. Since, however, נֶפֶשׁ has overtones of the mystery of life (what distinguishes a living person from a corpse), one can understand its use to refer to the part of man that departs at physical death (e.g., Gen 35:18; Jer 15:9) and that can be reunited with the resurrected body (1 Ki 17:21–22).

What little extrabiblical evidence we have might suggest that these activities were especially associated with pregnancy and childbirth—naturally the province of women.[26] But since the text itself does not pursue that issue, it is not germane to biblical exegesis.

הַנְּפָשׁוֹת—The verse continues with a rhetorical question, comparable to the one addressed to the male (false) prophets in 13:12. Normally, the *he* interrogative is not followed by a *daghesh forte*, but it is here (-נְּ-) and in 18:29; 20:30. All the versions render this clause as declarative, probably because they took the ה as the definite article.

לָכֶנָה—This is a unique lengthened form of the second feminine plural suffix with the preposition לְ (GKC, § 103 f; cf. וְאַתֵּנָה in 13:11).

תְחַיֶּינָה:—The Piel of חָיָה has a causative meaning, "keep/preserve alive."

13:19 It is grammatically possible to understand this verse as a continuation of the rhetorical question begun in 13:18 (so NKJV), but I agree with the majority, who take it as a very emphatic declaration of culpability.

בְּשַׁעֲלֵי שְׂעֹרִים וּבִפְתוֹתֵי לֶחֶם—The noun שַׁעַל, "hollow of the hand; handful," oc-

---

[25] Block, *Ezekiel*, 1:415.

[26] Compare the discussion in Nancy R. Bowen, "The Daughters of Your People: Female Prophets in Ezekiel 13:17–23," *JBL* 118/3 (Fall 1999): 417–33.

curs elsewhere only in 1 Ki 20:10; Is 40:12. Ezekiel's food included "barley" (שְׂעֹרִים) in 4:9, 12. פָּתוֹת occurs only here and means "bit, morsel," as does פַּת. The preposition בְּ (twice) probably indicates the price (BDB, III 3) that the prophetesses charge for carrying out their spells described here. See the commentary below.

בְּכַזֶּבְכֶם—The suffix on the Piel infinitive of כָּזַב, "to lie, deceive," is (second person plural) masculine, as are three more pronouns in 13:20–21 (אַתֶּם, זְרוֹעֹתֵיכֶם, and מִסְפְּחֹתֵיכֶם), in a context where Yahweh is speaking only to women. The substitution of masculine forms in place of expected feminine ones is common in the OT and especially frequent in Ezekiel 1.

13:20 לָכֵן plus the citation formula ("thus says the Lord Yahweh") marks the transition from the indictment (13:17–19) to the twofold announcement of judgment (13:20–21 and 13:22–23). Ezek 13:20–21 corresponds to the denunciation in 13:18 and 13:22–23 to the reproof in 13:19.

As in 13:8, the first announcement opens with the hostile orientation formula ("Behold, I am against … ," 13:20). While the general sense of 13:20 is clear enough, it is obscure in many details, and inevitably many emendations are proposed. Even Keil proposes a complicated one[27] (which I have not followed). Feminine second plural forms (like the elongated -כֶנָה and אַתֵּנָה, as in 13:11) alternate with masculine pronouns (like -יכֶם and אַתֶּם).

שָׁם—This spatial adverb ("there, where") implies that the "bands" are the precise point where the entrapment occurs (literally, "your magic bands which you entrap there the people"). The LXX attests to it, and some commentators defend it.[28] Others[29] and most translations, follow other ancient versions with an agential reading, "with/by which."

לְפֹרְחֹת … לְפֹרְחֹת:—The repeated enigmatic term occurs at the end of two of the verse's clauses. Most deem it to be from פָּרַח, "to fly," which occurs only here in the OT. This Qal feminine plural participle then means "flying things" or "birds." It is cognate to Aramaic and Syriac verbs and nouns meaning "to fly" and "bird." The use of the preposition לְ ("for, regarding") is unusual here. With others, I have adopted the expedient translation "like birds" (so NIV, RSV, NKJV). The LXX and Syriac omit the first instance of the word, but the Vulgate connects it with הַנְּפָשׁוֹת (animas volantes, "people as flying things/birds"). The LXX renders the second occurrence as εἰς διασκορπισμόν ("for dispersion, scattering"), as if it were an infinitive with לְ.

וְשִׁלַּחְתִּי—The Piel of שָׁלַח often has the sense "let go, set free," which fits perfectly here to describe Yahweh's deliverance from the spell or bondage under which the women had placed their victims.

אֶת־נְפָשִׁים—This is problematic for three reasons. First, it is redundant because אֶת־הַנְּפָשׁוֹת was in the preceding clause. Second, this masculine plural (נְפָשִׁים) of נֶפֶשׁ is found nowhere else. Third, it is unusual to have the sign of the direct object (אֶת־) before an indefinite noun. Many are attracted to a suggestion made by Cornill that the

---

27 Keil, *Ezekiel*, 1:173–76.

28 E.g., Zimmerli, *Ezekiel*, 1:289; Allen, *Ezekiel*, 1:186, 191.

29 Block, *Ezekiel*, 1:411.

original was אֹתָן חָפְשִׁים, "I will set ... *them free*" (cf. Is 58:6; Jer 34:9–16),[30] but then an errant ה must be accounted for. The words need not be reflected in translation and are not in mine. Their presence or absence does not change the meaning.

13:21 The verb קָרַע ("tear off") is repeated from 13:20, underscoring the forcefulness or violence of Yahweh's intervention. Here it is paralleled with the Hiphil of נָצַל, which will be repeated in 13:23. It might be translated either "rescue" or "save," which tends to have more theological connotations today. The repetition of "your hand" in the description of the rescue pictures in concrete terms the women's former grasp or clutches by which they entrapped people.

The recognition formula ("then you will know that I am Yahweh") will be repeated two verses later at the end of the chapter. Its inclusion here is partly for emphasis, no doubt, but it also signals the shift from the preceding specific denunciation of the women's magical practices to a more general statement about the deleterious impact of their activities in 13:22–23.

13:22 יַעַן הַכְאוֹת לֵב־צַדִּיק שֶׁקֶר—Literally, this is "because of grieving the heart of the righteous man [with] deception." The Niphal of the rare verb כָּאָה means "be disheartened, cowed," and it occurs with "heart" in Ps 109:16. The form here is the infinitive construct of the Hiphil, which occurs only here and has the corresponding causative meaning. "Dishearten" idiomatically captures the fact that its direct object here is לֵב. English requires rendering the infinitive as a finite verb in the second person ("you have disheartened").

In the next clause ("even though I have not aggrieved him"), Yahweh uses the Hiphil of כָּאַב (הִכְאַבְתִּיו) as an approximate synonym of הַכְאוֹת.[31] The LXX uses διαστρέφω, "to pervert," for both verbs, and KJV translated both as "made sad." The Hiphil of כָּאַב means "to cause pain, anguish." I have used "aggrieved" to distinguish it from the first verb.

God's intent in causing pain through the Law's condemnation is to drive a person to repentance. But for the "righteous man" who is already repentant, God does not want to dishearten or aggrieve him further; heaping on the Law will drive him to despair. Instead, he needs the comfort of the Gospel, which the false prophetesses do not provide.

The Hebrew contrasts the "righteous man" and the later "wicked man" in singular terms. Many recast them in the plural. Ezekiel is not thinking of isolated individuals, but of representatives of two classes of people: the righteous remnant and the masses involved in apostasy.

The noun שֶׁקֶר occurs only here in Ezekiel. It could be an adverbial accusative, "falsely, deceptively" (LXX: ἀδίκως). However, the usage of שָׁוְא in 13:6–9, 23 to re-

---

[30] Zimmerli, *Ezekiel*, 1:289, and Greenberg, *Ezekiel*, 1:241, both cite this suggestion by Cornill. See Carl Heinrich Cornill, *Das Buch des Propheten Ezechiel* (Leipzig: Hinrichs, 1886).

[31] Zimmerli, *Ezekiel*, 1:289, emends הַכְאוֹת to הַכְאִיב, so that the infinitive is of the same root as the following finite verb, because "we may conjecture that the original text used the same verb for the action of men and Yahweh." That logic is faulty, however; we may easily think of a play on two similar stems. (כָּאַב will reappear in 28:24.)

fer to the content of the prophecies as "vacuity" or "vacuous" visions suggests that שֶׁקֶר too refers to the content of the message of the false prophetesses, and probably also their magical practices, and is an accusative of means: "with/by deception, delusion." Jeremiah uses שֶׁקֶר often to describe false prophecy (see the textual notes on 12:24).

וּלְחַזֵּק֙ יְדֵי רָשָׁע—The infinitive construct (Piel of חָזַק) is grammatically parallel to the earlier infinitive הַכְאוֹת, and both are governed by the conjunction יַעַן ("because") at the beginning of the verse. The Piel of חָזַק with the object יָד, "to strengthen the hand," is a common idiom for "encourage" (BDB, s.v. חָזַק, Piel, 2).

לְבִלְתִּי־שׁוּב מִדַּרְכּוֹ הָרָע לְהַחֲיֹתוֹ—This description of the wicked man who persists in his evil "way" (דֶּרֶךְ) and does not "repent" (infinitive of שׁוּב) uses the same language used also in 3:19; 33:9, 11 (see also 18:23, 30). There Yahweh warns Ezekiel that if the prophet does not carry out his office, the wicked man will not repent, and "he shall die because of his iniquity" (3:19; 33:9). These clauses say much the same thing about the "ministry" of the false prophetesses: they do not cause the wicked man to repent, which would allow him to live.

The Hiphil of חָיָה (which occurs in Ezekiel only here) has the same meaning as the Piel of חָיָה in 3:18 and 18:27, namely, to "make someone live" or "save someone's life" by preaching God's Word, which elicits repentance and faith. Through faith in Yahweh come righteousness and eternal life, so the man then would be a "righteous man" (13:22; 18:5, 9, 20) who would "live."[d] See further the commentary on chapter 18. But the false prophetesses do not preach the Word, and thus they do not make the wicked man live or keep him alive. The negative particle לְבִלְתִּי governs both infinitives construct (שׁוּב and לְהַחֲיֹתוֹ). English requires changing the Hiphil infinitive לְהַחֲיֹתוֹ into a second person finite verb: "and thus you do not make him live/save his life." (The same was true of the translations of the infinitives הַכְאוֹת and וּלְחַזֵּק֙ earlier in the verse.) Most modern versions have "save his life," and KJV's "by promising him life" conveys that this would be done through preaching.

(d) Ezek 3:21; 18:9, 17, 19, 21–23, 28, 32

13:23 The vocabulary of this verse is similar to that in 13:6–7, 9, except that in those verses forms of קסם ("to divine" or "divination") were paired with כָּזָב, "lie, lying,"[32] while this verse uses a cognate accusative construction: וְקֶסֶם לֹא־תִקְסַמְנָה, literally, "and divination you shall not divine." The practitioners of divination no doubt thought their methods and messages dealt with what is true and were not prevaricating. However, from God's perspective, and in a Yahwistic context, all the occult arts are intrinsically evil and false because they seek truth apart from the one true God (cf. Jn 8:32, 44–46; 14:6).

Commentary

In chapter 12 Yahweh had answered the people's deluded views about prophecy. Now in this chapter Yahweh turns to the false prophets and prophetesses themselves who are misleading the people. The chapter contains two or-

---

[32] This is Zimmerli's reason for emending (*Ezekiel*, 1:289).

acles: the first addresses male false prophets and the second is directed to female practitioners. Both have the same structure:

I. False prophets (13:1–16)
    A. Charges against the imposters (13:1–7)
    B. Penalty (13:8–16)
        1. First announcement of judgment (13:8–12)
        2. Second announcement of judgment (13:13–16)
II. False prophetesses (13:17–23)
    A. Charges against the imposters (13:17–19)
    B. Penalty (13:20–23)
        1. First announcement of judgment (13:20–21)
        2. Second announcement of judgment (13:22–23)

The transition from the first to the second oracle is facilitated by the repetition of the signatory formula, "says the Lord Yahweh" (נְאֻם אֲדֹנָי יְהוִה), at the start and conclusion of the penalty announced to the false prophets (13:8, 16). Each of the four announcements of judgment includes the word "therefore" (לָכֵן, 13:8 [twice], 13, 20, 23).

The chapter has no indications of time or specific setting. We assume the two oracles were deliberately paired because of their similarity (a typical Ezekielian pattern). Modern commentators commonly assume that at least 13:2–9 was composed after the exile, at least in its present form. Even Greenberg is willing to entertain the possibility, partly because of the preponderance of perfect verbs (whereas the comparable material in Jeremiah 23, which is preexilic, has many participles and imperfects).[33] Especially if the "editor" was Ezekiel himself, this possibility cannot be ruled out a priori, but I remain unconvinced. Prediction is a hallmark of true prophecy, and there would be no better way of denouncing false prophets than by predicting their demise in ways that later are fulfilled precisely. (Hence the perfect verbs are to be understood as prophetic perfects.)

Since the role of women in the church has become such an important topic, we will preface the commentary on 13:17–23 with a brief overview of prophetesses in Scripture.

False Prophets (13:1–16)

Indictment against False Prophets (13:1–7)

13:2 Ezekiel begins his long denunciation of false prophets by all but mocking the title "prophet" by which they were known. The precise label he gives them, "prophets of Israel," should be high praise, but the context indicates that they have betrayed their privileged position. That label is unique to the book of Ezekiel (also in 13:16 and 38:17). It may distinguish these Israelite prophets in exile from their native Babylonian counterparts, who were more

---

[33] Greenberg, *Ezekiel*, 1:245–46.

diviners than prophets from a biblical perspective. That would accord with 13:9, which states that the Israelite "prophets" "will not [re-]enter the land of Israel." Or it may be targeted at false prophets still in the homeland, since 13:10 and 13:16 indicate they were proclaiming "peace" (i.e., that Jerusalem would not be captured), and 13:14 states that they "will perish within her" (i.e., in Jerusalem).

In principle, "prophets of Israel" would apply to all prophets who came under the umbrella of being Israelites. But as St. Paul would emphasize later, "not all who are descended from Israel belong to Israel" (Rom 9:6 ESV). Ethnic Israel was the "visible church" of the OT era, and then as now, the true "invisible church" consisting of believers comprised the real "Israel of God" (Gal 6:16). The same distinction can be made between all who claimed the title "prophet of Israel" versus those who truly were called by Yahweh and given his Word to preach. In the modern visible church, a similar distinction can be made between all men and women who hold the title "pastor" versus those men who actually carry out their prophetic and apostolic pastoral office in accord with God's call and Word.

The technically redundant phrase "the 'prophets' of Israel who are 'prophesying'" has sarcastic overtones of something like "prophesying at will," "ranting," or the like. But the most damning accusation (to be expanded in 13:3–7) is that the source of their utterances, and their only authority, is "their own heart" (13:2). The same accusation ("out of their own heart") will be leveled against the false prophetesses in 13:17. In OT usage לֵב ("heart") usually implies the faculties of what we call the "mind" and "will" and often is interchangeable with רוּחַ, a person's human "spirit," as in the next verse, which states that they "follow their own spirit" (13:3). We meet similar accusations elsewhere in the OT. In a parallel context Jeremiah denounces false prophets who "speak the vision of their own heart, not from the mouth of Yahweh" (Jer 23:16). Evil King Jeroboam of northern Israel devised idolatrous altars and a false worship festival at an unordained liturgical date he invented "from his heart" (1 Ki 12:33). Apostasy results in "uttering lying words from the heart" (Is 59:13).

The obvious contrast to their self-inspiration is a true prophet's inspiration by Yahweh (although the false prophets probably claimed that). Moses, a true prophet (Deut 18:15; 34:10), declared that he was sent by Yahweh to perform deeds that were "not from my own heart" (Num 16:28). The false prophets may even have been sincere in their delusion, but they were sincerely mistaken. In any case, Yahweh establishes that Ezekiel is an authentic messenger by ordering him to use the formula "Hear the Word of Yahweh."[34]

13:3 The essence of Ezekiel's denunciation of the false prophets comes in this verse. After intervening invective in 13:4–5, this denunciation will be

---

[34] For the distinction between true and false prophecy, see further "Introduction to Ezekiel 12:21–14:11" in the commentary on 12:21–28.

resumed and expanded slightly in 13:6–7. Three overlapping reasons are given for the initial "woe." First and most generally, the false prophets are "foolish." Especially in the Wisdom literature various Hebrew terms for "fool" and "fool-ish(ness)" describe all sorts of religious and moral deficiencies and misbehavior. The same term as used here, נָבָל, twice refers to a "fool" who "says in his heart, 'There is no God' " (Pss 14:1; 53:2 [ET 53:1]). The accent here is probably on the deceitfulness of their behavior and also on their failure to confess the true God and his ways. In particular, they encourage the people to believe they can have salvation without judgment, or that they deserve no judgment to begin with. A true prophet preaches Law and Gospel, but false prophets preach only a smug and self-confident "gospel."

Second, their god is ultimately a figment of "their own spirit." The Holy Spirit and divine inspiration play no role in their theology. Their "spirituality" is their own creation. This text says nothing about any evil spirit from Satan, but in total biblical context that might well be included. In principle, these "prophets" had succumbed to the spurious offer dangled before Adam and Eve in the garden, acting "like God, knowing good and evil" (Gen 3:5). This "spirit" they had followed, erecting their own norms.

The third indictment ("who follow ... that which they have not seen") seems to be a sort of sarcastic play on their claim to be true "visionaries." The verb for "see" used here (רָאָה) occasionally refers to prophetic sight (e.g., Is 30:10; Amos 7:8; 8:2), and the cognate nouns מַרְאָה (Ezek 1:1; 8:3; 40:2) or מַרְאֶה (8:4; 11:24; 43:3), "vision," refer to some of Ezekiel's prophetic visions, although חָזָה ("to see") and its cognate noun חָזוֹן ("vision") are more common terms for prophecy (e.g., Is 1:1; Ezek 12:27; 13:16). 1 Sam 9:9 indicates that the participle of the verb used here, רֹאֶה, "seer," was an older synonym of "prophet" (נָבִיא). The Christian church is still plagued by self-appointed "visionaries," who, if they have really "seen" anything at all, pursue a will-o'-the-wisp or a narcissistic reflection of themselves.

13:4 The association of jackals with ruins is frequent in the Bible, and the Israelites were probably acquainted with the reality underlying the metaphor. No explanation of the picture is offered, but to the original audience, it must have evoked a vivid picture of these scavengers who not only frequented ruins, but often enlarged the breaches or undermined the walls as they dug their own lairs. "Israel, a religio-moral ruin, teems with jackal-prophets who batten on the decay, and by telling the people what they want to hear, hasten the end."[35]

13:5 The two related metaphors in this verse (going up into the breaks in the wall and repairing it) are different than the one in 13:4, but both verses have to do with walls. Israel is defenseless because its "wall"—God's covenant, with its promises of grace and forgiveness[e]—has been demolished by the Israelites' own unbelief and faithlessness. That is why Jerusalem's (literal) walls will be breached by the enemy. A true prophet would stand in the (spiritual) breach to

(e) Cf. Is 26:1; 49:16; 60:18; Zech 2:9 (ET 2:5); Pss 51:20 (ET 51:18); 122:7

---

[35] Greenberg, *Ezekiel*, 1:236.

lead the defense or launch a counterattack. He would do something "constructive": rebuild the broken walls by warning the people, eliciting their repentance, reinstructing them in the true faith, and so on. A partial parallel is 22:30, which highlights the prophetic responsibility of intercession, and that may be applicable here also. Ps 106:23 uses the figure of standing in the breach to describe Moses' decisive action when confronted with the golden calf apostasy (Exodus 32). In contrast, the false prophets, if they recognized the danger at all, did nothing to deflect it but instead only looked after their own welfare.

The phrase "gone up into the breaks" (Ezek 13:5) probably is based on the tactics of siege warfare. The attacking army would erect ramps and run battering rams up them in order to break through the middle and upper courses of the wall, which were thinner than the wall's base. Hence the breaches would be in the higher portions of the wall, to which the defenders would need to ascend. After fending off the immediate attack, the defenders then would have "repaired the wall" (13:5), but the false prophets have not done that either.

The ministry of a true prophet has the goal that Israel "might stand in battle on the Day of Yahweh" (13:5). The battle is unavoidable; the Day of Judgment will come for all people. To "stand" on that day means to survive the judgment, not to be condemned, as "stand" is used in contexts of forensic justification.[f] The contrasting idiom of not standing (Mark 3:25; or "fall," Rom 14:4) means to be condemned. The war language applies not only to the imminent Babylonian assault on Jerusalem, but to the church in all ages. The church's strategy will always be both defensive and offensive. A church that has ceased to be the church militant is either a dying church or one that has already succumbed (become acculturated to its pagan surroundings). The war motif pervades all of Scripture, especially from the exodus ("Yahweh is a man of war," Ex 15:3) through Easter (the *Christus Victor* motif, as in church hymnody), all the way to the final showdown, accented especially in apocalyptic literature, as in Ezekiel 38–39 and Rev 16:16; 19:11–20:10.

(f) E.g., Mal 3:2; Lk 21:36; Rom 14:4; Eph 6:13; 1 Pet 5:12; Rev 6:17

The real enemy is not "flesh and blood" (cf. Eph 6:10–20), and in the case of judgment, the danger comes from Yahweh himself. Yahweh is the enemy of the sinful people, whom the prophetic "watchman" must warn so that they may repent and be saved (Ezek 3:16–21; see also 22:30; 33:7–9). The figure of the Day of Yahweh pervaded chapter 7. The idiom refers to any day when decisive, ultimate action is taken. The context here is not overtly eschatological, but those overtones should not escape us. Every day that Law and Gospel are preached is a judgment day, since sinners are condemned and eschatological salvation is proffered. But that existential dimension cannot eclipse the final and eternal judgment on the Last Day, when our Lord Jesus Christ returns to earth and all the dead are raised (Rev 20:11–15). The fall of Jerusalem is one of the major "types" of biblical history, portending the ultimate "Day of Wrath" (Zeph 1:15; see further the commentary on Ezek 7:8).

13:6 After the metaphorical interlude (13:4–5), Ezekiel now takes up where he had left off in 13:3. He sharpens his attack on the false prophets, who presume to use the signatory formula, "Yahweh says." Perhaps they had a rather magical conception of the formula, as though they could coerce God by its simple utterance. The statement that "they hope/expect" (יָחֵל) God "to fulfill [their] word" does indicate that they were sincere, not mere charlatans. In orthodox biblical piety that verb is a prominent one for the exercise of true, saving faith.[g] The use of standard Yahwistic language by the heterodox is a reminder that determining truth involves more than merely recognizing traditional words and rituals.

"Yahweh has not sent them" (13:6) negates a verb (שָׁלַח, "send") often used in Yahweh's commissioning of a prophet (e.g., Is 6:8 [twice]; 61:1; Jer 1:7), including Ezekiel himself (Ezek 2:3–4). In such passages, it is functionally equivalent to the NT ἀποστέλλω, "send" (e.g., Mt 10:5, 16; Mk 3:14), and the cognate noun ἀπόστολος, "apostle" (e.g., Mt 10:2; Lk 6:13).

13:7 By rephrasing 13:6 as a rhetorical question and switching to the second person ("Have you not … ?"), Ezekiel challenges his competitors to confront the truth question themselves. Precisely how they were to do this is not specified, but events would soon determine who was divinely inspired and who was deluded.

Announcements of Judgment on False Prophets (13:8–16)

13:8–9 The first announcement of judgment (13:8–12) begins with Yahweh answering in the affirmative (13:8) the rhetorical question he had posed in 13:7. Then he declares, "My hand will come upon the 'prophets' " (13:9). Yahweh's "hand" often came upon Ezekiel to empower him to prophesy (see the textual notes and commentary on 1:3). Perhaps the false prophets had claimed that same divine empowerment, but Yahweh now uses that phraseology ironically. They will, indeed, experience Yahweh's "hand," but in a way they have not expected, namely, in judgment.

Three negative results of Yahweh's "hand" upon them are specified in 13:9. First, they will not be included in the "council" (סוֹד) of God's people. The OT frequently uses the analogy of an earthly king surrounded by his council of advisors for Yahweh and his prophets, who are pictured as heralds or messengers of that council. The most fruitful parallel may be in Jer 23:18, 22, where Jeremiah asserts that the false prophets did not belong to Yahweh's heavenly "council" because if they did, they would have spoken his Word. Since here Yahweh denies the false prophets admittance to "the council of my people," not only is he seconding Jeremiah's expression about the heavenly council, but he is also proclaiming their exclusion from the communion of the faithful people on earth as well. "The council of my people" then is synonymous with "the house of Israel" in the following clause. A certain vertical typology of the church triumphant above and the church militant below may also be implied, and we shall note a similar vertical feature in the two parallel statements following.

The second negative result is that "they will not be recorded in the register of the house of Israel" (Ezek 13:9). If this register is an official list of true

(g) E.g., Is 42:4; 51:5; Micah 7:7; Pss 33:18, 22; 130:5, 7

(h) Ex 32:32–33; Pss 56:9 (ET 56:8); 69:29 (ET 69:28); 139:16; Dan 12:1; cf. Is 4:3

Israelites on earth, the closest analogy we have is the census lists of returnees from the exile in Ezra 2:62 and Neh 7:64. However, some OT passages refer to Yahweh having a heavenly "book (of life/the living)."[h] That suggests that Ezekiel may have a supernatural, eschatological register in mind as well. Ultimately, this points to the final Day of Judgment, when "the book of life" shall be opened, and "if anyone's name was not found written in the book of life, he was thrown into the lake of fire" (Rev 20:12, 15; see also Rev 3:5; 17:8; and "the Lamb's book of life" in 13:8; 21:27).

Third, and perhaps climactically, the false prophets "will not enter the land of Israel" (Ezek 13:9). This exclusion would be especially devastating to Ezekiel's immediate audience of exiles. Similarly, 20:38 will similarly exclude the wicked from the returnees. All indications are that the false prophets predicted—and the exiles expected—a speedy return to the land of Israel. Ezekiel asserts that even if the false prophets' predictions did come true, they themselves would not participate in that fulfillment. Even those still in Jerusalem would soon enter "the wilderness of the peoples" (20:35) like the generation of their ancestors who wandered in the wilderness for forty years and perished before Israel entered the Promised Land.

In this theme too, vertical and horizontal typology converge. Israel's crossing of the Red Sea and Jordan River and entrance into the earthly promised land was a type of the entrance into the new heavens and new earth promised to all believers by grace for Christ's sake (e.g., Isaiah 11; 65:17–25; Revelation 21–22). Christians too understand themselves as pilgrims on this earth and keep their eyes on the land above and beyond (cf. Gal 4:25–26; Heb 12:22; Rev 3:12), yet already now worship "with angels and archangels and with all the company of heaven."[36]

13:10 Ezekiel now zeroes in emphatically on the deceptive message of the false prophets, then introduces another metaphor, which will dominate the rest of the announcements of judgment (13:10–16), namely, that of a cover-up of a poorly constructed wall (repeated later in 22:28).

The metaphor is introduced by the charge that the false prophets "have misled my people" by preaching "peace." Micah issued a similar charge in the eighth century B.C. (Micah 3:5), and Jeremiah, Ezekiel's older contemporary, charged likewise in Jer 23:13–40 (in a chapter with many links to this one). As often in prophetic literature, we may hear an element of outrage in "my people." It would have been tragic enough if the false prophets had preached a false gospel to heathen, but to mislead the chosen, covenant people was incalculably worse. An application to pastors of baptized and confirmed Christians is at hand: judgment begins at the house of God (1 Pet 4:17; see the commentary on Ezek 9:6).

---

[36] For example, in the Prefaces in *LW*, pp. 146–48.

Again echoing earlier literature (Micah 3:5 and especially Jer 6:14; 8:11), Yahweh's denunciation is summarized in the objection that the false prophets preach, " 'Peace,' when there is no peace." It is commonly recognized that שָׁלוֹם has fuller connotations than the English word "peace" can capture. It is comprehensive enough that the word might be paraphrased as "divine favor" or "salvation." The immediate context here makes it likely that military peace was a prominent part of the word's intent, but Israel's security was a result of Yahweh's covenant of grace with her. The use of "peace" at the end of the Aaronic benediction (Num 6:26) after "Yahweh bless" and "be gracious" (Num 6:24–25) is a good reminder that spiritual aspects are always present with "peace" in any Israelite or Christian context.

The religious misguidance countered by Ezekiel and other true prophets was more serious than the false political and military hopes the false prophets aroused. In contemporary application, one thinks of preachers whose message could virtually be summarized in the slogan "Smile, God loves you," who seem to know much of God's love but little of his wrath over sin, and who do not preach Law *and* Gospel in proper balance and relationship to each other. Or in a worship context, when "the peace" is passed, one may ask whether the people have any idea what "peace" they are exchanging. The satisfaction of God's terrible wrath at our sin by Christ's bitter suffering, agony, and bloody death is the basis for divine love and peace.

A poorly built wall that could easily be plastered over with a little mud was undoubtedly familiar enough to Ezekiel's audience. If Jeremiah 23 underlies Ezekiel's oracle, as seems likely, one can probably see a wordplay between תָּפֵל ("mud plaster") here and the תִּפְלָה, "senselessness/nonsense" of which Jeremiah accused the false prophets in Jer 23:13. Especially if so, the "mud plaster" represents the same deceptive veneer called שָׁוְא ("vacuity/vacuous, emptiness, worthlessness," Ezek 13:6–9, 23) and כָּזָב ("lie, lying" Ezek 13:6–9, 19).

The application is clear: the people have a one-sided, naive optimism that Yahweh would protect Jerusalem indefinitely no matter how much they have sinned. Their fallacy is based on their misconceptions of the covenant,[37] which they have shattered, and of the inviolability of Zion, as preached especially by Isaiah (which they misinterpreted as the inviolability of Jerusalem; see the commentary on Ezek 8:12–13). Instead of exposing that fallacy as an unsteady "wall," the false prophets with their self-inspired predictions of "peace" have merely concealed the worthlessness of the structure (cf. Mt 23:27; Acts 23:3; 1 Cor 3:10–17).

13:11–12 Yahweh commands Ezekiel to tell the metaphorical plasterers (false prophets) that the wall, whose flimsy construction they had concealed

---

[37] See the excursus "Covenant" in Harstad, *Joshua*, 744–56.

(i) E.g., Is
8:8; 28:2, 15,
17–18;
30:28; 66:12

by a mere coat of mud plaster, will collapse under the onslaught of three kinds of violent, inclement weather. The first, "driving/flooding rain," uses the participle of a verb (שֹׁטֵף) that is common in prophetic oracles of divine judgment by means of flooding.[i] The second, "hailstones," recalls one of the plagues on Egypt (Ex 9:18–34, accompanied by rain; cf. Pss 78:47–48; 105:32) and also Yahweh's war against the Canaanites (Josh 10:11–14). Thus Israel will be treated no differently than those pagan nations were. The third, "a violent wind" (repeated in Ezek 13:13), uses the same Hebrew vocabulary as the theophany in 1:4, suggesting Yahweh's personal involvement, which will be made explicit in 13:13–14.

13:13–16 In this second announcement of judgment on the false prophets, two shifts take place. First, Yahweh makes explicit that the kinds of violent weather in 13:11 are no mere meteorological phenomena, but his personal wrath in action. The earlier clause was "a violent wind will break out" (13:11), but now Yahweh declares, "*I will make* a violent wind break out *in my wrath*" (13:13). The modern, secularized Western mind has been conditioned by our cultural construct of "science" to dissociate God from "acts of nature," but the biblical worldview sees all creation under the dominion and in the service of the Creator. Second, the metaphor of a hastily built field-wall shifts to Ezekiel's real point, the destruction of Jerusalem's walls ("you will perish within her" in 13:14 refers to Jerusalem) and the death of virtually all who had placed their confidence in them.

Ezek 13:15–16 wraps up the announcements of judgment, especially the reigning metaphor of the wall since 13:10. So no one will miss the application, Yahweh specifies the false prophets and their vacuous assurances that God would keep harm away from them. He attaches his own signature to the message (the signatory formula, "says the Lord Yahweh").

False Prophetesses (13:17–23)

Prophetesses in Scripture

The rest of the chapter (13:17–23) is directed against female practitioners of false prophecy. Rarely does the OT target a class of women as such (other examples are in Is 3:16–4:1; 32:9–13; Amos 4:1–3). Prophetesses were common in the pagan religions of Mesopotamia, Canaan, and also Greece. However, the OT evidence indicates they were quite rare in Israel. While the OT refers to many named and unnamed prophets and "sons of the prophets" (e.g., 1 Ki 20:35; 2 Ki 2:3), there are only five in the OT who are called a "prophetess": Moses' sister Miriam (Ex 15:20); Deborah (Judg 4:4); Huldah (2 Ki 22:14 ‖ 2 Chr 34:22); Isaiah's wife (Is 8:3); and in postexilic times, Noadiah (Neh 6:14). However, נְבִיאָה ("prophetess") may have substantially different meanings in these instances.

Since Noadiah was among the evil "prophets" who tried to intimidate Nehemiah (Neh 6:14), she clearly was a false prophetess. Miriam does not ever prophesy, and the sole verse that calls her a prophetess (Ex 15:20) immediately adds that she is "the sister of Aaron" (Moses' brother). She most likely is called a prophetess because of her relationship to Moses and Aaron, both of whom are called prophets (Aaron in Ex 7:1; Moses in Deut 34:10).[38] In her case "prophetess" may mean "sister of (a) prophet(s)." Likewise, Isaiah's wife never engages in prophetic ministry. Isaiah calls her a "prophetess" only when he describes his union with her ("I drew near to the prophetess") and the resulting son to whom she gave birth, who had a prophetic name ("Maher-shalal-hash-baz," Is 8:3). Thus in her case "prophetess" may mean "wife of a prophet" and perhaps also "mother of prophetic sons."

Only Deborah and Huldah actually engaged in leadership comparable to that of a prophet (Huldah) or judge (Deborah). Deborah's role is described as that of a judge (Judg 4:4–5). She attempted to persuade Barak to be the sole leader of Israel into battle, and only because of his request did she reluctantly accompany him (Judg 4:6–9). Hence her role as co-leader was due to the cowardice and default of men.

That leaves Huldah as the sole woman in the OT who truly prophesied. Probably within a few years of Ezekiel's birth,[39] after the Torah was rediscovered in the temple, King Josiah sent his men to inquire from Yahweh what would become of Israel since the nation had fallen into idolatry. Huldah prophesied that the covenant curses in the Torah would indeed be fulfilled by Israel's destruction (as happened during Ezekiel's ministry), but not until after repentant Josiah would die in peace (2 Ki 22:14–20 ‖ 2 Chr 34:22–28).

In the NT, the only woman called a true "prophetess" (προφῆτις) is Anna (Lk 2:36–38). In Rev 2:20 Christ condemns the church in Thyatira for tolerating a woman named (probably symbolically) Jezebel who called herself a "prophetess" and seduced some into sexual immorality and idolatry. The eschatological prophecy of Joel 3:1–2 (ET 2:28–29) includes women among those who will receive the Spirit and prophesy, and it is cited by St. Peter as fulfilled at Pentecost (Acts 2:17–18). Four unnamed virgin daughters of Philip are called "prophesiers" (participle of προφητεύω, Acts 21:9). Prophesying (προφητεύω), including that by women (1 Cor 11:4–5), becomes a major topic in 1 Corinthians 14. It may suffice to say here that the phenomenon to which

---

[38] Miriam led the Israelite women in a celebration of God's salvation with musical instruments and dancing (Ex 15:20). However, the words of the song of praise sung by Miriam and the women is taken from the song that Moses had first sung with the Israelites (Ex 15:21 echoes Ex 15:1). Critics often claim that Miriam composed the song in Ex 15:1–18 and led the worship celebration, but that is contrary to the text as it stands. Instructive is Numbers 12, where Miriam and Aaron challenge Moses' unique prophetic role by asking, "Is it indeed only through Moses that Yahweh has spoken? Has he not spoken also through us?" (Num 12:2). However, this kindled Yahweh's anger, and he struck Miriam with leprosy, though Aaron was not punished. The uneven punishment suggests that Yahweh had indeed spoken through Aaron at times (as other passages confirm), but Yahweh had never spoken through Miriam (no other passages support that he did).

[39] Based on "the thirtieth year" in 1:1, we estimated Ezekiel's birth at about 627 B.C. Josiah's reform, following the rediscovery of the Torah and Huldah's prophecy, is usually dated to about 622 B.C.

St. Paul refers may have been limited to the NT era, and the apostle expressly prohibits women from prophesying or speaking as worship leader in church (1 Cor 14:33–40). The church catholic has always understood this to prohibit women from the office of pastor.[40]

Indictment against False Prophetesses (13:17–19)

13:17 While details in the Hebrew text remain obscure to us, the ways in which the women Ezekiel denounces were "playing the prophet" (13:17) suggest that they were more like sorceresses, fortunetellers, or witches. They might be compared to the witch of Endor, who was a medium or channeler of spirits (1 Samuel 28), or to "Wiccans," the term preferred today for practitioners of ancient nature religion who claim to have good intentions and to use only "white magic." In any event, the fact that Ezekiel refrains from calling them "prophetesses" seems to be a deliberate show of disrespect for them (see the textual note on 13:17). It is impossible for us to determine whether the implication that they were witches (versus the description of the false prophets in 13:2–16 as pretenders to a sacred and noble office, that of a male "prophet") is another polemical insult because of their gender (Yahweh deemed it even worse that women should pretend to hold the sacred office) or whether it is an accurate depiction based on their actual activities. If the female type represented a special class or order among false prophets, we have no way of knowing.[41]

"*Set your face against* the daughters of your people" begins with the same Hebrew idiom used in 6:2, where Ezekiel prophesied against the mountains of Israel because of the idolatry performed on them. Allen calls it "a symbolic gesture" that "announces a virtual counterspell that puts the evil eye on these sorcerers,"[42] but since the formula is a common idiom in Ezekiel,[j] we must regard that as eisegesis, at best. Yahweh would not counter witchcraft with his own sorcery; his prophetic Word is more than sufficient to overcome evil.

(j) E.g., Ezek 21:2, 7 (ET 20:46; 21:2); 25:2; 28:21; 29:2; 35:2; 38:2

13:18 Our minimal understanding of key words in this verse makes it hard to exegete (see the textual notes). The use of an intensive stem (Polel) of the verb צוּד, "hunt," depicts the women's actions as predatory and destructive from an orthodox, Yahwistic perspective, even if they and their clients considered their intentions to be benign. It is commonly assumed that the "bands" were intended to symbolize the binding power of the spell or the incantation that accompanied it. That is plausible enough (so magic is always thought to "work"), but there is no explicit statement in the text to that effect.

---

[40] One may see the exposition of 1 Cor 14:33b–40 in Lockwood, *1 Corinthians*, 503–15, and the excursus "The Ordination of Women" on pages 516–44.

[41] A recent study of this pericope by Bowen begins by denying the validity of a distinction between religion and magic on the basis of "recent [secular] studies" (Nancy R. Bowen, "The Daughters of Your People: Female Prophets in Ezekiel 13:17–23," *JBL* 118/3 [Fall 1999]: 419). The article is largely a feminist screed and ultimately contributes little to the understanding of the passage.

[42] Allen, *Ezekiel*, 1:204.

The rhetorical question "Will you women entrap the lives of my people, but preserve your own lives?" implies that the women supposed that their own lives would be spared when God's judgment came even though they had trapped the lives of their victims by using their sorcery, which only confirmed and deepened the apostasy of God's people. Yahweh's implied answer is that they shall not preserve their own lives. Since they entrapped others, they too shall be entrapped in the divine punishment. Thus, this part of the verse parallels the prophecy in 13:14–16 that their male counterparts would perish within the city (Jerusalem).

13:19 The accusation "you women profane me" is doubly shocking. The verb itself (Piel of חָלַל, "to profane") implies some shockingly sacrilegious act. Usually the verb's object is something holy such as God's altar (Ex 20:25), the Sabbath (Ezek 20:13), the sanctuary (Ezek 23:39), or God's name (e.g., Lev 21:6; Ezek 20:39). Here the second shock is that the direct object is God himself (אֹתִי, "me"). This is the only verse in the OT to contain this expression. To profane Yahweh or his name means to deny his holiness, to put him on a par with other gods, and, in this context, probably to try to manipulate him by magic.

The most common understanding of the preposition (בְּ) is that it means "*for* handfuls of barley and scraps of bread," the meager payment that the diviners required to perform their services, although the commentators are not unanimous. Greenberg argues that the profanation of Yahweh involved offering these grain items to Yahweh as part of the divination (he compares it to the barley meal used in the ordeal ritual of Num 5:11–31) or that the divination ritual made use of these materials, perhaps throwing them on water, as in Babylonian rites. He mentions the Greek practices known technically as aleuromancy and alphitomancy, that is, "divination by wheat and barley meal."[43] Without further information in the biblical text, it is impossible to choose among these alternatives with any certainty, but the choice probably does not affect the exegesis of the entire passage.

The further accusation that the women were "killing people who should not die and keeping alive people who should not live" (Ezek 13:19) could be taken literally. The living conditions of some of the Israelites in exile, and certainly the conditions in Jerusalem when it was under Babylonian siege, were so dire that such little amounts of food could be a matter of life or death. More likely, however, the accusation refers to the spiritual condition of the people involved. The "people who should not die" are the Israelites ("my people," 13:18–19) who are seduced into apostasy ("those who listen to lies") by the prophetesses' act of "lying" (13:19). Those "who should not live" include the lying women themselves, as Yahweh had commanded, "You shall not allow a sorceress to live" (Ex 22:17; cf. Deut 18:10). The prophetesses may keep them-

---

[43] Greenberg, *Ezekiel*, 1:240, citing G. Contenau, *La Divination chez les Assyriens et les Babyloniens* (Paris: Payot, 1940), 296, for the second possibility and the Greek practices.

selves alive physically by the food they receive in payment, but nevertheless they should and shall die. Some may perish in the fall of Jerusalem or in the harsh conditions of exile, but for all of them the sentence of eternal death awaits on Judgment Day. "Sorcerers," along with idolaters, the sexually immoral, and all who love and do what is false, are consigned to the lake of fire and are excluded from the new Jerusalem (Rev 21:8; 22:15).

Announcements of Judgment on False Prophetesses (13:20–23)

13:20–21 Comparable to 13:13–16 on the male offenders, Yahweh here personally intervenes against the female charlatans. He will personally take away their magical paraphernalia, in which much of the populace was putting great stock. Again, even in the midst of a judgment oracle, we see Yahweh's overriding concern that his people ("my people," the recurrent refrain in 13:9–10, 18–19, 21, 23) not be victimized by quacks who peddle nostrums that cannot cure. He remains Redeemer at the same time that he must be Judge. The imposters will be held personally accountable by the personal God—all that is implied by the sacred, revealed name "Yahweh" ("then you will know that I am Yahweh," 13:21).

13:22–23 Somewhat echoing 13:19, this final pronouncement of judgment targets not merely the prophetesses' magical chicanery, but the general effect their parasitical behavior had on the morale of the community. Morale cannot be separated from morals, and morals cannot be separated from religion and theology. Again, the dichotomy between "the righteous man" (צַדִּיק) and "the wicked man" (רָשָׁע) is drawn sharply (cf. especially 3:16–21; 18:1–32; 33:1–9). Although behavior is clearly up front here, we need to keep the basically forensic orientation of the two vocables in mind. "The wicked man" (רָשָׁע) is a person who, though he may be an Israelite, does not trust Yahweh as his Creator and Redeemer; thus he stands apart from Christ and has been found guilty before God.

Conversely, "the righteous man" (צַדִּיק) is the person who is justified vicariously, by grace alone and through faith alone in the covenant promise, centering in Christ. On that basis (*propter Christum*), "the righteous man" has been declared innocent, and he bears the fruit of faith (good works). He will understand that, although he too may have to bear the cross because of his membership in Israel (the visible OT church, a mixed body of true believers and false brethren), the suffering he may endure as part of Israel under judgment is a manifestation of God's love toward him (cf. Rom 5:3–5; 8:28), not the capricious behavior of an implacable god, much less some impersonal fate or bad luck. Knowing that is much of what it means to "know that I am Yahweh" (13:23), all the more so as manifested in his Son, Jesus Christ.

Especially 13:17–23 gives occasion to remind ourselves of the hold that magic and the occult (Satanic arts) still have on our world, even in the so-called "enlightened" West. The loss of biblical and creedal certainty and doctrinal clarity in mainstream "Christian" churches has clearly abetted the revival of superstitious practices of the "New Age" variety and of notions that sometimes

insidiously coexist with more traditional, orthodox ones. Secular*ism* and spiritual*ism* are simply false religions that are incompatible with Christianity but
have infiltrated orthodoxy in various covert ways. One thinks of the many people who claim (nonsensically) that they are "spiritual" but not "religious"
(much less "Christian"). The template for much of the perennial battle is the
theory of evolution, which posits that human life is the result of random chance
(an accident of nature) and that events are governed by the natural laws of the
cosmos. That makes human life purely naturalistic, without any spiritual purpose. To the extent that people (including some Christians) buy into that theory, they find it harder to trust in the God of Israel and the Lord of the church
and are tempted to turn to alternative means to seek "spiritual" meaning and
security in life.

Ezekiel 14:1–23

Cases of Casuistry

Translation

14 ¹Some men from the elders of Israel came to me and sat down in front of me.
²Then the Word of Yahweh came to me: ³"Son of man, these men have set up their fecal deities in their heart, and they have put their iniquitous stumbling block in front of their faces. Should I let them consult me at all? ⁴Therefore, speak with them and say to them, 'Thus says the Lord Yahweh: Anyone from the house of Israel who sets up his fecal deities in his heart or puts his iniquitous stumbling block in front of his face and then comes to a prophet, I, Yahweh, will give an answer to him corresponding to it—to the multitude of his fecal deities, ⁵so that I may catch the house of Israel by what is in their heart, for all of them have alienated themselves from me with their fecal deities.'

⁶"Therefore, say to the house of Israel, 'Thus says the Lord Yahweh: Repent and turn away from your fecal deities, and from all your abominations turn your faces away. ⁷Certainly, anyone from the house of Israel or a proselyte who is residing in Israel, if he alienates himself from me and sets up his fecal deities in his heart and puts his iniquitous stumbling block in front of his face, and then he comes to a prophet to inquire for himself of me, I, Yahweh, will give an answer to him myself. ⁸I will set my face against that man, and I will make him into a sign and a byword, and I will cut him off from among my people. Then you will know that I am Yahweh.

⁹" 'If a prophet is misled and utters a prophecy, I, Yahweh, have misled that prophet. I will stretch out my hand against him, and I will destroy him from among my people Israel. ¹⁰They will bear their punishment; the punishment of the inquirer will be like the punishment of the prophet ¹¹so that the house of Israel will never again stray from [following] after me and they will never again defile themselves with all their rebellious actions. They will be my people, and I will be their God, says the Lord Yahweh.' "

¹²The Word of Yahweh came to me: ¹³"Son of man, when a land sins against me by faithlessly doing infidelity and I stretch out my hand against it, break its staff of bread and send famine against it, and cut off from it man and beast, ¹⁴even if these three men were in it—Noah, Daniel, and Job—they by their righteousness would save [only] themselves, says the Lord Yahweh. ¹⁵If I should cause wild animals to pass through the land and they bereave it so that it is a desolation without anyone passing through it because of the wild animals ¹⁶and these three men were in it, as I live, says the Lord Yahweh, neither sons nor daughters would they save. They alone would be saved, but the land would be a desolation. ¹⁷Or if I should bring a sword upon that land, and say, 'Let a sword go through the land,' and I cut off from it man and beast ¹⁸and these three men were in it, as I

live, says the Lord Yahweh, they would not save sons or daughters, for they alone would be saved. [19]Or if I should send a plague upon that land and I pour out my wrath upon it, with bloodshed to cut off from it man and beast, [20]and Noah, Daniel, and Job were in it, as I live, says the Lord Yahweh, neither son nor daughter would they save. They by their righteousness would save [only] themselves.

[21]"For thus says the Lord Yahweh: How much worse will it be when I send my four terrible judgments—sword, famine, wild beasts, and plague—upon Jerusalem to cut off from it man and beast! [22]Yet behold, a group of survivors will be left in it, those sons and daughters who will be brought out, and behold, they are coming out to you, and you shall see their behavior and their actions. Then you will be consoled concerning the disaster that I brought upon Jerusalem, everything that I brought upon it. [23]And they will console you because you will see their behavior and their actions. Then you will know that it was not without cause that I did everything that I did against it, says the Lord Yahweh."

Textual Notes

14:1 וַיָּבוֹא אֵלַי אֲנָשִׁים—The singular verb does not match its plural subject. However, the marginal Masoretic note indicates that there are eight (ח) instances in the OT where this verb is singular even though the context calls for a plural, and the Masoretic scribes state that it would be wrong to emend the text.[1] Three others are in Ezekiel (וַיָּבוֹא in 23:44; 36:20; and יָבוֹא in 20:38). Since they are spelled plene (with ו), some allege that they represent a scribal error for וַיָּבֹאוּ or יָבֹאוּ (the ו would be after the א rather than before it). However, when a verb begins a verse (as does וַיָּבוֹא in 14:1; 23:44; 36:20), it is common for Hebrew to use the masculine singular even if that does not agree with the later subject (Joüon, § 150 j).

14:3 הֶעֱלוּ גִלּוּלֵיהֶם עַל־לִבָּם—The intransitive Qal of עָלָה can refer to thoughts that "arise upon/in hearts" (we would say "enter the mind"). Here the Hiphil occurs in the transitive sense of "cause [thoughts about] their fecal deities to arise upon/in their heart." The Hiphil signals deliberate mental activity, not merely a stray, involuntary thought. The fact that these men make thoughts about these deities arise in their heart shows the intensity of their faith in these deities (and not in Yahweh). Other forms of the Hiphil (יַעֲלֶה and וְיָעַל) are used in this same idiom in 14:4, 7.

The plural of גִּלּוּל ("fecal deities") is used repeatedly in 14:3–7; see the textual note on it in 6:4.

The LXX translates this idiom by stating that the Israelites place their "thoughts" (διανοήματα, 14:3–4) or "desires" (ἐνθυμήματα, 14:7) upon their hearts. In these verses the LXX omits any term for their "fecal deities," perhaps to imply that the idolatry was more mental and spiritual than the crass worship of physical idols.

וּמִכְשׁוֹל עֲוֺנָם—See the textual note on this phrase in 7:19 and on מִכְשׁוֹל in 3:20.

---

[1] The marginal Masoretic *Sebirin* are alternative readings that the scribes declare to be "wrongly suggested" (סבירין ומטעין). See Yeivin, *Introduction to the Tiberian Masorah*, §§ 109–10, and Tov, *Textual Criticism of the Hebrew Bible*, 64. Yeivin translates the Masoretic note here as "eight times the plural is wrongly suggested" (§ 109).

נָתְנוּ נֹכַח פְּנֵיהֶם—This idiom with נָתַן ("put in front of their faces") occurs only here in the OT. The similar idiom with שִׂים in 14:4, 7 (יָשִׂים נֹכַח פָּנָיו) is synonymous. This action implies worship of the "iniquitous stumbling block."

הַאִדָּרֹשׁ אִדָּרֵשׁ לָהֶם:—The interrogative *he* (-הַ) indicates that this is a (rhetorical) question. The Niphal of דָּרַשׁ, "to seek," is used in a tolerative sense, "let myself be sought/consulted." Joüon (§ 51 c) explains: *To allow oneself to be asked*, and that effectively, hence practically = *to answer*" (cf. Waltke-O'Connor, § 23.4.f and g, including example 20). אִדָּרֹשׁ is the Niphal infinitive absolute, emphasizing God's indignation ("consult me *at all*"), but this form is unique. Normally the Niphal infinitive begins with ה, but here it is with א, probably to correspond to the consonants of the following finite verb, אִדָּרֵשׁ (GKC, § 51 k; for the form of the first singular imperfect beginning with -א, see GKC, § 51 p). Compare 1 Sam 20:6, where a Niphal infinitive absolute begins with נ to match the following perfect (Joüon, § 51 b). Another explanation is that the change is to avoid repetition of the consonant (-הַ).

The preposition לְ expresses the agent of the passive verb (לָהֶם, literally, inquired "by them").

14:4 דַּבֵּר־אוֹתָם—If the verb (Piel imperative) were taken transitively with אוֹתָם as the direct object, the phrase might be translated "lecture them." However, when the Piel of דָּבַר takes a direct object, normally the object is what is spoken (words, etc.). Ezekiel often uses the preposition אֵת in forms that appear to be the sign of the direct object (see the textual note on 2:1), and probably that is the case here, so אוֹתָם is equivalent to אִתָּם ("speak *with* them"). However, what follows is not a dialogue, as indicated by the following clause (וְאָמַרְתָּ אֲלֵיהֶם, "say *to* them").

כֹּה־אָמַר ׀ אֲדֹנָי יְהוִה—The citation formula is delayed until here because only now does Yahweh begin to address the elders.

אִישׁ אִישׁ מִבֵּית יִשְׂרָאֵל—This phrase reveals the priestly background of Ezekiel (1:3), as also does other phraseology in 14:7. Besides the repetition of this phrase in 14:7, it occurs only in Lev 17:3, 8, 10; 22:18, each time introducing a general law or rule that applies to all Israelites. Other passages in the Torah use אִישׁ אִישׁ in similar legal contexts, but outside the Torah אִישׁ אִישׁ is only in Ezek 14:4, 7. The translation "anyone" brings out its distributive force.

אֶל־הַנָּבִיא—The definite article with נָבִיא here and in 14:7, 9 (first occurrence), 10 denotes an office or class. English has the same idiom but deploys it on different occasions than Hebrew (cf. "the pastor" in a generic sense). English idiom requires the indefinite article in 14:4, 7, 9 ("a prophet"), but "the prophet" in 14:10.

אֲנִי יְהוָה נַעֲנֵיתִי לוֹ בָה—The Niphal of עָנָה may simply mean "to answer" (cf. BDB, s.v. עָנָה I, Niphal, 1), as does the common Qal, in which case לוֹ is the indirect object ("I will give an answer *to* him"). Or, here and in 14:7 the Niphal may be tolerative, "to allow oneself to be moved to answer" (*HALOT*, s.v. ענה I, Niphal, 1), similar to the tolerative Niphal in the question at the end of 14:3, in which case לוֹ is the agent, "I will be moved *by* him to answer." The (first common singular) perfect aspect of נַעֲנֵיתִי might be explained as indicating resolve (Waltke-O'Connor, § 30.5.1d) or as a prophetic perfect. Greenberg points to the use of the Niphal of עָנָה in the Mishnah, where it can imply a formal answer (in this case, also a sarcastic one): "oblige him with an answer."[2] In any event, the implication is that God will answer as he himself sees fit, not in accord with the inquirer's desire. The rest of the verse explains the way in which he will answer.

The Qere, בָא (in place of the Kethib, בָה), is the Qal third masculine singular perfect (or masculine singular participle) of בּוֹא and must refer to the man who "came" to the prophet, as stated earlier in the verse with the same verb (וּבָא אֶל־הַנָּבִיא). The Masoretic accents indicate that the words נַעֲנֵיתִי לוֹ בָא go together, and with the Qere, this would mean "I will give an answer to him [who] came."

I have opted, however, to remain with the Kethib in this instance. בָה apparently is the preposition בְּ with the third feminine singular pronominal suffix (which normally has *mappiq*: הָ-), "corresponding to it," and prospectively refers to the following phrase: "corresponding to it—corresponding to the multitude of his fecal deities." Such an anticipatory pronoun is common in Aramaic. The noun רֹב is masculine, but the feminine pronoun may be used for an abstract, referring to the entire idolatrous system. In both בָה and בְּרֹב, the בְּ is one of norm, "according to, corresponding to."

Critics commonly emend בָה to בִּי, "by myself," which is at the end of 14:7. Sometimes they also delete בְּרֹב גִּלּוּלָיו at the end of 14:4 because that phrase is absent in 14:7.

14:5 תְּפֹשׁ ... בְּלִבָּם—Literally, "to catch/seize by their heart," the verb is often used of capturing cities, prisoners, and the like. It is also used of catching someone in a secret sin (e.g., the suspected adulteress in Num 5:13), and that seems better to approximate the situation here. God's concern is with what is in their "heart," used here in the sense of spiritual allegiance and the seat of (idolatrous) faith (similarly in 20:16; 33:31). Yahweh discerns what is in the heart (Jer 12:3; 20:12; Ps 17:3). Yahweh must expose the people's secret (or even unacknowledged) duplicity in erecting idols in their heart (Ezek 14:3) and then inquiring of him through a prophet.

To retain the continuity with the use of "heart" in 14:3–4, I have translated, "by what is in their heart" here in 14:5. NIV ventures "*re*capture the hearts," which anticipates 14:6 nicely, but the overall thrust of the pericope is of God's judgment on hearts that do not repent. Already at Ezekiel's call, Yahweh declared that the Israelites were "hard-hearted" (חִזְקֵי־לֵב, 2:4; קְשֵׁי־לֵב, 3:7). Later he described theirs as a "whoring heart" (6:9) but also promised to remove their "heart of stone" and replace it with "one heart, and a new S/spirit ... a heart of flesh" (11:19). See also 18:31; 36:26.

אֲשֶׁר נָזֹרוּ מֵעָלַי—Since the verb is plural, the antecedent of אֲשֶׁר is "house of Israel" (the people) rather than "their heart." The Niphal of זוּר is used only here (third common plural perfect) and in Is 1:4. The reflexive sense of the Niphal here underscores the willful culpability of these disqualified petitioners, who "have alienated, estranged, disqualified themselves." Compare the Qal participle זָר, which can be used as a noun, "stranger, foreigner."

כֻּלָּם:—English idiom requires repositioning this last word ("all of them") to the start of the clause in the translation. Its final position in Hebrew may emphasize the

---

2 Greenberg, *Ezekiel*, 1:248. For rabbinic usage, Jastrow, עני, עָנָה I, Niphal, 2, includes the definition "to deliver an opinion" after being called upon to speak about some matter.

massiveness of the defection. Some critics delete the word because it is absent in the LXX. Others take it as referring to בְּגִלּוּלֵיהֶם ("with all their fecal deities"), but Zimmerli points out that in such instances ־כָּל always precedes the noun.[3]

14:6 שׁוּבוּ וְהָשִׁיבוּ מֵעַל גִּלּוּלֵיכֶם—The Qal of שׁוּב can have the intransitive meaning "repent" (BDB, 6 d). The following Hiphil imperative הָשִׁיבוּ too may be intransitive, and if so would mean "turn" (away from the idols) as a synonym of "repent." The Hiphil is used in that sense in the very similar שׁוּבוּ וְהָשִׁיבוּ מִכָּל־פִּשְׁעֵיכֶם ("repent and turn away from all your rebellious acts") in 18:30. Normally the Hiphil is transitive, and here it could be an incomplete anticipation of הָשִׁיבוּ פְּנֵיכֶם ("turn your faces away") at the end of the verse.

14:7 כִּי—This could simply function as a conjunction ("for"), but since the verse largely repeats 14:4, I have taken it as an asseverative ("certainly").

The compound subject, אִישׁ אִישׁ מִבֵּית יִשְׂרָאֵל וּמֵהַגֵּר אֲשֶׁר־יָגוּר בְּיִשְׂרָאֵל, is taken almost verbatim from Lev 17:8, 10 (cf. also Lev 17:13; 20:2; 22:18; Ezek 47:22). The use of phraseology from the Torah by Ezekiel, a priest (1:3), may "lend the pronouncement the aura of ancient, general authority and applicability,"[4] as does the phrase אִישׁ אִישׁ here and in 14:4 (see the second textual note on 14:4). In the Torah and early Israel גֵּר often referred to a "resident alien," and גּוּר referred to him "residing" among Israelites. Such an alien, if he was circumcised, could participate in worship and liturgical life, such as the Passover, and was treated the same as an Israelite according to the Torah (see, e.g., Ex 12:48–49).

But one must ask what this terminology means in the exilic context of Ezek 14:7. Allen allows that resident aliens in Israel may have been included in the deportation to Babylon in 597 B.C.,[5] but the evidence indicates that the deportation concentrated on the Israelite aristocracy. I judge that Block is closer to the mark when he argues that the contemporary reference is to proselytes who have attached themselves to Israel.[6] Considering the spiritual apostasy of the Israelites (both those still in Judah and those already in exile), a proselyte who has joined either group of Israelites would not necessarily be orthodox or faithful.

וְיִנָּזֵר מֵאַחֲרַי—This begins a long Hebrew protasis ("if he alienates himself from me …") with classical Hebrew parataxis (a series of coordinate *waw* clauses). The apodosis will be Yahweh's response at the end of the verse. The Niphal of נָזַר can mean "to dedicate, consecrate oneself" to a deity (to Baal in Hos 9:10) or "to abstain, hold oneself sacredly aloof from" something (from holy things in Lev 22:2). The Hiphil can mean "to live as a Nazirite," which requires some kinds of abstinence. If the sense of the Niphal here is that the person (sacredly) holds himself back from Yahweh so he can consecrate himself to his fecal deities, it is sarcastic, or an oxymoron.[7]

---

3   Zimmerli, *Ezekiel*, 1:301, citing 8:10; 16:36; 20:31; 23:7; 36:25.

4   Greenberg, *Ezekiel*, 1:249.

5   Allen, *Ezekiel*, 1:207.

6   Block, *Ezekiel*, 1:429. The LXX renders the phrase καὶ ἐκ τῶν προσηλύτων τῶν προσηλυτευόντων ἐν τῷ Ισραηλ.

7   The latter suggestion comes from Zimmerli, *Ezekiel*, 1:301–2.

HALOT (2) gives "withdraw from someone, **desert**." Greenberg,[8] endorsed by Block,[9] is probably correct in construing יִנָּזֵר as a back formation from נָזֹרוּ ("alienated themselves," Niphal of זור in 14:5), formed as though the *nun* in נָזֹרוּ were part of the root (hence יִנָּזֵר would be a Niphal of a Niphal). The combination here of וַיִּנָּזֵר מֵאַחֲרַי might be compared to the combination נָזֹרוּ אָחוֹר in Is 1:4 (the only other passage with the Niphal of זור besides Ezek 14:5, where נָזֹרוּ is followed by מֵעָלָי).

לִדְרָשׁ־לוֹ בִי אֲנִי יְהוָה נַעֲנֶה־לּוֹ בִּי:—This part of the sentence uses some of the same vocabulary as in 14:3–4. Since the second לוֹ refers to the petitioner ("I will give an answer *to him*"), probably the first לוֹ does too. The first would be a so-called dative of advantage, "inquire *for himself*." (Since Yahweh's answer will be condemnatory, it might even be a dative of disadvantage: by inquiring the petitioner incriminates himself.) The alternative is to understand the first לוֹ as referring to the prophet ("to inquire of me *by/through him*"). In terms of sense, that highlights the contrast with what follows, where Yahweh himself answers the petitioner directly (not through the prophet). But since הַנָּבִיא is the last word before this phrase, it seems superfluous for the first לוֹ to refer to the prophet again, so I take this understanding as less likely. In both instances here, לוֹ is connected to the preceding verb by a *maqqeph*, and the second is also connected to the preceding verb by a conjunctive *daghesh forte* (לּוֹ־).

The repetition of בִי is emphatic. Both times it refers to Yahweh. This use of the preposition and first common singular pronominal suffix (literally, "by me") functions almost like a personal pronoun, especially at the end of the verse (I, Yahweh, will give an answer to him *myself*").

14:8 וַהֲשִׁמֹתִיהוּ—This is the Hiphil of שִׂים (first common singular perfect with *waw* consecutive and third masculine singular suffix). Elsewhere the Hiphil occurs only in 21:21 (ET 21:16) and Job 4:20. It is synonymous with the Qal ("to set, place"), which occurred in 14:4, 7 (יָשִׂים). Here the Hiphil has a third masculine singular suffix as its direct object, followed by two nouns with לְ of product (לְאוֹת וְלִמְשָׁלִים), meaning "I will make him into a sign and a byword," as supported by the way the versions translate the verb. Many commentators emend the Hiphil verb to a Qal by deleting the initial ה and revocalizing it to וְשַׂמְתִּיהוּ, which would have the same meaning. Some manuscripts point the initial sibilant as שׁ, which would make it a Hiphil of שָׁמַם, "to devastate, make desolate," and Greenberg calls attention to Deut 28:37, where fallen Israel will be לְשַׁמָּה לְמָשָׁל, ("a desolation and a byword"). However, as Greenberg notes, the reading with שׁ fails to echo יָשִׂים in Ezek 14:4, 7 and also does not fit the following context.[10]

לְאוֹת וְלִמְשָׁלִים—See the textual note and commentary on אוֹת in 4:3. In 12:22–23 מָשָׁל referred to a "proverb." Here it means "byword," a proverbial object of derision and shame, a name used infamously as an example of judgment. There are several

---

[8] Greenberg, *Ezekiel*, 1:249. As another example of this phenomenon, Greenberg cites נְמַלְתֶּם ("you shall be circumcised") in Gen 17:11, backformed from נָמוֹל (Gen 17:26), a Niphal of מוּל.

[9] Block, *Ezekiel*, 1:428, n. 42.

[10] Greenberg, *Ezekiel*, 1:250.

possible explanations for the plural form of מְשָׁלִים, "proverbs, bywords." Critics often emend it to the expected singular, but Greenberg adduces other examples of noun pairs where the one is singular and the other plural (e.g., Is 43:28; 50:6).[11] Most likely it is to be taken as an intensive plural (cf. מַרְאוֹת in 1:1, and GKC, § 124 e; Joüon, § 136 f). The intensive would mean that the byword is particularly notorious. Or it could be a true plural if the idea is that the divine punishment will give rise to many proverbs about the offender. Or the final ם might be an enclitic *mem*, an antique stylistic flourish sometimes preserved in the consonantal text, but mispointed if not understood by the Masoretes. However, Ezekiel writes so late in the history of biblical Hebrew that one hardly expects to find it here.

14:9 וְהַנָּבִיא כִי־יְפֻתֶּה—The language is still that of sacral law. Instead of אִישׁ אִישׁ (as in 14:4, 7), an expression used in sacral law, here in the protasis the hypothetical subject הַנָּבִיא precedes the conditional כִי (literally, "the prophet, if he is deceived"). Compare the same construction in, for example, Lev 1:2; 2:1. Usually the verb פָּתָה involves evil intent and so is translated "entice, deceive, seduce," but it may be used of someone who is simply weak, naive, gullible, or foolish. Elsewhere the Pual means "be persuaded" (Prov 25:15) or "be deceived" (Jer 20:10). How we take the Pual here (and the following Piel, פִּתֵּיתִי) is partly a matter of exegesis (see the commentary below). I have chosen "misled" to indicate that the prophet's motivation is ultimately beside the point.

וְדִבֶּר דָּבָר—The cognate accusative construction is literally "he speaks a word," but the context demands that the "word" is an "oracle" or "prophecy," as I have translated it.

וְהִשְׁמַדְתִּיו—This Hiphil of שָׁמַד ("I will destroy him") parallels the Hiphil וְהִכְרַתִּיו ("I will cut him off") in 14:8.

14:10 וְנָשְׂאוּ עֲוֹנָם—In 4:4–6 Ezekiel was to "bear" (נָשָׂא) the "iniquity" (עָוֹן) of Israel by lying on his side (see the textual notes and commentary there). Here the emphasis is more eschatological, and so עָוֹן is rendered "punishment"; see the commentary below.

כַּעֲוֹן הַדֹּרֵשׁ כַּעֲוֹן הַנָּבִיא יִהְיֶה:—The clause translates, literally, "like the punishment of the inquirer, like the punishment of the prophet it will be." Such idiomatic repetition of כְ expresses the complete equivalence of the two. Ezekiel will use a variation of this idiom in 16:44. Cooke observes that usually in this idiom the first is like the second.[12] However, since this passage is about prophets, here Ezekiel emphasizes that "the prophet" who indulges the idolatrous "inquirer" is just as culpable as his client. (In most English translations "the prophet" precedes the inquirer.)

14:11 ... לְמַעַן לֹא־יִתְעוּ—This and the following clause are negative purpose clauses: God's equal punishment of both the inquirer and the (false) prophet (14:10) will accomplish these two goals, so Israel will never again stray or become defiled. The verb תָּעָה is rural vocabulary for livestock that "goes astray." In both Testaments

---

[11] Greenberg, *Ezekiel*, 1:250.

[12] Cooke, *Ezekiel*, 156, citing as examples Gen 44:18 and Deut 1:17.

such language is often used of covenant unfaithfulness, and Ezekiel will use the verb in that sense also in 44:10, 15; 48:11. Moreover, in chapter 34 Yahweh as shepherd will recover the lost sheep of Israel. Isaiah uses the verb in the simile "all we like sheep have gone astray" to convey universal human rebellion, which is rectified by Christ's substitutionary atonement, "Yahweh laid on him the iniquity of us all" (Is 53:6). Thus Isaiah proclaims the vicarious death of the Suffering Servant as the solution to the problem of human straying.

וְלֹא־יִטַּמְּאוּ עוֹד בְּכָל־פִּשְׁעֵיהֶם—The verb is the Hithpael of טָמֵא, which has a reflexive or middle meaning, "defile oneself, render oneself unclean." Various forms of the verb and cognate adjective are frequent in the Levitical laws of purity for Israel, including the Hithpael.[a] In the Hithpael the preformative ת is regularly assimilated and marked by the *daghesh* in the *tet* (-טַּ-; the unassimilated form here would have been יִתְטַמְּאוּ). "Rebellions" or "rebellious actions" brings out the specific nuance of פֶּשַׁע, one of the common and strong OT words for sin. Ezekiel's sacerdotal background (1:3) is apparent in his association of sin with defilement. The behavior is inseparable from the entire person, and evil actions defile the whole person. Accent on the pollution caused by sin in general (not merely certain specific sins) will recur in 37:23 (cf. the Day of Atonement in Leviticus 16).

וְהָיוּ לִי לְעָם וַאֲנִי אֶהְיֶה לָהֶם לֵאלֹהִים—This classic covenant formula is repeated verbatim from 11:20; see the textual notes and commentary there.

14:13–20 Syntactically, 14:13 and 14:14 together form one conditional sentence. The protasis describing a hypothetical situation extends from 14:13 (when a land sins and Yahweh punishes a land) through 14:14a (and if the three righteous men were in that land), and then the apodosis comes in 14:14b (only the three would be saved). That same pattern of a protasis (Yahweh's judgment of a land, and if the three were in it) and apodosis (salvation only for the three) is repeated three more times, forming three more long conditional sentences (14:15–16; 14:17–18; and 14:19–20).

14:13 לִמְעָל־מַעַל—The cognate accusative construction uses the verb מָעַל, "act unfaithfully" (BDB) or "violate one's covenant obligations" (cf. *HALOT*), and the corresponding noun מַעַל, "disloyalty, infidelity" (*HALOT*, 1). Ezekiel will use this cognate accusative (verb and noun) again in 15:8; 17:20; 18:24; 20:27; 39:26. Here the Qal infinitive לִמְעָל is used as a gerund after the preceding verb תֶחֱטָא, literally, "sins by acting unfaithfully [thereby doing] unfaithfulness." It is difficult to reproduce the combination in English idiom, but "faithlessly doing infidelity" attempts to reflect the verb and cognate noun.

The Torah uses this cognate accusative (verb and noun) for Israel or an Israelite violating the sacred law of God's covenant (e.g., Lev 5:15; 5:21 [ET 6:2]; 26:40) and specifically for a woman who is unfaithful to her husband (Num 5:12, 27). Hence when used of Israel, it may liken the covenant to a marriage between Yahweh and Israel, and picture Israel's covenant violations as marital infidelity. In Ezekiel 16 and 23 Yahweh will elaborate at great length on the image of the covenant as a marriage and of Israel's covenant violations as sexual infidelity. See also the textual note on קִנְאָה, "jealousy," in 5:13 and commentary on 5:13; 8:3, 5.

(a) Lev 11.24, 43, 18:24, 30; 21:1, 3, 4, 11

מַטֵּה־לֶחֶם—See the textual notes on this phrase ("staff of bread," i.e., bread as the staff of life) in 4:16. The next phrase (sending famine) clarifies what it means to break the "staff of bread."

וְהִשְׁלַחְתִּי־בָהּ—The Hiphil of שָׁלַח is uncommon, but the few passages that use it all speak of God sending forms of judgment: famine in Amos 8:11 and Ezek 14:13; wild beasts in Lev 26:22; the plague of flies in Ex 8:17; and enemy kings in 2 Ki 15:37. Elsewhere Ezekiel often uses the Piel in the same sense (e.g., 14:19, 21). Hence some critics wish to emend the Hiphil here to the Piel, but that is a clear case of trigger happiness!

The preposition בְּ with suffix means "against her/it" as also in 14:23. The suffix is feminine because אֶרֶץ is a feminine noun.

14:14 נֹחַ דָּנִאֵל וְאִיּוֹב—The names of Noah and Job are spelled the same as in Genesis and Job, respectively. Outside of Ezekiel the Hebrew name of Daniel is spelled דָּנִיֵּאל, which is the Qere here and also in 14:20 and 28:3. The Kethib in these three verses has the *ḥaser* (defective) spelling of the *hireq*, דָּנִאֵל. Both the Qere and Kethib obviously are pointed so as to agree with the pronunciation of "Daniel" as found in the canonical book by that name (דָּנִיֵּאל is also in Ezra 8:2; Neh 10:7 [ET 10:6]; 1 Chr 3:1). As such, nothing can be made of the Kethib's *ḥaser* orthography; the Qere and Kethib are simply variant spellings of the same name.

יְנַצְּלוּ נַפְשָׁם—The Hiphil of נָצַל commonly means "to save, rescue," as in 14:16, 18, 20. The Piel, used here, occurs only thrice elsewhere in the OT (Ex 3:22; 12:36; 2 Chr 20:25) and always means "to strip off, despoil," but that is too small a number of verses to rule out the possibility that here the Piel is synonymous with the usual meaning of the Hiphil (used in 14:16, 18, 20, and elsewhere in the book). For many other Hebrew verbs, the Piel and Hiphil can be essentially synonymous, as is the case with שָׁלַח (Hiphil in 14:13; Piel in 14:19, 21). The LXX translates almost all the instances of the verb נָצַל in 14:14, 16, 18 (Niphal, Piel, and Hiphil alike) by σωθήσονται ("shall be saved").[13] Keil defends the MT on the grounds that occasionally the Hiphil of נָצַל has the same meaning ("despoil") as the Piel does elsewhere.[14] Greenberg posits a patterned sequence of verbs, Hiphil then Piel, in 14:13–14 (הִשְׁלַחְתִּי ... יְנַצְּלוּ) matching the Piel-Hiphil order in 14:19–20 (אֲשַׁלַּח ... יַצִּילוּ).[15] Conclusion: there are insufficient grounds to emend, especially because the intended meaning is clear.

14:15 לוּ־חַיָּה רָעָה—The long protasis (continuing into 14:16) is introduced by לוּ. Ordinarily, this particle introduces contrary-to-fact conditions, but there are other exceptions (Gen 50:15 and Micah 2:11) where, as here, it simply means "if." It is essentially synonymous with אוֹ, "or (if)," which begins the parallel clauses in 14:17 and 14:19. There is no sufficient reason to emend it to אוֹ here.

---

[13] The only exception is that יַצִּילוּ in 14:18 is translated by ῥύσωνται. (In 14:16, יַצִּילוּ is translated by σωθήσονται.)

[14] Keil, *Ezekiel*, 1:187.

[15] Greenberg, *Ezekiel*, 1:258.

The direct object here, חַיָּה רָעָה, is feminine singular (collective or generic) in Hebrew, but English usage demands a plural translation, "wild animals" (also in 14:21). The adjective רָעָה often means "evil," but with חַיָּה, "wild" is the obvious English equivalent. See the textual note on the same phrase in 5:17.

אַעֲבִיר ... מִבְּלִי עוֹבֵר—The Hebrew clearly has a play on the root עָבַר, first in the Hiphil (אַעֲבִיר) with God as subject, literally, "I will cause wild animals to pass through," and then the Qal participle (עוֹבֵר) with an indefinite human subject, "without anyone passing through (it)." My English translation has retained that play.

וְשִׁכְּלָתָּה—The feminine singular direct object of the first clause, חַיָּה רָעָה, is the implied subject of this feminine singular verb, the Piel of שָׁכֵל with third feminine singular suffix, literally, "and she [wild beast(s)] bereaves her [the land]." The form is a pausal. The suffix lacks the usual *mappiq* (הָ-) apparently because of the recessive accent. The Piel usually means "to make (a father or mother) childless" by killing the children, sometimes by causing a miscarriage or stillbirth (Ex 23:26). Here it is used in an extended sense, probably anticipating the "sons and daughters" in the apodosis in 14:16 and also in 14:18, 20, 22. The LXX reads τιμωρήσομαι αὐτήν, "I will punish her," apparently understanding the consonants to be vocalized as first person singular, וְשִׁכַּלְתָּה. The LXX had also (inaccurately) used τιμωρήσομαι for a different form of the Piel in 5:17 (וְשִׁכְּלֻךְ).

14:16 The first part of the verse is still part of the protasis begun in 14:15, even though there is no connective on שְׁלֹשֶׁת. The parallels in 14:18 and 14:20 begin with the conjunction וְ, and the LXX (καί) and some Hebrew manuscripts have it here too. I have added it in English for idiomatic purposes. Without it a literal rendering would be "these three men being in it." The absence of the conjunction here may be a deliberate variation, as such variations often occur elsewhere in this pericope.

Both the oath formula (חַי־אָנִי, "as I live"; see the textual note on it in 5:11) and the signatory formula ("says the Lord Yahweh") precede and thereby emphasize the apodosis ("neither sons nor daughters would they save"). After an oath, אִם is an emphatic negative. The use of it twice in the apodosis means "neither ... nor." (Contrast its repetition in 2:5, not in an oath context, meaning "whether ... or.")

14:17–20 Two more examples of divine judgment, sword and plague, follow the pattern of the previous two, but with minor variations in phraseology, most of which are apparent in translation. For example, 14:18 uses לֹא instead of the אִם ... אִם idiom in 14:16 and 14:20. Ezek 14:20 uses the singulars בֵּן and בַּת instead of the plurals בָּנִים and בָּנוֹת in 14:16 and 14:18. The constructions with the verb נָצַל vary from the Piel (יְנַצְּלוּ נַפְשָׁם) in 14:14 to the Hiphil (יַצִּילוּ) in 14:16, 18, 20 and the Niphal (הֵמָּה לְבַדָּם יִנָּצֵלוּ) in 14:16 and 14:18. The "three men" (14:14, 16, 18) are named only in 14:14, 20.

14:21–23 Many critical scholars question the genuineness of 14:21–23 and consider these verses postexilic amendments, "prophecies after the event." That allegation arises because of the shift from the hypothetical situations in 14:14–20 to the specific judgments in 14:21–23 that actually took place, and even more because of the unexpected mention of and reference to survivors (14:22–23) after such emphatic predictions of total judgment. However, the lexical ties between 14:21 and other passages in Ezekiel (especially 5:15–17) support its authenticity and unity with the rest of the book.

Moreover, while imperfect verbs were repeatedly used in 14:14–20 when the hypothetical conditions were being introduced, Yahweh uses the perfect verb שִׁלַּחְתִּי in 14:21 precisely to make the point that his decision to "send" the four judgments has already been decided and now is decreed with a prophetic perfect. A hallmark of true, inspired prophecy is the accurate prediction of future events that indeed come to pass.[16] Ezek 14:21–23 as a whole makes a point we shall hear much more of in chapter 18: "Yahweh's judgment of Jerusalem is neither capricious nor arbitrary; it is more than deserved, and it is administered in precise fulfillment of the warnings issued long ago."[17]

14:21 כִּי—This initial conjunction ("for") signals the transition from theoretical possibilities to the immediate application.

כִּי אַף—This idiomatic combination is, literally, "*How much more when* I send my four evil judgments" (Waltke-O'Connor, § 39.3.4d, example 9). I have freely rendered it "how much worse will it be" to help bring out the sense. Since a temporal clause follows, we might have expected a second כִּי to follow: "How much worse [אַף כִּי] when [כִּי] I send … ," but just אַף כִּי is used elsewhere in a similar sense.

14:22 פְּלֵטָה—The context indicates that this refers to "a group of [unrighteous] survivors" left over after God's judgments, rather than a righteous "remnant" that is saved through faith. This noun occurs only here in Ezekiel, but related words are common: פָּלִיט, "escapee, survivor" in 6:8–9; 7:16; 24:26–27; 33:21–22 and the verb פָּלַט, "to escape," in 7:16.

הַמּוּצָאִים—This Hophal participle of יָצָא with the definite article means "who will be brought out." It modifies the following nouns בָּנִים וּבָנוֹת, so the "sons and daughters" are the ones "who will be brought out." Many commentators favor repointing it to the Hiphil participle הַמּוֹצִאִים based on the versions, which translate that the remnant/survivors will be the ones "leading out" the sons and daughters (LXX: οἱ ἐξάγουσιν; similar are the Syriac and Vulgate). The versional reading (with two groups: the survivors and the sons and daughters they lead out) has the advantage of paralleling the pattern in the hypothetical verses (14:14–20) of two groups, the three righteous men and the sons and daughters who would not be saved.

However, Greenberg probably has the better part of the argument by understanding the sons and daughters in the hypothetical verses as representing the undeserving.[18] They are ones who now turn out to be spared—but not saved (see the commentary below). That implies that the "son(s) and daughter(s)" (14:16, 18, 20, 22) are the same as the "group of survivors" (14:22). This does not contradict Yahweh's earlier assertion that he will "cut off" both man and beast (14:13, 17, 19, 21) because that can be accomplished by exile as well as by death. Understood that way, the verse makes perfect sense because it matches what certainly happened: some sur-

---

[16] See "Introduction to Ezekiel 12:21–14:11" in the commentary on chapter 12.

[17] Block, *Ezekiel*, 1:441.

[18] Greenberg, *Ezekiel*, 1:259.

vivors were brought out of the fallen city of Jerusalem by the Babylonians, and they came to Ezekiel's primary audience, joining the exiles at Tel Abib, thus fulfilling the following clause, יֹצְאִים אֲלֵיכֶם, "they are coming out to you."

אֶת־דַּרְכָּם וְאֶת־עֲלִילוֹתָם—These two nouns, דֶּרֶךְ and עֲלִילָה, are commonly paired (14:22–23; 20:43–44; 24:14; 36:17, 19. The first, often translated "way," is slightly more comprehensive in meaning, implying, as it does, not only actions, but the motivation or orientation underlying them. No wonder the first Christians called themselves followers of "the Way" (ὁδός, Acts 9:2)! I have translated it "behavior" here. Less common is עֲלִילָה, which can refer to any kind of "deed" (BDB, 2), but often elsewhere, and always in Ezekiel,[b] it has a pejorative sense and the plural refers to "evil deeds" (BDB, 2 c). Jeremiah never uses עֲלִילָה but prefers (eighteen times) its cognate and synonym, מַעֲלָל, which he almost always uses in a negative sense of "evil deed(s)."

(b) Ezek 14:22–23; 20:43–44; 21:29 (ET 21:24); 24:14; 36:17, 19

וְנִחַמְתֶּם—The meaning of the Niphal of נָחַם here is clear enough: "be comforted, consoled," as in, e.g., Gen 24:67; 38:12. The Piel of נָחַם beginning 14:23 (וְנִחֲמוּ) also is clear: "and they will console." The problem is one of interpretation (see the commentary below). As with many Hebrew verbs, the Niphal is the passive (or reflexive) of the Piel, especially when the Qal is not used. In older English translations, the Niphal was often confusingly translated "repent" even with God as subject. The Bible does speak of God "relenting" from executing judgment for various reasons, especially because of the satisfaction of his justice, ultimately accomplished by Jesus Christ, and the Niphal of נָחַם is often used in such OT contexts.

עַל־הָרָעָה—Here the nuance is hardly "evil," since Yahweh brought this on Israel, but something like "disaster," as I have rendered it. Compare the adjective רָעָה for the "wild" animals in 14:15, 21.

אֵת כָּל־אֲשֶׁר—The direct object marker אֵת can be used, as here, "before a noun [here כֹּל, 'everything'] in apposition to a noun with a preposition [עַל־הָרָעָה, 'concerning the disaster']" (Joüon, § 125 j 1). Thus "everything that I brought upon it" is in apposition to "the disaster" earlier in the verse. Critics often emend אֵת to אֶל, which can be equivalent in meaning to עַל, but there is no problem with the MT. The repetition of the verb "I brought" (הֵבֵאתִי ... הֵבֵאתִי) is parallel to the repetition of "I did" (עָשִׂיתִי ... עָשִׂיתִי) in the next verse (14:23).

Commentary

As noted earlier, 14:1–11 has affinities with chapter 13 since it too discusses abuses of prophecy.[19] Probably the reason for the chapter division at 14:1 is that the first section of the chapter (14:1–11) is addressed to the elders who came to the prophet (cf. the chapter division at 8:1, where elders have come to Ezekiel). While 14:1–8 concerns hypocrites who inquire of a true

---

[19] See "Introduction to Ezekiel 12:21–14:11" in the commentary on chapter 12. At one time, critical scholars generally dismissed Ezek 14:1–11 as inauthentic. However, Zimmerli, *Ezekiel*, 1:305–6, has defended the genuineness and unity of the section, and today a large measure of agreement with his basic position will be found among critical scholars.

prophet, 14:9–11 addresses false prophecy, and so it is most similar to chapter 13, which was about false prophets and prophetesses.

In form and style, however, chapter 14 differs markedly from chapter 13. This chapter is usually described as reminiscent of case law (laws of casuistry) in the Torah and hence "quasi-legal" or the like. If we can hear the label without immediately thinking "legalism," canon law would be the ecclesiastical counterpart, remembering that Israel was a theocracy and hence was both church and state at the same time. Casuistic laws predominate in the so-called "Book of the Covenant" (Ex 20:22–23:19), but they also appear throughout the legal portions of the Pentateuch. In form as well as particulars of vocabulary, Ezek 14:1–11 has much in common with Leviticus 17, the first chapter of the so-called "Holiness Code" (Leviticus 17–26), which, in general, has had a pronounced effect on the writing style and thought of Ezekiel, a priest (Ezek 1:3).

Typically the casuistic law form speaks hypothetically in the third person, for example, "If/when a man ..." Usually the case under discussion forms the protasis, introduced by a conjunction such as כִּי (14:9, 13), אוֹ (14:17, 19), or אִם, each of which might be translated as "when," "if," or "or" depending on the context. Then follows an apodosis describing the consequences. As this chapter will illustrate, however, there may be many variations on this basic form.

The chapter contains four cases of casuistry, arranged in two pairs:

I. Cases involving prophecy (14:1–11)
   A. When an idolater inquires of Yahweh (14:1–8)
   B. When a prophet is misled (14:9–11)

II. When Yahweh sends his four judgments on a land (14:12–23)
   A. If Noah, Daniel, and Job were in the land (14:12–20)
   B. How much worse it will be for Jerusalem (14:21–23)

Cases Involving Prophecy (14:1–11)

When an Idolater Inquires of Yahweh (14:1–8)

14:1 In contrast to chapter 8, where a similar delegation had come to Ezekiel's house, the group here is not called "the elders of Judah" (8:1) but "men from the elders of Israel" (14:1). The change is probably deliberate: "Israel" is the proper term for the theocracy, and case laws such as those in this chapter are stipulations of God for his kingdom. This accent is confirmed by the prominence of "Israel" a total of eight times in 14:1–11 (including "house of Israel" five times and "my people Israel" in 14:9).

We are not told explicitly why these elders had come. When we meet them again in 20:1, Ezekiel specifies that they came לִדְרֹשׁ אֶת־יְהוָה, "to consult/inquire of Yahweh." That vocabulary will also be used in chapter 14 (דָּרַשׁ, "consult/inquire," in 14:3, 7, 10). Therefore we may assume that the elders had asked some question, which is not recorded. That the elders were awaiting an answer is probably indicated by the statement that they "sat down in front of" Ezekiel

(14:1). Other uses of that phrase seem to imply some sort of official audience or meeting (so in 2 Ki 4:38; 6:32; cf. Num 22:8).

14:3 The reason why Yahweh does not answer their question emerges: God has read their minds and sees that their hearts are still full of idolatrous thoughts; their faith is at least partially in their fecal deities. We are not told whether these were old false gods they had brought along (at least in their hearts) from Jerusalem or new, syncretistic deities adopted from their Babylonian milieu, but that is really beside the point.

The implied answer to the rhetorical question is obviously negative: with their hearts still attached to other gods, Yahweh cannot and will not hear their prayer or respond to their inquiry. Yahweh rebukes the presumptiveness of the elders who think otherwise by referring to them rather disdainfully as "these men." They may be elders of Israel, but they are not sons of Israel in its theological sense.

Ezek 14:3 is obviously addressed to Ezekiel alone, and without the address to him as "son of man," it could pass for Yahweh's own soliloquy. The prophet has become, as it were, Yahweh's confidant as Yahweh considers how he shall respond, if at all, to such seekers.

Some commentators interpret the reference to idols as "on [עַל] their heart" and "in front of their faces" as implying concrete amulets or tattoos on the elders' bodies. The first term for idols, "fecal deities" (see the textual note on גִּלּוּל in 6:4), lends itself more readily to such an understanding than "stumbling block" (מִכְשׁוֹל). More likely, the phrases refer to some sort of "fine idolatry" in the heart and mind, as the LXX probably intends to imply (see the textual note). Although material images were more common in ancient idolatry than in modern apostasy, the real problem was internal, not in any physical realm.

14:4 Yahweh now directs Ezekiel to answer the elders for him, as indicated by the citation formula, delayed until now: "thus says the Lord Yahweh." The prophet is to speak using the casuistic law form of the Torah (see especially Leviticus 17), implicitly invoking its authority to emphasize his response. The use of legal language transforms the scene into that of a suit against those who would inquire of Yahweh. They must answer to him, not he to them.

14:5 The real problem is in the straying hearts of the elders and of the people they represent. Human laws cannot adjudicate what is in people's hearts, but God's laws do, for example, "you shall not covet" (Ex 20:17). See also Jesus' explication of the Decalogue in terms of what is in the heart in Matthew 5–6. Only God knows the content of the heart. Yahweh speaks his answer to the idolater through his prophet, and the answer echoes the case laws in the Torah. The prophetic Word exposes the deities in the idolaters' hearts so that God "may catch the house of Israel by what is in their heart." They must be caught red-handed, as it were, for the people to see that God is just and fair, and that their sin is not hidden from him. God's Law in the deeper, theological sense is operative.

14:6 The transitional לָכֵן ("therefore") introduces the second announcement of judgment that leads initially into an urgent call to repentance. Logically, it follows from 14:5b: because "all of them have alienated themselves" from the true God, they must be reconciled with him again. The urgency is expressed by a threefold repetition of שׁוּב, a common verb for "repent" or "return [to God]." The Qal imperative, "repent," is followed by two Hiphil imperatives, "turn away" from the idols. These imperatives underscore how deliberative an action the people's repentance must be, and one directly antithetical to their posture described in 14:3–5.

Superficially, this language poses theological difficulties. All descendants of Adam are by nature "dead in trespasses and sins" (Eph 2:1) and cannot by themselves repent, turn away from their idols, and turn back to God and thus live. God, working through his Word and Sacraments, raises the spiritually dead to life. For an Israelite, that vivifying work normally began with circumcision on the eighth day, just as for a NT believer it would begin with Baptism. Yet in some cases Israelites first heard God's Word, which led to their circumcision as adults, just as the NT narrates conversion through hearing the Gospel, which then led to Baptism into Christ.[20]

People do not of their own volition "make decisions for Christ" or decide to be "born again"; only God the Holy Spirit can move people to repent and create in their hearts faith in God, the only Savior. Yet the Scriptures (both the OT and NT) often issue calls for repentance and faith. Perhaps the apparent contradiction is best resolved by thinking of "two languages," that of our own limited, subjective experience or consciousness, and that of God himself. In this, as in many other respects, it is part of God's gracious condescension that he deigns to speak to us in language we can understand. The instructed and regenerate Christian knows that his experience is not a reliable basis for understanding what and how the Holy Spirit works within him; God's Word gives the trustworthy and accurate revelation of how conversion takes place.[21]

One might also perceive a problem in the immediate context because Yahweh's reply might be taken to contradict his rhetorical question in 14:3, "Should I let them consult me at all?" The implied negative answer to that question suggests that he would refuse to answer the apostate elders' inquiry, but now he rebukes the people (which is the kind of "answer" he promises in 14:4, 7). His reproof through the prophet might also be taken as a contradiction of his explanation of the reason for the prophet's speechlessness: "you will not be to

---

[20] Regarding God's Word and Sacraments, see "Our Christian Method of Interpretation" in the introduction, and "Ezekiel's Action Prophecies" and the following commentary on 4:1–3. For an example of Israelites who were circumcised as adults and for an exposition of the relationship between the OT rites of circumcision and the Passover and the NT Sacraments of Baptism and the Lord's Supper, one may see the commentary on Josh 5:2–3 and 5:10–12 in Harstad, *Joshua*, 224–27 and 240–44.

[21] For summaries of the biblical portrayal of repentance and the role of the human will, see, for example, AC XII; Ap XII; FC SD II.

them a man who reproves" (3:26). The solution to these apparent contradictions lies in the fact that there is both Law and Gospel in the situation. God is reminding Israel of its own responsibility for its faithlessness (Law), but his prophetic call for his people to repent emphasizes that Israel's willing faithfulness is his deepest desire, and by his gracious working at least a remnant will be saved (Gospel). Thus, he "opens the door just a crack to a new future for the immediate audience."[22]

14:7 Yahweh here returns to the realities of the situation: no matter how fervently he may desire Israel's repentance, he must deal with their present apostasy. To alienate themselves from him and then to inquire of him is an affront. Therefore, he will "answer" the apostates, but not in any way they hope. His rejoinder may not necessarily be verbal. Like ἀποκρίνομαι ("answer") in the NT (e.g., Mt 11:25; 17:4), the Hebrew עָנָה ("answer") does not have to be a direct reply to a prior question; often it implies some kind of response (verbal or otherwise) to a situation. God declares, "I, Yahweh, will give an answer to him myself [בִּי]," that is, in his own way, in accordance with his own nature, and directly, without any intermediary. The next verse spells out some details.

14:8 Four aspects of God answering in judgment are given. First, "I will set my face against that man" obviously implies hostility. This is a stronger expression than the so-called hostile orientation formula, "Behold, I am against (you) …"[c] The expression here must be understood as an action prophecy like previous ones where Ezekiel, representing Yahweh, was to "direct" or "set" his "face" toward the model of Jerusalem (4:3, 7) and Israel's mountains (6:2) and prophesy against them. Here Yahweh's hostile reaction corresponds to the idolatry of the people who "put their iniquitous stumbling block in front of their faces" (14:3; similarly 14:4, 7). The hostile sense of the clause contrasts with other OT idioms that describe God looking with favor upon his people.[23]

(c) Ezek 5:8; 13:8, 20; 21:8 (ET 21:3); 26:3; 28:22; 29:3, 10; 30:22; 34:10; 35:3; 36:9; 38:3; 39:1

Second, Yahweh will make them a "sign" (אוֹת). This word is often loaded (see the textual notes and commentary on 4:3). Here it apparently means "warning" or "lesson." Similarly, Aaron's sprouted rod was to be preserved as a "sign" (אוֹת) to the rebels that the house of Levi was the elected one (Num 17:25 [ET 17:10]). In this instance, the typological import that the word often carries is not present, but such a construal would be defensible: the judgment against such an apostate is a type of the judgment against apostate humanity that Christ

---

[22] Block, *Ezekiel*, 1:428, citing H. W. Wolff, "Das Thema 'Umkehr' in der alttestamentlichen Prophetie," *ZTK* 48 (1951): 129–48. The alternation of weal and woe is a characteristic of Ezekiel and all prophetic books; see "Outline and Theological Emphases" in the introduction.

[23] For example, God lifts up his face (נָשָׂא פָּנִים) in Num 6:26 and shows favor (נְשָׂא פָנִים) to people in Gen 19:21. Other expressions for God showing favor can use the verb רָצָה ("show favor"; Niphal: "be accepted, graciously received") and/or the derivative noun רָצוֹן ("favor, acceptance"), especially in contexts of sacrifice (e.g., Lev 1:3–4; 19:5; 22:19–21). Block, *Ezekiel*, 1:430, wrongly suggests that the phrase in Ezek 14:8 may be a deliberate contrast to שִׂים פָּנִים עַל, which he says is absent from Ezekiel. However, that phrase is present in Ezek 29:2 and 35:2 and connotes hostility.

suffered vicariously on the cross, and also a type of the everlasting judgment that God will administer on the Last Day upon all sinners who would presume upon God's grace without repentance (contrition and faith in Christ).

Third, partly parallel to "sign" (אוֹת) is "byword" (מָשָׁל). The name of that Israelite would become a shorthand for anyone who had deservedly borne God's judgment.[24] Within the Bible, "Sodom"[d] and "Babylon"[e] are examples of place names that have become infamous for the sinful behavior they typified and proverbial for the judgment God poured out on them. Likewise, "Judas" typifies betrayal of Christ and eternal perdition.

The fourth and climactic aspect of judgment is Yahweh's declaration, "I will cut him off from among my people." Similar statements about an offender being "cut off from his kinsmen" (e.g., Gen 17:14; Ex 31:14; Lev 7:20–21) are common in the Pentateuch, and the passive voice (Niphal of כָּרַת) usually has the implication of divine agency. In Lev 17:10 and 20:3, 5–6 we find very close parallels to the formulation of the idiom here: Yahweh uses the active verb (Hiphil of כָּרַת), "I will cut him off," and the singular עַם, "from the midst of his people," instead of the more common plural ("kinsmen"). These are the only verses in the Torah where God uses the active verb in this idiom. The offenses are all in contexts of idolatry and include the eating of blood (Lev 17:10), the sacrifice of children to Molech (Lev 20:3, 5), and the use of mediums or occult practices (Lev 20:6). Some of these offenses would be secret or outside the jurisdiction of human tribunals; Lev 20:4–5 deals with a situation in which an idolater who sacrifices his child(ren) to Molech is not prosecuted or punished by any human authority. Hence that resembles the contemporary situation with abortion, which is tolerated in many modern societies, but which nonetheless is the murder of children, and whose practitioners will be judged by God.[25]

Ezek 14:8, like many of the Torah verses, does not state exactly how the offender would be cut off, but "from among my people" (and "from his kinsmen" in many Torah passages) suggests that, at the very least, "excommunication" (to use the Christian counterpart) was involved. Sometimes the context suggests something even stronger, such as these parallels: "I will destroy him from among my people Israel" (Ezek 14:9). The one who sacrifices his child to Molech "shall certainly be put to death. The people of the land shall stone him with stones" (Lev 20:2). "I will exterminate that person from the midst of his people" (Lev 23:30). In all these cases, God's judgment has an eschatological dimension. Whether physical (capital punishment administered by Israel) or purely spiritual (excommunication in Israel or the church), the divine

(d) E.g., Deut 29:23; Is 1:9–10; Ezek 16:46–56; Mt 11:23–24; 2 Pet 2:6; Jude 7; Rev 11:8

(e) E.g., 1 Pet 5:13; Rev 14:8; 17:5; 18:2

---

[24] A rough parallel from the Cold War would be "Finlandization," where the country's name was used to describe any neighbor of the Soviet Union that was intimidated into a neutral, if not servile, stance as the price of independence.

[25] Kleinig, *Leviticus*, 442, states that "abortion is the closest modern equivalent to the Canaanite practice of parents sacrificing their children to the god Molech."

judgment executed during this life portends the eternal judgment and damnation on the Last Day. However, excommunication has the goal that the offender may be brought to repentance, be restored to communion with the church, and so "be saved on the Day of the Lord" (1 Cor 5:4–5).[26]

Against such a backdrop, the recognition formula, "then you will know that I am Yahweh" (Ezek 14:8), is like the tolling of a bell that takes on a terrible urgency.

When a Prophet Is Misled (14:9–11)

14:9 Ezekiel here moves on to a second case about prophecy that is related to the previous ruling about two-faced "seekers" (14:1–8), whom Yahweh refuses to answer through a (true) prophet, since he will answer them directly in judgment. In 14:9–11 the question is what to do "if a prophet is misled and utters a prophecy," that is, if a (false) prophet *does* give an answer to such idolatrous petitioners.

The textual notes on 14:9 observed that the passive verb translated "misled" leaves open what that prophet's motives might be. He might, indeed, be simply venal, or he might be trying to capitalize on the people's fears by proclaiming a phony peace (cf. 13:10). Out of ordinary human weakness, he may have simply allowed himself to be flattered into believing that he does indeed speak God's word. The "word" might not even have been an oracle of his own invention or a false prophecy "inspired" in him by an evil spirit (e.g., 1 Ki 22:19–23). Perhaps he merely repeats what he heard another would-be prophet say or articulates the (spoken or unspoken) hopes of the people.

Regardless of the source or motives , the spoken "prophecy" is the wrong word for the occasion. It is another "gospel" when "the Law" and "the Gospel" were required. It may be anything that, instead of requiring repentance and instilling faith, simply confirmed the sinner in his self-righteous security. Eichrodt summarizes quite nicely: such a "prophet" "lets himself be induced by the wish to please or by a calculated compromise … treating his client's deadly crime as if it were a venial weakness."[27]

The situation described in the protasis is an all-too-familiar one throughout the history of the church every bit as much as throughout the history of Israel. Every conscientious pastor is well aware of the constant temptation to say and do what the people will like (and hence what will bring him praise and promotion), and not to risk losing prospects or members by proclaiming "the whole counsel of God" (Acts 20:27). While God's Law is perennially offensive, it can be made to sound appealing in the form of moralism or certain kinds of legalism, but nothing is so offensive to human pride as the scandal of the cross—Christ crucified (see, e.g., 1 Cor 1:18–31).

---

26 On this goal of excommunication, see Lockwood, *1 Corinthians*, 164–70, 180–86.

27 Eichrodt, *Ezekiel*, 183.

The real shocker comes in the apodosis: "I, Yahweh, have misled that prophet"! We shall meet a similar, but even stronger assertion of God's *opus alienum* ("alien work" of judging sinners; cf. Is 28:21) in Ezek 20:25–26, where God says that he gave Israel "statues that were not good" so that he might "devastate them" (see the commentary there). The teaching that God intervenes in human "freedom" in order to punish is not peculiar to Ezekiel, but it does receive its most drastic expression there.

Major parallels to 14:9 appear in Jeremiah's autobiographical statements. In Jer 4:10 Jeremiah asserts that Yahweh has "completely deceived" (Hiphil of נָשָׁא) his people by promising them security when in fact they shall come under attack. Jeremiah seems to attribute to Yahweh himself the assurances of peace spoken in Yahweh's name by false prophets. In Jer 20:7, Jeremiah makes this accusation because of God's delay in executing the judgments Jeremiah had prophesied: "You deceived me, Yahweh, and I was deceived" (the Piel and Niphal of פָּתָה, the same verb as in Ezek 14:9).

Naturally, the commentary discussion on passages such as these tends to be long and often tortured because the passages appear to make God the author of evil. The easy way out is to dismiss such statements as expressing what God allows, not what he causes, but that is not what the text says, nor is it clear that that dodge exculpates God. Keil overstates somewhat but is essentially correct in asserting, "The Fathers and earlier Lutheran theologians are wrong in their interpretation of פִּתֵּיתִי ['I have misled,' Ezek 14:9], which they understand in a permissive sense, meaning simply that God allowed it, and did not prevent their [the false prophets] being seduced."[28] Even more simplistic than taking the text in a permissive sense is Cooke's explanation "that ancient habits of thought overlooked secondary causes, and attributed events directly to the action of God."[29]

(f) Ex 4:21; 9:12; 10:1, 20, 27; 11:10; 14:4, 8

Usually, the discussion turns to the illuminating episode recorded in 1 Ki 22:19–23. In Micaiah's famous vision of Yahweh in his heavenly throne room, Yahweh asks, "Who will deceive Ahab?" One of the "spirits" around him volunteers, "I will deceive him. … I will be a lying spirit in the mouth of all his [Ahab's] prophets," to which Yahweh replies, "You will deceive, and you will be able; go and do so" (1 Ki 22:20–22; the verb thrice translated "deceive" is the Piel of פָּתָה, as in Ezek 14:9). That passage says nothing about punishment for Ahab's lying court prophets, probably because it was not germane to the narrative (although, if it were to be pressed, one would imagine that their comeuppance came shortly in Jehu's revolt, if not before).

(g) Ex 7:13, 22; 8:15 (ET 8:19); 9:35

(h) Ex 8:11, 28 (ET 8:15, 32); 9:34

(i) E.g., Rom 11:7, 25; 2 Cor 3:14; Eph 4:18; Heb 3:13; 1 Jn 2:11

In a consideration of parallels, one must also recall the exodus narrative. Some passages state that Yahweh will or did "harden" Pharaoh's heart,[f] while others state that Pharaoh's heart "was hard"[g] or that Pharaoh "hardened" his own heart.[h] The NT too speaks of God's obduration,[i] which remains a legiti-

---

[28] Keil, *Ezekiel*, 1:182.

[29] Cooke, *Ezekiel*, 151.

mate, if sometimes minor, topic in classical Christian dogmatics.[30] Any pastor can attest to how much harder it often is to reclaim lapsed Christians or those alienated from the church than it is to gain new converts.

Thus that the "prophet is misled" (Ezek 14:9) is not merely a matter of divine permission (although it is that), but also of divine purpose and arrangement ("I, Yahweh, have misled that prophet"). Then those who are already deceived themselves readily become deceivers of others (whether or not they are aware of their own deception).

There is also an element of testing involved. Throughout this earthly life, the new man of faith in each believer gladly serves God by the power of the Spirit, but the believer's sinful flesh continually rebels against God (Rom 7:14–25). Only by the power of the Holy Spirit can any of us mortify the sinful flesh; otherwise, the old Adam (who only has the freedom to disbelieve, sin, and forfeit God's gift of salvation) will eventually triumph. Believers who have left the door ajar for Satan must ultimately decide (humanly speaking) whether they will use the power God offers through his means of grace to overcome the old, evil foe (and such a decision is only made with the aid of the Spirit), or whether they will allow Satan ultimately to become the undisputed master of their soul. As St. Paul says, "If you live according to the flesh, you are about to die, but if by the Spirit you put to death the deeds of the body, you will live" (Rom 8:13).

One also thinks of the close association of "test" and "tempt" (נָסָה or πειράζω), especially as we constantly articulate it in the Lord's Prayer: "Lead us not into temptation, but deliver us from evil" (Mt 6:13; cf. Lk 11:4; note that such deliverance comes from God alone). It is true indeed that God tempts no one (James 1:13), but the petition is that God will not put us to the ultimate test where we cannot stand (1 Cor 10:13).[31] St. Paul expounds Israel's temptation to idolatry as paradigmatic for the temptations faced by all Christians (1 Cor 10:1–13).

In the larger context of Ezek 14:9, "Yahweh answers insincerity with insincerity. ... By giving the people lying prophets, who proclaim to the people exactly what they want to hear, Yahweh ensures the people's judgment."[32] But as the last verse (14:11) of this case of casuistry will emphasize, "God's immediate punitive purpose has an educative final aim—to bring the errants back to him."[33] And the counterpart to God's "final judgment" here ("I will destroy him from among my people Israel" [14:9]) is the eschatological judgment imposed on Christ, Israel reduced to one, who was "destroyed" (cf. Mt 12:14; 26:61; 27:20, 40), thereby redeeming all humanity from all sin. All in him (OT

---

[30] See, for example, FC SD XI, especially § 83; Pieper, *Christian Dogmatics*, 3:473–503.

[31] See SC, Lord's Prayer, 18.

[32] Block, *Ezekiel*, 1:434–35, also citing (in n. 71) a comparable "poetic justice" in 2 Sam 22:26–27 ‖ Ps 18:26–27 (ET 18:25–26).

[33] Greenberg, *Ezekiel*, 1:255.

and NT believers alike) comprise the true Israel of God and receive the promise and gift of a "new heart" and a "new spirit" (Ezek 11:19–20; 36:26–27). In NT language, they have become new creations in Christ and have been raised with Christ to eternal life (cf. Rom 6:1–11; 2 Cor 5:17).

"Great is the mystery of godliness" (1 Tim 3:16), but there is also a "mystery of lawlessness" (2 Thess 2:7) to be reckoned with. (See also the commentary on Ezek 20:25–26.)

14:10 As Yahweh will "cut off" (14:8; cf. 14:13, 17, 19, 21) the idolater who inquires of the false prophet, so he will also "destroy" the "prophet" who "is misled and utters a prophecy" (14:9). "The punishment of the inquirer will be like the punishment of the prophet" (14:10) because the prophet has allowed himself to be an accomplice of the same unfaithfulness as the idolatrous client. Also in Lev 19:8 and 20:17, the excommunication formula ("that person/they shall be cut off") is accompanied by "he shall bear his iniquity/punishment," a clause that "implies certain retribution and has an eschatological dimension."[34] The noun עָוֹן can refer either to "iniquity" or to "punishment" for it, but in these passages, taken in the context of all Scripture, the emphasis is more on the eschatological "punishment" that both the idolater and the false prophet will bear throughout eternity (unless they repent before Judgment Day) than on their "iniquity" committed during earthly life.

14:11 The long diatribe (12:21–14:11) against false prophets and the abuse of true prophets ends on a beautiful note of Gospel. Weal following woe is a pattern we have noted before in Ezekiel and will note again.[35] Yahweh has no pleasure in the death of the wicked (18:23, a theme that chapter 18 will consider at length). Two "never again" statements will be followed by a positive one. The two "never again" statements, "so that the house of Israel will never again stray … and they will never again defile themselves," indicate that Yahweh is speaking of the realm of the eschatological, when we believers will no longer be *simul iustus et peccator* ("sinner and saint simultaneously"), but only *iustus* (saints in glory), risen bodily with Christ and beyond the present estate of temptation, sin, and death.

First, the redeemed will no longer "stray" like sheep (Is 53:6), constantly distracted by other gods and false gospels. Preachers who cater to our sinful, selfish desires will no longer receive a hearing. The Hebrew has "stray from [following] after me [מֵאַחֲרִי]," which evokes not only the picture of forsaking the Good Shepherd, but more specifically of forsaking the marriage covenant, anticipating the covenant language at the end of the verse. The same combination of prepositions is used in Hos 1:2, where Yahweh declares, "The land greatly whores [זָנָה] from after Yahweh [מֵאַחֲרֵי יְהוָה]," that is, goes a-whoring and so no longer follows after him. Hos 4:12 (literally, "a spirit of whoredom

---

[34] Kleinig, *Leviticus*, 106, commenting on that clause in Lev 5:1. See also the commentary on Ezek 4:4.

[35] See "Outline and Theological Emphases" in the introduction.

has caused them to stray, and they have whored from under their God") uses a similar prepositional phrase with זָנָה, "to whore," and the same verb תָּעָה, "to stray," as in Ezek 14:11. Ps 106:39 (literally, "they became defiled by their works, and they whored with their deeds") combines זָנָה, "to whore," with the same verb טָמֵא, "to be defiled," as in Ezek 14:11.

Second, the verb טָמֵא in "they will never again *defile themselves* with all their rebellious actions" is common in Leviticus (see the textual note) and reflects Ezekiel's priestly background (1:3). By his language in chapter 14, Ezekiel is giving his people a new Torah, a new covenant that will, in God's good time, be written on their hearts (the "new covenant/testament" prophesied in Jer 31:31–34). Following the verb "defile themselves" (טָמֵא) comes the strong noun "rebellion" (פֶּשַׁע, Ezek 14:11), often used of political insurrection against human lords to whom fealty had been sworn, but here it is against the Lord of life himself. No sins are mere peccadilloes, and especially not sexual ones, which involve the body, as our membership in the body of Christ also does (1 Cor 6:15–20).

Finally comes the positive promise, expressed in the words of the classical covenant formula, with its roots in the language of marriage and adoption (see Ezek 16:8): "They will be my people, and I will be their God" (see the commentary on 11:20, the first passage where Ezekiel employs that formula). It encompasses the full, undiluted dimensions of what it means to have Yahweh (that is, Jesus!) as our God, and, in turn, the full depths of the fact that we have been adopted as *his* people and are joined more closely to him than in Eden: "YHWH and the people are once again joined, as at the beginning, by a bond of mutual allegiance."[36]

The closing signatory formula ("says the Lord Yahweh") highlights the promise further.

When Yahweh Sends His Four Judgments on a Land (14:12–23)

The word-event formula ("the Word of Yahweh came to me," 14:12) and the address of the prophet as a creature ("son of man"; see the textual notes and commentary on 2:1) signal the beginning of an entirely different section of the book. A new chapter might well begin here. The section on false prophecy has ended (12:21–14:11),[37] and the prophet returns to the main theme of chapters 4–24: the inevitability of God's judgment on Jerusalem.

Perhaps the reason why a chapter break was not made here is that 14:12–23 continues with the same type of cultic case law as in 14:1–11, as evidenced in the initial case, literally, "a land, when …" (אֶרֶץ כִּי, 14:13) and by the repeated "or" (אוֹ, 14:17, 19). But the continuity is only formal: the subject is not human crimes against God (14:1–11), but four divine judgments. The language is heavily dependent on the covenant curses for Israel's disobedience, especially

---

[36] Greenberg, *Ezekiel*, 1:255.
[37] See "Introduction to Ezekiel 12:21–14:11" in the commentary on chapter 12.

Leviticus 26. Those same covenant curses were the background of Ezek 4:10–11, 16–17; chapters 5–6; and 12:19–20. The same four judgments in 14:12–23 were set forth in 5:16–17 (and three of them in 5:12; 6:11–12; 7:15; 12:16).

In many respects the remainder of chapter 14 might be joined to chapter 15 as one chapter, although the similarity may not be immediately obvious. In contrast to 14:12–23, chapter 15 is parabolic in nature. Although there is no reason to deny that they were originally independent oracles, they have enough in common that it seems they have been deliberately linked editorially, most likely by Ezekiel's own hand. They both begin with a theoretical situation, followed by a direct application to Jerusalem, and in both cases the transition is made by the citation formula, "thus says the Lord Yahweh" (14:21; 15:6). Stylistically, they both use these three expressions: (1) "how much worse/less" (אַף כִּי, 14:21 and 15:5);[38] (2) "faithlessly doing infidelity" (מָעַל מַעַל, 14:13 and 15:8); and (3) "desolation" (שְׁמָמָה, 14:15–16 and 15:8).

If Noah, Daniel, and Job Were in the Land (14:12–20)

Ezek 14:12–20 presents four hypothetical cases that each emphasize the same doctrine of divine retribution. Each case involves a divine agent of judgment: "famine" in 14:13–14; "wild animals" in 14:15–16; "sword" in 14:17–18; and "plague" in 14:19–20. Also in 14:19 is "bloodshed," which might possibly represent a fifth agent, murder through human violence, or it could represent death from the plague or be a corollary of the preceding case with the "sword." Since Ezekiel elsewhere favors the number four (see the textual notes and commentary on 1:6 and 7:1–4), most likely each of the four cases here should be understood to involve just one primary judgment. That is confirmed by 14:21, where Yahweh expressly lists "four" judgments, in the order of "sword, famine, wild beasts, and plague" (no "bloodshed" is included there).

Three of the four judgments here were in 5:12 ("plague," "famine," and "sword"). While 5:2, 12 pointed to three main judgments, the end of chapter 5 listed the same four (or five) as in 14:12–20: "famine and wild animals … plague and bloodshed … the sword" (5:17).

Jer 15:1–3 is similar to Ezek 14:12–20 in that Yahweh first declares that even if Moses and Samuel interceded, the people would not escape judgment (cf. Noah, Daniel, and Job in Ezek 14:14, 20). Then Yahweh lists four fates ("death," "sword," "famine," and "exile," Jer 15:2) and "four" means of death, "the sword to kill," "dogs to maul," "and the birds of the heavens and the beasts of the earth to eat and destroy" (Jer 15:3).

This oracle is even more tightly structured. Each of the four cases begins with phrases describing the scourge; then comes a statement of the inability of three righteous persons to save anyone's life but their own; and toward the end

---

[38] These are the only two times Ezekiel uses this idiom. (וְאַף כִּי in 23:40 has a different meaning.)

is the signatory formula ("says the Lord Yahweh"), in all but one instance also preceded by the oath formula ("as I live"). Even so, no two of the four examples are entirely alike.

No date is given for the oracle, but the subject matter is similar to that of chapter 18, where the topic receives extensive treatment. The topic is God's justice or fairness, which apostate Israelites were questioning in their desperate attempt to evade the judgment by any means but repentance.

14:13 The case-law pattern followed in all four examples is established immediately. All four cases are "when a land sins against me by faithlessly doing infidelity" (14:13), although that precipitating cause of the divine judgment is stated only here, at the beginning of the first case. The hypothetical land could be any land. Although the reader would readily guess that the prophet has the land of Israel in mind, that is not specified here. However, elsewhere in the OT the cognate accusative phrase מַעַל מַעַל ("faithlessly doing infidelity") always has an Israelite subject. Since the phrase refers not only to faithless behavior in general, but specifically to violations of things holy to Yahweh, it technically can be used only of offenders who at least nominally confess Yahweh (as clearly is the case in the preceding context, 14:1–11). When Yahweh applies the passage (14:12–20) later in 14:21–23, it is specifically to Jerusalem and the Israelites. Hence, the heinous perfidy implied by the phrase hangs over the rest of the chapter.

Yahweh's reaction to the infidelity is first described in a general phrase that is then illustrated in the four more specific scenarios that follow. He describes his first reaction to the infidelity as "I stretch out my hand against" the land. The same phraseology was in 6:14 (against the nation) and 14:9 (against a false prophet) and will recur later.[j] This phraseology is especially common in the exodus narrative, where Yahweh (or his agents, Moses and/or Aaron) stretched out his hand against Egypt in the form of the ten plagues and to enable Israel to cross the Red Sea, in which the Egyptians drowned.[k] Here Yahweh's "hand" of judgment results in famine, and the passage may imply that his hand is also manifest in the three other specific scenarios that will follow. Likewise, the general language of famine and breaking the staff of bread was met earlier in Ezek 5:16, echoing the curse in Lev 26:26 for breaking the covenant.

14:14 The second half of the compound protasis follows by adducing three paragons of righteousness. Continuing the generality of the formulation, at least two of the three worthies predate the exodus (fifteenth century B.C.) and thus are not "Israelite" in the later sense of the term (referring to the established nation). Perhaps the triad had a fixed, proverbial reputation.

Noah is well-known as the builder of the ark, in which his family alone was saved from the worldwide deluge, and 1 Pet 3:20–21 applies that typologically to salvation, conferred through Holy Baptism. In Gen 6:8–9 Noah is described as one who "found favor/grace in the eyes of Yahweh" and with the terms "righteous" (צַדִּיק), corresponding to the abstract noun "righteousness" here (צְדָקָה, Ezek 14:14, 20), and the synonym "blameless" (תָּמִים, Gen 6:9).

(j) Ezek 16:27; 25:7, 13, 16; 35:3; cf. 20:33–34

(k) Ex 7:5, 19; 8:1, 2, 13 (ET 8:5, 6, 17); 9:22; 10:12, 21, 22; 14:16, 21, 26, 27

Outside of Genesis 5–10 and here in Ezek 14:14, 20, Noah is mentioned elsewhere in the OT only in the chronicler's genealogy (1 Chr 1:4) and with specific reference to the flood in Is 54:9. St. Luke recognizes him as an ancestor of Jesus Christ (Lk 3:36), who refers to the universal flood in Noah's day as a type of the final judgment, which will take place at his return (Mt 24:37–39 ‖ Lk 17:26–27). The NT also names Noah in the catalog of saints by faith (Heb 11:7) and accords him the title "herald of righteousness" (2 Pet 2:5).

Modern scholars sometimes point out that the name "Noah" appears as the divine element of theophoric Amorite names in the Middle Bronze Age (nineteenth to eighteenth centuries B.C.). That observation is useful to counter critics who doubt the antiquity of the name, even though Ezekiel would not have had such personages in mind. Equally irrelevant are the other flood traditions known from the ancient Near East with various names for the survivor; all those myths probably represent garbled memories of the historical event accurately recorded in Genesis.

Job, listed third, is described elsewhere in the OT with the same kind of terms as Noah. He was "blameless and upright" (תָּם וְיָשָׁר, Job 1:1), "righteous and blameless" (צַדִּיק תָּמִים, Job 12:4).[39] In Job 27:6 he defends his own "righteousness" (צְדָקָה), the same term as in Ezek 14:14, 20. His name too is ancient, found in the Egyptian execration texts of ca. 2000 B.C., and frequently thereafter in the second millennium. Job's cultural milieu is usually described as "patriarchal." Like Abraham, Isaac, and Jacob, Job served as paterfamilias or priest for his family (Job 1:5), so he obviously predates the establishment of the priesthood and the tabernacle in Exodus. Outside of his book and Ezek 14:14, 20, Job is mentioned in the Scriptures only in James 5:10–11 as a paragon of endurance through suffering until the accomplishment of the Lord's gracious purpose or end (τέλος).

There is no certainty where Job's homeland, Uz, was located, and the language of the poetic bulk of the book varies enough from classical Hebrew that guesses about its precise date of composition and geographical provenance range virtually all over the horizon. The book has no real parallels in any literature. A composition often called the "Babylonian Job" from the last half of the second millennium is well-known, and there are scores of ancient Near Eastern complaints about perceived unfair treatment by the gods, but their "parallels" to Job are quite superficial.

Most debate turns on the identification of the "Daniel" mentioned here in Ezek 14:14, 20. As far as I know, until the rise of higher criticism, no one thought of anyone but the author of the sixth-century B.C. biblical book that bears his name. That "Daniel" was a fellow Israelite exile in Babylon who was contemporaneous with Ezekiel.

---

[39] In 12:4 Job with irony contrasts his friends' view of him as a laughingstock with his own estimation that he remains "righteous and blameless." Other passages that use derivatives of צדק to refer to Job as righteous (whether in fact or just in his own eyes) include 8:6; 9:15, 20; 10:15; 13:18; 29:14; 32:1–2; 34:5; 35:2, 7; 40:8.

When suspicions about the Daniel in Ezekiel did arise after the so-called Enlightenment, they initially could only be speculative. Thus Keil, writing almost a century and a half ago, could simply assert, "The fact that Daniel is named before Job does not warrant the conjecture that some other older Daniel is meant, of whom nothing is said in the history, and whose existence is merely postulated."[40] Suspicions might have arisen from the shorter spelling of his name according to the Kethib in the Hebrew text here, and also from the assertion in Ezek 28:2–3 that the king of Tyre thought of himself as a god and as (or was?) "wiser than Daniel."[41] There is also a Dan'el in the intertestamental book of *Jubilees* (4:20) who is described as the uncle and father-in-law of the antedeluvian Enoch. (*1 Enoch* 6:7 also speaks of another Dan'el as one of the leaders of the angels who cohabited with the daughters of men in Gen 6:1–4, but he would hardly be a candidate here!)

Scholarly opinion changed after the discovery in 1929 at Ugarit (Ras Shamra in northern Canaan, today coastal Syria)[42] of Canaanite mythological texts, including the Aqhat Epic. The tablets date from the latter part of the second millennium B.C., though the myths they record probably were older. The Aqhat Epic begins with the tale of a king named Dan'el (Ugaritic *dn'il*), who has no son or heir. Dan'el prepares a feast for the gods, and the fertility god Baal pleads Dan'el's case to the Canaanite pantheon, whereupon El, the head of the pantheon, grants the petition of Dan'el, whose wife conceives and bears Aqhat, who is the main character in the epic. Twice Dan'el is described as a ruler who sat in the city gate and "judged the cause of the widow, tried the case of the orphan."[43] Based on that description, some scholars have compared him to Solomon and have argued that Dan'el was a paragon of wisdom and righteousness. However, the actual text does not portray him as such. Therefore other scholars have argued that missing parts of the fragmentary epic or perhaps other versions of the tale must have supplied depictions of him that would match those in Ezekiel.[44]

The battle lines between advocates of the canonical Daniel and proponents of an extrabiblical Daniel quickly hardened and are still somewhat intact to

---

[40] Keil, *Ezekiel*, 1:185.

[41] While English Bibles include Daniel among the Prophets, the Hebrew canon includes it among the Writings, and the book's emphasis on Daniel's wisdom (e.g., Dan 2:48; 4:15 [4:18]) accords well with Ezek 28:3 (see the commentary there).

[42] See the map in the back of this book.

[43] Aqhat Epic, 17, column 5, line 8, and Aqhat Epic, 19, column 1, lines 24–25. The translation is from Gibson, *Canaanite Myths and Legends*, 107, 114.

[44] For example, Coogan, *Stories from Ancient Canaan*, 27, argues that the Daniel in Ezek 14:14, 20; 28:3 is to be identified as Dan'el, but Coogan concedes that "the three fragmentary tablets from Ras Shamra that deal with Danel and his son do not, unfortunately, illustrate his proverbial wisdom; we must presume that other parts of the cycle, as yet undiscovered, contained episodes similar to the biblical passages that show Solomon to be the quintessentially wise king." As for the description of Dan'el judging the widow and orphan, Coogan admits that "this was the ordinary task of an Oriental monarch. … The presentation of Danel as a judge is thus evidence for his royal status, but does not imply unusual sagacity."

day. For the critics, the Ugaritic tablets' description of the ancient Canaanite king was "proof" that there was some pre-Israelite figure named Daniel (or Dan'el) to whom the biblical legend (as they viewed it) could be attached and thereby exude greater authority.

Conservatives, however, quickly pointed out that the Ugaritic king was a polytheist of the typical Canaanite variety, and he venerated the Canaanite pantheon (Baal, El, and Anat are prominent in the Aqhat Epic, in which several lesser deities also play roles). Hence, how could a strict, orthodox priest of Yahweh like Ezekiel appeal to him? Block's interpretation is typical of conservatives:

> While the hero of the Aqhat story may have gained a reputation as a just ruler, he is a pagan, worshiping a foreign god, much more at home with the Canaanites and more like Ezekiel's audience than the people of Yahweh as the prophet envisions them. To see in him an internationally renowned paragon of virtue and devotion to Yahweh is too large a leap and probably wishful thinking—a way to avoid having to deal with Ezekiel's Daniel.[45]

Thus Block argues that "Daniel" in Ezekiel refers to the prophet's contemporary, the biblical Daniel of the sixth century B.C.:

> Based on the evidence of the book of Daniel, Ezekiel's contemporary meets the internal criterion. … If the Daniel of the book by this name was indeed a historical figure, it is inconceivable that Ezekiel's audience would not have been familiar with him, and it might even be surprising if Ezekiel had never mentioned him.[46]

Anyone who calls himself a conservative will surely resonate with what Block writes. Yet, in my judgment, he slightly overstates his case. Taking a different view is not necessarily a way to avoid having to deal with Ezekiel's Daniel. There can be no quarrel that the Ugaritic Dan'el is *not* the figure to whom Ezekiel refers; all that the Canaanite epic establishes is that the name was known in high antiquity. The historicity of the canonical book of Daniel and its sixth-century date[47] cannot be called into question even if Ezekiel is referring to someone else with the same name. (There are countless biblical examples of multiple figures bearing the same name.)

Ezekiel must be referring to a Daniel who was a believer in Yahweh and an example of righteousness through faith in the one triune God, just as Noah and Job were (and so Noah is extolled as "an heir of the righteousness that

---

[45] Block, *Ezekiel*, 1:448–49.

[46] Block, *Ezekiel*, 1:449.

[47] Critical scholars commonly date the canonical book of Daniel as late as the Maccabean era (early second century B.C.) because they deny predictive prophecy and believe that Daniel 2 and 7 envision the advent of God's kingdom and the Messiah during the Greek era. However, the book itself narrates events during the exile and claims to be from that period (sixth century B.C.). The traditional Christian view of Daniel 2 and 7 is that those chapters predict the advent of God's kingdom and the Messiah during the Roman era, and that those predictions were fulfilled by the first advent of Jesus Christ.

comes by faith," Heb 11:7). That there were orthodox Yahwists[48] outside the direct lineage of Israel is shown by the example of Melchizedek, "king of Salem [Jerusalem]" and "priest of God Most High," who, although mentioned quite briefly in Gen 14:18–20, became prominent in later biblical theology as a type of Christ, the great High Priest (Ps 110:4; Hebrews 5–7). Gen 4:26 indicates that only two generations after the expulsion from paradise, people (unnamed) "began to call on the name of Yahweh" (i.e., worship him under that name). On the other hand, Ex 6:3 indicates that in the pre-Mosaic era knowledge of the name "Yahweh" (or at least knowledge of all that the name conveys) was not widespread.

So dogmatism on the issue is not warranted as long as it remains a strictly exegetical question without compromising any tenet of biblical doctrine. The history of the pre-Mosaic era is not reported in the OT in anything approaching exhaustiveness. Ezekiel as a priest would surely have been well-versed in the "church history" preceding him, including narratives and personages God may not have seen fit to include elsewhere in Holy Scripture. It may be argued (humanly and historically speaking) that Ezekiel would be more likely to refer to an ancient Daniel in the same breath as the ancients Noah and Job than to put the name of a contemporary in that otherwise ancient list. Thus construed, it is no real problem if Ezekiel is referring to some ancient and otherwise unknown (but orthodox) "Daniel." Some may object that it is an argument from silence, but "absence of evidence is not evidence of absence."

Depending on the identification of Daniel, the three ancient righteous men, "Noah, Daniel, and Job" (Ezek 14:14, 20), may or may not be listed in chronological order. Ezekiel 14 does not state that the order is chronological, and there is no reason why Ezekiel should have felt obligated to list them that way.

In this entire section Ezekiel is surely correcting some particular theological misunderstanding, even though he uses case-law formulations to stress the universal application of the principle. No mention is made of it, but almost certainly the community was making implicit appeal to the narrative recorded in Gen 18:22–33, where Abraham bargains Yahweh down to the promise that Sodom will be spared if at least ten righteous men could be found in the city. Possibly, the common prophetic teaching that a righteous remnant of believers would be saved had even emboldened some to think that Ezekiel might on that basis intercede for them just as Abraham had for the inhabitants of Sodom, or that somehow the righteousness of a few could be transferred to the "accounts" of the many who were not righteous. Jeremiah apparently confronted a similar problem. In Jer 15:1, Moses and Samuel, two archetypical prophets, are cited as unable to prevent the destruction of the city even if they were to "stand before" (intercede with) Yahweh. There may even be a literary connec-

---

[48] The faith of OT believers can be called "Yahwism" and is essentially the same faith as the NT (Christianity); see under "Outline and Theological Emphases" in Introduction. Hence OT saints can be called "Yahwists" in that sense.

tion between the two passages, since Jer 15:2–3 lists almost the same four classical means of judgment that Ezekiel mentions (see the commentary above on the beginning of this section, Ezek 14:12–20).

A Christian can scarcely consider this text without recalling the Roman church's "treasury of merit" teaching, which precipitated the Reformation. The Council of Trent still obligates the church of Rome to cling to that doctrine, which is still quite evident in much Roman Catholic practice. According to that doctrine, prayers can be directed to Mary and other saints who have a surplus "treasury of merit" because of their righteousness, and the intercessions of such saints will grant "indulgences," which supposedly will lessen the time the praying sinner must spend in purgatory after death. (In fairness, it must be noted that this classical Catholic doctrine tends to be soft-pedaled in America, at least in practice, whereas it figures much more prominently in piety in other countries.)

Obviously, that teaching involves a kind of bookkeeping mentality and transfer of righteousness very similar to what Yahweh rejects in Ezek 14:12–20. Moreover, it is at odds with the biblical teaching of justification *sola gratia*, "by grace alone," and *sola fide*, "by faith alone," through the merits of Christ alone. Hence it subverts the biblical doctrines of Law and Gospel. Instead of directing sinners to seek righteousness or merit from other people, Scripture directs us to repent of our sins and trust the all-availing vicarious atonement of Jesus Christ, who promises the dying believer, "Today with me you shall be in paradise" (Lk 23:43, among the passages that refute the existence of purgatory).

That Yahweh cites *three* paragons of righteousness may symbolize comprehensiveness. If these three cannot save the Israelites, then neither can any number of others. As Taylor nicely summarizes it: "Ezekiel's message is that there are no party tickets to deliverance. The righteous man saves no-one but himself."[49]

The pivotal word in Ezekiel's argument is צְדָקָה, "righteousness" (14:14, 20), and it is all-important that it be heard in its full biblical sense. It is prominent in both Testaments and in Christian theology, but too often the word is heard only in the sense of morality or civic righteousness. Those dimensions are surely involved as part of its fruit, but in a sense, they are secondary.

When "righteousness" is considered as an innate personal possession, something to be achieved through human effort, the result can be a crass theology of salvation by merit or works. There is also the "righteousness" to be attained at least partly by human works, but not unaided by God's grace—a combination that results in the semi-Pelagianism that characterizes Judaism (and some brands of "Christianity") and distinguishes it from the Yahwism of the OT (and NT Christianity). If misinterpreted within that semi-Pelagian

---

[49] Taylor, *Ezekiel*, 128.

framework, many key parts of Scripture (for example, Psalm 1, contrasting the way of "the righteous" with that of "the wicked") can result in a theology of prosperity (the false gospel of health and wealth) that is often contradicted by experience and that conflicts with the biblical view of the life of faith under the cross. It is no contractual arrangement with some input from the human side.

It is as essential here, as in all theology, that we understand "righteousness" first of all in forensic terms: the repentant (contrite and believing) sinner is *declared* righteous for Christ's sake, in terms of the covenant promise initiated, maintained, and sealed on the cross by God himself.[50] God's undeserved favor is received by the empty hands of personal faith and emphatically is not transferable to any other person. (Yahweh will have much more to say about the justification of each person individually in chapter 18 and 33:10–20.)

14:15–16 The second hypothetical judgment is wild animals that would "bereave" the land, that is, leave it childless and a barren "desolation" (repeated in both 14:15 and 14:16 for emphasis). The phrase "these three men" undoubtedly refers to the three named in 14:14, 20. All ten of Job's first children were killed (Job 1:13–19) despite their father's righteousness and his sacrifices on their behalf (Job 1:1–5). Ezekiel may be implying that Jerusalem's fate will be like that of Job's first children, and not like those of Noah, whose sons and daughters-in-law were saved along with him (Genesis 6–9). (We have no information about a possible family of canonical Daniel.)

The major point is that "they alone [the three paragons of righteousness] would be saved" (14:16), which expresses with a passive verb (Niphal of נָצַל) the same conclusion expressed in 14:14 with an active verb, "they … would save [only] themselves" (Piel of נָצַל with נֶפֶשׁ as object).

14:17–20 Two more examples each drive home the same point as the previous two: the "righteousness" of the three men will avail to save nobody but themselves.

How Much Worse It Will Be for Jerusalem (14:21–23)

14:21 The chapter moves towards its climax with this verse: "How much worse will it be when I send my four terrible judgments … upon Jerusalem!" The symbolism of the numeral four may signify the completeness and universality of the judgment, as anticipated by, for example, "the end has come upon the *four* corners of the earth" (7:2).[51]

The four calamities, "sword, famine, wild beasts, and plague" (14:21), appear in a different order than in the preceding verses (famine, wild animals, sword, and plague in 14:13–19), than in 5:16–17, and than in the archetype,

---

[50] For the OT covenants in relation to the new covenant in Christ, see the excursus "Covenant" in Harstad, *Joshua*, 744–56

[51] For the judgment as a type of the universal and final judgment after Christ returns (Rev 20:11–15), see the commentary on 7:1–4. Regarding the biblical symbolism of the number four, see the textual note on וְאַרְבַּע כְּנָפַיִם, the "four wings" in 1:6, and Brighton, *Revelation*, 181–82.

the curses in Lev 26:21–26 for breaking the covenant. That no two listings have the same order indicates that the exact sequence has no significance. See also the four horsemen of the apocalypse (Rev 6:1–8) and the four means "to kill with sword and with famine and with death and by the beasts of the earth" (Rev 6:8; most English translations render "death" by "pestilence" or "plague").

As already in Ezek 5:10, 15 and 11:9, and again later (16:41), Ezekiel describes the impending disasters as שְׁפָטִים, "judgments," not just in the negative sense of punishments, but primarily in the sense of juridical decisions of the heavenly Judge, who determines history. If any one of the judgments would be catastrophic and "cut off ... man and beast" (14:13, 17, 19), how much more when Yahweh sends all four upon Jerusalem will they "cut off ... man and beast" (14:21).

14:22–23   Since not even Noah, Daniel, and Job could save sons and daughters from any one of the four judgments (14:12–20), how much more improbable would it be for the apostate Israelites to save sons and daughters when Yahweh sends all four (14:21). How surprising it is, then, that the final two verses promise "a group of survivors" consisting of "those sons and daughters who will be brought out" (14:22). The surprise is expressed in the text by הִנֵּה ("behold") at the beginning of two of the clauses in 14:22. Critics tend to eliminate 14:22–23 by regarding it as a later addition, but the surprise is not totally unexpected, since in earlier passages too Ezekiel had promised a remnant, and he will again later.[52]

Yet the remnant Ezekiel is plainly talking about in 14:22–23 is in a different sense: an "unspiritual remnant," as Block nicely labels it.[53] Careful note of Ezekiel's choice of words indicates this. Instead of the remnant being "saved" (נָצַל, "to save," figured prominently in the preceding hypothetical cases, 14:14, 16, 18, 20), this group "will be left,"[54] indicating mere existence, not salvation as usually understood. Similarly, פְּלֵיטָה ("a group of survivors") may carry theological freight as the righteous remnant (e.g., Is 4:2; Obadiah 17; Joel 3:5 [ET 2:32]), but very often does not (e.g., the plants that survived the hail in Ex 10:5). And in this context the two uses of יָצָא, "brought out" and "are coming out," suggest captives who are marched into exile (rather than something like the exodus deliverance, when Yahweh "brought out" his people [e.g., Ex 12:17]). Block calls our attention to the vivid pictures of earlier prophets who made a similar point about Israelites who would survive judgment: they would be like "gleanings ... like what is knocked down from an olive tree—two or three

---

[52]   See the textual notes on 5:10; the textual notes on 6:8, 12 and the commentary on 6:8; the discussion of whether there will be a remnant in "Introduction to Ezekiel 8–11" in the commentary on chapter 8; the commentary on 9:1–4; and the textual notes and commentary on 12:16.

[53]   Block, *Ezekiel*, 1:451.

[54]   The Niphal of יָתַר can occasionally refer to a righteous remnant that "remains" (e.g., Is 4:3), but usually, as here, it simply means "be left over" or "survive."

berries on the top of a bough" (Is 17:6) or "as the shepherd saves" parts of a carcass "from the mouth of the lion, two legs or a piece of an ear" (Amos 3:12).[55]

These random survivors have not been saved by anyone's righteousness. Ezekiel had already several times proclaimed that there would be survivors, but, now, by what Greenberg calls a "wry linguistic innovation," he gives that "article of faith" a novel twist.[56] When parents now in exile, worrying about their children still in Jerusalem, later see those children, now brought into exile too, exhibiting the same depravity of which they had been guilty in Jerusalem, they will realize that Yahweh had no alternative but to destroy that Sodom of a city (cf. Ezek 16:46–56). Thus, the parents "will be consoled concerning the disaster" (Ezek 14:22), yet not in the ordinary sense, but in the realization that all the "justice" and "righteousness" (words frequently paired) are on God's side.

Allen summarizes:

> Ironically, the very children who had been the focal point of theological hope for their worried parents would turn out to be agents of a different truth, witnesses to a divine necessity. ... The survival of beloved children would minimize the sense of shock at the downfall of Jerusalem. However, it would not be a case of human love bringing a measure of consolation. Rather, the factor of consolation is raised to a divine plane, the exiles' coming to understand the will of God and the constraint that triggered his radical action. The children would march as God's subdued prisoners in his victory procession.[57]

Very appropriately, then, this pericope ends with a modified recognition formula. Instead of the usual "then you/they will know that I am Yahweh" (e.g., 14:8), the formula here is "then you will know that it was not without cause that I did everything that I did against it" (14:23). The Israelites will not only "know" that he is Yahweh, but specifically that he had done nothing "without cause" (חִנָּם probably is a deliberate play on נִחַם, "console," in 14:22–23). The same adverb had been used in 6:10: "They will know that I, Yahweh, did not speak *in vain* [חִנָּם] about doing to them this disaster."

Here "not without cause" means that Yahweh's execution of the judgments is fully in accord with his very being and revealed character (cf. Job 1:9; 2:3, where חִנָּם is commonly translated "for nothing"). Specifically, Yahweh's cause is to teach that the "death" of the nation of Israel by means of the exile is necessary so that true repentance would be aroused in the survivors and a genuine "Israel" of faith could be resurrected (e.g., Ezek 37:1–14). That is the same message of Law and Gospel that is the *cantus firmus* ("constant melody") of all Scripture. The theology of the cross requires death with Christ and to sin in order to participate in Christ's resurrection (e.g., Romans 6–8).

---

[55] Block, *Ezekiel*, 1:451.

[56] Greenberg, *Ezekiel*, 1:261.

[57] Allen, *Ezekiel*, 1:219–20.

Jerusalem Is a Useless Vine

Translation

15 **¹The Word of Yahweh came to me: ²"Son of man, what becomes of the wood of the grapevine out of all trees—the vine branch that is among the trees of the forest? ³Can wood be taken from it to use for work? Can they take from it a peg, to hang on it anything? ⁴Instead, to the fire it is given for fuel. Its two ends the fire devours, and its middle is burned up. Is it then useful for any purpose? ⁵Since when it was intact it could not be used for any purpose, how much less after the fire has devoured it and it is burned up can it ever be used for work!**

⁶"Therefore, thus says the Lord Yahweh: Like the wood of the grapevine among the trees of the forest which I have given to the fire for fuel, so have I given the inhabitants of Jerusalem. ⁷I will set my face against them. From the fire they have come out, but the fire will still devour them. Then you will know that I am Yahweh when I set my face against them. ⁸I will make the land a desolation because they faithlessly did infidelity, says the Lord Yahweh."

Textual Notes

15:2 מַה־יִּהְיֶה עֵץ־הַגֶּפֶן מִכָּל־עֵץ—The noun עֵץ can mean "tree" (the plural at the end of 15:2) or the singular can be collective, "trees" (the second occurrence in 15:2 and second occurrence in 15:6). However, this first instance in 15:2 of עֵץ means "*wood, as material*" to be used for construction or an implement (BDB, 2 a), as also in 15:3 and the first occurrence in 15:6. (The multivalence of this word will confront us again in 37:15–28.) Here it is in construct with גֶּפֶן, the common noun for a "vine," especially the kind grown in a vineyard, which often serves as a metaphor for Israel (see the commentary below). "The wood of the grapevine" is soft and flexible, useless for anything except perhaps to make a fire (15:4).

Poetically or liturgically, Lutherans should be aware of the two meanings of עֵץ from the beautiful Proper Preface for Lent in *The Lutheran Hymnal* (in *Lutheran Worship* limited to Holy Week): "that he who *by a tree* once overcame might likewise *by a tree* be overcome."[1] The first instance refers to the tree of the knowledge of good and evil in Eden, while the second refers to the wooden cross. (The pastor must wonder how many parishioners get the point if they are not instructed.)

Most English translations take the מִן (on מִכָּל־) in a comparative sense: "How is the wood of the vine *better than* … ?" However, the ancient translations (beginning with the LXX) and most modern commentators take the preposition in a partitive sense, singling out the wood of the vine "from/out of all trees." That is supported by the most natural way to understand מַה־יִּהְיֶה, "what will become [of the wood]," not

---

[1] *TLH*, p. 25; cf. *Lutheran Worship Altar Book* (St. Louis: Concordia, 1982), 288, 324, 356.

"how is it [better]," which would normally be expressed in Hebrew with a phrase such as מַה טּוֹב rather than the phrase here. The imperfect of הָיָה often means "become" (BDB, II 2). The second half of 15:2 supports the partitive understanding of this first half. In addition, the following verse (15:3) does not pursue any comparison, but continues to ask whether the wood can be used for any constructive purpose. (In מַה־יִּהְיֶה the two words are joined by both *maqqeph* and a conjunctive *daghesh forte*.)

הַזְּמוֹרָה אֲשֶׁר הָיָה בַּעֲצֵי הַיָּעַר׃—This second half of the verse is in apposition to the question in the first half and is synonymously parallel to it. זְמוֹרָה refers to a "vine branch," probably a branch pruned off (as in Num 13:23), since the verb זָמַר in Lev 25:3–4 and Is 5:6 refers to pruning a vineyard. (The noun appeared in the enigmatic phrase at the end of Ezek 8:17, but that verse and this one shed no light on each other.) That feminine noun is followed by the masculine verb הָיָה, but biblical Hebrew commonly uses a masculine form in place of a grammatically "correct" feminine form. The parallel to הַזְּמוֹרָה ("the vine branch") here is עֵץ־הַגֶּפֶן ("the wood of the grapevine") in the first half of the verse—not the immediately preceding מִכָּל־עֵץ ("of all trees"), which would weaken the point of the question.

The sense of בַּעֲצֵי הַיַּעַר as *among the trees of the forest* affirms that the parallel in the first half of the verse, מִכָּל־עֵץ, has a partitive sense, "out of all trees." The phrase simply refers to the genus of trees, like "fish of the sea" or "birds of the air." Some commentators try to stretch the phrase to imply that Israel is no longer a cultivated vine, but a wild one, Israel having reverted to the wild by alliances with other nations.

15:3 הֲיֻקַּ֖ח מִמֶּ֥נּוּ עֵ֛ץ—The verb is the Qal passive third masculine singular imperfect with interrogative הֲ. The *daghesh* (-קַּ-) marks the assimilated ל from the root לָקַח, so the form is not a Hophal (contrary to older grammarians, e.g., BDB; cf. GKC, § 53 u). The Qal passive is a separate stem or conjugation than the Qal (active), but few examples of it (besides the fairly common Qal passive participle) survive in the OT (see Joüon, § 58). Some of the ancient versions (e.g., LXX) render הֲיֻקַּח as if it were a plural active Qal, "Will they take … ?" harmonizing it to אִם־יִקְחוּ in the second half of the verse. A few critics emend accordingly, but Greenberg points out that other verbs in this passage are used in both active and passive forms: עָשָׂה (Qal in 15:3; Niphal twice in 15:5) and נָתַן (Niphal in 15:4 and Qal twice in 15:6).[2] See also the Niphal, Piel, and Hiphil forms of נָצַל in 14:14, 16, 18, 20.

לַעֲשׂוֹת לִמְלָאכָה—Often מְלָאכָה means "work" in the sense of one's "business" or "occupation" (*HALOT*, 2), hence this phrase could mean "to make [the wood into something] for work," "to use for work." But the word can also refer to the concrete result(s) of one's labors, "objects, wares" (*HALOT*, 4), or to "service, use" in general (BDB, 5 [under the root לאך]), hence this phrase could mean "to use for any purpose/anything." It is hard to decide which of these nuances is most appropriate in each of the four instances of this noun in 15:3–5. A translation with "work" or "purpose" highlights the uselessness of the wood. In any event, there probably is a wordplay between לִמְלָאכָה and two words in 15:4, לְאָכְלָה ("for fuel") and אָכְלָה ("devours").

---

2 Greenberg, *Ezekiel*, 1:265.

יָתֵד most often refers to a tent peg (e.g., Judg 4:21; 5:26) but can refer to a hook, nail, or pin of virtually any sort. Here the obvious application is to a hook or peg in a wall on which "to hang" something (the infinitive construct לִתְלוֹת, from תָּלָה, as a purpose clause). Based on such use, יָתֵד can be used metaphorically of someone dependable, for example, of Eliakim (Is 22:23) or any leader (Zech 10:4).

15:4 הִנֵּה —Both this verse and the next begin with הִנֵּה, the very common Hebrew interjection. I have rendered it "instead" here and "since" in 15:5.

לָאֵשׁ נִתַּן לְאָכְלָה—Some translators take this and some or all of the following clauses as forming a long conditional or temporal sentence. However, this and the following clauses (except for the final rhetorical question in 15:4) are virtually proverbial, describing what in antiquity at least must have been everyday occurrences. The translation renders the verse as three separate sentences.

The Niphal of נָתַן (נִתַּן) anticipates the Qal twice in 15:6 with God as the subject. That is, this Niphal ("to the fire *it is given* as fuel") describes a "given" of life, "a law of nature, as it were," as Cooke comments on 15:6,[3] where God, the author of that "law," speaks. The Qal (נָתַתִּי) also begins the remaining verses of the chapter (15:7–8), although in different senses.

The noun אָכְלָה will recur in 15:6. Usually it means "food" or "devouring," but in English idiom "food" for the fire is "fuel."

אֵת שְׁנֵי קְצוֹתָיו אָכְלָה הָאֵשׁ וְתוֹכוֹ נָחָר—The order of these clauses is a natural one. Anyone who has watched a piece of wood in a bonfire or fireplace knows that "its ends" (קְצוֹתָיו is the plural of קָצֶה with suffix), the extremities of the logs or sticks, burn first, and later "its middle" (תוֹכוֹ) is reduced to a glowing ember. The Qal perfect אָכְלָה is feminine because its subject, אֵשׁ, is a feminine noun, and the verb plays on the preceding homographic noun אָכְלָה, "fuel." נָחָר is the pausal form of the Niphal perfect of חָרַר, "to be burned (up), charred," a less common by-form and synonym of חָרָה, "to be kindled" (usually of anger). The Niphal imperfect of חָרַר follows in 15:5 (וַיִּחָר).

הֲיִצְלַח לִמְלָאכָה:—The Qal of צָלַח (with interrogative -הֲ to form the rhetorical question) can mean "to be good for something, useful."

15:5 תָמִים—This adjective (from the root תמם) looks like a plural but is singular. In ethical contexts it often means "blameless," but for an inanimate object "whole, intact" is required.

אַף כִּי־—Here this combination means "*How much less*, when fire has consumed it …" (Waltke-O'Connor, § 39.3.4d, example 8). Compare the textual note on the combination in 14:21. The second half of the verse might be taken as the fifth in the series of rhetorical questions in 15:1–4. It might also be an exclamation, as I have punctuated it.

אֵשׁ אֲכָלָתְהוּ וַיִּחָר—The antecedent of the third masculine singular object suffix (הוּ-) on the third feminine singular verb אֲכָלָתְהוּ is עֵץ in עֵץ־הַגֶּפֶן back in 15:2. That עֵץ is also the subject of וַיִּחָר, a pausal Niphal imperfect with *waw* consecutive of חָרַר, "to be burned (up)," which was also in 15:4.

---

3 Cooke, *Ezekiel*, 157.

15:6 The syntax of this verse is unusual. Usually after a clause beginning with the conjunction כַּאֲשֶׁר (usually translated "as") a verb follows, but here a relative clause follows ("which I have given to the fire for fuel"). Rendering כַּאֲשֶׁר by "like" (which would normally translate כְּ) enables a literal English translation to make sense. The idea would be conveyed better in English by rearranging the syntax and wording to this: "Just as among the trees of the forest I have given the wood of the grapevine to the fire for fuel, so have I given the inhabitants of Jerusalem." The implication is that an additional phrase should be added to complete the thought: "so have I given the inhabitants of Jerusalem *to the fire for fuel.*"

Most English translations render נָתַן as "give(n)" both times here in 15:6, applying the metaphor to the inhabitants of Jerusalem. However, most do not so render it in 15:4, where it first occurred, but the ESV does, conveying the play on it here.

עֵץ בְּעֵץ הַיַּעַר uses עֵץ as a collective, whereas בַּעֲצֵי הַיַּעַר in 15:2 had the plural. Some manuscripts and the versions read the plural.

15:7 The verb נָתַן appears again here, but in a different sense. This display of hostility, "I will set my face against them," repeats the Hebrew idiom used in 14:8, where Yahweh warned the idolatrous seeker. It is similar to the action prophecy Ezekiel is commanded to perform in 6:2 and 13:17 (and later verses) with שִׂים, which is the verb in the restated formula at the end of 15:7.

15:8 The verb נָתַן appears one final time, but here in an entirely different idiom. For the cognate accusative construction with the verb מָעַל and noun מַעַל, see textual note on it in 14:13.

Commentary

15:2 In spite of the externally different subject matter, chapter 15 structurally has much in common with 14:12–23 (as discussed in the beginning of the commentary on 14:12–23). There is no reason to doubt that chapter 15 was originally a separate oracle, but was editorially linked with the preceding one, most likely by Ezekiel himself. The connections are especially clear in 15:7–8. The message of 15:7 recalls 14:22–23 (see the commentary below). The oracle's conclusion (15:8) uses vocabulary that was prominent in chapter 14, namely, "desolation" (שְׁמָמָה), as in 14:15–16, and "they faithlessly did infidelity" (מָעַל מַעַל), as in 14:13.

The metaphor of a useless vine is developed in a series of rhetorical questions and a concluding exclamation in 15:2–5, followed by "therefore" (לָכֵן) introducing the application of the metaphor to Jerusalem in 15:6–8.

The vineyard and grapevine are common biblical images for the church in both Testaments—for Israel, Judah, and Jerusalem in the OT, and for Christ and Christians in the NT.[4]

The metaphor appears already in two Pentateuchal poems, the blessing of Jacob (Gen 49:22) and the Song of Moses (Deut 32:32). In those two poems

---

4 For a brief study of the vineyard motif throughout the Scriptures, one may see "The Vineyard" in Mitchell, *The Song of Songs,* 299–311, and for some connections between the motif and the Lord's Supper, pages 311–54.

the Hebrew phrase that is literally "the blood of grapes/the grape" (Gen 49:11; Deut 32:14) alludes to the blood-red color of grapes and provides background for the association of juice from trampled grapes with human blood (e.g., Is 63:1–3; Rev 14:20; cf. Rev 19:13, 15) and for the use of "the fruit of the vine" (Mt 26:29; Mk 14:25; Lk 22:18) in the Sacrament of Christ's body and blood ("this is my blood," Mt 26:28; Mk 14:24). In Psalm 80, God is described as having transplanted the vine of Israel from Egypt to Canaan (Ps 80:9 [ET 80:8]) and is beseeched to restore it after its having been burned in the fire (Ps 80:15–20 [ET 80:14–19]). In the prophets, however, the imagery is used polemically of Israel's disobedience. Perhaps best known is Isaiah's Song of the Vineyard (Is 5:1–7) with its famous wordplays, stating that Israel yielded worthless grapes instead of a good harvest. Rather similar are Hos 10:1 and Jer 2:21. Yahweh in Is 28:23–29 uses agriculture (the sowing and harvesting of spices and grain) to describe his Law-Gospel mode of action, and in Ezekiel 15 he concentrates on the more common picture of viticulture to make the same point.

Thus those many aspects of the metaphor form this chapter's canonical background: Israel's "'congenital' baseness,"[5] the bad fruit it bore, and so on. Some of these themes, expressed in various ways, are prominent elsewhere in Ezekiel. Many commentators import those themes into the exegesis of this chapter. But for methodological reasons, it is important that they be excluded. This chapter may not be a parable in the strictest sense, but it is akin to one. And one of the cardinal principles of the interpretation of parables is that usually they have only one main point of comparison. Ezekiel's main point in this chapter is that the worthless wood is good for nothing except as fuel for the fire.

Christ uses the metaphor to convey the organic connection between himself and true believers. However, in Jn 15:1–8, instead of Israel/the church being the vine, Jesus himself is the vine, and believers in him are the fruitful branches. The phrase "fruit of the vine" is familiar from our Lord's use of it in describing the eschatological implications of the Eucharist (Mt 26:29; Mk 14:25; Lk 22:18), which unites communicants with him by furnishing his true body and blood (1 Cor 10:16–17; 11:17–34). Like Ezekiel 15, Christ states that unfruitful branches are to be thrown into the fire and burned (Jn 15:6). The description of the final judgment as a grape harvest (Is 63:1–6; Joel 4:13 [ET 3:13]; Rev 14:17–20; 19:15) has left its impress both on Christian hymnody and on English literature at large.

15:3–5 These verses develop the metaphor. To Ezekiel's audience, the answer to the rhetorical question in the previous verse ("What becomes of the wood of the grapevine?") would have been obvious. Ezekiel drives home the point with two more rhetorical questions: "Can wood be taken from it to use for work? Can they take from it a peg?" The obvious answer to both is nega-

---

[5] Greenberg, *Ezekiel*, 1:269.

tive. From its unsuitability as lumber (15:3), the next verse underscores its sole use: "to the fire it is given for fuel" (15:4). The climax comes in 15:5 with an a fortiori argument: since the intact wood is useless for work, how much more worthless it is once it has been reduced to ashes, since it has already been put to its sole use (as firewood).

15:6 "Therefore" (לָכֵן), often (as here) followed by the citation formula ("thus says the Lord Yahweh"), is Ezekiel's customary introduction to the part of the oracle that announces the divine judgment (see the textual note on it in 5:7). In prophetic usage it is not the conclusion of a syllogism (as "therefore" often is in Greek and classical Western logic), but simply a way of signaling that the point of the analogy is now being made. After the citation formula, "thus says the Lord Yahweh," Yahweh briskly makes the application to Jerusalem in the form of a simile ("like …").

Much of the point turns on the nuance of the verb נָתַן, "to give," which was used in 15:4; now is used twice in 15:6; and (in different senses) also begins each of the next two verses (15:7–8). Just as it is a "given," part of the order of creation, that the wood of the grapevine is good for nothing but fuel, so also in the order of redemption, apostate Jerusalem is fit for nothing but the fire. The analogy is not exact, of course. Jerusalem had not been created simply to be burned. King David had established it as the capital of Israel, God's "church and state" on earth.[6] But its refractoriness had disqualified it from continuing as the center of God's redemptive work, his new creation (promised and begun already in the OT). And so the fire of judgment had become, for now, just as much a "given" for her as it is for the wood of a vine.

This should not be misunderstood to imply determinism or predestination to damnation. There is no problem in understanding that God's purpose and intent is for a vine's wood to serve as fuel for fire, a law of nature explained in 15:4. But Jerusalem's consignment to the flames was no matter of God's eternal, immutable will (what theologians sometimes call his antecedent will), but of his consequent will (as theologians sometimes call it). His decree is a consequence of Jerusalem's violation of his covenant and rejection of him. At the time when Ezekiel prophesies chapter 15, God's decision to judge Jerusalem has been made final, and indeed the judgment had already commenced some years earlier with the first two waves of exiles having been taken from the city in 605 and 597 B.C. (the latter including Ezekiel). With this verb, "give(n)" (15:4, 6–8), as with everything in Holy Writ, Scripture must interpret Scripture.

The Christian reader knows, of course, that Jerusalem's destruction in 587 B.C. by no means marked the termination of her role in salvation history. A less glorious city and temple would be rebuilt after the exile, and Jerusalem would be the site of the greatest acts of redemption: Christ's suffering, death, and res-

---

[6] For a sketch of Jerusalem's history and purpose, see the excursus "Jerusalem" in Harstad, *Joshua*, 443–48.

urrection in fulfillment of all that was written by the prophets (Lk 24:25, 27, 44). Jerusalem even serves as the earthly type of the eternal city in the new heavens and new earth that shall be the home of all believers: the new Jerusalem (Revelation 21; cf. Gal 4:25–26; Heb 12:22). Yet ethnic Israel as a whole rejected the Messiah at his first advent, and the consequence was yet another destruction of the city, in A.D. 70, which serves as a type of the final destruction at the end of the world upon Christ's return (Mt 23:37–25:46).

15:7 Twice a formula expressing hostility, in which Yahweh declares, "I will set my face against them," underscores what was already clear in 15:6, namely, that Jerusalem's consignment to the fire of destruction is not simply another instance of the "horror of history." The destruction of an ancient city by fire was an event that has happened countless times throughout history (see, e.g., Josh 6:24; 8:8, 19; 11:11). But in the case of Jerusalem in 587 B.C., the event would be by God's deliberate design and of a piece with his overarching purpose in history. He "desires all people to be saved" (1 Tim 2:4), and he accomplishes salvation for all in a cruciform way. The people's sin led to the city's well-deserved judgment by fire, though a remnant would be preserved by grace and the people would experience a kind of "resurrection" to new life by the Spirit (Ezek 37:1–14). Even so, outside that same city the sinless Christ vicariously suffered the judgment for the sin of the world, and after his baptism by fire (Lk 12:49–50) he rose in power according to the Spirit of holiness (Rom 1:4).

Yahweh's statement here that some Israelites already "have come out" (Ezek 15:7) of the "fire" (see below) most naturally refers to the siege of Jerusalem in 597 B.C., when Ezekiel and probably most of his present audience,[7] which he will address shortly, were taken into exile. That "the fire will still devour them" refers to the conflagration coming in 587 B.C. As in 14:22–23, the people dare not consider their escape from the first "fire" a sign of God's favor. It was only a temporary reprieve, and since they had not repented, the fire of his well-deserved wrath would eventually overtake them.

The momentary shift to the second person plural in the recognition formula, "then *you* will know that I am Yahweh," makes plain that Ezekiel's first audience is his fellow exiles, although the "final judgment" of which he prophesies will more immediately affect their compatriots who were still in Jerusalem—who, however, may well have become his "second audience." By indirection, the recognition formula may intimate that a remnant of believers ("know" as a synonym for "faith") will survive, but its major accent in this context is surely Law: the people's recognition, however begrudging, of Yahweh's omnipotence and the justice of his judgment.

It is not known whether fire had literally played much of a role in the siege preceding the deportation of 597 B.C., but it certainly did in 587 B.C. (2 Ki 25:9).

---

[7] Some of Ezekiel's audience may have been part of the deportation in 605 B.C., of which Daniel was a part (see Dan 1:1–7).

Ezekiel may be using the word more figuratively to make an immediate connection between the two events. Keil argues that the reference is not merely to those two events, but also "to all the judgments which fell upon the covenant nation, from the destruction of the kingdom of the ten tribes to the catastrophe in the reign of Jehoiachin."[8] Ultimately, no doubt, all those other judgments illustrated the same problem of Israel's faithlessness, but the immediate accent is clearly on the end of monarchial Israel in 587 B.C. (the brief respite under Zerubbabel after the exile notwithstanding).

The conflagration of Jerusalem in 587 B.C. with fire, like that of Sodom and Gomorrah (Jude 7), serves as a type of the final judgment of all unbelievers at the end of the world, pictured as the burning of the city "Babylon" in Rev 18:8. Many Scripture passages depict that eternal judgment as by fire.[a]

(a) E.g., Is 66:15–16, 24; Mt 3:12; 5:22; 13:40; 18:8–9; Heb 10:27; 2 Pet 3:7, 12; Rev 20:14–15

15:8 This verse might appear redundant at first glance, but its connections with 14:12–23 (see the beginning of the commentary on 15:2) appear to be a deliberate attempt to weld the two chapters together. It supplies the prophetic indictment or reason for the judgment which had not been developed explicitly in this chapter. Ultimately, Jerusalem's burning is not the result of some ineluctable order of creation (see the textual note and commentary on 15:6), but of its own sacrilegious deportment.

---

[8] Keil, *Ezekiel*, 1:193.

Ezekiel 16:1–63

Jerusalem the Whore

Translation

16 ¹The Word of Yahweh came to me: ²"Son of man, make Jerusalem know her abominations, ³and say, 'Thus says the Lord Yahweh to Jerusalem: Your ancestry and your birth were from the land of the Canaanites. Your father was an Amorite and your mother a Hittite. ⁴As for your birth, on the day you were born, your navel cord was not cut, and you were not washed with water for oiling; you were not rubbed thoroughly with salt, nor were you tightly swaddled. ⁵An eye did not have pity on you to do for you one of these things, to show compassion for you. You were thrown out in the open field in disregard for your life on the day you were born. ⁶I passed by you and I saw you thrashing about in your blood. I said to you, "In your blood, live!" and I said to you, "In your blood, live!" ⁷I made you thrive like a sprout of the field. You grew up, you developed, and you became very beautiful. Your breasts were well formed and your pubic hair sprouted, but you were naked and nude. ⁸I passed by you and I saw you, and behold, your time was the time of love. I spread my robe over you and I covered your nakedness. I swore [an oath] to you and entered into a covenant with you, says the Lord Yahweh, and you became mine. ⁹I washed you in water; I washed off your blood from you; and I anointed you with oil. ¹⁰I clothed you with finest woven material and gave you sandals of luxury leather. I wrapped your head in the best linen and covered you in exquisite fabric. ¹¹I adorned you with jewelry: I put bracelets on your wrists and a necklace on your neck. ¹²I put a ring on your nose, earrings on your ears, and a crown of glory on your head. ¹³So you were adorned with gold and silver, and your clothing was of the best linen, exquisite fabric, and finest woven material. Fine flour, honey, and oil you ate. You were extraordinarily beautiful and you attained royalty. ¹⁴Your fame spread throughout the nations because of your beauty. In fact, it was perfect because of my splendor which I had bestowed upon you, says the Lord Yahweh.

¹⁵" 'But you trusted in your beauty and played the whore in reliance on your fame. You lavished your whorings on every man passing by—his you became. ¹⁶You took some of your clothes and made for yourself multicolored high places and played the whore on them. Such things should not happen and it should not be! ¹⁷You took your articles of glory from my gold and my silver which I had given to you, and you made for yourself images of the male and you played the whore with them. ¹⁸You took your clothes of finest woven material and covered them, and you set my oil and my incense before them. ¹⁹Also my bread which I gave you—the fine flour, oil, and honey which I fed you—you set before them as a fragrant sacrifice, and it was [so], says the Lord Yahweh. ²⁰You even took your sons and your daughters which you bore for me and sacrificed them to them [the images] to eat. Were your whorings not enough ²¹that you slaughtered my chil-

dren and offered them by making them pass through [the fire] to them [the images]? ²²With all your abominations and your whorings, you did not remember the days of your youth, when you were naked and nude; you were thrashing about in your blood. ²³And after all your wickedness—woe, woe to you, says the Lord Yahweh!— ²⁴you built for yourself a domed tent, and you made for yourself a platform in every city square. ²⁵At the head of every street you built your platform and made your beauty abominable. You spread your legs for every man passing by and you multiplied your whorings. ²⁶You played the whore with the sons of Egypt, your neighbors with their enlarged penises, and you multiplied your whoring to enrage me! ²⁷So behold, I stretched out my hand against you, and I reduced your territory. I gave you up to the desire of those who hate you, the daughters of the Philistines, who were embarrassed by your way of lewdness. ²⁸You played the whore with the sons of the Assyrians because you were insatiable. Even after whoring with them, you were not satisfied. ²⁹So you extended your whoring to the land of merchants, to Chaldea, but even with this you were not satisfied.

³⁰" 'How feverish is your heart, says the Lord Yahweh, that you did all these things, the behavior of a woman who is a whore dominatrix. ³¹When you built your domed tent at the head of every street and you made your platform in every city square, you were not like an [ordinary] whore by [your] refusing payment. ³²O adulterous wife, who instead of her husband procures strange men! ³³To all whores men give a fee, but you gave your gifts to all your lovers. You bribed them to come to you from all around for your whorings. ³⁴There was in you an oppositeness from the [other] women in your whorings. You were not solicited for prostitution, but by your giving payment, instead of payment being given you, you were the very opposite.

³⁵" 'Therefore, whore, hear the Word of Yahweh! ³⁶Thus says the Lord Yahweh: Because your vaginal fluid was poured out and your nakedness was exposed in your whoring with your lovers, because of all your abominable fecal deities, and in accordance with the blood of your children, whom you gave to them [false deities], ³⁷therefore behold, I am about to gather all your lovers to whom you were pleasing—all those you loved in addition to all those you hated. I will gather them against you from all around. I will expose your nakedness to them, and they will see your nakedness. ³⁸I will judge you with judgments for women who commit adultery and who shed blood; I will make you blood(y) in [my] wrath and passion. ³⁹I will deliver you into their hands, and they will tear down your domed tent, demolish your platforms, strip you of your clothes, take your jewelry of glory, and leave you naked and nude. ⁴⁰They will bring up against you a mob, and they will stone you with stones and hack you to pieces with their swords. ⁴¹They will burn down your houses with fire and execute on you judgments in the sight of many women. I will make you cease from being a whore, and you will never again give a payment. ⁴²Then I will lay to rest my wrath against you, and my passion will subside. I will be calm and no longer be vexed.

⁴³" 'Because you did not remember the days of your youth and did not dread me in all these [activities], I myself will surely place your conduct upon [your] head, says the Lord Yahweh. Have you not done lewdness in addition to all your abominations? ⁴⁴Behold, everyone speaking a proverb about you will say proverbially, "Like her mother is her daughter." ⁴⁵You are a true daughter of your mother, who disregards her husband and her children; and you are a true sister of your sisters, who disregard their husbands and their children. The mother of all of you was a Hittite and your father an Amorite. ⁴⁶Your big sister is Samaria (she and her daughters), who lives north of you, and your sister who is smaller than you and who lives south of you is Sodom and her daughters. ⁴⁷You did not [even] walk in their ways and act according to their abominations, [since] in a very short time you became more depraved than they in all your ways. ⁴⁸As I live, says the Lord Yahweh, Sodom your sister (she and her daughters) has not done what you have done (you and your daughters). ⁴⁹Behold, this was the iniquity of Sodom, your sister: pride, surfeit of food, and complacent ease belonged to her and her daughters, and she failed to strengthen the hand of the poor and needy. ⁵⁰They were haughty and committed abomination before me, and so I removed them when I saw. ⁵¹Samaria did not sin like even half of your sins. You multiplied your abominations more than they, and you made your sisters appear righteous by all your abominations which you did. ⁵²So also you—bear your disgrace, by which you appeared to intercede for your sisters. Because of your sins, which you did more abominably than they, they appear more righteous than you. So also you—be ashamed and bear your disgrace, because you made your sisters appear righteous. ⁵³I will bring about their restoration—the restoration of Sodom and her daughters, and the restoration of Samaria and her daughters—and your complete restoration in their midst, ⁵⁴so that you will bear your disgrace and you will be ashamed of everything you did in apparently giving them comfort. ⁵⁵Your sisters Sodom and her daughters will return to their former state, and Samaria and her daughters will return to their former state, and you and your daughters will return to your former state. ⁵⁶Did not Sodom your sister become a byword in your mouth in the day of your great pride, ⁵⁷before your own wickedness was exposed, so now you are a reproach to the daughters of Edom and all those around her and to the daughters of the Philistines, who scorn you from all around? ⁵⁸Your lewdness and your abominations you must now bear, says Yahweh.

⁵⁹" 'For thus says the Lord Yahweh: Shall I do with you as you have done, [you] who despised the oath, thereby breaking the covenant? ⁶⁰On the contrary, I myself will remember my covenant with you in the days of your youth, and I will establish for you an everlasting covenant. ⁶¹Then you will remember your ways and be ashamed when you receive your sisters who are bigger than you in addition to those who are smaller than you, and I will give them to you as daughters, and not outside my covenant with you. ⁶²I myself will establish my covenant with you; then you will know that I am Yahweh, ⁶³in order that you may remember and be ashamed and never again open your mouth because of your

disgrace, when I make atonement for you for all you have done, says the Lord Yahweh.' "

Textual Notes

Chapters 16 and 23, besides a certain similarity in theme, also seem to provide a framework or "inclusion" for the intervening chapters. The six chapters in between seem to be deliberately ordered in an ABABAB pattern. Chapters 17, 19, and 21 are oracles concerning the role the Babylonians played in the last days of Judah, while chapters 18, 20, and 22 reiterate the manifold sins of Judah that have triggered God's inevitable judgment.

Chapter 16, at sixty-three verses, by itself is longer than half of the minor prophets, yet it contains textual and translational challenges out of proportion to even its outsized length. Depending on how one counts, the chapter contains over a dozen unique words (hapax legomena), a large number of obscure words and usages, and various anomalous grammatical forms. Some of these may be due to the topic treated. Others can be attributed to Akkadian or Aramaic influences on the language, while in other cases archaic verbal endings are preserved.[1] I shall consider them when encountered.

The fact that these difficulties are distributed more or less evenly throughout the chapter is one indication of its unity—that it is all from Ezekiel's hand and was written at essentially the same time. The structure and thematic development of the chapter also argue for its unity.[2] In defense of the chapter's unity, the word-event formula in 16:1 does not recur until 17:1. The intervening material divides itself into these uneven sections: (1) 16:2–42, the extended metaphor of the nymphomaniacal adulteress; (2) 16:43–58, a comparison of Jerusalem with her "sisters," Sodom and Samaria; and (3) 16:59–63, Yahweh's renewal of the covenant with a regenerated Israel.

A family theme runs throughout the chapter. The leading motif is marriage: an infant girl grows up and is taken as a wife by Yahweh, though she proves unfaithful. The chapter also gives attention to the girl's parents and sisters. The woman's descent into ever more flagrant depravity is unified by the use of derivatives of the root זָנָה, "to be a whore, prostitute," over twenty times (twelve instances of the verb, including the participle זוֹנָה, "whore," and nine of the noun תַּזְנוּת, "whoring").

Stark contrasts characterize the entire chapter: Yahweh's faithful love versus Israel's rebellious infidelity; the fallen woman's shamelessness versus the shame she feels upon repentance; and her forgetfulness versus Yahweh's remembering.

Certain key expressions recur: God "passed by," both after the woman's birth (16:6) and again when she came of age (16:8; cf. "every man passing by," 16:15, 25); her stark "nakedness" at her coming of age (16:8); in her whoring (16:36); and twice

---

[1] See the lists in Greenberg, *Ezekiel*, 1:296–97, and in Block, *Ezekiel*, 1:464–65, nn. 19–21.

[2] Of course, critical commentators generally deny the unity of the chapter and its authorship by Ezekiel. Rather typically, Zimmerli, *Ezekiel*, 1:349–53, attributes 16:44–58 to sometime after the fall of Jerusalem (although possibly appended by Ezekiel himself), while he credits 16:59–63 to Ezekiel's disciples.

when Yahweh strips her prior to execution (16:37); "abomination(s)" nine times in this chapter (and often elsewhere in Ezekiel).

16:2 הוֹדַע אֶת־יְרוּשָׁלַ͏ִם אֶת־תּוֹעֲבֹתֶיהָ—The Hiphil (imperative) of יָדַע with a double accusative (each marked by אֶת) is, literally, "to cause (someone) to know (something)." The idiom implies divine revelation, as in 20:11, where Yahweh made Israel to know his judgments, that is, the Torah (see it also 39:7; 43:11), but here it is a revelation of the extent of Israel's depravity, which she apparently did not know or acknowledge. The verb also evokes a forensic context, as in the similar passages 20:4 and 22:2, where Ezekiel is to "judge" Israel and "make known … abominations." A forensic metaphor underlies justification, but here we have not a verdict of righteousness and acquittal, but a charge or indictment of guilt that continues until 16:35, where the guilty sentence is pronounced. A priest had the responsibility to make God's Word known to Israel, both in pronouncing verdicts about liturgical matters, such as clean versus unclean (see 22:26; 44:23), and pedagogically (teaching the Torah). Here we may see Ezekiel as the priest-prophet he really was.

The accusation is addressed to "Jerusalem," who, as the capital, represents the entire nation. Since cities are feminine (as indicated by the feminine suffix on תּוֹעֲבֹתֶיהָ), the address to Jerusalem easily leads into the metaphor of her as a girl and woman throughout the rest of the chapter. The fact that Jerusalem originally was a pagan Canaanite city facilitates the description of the people's pagan "genealogy," which follows in 16:3.[3]

The noun תּוֹעֵבָה occurs nine times in the chapter (out of forty-three times in Ezekiel). In the OT an "abomination" refers to a vile act that is reprehensible to Yahweh and incompatible with faith in and worship of him. See chapter 8, which describes four abominations in the temple precincts that cause Yahweh to kill the idolaters (chapter 9). While in the OT an abomination frequently pertains to liturgical matters, it can also refer to what we would distinguish as a moral issue, and that dimension takes precedence in this chapter. As the NT reminds us, sexual behavior is a matter of highest concern to God and the church (e.g., 1 Cor 5:1–13; 6:12–7:40). Theology and morality cannot be divorced from one another.

16:3 מְכֹרֹתַיִךְ וּמֹלְדֹתַיִךְ—The etymology of מְכוּרָה is unknown. In the OT it occurs only here and in 21:35 (ET 21:30); 29:14. Its following synonym here, מוֹלֶדֶת ("descent" by birth, from יָלַד), and the other two passages indicate that it must mean something like "ancestry, parentage, origin." The LXX translates it by ῥίζα, "root," which captures the idea.

Both nouns are plurals. The first might be translated "origins," but it is impossible for a person to have multiple physical births. The plurals thus indicate that Ezekiel is not attempting a precise biological genealogy, but a spiritual one, and the words underscore Israel's mixed ancestry.

מֵאֶרֶץ הַכְּנַעֲנִי—"Canaanite" is singular. The gentilic ending ("land of *the Canaanite*" versus "land of Canaan"; cf. the textual notes on 16:29) emphasizes ethnicity

---

[3] See the excursus "Jerusalem" in Harstad, *Joshua*, 443–48.

rather than geography. The Canaanites were just one of several ethnic groups that inhabited the land of Canaan before Israel's conquest.[4] "Canaanite" is probably almost sarcastic, virtual shorthand for moral decadence, representative of everything antithetical to Yahwism and to Israel as God intended her to be.

אָבִיךְ הָאֱמֹרִי וְאִמֵּךְ חִתִּית:—"Amorite" and "Hittite" are two more gentilic nouns. The first has a definite article, while the second does not. The LXX translates both anarthrously, and both are anarthrous when they are repeated (in reverse order) in 16:45. Articles are common before gentilics when they are collective. A collective sense here would point to a metaphorical and spiritual ancestry, rather than a biological one. Compare the first textual note on 16:3, about the plurals. The inconsistency in the use of the article here is hard to explain, but the article on הַכְּנַעֲנִי in the previous phrase may have led to the use of the article on הָאֱמֹרִי in the first part of this clause.

The Amorites and Hittites, like the Canaanites, were members of the original, non-Israelite population of Canaan. The Amorites, Hittites, Girgashites, and Jebusites all were descended from Canaan, son of Ham (Gen 10:15–16), and so these terms sometimes overlap in biblical usage.[5] Often the OT lists seven different ethnic or cultural groups in Canaan (e.g., Deut 7:1; Josh 3:10), and it is not clear whether each group occupied a specific part of the land or whether the groups mingled with each other.

The Amorites ruled various city-states centered along the middle Euphrates in the middle of the second millennium. One common hypothesis attempting to locate Abraham's migration to Canaan in the wider historical scene associates him with a great Amorite invasion of Canaan at the time, but the connection remains unproven. At the time of Moses (fifteenth century B.C.), some of the Amorites were centered in Transjordan, since there the two Amorite kings Sihon and Og were defeated by Israel (Num 21:21–35). Sometimes "Amorite" is used as a general term for all the (non-Israelite) inhabitants of Canaan (e.g., Gen 15:16; Josh 24:15).

Israel's ancestors associated with Hittites. Abraham purchased the region around the cave of Machpelah near Hebron from Hittites (ca. 2000 B.C.; Genesis 23). Esau married Hittite women (Gen 26:34). The Hittites once had a major empire centered in Anatolia toward the end of the second millennium, but it fell to the Sea Peoples about 1200 B.C., and the Hittites were widely dispersed after that. In David's time (ca. 1000 B.C.), Uriah the Hittite (Bathsheba's husband) lived in Jerusalem and was a Yahwist (2 Samuel 11–12). But the Bible attests to the presence of Hittites much farther south in Canaan and much earlier—under circumstances about which we can only speculate.

---

[4] See the excursus "The Seven Peoples of Canaan" in Harstad, *Joshua*, 175–79.

[5] For example, in Josh 10:5 the king of Jerusalem was one of five kings called Amorites who allied against Joshua, but after those kings were defeated and the land as a whole was conquered, Josh 15:8 associates Jerusalem with Jebusite territory, and several hundred years later 2 Sam 5:6–10 recounts David's capture of Jerusalem from the Jebusites, who had retained a stronghold there.

16:4 וּמוֹלְדוֹתַ֫יִךְ—This word (here written plene) is repeated from 16:3 as a *casus pendens*, standing independently at the beginning of the sentence, apparently for emphasis.

בְּי֨וֹם הוּלֶּ֣דֶת אֹתָ֗ךְ—The verb is the Hophal infinitive construct of יָלַד, "to give birth," the root of the noun at the beginning of the verse. The Hophal infinitive construct recurs in the form הֻלֶּ֫דֶת in 16:5. In both, the *daghesh* (-לּ-) marks the assimilated root letter י (see GKC, § 71). Joüon, § 58 c, suggests that the form may be a Qal passive infinitive, but Waltke-O'Connor states that the Qal passive infinitive is "a problematic form altogether" (§ 22.6d, footnote 38). The Hiphil is well attested, and the Hophal has the passive of the Hiphil's meaning.

The passive verb ("be born") does not take a pronominal suffix here, but is followed by the direct object sign with suffix, אֹתָ֗ךְ. This usage of אֶת introducing the *subject* of a passive verb is well attested in biblical Hebrew (GKC, § 121 a, b). It is a reminder of how ill-fitting Western grammatical categories are to Semitic languages.

לֹא־כָרַּ֣ת שָׁרֵּ֗ךְ—The verb is a Qal passive perfect (third masculine singular) of כָּרַת, "to cut." Two later verbs in the verse, רֻחַ֫צְתְּ and חֻתָּ֫לְתְּ, are also Qal passive perfects (but second feminine singular). Older grammarians regarded these forms as Pual (e.g., GKC, § 64 d, e), but the Piel of these verbs is not used in the OT, and the meanings of כָּרַת and רֻחַ֫צְתְּ are the passives of the Qal meanings. Modern grammarians generally agree that Hebrew once had a complete Qal passive conjugation (as do some other Semitic languages), but it fell into disuse, and the OT preserves only a few examples besides the common Qal passive participle (Joüon, § 58; Waltke-O'Connor, § 22.6).

The noun שֹׁר is from the root שׁרר as one can see from שָׁרְרֵ֫ךְ in Song 7:3 (ET 7:2), which is the same form as שָׁרֵּ֫ךְ except that here the second ר is assimilated and marked by *daghesh*. In the only other OT occurrence it has the masculine pronoun, שָׁרֶ֫ךָ (Prov 3:8). It means "navel" (Song 7:3; Prov 3:8) or "umbilical cord" (Ezek 16:4).[6] Normally the umbilical cord is tied or clamped before being cut so that the baby will not bleed through it, but neither is done for this infant.

It is rare for the consonant ר to be doubled (-רּ-), but the OT has other instances (GKC, § 22 s; Joüon § 23 a). Its doubling in the verb is a result of the Qal passive conjugation (or of the Masoretes assumption that it is Pual). Its doubling in the noun is the result of the noun's root.

The Talmud (*Shabbath*, 129b) quotes 16:4 and allows that even on the Sabbath a newborn should have the umbilical cord cut and be washed, "salted," and swaddled.

וּבְמַ֥יִם לֹא־רֻחַ֖צְתְּ לְמִשְׁעִ֑י—The verb is another Qal passive perfect (second feminine singular), from רָחַץ, "to wash, bathe." There is no consensus whatsoever on the derivation or meaning of לְמִשְׁעִי, nor apparently was there in antiquity. The LXX and Syriac do not translate it at all, probably because they did not understand it.[7] Some

---

[6] One may see the discussion in Mitchell, *The Song of Songs*, 1055–57, 1096, 1106–8.

[7] Some moderns interpret the omission as confirmation of their suspicion that it is a later addition. For example, Zimmerli, *Ezekiel*, 1:323, omits it and alleges that "it disturbs the rhythmic balance of the four negative clauses." However, it is difficult to see why a scribe would

Greek translations have τοῦ χριστοῦ μου, "you were not washed in the water *of my Christ*," which apparently was added by Christian copyists who intended an allusion to Holy Baptism. Apparently they equated לְמִשְׁעִי with לִמְשִׁיחִי, the noun מָשִׁיח ("Messiah/Christ, anointed one") with preposition לְ ("belonging to") and first common singular suffix.

The Vulgate's translation of לְמִשְׁעִי by *in salutem*, "you were not washed in water *into salvation*," may also allude to Christian Baptism and seems to presuppose that the term is derived from יָשַׁע. The Targum's paraphrase is "to cleanse him," which is somewhat tautological (since washing obviously would be to cleanse), and surprisingly, a majority of modern English translations follow that.

Grammatically, לְמִשְׁעִי could be the Aramaic Peal infinitive of שְׁעַי, "to daub, smear, cover," with preposition לְ. (Aramaic infinitives with preformative -מ occasionally appear in the Hebrew portions of the OT; see GKC, § 45 e.) Driver[8] is influential in suggesting that it is an Aramaic form of verbal noun from שְׁעַי, cognate with Hebrew שָׁעַע, "to smooth, smear, seal," attested in the OT and in rabbinic Hebrew (also cognate with Aramaic שְׁעַע and Syriac ܫܥܐ). According to Greenberg,[9] already Rashi explained לְמִשְׁעִי as a by-form of שׁעע. Many other suggestions have been tendered, but I, with Greenberg, Block,[10] and Allen,[11] am attracted to this one. Driver interprets it as a rubbing with *oil*, and so Allen tentatively translates "you were not washed with a view to oiling (?) you,"[12] an interpretation reflected in my translation. Driver writes (ca. 1950) that "a new-born infant is to this day washed and oiled and then salted in Palestine."[13] Greenberg (ca. 1983) remarks that even in modern times Arab midwives in Palestine have been known to cover the infant's body with a mixture of salt and oil, and that salt was thought to toughen the skin.[14]

The sequel in 16:9 offers a possible contextual guide to the meaning of the Hebrew here. There Yahweh states that he washed her, washed off her blood, and anointed her with oil. It is plausible that after bathing in water, oil would be rubbed on the infant (cf. modern baby oil). If so, early Christian translators and copyists may have thought of the rite of chrismation: especially in the Eastern Orthodox rite, oil is applied after Baptism as a sign of the gift of the Holy Spirit. The practice of chrismation is drawn from NT passages that allude to Baptism as the Sacrament by which one is "sealed" with the gift of the Holy Spirit (e.g., 2 Cor 1:22; Eph 1:13; 4:30; cf. Eph 4:5). The very title "Christ" and the idiom of a "*Christian* name" conferred when a person is "*christened*" (baptized) are all derived from the same Greek verb, χρίω, "to

---

add a term whose meaning is unknown, and it is far more plausible that the ancient translators were as baffled by it as modern ones are.

8   Driver, "Difficult Words in the Hebrew Prophets," 63–64.

9   Greenberg, *Ezekiel*, 1:275.

10 Block, *Ezekiel*, 1:473, including n. 57.

11 Allen, *Ezekiel*, 1:226–27.

12 Allen, *Ezekiel*, 1:224.

13 Driver, "Difficult Words in the Hebrew Prophets," 64.

14 Greenberg, *Ezekiel 1–20*, 274, citing several ethnographic studies.

anoint." The association of oil with baptismal incorporation into Christ may have given rise to the variant Greek translation of Ezek 16:4 ("washed in the water of my Christ") and the Vulgate's "washed in water into salvation."

וְהָמְלֵחַ֙ לֹ֣א הֻמְלַ֔חַתְּ וְהָחְתֵּ֖ל לֹ֥א חֻתָּֽלְתְּ׃—These final two clauses are grammatically parallel to each other. Both begin with a Hophal infinitive absolute (GKC, § 53 t) and end with a corresponding (second feminine singular) perfect verb. The four similar verb forms (the first three of which are Hophal) create assonance. The infinitive absolute usually conveys emphasis, and here it would reinforce the neglected condition of the pathetic infant: *"To be sure*, you were not rubbed with salt or wrapped in cloth" (Waltke-O'Connor, § 35.3.1f, example 5; see also § 28.4a, example 3b). I have translated "thoroughly," parallel to "tightly" in the next clause. The rare verb מָלַח is denominative from מֶלַח, "salt," and the Qal means "to salt" in Lev 2:13. The Hophal occurs only here (twice) and means "to be rubbed with salt" or "to be washed with salt water." Since salt was widely used as a preservative, salt or salt water probably would serve as an antiseptic.

The verb חָתַל occurs (twice) only here in the OT, and rare cognate nouns in Hebrew (חֲתֻלָּה, חִתּוּל) and Ugaritic (*ḥtl*) mean "swaddling cloths" or "bandage." The verb means "to swaddle, wrap in cloths." הָחְתֵּל is the Hophal infinitive absolute, for which I have used "tightly." חֻתָּלְתְּ probably is the third Qal passive perfect in the verse, rather than a Pual. Some suggest emending it to a Hophal, but the OT contains many other examples where an infinitive absolute and the finite form of the same verb are in different stems. Possibly the desire for assonance called for the Hophal infinitive here, just as in the preceding clause.

16:5 לֹא־חָ֧סָה עָלַ֣יִךְ עַ֗יִן ... לְחֻמְלָ֖ה עָלָ֑יִךְ—This is phrased somewhat differently than the usual idioms in Ezekiel with עַיִן ("eye") and the verbs חָסָה and חָמַל. See the last textual note on 5:11. לְחֻמְלָה is one of several so-called feminine forms of the Qal infinitive construct (GKC, § 45 d).

וַתֻּֽשְׁלְכִ֞י אֶל־פְּנֵ֤י הַשָּׂדֶה֙—The verb שָׁלַךְ, "to throw (out)," occurs only in the Hiphil and (as here) Hophal, and it can be a technical term for abandonment or, in the case of infants, exposure to the elements for the purpose of causing the death of unwanted children, a common practice in antiquity.[15] That meaning is reinforced by the following phrase בְּגֹ֖עַל נַפְשֵֽׁךְ. The noun גֹּעַל, "loathing, **disdain**" (*HALOT*) occurs only here but is cognate to the infrequent verb גָּעַל, "to **loathe**, to feel disgust" (*HALOT*), which sometimes seems to have the technical sense of rejecting or repudiating a legal or covenantal obligation, in addition to the emotional overtones of "despise, abhor, reject." In 16:45 גָּעַל will be used twice to refer to women who repudiate their obligations to their husbands and their children.

16:6 וָאֶעֱבֹ֤ר עָלַ֙יִךְ֙— This clause will also begin 16:8. The combination of עָבַר and preposition עַל can have various nuances, including "(happen to) pass by" (Judg 9:25) unintentionally; "come upon" (e.g., Num 5:14); and "cross over to, come to" someone deliberately (e.g., 2 Sam 24:20; 2 Ki 4:9). For the implications here, see the com-

---

[15] See the references in Greenberg, *Ezekiel 1–20*, 275.

mentary below. (In 16:15, 25 the participle עֹבֵר clearly has the sense of "passerby," any man that just happens to pass by at random.)

וָאֶרְאֵךְ מִתְבּוֹסֶסֶת בְּדָמָיִךְ—The verb רָאָה has the second feminine singular object suffix. The Qal of בּוּס means "to tread, trample under foot." The form here (repeated in 16:22) is the feminine singular participle of the Hithpolel (found only in these two verses), which suggests "the blind movement of [an] infant's limbs, *kick out* (this way and that)" (BDB), as infants do reflexively. "In your blood" could refer to blood from the mother on the newborn, unwashed baby, but the pronoun "your" may suggest that the infant is bleeding, perhaps from her uncut (and untied, unclamped) umbilical cord.

דָּם (בְּדָמָיִךְ) is plural throughout this verse, but singular in 16:22 (בְּדָמֵךְ). The plural accords with the usage in priestly laws concerning bloody bodily discharges (Lev 12:4, 5, 7; 20:18; cf. the singular in Lev 15:19, 25). A comparable variation in number occurs with תַּזְנוּת in Ezek 16:15 and 16:26 and other places in the book.

וָאֹמַר לָךְ בְּדָמַיִךְ חֲיִי—The Masoretic accents punctuate this as "I said to you, 'In your blood, live!' " Keil prefers that understanding as allegedly more emphatic: "Although lying in thy blood, in which thou wouldst inevitably bleed to death, yet thou shalt live."[16] Most translations and commentators abandon the Masoretic accents and punctuate it as "I said to you [while you were] in your blood, 'Live!' " In 16:9 Yahweh will wash her blood off of her, after she has reached physical maturity. If the blood in that verse is the same as the blood here, it seems that Yahweh here commands her to live in her blood (covered by it) until that later time. The blood in 16:6 may connote her uncleanness or neglected condition, which would continue until God's actions in 16:9. Despite her abject condition, Yahweh grants her continuing life by the power of his spoken Word.

The view that she remains covered by her blood until it is washed off in 16:9 is supported by the parallel delay in applying oil (if the difficult Hebrew in 16:4 refers to the lack of "oiling" at her birth), since she is not anointed with oil until 16:9. Alternatively, the blood in 16:9 might be menstrual blood, but even if so, there is no indication that Yahweh removed her birth blood (16:6) until he washed her in 16:9. The Targum interprets the first "blood" in 16:6 as that of circumcision with its saving significance for Israel (even though the metaphorical infant is a girl) and the "blood" in the repeated clause in 16:6 as that of the Passover, which delivers Israel.

Since the LXX does not repeat the clause, some consider its repetition secondary,[17] and many modern translations (RSV, NRSV, NIV) omit it. While scribal dittography in the MT is possible, the generally shorter character of the LXX diminishes the force of its testimony, and if textual error is involved, we should think instead of haplography in the LXX. Greenberg makes a good case for understanding the repetition as emphatic; he aptly compares the more familiar example in Ps 130:6.[18] KJV adds "yea" before the repetition, and NKJV modernizes to "yes."

---

[16] Keil, *Ezekiel*, 1:200.

[17] For example, Zimmerli, *Ezekiel*, 1:323.

[18] Greenberg, *Ezekiel*, 1:276.

16:7 רְבָבָה כְּצֶמַח הַשָּׂדֶה נְתַתִּיךְ—**רְבָבָה**—Ordinarily, the noun רְבָבָה means "multitude" or "myriad." Here it is used idiomatically as a second direct object after נָתַן with its object suffix, literally, "I have made you [to be] a myriad," which is appropriate for the growing population of Israelites, but is hard to translate in reference to the metaphorical girl, especially with the following simile "like a sprout of the field" (see the commentary). It requires an English idiom such as "I made you grow prolifically/ luxuriantly." I have translated, "I made you thrive." The accent is not merely on quantity, but also quality, as reinforced by the simile. Wild plants (and weeds) always seem to thrive more readily than cultivated plants, as farmers and gardeners can attest. The Piel of צָמַח, cognate to the noun צֶמַח, "sprout," appears later in the verse with reference to her hair sprouting.

Critical commentators commonly perform radical surgery on רְבָבָה, often emending it to רְבִי (imperative of רָבָה), parallel to the previous imperative חֲיִי in 16:6. Some connect this clause with the last clause of 16:6, except for נְתַתִּיךְ, which they delete, even though it is attested in the LXX.[19]

וַתִּרְבִּי וַתִּגְדְּלִי—The verb רָבָה usually means "become numerous, increase," but only here (and in reference to animals in Job 39:4) it must mean to "grow up" (BDB, 2 b (1); *HALOT*, 2 c). As with the related preceding noun רְבָבָה, it certainly could have the numerical meaning in the application of the metaphor to Israel's population. The verb גָּדַל often is used in reference to a child, meaning to "grow up" (BDB, 1 a). RSV and NRSV have "became tall," but that is more specific than גָּדַל warrants. "Matured" is a common rendition, and the context certainly refers to physical maturation, but that English word is much broader. With NIV, I have settled on "developed" as being neither broader nor narrower than the original.

וַתָּבֹאִי בַּעֲדִי עֲדָיִים—This difficult clause literalistically translates as "you came with jewelry of jewelries," but the construct phrase is a superlative, "with most excellent ornaments/jewelry" (cf. "Song of Songs," i.e., the best song). The noun עֲדִי, "ornament, jewelry," occurred in 7:20, and it will recur in 16:11 (the pausal form עֶדִי), where Yahweh will describe in detail how he adorned her with various kinds of jewelry (16:11–13). Elsewhere in the OT, the noun is always singular, but a plural form was required here to form the superlative construction.

The clause here may be proleptic, stating that Israel "came by" or "acquired" the jewelry, and the later verses (16:11–13) would then explain that it was Yahweh who gave the jewelry to her, and enumerate the specific kinds. Slightly different is NIV's "became the most beautiful of jewels," which takes the "jewelry" as metaphorical for the pubescent girl herself (cf. also ESV's "arrived at full adornment"). That may have some support in the metaphorical use of עֲדִי in 7:20, where "his ornament" probably refers to Yahweh's temple (though other metaphorical meanings are possible there).

Most convincingly in my judgment, Greenberg cites Mesopotamian and Mishnaic parallels where similar language describes puberty, specifically the growth of

---

[19] See, for example, Zimmerli, *Ezekiel*, 1:324; Allen, *Ezekiel*, 1:224, 227; and the RSV. Zimmerli suggests that the emended text echoes פְּרוּ וּרְבוּ in Gen 1:22, which is rather venturesome, to say the least.

breasts and body hair. He rejects the common emendation (see below) by noting that Jewish commentators never include menarche among the signs of puberty, and that its mention here does not "suit the erotic context."[20] With NKJV I have paraphrased "became very beautiful."

Many commentators propose emendations, most commonly to וַתָּבֹאִי בַּעֲדִים, "and you came into menses" (or some variant reconstruction).[21] RSV paraphrases "arrived at full maidenhood" (similar is NRSV: "arrived at full womanhood"). This fits the context, but at the cost of radical textual surgery. The LXX has εἰς πόλεις πόλεων, "into cities of cities," which essentially testifies to the MT but evidently confused ד for ר (as if the text were בְּעָרֵי עָרִים). Block thinks that the LXX points to the original consonants, and he posits an original text of בַּעֲרִי עֶרְיִים, "completely nude,"[22] but his proposed noun forms (based on the verb עָרָה, "be naked") never occur elsewhere in the OT, and his phrase virtually duplicates the final clause in the verse.

שָׁדַיִם נָכֹנוּ—The dual שָׁדַיִם (two "breasts") does not have a pronominal suffix, but there are other examples of its omission, which may be for stylistic variation, and a pronoun ("your") can easily be supplied from the context. Usually nouns for body parts that occur in pairs are feminine, but oddly שַׁד is masculine, and so שָׁדַיִם takes the third masculine plural verb נָכֹנוּ (Niphal of כּוּן), "be established, prepared," which might mean "be firm" (BDB, 1 a; *HALOT*, 1), but with many I have rendered it "well formed."

וּשְׂעָרֵךְ צִמֵּחַ—The verb is, literally, "sprouted," echoing the cognate noun צֶמַח earlier in the verse. Some translate ingressively, "began to grow," although the Piel may be intensive: "grew thickly." שֵׂעָר can refer to various kinds of "hair," including on the scalp, the beard, the eyebrows, body hair, and "hair of the legs," probably pubic hair (of men in Is 7:20). Here it might refer to the "long *hair* of [a] woman" (BDB, 2). However, the statement that hers now "sprouted" at puberty implies that it is a secondary sexual characteristic, which would include underarm and "pubic hair" (*HALOT*, 2 b). If so, this would be the only passage in the Bible that refers to a woman's in an amorous context. In contrast, the Song of Songs never refers to the region of the genitalia of either Solomon or the Shulammite.[23]

וְאַתְּ עֵרֹם וְעֶרְיָה:—Literally, "you were naked and nakedness," this alliterative hendiadys (idiomatically in English, "bare/stark naked") uses a predicate adjective and a predicate noun. עֵירֹם is from עוּר and עֶרְיָה is from עָרָה. The verbs עוּר and עָרָה both mean "be naked, bare," and they are by-forms; both seem to be derived from a biliteral root ער.

16:8 The first three Hebrew words repeat verbatim the opening words of 16:6.

וְהִנֵּה עִתֵּךְ עֵת דֹּדִים—The noun עֵת can refer to "time" with various nuances. The first instance here refers to her "time" or "stage" of life, namely, that she has attained marriageable age, and the second refers to the "proper, suitable time" (BDB, 2 b) for

---

[20] Greenberg, *Ezekiel*, 1:276–77.

[21] So, for example, Cooke, *Ezekiel*, 166; Zimmerli, *Ezekiel*, 1:324.

[22] Block, *Ezekiel*, 1:478, n. 84.

[23] See the analysis in Mitchell, *The Song of Songs*, 287–90, 807–10.

"love." דֹּדִים (the plural of דֹּד, "lover") is an abstract plural, usually referring to married "love" (e.g., Song 1:2; 4:10), and sometimes connoting married lovemaking (e.g., Song 5:1; 7:13 [ET 7:12]), though some commentators err by overemphasizing the sexual aspect of married love.[24] Here it probably implies both the marriage relationship and lovemaking. In some passages דֹּדִים refers to adulterous sexual "love" (Ezek 23:17; Prov 7:18).

וָאֶפְרֹשׂ כְּנָפִי עָלַיִךְ—Literally, "I spread my wing over you," this is an undisputed idiom for taking a wife in marriage; see Ruth's request to Boaz, וּפָרַשְׂתָּ כְנָפֶךָ עַל־אֲמָתְךָ (Ruth 3:9). In Ezek 5:3 the same noun ("wings") referred to folds in Ezekiel's robe, and in the idiom here in 16:8 it is commonly rendered "robe." It is not certain whether the metaphor is only verbal or describes some symbolical action (e.g., spreading a robe over a woman) that may have been part of a marriage pledge or ceremony. In either case, the next clause (וָאֲכַסֶּה עֶרְוָתֵךְ) makes the meaning of the symbolism explicit: the husband covers the woman's nakedness, so that henceforth she will be "covered" (unavailable) to any man except her husband. (An opposite idiom appears in Deut 23:1 [ET 22:30], where a man who takes his father's wife "uncovers the wing of his father," that is, violates his father's marriage.)

וָאֶשָּׁבַע לָךְ וָאָבוֹא בִבְרִית אֹתָךְ—These two synonymous statements come close to temporarily abandoning the marriage metaphor in favor of Yahweh's covenant oath. The Hebrew has only "I swore to you," but I have added "an oath" because I fear that in the English vernacular "swear" by itself has come to be used interchangeably with "curse." "I entered into a covenant with you" is not among the common expressions for making a covenant. Perhaps, like the wedding formula at the end of the verse, it emphasizes that the action was unilateral on Yahweh's part, not a mutual covenant between equal partners. Other passages use הֵקִים or נָתַן to emphasize the unilateral aspect of the covenant that Yahweh "established" or "gave" to Israel. Ezekiel usually uses the verb כָּרַת ("to cut a covenant"), which can also be used for a bilateral pact between people. This verse in Ezekiel may be unique in the OT in referring to the wedding vow as an oath to which the spouse swears, though other passages depict marriage as a "covenant" (e.g., Mal 2:14 and perhaps Prov 2:17).[25]

Greenberg is probably correct in understanding the language here as encompassing both Yahweh's repeated sworn oaths to the patriarchs to give them the land of Canaan and the Sinai "covenant."[26] Ezekiel himself in 20:5–6 connects God's oath ("I swore with uplifted hand") with the patriarchal promise, which includes the "Seed" or descendants culminating in Jesus Christ (Galatians 3). In the Torah, when God is the subject of this verb "to swear" (Niphal of שָׁבַע), some passages (e.g., Gen

---

[24] For the biblical usage and meaning of דֹּד, "lover," in the context of marriage, see Mitchell, *The Song of Songs*, 386–93. For the meaning of the abstract plural דֹּדִים, "love," throughout the OT, see Mitchell, *The Song of Songs*, 562–63. When discussing the meanings of these terms many commentators disregard that the lovers in the Song are married (Song 3:11). See Mitchell, *The Song of Songs*, 279–81.

[25] See further Hugenberger, *Marriage as a Covenant*.

[26] Greenberg, *Ezekiel*, 1:277–78.

22:16–18; 26:3–4) affirm God's original promise to Abraham (Gen 12:1–3) of this Seed and that through this Seed all nations of the earth would be blessed. Others quote the promise of the land (Gen 24:7; 26:3; Ex 13:5). Still others (not necessarily with "swear") quote God as saying, "I am Yahweh, your God" (e.g., Ex 6:7; cf. Gen 15:7; 28:13), alluding to the basic covenant formula, "I will be your God, and you will be my people" (e.g., Lev 26:12; cf., e.g., Ezek 11:20; 14:11).

וַתִּֽהְיִי לִי׃—While the preceding emphasized the divine side of the covenant, this concluding assertion, "and you became mine," brings out the human side. This use of the preposition לְ for possession in marriage is similar to language found in marriage contracts throughout the ancient Near East. The formulation may sound to modern Westerners as though the husband is claiming his bride as though she were chattel, but in total biblical context, this clearly is not the case. Israelite marriages, like most of those in antiquity, had a "patriarchal" cast to them, but the husband's headship was to be exercised in love, recalling Adam's headship over Eve in Eden before the fall, and anticipating the headship of Jesus Christ over his church. The following verses will show that the divine Husband goes to great lengths to enhance his wife's status and wellbeing. As for other specific texts, Hos 2:18 (ET 2:16); Song 2:16; 6:3; 7:11 (ET 7:10); 1 Cor 7:1–7; and Eph 5:21–33 stand out.[27]

16:9 Yahweh does what can be done only by him. The three actions mentioned here reverse the deprivations mentioned in Ezek 16:4. It is doubtful if these actions reflect ceremonies in OT wedding rites. The source of her blood that Yahweh washes away is disputed. Greenberg understands it as the birth blood (16:6), which "in the tele-scoped vision of the allegory" still clung to her.[28] Those who emended 16:7 to עֲדָיִם think of menstrual blood, but according to Levitical law this would have precluded consummation of the marriage (Lev 15:19–24; cf. Ezek 18:6). Block thinks of a virgin's bleeding at first coitus (cf. Deut 22:13–21).[29] There are other suggestions, but we need not decide.

The verb וָאֲסֻכֵךְ is the Qal of סוּךְ, "to anoint," usually (as here) with "oil" (שֶׁמֶן), which is associated with marital intimacy in Song 1:3 and 4:10, and perfumed oil is also part of the bridal preparations in Esth 2:12. See also סוּךְ in Ruth 3:3 as part of Ruth's preparations before offering marriage (Ruth 3:4, 9).

16:10 The general picture Yahweh paints here is very clear. He provides the attire appropriate for princesses (cf. Ps 45:14–15 [ET 45:13–14] in the messianic/royal wedding psalm) or the spoils of war received by upper-class women (Judg 5:30). Unfortunately, many of the words in Ezek 16:10–13 (especially 16:10) are not totally understood, so there is an element of conjecture in any translation. Some of the words appear also in the descriptions of the tabernacle's construction (Exodus 25–28). While those descriptions

---

27 One may see the discussion "The Progressive Covenantal Affirmations in Song of Songs 2:16; 6:3; 7:11 (ET 7:10)" in Mitchell, *The Song of Songs*, 404–8, and also "The Headship of the Lord Jesus Christ" on pages 395–99.

28 Greenberg, *Ezekiel*, 1:278.

29 Block, *Ezekiel*, 1:484.

usually do not clarify the meanings of the vocables themselves, they remind us that the finest materials were used in the building of that elaborate sanctuary. Compare Song 1:5, where the Shulammite bride of Solomon is likened to the temple curtains.

וָאַלְבִּישֵׁךְ רִקְמָה—The noun רִקְמָה (also in 16:13, 18) is often translated "embroidered cloth," but that is misleading because it suggests decorative touches on the exterior or borders of the material. I have rendered it "finest woven material." It is cognate to the verb רָקַם, "to weave," used often for weaving for the tabernacle an elaborate material, probably of multicolored strands and displaying the same finished composition on both front and back.[a] The same noun (רִקְמָה) is used in the messianic Ps 45:15 (ET 45:14), where the bride apparently in woven robes is led to the king for her wedding (cf. Revelation 21). In Ps 139:15 the psalmist uses the verb רָקַם figuratively to say that he was masterfully "woven" or "knit" by God together as a baby in the womb, an oft-cited verse for the Christian view of the sanctity of human life from conception.

(a) E.g., Ex 26:36; 35:35; 38:18, 23

וָאֶנְעֲלֵךְ תָּחַשׁ—The verb נָעַל occurs only here and in 2 Chr 28:15 but obviously is denominative from נַעַל, "sandal," and hence means "to furnish with sandals" (BDB). תָּחַשׁ ("luxury leather"), the material of which her sandals were made, was also used for the cover of the tabernacle (Ex 26:14; Num 4:6). Its meaning has long been debated, and no definitive solution is in sight. KJV's "badgers' skin" is no longer defended because of its unsuitability for shoes and for the tabernacle covering. Modern scholars have favored leather from a dolphin, dugong, or manatee, both because of the abundance of a creature of this sort in the Red Sea and because the Bedouin were known to use its hide for shoes. The best recent evidence prefers an Akkadian cognate, *dushu*, which described goat or sheep leather dyed and tanned the color of a *dushu* stone and used for luxury footwear or for decorating harnesses.

וָאֶחְבְּשֵׁךְ בַּשֵּׁשׁ—When the verb חָבַשׁ, "bind up," is used of putting on clothing, it refers to winding on headgear of some sort (so again in 24:17; and of the priests' turbans in Ex 29:9; Lev 8:13). שֵׁשׁ is an Egyptian loanword used for the highest quality linen. It was used both for the priestly headdress (Ex 28:39; 39:28) and for certain tabernacle curtains (e.g., Ex 36:8; 38:9). Later it tended to be replaced by the native Semitic word בּוּץ (e.g., Ezek 27:16), which too contrasts with בַּד, ordinary linen.

וָאֲכַסֵּךְ מֶשִׁי:—This appears to be a summary statement about the woman's wardrobe. The noun מֶשִׁי occurs only here and in 16:13. Its traditional translation is "silk," but that fabric does not appear to have been known in the western part of the fertile crescent until a couple of centuries after Ezekiel. A possible Hittite derivation suggests a veil or shawl. A possible Egyptian cognate indicates only some kind of exotic cloth. "Exquisite fabric" is an appropriate guess.

16:11 וָאֶעְדֵּךְ עֶדִי—Usually the verb עָדָה is intransitive (see the textual note on it in 16:13), but here it is transitive with an object suffix (ךְ—[d]) and a second accusative: "I adorned you (with) jewelry." The noun עֶדִי, "jewelry," is used literally, whereas it may have been figurative in 16:7.

צְמִידִים עַל־יָדַיִךְ—Hebrew יָד can include the forearm, but "wrists" are the natural location of "bracelets." The same vocabulary is used for the wedding gift of "bracelets" given to Rebekah to wear on her "wrists" (Gen 24:22, 30, 47). They are also given to the sisters in Ezek 23:42.

וּרְבִיד—The only other OT occurrence of this word is in Gen 41:42, where Joseph was given a gold "necklace."

16:12   A נֶזֶם can apparently be any kind of ring, but its use with אַף here implies that it is a nose ring. The same vocabulary is used when Abraham's servant placed a "ring" on Rebekah's "nose" as a wedding gift (Gen 24:47; see also נֶזֶם in Gen 24:22, 30). While nose rings in the modern West are often associated with the counterculture, they were an elegant form of female jewelry in the ancient Orient (Is 3:21; but cf. Prov 11:22) and are still frequently to be seen on Bedouin women.

וַעֲטֶרֶת תִּפְאֶרֶת—The list of jewelry lavished on the woman climaxes in "a crown of glory" (also in 23:42). The Hebrew phrase is assonant. עֲטָרָה ("crown") is placed in construct with תִּפְאֶרֶת instead of an adjectival modifier ("glorious crown"). This phrase appears also in Is 62:3; Jer 13:18; Prov 4:9; 16:31.

16:13   וַתַּעְדִּי—Usually the verb עָדָה is intransitive and reflexive, "adorn oneself." However, the emphasis throughout this section has been that Yahweh has given the woman everything she has, so it would be inconsistent to make her the actor. Many translations use a passive ("you were adorned"), which conveys the graciousness of Yahweh's actions toward her, even though grammatically the precise sense of the Qal probably is "you wore jewelry/finery."

The first part of the verse reiterates the expensive material used for her clothing in 16:10, only in a different order and with the addition of "gold and silver" (and the omission of "sandals"). The Kethib שֵׁשִׁי has acquired a superfluous *yod*, apparently by attraction to the following מֶשִׁי, and the Qere has שֵׁשׁ as in 16:10.

סֹלֶת—"Fine flour" refers to seminola, essentially our "cream of wheat." Everyday flour was more coarsely ground.

אָכָלְתִּי—The Qere is the regular second feminine singular perfect in pause, אָכָלְתְּ. The ending of the Kethib (תִי-) retains the archaic form of the second singular feminine afformative (Joüon, § 42 f). Eight more times in this chapter the Kethib will be a second feminine singular perfect verb with that same archaic ending (16:18, 22a, 31 [twice], 43 [twice], 47, and 51). Why these archaisms, and so many of them, appear here is impossible to say. In the passage many other second feminine singular perfect verbs (e.g., those in 16:22b, 28, 29) have the usual, later ending (תְּ-).

וַתִּיפִי בִּמְאֹד מְאֹד—The verb יָפָה means "to be beautiful" and can be used of a man (the reduplicated form in Ps 45:3 [ET 45:2], the wedding psalm, pointing to Christ) as well as a woman (here and Song 7:7 [ET 7:6]; cf. Song 4:10; 7:2 [ET 7:1]). See the textual note on the repeated adverbial phrase בִּמְאֹד מְאֹד (literally, "with muchness, muchness") in 9:9.

וַתִּצְלְחִי לִמְלוּכָה:—Literally, "and thou didst prosper to royalty" (BDB, s.v. צָלֵחַ II, Qal), this does not mean that she deserved or somehow worked her way up to be queen. Rather, royal status was given to her by virtue of her union with the King. This same "great reversal" theme of a lowly maiden elevated to royalty purely by the King's grace is part of the Gospel message of the Song. See especially Song 6:8–9, 12.[30]

---

[30] One may see the discussion of the great reversal theme in Mitchell, *The Song of Songs*, 372–80.

Some question the genuineness of those final two words, largely because of their omission in most LXX manuscripts and some other early translations. Various reasons are advanced for its alleged addition. Zimmerli thinks it was "provoked by v 12b, which points to Jerusalem as a royal city."[31] But his logic seems poor. Already Cooke defended the words as necessary "to bring the story to its climax."[32]

16:14 וַיֵּצֵא לָךְ שֵׁם—Literally, "a name went out for you," שֵׁם ("name") often implies "reputation, fame," as also in 16:15 (cf. 1 Ki 10:1).

בְּיָפְיֵךְ—The noun יֳפִי[d], "beauty," will be repeated in 16:15, 25 and is cognate to the verb יָפָה in 16:13.

כִּי ׀ כָּלִיל הוּא—I have taken כִּי as asseverative: "in fact, indeed." כָּלִיל can mean "whole, complete," but in reference to "beauty" (יֳפִי[d]) here and in 27:3; 28:12, it is best translated "perfect" (*HALOT*, 1 b).

16:15 וַתִּבְטְחִי בְיָפְיֵךְ—The common combination בָּטַח בְּ means "to trust in" someone or something, and especially in the Psalms it is often used of trusting in Yahweh. Here the context demands that the initial *waw* be adversative: "*But* you trusted …"

וַתִּזְנִי עַל־שְׁמֵךְ—This form (second feminine singular Qal imperfect with *waw* consecutive) of זָנָה will be repeated in 16:16, 17, 26, 28, and the participle, זוֹנָה, will be in 16:30, 31, 33, 35, 41. Every language is rich in renditions of the verb. "Play the harlot" and "be a prostitute" are common, but the verb itself is broader than that, and the woman's behavior in this chapter exceeds that of typical prostitution and verges on pathological nymphomania. "Be sexually promiscuous" is a possibility but seems weaker than required by the context.

I have settled on the Anglo-Saxon "play the whore" for finite forms of the verb and "whore" for the participle, not least because of Ezekiel's own penchant for earthy language. Likewise, the cognate noun תַּזְנוּת is rendered "whoring" (see the next textual note).

I have taken עַל in the sense of "*in reliance on* your fame," parallel to " you trusted in your beauty."

וַתִּשְׁפְּכִי אֶת־תַּזְנוּתַיִךְ—Usually שָׁפַךְ means "to pour out," but that hardly produces idiomatic English, so, with many, here I have used "lavish." Possibly, there is an anticipation of the verb's use in 16:36.

The noun תַּזְנוּת, "whoring," has the וּת- ending common for abstract nouns (concepts). However, here and in 16:22, 33, 34, and 36, the abstract ending is treated as though it were the feminine plural ending וֹת- and so the second feminine singular suffix is the form used on plural nouns (יִךְ-). Even though the noun remains singular, the intent of the suffix may be to suggest that it is an intensive plural, for example, "profligate whoring." Yet the noun takes the form of the suffix used for singular nouns (ךְ-[d]) in 16:26 and 16:29, and in 16:20 and 16:25 the Kethib has the singular form, while the Qere directs reading the form as plural. A similar variation will occur with the use of this noun in chapter 23. I know of no explanation for this inconsistency and alternation.

---

[31] Zimmerli, *Ezekiel*, 1:325.

[32] Cooke, *Ezekiel*, 165.

כָּל־עוֹבֵר—Since the participle is masculine, this can be rendered "every man passing by." The phrase recurs in 16:25. It contrasts with Yahweh, who "passed by" her in 16:6, 8.

לוֹ־יֶהִי:—Grammatically this clause resembles the one at the end of 16:8, where Yahweh says לִי וַתִּהְיִי, "and you became mine." Probably its message is the opposite: the woman came to belong to others. Here too לְ denotes possession (belonging to someone). Its pronoun (לוֹ) must refer to the preceding participle, עוֹבֵר, "every man passing by." יְהִי is the third masculine singular jussive, so the clause is, literally, "to him let it be." We would have expected the verb to be וַתְּהִי (second feminine singular): "and you became his."

The ancient versions vary widely, apparently reflecting either textual or exegetical uncertainty, and the uncertainty continues in modern commentaries and translations. Origen's Hexapla preserves a Greek reading, "his you were," and the Vulgate similarly has the purpose clause *ut eius fieres*, "so that you would be made his." Of all the possibilities, this one appeals most to me because of its sharp contrast with the end of 16:8.

Keil,[33] Block,[34] NIV, and ESV take the subject of the masculine verb to be her "beauty" (בְיָפְיֵךְ near the start of the verse), since the noun יֳפִי is masculine (NIV and ESV: "your beauty became his"). That surely is possible, although "beauty" is quite distant.

Greenberg notes that a jussive occasionally stands for an imperfect, and that especially with הָיָה לְ a feminine subject sometimes occurs with a masculine verb and so translates as "it was his"[35] (similar to KJV). But what is the antecedent of "it"?

The clause וְלֹא יִהְיֶה ("and it should not be") at the end of 16:16 is similar (but negated). Also, the similar verb form וַיֶּהִי occurs near the end of 16:19 with no clear subject, apparently meaning "and it was [so]." Allen[36] along with others thinks of some confusion between the final words of 16:15 and 16:16 and suggests either not translating the end of 16:15 at all (RSV and NRSV omit it) or emending both texts. Zimmerli finds all such efforts unconvincing.[37]

16:16 בָּמוֹת טְלֻאֹת—The plural of בָּמָה, common in the prophets and historical books, is traditionally rendered "high places." See the lengthy textual note on it in 6:3. Apparently the woman's clothes were spread out on the floors of the shrines as mattresses or bedding. In the following clause וַתִּזְנִי עֲלֵיהֶם the masculine plural suffix ("on them") must refer to מִבְּגָדַיִךְ (sex would have taken place on her clothing).

The Qal passive participle טְלֻאֹת, serving as an adjective modifying בָּמוֹת, apparently means "multicoloured" (*HALOT*, s.v. טלא, 2) . The verb is used in only two other passages. The Qal passive participles in Gen 30:32–39 referring to the sheep

---

[33] Keil, *Ezekiel*, 1:204.

[34] Block, *Ezekiel*, 1:486, including n. 134.

[35] Greenberg, *Ezekiel*, 1:280, citing GKC, § 109 k; Joüon, §§ 114 l; 150 k, l.

[36] Allen, *Ezekiel*, 1:228.

[37] Zimmerli, *Ezekiel*, 1:325–26.

and goats of Jacob and Laban apparently mean "spotted," and the Pual participle in Josh 9:5 refers to the Gibeonites' sandals as "patched."

Even though different vocabulary is used in Prov 7:16, the scene there is similar as the adulteress entices passers-by, saying that she has spread colored Egyptian linens on her couch as preparation for sinful liaisons there.

לֹא בָאֹות וְלֹא יִהְיֶה׃—This ending of 16:16 is as difficult as the ending of 16:15 (see the textual note on it above). Some ancient versions attest to the presence of these words in their original text, but render them differently. If בָאֹות is the Qal feminine plural participle of בֹּוא, a literalistic reading would be "things not coming/entering, and it will not be." Alternatively, בָאֹות could be the noun אֹות, "sign" (as in 4:3; 14:8), with the preposition בְּ, in which case the first part would mean "not by the sign."

The translation "such things should not happen and it should not be" is partly dependent on Keil's treatment of בָאֹות as a participial substitute for a modal use of the imperfect, chosen, he argues, for the sake of paronomasia with בָּמֹות. He associates בֹּוא with the erection of the בָּמֹות, and יִהְיֶה with the clause with זָנָה. However, Keil denies that בֹּוא can mean "happen,"[38] but "come to pass" (BDB, 2 c) is one of its well-established meanings (cf. *HALOT*, 2 h, and הַבָּאֹות in Is 41:22, meaning "coming/future things"). My translation agrees essentially with NKJV and NIV. But also defensible is the view that the first clause refers to past things that had already come or happened: "The like has never been, nor ever shall be" (RSV and ESV). Many commentators either give up or resort to some emendation.

16:17 כְּלֵי תִפְאַרְתֵּךְ—The plural of the generic word כְּלִי ("thing, article") is in construct with תִּפְאֶרֶת, the same term describing the "crown of glory" Yahweh gave her in 16:12. The phrase here will be repeated in 16:39 and 23:26.

צַלְמֵי זָכָר—The noun צֶלֶם, "image," can have a variety of nuances, depending on what the image reproduces, for example, "the image of God" in Gen 1:27 and 9:6. The context here indicates that these were idolatrous or obscene "images." See the textual note on צֶלֶם in 7:20 and the commentary on 16:17. זָכָר can serve as a noun, "a man, a male," or as an adjective, "male." Some argue that the phrase may not necessarily be intended to exclude female images. Archaeological evidence, if relevant here, would strengthen that, since female fertility figurines are well-nigh ubiquitous in Iron Age strata, while male ones are almost totally absent.

If the phrase simply had זָכָר in apposition as an adjective, it would mean "male images." However, the construct phrase here is literalistically "images of male," and that makes it more likely that the images were of (or had) "phalli" (*HALOT*, s.v. זָכָר, 1). BDB cites an Arabic cognate that means "male organ," and in rabbinic Hebrew זָכָר can mean "phallus" (Jastrow, 3, gives *membrum*). In pagan art, phallic (often ithyphallic) images are common. The following clause, "and you played the whore with them," indicates that these images served as her consorts. Ezek 16:18–20 will describe her worship of them.

---

[38] Keil, *Ezekiel*, 1:205.

16:18 נָתַתִּי—The Kethib again has the archaic second feminine singular ending (נָתַתִּי), while the Qere reads the classical form (נָתַתְּ). See the textual note on אֲכַלְתִּי in 16:13.

16:19 וְלַחְמִי—The direct object ("my bread") of the verb נָתַתִּי is placed first, apparently for emphasis. Since "bread" had not been mentioned earlier, it is paralleled by a relative clause in apposition (without אֲשֶׁר) that lists the fare, "fine flour, oil, and honey," repeated from 16:13, but with the Hiphil verb הֶאֱכַלְתִּיךְ ("I fed you") rather than the Qal in 16:13 (אָכַלְתְּ, "you ate").[39]

וּנְתַתִּיהוּ—The third masculine singular object suffix is resumptive and refers back to וְלַחְמִי at the start of the verse.

לְרֵיחַ נִיחֹחַ—See the textual note on this technical phrase in 6:13. It removes any doubt that Ezekiel is talking about sacrificial offerings to idols.

וַיֶּהִי—This isolated verb is similar to the isolated clauses at the end of 16:15 and 16:16. Cooke[40] and Zimmerli[41] think it might be a dittograph of the preceding word, but the two forms differ too much to even make that plausible. The LXX and Vulgate attest to its presence. Allen suggests that if the preceding perfect consecutive has the modal sense ("you wanted to place before them") sometimes associated with the imperfect, this final statement would indicate achievement.[42] In Genesis 1 the repeated clause וַיְהִי־כֵן, "and it was so" (Gen 1:7, etc.) follows God's creative commands. At any rate, the gist of the word here seems to be "and it was so" or "and that happened," surely spoken in deep disappointment and disgust.

16:20 וַתִּזְבָּחִים לָהֶם לֶאֱכוֹל—The antecedent of the third masculine plural suffix on the verb ("you sacrificed them") is the "sons" and "daughters." The antecedent of לָהֶם ("to them") must be the "images" from 16:17. The same is true for לָהֶם at the end of 16:21. As in all pagan religions, here the sacrifices are offered as food for the gods "to eat" (infinitive of אָכַל), but Yahweh specifically renounces any such need for food; all belongs to him (Ps 50:12–13).

הַמְעַט מִתַּזְנוּתָיִךְ:—The interrogative הַ- with מְעַט, "a little, few," begins a question that extends into 16:21. The verse division is infelicitous. הַמְעַט is often followed by the preposition מִן in this sense: "Is [something] too little/not enough for you?" (see BDB, s.v. מְעַט, 1 e). The Qere again directs reading the form of the pronoun as if the noun were plural (מִתַּזְנוּתָיִךְ, "from your whorings"), whereas the Kethib considers it singular (מִתַּזְנֻתֵךְ).

16:21 וַתִּתְּנִים—This is the first of two clauses used elsewhere in the OT for human sacrifice. The verb נָתַן often means "to offer" a sacrifice (see BDB, 1 k), including the offering of children to Molech (Lev 18:21; 20:2–4). Whoever did so was to be stoned for profaning Yahweh's sanctuary and name (Lev 20:2–4). That same context (Lev

---

[39] Many critics would delete the whole appositional clause; see Zimmerli, *Ezekiel*, 1:326.

[40] Cooke, *Ezekiel*, 168.

[41] Zimmerli, *Ezekiel*, 1:326.

[42] Allen, *Ezekiel*, 1:228; his translation is on page 224.

20:5) describes such worship as "whoring" (זָנָה) after Molech. Since Ezekiel was a priest (Ezek 1:3), he would have been well versed in this terminology in Leviticus.

בְּהַעֲבִיר אוֹתָם לָהֶם:—This clause literally states that she offered her children "by making them pass through/cross over to them [to the images]." The Hiphil of עָבַר with בָּאֵשׁ, meaning "to cause [children] to pass through the fire" to Molech, occurs in 2 Ki 23:10. The Hiphil of עָבַר with בָּאֵשׁ but without reference to Molech is used for child sacrifice in Deut 18:10; 2 Ki 16:3; 17:17; 21:6; 23:10; Ezek 20:31; 2 Chr 33:6. Many of those passages associate that practice with other Satanic occult arts, such as divination, fortunetelling, mediums (channeling), and necromancy.

Here Ezekiel refers neither to fire nor to Molech. Nevertheless, in this context the clause clearly refers to sacrificing children, probably by causing them to pass through fire, that is, by burning them, and so the translation adds "the fire." But we are poorly informed on the details of such rites (see the commentary below).

16:22 וְאֵת—Apparently this is the preposition "with," linking the horrors of child sacrifice in 16:21 with "all your abominations and your whorings."

זָכַרְתִּי—The Kethib has the archaic second feminine singular ending, whereas the Qere (זָכַרְתְּ) has the usual classical spelling (see the textual note on אָכַלְתִּי in 16:13).

הָיִית:—This verb is unnecessary because the infinitive בְּהִיוֹתֵךְ began the second half of the verse. However, the LXX attests to the presence of a verb here. The LXX reads ἔζησας ("you lived"), as if it were חָיִית, which would be an obvious echo of 16:6. That would change the point from the infant's mortal danger after abandonment (kicking about in blood, in danger of bleeding to death) to Yahweh's intervention, which enabled her to live, even in her blood (16:6), but that theme seems intrusive and unlikely at this point.

16:23 רָעָתֵךְ—Instead of this singular noun, the LXX, Syriac, and one Hebrew manuscript read the plural. The difference in meaning is not substantial, but earlier Ezekiel used the singular ("evil, disaster") for punishment sent by God (6:10; 7:5; 14:22) and the plural for "evils" done by people (6:9, 11). However, he will use the singular again in 16:57 to refer to the woman's "wickedness."

אוֹי אוֹי לָךְ נְאֻם אֲדֹנָי יְהוִה:—The LXX does not have the exclamation "woe, woe to you," and so some critics allege that it is not original.[43] However, Yahweh uses אוֹי in exclamations against Jerusalem again in 24:6, 9. Here the signatory formula "says the Lord Yahweh," which the LXX attests, reinforces that the exclamation is uttered by Yahweh himself.

16:24 The precise meaning of two key words eludes us. גַּב occurs in Ezek 16:24, 31, 39 and רָמָה in 16:24, 25, 31, 39. The context indicates that they were structures of some sort that were readily recognized as places of prostitution. The LXX translates גַּב in 16:24 as οἴκημα πορνικόν, "house of fornication," and in 16:31, 39 as πορνεῖον, "brothel" (LEH). In 16:24 it renders רָמָה as ἔκθεμα, a "public notice" or "notice of directions" (how to get to the brothel), but in 16:25 as πορνεῖα, "brothels," and in 16:31, 39 as βάσις, "base, pedestal." These varied translations reflect their

---

43 For example, Zimmerli, *Ezekiel*, 1:327, who labels it "a passionate interjection of a reader."

function, but offer no reliable details. Both Hebrew words are often taken as synonyms of the common term בָּמָה, traditionally rendered "high place" (see the textual note on it in 6:3). Although these three terms doubtlessly were functionally related, and Ezekiel uses all three in this chapter (בָּמָה in 16:16), they probably are distinct from each other. One gets the impression that a "high place" was more complex and served as an established cultic installation, while in 16:24–39 Ezekiel seems to be describing simpler, impromptu, freelance constructions.

Seven of the twelve OT occurrences of גַּב occur in Ezekiel. The word is used in quite a variety of senses, including the rim of the wheels under the Glory (twice in 1:18); the back of the cherubim (10:12); a man's back (Ps 129:3); and the rounded molding of an altar base (Ezek 43:13). All uses seem to have a common reference to something convex, rounded, or domed. Hence I have rendered it here as "domed tent."

The pausal form here in Leningradensis is גָּב, whereas in 16:31, 39 the form (not in pause) is גַּב, whose pausal form would be גָּב. Many other manuscripts have גַּב here. A possible parallel would be עַד, "forever," whose pausal form is עָד in the frequent formula לְעוֹלָם וָעֶד ("forever and ever," e.g., Ex 15:18; Ps 9:6 [ET 9:5]).

Probably רָמָה is from the verb רום, and hence it is usually translated as "height, elevated place." Since the verb עָשָׂה is used with it, the reference must be to something manmade, and in a city "platform" seems more likely than a mound.

16:25 וַתְּתַעֲבִי אֶת־יָפְיֵךְ—The verb תָּעַב is related to the noun תּוֹעֵבָה, "abomination," which is frequent in Ezekiel. The Piel usually means "abhor, regard as an abomination," but here it must mean "cause [her beauty] to be an abomination" (BDB, 2). The most beautiful woman can be abhorrent (Prov 11:22).

וַתְּפַשְּׂקִי אֶת־רַגְלַיִךְ—The verb פָּשַׂק is used only one other time in the Bible, the Qal in Prov 13:3, for a garrulous person who "parts" or "opens wide" his lips. Here it is Piel, probably in a frequentative sense: "you kept spreading your legs for every man passing by."

וַתַּרְבִּי אֶת־תַּזְנוּתָיִךְ:—This clause, with the Hiphil of רָבָה and "whoring(s)," will be repeated in 16:26, 29, and with "abominations" in 16:51. This is the last time the Kethib is the singular תַּזְנֻתֵךְ whereas the Qere (תַּזְנוּתַיִךְ) has the suffix form for a plural noun ("whorings"). In the next verse, the text is singular with no Kethib/Qere variants.

16:26 גִּדְלֵי בָשָׂר—In a number of OT passages בָּשָׂר is "euphemistic for the pubic region," and here it specifically means "penis" (*HALOT*, 5 b), as also in Lev 15:2–3, 7, and Ezek 23:20, where size seems to be the distinctive feature of the woman's paramours (their penises were like those of donkeys). The verbal adjective here, גָּדֵל, occurs in just a few other OT passages, where the contexts indicate it means "becoming great, growing up" (BDB). The Hebrew phrase may not necessarily mean that the Egyptians had larger members than other peoples; instead, literally, "enlarged of penis," it more likely depicts the Egyptians' penises as growing erect. That suspicion is not dampened by an acquaintance with Egyptian art, which often shows ithyphallic men. Erect penises are evident sometimes even on fully clothed Pharaohs. One Egyptian papyrus shows ithyphallic men with enormous organs in the company of receptive women; such art is not meant to be realistic, but reflects the erotic content of much of their cults and culture.

Here the LXX has the plural of μεγαλόσαρκος, literally, "great of flesh," meaning "with a great member" (LEH). But most English renditions avoid literal translation and so weaken the shocking forcefulness of the prophecy. For example, RSV, NIV, and ESV simply have "lustful."

לְהַכְעִיסֵנִי—See the textual note on this in 8:17. The Hiphil infinitive with לְ can denote either purpose or result, which is more likely in both passages. The verb ranges from "offend" to "provoke," "insult," and "enrage." Together with the exclamation of "woe" in 16:23, the text builds up to God's punishment in reaction, beginning in the next verse, and coming full force in 16:35–58.

16:27 וָאֶגְרַע חֻקֵּךְ^{ddd}—The noun חֹק often refers to a legal "statute," but it can also refer to a "prescribed limit, boundary" of land, water, and so forth (BDB, 5). If so, here "I diminished your boundary" means "I reduced your territory." After the reign of Solomon, Israel's territory shrank, especially after the Assyrian conquest of the northern territory in 722 B.C. Also possible here is that חֹק refers to Israel's allowance or portion of food (BDB, 2), but that seems less appropriate for this context. Translation is inseparable from interpretation; see the commentary below.

"Desire" renders נֶפֶשׁ. From its basic physiological meaning of "throat, gullet" comes its semi-figurative meanings, "appetite, desire, greed." The word is used in that or a similar sense elsewhere (e.g. Ex 15:9). Here it expresses the Philistines' eagerness to gobble up the territory of neighboring Israel, as recounted in the OT historical books.

שֹׂנְאוֹתַיִךְ בְּנוֹת פְּלִשְׁתִּים—The participle of שָׂנֵא, "to hate," is feminine plural, matching בְּנוֹת. In the allegory the lovers of (female) Jerusalem naturally have been masculine, while her "haters" would be other women who competed for her paramours' attentions. The theme of "hate" in the same metaphorical sense will reappear in 16:37.

"Daughters of the Philistines" is, in part, idiomatic for Philistine "cities" as well. "Daughters" (בְּנוֹת) is often used of the satellite towns and unwalled villages surrounding larger cities (e.g., Josh 15:45, 47; 17:11, 16). The bulk of the population typically lived in such "daughters," while the royalty, priests, and other privileged people resided inside the walls. The Philistines were governed by a pentapolis, and their five major cities were undoubtedly surrounded by "daughters" (what we might call "suburbs"). Ezekiel probably has no particular ones in mind.

הַנִּכְלָמוֹת מִדַּרְכֵּךְ זִמָּה:—The Niphal of כָּלַם recurs in 16:54, 61; 36:32; 43:10, 11, all referring to Israel. But here, the depth of her depravity is shown by the fact that it is the heathen Philistines who would be "ashamed" or "embarrassed" because of (מִן) Israel's "way, behavior, conduct" (singular דֶּרֶךְ as in 7:27) of "lewdness, depravity" (זִמָּה). Ezekiel uses זִמָּה, a rather extreme word for wickedness, a total of fourteen times, usually, though not exclusively, for sexual lewdness (as also in 16:43, 58; 22:9, 11; and often in chapter 23). It augments Ezekiel's more common terms, תּוֹעֵבָה and תַּזְנוּת. Here זִמָּה is in apposition to מִדַּרְכֵּךְ and is epexegetical; the phrase (מִדַּרְכֵּךְ זִמָּה) probably means "[ashamed] *of thy conduct in lewdness*" but could mean "[ashamed] *of thy conduct*, which is *lewdness*" (GKC, § 131 r). Ezekiel has a similar syntactical construction with זִמָּה in 24:13 and with other words in 18:7. A more common construction for expressing such an idea is a construct chain with the suffix on the last member (מִדֶּרֶךְ־זִמָּתֵךְ, "of your lewd conduct").

16:28 בְּנֵי אַשּׁוּר—Instead of a gentilic noun (such as אַשּׁוּרִי, "Assyrian," whose plural could have been used here), a construct phrase with the country's name, "sons of …" can be used for various peoples. "Sons of Israel" is common; usages with other countries are relatively rare.

מִבִּלְתִּי שָׂבְעָתֵךְ—The noun שָׂבְעָה means "satiation" or "satiety" and often refers to a full and satisfied condition after eating one's fill (e.g., 39:19). It is derived from the verb שָׂבַע, "to be full, satisfied," which occurs at the end of this verse and the next (16:28, 29). The preposition מִן (with negative particle בִּלְתִּי) is causative: "because of no satiety for you" or "because there was no satisfying you."

וַתִּזְנִים—Here זָנָה takes an object suffix where English would use a prepositional phrase ("you whored *with* them"). The verb takes a direct object also in Jer 3:1 and possibly Is 23:17. Ezekiel uses the preposition אֶל with this verb in Ezek 16:26, 28a, and other prepositions elsewhere. If there is any difference in nuance, it cannot be reproduced in English translation.

16:29 וַתַּרְבִּי אֶת־תַּזְנוּתֵךְ—This clause is repeated from 16:25 (see the textual note there), but here instead of "you multiplied" the spatial context requires the Hiphil of רָבָה to be translated "you extended."

אֶל־אֶרֶץ כְּנַעַן כַּשְׂדִּימָה—While the construct phrase normally means "the land of Canaan," in its two occurrences in Ezekiel (16:29; 17:4), it means "the land of merchants." (In both "the land of Canaan" would make no sense.) The secondary, non-geographical meaning of כְּנַעַן, "trader(s), merchant(s)," developed from the commercial renown of the Phoenicians, who were also "Canaanites" (residents of Canaan). כְּנַעַן is used in the derivative sense of "merchant(s)" a number of times in the OT. Its geographical meaning is attested in the earliest (non-biblical) texts at our disposal. If, as a few speculate, its geographical sense was the secondary one, that development occurred before any literary attestations of the term.

In apposition to "to the land of merchants," governed by אֶל, stands כַּשְׂדִּימָה, "to Chaldea/Babylon," with the *he* directive (as in 11:24).

16:30 מָה אֲמֻלָה לִבָּתֵךְ—The ancient versions support this consonantal text, but there is no unanimity about what it means, neither in the ancient versions nor among modern commentators. Both אֲמֻלָה and לִבָּה are hapax legomena. אֲמֻלָה appears to be the feminine singular Qal passive participle of אָמַל. The Pual of אָמַל means "to wither, languish," but the Qal is unattested elsewhere. The subject of the participle, לִבָּה is unique but could be a feminine form of the common noun לֵב or לֵבָב, "heart." KJV understood the clause as "How weak is thine heart" (similar is BDB, s.v. אָמַל), but NIV paraphrased, " How weak-willed you are."[44]

---

[44] Using different vocabulary, the Shulammite declares, "I am sick/weak with love" (חוֹלַת אַהֲבָה אָנִי, Song 2:5; 5:8), but that is a positive quality that results from overpowering, faithful love from and for Solomon, whereas the woman here is characterized by infidelity.

Some, including *HALOT* (s.v. אמל II), consider this אָמַל to be a different, homographic verb related to an Arabic cognate *malla*, meaning "be hot, feverish, ill with fever," and this probably is reflected in "How lovesick is your heart" (RSV, ESV), Zimmerli's "feverish,"[45] NRSV's "sick," and Greenberg's "How hot your ardor is."[46] Thus the woman's heart is hot with lust, and her extreme licentiousness is feverishly pathological. This fits best with the rest of the verse.

Some follow the Akkadian idiom *libbati malu* and the Aramaic מְלָא לְבָת, both of which mean "to be full of wrath," and both take an object suffix, as noted already by Cooke.[47] Thus לְבָתֵךְ would mean "anger" (BDB, s.v. לְבָה, under the root לבב) or "rage" (*HALOT*, s.v. לְבָה) "at you" (ךָ-ᵈ). However, this understanding requires emending the vowels of אֲמָלָה to אֻמְלֵה and the assumption that the resulting form is equivalent to אֻמְלָא (Niphal of מָלֵא; the interchange of א and ה as the final weak root letter is not unusual). Thus Block[48] translated, "How furious I am with you!" Zimmerli objects that such a note of anger comes too soon in the chapter.[49] It may follow Yahweh's partial reaction in 16:26–27 and prepare for his full reaction, beginning in 16:35–37, the execution of which will finally satisfy his anger (16:42). However, the rest of the verse and the following verses continue to describe the woman's actions.

שַׁלֶּטֶת:—This word too is a hapax legomenon, but much less problematic. Cognates in many Semitic languages mean to "exert force, dominate," and even "rape, sleep with someone" (see *HALOT*, s.v. שלט). There is general agreement that this form is an Aramaism. The verb שָׁלַט, "domineer, be master," and the adjective שַׁלִּיט, "domineering, ruling," occur in some OT passages (in both Hebrew and Aramaic).[50] The words are cognate to the Arabic "sultan." The more common classical Hebrew verb for "rule" is מָשַׁל. Originally, שָׁלַט may have been a relatively neutral word, "rule," but increasingly it took on the more negative overtones of "domineer, tyrannize." In this context, the "dominatrix" thinks she is answerable to no one and does completely as she pleases. This represents Israel's defiant rebellion against Yahweh and his covenant norms for behavior. Compare the description of Israel in 2:3–7 and 3:7–11.

16:31 בִּבְנוֹתַיִךְ—The first half of Ezek 16:31 is a circumstantial clause, repeating language found in 16:24–25. Oddly, this infinitive construct of בָּנָה ("when you built") takes the form of (second feminine singular) suffix normally used for feminine plural nouns, as if the וֹת- termination were that of a feminine plural noun (cf. GKC, § 91 l). The same oddity was in 6:8 (בְּהִזָּרוֹתֵיכֶם).

עָשִׂיתִי—Again, the Kethib עָשִׂיתִי has the archaic second feminine singular ending while the Qere (עָשִׂית) is the usual classical form. The same is true about the Kethib הָיִיתִי and Qere הָיִית later in the verse. We have met this phenomenon before (16:18,

[45] Zimmerli, *Ezekiel*, 1:328.

[46] Greenberg, *Ezekiel*, 1:271, 283.

[47] Cooke, *Ezekiel*, 173.

[48] Block, *Ezekiel*, 1:492, 496–97.

[49] Zimmerli, *Ezekiel*, 1:328.

[50] On the basis of שָׁלִיט used of Joseph in Gen 42:6, Greenberg, *Ezekiel*, 1:284, suggests that the ancient word was revived in and after the exile under Aramaic influence.

22) and will do so again four more times in this chapter (16:43 [twice], 47, 51). This feature may reflect Ezekiel's own predilection.

כְּזוֹנָה לְקַלֵּס אֶתְנָן:—The context requires adding "ordinary" ("like an [ordinary] whore") to distinguish the typical whore here from Jerusalem (called a "whore" in 16:30, 35, 41). In its three other OT appearances, קָלַס is used in the Hithpael in the sense of "to ridicule." The Piel occurs only here and probably means "to spurn" (*HALOT*) or "to scorn, disdain," that is, to refuse to accept payment. The infinitive construct with לְ functions adverbially. (The word occurs on a fragment of the book of Ezekiel found at Qumran.) The noun אֶתְנָן (probably related to נָתַן) may have the underlying sense of an ordinary "gift," but in the OT the word is used exclusively of a prostitute's fee or the payment she received for her services.

16:32 Some critics question the genuineness of this exclamation. Zimmerli takes it as a redactional comment,[51] and Greenberg suggests it might be an alternative to 16:33a in a conflated text.[52] The verse does have its internal difficulties (see below), but these are characteristic of Ezekiel's text. There have been other outcries or interjections in the pericope. The ancient versions vary considerably but do attest to its existence in their texts. The syntactical problem is that the second person address implied by the opening vocative phrase (הָאִשָּׁה הַמְּנָאָפֶת, "O adulterous wife") is followed by תִּקַּח, a third person verb ("[she] who … procures"). There are near parallels to this (Is 22:16; 47:8a; 54:1), but only in this one is the vocative composed of a noun phrase with definite articles. It seems best to construe the following clause as relative even though it lacks אֲשֶׁר, something with many parallels (e.g., in 16:19).

הָאִשָּׁה הַמְּנָאָפֶת—This phrase with definite articles is a vocative. נָאַף is the specific verb for "commit adultery" in the Sixth Commandment (Ex 20:14), where it is Qal. Here the Piel (feminine singular participle) is used, but the Qal is also common, and Ezekiel uses both. There appears to be no difference in meaning. Used with that word, אִשָּׁה must be translated "wife," not merely "woman," and correspondingly, the following אִישָׁהּ as "her husband."

תִּקַּח אֶת־זָרִים:—Usually לָקַח is simply "take, receive," but in the light of the next verses, the stronger "procure" seems appropriate. See the textual note on זָרִים in 7:21. The use of the sign of the accusative (אֶת) before an indefinite object is unusual, but not unparalleled. In place of אֶת־זָרִים, the LXX seems to have read אֶתְנַנִּים (she receives "payments"), either translating freely from the context or by homoioteleuton from the previous verse. But this does not fit; this is precisely what the context says the adulteress does *not* do.

16:33 In this verse Ezekiel uses two unique words that both apparently refer to a prostitute's fee, נֵדֶ֜ה ("fee") and the plural of נָדָן (with suffix), "gifts." Both may be derived from the same root. (Likewise, אֶתְנַן in 16:31 and אֶתְנָה in Hos 2:14 [ET 2:12] both may be related to נָתַן and both refer to a "payment" given to a prostitute.) In any case, נֵדֶ֜ה and נָדָן are functional equivalents of אֶתְנַן. In context, however, they may have different nuances, as indicated in my translation. See the commentary below.

---

[51] Zimmerli, *Ezekiel*, 1:329.

[52] Greenberg, *Ezekiel*, 1:285.

יִתְּנוּ—The implied subject of the impersonal verb must be specifically "men."

מְאַהֲבַיִךְ—On the whole, the verb אָהַב is about as multivalent a word as the English "love." However, in the OT the Piel is used only in the participle and only for adulterous "lovers," except in Zech 13:6, where it refers to pseudo-friends. The Piel masculine plural participle will be used again in the same sense in Ezek 16:36, 37; 23:5, 9, 22.

וַתִּשְׁחֲדִי אוֹתָם—The verb שָׁחַד, "to bribe," occurs elsewhere only in Job 6:22 (some emend Is 47:11 to include it), but the cognate noun שֹׁחַד, "bribe," is quite common, and 2 Ki 16:8 uses the noun in the context of international diplomacy, which fits the metaphor here of the woman hiring lovers from foreign countries.

16:34 The noun הֵפֶךְ is used in only one other verse, Is 29:16, which also speaks of an inversion of the natural order. The related verb is common, often used of the overthrow of cities or kingdoms, or otherwise transforming things into their opposite. The noun is used both at the beginning and end of this verse, apparently with intensification the second time. Initially, we have "there was in you an oppositeness." The verse ends with, literally, "you were/became oppositeness," that is, a veritable incarnation of that perverse state of being.

וְאַחֲרַיִךְ לֹא זוּנָּה—The impersonal verb זוּנָּה is either a Qal passive or Pual third masculine singular perfect. (The fact that the Piel does not occur in the OT favors the view that this is a Qal passive.) The clause, literally, is *fornication was not done* (in going) *after thee*" (BDB, Pual), meaning "you were not solicited for prostitution."

16:35 לָכֵן—"Therefore" signals a major transition in the chapter (see the textual note on it in 5:7). What follows is Yahweh's sentence or announcement of punishment. This is the climax of the preceding indictment, as indicated by the heaping up of formulae: "hear the Word of Yahweh" in 16:35; "thus says the Lord Yahweh" in 16:36; and another "therefore" followed by "behold" in 16:37.

זוֹנָה—Usually a vocative noun has the article, making its absence here somewhat unusual.

16:36 Before the sentence is pronounced, all her infractions, on which it will be based, are summarized, introduced by יַעַן, "because" (see the textual note on it in 5:7). There seem to be four charges. The first two, somewhat parallel, refer to her insatiable sexual pursuits described in 16:15–34. The third broadens out to include all idolatrous activity, and the fourth alludes to the people's sacrifice of children denounced in 16:20–21.

יַעַן הִשָּׁפֵךְ נְחֻשְׁתֵּךְ—This first charge is the most difficult to translate and understand. נְחֹשֶׁת is a common word for "bronze," and so the LXX and Jerome translated it. The verb שָׁפַךְ, "pour out" (here the Niphal infinitive construct: "to be poured out") seems strange with "bronze." If "bronze" refers to money, the verb could refer to her payments being "poured out" to her lovers, as 16:33–34 says. Keil vigorously defended that interpretation,[53] and it is reflected in NIV's "wealth" (with a footnote offering "lust"). However, it seems that bronze coinage did not yet exist in Ezekiel's

---

[53] Keil, *Ezekiel*, 1:215–16.

day, and the noun is never used for money elsewhere in the OT. An added problem is that such a translation does not make a good parallel with the following clause.

The נְחֹשֶׁת here may be a homograph with an entirely different meaning than "bronze." Fredrich Delitzsch and G. R. Driver called attention to a possible Akkadian cognate that can refer to overflowing liquid (rain or floods) and might refer to sexual excess or extravagance.[54] Cooke endorsed the connection.[55] Greenberg was a bit more explicit in explaining that the term refers to an excessive flow "produced by sexual arousal" and that the verse "may be the earliest instance of what became a motif of hypersexuality in erotic literature."[56] Virtually all important commentaries since[57] (with the notable exception of Zimmerli[58]) have agreed that we have here a homograph that refers to some kind of female genital discharge. Perhaps it could refer to a heavy flow during menstruation (cf. *HALOT*, s.v. נְחֹשֶׁת II). But most likely it refers to abundant lubrication flowing from female sexual arousal. The reference may or may not refer to some abnormal or pathological condition. If it does, then Block may be right that "Ezekiel has changed a pathological expression into an erotic image."[59]

Most English versions follow the view that נְחֹשֶׁת here is a sexual term, but they avoid any literal translation: "because thy filthiness was poured out" (KJV, similarly NKJV); "shame" (RSV); "lust" (ESV, NRSV). Already the Targum paraphrased, "You uncovered your genitals," and most medieval Jewish scholars offered something similar.

וַתִּגָּלֶה עֶרְוָתֵךְ—This second charge uses language common in the Torah in prohibitions against exposing nakedness (e.g., Ex 20:26), especially in Leviticus, where one "exposes nakedness" by improper sexual relations (e.g., Lev 18:6–19; 20:11, 17–21). The sentence of punishment uses this same terminology to state that Yahweh will expose her nakedness (Ezek 16:37; the terminology is used also in 23:10, 18, 29).

וְעַל כָּל־גִּלּוּלֵי תוֹעֲבוֹתָיִךְ—Since Ezekiel has used language we might deem nearly pornographic, it is not surprising that this third charge uses scatological language, literally, "the turds of your abominations." We first met גִּלּוּלִים in 6:4 ("fecal deities"); see the textual note on it there. It is one of Ezekiel's favorite expressions of consummate contempt for idols. Nothing more is said about them, as such, in the immediate context of chapter 16. But as mentioned, "affairs" with foreign nations inevitably involved religious syncretism. The prosecutorial content is apparently to make the indictment as comprehensive as possible. It was not just a matter of isolated indiscretions, but an entire lifestyle.

[54] Fredrich Delitzsch, "Specimen Glossarii Ezechielico-Babylonici," in *Liber Ezechielis* (ed. S. Baer; Leipzig: Tauchnitz, 1884), xiv–xv, and G. R. Driver, "Linguistic and Textual Problems: Ezekiel," *Biblica* 19 (1938): 65.

[55] Cooke, *Ezekiel*, 174.

[56] Greenberg, *Ezekiel*, 1:285–86.

[57] E.g., Allen, *Ezekiel*, 1:230; Block, *Ezekiel*, 1:498, including n. 208; 500.

[58] Zimmerli, *Ezekiel*, 1:329–30.

[59] Block, *Ezekiel*, 1:500.

וְכִדְמֵי בָנַיִךְ אֲשֶׁר נָתַתְּ לָהֶם:—This fourth charge recalls 16:20–21, where she sacrificed her children to images of false deities, who must be the referent of לָהֶם ("to them"). The LXX and other ancient witnesses read "*in* the blood of" as if their text had the preposition בְּ (וּבְדְמֵי) instead of כְּ (וְכִדְמֵי), but the two prepositions sometimes interchange, and Ezekiel seems to prefer כְּ in relating offense to punishment (see, for example, 7:3; 24:14).

16:37 לָכֵן הִנְנִי מְקַבֵּץ—Again, "therefore" introduces the sentence of punishment. הִנֵּה followed by a participle can serve as a *futurum instans* denoting something imminent or on the verge of happening (GKC, § 116 p). The first two-thirds of the verse is structured chiastically, with a Piel of קָבַץ at the start and the finish, and in between are two phrases describing all those who will be gathered: "I am about to gather [מְקַבֵּץ] … all those you loved … all those you hated. … I will gather [וְקִבַּצְתִּי] them."

אֲשֶׁר עָרַבְתְּ עֲלֵיהֶם—The OT has several homographic verbs עָרַב, and this one can mean "to be pleasant, pleasing" to someone (see BDB and *HALOT*, s.v. עָרַב III). This verb is nowhere else used in the sense of giving sexual pleasure (which if present here, the clause could mean "you were pleasing [while] upon them"). Since it is also used for worship offerings that are (or are not) pleasing to God (Jer 6:20; Hos 9:4; Mal 3:4), perhaps here it connotes that the woman's idolatry was worship that was pleasing to the false deities. Many critics emend to עָגַבְתְּ ("lust after"), used, for example, in 23:5, but the change is unnecessary.

עַל כָּל־אֲשֶׁר שָׂנֵאת—In 16:27, the same verb was applied to the Philistine women hating the woman because they were her competitors in promiscuous behavior, competing for the attention of the same men. If the Philistines are still in view, see 25:15–16, where they are condemned for taking vengeance on Judah. Here, however, "all those you hated" apparently are former (male) lovers, as in 23:28 (in light of 23:22), where the woman hates former paramours.

16:38 The forms of שׁפט ("judge," "judgments") could also be translated "sentence(s)."

וּנְתַתִּיךְ דַּם חֵמָה וְקִנְאָה:—Literally, Yahweh states, "I will make you blood of wrath and jealousy." As confirmed by the violent imagery in 16:40 and the similar language in 35:6, this means that Yahweh will make her bloody. For the theme of Yahweh's "wrath" (חֵמָה), see the commentary on 7:8. For his "jealousy" (קִנְאָה), see the textual notes and commentary on 5:13 and commentary on 8:3, 5.

16:39 גַּב ("domed tent") is singular, as earlier (16:24, 31). However, רָמֹתַיִךְ רָמָה, "your platforms") is plural, whereas it had been singular previously (16:24, 25, 31). The ancient versions harmonize by making both here either singular or plural. Some English translations harmonize (usually making both plural). Others retain the MT, as I have, as the *lectio difficilior*. The issue is insignificant.

16:40 וְהֶעֱלוּ עָלַיִךְ קָהָל וְרָגְמוּ—The noun קָהָל is common and can refer to a "crowd, assembly" of various sorts. Sometimes, however, it takes on a technical meaning such as "congregation" for worship. Some Torah passages that prescribe capital punishment by stoning state that the "congregation" (but denoted by עֵדָה) is to do the stoning (e.g., Lev 24:14, 16; Num 15:35–36). If קָהָל here and in 23:47 is a legal assembly constituted to carry out the stoning, then "mob" would wrongly connote anarchy. But the next verse may picture the chaos inflicted by an invading army, and that picture may begin here. The Qal of עָלָה often is used for attacking in war (see BDB, 2 c), and the Hiphil here (וְהַעֲלוּ, "bring up") may be the causative counterpart.

וּבִתְּקוּךְ בְּחַרְבוֹתָם—The verb בָּתַק occurs only here in the OT, but it is well-attested in cognate languages and means "cut in pieces."

16:41 וְגַם־אֶתְנַן לֹא תִתְּנִי־עוֹד:—This must be understood in light of 16:31–34, which states that in her whoring she gave "payment" or bribes to her lovers, contrary to the normal practice of prostitution.

16:43 One must decide upon the role of this verse in the structure of the entire chapter. Usually it is taken as a concluding summary of virtually the entire oracle up to this point and almost a concluding theodicy to the effect that ingrate Israel's behavior had left Yahweh no alternative but terrible punishment. (Hence most consider 16:35–43 to be a unit.) But that view is disputed, nowhere more vigorously, as far as I am aware, than by Keil.[60] Keil considers 16:42 to conclude the preceding paragraph. He perceives 16:43–52 and 16:53–63 as units. Thus he connects all of 16:43 with the following verses, and in that much, he probably intuits correctly. He argues that יַעַן אֲשֶׁר at the beginning of the verse signals a new train of thought, as יַעַן had in 16:36. (There is, however, no אֲשֶׁר in 16:36, nor is there a following לָכֵן here as there had been in 16:37.)

לֹא־זָכַרְתְּי אֶת־יְמֵי נְעוּרַיִךְ—This clause is repeated from 16:22. Regarding the Qere זָכַרְתְּ for the Kethib זָכַרְתִּי, see the textual notes on 16:13.

וַתִּרְגְּזִי־לִי בְּכָל־אֵלֶּה—In the Qal רָגַז is intransitive, "to tremble, quake with fear," and לִי means "at me [Yahweh]," just as in Is 14:9, where the Qal takes the preposition לְ attached to the person who causes the agitation ("Sheol below trembles at you"). For Israel to have trembled at Yahweh would have been a sign of faith, as in Jer 33:9, where the people shall tremble (רָגַז) because of all the good Yahweh will do for them, but here Israel has been faithless. Therefore this context requires the earlier negative לֹא (לֹא־זָכַרְתְּי) to do double duty and negate this verb too.[61]

The versions translate this clause transitively, for example, "you grieved me by all these (activities)" (LXX; Vulgate: "you have provoked me …"), presumably because they read their unpointed text as a Hiphil (תַּרְגִּזִי), which can mean "to enrage, excite, cause to tremble." That would be a unique idiom in the whole OT for agitating Yahweh. Hence, and because of my disinclination to emend, my translation follows the Hebrew.

וְגַם־אֲנִי הֵא—הֵא is an Aramaic equivalent of הִנֵּה. It occurs in the Hebrew OT otherwise only in Gen 47:23. Its position in the sentence is unusual; often הִנֵּה comes at the beginning, as in numerous other verses in Ezekiel. I have tried to retain its force by translating it "surely." The evidence of the versions for it is divided.

דַּרְכֵּךְ | בְּרֹאשׁ נָתָתִּי—See the textual note on the similar clause in 9:10 (also 11:21; 22:31). While the two words רֹאשׁ and דֶּרֶךְ are used in a different sense here than in

---

[60] Keil, *Ezekiel*, 1:220–21.

[61] So also Greenberg, *Ezekiel*, 1:288.

16:31, they sound like a deliberate reminiscence of בְּרֹאשׁ כָּל־דֶּרֶךְ in 16:31 ("you built your domed tent at *the head of every street*"). That may explain why here there is no suffix on רֹאשׁ (the translation supplies "your"), whereas the idiom in 9:10; 11:21; 22:31 has a suffix ("their head"). This punishment will mirror the crime. The same idiom in 9:10; 11:21; 22:31 uses a prophetic perfect ("I *will* place"), and that is the most natural way to take נָתַתִּי here, as I have translated it: "I myself will surely place." A prophetic perfect is a common idiom describing what God will do as so certain, based on his Word, that God can say he has already done it.[62]

וְלֹא עָשִׂיתִי אֶת־הַזִּמָּה עַל כָּל־תּוֹעֲבֹתָיִךְ:—Regarding the Qere עָשִׂית for the Kethib עָשִׂיתִי, see the textual notes on 16:13. See the textual note on the noun זִמָּה in 16:27. The preposition עַל has the meaning "in addition to," as also in 16:37 (the second instance). If the verb in the preceding clause is taken as a prophetic perfect (נָתַתִּי, "I will surely place"), then עָשִׂית could be too: as a result of the divine punishment placed on Israel's head, "you will not do lewdness in addition to all your abominations" (essentially KJV, NKJV).

However, both the meaning of the final clause and its syntactical relationship to the rest of the verse are much debated. Some regard it as a simple declarative conclusion to the verse and to the preceding paragraph (which they define as 16:35–43) and then argue that it is lame, redundant, or attempting to make a distinction (between "lewdness" and "abominations") where there is none. If it were a conclusion, we might have at least expected עוֹד to be included ("you will never *again* …"). However, I have followed Keil's view that the preceding paragraph (16:35–42) ended with 16:42 and that 16:43 begins a new unit.[63]

A common expedient is to take וְלֹא as introducing a rhetorical question (as is possible for וְלֹא in 16:47 and 16:56). In Hebrew a question does not have to be marked with an interrogative particle (GKC § 150 a; Joüon § 161 a). The question here ("Have you not … ?") refers to the past and could aptly conclude the verse and conclude a paragraph consisting of 16:35–43 (so ESV). But in my judgment, it is better to consider the question to be connected with the following verses, and to be part of the paragraph consisting of 16:43–58, since the question leads easily into 16:44. RSV and NRSV consider this question to begin a new paragraph (consisting of 16:43b–52). The woman's past moral degradation is a natural introduction to a discussion of the proverbial destructions of Samaria and Sodom in the past (16:44–58) and the popular sayings those destructions apparently spawned, one of which Ezekiel quotes in 16:44.

Keil proposes a much more radical solution. He disregards the Qere and, following Symmachus and the Vulgate, reads the Kethib עָשִׂיתִי as *first* person, with Yahweh as the subject: "Behold, I also give thy way upon thy head … that I may not do that which is wrong above all thine abominations." He appeals to Lev 19:29, where a father is forbidden to prostitute his daughter, lest the whole land fall into זִמָּה ("lewd-

---

[62] Block, *Ezekiel*, 1:499, uses a future perfect ("I will have brought"), although he makes no comment about it.

[63] Keil, *Ezekiel*, 1:220.

ness," the same term in Ezek 16:43). Thus Keil reads the clause in Ezek 16:43 as saying that if Yahweh had not punished Israel's degeneracy, he himself would have committed lewdness by becoming an accessory to Israel's sins.[64] Textually, such an exegesis could stand if the Kethib were a first common singular variant reading to the second feminine singular Qere, but throughout this chapter we have seen that this Kethib is an archaic spelling of the second feminine singular, not a first common singular variant. Moreover, Keil's explanation that Yahweh might have committed lewdness is so novel and without any real biblical analogy as far as I know (and without endorsement by any other exegete, to the best of my knowledge) that it can hardly be accepted.

16:44 As explained in the first textual note on 16:43, I follow Keil in taking the previous verse as the beginning of a new theme in the oracle, developed in 16:43–58. Yahweh introduces the allegory of a mother, her daughter (Israel), and the daughter's sisters (Samaria and Sodom). However, this allegory is not completely new. Ezekiel links it to the first part of the chapter by referring again (as in 16:3) to Israel's mixed parentage, which makes this an expansion of that aspect of the allegory of Israel as a girl.

הַמֹּשֵׁל ... יִמְשֹׁל—The verb מָשַׁל, "quote a proverb, speak proverbially," occurred in 12:23 (see the first textual note on 12:22, which has the cognate noun מָשָׁל).

כְּאִמָּה בִּתָּהּ—Proverbs appear in various forms (see Proverbs), but what we have here is quite typical. This is a nominal sentence (no verb). The predicate noun is first, with the preposition כְּ, indicating that she is the standard of comparison, and the third feminine singular suffix: "like her mother." The suffix (הָ-) lacks *mappiq*, but that is not unusual before *bgdkpt* letters (ב follows). The subject noun with suffix ("her daughter") comes second. In usual English subject-predicate order this would be "her daughter is like her mother," but the sense and proverbial ring are better in inverted English order (following the Hebrew order): "Like her mother is her daughter." Some translations paraphrase by dropping the suffixes and adding another "like" (כְּ): "like mother, like daughter" (RSV, NIV, ESV).

16:45 With NIV, I have twice added "true" to help bring out the intended emphasis.

גָּעֲלָה ... גָּעָלוּ—For the verb גָּעַל, used twice here, see the last textual note on 16:5, which has the cognate noun גֹּעַל. I have been able to reproduce that parallel by translating with "disregard" again, this time as a verb. As the floundering infant had been cast out with "disregard" for her life (16:5), so the three sisters "disregard" their families and their responsibilities.

וַאֲחוֹת אֲחוֹתֵךְ אַתְּ אֲשֶׁר גָּעֲלוּ אַנְשֵׁיהֶן וּבְנֵיהֶן—The form of אֲחוֹתֵךְ appears singular (and the identical form in 16:46, 48, 49, 56 is singular), but here (and the first instance in 16:52), it is actually plural and so is translated "your sister*s*." The following context, including the plural verb (גָּעֲלוּ) and plural pronouns (יהֶן-[d]) on the nouns (אַנְשֵׁיהֶן וּבְנֵיהֶן) confirm that אֲחוֹתֵךְ is plural. The expected "textbook" form here would be אַחְיוֹתַיִךְ (which is the form that a few manuscripts have at the end of 16:52, but most manuscripts have אַחְיוֹתֵךְ there). Here and in 16:51, 52 (first instance), 55,

---

61, the plural of אָחוֹת with suffix is spelled אַחוֹת- because the י (in the hypothetical plural absolute form אֲחָיוֹת) has been syncopated. The form here has the further oddity that the expected י in the suffix for the plural (יִךְ-) is absent. The forms in 16:51 (the Qere), 55, 61 have the expected י in the suffix (אַחוֹתַיִךְ). See the paradigm of אָחוֹת and the "Remarks" on אָחוֹת in GKC, § 96.

אִמְּכֶן חִתִּית וַאֲבִיכֶן אֱמֹרִי:—The suffixes are plural: "you" refers to Israel and her two sisters, Samaria and Sodom. In Elizabethan English, KJV is still able to distinguish singular "thy/thine" from the plural "your." In modern English both have coalesced into "your," so I have added "of *all* of you."[65] Whereas 16:3 referred to the woman's Amorite father first, here her Hittite mother is mentioned first, probably because this section of the chapter concentrates on the female members of the family.

16:46 The adjectives גָּדוֹל and קָטֹן ordinarily mean "big(ger)" and "little(r), small(er)," respectively. There is disagreement among commentators and translators whether here they should be rendered "old(er)" and "young(er)," respectively. It seems to me that the reasons for retaining the ordinary translations far outweigh the alternative. The northern kingdom, represented by Samaria, certainly was not "older" than Judah, represented by Jerusalem; it apostatized from Jerusalem and the Davidic dynasty ca. 930 B.C., almost five hundred years after the conquest of Canaan, and perhaps seventy years after David made Jerusalem the capital of (united) Israel. However, the territory of the northern kingdom was considerably larger than the southern kingdom (Judah, incorporating Benjamin), and so it was "bigger" in that sense. Sodom certainly was not "younger" than Jerusalem, since it was destroyed ca. 2000 B.C. (Genesis 19), but its territory probably was "smaller" than that of Judah, judging from Genesis 14, where it is a city-state adjacent to (not encompassing) the city-states of Gomorrah and three other nearby cities.

וּבְנוֹתֶיהָ—As in 16:27, the "daughters" are "suburbs" or satellite villages. The term will be repeated at the end of the verse in reference to those of Sodom. In Genesis 14 Sodom seems to be the leader of the league of five city-states, consisting in addition of Gomorrah, Admah, Zeboiim, and Zoar. All five cities were in the same general vicinity, near the southeastern shore of the Dead Sea. How closely they may have been allied when not under attack and whether they constituted a pentapolis of the sort the Philistines had we do not know.

שְׂמֹאולֵךְ ... מִימִינֵךְ—When one is oriented ("east-facing") to the east, north is to the "left" (שְׂמֹאל) and south is to the "right" (יָמִין). This is a common way to designate these geographical directions in the OT.

16:47 וְלֹא—This might be taken as introducing a rhetorical question ("Did you not walk … ?"), as וְלֹא apparently does in 16:43 and might in 16:56. However, the comparative construction at the end of the verse (Israel became "more depraved" than her sisters) implies that וְלֹא introduces a negative indicative statement: Israel "did not walk in their ways" because her ways were even worse (as most English versions

---

[65] Block (*Ezekiel*, 1:504, n. 237) supposes that the plural suffixes are due to attraction to the third plural suffixes on the preceding nouns אַנְשֵׁיהֶן and בְּנֵיהֶן, but it is more likely that they include Israel's two sisters, described in the following verses.

translate). This is confirmed by 16:48. The sense is the same as in 5:7, "you have not even acted according to the ordinances of the nations around you" (see the commentary there).

וּבְתוֹעֲבוֹתֵיהֶן עָשִׂיתי—Allen points out that the preposition בְּ in *BHS* is a printing error for כְּ,[66] which other modern printed editions have. On the Qere (עָשִׂית)/Kethib (עָשִׂיתי), see the textual note on אָכַלְתִּי in 16:13.

כִּמְעַט קָט—The idiomatic "like [כְּ] a little [מְעַט]" is used in various senses. Here the most likely one is temporal, "shortly, soon, quickly," as also in Ps 81:15 (ET 81:14); Job 32:22; 2 Chr 12:7 (cf. *HALOT*, s.v. מְעַט, 6 a). The term קָט is a hapax legomenon.[67] An Ethiopic cognate supports the meaning "small" (*HALOT*), while an Arabic cognate suggests that it means "soon,"[68] so it probably is an intensifier of כִּמְעַט, and I have translated the two together as "in a very short time." Compare כִּמְעַט־רֶגַע, "shortly for a moment," in Is 26:20 and Ezra 9:8.

וַתַּשְׁחִתִי מֵהֶן—In the parallel clause in 23:11 the Hiphil of שָׁחַת is transitive, "to make (something) corrupt," but here and in a number of other OT passages it is "internally factitive," that is, "to make oneself corrupt," but normally translated "behave corruptly" or simply "be corrupt" (cf. *HALOT*, Hiphil, 1 c). With the preposition מִן and suffix (מֵהֶן) it forms a comparative construction: "you became more corrupt/depraved than they." The suffix is third feminine plural, referring to her two sisters.

16:48 חַי־אָנִי נְאֻם אֲדֹנָי יְהוִֹה אִם־—The oath formula with חַי and אִם is a strong negative, as in 14:16, 20.

עָשִׂית אַתְּ וּבְנוֹתָיִךְ:—The verb is singular ("you have done") even though the subject is compound ("you and your daughters"), so the emphasis is on Jerusalem herself (rather than her daughters or surrounding towns) as the offender. (The preceding clause in 16:48 about Sodom and her daughters also has a singular verb despite the compound subject, but plural verbs are used in 16:50 with Sodom and her daughters in 16:49 as their compound subject.)

16:49 גָּאוֹן—This noun, from the root גאה, can mean "height" or "eminence." It can be used positively of those who rightly are exalted, especially God (Ex 15:7; Is 2:10), but far more often it is used, as here, of the "presumption, pride" of those who have arrogantly abused their lofty position. In Ezek 7:20 it seems to indicate that Yahweh's temple became an object of sinful pride for Israel (cf. 7:24).

שִׂבְעַת־לֶחֶם וְשַׁלְוַת הַשְׁקֵט—The next two phrases fill out the picture of Israel's idle luxury. Each is a construct phrase. The noun שִׂבְעָה means "satiety, surfeit." The noun שַׁלְוָה means "ease, rest." הַשְׁקֵט is the Hiphil infinitive absolute of שָׁקַט, "to have peace, tranquility," used as a noun (see GKC, § 113 a). The description is obviously intended as a contrast to the people's failure to help those less fortunate.

וְיַד־עָנִי וְאֶבְיוֹן לֹא הֶחֱזִיקָה:—The idiom with the Hiphil of חָזַק and יָד, literally, "to strengthen (someone's) hand," means "to support, help, aid," as also in Job 8:20. More common is the synonymous idiom with the Piel of חָזַק with either יָד (as in Ezek

---

[66] Allen, *Ezekiel*, 1:231.

[67] Zimmerli, *Ezekiel*, 1:331, dismisses it as "probably ... an incorrectly written dittography."

[68] Greenberg, *Ezekiel*, 1:289; cf. BDB.

13:22) or זְרוֹעַ (as in 30:24), "to strengthen (someone's) hands/arms." Stative verbs often use the Piel to express the transitive, but otherwise both conjugations frequently have causative or factitive force. עָנִי וְאֶבְיוֹן is a stock phrase. The two words are virtual synonyms.

16:50   וַתִּגְבְּהֶינָה וַתַּעֲשֶׂינָה תוֹעֵבָה לְפָנָי—The Qal of גָּבַהּ, "be high, lofty," can have the negative sense "become haughty, arrogant." Since its final *he* is an original root letter, its textbook form would be תִּגְבַּהְנָה, but the form here apparently was assimilated to that of the following verb (cf. GKC, § 47 l).

וָאָסִיר אֶתְהֶן—The Hiphil of סוּר is a rather ordinary verb for "remove, take away." It suggests that Yahweh had effortlessly, or in a mere instant, brushed aside a bothersome nuisance. The details of the biblical account of how Yahweh "removed" Sodom (Genesis 19) was too well-known to require any detailed recounting by Ezekiel.

כַּאֲשֶׁר רָאִיתִי:—The LXX (καθὼς εἶδον) reads the verb as first person singular ("when I saw"). However, two Hebrew manuscripts have the second person feminine singular רָאִית ("when you saw"). The Vulgate (*vidisti*), and some Greek versions have a second person singular verb, either because their Hebrew text had ראית or because they regarded ראיתי as yet another archaic second feminine singular perfect (see the textual note on אָכַלְתִּי in 16:13), many examples of which are the Kethib in this chapter. The meaning then would be "as you [Jerusalem] have seen." Abraham saw the destruction of Sodom (Gen 19:28), and all Israelites knew of its destruction because of the inclusion of the account in their Scriptures (Genesis 19). "As you [Jerusalem] have seen" could be an anticipation of the allusion in 16:56 to Jerusalem using Sodom as a byword. However, since there is no Qere identifying the Hebrew verb as second feminine singular, it is most likely first common singular, which has a more theocentric emphasis, especially after the preceding לְפָנָי. This may allude to Gen 18:21, where Yahweh says וְאֶרְאֶה ("I will see") whether the situation in Sodom is as grave as its outcry would indicate.

16:51   וַתְּצַדְּקִי אֶת־אֲחוֹתֵיךְ—Elsewhere the Piel (spoken by Elihu in Job 32:2; 33:32) and the Hiphil of צָדֵק usually mean "to justify, declare righteous." However, the Piel in Ezek 16:51–52 (also Jer 3:11) means "make [someone] to appear righteous" (BDB) in a comparative sense: Jerusalem, by her greater depravity, made Sodom and Samaria only *seem* more righteous in comparison. The idea is anticipated in Jer 3:11, where Yahweh states, "Apostate Israel made herself seem more righteous than treacherous Judah." Similar is the use of the Qal of צָדֵק by Judah, who admitted that his daughter-in-law, who had posed as a prostitute, was "more righteous than me" (צָֽדְ֨קָה^{dd} מִמֶּ֔נִּי) since he had employed her services (Gen 38:26).

To translate the verb here as "justify" (KJV, NKJV) is misleading. None of the women here are justified or righteous. The intent of the comparison is to shame Jerusalem by stating ironically that her degenerate sisters seemed better than she.

See also the textual notes on פִּלְלְתִּ in 16:52 and בְּנַחֲמֵךְ in 16:54, which are used in a similar, ironic sense.

The Qere, אֲחוֹתַיִךְ (the sole reading in 16:55, 61) has the suffix appropriate for a plural noun, and the context here indicates that אֲחוֹת- is plural (hence "your sister*s*"). See the second textual note on 16:45.

עָשִׂיתִי—See the textual note on אָכַלְתִּי in 16:13.

16:52   שְׂאִי כְלִמָּתֵךְ—This clause, "bear your disgrace," occurs twice in 16:52. The imperative of נָשָׂא may be tantamount to a prediction; imperatives are commonly used as such in prophetic discourse. This kind of use of נָשָׂא is not unique to Ezekiel, but is typical of him. To "bear iniquity" (4:4–6; see the textual notes and commentary there) means to bear responsibility for it and to suffer its consequences in punishment. However, to "bear disgrace" here and also in 39:26 is to lead to remorse over former sins as the first step in repentance (contrition, followed by faith).

אֲשֶׁר פִּלַּלְתְּ לַאֲחוֹתֵךְ—Yahweh's rhetoric of Jerusalem making her sisters seem more righteous than herself becomes even more hyperbolic here. Literally, he says, "by which you interceded for your sister(s)." The Piel of פָּלַל can mean "mediate, arbitrate, intercede," and the force of לְ is a dative of advantage, "for" someone. The idea is to interpose oneself in defense of someone else. While not used here, the Hithpael often refers to intercessory prayer, which avails much (James 5:16), and a prime OT example is Solomon's prayer at the consecration of the temple (1 Ki 8:22–53). But the kind of intercession here is the opposite of that. The relative אֲשֶׁר has the antecedent כְּלִמָּתֵךְ, so it was by her "disgrace" (egregiously disgraceful conduct) that Jerusalem "interceded for" her sisters. As the rest of Ezek 16:52 shows, Yahweh means that she was so bad that she made her sisters appear more favorable before the heavenly Judge in comparison to her. This action of hers was inadvertent and unintentional, of course. The idiom is not easy to translate. "You appeared to intercede" is close to literal and uses the same English modification as "you made your sisters *appear* righteous" (16:51). Allen's looser translation is "since you have been an argument in your sisters' defense."[69]

בְּחַטֹּאתַיִךְ אֲשֶׁר־הִתְעַבְתְּ מֵהֵן—The Hiphil of תָּעַב may have a causative force, as the Piel does in 16:25, in which case the meaning would be "by your sins, which you made more abominable than they [did]." However, since there is no stated direct object here, the Hiphil may be "internally factitive" and have the intransitive meaning "do/act abominably." In either case, מֵהֵן refers to her sisters and forms a comparative construction ("than they [did]").

בּוֹשִׁי[d]   The Qal of בּוֹשׁ (16:52, 63; 32:30; 36:32) is a synonym of the Niphal of כָּלַם (16:27, 54, 61; 36:32). Both mean "be ashamed, humiliated, embarrassed."

בְּצַדֶּקְתֵּךְ אַחְיוֹתֵךְ—The verb is a feminine form of the Piel infinitive construct, used in a gerundival construction for a circumstantial clause. In his book only here does Ezekiel use the "textbook" plural of the noun אָחוֹת, which includes the י (in אֲחָיוֹת-). However, here it has the suffix appropriate for a singular noun; the expected form would be אַחְיוֹתַיִךְ. See the second textual note on 16:45.

16:53   וְשַׁבְתִּי אֶת־שְׁבִיתְהֶן—This idiom with the verb שׁוּב and noun שְׁבִית or שְׁבוּת is one of the most important expressions in the OT prophets for the Gospel, expressed as an eschatological great reversal. In Ezekiel it occurs only here, in 39:25, and in 29:14 referring to Egypt. Its precise meaning is much debated and somewhat uncer-

---

[69] Allen, *Ezekiel*, 1:226.

tain. Usually the Qal of שׁוּב is intransitive and can mean "turn back to God" or "be restored." In this idiom, the verb is transitive and today the phrase is usually rendered "restore the fortunes" (see BDB, s.v. שׁוּב, 9; BDB, s.v. שְׁבִית, 2 [under the root שׁבה]; *HALOT*, s.v. שְׁבוּת, 3 c).

The literature on the subject is vast, and the conclusions are often contradictory. An initial question has always been whether the noun is derived from שׁוּב, "return, restore," or from שָׁבָה, "take captive." The noun is more commonly in the form שְׁבוּת (twenty-one times in the OT versus eleven for שְׁבִית), and it could derive from either verb, but שְׁבִית would more likely be from שָׁבָה. The OT has mixed forms where the Kethib/Qere is שְׁבִית/שְׁבוּת or vice versa. (Three times later in this verse the Kethib, pointed שְׁבִית, is to be read as שְׁבוּת.) The ancient versions were uncertain which derivation to favor, but since the LXX and Vulgate, the two most influential ones, generally favored the etymology from שָׁבָה, the traditional view became that the phrase meant "return the captivity of," that is, to restore or free someone from captivity. KJV and NKJV still clearly reflect this understanding.

A handful of passages clearly favors a more general meaning for the noun, such as "restoration" (Job 42:10 and Ezek 16:53), since the people to be restored were not in captivity in any literal sense (Job was sick; Sodom and her daughters were destroyed; but the surviving Israelites from Samaria and her daughters would have been in captivity, either still in northern Israel or deported into exile). Another handful of passages favors the "captivity" theory (Jer 29:14; Ezek 29:14; Zeph 3:20). Most passages are, theoretically at least, capable of either rendition.

A related conundrum for which there is no satisfactory explanation is that the verb appears in about equal numbers in both Qal and Hiphil forms, without discernible difference in meaning, and except for this idiom there are no other instances where the Qal of שׁוּב has transitive force.

Since the discovery of the same idiom in the Aramaic inscription at Sefire (northwestern Syria) from the eighth century and the indication that the phrase was common in Northwest Semitic, scholarly opinion has shifted overwhelmingly in favor of the "restoration" understanding, reflected in most recent translations by the phrase "restore the fortunes." However, this strikes me as an unfortunate (no pun intended) turn of a phrase. As any English dictionary will confirm, "fortune" implies unpredictable luck, destiny, fate, or the like. That conceptually would befit the Greek τύχη ("chance, luck") or μοῖρα ("fate"), both commonly divinized in paganism, but hardly "the Lord Yahweh" (e.g., 16:48)!

Hence, my rendition of the phrase is simply "bring about the restoration," with Yahweh clearly the author and finisher. That uses two words, as the Hebrew does. The phrase commonly has eschatological connotations (see the commentary), but it can be ambivalent in the nature of the restoration.

Ezek 16:55 has a phrase that appears to be a virtual synonym of this idiom: תָּשֹׁבְןָ לְקַדְמָתָן, "they will return to their former state/condition."

וּשְׁבִית שְׁבִיתַיִךְ בְּתוֹכָהֵנָה:—As it stands, this phrase is, literally, "and the restoration of your restorations in their midst." The construct phrase might be a superlative that indicates that her restoration is the best compared to the restorations of the others (a "comparative superlative"; see Waltke-O'Connor, §§ 9.5.3j and 14.5a) or that indicates that her restoration is complete (an "absolute superlative"; see Waltke-O'Connor, § 14.5b). The ancient versions translated as if the initial noun וּשְׁבִית instead were the verb וְשַׁבְתִּי, "and I will restore," which only requires transposing the last two consonants and repointing. KJV (similarly NKJV) adds that verb: "then *will I bring again* the captivity of thy captives," but other English translations emend the noun to the verb (RSV, ESV).

16:54 כְּלִמָּתֵךְ וְנִכְלַמְתְּ—The noun כְּלִמָּה is again translated "disgrace," as in 16:52, but the cognate verb (Niphal of כָּלַם) is rendered "be ashamed." English style seemed to require two near synonyms.

בְּנַחֲמֵךְ אֹתָן:—Normally the Piel of נָחַם means "to comfort, console." Here the infinitive construct is used in the same kind of ironic way as the Piels of צָדַק in 16:51–52 and פָּלַל in 16:52: because Jerusalem was so much worse than her sisters, she appeared to console them by making them appear more righteous before God than she herself was. This form of the sign of the direct object with third feminine plural suffix, אֹתָן, occurs only here in the OT, but it is analogous to the common masculine אֹתָם. The usual feminine form is אֶתְהֶן (e.g., 16:50, 61), but Ezekiel also uses אוֹתְהֶן (23:47) and אוֹתָנָה (34:21). This is one of many examples where biblical Hebrew continued to use different but synonymous forms without standardizing them.

16:55 The verse repeats the message of 16:53 but thrice using a different idiom, the Qal of שׁוּב in the intransitive sense of "return" or "be restored," and the noun קַדְמָה, "former state" (BDB, 2), also in 36:11. In the OT the third and second person feminine plural Qal imperfect of שׁוּב occurs only in this verse and 35:9. For most Hebrew verbs the same form serves for both third and second person. The unusual orthography (ddתְּשֹׁבְןָ) twice in the first two parts of this verse may distinguish that form, used for the third person, from the more customary תְּשֹׁבֶינָה at the end of the verse, where it is second person with Jerusalem as the antecedent of the subject pronoun.

16:56 וְלוֹא—As in 16:43 (cf. 16:47), I take וְלוֹא as introducing a question expecting an affirmative answer (so also RSV, ESV). KJV, NKJV, and NIV, all in their own way, construe it as declarative negative statement, which, in my judgment, makes no sense and contradicts other biblical testimony. To declare that Jerusalem never spoke of Sodom is contradicted by the frequent mention of Sodom as proverbial of depravity and God's judgment in the OT Scriptures of Israel,[b] including this chapter (Ezek 16:46–56), as it will also be in the Scriptures of the new Israel.[c] As long as Jerusalem thought of herself pridefully, Sodom was a handy byword for excusing whatever little peccadilloes Jerusalem might have admitted—precisely as Jerusalem had now become for the Edomites and Philistines (16:57).

לִשְׁמוּעָה בְּפִיךְ—Usually the noun שְׁמוּעָה means a "report" that one hears (שָׁמַע) with the ears, but here it is "in your mouth," that is, it is spoken by Jerusalem. (In Is 53:1 it may refer to a prophetic message that is spoken.) The apparent explanation is that in ordinary conversation one person hears what another speaks, so the same word might be used for both.

(b) Deut 29:23; 32:32; Is 1:9–10; 3:9; 13:19; Jer 23:14; 49:18; 50:40; Amos 4:11; Zeph 2:9; Lam 4:6

(c) Mt 11:23–24; 2 Pet 2:6; Jude 7; Rev 11:8

בְּיוֹם גְּאוֹנָיִךְ:—All translations and versions, ancient and modern, to the best of my knowledge, translate the anomalous plural גְּאוֹנָיִךְ ("your prides") as though it were singular ("your pride"). The plural may be intensive, hence "your great pride."

16:57 בְּטֶרֶם תִּגָּלֶה רָעָתֵךְ—These words continue the rhetorical question begun in 16:56. Some translations ignore the verse division and take them as the end of the question: "… before your wickedness was uncovered?" (e.g., RSV, ESV). However, it is more likely that the sentence continues through the end of 16:57 (as KJV translates, though as a statement, not a question). This phrase is semantically connected to the rest of 16:57: because her "wickedness was exposed" she has now become a "reproach" to other nations. That exposure has fulfilled God's judgment in 16:37 ("I will expose your nakedness"). Zimmerli[70] and a few others follow a few Hebrew manuscripts in reading עֶרְוָתֵךְ ("your nakedness," as in 16:37) in place of רָעָתֵךְ, but the LXX supports the MT, and there is no reason to emend.

כְּמוֹ עֵת—This is, literally, "like the time," but by necessity it is translated with "so now you are." כְּמוֹ is an independent, semi-poetic and possibly archaic form of the preposition כְּ. Greenberg compares the phrase here to כָּעֵת in Judg 13:23 and translates both "now,"[71] which is supported by the LXX (νῦν). Many emendations have been proposed; Zimmerli gives a list of them.[72] The emendation apparently attracting the most support is כָּמוֹהָ עַתָּ, "like her, now [you are] …" (The abbreviated form of the temporal adverb, עַתָּ for עַתָּה, is the Kethib in Ezek 23:43 and Ps 74:6.) Whether or not the text is emended, one must supply (at least in thought) הָיִית, "you are," to complete the sense, as the LXX does (εἶ).

חֶרְפַּת בְּנוֹת־אֲרָם וְכָל־סְבִיבוֹתֶיהָ—Already in 5:14–15 Yahweh had declared that he would make Israel a "reproach" (חֶרְפָּה) to the other nations. The LXX reflects אֲרָם ("Aram") in Leningradensis but, as usual, renders it as "Syria" (Συρία), as do some English translations (e.g., KJV, ESV). However, many Hebrew manuscripts have אֱדֹם ("Edom"), which is supported by the Syriac. Since *resh* and *dalet* are so similar in Hebrew, both in the ancient (Phoenician) script and the "square" Aramaic script (used for Hebrew from the postexilic period down to the modern era), there are many scribal confusions of the two letters, including other examples of the names of these two countries. Aram had ceased to be a threat since its annexation by Assyria over a century before, a decade before the fall of Samaria in 722. However, Edom was still a threat to Israelites at the time of Ezekiel. Philistia (cf. 16:27) and Edom are condemned in adjacent Gentile oracles in Ezekiel 25, and Edom will be heartily condemned again in 36:5.

בְּנוֹת פְּלִשְׁתִּים—This phrase is asyndetic and prepositionless, which makes for awkward syntax. The translation supplies "and to …" In 16:27 Yahweh had warned that he would hand Jerusalem over to "the daughters of the Philistines, who were em-

---

[70] Zimmerli, *Ezekiel*, 1:333.

[71] Greenberg, *Ezekiel*, 1:273, 290.

[72] Zimmerli, *Ezekiel*, 1:333.

barrassed by your way of lewdness," so the phrase here indicates that that judgment has been fulfilled.[73]

הַשָּׁאטוֹת אוֹתָךְ מִסָּבִיב:—This refers to the daughters of Edom and her neighbors in addition to the daughters of the Philistines. The verb is the Qal feminine plural participle of שׁוּט II, "to deride, despise, scorn," which occurs only in Ezekiel (16:57; 28:24, 26; all as a participle), but there are cognates in Akkadian, Aramaic, and Syriac. The related noun שְׁאָט, "derision, scorn, contempt," also occurs only in Ezekiel (25:6, 15; 36:5). In הַשָּׁאטוֹת the א is a vowel letter (אָ-). This use of א in the participle of a "hollow" (*'ayin-waw* or *'ayin-yod*) verb may be due to Aramaic influence, as also with the noun (שְׁאָט). See GKC, § 72 p, and Joüon, § 80 k.

16:58 נְשָׂאתִים—The antecedents of the redundant third masculine plural suffix are זִמָּתֵךְ (see 16:27, 43) and תּוֹעֲבוֹתַיִךְ, both of which are feminine nouns, but masculine forms are often used in place of feminine ones. Cooke aptly calls the form of נָשָׂא a perfect "of future certainty."[74] It is akin to a prophetic perfect and indicates the certainty that she will bear her punishment (the shame she will feel in 16:61, 63). Earlier verses had used other forms of נָשָׂא to describe her punishment: the imperative ("bear your disgrace") twice in 16:52 and the imperfect ("you will bear your disgrace") in 16:54.

16:59 כִּי כֹה אָמַר אֲדֹנָי יְהוִה—"Finally, the longest single oracle in the OT draws to a close." So Block begins his exegesis of 16:59–63, which he and most other commentators regard as a distinct, final section.[75] The signatory formula ("says Yahweh") at the end of 16:58 and the citation formula ("thus says the Lord Yahweh") beginning 16:59 certainly suggest a major transition, at least formally, between 16:58 and 16:59. Materially, the "covenant" theme reintroduced in 16:59 (previously in 16:8) continues in 16:60–63, where the term occurs four more times, so these verses (16:59–63) properly go together.

However, the initial כִּי, "for," indicates at least some connection between 16:59 and the preceding. If the next clause in 16:59 (see the next textual note) is taken as a statement, "I shall do …" rather than a question, "Shall I do … ?" then its Law tone would make 16:59 fit better as a conclusion of the previous section, as in the NASB,[76] but that is a minority position. I agree with Allen[77] that the next clause should be taken as a question and that 16:59 goes with 16:60–63.

וְעָשִׂית אוֹתָךְ כַּאֲשֶׁר עָשִׂית—Here אוֹתָךְ is (or is equivalent to) the preposition (with suffix: "with you") rather than the sign of the direct object. The Qere וְעָשִׂיתִי makes

---

[73] Critics generally have an aversion to predictive prophecy, and so some consider this and the rest of the verse a secondary addition inspired by 16:27. See, for example, Zimmerli, *Ezekiel*, 1:333.

[74] Cooke, *Ezekiel*, 178.

[75] Block, *Ezekiel*, 1:515.

[76] NASB takes the next clause as a statement and has 16:59 conclude one paragraph (16:53–59), while 16:60–63 constitutes another paragraph.

[77] Allen, *Ezekiel*, 1:232, argues that the next clause should be taken as a question because it fits poorly with 16:60–63 if taken as a statement.

explicit that the initial verb is first common singular, as the context requires. The Kethib may be a defectively written equivalent (וְעָשִׂית) since a repetition of the second feminine singular form at the end of the phrase (עָשִׂית) would make no sense. Contrast this Kethib/Qere with the nine previous ones where the Kethib of a second feminine singular verb had a final י but the Qere omitted it (see the textual note on אָכַלְתִּי in 16:13).

This clause has no interrogative or other overt indication that it is a rhetorical question, but some commentators take it as such. Allen considers 16:59 to be a deliberate counterpart to the question at the end of 16:43.[78] In Hebrew it is often enough for the context to require taking a phrase or clause as a question (GKC, § 150 a; Joüon, § 161 a), and unmarked questions are in 16:43, 56; 18:13, 24; and the last clause of 17:15, which likewise is about the consequences of breaking a covenant. Since 16:56–58 is Law (condemnation), and 16:60–63 has some Law but mostly is rich Gospel, a transition is necessary at some point. Most English translations take 16:59 as a declaration and as the start of a paragraph consisting of 16:59–63, but 16:59 forms a better transition to 16:60–63 if it is taken as a question (as in my translation).

אֲשֶׁר־בָּזִית אָלָה לְהָפֵר בְּרִית:—These phrases refer to the Mosaic covenant. אָלָה, "oath," is specifically a covenantal oath, as also in 17:13, 16, 18, 19 (see also, e.g., Gen 26:28; Deut 29:11, 13 [ET 29:12, 14]). The Hiphil of פָּרַר is a technical term for "breaking" God's "covenant" (בְּרִית) in Gen 17:14; Lev 26:15, 44; Deut 31:16, 20. The same language as here is used for covenant violation in Ezek 17:15–19.

16:60 וְזָכַרְתִּי אֲנִי אֶת־בְּרִיתִי—Most English translations render the initial *waw* as adversative, for example, "nevertheless" (KJV) or "yet" (NIV, ESV), so that it is part of the transition from the previous Law condemnations (16:56–58, and 16:59 if taken as a declaration) to the following Gospel promises. For Yahweh to "remember" (זָכַר) his "covenant" (בְּרִית) is a strong expression of the Gospel.[d] The redundant, emphatic pronoun אֲנִי reinforces that Yahweh himself (in contrast to Israelite perfidy and unaided by any human compliance) will remember his covenant. See it also in the first clause of 16:62. In biblical usage "to remember" is no mere intellectual act, but also involves carrying out present action in accord with the memory.

וַהֲקִמוֹתִי לָךְ בְּרִית עוֹלָם:—The Hiphil verb with Yahweh as subject and the preposition with suffix, לָךְ ("*for* you"), indicates that Yahweh himself will establish this everlasting covenant unilaterally by his grace. It will not be a bilateral covenant, as might have been suggested by "with you." The phrase בְּרִית עוֹלָם, "(ever)lasting covenant," is used to refer to the Noahic covenant (Gen 9:16), the Abrahamic covenant (Gen 17:7, 13, 19), the Mosaic covenant (Ps 105:10 ‖ 1 Chr 16:17) with its provision of the Sabbath (Ex 31:16; Lev 24:8), Israel's violation of the Mosaic covenant (Is 24:5), and to the new covenant in Christ, the Son of David (2 Sam 23:5; Is 55:3; Ezek 37:26), which Yahweh promises to establish (Is 61:8; Jer 32:40; Ezek 16:60; cf. Jer 50:5).[79]

(d) E.g., Gen 9:15–16; Ex 2:24; 6:5; Lev 26:42, 45; Jer 14:21; Pss 105:8; 106:45; 111:5

---

[78] Allen, *Ezekiel*, 1:226, 232, who also cites Calvin (*Ezekiel*, 2:172) as being aware that some interpreters translated the phrase in 16:59 as a question.

[79] For these covenants and their connections, see the excursus "Covenant" in Harstad, *Joshua*, 744–56.

16:61 וְזָכַרְתְּ אֶת־דְּרָכַיִךְ וְנִכְלַמְתְּ—In 16:27, the Philistines were "ashamed/embarrassed" at Jerusalem's "way/conduct," but now she will be "ashamed" at her own "ways," indicating true repentance. "Godly sorrow works a repentance unto salvation" (2 Cor 7:10).

אֶל־ ... בְּקַחְתֵּךְ—Jerusalem will "receive" (infinitive of לָקַח) her larger sisters "in addition to" her smaller sisters. Ezekiel often uses אֶל with one of the meanings of עַל. The plural forms apparently include both Samaria and her daughters as "your sisters who are bigger" (אֲחוֹתַיִךְ הַגְּדֹלוֹת) and both Sodom and her daughters as the sisters "who are smaller" (הַקְּטַנּוֹת).

A couple of LXX manuscripts and the Syriac translate "when I receive," apparently reading בְּקַחְתִּי instead of בְּקַחְתֵּךְ. Some commentators and translations (e.g., RSV, NRSV) follow that reading, which leads more smoothly to the following verb, וְנָתַתִּי, "I will give ..." It also emphasizes God as the one who first receives the heathen nations, then reconciles them with his elect people.

However, Yahweh's promise that Jerusalem will receive the heathen nations presupposes that he will have reconciled them to himself; compare the Fifth Petition of the Lord's Prayer (Mt 6:12). The MT makes sense and so qualifies as a *lectio difficilior*. More may be lost than gained by emending it. Here לָקַח may be used (as in 16:16–18, 20) "as preliminary to further action" (BDB, s.v. לָקַח, Qal, 4 g), namely, Yahweh giving the sisters to the woman as daughters. Or לָקַח may be used in the sense of receiving an inheritance or a gift (e.g., Num 34:14–15; Josh 13:8; 18:7; see BDB, 4 f). Other possibilities are that לָקַח reflects the language of adoption of children or is akin to its use for taking a spouse in marriage (BDB, 4 e).

וְלֹא מִבְּרִיתֵךְ:—This phrase, literally, "and not from your covenant," is highly debated; see the commentary. All translation involves interpretation, and mine reflects my conclusions. Since Yahweh unilaterally initiated the prior covenants (with Noah, Abraham, and Moses) and unilaterally will establish the new "everlasting covenant" (16:60), בְּרִיתֵךְ ("your covenant") is rightly understood and translated as "my covenant with you." It is not a covenant that Jerusalem would establish, either with Yahweh or her sisters.

16:62 וַהֲקִמוֹתִי אֲנִי אֶת־בְּרִיתִי אִתָּךְ—As in the first clause of 16:60, the redundant pronoun אֲנִי emphasizes divine monergism in salvation (in contrast to Israel's synergism or outright paganism): Yahweh ("I myself") establishes the covenant.[80]

16:63 פִּתְחוֹן פֶּה—This phrase, literally, "opening of mouth," uses the noun (פִּתְחוֹן) cognate to the usual verb (פָּתַח) for opening one's mouth. In the OT the noun and the phrase recur only in 29:21, which relates to Ezekiel's speechlessness (see the textual notes and commentary on 3:25–27; 4:8). Here, however, the phrase clearly refers to Israel and apparently means opening the mouth for arrogant or prideful speech. Compare 16:56–57, when Jerusalem, in the days of her pride, used Sodom as a byword.

בְּכַפְּרִי־לָךְ לְכָל־אֲשֶׁר עָשִׂית—The Piel verb כָּפֶּר is especially prominent in Leviticus in the sacrificial liturgies of the OT divine service, and its use here by Ezekiel, a

---

[80] Again, one may see the excursus "Covenant" in Harstad, *Joshua*, 744–56.

prophet-priest (1:3), should be interpreted in that light. It means "make atonement, expiate," and in Leviticus invariably involves a sacrificial rite. A cognate noun is used for the "Day of Atonement," יוֹם־(הַ)כִּפֻּרִים (Lev 23:27–28; 25:9), and the comprehensive atonement made on that day for the sins of all Israel (Leviticus 16) is the closest OT parallel to Yahweh's statement here that he would atone "*for all* [לְכָל] you have done." Translations such as "forgive, absolve, propitiate," while not totally incorrect, lose the specific coloration of the word.

In this eschatological context, Ezekiel's use of this word associated with the tabernacle and temple, liturgy, and sacrifice points toward his full elaboration of these themes in chapters 40–48, where he will use the verb again (43:20, 26; 45:15, 17, 20). There we will be fully alerted to its fulfillment in Christ's atonement, effected on Calvary.

Commentary

Taken on its own terms, this longest single oracle in the whole OT is one of Scripture's most powerful expressions of both God's wrath and his love— of Law and Gospel.

In form, it is an allegory of Jerusalem as an abandoned girl who is rescued by Yahweh, and when grown into a beautiful woman, she is married to him and made a queen, richly clothed and fed. But she repays Yahweh's gratuitous largesse by pathological infidelity, even paying lovers to sleep with her and surpassing even Sodom and Samaria in lewdness. Hence, judgment is unavoidable, but, after that, Yahweh will repay her faithlessness with faithfulness to his ancient covenant. Moreover, Yahweh will establish an "everlasting covenant" that includes not only Israelites, but also former pagans: Samaria, Sodom, and their children (16:60–62). Read in light of the NT, this is nothing less than the promise of the new covenant in Jesus Christ and the ingrafting of Gentiles into "the Israel of God" (Gal 6:16), the Christian church. All this shall take place "when I make atonement for you for all you have done" (Ezek 16:63) through Christ's unblemished life, atoning death, and victorious resurrection.

We can easily view the entire pericope as a unit with one major point of comparison: Israel's gross unfaithfulness in contrast to God's gracious love. Thus it may be more of a parable than an allegory, although one can find both labels for it in secondary literature. Subsumed under the one main point are various correspondences. As the capital city of united Israel and then Judah, "Jerusalem" represents Israel, the people God had called out of heathenism (16:3, 45; see also Gen 12:1–3) to be his own according to his covenant of grace. "Samaria" represents the northern kingdom, which had apostatized under Jeroboam and had been conquered by Assyria in 722 B.C. (about 129 years before Ezekiel's ministry began). "Sodom" had been destroyed over a millennium earlier (Genesis 19), but its name lived on as a byword representing the ultimate in depravity. The extended picture of Jerusalem's harlotry has the historical and political referent of Israel's flirtations (alliances) with her pagan neighbors, liaisons that inevitably entailed worship of pagan gods. Exact connections between the specific acts of whoredom and particulars in Israel's history are sometimes impossible to establish and probably should not be expected.

Throughout the Bible God often portrays his covenant relationship with his people as a spiritual marriage.[81] The OT suggests that Yahweh wedded Israel as his wife through his exodus redemption of her. The marriage metaphor appears frequently already in the Torah of Moses (Ex 34:15–16; Lev 17:7; 20:5; Deut 32:15–18; and elsewhere). According to traditional Jewish and Christian interpretation, the Song of Songs relates the marriage of Solomon and one Shulammite to that between Yahweh and Israel, typifying (in Christian interpretation) that of Christ and his body and bride, the church. Psalm 45, a royal wedding psalm, shares many affinities to the Song of Solomon. In the eighth-century B.C. Isaiah employs the theme (Is 61:10; 62:1–5), and the marriage of Hosea and Gomer embodies it (Hosea 1–3). Ezekiel's older contemporary uses it especially in Jeremiah 2–3.

The picture in Ezekiel 16 and 23 of Israel's marriage to Yahweh anticipates the NT depiction of the church as the bride of Christ—already betrothed through the washing of Baptism (Eph 5:25–27), but awaiting the consummation after his second coming, whereupon "the bride" shall become "the wife of the Lamb" (Rev 21:9). That NT theme appears in Jesus' wedding parables (Mt 22:1–14; 25:1–13) and sayings such as Lk 5:34–35; Jn 3:29–30 (cf. Jn 2:1–11). Of the many passages that portray the church as the body and bride of Christ, Eph 5:21–33 is the best known. And the canon of Scripture ends with an extended picture of Jerusalem as the virgin bride finally united with her Bridegroom (Revelation 21; cf. Rev 22:17).

The depiction of idolatry as adultery likewise is found throughout the Scriptures. It is implicit in Ezekiel's references to divine "jealousy" (קִנְאָה in 5:13; 8:3, 5), as confirmed by the use of the same term in 16:38, 42; 23:25 (see also 6:9). The NT too correlates idolatry and spiritual infidelity with sexual sins (e.g., Rom 1:18–32; 1 Cor 6:12–20; Gal 5:16–26).

As a priest (Ezek 1:3), Ezekiel no doubt was familiar with those OT texts that predated him, yet he develops and elaborates the marriage theme in a unique way in two extensive chapters (16 and 23).[82] No other biblical book depicts the divine relationship with such explicitly sexual language (e.g., 16:7–8). Nor will anyone who has read this far in the book be surprised by the explicitness with which Ezekiel discusses sexual matters in chapters 16 and 23. (Such explicitness may reflect his priestly background, since comparable directness

---

[81]　For a fuller survey of OT and NT passages and their theological significance, see Mitchell, *The Song of Songs*, 29–66.

[82]　The marriage theme also underlies 24:15–27, where the death of Ezekiel's wife portends the destruction of Jerusalem, but the tone of that passage is one of austere mourning and sadness (for both Yahweh and Ezekiel) in contrast to the outrage provoked by the lewdness in chapters 16 and 23.

can be found in parts of Leviticus.) Were Ezekiel not divinely inspired for the purpose of eliciting repentance and faith, one might call chapters 16 and 23 pornographic. Perhaps the grossness of our contemporary culture makes it less shocking today than the chapters might have seemed even a generation ago. But still, the ordinary Christian reader may not expect to find such language in the Bible. The fact that most English translations avoid rendering some of the language literally (e.g., 16:25–26, 36) shows that it continues to offend.

Why has Yahweh inspired Ezekiel to use such scandalous language in a book of Holy Scripture? His immediate intent is to provoke a strong emotional response of revulsion in the audience. But his aim is not shock simply for the sake of shock. Sin is ugly and offensive to God, and none more so than the spiritual adultery of his people, and all the more when they seem to be unaware that they are even sinning and so persistently fall from bad to worse. Probably no reader who is aware of his sinfulness and has a functioning conscience can read this chapter without feeling a sense of shame. Yahweh's repeatedly stated goal is that the audience will "be ashamed" (16:61, 63) of their sin and receive in faith the "atonement" he makes "for you for all you have done" (16:63).

To liberals today, Ezekiel 16 is offensive for additional reasons. A conservative might easily dismiss these liberal objections as anachronistic and irrelevant, and in a sense they are, but our cultural context demands that we not simply ignore them. In this third millennium A.D. many desire to leave behind the framework of biblical faith in the Trinity (Father, Son, and Holy Spirit) and the constraints of biblical morality and to recast God and religion in more egalitarian (tolerant, inclusive, pluralistic) terms. The modern "ecumenical" agenda, which advocates the ordination of women and now the acceptance and even the ordination of gays and lesbians, takes offense at the condemnation of Sodom in 16:46–50 and the thoroughly patriarchal and heterosexual nature of the imagery throughout Ezekiel 16 and 23. To those who perceive themselves as "liberated" (but who, from a biblical perspective, are enslaved!), Yahweh as depicted in Ezekiel 16 and 23 is an abusive husband who resorts to violence to control female sexuality for his own ends. Such a God they will not abide, and so they construct a god (or goddess) made in their own image (as the German philosopher Feuerbach once famously advocated doing).

In Ezekiel 16 and 23 Yahweh is not acting capriciously, but in accordance with the curses for covenant-breaking that were intrinsic to the divine covenant.[83] And "covenant," like "jealousy" (קִנְאָה, which Block especially highlights[84]), has two sides. First, Yahweh's righteous jealousy brings just retribution for unfaithfulness, and Israelite law knew no double standard; adul-

---

[83] The commentary on earlier chapters repeatedly pointed out how many of the judgments Yahweh pronounces are specific fulfillments of the covenant curses, especially in Leviticus 26. See, for example, the textual notes and commentary on 4:10–11, 16–17; chapters 5–6; 12:19–20; 14:12–23.

[84] Ezek 5:13; 8:3, 5; 16:38, 42; 23:25. Block, *Ezekiel*, 1:13–15, 469.

tery was a capital crime regardless of the gender of the offender (Lev 20:10). But second, the ultimate purpose of such punishment is to evoke repentance, restore the original relationship, and even establish something more—the new covenant in Christ, with which the chapter ends (Ezek 16:59–63). "Where sin abounded, grace did much more abound" (Rom 5:20 KJV). Rather than an oppressive male taking advantage of a vulnerable female, Yahweh appears here as the gracious Savior who first saves the foundling's life, then lavishly showers all kinds of gifts on her. He who created male and female is no misogynist, and neither is his prophet Ezekiel, as we can see from Yahweh's own reference to Ezekiel's wife as "the desire of your eyes" (Ezek 24:16).

The long chapter may be subdivided as follows. Doctrinally, the first and last sections emphasize the Gospel (Jerusalem's original calling and her eschatological restoration), while the middle sections are Law (her whoring and appropriate punishment). The chapter begins with the abject condition of the helpless baby, upon whom Yahweh lavishes gifts purely by grace and takes in marriage. The "whorings" of the ingrate are described in sordid detail in 16:15–34. Then in 16:35–42 we hear the first part of her sentence and judgment (more judgment pronouncements come at various places in 16:43–63). Ezek 16:43–58 introduces an invidious comparison to Sodom and Samaria to underscore how deserving Jerusalem is of her impending destruction. That comparison finally morphs into the theme of the eschatological great reversal in 16:59–63. These themes are summarized in the following outline:

I. Jerusalem's infancy, rescue, puberty, marriage, and adornment by grace (16:1–14)
II. Jerusalem exchanges her glory for idols, sacrifices Yahweh's children, and spreads her legs for every man passing by (16:15–29)
III. Jerusalem pays to be a whore dominatrix (16:30–34)
IV. Yahweh announces the whore's judgment (16:35–42)
V. Jerusalem is like her mother and sisters (16:43–58)
VI. Yahweh shall restore Jerusalem, establish an everlasting covenant, and make atonement for all sin (16:59–63)

Jerusalem's Infancy, Rescue, Puberty, Marriage, and Adornment by Grace (16:1–14)

16:2 While this first section of the chapter accents Jerusalem's original calling by grace, this review of covenant history is recited for the purpose of highlighting her current degradation, as Yahweh commands Ezekiel, "make Jerusalem know her abominations."

16:3 Yahweh begins his long, searing indictment of the current depravity of Israel by exposing the hollowness of the people's pride in allegedly being descendants of Abraham. He is not challenging the Genesis account of Israel's origins; rather, his concern is with her spiritual descent. There may well have been some in Ezekiel's audience who could trace their physical descent back to Abraham himself. Even so, Yahweh had led a mixed multitude out from

Egypt (Ex 12:38). Through mixed marriages, a large proportion of the population had Canaanite, Amorite, and/or Hittite blood in their veins. Even Moses had married a Cushite (Num 12:1), and by grace various foreigners had been incorporated into Israel (e.g., Rahab, the Gibeonites, Ruth).

The problem was that Israel had adopted many of their pagan neighbors' religious beliefs and practices. The three peoples Yahweh names ("Canaanites … Amorite[s] … Hittite[s]") are symbols of all that "Israel" was called to oppose. The "land of the Canaanites" had a reputation as the locus of the worst heathen "abominations" (16:2), of human depravity at is worst (16:44–52). It was for that reason that the invading Israelites were commanded to treat the previous inhabitants so harshly, to exterminate those who were not driven out (e.g., Deut 7:1–5; Joshua 1–12). But the Israelites had failed to carry out that covenant command completely (e.g., Josh 13:1–7; Judges 1–3). They often tolerated and intermarried with the remaining Canaanites, and in spite of brief reformations, they had persistently adopted their religious practices. Thus one could say that "Jerusalem had paganism in its blood."[85]

Ezekiel's confrontation here with his Israelite audience is phenomenally similar to one Jesus had with the Jews of his day, as recorded in Jn 8:31–59. To the Jews' boast that "Abraham is our father," Jesus responds, "If you were Abraham's children, you would do what Abraham did. … You are of your father, the devil, and your will is to do your father's desires. He was a murderer from the beginning and has nothing to do with the truth, because there is no truth in him" (Jn 8:39, 44).

Christians today are unlikely to pin their hope for salvation on their ancestry, although nationalistic pride or separatism based on ethnic origin may virtually become a religion. More likely today is the narcissistic conceit that some "spark of the divine" is each individual's birthright, enabling him to embark on his own "faith journey" and forge his own "spirituality." Arminian decision theology and semi-Pelagianism are prominent in many Protestant churches. Appeals to the transferable merit of saints are still part of official Roman Catholic doctrine (see the commentary on 14:12–20). No Christian is immune from the temptation to think that his place in heaven is secure because of his pedigree of past faithfulness or good works (based on what Lutheran theologians call the *opinio legis*, the Law-based thinking that persists in all sinful people).

16:4–5 The topic shifts from genealogy to circumstances of birth, which were just as inauspicious. The two verses are framed by the inclusio "on the day you were born."

Ezek 16:4 is simply a list of four (or five) things normally done for a newborn in the ancient Near East. The first two are universal, while the last two (alien to us in the modern West) are still attested in remote parts of the Near

---

85 Allen, *Ezekiel*, 1:236.

East. If the umbilical cord is not tied and cut relatively soon after birth, the infant can bleed to death. Bathing the newborn would follow almost instinctively. The Hebrew may refer to a subsequent application of oil ("for oiling"; see the textual note), or the oil and salt may have been mixed together. Rubbing with salt probably was for cleansing or hygienic reasons. The Hebrew text actually does not refer to rubbing, but simply to salting with salt—possibly applied to the swaddling clothes to inhibit bacteria. Some commentators give it an apotropaic meaning, seeing it as a superstitious practice to ward off demons or evil spirits, and in the light of Ezekiel's general picture of Israelite "spirituality," such notions might well have been part of the action. Wrapping tightly in swaddling clothes comforts a newborn, and in the ancient world doing so (sometimes on a straight board) was apparently thought to help limbs develop straightly.

That last act not done for infant "Jerusalem" was done for the infant Lord, since the Gospel of Luke records that at Christ's nativity the Virgin Mary wrapped him in swaddling cloths (Lk 2:7), showing her care for him and serving as part of the divine "sign" to the shepherds (Lk 2:12).[86]

In contrast, Ezek 16:5 spells out the malevolent motivation behind not doing those things for infant "Jerusalem." Her neglect implies not only the repression of natural parental compassion, but the repudiation of the offspring by abandonment. Parents who abandoned a baby officially rejected all their parental rights and obligations and renounced the child as their own. If the baby happened to be rescued before death, he or she could then legally be adopted, but most likely the child, even if discovered by others, would be left to die.

It must be remembered that the exposure of unwanted babies (especially girls) was widespread throughout the ancient world. Even classical philosophers and lawgivers such as Plato and Plutarch recommended the practice, whatever the reason or motivation.[87] However, given the sanctity of all human life according to the OT and NT, orthodox Israel did not tolerate that practice, nor did subsequent Christianity. The founding of orphanages and other eleemosynary institutions by Christians in the late Roman Empire is well documented.

The parallel to abortion must not go unnoticed. The *Didache* (second century A.D.) elaborates the Fifth Commandment (οὐ φονεύσεις, "you shall not murder," LXX Ex 20:15 [MT/ET 20:13]) by including the command "you shall not murder a child by abortion" (οὐ φονεύσεις τέκνον ἐν φθορᾷ, *Didache* 2:2). Today in many Western countries, a parent who abandons (or even "abuses")

---

[86] Just, *Luke 1:1–9:50*, 110, comments that "Luke will frame his gospel with reference to Jesus' clothes, beginning with the strips of cloth for the infant Jesus as a sign of the Messiah's birth and concluding with his dead body wrapped in a shroud at his burial (23:53), which will be 'the linen clothes alone' discovered by Peter as a sign of the Messiah's resurrection (24:12). By this frame, Luke connects Jesus' birth, death, and resurrection."

[87] Plato, *Republic*, 5.459–61; Plutarch, *Lycurgus*, 16, cited in Greenberg, *Ezekiel*, 1:275.

children after birth will be prosecuted, but murder in the womb before birth is excused under sophistries about "choice," when exactly "life" begins, and so on. As in antiquity, many of this world's "wise" approve (cf. 1 Corinthians 1), and even more tragically, many churches, which have become conformed to the world (Rom 12:2) and whose salt has lost its saltiness (Mt 5:13), follow suit. This practice is equivalent to the sacrifice of children to Molech by apostate ancient Israelites (see the textual note and commentary on Ezek 16:20–21).

In Israel's actual history, it is not easy to find a counterpart to the abandonment of the infant in Ezekiel's extended metaphor, and perhaps we should not try. Occasionally an attempt is made to match this part of the oracle with the Egyptian command to the Hebrew midwives to kill all newborn male infants, but the midwives feared God rather than man, and so both they and the children were preserved (Ex 1:15–22), and thus that connection seems forced. The example of Moses' birth shows that even under the most extreme circumstances faithful Israelites would seek any way to sustain a baby's life, even feigning abandonment (Ex 2:1–10).

The absence of parental care serves as a negative foil to Yahweh's positive intervention which follows in the narrative. Without God's rescue the infant surely would have died, and such is the natural condition of all children of Adam and Eve (except Jesus), who, as sinners, stand under God's judgment. Neither infant Jerusalem nor any person can do anything to save himself. This underscores the sheer grace underlying the election of ancient Israel—and of all believers in all ages. Deut 7:7–8 is perhaps the classical OT expression of the fact that the choice of Israel was not the result of anything attractive to God in her, but only "because Yahweh loves you." In the NT, one might cite Rom 5:8: "God shows his love for us in that while we were yet sinners Christ died for us."

Beyond such statements of God's pure grace and unmerited love, the Scriptures never say why God chose Israel instead of any other people, or why he has chosen to elect or predestine some to eternal life (e.g., Acts 13:48; Rom 8:29–30; Eph 1:5, 11). From the human side, there is no answer for the ancient dogmatic conundrum *cur alii, alii non*?[88]

16:6 Yahweh's description of his compassionate love for Jerusalem is divided into two sections, her childhood (16:6–7) and her married life (16:8–14), each beginning with "I passed by you and I saw you" (16:6, 8). The Hebrew might imply that Yahweh came upon her unintentionally ("I happened to pass by"[89]), and if pressed, that could be misunderstood as denying God's prior salvific intent to choose Israel—as well as Christ and his church. But the Hebrew can also be used of deliberately coming to a person (see the textual notes), and the Scriptures teach that God willed and planned our salvation from all eternity! The clause in this context must underscore again the element of sheer grace. A person who finds a helpless infant will feel compassion (as did

---

[88] See FC SD XI, "Eternal Foreknowledge and Divine Election."

[89] Block, *Ezekiel*, 1:477.

Pharaoh's daughter, Ex 2:6), but not because the baby somehow merits or has earned it. There is no historical or logical, "worldly" or Law-based reason why God chose Israel, or why he has chosen any of us to believe in Christ and so to be saved. The doctrine of election is a mystery that must be filled out according to the Gospel alone. If any idea of merit, worthiness, anything at all in a person (*aliquid in homine*), or even *intuitu fidei*, is allowed into the equation, it will lead to some form of works-righteousness. On the other hand, if the doctrine of election is filled out wrongly with appeal to God's punitive judgment, that can lead to the error of double predestination, namely, that God not only elected some to salvation, but also others to damnation.[90]

That God "saw" the infant (16:6; cf. 16:8) reverses the human neglect expressed by "an eye did not have pity on you" in 16:5. God provides what no human did or, from a theological perspective, could. Theologically, from where else could salvation come?

Yahweh's repeated statement, "I said to you, 'In your blood, live!' " (16:6), refers first of all to biological life. Physical life is always the first of God's gifts, and he gives it to all people, even to unbelievers, even though they do not acknowledge him as the giver or receive the gift with thanksgiving (cf. Mt 5:45). Allen's instinct is sound when he senses here a certain analogy to the doctrine of creation.[91]

Yet the ancient Near Eastern context gives this statement a greater depth of meaning. To take a baby in his or her amniotic fluid and birth blood implied a legal adoption of the child, who then could not be reclaimed by the natural parents.[92] In the biblical context, "live" implies also spiritual life in this world and bodily resurrection followed by eternal life in the world to come (cf. Jn 10:10; 11:25–26). That God here enables the girl to "live" simply by speaking his Word points toward the rebirth by the power of the Word in, for example, 1 Pet 1:3–5, 23, and to Baptism, wherein the water is accompanied by God's Word ("the washing of water with the Word," with bridal imagery in Eph 5:26; see the commentary on Ezek 16:9 below). On a theological level, this OT imagery corresponds to the NT portrayal of the second birth and adoption as children of God that takes place in the Sacrament of Holy Baptism (e.g., Jn 3:3–8; Gal 3:26–29; Titus 3:4–7).

---

90 Again, see FC SD XI, "Eternal Foreknowledge and Divine Election." See also Pieper, *Christian Dogmatics*, 3:473–503; Robert Preus, "Predestination and Election," in *A Contemporary Look at the Formula of Concord* (St. Louis: Concordia, 1978), 271–77. *Intuitu fidei* refers to the idea (popular in some branches of Lutheranism in the late nineteenth century) that God elected people to salvation at least partly because he knew they would respond to the Gospel and believe it. However, orthodox Lutheranism rejected that idea because it bases salvation at least in part on some quality in a person (*aliquid in homine*) or on something a person does, rather than solely on the grace of God.

91 Allen, *Ezekiel*, 1:237.

92 See the Mesopotamian sources cited in Malul, "Adoption of Foundlings in the Bible and Mesopotamian Documents," 106–10, including his translation of section 185 of the Code of Hammurabi.

16:7 The idiomatic Hebrew rendered "I made you thrive" again finds a parallel in section 185 of the Code of Hammurabi, where it describes the rearing of an adopted child by his or her legal parents.[93] Thus the adoption metaphor of the previous verse is continued. The subsequent simile ("like a sprout of the field") indicates how excellent the parenting was. Some have seen in this clause an allusion to the rapid growth of the Israelite slaves in Egypt (Ex 1:7, 12, 20–21), and if such an allusion is intended, one might also think of the rapid growth of the early church despite fierce persecution (e.g., Acts 2–12), but I judge that one must be cautious in seeking such specific parallels. In any event, the newborn had been left to die in the "field" (שָׂדֶה, 16:5), but after Yahweh's intervention, here the "field" (שָׂדֶה, 16:7) becomes the place where the girl thrives. This hints at the great reversal, a central theme of biblical soteriology and eschatology ("the last shall be first," Mt 20:16; God chooses the weak and lowly, 1 Cor 1:26–28).

With unblushing frankness, Ezekiel depicts the onset of puberty and the girl's growth into womanhood. It is probably as futile as elsewhere to seek a historical analogue in Israel's history for the woman's stark nakedness even after maturing. If it can be pressed, it possibly implies that Israel's status as the chosen people was no birthright nor a product of her "search for truth" nor of any other action by her or quality in her. She was nothing before God and had nothing until he gave her his covenant and promises, as the following verses will emphasize. (Later in the chapter, nudity will be associated with promiscuity and prostitution, but that theme is not yet on the horizon here.)

16:8 The spiritual wedding takes place here as Yahweh "swore [an oath]" and "entered into a covenant" with her. Since this is not ordinary nuptial language (see the textual note), we begin to see a little of the underlying reality to which the allegory points. That Yahweh initiates the covenant at this point suggests that the metaphorical wedding occurred in Israel's history at the time of the exodus redemption and Sinai covenant, as affirmed by Jeremiah's comparable allegory (Jer 2:2–6) and the traditional Jewish interpretation of the Song of Songs.[94] It might also be supported by the "field" in Ezek 16:5, 7 if that hints at Israel's wilderness wanderings. "You became mine" (16:8) alludes to the frequent OT covenant formula "I shall be your God and you shall be my people," expressed in wedding language (see the commentary on 11:20; 14:11).

The background of Yahweh's gracious oath, covenant, and wedding provides much of the pathos and poignancy during the following picture of her gross amnesia, ingratitude, and whoredom (16:15–58). It also provides the basis for the anthropopathism that pervades most of the book of Ezekiel: God suffers (described in human terms) at such a base response by his bride (e.g., Hos 11:8). This suffering culminates in that of Jesus Christ, God incarnate, who

---

[93] Malul, "Adoption of Foundlings in the Bible and Mesopotamian Documents," 106–7, 112.

[94] See "Traditional Jewish Interpretation" in Mitchell, *The Song of Songs*, 463–67.

(like Yahweh in Ezekiel 16) lamented over Jerusalem's rejection of him (Mt 23:37; Lk 13:34).

No matter how unfaithful his people may be, God does not lie (2 Tim 2:13). He will not break his oath or abandon the promise of life and eternal blessing intrinsic to his covenant. Yet the oath and covenant also entail judgment if his faithfulness is not believed and reciprocated in a life of faith in him. The gracious God is also just, and his justice requires that aspect of the covenant promises now to be carried out, so that a righteous remnant might be preserved. At this point, however, Ezekiel does not spell out all the implications, both positive and negative. The ultimate resolution of the "tension" between God's love and his justice comes only at Calvary, where the entirety of divine punishment for human sin was borne by the sinless Son of God, whose vicarious atonement (see 16:63) procured mercy for all. In the new covenant too, the benefits of God's faithfulness are appropriated through faith and are reciprocated in a life of faith in him; without such faith a person forfeits God's mercy and stands under his judgment.

16:9 If 16:8–13 is taken as strictly sequential, it might seem strange from a human standpoint that Yahweh cleanses, anoints, and adorns his bride *after* the wedding. According to the cultural customs to which the metaphors refer, the cleansing, clothing, and adornment may have been done first as preparation for the wedding or as part of the ceremony itself. The textual notes above pointed out that much of the same vocabulary was used in Genesis 24 for jewelry given to Rebekah prior to her wedding to Isaac, and women in Esth 2:9–13 were given choice food, anointed, and adorned before union with the king. Also in the royal wedding psalm (Ps 45:14–16 [ET 45:13–15]) and the Song (1:9–11; 4:1–7), the bride is adorned with jewelry for or at her wedding.[95]

However, on the theological level, the literal sequence in these verses is all important. God does not demand holiness or cleanness as a prerequisite for those who would enter his covenant of grace. On the contrary, he bestows these unmerited gifts upon his bride *sola gratia*, "by grace alone." Thus the washing of Israel with water may allude to her exodus redemption through the Red Sea waters, which St. Paul expounds as a type of Holy Baptism in 1 Cor 10:1–2. The NT too speaks of the Lord washing his bride: Christ "gave himself up" for his bride, the church, "so that he might sanctify her, having cleansed her by the washing of water with the Word, so that he himself might present the church to himself as glorious … holy and blameless" (Eph 5:25–27). The Christian Sacrament of Baptism is the "washing of rebirth/regeneration" (Titus 3:5). In a new act of creation, God makes his redeemed people into a *"holy* nation" (Ex 19:6; cf. 1 Pet 2:9). Thus, we can confess belief "in one *holy* catholic and apostolic church … one Baptism for the remission of sins" (Nicene Creed).

---

[95] Song 1:11 emphasizes that this jewelry was given to her. For the view that these passages depict her adornment for the wedding ceremony (3:11), see Mitchell, *The Song of Songs*, 148–52.

Anointing with oil accompanied Baptism as a sign of the "unction" of the Holy Spirit, perhaps already in NT times (if that is part of the sealing in, e.g., Eph 1:13; 4:30) and certainly at an early date in church history, as it still does in some baptismal liturgies. That probably explains why the Vulgate and a Greek translation related the "oiling" in Ezek 16:4 to salvation in Christ (see the textual notes on 16:4).

16:10–13 In great detail, Ezekiel continues to describe the lavish clothing and expensive jewelry showered upon the bride, not to speak of the stunning natural beauty with which God endowed her. It is a minor point, but these gifts are probably best not thought of as specifically wedding gifts (the wedding is past, so 16:8), but rather as the boundless demonstrations of love by a devoted and faithful husband "as long as [they] both shall live."[96]

In my judgment the application of the metaphor peers through the words also here. We cannot overlook the many correspondences between 16:10–13 and the objects and vocabulary associated with the tabernacle, the priestly vestments, and the liturgical sacrifices (see the textual notes on the first three words listed below). These correspondences include the "finest woven material" (רִקְמָה, 16:10, 13, 18), "luxury leather" (תַּחַשׁ, 16:10), "the best linen" (שֵׁשׁ, 16:10, 13), "fine flour" (סֹלֶת, 16:13, 19), "oil" (שֶׁמֶן, 16:13, 18, 19), and "incense" (קְטֹרֶת, 16:18). "Fine flour" and "oil" are especially prominent in the grain offerings of the sacrificial rituals. Gold was abundant in the tabernacle and temple, especially as one approached the Holy of Holies. While we are not told any specifics about articles of silver in the temple, there were ones of silver in the tabernacle. The temple also served as the national treasury of gold and silver.[97]

As Jerusalem in these passages is synecdochical for all of Israel, so the temple is synecdochical for God himself. There God was "incarnationally" present among his people, and only his holy presence and sanctifying work through the means of grace enabled Jerusalem to be a holy city.

Analogically, the treasures of the holy church are God's means of grace: his Word, which is preached in the sermon and spoken in the absolution, and the Sacraments, by which the Gospel is conveyed to members of the body of Christ.

That she "attained royalty" (16:13) explains the significance of the "crown of glory" placed on her head by Yahweh (16:12). Her royal status was due to her union with her God and King. This too is part of the great reversal theme: the ignoble infant of heathen lineage (16:3) is privileged to become not just a member of God's kingdom, but his queen. (NIV translates the last phrase of 16:13 with "queen," but the Hebrew does not use that term, perhaps to avoid any thought that she deserved the position by her birth.) The Christological

---

[96] *Lutheran Worship Agenda* (St. Louis: Concordia, 1984), 122.

[97] For example, 1 Ki 7:51; 15:15. See the second textual note on Ezek 7:20.

wedding psalm (Ps 45:11–16 [ET 45:10–15]) and the Song of Songs (6:8–9) contain this same theme that the woman married by grace to the king is thereby elevated and given the gift of royalty.[98] The NT affirms that all baptized believers in Christ are members of the kingdom of God by grace and shall reign with Christ in eternity,[e] and in a sense even now reign with him during the church age (Rev 20:4, 6).

(e) E.g., Mt 19:28; Rom 5:17; Rev 4:4; 5:10; 22:5

16:14 The picture of God's boundless gifts comes to a climax with the bride's unparalleled fame, beauty, perfection, and splendor. As Ezekiel wrote and preached, Jerusalem was threatened, and his audience would hear in such language an evocation of the so-called "theology of Zion" (see, e.g., Lam 2:15; Pss 48:3 [ET 48:2]; 50:2). Unfortunately, his audience probably heard such language as describing the "inviolability of Zion," that is, that Jerusalem could not be destroyed, no matter how much she sinned.[99] That was a confusion of "Jerusalem" as merely another earthly city with "Zion" as the holy city wherein God dwelt (to the extent that the two terms are distinguishable).

Zion/Jerusalem as a type of the Christian church receives language similar to Ezek 16:14, as in the hymn "Glorious Things of You Are Spoken" (*LW* 294), or in a more eschatological vein, "Jerusalem the Golden" (*LW* 309) and "Jerusalem, O City Fair and High" (*LW* 306). These portraits reflect that of the new Jerusalem (the church triumphant) as the bride adorned for her Bridegroom in Revelation 21, and that of the church as the cleansed bride of Christ, who even now by virtue of his gracious baptismal washing is "glorious, not having a spot or wrinkle or any of such things, but … holy and blameless" (Eph 5:27).

Finally, this section of the chapter ends with the salutary reminder that everything the woman had and all she had become was that "which I had bestowed upon you, says the Lord Yahweh " (Ezek 16:14). She would quickly forget what we too so easily forget—that this absolute, perfect beauty was not innate, but bestowed, a righteousness imputed solely for Christ's sake, a holiness which by nature is God's alone. In the NT, see, for example, 1 Cor 4:7–8; Rev 1:5b–6. This final reminder that "we are unworthy servants" (Lk 17:10), or, according to Luther's last written words, "we are beggars" (AE 54:476), serves as a foil for the abrupt transition to follow.

Jerusalem Exchanges Her Glory for Idols, Sacrifices Yahweh's Children, and Spreads Her Legs for Every Man Passing By (16:15–29)

16:15 That Jerusalem "played the whore" is a summary of the rest of the chapter from 16:15–58 down to the eschatological reversal at its end (16:59–63). The initial division in 16:15–22 deals with the origin and nature of Israel's apostasy, described in terms of whoring. The verb זָנָה, "play the

---

98 On the great reversal theme in the Song, see Mitchell, *The Song of Songs*, 372–80.

99 See further the commentary on 8:12–13.

471

whore," its participle, זֹנָה, "whore," and the noun תַּזְנוּת, "whoring, whoredom," together occur twenty-one times in 16:15–41. This language refers not only to literal sexual sins, but also to spiritual unions with false gods (idolatry). The reader must remain aware of this double entendre, even if we are unable to match precisely the actions here with specific events in Israel's history.

In short, Israel's new status and power "went to her head." I cannot improve upon two expositions, the first from Block:

> For Jerusalem the newly found beauty and fame were intoxicating. In her inebriation she lost all sense of history, perspective, and propriety; the temporal and ephemeral replaced the eternal; the gift displaced the giver.[100]

That Jerusalem "trusted in [her] beauty" (16:15) is remarkably similar to the sin of Tyre and her prince (27:3–4, 11; 28:12, 17) and that of Assyria (31:8–9), and in both cases the sin is likened to the primeval hubris of Satan, who sought to elevate himself above God (28:2, 6, 9, 12–19; 31:8–9, 15). Hence Zimmerli is also worth quoting. He characterizes Israel's behavior as an attempt to seize equality with God—the very thing of which the sinless Christ was not guilty (οὐχ ἁρπαγμὸν ἡγήσατο τὸ εἶναι ἴσα θεῷ); instead he emptied himself and became a servant (Phil 2:6–7). Zimmerli says of Ezekiel's prophecy:

> This is not addressed to the "world," but to the people of God, the Church. Thereby it is laid down that nothing is so holy, even the sacramental inheritance of the Church, that it cannot become a means of the worst abuse when it is used selfishly.[101]

Thus when we Christians, especially Gentile believers, read of Israel's degeneracy, we must not think that the Israelites were any more susceptible to the temptations to which they succumbed than we are. Instead, we must read Israel's history as a warning for us not to do the same, as St. Paul explains in 1 Cor 10:1–13. What is more, we read knowing that the prophetic promises (Ezek 16:59–63) have now been fulfilled in Christ, and in us—if we remain in Christ.

Israel's promiscuous liaisons with "every man passing by" (כָּל־עוֹבֵר, 16:15, 25) are clearly intended as a contrast with the One who passed by earlier (וָאֶעֱבֹר עָלַיִךְ, "I passed by you," 16:6, 8), first to save her life (16:6), and then to make her his wife and share his splendor with her (16:8). That she gave herself to these lovers (the apparent meaning of the Hebrew translated "his you became," 16:15) meant that she had flagrantly and repeatedly broken the marriage covenant.

Ezekiel does not specify any specific situation or period in Israel's history, but "trusted in your beauty" and "reliance on your fame" (16:15) might allude to the era of David and Solomon, when Israel was at the height of her outward

---

[100] Block, *Ezekiel*, 1:488.

[101] Zimmerli, *Ezekiel*, 1:349.

prosperity. Nevertheless, apostasies and rebellions punctuated Israel's history from the wilderness era down to the fall of Jerusalem. The same can be said about church history from the betrayal of Christ down to the present.

16:16–17 The verb וַתִּקְחִי, "and you took," begins 16:16, 17, 18, 20. All of 16:16–22 describes Israel's whorish misuse of God's gifts, even of her children (16:20), as if, instead of gifts to be received with thanksgiving, they were hers alone to take and use as she pleased without responsibility or accountability to anyone. These verses set the rebellion of the Israelites in sharp relief by their repeated contrast between Yahweh's original gift of the objects (which really were still his) and her taking of them to devote to pagan uses.

As St. Paul states about humanity in general in Rom 1:23, she exchanged the glory Yahweh gave her for inglorious images for harlotry: "You took your articles of glory from my gold and my silver which I had given to you, and you made for yourself images of the male and you played the whore with them" (Ezek 16:17). This recalls the "crown of glory" Yahweh had given her in 16:12, and also 7:19–20, where Israel made idols out of gold and silver, perhaps taken from the temple treasury (see the commentary there). It may also recall how the Israelites made the golden calf from personal jewelry at the very start of Israel's national history (Ex 32:2–4). Here, the statements that the "images" were "of the male" and that she "played the whore" with them leads to speculation that they were phallic symbols (to which the Hebrew of Is 57:8 also seems to refer). The centrality of ithyphallic processions and festivals are well-known in the ancient pagan world. Possibly, the specification that the images were "of the male" refers to Baal (Hadad). Baal was the dominant male fertility god in Canaanite religion, and many statues and engravings of him, often as a bull, have been found in Canaan. The Bible repeatedly refers to the ongoing battle between the true worship of Yahweh and the seduction of God's people into worship of Baal, most famously in 1 Kings 18. The NT equates the faithful remnant who did not worship Baal with the Christian church, comprised of believing Jews and Gentiles in Christ (Rom 11:4 in its larger context).

In the following verses (Ezek 16:18–21), the woman clothes the images and offers worship to them, and the descriptions are of more general pagan cultic practices, not strictly lascivious behavior as such. Hence in those verses the images seem to be of false gods in toto, not specifically phallic symbols, and her harlotry with them points to the basic metaphor of pagan worship in general.

16:18–19 These two verses continue the theme of the repudiation of the true Giver of all gifts by the dedication of his gifts to the glory of non-gods. Only rarely does the Bible give such specific allusions to Israelite idolatrous rituals. Much of the vocabulary and details parallel those of the orthodox Israelite cultus according to the Torah. For example, "oil," "incense," "fine flour," and "bread" were all used in the divine service according to the Torah. The casual observer of some of these actions perhaps would no more be able to tell what religion was being practiced than a visitor to many churches today could be sure, based on the outward forms of worship, of what is really believed, taught, and confessed there.

Yet closer scrutiny reveals differences in detail, and certainly in underlying theology, between the rites described here and those in the Torah. In orthodox Israelite worship there was no image of Yahweh, so the covering of an image with clothing was a heterodox act. The notion that the deity needed to be fed is prominent in Mesopotamian and Egyptian ritual (probably that of Canaan too), but it is mocked in the Scriptures (e.g., Ps 50:7–15).

"A fragrant sacrifice" (רֵיחַ נִיחֹחַ, Ezek 16:19) is a frequent phrase in Leviticus (e.g., Lev 1:9, 13) describing God's favor toward the divinely prescribed rituals, but Ezekiel uses the phrase only three other times besides here (see the textual note on it in 6:13). Ezekiel uses it for pagan rituals in 6:13; 16:19; 20:28, but in 20:41 he uses it metaphorically for the Israelites themselves after they have been regathered in an eschatological act of redemption. Although sacrifice and incense as "a pleasing fragrance," "a soothing odor," or "a tranquilizing scent" (as the Hebrew phrase might also be translated) were understood in a propitiatory sense in both Yahwism and paganism, in heathen religions it is a matter of attempting by human works to placate an often capricious deity, whose relationship with his people is based on law. In Yahwism, on the other hand, it was simple obedience to God's command to make use of the "sacramental" means by which his justice might be satisfied. Thus it is comparable to the sacrifice of Christ on the cross and the doctrine of Christ's vicarious satisfaction in the Christian doctrine of atonement.[102]

The use of "honey" in sacrifice is explicitly forbidden in Lev 2:11. Possibly it is mentioned in Ezek 16:19 as an introduction to the sacrifice of children (worship of Molech) in 16:20–21; compare Is 57:9.

The concluding signatory formula, "says the Lord Yahweh," perhaps is intended to help the reader catch his breath, as it were, before the most monstrous apostate act, which comes next.

16:20–22 The list of offensive practices in idolatrous worship obviously climaxes in these verses. Children had not been mentioned in the earlier list of Yahweh's gifts in Ezekiel 16, but from the very start of the Scriptures (e.g., Gen 1:28; 9:1) and the beginning of covenant history (e.g., Gen 12:1–3; 15:4–6; 17:1–8), children were chief among God's blessings. Childlessness was considered a great tragedy, as many biblical narratives attest. In the Hebrew language, as in those of many of Israel's neighbors, the frequency of theophoric personal names formed by the name or title of the deity (El or Yahweh in Hebrew) plus נָתַן, "give," or a similar verb or noun, witnesses to the common belief that children were gifts of God, for example, "Nathaniel" ("God gives"), "Jonathan" ("Yahweh gives"), and "Matthew" ("gift of Yahweh"). Because children were considered among the greatest of Yahweh's gifts (cf. Abraham's

---

[102] See Kleinig, *Leviticus*, 42–43, 57–58, 66–68.

anguish in Genesis 15–17 before Isaac's conception), they were also, potentially at least, the greatest possible sacrifice (cf. the rhetorical question in Micah 6:7b). That children were born *for* or *to* the husbands (in this metaphor, Yahweh) is indicated by the common idiom לְ יָלַד, as in Ezek 16:20 (אֲשֶׁר יָלַדְתְּ לִּי, "which you bore for me").

After circumcision on the eighth day (of males), babies (of both genders) were presented at the tabernacle/temple (on the fortieth day for males and the eightieth for females, Lev 12:1–8).[103] In addition, there were special requirements for the "redemption" of the firstborn, connected with the exodus (Ex 13:1, 11–16; Num 3:40–51; 18:15–16). However, instead of Israel dedicating her offspring to Yahweh, here she sacrifices them to other gods by slaughtering them and making them pass through fire (Ezek 16:20–21). And she offers them to idols "to eat" (לֶאֱכוֹל, 16:20), something unthinkable in any presentation to Yahweh, who needs no food of any sort from humans, and that humans would be his food elicits utter revulsion.

Three expressions are used to describe the ritual practice. Ezek 16:20 uses זָבַח, "to sacrifice," in its pagan sense of slaughtering a victim to propitiate a deity and to provide a meal for the god(s)—and Israel's children are the pièce de résistance. In orthodox Israelite liturgy, this verb may be used quite generally for any type of sacrifice. The cognate noun (זֶבַח) can refer specifically to the one "sacrifice" in which part of the victim was returned to the sacrificers to be used as a meal to be eaten in the tabernacle/temple precincts (Leviticus 3; 7:11–21). The full nominal expression is זֶבַח שְׁלָמִים or זֶבַח הַשְּׁלָמִים, and apparently because of the similarity of the second element with שָׁלוֹם, this type of sacrifice has traditionally been referred to as "the peace offering." A much more descriptive label would be "communion sacrifice," because in the meal before Yahweh the worshipers celebrated what they had in common/communion with him.

The analogy with the Christian Sacrament of Holy Communion is obvious and not only verbal. The location of the sacrificial meal is not prescribed in Leviticus 3 and 7:11–21, but it could have been in the forecourts of God's house or in the worshiper's home[104] (the location of celebrations of the Sacrament in Acts 2:46; cf. Lk 24:30, 35; Acts 2:42; 20:7). In either case Yahweh was present at the meal in some sense and surely was acknowledged as such by the worshipers, although Yahwism repudiated any notion of alimentation of the deity (a thought so prominent in pagan sacrifice; see above on 16:18–19) so the meal itself was in no sense an offering of food for Yahweh. It probably was taken for granted, but the OT says nothing explicitly about Yahweh being the host of the meal, perhaps to prevent pagan misunderstanding. In the NT, Christ

---

[103] Liturgical churches annually commemorate our Lord's circumcision on January 1 and his presentation in the temple (Lk 2:22–24) on February 2.

[104] Kleinig, *Leviticus*, 90, 170, believes that the meal would have been eaten in the worshiper's home if it wasn't too far away from the sanctuary.

was the host of the Last Supper and is the host (both literally and spiritually) in every celebration of the Sacrament, in which communicants receive his true body and blood, given and shed for the forgiveness of sins (the Words of Institution).

Ezek 16:21 introduces the verb שָׁחַט, "to slaughter," sometimes used of everyday butchering of livestock, but usually with sacrificial overtones. Ezekiel will use the verb again in 23:39 for sacrificing children to idols. There is no way to combine the ideas of "sacrifice" and "slaughter" in any one English word, but "slaughter" does convey the crescendo of repugnance in the passage.

The climax comes in 16:21 in the summary statement that the woman "offered" Yahweh's children "by making them pass through [the fire] to them [the images]" (see the textual notes; cf. 23:37–39). A similar phrase with "fire" is in 2 Ki 16:3. A few scholars try to limit the meaning to a mere purification by fire, as in Num 31:21–23, where metallic spoils of war are made to pass through fire and then water is applied in a rite of lustration to render them clean. But the context here, as well as other biblical and archaeological evidence, makes plain that nothing quite so benign is in view here.

As is true of most other pagan rituals, we know only the basic outline of the ceremony, even though there is considerable modern literature on the subject.[105] The god involved is usually referred to as Molech, which may simply be an honorific title of Baal (since he is the god to whom children are sacrificed in Jer 19:5; see also Jer 32:35) as "king" (מֶלֶךְ) contemptuously supplied with the vowels of בֹּשֶׁת ("shame"). The place where the rites took place and where the remains of the children were buried is usually referred to as a *topheth*, after תֹּפֶת in 2 Ki 23:10; Jer 7:31–32; 19:6, 11–14. The *topheth* at Carthage in North Africa has been excavated, and apparently some others on the Phoenician coast. Indications are that the rites varied in different places, so the external evidence is of arguable value for illuminating apostate Israelite practice. The Bible consistently locates Jerusalem's *topheth* in the Valley of Hinnom (e.g., 2 Ki 23:10; Jer 7:31), running on the south side of ancient Jerusalem, a tributary of the Kidron on the east. Later, the area seems to have simply become the city's dump, and because of the continuous fires there, it became a symbol of hell, or "Gehenna" (the Greek and Latin adaptation of גֵּי הִנֹּם, "Valley of Hinnom").

The giving of children to Molech is prohibited in Lev 20:2–5, which indicates that the practice was present among the Canaanite population already in Mosaic times. 2 Ki 17:17 indicates the cult's presence among the Israelites in the northern kingdom, but it apparently first became popular in the south under Ahaz (2 Ki 16:2–3; 2 Chr 28:1–3) and became even more widespread un-

---

[105] See, for example, John Day, *Molech: A God of Human Sacrifice in the Old Testament* (Cambridge: Cambridge University Press, 1989), and George C. Heider, *The Cult of Molek: A Reassessment* (JSOTSup 43; Sheffield: JSOT, 1985).

der Manasseh (2 Chr 33:6). Josiah attempted to eliminate it in his reformation in about 622 B.C. (2 Ki 23:10), but subsequently Jer 32:35 refers to it, so it may have returned. The supposition that, despite Josiah's reformation, it continued until Jerusalem's fall would explain why both Jeremiah (7:31; 19:5; 32:35) and Ezekiel (16:20–21; 23:37–39) vociferously denounce it. Jeremiah emphasizes that Yahweh had never commanded it or even imagined it (Jer 7:31; 19:5; 32:35), so we might surmise that syncretistic or "ecumenical" circles in Jerusalem taught that Yahweh had instituted it. That would represent complete amnesia of the Torah of Moses, explaining why Yahweh states, "You did not remember the days of your youth" (Ezek 16:22).

In her slaughter of Yahweh's children, as well as her harlotry and adornments, apostate Jerusalem is like Babylon the Great Harlot, who is the antithesis of the church, the virgin bride of Christ, and who will receive her just judgment when Christ returns:

> The woman was clothed in purple and scarlet and was gilded with gold and precious stone and pearls, holding in her hand a golden cup full of abominable things, indeed, the unclean things of her immorality. And on her forehead a name had been written, a mystery: "Babylon the great, the mother of harlots and of the abominable things of the earth." And I saw the woman in a drunken stupor from the blood of the saints and from the blood of the witnesses of Jesus. (Rev 17:4–6)[106]

Just as abortion is a modern counterpart to killing infants by abandonment (see the commentary above on Ezek 16:4–5), so too apostate Jerusalem (Ezekiel 16) and Babylon the Harlot (Revelation 17–19), who slaughters God's children, embody those who condone abortion and sexual immorality, including homosexuality and lesbianism, which are currently gaining acceptance in some nominally Christian denominations. (See also the commentary on 16:30–34.)

16:23–25 Jerusalem's harlotry becomes more brazen, and Yahweh's exasperation increases, as indicated by the outburst at the beginning, "Woe, woe to you, says the Lord Yahweh!" Some of the details of her increasingly flagrant behavior are obscure (see the textual notes on the "domed tent" and "platform"), but the general picture is clear: she conducts her whoring in the most public places and is accessible to all. She made abominable her "beauty," and trust in her "beauty" had begun her downward spiral in 16:15. Whereas 16:15 used more general language, "you lavished your whorings on every man passing by," 16:25 leaves nothing to the imagination: "you spread your legs for every man passing by." (Both verses contrast the passers-by with Yahweh, who "passed by" her in 16:6, 8.) כֹּל ("every, all") is repeated three times in 16:24–25, adding to the tone of excess, painting a picture of a nymphomaniac out of control. "You *multiplied* your whorings" (16:25) will be repeated in 16:26 and

---

[106] The translation is from Brighton, *Revelation*, 431. For the interpretation of who the great harlot represents, see pages 434–45.

16:29 (where it is translated somewhat differently). Ezek 16:24–25a will be largely repeated in 16:31a.

16:26–29   The public setting of her whoring in places of commerce in 16:24–25 may hint at what these verses make explicit: Israel's sexual partners are the neighboring nations. Political and economic entanglements with foreign countries were part and parcel of the whoredom. "Alliance meant dalliance."[107] Objections to foreign alliances were especially central to Isaiah's preachments over a century earlier. They must not be read as some sort of isolationist foreign policy, but intrinsic to the character of Israel in the ancient world. Israel, like other nations in the ancient Near East, knew nothing of "the separation between church and state" and would have considered the idea heretical. Every nation fostered worship of its god(s) for protection and prosperity. Political alliances inevitably involved recognition and veneration of the deities of the partner nations; sometimes the deities of the two countries were simply equated with each other, which was generally easy in paganism, where the different pantheons were personifications of the same forces of nature, merely calledy by different names in the various languages. In terms of religious influence (as well as military and economic influence), smaller nations were unequal partners with great empires, whose religions would take precedence. For Israel to ally with or rely on another nation always involved the underlying failure to "let God be God," to fail to trust his promises and to succumb to the basic human conceit that we are really the ones who make and control history.

The order in which Ezekiel mentions nations with which Jerusalem made unholy alliances roughly reflects the historical order in which Israel came into close contact with them. The liaison with Egypt (16:26) began with Israel's sojourn there for four centuries (Gen 15:13; Ex 12:40), from the time of Joseph to that of Moses. Ever since Assyria rose to be a threatening world power in the ninth century B.C., both the northern and southern kingdoms had appealed to Egypt for military help against her. But Egypt was no longer the power she pretended to be, and so Sennacherib's general taunts Hezekiah for his reliance on "that broken reed of a staff, which will pierce the hand of any man who leans on it" (Is 36:6 ‖ 2 Ki 18:21). Ezekiel is especially concerned with Zedekiah's alliance with Pharaoh Psammetichus II, a topic to which he will return in the next chapter. Egypt will also figure in oracles in Ezek 20:7 and 23:3.

The Philistines (16:27) had apparently invaded the Mediterranean coast shortly after Joshua led the Israelite incursion from the east to secure the promised land (ca. 1400 B.C.). Israel and the Philistines had been competitors for control of Canaan until David's victories. But the Philistines did not disappear for a long time, and 16:57 will mention them as contemporaries of Ezekiel. In fact, Neh 13:23–24 indicates that, at least culturally and religiously,

---

[107] Allen, *Ezekiel*, 1:240.

some of them continued to menace even the Israelites returning from exile, and 1 Macc 5:68 and 10:84 show that the problem continued even in Maccabean times.

The best commentary on "I gave you up to the desire of those who hate you, the daughters of the Philistines" (16:27) appears to come from an extra-biblical account. The Bible records only the miraculous failure of the Assyrians to capture Jerusalem at the end of the eighth century (Is 37:36–37 ‖ 2 Ki 19:35–36). Sennacherib fails to explain that failure but does record that he awarded some adjacent Judean territories to three Philistine cities, Ashdod, Ekron, and Gaza, who had not joined Hezekiah in his revolt.[108] Those three cities must be the "daughters of the Philistines" mentioned here (16:27).

Yahweh's assertion that the Philistines, Israel's historic enemies, "were embarrassed by your way of lewdness" (16:27) would have been taken by Ezekiel's audience as a biting comment. All evidence indicates that the Philistines acculturated to Canaanite ways shortly after they invaded Canaan, and surely they were no paragons of virtue. We may think of the similar way St. Paul shames a Christian church:

> It is actually heard that there is a sexual sin among you, and this sort of sexual sin is not even among the pagans. (1 Cor 5:1)

By Ezekiel's time (sixth century B.C.), the once-mighty empire of the Assyrians (Ezek 16:28) had ceased to exist, but in much of the ninth–seventh centuries it had been an almost constant menace. It began to eliminate Judah when Ahaz offered vassaldom to Tiglath-Pileser III in return for protection from a feared Israelite-Damascene attack (2 Ki 16:7–18; Isaiah 7–8), and it conquered the northern kingdom of Israel in 722 B.C.

Judah's last "affair" was with Babylon, not referred to by that name, but as "the land of merchants, … Chaldea" in Ezek 16:29. The relationship began with Hezekiah's favorable reception of Merodach-Baladan's envoys (2 Ki 20:12–19 ‖ Is 39:1–8) in an unsuccessful attempt to thwart Assyria (ca. 703 B.C.). Babylon had become a major force only after Assyria fell, and it bested the Egyptians in the contest at Carchemish in 605 B.C. over who would replace the fallen tyrant. Babylon was Jerusalem's major current "lover" in Ezekiel's own time. The implication is that the insatiable, incorrigible city of Jerusalem would continue her dissolute behavior indefinitely if God's judgment did not bring it to a halt.

Jerusalem Pays to Be a Whore Dominatrix (16:30–34)

16:30–31 With another expression of Yahweh's increasing ire, a new paragraph begins. As in 16:20–22, the portrait of apostate Jerusalem resembles that of Babylon the Great Harlot in Revelation 17–19. She is not just rebellious, but a dominatrix, even as Babylon the Harlot, together with the beast on

---

[108] *ANET*, 288.

which she rides (Rev 17:3, 7), dominates the nations using political and economic pressure (as well as other means of oppression) especially against Christians.[109] That Jerusalem does not receive a harlot's pay but actually hires lovers from foreign countries undoubtedly refers to the commerce Israel conducted with pagan nations, which profited those other nations and impoverished Israel. Similar is the picture of the international trade of Babylon the Harlot, which made many other merchants rich, so that they lament her demise (Rev 18:3, 11–19).

16:32 This verse (perhaps in conjunction with 16:30b, since "woman" there could also be translated as "wife") reintroduces a somber theological note. The woman is not only a pathologically immoral harlot, but specifically a philandering "wife," and "her husband" (16:32) is no less than Yahweh, as the earlier part of the allegory had emphasized (16:8). She compulsively breaks her marriage vow to Yahweh and even pays for her clients, instead of being paid by them.

"Strange men" (זָרִים) may underscore the point. Solomon used the same term for "strange men" who could adulterously enjoy a man's wife (Prov 5:17), metaphorically pictured as a spring of water (Prov 5:15). Proverbs also uses the feminine form (זָרָה) for the "strange/foreign/forbidden woman," who is any partner outside the marriage bond (Prov 2:16; 5:3, 20; 7:5; 22:14). The masculine is also used more generally for foreigners and foreign nations (Ezek 7:21; 11:9; Lam 5:2) and for foreign gods (e.g., Deut 32:16). Thus it evokes the whole range of infidelities referred to in this context.

16:33 The "gifts" the woman uses to solicit customers are more than merely the reverse of the fees a prostitute would ordinarily charge. These "gifts" were the ones originally given to her by Yahweh, the Creator and Redeemer: her physical life and natural sexual development (16:6–7) as well as her "beauty" (16:14, 15, 25) and her dowry of other possessions and promises (16:8–14) which she has squandered on illicit pursuits.

16:34 The emphasis specifically on adultery in 16:32 has reverted to a more general emphasis on the woman's abnormal promiscuity. This verse does not just describe an inversion of the natural created order, in which sexual fidelity is the norm (and is outwardly maintained by many, even after the fall into sin), but an inversion of the usual practice of prostitution within reprobate humanity after the fall. Zimmerli appropriately compares it to St. Paul's phrase "contrary to nature" (παρὰ φύσιν) in Rom 1:26,[110] speaking of lesbianism. Instead of normal sexual relations with her husband, the woman had become like an animal in frenzied heat. *Corruptio optimi pessima*: "the corruption of the best is the worst of all." The church of Jesus Christ easily becomes a "synagogue of Satan" (Rev 2:9).

---

[109] The description in Rev 17:7 of the beast she rides matches the beast from the sea in Rev 13:1–10. See Brighton, *Revelation*, 436.

[110] Zimmerli, *Ezekiel*, 1:329.

Yahweh Announces the Whore's Judgment (16:35–42)

16:35–36 Before Yahweh pronounces her just judgment, he first addresses her as "whore" (16:35) and issues a comprehensive, four-part indictment (16:36), beginning with the strongest and most graphic language imaginable (which English Bibles do not translate literally): "your vaginal fluid was poured out." Since she has relinquished what her Husband had given and made her, before God she retains nothing desirable. Such was ancient Jerusalem, and such are those called to be the bride of Christ who forsake Christ's gifts of grace to prostitute themselves with the world in order to gain human praise.

16:37 Somewhat corresponding to the four charges against Jerusalem in 16:36, there now follow four stages of Yahweh's sentence, his response to Jerusalem's behavior. The first and second appear in 16:37; the third in 16:38; and the fourth (with three subdivisions) takes up 16:39–41.

The punishment will fit the crime as the tables are turned. First, as she had gathered her neighbors for assignations, now Yahweh will gather them as agents of his wrath, both "all those [men] you loved" and "all those [rival women; cf. 'many women' in 16:41] you hated" (16:37). But that they are Yahweh's agents, albeit unwittingly, does not exculpate them. Since they too fail to recognize his lordship and instead act with human arrogance and seek absolute power, they, in turn, will pay for their own behavior. So Isaiah had spoken of the Assyrians, both as "the rod of my anger" to punish Judah (Is 10:5) and as a people to be devastated by Yahweh in his good time (Is 10:12–34). In the political application of Ezekiel's metaphor, the application will be to the Babylonians and to all those scored in the Gentile oracles of the book, Ezekiel 25–32. (In the punishment of Babylon the Great Harlot too, the kings who first were in league with her turn and help destroy her [Rev 17:16–17].)

Second, Yahweh will publicly strip the woman naked (Ezek 16:37). She who exposed herself so readily for sin will now be publicly exposed in punishment. This action is a reversal of the symbolic gesture of Yahweh spreading the edge of his robe over the woman as a gesture of marital commitment (16:8). Now it was a matter of the annulment of the woman's married identity, that is, a divorce. There is copious evidence, both biblical and extrabiblical, that such exposure was a common practice in the ancient Near East as a gesture of punishment for unfaithfulness, leading to divorce. Probably the most vivid biblical parallel is Hos 2:4–5 (ET 2:2–3), but it is also alluded to in Nah 3:5 and Jer 13:22, 26. The exact relationship between the stripping mentioned in this verse and that in Ezek 16:39 is not clear. Conceivably, they are identical, or Ezekiel may have telescoped them. But Greenberg may be correct in distinguishing the momentary turning back of the woman's clothing in this verse before the trial from the permanent stripping after the trial and before her execution in 16:39–40.[111]

---

[111] Greenberg, *Ezekiel*, 1:286.

A context like this inevitably occasions consideration of the "social issue" of rampant divorce. The Bible is universal in its condemnation of the practice. Evidently stripping of the divorcee or adulteress had ceased by NT times and has never been a part of the Christian ethos. But the NT is no more approving of divorce than the OT. The key NT text is Mt 5:31–32, our Lord's endorsement of the strict understanding of Deut 24:1–4 by the early rabbinical school of Shammai and a repudiation of the laxity of Hillel. The topic is, of course, too broad to pursue further here, but this aspect of Ezekiel's metaphor is another warning sign to churches that have accommodated and conformed to the pagan culture (perhaps attempting to justify their resignation in the guise of "tolerance" and "love").[112] And such a spirit of accommodation readily metastasizes until both Law and Gospel disappear. "A little leaven leavens the whole lump" (1 Cor 5:6; Gal 5:9).

The theological application of the metaphor of stripping is not developed here, but it is no stretch to make the soteriological application: stripped of the cloak of Yahweh's promise and the gift of righteousness won by Christ, the unbelieving sinner stands naked and defenseless before the righteous Judge (cf. Rev 3:17). The divorce, in effect, takes place already at the death of the unbeliever, but will be made public on the Last Day and will necessarily end in eternal damnation (Rev 20:11–15). Church art traditionally shows the damned as naked and the saints in glory as clothed in white garments (see, e.g., Rev 3:4–5; 4:4; 6:9–11). Christ himself exhorts:

> I counsel you to acquire from me gold which has been refined by fire so that you may be wealthy and white garments so that you may clothe yourself and the shame of your nakedness may not be seen. (Rev 3:18)

16:38 In the third part of the judgment, the metaphor shifts back again to more specifically the offense of "adultery," as well as the shedding of blood, a reference to the woman's sacrifice of the children she bore for Yahweh (16:20–21, 36). Yahweh pronounces capital punishment: "I will make you blood(y)." That this refers not just to injury, but to her blood being shed, is affirmed by the references to the shedding of "blood" in 16:36 and immediately preceding in 16:38. The accent on blood brings us full circle to the chapter's beginning, where the newborn girl had been found "thrashing about in [her] blood" (16:6, 22). Her life will end as it began, forsaken by all.

Capital punishment in no way conflicts with the Fifth Commandment. Churches err if they try to equate capital punishment with abortion in some allegedly unified "ethic of life." Scripture's high view of the sanctity of life requires capital punishment for capital offenses.[113] Adultery was a capital crime for both men and women (Lev 20:10; Deut 22:22), as was murder, in this case

---

[112] For a recent exegetical treatment of divorce and remarriage based on 1 Corinthians 7, see Lockwood, *1 Corinthians*, 237–39, 243–44.

[113] See, for example, Joshua 20 and Harstad, *Joshua*, 643–48.

of the woman's own children (Ezek 16:20–21, 36). Yahweh, as both cuckolded husband and sovereign judge will pass the sentence "in wrath and passion" (16:38). As noted at the start of the commentary on this chapter, the monogamous image of Yahweh's righteous jealousy permeates Ezekiel and indeed the whole Bible, even when the vocabulary is more subtle.

16:39 The fourth and final part of Yahweh's verdict upon Jerusalem for her abominations is that he "deputizes" her former "lovers" as his agents to carry out his *opus alienum* (a favorite phrase of Luther, based on Is 28:21), his alien work of judgment under the Law. In this way he destroys the unholy liaisons she had sought to establish by her whorings. Her paramours turned executioners carry out her execution in three phases (16:39–41), and it becomes increasingly difficult to separate the metaphor itself and what it relates to, namely, the physical destruction of Jerusalem.

Phase 1 is that her former clients will destroy the facilities she built for her whorings (the "domed tent" and "platform(s)" she built in 16:31) and strip her of Yahweh's remaining gifts, her "clothes" and "jewelry of glory" (which he gave her in 16:10–13), so that she is "naked and nude," just as she was in 16:7, before Yahweh married her. Thus, once again we are returned to the chapter's beginning: a stark naked woman, this time, however, not because of helpless neglect, but in judgment for her abuse of God's gifts.

16:40 Phase 2 is that a mob will stone her to death, following the prescription of Deut 22:23–24. There is no biblical parallel to the subsequent hacking of her body to pieces, but it graphically illustrates the fury of Yahweh's judgment. Her dismemberment would make burial difficult or impossible and suggests that she would not be raised to eternal life (cf. 2 Ki 9:10, 36–37).

16:41 The third and final phase is that "they will burn down your houses with fire and execute on you judgments in the sight of many women." The language of this verse almost breaks away from its metaphorical packaging into an explicit politico-military prediction of what happened to Jerusalem in 587 B.C. The metaphor with both men and women is continued consistently with earlier parts of the chapter: her former male allies are the ones who torch her dwellings and execute judgments on her, while rival women (called "those who hate you" in 16:27 and "those you hated" in 16:37) look on with glee at her elimination. She who had been so open in her depravity will be a public spectacle in open view of the whole world when, Yahweh says, "I will make you cease from being a whore."

16:42 In the anthropopathic language of the verse, God will find emotional satisfaction only after his righteous justice has been satisfied and Jerusalem has paid the full penalty. Similar anthropopathic language occurred before (especially 5:13) and will occur later (e.g., 24:13). She could have avoided this punishment had she repented and cast herself upon God's free grace, but she had long ago hardened her heart against that.

Zimmerli considers Yahweh's words in 16:42 to introduce a note of consolation here, an assurance of salvation beyond the judgment, anticipating

16:60–63.[114] Although that might be defensible theologically as a proleptic thought (God's ultimate salvific intent), the immediate context indicates that Yahweh's words have the opposite force: he will not be satisfied until he has completely executed judgment on the woman. Ultimately, the full severity of his wrath will fall upon the sinless Christ on the cross, and in that way Christ's vicarious sufferings will make full satisfaction for humanity's sins.

Jerusalem Is Like Her Mother and Sisters (16:43–58)

16:43 See the textual notes on this verse, which could be a concluding summary of the chapter thus far (as most take it), the preface to a collateral theme that extends through 16:58 (as I take it), or a transition between the two.[115] In any case, its warning of judgment ("I myself will surely place your conduct upon [your] head") prepares for the announcements of judgment that punctuate the rest of the chapter. Its reference to Jerusalem's "lewdness" leads into the development of Jerusalem's comparatively better "mother" and "sisters," especially in 16:44–52, although they also appear later in the chapter.

16:44 Israel's wild behavior had been so open and flagrant that everyone knew and talked about it, distilling their revulsion into a popular proverb, "Like her mother is her daughter." The mother, called a "Hittite" in 16:3 and 16:45b, represents the heathen Canaanites, while her daughter is Jerusalem, representing, as throughout the pericope, all Israel.

16:45 This verse expands the basic metaphor of the chapter: Jerusalem is not the only child of her pagan mother and father (16:3, 45) but has two sisters. All three sisters exhibit the same congenital defect as their mother: neglect of their responsibilities to their husbands and children. Where is the evidence of this neglect? Since the genre of the material is quasi-allegorical metaphor, we must not try to "squeeze blood out of a turnip." The "family" relationship is not biological or genealogical, but theological, with sociological and moral implications. From that viewpoint, values and behavior, which reveal the underlying theology, are the real indicators of family ties.

The text does not indicate who the sisters' husbands might represent metaphorically, but the verse should not be taken to mean that God expects each people to worship their patron deity faithfully. Instead, all three sisters are guilty of idolatry, even though Jerusalem has greater culpability because of the privileged position she had. The children abused by Jerusalem's sisters may well be victims of Molech worship (even though evidence about the cult's antiquity and extent is scanty), since Jerusalem slaughtered her own children, apparently to that deity (see the commentary on 16:20–21). We have even less specific information along those lines about the Hittites (the sisters' "mother,"

---

[114] Zimmerli, *Ezekiel*, 1:347. He considers 16:42 to be secondary, added to attempt to provide some consolation.

[115] NIV formats 16:43 as its own one-verse paragraph so that it could be taken with either the preceding or following paragraphs.

16:3, 45), although their pantheon is by now fairly well-known. Regardless of details, the implication is surely that the veneration of any other deity is idolatry and defection from Yahweh, who is the one true God, and who rules over all peoples, whether or not they know it and acknowledge him in worship. Keil quotes from the fifth-century church father Theodoret to that effect:

> He shows by this, that He is not the God of Jews only, but of Gentiles also; for God once gave oracles to them, before they chose the abomination of idolatry. Therefore he says that they also put away both the husband and the children by denying God, and slaying the children to demons.[116]

Block nicely compares Yahweh's argumentation here with that of Jesus in Jn 8:39–47, where the Lord declares that the Jewish leaders are descendants of the devil rather than of Abraham and God.[117] The NT makes plain that all peoples are called to forsake their idols (e.g., Acts 17:22–31) and worship the one true God through faith in Jesus Christ, who is the sole way to God the Father (e.g., Jn 14:6). Christ is "the true God and eternal life"; all others are idols (1 Jn 5:20–21).

16:46–47   These two verses express in brief what 16:48–51 will expatiate upon. Both Sodom and Samaria were notorious for their behavior, which had led to their downfall. The use of them as bywords was not new. Already Isaiah had called Jerusalem "Sodom" (Is 1:10), and Jeremiah had likened the false prophets of Jerusalem to those of Sodom and Gomorrah (Jer 23:14). For further examples about Sodom, see the textual notes on Ezek 16:56. As for Samaria, in Micah 6:16 Jerusalem is accused of adopting the practices of Omri and Ahab, and in Jer 3:11 the same charge was made as here: Judah (here Jerusalem) is more guilty than Israel (her sister Samaria).

16:48–50   Jerusalem is first compared unfavorably with Sodom (reversing the sequence of Samaria then Sodom in 16:46). Yahweh affirms on oath that even Sodom, the very archetype of wickedness, was no match for that now found in Jerusalem. Ezekiel is engaging in a little "shock therapy" here, but it was not immediately effective. In the indictment of Sodom, the initial term "iniquity" is singular and all encompassing: "this was the iniquity [עֲוֹן] of Sodom" (16:49). Similarly, Christian theology speaks first of all of "sin" in the singular (sinful nature; the state of sin) before speaking of individual sins. The overriding issue with "sin" or "iniquity" is basic orientation: the failure to fear, love, and trust the one true God above all things, and the worship of others in his place (thus the First Commandment is a summary of the Decalogue). The same point can be made about the singular "abomination" (תּוֹעֵבָה) in 16:50.

The picture limned here of Sodom's sin does not recount the attempted homosexual gang rape in Genesis 19 for which the city lives on in infamy, even

---

[116] Keil, *Ezekiel*, 1:222, n 1, quoting Theodoret, *In Divini Ezechielis Prophetiam Interpretatio*, on Ezek 16:45 (PG 81:948–49).

[117] Block, *Ezekiel*, 1:508, n. 263.

though it is a classic example of the depravity Ezekiel so often condemns. Instead we have a picture of arrogance, complacency, gluttony, and shirking of social responsibilities toward the poor. Critics have often hypothesized some alternate, even contradictory tradition about why Sodom was destroyed. The homosexual lobby has been only too happy to champion that supposition and to declare this passage, not Genesis 19, to present the real reasons (as if the Bible does not have enough additional condemnations of homosexuality as an abomination).[118]

However, the view of Sodom here is fully consistent with that in Genesis 19, and the Hebrew texts indicate how readily the "two traditions" are really one. Ezekiel states that Sodom and her daughters committed "abomination" (תּוֹעֵבָה, 16:50), and in Lev 18:22 and 20:13 homosexuality is specifically labeled an "abomination" (תּוֹעֵבָה), so Ezekiel's language easily encompasses that particular sin. Moreover, the luxuriant apathy in Ezek 16:49 could be encompassed by the Hebrew terminology in Genesis 19. Thrice the Genesis text refers to the "outcry" from Sodom that had reached heaven (זְעָקָה, Gen 18:20; צְעָקָה, 18:21; 19:13). This "outcry" would be from people suffering from the misbehavior of their fellow residents and could be from the oppressed poor as well as those grieving at the abomination of homosexuality (cf. Ezek 9:4). Other OT passages use the same nouns (and cognate verbs) to refer to the "outcry" of the oppressed poor (e.g., זְעָקָה in Prov 21:13; צְעָקָה in Ex 22:22 [ET 22:23]; Job 34:28). Isaiah's wordplay on צְדָקָה ("righteousness") and צְעָקָה ("outcry") shows that "outcry" can be used as a comprehensive term for all kinds of human sin and as the very antithesis of Yahweh's "righteousness" (Is 5:7).

The Bible never advocates any simplistic equation of wealth with profligacy, nor is the Gospel a manifesto to attempt to correct the gross imbalance in the distribution of wealth in this life (as recent liberation theology often intimates). Nevertheless, history provides many examples where prosperity has led to arrogance and ungodliness, including Jerusalem in this chapter (see also Tyre and its prince in Ezek 27:27–28:19; and Babylon the Harlot in Rev 18:7–20). Even today statistics indicate that the poor generally give a higher percentage of their income to charity, including the church, than do the rich. Nevertheless, it is a timely reminder (perhaps especially to Lutherans, who are so often accused of being weak on sanctification by those who do not really grasp their theology) that the "sins" we too must confess are not only heinous outrages, but the more subtle ones of middle-class security (cf. James 2:15–26).

"So I removed them [Sodom and her daughters]" (Ezek 16:50) alludes ever so briefly to the fiery conflagration in Gen 19:23–29, which Jude 7 describes as "a judgment of eternal fire" (πυρὸς αἰωνίου δίκην).

16:51–52 Without specifying northern Israel's faults, Yahweh only states that "Samaria did not sin like even half of your sins." Since the chapter

---

[118] See the excursus "Homosexuality" in Lockwood, *1 Corinthians*, 204–9.

spends so much time on Jerusalem's ("your") sins, the reader can easily infer what Samaria's were. Chapter 23 will more than make up for this imbalance by describing Samaria's sins and comparing hers to Jerusalem's in great detail!

"Characteristically, Ezekiel carries the thought to an extreme"[119] by saying, "You made your sisters appear righteous by all your abominations" (16:51). Among sinners one can distinguish between relative degrees of manifest sinfulness, and the worst are those who have the greatest exposure to the Gospel but reject it. Thus the Lord stated about Capernaum and the cities who rejected him, "It will be more tolerable on the day of judgment for the land of Sodom than for you" (Mt 11:24). Samaria and Sodom will certainly not be excused or "justified" in the proper theological sense, but they could use the alibi that the accused employ almost instinctively: "I am not as bad as he/she is." This completely deflates the self-righteousness of Jerusalem, who misunderstood the grace of election as some sort of magical guarantee of her superiority over her neighbors. When the scales finally fall from her eyes and she realizes that hers is the greater guilt, the result can only be disgrace in the eyes of others and shame in her own eyes. When she must own the greater shame, she will only be able to confess about her reprobate sister (as Judah did about Tamar), "She is more righteous than I" (Gen 38:26; see the textual notes on Ezek 16:51). Only when the Law has brought her to that point, so that she can only throw herself on the mercy of the heavenly court, is there an opening for the Gospel, the true justification of the ungodly (Rom 4:5). That point will come with the fall of Jerusalem in Ezekiel 33.

"Be ashamed and bear your disgrace" (16:52) may be a flashback to Ezekiel's earlier forecast that the Israelites will eventually come to regard their past with revulsion (6:9). Ezekiel does not explicitly use Jeremiah's metaphor of a "whore's forehead," which knows no shame (Jer 3:3), but the picture is clearly of one who can now only approach in sackcloth and ashes, and by the miracle of justification and regeneration (Ezek 11:19–20; 16:59–63) regain in a new creation the birthright that was hers by adoption and marriage (16:6–9), which correspond to Holy Baptism: Baptism effects adoption (Gal 3:26–29) and is the betrothal of the church to Christ (Eph 5:25–27).

16:53 What all is implied by the language of "restoration" (see the textual notes) must be determined from the context. Even though the phraseology (שׁוּב שְׁבוּת/ שְׁבִית) itself is not used all that often, one must be aware of its pivotal significance in the history of biblical thought. Much like Ezekiel's use of it here, Job 42:10 illustrates its basic meaning: restoration in the fullest sense, not just to the previous state (the status quo ante), but to something much better. Hence restored Job had twice as much of everything as he did in the beginning (Job 1), and most importantly, he had a far greater faith in Yahweh than he did before he lost everything and endured prolonged suffering.

---

[119] Greenberg, *Ezekiel*, 1:289.

Unless Job predates Moses, Deut 30:3 would be the first appearance in the Bible of this phrase for restoration (שׁוּב שְׁבוּת). In either case, it is a phrase of great antiquity. So malleable a phrase would easily be subject to various adaptations and even a certain development as time went on. Jeremiah especially seems to develop the eschatological significance of the restoration of a true "Israel of God" (Gal 6:16) to its primal glory (Jeremiah 29–33). While the phrase does not specifically refer to the Messiah, inevitably the theme of "restoration" is bound up with the promise of Christ, as also are the themes of the "remnant," the "Day of Yahweh," and so on, as a staple of biblical language about the future. For example, Amos 9:14 promises restoration (שׁוּב שְׁבוּת) in conjunction with the rebuilding of the tent of David (pointing to Christ, the Son of David and the incarnation of God) and the remnant, including ingrafted Gentiles (Amos 9:11–12, quoted in Acts 15:16–17).

Once Jerusalem actually did fall in 587 B.C. (Ezekiel 33) and captives were taken (as, indeed, Ezekiel and his audience already had been in 597 B.C.), it is understandable that "restoration" would focus on a return to a new Jerusalem (e.g., Jer 30:3, 18) and a defeat of those who had taken her captive. Hence St. Paul states that the risen and ascended Christ "took captivity captive" (Eph 4:8, quoting שָׁבִיתָ שֶּׁבִי in Ps 68:19 [ET 68:18]). And if "restoration" could come to be almost synonymous with "release of captives," it must also be borne in mind that "exile" or "captivity" itself was readily capable of a transferred or typological meaning: the release effected by Christ from the power of sin and finally from the "last enemy," death itself. In fact, Christians still use the language, at least in their hymnody, of our captivity ("Israel," that is, the church) until the second coming of Christ, even as OT Israel awaited his first advent:

> Oh, come, oh, come, Emmanuel,
>   And ransom *captive* Israel,
> That mourns in lonely *exile* here,
>   Until the Son of God appear.
> Rejoice! Rejoice! Emmanuel
>   Shall come to you, O Israel![120]

Thus the language of eschatological restoration and release leads into the "now–not yet" or "Law-Gospel" paradox that is constitutive of all orthodox theology.

The NT speaks often of the new creation, sometimes in terms of renovation of the fallen order and at other times of beginning anew *ex nihilo*, "out of nothing." The general pattern between type and antitype involves both continuity and discontinuity, as, for example, with the resurrection of the body—the same body we now have, but to be a new "spiritual" body (1 Corinthians 15). The only place where the NT specifically reflects the Hebrew phrase שׁוּב שְׁבוּת is in (literally) "the restoration of all things" (ἀποκατάστασις πάν-

---

[120] *LW* 31:1; emphasis added.

των) upon Christ's second coming, described in Acts 3:20–21: God will "send the Christ appointed for you, Jesus, whom heaven must receive until the time for restoring all the things about which God spoke by the mouth of his holy prophets long ago" (ESV). The Greek phrase there was intended to be understood in a thoroughly biblical way, that is, teleologically, but unfortunately in some parts of the early church it soon became confused with the circular pagan "myth of eternal return," of endless recurrence, of quasi-astrological notions of the return of the constellations to their original position (a "great year" usually reckoned to be some 25,000 years). In the semi-philosophical schools of early Christianity, the fusion easily led into some form of universalism, especially associated with Origen (or at least his later disciples), who as a result was anathematized in A.D. 553 by the Fifth Ecumenical Council. For orthodox Christians, who are not universalists, the biblical picture is not merely that the eschatological state is like the primeval state, since more is gained through Christ, the "second Adam" (Rom 5:12–21), than was lost by the sin of the first Adam.

That issue (still debated in the church, in one form or another) leads us directly back to the question of what Ezekiel had in mind in 16:53. Some might deem it premature to label this verse as "eschatological," but it certainly is leading into what can only be so labeled in 16:60–63. Ezekiel prophesies a restoration of both Jerusalem (Judah) and Samaria (Israel) in other passages (4:4–6; 37:15–22), but elsewhere neither he nor any other biblical writer envisions a restoration of Sodom. It is inconceivable that Yahweh is promising a restoration of the ancient city as it was in Abraham's day, full of its vice and depravity. Among the various answers that have been offered is that it might simply be a rhetorical device, not to be pursued literally. Block suggests that "Sodom" is metonymic for the Canaanite part of the population, the other two parts being represented by Samaria and Jerusalem.[121]

Since we are edging into eschatological discourse, the best solution is probably to be sought in that direction. The restoration even of Sodom points toward the inclusion in the church of Christ of even the worst of sinners, and of Gentiles from all nations, beginning particularly on Pentecost (Acts 2; cf. the description of the saints in glory in Rev 7:9–14). Neither the NT nor Ezekiel teaches universalism, however. The abundant biblical condemnations of Sodom, including the consignment of its wicked inhabitants to "eternal fire" (Jude 7), require the view that the unbelievers who perished in it are damned to hell for eternity (see also the other verses cited in the textual notes on Ezek 16:56). Any thought of a universal restoration of all created things—including those who died in the state of unbelief, exemplars of wickedness like the people of Sodom, and even Satan himself and his minions—is as alien to OT theology as it is to that of the NT. Nor does the Bible permit the theory of

---

[121] Block, *Ezekiel*, 1:513–14.

"anonymous Christianity"—that people who do not believe in Christ (and may belong to other religions) can be saved because of their sincere search for truth and their faith in the "truth" revealed in other religions.

To be sure, the Scriptures emphasize the universal atonement of Christ and the objective justification of the whole world (e.g., Jn 1:29; 1 Jn 2:2). Ezekiel and the other prophets express the hope that a remnant will return from many quarters, yet the Lord warned that "many are called, but few are chosen" (Mt 22:14). Elsewhere restoration (שׁוּב שְׁבוּת) includes the idea that God's gracious work will bring about a transformation that removes the causes of the original judgment (Deut 30:1–10; Jer 33:6–9; Ezek 39:25–26). There may be some connection between Ezek 16:53 and Ezekiel's vision of a new creation that includes the revivification of the entire Dead Sea area, where Sodom once stood (47:3–12). Here in 16:53 Yahweh is promising that mercy will be extended to others beyond Israel, and if Sodom can be included, so can any other people or nation. At the same time, the actual restoration of such as Sodom only takes place through God bringing about a new creation, with a new orientation of faith and a new way of life, such as St. Paul describes:

> Don't you know that unrighteous people will not inherit God's kingdom? Stop deceiving yourselves: neither the sexually immoral nor idolaters nor adulterers nor catamites nor sodomites … will inherit the kingdom of God. And such were some of you. But you were washed, but you were sanctified, but you were justified in the name of the Lord Jesus Christ and by the Spirit of our God. (1 Cor 6:9–11)[122]

That Jerusalem will also be restored is added at the very end, almost as an afterthought (a pattern to be repeated in 16:55). If Jerusalem is to be restored, it is only fair that the lesser offenders, Samaria and Sodom, should not only share in the restoration, but even participate first (cf. Mt 21:31). Israel is not allowed to forget that she, in a sense, is in special need of sheer grace, because, as heir of the promises, she has transgressed much more.

16:54 This verse is a continuation of the sentence begun in 16:53. It stresses that the immediate reason for mentioning Sodom's and Samaria's restoration is negative: pure Law to impress upon Jerusalem the destructive results of her rebellion. A comparable point had already been made in 16:51–52 and will be explained further in 16:56–57, as well as in 16:63 and 20:43. Anyone who, like apostate Jerusalem, gives comfort to such as Samaria and Sodom, that is, anyone whose flagrant sin makes it possible for others to extenuate their own sinfulness, must realize how damaging to God's purposes his behavior is. Through the ages, the misdeeds of church members have always been a major alibi for unbelievers to reject any missionary invitation to the Gospel.

16:56–58 These verses continue the great reversal theme involving restoration (16:53) and represent a "turning of the tables," but they are still very much part of the condemning work of the Law that is prerequisite for full

---

[122] The translation is from Lockwood, *1 Corinthians*, 196.

restoration by the Gospel. She who once in her conceit had fancied herself especially blessed and had found her neighbors convenient objects of gossip and derision will now find herself at the receiving end of the same kind of ridicule. To be a public laughingstock is part of God's direct judgment upon the people. Just as Sodom is a byword throughout the Scriptures (see the textual notes on 16:56), so apostate Jerusalem shall become.

There is a Gospel side implicit in this situation, but it does not surface until 16:59–63. If Yahweh can restore someone who has fallen as far as Jerusalem has, he can restore anybody. The church, individually and collectively, prays that it will not have to learn the hard way that it is indeed "chief of sinners."[123]

Yahweh Shall Restore Jerusalem, Establish an Everlasting Covenant, and Make Atonement for All Sin (16:59–63)

16:59 Whether this verse is a question or a statement (see the textual notes), it makes an emphatic transition to the powerful Gospel section in 16:60–63. The Law aspect of 16:53–58 is well summarized in the severe assertion here of all that Jerusalem was guilty of doing: "who despised the oath, thereby breaking the covenant" (16:59). The same phraseology reappears in 17:13–19, referring to Zedekiah's rebellion against Nebuchadnezzar, which is the political counterpart to the religious rebellion Ezekiel is describing metaphorically in this chapter. If Yahweh operated strictly on the principle of reciprocity, Jerusalem, of all the cities of the world, would bear the brunt of Yahweh's wrath.

While אָלָה, "oath," is a common, generic word, in the OT it is usually used in covenantal contexts. Sometimes the word is simply paired with בְּרִית, "covenant" (e.g., Deut 29:11, 13 [ET 29:12, 14]). The oath played a prominent role in the ritual of covenant making, which would include both positive oaths (promises, blessings) and negative oaths (imprecations to be implemented if either party broke the covenant). Human "covenants" or contracts were usually bilateral, and some of this feature continues in the Sinaitic covenant. But the Abrahamic covenant was prior (Gal 3:17), and it was unconditional and unilateral (God alone issued his promise).[124] Yahweh's description of his original "marriage" to Jerusalem alluded to his unconditional, unilateral oath: "I swore [an oath] to you and entered into a covenant with you" (16:8).

The Hiphil of פָּרַר and the noun בְּרִית form the usual OT idiom for "break a covenant." Jeremiah's famous "new covenant" prophecy (Jer 31:31–34, the OT Lesson for Reformation Day) uses this idiom for the old, Sinai covenant ("they broke my covenant," Jer 31:32). The affinities between the prophecies of Jeremiah and Ezekiel will be even more evident in 16:60.

16:60 Regardless of whether 16:59 is a question or a statement (see the textual notes on it), the transition to Gospel promises requires translating with

---

[123] See 1 Tim 1:15 and "Chief of Sinners Though I Be" (*LW* 285).

[124] See the excursus "Covenant" in Harstad, *Joshua*, 744–56.

a major disjunctive: "*On the contrary*, I myself will remember my covenant …" (16:60). The rest of the chapter looks forward to the new eon after Yahweh heals the rupture caused by human sin. The language and theology have many antecedents, and the theology will be developed in greater detail in chapters 34, 36, and 37. Only a few retrospects will remind Ezekiel's first audience (and us) of the "not yet." Coming as it does at the end of so long and so lurid a chapter, the words here make an even greater impact, expressing the magnitude of God's grace almost beyond what human language can express.

The anthropomorphism of Yahweh "remembering" his covenant occurs only here in Ezekiel, but the idiom frequently occurs elsewhere (e.g., Gen 9:15–16). See especially Lev 26:42, 45, because of that chapter's many reverberations in Ezekiel.[125] As usual in biblical idiom, "remembering" is no mere intellectual activity but implies implementation as well.

In "I will establish for you an everlasting covenant" (16:60), instead of the common verb כָּרַת, literally, "to cut" a covenant, Ezekiel uses הֵקִים "to establish, institute." Older source criticism once used these two verbs to distinguish Pentateuchal sources, alleging that הֵקִים was a sure sign of "P" (the priestly source). The only grain of truth in that is that הֵקִים usually appears in more liturgical contexts, with which priest-theologians would be especially familiar. But Ezekiel, himself a priest (1:3) and prophet, gives the lie to any pitting of the two verbs against each other by his use of כָּרַת ("cut" a covenant) in 17:13; 34:25; 37:26.

Nevertheless, the two verbs often may have different nuances. כָּרַת ("cut"), probably derived from the world of commerce and its contracts (as the plural of בְּרִית could then often be translated), had a more bilateral tone to it (*do ut des*, "I give in order that you give"), and it was the normal word to use for brand-new agreements. With careful qualifications, Yahweh's covenant with Israel could be called "bilateral" in that God had expectations and obligations for his people, but such language is best avoided since it can easily leave the door open for the fatal misunderstanding that Israel (or we) must or even could do something to earn, deserve, or qualify for God's gifts.

In contrast, הֵקִים ("establish, institute") more clearly conveys divine monergism in salvation and the divine initiative in all of God's covenant making. Sometimes נָתַן too can be used to underscore the sheer gift quality when God literally "gives a covenant" (e.g., Gen 17:2; Num 25:12; cf. Is 42:6; 49:8). In addition to its initiation, הֵקִים ("establish") can also imply the maintenance of a covenant, and some prefer to translate the verb "maintain" here. Certainly there are elements of continuity as well as discontinuity here, as also in the climactic application of "covenant" to the two Testaments that constitute our Bible. The continuity of the "covenant [made with Israel] in the days of [her]

---

[125] The covenant curses from Leviticus 26 are reflected especially in Ezek 4:10–11, 16–17; chapters 5–6; 12:19–20; 14:12–23.

youth" with the "everlasting covenant" (16:60) is evidenced by the fact that Yahweh remembers the former when he establishes the latter. Note well that Yahweh's motive is *not* his remembrance of Israel's youth nor any time or act of her fidelity, but rather his own promises that he issued to her in her youth. Yahweh remains faithful to his Word despite all human infidelity (2 Tim 2:13). Thus הָפֵר (that his people were "breaking" his covenant) in 16:59 and הָקִים (that he himself will "establish" the everlasting covenant) in 16:60 are precise antonyms.

The message in 16:60 may well echo Leviticus 26, which summarizes the blessings and curses of the Sinaitic covenant. After a recital of the terrible curses that would befall a disobedient Israel, Lev 26:40–45 nevertheless concludes that the blessings of the covenant would return once the people repented. The *"everlasting covenant"* (Ezek 16:60) cannot be forgotten or annulled, but its benefits may be suspended or forfeited entirely if the receiving party refuses to acknowledge them. We may compare Is 55:3: "And I will make [וְאֶכְרְתָה] for you an everlasting covenant, [fulfilling my] faithful mercies to David [חַסְדֵי דָוִד הַנֶּאֱמָנִים]." And the Davidic covenant (2 Samuel 7; cf. Psalm 2), with the promise of the Son who would build God's house and rule on his throne forever, is simply an extension of the one with the patriarchs (see also Is 7:14; 9:5 [ET 9:6]; 59:21; 61:8). In 2 Sam 23:5 David himself calls the covenant God had made with him "everlasting." And as Ezek 16:63 will shortly emphasize even further, its eternalness does not depend upon any human attempt to fulfill the Law, but solely on God's forgiving grace. Jer 31:31–34, the *locus classicus* of the "new covenant," with its links to Ezek 16:60, makes the same point in its own way. Ezekiel will expand on the role of the new David (Jesus Christ) in establishing the new covenant in 34:23–25 and 37:25–26.

16:61 The continuity between God's remembering in the previous verse and Israel's here is obvious. Not only will there be a reversal of the almost total amnesia from which she seemed to suffer before, but her memory will be sharpened and more focused. The memory of the people's depraved past will not only evoke "a Lenten memorial"[126] in their hearts, but God, far from holding a grudge, will grant them even greater blessings. "Where sin abounded, grace did much more abound" (Rom 5:20 KJV), thus, in one sense, intensifying their shame. In this eschatological era, we may take Sodom and Samaria as representing heathen nations generally—Sodom perhaps those who previously had never heard the Gospel and who had sunk into the deepest moral degradation, and Samaria those who had fallen from the state of grace.[127] These cities that had previously been "sisters" are now received as "daughters." That is, they will now be dependencies, not in any political or imperialistic sense, but in the recognition that there is but "one God and Father of all" (Eph 4:6).

---

[126] Allen, *Ezekiel*, 1:248.

[127] Keil, *Ezekiel*, 1:231.

Presumably, that thought should lead into the final phrase of the verse, but the Hebrew has been understood in many different ways. "And not without your covenant" is a literal translation, but like any translation, it also interprets. The conjunction *waw* ("and") is elastic. Does the preposition מִן indicate separation ("without, apart from") or source? And who is the antecedent of "your"? The various possibilities finally boil down to two sets of options: (1) whether or not Sodom and Samaria will be a part of the covenant and (2) whether the covenant is the old one ("in the days of your youth," 16:60) or the "everlasting covenant" (16:60). We mention four possible combinations of those options.

First, Keil, by making the phrase refer to the "daughters" (16:61), not to Israel, can take the passage to mean that Sodom and Samaria will *not* be included in the everlasting covenant to be established.[128] That interpretation is difficult to harmonize with the tenor of the previous verse, which clearly includes the cities as members of the family, although in a different relationship than before.

Second, Block splits the difference, as it were: by taking the initial conjunction concessively ("even though they are not your covenant partners"), he makes the phrase say that the cities will be benefactors of the covenant, but will have no covenantal ties with Jerusalem. He judges that approach to explain best the final suffix ("your").[129] In my judgment, that is possible but seems rather forced.

The third and fourth possibilities are compatible with each other. Both include the cities in the covenant, and both assume Yahweh is talking about the new, "everlasting" covenant. Throughout the Bible, a "covenant" usually is Yahweh's. The reference here to an "*everlasting covenant*" (16:60) implies a relationship founded anew by God's grace on the ashes of the old. The various similar prophecies elsewhere, as cited above (e.g., Jer 31:31–34), usually emphasize the breach made by Israel with the old covenant, but also the covenant's reinstitution on another plane by Yahweh. Furthermore, covenants with the patriarchs and with Israel always include the children as well. From the very first promise (Gen 3:15) and continuing in the patriarchal promises, the children or "seed," culminating in Jesus Christ (Galatians 3), are central to the covenant.

The third understanding of the phrase is possibly the oldest and is the traditional one, advocated by both Jewish and Christian commentators. It takes the מִן causatively and the entire phrase in the sense of "and not because you have kept the covenant."[130] This fits the context well and may even follow from the previous mention of the people's shame: in spite of their contumacy,

---

[128] Keil, *Ezekiel*, 1:232.

[129] Block, *Ezekiel*, 1:518.

[130] So, for example Greenberg, *Ezekiel*, 1:292; Taylor, *Ezekiel*, 142; and apparently Allen, *Ezekiel*, 1:226, by his translation (although without comment): "even though I am not obliged by my covenant with you."

Yahweh has gone far beyond the letter of the law and has now given them even more than he had promised.

A fourth possibility (reflected in my translation), with a similar upshot, is to treat the מִן privatively. Following the initial negative ("and not"), the privative מִן results in a double negative or litotes: "and not outside/apart from/without my covenant with you." This makes the explicit statement that Samaria and Sodom will not be second-class citizens but will be fully incorporated into the people of the new covenant. The phrase safeguards against any assumption of a qualitative difference in the divine favor shown to mother and daughters. "There is neither Jew nor Greek ... for you are all one in Christ Jesus" (Gal 3:28).

16:62 It is almost surprising that the recognition formula ("then you will know that I am Yahweh"), which is so prominent throughout the book, does not come until the penultimate verse of this long chapter. Israel did not come by that confession easily, nor do we. There may be the implication that only in eternity will we fully "know" all that is involved in the divine name—as can also be said about the name of Jesus (Mt 1:21; Phil 2:6–11; Rev 19:16). Nor should we overlook the use here again of the emphatic pronoun: "*I myself* will establish my covenant with you." Since he will do this through the incarnate and crucified One, the pronoun summarizes the *sola gratia* import of the entire chapter.

16:63 The last verse in the chapter is an expansion of the recognition formula in a complex purpose clause. In retrospect, after acquiring the full knowledge of Yahweh, the shame and awakened memory can only lead the people to "never again open [their] mouth." It is hard to say whether their silence is in contrast to earlier specific circumstances or whether Yahweh is making a more general theological statement. Their silence may be in contrast to the arrogance they had once shown in speaking of Sodom (16:56). Chapter 18 will confront their vocal complaints that God has not treated them fairly and has reneged on his covenant commitment. Chapter 37 addresses their lament that, like dry bones, they have no future. The book of Habakkuk, written not too long before Ezekiel, shows that even among the faithful, the cry of the saints "How long?" readily arises. In the interim between Christ's first and second advents, even the saints in heaven ask that question (Rev 6:10) as they await the final defeat of all evil on earth, the resurrection of their bodies, and their entrance into the new heavens and new earth (Revelation 21–22).

Any or all of these interpretations of "never again open your mouth" (Ezek 16:63) amount to an assertion by Yahweh that self-assertion by a regenerate Israel will be impossible. The thought is not far from St. Paul's dictum that the full weight of the Law (Rom 3:9–20) achieves God's purpose "that every mouth may be stopped" (Rom 3:19) because of the realization that no one is innately righteous, not even one; no one has any claim whatsoever on God, and no meritorious deeds or qualities with which to impress him. While God's Law silences every sinner's complaining, his free gift of righteousness solely through

faith in Christ also leaves sinner-saints (Christians) with no grounds on which to complain about the theology of the cross and resurrection into which they have been baptized (Rom 6:1–4).

Perhaps it is no coincidence, then, that after "every mouth may be stopped" (Rom 3:19), St. Paul goes on to speak of the ἱλαστήριον, the "expiation" achieved through Christ's blood (Rom 3:25). The Greek word is technically the name of the "mercy seat" (כַּפֹּרֶת in Hebrew), the lid of the ark of the covenant, and brings us into the same theology that Yahweh introduces with the verb כָּפֶּר, "atone" (Ezek 16:63). Usually in the OT, Yahweh accomplishes atonement through the ministrations of the priests, especially the high priest (e.g., Leviticus 16), but here in Ezek 16:63 he declares he will act directly "when I make atonement for you." It is Christ, the great High Priest, the God-man, who effects the once-for-all atonement for all sin.[131]

Commentaries often remark that instead of the usual Law-Gospel order, with shame leading to repentance followed by the conferral of the forgiveness of sins, here the sequence is reversed: Yahweh's atonement occasions the shame. The usual order (Law followed by Gospel) must not be misunderstood, as though some human sentiment or action can ever be a cause of the bestowal of God's grace. Nor must the usual order lead us to imagine that once a person believes the Gospel, he no longer needs the Law and the repentance worked by the Law. The usual order speaks from the human or experiential perception, but Ezekiel stresses that repentance, just like faith, does not originate from anything in man; repentance and faith are God's work alone, even as the entirety of salvation is his alone. The thought is in line with the entire context from 16:61 on: only the realization of the all-availing, free grace given in the blood of the Lamb can evoke a genuine response of repentance and faith, followed by thanksgiving in worship—now and into the eschaton, which, paradoxically, has already begun. Hence the church on earth already now sings the same hymns to God and to the Lamb that the church in glory sings, continuing throughout eternity (e.g., Rev 4:8, 11; 19:6–8).

---

[131] One may see Kleinig, *Leviticus*, 345–50.

The Allegory of the Cedar Sprig
and the Messiah Planted by Yahweh

Translation

17 ¹The Word of Yahweh came to me: ²"Son of man, pose a riddle and compose an allegory for the house of Israel. ³Say, 'Thus says the Lord Yahweh:

> A great eagle with powerful wings,
>> long feathers,
>
> full of plumage and multicolored,
>> came to Lebanon.
>
> He took the crown of a cedar;
>> ⁴the topmost of its shoots he plucked off,
>
> and he carried it to a land of merchants;
>> in a city of traders he set it.
>
> ⁵He took one of the seeds of the land
>> and planted it in a fertile field—
>
> as a slip beside abundant water,
>> like a willow twig he set it out,
>
> ⁶so it would sprout and become a spreading vine,
>> low in height,
>
> so its branches would turn toward him,
>> and its roots remain under him.
>
> So it became a vine,
>> produced shoots,
>> and sent out foliage.
>
> ⁷But there was another great eagle
>> with powerful wings
>> and much plumage.
>
> Surprisingly, this vine bent its roots toward him
>> and stretched out its branches toward him—
>
> so that he might water it—
>> from the bed where it had been planted.
>
> ⁸It had been planted in good soil beside abundant water
>> to grow branches,
>> to bear fruit,
>> and to become a magnificent vine.'

⁹"Say, 'Thus says the Lord Yahweh:

> Will it thrive?
> Will he not pull up its roots
>> and cause its fruit to rot and wither?

Will not all its new growth dry up?
No strong arm or mighty army will be needed
    to pluck it from its roots.
¹⁰Although it has been planted,
    will it thrive?
When the east wind touches it,
    will it not shrivel completely?
On the very bed where it had sprouted
    it will wither away.' "

¹¹The Word of Yahweh came to me: ¹²"Say to the rebellious house, 'Do you not know what these things mean?' Say, 'Behold, the king of Babylon came to Jerusalem, took its king and its officials, and brought them back with him to Babylon. ¹³Then he took a member of the royal family, made a covenant with him, and brought him under an oath. He took away the leading men of the land ¹⁴so that it would be a lowly kingdom, would not lift itself up, but would keep his covenant that it might stand. ¹⁵But he rebelled against him by sending his envoys to Egypt to obtain horses and a large army. Will he succeed? Can one who does such things escape? Can he break a covenant and still escape? ¹⁶As I live, says the Lord Yahweh, in the land of the king who made him king, whose oath he despised, and whose covenant he broke, with him in Babylon he shall die. ¹⁷Pharaoh with a mighty army and great force will not join him in the war when they heap up ramps and build siege walls in order to cut off many lives. ¹⁸He despised the oath by breaking the covenant. Even though he had given his hand, he did all these things. He shall not escape!

¹⁹" 'Therefore, thus says the Lord Yahweh: As I live, my oath which he despised and my covenant which he broke I will bring down on his own head. ²⁰I will spread for him my net, and he will be caught in my trap. I will bring him to Babylon, and I will enter into judgment with him there for the treason he has committed against me. ²¹All his fugitives with all his troops will fall by the sword, and the rest will be scattered to every wind. Then you will know that I, Yahweh, have spoken.

²²" 'Thus says the Lord Yahweh: I myself will take part of the high crown of the cedar and set it out. From the topmost of its shoots I will pluck off a tender [sprig], and I myself will plant it on a high and lofty mountain. ²³On the high mountain of Israel I will plant it. It will produce branches, bear fruit, and become a magnificent cedar. Every kind of winged bird will live under it; in the shelter of its branches they will nest. ²⁴Then all the trees of the countryside will know that I, Yahweh, bring down the high tree and exalt the low tree, that I make the green tree wither and I make the withered tree blossom. I, Yahweh, have spoken, and I will accomplish it.' "

Textual Notes

17:1 The chapter opens with the word-event formula, "The Word of Yahweh came to me," and the "Word" applies to the entire chapter, although the formula is repeated in 17:11, tying together the two main parts, the allegory (17:1–10) and its interpretation (17:11–24, consisting of three sections: 17:11–18; 17:19–21; and 17:22–24). The chapter will close (as chapter 16 had) with an expanded recognition formula, "Then all the trees of the countryside will know that I, Yahweh, …"

17:2 חוּד חִידָה וּמְשֹׁל מָשָׁל—The genre of the first unit (17:1–10) is introduced by two expressions, both of which begin with an imperative (חוּד, וּמְשֹׁל) followed by a cognate noun (חִידָה, מָשָׁל) as the direct object. Both expressions are virtually impossible to translate satisfactorily, because neither corresponds precisely to any English equivalent. The two nouns appear in parallelism elsewhere but are not interchangeable. A חִידָה is some opaque or obscure saying or story that requires interpretation to be understood. Nearly half of its OT uses appear in Judg 14:12–19, the account of Samson and his riddle. It may be a fable (as the word is often translated here), where plant or animal figures are personified. It may also be an allegory, but I have used that translation for the next word.

The terms in the second pair are far more common. The basic meaning of the verb מָשַׁל is "to be like" or "to compare." The purpose of a מָשָׁל (in contrast to that of a חִידָה) is to illuminate and explain, and "proverb" and "parable" are both common translations (as in 12:22–23; 18:2–3). Ezekiel apparently used such forms quite frequently, because in 21:5 (ET 20:49) he is called "a teller of מְשָׁלִים," and 33:30–32 reveals a common perception of him as an entertainer. Here I have chosen the translation "allegory," because each detail is worked out quite carefully. That word often has a bad reputation today because texts are often allegorized arbitrarily by interpreters, but hermeneutically it must be stressed that allegory is the *literal* sense if that is the writer's intent.

Greenberg has observed that, following the pairing of these two near synonyms in 17:2, a certain twinning pattern pervades the entire chapter:[1] two eagles; two plants; "the house of Israel" here versus "the rebellious house" of 17:12; and so on.

17:3 הַנֶּשֶׁר—The noun נֶשֶׁר can refer to a vulture, which is not a very attractive bird, but the language later in the verse (הָרִקְמָה) indicates that this is a "golden eagle" because of the color of its neck feathers. If symbolically significant, the color probably refers to the wealth and splendor of a royal court. The metaphor of an "eagle" is common in the OT. In Ex 19:4 and Deut 32:11–12 it is even used of God's watchfulness over his people. Here it refers to Nebuchadnezzar (Ezek 17:12). It has the definite article in Hebrew, which simply indicates the species. English uses an indefinite article. Greenberg thinks the article indicates "incomplete determination," that is, "*a certain* eagle," in contrast to the second eagle in 17:7.[2] Whatever the translation, it probably forms the first part of a Hebrew idiom meaning "one … another/a second …" and the second member appears in 17:7 (see the first textual note on that verse).

אֵבֶר is a poetic word for "wing" that is used elsewhere only in Is 40:31 and Ps 55:7 (ET 55:6). Thus it is a synonym of the more common noun כָּנָף, whose dual form

---

[1] Greenberg, *Ezekiel*, 1:317.

[2] Greenberg, *Ezekiel*, 1:309–10; emphasis added.

is in the preceding phrase. (A related feminine noun, אֶבְרָה, is always parallel to כָּנָף.)
Even if it is an allegory, we need not exploit every little detail, but the long, strong
wings might refer to the fact that the great bird has already flown triumphantly over
many countries.

מָלֵא הַנּוֹצָה אֲשֶׁר־לוֹ הָרִקְמָה—The bird is described, literally, as "full of feather(s)"
and "which has multicolored weave." The noun רִקְמָה, indicating fabric of finest
weave and probably also multicolored, was used for the clothing Yahweh gave to
Jerusalem, his wife and queen, in 16:10, 13, 18 (see the textual note on it in 16:10).

"Lebanon," by extension, must refer to Jerusalem, which too was located on a
mountain. Cedar was prominent in the construction of the temple by Solomon, and
one of his nearby buildings was even called "the House of the Forest of Lebanon"
(1 Ki 7:2; 10:17, 21). Because of the close association between the tree and the mountain (still true of the modern country of Lebanon), the "cedar" may represent the royal
house of David.

וַיִּקַּח אֵת־צַמֶּרֶת הָאָרֶז:—This clause is parallel to the first clause of 17:4, so the
versification splits the natural parallelism. The noun צַמֶּרֶת occurs only in Ezekiel. In
17:22 it also parallels רֹאשׁ, and in 31:3, 10, 14 it refers to the part of the tree that
reaches into the clouds. The reference is clearly to the royal dynasty, the pinnacle of
the country, hence my translation, "crown."

17:4 אֵת רֹאשׁ יְנִיקוֹתָיו קָטָף—The construct phrase רֹאשׁ יְנִיקוֹתָיו (literally, "the top
of its shoots") is the counterpart to צַמֶּרֶת in the preceding colon. The noun יְנִיקָה occurs only here in the OT. Already Cooke suggested that the form here was a mistake
for יְנָקוֹתָיו,[3] the plural of יוֹנֶקֶת (in form the feminine participle of יָנַק), since יְנִקוֹתָיו
occurs in 17:22 and יוֹנֶקֶת is used elsewhere (in singular and plural) meaning "shoot,
branch."[a] The masculine noun or participle יוֹנֵק in Is 53:2 has a similar sense ("young
plant, shoot"). Literally, יוֹנֵק means "sucker, suckling," and often in the OT it refers
to a nursing (unweaned) infant (e.g., Num 11:12; Is 11:8). Metaphorically יוֹנֶקֶת was
applied to a very young or recent shoot of a plant, which sucks sap from the main
stem (and which corn farmers still call a "sucker"). Here with רֹאשׁ, it must refer to
the very latest growth at the top of the tree, and metaphorically it undoubtedly refers
to a king or prince at the head of the royal family.

(a) Hos 14:7
(ET 14:6);
Ps 80:12 (ET
80:11); Job
8:16; 14:7;
15:30

אֶרֶץ כְּנַעַן—As in 16:29 (see the textual note there), this does not refer to "the
land of Canaan" but "the land of merchants," as confirmed by the participle רֹכְלִים,
"traders, merchants," in the following parallel phrase. The reference is to Babylon, as
17:12 will state explicitly. Transplanted cedars were a common feature in Assyrian
royal parks.

17:5 מִזֶּרַע הָאָרֶץ—The מִן is partitive, and זֶרַע is collective ("seeds"). If we anticipate interpretation, this must refer to a native Israelite king (Zedekiah), not a foreign,
Babylonian regent.

בִּשְׂדֵה־זֶרַע—Literally, "in a field of seed," this refers to a carefully prepared and
"fertile" plot of land. Vines are not normally started from seeds (although that is pos-

---

[3]   Cooke, *Ezekiel*, 186.

sible), but from seedlings or slips. The metaphor has changed slightly: the eagle is now a gardener.

קָח עַל־מַיִם רַבִּים צַפְצָפָה שָׂמוֹ׃—This is very difficult, and all translations are tentative. Critics easily dismiss the obscure word קָח as a partial vertical dittograph of וַיִּקַח from the line above.[4] Many think that it is absent in the LXX and Syriac, but some find it reflected in the free translations of those versions. Some English translations have "he placed it" (KJV, NKJV, RSV), apparently because they took קָח as a (corrupted?) form of לָקַח, while others ignore it (NIV's "he planted it" probably translates שָׂמוֹ). A more positive possibility is provided by apparent Akkadian, Syriac, and modern Ethiopic cognates with meanings like "plant/stem/stalk."[5] If it has a meaning like that, קָח may be parallel to צַפְצָפָה, and each of the nouns would serve as a second direct object (complement accusative) of the verb שָׂמוֹ with its rather redundant suffix. The noun צַפְצָפָה is a hapax too. In Mishnaic Hebrew and Arabic it refers to some tree like a willow or poplar that is commonly found on riverbanks and usually grows rapidly. That is the most common understanding of the noun, and it certainly fits the context.

17:6 וַיִּצְמַח וַיְהִי—Many commentators (but no major English translations) change the *waw* consecutives into *waw* conjunctives and understand the verbs as jussive instead of indicative. However, even without that emendation, these verbs form a purpose clause connected with 17:5: "he set it out, ⁶so it would sprout and become …" The eagle clearly was the subject in 17:5. The first four lines of 17:6 express the eagle's purpose, and the final three lines (beginning "so it became …") describe the successful accomplishment of that purpose. With that understanding, the first two poetic lines lead smoothly into the third line, since the infinitive לִפְנוֹת at the start of the third line denotes purpose, and וַיְהִי לְגֶפֶן in the first line is not redundant with וַתְּהִי לְגֶפֶן in the fifth line. This understanding also accords with the intention of the overlord in the interpretation in 17:14.

סֹרַחַת—The verb סָרַח means to grow luxuriantly, even rankly. My rendition of the participle as "spreading" may be too weak. A noun from the same root is also used in Ex 26:12 of the overhang of the tabernacle curtains.

שִׁפְלַת קוֹמָה—"Low in height" corresponds to the nature of Near Eastern viticulture. Because of the unrelenting summer heat, the vines are usually trained to hug the ground, whereas in more northerly climates they usually grow several feet high. The metaphorical point is political subservience, as continued in the next part of the verse.

לִפְנוֹת דָּלִיּוֹתָיו אֵלָיו—The infinitive construct with לְ forms a purpose clause, which supports the interpretation that the first two verbs of the verse also are part of a purpose clause (see the first textual note on 17:6). In the OT the noun דָּלִית, "branch, bough," always occurs in the plural and always metaphorically, either for Israel (Jer 11:16; Ezek 17:6, 7, 23; 19:11) or Assyria (Ezek 31:7, 9, 12).

---

[4] See, for example, Zimmerli, *Ezekiel*, 1:355.

[5] Greenberg, *Ezekiel*, 1:310–11.

וְשָׁרָשָׁיו תַּחְתָּיו יִהְיוּ—Cooke[6] and others take תַּחְתָּיו reflexively, "under itself," that is, rather than growing underground in all directions. While this makes sense, it is better to take the eagle (נֶשֶׁר, 17:3) as the antecedent of the suffix here ("under him"), just as the eagle must be the referent of the suffix on אֵלָיו in the preceding phrase ("toward him"). Thus the plant is oriented toward the eagle and dependent on him, since his roots are under the eagle. Both the contrast in the next verse and the subservience expressed in 17:14 point in this direction.

וַתְּהִי לְגֶפֶן וַתַּעַשׂ בַּדִּים וַתְּשַׁלַּח פֹּארוֹת:—The first verb is feminine, probably because of the following feminine product noun, גֶּפֶן, rather than because of any feminine subject. The following two verbs also are feminine. The verbs at the beginning of 17:6 were masculine. Because of all the complexities of 17:5, it is unclear exactly what term from 17:5 becomes the subject in 17:6, but זֶרַע and probably קָח are masculine, whereas צַפְצָפָה is feminine.

The noun פֹּארָה, "bough, branch," is peculiar to Ezekiel and occurs several times in chapter 31. A related synonym, פֻּארָה, is used in Is 10:33.

The upshot of the verse is that the transplant behaves exactly as the gardener had intended. If nothing else had intervened, it would have continued to flourish.

17:7 וַיְהִי נֶשֶׁר־אֶחָד גָּדוֹל—The ancient versions translate as if אֶחָד were אַחֵר ("another") as it virtually has to be rendered in English. Some advocate emending to אַחֵר, and a scribal confusion between ד and ר would be easy to understand. But אֶחָד appears to be the second member of a distributive idiom ("the one … another/the other"). The idiom אֶחָד … אֶחָד is found in 37:16 and probably also in 19:3, 5, and perhaps here that idiom is abbreviated, with only the second אֶחָד appearing here, since there is no אֶחָד earlier in the chapter. Instead, the definite article on הַנֶּשֶׁר in 17:3 (see the textual note there) functions like a first אֶחָד, and there English idiom requires an indefinite article, "an/one eagle."[7]

The shorter description of this second eagle may indicate that the Egyptian Pharaoh (Hophra) had not attained the status and renown of Nebuchadnezzar, who is represented by the first eagle.

וְהִנֵּה הַגֶּפֶן הַזֹּאת כָּפְנָה שָׁרָשֶׁיהָ עָלָיו—"Surprisingly" is my free rendering of וְהִנֵּה. The verb כָּפַן is a hapax. The context establishes its general sense as "turn toward, bend," but greater precision is impossible. Various cognates are available, which also point in various directions. The LXX and Targum, an Arabic cognate, and the verb's meaning in postbiblical Hebrew and Jewish Aramaic all support some meaning such as "bend, twist, turn." However, an Aramaic cognate and the noun כָּפָן ("hunger, famine") in Job 5:22 and 30:3 could suggest "hunger for, stretch out hungrily." An Oriental Qere assumes metathesis of the last two radicals and reads כָּנְפָה, related to an Aramaic root that means "gather."

וְדָלִיּוֹתָיו—The suffix is masculine even though the antecedent is the feminine noun גֶּפֶן, but perhaps it was influenced by the suffix on the preceding עָלָיו. This is

---

6   Cooke, *Ezekiel*, 186.

7   Cf. Keil, *Ezekiel*, 1:237; Zimmerli, *Ezekiel*, 1:355.

just one more example of many gender inconsistencies in Ezekiel. Since דָּלִית derives from דָּלָה, "to draw water," and the context is about a different water source, Block thinks of a "literary license" that shifts the word's meaning from "branch" (which דָּלִית meant in 17:6) to something like "suckers, rootlets" here.[8] However, 17:6 had two successive lines about "its branches" and "its roots," so after the preceding line in 17:7 about "its roots," וְדָלִיּוֹתָיו probably refers to "its branches."

שִׁלְחָה־לּוֹ—The two words are connected both by a *maqqeph* and a conjunctive *daghesh forte* (לּ), perhaps for metrical reasons. לוֹ ("toward him") refers to the second eagle.

לְהַשְׁקוֹת אוֹתָהּ—The dashes in my translation indicate that this clause is intrusive. As Keil argues,[9] and many agree, the intrusiveness brings out the main point: the vine already had all the water it needed. As 17:5 has already indicated and 17:8 will state clearly, there was no need for the vine to turn to another source of water. The historical application is this: if Zedekiah had remained quiet and subservient under Nebuchadnezzar, he and his government would have prospered and continued; there was no need for him to turn to Egypt (Pharaoh Hophra).

מֵעֲרֻגוֹת מַטָּעָהּ:—This phrase (literally, "from the beds of its planting") follows the clause two lines earlier ("stretched out its branches … from the beds") rather than the immediately preceding line ("so that he might water it"), which is set off by dashes in the translation. Some translations (e.g., NIV, ESV) transpose lines to make the syntax clearer. The preposition מִן indicates "the point of departure for an action" (*HALOT*, 1 a), hence "stretched out its branches … *from* …" The noun עֲרוּגָה, a garden "bed," occurs in the OT only in Ezek 17:7, 10, and Song 5:13; 6:2. It is plural here in Ezek 17:7 and also in 17:10, but both times we might expect the singular for a bed or plot of land. Perhaps some Hebrew idiom explains the plural. In both verses the LXX (τῷ βώλῳ) and Syriac (ܠܐ) translate with a singular. That leads some to propose that עֲרֻגוֹת is the result of scribal metathesis from an original עֲרוּגַת, but metathesis cannot explain the plural עֲרֻגֹת in 17:10.

RSV and NRSV ignore the Masoretic accents and verse division and emend שְׁתוּלָה in 17:8 to שְׁתָלָהּ ("he transplanted it") so that a new sentence begins with "From the bed …" and the *second* eagle is the subject of "*he* transplanted it" in 17:8. This changes the meaning drastically. It relies on the questionable translation of שָׁתַל in 17:8 as "*trans*plant" (see below) and introduces the alien idea that the vine had reason to be discontented. A look ahead at 17:23 indicates that God's will was for the vine to thrive under the first eagle, but the vine's defection forced God to take matters into his own hands.

One other variation in interpretation must be noted. Some recent commentators and translators take the preposition מִן comparatively. This yields a translation like "That he [the second eagle] might water it more than the bed where it was [originally] planted." Grammatically, this is conceivable, but Greenberg points out that the com-

---

8 Block, *Ezekiel*, 1:529, n. 34.
9 Keil, *Ezekiel*, 1:239–40.

parative use of מִן usually appears with expressions that contain or imply quality.[10] Obviously, translation is again bound up with interpretation.

17:8 Exactly how one translates the verse, and specifically how one relates the first clause of 17:8 with the subsequent phrases in the verse, depends upon how one connects 17:8 with 17:7, which, in turn, depends on one's understanding of what is being described. As my translation shows, I understand the first eagle to be the implied agent of the passive verb שְׁתוּלָה, describing what the eagle had done with the vine in the past. The rest of the verse summarizes what he expects of the vine in the future.

Much turns on whether שָׁתַל means "to plant" or "to *trans*plant." The (active) Qal appears in 17:22–23 and the Qal passive participle (שְׁתוּלָה) in 17:8, 10 has the corresponding passive meaning. By Greenberg's reckoning, nowhere (with the possible exception of 19:13) does the verb *require* the translation "to transplant"; sometimes "to plant" is necessary (e.g., 17:22); and usually an undifferentiated "to plant" (synonymous with נָטַע) is adequate.[11]

The consequences of the vine's disloyalty are not yet explicit, but the series of rhetorical questions in the next two verses will introduce that theme, before the detailed consequences are spelled out in 17:11–24.

17:9 The imperative אֱמֹר (anacrusis or extrametrical if 17:3–10 is poetry) apparently signals a new accent in the account. As the following citation formula ("thus says the Lord Yahweh") will emphasize, although the prophet is still nothing but Yahweh's obedient mouthpiece, he will not explain the allegory yet but simply focus all the attention on the prospects of the vine.

תִּצְלָח—A few Hebrew manuscripts prefix the interrogative *he*, as in 17:10 (also 17:15), where Yahweh will ask, הֲתִצְלָח. Here the interrogative *he* might have dropped out by haplography after the preceding יְהֹוָה, but it does not have to be present. In Hebrew it is sufficient for the context to require an interrogative sense.

וְאֶת־פִּרְיָהּ ׀ יְקוֹסֵס—The text does not state whether the subject is the first or second eagle, but the historical application is that it is the first eagle (Babylon, 17:3–6), rather than the second (Egypt, 17:7–8), who destroys the vine (Jerusalem). Block intriguingly proposes that the ambiguity of the subject in 17:9 is a deliberate anticipation of the bifurcation of the interpretation (the historical plane in 17:11–18 and the theological restatement in 17:19–21).[12]

The verb יְקוֹסֵס is clearly the Polel imperfect of קָסַס, but that root is otherwise unknown in the OT. Traditional translations thought of some connection with קָצַץ, "cut off," and so translate יְקוֹסֵס as "cut off" its fruit (KJV, NKJV, RSV, ESV). However, the LXX and Syriac translate that "its fruit will rot," and the Mishnah uses the Qal (and in some manuscripts, the Piel and Hiphil) of קָסַס for "wine that has turned sourish" (Jastrow). Therefore some now favor a translation such as mine, "cause its fruit to rot" (e.g., NRSV). Polel verbs normally are transitive, and so וְאֶת־פִּרְיָהּ must

---

[10] Greenberg, *Ezekiel*, 1:312.

[11] Greenberg, *Ezekiel*, 1:312.

[12] Block, *Ezekiel*, 1:546.

the movement from the historical
logical interpretation in 17:19–21.
fter a finite form of the same verb

its planting" in 17:7, here we have
plural, presumably to parallel the

ory now commences, continuing

know?") as emphatic ("Surely you
troduce rhetorical questions makes
idience knew the answer only too
events to the "rebellious house."
ranslated "prince," but unless that
in 11:1, here too it means "leader,
zar's design was to remove anyone
d cause him any further trouble, as

he seed of royalty." The historical
whom Nebuchadnezzar renamed

have been a better rendition than
but in 17:19 the chapter brings out

) was sealed with an "oath" (אָלָה).

this last clause of the verse is curi-
"its king and its officials" in 17:12.
e beginning of a sentence that con-
lauses into which it leads naturally.
animal is used metaphorically for a
exts. "The leading men of the land"
7:12. 2 Kings 24 uses various other
deportation: כָּל־גִּבּוֹרֵי הַחַיִל (2 Ki

low kingdom" implies that what re-

Hithpael infinitive construct proba-
el, hence "would not lift *itself* up."
ing (17:13). It probably is a distinc-
together would lift themselves up

sitively,
ceding
though

iterally,
) omits
פִּרְיָה f
ns fol-

טָרָף h,
rs to a
ransla-
טָרַף) is
clause
it [the

almost
upport
a year
below.
נָ֫ to",
a pre-
ות he-
ut oc-
oüon,

even'
it that
d" in
of the

e in-

e and
n in-
role
it as
iabi-
Ana,
ider-
piri-

tual' instrumentality than [17:]9,"[14] corresponding
interpretation of the allegory (17:11–18) to its the

תִּיבַשׁ יָבֹשׁ—The use of an infinitive absolute
is rare.

עַל־עֲרֻגֹת צִמְחָהּ—Instead of (literally) "beds o
"beds of its sprouting." Again, the form of עֲרוּגָה
plural in 17:7 (see the textual note there).

17:11 The historical interpretation of the alle
through 17:18.

17:12 הֲלֹא יְדַעְתֶּם—Some take this ("Do you no
know!"). However, the use of הֲלֹא in 17:9–10 to ir
the same sense more likely here too. Ezekiel's a
well, but Ezekiel proceeds to rehearse the salien

שָׂרֶיהָ—The noun שַׂר was traditionally often
word is used rather poetically, it is imprecise. As
official." As 2 Ki 24:14–16 details, Nebuchadnez
with power, wealth, or authority, anyone who cou
Ezek 17:14 will specify shortly.

17:13 מִזֶּרַע הַמְּלוּכָה—This is, literally, "from
reference is to Jehoiachin's uncle Mattaniah,
Zedekiah (2 Ki 24:17–18).

בְּרִית—In this verse "treaty" or "pact" migl
"covenant," which for us is theologically laden,
the theological implications of the word.

בְּאָלָה—Normally a treaty or covenant (בְּרִית
See the textual notes on 16:59.

וְאֶת־אֵילֵי הָאָרֶץ לָקָח׃—The positioning of
ous. It would seem to fit more naturally right afte
It must almost certainly be taken as, in effect, th
tinues in 17:14, which contains a series of result
אַיִל is literally a "ram" (e.g., 43:23, 25), but the
human leader in the OT[b] and also in Canaanite t
is somewhat parallel to "its officials" (שָׂרֶיהָ) in
similar expressions to describe the scope of the
24:14); סָרִיסָיו (24:15); and אַנְשֵׁי הַחַיִל (24:16).

17:14 לִהְיוֹת מַמְלָכָה שְׁפָלָה—Literally, "to be a
mained of Israel would be a vassal state.

לְבִלְתִּי הִתְנַשֵּׂא—The implied subject of the
bly is the preceding "kingdom" (מַמְלָכָה) of Isr
But the implied subject could also be its vassal
tion without a difference. The king and kingdo
by rebelling against the Babylonian overlord.

(b) Ex 15:15;
2 Ki 24:15;
Ezek 17:13;
31:11; 32:21

---

[14] Greenberg, *Ezekiel*, 1:314.

לְעָמְדָה:—The antecedent of the feminine subjective suffix ("that *it* might stand") on the Qal infinitive might be either the immediately preceding "covenant" (בְּרִיתוֹ) or the earlier "kingdom" (מַמְלָכָה), both of which are feminine in Hebrew. Commentators defend both, but "covenant" is probably preferable, as already the Targum and the Vulgate understood it. Ps 105:10 uses the Hiphil of עָמַד to say that Yahweh "established" the covenant with Israel, and the Qal is used in 2 Ki 23:3 to state that the Israelites "stood in the covenant," that is, promised to keep and continue in it.

17:15 וַיִּמְרָד־בּוֹ לִשְׁלֹחַ מַלְאָכָיו מִצְרַיִם—Following a finite verb (וַיִּמְרָד), an infinitive construct with לְ (לִשְׁלֹחַ) can serve as a gerund (Joüon, § 124 o): "he rebelled ... by sending." For this rebellion, see the commentary below.

הֲיִצְלָח—In 17:15b, Ezekiel interrupts his interpretation of the allegory to pose a series of three rhetorical questions, similar to those in 17:9–10. The first question consists of this one verb, used also in 17:9–10, but this context refers to a man (Zedekiah) instead of a vine, hence "Will he succeed?" instead of "Will it thrive?" (17:9–10).

הֲיִמָּלֵט הָעֹשֵׂה אֵלֶּה—The Niphal imperfect that begins this second question is not simply about the future ("Will he escape?") but about the possibility, "*Can* he escape?" (so also with the Niphal perfect with *waw* consecutive in the next question). The following participle with article (הָעֹשֵׂה instead of the usual הָעֹשֶׂה) is pointed as though in construct with אֵלֶּה, the direct object ("the one doing these"). עֹשֵׂה אֵלֶּה occurs also in Deut 18:12; 22:5; 25:16; Ps 15:5 (cf. Is 45:7).

וְהֵפֵר בְּרִית וְנִמְלָט:—The previous two questions with the interrogative -הֲ imply that this too is a rhetorical question, even though it lacks the interrogative. The first part could be hypothetical, "Can he break a covenant and still escape?" or it could be factual, "*Since* he broke a covenant, can/should he escape?"

17:16 The Hebrew deliberately delays the climax of the sentence, Zedekiah's death in Babylon, until the very end of the sentence. Fortunately, that same word order can easily be retained in English.

אִתּוֹ בְתוֹךְ־בָּבֶל יָמוּת:—The Masoretic accents on this clause and the previous word (בְּרִיתוֹ) indicate that אִתּוֹ is part of this clause, "with him [Nebuchadnezzar] in Babylon he [Zedekiah] shall die." Zedekiah did in fact die in Babylon (Jer 52:11), where presumably Nebuchadnezzar died too.[15] Ezekiel has often alluded to the covenant curses in Leviticus 26, which warn that the Israelites would die in the foreign lands of their enemies (Lev 26:38–39).[16] If one disregards the accents, בְּרִיתוֹ אִתּוֹ could mean "his [Nebuchadnezzar's] covenant with him [Zedekiah]." The Vulgate translates "the pact he had with him," and בְּרִית is paired with -אֶת in Lev 26:44, a possible parent phrase.

17:17 Most translations agree substantially with mine, but there is considerable commentary skirmishing about who is doing what in this verse. In light of what we

---

[15] Greenberg, *Ezekiel*, 1:315, argues that it would mean they would die at the same time, but then, "since this precision seems pointless," he follows the view that אִתּוֹ should go with the preceding בְּרִיתוֹ.

[16] For other allusions to Leviticus 26, see the textual notes and commentary on Ezek 4:10–11, 16–17; chapters 5–6; 12:19–20; 14:12–23.

know actually happened, the text must describe the failure of Pharaoh Hophra to field more than a token force to aid Zedekiah; therefore the verse accurately predicts what happened in 588–587 B.C. The verse parallels Jer 37:5–10: when Hophra challenged Nebuchadnezzar's movement into the region, Nebuchadnezzar did temporarily lift the siege of Jerusalem, but when Hophra retreated, Jerusalem faced mighty Babylon alone. Therefore Ezek 17:9 and 17:17 complement one another: 17:9 describes the relative ease with which Zedekiah was uprooted, and 17:17 describes the failure of Zedekiah's hopes that Egypt would effectively aid him.

Much turns on the meaning of וְלֹא ... יַעֲשֶׂה אוֹתוֹ, literally, "he will not do with him." Here, as often in Ezekiel, אוֹת- is the preposition "with" with suffix, which usually is spelled אֶת- in other biblical books (see the last textual note on 2:1). The clause has a positive sense in 20:44 (עָשָׂה אֶת-), and I have taken it here to refer to joining someone as an ally: "Pharaoh ... *will not join him* in the war," that is, Hophra will not aid Zedekiah when the Babylonians "heap up ramps and build siege walls" to attack Jerusalem. Similar are RSV, NIV, and ESV. My reading of the entire context makes the unfaithful Zedekiah the all-encompassing concern.

KJV took the Egyptians (rather than the Babylonians) as the actors in the latter part of the verse: Pharaoh shall not "make for him in the war, by casting up mounts, and building forts." NKJV's translation, that Pharaoh would not "do anything," is not historically accurate.

Greenberg argues that עָשָׂה אוֹת- means "deal hostilely with" and refers to "the small force to be supplied by Pharaoh to oppose Nebuchadnezzar at the siege of Jerusalem." Moreover, he considers "Pharaoh" to be a gloss and construes his version of the "original" text as a reference to the relative ease with which Ezekiel thought Nebuchadnezzar would dispose of Zedekiah, and so 17:17 originally would have said the same thing as 17:9, but both verses would have been inaccurate predictions.[17]

בִּשְׁפֹּךְ סֹלְלָה וּבִבְנוֹת דָּיֵק—The same verbs and nouns in these two clauses describing siege warfare were in 4:2 (which see), where Ezekiel builds a model of Jerusalem under siege. They will recur in 21:27 (ET 21:22).

17:18 וְהִנֵּה נָתַן יָדוֹ—On וְהִנֵּה, see the textual note on 17:10. Giving the hand (נָתַן יָד) is a gesture showing allegiance (sometimes submission), often in connection with promises and treaties,[c] not unlike our handshake.

לֹא יִמָּלֵט:—This final clause is an exclamation ("He shall not escape!") and the direct answer to the rhetorical question "Can he escape?" (twice in 17:15).

17:19 The shift to an explicitly theological perspective in this third part of the chapter (17:19–21) is immediately evident in that the subjects are no longer human

(c) E.g.,
2 Ki 10:15;
Jer 50:15;
Lam 5:6;
Ezra 10:19;
1 Chr 29:24;
2 Chr 30:8

---

[17] Greenberg, *Ezekiel*, 1:314–15. Doubting the originality of "the prescient anticipation of Pharaoh Hophra's futile sally," Greenberg argues that, after the failure of Jerusalem to capitulate easily, "Pharaoh" was added to change the verse's original agreement with 17:9 to make it agree with the historical fact of Hophra's ineffectual intervention. However, aside from the issue of prescience (to say nothing of God's ability to inspire predictive prophecy), the inclusion of "Pharaoh" in 17:17 is supported by all the versions. Moreover, the combination of עָשָׂה and the preposition אוֹת-/אֶת- ("do/deal with") does not always have a hostile meaning; Greenberg cites 7:27; 16:59; 22:14; 23:25, 29; 39:24, where it does, but in 20:44 it pertains to Yahweh acting in grace toward Israel.

(Zedekiah, Nebuchadnezzar, and Hophra in 17:11–18) and their covenants (17:13–16), but rather God, who speaks of "*my* oath" and "*my* covenant" being rejected. The suffixes must be understood as subjective genitives: "the oath I swore" (by Yahweh's invocation of his own name) and "the covenant I made" (by issuing his blessing promises and curses for disobedience).[18]

Somewhat of a parallel to this verse appears in 2 Chr 36:13, which states that when Nebuchadnezzar imposed his vassal covenant on Zedekiah, he made him swear by "God" (probably Israel's). There is ample evidence that this was no exceptional practice. In a polytheistic environment, it would be only natural for the conqueror to assimilate the local god(s) of the vassal into his own pantheon even as he assimilates the vassal's territory into his own, and to have the vassal invoke the vassal's own god(s) in the swearing of any oath or covenant, since the vassal would be most loyal to his own god(s). A comparable invocation will happen roughly a half century later (538 B.C.) when Cyrus' edict of restoration names Yahweh (Ezra 1:2–4; cf. 6:2–5).

הֵפִיר—The Hiphil of פָּרַר is regularly used for "breaking" a covenant. The normal third masculine singular perfect form is הֵפַר (17:15–16). The form in this verse apparently is the third masculine singular Hiphil perfect of the by-form פּוּר, which occurs elsewhere only in Pss 33:10 (הֵפִיר); 89:34 (ET 89:33; אָפִיר). Biblical Hebrew has other examples of geminate verbs that also have a hollow (*ayin-waw* or *yod*) by-form.

וּנְתַתִּיו בְרֹאשׁוֹ:—See the textual note on the similar idiom in 9:10. The masculine suffix on וּנְתַתִּיו clashes with the antecedents אָלָה and בְּרִית, both of which are feminine. Zimmerli wishes to emend,[19] but there are better explanations. "The masculine pronoun is often used for a feminine antecedent" (Waltke-O'Connor, 16.4b). The clause here may be an abbreviation of the fuller idiom "I will place his *conduct* [דֶּרֶךְ] on his head" (cf. 9:10; 11:21; 16:43; 22:31), or it may refer generally to the offense ("it") against the oath and covenant.

17:20 This verse echoes 12:13; see the textual notes there. Here too עָלָיו should be translated "for him," rather than its more usual sense, "over/upon him." The actual capture is described in the following parallel metaphor.

וַהֲבִיאוֹתִיהוּ—This is a longer form of the Hiphil of בוֹא, with וֹ and an object suffix (cf. GKC, § 76 h). Ezekiel uses וַהֲבִיאוֹתִי with suffixes also in 38:16; 39:2. The shorter form with direct object, וְהֵבֵאתִי אֹתוֹ, had been used in 12:13.

וְנִשְׁפַּטְתִּי אִתּוֹ—The Niphal in a reciprocal sense implies some sort of a "dialogical" situation, and this verb implies a courtroom setting, hence "*I will enter into judgment* with him." Since God is clearly the judge (and the verdict of "guilty" is not in doubt) "I will put on trial" or even "I will condemn" would be appropriate translations.

מַעֲלוֹ אֲשֶׁר מָעַל־בִּי:—See the textual note on the cognate accusative מָעַל מַעַל in 14:13. Syntactically this whole phrase is an accusative of specification. Some suggest

---

[18] Waltke-O'Connor calls "my covenant" a subjective genitive suffix of "authorship" (§ 16.4d, including example 6, citing the phrase in Gen 9:9).

[19] Zimmerli, *Ezekiel*, 1:358.

adding a preposition before מַעֲלוֹ, either בְּ (as reflected in the Vulgate) or עַל (as reflected in the Syriac), but like English, those languages could not idiomatically reproduce the Hebrew accusative of specification (which, as is, means "*for* the treason …"). The verb מָעַל is quite strong and is used of quite a variety of perfidies and infidelities, for example, adultery (e.g., Num 5:12) and breaking the חֵרֶם ban (e.g., Josh 7:1). The cognate noun מַעַל usually involves some kind of infidelity against God, but "treason" retains contact with the political situation. Nebuchadnezzar would punish Zedekiah severely at Riblah (2 Ki 25:6–7 ‖ Jer 52:9–11), but Ezek 17:20 affirms that there it is Yahweh who is executing the final judgment on him for his treachery.

17:21 וְאֵת כָּל־מִבְרָחָו—The nominative use of אֵת (ordinarily the sign of the direct object) before the subject of the verb (יִפֹּלוּ) apparently serves to emphasize the subject (cf. Joüon, § 125 j (3)).

Between the Kethib, מִבְרָחוֹ, "his refugee(s)/fugitive(s)" (a singular collective) and the Qere, מִבְרָחָיו, "his fugitives" (a true plural), the Qere is probably the preferable reading. But there is another reading, מִבְחָרָיו, "his choice/elite (troops)," in many Hebrew manuscripts that is also supported by many of the ancient versions. What is involved is metathesis of the two middle consonants (-רח- or -חר-). מִבְרָח is a hapax, although the verbal root בָּרַח, "to flee," is common. Such a unique word is not at all surprising in Ezekiel, and is perfectly intelligible. On the other side of the ledger, מִבְחָר appears elsewhere in Ezekiel (23:7; 24:4–5; 31:16). It also finds support in one Greek translation (although the mainstream LXX omits the phrase), the Targum, and the Syriac. But other Greek versions and the Vulgate agree with the MT. The split in the linguistic evidence is paralleled almost exactly by a split among commentators and translators. Seeing no overriding reason to abandon the MT, I have opted to translate "fugitives."

לְכָל־רוּחַ יִפָּרֵשׂוּ—Yahweh used לְכָל־רוּחַ in 5:10, 12; 12:14 for scattering Israel "to every wind," that is, in every direction. This is the only instance of the Niphal of פָּרַשׂ ("be scattered"). Presumably, it was chosen to form an inclusion with the Qal at the beginning of 17:20 (וּפָרַשְׂתִּי, "*I will spread out* … my net"). (The Qal is also commonly used of the OT gesture of prayer: "*spread out* the hands." The Piel is similarly used twice.)

17:22 To a large extent, the verse is a reworking, with Yahweh as the subject, of elements in 17:3–4 (which see on certain details). Twice אָנִי is added redundantly after a first singular verb, putting the accent on Yahweh, the speaker ("I myself").

הָרָמָה וְנָתָתִּי—A translation of these two words ("high … and set it out") is missing in the LXX, and since the verse can be read without them, a widespread tendency among critics is to excise them.[20] Block suggests an expanded reconstruction on the basis of 17:5, but that is inevitably speculative, and he finally concedes that "the truncated sentence has the rhetorical effect of heightening audience expectation."[21] Most modern translations take the feminine adjective (with article) הָרָמָה ("high") as mod-

---

[20] Zimmerli, *Ezekiel*, 1:358–59. Allen, *Ezekiel*, 1:251, 253, and Greenberg, *Ezekiel*, 1:309, 316, advocate deleting the second word only.

[21] Block, *Ezekiel*, 1:548, n. 134.

ifying the preceding feminine noun צַמֶּרֶת, "crown" (see the last textual note on 17:3). An older view is that אֶרֶז, which usually is masculine, here is feminine (so BDB), hence "high cedar" (KJV).

רָךְ—The LXX translates the middle part of the verse freely and does not reflect this adjective ("tender"), but it is common in the rest of the OT and relates to other horticultural prophecies of Christ (see the commentary below). There is no Hebrew noun modified by this adjective, but the context implies that from the top shoots Yahweh plucks off a "tender" sprig, so the translation adds "sprig" in brackets.

הַר־גָּבֹהַּ וְתָלוּל:—Many manuscripts and editions add a *mappiq* in the *he* of גָּבֹהַּ, which is expected because the *he* is a consonant, not a vowel letter. The *mappiq* is absent in Leningradensis. תָּלוּל is a hapax, and the translation "lofty" is a traditional guess. It may be related to תֵּל, "mound, hill." Its form appears to be a Qal passive participle of תָּלַל, but that Qal verb is otherwise unknown. (The OT contains a תָּלַל whose Hiphil means "to deceive.")

17:23 בְּהַר מְרוֹם יִשְׂרָאֵל אֶשְׁתֳּלֶנּוּ—The noun מְרוֹם can refer to any kind of "height." Sometimes it is used specifically of heaven, but because of its association with הַר, "mountain," which occurs here and in the last phrase of 17:22, its main thrust in this verse is God's redemptive work in Jerusalem. See the commentary below on 17:22–23. For the meaning of שָׁתַל (אֶשְׁתֳּלֶנּוּ is the Qal imperfect with suffix), see the textual note on it in 17:8.

וְעָשָׂה פֶרִי—Prosaic minds, ancient and modern, have tried to explain by midrashic tales or by textual emendation how a cedar tree might "bear fruit"! But in this kind of context, natural realities are transcended, both literarily and theologically.

וְשָׁכְנוּ ... תִּשְׁכֹּנָה:—Most translations vary their rendition of the repeated verb שָׁכַן ("live, dwell"). I have rendered the second one with "nest." Both forms are plural *ad sensum* even though the (usually) feminine noun צִפּוֹר is singular ("every kind of bird" implies "birds").

תַּחְתָּיו—Prosaic minds have also caviled that birds do not live "under" trees. Some LXX manuscripts have θηρίον (collective: "animals") for צִפּוֹר ("bird"), broadening the picture to include terrestrial animals under the tree. That LXX reading has provided an alibi for various ingenious reconstructions of the history of the text.

כֹּל צִפּוֹר כָּל־כָּנָף—This is, literally, "every bird of every wing." The phrase occurs also in Gen 7:14 and without the first כֹּל also in Ezek 39:4, 17 (cf. Deut 4:17; Ps 148:10).

בְּצֵל דָּלִיּוֹתָיו—Birds do live among the "branches" of a tree. Sometimes צֵל means "shade, shadow," but often it is used metaphorically of "shelter" or protection, which seems appropriate here.

17:24 גָּבֹהַ—As in 17:22, the adjective גָּבֹהַ lacks a *mappiq* in Leningradensis.

Commentary

Material very similar to chapter 16 will reappear in chapter 23. The intervening chapters have quite a variety of material. Some commentators think they perceive that chapters 17–22 are a deliberately constructed unit. I, for one, am not convinced; the material is too varied to fit easily into any one overarching framework. Chapter 17 and chapter 19 have enough similarities that some think they were originally joined and chapter 18 was redactionally inserted at a later point.[22] The rest of the material in chapters 20–22 somewhat alternates between oracles of judgment on Israel and oracles that Babylon is God's designated agent in the judgment. But such an observation does little more than summarize much of the message of the book so far.

Structurally, many have observed a phenomenal similarity between 12:1–16 and 17:1–24.[23] While 12:1–16 was an action prophecy or pantomime, followed by an explanation, here we have a verbal presentation. Much of the language in 17:3–10 has a distinct poetic cast about it. Note the poetic typography in many modern Hebrew Bibles and English translations. Greenberg offers an interesting metrical analysis.[24] It is difficult, however, simply to label the section as typical poetry, especially in 17:9–10. It is probably safer to agree with Hals and call the material "elevated prose."[25] There is extensive use of parallelism, often in bicola with three words in each of the two lines, or in triads with two words in each of the three lines.[26] It is conceivable that Ezekiel has reworked some older, preexisting poem, but there is no evidence of that.

This chapter is more specifically anchored in current political events (Zedekiah's rebellion) than anything in the book so far, and its contents indicate that it must have been uttered (and probably written) not long before the actual fall of Jerusalem in 587 B.C., but it is impossible to be more precise than that. It is also noteworthy that, for the first time in the book, we meet specifically "messianic" prophecy in the narrow, that is, royal sense of that word (17:22–24).

The chapter consists of two main parts, the allegory (17:1–10) and its interpretation (17:11–24). The interpretation quite naturally divides into three discrete sections: (1) the allegory's historical meaning (17:11–18); (2) its theological meaning (17:19–21); and (3) the messianic kingdom (17:22–24).

The Allegory of Two Eagles and the Cedar Sprig that Grew into a Vine (17:1–10)

In the nature of the case, there is little, if any, explicit theological content in the "riddle" or "allegory" (17:2) narrated in these verses. Yet, of course, the rest of the chapter hangs on them. Because of the inseparable interrelation between translation and interpretation, occasionally a matter of interpretation was interjected into the textual notes above in order to explain or defend a particu-

---

[22] For example, Allen, *Ezekiel*, 1:285.

[23] See the table in Block, *Ezekiel*, 1:523.

[24] Greenberg, *Ezekiel*, 1:317–20.

[25] Hals, *Ezekiel*, 115.

[26] In Hebrew poetry, separable prepositions and particles often are not counted as separate words, and words in construct may be counted as one word. As always, English translations have far more words than the Hebrew.

lar translational decision. For the most part, however, explicit theology does not emerge until 17:19.

The image of "cedar" and the image of a "vine" as representing God's people are motifs that are prominent in other biblical passages, the most famous "vine" passage being John 15 (cf. also Is 5:1–7; Mt 20:1–16; 21:33–46).[27]

The Allegory's Historical Meaning (17:11–18)

The nature of the material continues to be non-theological, at least on the surface, as these verses present historical interpretation of the allegory in 17:1–10. The "surface" qualifier is necessary because of the ever-present temptation to divorce theology from history in one direction or the other. History unilluminated by revelation is, at best, mute and certainly does not disclose anything but an inscrutable *Deus absconditus*.[28] Various theologies or philosophies may (and do) attempt to fill the void, but the Gospel will never be discerned from history alone.[29]

Just as great a danger is "docetic" theology,[30] which fails to see that God is the final author of all history and is directing it toward its conclusion at Christ's return (as especially Revelation affirms). "Docetic" theologies allege that God is not involved in flesh-and-blood history, either because of his indifference to human affairs or because of his impotence (so history is out of his control). Such theologies are anti-incarnational in essence. In them the OT, because of its enormous historical content, will be one of the major casualties, and all that will be left is some purely intellectual or emotional enterprise. They deny that God's redemptive actions at Bethlehem (Christ's incarnation of the Virgin Mary) and Calvary (his physical agony and atonement, death, and bodily resurrection) took place in real, physical history, and so in them those events at best retain only symbolic value.

All this means that 17:11–18 is an indispensable part of the exegesis of the chapter. The basic historical details they relate about Israel are just as integral

---

[27] One may see the exposition of the biblical motif of "The Vineyard" in Mitchell, *The Song of Songs*, 299–311. For cedar, one may see pages 658–64, 1261–64, and for the cedar temple, pages 104–10.

[28] By "the hidden God" Lutheran theology refers to those aspects of God (including his actions and will) that have only been revealed according to nature. Thus for sinful man the *Deus absconditus* can only result in human ignorance, frustration, condemnation, and death (Law). The Gospel of God's grace is only to be found in the *Deus revelatus*, God as he has revealed himself in the Scriptures and supremely in the vicarious atonement (suffering, death, and resurrection) of Jesus Christ. See Pieper, *Christian Dogmatics*, 1:377–81.

[29] Likewise, the creation itself, properly viewed, can reveal God's glory and power (as well as the pernicious effects of sin, which is the cause of suffering and death), but it can never reveal the Gospel—the forgiveness of sins and the gift of eternal life in Jesus Christ. Again, see Pieper, *Christian Dogmatics*, 1:377–81.

[30] Docetism (from δοκέω, "to seem") is the ancient heresy that Christ only "seemed" to be a man with a human body and only "seemed" to suffer and die on the cross. It is related to Gnosticism, which has become popular in modern academic circles, and various forms of Docetism too remain prevalent today.

to salvation history as the historical facts of the Gospel, traditionally summarized in the (baptismal) Apostles' Creed. Among those facts, one also included in the Nicene Creed is that Christ's vicarious atonement took place "under Pontius Pilate," a historical detail that anchors the Gospel in actual history.

The first eagle (17:3–6) is Nebuchadnezzar, king of Babylon (605–562 B.C.). The "cedar" is said to be in "Lebanon" (17:4), the land famous for its cedars, but the tree represents Jerusalem. That the eagle breaks off "the topmost of its [the cedar's] shoots" (17:4) refers to Nebuchadnezzar removing King Jehoiachin, whom he took to Babylon along with the other leading Israelites in the deportation recorded in 2 Ki 24:10–16 and 2 Chr 36:9–10 (597 B.C.). The "member of the royal family" (17:13) was Jehoiachin's uncle Mattaniah, whom Nebuchadnezzar renamed Zedekiah and stationed as his vassal king over Judah (2 Ki 24:17–18; 2 Chr 36:10–11). The act of renaming him probably was intended as a reminder that the real power lay with Nebuchadnezzar.

That Zedekiah rebelled against Nebuchadnezzar (Ezek 17:15; cf. 17:7) is recorded also in 2 Ki 24:20 and elaborated in 2 Chr 36:13–16. Not all the details of the rebellion are known, but it is clear that it was no sudden impulse by Zedekiah, but probably had been brewing almost since his accession. Jeremiah 27 records an order from Yahweh to Jeremiah to denounce Zedekiah in the fourth year of his reign (593 B.C.; cf. Jer 28:1) for joining four neighbors who had met to conspire against Babylon, and Jer 51:59 mentions a visit by Zedekiah to Babylon, presumably to defend his behavior, which apparently he did successfully (since he retained his office for a while longer). At about the same time, Psammetichus II (594–589) assumed power in Egypt and may well have encouraged Zedekiah to revolt, promising him assistance if needed. Clearly, when the Babylonian siege of Jerusalem began, Judah looked for assistance from Psammetichus' successor, Hophra (589–570), but to no avail (Jer 37:5–10). Thus Egypt is the second "great eagle" toward which the "vine" turned (Ezek 17:7).

The uprooting of the vine and its desiccation by the east wind (since Babylon is east of Israel) in 17:9–10 correspond to the punishment described in 17:16–18 and refer to the destruction of Jerusalem by Nebuchadnezzar in 587 B.C. (2 Ki 25:1–21; 2 Chr 36:17–21). Zedekiah fled, but he did "not escape" (Ezek 17:18; cf. 17:15). His sons were slaughtered in his presence before he was blinded and brought to Babylon (2 Ki 25:7), where he died (Jer 52:11), fulfilling Ezek 17:16.

The Allegory's Theological Meaning (17:19–21)

17:19 In the Bible's (and Christianity's) "two storied" view of history, the focus now shifts to the upper, heavenly one, where earthly history is really made. It has often been noted that the Bible really has no vocable corresponding to our "history," which, as a discipline divorced from theology, is a child of the Enlightenment. It is not that what people call and know as "history" is illusory or some Platonic shadow of reality outside the cave, but that it is the only part of the totality that, apart from the Scriptures, is accessible to human reason and the senses. Thus, it is no accident that in many respects the theological interpretation of the allegory does little more than restate what has already been explained in the preceding verses, except that God now becomes the constant subject. Everything is now viewed *sub specie aeternitatis*, as part of God's eternal plan. The divine revelation about the purpose and goal of history moves us from the *Deus absconditus* to the *Deus revelatus*.[31]

The theme of Israel breaking the covenant recalls 16:59, and the result, that Yahweh will impose the proper punishment on the head of the offender, recalls 9:10; 11:21; 16:43.

17:20 This verse momentarily introduces the twin metaphors of Yahweh's "net" and "trap" (see the textual notes and commentary on 12:13), which were not mentioned in the allegory at the beginning of the chapter (17:1–10). Apparently they are a vivid way of underscoring that Zedekiah ultimately receives his comeuppance, not from Nebuchadnezzar, but from Yahweh. The very lack of details, especially the silence about the sad scene at Riblah (2 Ki 25:6–7 ‖ Jer 52:9–11), indicates that the concern here is not with earthly history, but with theology. It also militates against those who propose that the prophecy is *ex eventu* (after the event), since an after-the-fact writer would be tempted to add details to make the "prophecy" more credible.

17:21 The sword and the scattering of the fugitives "to every wind" recalls chapter 5 (5:2, 10, 12, 17). With the theme of God's demolition of all human hubris, the chapter moves at once into a poetic description in the following verses of how Yahweh will rebuild his kingdom. The recognition formula common elsewhere ("then you will know that I am Yahweh") is modified here with an emphasis on God's spoken Word: "then you will know that I, Yahweh, have spoken" (17:21), pointing to the fulfillment of this particular prophetic chapter. The clause is similar to that at the end of the chapter ("I, Yahweh, have spoken," 17:24) and virtually forms an inclusion with it. Together with the citation formula at the beginning of the next verse ("thus says the Lord Yahweh," 17:22), on a literary level alone, it provides an unmistakable sense of contrast between the demolished vine/kingdom of Israel and the new sprig Yahweh will plant, which shall bear fruit and provide refuge.

The Messianic Kingdom (17:22–24)

17:22 To the casual reader it may not be immediately apparent that this is a messianic prophecy. (I personally can recall no churchly use of the verse as such in any context, not even in children's Advent or Christmas Eve programs, which tend to include long series of messianic prophecies.) But the cedar from which Yahweh will pluck off a shoot is growing in a land that 17:3

---

[31] See the preceding footnote that discusses these terms.

had poetically called "Lebanon," that is, Jerusalem or Zion. Cedar had played a prominent role in the construction of the temple and palace there (e.g., 1 Kings 5–7). Jerusalem was the home of the Davidic dynasty, and the oracle (almost depicting Yahweh as a true eagle) virtually reaffirms the key messianic oracle of 2 Samuel 7 (∥ 1 Chronicles 17; Ps 89:20–38 [ET 89:19–37]) of the perpetuity of the Davidic line through the "son/Son" of David and of God the Father (2 Sam 7:14). Especially Pss 78:68–73 and 132:10–18 will juxtapose God's election of David and his dynasty with his choice of Mount Zion as his dwelling place. And here the cedar would achieve the growth that had eluded the rebellious house of Israel (Ezek 17:2, 12) and Zedekiah. This new growth would ultimately be achieved in the transhistorical sphere.

And the sprig that will be broken off is a very special one, characterized as "tender, soft" (רַךְ, 17:22). The word itself is unparalleled in a context such as this, but it belongs together with a number of other horticultural expressions used to describe the eschatological climax of the line of David in Jesus Christ, apparently beginning with the חֹטֶר ("shoot") and נֵצֶר ("branch") of Is 11:1 and expressed so prominently in the צֶמַח ("branch/shoot") of Jer 23:5; 33:15; Zech 3:8; 6:12 that at times it almost becomes a personal name. Related are the "shoot" (יוֹנֶק, similar to יְנִיקוֹתָיו in Ezek 17:4 and יְנִקוֹתָיו in Ezek 17:22) and "root" (שֶׁרֶשׁ, also in Ezek 17:6, 7, 9) that improbably grow from arid ground and represent the Suffering Servant in Is 53:2, although there the accent may be more on the Messiah's lowly origin than on his tender youthfulness. The OT prophecies of the Messiah as a "branch" (*netser*) may explain St. Matthew's statement that when the young Jesus settled with his family in *Nazareth*, it was "so that what was spoken through the prophets might be fulfilled: 'He shall be called a Nazarene [Ναζωραῖος]' " (Mt 2:23).[32]

Since the free rendition of the LXX omits a translation of רַךְ ("tender") in Ezek 17:22, our earliest versional attestation of a specifically messianic interpretation may be in the Vulgate, "I will break off from the topmost of its branches a tender one and stretch it out [*tenerum distringam*] and plant it on the most high and prominent mountain," which seems to allude to Jesus' arms being stretched out on the cross.

By the repeated, emphatic "I myself" and the contrast with the machinations of the two eagles, Yahweh puts great accent on the antithesis between his free divine action and all human activity. What he promises is not the result of some new and clever human plan, but solely a new, free act of God in faithfulness to his ancient promises.

---

[32] The exact term that St. Matthew uses, Ναζωραῖος ("Nazarene"?), does not occur in the Greek OT. Clearly it is related to "Nazareth" (Ναζαρέτ), but it may refer to more than just the town's name. It is also related to, but not identical with, the LXX term for "Nazirite" (ναζιραῖος, e.g., Judg 13:5, 7; 16:17). It is similar to a transliteration of נֵצֶר (*netser* or *nezer*), "branch." "Through the *prophets*" (Mt 2:23) suggests that Matthew did not have just one prophecy in mind, but perhaps a composite idea supported by a number of prophetic passages, such as the collection of horticultural prophecies of Christ.

The shoot used as a scion will be planted on a "high and lofty mountain"—a picture that will be expanded a bit further at the beginning of 17:23. The metaphor of a "world mountain" (a mountain so high and important it dominates the whole earth) flits about the edges of biblical imagery but is never fully developed. Protologically, 28:13–16 will picture the king of Tyre (as a type of Satan before his fall) in "Eden, the garden of God," which was on "the holy mountain of God." Sometimes the "holy mountain" is applied to Zion in terms that transcend the geographic reality (Ps 48:2–3 [ET 48:1–2]). Jerusalem with the temple as הַר קָדְשִׁי, "my [God's] holy mountain" (or a variant; e.g., Is 27:13; 56:7), is a recurrent refrain. The eschatological feast of Is 25:6–8 will be celebrated "on this mountain." In Is 11:9, "paradise restored" is described as "my holy mountain."

Christianity found the "mountain" image useful to describe Calvary as the focal point of all history and existence. The site of the reconciliation of God and sinners is the highest "mountain," one that connects heaven to earth by God's grace—a picture filled out by Christ's descent to earth at his incarnation[33] and his ascension to heaven from the Mount of Olives after his resurrection (Lk 24:50–51; Acts 1:9–12). Perhaps the mount of transfiguration (Mt 17:1–13 and parallels) and the "very high mountain" of our Lord's temptation (Mt 4:1–11 and parallels), both tantalizingly imprecise about geographic location, are relevant here too. One might say that "Mount Calvary" connects the original paradise lost to the future paradise opened to all believers in Christ (e.g., Lk 23:43).[34] Since rivers may have their source in the mountains (as the Jordan begins near Mount Hermon) and four rivers flowed out of Eden (Gen 2:10–14), which is pictured as a mountain in Ezek 28:13–16, Christian artists have tended to paint the first paradise so. Correspondingly, the apostle John sees that the new Jerusalem is on a "great, high mountain" (Rev 21:2, 10), as reflected in Christian hymnody, for example, "Jerusalem, O City Fair *and High*."[35] Already Ezekiel will see that a renewed Israel will worship Yahweh on "my holy mountain" (Ezek 20:40), and in his concluding eschatological vision, the new temple, city, and land in Ezekiel 40–48 (anticipating Revelation 21–22) will be on "a very high mountain" (Ezek 40:2).[36]

17:23 The "mountain" motif continues in the first part of the verse. Then the verse leaves that metaphor and develops another one, which extends somewhat into 17:24. This one may be labeled "exmythological" because it is widespread in the myths of world religions, but in biblical speech it is free from pagan theology and is used to convey divine truth (whether or not the Israelites

---

[33] One may compare the similar refrains at Christ's incarnation (Lk 2:14) and at Palm Sunday as he ascended toward Calvary (Lk 19:38). See Just, *Luke 1:1–9:50*, 111

[34] One may see "The Garden Paradise" in Mitchell, *The Song of Songs*, 263–74.

[35] *LW* 306; emphasis added.

[36] See also the sketch of Ezekiel's mountain motif in "Outline and Theological Emphases" in the introduction, and the introduction to the commentary on chapter 6.

were aware of its pagan origins and/or parallels). Ezekiel's more immediate sources may have been other prophetic pictures of the Messiah as a "Branch" and so on (see the commentary on 17:22).

This is the picture of a "cosmic tree," which depicts the living world as an enormous tree with its roots in the subterranean depths and its tops in the clouds, thus providing shelter for every living creature. In 31:1–18 (which see), Ezekiel will develop the metaphor in much greater detail in a Gentile oracle against Egypt, and especially against the very Pharaoh Hophra who figures marginally in this chapter. While Hophra is not named in Ezekiel, he is the second "eagle" in 17:7 and the "Pharaoh" in 17:17 and chapters 29–32. (Hophra is named in Jer 44:30.) In Daniel 4 the cosmic tree becomes a representation of Nebuchadnezzar. Jesus uses the motif in his parable of the mustard seed (Mt 13:31–32, quoted below, and parallels).

The same triad of words appears here as in Ezek 17:8: "branches" (collective use of עָנָף), "fruit" (פְּרִי), and "magnificent" (אַדֶּרֶת, 17:8; אַדִּיר, 17:23). In 17:8 they described human aspirations (Nebuchadnezzar's intent for Israel as his vassal state), which would come to naught. Here the words have been transmuted into a description of what only God can accomplish by his grace.

The immediate point is that God's removal of Zedekiah will not be the end of the Davidic kings. His new planting will keep the ancient messianic promise (specifically in its Davidic manifestation) alive, so that in the fullness of time (Gal 4:4) its influence will truly be cosmic. The tiny, "tender" sprig or scion— the infant Messiah (see the commentary on 17:22)—grows into a beautiful, stately tree under which "every kind of winged bird" will find both food and protection. In the next verse the trees will symbolize the nations, but here the point is the tree's expansiveness. The Lord's parable clearly alludes to the verse:

> The kingdom of heaven is like a grain of mustard seed that a man took and sowed in his field. It is the smallest of all the seeds, but when it has grown it is larger than the garden plants and becomes a tree, so that the birds of heaven come and dwell in its branches. (Mt 13:31–32)

17:24 The chapter closes climactically with an expansion of the usual recognition formula ("then you/they will know that I am Yahweh"), put into the mouths, as it were, of all the personified trees of the world, representing all nations: "then all the trees of the countryside will know that I, Yahweh, …" Most of the verbs are perfects and the nouns are anarthrous, thus formulating a proverbial (or better: dogmatic!) assertion of the great reversal theme that runs throughout the Scriptures: "… will know that I, Yahweh, bring down the high tree and exalt the low tree, that I make the green tree wither and I make the withered tree blossom" (17:24). Ezekiel's deft contrast of "bring down" (Hiphil of שָׁפֵל) and "high" (גָּבֹהַּ); of "wither" (Hiphil of יָבֵשׁ) and "green" (לַח); and of "withered" (יָבֵשׁ) and "make blossom" (Hiphil of פָּרַח) gives a vivid, poetic expression to the theology of the cross, the way of the Gospel, the administration of the kingdom of God versus the kingdoms of this world (cf. the request of the sons of Zebedee in Mt 20:20–28 ‖ Mk 10:35–45). The theme of the great reversal is seen most clearly in Christ himself, who suffered the most shameful death as he bore the world's sins, but then was raised in glory on the third day. Some of the very language in Ezek 17:24 is cited by Christ on his way to the cross:

> For if they do these things when the wood is green, what shall happen when it is dry? (Lk 23:31; cf. also Ezek 21:3 [ET 20:47])

The immediate historical application of the great reversal in 17:24 is to the presumptuous King Zedekiah, who is still in power as Ezekiel prophesies, but whom God will soon bring low (2 Ki 25:6–7 ‖ Jer 52:9–11), versus King Jehoiachin, who is already captive in Babylon as Ezekiel prophesies, but who, after thirty-seven years in prison, will be released and spend the rest of his life dining at the table of the king of Babylon (2 Ki 25:27–30, thus ending 1–2 Kings on the Gospel note of hope for the restoration of the line of kings in the Son of David). But the great reversal theme is strongly eschatological, and often what it describes will not happen until the Last Day, when downtrodden believers enter the glory of their Lord and powerful unbelievers are laid low for eternity.

One could cite biblical parallels or expressions of the great reversal theme almost without end. I think immediately of Hannah's psalm (1 Sam 2:1–10), recycled in the Magnificat (Lk 1:46–55). St. Paul develops the theme at length in 1 Corinthians 1–2. Let a Reformation era hymn summarize Luther's theme of the "blessed exchange" wherein Christ takes on humanity's sin and imputes his own righteousness to all believers:

> He serves that I a lord may be;
> A great exchange indeed!
> Could Jesus' love do more for me
> To help me in my need?[37]

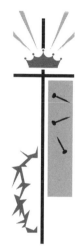

---

[37] From "Praise God the Lord, Ye Sons of Men" (*TLH* 105:7; cf. *LW* 44:5).

The Wicked Will Die
and the Righteous Will Live

Translation

18 ¹The Word of Yahweh came to me: ²"What do you mean, you who keep repeating this proverb concerning the land of Israel: 'Fathers eat sour grapes, and the teeth of their sons are set on edge'? ³As I live, says the Lord Yahweh, you will never again use this proverb in Israel. ⁴Behold, all persons are mine. The person of the father just like the person of the son is mine. The person who sins is the one who will die.

⁵"If a man is righteous and he practices justice and righteousness, ⁶if he does not eat on the mountains and does not lift up his eyes to the fecal deities of the house of Israel, if he does not defile his neighbor's wife and does not approach a menstruous woman, ⁷if he does not exploit anyone but returns the collateral given him for a loan, if he does not seize another's property by force but gives his own food to the hungry and covers the naked with clothes, ⁸if he does not demand that interest be paid in advance of a loan and then refuse to return it when the loan is repaid, if he withdraws his hand from unrighteousness and performs faithful arbitration between men, ⁹that is, if he keeps walking in my statues and keeps my ordinances by acting faithfully, that man is righteous and he will surely live, says the Lord Yahweh.

¹⁰"Now if he fathers a violent son, a shedder of blood, who does any one of these things ¹¹(although he [the father] did not do all these), but he [the son] even eats on the mountains and defiles his neighbor's wife, ¹²exploits the poor and the needy, seizes others' property by force, does not return the collateral on a loan, lifts up his eyes to the fecal deities, does what is an abomination, ¹³and demands that interest be paid in advance of a loan but then refuses to return it when the loan is repaid—will he live? He will not live! He did all these abominations, so he will surely be put to death. His blood will be upon him.

¹⁴"But if he [that son] should himself father a son who sees all the sins that his father has committed, and he sees and does not do like them— ¹⁵he does not eat on the mountains, does not lift up his eyes to the fecal deities of the house of Israel, does not defile his neighbor's wife, ¹⁶does not exploit anyone, does not require collateral for a loan, does not seize another's property by force, gives his own food to the hungry and covers the naked with clothes, ¹⁷takes care not to harm the poor, does not take interest in advance and then refuse to return it, but keeps my ordinances and walks according to my statutes, he will not die because of his father's iniquity; he will surely live. ¹⁸But his father, if he practices extortion, seizes his brother's goods by force, and does what was not good among his kinsmen, behold, he will die because of his own iniquity.

¹⁹"But you ask, 'Why does the son not share in the guilt of the father?' [Answer:] The son did justice and righteousness; he kept all my statutes and did them, so he will surely live. ²⁰The person who sins is the one who will die. The son will not share in the guilt of the father, and the father will not share in the guilt of the son. The righteousness of the righteous person shall be upon him alone, and the wickedness of the wicked person shall be upon him alone.

²¹"A wicked man, if he repents of all his sins that he has committed and keeps all my statutes and does justice and righteousness, he will surely live; he will not die. ²²All of the rebellious acts that he had committed will not be remembered against him. Because of his righteousness that he has done, he will live. ²³Do I really find any pleasure in the death of the wicked man, says the Lord Yahweh? Is it not rather when he repents of his ways and lives?

²⁴"But if a righteous man turns away from his righteousness and practices unrighteousness—like all the abominations that the wicked man practices, he practices—will he live? All the righteous deeds that he did will not be remembered. Because of the faithless infidelity he did and because of the sin that he has committed, because of them he will die. ²⁵But you say, 'The Lord's way is unpredictable.' Listen now, house of Israel. Is it my way that is unpredictable? Is it not your ways that are unpredictable? ²⁶If a righteous man turns away from his righteousness and practices unrighteousness, he will die because of them; because of the unrighteousness that he has practiced, he will die.

²⁷"And if a wicked man repents of his wickedness that he had done and does justice and righteousness, he will save his life. ²⁸Because he has seen and repented of all the rebellious acts that he had committed, he will surely live and he will not die. ²⁹But the house of Israel says, 'The Lord's way is unpredictable.' Is it really my ways that are unpredictable, O house of Israel? Is it not your ways that are unpredictable?

³⁰"Therefore, I will judge you, each one according to his ways, O house of Israel, says the Lord Yahweh. Repent and turn away from all your rebellious acts, so that you will not have an iniquitous stumbling block. ³¹Throw off from upon yourselves all your rebellious actions by which you have rebelled, and get for yourselves a new heart and a new S/spirit. For why should you die, O house of Israel? ³²For I have no pleasure in the death of the dead man, says the Lord Yahweh. So repent and live!"

Textual Notes

18:2 מַה־לָּכֶם—This interrogative expression is not easy to render precisely. Literally, it translates, "What [is it] to you?" The *maqqeph* and conjunctive *daghesh forte* (-לָּ) join the words closely together. Sometimes the expression connotes "What do you want?" or "What is your problem?" (cf. BDB, s.v. מָה, 1 a (c), and s.v. לְ, 5 a (d)). Usually its sense is clarified by what follows, which here is the Israelites' use of a proverb.

אַתֶּם מֹשְׁלִים אֶת־הַמָּשָׁל הַזֶּה—The first three words (including the sign of the direct object) are not reflected in the LXX. I have translated אַתֶּם as underscoring the suffix on לָכֶם. Zimmerli retains it too, but takes it as the subject of an asyndetic nominal clause related to לָכֶם.[1] Greenberg thinks it was added to indicate the inappropriateness of the proverb to them ("you").[2] The cognate accusative construction uses the verb מָשַׁל (the participle possibly indicating virtually constant activity) and the noun מָשָׁל, as in 12:22–23 (see the textual notes there). The verb and/or noun also occurred previously in 14:8; 16:44; 17:2. Here, the usual translation, "proverb, saying, slogan," works well for the noun.

עַל־אַדְמַת יִשְׂרָאֵל—The preposition probably means "*concerning* the land of Israel" rather than just "upon," since there is no reason why the proverb should not have been current among Israelites in exile (who were not "upon" the land) as well as among those still in Jerusalem. (The LXX has "among [ἐν] the sons of Israel.") The end of 18:3 has בְּיִשְׂרָאֵל, probably in a local sense (the proverb will no longer be used "in" Israel).

אָבוֹת יֹאכְלוּ בֹסֶר וְשִׁנֵּי הַבָּנִים תִּקְהֶינָה:—Jer 31:29 too quotes this proverb, with only minor differences.[3] In both verses (Jer 31:29; Ezek 18:2) the asyndetic form of אָבוֹת indicates its broad applicability to all "fathers," that is, everyone's progenitors, although it has an unusual urgency in the present circumstances, shortly before the fall of Jerusalem. It goes without saying that mothers are not to be excluded, but it is "inclusiveness" *ad absurdum* to translate "parents"[4] or to feel the need to apologize for the masculine forms here and in the following verses.[5]

The imperfect יֹאכְלוּ is the expected form in maxims, indicating timeless action. In Jer 31:29 the verb אָכְלוּ is perfect, as often in other proverbs, a classical "proof" that Hebrew really has no "tenses" in the Western sense. But Jeremiah's different application of the proverb may affect the form chosen (see the commentary below).

The noun בֹסֶר probably signifies unripe fruit in general, but there is no reason to question its traditional application to grapes. Many sources, ancient and modern, attest to the custom of eating unripe grapes in the Near East, and anyone who has spent time there is aware that the custom applies to other fruits as well (figs, dates, pomegranates).

The article with בָּנִים probably has possessive force ("*their* sons"). The article is lacking in the Jeremianic version, without significant change in meaning.

The Qal of קָהָה occurs only in Jer 31:29–30; Ezek 18:2, always in this identical form, תִּקְהֶינָה, with the final *he* reverting to the original *yod*. The Piel occurs only in Eccl 10:10, where it describes an iron tool becoming blunt or dull. The verb's use in Rabbinic Hebrew as well as Aramaic and Syriac cognates confirm that the Qal literally means "be blunt, dull," but the traditional translation that the teeth are "set on

---

[1] Zimmerli, *Ezekiel*, 1:369.

[2] Greenberg, *Ezekiel*, 1:327.

[3] Jeremiah's version reads as follows:

אָבוֹת אָכְלוּ בֹסֶר
וְשִׁנֵּי בָנִים תִּקְהֶינָה:

[4] As does Block, *Ezekiel*, 1:557.

[5] For example, Allen, *Ezekiel*, 1:265.

edge" really cannot be improved upon. It is one of those unpleasant experiences that defies verbalization.

18:3 God's self-adjuration חַי־אָ֫נִי is followed by אִם, forming a powerful prohibition, as is even clearer in Jeremiah, where Yahweh prefaces the proverb with לֹא־יֹאמְרוּ עוֹד ("they shall never again say," Jer 31:29). God will see to it that his judgments will convince the people of the fairness of his acts.

18:4 This is the only place where Ezekiel uses הֵן instead of הִנֵּה, and it too is traditionally translated "behold" (*HALOT*, 1). Four times in this verse we confront נֶפֶשׁ, which has no simple English equivalent. The traditional "soul" is completely misleading to the modern ear. As is evident already in Gen 2:7, a "living soul/being" (נֶפֶשׁ חַיָּה) is not just something a person has, it is what a person *is*. The dichotomy of the corporeal and non-corporeal parts of a person is entirely alien to Hebrew thought. The usage of "soul" for the non-physical aspect of a person apparently entered Christian language when the church started talking about the "immortality of the soul" as essentially synonymous with the creedal "resurrection of the body," but that usage is in almost total opposition to the original sense of "soul" in Hellenistic paganism. But since part of the force of נֶפֶשׁ is that mysterious quality that distinguishes a living person from a corpse, it is easy to understand how, in Christian contexts after Easter, it took on its later sense familiar to us. Subsequently in the chapter Ezekiel himself resolves some of the difficulty by using אִישׁ ("man, person," 18:5), צַדִּיק ("righteous man," 18:20, 24, 26), and other words as synonyms of נֶפֶשׁ. I have settled on the translation "person" as the least misleading equivalent of נֶפֶשׁ.

הַנֶּפֶשׁ הַחֹטֵאת הִיא תָמוּת׃—This will be repeated at the beginning of 18:20. Since נֶפֶשׁ is feminine, it takes a feminine form of the participle (הֹטֵאת ; see GKC, § 74 i) and finite verb (תָמוּת).

18:5 וְעָשָׂה מִשְׁפָּט וּצְדָקָה:—Syntactically, the entirety of 18:5 is the summary protasis for the whole section of 18:5–9. The qualities of "justice" and "righteousness" will be itemized in various ways in the following verses, with the apodosis not coming until the very end (18:9). Most of the time in Ezekiel מִשְׁפָּט is plural and refers to God's "ordinances" in the Torah (e.g., 5:6–7; 11:12, 20; see the textual note on it in 5:6). Conversely, most of the occurrences of צְדָקָה refer to "righteousness" done by believers[a] or as a quality possessed by believers (14:14, 20). The two are paired often in Ezekiel[b] and many other OT passages,[c] where they may be virtual synonyms or at least two sides of the same coin. As long as the two nouns are understood as referring to characteristics of God, which he reveals in his Word and imparts to his people through faith (not to status achieved through human effort), possible translations of this clause would include "he practices justice and righteousness" or even "he does what is just and right."

18:6 וְאֶת־אֵשֶׁת רֵעֵהוּ לֹא טִמֵּא וְאֶל־אִשָּׁה נִדָּה לֹא יִקְרָב:—The verb "defile" (Piel of טָמֵא, also in 18:11, 15) is used for violations of chastity of various sorts. It and "to approach" (קָרַב) a woman are obviously both semi-euphemistic for sexual relations. Both are used in their primary senses here, although both have various metaphorical applications in other contexts. נִדָּה is technically an abstract noun meaning "menstrual impurity," but in the phrase אִשָּׁה נִדָּה it is best rendered as an adjective

(a) Ezek 3:20; 18:5, 19–22, 24, 26, 27; 33:12–14, 16, 18–19; 45:9

(b) Ezek 18:5, 19, 21, 27; 33:14, 16, 19; 45:9

(c) E.g., Gen 18:19; 2 Sam 8:15; Is 1:27; 9:6 (ET 9:7); 33:5; 58:2

523

("menstruous woman"). This is an abbreviation of the full idiom found in Lev 18:19: אִשָּׁה בְּנִדַּת טֻמְאָתָהּ.

18:7 The vocabulary is economic, but the entire verse exudes a sense of genuine concern by the strong for the weak, not mere legalistic "rights." יוֹנֶ֔ה, Hiphil of יָנָה, "to oppress, exploit" (which recurs in 18:12, 16), is quite generic; it tends to imply conning someone (usually helpless or naive) out of what is really his by some chicanery or the other.

חֲבֹלָתוֹ חוֹב יָשִׁיב—This second clause, containing two hapax legomena, is more difficult. The feminine חֲבֹלָה occurs only here but the masculine חֲבֹל is in 18:12, 16; 33:15. Both are often translated "pledge," but I think "collateral" (given someone for a loan) communicates better today. (Other Hebrew terms for collateral are עֲרֻבָּה and עֵרָבוֹן.) The suffix on חֲבֹלָתוֹ is objective: "collateral [given to] him [the creditor]." חוֹב too is a hapax legomenon in the OT, but is well-known from later Hebrew and Aramaic. Syntactically, it appears to be used as an adverbial accusative: "the collateral given him *for a loan*." The sense is that the righteous creditor "returns" (יָשִׁיב) the collateral the debtor had given him once the debt is paid off. Similar idioms will recur in 18:12 (negated) and 18:16.

גְּזֵלָה לֹא יִגְזֹל—The cognate accusative construction with the verb גָּזַל and noun (direct object) גְּזֵלָה emphasizes an already emphatic root. The verb overlaps with גָּנַב, "to steal" (used in the Seventh Commandment, Ex 20:15 ‖ Deut 5:19) but emphasizes taking something violently or by force, not by stealth or guile, hence "seize another's property by force." A clause with the same two cognates occurs in 18:16, and similar clauses are in 18:12 and (with the noun גֵּזֶל) 18:18.

18:8 בַּנֶּשֶׁךְ לֹא־יִתֵּן וְתַרְבִּית לֹא יִקָּח—The meaning of these clauses has long been debated, and still is. Inevitably, translation reflects exegesis, as does mine. The precise meanings of נֶשֶׁךְ (*HALOT:* "interest") and תַּרְבִּית (*HALOT*: "profit" or "usury") are uncertain, especially in their relation to each other. To "give" נֶשֶׁךְ probably means "to determine, establish" it. On the other hand, תַּרְבִּית is something the righteous man does not "take."

Three times Israelites are forbidden to lend with interest to fellow Israelites (Ex 22:24 [ET 22:25]; Lev 25:36–37; Deut 23:20 [ET 23:19]). The Deuteronomy 23 passage adds the qualification that it is permissible to require interest on a loan to a foreigner (נָכְרִי, Deut 23:21 [ET 23:20]). Lending to a "brother" (Deut 23:20 [ET 23:19]) was not considered a commercial transaction, but simply a kindly act of helping out someone in the community of faith who was temporarily in need. Thus, if the transgression here (which the righteous man does not do) involves a fellow Israelite (as seems most likely), the offender would be doubly guilty, while if the other party is a foreigner, he may have simply violated the "natural law" of fairness written on the human conscience (but not in the Torah).

The noun נֶשֶׁךְ is related to the rare verb נָשַׁךְ, "to lend on interest" (*HALOT*, s.v. נשׁך II), which occurs only in Deut 23:20–21 (ET 23:19–20); Hab 2:7, and both may be related to the more common verb נָשַׁךְ, "to bite." If so, the offender is taking a "bite" out of someone's property. תַּרְבִּית is from the root רבה, so apparently it refers to the lender obtaining an "increase" in his own property by taking a bite out of another's.

Generally נֶשֶׁךְ appears to be related to the act of lending, and תַּרְבִּית to collecting. Thus, the interpretation follows that an unrighteous lender would take a "bite" by requiring the debtor to give him an advance payment, and then the lender either refuses to repay the advance, or he refuses to give the debtor credit for the advance, and so he demands payment of the full original amount upon maturation of the loan. This line of thought underlies the NRSV's "take advance and accrued interest," which I have substantially followed but attempted to restate in more everyday language.

It is worth noting the history of application of biblical passages forbidding interest. In the Middle Ages the fact that Jews could serve as money lenders only to Gentiles, plus Gentile prohibitions on Jews owning land or serving in other professions, led to "Shylock" stereotypes and the anti-Semitic myths of unusual Jewish economic power (myths that still beset us). Generally, modern Jews and Christians have learned to distinguish legitimate interest and usury, no matter who is involved. But reportedly, Muslim immigrants to the West (who no doubt inherited anti-interest laws from Jews and/or Christians) still struggle with it. Some system of cooperatives seems to be the most common type of attempted solution.

מֵעָוֶל יָשִׁיב יָדוֹ—The rest of 18:8 presumably is continuing to concentrate on economic matters. The noun עָוֶל, repeated in 18:24, 26 (also 28:18; 33:13, 15, 18), means "unrighteousness"; see the textual note on it in 3:20. It may be quite generic for any "wrong" or "injustice," from which the righteous man, literally, "causes his hand to return," that is, "withdraws his hand," that is, refuses to practice. The next phrase will state what he does practice.

מִשְׁפַּט אֱמֶת יַעֲשֶׂה בֵּין אִישׁ לְאִישׁ:—This unusual idiom, literally, "he practices justice of faithfulness between a man and another," means "he performs faithful arbitration between men" or "he judges fairly" when a court decision or arbitration is required. **18:9** בְּחֻקּוֹתַי יְהַלֵּךְ—Similar clauses with the Piel of הָלַךְ for walking in God's ways, light, and so on are in Pss 81:14 (ET 81:13); 86:11; 89:16 (ET 89:15); Prov 8:20. Similar clauses with the Qal are much more common. The Piel here may well be a semi-poetic change to avoid monotony and/or may reflect a general shift from classical to late Hebrew idioms. Zimmerli wants to delete the initial י of יְהַלֵּךְ as due to dittography,[6] but that is hypercritical.

וּמִשְׁפָּטַי שָׁמַר לַעֲשׂוֹת אֱמֶת—The similar clause in 18:19 has וַיַעֲשֶׂה אֹתָם (אֹתָם) instead of אֱמֶת), to which many scholars, following the LXX, wish to emend this passage. But, at best, this is unnecessary. The idiom עָשָׂה חֶסֶד וֶאֱמֶת is found in old portions of the OT (e.g., Gen 24:49; 32:11 [ET 32:10]; 47:29) and עָשָׂה אֱמֶת is found in late passages (Neh 9:33; 2 Chr 31:20). Fortunately, most modern English translations do not emend. The infinitive לַעֲשׂוֹת acts as a gerund (literally, "by doing faithfulness"), and NIV, NKJV, and ESV all render the direct object with the adverb "faithfully." **18:10** וְהוֹלִיד בֶּן־פָּרִיץ שֹׁפֵךְ דָּם—The long conditional sentence in 18:10–13a will generally use perfect verbs (except for יָשִׁיב in 18:12). The Qal of יָלַד, "to give birth," usually is feminine, referring to the mother (as in 16:20), although there are exceptions, as in Ps 2:7, which refers to God the Father's eternal generation of God the Son

---

[6] Zimmerli, *Ezekiel*, 1:370–71.

("begotten of his Father before all worlds," Nicene Creed). The Hiphil generally is masculine and refers to the father as the one who "causes a son to be born." The connective is not *waw* consecutive, as one would expect in classical Hebrew, but a simple *waw* conjunctive, which later Hebrew increasingly preferred. הוֹלִיד will be repeated in 18:14.

The ordinary antonym to צַדִּיק (18:5, 9) would be רָשָׁע, but for the "son" (18:10) Ezekiel uses the much stronger term פָּרִיץ, "breaker [and enterer]," a robber, a thoroughly violent and dangerous person (cf. Jer 7:11, "a den of *thieves*," applied to the temple of his day by Jeremiah and again by Jesus in Mt 21:13 and parallels). As a virtual synonym, Ezekiel also uses "shedder of blood" (שֹׁפֵךְ דָּם), a frequent phrase in prophetic condemnations of Israel, which is rooted in the Noachide command of Gen 9:6 (שֹׁפֵךְ דַּם הָאָדָם). An inclusion is formed when in 18:13 the violent son's own blood (דָּמָיו) will be required of him.

וְעָשָׂה אָח מֵאַחַד מֵאֵלֶּה:—This is, literally, "and does a brother from one of these." KJV has "and that doeth the like to any one of these things," but most other translations disregard אָח (which will occur in 18:18) here as the result of textual corruption. If so, the most likely explanation is to assume that the scribe began to write אַחַד, but after writing אַח, he realized that the preposition מִן should have been prefixed, and so without deleting אח (later vocalized to אָח), he then proceeded to write the correct word, מֵאַחַד. The phrase מֵאַחַד מֵאֵלֶּה is patterned after two phrases with the feminine numeral, מֵאַחַת מֵהֵנָּה in Lev 4:2 and מֵאַחַת מֵאֵלֶּה in Lev 5:13. The repeated preposition מִן has a partitive sense, so that these phrases mean "any one of these things" (GKC, § 119 w, footnote 2). The antecedent of אֵלֶּה, both here and in 18:11, must be the violent acts of bloodshed in 18:10.

The idea is comparable to James 2:10: he who keeps the whole Law but fails in one point is guilty of violating all the commandments.

18:11 The verse division is not the happiest. What I have put in parentheses is an independent circumstantial clause in Hebrew, serving to underscore the difference between the righteous father and the violent son. (וְהוּא, "although he," must refer to the father.) The contrast is further highlighted by the adversative כִּי גַם, "but even," introducing further atrocities (beyond those in 18:10) by the son who does none of his father's righteous deeds.

In 18:11b–13a, Yahweh generally proceeds by changing statements that were positive in the case of the father (18:5–9) into negatives and vice versa. In 18:12, we encounter two minor phraseological variations.

18:12 The exploited parties are עָנִי וְאֶבְיוֹן, "the poor and needy," a stock phrase used already in 16:49, but especially characteristic of the Psalter. Here the phrase seems to emphasize that the son picks on those already down and out to take further advantage of them.

גְּזֵלוֹת גָּזָל—The parallels in 18:7, 16, 18 have singular nouns, which inevitably tempts some (e.g., Zimmerli[7]) to emend גְּזֵלוֹת to a singular. But late biblical Hebrew

---

[7]   Zimmerli, *Ezekiel*, 1:371.

shows a pronounced tendency to replace singulars with plurals, so that we need entertain no change here.

The last two clauses, with "fecal deities" and "abomination," are characteristic Ezekielianisms.

18:13 The long conditional sentence (18:10–13a) ends in the middle of the verse.

וָחָ֔י—This is the apodosis of the conditional sentence that began in 18:10. We meet this apocopated *waw* consecutive perfect of חָיָה again in 18:24 and several times in chapter 20. (It was used already in, for example, Gen 3:22; Ex 33:20; Lev 18:5; 25:35.) The unapocopated form would be וְחָיָה, which we meet in 18:23 and 33:11.

Already the LXX and some modern translations harmonize וָחָ֔י to the infinitive absolute (חָיֹה) in the clause חָיֹה יִחְיֶה in 18:9, 17, 21. Thus they read וָחַי לֹא יִחְיֶה as if it were וְחָיֹה לֹא יִחְיֶה, "he surely will not live." However, as the text stands, the context demands that וָחָ֔י be taken interrogatively, and in the context of the entire chapter, it is a rhetorical question: "Will he live?" The same is true of וָחָ֔י in 18:24. In Hebrew it is often enough for the context to require taking a phrase or clause as a question; other examples that could possibly be taken that way are in 16:43, 56, 59; 17:15. The answer to the rhetorical question then follows: לֹא יִחְיֶה, "he will not live!"

18:14 וְהִנֵּה֙ הוֹלִ֣יד בֵּ֔ן וַיַּ֗רְא—The interjection (translated "but if …") introduces the new case: the righteous grandson (18:14–17). The subjects of the two verbs are not specified, but in this context the subject of הוֹלִיד must be the wicked son (18:10–13) who now fathers his own son, and that son is the subject of וַיַּרְא, the one who "sees" the sins of his wicked father (who, in turn, was the son of the righteous man in 18:5–9).

חַטֹּאת—In this chapter the generic word for sin, חַטָּאת, appears here for the first time (also 18:21, 24). The feminine plural ("sins") is the antecedent for the feminine plural suffix at the end of the verse (כָּהֵן, "like them").

וַיִּרְאֶה—Instead of this second instance in the verse of "and he sees," many Hebrew manuscripts have וַיִּרָא, "and he was afraid," which is reflected in the LXX and Vulgate. Many critics happily emend, but even Zimmerli notes that יָרֵא, "to fear," is rare in Ezekiel.[8] "Fear" suggests a rather craven "righteousness," living correctly out of fear of consequences (perhaps witnessed in his own father) rather than out of any conviction. Furthermore, the use of two different forms of the imperfect of רָאָה so close together in the verse (וַיַּרְא … וַיִּרְאֶה; the first is apocopated) suggests a slightly different nuance. First he "sees" his father's sins, then the second use of "sees" implies spiritual discernment. He perceives the consequences of a life of sin and so refrains from his father's behavior. His positive actions are done out of love for God with all his heart, mind, and soul (Deut 6:5). It is a reminder that the OT is no more satisfied with mere exterior conformity to the letter of the Torah than is the NT (Rom 2:29; 2 Cor 3:6).

18:17 מֵעָנִ֞י הֵשִׁ֣יב יָד֗וֹ—This difficult clause is, literalistically, "from the poor he turned back his hand." The vast majority of modern commentators and translations

---

8   Zimmerli, *Ezekiel*, 1:372.

(except KJV and NKJV) follow the LXX and emend מֵעָנִי to מֵעָוֶל, producing the identical clause as in 18:8, where the righteous man "withdraws his hand from unrighteousness" (עָוֶל is also in 18:24, 26). But to me that general statement seems premature here; the generalities will come after stating the man's avoidance of one more particular offense (dealing with "interest"). A translation such as "he refuses to hurt/desists from harming the poor" makes better sense at this position in the verse.

הוּא לֹא יָמוּת בַּעֲוֺן אָבִיו—For the causal meaning of בְּ in the similar phrase בַּעֲוֺנוֹ, see textual note on it in 3:18.

18:18 אָבִיו כִּי־עָשַׁק עֹשֶׁק—As in 18:5, כִּי is the second word of the verse, and the entire verse is to be taken conditionally ("if"). The cognate accusative construction with עָשַׁק ("extort") and עֹשֶׁק ("extortion") is similar in meaning to those with גָּזַל and cognate nouns (18:7, 12, 16, 18) except that it may refer to something that at one time had been in the offender's possession legally; for example, "extortion" may consist of illegally withholding the wages due a laborer. The two verbs are frequently paired.

בְּתוֹךְ עַמָּיו—The plural of עַם technically refers to a father's relatives and is often translated "kinsmen." It is mainly found in fixed, traditional formulae, such as this one. It may be a homonym of the common עַם, "people" (so BDB, s.v. עַם II), or it may be a nuance of that same word (so *HALOT*, s.v. עַם; see meaning B).

לֹא־טוֹב—The litotes "not good" can be found throughout the OT (e.g., Gen 2:18), but it is especially found in Proverbs. See the plural phrase in Ezek 20:25; 36:31.

18:19 At this point, Yahweh quotes an objection from the audience. Whether it is hypothetical or was actually spoken by the Israelites, it probably does accurately reflect the original disagreement triggering the entire chapter. Another objection will be quoted in 18:25, and the question in 18:23 ("Do I really find any pleasure in the death of the wicked man?") may address an allegation of the audience. Ezekiel uses לָמָּה only in 18:31 ‖ 33:11, whereas only here he uses מַדּוּעַ. Attempts have been made to distinguish the two interrogatives, but they are hard to sustain. Yahweh's question and the answer he supplies must be distinguished, and since Hebrew punctuation does not clearly do that, I have differentiated them in the translation by inserting "answer."

Most commentators include 18:19–20 with the preceding two case studies (18:5–9 and 18:10–18), but Block, on the basis of the interjected question, more plausibly understands 18:19–24 as transitional.[9] Initially now in 18:19b–20 Yahweh parries the audience's objection (18:19a) by repeating his argumentation from 18:3–18. Then, in 18:21–24, he brings in new possibilities not considered so far, which, after a second audience query in 18:25, lead into the climactic option of repentance versus death in 18:25–32.

לֹא־נָשָׂא הַבֵּן בַּעֲוֺן הָאָב—The idiom נָשָׂא עָוֺן ("bear iniquity/punishment") without a preposition is used for a person who suffers the consequences of his own sin (e.g., 14:10). Here and twice in 18:20 that idiom is modified by the addition of בְּ to עָוֺן, meaning that one person does or does not "share in" the guilt of another (BDB,

---

9   Block, *Ezekiel*, 1:579–80.

s.v. נָשָׂא, Qal, 2 b). Hence בְּ has a partitive sense. I take the idiom in the direction "bear any of the consequences of."

18:20 צִדְ⸺קַת הַצַּדִּיק֙ עָלָ֣יו תִּֽהְיֶ֔ה—Both here and in the corresponding case of the wicked man, the Hebrew, literally, has "the righteousness/wickedness … shall be *upon* him." It is tempting to translate this as though God were keeping accounts with two ledgers, "credit" and "debit." Some translators do just that. As a metaphor that might be unobjectionable, but it lends itself too easily to an atomistic, legalistic misreading of the way God's "justice" is reckoned. See the pivotal expression of righteousness through faith alone in Gen 15:6, and the many NT affirmations and applications of *sola fide*, some of which cite Gen 15:6 (e.g., Rom 4:3, 9; Gal 3:6; James 2:23). A simple possessive translation ("the righteousness of the righteous person") seems best. Here Ezekiel is not answering recondite questions about precisely how God administers his מִשְׁפָּט.

רֶשַׁע,—The Qere (הָרָשָׁע) has the definite article, matching הַצַּדִּיק֙ earlier in the verse. The article on רָשָׁע is not strictly necessary but seems likely. For that matter, the sense would have been the same if both of the words had been anarthrous.

Greenberg notes the similarity of this verse with Deut 24:16, although Ezekiel reverses the sequence of the three parts, putting the summary statement first (in Ezekiel: "the person who sins is the one who will die"), then mentioning the case of the son before that of the father. Greenberg, citing what he calls "Seidel's rule," asserts that this reversal indicates a quotation or allusion to earlier Scripture. Since Deuteronomy has the more common sequence, discussing the case of fathers, then that of sons, the reverse order here would indicate that Ezekiel is borrowing from Deuteronomy. There is certainly nothing problematic about that. Exegetically more significant is Greenberg's understanding that the balancing of the two generations is another rhetorical device for dissociating one generation's guilt from another's.[10]

18:21 The Qal of שׁוּב can have the positive meaning "repent" (as here and in 18:23, 27, 28, 30) or the negative meaning "apostatize, turn away," as in 18:24, 26. The believer, who is righteous through faith, can apostatize/turn away from his righteousness and so forfeit salvation. If he persists in his unbelief until death, he will be damned for eternity. Hence Ezek 18:21, 24, 26 are among the Scripture passages that show the Calvinistic doctrine "once saved, always saved" is false.

חַטֹּאתָו֙—The Qere (חַטֹּאתָיו) reads the plural, "his sins," while the Kethib (חַטֹּאתוֹ) has the singular, "his sin." The Qere is probably correct after the preceding כָּל־.

18:22 פֶּשַׁע, "rebellion," is one of the three most common words the OT uses for "sin." The plural here (פְּשָׁעָיו) indicates the external manifestations of the underlying sinful nature and old spirit (contrast the "new S/spirit" in 18:31; also 11:19; 36:26). "Will not be remembered against him" may not be the most felicitous English, but it directly translates לֹא יִזָּכְרוּ לוֹ. For Yahweh not to "remember" sin is a common biblical anthropomorphism (e.g., Jer 31:34). The לוֹ is a dative of disadvantage (used

---

[10] Greenberg, *Ezekiel*, 1:332–33.

again in 33:16). Together with the Niphal of זָכַר, it implies "will not be held/charged against him." The forensic scene evoked keeps us from misconstruing the last clause in the verse as crass works-righteousness. In an essentially parallel passage, Hab 2:4 has וְצַדִּיק בֶּאֱמוּנָתוֹ יִחְיֶה, "and the righteous man by his faith shall live," cited in Rom 1:17; Gal 3:11; Heb 10:38.

18:23   The verb חָפֵץ is relatively rare in Ezekiel (elsewhere only in 18:32 and 33:11). It is used of Yahweh in many other OT passages. It may either be used with the preposition בְּ (as in the English idiom, "take pleasure in") or with a direct object. Here both constructions are used: after הֶחָפֹץ אֶחְפֹּץ first comes the construct phrase מוֹת רָשָׁע as a direct object, then follows בְּשׁוּבוֹ with the preposition. Since בְּמוֹת is used in 18:32 and 33:11, a number of Hebrew manuscripts have the preposition on מוֹת here too. The sense is unaffected.

18:24   וְחָי has an interrogative sense ("will he live?") also in 18:13. A translation of וְחָי (and of the preceding יַעֲשֶׂה) is missing in the LXX and Syriac, and so many critics delete it from the MT as a gloss, but there are insufficient grounds for omitting it. Allen, following Eichrodt, observes that "Will he live?" at the midpoint of 18:24, to be followed by the declaration "he will die" at the end of 18:24, is parallel to "he will surely live" at the midpoint of 18:21–22 (near the end of 18:21), which is followed by the declaration "he will live" at the end of 18:22.[11]

צִדְקֹתָו—The Qere is the plural צִדְקֹתָיו, which agrees with the following plural verb תִּזָּכַרְנָה.

בְּמַעֲלוֹ אֲשֶׁר־מָעַל—See textual note on the cognate accusative מָעַל מַעַל in 14:13.

18:25   לֹא יִתָּכֵן—The meaning of this entire verse and 18:29, which repeats much of it (also of the parallel verses 33:17, 20), turns on the meaning of the Niphal of תָּכַן. Translations vary widely. The Qal means "to examine, determine" the character of a person, which only God can do; Yahweh "examines/assays/weighs" a person's heart and spirit (Prov 16:2; 21:2; 24:12). Outside of Ezekiel the Niphal occurs only in 1 Sam 2:3, which has the corresponding sense: deeds are "examined/assessed" by Yahweh. The Piel is used to say that Yahweh alone can "measure" or "fathom" the heavens or ocean (Is 40:12; Job 28:25) and also to state that no one can "discern" or "understand" the Spirit of Yahweh (Is 40:13), which could give some credence to the charge Yahweh refutes here. In Ezekiel (18:25, 29; 33:17, 20), the Niphal seems to have a tolerative sense, as is often implied in Niphals: Yahweh does not "allow himself to be examined, determined, understood." The charge here, then, is that God's behavior follows no discernable norm or standard, is "unpredictable" (as I have translated it), "arbitrary," "unscrupulous," perhaps even "nonsensical." The common alternative renditions, "unfair," "unjust," and so on make the present complaint into an alternative expression of the initial "sour grapes" protest that sons are punished for their fathers' sins (18:2). If that is true, it must be related to the deterministic understanding of the proverb.

---

[11]   Allen, *Ezekiel*, 1:266, citing Eichrodt, *Ezekiel*, 234.

The charge here, then, is that a vindictive God does not care whether the person punished is righteous or wicked—just so somebody gets punished. That would be a conception of Yahweh similar to pagan deities, whose whims and moods one could never know.

18:26 וְעָשָׂה עָוֶל וּמֵת עֲלֵיהֶם—The suffix is plural ("will die because of *them*"; cf. בָּהֶם in 33:18) although עָוֶל is singular (or collective). The plural suffix apparently means to make a theoretical distinction between (singular) "unrighteousness" and its result: many unrighteous deeds, which are fatal.

18:27 הוּא אֶת־נַפְשׁוֹ יְחַיֶּה׃—The Piel of חָיָה can have various nuances. It can mean "restore to life, resurrect," but Ezekiel's theology is not Pelagian. "Save his life" or the like is required by the context. Perhaps this expression puts greater emphasis on the individual's responsibility than a mere "will live," and so it too (like 18:25, 29) combats any notion of an impersonal, inscrutable fate.

18:28 וַיִּרְאֶה—This harks back to the identical word in 18:14 (the second "he sees" in 18:14), which connotes spiritual discernment and recognition of the eschatological result of unrighteousness.

18:29 הֲלֹא דַרְכֵיכֶם לֹא יִתָּכֵן׃—The subject, דַרְכֵיכֶם, is plural, while the verb, יִתָּכֵן, is singular. Other manuscripts and versions make a grammatical adjustment one way or the other. With one exception in 18:29, the divine "way" in 18:25, 29 has been expressed in the singular, while the people's "ways" are in the plural. Defending the singular verb with plural subject, Keil suggests that the "ways" of the people are here summed up into one, as if to say, "What you say of my way applies to your own ways."[12]

18:30 אֶשְׁפֹּט—"Judge" must not be understood as "condemn." "Render a verdict" or the like would cause fewer exegetical problems. Similarly, each man's "ways," which Yahweh will judge, are easily misunderstood to refer only to actions (to the exclusion of faith), but the word hardly permits the exclusion of actions either; thus, it refers to faith *and* good works (or unbelief and evil works).

שׁוּבוּ וְהָשִׁיבוּ—See the textual note on the identical phrase in 14:6. At the end of the chapter, we will meet the Hiphil imperative alone (וְהָשִׁיבוּ, 18:32). Usually Hiphil verbs are transitive, but Hebrew has various intransitive Hiphil verbs, sometimes called "internal" or "elative" Hiphils, and in these verses (Ezek 14:6; 18:30, 32), the Hiphil of שׁוּב means "turn away" (BDB, Hiphil, 10, including Ps 85:4 [ET 85:3], of Yahweh) or "repent." Most likely, we have the same phenomenon here that we often meet in the synonymous parallelism of Hebrew poetry: the matching word in the second colon (here: וְהָשִׁיבוּ) is slightly more emphatic or expansive than its counterpart in the first colon (here: שׁוּבוּ). That understood, however, a more intensive counterpart to "repent" in English is hard to find!

לְמִכְשׁוֹל עָוֺן׃—We have also struggled before with this phrase. See the textual note on the similar phrase in 7:19, and also on מִכְשׁוֹל in 3:20. The phrase is peculiar to Ezekiel. The issue is whether the genitive is objective (something causes a person

---

[12] Keil, *Ezekiel*, 1:257.

to stumble into iniquity) or subjective (a person's iniquity causes him to stumble). Since Yahweh has just called for the Israelites to turn from their "rebellious acts," it seems preferable to understand עָוֹן as a collective restatement of the same thought, and the genitive as subjective: their "rebellious acts" are the "iniquity" that will cause them to stumble, unless they repent. "An iniquitous cause of stumbling" would then be a literal translation—that is, lest there be another, later relapse into apostasy.

18:31 הַשְׁלִיכוּ מֵעֲלֵיכֶם—The verb שָׁלַךְ (occurring only in Hiphil and Hophal) is quite general for "throw off/away, discard" and so forth. Keil suggests that the verb was used because the people's sins were mostly idols,[13] but idols were not normally carried around. The Hebrew adds "from upon yourselves," which suggests an unwelcome load or burden.

כָּל־פִּשְׁעֵיכֶם אֲשֶׁר פְּשַׁעְתֶּם בָּם—The suffix on בָּם must be construed as a resumptive pronoun, literally, "all your rebellions, which you have rebelled by them." Since the LXX, a similar text in Jer 33:8, and some other minor witnesses seem to have read בִּי ("rebelled *against me*"), many (e.g., RSV, NRSV) emend accordingly. The change might be considered stronger, but is by no means necessary.

וַעֲשׂוּ לָכֶם—Because the objects are "a new heart and a new S/spirit," almost any translation of this phrase risks being theologically problematic (see the commentary). Of the main alternatives, "get/acquire for yourselves" is much to be preferred over "make/create for yourselves," since sinful humans cannot do that. In some passages (e.g., Deut 8:17; 2 Sam 15:1; 1 Ki 1:5; Ezek 28:4), the idiom עָשָׂה לְ has the sense "acquire for oneself" (cf. BDB, s.v. עָשָׂה, Qal, 7) and is used with objects such as wealth, property, and attendants—things that one *obtains* but does not create.

Both in this verse and in 18:32b, the first imperative functions, in effect, as a condition, while the second describes the result if that condition is met. Thus we might phrase 18:31 as Yahweh's promise, "*If* you throw off from upon yourselves ... *then* you will receive ..."

Likewise, the end of 18:32 could be phrased, "If you repent, you will live!"

Commentary

Justification of the Individual

Theologically, this chapter must rank as one of the most important in the book. Its theme of the justification (or damnation) of the individual, expressed in 18:4 and 18:20 ("The person who sins is the one who will die"; 18:20 continues: "The righteousness of the righteous person shall be upon him alone, and the wickedness of the wicked person shall be upon him alone"), is one of those most immediately recognizable as Ezekielian. Equally important, but perhaps not as familiar, is that God desires all people be saved, as expressed in Ezek 18:23 as well as 18:32: "For I have no pleasure in the death of the dead man, says the Lord Yahweh. So repent and live!" However, this chapter's theme is subject to misinterpretation from two directions.

---

[13] Keil, *Ezekiel*, 1:257.

The first misinterpretation is highlighted by its history in modern higher criticism. In the early days of criticism, when Israel was thought to have gradually matured and outgrown its earlier primitive or even quasi-pagan views, it was common to assign to each biblical writer or tradition a particular "contribution" to "true" religion (defined by critics as "liberal, Protestant" religion). Ezekiel's enduring "contribution" was supposed to have been that of "individual responsibility." Allegedly, before Ezekiel, Yahweh and the people related to each other almost exclusively on a communal, collectivistic basis.

There is somewhat greater accent in Ezekiel on individual accountability, no doubt. In the fragmenting circumstances of the exile and the Diaspora, when many of the old bonds of family, community, and so on disintegrated, the environment of "every man for himself" almost inevitably required greater accent on an individualistic dimension of faith. But a greater accent in Ezekiel is a far different matter than a fundamental change in doctrine. It really is quite easy to demonstrate an individual accent in the Bible from the very outset: the individual creations of both Adam and Eve, and their individual punishments; the salvation of Noah and his family when the rest of humanity perished in the flood; the promises to individual patriarchs; the formulation of the Ten Commandments, in which "you" is singular in Hebrew; the frequent legal constructions with אִישׁ אִישׁ ("each person," e.g., Lev 15:2; 17:3; 20:2); and so on.

That the communal element is also prominent in Ezekiel (as in ancient Israel) needs no further demonstration than Ezekiel's frequent references to "the house of Israel" (e.g., 3:1, 4, 5, 7), "a/the rebellious house" (e.g., 2:5, 6, 8), the "people" (עַם, e.g., 3:5; 11:1), and so forth. But there is one well-known passage in the Torah that may have seemed to clash with the overriding accent of Ezekiel 18 in a special way. That passage, Ex 20:5–6 ‖ Deut 5:9–10, is part of the explanation for the First Commandment, but is known to Lutherans, following Luther's repositioning of it in the Small Catechism, as the "Close of the Commandments." In the traditional rendering of the RSV, Yahweh declares:

> I the LORD your God am a jealous [קַנָּא] God, visiting [פֹּקֵד] the iniquity of the fathers upon the children to the third and the fourth generation of those who hate me, but showing steadfast love [חֶסֶד] to thousands [although that could be another ordinal: "the thousandth (generation)"] of those who love me and keep my commandments.

In its original context, the passage serves partly as a proleptic warning to adults to watch their conduct because of the possible implications for their children. The accent is undoubtedly primarily vertical (*coram Deo*), but there may also be a horizontal dimension: "third" or "fourth" may be the maximum number of generations living together in an extended family. The passage does not teach an automatic transgenerational transmission of either God's jealousy or his love. In biblical history it may sometimes appear so (as, for example, the kings of northern Israel who continued in the sins of Jeroboam), but the determinative verbs (participles) remain "those who hate me" and "those who love me," which indicate that the subsequent generations continue in unbelief or in faith, respectively, and so are requited by God accordingly. It might have been very easy for Ezekiel's contemporaries to miss that aspect of Ex 20:5–6 (|| Deut 5:9–10) and use their misinterpretation of it as a convenient alibi and an accusation of divine injustice.

Nor should we forget the prohibition of transgenerational punishment in Deut 24:16. On its face, it might appear to contradict Ex 20:5–6 (|| Deut 5:9–10). But apparently Deut 24:16 was speaking of *human* judicial decisions, while Exodus 20 spoke of the divine administration of justice. In Ezekiel 18 Yahweh merely extends the principle of Deuteronomy 24 into a universal law.

Ezekiel 18 also was and is subject to a second misinterpretation from the opposite direction: an *individualism* as a virtual theology or ideology. Since the fall there probably never has been a time when the "old Adam" did not exhibit the tendency to exculpate himself by trying to transfer the fault for his sin to someone else, just as Adam did in Eden ("*the woman*, whom *you* put with me, *she* gave to me from the tree, and I ate," Gen 3:12). The nineteenth-century critics rallied around Ezekiel 18 and other allegedly supporting passages because they took the "individualism" in them to be of the essence of "true religion." Many philosophical and cultural currents contributed to this ever-strengthening movement, and we cannot begin to trace them all here.

Pietism's one-sided accent on the universal priesthood of all believers (and its minimization and even exclusion of the distinctive office of the ministry established by Christ) played a prominent role in religious dimensions of it. We still hear it in various versions in Evangelicalism's one-sided emphasis on a "direct, personal relationship with Jesus," and on the necessity of an individual's subjective experience of conversion or of being "born again" apart from Holy Baptism, the Sacrament by which God promises to effect rebirth (Jn 3:5; Titus 3:5–6). There is, allegedly, no need for the mediation of clergy, and "church" has a hard time becoming more than a sociological term (both larger issues, into which we cannot delve here). To be sure, every Christian does believe in Christ personally, but not in isolation from the rest of the church, and conversion is not just an experience (let alone a private, self-centered one), but incorporation into the body of Christ, frequently through infant Baptism, or if later in life, through hearing the Word, which then leads to participation in the Sacraments of the church (Baptism and the Lord's Supper). The many conversion accounts in the book of Acts confirm the corporate and Sacramental aspects of conversion and the ecclesiastical offices (especially apostle and evangelist).

Secularism, again fed by many streams, has made radical individual autonomy a hallmark of our age. "Spirituality" (usually eschewing orthodox Christianity) means an individual is free to select from a veritable cafeteria of religious options before him. "Pluralism," "unity in diversity," "tolerance" (a euphemism), "reconciled in Christ" (code for acceptance of homosexuals and lesbians), and "relativism" have become the new absolutes, from which significant divergence (including adherence to the absolutes of biblical Christianity) is impermissible. Individual or personal "choice" has almost become *the* synonym for religion, and by no means only as the rallying cry of those who wish to "take charge of their own bodies" (shorthand for the exaltation of individual autonomy to such an extent that a mother is even free to kill her unborn child). Any sense of religious obligation to any ends that we have not chosen for ourselves is renounced. But there is no point in extending this essay and belaboring the obvious.

Structurally, Ezekiel 18 is quite unique, as is evident at a glance. Between the initial word-event formula ("the Word of Yahweh came to me," 18:1) and "therefore" at the end of the chapter (18:30), there are hardly any of the usual prophetic markers or formulae. There is no command to the prophet to speak. The signatory formula "says the Lord Yahweh" occurs in 18:3, 9, 23, 30, and 32, but only in 18:9 does it close a subunit. The citation formula ("thus says the Lord Yahweh") and the recognition formula ("then you/they will know that I am Yahweh") never appear. We are given no clue as to precisely when the oracle was given or any information on what specific circumstance occasioned it. Apparently, we are to conclude that it represented an ongoing debate or discussion—and *mutatis mutandis*, it summarizes a perennial problem also for the Christian church. Such a conclusion is strengthened by the affinities the chapter has with chapters 3 and 33.

Were the chapter not located in the book of Ezekiel, one could almost forget that it has anything to do with the imminent destruction of Jerusalem and the Babylonian captivity. There is minimal reference to the community. Rather, the concern is with the individual person in his relationship before God. Some have suggested that the trigenerational scheme that follows (see the commentary on 18:5–18) represents the reigns of the previous three major kings, Josiah, Jehoiakim, and Jehoiachin; just as the tragic end of their reigns had not meant the end of the monarchy, so the present judgments should not be viewed too fatalistically. But that interpretation of the reason for the chapter's placement here strikes me as over imaginative, at best, and will be called into question by the next chapter.

As for its form, the chapter is a complex disputation speech, as its postulation of cases and legal terminology indicates. Typically in such a speech, we find a thesis, counterthesis, and ruling. That it is a priestly version of the form is evident by the large number of specifically ritual or cultic examples cited.

The chapter is commonly divided into two parts: 18:1–20 and 18:21–32. Another helpful division is offered by the three quotations of popular opinion in the chapter (18:2, 19, and 25), each of which occasions a long prophetic speech.

The Proverb about Sour Grapes (18:2–4)

18:2–3 Yahweh's question begins abruptly: "What do you mean … ?" It is addressed to the Israelites ("you" is plural in Hebrew). In the LXX Yahweh first addresses Ezekiel as "son of man" (see on 2:1) before addressing the Israelites. Except perhaps for rhetorical effect, it is doubtful if any significance can be attached to its absence in the MT.

The general import of the popular proverb ("Fathers eat sour grapes, and the teeth of their sons are set on edge"), which the people apparently love to quote, is clear even without much of a context. The Israelites do not question the principle that sin deserves punishment and that it is in fact punished. Rather, their complaint is that God is punishing the wrong people.[14] The immediate plea is perhaps not so much the people's innocence as it is an expansion of a certain cosmic determinism or fatalism by which they are being victimized. (The true gnomic sense of the imperfect verbs that Ezekiel uses suggests that.) Allegedly, God does not care who suffers so long as the balance of sin and punishment is kept. The thought approaches one common in paganism, that even the high gods are not totally free agents but are themselves bound to certain immutable laws of the universe.

While there is much to be made of this point of departure for understanding the exiles' use of the proverb, I doubt if the traditional interpretation can be dismissed completely. That traditional interpretation is that the issue in the proverb is theodicy, and those who use the proverb are protesting that they are suffering for sins they did not commit; hence they are accusing God of injustice. That issue of theodicy is given classical expression in Lam 5:7, and much of Ezekiel's counterargumentation in 18:4–32 seems to me to be best understood with that as its antithesis. People today may issue the same basic protest against God's justice, often with some appeal to genetics or the like as the cause of their suffering or of their sins—although the "nurture" side of the old "nature versus nurture" debate has not yet been completely silenced.

It is instructive to compare Jeremiah's use of the proverb (31:29) with Ezekiel's. Jeremiah's context is totally eschatological. There will be no more occasion to use the proverb because God will have fulfilled his promise to Jeremiah in his call (Jer 1:10; 31:28), and the "new covenant" with the Torah written on the people's hearts will have been established (Jer 31:31–34).

In Ezekiel, in contrast, Yahweh contents himself with simply making a dogmatic statement: people will no longer use the proverb because he sets forth his justice in the rest of the chapter. In the broader context of the book, the eschatological element cannot be said to be absent from this chapter, but it recedes very much into the background, except for the implications of the verdicts that the righteous will "live" (18:9, 17, 19, 21–22, 27–28) and the wicked will "die" (18:4, 13, 18, 20, 24, 26; see further the commentary on 18:4). After the inevitable judgment comes at the fall of Jerusalem (Ezekiel 33), God will manifest his grace so thoroughly in the new covenant (34:25; 37:26) that the pardoned sinner will no longer have any doubts about God's forgiveness, and the eschatological emphasis is especially pronounced in Ezekiel 40–48. But its rel-

---

[14] Greenberg, *Ezekiel*, 1:328, citing private communication with David Noel Freedman.

ative absence here is simply a reminder that Ezekiel, like other prophets, was not writing systematic theology.

18:4 In spite of the unusual syntax of the verse (see the textual note), its point is crystal clear. God relates to each individual personally, and he treats all alike: father, son, and any other human in any relationship to others.

"Die" appears in 18:4 for the first time in this chapter as the punishment for "the person who sins." It and its opposite, "live," form the two poles of justice throughout the rest of the chapter (as, for that matter, throughout the Bible). The words obviously may have many applications, depending on context. Especially with the destruction of Jerusalem looming, the simple issue of physical survival through the catastrophe may loom large. But the many cultic and ethical details that Ezekiel will detail shortly make it unlikely he is limiting himself to such a temporal conception. Just as exclusion from the community could be a form of living death (as when Adam and Eve were excluded from Eden; cf. Gen 2:17), it is much more so with God and the family of the righteous, the covenant people (hence excommunication is handing a person over to Satan, 1 Corinthians 5). Similarly, life involves inclusion in the family of God with all the promises of which the people are heirs (hence the Third Article of the Apostles' Creed confesses "the communion of saints" and "the life everlasting").

Special hermeneutical problems inevitably arise for the Christian understanding of such terms. I like to formulate the interpretive principle as one of *neither* "reading *into*" what the passages meant in their original context *nor* of failing to "read *out*" of them all that they must mean in the light of *all* of Scripture, including the fulfillment in the NT, specifically in Christ. And here exegesis may stop short of homiletics. The exegete *qua* exegete must strive to reproduce the original grammatical yield. While the homiletician may begin with his text's B.C. context, his primary obligation is to proclaim what the text says in its Trinitarian fullness, as fully revealed in the NT, so as to call his hearers to repentance and faith in Jesus Christ—and thus to eternal life in him.

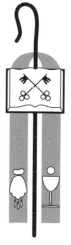

How much the OT saints knew about the details of eternal life and eternal perdition is not easy to nail down. But plainly their hope for the afterlife was not merely some shadowy quasi-existence in Sheol, as "critical orthodoxy" depicted it. In addition to bodily resurrections (1 Ki 17:17–24; 2 Ki 4:8–37; 13:21) and assumptions into heaven (Gen 5:24; 2 Kings 2), one must consider OT promises such as Is 25:6–9; 26:17–19; Dan 12:1–3; and the implication of passages such as Ezek 37:1–14. At the same time, OT saints plainly did not know all that we are now able to confess since Christ has risen from the dead. The faith of the OT ("Yahwism") is the same religion as that of the NT ("Christianity").[15] The two may be distinguished, but must not be divorced, lest we end up with two fundamentally different religions, sharing only a little "Judeo-

---

[15] See further under "Outline and Theological Emphases" in the introduction.

Christian" ethical idealism. If we wish to press the word "know," we may compare the difference between the OT faith and that of the NT to the difference between our present knowledge and that we will have in the eschaton, as we confess with St. Paul that "now I know in part; then I shall understand fully, even as I have been fully understood" (1 Cor 13:12).

Three Cases of Individual Retribution (18:5–18)

If we understand 18:4 as Yahweh's thesis, he plainly is not content simply to state it. He illustrates that thesis at great length by presenting three case studies in divine justice. Possibly the number three was chosen as symbolic of completeness, or it might reflect the Deuteronomic rule that two or three witnesses were required to prove a criminal case (Deut 17:6; 19:15). The three cases are as follows: (1) Ezek 18:5–9, the righteous man; (2) 18:10–13, his wicked son; and (3) 18:14–17, the righteous grandson. With only minor variations, the same standards are applied to all three groups. As many have noted, there are structural similarities with other OT passages that list standards for righteousness or requirements for a particular office,[d] especially in the priestly legislation of Leviticus (e.g., Leviticus 18–21), and also to lists outside of Israel, at entrances to temples (cf. Ps 24:3–6) or for positions of leadership. The wicked shepherds of Ezekiel 34 will be accused of failing to observe similar standards.

(d) E.g., Deut 17:14–20; Job 22:1–9, 29–30; Prov 31:5–9; Is 33:14–16

Formally, the style of the priestly legislation in the Pentateuch reflects Ezekiel's own background and training. Some of the most noteworthy are the forms of the verdicts. For example, just as Leviticus 13 gives extensive criteria based upon which the priest is to declare a person either "clean" or "unclean," so Ezek 18:5–18 gives the criteria based upon which Yahweh declares a person either "righteous" (e.g., צַדִּיק הוּא in 18:9) or unrighteous ("wicked," 18:20), with the corresponding verdicts (with infinitives absolute), either that "he will surely live" (חָיֹה יִחְיֶה, 18:9, 17, 19, 21, 28) or "he will surely be put to death" (מוֹת יוּמָת, 18:13; cf. 18:18). The Torah has similar verdicts or promises with forms of "live" (חָיָה).[e] Far more frequent is the same verdict of death as in Ezek 18:13 (מוֹת יוּמָת).[f]

(e) E.g., Lev 18:5; Num 21:8–9; Deut 8:1, 3; 16:20; 30:16, 19

(f) E.g., Ex 21:12, 15–18; Lev 20:2, 9, 10, 15; 24:16–17

The lists of standards in 18:5–18 contain both positive and negative statements. Most of the statements in 18:5–9 and many of the ones in 18:10–13 and 18:14–18 have pairs of related behaviors, and each such pair is demarcated by a comma in the translation. For example, "he does not eat on the mountains and does not lift up his eyes to the fecal deities of the house of Israel" is one pair, and the two actions are related because of the association of the "fecal deities" with the "mountains" (see Ezekiel 6). Most of the standards by which the righteous man and the wicked man are identified are what Christians would regard as part of the "moral" law, still valid after Christ, although a few are "ceremonial" and no longer operative after the all-encompassing ceremony of the sacrifice of God's own Son on Calvary. (St. Paul spends considerable time on this point, especially in Romans and Galatians.)

Some Protestant commentators see the stress on the moral law here as evidence for the allegation that the prophets preferred ethical over ritual action,

but the more radical anti-sacramental and anti-ritual reaction of the Calvinistic-Zwinglian Reformation betrays itself there, and one notes that liturgical infidelity evidenced in pagan worship is not overlooked, although usually dealt with quite summarily. The OT itself does not make a rigid distinction between moral and ceremonial laws, no doubt partly because the two were (and to some extent still are!) so intertwined in practice.

Another way of saying that is to stress, as we have repeatedly, that "righteousness" (צְדָקָה, 18:5, 19–22, 24, 26–27) in the OT, as in the NT, is primarily a forensic, vertical relationship of justification *coram Deo* ("before God"). Sanctification inevitably follows and displays the relationship *coram hominibus* ("before men"). If this is lost sight of, the OT, more so than the NT, will be misread moralistically. See AC IV, VI, and XX.

The Righteous Man (18:5–9)

18:5–6 The first pair of transgressions (here avoided by the "righteous" man, 18:5) involve "the mountains" and "the fecal deities" (18:6). In chapter 6 Ezekiel had prophesied against the "mountains" of Israel because of the false worship practiced there. The verb "eat" (אָכַל) was not used in that chapter, but eating on the mountains (18:6, 11, 15) probably refers to eating sacrifices offered to "fecal deities" (18:6, 12, 15), who are associated with (but not limited to) the mountains (for "fecal deities," see the last textual note on 6:4). The idolatrous sacrificial meals were often eaten on the "high places" (בָּמוֹת; see on 6:3), which apparently were not necessarily, but preferably, located on physical heights. Eating on the mountains occurs in no legal codes and nowhere else in the OT except Ezekiel (18:6, 11, 15; 22:9).[16]

The parallel clause, "… lift up his eyes to the fecal deities," appears in no legal codes either, but it too is typically Ezekelian. It may refer more to "fine idolatry" (committed in the heart) in contrast to the more overt, public act of eating idolatrous sacrifices, mentioned first. "Lift up his eyes" implies looking for help, trusting in, and perhaps making supplication to the deities, rather than to the Creator and Redeemer. Similar phrases appear famously in Psalm 121:

I lift up my eyes to the mountains.
From where shall my help come?
My help is from Yahweh,
Maker of heaven and earth. (Ps 121:1–2)

The second pair of offenses in the verse ("defile his neighbor's wife … approach a menstruous woman") highlights sexual transgressions. It is an alternate wording and slight abbreviation of Lev 18:19–20. Block plausibly

---

[16] In 33:25, eating "on/over the blood" (עַל־הַדָּם ׀ תֹּאכֵלוּ) is associated with lifting up the eyes to the fecal deities, and so some needlessly wish to emend eating "on the mountains" (אֶל־הֶהָרִים in 18:6, 11 and עַל־הֶהָרִים in 18:15) to "on the blood." The expression in 33:25 undoubtedly refers to the practice prohibited by Lev 19:26 (about which see Kleinig, *Leviticus,* 399–400). That practice might be the offense of eating meat with blood still in it or (as Kleinig deems most likely) the pagan, occult practice of eating beside a pit that contained the blood of the sacrificed animal.

suggests that Yahweh alludes to that passage because that chapter goes on to speak of the land vomiting out its Canaanite inhabitants because their sexual sins defiled the land, and warns that the same will happen to Israel if the Israelites defile themselves in the same ways (Lev 18:24–30).[17] As Ezekiel prophesies, the land would soon vomit out those Israelites to be exiled to Babylon.

To "defile" (Piel of טָמֵא) a woman refers to intercourse outside of marriage (Gen 34:5, 13, 27). Extramarital intercourse also causes the man to become "defiled" (Qal of טָמֵא, Lev 18:20), as also do bestiality and homosexuality (Lev 18:22–24). These sexual sins are to be punished by death (Lev 20:10–16).

This part of the verse considers adultery and intercourse with a woman during her period as equally heinous. There has never been a moment's doubt that the prohibition of adultery is part of the eternal moral law written on the conscience and obvious from creation, as well as part of the Ten Commandments, and the prohibition of adultery (and also of homosexuality) is reiterated in the NT (e.g., Mt 5:27–32; 19:9; Rom 13:9; 1 Cor 6:9–20; Gal 5:19–21), which also affirms that the perpetrators deserve to die (Rom 1:18–32). But to the best of my knowledge, abstention during menstruation has never been considered an ethical issue in Christendom, since it was deemed part of the OT ceremonial law fulfilled and abolished in Christ.

18:7–8 After the sampling in 18:6 of activities that the man who is "righteous" (צַדִּיק, 18:5) refrains from doing because they are incompatible with "justice" and "righteousness" (צְדָקָה, 18:5), the next two verses turn to a list of virtues that exemplify the behavior of the righteous man. They especially include activities that would impact the weaker members of the covenant community. Ezek 18:7–8 reflects the spirit (if not the exact wording) of the Torah (e.g., Lev 5:21–23 [ET 6:2–4]; 19:9–18; Deut 24:10–15), both in avoiding sins against the neighbor and in the positive witness of caring for the hungry and homeless.

The "logic" at work in Ezek 18:7–8 may be fruitfully related to the often misunderstood negative formulation of most of the Decalogue ("you shall not … ," e.g., Ex 20:7). Positively formulated mandates offer only two alternatives: obedience or disobedience. In contrast, a negative formulation outlines a perimeter or circumference beyond which one cannot go without self-exclusion from the community. Within those boundaries, however, one is free to do whatever the regenerate heart or the "law of love" invites (Lev 19:18; Rom 13:8–10). After listing "the fruit of the Spirit," beginning with "love," St. Paul declares that "against such things there is no law" (Gal 5:22–23); how could there be? Attributed to St. Augustine is the maxim "Love God, and do whatever you please," a striking affirmation of the *iustus* ("saint") part of the paradox of biblical righteousness.[18]

---

17 Block, *Ezekiel*, 1:572.

18 Justified through faith, believers are "saint and sinner simultaneously." Of course, "do as you please" refers to the desires of the regenerate, new nature in Christ (corresponding to what

While these behaviors are in accord with Yahweh's self-revelation in the Scriptures (a point made more explicit in Ezek 18:9), it may also be said that all societies have laws, or at least ideals, that recommend such charitable and philanthropic actions. Those outside God's covenant community still have what is often called God's "natural law": the principles of fairness to which even the creation itself testifies, and the law written on the heart, even though after the fall into sin that knowledge of right and wrong has become corrupted and people often flout or ignore it (Rom 1:18–32).

Since Ezekiel here is speaking of the "righteous" man (18:5), it is important that we recognize his actions as the good fruit produced by a good tree, not fruit that will make a bad tree good (Mt 7:15–20). The righteous man's deeds, also in the civil realm, are the fruit of his faith—the product of the Gospel, which he believes. The righteousness God imputes to him as a member of his kingdom spills over into deeds of justice and righteousness in society. OT Israel was both "church" and "state," but even so, we can see the resemblance between the situation here and that in the NT era, where the Christian, as a member of God's (right-hand) kingdom of grace (the church), "practices justice and righteousness" (Ezek 18:5) also in society and the world (God's left-hand kingdom).

The unrighteous man in 18:10–13 does not perform these same deeds. Nevertheless, we must concede that an unbeliever too can do acts of "civic righteousness," that is, things that society and the natural law teach are good and right. When he does, his acts are commendable enough as judged by other people, and they do benefit society, but any "righteousness" he thereby possesses or attains is only before men (*coram hominibus*), and does not avail before God (*coram Deo*). His deeds are only relics of God's good gifts in creation; they do not render the man righteous before God and do not lead the man (or the beneficiaries of his actions) toward God. We can, do, and must join hands with those of all religions—or of no religion—in humanitarian efforts. But we dare not forget to emphasize that the external cooperation itself does not bridge the theological chasm between those involved; only concord in the Gospel provides true unity.

Lutherans affirm the biblical doctrine that general revelation (the "natural law") does not reveal God's grace in Jesus Christ, and it condemns the sinner. Natural man wrongly imagines that sufficient effort will eventually satisfy God and lead to eternal life, but the result of works-based "religion" is either despair or self-satisfied delusion. Sinners can even abuse general revelation to manufacture their own gods, for example, by personifying the forces of nature, resulting in fertility gods or the earth mother-goddess. The Law in Scripture (special revelation) shows that such "religion" actually leads away from the triune God and is cause for the unbeliever to be damned to hell. The necessary

---

Ezekiel calls the "new heart" and "new S/spirit," 11:19; 18:31; 36:26), not to gratification of the sinful nature, which the believer is to mortify (Rom 8:13; Col 3:5).

(g) E.g.,
Rom 6:1–4;
1 Pet
3:18–22; see
also Ap IV
7–47; LC II
34–46; FC
SD XI 33–42

work of the Law is to "kill" the sinner and all his hopes in such "religion," so the Gospel (special revelation, Word and Sacrament) can raise the sinner to new and eternal life in Christ.[g]

18:9 This verse summarizes all the preceding. The man is not righteous because of atomistic adherence to so many stipulations; rather, his righteous actions are manifestations of a comprehensive right relation to Yahweh. Justification by grace and through faith logically precedes sanctification. Finally comes the apodosis—a double one: "that man is righteous and he will surely live." Yahweh's verdict pronounces him truly righteous and bearing the promise of eternal life. The paragraph thus comes full circle, forming an inclusion parallel to 18:5.

The Wicked Son (18:10–13)

18:10–13 This is Yahweh's second case study, that of the wicked son. It is the shortest of the three cases (nine discrete points are made, in contrast to sixteen in the first and twelve in the third). In general, the illustrations are the same as in the first, although in different order. Above all, the behavior of the son is at every point the polar opposite of his father. The strong language used in these verses paints a picture of one whose attitude toward other people, even toward their lives, is the farthest removed from his father's. Far from being concerned about the poor, the son even has no compunctions about taking the life of anyone who stands in the way of his own goals.

After the long list of outrageous actions by the son who is the very antithesis of his father, we suddenly meet the apodosis in the form of a question, "Will he live?" which is immediately answered negatively: "He will not live!" (18:13). The emphatic infinitive absolute of "live" (חָיֹה) is not used here (see the textual note), but the infinitive absolute מוֹת, "die," is used with one of the main parallel verbs that follow, "he will surely be put to death" (מוֹת יוּמָת). That clause is found in decrees by kings (e.g., Gen 26:11) and is especially common in God's decrees for execution.[h] Whether or not the passive clause in Ezek 18:13 implies human agency in the execution is uncertain—and perhaps, being considered beside the point here, is left unspecified. The form יָמוּת ("he will die") is used in the comparable situations of 18:24, 26 (and also in 18:17, 21, 28); those verses likewise do not specify the cause of death.[19]

(h) E.g., Ex
21:12,
15–17; 22:18
(ET 22:19);
Lev 20:2,
9–10, 15;
24:16–17

The original force of the final expression, "his blood will be upon him," was apparently to exculpate legal executioners of blood guilt (cf. "his blood will be upon his head" in Josh 2:19; Ezek 33:4; cf. 2 Sam 1:16; 1 Ki 2:32–33, 37). But since (as just noted) Ezekiel 18 does not indicate whether human executioners would carry out the death sentence, probably the clause's force here is to say that the son has no one but himself to blame since he spurned the ex-

---

[19] A few Hebrew manuscripts have יָמוּת in 18:13 and most of the major versions support that reading, so many prefer to emend the verb here. However, since יָמוּת is used in those other verses, יוּמָת is the *lectio difficilior.*

cellent example of his father and chose to go about as far down the opposite path as possible.

The Righteous Grandson versus His Wicked Father (18:14–18)

18:14–17   These verses form Ezekiel's third case study, the righteous *grandson* (the son of the original righteous man's wicked son). It is slightly shorter than the first case study, that of the righteous grandfather (18:5–9), but the changes are minor and largely only stylistic.

It is a parenthetical observation here, and certainly not Ezekiel's main point, but one can hardly help but note how often in history intergenerational shifts move just as Ezekiel describes them. It often seems to be an innate manifestation of adolescent original sin that the second generation rejects the values and principles of the parents. It may be only indifference, but often it flares into open rebellion. One notices this pattern in church life as much or more than elsewhere. If some minimal contact can be maintained with that second generation, the third generation may once again be open to God's Word. Painful as the falling away of the second generation is, the church can take hope that at least some of the grandchildren will exemplify God's promise that "the Word of our God shall stand forever" (Is 40:8).

As in Ezek 18:13, the apodosis or conclusion appears very suddenly in 18:17: "he will not die because of his father's iniquity; he will surely live." There is an organic connection between faith and works. The main point is that the grandson lives in his own faithfulness, regardless of the faithlessness of his father.

18:18   Ezekiel makes yet a quick retrospective glance back at the unrighteous example of the middle generation (18:10–13). The point is to nail down one final time that each individual, and he alone, is answerable for his own faith and life. A slight novelty appears, however, in the pronounced accent here on the community (אָח, "brother," and the plural of עַם, "kinsmen"), "the entire nation as a consanguineous extended family."[20] Not that his membership in a covenant community makes him any less answerable before the divine Judge, but since "no man is an island,"[21] his behavior, whether righteous or unrighteous, inevitably affects many more than himself. This is also a reminder that although, as we noted, many of Ezekiel's examples involved standards of conduct that can be considered part of general revelation, the prophet's focus here is on the elect family of God created by his Word (special revelation) and covenant, with all its promises and commandments.

Individual Justification Reiterated (18:19–20)

18:19–20   A question that Yahweh knows the audience is asking provides the springboard for him both to summarize the point he has been emphasizing

---

[20]   Block, *Ezekiel*, 1:579.

[21]   John Donne, *Devotions upon Emergent Occasions* (1624), no. 17.

all along and to begin a transition to a slightly different emphasis. The people's question, "Why does the son not share in the guilt of the father?" contains the potential for a contradiction if it is not understood correctly. The original charge against God in the proverb ("Fathers eat sour grapes, and the teeth of their sons are set on edge," 18:2) appears to express a deterministic notion that God punishes the innocent. The "sour grapes" proverb was virtual dogma for the people: they preferred to accuse Yahweh of injustice rather than to admit any guilt on their part. Since they regarded themselves as innocent, they argued that their suffering must be the punishment for their fathers' sins. Their incredulous question in 18:19 flows from their presumption that their proverb in 18:2 was true.

Part of Yahweh's answer simply reiterates the revealed divine rule of retribution. "The person who sins is the one who will die" (18:20) is a verbatim repetition of the end of 18:4. But the rest of the answer is more extensive than 18:4 since it first includes the case of the righteous grandson (18:19b) and then generalizes to include other righteous people ("the righteousness of the righteous person shall be upon him alone") as well as the wicked ("and the wickedness of the wicked person shall be upon him alone"). In saying this, Yahweh is repeating the point he made in chapter 14: if the three eminently righteous men Noah, Daniel, and Job were among the wicked Israelites, those three alone would be saved because of their righteousness, which would not avail for any others (14:14, 20).

In Case of Repentance or Apostasy (18:21–28)

If a Wicked Man Repents (18:21–23, 27–28)

The reader should not miss the fundamental shift in tone beginning with 18:21. God is not an unfeeling, legalistic bookkeeper in his judgments. The following verses (18:21–32) must be added to the many others in the book (many of them easily overlooked) that correct the mistaken portrait of the God of Israel as simply judgmental and vindictive, rather than as the same triune God whose love is fully revealed in Christ and the NT. Block aptly entitles the remainder of this chapter "Opening the Door to Divine Mercy," and the immediately following verses (18:21–24) "The Two Ways"[22]—a major biblical theme in Deuteronomy and almost constitutively in the Wisdom literature (e.g., Psalm 1; Proverbs).

So far in the chapter, and clearly in the three cases presented by Yahweh in 18:5–18, a person has been *consistently* either righteous or unbelieving. But what about cases where a person's orientation to God and their course of life are completely reversed—a wicked man becoming a believer or a faithful man apostatizing? It is these possibilities that are considered now in 18:21–28.

18:21–22   The first example, that of the repentance of the wicked, is a sort of a fortiori argument from the question of 18:19: if a repentant and reformed reprobate will not be punished for his former deviancy (18:22), how

---

[22]   Block, *Ezekiel*, 1:581.

much less should a son who has always been faithful suffer for the evil deportment of his father, an entirely different person (18:19)?

By the three conditional clauses in 18:21, Ezekiel summarizes what the Bible understands by repentance: (1) a person "returns" (שׁוּב, the usual OT term for repentance) to the God from whom he had been estranged; (2) his new life is characterized by specific creeds and deeds (Ezekiel's accent on the latter does not imply a minimization of the former); and (3) beyond what can be tabulated by any list, his entire demeanor and desire have a different fulcrum.

18:23 This emphatic question by Yahweh between the two examples (18:21–22 and 18:24) almost takes one by surprise: "Do I really find any pleasure in the death of the wicked man, says the Lord Yahweh? Is it not rather when he repents of his ways and lives?" Even though expressions such as these are relatively few statistically, they really are far closer to the heart of Ezekiel's message (and that of all Scripture) than the many thunderous threats of judgment that punctuate the book. It really needs to be quoted much more than "the person who sins is the one who will die" (18:4, 20).

As already Moses had stressed in Deuteronomy, God desires to bestow blessing and life on his people, not the curse and death (Deut 30:15–20). Compare the very similar affirmation of St. Paul: God "desires all people to be saved and to come to a knowledge of the truth" (1 Tim 2:4). There is no *Schadenfreude* ("malicious joy at another's misfortune") in God. Accordingly, he is not only just and fair, but merciful and gracious, and he punishes only those who do not believe. The state of grace is open for all who desist from trying to play God themselves. Obviously, this line of thought needs to be filled out Christologically;[23] it lies at the very heart of the Gospel and can scarcely be emphasized too much. And this sudden exclamation of pure grace is uttered through Ezekiel on the eve of the fall of Jerusalem (587 B.C.) to an obdurate crowd of exilic rebels who are not only blaming their predicament on God himself, but accusing him of enjoying the exercise of judgment!

If a Righteous Man Apostatizes (18:24, 26)

18:24 Here we have the obverse of the situation described in 18:21–22. The vocabulary is somewhat a reprise of that used in 3:20. The faith and good behavior of a formerly righteous man are no more transferrable to the other side of God's ledger than are the evil deeds of the former unbeliever. Since all depends on God's free grace, his "memory" does not calculate debits versus credits at the moment of judgment. Everyone will be judged in that state in which he is found before God at the moment of judgment. Hence the recurrent admonition of especially the Gospels for Christians to "watch" and "be ready" (e.g., Mt 24:42–46; 25:13).

---

[23] Since Christ is the one who died and rose, he holds the keys to death and life. He offers life freely and grants it to all who believe. See, for example, 1 Jn 1:5–10; Rev 1:17–18; 2:7–8, 11; 20:12–15; 22:17.

Israel's Ways, Not Yahweh's, Are Unpredictable (18:25, 29–32)

The last part of the chapter turns on the people's new charge that Yahweh's behavior is unpredictable or arbitrary. Yahweh vigorously refutes the charge by insisting that it is the other way around. In so doing, he simply reiterates his previous pronouncements that he does not judge by a person's past, but by his disposition and behavior when the Judge is at the door (cf. Mt 24:33; James 5:9; Rev 3:20).

18:30 The first half of the verse simply restates and summarizes the message of the entire chapter: each person will be judged individually according to his own standing before his Creator and Redeemer at the moment of judgment—never mind his past faith and life, or that of any of his relatives. A typical judgment oracle would end here with "therefore" (לָכֵן) plus the verdict and the signatory formula "says the Lord Yahweh" (18:30). But matters do not end with some capricious or ineluctable fate. The door of mercy is still wide open—to all who will repent, as emphasized by the repetition of the Hebrew verb in a more emphatic form (שׁוּבוּ וְהָשִׁיבוּ, "repent and turn away"). The remaining verses of the chapter (the summary and climactic ones) will repeat and expand upon the thought.

18:31 As elsewhere, Ezekiel pinpoints the real problem as one of the לֵב, "heart," and the רוּחַ, "spirit." Juxtaposed as they are here, the two words are virtually synonymous. The real problem is interior, a matter of the will and of the mind. But in 11:19 and 36:26 such a radical moral and spiritual transformation is clearly presented as a miraculous, divine act and gift of a "new heart" and "new S/spirit" (see the commentary on 11:19). Here, on the surface at least, the change is recast as a command.

If we were to isolate this and the following verse and have Ezekiel, in effect, telling the dead to raise themselves, we would not only involve him in self-contradiction but also raise questions about his theological soundness in general. We must let Ezekiel interpret Ezekiel as the immediate example of the basic hermeneutical principle of interpreting Scripture by Scripture.

The problem might be described in various ways, but I am often tempted to speak of two "languages": first, the language of human experience and rationality, and second, the language of revelation and theology. We struggle with the issue of language all the time ourselves, and countless parallels could be found in the Bible itself. When we say "believe," "repent," and so on in the imperative, who else could possibly respond positively—humanly speaking—other than the person addressed? To his consciousness, it will indeed appear as though he, of his own free will, has made the decision to repent and believe in Christ.

Yet, theologically, we will stress increasingly that the decision was not really his—that a fallen sinner is by nature simply incapable of making that choice. Fallen man retains the "freedom" to refuse and reject, but has lost the ability to "get … a new heart and a new S/spirit" (18:31). That he obtains only by God's action, by dying and rising with Christ in Word and Sacrament, in the dual operation of both Law and Gospel. God does not impose his grace on the unwilling; only after the will has been changed by God can one speak theologically of a person's "freedom" to believe and live accordingly. Without repentance and the perfect righteousness of Christ, which is imputed to the sinner through faith, the just and predictable God cannot forgive the sinner, and the death sentence remains inevitable.[24]

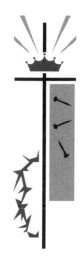

A probable parallel in Jeremiah (21:8–9) speaks more concretely to the historical situation of those trapped in Jerusalem under siege: either to remain in the city (and die) or surrender to the Babylonians (and live). We have no way of knowing to what extent Ezekiel's debate with his audience of exiles involved those still back in Jerusalem, but as we have seen at many points, those already exiled were at one with them in spirit, and the theological principles remain the same. Ezekiel's prescinding from historical specifics facilitates theological exegesis, but we easily change biblical revelation into a philosophy of religion if we forget that the issues of life and death, of belief or unbelief, always operate in this world of space and time into which God has placed us.

The rhetorical question at the end of Ezek 18:31, together with the repetition of the thought of 18:23 in 18:32, poignantly ends the chapter with an emotional (anthropopathic) and standing divine invitation to all to repent and live in the life for which God created them before the fall—and who, through his Son, has provided the means for them to do so.

---

[24] See AC XVIII, "Free Will." One may also see the exposition of Josh 24:15, a favorite text for those who advocate decision theology, in Harstad, *Joshua*, 783–87.

A Lament for Israel's Princes

Translation

19 ^{1}"As for you, take up a lament for the princes of Israel: ^{2}You shall say,

" 'What a lioness was your mother!
    Among the lions she crouched.
In the midst of the young lions
    she reared her cubs.
^{3}She raised up one of her cubs,
    and as he became a young lion,
he learned to tear prey;
    he even ate people.
^{4}When the nations heard about him,
    he was trapped in their pit,
and they brought him in hooks
    to the land of Egypt.

^{5}" 'When she saw that she waited in vain,
    that her hope was lost,
she took another of her cubs
    and made him a young lion.
^{6}He prowled around the lions,
    for he too had become a young lion.
He learned to tear prey;
    he even ate people.
^{7}He knew how many widows he made
    as he ravaged their cities.
The land and its contents were desolated
    by the noise of his roaring.
^{8}Nations set upon him
    from the surrounding provinces.
They spread their net for him,
    and he was trapped in their pit.
^{9}They put him in a wooden collar with hooks
    and brought him to the king of Babylon.
They brought him into prison
    so that his roar would not be heard again
    on the mountains of Israel.
^{10}" 'Your mother was like a vine in your vineyard.
    Planted by water,
fruitful and full of branches
    it was because of abundant waters.

¹¹The strong branches became for her
     scepters of rulers.
His stature soared high among the clouds,
     and in his height he was visible with the abundance of his branches.
¹²But it [the vine] was uprooted in wrath
     and to the ground it was hurled.
The east wind dried up its fruit.
Its strong branch was torn off so that it withered,
     and the fire devoured it.
¹³Now it is planted in the desert,
     in a dry and thirsty land.
¹⁴Fire has come out from its main branch
     and consumed its fruit,
so that it no longer has a strong branch,
     a scepter for ruling.'
"This is a lament, and it became a lament."

Textual Notes

19:1 וְאַתָּה֙ שָׂ֣א קִינָ֔ה—For the significance of this beginning of the chapter and for the definition of קִינָה, see the commentary below. After "you" the Peshitta adds ܟ‍ܒ‍ܪܢ‍ܫ‍ܐ ("son of man") to harmonize with the characteristic beginning of Ezekielian units (וְאַתָּה בֶן־אָדָם, e.g., 2:6, 8; 3:25; 4:1; 5:1; 7:2), but that is almost certainly secondary. נָשָׂא can mean "to lift up the voice," implying a loud utterance, often with weeping (see BDB, 1 b (5)).

אֶל־נְשִׂיאֵי יִשְׂרָאֵל:—The preposition could mean "for," "over," or "about." The latter two meanings are more commonly expressed by עַל, but Ezekiel uses the two prepositions rather interchangeably. For the significance of נָשִׂיא (here plural), see commentary below. The LXX has the singular (τὸν ἄρχοντα, "the ruler"), which some critics find attractive because of the singular pronominal suffix on אִמְּךָ in 19:2. The LXX reading may be due to haplography of one of the two contiguous *yod*s. The plural in the MT better reflects the content of the chapter: the lioness in 19:2–9 had (plural) "cubs" and the vine in 19:10–14 had (plural) "branches."

19:2 מָה אִמְּךָ֙ לְבִיָּ֔א—The exclamatory translation I have given to the initial clause agrees with RSV, NRSV, NIV. Others take it as a question and answer, "What was your mother? A lioness" (ESV; similarly KJV, NKJV), and adduce that when מָה is used as an exclamation, it usually accompanies either an adjective or a verb (see BDB, 2 b), not a noun, as here. Some claim that the Masoretic accents support understanding it as a question, but the same accents on the three words in this clause are used in the three-word exclamation beginning with מָה in 16:30. Likewise, some claim that the LXX took it as a question, but τί can also be used as an exclamation (see LEH, citing 2 Sam 6:20). The debate is legitimate, but to my mind, the question (immediately answered!) is jejune.

Ezekiel uses four different words for "lion" in 19:2 alone. As far as we know, the distinctions between them are fluid. Probably the major motive for using the different terms is the desire for variety in vocabulary (rather than contrasting meanings). Likewise, Job 4:10–11 uses five different terms all meaning "lion."

לְבִיָא is a unique Aramaized feminine form of לָבִיא, which is used primarily in poetic contexts and for both masculine ("lion") and feminine ("lioness"). The "mother" who is a לְבִיָא probably is the queen mother (the mother of the ruling Davidic king; see the textual note on 19:3).

אֲרִי is the most common and general Hebrew word for "lion." It has two plural forms: אֲרָיִים appears to be masculine, and אֲרָיוֹת appears to be feminine. But אֲרָיוֹת can be grammatically masculine, and in 19:2, 6 it is translated "lions" (cf. the masculine parallel כְּפִרִים in 19:2).

On the basis of this verse, כְּפִיר is thought to refer to a "*young* lion," but except in Judg 14:5 it is always used rather figuratively.

גּוּר is a general word for "cub," but is also used of young jackals. That they are young is clear from the verb used with them, the Piel of רָבָה (רִבְּתָה), to "bring up, rear" (BDB). The "young lions" and "cubs" here probably represent the royalty and nobility of Judah.

19:3 The queen mother can in this case be identified as Hamutal (2 Ki 23:31; 24:18; Jer 52:1), widow of Josiah and mother of Jehoahaz and Zedekiah. This identification is certain because of the reference to Jehoahaz's deportation to Egypt in Ezek 19:4 (see the next textual note). She "raised up" Jehoahaz (19:3), evidently singling him out by training him or elevating him in rank, as the Hiphil of עָלָה (וַתַּעַל) may mean here. It is nowhere else attested in the sense of "train" (the definition given in BDB, Hiphil, 3), but elsewhere it can mean "exalt" (BDB, 7). (The Syriac has "one of her cubs grew," as though reading וַיַּעַל.) Ezek 19:5 indicates that the queen mother played a prominent role in king-making. 2 Ki 23:30 attributes the accession of Jehoahaz to "the people of the land," but that really does not conflict with the role of the mother here. The translation "raised up" fits known leonine behavior, where cubs are known to learn hunting from older animals, especially their mothers. Most of Ezek 19:3 will be repeated in 19:6.

אָדָם אָכֵל:—Depictions of lions eating humans is a common motif in ancient Near Eastern art. Early church art pictures the martyrdom of Christians in this way in the Roman Colosseum.

19:4 The poetic language, still depicting the prince as a lion, must be compared to the historical detail given in 2 Ki 23:30b–34 ‖ 2 Chr 36:1–4. For one thing, in the mere three months Jehoahaz reigned, he would hardly have had time to develop such a fearsome reputation among the nations. He was deposed after only three months because he was sympathetic with the pro-independence policies of his slain father, Josiah. When the Egyptians gained control of Canaanite territory for a few years after the battle of Megiddo (609 B.C.), they preferred to have their own compliant puppet on the throne of Judah. 2 Kings reports only that Jehoahaz "did what was evil in the eyes of Yahweh" (2 Ki 23:32; unlike his father in this respect) and that Pharaoh Neco "bound" him at Riblah in Syria and eventually took him to Egypt, where he died (2 Ki 23:33–34).

וַיִּשְׁמְעוּ אֵלָיו—The idiom שָׁמַע אֶל/עַל, meaning "to hear about," makes perfect sense, and one can compare, for example, Gen 41:15; 2 Ki 19:9; and Is 37:9. Many critics emend the Qal to a Hiphil with some sense like "sound an alarm" (see RSV, NRSV), as does Zimmerli,[1] who also wants to take the nations as the object, but there is no versional or manuscript evidence for emendation, and such unnecessary changes strike me as emendation for the sake of emendation.

בְּשַׁחְתָּם נִתְפָּשׂ—This will be repeated in 19:8. שַׁחַת is usually translated "pit"; it was concealed by some kind of covering until the animal fell or could be lured into it. The word is used in that sense in various other biblical and extrabiblical texts. Some translate "net/snare," but a separate word refers to a "net" in 19:8. Lions were, in fact, hunted in both ways, and both methods are documented in ancient literature. The Niphal of תָּפַשׂ referred to people being "caught" also in 12:13 and 17:20.

בַּחַחִים—This will be repeated in 19:9, where too this implement is used to deport a person to a foreign country. Some suggest "shackles," "muzzles," "manacles," or the like. More likely are some type of piercing objects, "hooks" of some sort. Later Yahweh declares that he will put "hooks" (חַחִים) in the jaws of the Nile monster (29:4) and of Gog (38:4). In Is 37:29 ‖ 2 Ki 19:28 Yahweh declares to Sennacherib, "I will put my hook [חַחִי] in your nose," suggesting that he will receive the same treatment he had inflicted on others. Extrabiblical sources attest the leading of captives pierced with hooks, and also with shackles.

Probably all this language is conventional and poetic, not necessarily a literal, "photographic" report of Jehoahaz's treatment. But since he was the only king of Judah exiled in Egypt, we do briefly touch certain historical ground here (as opposed to historical symbolism with uncertain referents).

19:5 וַתֵּרֶא כִּי נוֹחֲלָה—The common Piel of יָחַל means "to wait (for, patiently)." The Niphal occurs only here and in Gen 8:12 and 1 Sam 13:8 (both contested texts). Various emendations have been suggested, but taking it in the passive sense with the mother as subject, "she saw that *she was made to wait [in vain]*," seems to be the best expedient.

An alternative view is that the subject of both נוֹחֲלָה and אָבְדָה is the following feminine noun תִּקְוָה, so that the first poetic line leaves the reader in suspense until the subject is supplied at the end of the second line. English would require rearranging the word order: "She saw that her hope tarried and perished" (see BDB, s.v. יָחַל, Niphal).

19:6 וַיִּתְהַלֵּךְ—Various nuances could attend the Hithpael of הָלַךְ, which by itself merely indicates walking back and forth. I have chosen "prowled" (so also BDB, 1 b; ESV; NIV).

19:7 The first half of this verse is a notorious crux. There are ancient variants for every word and modern proponents of diverse meanings. The list of proposed emendations and alternate interpretations is long.

---

[1] Zimmerli, *Ezekiel*, 1:389.

וַיֵּדַע אַלְמְנוֹתָיו—This is, literally, "and he knew his widows." Many medieval commentators took יָדַע in its common euphemistic sense, "to know (sexually)," and so interpreted the clause to mean that he raped widows. Keil essentially agrees ("He [Jehoiachin] not only devoured men, but laid hands on defenceless widows").[2] Similar is ESV.[3] Block translates "consorted with" and, following the leonine imagery, explains that the now-dominant male consolidates his status by copulating with the females of the previously dominant male.[4] Support for this view can be adduced in the common ancient practice of conquerors more or less openly appropriating the predecessor's wives and concubines. Absalom's behavior when he temporarily overthrew David (2 Sam 16:20–22) makes plain that the custom was known in Israel also. The idea would be that the second cub (Ezek 19:5–9) was far more cruel than his predecessor (the first cub, in 19:3–4), menacing also the non-combatant female part of the population. The Vulgate has *didicit viduas facere*, "he knew the widows he has made," and Greenberg explains that "his widows" does not mean simply the widows within his reach, but "the women made widows by him" (comparing חַלְלֵיכֶם in 11:6, which has the sense of "those whose death you have caused").[5]

I have adopted "he knew how many widows he made," which in part follows the Vulgate and Greenberg, but does not take the verb in a sexual sense. Finally, the exegete must choose his translation/interpretation. Mine I believe to be defensible, but I would not care to be dogmatic about it.

In place of וַיֵּדַע, many of the ancient versions apparently read a verb form with ר instead of ד. In both the ancient Canaanite script and the square Aramaic script later used for biblical Hebrew, *dalet* and *resh* are similar enough to be easily confused. The mainstream LXX translated καὶ ἐνέμετο τῷ θράσει αὐτοῦ, "and he fed in his boldness," as if the verb were a form of רָעָה, "graze, feed on." Aquila translated the verb as ἐκάκωσε, as if it were וַיָּרַע, a Hiphil of רָעַע, "do harm to," probably reflected by "he ravaged their strongholds" (RSV and NRSV). These variations have the merit of continuing an idea expressed in the previous verse of tearing prey and eating. The Targum has ואצדי בירנייתיה ('aphel of צְדִי), "he made desolate his castles," which may be reflected in the NIV ("he broke down their strongholds").

While the Vulgate supports אַלְמְנוֹתָיו as meaning "widows," the Targum and Theodotion have "his castles/fortresses," perhaps reading the word as אַרְמְנוֹתָיו (with *resh* instead of *lamed*). The confusion or dialectical variant between *l* and *r* is common in many languages, including apparently those spoken in Ebla in northern Syria and in modern Japan. In Is 13:22 אַלְמְנוֹתָיו apparently means "his fortresses," and so the Targum and Theodotion may have read אַלְמְנוֹתָיו, but as a dialectical variant meaning "his fortresses." The conquest of "fortresses/citadels" (plural of אַרְמוֹן) is part of

---

[2]   Keil, *Ezekiel*, 1:261.

[3]   ESV has "he seized their widows" with a footnote on "seized" explaining that the Hebrew means "knew" (the antecedent of "their" is the "men" at the end of 19:6).

[4]   Block, *Ezekiel*, 1:596, 596–97, nn. 29–30, 602.

[5]   Greenberg, *Ezekiel*, 1:351.

prophecies of defeat in, for example, Is 23:13; 34:13; Amos 1:4, 7, 10, 12, 14. At any rate, RSV, NRSV, and NIV have "strongholds," which is usually defended as a better parallel with "cities" in the next colon.

וְעָרֵיהֶם הֶחֱרִיב—There is no textual problem with this clause. Greenberg suggests taking the Hiphil of חָרַב not merely in its general sense of "devastate," but as specifically meaning "depopulate," as in Zeph 3:6.[6] (The Qal in Ezek 6:6 [first occurrence] and 12:20 may mean "be depopulated.") Assyrian kings sometimes boast of a plague of lions devastating territory. Thus this colon would speak of the consequence of the young lion eating human flesh (19:6).

וַתֵּשַׁם אֶרֶץ וּמְלֹאָהּ—See the textual notes on the similar clause with the identical verb in 12:19. Here the verb has a compound subject and is feminine to agree with אֶרֶץ (but not with the masculine noun מְלֹא).

19:8 וַיִּתְּנוּ עָלָיו—The combination נָתַן עַל can be a military idiom for "set upon, attack"; see the fuller idioms in 4:2. Likewise, שִׂים עַל (e.g., 23:24) and שִׁית עַל (Ps 3:7 [ET 3:6]) can mean "set upon, attack."

מְדִינָה is an Aramaism, "satrapy" in the Persian period, but it was also used earlier in the more general sense of "administrative district." It apparently entered the Hebrew vocabulary in the era of Solomon (Eccl 2:8; 5:8), and it was used in the era of the divided monarchy (see 1 Ki 20:14–19).

וַיִּפְרְשׂוּ עָלָיו רִשְׁתָּם—The same idiom was in 12:13 (see the textual note on it there) and 17:20.

19:9 In general terms, this verse parallels the second half of 19:4, but many details are unclear. סוּגַר is a hapax legomenon. It is usually associated with the common verb סָגַר, "to close," and so most English translations render it "cage" (NKJV, RSV, NRSV, NIV; KJV is apparently being free with its "ward"). However, newer archaeological discoveries have convinced most commentators that it is cognate to Akkadian *sigaru*, a sort of "neck stock" or ladder-like "wooden collar," known both from written texts and pictorial representations to have been used to transport both people and animals. Precisely how its use was combined with חַחִים, "hooks" (used also in 19:4), is unclear, but that probably only reflects our partial understanding of the practices of the day.

וַיְבִאֻהוּ ... יְבִאֻהוּ—The second use of the (third masculine singular) Hiphil of בּוֹא (with third masculine singular suffix) lacks the expected *waw* consecutive. Presumably the conjunction on the first one does double duty. The action denoted by the second verb is clearly contemporaneous with that of the first.

בַּמְּצֹדוֹת—The noun מְצוֹדָה in Eccl 9:12 means "fishnet," while in Is 29:7 it means "stronghold." Closely related nouns (מְצָד, מְצוּדָה) can mean "stronghold." The ancient versions generally have "prison" here, which may be a meaning of the Hebrew word, and my translation follows that understanding. It is possible that the versions might have read the word with a *resh* rather than *dalet*, and so as a noun from צָרַר, "bind, shut up, restrict," although there is no common Hebrew noun for "prison" from

---

[6] Greenberg, *Ezekiel*, 1:352.

that root. NKJV translates "nets" (KJV, curiously, "holds"), and Greenberg defends it ("toils").[7] However, that seems to be a strange parallel to the first half of the verse.

לְמַ֫עַן לֹא־יִשָּׁמַע קוֹל֖וֹ ע֑וֹד—This can be taken as either a purpose or a result clause. If we take it in the first sense, as I have, it might imply that the Babylonian conquerors of Judah were posing as liberators (as conquerors often have done throughout history and still tend to do).

19:10   אִמְּךָ֙ כַגֶּ֫פֶן בְּדָמְךָ֖—As in 19:2, this second section of the chapter (19:10–14) opens abruptly with a reference to "your mother." However, the leonine metaphor of the previous section is abandoned and replaced by a simile, literally, "like the vine." The definite article may be generic (characteristic of the genus, "vine"), or it may refer specifically to the Davidic dynasty as *the* vine." The latter seems more likely.

A major crux is בְּדָמְךָ֖, literally, "in your blood," a text attested in some ancient Greek translations and in the Vulgate. (The mainstream LXX strangely has ὡς ἄνθος ἐν ῥόᾳ, "like a flower in a pomegranate.") KJV translates "in thy blood," but NKJV ventures "in your bloodline," apparently attempting to cement the association between the vine and the entire dynasty.[8] A more likely sense would be "on account of the blood you shed." Such an understanding was once common, and it fits with the opprobrium associated with the vine in chapter 17. While "blood" does not occur in chapter 17, the rebellion of the "vine" (Zedekiah) causes the death of many Israelites (17:17, 21). One may also think of the "blood" throughout chapter 16 in reference to Jerusalem (16:6, 9, 22, 36), including the shedding of blood (16:38). However, the picture in 19:10 is of a vine yielding fruit as God intended, so a reference to bloodshed seems out of place here (it might fit better in 19:12–14).

Another possibility is to take "blood" as figurative of red grape juice, as in Gen 49:11, Jacob's blessing of Judah, with which this section continues to have connections.

Two Hebrew manuscripts read כַּרְמְךָ ("your vineyard"), which plausibly could be the original because of the common confusion of ד and ר (see the first textual note on 19:7) and the similarity of ב and כ. Most contemporary English versions follow this expedient (NIV: "in your vineyard," often arbitrarily omitting the suffix as in RSV, NRSV, ESV: "in a vineyard"), and so have I.

A more radical solution, which has found favor with Block and tentatively in Greenberg, proposes a faulty word division in the MT and reads כַּגֶּ֫פֶן בַּדִּים כִּי, "like a vine full of shoots, because …"[9] Text critically, this is not out of the question, because words often were not divided in ancient manuscripts. But it is somewhat more venturesome than the solution I have adopted, and the result is a redundant parallelism with עֲנָפָה in the next line.

---

[7]   Greenberg, *Ezekiel*, 1:352.

[8]   The commentary below contends that the lions and the vine are best understood in reference to the entire Davidic dynasty.

[9]   Block, *Ezekiel*, 1:607, n. 68, and Greenberg, *Ezekiel*, 1:353, both citing Julius A. Bewer, "Textual and Exegetical Notes on the Book of Ezekiel," *JBL* 72 (1953): 159.

שְׁתוּלָה—For the meaning of שָׁתַל, see the textual note on it in 17:8. Here, the passive participle is feminine (as are later forms in the verse) because גֶּפֶן is a feminine noun.

פֹּרִיָּה֙ וַעֲנֵפָ֔ה—The feminine singular participle of פָּרָה retains the original *yod* as the third radical. The adjective עָנֵף ("full of branches") occurs only here, but the noun עָנָף ("branch") is more common.

מִמַּיִם רַבִּים:—In the Psalms "many waters" are often symbolic of the forces of chaos and evil (e.g., Pss 18:17 [ET 18:16]; 32:6), but there is no hint of such overtones here.[10]

19:11 Virtually every detail in the translation of this verse is disputed. There are inconsistencies in number and gender. The most likely explanation is that the text moves from the many kings in David's line ("rulers" and the other plurals in the first part of the verse) to the one final king under whom the state collapsed (the masculine singular forms, e.g., "his stature" and "his height," in the latter part of the verse).

וַיִּהְיוּ ... אֶל־—Instead of saying that her branches "became" rulers' scepters (a metaphorical statement of fact), NIV and some others take this to mean that her branches were "fit for" being (a) royal scepter(s). However, that shifts the emphasis to the competence or worthiness of the Davidides to be kings, and the history of Israel does not bear witness to their merit. Usually in Hebrew "become" is expressed with הָיָה and לְ (BDB, s.v. הָיָה, II 2 d, e) instead of אֶל. However, Ezekiel uses הָיָה אֶל for "be/become" in, for example, 45:2, 11. I have retained a literal translation of the idiom.

The MT has plural nouns (מַטּוֹת ... שִׁבְטֵי) for "branches" and "scepters," whereas the LXX has singular nouns. The same Hebrew words are singular later (מַטֶּה in 19:12 and twice in 19:14; שֵׁבֶט in 19:14). Later in the verse, the verb וַתִּגְבַּהּ and the suffixes on קוֹמָתוֹ and בְּנִבְהוֹ are singular, which assume a singular antecedent. Hence some critics emend the initial verb (וַיִּהְיוּ) and the two nouns (שִׁבְטֵי ... מַטּוֹת) to singulars, as in the interpretive translations of RSV and NRSV: "Its strongest stem became a ruler's scepter." NIV also has "a ruler's scepter." Some have suggested that at least some of the plural forms in the MT are plurals of majesty or of amplification. However, מֹשְׁלִים is plural ("rulers"), and indeed many kings emerged from the Davidic line (the vine).

Then there is the matter of gender. The suffixes on קוֹמָתוֹ and בְּנִבְהוֹ are masculine, but גֶּפֶן ("vine," 19:10) is virtually always feminine, and 19:12 refers to it as feminine. Masculine forms are often used in place of feminine ones, but the more likely explanation is that the masculine suffixes do not refer to the vine, but to one king as one of the vine's shoots or tendrils (cf. בַּדֶּיהָ in 19:14), hence קוֹמָתוֹ and בְּנִבְהוֹ are rendered "his stature" and "his height," respectively. Zimmerli would "solve" the problem by eliminating the whole last half of the verse as an addition inspired by 31:3–5,[11]

---

[10] The phrase is used in contexts of both judgment and salvation, including Song 8:7. One may see the study in Mitchell, *The Song of Songs*, 1192–97, 1227–29.

[11] Zimmerli, *Ezekiel*, 1:390–91.

but as Greenberg points out, 19:12 speaks of the vine being hurled to the ground, so it must previously have risen above it, as described in the second half of 19:11.[12]

עַל־בֵּין עֲבֹתִים—There is disagreement about the meaning of עֲבֹתִים. The noun עֲבֹת usually refers to a rope. The form here is its masculine plural, which is rarer than עֲבֹתוֹת, its feminine plural form (Joüon, § 90 e). Already BDB (s.v. עֲבֹת, 2) included the possibility that עֲבֹתִים in 19:11; 31:3, 10, 14 means "interwoven foliage." The adjective עָבֹת in Ezek 6:13; 20:28 (and other verses) means "leafy," and עֲבֹתִים might be the masculine plural of that adjective. *HALOT* (s.v. עָבֹת I) proposes that עֲבֹתִים here is the plural of an otherwise unattested noun עָבֹת, "branch," and that עֲבֹתִים in 31:3, 10, 14 should be emended to עָבוֹת, which would be the plural of עָב, "cloud" (the OT attests both עָבוֹת and עָבִים as plurals of עָב, "cloud"). Almost all English versions beginning with KJV (also RSV, NIV, ESV) translate it here as "thick branches" or the like. However, the metaphor of the towering plant in 19:11; 31:3, 10, 14 makes the most sense if the term means "clouds."[13] (The more common Hebrew word for "cloud" is עָנָן, e.g., 1:4, 28.) Those who defend the translation "branches" appeal to 31:3, 10, 14, but partisans of "clouds" appeal to the same verses!

וַיֵּרָא בְגָבְהוֹ בְּרֹב דָּלִיֹּתָיו׃—This is, literally, "he was seen in his height in the abundance of his branches." If עֲבֹתִים means "clouds," then its meaning is not duplicated by דָּלִיֹּתָיו at the end of the verse, since דָּלִית clearly means "branch, bough" (as also in 17:6, 7, 23). Instead, the slight variation between "clouds" and "branches" is rather typical of Hebrew poetic parallelism, which here might be called synthetic (not strictly synonymous, but not antithetical either).

19:12 וַתֻּתַּשׁ בְּחֵמָה—The verb probably is a Qal passive (third feminine singular imperfect) of נָתַשׁ (so *HALOT*) rather than a Hophal (BDB) because the Hiphil is not used in the OT. The Qal commonly means "to pull/pluck up." Following the initial imperfect with *waw* consecutive, the rest of the verbs in the verse are perfects. That probably reflects the tendency in later biblical Hebrew not to employ the *waw* consecutive (cf. their absence in 21:12; 39:8). חֵמָה referring to divine "wrath" is common in Ezekiel. For the "day of wrath" theme, see the commentary on 7:8.

הִתְפָּרְקוּ וְיָבֵשׁוּ מַטֵּה עֻזָּה—The verbs, which I have rendered "was torn off so that it withered," are plural, even though the subject, מַטֵּה עֻזָּה ("its strong branch"), is singular. (At least the verbs agree with מַטֶּה in being masculine.) The plural verbs may have been influenced by the plural מַטּוֹת ("branches") in 19:11. As Zimmerli points out, since the vine's fruit and branches were introduced together in 19:10, it is not out of place to link the two together in the account of their destruction, so the implied subjects of the verbs could include the preceding word, פִּרְיָה ("its fruit," a collective).[14]

---

[12] Greenberg, *Ezekiel*, 1:353.

[13] So also Keil, *Ezekiel*, 1:262, and Block, *Ezekiel*, 1:607.

[14] Zimmerli, *Ezekiel*, 1:391. His comment is intended to explain the mention of "fruit" alone in the preceding phrase. He rejects the emendation of פִּרְיָה to בַּדֶּיהָ, "tendrils," which occurs in 19:14—an emendation favored by Allen (*Ezekiel*, 1:285) and others. But Zimmerli is ultimately much more radical; he would delete the two verbs as "syntactically unrelated to the context" and thus "a later interpretative addition."

19:13 בְּאֶרֶץ צִיָּה וְצָמָא—This is, literally, "in a land of dryness and thirst," but almost all translations render the nouns as adjectives ("in a dry and thirsty land"). Since the LXX has no translation of the second noun with *waw*, וְצָמָא, many wish to delete it.[15] Often part of their argument is metrical (the first line of the verse has three words, and deleting one here makes a two-word line). However, that is a very iffy criterion, especially since 19:10–14 conforms to the supposed 3:2 קִינָה meter even less regularly than 19:2–9. See "Introduction to Ezekiel 19" below.

19:14 בַּדִּים can mean "rods" or "shoots" of vines (BDB, s.v. בַּד II, 3 (b)), so the construct phrase מִמַּטֵּה בַדֶּיהָ ("its main branch") is, literally, "the branch of its shoots." The routine critical doubts and speculations about the rest of the verse could be noted, but none affect the sense (intrinsically debatable because of the poetic form). Formally, however, we cannot fail to note two inclusions: קִינָה in both 19:1 and 19:14, framing the chapter, and the similarity between מַטּוֹת עֹז אֶל־שִׁבְטֵי מֹשְׁלִים in 19:14 and מַטֶּה־עֹז שֵׁבֶט לִמְשׁוֹל in 19:11, framing most of the second section of the chapter (19:10–14).

Commentary

Introduction to Ezekiel 19

With this chapter, we are abruptly plunged back into the political circumstances of Judah's last days, where we were in chapter 17. That the chapter begins with Yahweh's simple address to Ezekiel, "as for you" (וְאַתָּה),[a] makes it sound more like a section within a unit than the beginning of a new unit. Indeed, Ezekiel, as the likely editor of his book, may well have placed chapter 19 here deliberately, as the last section of a unit that began with 17:1 and clearly ends at the close of chapter 19.

(a) As in, e.g., Ezek 2:6, 8; 3:25; 4:1, 3, 4, 9; 5:1; 7:2

If so, why does chapter 18, which is about individual justification, intervene between chapters 17 and 19, which are about the kings of Judah? Perhaps the best explanation is that the placement of chapter 19 here with its simple beginning forces the reader to connect the last kings of Judah (the subject of this chapter) with the hypothetical individuals whose retribution is described in chapter 18. That chapter's depiction of individual retribution for the wicked man (18:10–13) and for the righteous man who apostatizes (18:24, 26) gives the rationale for the harsh judgment coming upon the Davidic dynasty. Chapter 19 applies the principles of God's consistent justice more concretely to the kings themselves, demonstrating that Yahweh does indeed operate predictably (see 18:25, 29) and fairly in the administration of justice.

Ezekiel is to raise a קִינָה ("lament," 19:1) over Israel's rulers. The word is not easy to translate, especially in this context, and considerable ink has been used in discussion of its form, content, and meaning. Usual translations are "lament(ation)" or "dirge." Evolutionistic thought once dogmatized that the form originated in pagan rites of the death and resurrection of a vegetation deity. If there is any truth to such a hypothesis, the form was thoroughly demythologized and desacralized in Israel.[16] The "lament" (קִינָה) form has a

---

[15] For example, Zimmerli, *Ezekiel*, 1:391.

[16] Block, *Ezekiel*, 1:593; Zimmerli, *Ezekiel*, 1:392.

demonstrable connection with the death of an individual or nation, but this evinces no necessary connection with paganism. The association of the "lament" with death is established by passages such as 2 Sam 1:17, where David composes a "lament" (קִינָה) over Saul and Jonathan after their deaths, and the "lament" (קִינָה) for King Josiah at his death, mentioned in 2 Chr 35:25. Those two passages also use the cognate verb קִין, "to sing a funeral song" (*HALOT*). Ten of the eighteen uses of "lament" (קִינָה) in the OT occur in Ezekiel, usually in connection with prophecies of judgment and death.[17]

At its acme in the history of higher criticism, form criticism posited a quite rigid pattern which the genre originally was supposed to have followed. Most characteristic was the 3:2 meter it was supposed to have (a line of three Hebrew words, followed by a line of two Hebrew words), sometimes styled the "limping meter," supposing a necessary connection between the metrical imbalance of the line and a certain bodily motion. Less prejudiced analysis demonstrates that there is indeed a connection, but not so mandatorily as once supposed. Many laments do not use 3:2 meter, and 3:2 meter often appears in non-lament material. Ezekiel will frequently employ 3:2 meter in his oracles against Tyre and Egypt throughout chapters 26–32, and several of those oracles are called a "lament."[18]

Critics formerly also alleged that another necessary characteristic of a "lament" (קִינָה) was the use of אֵיךְ or אֵיכָה ("how!") as its opening word. Neither of those words appears in Ezekiel 19, but אֵיךְ does begin the "lament" (קִינָה) that starts in 26:17 (it is also in 33:10). The book of Lamentations begins with אֵיכָה ("How lonely sits the city … !"), and substantial parts of that book are in a 3:2 meter, though it is never called a "lament" (קִינָה). Hebrew tradition tends to use incipits as names of books, and so the Hebrew title for Lamentations is אֵיכָה.

Finally, laments were supposed to follow a "once versus now" pattern, contrasting former glories with present ignominy. That pattern does hold true here (and for the depiction of Jerusalem in Lamentations).

There still is no unanimity on precisely what to label the form(s) employed in Ezekiel 19—nor, I suppose, does there have to be. Pointing to the way it treats plants and animals practically as human, Block notes the chapter's similarity to fables and labels the whole composition as a "parody" that uses the "lament" (קִינָה) form in an incongruous way to arouse attention.[19] Allen notes

---

[17] The plural is in 2:10, describing the scroll Ezekiel is to eat as containing "laments." The singular is in 19:1, 14; 26:17; 27:2, 32; 28:12; 32:2, 16.

[18] Ezek 26:17; 27:2, 32; 28:12; 32:2, 16. The editors of *Biblia Hebraica Stuttgartensia* attempted to format all of chapter 19 in a 3:2 meter. If one disregards the Masoretic accents, this can be accomplished in most of 19:2–9 (the first section of the chapter; see below) but it can be maintained in 19:10–14 only by radical emendation of the received text. The forthcoming *Biblia Hebraica Quinta* (the fascicle on Ezekiel is not yet published as of this writing) is supposed to follow the lineation of the Masoretic text, which my translation reflects.

[19] Block, *Ezekiel*, 1:594–95.

that the traditional time perspective of the form has been changed: usually a "lament" (קִינָה) mourns a death that has already taken place, but Ezekiel turns the genre into an oracle of impending judgment that represents future doom as having already taken place (a sort of prophetic perfect).[20] Greenberg does not hesitate to speak of the chapter as containing two allegories.[21] It is probably most helpful to approach the chapter as an extended metaphor, possibly even as an allegory, if that term is not misunderstood as negating the underlying historicity of the events described.

We might as well note at the outset that in neither ancient nor modern times has any consensus been reached as to which kings the figures represent. The only exception is the first lion cub, which is forcibly brought to Egypt (19:4), and which undoubtedly represents Jehoahaz (2 Ki 23:34). The problem is probably a case, however, of asking the wrong question. Let Greenberg (speaking initially of the second "allegory" in the chapter, 19:10–14) summarize:

> The allegory appears to be schematic, with fidelity to history subordinated to the elegiac theme of onetime glory turned into disgrace and ruin. The lioness and the vine stand for the glorious source out of which calamitous issue sprang. ... [To take them as a particular person] needlessly commits one to a specificity in interpretation ... beyond that which the data allow, thus shifting attention from their typical features to historical details that the allegory is not meant to illumine.[22]

The "lament" is "for the *princes* of Israel" (19:1). Consistent with his practice throughout the book (see the commentary on 12:10), Ezekiel refuses to dignify Israel's kings with their ordinary title, "king" (מֶלֶךְ), and instead uses נָשִׂיא (as in, e.g., 12:10, 12; 21:12, 25), which is ordinarily translated "prince." Here it almost certainly does refer to the last kings of Judah, although it might include other nobility as well. Originally, it referred to premonarchical leaders of Israel, perhaps tribal chieftans. Not that Ezekiel is anti-royalist in principle: he will use "king" (מֶלֶךְ) later of the second David, the eschatological, messianic King (37:24), although even in such contexts he retains a certain preference for prophesying about Christ as the "Prince" (נָשִׂיא, 34:24; 37:25; see the word's use also in, e.g., 44:3; 45:7–9, 16–17). The main point is that the present occupants of the throne have so sullied it by their behavior that they no longer deserve the honorable title. The royal (messianic) promises have not been abrogated, merely suspended until the advent of "the King of Israel" (Mt 27:42; Mk 15:32; Jn 1:49; 12:13).

The chapter readily divides itself into two sections (Ezek 19:2–9 and 19:10–14), each of which has "your mother" in Hebrew at or near the beginning of the first verse (מָה אִמְּךָ, 19:2; אִמְּךָ, 19:10). In the first section, the dominant figure is that of a lioness. In turn, the first section is easily subdivided into

[20] Allen, *Ezekiel*, 1:286.

[21] Greenberg, *Ezekiel*, 1:355 and passim.

[22] Greenberg, *Ezekiel*, 1:356–57.

two parts: (1) the lioness and her first cub (19:2–4) and (2) the lioness and her second cub (19:5–9). Readers will probably find it more opaque than the second section, 19:10–14, where the dominant figure is that of a (grape)vine.[23] Ezekiel 17 too had used the image of the planted vine, and 19:10–14 has certain other affinities with that chapter. As an "inclusion," both the first and last verses of chapter 19 label the chapter a "lament" (קִינָה).

On its surface, at least, chapter 19 is almost totally devoid of any "theology" in the ordinary sense of the term. Ezekiel's original audience may well have grasped the metaphors and some of the vocabulary more readily than we. Only careful analysis and meditation will yield theological fruit for the contemporary reader.

The Allegory of the Lioness and Her Cubs (19:2–9)

We turn our attention first to the lion metaphor of the first and larger portion of the chapter. A poetic figure like a lion can and will naturally be used to represent various things. In the Psalter, lions are usually emblems of a ferocious enemy (e.g., Pss 7:3 [ET 7:2]; 17:12). Similarly, in much of prophecy, lions represent fierce cruelty, especially in Nahum 2:12–14 (ET 2:11–13), representing Assyria. A number of other terms are shared by Nahum 2 and Ezekiel 19.

The lion was a common symbol of royalty in the ancient Near East—in Israel as well as Egypt and Assyria.[24] Even though Yahweh refuses to dignify the kings of Ezekiel's day with the title מֶלֶךְ, "king" (in 19:1 he uses נָשִׂיא, "prince," instead), there is no doubt that he is talking about kings in the text before us. In connection with royalty, the lion metaphor had special significance, going back to the earliest times. In Balaam's oracles, the nation of Israel itself is compared with a lion (Num 23:24; 24:9). In Moses' blessing, the figure of a lion is used of the tribe of Gad (Deut 33:20).

However, the main predecessor source of Yahweh's present oracle is indisputably Jacob's blessing of Judah in Gen 49:8–12. So much of the vocabulary is shared that there must be a genetic relationship between the two pericopes: "lion cub" (גּוּר, Gen 49:9; Ezek 19:2, 3, 5); "prey" (טֶרֶף, Gen 49:9; Ezek 19:3, 6); "crouch" (רָבַץ, Gen 49:9; Ezek 19:2); the similar Hebrew terms for "lion" (לָבִיא, Gen 49:9) and "lioness" (לְבִיָּא, Ezek 19:2); and the similar terms for "lion" (אַרְיֵה, twice in Gen 49:9) and "lions" (אֲרָיוֹת, Ezek 19:2, 6). (There are additional correspondences between Gen 49:8–12 and Ezek 19:10–14; see the commentary below.)

---

[23] Critics, who generally disparage predictive prophecy, widely view the second section (19:10–14) as a postexilic expansion. See, for example, Zimmerli, *Ezekiel*, 1:397. However, there is no reason why Yahweh could not have inspired that section prior to Jerusalem's fall in 587 B.C.

[24] For Israel, see a seal found at Megiddo belonging to a servant of Jeroboam II in *ANEP*, § 276.

Since Jacob had assigned to Judah dominance over his enemies and over the other tribes (Gen 49:8–9), the lion in Ezekiel 19 is obviously a symbol of rule. But this chapter describes a rule that had miscarried and become a caricature of God's intent. We first hear that theme in Zeph 3:3, written perhaps a half century before Ezekiel. Here, however, it has become all encompassing, and only judgment could silence it until Yahweh caused a thorough change of heart to take place (Ezek 11:19; 18:31). As often in Scripture, God uses judgment upon his own people not only to renovate them, but to accomplish his larger salvific purposes. The church has never had difficulty understanding the blessing of Judah as messianic, and remaining cognizant of that, 19:1–9 can only be read as a prediction of a certain eclipse of the application of that prophecy until its ultimate and climactic fulfillment appears in the "Lion of the tribe of Judah" (Rev 5:5), Jesus Christ himself.

The nagging question that still remains is that of which specific royal figures the lioness and her cubs represent. The first such figure we meet (Ezek 19:2) is some queen mother. Which one(s) depends, of course, on which kings we understand the cubs to portray. In this case we can identify her historically with Hamutal, mother of Jehoahaz and Zedekiah.[25] Although Israel's queens are mentioned frequently in the OT, we should not attach excessive significance to any particular queen. Rather, the ultimate "mother" is the entire Davidic line, from which all the legitimate individual kings emerged. This understanding will be quite explicit in 19:10, where the image shifts to portray "your mother" as "like a vine," from which all the branches emanate. But already in the first part of the chapter "your mother" has several cubs (19:2–3, 5), and so the figure is not limited to Hamutal.

The picture here is not identical with, but ultimately can and must be integrated with St. Paul's reference to "the Jerusalem above [which] is free, which is the mother of us all" (Gal 4:26).

The larger question perhaps is which kings are in view. The first lion cub (Ezek 19:3–4) is obviously Jehoahaz, the only royal scion to be exiled in Egypt (see the textual notes on 19:4). If nothing else, that undebatable datum assures us that Ezekiel is speaking of real history and is not inventing mythological allegories.

As for the second cub (19:5–9), we have three remaining possibilities: Jehoiakim, Jehoiachin, and Zedekiah. The second cub was brought "to the king of Babylon" (19:9), which may mean that he was brought to Babylon itself. It is clear that both Jehoiachin (2 Ki 24:12–15) and Zedekiah (2 Ki 25:7) were taken to Babylon. As for the earlier King Jehoiakim, 2 Chr 36:6 and Dan 1:1 suggest that Nebuchadnezzar himself was in Jerusalem after the battle at Carchemish (605 B.C.), when Babylon had defeated Egypt and so Babylon's hegemony over Israel had replaced that of Egypt. 2 Chr 36:6 describes

---

[25] See the textual note on 19:3. For more information about Zedekiah, see "The Allegory's Historical Meaning (Ezek 17:11–18)" in the commentary on Ezekiel 17.

Nebuchadnezzar as binding Jehoiakim in bronze shackles "to take him to Babylon." However, 2 Ki 24:6 states that Jehoiakim "slept with his fathers," which may suggest that he was buried in Jerusalem. Neither text explicitly reports a deportation of Jehoiakim to Babylon, so the exile Nebuchadnezzar intended (2 Chr 36:6) may not have been carried out. If Jehoiakim was not taken to Babylon, and if Ezek 19:9 implies that the second cub was, that would eliminate Jehoiakim from consideration as the second cub. However, 19:9 may simply mean that the second cub was brought before the king of Babylon, as Jehoiakim apparently was in Jerusalem (2 Chr 36:6).

Be that as it may, all three of the possible kings are vigorously championed by various commentators, who advance seemingly persuasive arguments in favor of the king they prefer.[26]

As I indicated above (in "Introduction to Ezekiel 19"), I believe all of these arguments are somewhat beside the point. What gives a certain verisimilitude to all the proposals is that there probably *is* an element of truth in all of them. But Ezekiel's figurative and generalized language indicates that his purpose is not to rehearse details of a history already too familiar to his audience. Instead, he wishes to stress that the entire Davidic line in recent times has substituted its own purposes for God's (with the exception of Josiah [640–609 B.C.], who initiated reformation after rediscovering the Torah in the temple, but who does not enter into Ezekiel 19). It is not explicit in 19:9, but "Babylon" often functions in the Bible as a symbol of death and the grave (preeminently in "Babylon, the Great Harlot" in Revelation 14–18, "drunk with the blood of the saints, the blood of the martyrs of Jesus," Rev 17:6). Like the remainder of Ezekiel 19, the imminent overthrow of the royal house and the destruction of Jerusalem and the temple were intended "to annihilate every hope that things might not come to the worst after all."[27] Only when resurrected from that grave in ways that only God could foresee and accomplish would his kingdom really come, ruled by the crucified and risen "King of kings" (1 Tim 6:15; Rev 17:14; 19:16).

The Allegory of the Uprooted Vine (19:10–14)

The image shifts abruptly from "your mother" as a "lioness" (19:2, a metaphor) to "your mother" being "*like* a vine" (19:10, a simile). That the shift from imagery derived from the animate world to the inanimate has any great significance is doubtful. But it is evident that in this section more attention is paid to the mother herself (the Davidic dynasty) and less to her individual offspring (particular kings), although obviously the two cannot be divorced.

Even a cursory reading will discern that the general import in the application of the two figures is the same: the vine and her branches correspond to the lioness and her cubs, respectively. But a thorough acquaintance with Scripture

---

[26] A convenient summary can be found in Block, *Ezekiel*, 1:604–6. Block himself prefers Jehoiakim.

[27] Keil, *Ezekiel*, 1:258.

(as at least some in Ezekiel's audience of Israelite exiles must have had) will recognize not only a surface parallelism, but an organic unity. The bond is evident in the specific lexical connections with Gen 49:8–12, which continue to be evident in Ezek 19:10–14. (The commentary above noted connections between Gen 49:8–12 and Ezek 19:2–9.) These include the central motif of the "vine" (גֶּפֶן, Gen 49:11; Ezek 19:10; see also 15:2–6; 17:6–8), the "scepter" (שֵׁבֶט, Gen 49:10; Ezek 19:11, 14), and perhaps also "blood" (דָּם), if the "blood of grapes" in Gen 49:11 (cf. "wine" in Gen 49:11–12) explains the crux of בְּדָמְךָ (translated as "in your vineyard") in Ezek 19:10 (see the textual note on it above).

Gen 49:8–12 is "messianic" because it expresses the promise that the Messiah will come from the tribe of Judah. Therefore Ezekiel's use of the same vocabulary and imagery in chapter 19 may be labeled "de-messianic" (if we may coin that word), that is, seriously qualifying the hope and the confidence Gen 49:8–12 enshrined, at least in the illegitimate form which that hope had assumed in Ezekiel's day. God was not unfaithful to his promises (cf. chapter 18), but his people had proved themselves totally unfaithful to him. They presumed that despite their personal unbelief and infidelity the Davidic kingship (also the temple, Torah, and other divine promises) would protect them from harm and from individual accountability (contra Ezekiel 18 and 33:10–20). Therefore Yahweh, through Ezekiel, declares that their kind of "hope" (19:5) in the figures of the lion and vine will not avail; the apostate Davidic kings will be exiled (19:4, 9), and the monarchy will be "uprooted in wrath" (19:12) "so that it no longer has a strong branch, a scepter for ruling" (19:14).

This chapter constitutes the third time Ezekiel makes use of the vine metaphor (previously, see chapters 15 and 17). In many respects, its use here is particularly close to the allegory of the eagles, cedar, vine, and new messianic planting in chapter 17. Some have taken chapter 19 to be a continuation of chapter 17, but there are signal differences that veto that view. This chapter distinguishes between generations (the "mother," 19:2, 10, and her children) and emphasizes moral grounds (e.g., cruelty in 19:3, 6–7, and pride in 19:11) for the imminent punishment instead of the political (theocratic) grounds for judgment in chapter 17.

The symbol of the vine and the vineyard is found not only in Ezekiel, but in other biblical writers also, notably Is 5:1–7 ("the Song of the Vineyard"); 27:2–6; Song of Songs;[28] Ps 80:9–17 (ET 80:8–16); and in the NT, Mt 21:33–41 and Jn 15:1–8.

19:10 This section of the chapter begins with the theme already familiar from 17:5–8 of a vine planted by a copious supply of water. As a result, it produces many branches and much fruit. Superficially, it was a beautiful picture of perfect health, pleasing to both God and man. The picture resembles many

---

[28] One may see "The Vineyard," a the survey of the motif throughout the OT and NT, in Mitchell, *The Song of Songs*, 299–311.

(b) E.g., Gen
2:10–14; Ex
15:27;
Psalm 1;
Song 4:12–16;
Rev 22:1–2;
cf. Jn 4:10–14;
7:37–39;
Rev 22:17

other biblical passages with fruitful plants beside flowing water,[b] including 47:1–12, where Ezekiel himself will later expatiate upon the theme eschatologically.

19:11 This verse appears to say that the royal family was large. "The strong branches" (עֹז מַטּוֹת) uses the noun מַטֶּה, "branch; staff, scepter," which originally may have been an official insignia for a tribal chieftan (consistent with Ezekiel's use of premonarchical נָשִׂיא, "prince," in place of "king"; see "Introduction to Ezekiel 19" above). Here the "branches" refer to members of the royal family. Messianic overtones are closely connected with the Hebrew phrase rendered "strong branches." For example, in Ps 110:2, a pivotal Christological text, the same (singular) Hebrew phrase (מַטֵּה־עֻזְּ) refers to Christ's "mighty scepter," which extends from Zion (Calvary; see the commentary on 8:5, 12–13) and enables him to rule over his enemies. Thus while the context requires the translation "strong branches," the Hebrew term (מַטֶּה, "branch") can be a synonym of the term in the parallel phrase "scepters [plural of שֵׁבֶט] of rulers." "Scepter" derives directly from Gen 49:10:

> The scepter shall not depart from Judah,
>> nor the ruler's staff from between his feet,
> until *shiloh* comes,
>> and to him shall be the obedience of peoples.

In Ezek 21:32 (ET 21:27) Yahweh seems to allude to Gen 49:10 and to interpret *shiloh* as meaning "the one to whom justice/justification belongs."[29] And in the NT Psalm 110 is one of the most frequently cited and alluded to OT passages regarding Christ's victorious reign after his suffering, death, resurrection, and ascension to procure justification for sinners.[c]

In the second half of Ezek 19:11 comes what is undoubtedly the key to the understanding of this entire section of the chapter. The vine (the "mother" of the Davidic dynasty, 19:10), from which the ruling Davidides sprouted (with many other potential ones in the wings) abandoned its God-given role of producing grapes and acted like a towering tree, arrogant as could be: "His stature soared high among the clouds." (The motif will reappear in chapter 31, where Egypt and Assyria are depicted as a huge cedar guilty of hubris.) Here the picture moves from an allusion to the many kings of Davidic descent to the one final king, whose self-aggrandizement is ended by God's overthrow of Judah by means of Babylon, thus ending the era of Israel's monarchy.

(c) E.g., Mt
22:44 and
parallels;
26:64 and
parallels;
Acts
2:34–35;
Rom 8:34;
1 Cor 15:25,
27; Eph
1:20; Col
3:1; Heb 1:3,
13; 2:8; 8:1;
10:12

The picture of the vine's mighty bough towering among the clouds sounds an ominous note of human attempts to play God (cf. Gen 11:4). In the prophets, "highness" by itself evokes the idea of forgetting God and usurping his place (e.g., Ezek 16:50; 17:24; cf. Deut 8:14). To God alone belongs "height." That

---

[29] See the commentary on Ezek 21:32 (ET 21:27). Regarding Gen 49:10 and Ezek 21:32, as both are fulfilled in Christ, one may also see Harstad, *Joshua*, 522–23, and for Gen 49:10, Harstad, *Joshua*, 574–75.

is why his temple mount is "a high and lofty mountain" (Ezek 17:22; cf. 40:2; Ps 48:3–4 [ET 48:2–3]).

19:12–14   In a sudden act of destruction, the vine is "uprooted in wrath" and "hurled" to the ground (19:12). The real agent behind the passive verbs is Yahweh himself. Some of the same language is also used in Lam 2:1:

> How the Lord in his anger has set the daughter of Zion under a cloud!
> He hurled from heaven to earth the glory of Israel.

Not only is the vine's height reversed, but what had been its legitimate glory, its "fruit," is destroyed by the "east wind" (Ezek 19:12; see also 17:10). Then it is planted "in a dry and thirsty land" (19:13), which undoubtedly refers to Babylon. Physically, Babylon is a harsh environment for a vine to flourish, let alone a mighty tree, and metaphorically for the Israelites exiled there, life itself will be difficult.

What is more, "its strong branch" is torn off and devoured by fire (19:12)—a theme to which 19:14 will return (see also 15:4–7; 21:3 [ET 20:47]). This being poetry, we should not expect to be able to associate every detail with known history, but a few comments can be made. The "strong branch" in 19:12 (the phrase is repeated in 19:14) and the "main branch" in 19:14 refer to Israelite kings. Probably it is futile to try to limit the identification of each branch to any one king. As in the previous section (19:2–9), we have an amalgam of Israel's kings, especially the last three before the destruction of Jerusalem in 587 B.C., namely, Jehoiakim, Jehoiachin, and Zedekiah (for their ends, see the commentary on 19:2–9).

We are not certain how or where Jehoiakim died. Jehoiachin was torn off the throne and deported to Babylon, so 19:12–13 would apply to him. The "main branch" that emerges in 19:14 apparently is a different king than the one in 19:12. Many commentators have noted that the fact that the destroying fire comes out from the "main branch" in 19:14 is reminiscent of Jotham's historical fable, where a worthless bramble starts a fire that destroys the cedars of Lebanon (Judg 9:7–20, especially 9:15, 20). The point in Ezek 19:14 appears to be that the conceited king is himself the immediate cause of the people's plight. They were all implicated in his arrogance, and all suffer, in effect, his own fate. In 19:12, the fire that destroyed the "strong branch" represented God's wrath executed by external forces (the Babylonian invasion). The destroying fire in 19:14 represents divine wrath triggered by the king himself, and this likely points to Zedekiah's conniving and subversive behavior.[30] But the very vagueness of the language permits any number of applications.

While the divine wrath is a consuming fire, Ezekiel does *not* say that the "scepter" would indeed depart from the royal house of Judah until God's final judgment came; he does not negate the ancient messianic promise in Gen 49:10.

---

[30] See also "The Allegory's Historical Meaning (Ezek 17:11–18)" in the commentary on Ezekiel 17.

Ezekiel describes the result as "that it [the vine] no longer has a strong branch"—but here he leaves open the possibility that is explicitly added in Ezek 17:22–24, namely, that Yahweh will one day plant a new sprig that will indeed bear fruit (cf. Mt 21:33–41; John 15).

Naturally, nearly all critics take at least Ezek 19:12–14 as "prophecies after the event" composed after 587 B.C. Since critical dogma is involved, there is no point in attempting a refutation using critical logic. For many critics it is axiomatic that genuine predictive prophecy cannot occur, and for them none will be admitted "even if a man should rise from the dead" (Lk 16:31).

Orthodox exegesis takes the verbs in Ezek 19:12–14 (mostly perfects and some imperfects with *waw* consecutive) as prophetic perfects, especially common in laments or dirges (e.g., Amos 5:2). This enables us to understand even the independent little "colophon" or postscript at the very end of the chapter ("This is a lament, and it became a lament") as words composed by Ezekiel himself before 587 B.C., emphasizing the credibility of the prediction the chapter contains. As Yahweh communicated to Ezekiel already in 19:1, the entire chapter is a "lament" (קִינָה), and using a final "prophetic perfect" (וַתְּהִי) in anticipating that reality, Ezekiel prophesies that it will be used as a "lament" when it is fulfilled. Mere lamentation over the loss of vain hopes does not imply repentance, but it does invite it.

Less likely is a common guess that the elders came seeking permission to estab-lish some syncretistic cult in the absence of a temple, possibly even to fashion an idol. That hypothesis arises from reading back from the contents of Yahweh's speech to the kind of question that might have triggered it. But a pure hypothesis it remains, nonetheless. The logic is weak, and such a supposition appears intrinsically unlikely to me. And even if so, the elders surely knew Ezekiel well enough by this time to re-alize that they did not stand the faintest chance of getting a positive reply from him for such a request.

לִדְרֹשׁ אֶת־יְהוָה—The Qal of דָּרַשׁ had been used to "consult, inquire" of Yahweh also in 14:7, 10, and will reappear in 20:3. In these verses the translation "seek" would be misleading; the apostate Israelites did not really "seek" Yahweh, anymore than modern "searchers for truth" do. What they find, if anything, is a reflection of them-selves, an idol. God is the genuine seeker; as Shepherd, he is the one who will "seek" (דָּרַשׁ) his sheep (34:10–11). But as we see in this chapter, people first must be con-vinced of the futility of their own searches. The translation "consult" enables the re-tention of אֶת־יְהוָה as the direct object and probably better reproduces the breadth of possible meanings of דָּרַשׁ with Yahweh as the object.

The Qal idiom in 20:1, 3 means to seek some revelation from Yahweh (as also in, e.g., Gen 25:22; Ex 18:15; Jer 21:2). The Niphal of דָּרַשׁ in 20:3, 31 (אִדָּרֵשׁ) will have the corresponding tolerative sense: Yahweh does not "allow himself to be con-sulted/inquired of," that is, if idolaters inquire, he refuses to provide a revelation or answer for them. See the textual note on the Niphal in 14:3.

In other contexts the Qal of דָּרַשׁ can refer to a response of faith: prompted by Yahweh's Word and invitation, the repentant believer is called to "seek" Yahweh (e.g., Is 55:6; Amos 5:4, 6; Ps 105:4; cf. the Niphal in Is 65:1), and often in the Psalms, be-lievers are those who "seek" Yahweh.[a]

20:3 דַּבֵּר אֶת־זִקְנֵי יִשְׂרָאֵל—Here אֶת is the preposition, so this is, literally, "speak with the elders." However, since Yahweh refuses to dialogue with the inquirers, I have translated "speak to," which agrees with the many other Hebrew manuscripts that have the more common אֶל and with the LXX, which has πρός.

20:4 הֲתִשְׁפֹּט אֹתָם הֲתִשְׁפּוֹט—The repeated imperfect with interrogative *he* implies impassioned affirmation: "Will you arraign?" is thus an earnest way of commanding Ezekiel to "arraign" Israel.[2] That this is its force is indicated by the imperative with which the sentence continues (הוֹדִיעֵם; see the next textual note). הֲתִשְׁפֹּט will be re-peated in 22:2 and 23:36. The verb שָׁפַט, whether in the human or divine realm, is multivalent enough to cover the entire judicial process. Since Yahweh is the one who will "judge" Israel, "arraign" is probably the appropriate translation for the verb here, since it refers to Ezekiel's activity. The prophet is pictured as a lawyer bringing a bill of indictment.

אֶת־תּוֹעֲבֹת אֲבוֹתָם הוֹדִיעֵם:—Similarly, Yahweh used the Hiphil imperative of יָדַע also in 16:2 to command Ezekiel to "make Jerusalem know her abominations"

(a) E.g., Pss 9:11 (ET 9:10); 22:27 (ET 22:26); 34:5, 11 (ET 34:4, 10); 119:2, 10

---

2   Greenberg, *Ezekiel*, 1:363.

Review of the Old Covenant and Promise of the New

Translation

20 ¹In the seventh year, in the fifth [month], on the tenth [day] of the month, men came from the elders of Israel to consult Yahweh, and they sat in front of me. ²Then the Word of Yahweh came to me: ³"Son of man, speak to the elders of Israel and say to them, 'Thus says the Lord Yahweh: Are you really coming to consult me? As I live, I will not let myself be consulted by you, says the Lord Yah-weh.' ⁴Will you arraign them? Will you arraign, son of man? Remind them of the abominable practices of their fathers.

⁵"You shall say to them, 'Thus says the Lord Yahweh: On the day when I chose Israel, when I swore with uplifted hand to the descendants of the house of Jacob and I made myself known to them in the land of Egypt, then I swore to them with uplifted hand, saying, "I am Yahweh, your God." ⁶On that day I swore to them with uplifted hand to bring them out of the land of Egypt to a land that I had searched out for them, flowing with milk and honey; it was the most glo-rious of all the lands. ⁷I said to them, "Each man must throw away the loathsome things before his eyes, and do not defile yourselves with the fecal deities of Egypt; I am Yahweh, your God." ⁸But they rebelled against me and were not willing to listen to me. Each of them did not throw away the loathsome things before their eyes, nor did they forsake the fecal deities of Egypt, so I resolved to pour out my wrath on them and exhaust my anger against them in the midst of the land of Egypt. ⁹Instead, I acted for the sake of my name so that it would not be profaned in the sight of the nations they were among, to whom I had made myself known in their sight by bringing them [the Israelites] out of the land of Egypt.

¹⁰"'So I brought them out of the land of Egypt and led them into the desert. ¹¹I gave them my statutes, and my ordinances I made known to them, by which man will live if he observes them. ¹²I also gave them my Sabbaths to be a sign be-tween me and them, so that they might know that it is I, Yahweh, who sanctifies them. ¹³But the house of Israel rebelled against me in the desert. They did not walk in my statutes, and they rejected my ordinances (by which man will live if he observes them), and they utterly profaned my Sabbaths. So I resolved to pour out my wrath on them in the desert to annihilate them. ¹⁴Instead, I acted for the sake of my name so that it would not be profaned in the sight of the nations in whose sight I had brought them out [from Egypt]. ¹⁵So I also swore to them with uplifted hand in the desert not to bring them into the land that I had given [to them], flowing with milk and honey—it is the most glorious of all the lands—¹⁶because they rejected my ordinances and did not walk in my statutes, but pro-

faned my Sabbaths, for their heart goes after their fecal deities. [17]Yet my eye had pity on them so as not to destroy them, and I did not make a complete destruction with them in the desert.

[18]" 'Then I said to their sons in the desert: "Do not walk in the statutes of your parents, do not observe their ordinances, and do not defile yourselves with their fecal deities. [19]I, Yahweh, am your God. Walk in my statutes, and observe my ordinances and practice them. [20]Keep my Sabbaths holy that they may be a sign between me and you, so that you might know that I, Yahweh, am your God." [21]But the sons rebelled against me. They did not walk in my statutes, they did not observe my ordinances by practicing them, by which man will live if he observes them. They profaned my Sabbaths, so I resolved to pour out my wrath on them and exhaust my anger on them in the desert. [22]Nevertheless, I withdrew my hand and acted for the sake of my name so that it would not be profaned in the sight of the nations in whose sight I had brought them out [from Egypt]. [23]However, I swore to them with uplifted hand in the desert to scatter them among the nations and to disperse them among the countries, [24]because they did not observe my ordinances, they despised my statutes, they profaned my Sabbaths, and on the fecal deities of their fathers they fixed their eyes. [25]Moreover, I gave them statutes that were not good and ordinances by which they could not live. [26]I defiled them through their gifts when they made every issue that opened the womb pass through [the fire] so that I might devastate them, so that they might know that I am Yahweh.'

[27]"Therefore, speak to the house of Israel, son of man, and say to them, 'Thus says the Lord Yahweh: In this too your fathers blasphemed me by their faithless infidelity toward me. [28]When I brought them to the land which I had sworn with uplifted hand to give it to them, when they saw any high hill or any leafy tree, there they offered their sacrifices, there they placed their vexatious offerings, there they set their fragrant sacrifices, and there they poured out their libations. [29]Then I said to them, "What is the high place to which you are going?" ' " So it is called *Bamah* [High Place] to this day.

[30]"Therefore, say to the house of Israel, 'Thus says the Lord Yahweh: Are you continuing to defile yourselves in the way your fathers did? Are you still whoring after their loathsome idolatries? [31]When you offer your gifts and make your sons pass through the fire, you continue to defile yourselves by all your fecal deities to this day. So should I let myself be consulted by you, house of Israel? As I live, says the Lord Yahweh, I will not let myself be consulted by you.

[32]" 'What has arisen in your mind will definitely never happen, that is, you are saying, "Let us become like the nations, like the families in other countries, by worshiping wood and stone." [33]As I live, says the Lord Yahweh, with a mighty hand, with an outstretched arm, and with wrath outpoured, I will rule over you! [34]I will bring you out from the nations, and I will gather you from the countries among which you have been scattered, with a mighty hand, with an outstretched arm, and with wrath outpoured, [35]and I will bring you into the wilderness of the peoples and enter into judgment with you there face to face. [36]As I entered into

judgment with your fathers in the wilderness of the land of Egypt, so will I enter into judgment with you, says the Lord Yahweh. [37]I will make you pass under the staff, and I will bring you into the bond of the covenant. [38]I will purge out from you those who revolt and rebel against me. From the land of their sojourning I will bring them out, but into the land of Israel they shall not come. Then you will know that I am Yahweh.

[39]" 'As for you, O house of Israel, thus says the Lord Yahweh: Each man go and worship his fecal deities, but henceforth if you will not listen to me … ! My holy name you shall no longer profane with your gifts and your fecal deities. [40]For on my holy mountain, on the high mountain of Israel, says the Lord Yahweh, there the whole house of Israel will worship me—all of it in the homeland. There I will accept them, and there I will request your offerings and your choice gifts together with all your holy things. [41]As a fragrant sacrifice I will accept you when I bring you out from the nations and I gather you from the lands among which you were scattered, and I will show myself holy through you in the sight of the nations. [42]Then you will know that I am Yahweh when I bring you to the ground of Israel, to the land that I swore with uplifted hand to give to your fathers. [43]There you will remember your ways and all your deeds by which you defiled yourselves, and you will loath yourselves in your own sight for all your evils which you did. [44]Then you will know that I am Yahweh when I deal with you for the sake of my name and not according to your evil ways and your corrupt deeds, O house of Israel, says the Lord Yahweh.' "

Textual Notes

20:1 For the first time since 8:1, we encounter a precise date, which is August 14, 591 B.C., according to a common chronological calculation. Jewish scholars have long observed that the date, the tenth of the month Ab, is also the date of the destruction of the temple five years later (cf. Jer 52:12–14), and according to tradition, also of the second temple in A.D. 70. This date is only eleven months and five days after the one given in Ezek 8:1. It is also two years, a month, and five days after Ezekiel's call (1:2), and two years and five months before the beginning of the final siege of Jerusalem (24:1). Therefore this date is close to the middle of the first part of Ezekiel's total recorded ministry (from his call to the fall of Jerusalem in 587 B.C.).

Possibly, the date applies not only to chapter 20, but also to chapters 21–23, since the next date is given in 24:1. As evidence for that possibility, Keil adduces the repetition of the interrogative "Will you arraign/indict?" not only in 20:4 but also in 22:2 and 23:36.[1] That conclusion may be correct but can hardly be regarded as certain.

We are not told why the elders came in 20:1 (nor in 8:1 and 14:1), but one intriguing proposal is to connect their visit with the prediction of the false prophet Hananiah (made in 593 B.C.) that the exile involving the elders and Ezekiel would be over by this time (Jer 28:1–4). Again, this is possible but speculative.

---

[1] Keil, *Ezekiel*, 1:263.

[תוֹעֵבוֹת]." Here too a summary of Israel's history follows, narrated from God's perspective, which gives the theological basis for the historical events (historical theology). Presumably the elders already "knew" the historical record in a superficial, intellectual sense, but they were ignoring the theology behind it or were humanistically misconstruing history somehow in their favor (see the commentary below). I have rendered the literal "make them know" as "remind them of," which in this context implies theological review to move them to repentance and faith.

20:5 The Hebrew of this verse is rather prolix (no novelty in Ezekiel) and could be punctuated in various ways.

וָאֶשָּׂא יָדִי—Twice Yahweh declares, literally, "I lifted up my hand." The idiom's use undoubtedly echoes Ex 6:8 (see the commentary below). The gesture, still followed in courts today, refers to the making of an oath. I have added "swore" to the translation for clarity, and that alone could have sufficed as an accurate translation, but "with uplifted hand" retains the picture embedded in the original text. (Only in 16:8 does Ezekiel use the usual Niphal verb for "swear," נִשְׁבַּע.) The idiom will be repeated with the perfect נָשָׂאתִי and יָדִי in 20:6, 15, 23, 28, 42.

לֵאמֹר—This is one of the few times when it seemed necessary to translate לֵאמֹר with "saying." Usually English idiom uses only a colon or comma and quotation marks.

20:6 "Bring out from the land of Egypt" (Hiphil of יָצָא, as also in 20:9, 10, 14, 22) and "flowing with milk and honey" (also 20:15) are almost stock phrases throughout the Pentateuch (the former also in Josh 24:5–6 and the latter also in Josh 5:6), but in the prophetic literature they appear only in Jeremiah and Ezekiel. However, the Hiphil of יָצָא will be used for a new exodus redemption in Ezek 20:34, 38, 41, as previously in Isaiah (Is 42:7; 48:20; 65:9).

צְבִי הִיא לְכָל־הָאֲרָצוֹת:—Yahweh will repeat this clause about the land of Israel in 20:15. צְבִי can mean "beauty, glory," or perhaps "ornament," hence literally, "It is an ornament/glory to all the lands." Such a description of Israel does not appear in the Torah, but is first used by the sixth-century prophets: Jer 3:19; Ezek 20:6, 15 (in 25:9 of the cities of Moab); Dan 8:9; 11:16, 41, 45. The clause refers not only to something's appearance, but also to Yahweh's high regard for it.

20:7 But the other side of the coin is that Yahweh's high regard for Israel cannot continue unless the people worship him exclusively. Contrary to the spirit of modern liberalism, Yahweh's injunction is that they must stop being "inclusive" and "pluralistic." The verse uses two of Ezekiel's favorite and strongest terms for condemnation of idols, the plurals of שִׁקּוּץ ("loathsome/detestable/disgusting things"; see the textual notes on it in 5:11; 7:20; 11:18, 21) and גִּלּוּל (see the textual note on "fecal deities" in 6:4). שִׁקּוּצִים will recur in 20:8, 30 and גִּלּוּלִים in 20:8, 16, 18, 24, 31, 39.

אִישׁ שִׁקּוּצֵי עֵינָיו הַשְׁלִיכוּ—Following the distributive אִישׁ and the singular pronoun on עֵינָיו, one would expect the imperative הַשְׁלִיכוּ to be singular, but Hebrew usage is not rigid in that respect, and the same kind of construction occurs in 20:39 (אִישׁ גִּלּוּלָיו לְכוּ עֲבֹדוּ). The inclusion of "each man ... his" makes for a much harsher accusation that targets each Israelite. Most of the ancient versions translate אִישׁ here but not in the parallel clause in 20:8 (where the pronoun on עֵינֵיהֶם is plural), so most commentators delete it in 20:8 as a secondary insertion from 20:7, but the parallelism between the two verses supports its presence in 20:8 too.

Here and in 20:8 שִׁקּוּצֵי is in construct with "eyes," and the clauses are usually translated so that the idols are "before his/their eyes," although RSV, NRSV, and ESV have "the detestable things your eyes feast on" (20:7; similarly in 20:8), which is possible. Ezek 18:6, 12, 15; 33:25 refer to Israelites lifting up their eyes to gaze at idols, which might echo Deut 4:19. Greenberg proposes associating "eyes" here with "heart" in Ezek 20:16 ("their heart goes after their fecal deities") and "whoring after their loathsome things/idolatries" in 20:30, and deriving all three from Num 15:39: when the Israelites see the צִיצַת ("tassels" on the fringes of their garments), they should remember Yahweh's commandments and not go whoring after their eyes (idols, which their eyes see).[3] We need not decide on the precise source of Ezekiel's expressions, but this one, like so many others, demonstrates how steeped in earlier Scripture Ezekiel actually was.

אַל־תִּטַּמָּאוּ—The Hithpael of טָמֵא has a reflexive or middle meaning, "defile oneself, render oneself unclean." The term echoes the Levitical laws of purity for Israel; see the textual notes and commentary on Ezek 4:13–14. The preformative ת (תִּתְטַמָּאוּ) has been assimilated and is marked by the *daghesh* (-מָּ-). The identical form recurs in 20:18.

20:8 וַיַּמְרוּ־בִי—This clause (repeated in 20:13, 21) with the Hiphil of מָרָה recalls 5:6 and is redolent of Israel's appellation as (literally) the "house of rebellion" (with the cognate noun מְרִי) already in Ezekiel's call (2:5–6, 8; 3:9, 26–27). The following clause too (וְלֹא אָבוּ לִשְׁמֹעַ אֵלַי) recalls Yahweh's prediction at Ezekiel's call that the Israelites would not listen to the prophet because they do not listen to him (3:7). In Deut 1:43 and 9:23, Israel's rebelling (מָרָה) is combined with the people not listening (לֹא שָׁמַע) to Yahweh, and that may be the background here. Compare also Israel rebelling (מָרָה) by not being willing (לֹא אָבָה) to take the land in Deut 1:26, and the rebellious son (participle of מָרָה) who does not listen (לֹא שָׁמַע) to his parents in Deut 21:18, 20.

(b) Ezek 7:8;
9:8; 14:19;
20:8, 13, 21,
33, 34;
22:22;
30:15; 36:18

וָאֹמַר לִשְׁפֹּךְ חֲמָתִי עֲלֵיהֶם לְכַלּוֹת אַפִּי בָּהֶם—This will be repeated (with one significant difference) in 20:13 and almost verbatim in 20:21. "Resolve" translates אָמַר (usually "say," sometimes "think"), which, when followed by the infinitive construct with לְ, often expresses intention. Ezekiel often refers to Yahweh "pouring out" (שָׁפַךְ) his "wrath" (חֵמָה).[b] See especially the commentary on 7:8. For Yahweh "to fulfill/exhaust" his "anger" (Qal or Piel of כָּלָה and אַף) means he would express it fully; this idiom too is common in Ezekiel (see 5:13 and the similar expression in 6:12).

20:9 וָאַעַשׂ לְמַעַן שְׁמִי לְבִלְתִּי הֵחֵל—This will be repeated almost verbatim in 20:14, 22. הֵחֵל is the Niphal infinitive construct of חָלַל (GKC, § 67 t), meaning "to be profaned."

20:12 לָדַעַת כִּי אֲנִי יְהוָה מְקַדְּשָׁם:—There is no expressed subject of the infinitive of יָדַע here and in 20:20, but the immediate context refers to the Israelites as the ones who will "know." However, other nations too will know from Israel's Sabbath that

---

[3] Greenberg, *Ezekiel*, 1:365.

Yahweh is the one who sanctifies Israel (cf., e.g., Deut 28:9–10). In Ezek 37:28 Yahweh promises evangelistically, "The nations will know that I, Yahweh, sanctify Israel when my sanctuary is in their midst forever."

Since Ezekiel was a priest (1:3), it is no surprise that here again, as throughout his book, he reflects the language and theology of Leviticus. The phrase here in 20:12 (אֲנִי יְהוָה מְקַדְּשָׁם) quotes verbatim Lev 21:23; 22:9, 16, and with only a change in the pronominal suffix ("it is I, Yahweh, who sanctifies you/him"), Ex 31:13; Lev 20:8; 21:8, 15; 22:32.[4] God sanctified his people in the OT era in essentially the same way as he sanctifies his people in the NT era, namely, by forgiving their sins, and thus they are "saints."[c] The "Word and Sacraments" that God used for this purpose in the OT era differed from those of the NT era only in form. In both eras, the means of grace receive their efficacy by their bond with Christ's death and resurrection—in the OT prospectively, and in the NT retrospectively. The sacrifices and sacred institutions (circumcision, the Passover, etc.) were the "sacraments" of the OT. Priests/pastors are instrumental in both eras. The OT gives us much detail about the sacrifices, but little about the priests' verbal proclamation of the Gospel, although plainly that was one of their obligations.

20:13   The verse is basically a reworking of material we have met earlier, especially 20:8, 11.

וְאֶת־שַׁבְּתֹתַי חִלְּלוּ מְאֹד—This will be repeated almost verbatim in 20:16, 21, 24. While Yahweh protected his name from "being profaned" (20:9, 14, 22), the Israelites "utterly profaned" his Sabbaths. The adverb מְאֹד, usually translated "very," forms a sort of superlative: their desecration of the Sabbaths could not have been worse.

לְכַלּוֹתָם:—In 20:8, 21 the Piel of כָּלָה has אַפִּי as its object (Yahweh would exhaust his anger at Israel). Here the Piel of כָּלָה has an object suffix referring to the Israelites themselves: God thought of ending/exterminating them. Compare also the noun כָּלָה in 20:17.

20:15   This verse is an updated version of 20:6.

אֶל־הָאָרֶץ אֲשֶׁר־נָתַתִּי—There is no indirect object after נָתַתִּי, but the translation adds "to them," as do the ancient versions. Normal Hebrew usage would have an indirect object. Zimmerli suggests emending נָתַתִּי to תַּרְתִּי to match 20:6 (אֶל־אֶרֶץ אֲשֶׁר־תַּרְתִּי לָהֶם) because an omission of לָהֶם is easier to explain after תַּרְתִּי than after נָתַתִּי.[5] In both verses the phrase about the land ("flowing with milk and honey") immediately follows.

20:16   Several Hebrew manuscripts add מְאֹד after חִלֵּלוּ to agree with 20:13, 21.
20:17   וַתָּחָס עֵינִי עֲלֵיהֶם מִשַּׁחֲתָם—Yahweh's affirmation that his eye *did* have pity on them in the past contrasts with his repeated assertion through Ezekiel about the future judgment, "My eye will not pity" (see the textual notes on 5:11). Likewise, that he did not "destroy" them (Piel infinitive of שָׁחַת with privative מִן) contrasts with other passages in the book where Yahweh threatens to do so (Piel of שָׁחַת in 5:16; 22:30; 43:3; cf. the Hiphil in 9:8).

(c) E.g., Pss 16:3; 34:10; Dan 7:18, 27; Mt 27:52; Rom 1:7; 1 Cor 1:2

---

4   For this formula, cf. Kleinig, *Leviticus*, 11.
5   Zimmerli, *Ezekiel*, 1:400–401.

וְלֹא־עָשִׂיתִי אוֹתָם כָּלָה—The idiomatic construction with the verb עָשָׂה, the noun כָּלָה ("complete destruction"), and the preposition אֵת ("with"; see the last textual note on 2:1) is similar to ones in 11:13 and Jer 5:18.

20:18 בְּחוּקֵּי אֲבוֹתֵיכֶם—Allen suggests that the phrase implies "a do-it-themselves approach to human existence."[6] The masculine noun חֹק is used here, instead of the feminine חֻקָּה, which is the usual term for God's "statutes." The masculine was used already in 11:12 and will be again in 20:25 and 36:27. Zimmerli wonders whether the masculine is meant to distinguish the human statutes of the ancestors from Yahweh's statues.[7] When the masculine is used again in 20:25, it may be exegetically significant, but in 36:27 the masculine clearly refers to divine "statutes." Especially considering the apparent interchangeability of the two forms elsewhere in the OT, in my judgment the distinction is too slender a thread on which to hang any argument.

20:22 וַהֲשִׁבֹתִי אֶת־יָדִי—This first clause is not attested in the LXX and Syriac. A number of factors lead to a wide consensus among critical scholars that the clause is a later gloss.[8] It is absent from the parallel statements in 20:9 and 20:14, and elsewhere Ezekiel never uses the idiom (Hiphil of שׁוּב and יָד, "withdraw the hand") for Yahweh, although it describes people in 18:8, 17; 38:12. Similar language in reference to Yahweh does appear in Lam 2:8; Pss 74:11; 78:38 (in the last verse with "anger" as the object, but with the verb negated, speaking of God sparing the rebels in the wilderness).

The penultimate accent on וַהֲשִׁבֹתִי indicates that it is a perfect with ordinary *waw* (here with adversative meaning), not *waw* consecutive. One might expect the verb to be imperfect with *waw* consecutive (which would be וָאָשֶׁב) since in the preceding verse the last main verb was an imperfect with *waw* consecutive (וָאֹמַר in 20:21), as is also the following main verb (וָאַעַשׂ in 20:22). But Greenberg convincingly points to comparable instances of a perfect with conjunctive *waw* in Ezekiel which are the result of his loose style and may reflect the incipient influence of Aramaic, which does not use *waw* consecutives. Greenberg labels וַהֲשִׁבֹתִי an "out-of-pattern parallel" to וַתָּחָס ("yet my eye *had pity* on them") in 20:17, since it is parallel in meaning,[9] but וַתָּחָס is an imperfect with *waw* consecutive.

20:25 חֻקִּים לֹא טוֹבִים—Note that "statutes" is masculine (plural of חֹק) as in 20:18. This may or may not be exegetically significant; see the textual note on it in 20:18 and the commentary on 20:25. The combination "no(t) good" (לֹא טוֹבִים) is used instead of "evil" (רָעִים).

20:26 וָאֲטַמֵּא אוֹתָם בְּמַתְּנוֹתָם—This is the only place in the OT where Yahweh is the subject of "defile" (Piel of טָמֵא), which is one sign of how radical the message is in 20:25–26. God gave Israel the Levitical laws of purity so as to prevent Israel from becoming defiled (see the textual notes and commentary on 4:13–14). NIV apparently

---

6   Allen, *Ezekiel*, 2:11.

7   Zimmerli, *Ezekiel*, 1:410.

8   For example, Zimmerli, *Ezekiel*, 1:401.

9   Greenberg, *Ezekiel*, 1:368.

feels that this literal translation is too offensive and paraphrases, "I let them become defiled" (shifting the meaning toward the Hithpael of טָמֵא in 20:7, 18 and the Niphal in 20:30, 31, 43). But as far as I know, the Piel is never passive in meaning, nor does it ever have a tolerative sense (as the Niphal can, e.g., אִדָּרֵשׁ in 20:3). The radicalism here is of a piece with the theological issue of both 20:25 and 20:26 (see the commentary below).

The noun מַתָּנָה, "gift, offering" (a derivative of נָתַן), will be used again in 20:31, 39 (also 46:16–17). It is a general term for all sorts of gifts to God, including those specified in the Torah (e.g., Ex 28:38; Lev 23:38), but the following clause indicates that in 20:26, 31, 39 it refers to "rejected (idolatrous) offerings" (BDB).

בְּהַעֲבִיר כָּל־פֶּטֶר רֶחַם—This circumstantial clause is, literally, "when making pass through [fire] all that opens the womb." The Hiphil infinitive of עָבַר will be used again in 20:31 with בָּאֵשׁ (literally, "when making pass through the fire"), and "fire" is implied here (as also in 16:21). This is a technical idiom for child sacrifice, used earlier in 16:20–21 and again in 23:37. Other verbs or idioms are sometimes used for the rite. פֶּטֶר רֶחַם is used exclusively of the firstborn of a mother.[d] The more common noun בְּכוֹר is used of the "firstborn" of the father, and of Israel as the "firstborn," elect people of the heavenly Father (Ex 4:22).

לְמַעַן אֲשֶׁר יֵדְעוּ אֲשֶׁר אֲנִי יְהוָה:—In later biblical Hebrew, אֲשֶׁר often replaces כִּי as a relative particle. The recognition formula usually uses כִּי ("then you/they will know *that* I am Yahweh," e.g., Ezek 20:38, 42, 44). For that reason, and because here it is introduced in an unusual way (לְמַעַן אֲשֶׁר followed by the simple imperfect יֵדְע֫וּ[d] instead of the perfect with *waw* consecutive), and also because it is missing in the LXX and other versions, critics commonly consider it here to be a gloss or early addition to the text.[10]

20:27 לָכֵן דַּבֵּר—A new section begins here with "therefore." לָכֵן דַּבֵּר occurs otherwise in Ezekiel only in 14:4, although לָכֵן אֱמֹר is quite common (e.g., 11:16–17) as is לָכֵן הִנָּבֵא (e.g., 11:4; 36:3, 6).

Critics widely regard 20:27–29 (up until another לָכֵן in 20:30) as a redactional supplement.[11] Some of the reasons are linguistic: the use of דַּבֵּר instead of אֱמֹר; the opening words of what Ezekiel is to say, עוֹד זֹאת (but they are also in 23:38; 36:37); and the similarity in language in 20:28–29 to 6:13–14, on which these verses might be based. Thus, this passage allegedly breaks the pattern of the previous indictments. Supposedly a redactor noticed the lack of mention of Israel's occupation of Canaan (the period immediately relevant to Israel's plight) and added it (20:27–29). But in the latter fact is also a major argument for the integrity of the material. And why should Ezekiel not use somewhat different vocabulary while speaking of the more recent past and the present?[12]

(d) Ex 13:12, 15; 34:19; Num 3:12; 18:15; cf. Ex 13:2

---

[10] See, for example, Zimmerli, *Ezekiel*, 1:401, and Allen, *Ezekiel*, 2:4.

[11] Zimmerli, *Ezekiel*, 1:404–5, 412; Allen, *Ezekiel*, 2:12–13; and others. In fact, Zimmerli thinks he detects three stages of redaction.

[12] Block, *Ezekiel*, 1:642, points out that even if these verses were a sort of afterthought, Ezekiel remains as likely to be the writer as anyone.

גִּדְּפוּ אוֹתִי אֲבוֹתֵיכֶם—The verb גָּדַף occurs only in the Piel in the OT and means "blaspheme (God)" or "revile (men)." Usually it refers to utterances, but here and in Num 15:30 it refers to blasphemous actions: here the illegitimate worship on the high places described in Ezek 20:28. The uncommon verb occurs only here in Ezekiel, although the cognate noun גְּדוּפָה was in 5:15.

בְּמַעֲלָם בִּי מָעַל׃—See the textual note on this cognate accusative construction in 14:13. בְּמַעֲלָם is the Qal infinitive of מָעַל and מָעַל is the pausal form of the noun מַעַל.

20:28 The liturgical terminology used in this verse is generic enough that Ezekiel is probably giving us only a general overview of idolatrous rites on the high places (cf. the textual notes and commentary on 6:3; 16:16).

וַיִּזְבְּחוּ־שָׁם אֶת־זִבְחֵיהֶם—The noun זֶבַח can refer specifically to a "peace offering" (better: "communion sacrifice"), especially when שְׁלָמִים is added (e.g., Lev 3:1), but it and the cognate verb used here (זָבַח) are often general terms for "sacrifice" of any sort.

כַּעַס קָרְבָּנָם—This is, literally, "the vexation/provocation of their offering," with the idiomatic Hebrew preference for a construct chain instead of an adjectival modifier, hence "vexatious offerings," that is, offerings that vexed and provoked God. קָרְבָּן may be the most general word for any and every kind of offering that was "brought near" (הִקְרִיב, Hiphil of the verb from which the noun is derived), and the word is transliterated in Mk 7:11 (κορβᾶν). Besides Ezek 20:28; 40:43, קָרְבָּן occurs only in Leviticus (e.g., 1:2–3, 10, 14) and Numbers (e.g., 5:15; 6:14, 21).

רֵיחַ נִיחוֹחֵיהֶם—See the textual note on the similar phrase in 6:13.

וַיַּסִּיכוּ שָׁם אֶת־נִסְכֵּיהֶם׃—This is a cognate accusative construction with the Hiphil of נָסַךְ ("pour out") and noun נֶסֶךְ, "libation, drink offering." We know little about the precise ritual use of libations, which had their proper place in Israel's orthodox worship (e.g., Ex 29:40–41; Lev 23:13, 18, 37), but here are part of idolatry. Ezekiel uses the term only once elsewhere, in a prophecy of Christ and his atoning sacrifice for the world's sin: in Ezekiel's eschatological vision it will be the Prince who furnishes the sacrifices and libations (Ezek 45:17).

20:29 מָה הַבָּמָה אֲשֶׁר־אַתֶּם הַבָּאִים שָׁם—There is no way to reproduce in translation the alliterative pun: the interrogative מָה, "what?" is also the second half of בָּמָה, "high place," and rearranging the consonants of בָּמָה (and adding אי) yields הַבָּאִים, "going." Many commentaries cite Moffatt's attempt to reproduce the original wordplay, "What is the high place you hie to?"[13] But that almost requires translation itself. The artistry of the Hebrew is heightened by the addition of an unnecessary article on הַבָּאִים in order to provide assonance with הַבָּמָה.

Many translations render the definite article on הַבָּמָה by "*this* high place." Since the article is a sort of weak demonstrative, such a translation is technically possible. "This" would seem to indicate reference to some specific shrine (one erected by the exiles in Babylon?), but we lack context for such an assumption. (Translation, as of-

---

[13] James Moffatt, *A New Translation of the Bible Containing the Old and New Testaments* (New York: Harper & Brothers, 1935).

ten, is inseparable from exegesis.) Keil may be on the right track when he takes הַבָּמָה collectively and explains the singular as an antithesis to the legitimate place of worship, the Holy of Holies in the temple on Mount Zion.[14] Something of that sort appears to me to be at least implicit in the question.

Critics commonly dismiss 20:29 as too frivolous to be original. Even Allen is needlessly pejorative: "It uses the culturally popular device of wordplay in a propagandist attack on unorthodox religion."[15] Greenberg provides balance by citing other examples of the use of paronomasia in serious literature.[16]

I have simply transliterated the second instance of בָּמָה and put the usual translation in brackets. In fact, we have no clue to the actual etymology or even precise meaning of בָּמָה. The literature on the entire subject is immense; see earlier comments on 6:3–7. This verse is not an attempt to explain the word's etymology. The association between בָּמָה and the other words (הַבָּאִים, מָה) is assonantal rather than etymological. Some biblical wordplays using etymology are really just that: wordplays (e.g., Gen 26:33), and so they should not be criticized as giving a linguistically false etymology. (Etymologies are more of a modern concern, especially when we are ignorant about a word's contextual meaning.) The text dare not be interrogated about issues it does not address.

20:30 הַבְּדֶרֶךְ—The noun דֶּרֶךְ ("way") has overtones of total orientation, a way of living, believing, and worship (hence Christianity is "the Way," e.g., Acts 9:2; 19:9, 23). My translation manages to retain "way" as part of the horizon of the original. Here שִׁקּוּץ may have a more general meaning than in Ezek 20:7–8 and refer to everything connected with loathsome idolatry.

20:31 וּבִשְׂאֵת—The Qal infinitive of נָשָׂא ("lift") used as a gerund may imply some gesture of presentation to the deity, but the verb is used quite generally of sacrificing or offering. The first part of the verse echoes 20:26, while the last part returns us to 20:3, thus framing the entire indictment (20:5–31).

The verse implies that child sacrifice was still being practiced by Israelites, and now in Babylon (cf. the references to it in the past in Israel in 16:20–21; 20:26; 23:37). It is possible that Ezekiel is again lumping together those in exile with those still in Jerusalem (and only those back in Israel were actually committing the abomination), but the alternative cannot be ruled out. Those already exiled had so often showed themselves to be of the same mind and spirit (20:32) as those left behind that it is entirely possible that they also continued this most heinous abomination. We have no external evidence for answering the question more definitely.

20:32 וְהָעֹלָה עַל־רוּחֲכֶם—The more common idiom for thoughts is that they "arise upon the heart" (עָלָה עַל־לֵב), that is, arise in consciousness, but here רוּחַ is used instead, as in 11:5, and "spirit" is essentially what we call "mind" or "consciousness."

---

[14] Keil, *Ezekiel*, 1:277.

[15] Allen, *Ezekiel*, 2:13.

[16] Greenberg, *Ezekiel*, 1:370.

הָיוֹ לֹא תִהְיֶה—The infinitive absolute is reproduced by "definitely," a determination on God's part that is clearly reflected in the following verses.

נִהְיֶה—The imperfect can have the meaning of a cohortative, as I have translated it: "let us become …" It could also be a simple declarative ("we will be …"). The cohortative implies defiance toward Yahweh and deliberate apostasy. A declarative could be an expression of resignation or even despair: the people might lament that if their fate is to be scattered among the nations, they will lose their identity as the people of Yahweh and become indistinguishable from the heathen.[17] However, the general picture of the Israelites as having already become virtual pagans even before the exile makes it unlikely that they would have enough Yahwistic loyalty to lament their impending assimilation into the other heathens (see further the commentary below).

לְשָׁרֵת עֵץ וָאָבֶן:—The Piel of שָׁרֵת here is used in the sense of "worship," more commonly expressed by עָבַד (20:39–40). The Torah uses שָׁרֵת frequently for the service of Yahweh by priests and Levites, and Ezekiel will use it for orthodox worship often in chapters 40–46. Only here in the OT is it used for idolatry, and so it may be sarcastic.

20:33 וּבְחֵמָה שְׁפוּכָה—This phrase, repeated in 20:34, uses the Qal passive participle of שָׁפַךְ, with חֵמָה as its subject, to express the same thought (the outpouring of Yahweh's wrath) as the phrase with the infinitive and direct object (לִשְׁפֹּךְ חֲמָתִי) in 20:8, 13, 21.

אֶמְלוֹךְ עֲלֵיכֶם:—The predication of Yahweh reigning as king (the verb מָלַךְ) is found only here in Ezekiel. Because of all the exodus language in the verse, one might conceivably look to Ex 15:18 ("Yahweh will reign forever and ever," the coda of what is often called Israel's Te Deum) as the ultimate reason for the verb's appearance here too. Ezekiel frequently uses the corresponding noun מֶלֶךְ for pagan kings, and the verb is used in 17:16 in a secular sense, but Ezekiel avoids using מֶלֶךְ for Yahweh, and normally avoids using it for OT Israel's kings (except in 1:2 and the condemnations in 43:7, 9). Reasons why he avoids it for the kings are discussed in "Introduction to Ezekiel 19" in the commentary on chapter 19. Ezekiel does use other regal terminology for Yahweh. For example, in chapter 34, Yahweh will "shepherd" Israel (רָעָה in 34:12–16; cf. Psalm 23). "Shepherd" is a common epithet of kings throughout the ancient Near East, and the new David (Jesus Christ) will be Israel's "Shepherd" (רֹעֶה, 34:23; 37:24) and "King" (מֶלֶךְ, 37:22, 24).

20:35 Elsewhere (other than 20:35–36) I have consistently rendered מִדְבָּר as "desert" instead of "wilderness" because according to modern usage "desert" more accurately conveys the nature of the terrain involved. Here I have made an exception for "the *wilderness* of the peoples" because the reference is not to any particular terrain or geographical location, but to the regathered people experiencing God's judgment in the same way that the Israelites did during their forty years of wilderness

---

[17] Cf. Zimmerli, *Ezekiel*, 1:417–18, and Allen, *Ezekiel*, 2:13–14. Critics who tend to consider virtually all of the rest of the chapter as a postexilic supplement usually understand the words in that way.

wandering after the first exodus (and the use of "wilderness" for that is part of the vernacular of biblically literate people). To convey that typology clearly, מִדְבָּר is translated the same way in 20:36 ("the *wilderness* of the land of Egypt," meaning the wilderness they entered after leaving Egypt).

וְנִשְׁפַּטְתִּי אִתְּכֶם—The Niphal of שָׁפַט in 20:35–36 (also 17:20; 38:22) with preposition (אֵת) has a middle sense, "I will enter into judgment with you," and implies more personal involvement than would the Qal with a direct object ("I will judge you"). It suggests more than just the beginning of juridical proceedings. Especially together with "face to face," it may signal a dialogic situation: the accused stands before the judge. If the accused says anything, it would be to confess his guilt (perhaps corroborated by other witnesses), based on which the judge pronounces the sentence. It is plain that before God the people can do nothing but plead guilty and receive his justice. The same kind of helplessness before God is envisioned in "Just as I Am, without One Plea" (*LW* 359).

20:37 וְהַעֲבַרְתִּי אֶתְכֶם תַּחַת הַשָּׁבֶט—To "cause to pass under the staff" refers to the shepherd's practice of counting off, separating, and/or selecting members of a flock. Lev 27:32–33 (for the tithe) and Jer 33:13 mention counting animals in that way. But instead of enumeration, the practice often was for the purpose of culling: the rejection of the inferior or unsuitable and the selection of those usable or fit for a purpose. Probably such separation is implied here, anticipating the purge in the following verse.

בְּמָסֹרֶת הַבְּרִית:—The noun מָסֹרֶת is a hapax legomenon and inevitably precipitates major debates. Already the ancient versions had difficulty with it and vary widely. The most common understanding, which I have also followed, is that it is derived from אָסַר, "bind," so the phrase means "the bond of the covenant" (so BDB, s.v. מָסֹרֶת). The fuller form of a noun derived from that root would be מַאְסֹרֶת, but the weak א apparently became quiescent and was elided. Likewise, the common noun מוֹסֵר, "bond, fetter," probably is from that same root with the elision of א (see also הָאֲסוּרִים for הָאֲסוּרִים, "fetters," in Eccl 4:14). This understanding was followed in antiquity by the Vulgate and Aquila, who translate "bond," and among modern translations, by KJV, NKJV, NRSV,[18] NIV, and ESV.

The Syriac translated ܒܡܪܕܘܬܐ ܕܕܝܬܩܐ, "into the discipline/chastisement of the covenant" (ܕܕܝܬܩܐ is a transliteration of διαθήκη), and so it apparently understood מָסֹרֶת to be synonymous with מוּסָר, "discipline, chastisement" (a derivative of יָסַר), since the Syriac often uses ܡܪܕܘܬܐ to translate מוּסָר. Such a route may be supported by שֵׁבֶט ("staff") earlier in the verse because מוּסָר is parallel to שֵׁבֶט in Prov 13:24; 22:15; 23:13. A few others have taken מָסֹרֶת as derived from יָסַר.

---

[18] NRSV has "within the bond of the covenant." Why does it render בְּ by "within" instead of "into"? Even if the sense may not be much different, one may be excused for wondering whether a semi-universalistic impulse cannot be detected. Compare the "two covenant" theory, so popular among ecumenists, according to which the NT covenant did not supersede or fulfill that of the OT, but is an entirely separate covenant for Gentiles, while Jews continue to be saved by the old covenant apart from Christ. That theory, of course, directly contradicts the claims of Christ himself and the rest of the NT.

Still another theoretical possibility is to derive the noun from מָסַר, "deliver, transmit (a tradition)" (the verb from which the name for the "Masoretes" is derived). While מָסַר is common in postbiblical Hebrew, it occurs only twice in the OT (Num 31:5, 16; see *HALOT*). Greenberg cites the rare Tannaitic idiom מסרת ביד- meaning "be under obligation" (or "have a tradition"), which in a rabbinic passage alternates with another phrase meaning "be bound by oath."[19] The LXX's ἐν ἀριθμῷ probably is related to מָסַר, which can mean "count" (cf. *HALOT*, Niphal), and the LXX is followed by RSV: "I will let you go in by number," taken as a parallel to the first half of the verse.[20]

Since the LXX lacks a translation of הַבְּרִית, some critics take it as a dittograph of the first word of the next verse, וּבָרוֹתִי, but its absence in the LXX is more likely to be a result of haplography.

20:38 וּבָרוֹתִי מִכֶּם—The verb בָּרַר occurs only here in Ezekiel and in the Qal means "purge out, purify" (BDB, 1).

לֹא יָבוֹא—The singular verb has the plural compound subject הַמֹּרְדִים וְהַפּוֹשְׁעִים. Yet the marginal Masoretic *sebir* warns against emending the verb to the plural. See the textual note on 14:1, which begins with וַיָּבֹא, followed by a plural subject.

20:39 By almost any reckoning, 20:39 is difficult, both in syntax and in theology. Translators and commentators disagree, and many emendations are suggested. Finally, one must simply "sin boldly."

אִישׁ גִּלּוּלָיו לְכוּ עֲבֹדוּ—This is the same kind of construction as in 20:7; see the textual notes there. There are parallels to the ironical imperative, for example, Amos 4:4 ("come to Bethel and sin") or Jer 44:25 ("confirm your vows and fulfill your vows" to the queen of heaven). The LXX removed the irony here by rendering with ἐξάρατε, perhaps reading הַעֲבִירוּ, "remove," or בַּעֲרוּ, "burn down/destroy," instead of עֲבֹדוּ ("worship"). However, other versions support the MT, and there may be a deliberate correspondence with יַעַבְדֻנִי ("they will worship me") in 20:40.

וְאַחַר אִם־אֵינְכֶם שֹׁמְעִים אֵלָי—If we eschew speculative emendations,[21] this clause (clear enough itself) raises a hard issue of Hebrew syntax. The first issue is whether this clause belongs with what precedes or with what follows. If we follow the Masoretic accents, as I and probably a majority of translators do, it continues the preceding clause (see the preceding textual note), and the major break comes at its end (אֵלָי with *athnach* ends the first half of the verse). But then the second issue is that the conditional clause introduced by אִם appears to be incomplete. The best solution seems to be to assume that the needed apodosis has been omitted, perhaps the implied

---

19 Greenberg, *Ezekiel*, 1:372–73.

20 Zimmerli, *Ezekiel*, 1:403, following the LXX, emends מָסֹרֶת to מִסְפָּר (and *HALOT* follows Zimmerli), but that emendation is unnecessary.

21 Zimmerli, *Ezekiel*, 1:403, mentions the possibility of following the LXX but, more radically, thinks he perceives in לְכוּ a remnant of an original הַשְׁלִיכוּ (as in 20:7, "throw away"). He then skips to וְאֶת־שֵׁם קָדְשִׁי, dismissing what intervenes (usually considered the most problematic part of the verse) as a stray fragment from elsewhere. But all of this is entirely arbitrary.

dire threat being considered obvious: if you will not listen to me then I will annihilate (cf. 20:13), destroy (cf. 20:17), devastate (cf. 20:26) you!

Some who connect this clause with what follows interpret אִם as the sign of an oath ("surely"). NIV[22] and Keil[23] follow this option. But as Greenberg correctly points out, when אִם is used as an oath particle with a negative, the usual phrase is אִם לֹא followed by a finite verb, not אִם אֵין- with a participle.[24]

20:41 בְּרֵיחַ נִיחֹחַ—On the nuance of the preposition בְּ here, see the commentary. On רֵיחַ נִיחֹחַ, see the textual note on it in 6:13.

20:43 דַּרְכֵיכֶם וְאֵת כָּל־עֲלִילוֹתֵיכֶם—"Way(s)" and "deeds" are parallel, as also in 14:22–23; 20:44; 24:14; 36:17, 19; Ps 103:7. The two words could easily be taken as a hendiadys. עֲלִילָה can refer to good deeds or even God's deeds (Ps 103:7), but Ezekiel always uses it in a negative sense of sinful human deeds. (See the last textual note on 20:44.)

אֲשֶׁר נִטְמֵאתֶם בָּם—The Niphal of טמא (also in 20:30–31) could be translated either as passive or reflexive. I have chosen the latter because the sense is not that the Israelites were hapless victims of circumstances over which they had no control. On the contrary, they had actively rejected Yahweh and chosen another way. The next verb (see the next textual note) must be translated reflexively, and the two reflexives fit well together.

וּנְקֹטֹתֶם בִּפְנֵיכֶם—The verb קוט occurs mostly in the Niphal (as here) and has a very strong meaning, "to loathe, detest, abhor oneself." Like the related verb קוץ, the sense is not only psychological, but also psychosomatic, implying nausea or retching. Most translations render the verb reflexively ("you will loath yourselves"). Many translations do not reflect בִּפְנֵיכֶם ("in your own sight"). בִּפְנֵיכֶם is a less common, but probably stronger reflexive idiom than the use of נֶפֶשׁ to mean "oneself." Literalistically it is "at your faces," and it almost implies that, at least spiritually, they could not stand to look at themselves in the mirror. Compare our frequent description of the second use of the Law as a mirror. Rendering it as "in your own sight" provides a contrast to "in the sight of the nations" (with לְעֵינֵי, 20:9, 14, 22, 41) and to the idioms about the Israelites' "eyes" (עֵינַיִם) being directed toward their idols (20:7, 8, 24).

20:44 בַּעֲשׂוֹתִי אִתְּכֶם—The idiom עָשָׂה אֵת־, to "deal with" someone, can have either positive or negative connotations, depending on the context (BDB, s.v. עָשָׂה I, 2; cf. *HALOT*, s.v. עָשָׂה, 12). It has a hostile connotation in 7:27; 16:59; 22:14; 23:25, 29; 39:24, but refers to fighting as Israel's ally against a common enemy (Babylon) in 17:17 (which, however, predicts that Pharaoh will fail to aid Israel in that way). Here the context implies that Yahweh's action will be gracious, because it is "for the sake of my name and not according to your evil ways." Greenberg's "act on your behalf" is rather free but in the right direction.[25]

---

[22] "But afterward you will surely listen to me and no longer profane my holy name."

[23] Keil, *Ezekiel*, 1:284.

[24] Greenberg, *Ezekiel*, 1:374.

[25] Greenberg, *Ezekiel*, 1:363 and 376.

לְמַעַן שְׁמִי—In 20:9, 14, 22 God acted "for the sake of [his] name" by refraining from executing judgment on Israel, but here the phrase refers to his beneficent fulfillment of his promises.

וְכַעֲלִילוֹתֵיכֶם הַנִּשְׁחָתוֹת—"Your deeds" (עֲלִילוֹתֵיכֶם) in 20:43 referred to evil deeds, and here the expression is even stronger. The Niphal of שָׁחַת (the Qal is not used) means "corrupt(ed)" and appears, for example, in the flood narrative, where the whole earth became corrupt (Gen 6:11–12; see also Ex 8:20; Jer 13:7; 18:4). The meaning of the phrase here corresponds to the Hiphil of שָׁחַת with עֲלִילָה in Zeph 3:7 and Ps 14:1 and with דֶּרֶךְ in Ezek 16:47 ("you became more depraved … in all your ways"). Again, the corruption of the people is no accident, but the result of their deliberate actions. Ezekiel uses the Piel and the Hiphil of שָׁחַת, both meaning "destroy," for the divine judgment well deserved by the people (5:16; 43:3) but which God previously refrained from carrying out (20:17; cf. 9:8; 22:30).

Commentary
Introduction to Ezekiel 20

This is a long and polymorphous chapter. It is immediately divisible into two very uneven parts: an introduction (20:1–4), which gives us the context for the long divine speech (20:5–44). The latter is usually divided into two segments: a homiletical review of Israel's history that serves as the indictment of Israel (20:5–31) and the future redemption that will bring forth a new Israel (the Christian church), couched in typological terms of a second exodus (20:32–44).

The diatribe divides Israel's past history into four epochs addressing the people's rebellion: (1) in Egypt (20:5–9); (2) in the desert by the original generation brought out from Egypt (20:10–17); (3) in the desert by the second generation (20:18–26); and (4) after the conquest, in the land (20:27–29). In a fifth section Ezekiel considers briefly the present exilic situation (20:30–31).

Then in 20:32–44, he considers Israel's future transformation. Those promissory verses may, in turn, be subdivided into two parts. First is the description of the new exodus as Yahweh brings his scattered people out from the nations with his outstretched arm (20:32–38). He enters into judgment with them in "the wilderness of the peoples" (20:35) as an antitype of the earlier forty years in the wilderness following the first exodus (20:36). Second (20:39–44) is the description of the transformed Israel that is accepted by Yahweh and that offers acceptable worship on his "holy mountain" (20:40), which is an antitype of Solomon's temple on Mount Zion, and in some ways an adumbration of Ezekiel 40–48, since the eschatological city and temple are on a high mountain (40:2; 43:12). Yahweh will finally fulfill his ancient promise, but this time he will not let human sinfulness stand in his way. Nevertheless, those who continue to revolt against him will pay a terrible price. Thus we may outline the chapter as follows:

I. Introduction to Israel's history (20:1–4)
II. Indictment of Israel and promise of redemption (20:5–44)
  A. Indictment: Homiletical review of Israel's history (20:5–31)
    1. Israel in Egypt before the exodus (20:5–9)
    2. The original generation of Israelites who participated in the exodus and received the Torah for life, but rejected it (20:10–17)
    3. The second generation of Israelites, born during the forty years of wilderness wandering (20:18–26)
    4. Israel in the land after the conquest (20:27–29)
    5. Israelites who are Ezekiel's contemporaries (20:30–31)
  B. Yahweh's future redemption creates a new Israel that offers acceptable worship (20:32–44)
    1. The new exodus from the wilderness of the peoples (20:32–38)
    2. The acceptance and worship of the new, transformed Israel (20:39–44)

What is labeled in English Bibles as 20:45–49 is 21:1–5 in the Hebrew, and so it will be covered in the commentary on chapter 21. While those verses may be related to this chapter, they record a separate "Word of Yahweh" (21:1 [ET 20:45]) and a response by Ezekiel (21:5 [ET 20:49]), making the Hebrew chapter division the better of the two.

Even when the facts of history are undisputed, they are subject to interpretation. God's own explanation for the way he has guided history may differ radically from human perspectives on the same events. Human historians are selective: they choose the events they want included in their rehearsals of history in order to paint the picture the way they want it painted. God's narration of history (in Ezekiel 20 and elsewhere in Scripture) is selective too, but the resulting painting is authoritative because God is the author of all history. (One may compare the apostle John's salvific reason for selecting some events and excluding many others from his Gospel in Jn 20:30–31.)

The institutional church on earth is *simul iustus et peccator*, just as its individual members are. And just as individuals tend to gloss over their sins (if they are even aware of them), so the church tends to paint an idealized picture of itself, ignoring or burying in obscure footnotes its failings—sins of both omission and commission. It is against such an idealized picture of the OT church (Israel) that 20:5–31 is directed, and it could easily be recast so as to apply to the NT church.[26]

Critics often label Ezekiel's history "revisionist," but that implies historical inaccuracy. Rather, it is a true and tendentious history, told to make a certain point (as all presentations of history are). Even if one admits (as most will

---

[26] It would be a fruitful exercise to have a faithful member of the church (not, of course, some hostile agnostic) do his best to write an "objective" history of the church—of any focus, whether of Christendom at large, of Lutheranism as a whole, of The Lutheran Church—Missouri Synod, or of any local congregation. The picture that would emerge would not be the prettiest, not one the public relations departments would advertise. See Block's observations along the same line (*Ezekiel*, 1:658).

today) that any purely "objective" history is impossible, the label "tendentious" applies to Ezekiel's account of history like no other in the Bible. In a way, it is of a piece with the extreme, hyperbolic statements and portraits throughout the book. Ezekiel makes assertions unmentioned in the historical books. Even humanly speaking, he might have had access to information we no longer have, or it may be his rhetorical way of making the point that, in principle, Israel has always been refractory. All phases of Israel's sin are essentially alike: defying God's will *and* substituting the people's own will for God's. "Contra all their creedal affirmations, Israel's story is no *Heilsgeschichte* ('history of salvation'); it is a story of apostasy and rebellion from beginning to end."[27]

Certain themes especially stand out in chapter 20, most of which correspond to the eschatological era predicted in chapter 36. Perhaps most prominent of these is Yahweh's great concern for his "name," a motif especially associated with Deuteronomy and that appears in Ezekiel most prominently in chapters 20 and 36 (and elsewhere only in chapters 39 and 43).[28] Three times Yahweh said, "I resolved to pour out my wrath on them" (20:8, 13, 21), but instead, each time "I acted for the sake of my name" (20:9, 14; similar is 20:22), and concern for his name caused him to modify his punishment of Israel. It will also be Yahweh's motivation for Israel's restoration, "when I deal with you for the sake of my name and not according to your evil ways" (20:44).

Usually "name" is taken merely as concern for God's reputation (an idiom also present in English), and no doubt, that is a part of it. But God's "name" is a far more loaded term than that. Often it is what I call a "hypostasis" of Christ (as also is Yahweh's "Glory"). Thus Yahweh's "name" is a way of expressing Christ's incarnational or "sacramental" presence on earth, even before his incarnation of the Virgin Mary (Is 7:14; Mt 1:23). This "hypostasis" of Christ is what dogmaticians call the λόγος ἄσαρκος, "the Word not yet made flesh" (cf. Jn 1:14).[29]

Since Yahweh's very character is involved in his "name," his judgments are not arbitrary, but follow fixed rules, and his promises are just as certain. The promise of Israel actually living in a covenant relationship with Yahweh is affirmed in 20:5 ("I am Yahweh, your God") and reaffirmed in terms of the new covenant in 36:28 ("You will be my people, and I will be your God"; see also "covenant" in 20:37; 34:25; 37:26). The theme of the Israelites defiling themselves (Hithpael of טָמֵא in 20:7, 18; Niphal in 20:30, 31, 43; cf. the Piel in 20:26) is finally solved by Yahweh himself cleansing them (Piel of טָהֵר in 36:25, 33; 37:23). That priestly vocabulary characteristic of Leviticus (hence

---

[27] Block, *Ezekiel*, 1:614.

[28] For the theme in Deuteronomy, see, for example, Deut 5:11; 6:13; 10:8, 20; 12:5, 11, 21; 14:23–24; 16:2, 6, 11. In Ezekiel שֵׁם refers to God's "name" in 20:9, 14, 22, 39, 44; 36:20–23; 39:7, 25; 43:7–8.

[29] See further the textual notes on 1:28 and the commentary on 1:3, 25–28.

familiar to Ezekiel, the priest, 1:3) is but one sample of the extent to which this chapter focuses on cultic (in contrast to political) issues: "fecal deities" (idols), "abominations," child sacrifice, and improper sites of worship.

Ezekiel 20 puts great accent on the promised "land"[e] versus other lands.[f] There is special stress on the Sabbath as a sign of the covenant (20:12–24). God's raising of his hand in oath is a recurrent refrain.[g] Other special features of the chapter will be noted in the course of the exegesis.

The reference to the "fathers" (אָבוֹת) at the end of 20:4 is, in a backhanded way, transitional to 20:5 since it is their "abominable practices" (20:4) that are the topic of the sermon in 20:5–31. The word must be heard in the generalized sense of "ancestors," not "patriarchs," as it sometimes implies. It is not entirely clear why Ezekiel does not begin his survey of Israel's history with the patriarchs. He clearly was familiar with them, as is proven, for example, by his use of the phrase "house of Jacob" in 20:5 and the reference to Abraham in 33:24. Perhaps the patriarchs were too archetypal of faithful reception of God's blessing. More likely, Ezekiel wishes to begin with Israel's first encounter with Yahweh as a nation, which occurred in Egypt, and the following verse (20:5) indicates some accent on the revelation of his *name* there. This alludes to the "I Am" passage in Ex 3:14 and to Ex 6:3, where Yahweh contrasts the patriarchs knowing him as "El Shaddai" ("God Almighty"?) with his revelation of (the fuller meaning of) his name "Yahweh" to Moses (see further the commentary on Ezek 20:5–6).

One other related issue probably should engage us topically before we proceed with the verse-by-verse exegesis. It will be immediately obvious that Ezekiel presents Israel's time in Egypt, even before she was constituted as a nation (through the exodus and conquest of the land), as an evil time (so also in 23:19). In fact, he makes no mention of a prelapsarian period. If Ezekiel were writing a dogmatic treatise, one might describe this as his "doctrine" of original sin (cf. also 16:3–5, where "Jerusalem" is conceived by pagan Canaanites and rejected at her birth). From the outset to the present day, she "could not not sin" (to reproduce the double negative of a classical Latin formulation *non posse non peccare*).[30]

That construal of Israel's time in Egypt clashes frontally with other prophetic views. For those who operate with a hermeneutic of suspicion, Ezekiel 20 has always been a famous example of inconsistency or outright contradiction in Scripture. The disparity is sharpest with Hosea and Jeremiah. Jeremiah depicts the wilderness period (after the exodus, before the conquest) as a sort of honeymoon (Jer 2:2–3). Similarly, Hosea localizes Israel's fall at Baal Peor (Hos 9:10; see also Numbers 25; 31:8, 16), its last desert encampment before

(e) Ezek 20:6, 15, 28, 38, 40, 42

(f) Ezek 20:5–10, 23, 32, 34, 36, 38, 41

(g) Ezek 20:5, 6, 15, 23, 28, 42

---

[30] Johann Gerhard, "De libero arbitrio," § 29, *Loci Theologici*, vol. 2 (ed. Eduard Preuss; Berlin: Gustav Schlawitz, 1864), 241, translated in Pieper, *Christian Dogmatics*, 3:555. See also FC Ep and SD II, "Free Will."

crossing the Jordan (toward the end of the forty years of wilderness wandering). Those other prophets seem to regard Israel as having been pure until she approached or entered Canaan and was contaminated by its cult and culture. Perhaps comparable to Hosea and Jeremiah is Isaiah's description of Jerusalem having once been characterized by faithfulness and righteousness (Is 1:21, 26).

However, the Pentateuchal narratives themselves support Ezekiel. The accounts of Exodus through Deuteronomy are full of records of Israel's grumbling, rebellion, and idolatry (climactically, the golden calf incident in Exodus 32).

How does one harmonize all these disparate accounts? Perhaps an attempt to "harmonize" pinpoints the problem. All the perspectives are true, but as is normally the case in all real history, the whole picture was far more complicated than the aspect any one writer accented. One must not ask the accounts to answer questions they were not trying to answer. None of the viewpoints pretends to give a comprehensive, exhaustive narration of Israel's history. Since God's people ever remain both saints and sinners throughout earthly life (if indeed they remain God's people and are not totally apostate), their history will always provide examples of at least some fidelity and also plenty of infidelity. The details of Israel's disobedience varied from age to age, yet it was all disobedience (cf. Gal 5:3; James 2:10).

Whether one form of rebellion or one era of infidelity should be considered more offensive than another depends on perspective, on the particular point Yahweh wants to make through the writer at that time. Thus when through Hosea, Isaiah, and Jeremiah, Yahweh calls his people back to the covenant he once established with them, he pictures that time as one of divine favor and relative faithfulness, compared to the increasing apostasy of later times (cf. Christ calling the church at Ephesus back to her first love, Rev 2:4). Ezekiel 20, on the other hand, is preparing the people for the impending judgment (the destruction of Jerusalem in 587 B.C.) by demonstrating how it is fully justified. No longer is Yahweh calling his people to return to the old covenant; rather, he will establish a new one (20:32–44; cf. 34:25; 37:26).

Introduction to Israel's History (20:1–4)

20:1 We are given no clue as to why the elders of Israel came to Ezekiel. That they came to him at all suggests that, however skeptically or reluctantly, they do consider him a genuine prophet. However, their response as summarized by Ezekiel in 21:5 (ET 20:49) may indicate not only disappointment at the harsh reply, but also doubts about the authenticity of his claims to be an accredited spokesman of God. That the elders are "of Israel" implies that they spoke—or at least claimed to speak—for all Israelites, including those not yet exiled. Throughout the book it is evident that Ezekiel himself often does not distinguish between those already exiled with him in Babylon and those soon to be. Both were equally guilty of the same abominable ideas and practices. (Some critical attempts to distinguish the two by appealing to additional editors easily approach the ludicrous.)

20:2–3 The elders are rebuffed in about the strongest possible language. The rhetorical question "Are you really coming to consult me?" casts doubt on the sincerity of the elder's request and probably implies that Yahweh's answer will be negative, if he answers at all (cf. 7:26). Whatever was in their hearts, they were not consulting him with their whole heart and being (cf. Deut 4:29). A similar rebuff had come in Ezek 14:3–11, where the reason Yahweh gave was that they had "fecal deities [idols] in their hearts." It is undoubtedly for the same reason here, but Ezekiel does not make it explicit.

In the second part of the reply, "As I live, I will not let myself be consulted by you" (20:3), Yahweh emphatically states that he is not available for consultation by such skeptics. He emphasizes this by an oath by his own life (his very being and will), and the concluding signatory formula, "says the Lord Yahweh." Answer to prayer is a gift to the contrite, not a "right" available also to "dogs ... and whoever loves and practices a lie" (Rev 22:15).

As our Lord Jesus Christ himself teaches in the fullness of revelation, "no one comes to the Father except through me" (Jn 14:6). Hence, the most precise Trinitarian form of prayer is *to* the Father (e.g., Phil 4:6; Jude 25), *through* the Son (e.g., Rom 1:8; 16:27), and *in* the Holy Spirit (e.g., Eph 6:18). The same thought is summarized when prayers begin with the baptismal formula (Mt 28:19), also used for the Invocation: "In the name of the Father and of the Son and of the Holy Spirit."[31] The Scriptures and the liturgy and hymns of the church include prayers addressed to God the Son and to God the Holy Spirit as well as to the Father, but always with the full Trinity in mind, never in the sense of confessing a "unitarianism" of any one person, which arguably would be little better than prayer addressed to some indeterminate "God." In practice, my perception is that this is a problem especially with prayers addressed only to Jesus; the Trinitarian context must be explicitly verbalized. All valid prayers are in Jesus' name, that is, spoken with faith in Christ and in reliance on the divine mercy he has procured by his atonement on the cross, which is what makes us and our prayers acceptable to God (cf. Rev 5:8; 8:3–4).[32]

20:4 Yahweh will not give the elders whatever they may have wanted to gain by approaching the prophet, but he will seize the opportunity to impress upon them the terrible legacy of flagrant disobedience they were affirming by continuing on the same path. The tenor of the searing sermon that follows (especially Ezek 20:5–31) is clearly indicated by the question that directs Ezekiel to "arraign/indict" them and by the command to "remind them of the abominable practices of their fathers." In the Torah, this terminology (תּוֹעֵבֹת, "abominations, abominable practices") predominantly refers to the pagan practices of the peoples Yahweh was going to destroy so that Israel could inherit the land (e.g., Lev 18:22–30; Deut 7:25–26; 18:9–12). Now, severed from the covenant, Israel was in God's eyes only another Canaanite nation.

---

[31] For example, SC, Morning Prayer and Evening Prayer.
[32] Cf. Ap XXI 20; LC III (Lord's Prayer) 1–34.

Indictment: Homiletical Review of Israel's History (20:5–31)

Israel in Egypt before the Exodus (20:5–9)

20:5 The bill of indictment begins with God's unmerited election of "Israel." The reference is not to the patriarch Jacob, but to the nation or people, as evidenced by the following parallel phrase "house of Jacob." (The LXX adds "house" also to make "house of Israel.")

It is striking that this is the only place in the book with the key verb בָּחַר, "choose, elect." Just why is not certain, but the best guess is that Ezekiel avoids it elsewhere because of the tendency of sinful people to presume that their election by God allows them the luxury of responding with complacency and failure in sanctification—something Moses keenly warned against in his farewell sermon (בָּחַר in Deut 4:37; 7:6–7; 10:15; 14:2; see also 9:4–29).

Even though Ezekiel does not develop it, the vocabulary of election is useful in summarizing biblical typology and the unity of the church of both Testaments in Christ. In the NT, ἐκλέγομαι, "choose, elect," is used of God choosing Israel's patriarchs (Acts 13:17); of Christ himself as chosen/elected by the Father (Lk 9:35); of Christ choosing the apostles (Lk 6:13; Acts 1:2); and of all Christians as the elect (Mk 13:20; 1 Cor 1:27–28; Eph 1:4; James 2:5). The typological connection between those chosen in the OT and Christ, and between Christ and the elect in him, pervades the patristic writings.[33] One can diagram this by two triangles with their apexes meeting in *the Elect One*, Christ himself, in whom the elect of both Testaments find their unity.[34] The history of the "chosen people" in the OT finds its fulfillment in Christ and then is continued with the church as the new Israel until the consummation, when all the elect ("all Israel," Rom 11:26, that is, all believers in Christ) shall be saved.

In the phrase "descendants [literally, 'seed'] of the house of Jacob," which occurs only here in the OT (cf. Jer 23:8; Ezek 44:22), Ezekiel has combined the very common "house of Jacob" (twenty-one times in the OT) with the less common "seed of Jacob" (only Is 45:19; Jer 33:26; Ps 22:24 [ET 22:23]). Perhaps the point is to underscore the congenital and common complicity of the whole people in their history of sin. "Jacob" and "Israel" are often used in parallelism and indistinguishably, but sometimes, as perhaps here, "Jacob" refers to the unregenerate shyster the patriarch initially was (and his descendants were), while "Israel" reflects the conversion affected in connection with the change of name (Gen 32:23–29 [ET 32:22–28]).

Yahweh's statement "I made myself known to them" (וָאִוָּדַע לָהֶם, Ezek 20:5) in connection with the exodus from Egypt is a direct reference to the revelation of the meaning of his name to Moses in Ex 3:14 and to Ex 6:3, where Yahweh told Moses, "(By) my name Yahweh I did not make myself known to

---

[33] The relevant literature is large, but one of the best introductions can be found in Woollcombe, "The Biblical Origins and Patristic Development of Typology."

[34] This is illustrated in Mitchell, *Our Suffering Savior*, 39.

them [the patriarchs]" (וּשְׁמִי יְהוָה לֹא נוֹדַעְתִּי לָהֶם). In addition to the verbal explanations Yahweh gave to Moses, the meaning of his name would be shown by his acts of salvation as he redeemed Israel from Egypt.[35] The Hebrew יָדַע, "to know," often implies far more than mere cognition and hence is not easy to translate (cf. its idiomatic use for the act of marriage). In a covenantal context such as this, it implies more than mere awareness of the existence of the divine name ("Yahweh," the Tetragrammaton); it also signifies an awareness of all that the name conveys (election, covenant, etc.) and an intimacy with the God who bears the name. By revealing his name to them, God allows himself to be invoked by them, but at the same time opens up the possibility that his name will be misused. It is no accident that the "preamble" to the Decalogue[36] opens by citing the name (Ex 20:2 ‖ Deut 5:6), and later the entire Second Commandment is devoted to "the name of Yahweh, your God" (Ex 20:7 ‖ Deut 5:11).

To emphasize that the initiative for Israel's special covenantal relationship lay with God alone, Yahweh twice affirms in Ezek 20:5 that "I swore with uplifted hand." Also emphasizing divine monergism in salvation is Yahweh's citation of only part ("I am Yahweh, your God") of the common covenant formula that summarizes the meaning and benefit of the covenant. The formula normally also continues with a clause like "and you will be my people,"[h] but it was precisely that part Israel had neglected and spurned. The establishment of the covenant is a unilateral gift of God, but it is not enforced upon anyone without reception in faith, nor is it some sort of magic.

(h) E.g., Ex 6:7; Lev 26:12; Ezek 36:28; Ezek 11:20; 14:11; 34:30; 37:23, 27

20:6 The reiteration of the oath now brings it into connection with a choice land. Here the promise is to the Israelites in Egypt, not to the patriarchs (whom Ezekiel skips over; see "Introduction to Ezekiel 20" above). The reference, if we look for a specific one, is probably Ex 6:8, where Yahweh extends the patriarchal promise ("the land which I swore with uplifted hand to give to Abraham") to the Israelites in Egypt ("I will give it [the land] to you as a possession"). Yet Ezek 20:6 is so much in line with the general thrust of the exodus narrative that we do not need a more specific reference to that effect.

---

[35] Thus Ex 3:14 and 6:3 speak of Yahweh revealing more fully the significance of his name, which the Israelites came to know as he saved them (cf. Mt 1:21). Failure or refusal to understand "know" (יָדַע) in this sense played a prominent role in the old critical documentary hypothesis (JEDP): Since God had repeatedly identified himself as "Yahweh" in Genesis (in the "J" source), Ex 6:3 must have been about the patriarchal history according to the "E" source (which only referred to God as Elohim). Two different documents with two different histories of Israel's religion must have (supposedly) been involved!

[36] According to the Jewish numbering of the commandments, this (Ex 20:2 ‖ Deut 5:6) is the First Commandment (even though it is Yahweh's self-identification, and not a command). In many ways that numbering system is superior to either of the two used by Christians (one is used by Roman Catholics and Lutherans, the other by Eastern Orthodox and Reformed churches) because the preamble sets forth the Gospel basis for Israel's response in faith (obeying all the commandments). The OT calls the Decalogue the "ten words" (עֲשֶׂרֶת הַדְּבָרִים, Ex 34:28; Deut 4:13; 10:4) but does not specify how they are to be divided or counted.

Apart from the covenant oath, Ezekiel does not dwell on the redemptive activity in connection with the exodus. Zimmerli has noted that nowhere in the book does Ezekiel ever even use גָּאַל or פָּדָה, verbs for "redeem, ransom" that the Torah uses to summarize Yahweh's redemption of Israel through the exodus.[37]

Instead of the usual verb נָתַן, "give," in reference to the gift of the land (as in 20:15, 28, 42), in 20:6 we have תּוּר, "search out, spy out, reconnoiter." The reference is to Num 10:33 and Deut 1:33 (both use תּוּר), where God scouts for Israel's campsites as he leads them by means of his ark (Num 10:33–36), "the cloud of Yahweh" (Num 10:34; cf. Deut 1:33), and the pillar of fire by night (Deut 1:33). Perhaps, however, there is also a deliberate allusion to one of the tragic examples of Israel's disobedience during the journey. After the twelve spies reconnoiter Canaan, all the spies but Caleb and Joshua bring a negative report and the people mutiny, with the result that Yahweh threatens to annihilate them and start anew (תּוּר is used throughout Numbers 13–14, including the participle for the "spies" in 14:6). Moses' intercession commutes the sentence to the fact that all the unfaithful would die in the desert without themselves setting foot in the promised land, and the forty days of spying translates into the forty years in the desert (Num 14:33–34). The whole episode is so similar to Ezekiel's pattern of recounting Israel's history as one of apostasy, with complete annihilation threatened and just barely averted,[i] that one is almost surprised that he does not dwell on it a bit longer.

Let us observe parenthetically that the theme of the "land" is difficult typologically. With its eschatological component we have no difficulty: the new heavens and new earth with the new Jerusalem, to be created after Christ's second coming, are the promised land for Christians (e.g., Isaiah 11; 65; Ezekiel 40–48; Revelation 21–22). But what of the interim between the first and second comings of Christ? For now Christianity has no specific "land" in a geographical sense, and the NT refrains from speaking in such terms. But anywhere on this globe we still occupy space and time, and if we have not totally spiritualized or privatized the concept of the church as the "*body* of Christ" (not merely a metaphor), its pre-eschatological counterpart is to be sought there. Of that, the physicality of the Sacraments (Baptism and the Lord's Supper) should be a major reminder, and we look forward to "the resurrection of the *body*" for "the life everlasting" (Apostles' Creed).

20:7 Except for Josh 24:14, we have no explicit record of Israelite idolatry in Egypt, nor of an explicit demand there that they cease and desist. But there is nothing intrinsically unlikely about either, and in fact, both can be inferred by the Israelites' interactions with Moses: their initial rejection of the very idea of leaving Egypt with Moses (Ex 6:9, 12), their reaction when they feared that the Pharaoh had them trapped at the Red Sea (Ex 14:11–12), their

(i) E.g., Ezek 9:8; 11:13; 20:8–9, 13–14, 17, 21–22

---

[37] Zimmerli, *Ezekiel*, 1:408. On פָּדָה used for God "redeeming" Israel from Egypt, see, for example, Deut 7:8; 9:26; 13:6 (ET 13:5). For גָּאַל see, for example, Ex 6:6; 15:13.

repeated expressions of a desire to return to Egypt (e.g., Num 11:4–5, 18, 20; 14:2–4), and the golden calf incident (Exodus 32).[38]

The last clause in Ezek 20:7, "I am Yahweh, your God," is a repetition of its use in connection with the revealing of the covenant name in Ezek 20:5. The clause (and the shorter "I am Yahweh") is common in much Pentateuchal legislation. Yahweh had no need to offer a rationale of every command; often he begins (e.g., Ex 20:2 ‖ Deut 5:6; Lev 18:2; 19:3; 26:1) and/or ends (e.g., Lev 18:30; 19:36; 25:55) a block of legislation with this statement of his name. It was Yahweh's will, consonant with his revealed nature, and the faithful need no other explanation. The principle still applies! (Compare the "name" of the Lord Jesus in the NT [e.g., Acts 2:38; 3:6; 1 Cor 1:2, 10].)

20:8 Such a resolve by God against the Israelites while still in Egypt is not attested elsewhere, but compare Ex 32:10 soon afterward, and Ezek 20:9 may suggest that Ezekiel is condensing events after the reference to "bring[ing] them out of the land of Egypt" (20:6). The resolve here may be partly formulaic, because almost identical language will be repeated in 20:13, 21 regarding Israel's later sins, which are attested elsewhere. Formulaic patterning will also be true of the next verse.

20:9 The themes of covenant making (Yahweh making his name known) and of the exodus are somewhat telescoped here, but that only illustrates how cursorily Ezekiel is rehearsing past history. The viewpoint, at the heart of Ezekiel's theology, is radically theocentric. Yahweh's action was not sought by the Israelites (let alone merited), but it was imposed upon them for his purpose. Having sworn by his own name, the election of Israel becomes irrevocable, because it was done for Yahweh's sake, not Israel's. This rhetoric of what might sound like historical determinism can easily be misconstrued as contradicting the accent on individual accountability in chapters 18 and 33. By nature, all of us were rebels (Rom 5:6–10) and partly remain so *(simul iustus et peccator,* Romans 7). Only the miracle of God preserving us in the faith (Rom 8:28–39; Eph 1:3–23; 2 Thess 2:13–17) keeps any of us from lapsing into an absolute incorrigibility (cf. Heb 6:4–14) and being damned along with those who never believed. In Ezek 20:32 Yahweh will express to Ezekiel's contemporaries that he will prevent them from becoming completely assimilated into the heathen nations, and Yahweh even offers that prevention as part of the motive for the future redemption in 20:33–34.

The Exodus Israelites Who Received the Torah for Life but Rejected It (20:10–17)

20:10 With this verse begins the second phase of Israel's past: the original generation of Israelites who participated in the exodus (ca. 1440 B.C.) and their relationship to Yahweh in the desert. While 20:11–12 certainly refers to

---

[38] Cf. Harstad, *Joshua,* 781, who also cites Lev 17:7; Deut 32:16–17; as well as Ezek 20:7–8; 23:3, 8.

the Torah God gave Moses at Sinai, one cannot help but note that Yahweh says nothing specifically about Mount Sinai or Horeb, neither here nor anywhere else in the book. The concern here is not the geographical location but the Israelites' encounter with their God.

20:11 The key terms "statutes," "ordinances," "live," and "observes/keeps" are found throughout the Torah in abundance. The verse is very similar to Lev 18:5. The accent on faithfulness to Yahweh as the key to life repeats the emphasis of Ezekiel 18, where the man who keeps Yahweh's "statutes" and "ordinances" (the same terms used in 20:11 are also in 18:9, 17; "statutes" is also in 18:21) will "live."[j] The use of הָאָדָם ("man" in the generic sense, "mankind, humanity") suggests a universal aspect. While the passage is about OT Israel, the promise of life also applies to all those incorporated into the new Israel through faith and Baptism into Christ (e.g., Gal 3:26–29; 6:16). We have earlier discussed the multivalence of "statutes" and "ordinances" (see the textual notes on Ezek 5:6 and 11:12), as well as the eschatological meaning of "live" in such contexts, which points to eternal life (see the commentary on 18:4 and also on 18:7–9). The proper understanding of all these terms in the light of all Scripture (including the NT) will keep them from being misunderstood as sheer legalism. Far from onerous demands, the Torah was God's gracious gift, along with the land.

(j) Also in Ezek 18:9, 13, 17, 19, 21–24, 27, 28, 32

20:12 Yahweh revealed the general principles of his covenant relationship with his people, and here he highlights the Sabbath as a special "sign" or distinguishing mark of that closeness. "Sign" is not quite an adequate reproduction of אוֹת. In some contexts it might be called "incarnational" (e.g., Is 8:18) or "sacramental" (see further the last textual note and the commentary on Ezek 4:3). The word connotes an outward, visible indication of divine power or truth. If Block is correct in applying the plural "my Sabbaths" to the extensions of the seventh day of the week (to Sabbatical Years, the Jubilee, and other occasions when all work ceased),[39] its application not only to time, but also to space and matter, that is, to all dimensions of life, is even more obvious.

The two versions of the Decalogue give two complementary reasons for the Sabbath command. Ex 20:11 relates it to God's own rest at the end of his six days of creative work, when he "sanctified" ("made holy," factitive Piel of קָדַשׁ) the seventh day, while Deut 5:15 bases the observance of the Sabbath on the exodus, when Yahweh saved Israel from slavery in Egypt. That is, in both the orders of creation (Ex 20:11) and of redemption (Deut 5:15), the believer renounces his claim to autonomy over his time and space, abstaining from his own concerns to confess God's domain over his whole life.

The Third Commandment enjoins the faithful to "remember" (זָכוֹר) the Sabbath to "*keep* it holy" (לְקַדְּשׁוֹ, Ex 20:8; cf. Deut 5:12). That is possible only because God had originally "*made* it holy" when he established it (וַיְקַדֵּשׁ אֹתוֹ,

---

[39] Block, *Ezekiel*, 1:632.

Gen 2:3). The same Piel verb is used in both passages, but with those different nuances. It is to the divine, factitive sense of Gen 2:3 and the Leviticus passages he is quoting (see the textual note) that Yahweh returns by his use of the Piel participle at the end of the verse: "It is I, Yahweh, who sanctifies them [מְקַדִּשָׁם]." God sets aside or sanctifies not only the day as such, but all who participate in it and confess its meaning. His sanctification of it occurred once in primordial time, and its sanctifying, "sacramental" power also continues throughout time, particularly through the means of grace in the worship service on the Lord's day, unto the final rest at the end of time—the eternal Sabbath furnished by Christ (e.g., Heb 4:4–11).

Keeping the Sabbath was a sign that God had sanctified or consecrated Israel to himself to be a holy people, set apart and endowed with his own holiness, which he imparts through his appointed means. It is noteworthy that when the final purpose clause in Ezek 20:12 is recast in 20:20, the last part is replaced by "... that I, Yahweh, am your God." Thus, having him as God, his consecration of his people, and their dedication or consecration of their lives to him (epitomized on the Sabbath day) are all of a piece.

Mutatis mutandis ("with the necessary changes having been made"), it is not all that different for Christians. Rejection of a legalistic view of the OT Sabbath (especially as it was burdened with ever-increasing rabbinical regulations) was from the very beginning a major distinction between Jews and Christians, evident already in the ministry of Jesus himself (e.g., Mt 12:1–12; Jn 9:13–16) and sharply in St. Paul versus the Judaizers (especially in Galatians; see, e.g., Gal 4:10; Col 2:16). Yet the NT does not expunge the Third Commandment from the Decalogue. Rather, the NT church proclaimed that Christ has ushered in the beginning of the eschatological "rest," both in terms of the new creation in Christ (2 Cor 5:17) and arrival at the promised "land" through Christ as the new Joshua (cf. Heb 4:8),[40] and so sanctified the first day of the new week (the eighth day, the day after the old Sabbath), when our Lord rose from the dead, as the day of Christian worship (Jn 20:1, 19; Acts 20:7; 1 Cor 16:2).

Although in Christian freedom any day of the week could serve (Acts 2:46; Col 2:16), the NT custom has largely continued until the present day, and Sunday is formally a "holiday" even in secularized parts of the West. Among those who claim membership in Christendom, only Seventh-Day Adventists separate themselves by insisting that the OT Sabbath (along with certain dietary laws) is still mandatory. The term "Sabbath" is used by many Reformed groups when speaking of Sunday—a usage virtually unknown in Lutheranism, but which would facilitate the teaching of the Third Commandment in catechesis.

---

[40] "Joshua" and "Jesus" are the Hebrew and Greek forms of the same name. For Jesus as the new Joshua, see Harstad, *Joshua*, 12–14, 413–14 (and other pages listed in the index of subjects under the entry "Christ, as new Joshua").

Often attached to that Reformed idiom were various "blue laws" that kept stores closed and prohibited various other activities on Sunday. Today, however, secularism has largely succeeded in erasing most "Sabbath" restrictions, and so the church faces the problem of competition from other Sunday activities, including work schedules that prevent Sunday morning church attendance, as well as sports and other recreational activities. Increasingly, observance of the Sabbath is one of those areas where the intrinsic *counter*cultural nature of the church must manifest itself. It must remain high on our agenda that we not abuse our freedom in Christ, but concern ourselves with keeping our *day* of worship "holy"—not only one hour of that day—as a concentrated expression of our lives every day, until the "Day of the Lord"[k] finally arrives, and Christ's second advent ushers in the eternal Sabbath rest.

(k) Acts 2:20; 1 Cor 5:5; 1 Thess 5:2; 2 Thess 2:2; 2 Pet 3:10; see also 1 Cor 1:8; 2 Cor 1:14

It should be noted, finally, that critical opinion has long inclined to the view that in ancient Israel, the Sabbath, in whatever form it existed (if it even existed at all), was observed only desultorily until the time of the exile. There may be a half truth there. During the great periods of apostasy that the OT itself records, there is no reason to suppose that the Sabbath was kept with any greater zeal than the rest of the Torah. In fact, that seems to be the very sort of atmosphere Yahweh is confronting in this chapter. For whatever reason, accent on the Sabbath as a major distinguishing feature of God's people is most prominent in later texts of the OT (Ezekiel here, paralleled by Jer 17:19–27 and Neh 13:18). Qualifying such a statement might be Is 56:2–7 (notwithstanding that critics wrongly date chapters 56–66 of that eighth-century prophet to a late postexilic "Third Isaiah"). But it stands to reason that in the exile and the Diaspora, when national and communal marks of identity disappeared, the Sabbath would assume greater importance as a touchstone of loyalty to Yahweh and a mark of an authentic member of his community—something that is still true of observant Judaism today.

20:13–14   Even though the scene has shifted to the Israelites in the desert who had been redeemed through the exodus, it is déjà vu, as evidenced partly by the nearly verbatim repetition of portions of previous verses (especially 20:8) describing Israel's rebellion while still in Egypt. The major difference is the addition of the people's utter desecration of the Sabbath, which had been introduced in 20:12. That addition attests to the supreme importance Yahweh in Ezekiel attaches to its observance.

Two obvious parallels between 20:13–14 and the Pentateuchal record are Ex 32:10–14 and Num 14:11–19. Both times Yahweh threatens to annihilate (the exodus generation of) the people, but relents after Moses intercedes with appeals to Yahweh's reputation among the nations and his promises to the patriarchs (as Ezekiel summarizes: "for the sake of my name so that it would not be profaned in the sight of the nations," Ezek 20:14). Major examples of the Israelites' rebellion are the golden calf incident (Ex 32:1–6) and the pagan orgy at Baal Peor (Num 25:1–3). Desecration of the Sabbath is mentioned in Ex 16:27 and Num 15:32. An assertion parallel to Ezek 20:13 (also to 20:21 and possibly also to Jeremiah's sarcastic rhetorical question in Jer 7:22) appears in Amos 5:25–27.

Ezek 20:14 is nearly identical with 20:9. There is consistency in the people's behavior, but also a consistency in God's concern for his "name"—his character of keeping his Word, of not being arbitrary and impetuous, as the heathen gods were and are thought to be. (See the commentary on 18:25, 29.)

20:15–16 Numbers 14 attributes Israel's failure to enter Canaan to their unbelief of God's promises, leading to their cowardly refusal to attempt to take the land. Ezekiel follows his formula of attributing their failure to the four kinds of sins specified in 20:16. Obviously, there is not contradiction, only complementarity. As usual, Ezekiel has no interest in repeating specific historical details that would have been familiar to him (as a priest, 1:3) and to his audience from the Torah.

20:17 "My eye had pity on them," with the verb חוס ("pity, look upon with compassion"), may mislead a reader into understanding Ezekiel to be speaking about a sudden outburst of sentimentality by God for his people that overrides all other considerations. The verb itself can sometimes have such emotional connotations, but in the context there is room for no motive other than Yahweh's concern for the sanctity of his name. Hence the idiomatic phrase could be paraphrased as "I spared them," that is, God did not inflict the deserved and expected punishment. Only once in the entire book does Ezekiel attribute tender sentiment to God with רחם, "have compassion for" (39:25), and even there (as here) it is for the sake of "my holy name." Of course, Ezekiel would not have denied that Yahweh is compassionate and merciful, but he is not writing a comprehensive "biblical theology." His concern throughout the book is the necessity for God to manifest his love in judgment.[41] Therefore Ezekiel is a needed corrective to the constant temptation for the pastor and theologian to sweep all sorts of aberrations, moral and doctrinal, under the rug in the name of sentimentalistic "love."

The Second Generation of Israelites in the Wilderness (20:18–26)

20:18–21 Ezekiel now turns to the next generation of Israel, the children born in the desert to the parents who had participated in the exodus. To a large extent, the language is simply a recasting of what we have met before. Block argues that the changes suggest a growing impatience on Yahweh's part.[42] This is surely plausible, and Block's intuition may be correct, but in my judgment, he overstates his case. He notes that there is no opening summary of God's ear-

---

[41] As another sign of Ezekiel's emphasis, one may note that the (italicized) key terms (including a cognate adjective) in the common OT creedal affirmation that Yahweh is "*merciful* [רחום] and *gracious*, slow of anger and abounding in *steadfast love*" (Ex 34:6; see also Joel 2:13; Jonah 4:2; Pss 86:15; 103:8; 145:8; Neh 9:17) never occur in Ezekiel. The term in it for divine "anger" (אף) is common in Ezekiel, but as imminent or already demonstrated (not "slow of" or postponed).

[42] Block, *Ezekiel*, 1:635.

lier acts of grace, and the use of the imperatives throughout suggests to him that they are presented as demands rather than gifts to be received. Since the recognition formula in 20:20, "so that you might know that I, Yahweh, am your God," echoes that in 20:12 but omits "who sanctifies them," Block thinks the Sabbaths likewise have simply become days for the people either to keep holy or desecrate (not days on which God performs his sanctifying work). And he thinks the absence of the promise that the faithful will "live" (which was in 20:11 and 20:13) is significant. In contrast, I am inclined to construe the differences as more a matter of stylistic variation.

The addressees in the latter part of the Torah (especially after Numbers 14) would have included those of this second generation. Particularly Deuteronomy has many exhortations to faithfulness of the sort that could be summarized by Ezek 20:18–20. Additionally, throughout the historical books and Jeremiah, there is ample record of God continually summoning his wayward people to return to him. A general parallel to Ezekiel's charges here can be found in Numbers 16, the rebellion of Korah and his followers, and after their annihilation, the murmuring of the entire congregation against Moses and Aaron. The Pentateuch does not indicate that these events no longer included the first exodus generation, so perhaps these precise incidents should not be highlighted too much. But Moses (with Aaron) does dissuade God from destroying the people (Num 16:22, 44–50; cf. 17:10), as Moses did earlier (Ex 32:10–14; Num 14:11–19).

20:23–24 The Pentateuch is silent about any oath by Yahweh to exile the people even before they entered the land. The possibility that it could happen if they were disobedient is mentioned in both Lev 26:33 and Deut 28:64, but Ezekiel speaks of more than possibilities. In both the Pentateuchal texts, the nation is regarded as a whole; no distinction is made between successive generations. The Pentateuch's perspective is prospective, while Ezekiel's is retrospective. By placing this oath after the apostasy of the second desert generation, Ezekiel implies that it is punishment also for the rebellions described in Ezek 20:8 and 20:13. The people's fate was sealed in God's mind long before they reached Canaan; it was only a matter of time before it would actually be executed. Greenberg compares it to the implicit condemnation of the Amorites in Abraham's time (Gen 15:13–16); their iniquity was "not yet complete," but by the fourth generation the time would be ripe for their destruction by the invading Israelites.[43]

20:25–26 By almost any measure these two verses rank as among the most difficult theologically in the entire book. Not surprising, the literature on them is considerable and the interpretations diverse. Yahweh is not only decrying Israel's persistent rebelliousness, but seems to be attributing to himself laws that could only damn ("ordinances by which they could not live," the opposite of "ordinances … by which man will live" eternally in 20:11, 13). Some

---

[43] Greenberg, *Ezekiel*, 1:368.

interpreters even take 20:26 as implying that Yahweh commanded the Israelites to sacrifice their children to Molech, but it is clear in 16:20–21 that Jerusalem acted against Yahweh's will and express command when, as the foundling baby girl turned whore, she slaughtered the children she had borne to Yahweh by making them pass through the fire (the same act of which the people are accused here).

It is not the first time in Ezekiel that Yahweh has made similar assertions about himself. In 14:9, for example, we met the deceived prophet, about whom God declared, "I, Yahweh, have misled that prophet. ... and I will destroy him." But the assertions here are easily the most extreme in the book.

It is very tempting, especially to Lutherans, to hear these verses as the second use of the Law: *lex semper accusat*, "the Law always accuses" (cf. Rom 3:19–20; 7:7). While that is true, it would be wrong to interpret the "statutes" and "ordinances" (Ezek 20:25) of the Torah as pure Law in that sense and as devoid of any Gospel content. Since Torah (תּוֹרָה) is so frequently mistranslated as "law" and misinterpreted as consisting only of Law in the doctrinal and accusatory sense, it is only a short step to apply that conception to the OT as a whole, which then becomes, at best, subcanonical, and the result is a crypto-Marcionite interpretation.[44] Even Zimmerli seems open to this interpretation: "The Pauline recognition of the nature of the law (Rom 5:20; 7:13; Gal 3:19) is here hinted at a distance in a specifically limited formulation (in a different way Jer 31:31–34)."[45] But that Ezekiel, of all the prophets, should entertain such thoughts seems to me almost unthinkable. The priests (of which he was one, Ezek 1:3) were called to teach Israel the Torah (Lev 10:11; Deut 33:10), that is, the totality of God's revelation (in dogmatic terms, both Law and Gospel), as its very lifeblood.

It is my sense that the failure to recognize the multivalence of "Torah" in the Bible (and of its translation as "Law" in dogmatics) is one of the major causes of the failure to understand the OT. I am still waiting for the translation that will have the courage to translate תּוֹרָה, whenever appropriate, as God's "Word" (תּוֹרָה, "Torah," is often parallel to דָּבָר, "Word") or even as "Gospel."[46]

Lutherans were not the first to interpret Ezek 20:25–26 as a negative teaching about the Torah. Some version of that interpretation seems to have been almost standard in patristic polemics with Jews. Already Justin Martyr tells Trypho that God gave the laws to Israel not because they were his chosen peo-

---

[44] A recent expression of this orientation can be found in John H. Sailhamer, *Introduction to Old Testament Theology: A Canonical Approach* (Grand Rapids: Zondervan, 1995), 282–83. He advocates the critical theory that Exodus 19 records two different views of the Sinai covenant. The one, which he seems to view favorably, is that faith, along with a simple, undefined obedience to God, is the basis of Israel's keeping of the covenant. The other view is that the Decalogue and the Covenant Code are the basis of the covenant. Sailhamer finds that position (which he seems to view in a fundamentally negative way) reflected in Ezekiel.

[45] Zimmerli, *Ezekiel*, 1:412.

[46] The Gospel content of תּוֹרָה, "Torah," is accented by Kleinig, *Leviticus,* 1–2, and Harstad, *Joshua,* 81–87.

ple but as punishment for their sin and hardness of heart.[47] Irenaeus writes that God already wrote the natural law on human hearts and codified it in the Decalogue, but after the golden calf incident (Exodus 32, often the presumed context of the "not good" statutes mentioned in Ezek 20:25), God gave Israel the other commandments in order to reduce them to slavery.[48] Chrysostom (very vocal in his anti-Jewish views) argued that the laws were never intended to foster virtuous living but were intended as a curb on natural Jewish license.[49] Origen, true to his generally allegorical approach, asserted that because the Jews took the laws literally, they led to death, but if interpreted "spiritually," they would bring life.[50] Some of the fathers and many commentators after the Reformation, as far as I know, considered the "ordinances by which they could not live" (20:25) to be the ceremonial laws of the OT.

Judaism initially showed little interest in these verses until Jews felt the need to counter Christian argumentation. The Targum simply paraphrases the passage into another statement of Israelite rebellion. The earlier rabbis pointed to the inapplicability of many of the laws in the Diaspora or considered the laws "not good" if they were merely read in the synagogue, not chanted. In the Middle Ages Jews often argued that Ezekiel was not talking about Jewish laws at all, but about the Christian statutes which often were not congenial.

The rise of the historical-critical method in the eighteenth and nineteenth centuries inevitably refocused the discussion. It held that syncretism was accepted in Israel before the exile and that Ezekiel was a champion of an exclusive version of Yahwism that was only then emerging and that later became normative in Israel and Judaism. Since the historical-critical method is inherently inimical to the traditional, orthodox view of Scripture, its results are usable, if at all, only with caution. We prefer to speak of the "historical grammatical" method, which pays greater attention to the biblical writers' original intent in their historical circumstances, as nearly as that can be ascertained. Thus we reject the critical versions of "history" that conflict with Scripture, but affirm genuine history. Of course, while we conservatives agree on the axioms of biblical inspiration and inerrancy, that does not magically mean unanimity in exegetical specifics.

A common reaction among conservatives is to try somehow to mitigate the harshness of the verses and the obvious theological problems they raise. One stratagem is to transmute the face assertion of the verses that God actually *gave* such statutes into a statement of what God *permitted.* Now, indeed, dogmatic theology affirms, on the basis of Scripture, that God himself never is the author of evil; he only permits it (e.g., FC SD XI 6–7). Yet the Bible often speaks

---

[47] Justin Martyr, *Dialogue with Trypho*, chapters 18–22 (*ANF* 1:203–6).

[48] Irenaeus, *Against Heresies*, 4.15.1, citing Ezek 20:24–25 (*ANF* 1:479).

[49] Chrysostom, *Homilies on 1 Corinthians*, homily 7.9, citing Ezek 20:25 (*NPNF*[1] 12:38).

[50] Origen, *Selecta in Ezechielem* (PG 13:820).

of God as if he were the cause of what he permits (e.g., Is 45:7: "I form light and create darkness; I make weal and create woe"). Polytheism could always blame misfortunes on fickle or malicious god(s), but in the monotheistic faith of the Scriptures only the one true God must ultimately be responsible. Even Satan is not a completely free agent apart from God's control (Job 1–2).

However, to try to exculpate God by attributing the "not good" statutes to some other agent (human or demonic) finally shortchanges what God is saying through Ezekiel. The "not good" statutes were "independent of Yahweh's positive will" but yet were "enclosed within the purview of his punitive will" and were indeed given by God.[51] Impervious to positive attempts to teach them to know and recognize God (Ezek 20:5, 7, 12, 19), the people finally had to encounter God in a life-negating judgment "so that they might know that I am Yahweh" (20:26). "In the mystery of such strange actions, Yahweh can be recognized in the mystery of his being, which here means the incomprehensibility of the holy Judge."[52] It is God's *opus alienum*, his "alien work" (Is 28:21).[53]

Another attempt at mollifying the shock of Ezek 20:25–26 is to translate in some softer way God's statement of purpose, "so that I might devastate them." While ESV agrees with my translation of לְמַעַן אֲשִׁמֵּם (with the Hiphil of שָׁמֵם), many other translations offer "that I might horrify them."[54] Those versions might appeal to the meaning of the Niphal (וְנָשַׁמּוּ) in 4:17, "be horrified," but the Hiphil usually means "devastate." The evasion leaves God as a sort of practitioner of aversion therapy. Still others translate, "that I might make them desolate" (KJV and NKJV), perhaps understanding it to say only that God made the land of Israel desolate by driving the Israelites into exile, where they adopted pagan practices, including child sacrifice (20:26). A still more radical step is taken by a few who arbitrarily venture to delete most of 20:26.

Ezekiel's assertion here is, in fact, not as unique as might appear at first blush; see the commentary on 14:9–11. In the prophetic literature, a close parallel appears in the bleak terms of Isaiah's call, where Yahweh orders him:

> Make the heart of this people fat/dull,
>> and make its ears heavy,
>> and smear over its eyes,

---

[51] Allen, *Ezekiel*, 2:12.

[52] Zimmerli, *Ezekiel*, 1:412.

[53] Lutherans speak of God's "alien work" as his condemnation of sinners through the Law. His "proper work" is the justification of sinners through the Gospel, by grace alone for Christ's sake. God's "alien work" is indeed good (as the Law itself is good, Rom 7:12; cf. 1 Tim 1:8), and it is necessary to drive sinners to repentance, but it is preparatory to God's goal of justifying the sinner. This conception of God's alien and proper work is affirmed by, for example, Ezek 18:23, 32.

[54] So RSV and NRSV. NIV has "that I might fill them with horror." As possible meanings for the Hiphil, *HALOT* (s.v. שָׁמֵם, 2) gives "to cause people to be dumbfounded, disconcerted, awestruck," and cites 1 Sam 5:6; Ezek 20:26; 32:10.

> lest it see with its eyes
>> and with its ears hear
>> and its heart discern,
> and it repent and be healed. (Is 6:10)

Our Lord quoted from those words in answer to the disciples' query as to why he spoke in parables (Mt 13:14–15 and parallels). They are also quoted in Jn 12:39–41 and Acts 28:25–27 (among the last words of the apostle Paul in that book). God's ultimate hardening of Pharaoh's heart (Ex 9:12; 10:20) is often appropriately cited. Isaiah asks, "Why Yahweh, do you ... harden our hearts not to fear you?" (Is 63:17). The NT often speaks similarly: "God sends upon them a strong delusion to make them believe what is false" (2 Thess 2:11). St. Stephen tells the mob that God "gave them [their ancestors] over to worship the host of heaven" (Acts 7:42). Similarly, St. Paul asserts that "God gave them [the ungodly] up in the lusts of their hearts to impurity" (Rom 1:24; the immediate reference is to homosexuality!). One could cite many other similar passages. Is this connected with the unforgivable sin, blasphemy against the Holy Spirit (Mt 12:31–32)?

To get the particular reference of Ezek 20:26, one must refer back to Exodus 13, where "every issue that opened the womb" (כָּל־פֶּטֶר־רֶחֶם) occurs several times (Ex 13:12, 15; also 34:19; cf. 13:2). "Every issue that opened the womb" of animals must either be sacrificed to Yahweh or "redeemed" by substitutionary sacrifice, but children "you shall redeem" (Ex 13:13; 34:20; cf. 13:15). The repeated insistence of Jeremiah (7:31; 19:5; 32:35) that Yahweh had not commanded the sacrifice of firstborn *children* makes plain that the Israelites had misinterpreted or ignored those passages in Exodus and by some syncretistic confusion had concluded that Yahweh permitted, and perhaps even commanded, such behavior. The polemic against the practice in Deut 12:29–31 makes plain that the aberration was known already in Mosaic times, but the evidence is that it had become especially common since the days of the reign of Manasseh in the seventh century.

The "Topheth" was Jeremiah's name for the place in Valley of Hinnom (just south of Jerusalem) where the rite was practiced in his time (e.g., Jer 7:31–32). Archaeologists have applied that name to other sites of child sacrifice, and a famous one at Carthage has been excavated; others are known. Excavation cannot tell us whether the infant bones found were those of firstborn or not, but that is entirely plausible in the light of the special status and privileges accorded the firstborn as the "beginning of ... strength" (Gen 49:3; Deut 21:17; cf. Micah 6:7) throughout the ancient Near East. Especially in times of crisis, the firstborn would naturally be viewed as an especially potent means of propitiating the deity. Many details of the actual practice and meaning of the rite are unclear or debated but need not detain us here.[55]

---

[55] See further the textual notes and commentary on 16:20–21.

Israel in the Land after the Conquest (20:27–29)

20:27 This short section (20:27–29) provides a brief review of the more recent past, Israel in the land, to be followed by an address to at least some of the people now in the exile (20:30–31). In many respects, it is the climax of Israel's provocations, as may be indicated by the idiomatic "therefore, speak ..." (לָכֵן followed by a command to speak, as also in 20:30). Most often לָכֵן ("therefore") indicates consequence, but here it may express climax. The relatively unusual vocabulary employed may connote the same thing (see the textual notes on 20:27).

20:28 In this verse is summarized the gravamen of Ezekiel's entire indictment. Instead of gratitude and thanksgiving for bringing them to the promised land, the people repaid Yahweh with pagan worship in every suitable place. If it were not for כַּעַס ("their *vexatious* offerings"), there would be no way to tell from the vocabulary itself whether Yahwistic or pagan (probably syncretistic) worship was being spoken of. The shared vocabulary probably indicates a considerable amount of similarity in the items and rituals used in both. But even if the words and actions were identical, there would be great differences in how they were understood. For example, the "fragrant sacrifices" (literally, "soothing odor") in a pagan cult would be offered in the hope of pacifying or propitiating unpredictable gods. Ezekiel himself usually uses the idiom for idolatrous worship (6:13; 16:19; 20:28), although Leviticus and other OT texts make plain that it was prominent in orthodox ritual too (as in Ezek 20:41). We know little about the role of "libations" in Yahwistic ritual, but the term is used in worship of Yahweh in, for example, Gen 35:14; Ex 29:40; Lev 23:13, 18, 37. Scholars usually suppose that the liquid used was wine and that the ritual was most prominent in the meals of the communion sacrifices (שְׁלָמִים, often translated "fellowship" or "peace offerings"). Pagan sacrifices attempted to rectify the sinful human condition by offering alimentation to appease the god(s), so that was probably the intent of the libations on the high places (suggested by Jotham's reference in Judg 9:13 to "wine that cheers gods and men").

20:29 The pun constituting this verse is contemptuous (see the textual notes). What one believes is witnessed by where and how one worships (cf. contemporary "worship wars"). The issue all along had been Yahweh versus the gods, and "to this day" (a phrase frequently associated with OT wordplays) indicates that degenerate worship on the high places was still very much a live question when Ezekiel wrote. Yahweh now turns his attention to the continuing rebellion of the Israelites in the exile. At the same time, together with the questions in the next two verses, 20:29 facilitates the transition to the rest of the chapter. Since Ezekiel's contemporaries were continuing to patronize the high places they were implicated in all the infidelities of their ancestors. The high places, at least since the building of Solomon's temple, had been the foci of repudiation of the place where Yahweh had chosen for "his name to dwell" (e.g., Deut 12:11; 14:23; see the textual notes and commentary on Ezek 6:3; 16:16).

Israelites Who Are Ezekiel's Contemporaries (20:30–31)

20:30–31 Here we have the climax of the entire indictment, even repeating earlier language. All of it is applied to the contemporary generation. Thus, for the first time in Yahweh's speech (20:5–44) he uses the second person ("you"). The "house of Israel" is confronted directly. The two questions in 20:30 are obviously rhetorical. The present generation is not responsible for the misbehavior of previous generations (a point chapter 18 had established), but the people of this generation are accountable for continuing the same pattern of defiant disobedience. Ezek 20:31 then answers both questions. The repetition of "to this day" (20:31, from 20:29) emphasizes that they cannot evade their answerability and deflect God's wrath away from themselves.

Yahweh's Future Redemption Creates a New Israel That Offers Acceptable Worship (20:32–44)

The second major part (20:32–44) of the divine speech (20:5–44) begins here and constitutes the rest of the chapter (according to the Hebrew chapter division). Instead of continuing to excoriate the almost congenital rebelliousness of Israel in the past, Yahweh now turns to the future. To safeguard his "name" (20:39, 44; previously 20:9, 14, 22, 29) and be true to his covenant promises, he must and will restore "the Israel of God" (Gal 6:16). But he will display "tough love" to purge Israel before the eschatological restoration will occur.

The rest of the chapter might be divided in various ways, but those two movements seem to invite its division into (1) Israel in the "wilderness of the peoples" (20:32–38) and (2) the new, transformed Israel (20:39–44). Since these verses (20:32–44) are promissory, many critics assume that they are later supplements, since they allegedly presuppose the fall of Jerusalem.[56] However, able defenses of the original unity of the material can be found in Cooke, Greenberg, and Block.[57]

The New Exodus from "the Wilderness of the Peoples" (20:32–38)

20:32 Ezekiel's contemporaries were saying, "Let us become like the nations, like the families in other countries, by worshiping wood and stone." In contrast to those who interpret this wish as an expression of despair, or, at least, resignation (see the textual notes), it seems clear to me that it is a defiant wish or statement of intent to apostatize. It is very comparable to liberal Christianity's tendency today to become nothing more than a "cultural religion" by simply blessing the norms and ideals of the surrounding pagan society. As the earlier part of the chapter made plain, a desire for conformity with the heathen nations had been the people's attitude or motivation in their persistent rebellions all along. And the very next verse (20:33) is one of God's indignant re-

---

[56] For example, Zimmerli, *Ezekiel*, 1:414, and Allen, *Ezekiel*, 2:8.

[57] Cooke, *Ezekiel*, 212–14; Greenberg, *Ezekiel*, 1:376–88; Block, *Ezekiel*, 1:612–13.

action—not encouragement, as when he later responds to genuine expressions of despair (33:10–20; 37:11–14).

The parallel with 1 Sam 8:5, where an earlier generation had given the same rationale for their desire to have a king, is too close to be coincidental. In the earlier case, Yahweh had overruled Samuel and conceded to their request, granting them Saul. In this case, he refuses even to listen. Both cases have to do with kingship, but a kingship with less than happy results. Samuel, after conveying to the people God's positive answer to their request, gave a harsh preview of what life under a monarchy would be like (1 Sam 8:10–18)— a virtual prediction that came true many times over in the following centuries. Here, in the very next verse (Ezek 20:33), God promises (or should we say threatens?) to be their king with "wrath outpoured." In fact, one may wonder whether we do not find here part of the reason for Ezekiel's coolness toward the whole concept of kingship and his reluctance even to use that vocabulary. In Ezekiel Yahweh customarily refers to Israel's kings as mere princes,[58] and even in the next verse, speaking of himself, he uses the verb "to reign, rule" (20:33) rather than the noun "king."

In 1 Samuel 8 too, in the context of the people's request for a king, Yahweh had noted that they had rejected him as their king and they had "worshiped other gods" (1 Sam 8:8). "Worshiping wood and stone" (Ezek 20:32) would hardly be the way the people would perceive or describe their actions, but it is a derisive truth added to the preceding quote of them. The concept of idols being nothing more than wood and/or stone also appears in earlier texts: in Deut 4:28 after an extended warning against any sort of idolatry in Israel (Deut 4:15–28), and in an extended satire on worshiping idols made of wood and metal (Is 44:9–20). Paganism itself thought its statues were indwelt by the spirit of the gods they represented, but to a monotheist, they could be no more than mere "wood and stone," fashioned out of products of the one triune God's creative activity, but totally separate from the Creator himself.

It must be noted finally that the temptation to be "like the nations" (20:32) has not disappeared in modern times, but still thrives in something more like "fine idolatry " (without the statues, but desires and actions that are nonetheless idolatrous). A good case can be made that many aspects of the modern "ecumenical" impulse are not all that different in principle from ancient syncretism, which often eventuated in gross idolatry. Agreement among denominations and Christians is relatively easy if all differences are simply declared "not divisive of church fellowship" and concern for church discipline disappears or is derided as "sectarian." The particularity of the faith dissolves under the broad rubric of "religion." At its most extreme, what is lost is *the* scandal of particularity that is at the heart of biblical religion: salvation only through Christ crucified, and the result is plain (pagan) universalism.

---

[58] See "Introduction to Ezekiel 19" in the commentary on chapter 19 as well as "Outline and Theological Emphases" in the introduction.

More subtle versions of syncretism and idolatry submerge denominational particulars under slogans of "inclusiveness," "unity in diversity," "tolerance," or "pluralism of faiths" under one organizational roof. Statements of unity may be couched in language elastic or ambiguous enough that both parties can interpret them on their own terms. It is significant that historical confessions, such as the Augsburg Confession, not only state the positive (the truth that is being confessed) but also the negative (the errors that simultaneously must be condemned). Whether a denomination still adheres to its historical confessions (such as the Lutheran Confessions) may be revealed by whether they are taught, at the seminary level, as part of dogmatic theology (as expressions of the Christian faith that continue to be normative) or as part of historical theology (as historical documents that may be relevant no longer).[59]

20:33 The phrases "with a mighty hand" and "with an outstretched arm" are almost inextricably associated with the exodus; they are used frequently in Exodus and again in Deuteronomy.[l] Their repetition at the end of the next verse (20:34) makes of them an inclusion or frame around the thought expressed in 20:33–34: the drastic steps God will take to countermand the people's determination to be "like the nations" (20:32). The startling novelty here is that those phrases traditionally described God's ferocity toward Egypt in order to free Israel, but here they are turned against Israel itself in order to force the people finally to accept God's kingship once and for all.

That inversion of redemption language is reinforced by the addition of "wrath outpoured" (20:33–34; cf. 20:8, 13, 21). That Hebrew terminology was not used in the Torah in connection with the exodus deliverance, but already there Yahweh had threatened to unleash his "wrath" against disobedient Israel (Lev 26:28; Num 25:11; Deut 9:19), and the outpouring of God's wrath is used repeatedly in Ezekiel of God's fury toward Jerusalem.[m] Earlier in this chapter (20:8, 13, 21), Yahweh had desisted from pouring out his wrath, but in 36:18 and Lam 2:4 he will declare that he has poured it out . (The language of this verse, 20:33, may have been anticipated by Jer 21:5.)

In 20:34 it will become even more clear that Ezekiel is here employing considerable typological imagery. "Typology" implies that it is not mere "imagery." "Typology" is a near synonym of "prophecy," accenting prophetic events (e.g., the action prophecies in chapter 4) more than just words. It always involves both continuity and discontinuity, that is, it is neither mere analogy nor simple repetition (which, if we are speaking of history, is impossible). The "antitype" or fulfillment is a "recapitulation" (there is no adequate term for

(l) E.g., Ex 3:19; 6:6; 32:11; Deut 3:24; 4:34; 5:15

(m) Ezek 7:8; 9:8; 14:19; 22:22; 36:18

---

[59] The Lutheran church has always taught as the "formal principle" of theology that the Scriptures are the *norma normans* ("norming norm"), the sole source and norm for the Christian faith and life (doctrine and practice; see FC Ep and SD, Rule and Norm), and the Lutheran Confessions are the *norma normata* ("normed norm"), a true exposition of teachings in the Scriptures that is normed by the Scriptures. The Lutheran Confessions are normative "because" (*quia*, not *quatenus*, "in so far as") their doctrine is derived from the Scriptures. However, not all "Lutheran" denominations continue to adhere to this formal principle.

something miraculous) on a higher level of the implicit intent of the "type." One fulfillment often becomes a sort of springboard for still further "recapitulation" until the "consummation" is finally achieved. (This understanding of typology was advocated already by Irenaeus).[60] In 20:39–44 Ezekiel will speak of a consummation according to OT vistas (just as all OT prophecy uses B.C. language), but the final antitype is Christ and his "exodus" (Lk 9:31).[61] NT precedents mandate that the Christian exegete factor in that climactic event—Christ's death and resurrection—although, in this interim between his first and second advents, we too await a consummation at the end of time, all the while receiving and celebrating the benefits of the divine action in Christ by means of God's Word and Sacraments.

In this verse (Ezek 20:33), salvation and judgment are mingled in one event. What better "type" could one desire of the cross, where the entirety of God's wrath at humanity's sin was poured out on the sinless Christ, who by his atonement procured salvation for all? Ezek 20:33 does not specify exactly what action(s) or event(s) will take place, but obviously some are implicit in "with a mighty hand, with an outstretched arm, and with wrath outpoured," which will accomplish his purpose, "I will rule over you!" We confess the cross of Christ to be the locale of God's maximal judgment on sin, there visited on his Son vicariously for the sins of all, who must surely perish unless they believe and are baptized into Christ's death and resurrection. And concurrent in that judgment is total salvation for the believer, with supplementation neither needed nor possible.

Is it not cause for concern that the first part of that equation, judgment, so easily gets muted or even lost in our teaching and preaching—which means that Law *and* Gospel are not really proclaimed and a reductionist or even false "gospel" of an undefined "God loves you" is broadcast in their place?

20:34 The typology of a new, second exodus is explicit in this verse. Yahweh's assertion of his kingship in the previous verse is here made historically concrete. In fact, this second exodus will involve more than the first exodus from Egypt: the first concerned only deliverance from one land, but here many lands are in view and from them all God's reconstituted Israel is to be gathered. The same assertion is made in 20:41 and 34:13. Which lands are these? Besides Babylon, where most of the captives went in Ezekiel's day, Yahweh may also have in mind the exiles from the northern kingdom (2 Ki 17:6) and the groups that would flee to Egypt with Jeremiah (Jeremiah 43–44). It may

---

[60] Woollcombe, "The Biblical Origins and Patristic Development of Typology," 42–49, explains the view of Irenaeus that much OT prophecy is "recapitulative" and has two aspects, "consummative" and "reiterative." Woollcombe argues that Irenaeus did not invent this typological view of prophecy. Rather, Irenaeus "found [it] entrenched in the Old Testament eschatological prophecies" (p. 43) and "in the way the New Testament writers handled the Old Testament prophecies" (p. 49).

[61] In terms of the Lutheran hermeneutical accent on "one literal sense," we would insist that these are not different senses, but "levels" or "phases" of a unified sense.

well even be that the Diaspora throughout the ancient Near East was well under way by this time.

But when dealing with prophecy, the horizons are often much larger than the merely "historical" (in its usual modern, positivistic sense). They often include the transhistorical and eschatological as well. The rest of the chapter indicates that Yahweh is envisioning far more than the return to Canaan after Cyprus' edict in 538 B.C. "Exile" has become a type of all those who remain afar from their true homeland in Christ. These are not the ones who are still in spiritual slavery and whose allegiance is to the Jerusalem below (Gal 4:21–25, 30), but rather all children of the Jerusalem above (Gal 4:26–31)—all baptized believers in Christ, who are sons of Abraham, children of God, and heirs of all the promises (Gal 3:26–29).

Thus, in a well-known Advent hymn, even we in this time of the "not yet" sing, "Oh, come, Oh, come, Emmanuel, And ransom captive *Israel*, That mourns in lonely *exile* here."[62] The return from the exile began with the Great Commission (Mt 28:19–20) and Pentecost (Acts 2). God's new Israel consists of all in Christ, gathered from all nations (Romans 9–11), the end of whose exile will take place with the realization of the vision of the Seer of Patmos of "a great multitude … of all nations, tribes, peoples, and tongues standing before the throne and before the Lamb" (Rev 7:9).

We should note finally that in the eighth-century B.C. poetic prophecy of Isaiah 40–66 we find an OT counterpart to this cosmic perspective, also replete with second exodus language.

20:35–36 It is just as futile to try to locate or limit geographically the "wilderness of the peoples" (20:35) as it was the "countries" of 20:34. The expression is obviously a typological counterpart to the "wilderness of the land of Egypt" (Sinai) in 20:36. The great Syro-Arabian desert, which those exiled in Babylon had to traverse on their return to Canaan, may provide a point of departure for the prophetic imagery. The expression "wilderness of the peoples" refers to a sort of no-man's land that nobody calls home, where the plethora of religious options provides just as bleak a terrain as a desert, where the people must make spiritual choices, and where God will confront his people. God is described as meeting people "face to face" several times in the OT, but the past precedent for 20:35–36 must be the theophany at Sinai (Deut 5:4). Then the people tried to run away; this time there will be no escape.

Typologically, we finally must refer the action here to the great assize at the end of time:

> At [Christ's second] coming all men will rise again with their bodies and will give an account of their own works. And they that have done good will go into life everlasting; and they that have done evil, into everlasting fire.[63]

---

[62] *LW* 31:1; emphasis added.

[63] Athanasian Creed (*LW*, p. 135).

As those words make plain, the references to God's people as a whole must be interpreted in light of the teaching of Scripture (e.g., Ezekiel 18) that each individual cannot delegate to anyone else the necessity to confront the Judge and receive his verdict, which will be determined by whether or not the void of his fallen human soul has been filled with the Gospel of Christ as his substitute, for the Christ who lives in the believer does indeed produce good works (Gal 2:20).

The phrase "wilderness of the peoples" (Ezek 20:35) is a suggestive one whose applications extend far beyond the limits of exegesis. That non-Christian Jews have today been scattered to the four corners of the earth is irrelevant, as is the fact that many make *'aliyah* (immigration) to the modern state of Israel. Christians (Jews and Gentiles alike in Christ) also now are scattered throughout the world, though not as a divine judgment, but as an opportunity for proclaiming the one saving Gospel to all peoples. The "wilderness of the peoples" takes on increasing cogency now as multicultural and multilingual populations are present especially in metropolitan centers, but also throughout most of the world.

20:37 In spite of the uncertainty about the Hebrew word in "the *bond* [?] of the covenant" (see the textual note), the verse proclaims that those who survive the sifting will be brought into the covenant relationship. The expression parallels the covenant oath Yahweh swore in 20:5 and the revelation of his "statutes" and "ordinances" (Torah) in 20:11. By "bond of the covenant" we must understand not only the covenant punishments, but also the covenant promises (Law and Gospel). Also the promises of the covenant are bonds by which God trains and educates his people.[64]

20:38 This verse returns to the theme of 20:37a and amplifies it. "Land of sojourning" (אֶרֶץ מְגוּר) is an expression that referred to the land of Canaan,[n] which God promised to the patriarchs, but in which they resided only temporarily without actually taking full possession of it. Only here is it applied to the lands of exile, from which "those who revolt and rebel against [God]" will be brought out. But like most of the original exodus generation, and also like the false prophets of 13:9, the rebels will not be allowed to enter the promised land. Just exactly what will happen to them is not made clear. Perhaps Ezekiel could not press the underlying typology of the section farther. Or perhaps it was irrelevant to his main point, that God will have rid the faithful of the faithless. In the faithful remnant, Yahweh will have finally accomplished his goal

(n) Gen 17:8; 28:4; 36:7; 37:1; Ex 6:4

---

[64] Compare "a king is captivated by the tresses" in Song 7:6 (ET 7:5), where Solomon uses אָסוּר, "bound, captivated," which is related to "bond" (בְּמָסֹרֶת) in Ezek 20:37, to express how his wife's tresses hold him captive with bonds of love. For exegesis of the verse, one may see Mitchell, *The Song of Songs*, 1070–71, who comments, " 'Captivated' ... expresses both the idea of captivity and also the implication that what binds the king to the Shulammite is not force or compulsion (Law) but love that seeks its object (Gospel). ... The bond is created by divine love, which surpasses even death and hell in its strength ([Song] 8:6)" (p. 1070).

of having a purified, holy people who truly "know" him. Here it is plain that the emphasis has begun to shift to an eschatological focus, as is apparent in most of the rest of the Hebrew chapter (20:39–44).

This theme of "holy things for holy people" (applied to the Lord's Supper in the Eastern Orthodox liturgy) pervades Scripture; see, for example, Is 35:8–9; Rev 22:14–15. It can be taken as an expression of the goal of Christ's redemptive activity, with the understanding that we sinners become God's holy people in Christ (e.g., 1 Pet 2:5, 9–11, which also calls Christians "sojourners and exiles"; compare 1 Pet 2:11 to Ezek 20:38). It also underlies the practice of closed Communion (required to prevent *manducatio indignorum*, "eating by the unworthy"),[65] the use of private and/or corporate confession and absolution (so that our sins are forgiven) before our main worship services, and the opening versicles of many minor services, "O Lord, open my lips, and my mouth shall declare your praise" (Ps 51:17 [ET 51:15]; only after God has opened our lips can we truly sing his praise).

The Acceptance and Worship of the New, Transformed Israel (20:39–44)

20:39 Besides the challenges of the Hebrew (see the textual notes), another difficulty is that we might think the verse is positioned inappropriately. Ezek 20:38 had begun to move in a strongly eschatological direction (looking toward the final gathering of all Christians at Christ's second coming), but here we have an obvious recognition of continued idolatry at the present time, expressed in a satirical command to continue it. In a similar vein is Rev 22:11: "Let the evildoer keep doing evil, and let the filthy man still remain filthy, and let the righteous man keep doing righteousness, and the holy man still be sanctified."

The injunction for idolatry is all the more curious since we probably have here the beginning of a subsection describing Israel's purified, eschatological worship. Perhaps we understand the verse best if we take it as transitional. If we are labeling it "eschatological," it is an inaugurated eschatology, but not yet consummated. Ezekiel apparently still has in view those who have come close to the promised land but have not entered it, and if they persist in their past idolatries, they never will. I would understand the verse as a sort of summary of the church on earth, in the time of the "now-not yet," which will always have hypocrites in its midst (even if they are known only to God). The dream of a

---

[65] All communicants eat and drink the true body and blood of Christ in the Lord's Supper according to the Words of Institution (e.g., 1 Cor 11:23–26). Unworthy communicants do so to their condemnation (1 Cor 11:27–30). That is why, from the early church era to the present day, the Christian church has followed the evangelical practice of excluding from the Supper the impenitent, those who do not discern the body and blood of the Lord in it, and those who do not profess agreement in Christian doctrine. See, for example, Werner Elert, *Eucharist and Church Fellowship in the First Four Centuries* (St. Louis: Concordia, 1966), and "Closed Communion" in Lockwood, *1 Corinthians*, 400–405.

"pure" church on earth is utopian and finally contrary to the Bible's own descriptions. As each Christian remains sinner and saint throughout earthly life (e.g., Romans 7), so too the visible church on earth remains a mixture of wheat and weeds until the harvest (Mt 13:29–30).

The last clause of the verse makes plain that the offensive forms of worship were directed against Yahweh. "My holy name" is used here for the first time in the book; it is developed more fully in 36:20–22 and mentioned in 39:7, 25 and 43:7–8, as well as elsewhere in Scripture. The defiling of Yahweh's name (20:39) and of the idolaters themselves through their gifts and offerings had started long ago by divine decree (20:26) and has lasted into the present. By claiming to honor Yahweh while worshiping idols, the people had reduced him to the level of any other god. Whatever their rationalizations, they did not really "know" him (20:38, 42). Ezek 20:39 has described the negative correction of such delusions (by God's judgment), while 20:40 will begin to describe the positive correction (by his grace). Whether before or after the people's transformation, it is noteworthy that Yahweh's measure of their faithfulness is the quality of their worship—whether idolatry or acceptable worship (20:40), which, he makes plain, is a gift to them that only he can enable.

20:40 Thus, it is no surprise that 20:40–41 is full of traditional, sometimes technical, liturgical language. First of all, true worship must take place on Yahweh's "holy mountain"—in contrast to every "high hill" (20:28, sites of idolatrous devotion). The obvious reference is to Zion, the temple mount. It is "holy," not by nature, as pagan sites were often thought to be, but by God's election or choice. Even as he "chose" Israel (20:5), culminating in Jesus Christ, then spreading out to all believers (see the commentary on 20:5), so also he "chose" Zion as the one location for OT worship and his temple (e.g., Deut 12:5–26). It is a "high" mountain (Ezek 20:40) because it towers above all competitors, and all who would be saved must make the pilgrimage to it (Is 2:2–4 ‖ Micah 4:1–3). It is the site of God's "incarnational" presence on earth (cf. Christ as the new temple, e.g., Jn 2:18–22). Located there is as much of paradise restored as is possible until the new creation, in which its worshipers already participate (2 Cor 5:17). It manifests a transcendence of all earthly desires (Pss 42:2–4 [ET 42:1–3]; 122:1; cf. Ezek 24:21), a transcendence that Christian worship replicates in its antitypical way.

The importance of *place* of worship is underscored by the repetition of "there" (שָׁם) thrice in 20:40 (contrast its five occurrences in 20:28–29 for places of idolatrous worship). Christian worship is not bound to one geographical mountain, but takes place "in Spirit and truth" (Jn 4:20–24). Yet neither can it be divorced from Bethlehem (in the hill country), Mount Calvary, the Mount of Olives, and what occurred in those places (Christ's incarnation, passion, death, resurrection, and ascension). As long as we are in this world of time and space, worship will take place at some specific time and place where God's Word is proclaimed truly and his Sacraments administered rightly, and not merely in the privacy of the individual heart, apart from the body of Christ—

the church. It has been said that he who does not worship at specific times and places probably does not worship at all.

The verb עָבַד (20:40) is often translated "serve," but here (and often) "worship" is most appropriate. It is a happy coincidence that in both Hebrew (the noun cognate to עָבַד) and English the same word can be used both of a liturgical "worship service," as well as in the broader sense of Christian conduct (e.g., Rom 12:1), because neither activity has integrity apart from close association with the other. It is perverse to pit worship and missions against each other; Christian "service" requires both to be done rightly.

"There the *whole* house of Israel will worship me—*all* [כֹּל] of it" (Ezek 20:40) appears to say that a complete restoration of right worship will only be accomplished when all the people have been restored, that is, when all who shall be saved will be gathered in at the final judgment (Revelation 20–22). Here it is bound with בָּאָרֶץ, which, with only slight freedom, I have translated "in the *home*land." אֶרֶץ "land," can be used more broadly, but often it refers specifically to the land of Israel, as here. The boundaries of spiritual and physical Israel will finally coincide when all the chaff has been blown away, that is, only eschatologically, when the wheat and the weeds are no longer intermingled, as they inevitably are on earth. As Ezekiel describes the ultimate normalization of all covenant relationships—God, nation, and land/mountain—he inevitably predicts the future through his OT lens, the future in terms of his present, just as St. John envisions the consummation through his contemporary NT lens in Revelation 21–22 (and we too view the future through the lens of our present). What was said above about the Spiritualization of "mountain" via the Holy Spirit—not "spiritualization" (untethered interiority)—also applies here of the "land."

"There I will accept them" uses the verb רָצָה, "to be pleased with, accept, show favor/grace," which occurs in Ezekiel only in 20:40–41. Along with its related noun רָצוֹן, "favor, acceptance, grace," it is sometimes used in a more general sense, but often has a specialized, liturgical sense. It is used of God's acceptance of the worshiper, as here, or of the sacrifice.° The worshiper has no natural right to claim acceptance by God, except through God's grace for Christ's sake, in view of his atoning sacrifice. Similarly, our offerings are not pleasing to God if they are offered in any other spirit than gratitude for God's grace. The Lutheran definition of justification by faith as the *favor Dei*, earned vicariously by Christ, is as fully applicable to the OT church as to the new. Any other doctrine of "favor" from God is chimerical and heterodox.

(o) E.g., Lev 1:4; 7:18; 19:7; 22:23, 25, 27

"There I will *request* your offerings" (20:40) uses דָּרַשׁ, obviously a play on its use in 20:1, 3, 31 (also 14:7, 10), where idolatrous Israelites attempt to "consult" Yahweh or "inquire" of him through Ezekiel, but Yahweh refuses to answer their inquiry. People do not "seek" God of their own volition (and if they look for him apart from where he has promised to be found, in his Word and Sacraments, they will never find his grace). But Yahweh seeks them out (Ezek 34:10–16; Mt 18:10–14; Jn 6:44; 12:32) and requests their thank offerings. Here the verb might have been translated "demand, require," as it often implies, but in this evangelical context "request" seems more appropriate.

Three terms ("offerings … choice gifts … holy things") follow in 20:40, all of them fairly technical and at least partly synonymous. The precise meaning of תְּרוּמָה (plural here: "offerings") has long been debated. In the Torah it traditionally was rendered as "heave offering" and was associated with תְּנוּפָה, traditionally rendered as "wave offering" (the two occur together in, e.g., Ex 29:27; Lev 7:34; 10:14–15). Since the "heave offering" was thought to be presented to God with vertical motion and the "wave offering" with horizontal waving, thus, in effect, making the sign of the cross, it was often interpreted as a prediction or premonition of the cross of Christ. But recent expositors argue that תְּרוּמָה does not mean "heave offering" because it is not derived from the Qal of רוּם, "be high, lifted up," but rather from the Hiphil of רוּם in its specialized sense "dedicate, reserve" (a portion of the sacrifice), and there is a cognate Akkadian noun with that meaning. Sometimes it is used almost generically of any "contribution" to Yahwistic ritual. The theory of Milgrom is widely accepted, namely, that the תְּרוּמָה was a gift dedicated *to* Yahweh outside the sanctuary without a ritual, in contrast to the תְּנוּפָה ("wave offering"), which was presented *before* Yahweh in the sanctuary by ritual.[66]

The following phrase (רֵאשִׁית מַשְׂאוֹתֵיכֶם, 20:40), literally, "first of your gifts," is unique in the OT. The first term, רֵאשִׁית, often means "first," and "first-fruits" (designated by the different Hebrew term בִּכּוּרִים) were often thought of as the best of a crop, offered in recognition that the entire crop was really a divine gift. Milgrom, perhaps correctly, distinguishes between בִּכּוּרִים ("first-fruits") as "first ripe" gifts, and רֵאשִׁית ("first") as "first processed."[67] The second term of the phrase in 20:40 is the plural of מַשְׂאֵת, which normally designates a "portion, contribution, gift" given from one person to another, and only here refers to a gift to God. In any case, these "choice gifts" will be a God-pleasing alternative to all the futile, pagan offerings mentioned previously (20:26, 28, 31, 39). The literal "first of your gifts" here probably also implies a God-pleasing alternative to "every first issue that opened the womb" (20:26), which, incredibly, the Israelites had perverted to justify infant sacrifice.

The most comprehensive of the three terms in 20:40 is "holy things" (קֳדָשִׁים, plural of קֹדֶשׁ, which is common in Ezekiel 41–48). The primary reference is, no doubt, to offerings, but since everything about the Yahwistic cultus was to be holy (also objects, personnel), the nonspecific translation "holy things" seems best. If so, the בְּ (בְּכָל־קָדְשֵׁיכֶם) is not a *beth essentiae*, as some[68] take it, which would make the phrase essentially synonymous with the pre-

---

[66] Jacob Milgrom, *Leviticus 1–16* (Anchor Bible 3; New York: Doubleday, 1991), 415–16, cited by Block, *Ezekiel*, 1:653, n. 200. See also the note on תְּרוּמָה in Lev 7:14 in Kleinig, *Leviticus*, 161.

[67] Milgrom, *Leviticus 1–16*, 190–91, cited by Block, *Ezekiel*, 1:653, n. 201.

[68] Zimmerli, *Ezekiel*, 1:403, citing GKC, § 119 i; Block, *Ezekiel*, 1:653, n. 202.

ceding two expressions. Instead, "with all your holy things" subsumes the previous two phrases and also is broader, since it includes everything and everyone involved in the divine liturgy. "Worship Yahweh in the splendor of holiness!" (Pss 29:2; 96:9; 1 Chr 16:29; cf. 2 Chr 20:21). The Christian conception of authentic worship is essentially the same.

20:41 The interpretation of the pliable preposition בְּ in two phrases will determine how we understand the verse. Elsewhere it sometimes is used as a *beth pretii* (of price). If that were the case here, the first phrase would mean "by [בְּ] a fragrant sacrifice I will accept you" and would refer to a sacrifice by which the people would purchase God's favor,[69] but that flies directly in the face of *sola gratia* (salvation "by grace alone" is the teaching of the OT as much as of the NT). Rather, the preposition here should be taken as a *beth essentiae*, pointing to the heart of the matter: Yahweh will accept the purified worshipers *themselves "as a* fragrant sacrifice," smelling, as it were, good before both God and people because of their faith and lives.

This is the only time in the OT where people themselves are described as a "fragrant sacrifice." It is also the only time Ezekiel himself uses the phrase positively, although it is frequently used in that way elsewhere in the OT (especially of God-pleasing sacrifices prescribed in Leviticus). Undoubtedly Ezekiel tends to avoid the phrase for the polemical reason that it was misappropriated by apostate Israelites for idolatrous worship (to which it refers in 6:13; 16:19; 20:28).

It is often forgotten or overlooked that the NT uses corresponding Greek similarly:

> Christ loved us and gave himself up for us as an offering and sacrifice to God for a pleasing aroma [ὀσμὴν εὐωδίας]. (Eph 5:2)

Christ himself is the ultimate sacrifice that satisfied God's wrath once and for all. In 2 Cor 2:14–16 St. Paul declares that the "aroma" (ὀσμή) of Christ perfumes the church and is an "aroma from death to death" for unbelievers, but an "aroma from life to life" for believers. St. Paul calls the gifts sent to him by the Philippians via Epaphroditus "a pleasing aroma [ὀσμὴν εὐωδίας], an acceptable sacrifice, well pleasing to God" (Phil 4:18). Compare also the apostle John's vision of the prayers of the faithful as plentiful incense in the celestial liturgy in Rev 5:8 and 8:3–4. These scriptural depictions should be called to the congregation's attention when our worship services use the "fragrant aroma" of incense, which is employed in the greater part of Christendom. There is no reason why it should not be used in Lutheran churches, especially on festive occasions, except because of Protestant anti-Catholic and anti-ritual prejudices.

---

[69] As one might expect from a Jewish commentator, Greenberg, *Ezekiel*, 1:375, explains: "By means of the sacrificial offerings—properly made (contrast [20:]28)—you will win my favor."

The second phrase in Ezek 20:41 in which the meaning of the preposition בְּ is disputed (וְנִקְדַּשְׁתִּי בָכֶם) revolves around the translation of the Niphal verb with Yahweh as subject. A purely passive translation ("I will be made holy") is out of the question; he who is holiness itself cannot be made more holy. Some type of reflexive is the only alternative: "I will hallow myself, show myself to be holy." A reflexive force is clinched by the Hithpael instead of the Niphal in 38:23, where Yahweh says, "I will prove myself holy and I will make myself known in the sight of many nations." In virtually every instance of the Niphal with a following בְּ, the preposition is a *beth personae*.[70]

That still allows three possible translations here, all of which have been proposed: Yahweh says, "I show myself holy in you," "among you," or "through you." The first two suggestions seem tautologous in the light of the context, which seems already to be assuming that the new Israel has been made holy by the holy God, and Israel confesses that fact. Yahweh says, "I will show myself holy through you in the sight of the nations" (similar to 38:23), which seems to require that the new Israel will serve as a "light to the nations" (Is 49:6), as a conduit through whom Yahweh will proclaim his saving Gospel (through which God imparts the very righteousness and holiness of Christ to all who believe). This is in contrast to former times, when his name and holiness were desecrated through Israel (20:13–16, 21–26, 39). Instead, Yahweh will have shown himself holy, both by his purifying judgment on his people and by his ability to effect a new exodus, gather a new Israel, and restore his people to their homeland.

20:42 The remaining verses in the chapter reaffirm the new creation that will have taken place in the hearts of all Israel and will give the people a new vantage point from which to survey and evaluate their past relationship with Yahweh.

20:43 *"There* [שָׁם] you will remember … and you will loath yourselves" stresses that such repentance and faith will not occur in the exile, but only after the restoration, as 16:61 and 16:63 (cf. 6:9) have already asserted. (Compare the commentary above on "there" in 20:40.) The self-loathing is not some neurosis, but genuine contrition or repentance. Anyone can regret his past mistakes, but only those who have been overcome by the Law and who now know the comfort of the forgiving Gospel can recognize the depths of the depravity from which they have been delivered—and to which the old Adam in them is still prone throughout earthly life. This verse bears witness to the ongoing role of the Law and repentance in the life of believers, even after they have been converted and regenerated by the power of the Gospel.[71]

---

[70] The Niphal of קָדַשׁ is used with בְּ in, for example, Ex 29:43; Lev 10:3; Num 20:13; and Ezekiel 28:22, 25; 36:23; 38:16; 39:27.

[71] Cf. Romans 6–7; FC VI; and the first of Martin Luther's Ninety-five Theses: "When our Lord and Master Jesus Christ said, 'Repent' [Mt 4:17], he willed the entire life of believers to be one of repentance" (AE 31:25).

20:44 The final verse of the oracle has a climactic use of the recognition formula: "Then you will know that I am Yahweh when I deal with you for the sake of my name and not according to your evil ways and your corrupt deeds." Zimmerli summarizes:

> The mystery of Yahweh's being, however, will then clearly be the mystery of one who is not compelled to follow the law of human activity, in its scheme of retribution, but of one whose inner loyalty maintains what it has promised and thereby demonstrates his holiness.[72]

The new Israel's knowledge of Yahweh fulfills his desire that people not remain obstinate to the end and die, but repent and live (18:23, 32). The people's recognition that Yahweh has acted for the sake of his name (20:44) is also a confession of faith that their salvation is solely by his grace (the only human works in view are "your evil ways and your corrupt deeds"). Eternal life comes through the knowledge of the one true God and the One he has sent, who has revealed God's name to the new Israel he has gathered (Jn 17:3, 6, 11–12, 26; Rom 1:5; 3 John 7).

---

[72] Zimmerli, *Ezekiel*, 1:417.